Fodor's

THAILAND

11th Edition

Fodor's Travel Publications New York, Toronto, London, Sydney, Auckland
www.fodors.com

Be a Fodor's Correspondent

Your opinion matters. It matters to us. It matters to your fellow Fodor's travelers, too. And we'd like to hear it. In fact, we need to hear it.

When you share your experiences and opinions, you become an active member of the Fodor's community. That means we'll not only use your feedback to make our books better, but we'll publish your names and comments whenever possible. Throughout our guides, look for "Word of Mouth," excerpts of your unvarnished feedback.

Here's how you can help improve Fodor's for all of us.

Tell us when we're right. We rely on local writers to give you an insider's perspective. But our writers and staff editors—who are the best in the business—depend on you. Your positive feedback is a vote to renew our recommendations for the next edition.

Tell us when we're wrong. We're proud that we update most of our guides every year. But we're not perfect. Things change. Hotels cut services. Museums change hours. Charming cafés lose charm. If our writer didn't quite capture the essence of a place, tell us how you'd do it differently. If any of our descriptions are inaccurate or inadequate, we'll incorporate your changes in the next edition and will correct factual errors at fodors.com immediately.

Tell us what to include. You probably have had fantastic travel experiences that aren't yet in Fodor's. Why not share them with a community of like-minded travelers? Maybe you chanced upon a beach or bistro or B&B that you don't want to keep to yourself. Tell us why we should include it. And share your discoveries and experiences with everyone directly at fodors.com. Your input may lead us to add a new listing or highlight a place we cover with a "Highly Recommended" star or with our highest rating, "Fodor's Choice."

Give us your opinion instantly at our feedback center at www.fodors.com/feedback. You may also e-mail editors@fodors.com with the subject line "Thailand Editor." Or send your nominations, comments, and complaints by mail to Thailand Editor, Fodor's, 1745 Broadway, New York, NY 10019.

You and travelers like you are the heart of the Fodor's community. Make our community richer by sharing your experiences. Be a Fodor's correspondent.

Happy Traveling!

Tim Jarrell, Publisher

FODOR'S THAILAND

Editor: Joanna G. Cantor
Editorial Contributor: Shannon Kelly
Writers: Hana Borrowman, Karen Coates, Robin Goldstein, Alexis Herschkowitsch, Christina Knight, Emmanuelle Michel, Lee Middleton, Howard Richardson, Dave Stamboulis, Simon Stewart, Brian Thomson, Robert Tilley, Martin Young

Production Editor: Evangelos Vasilakis
Maps & Illustrations: Henry Colomb and Mark Stroud, Moon Street Cartography; David Lindroth, *cartographers*; Bob Blake, Rebecca Baer, *map editors;* William Wu, *information graphics*
Design: Fabrizio LaRocca, *creative director*; Guido Caroti, Siobhan O'Hare, *art directors*; Tina Malaney, Chie Ushio, Ann McBride, Jessica Walsh, *designers*; Melanie Marin, *senior picture editor;* Moon Sun Kim, *cover designer*
Cover Photo (Floating market, Thailand): Chederros/Nomad/age fotostock
Production Manager: Steve Slawsky

COPYRIGHT

11th Edition

ISBN 978-1-4000-0829-2

ISSN 1064-0993

SPECIAL SALES

This book is available at special discounts for bulk purchases for sales promotions or premiums. Special editions, including personalized covers, excerpts of existing books, and corporate imprints, can be created in large quantities for special needs. For more information, write to Special Markets/Premium Sales, 1745 Broadway, MD 6-2, New York, New York 10019, or e-mail specialmarkets@randomhouse.com.

AN IMPORTANT TIP & AN INVITATION

Although all prices, opening times, and other details in this book are based on information supplied to us at press time, changes occur all the time in the travel world, and Fodor's cannot accept responsibility for facts that become outdated or for inadvertent errors or omissions. So **always confirm information when it matters,** especially if you're making a detour to visit a specific place. Your experiences—positive and negative—matter to us. If we have missed or misstated something, **please write to us.** We follow up on all suggestions. Contact the Thailand editor at editors@fodors.com or c/o Fodor's at 1745 Broadway, New York, NY 10019.

PRINTED IN SINGAPORE

10 9 8 7 6 5 4 3 2 1

CONTENTS

Fodor's Features

CONTENTS

MAPS

ABOUT THIS BOOK

Our Ratings

Sometimes you find terrific travel experiences and sometimes they just find you. But usually the burden is on you to select the right combination of experiences. That's where our ratings come in.

As travelers we've all discovered a place so wonderful that its worthiness is obvious. And sometimes that place is so unique that superlatives don't do it justice: you just have to be there to know. These sights, properties, and experiences get our highest rating, **Fodor's Choice,** indicated by orange stars throughout this book.

Black stars highlight sights and properties we deem **Highly Recommended,** places that our writers, editors, and readers praise again and again for consistency and excellence.

By default, there's another category: any place we include in this book is by definition worth your time, unless we say otherwise. And we will.

Disagree with any of our choices? Care to nominate a place or suggest that we rate one more highly? Visit our feedback center at www.fodors.com/feedback.

Budget Well

Hotel and restaurant price categories from ¢ to $$$$ are defined in the opening pages of each chapter. For attractions, we always give standard adult admission fees; reductions are usually available for children, students, and senior citizens. Want to pay with plastic? **AE, D, DC, MC, V** following restaurant and hotel listings indicate whether American Express, Discover, Diners Club, MasterCard, and Visa are accepted.

Restaurants

Unless we state otherwise, restaurants are open for lunch and dinner daily. We mention dress only when there's a specific requirement and reservations only when they're essential or not accepted—it's always best to book ahead.

Hotels

Hotels have private bath, phone, TV, and air-conditioning and operate on the European Plan (aka EP, meaning without meals), unless we specify that they use the Continental Plan (CP, with a Continental breakfast), Breakfast Plan (BP, with a full breakfast), or Modified American Plan (MAP, with breakfast and dinner) or are all-inclusive (including all meals and most activities). We always list facilities but not whether you'll be charged an extra fee to use them, so when pricing accommodations, find out what's included.

Many Listings

- ★ Fodor's Choice
- ★ Highly recommended
- ✉ Physical address
- ✥ Directions
- 📫 Mailing address
- ☎ Telephone
- 📠 Fax
- 🌐 On the Web
- ✎ E-mail
- 🎟 Admission fee
- ⊙ Open/closed times
- Ⓜ Metro stations
- ▭ Credit cards

Hotels & Restaurants

- 🏨 Hotel
- 🛏 Number of rooms
- 👍 Facilities
- 🍽 Meal plans
- ✕ Restaurant
- ✍ Reservations
- 🚬 Smoking
- 🍷 BYOB
- ✕🏨 Hotel with restaurant that warrants a visit

Outdoors

- 🏌 Golf
- ⛺ Camping

Other

- ☺ Family-friendly
- ⇨ See also
- ✉ Branch address
- ☞ Take note

Thailand,
Cambodia & Laos
CHINA
Jinghong
Phongsali
VIETNAM
HANOI
Hai Phong
Dien Bien Phu
Muang Sing
Luang Namtha
Xam Nua
Gulf of Tonkin
HAINAN ISLAND
Mae Sai
Chiang Khong
Luang Phrabang
BURMA (MYANMAR)
Chiang Rai
LAOS
Vinh
Muang Xaignabouri
Mae Hong Son
Phayao
Nan
Chiang Mai
Lamphun
VIENTIANE
Lampang
Phrae
Nong Khai
Nakhom Phanom
Muang Khammouan
Uttaradit
Loei
Udon Thani
Hue
Sukhothai
Phitsanulok
Khon Kaen
Kalasin
Savannakhet
Phetchanburi
Roi Et
Da Nang
Yasothon
Saravan
Chaiyaphum
Pakxé
THAILAND
Champasak
Attapu
Gulf of Martaban
Nakhon Sawan
Ubon Ratchathani
Buriram
Nakhon Ratchasima
Surin
Sangklaburi
Lopburi
Ayutthaya
Kanchanaburi
Stoeng Treng
BANGKOK
Siem Reap

Kanchanaburi
BANGKOK
Ratchaburi
Chon Buri
Phet Buri
Pattaya
Rayong
Siem Reap
Batdambang
CAMBODIA
Stoeng Treng
Kampong Thum
Kracheh
Kampong Cham
Chanthaburi
Pouthisat
Trat
Ko Chang
Ko Kut
Krong Kaoh Kong
Kaoh Kong
PHNOM PENH
Svay Rieng
Takev
Kampot
Ho Chi Minh City
Mekong Delta
VIETNAM
Hon Khoai
SOUTH CHINA SEA
Gulf of Thailand
MERGUI ARCHIPELAGO
ISTHMUS OF KRA
Mergui
Prachuap Khiri Khan
Chumphon
Ko Tao
Ranong
Lang Suan
Ao Ban Dan
Koh Pha Ngan
Ko Samui
Ko Surin Nua
Surat Thani
SIMILAN ISLANDS
Nakhon Si Thammarat
Ko Similan
Phangnga
Krabi
Phuket
Ko Phuket
Ko Lanta Yai
Trang
Phatthalung
Songkhla
Pattani
Narathiwat
Yala
Satun
MALAYSIA
Andaman Sea
0
200 mi
0
200 km

Experience Thailand

WHAT'S WHERE

1 Bangkok. In this boomtown of contrasts where old-world charm meets futuristic luxury, you can dine at street stalls or ritzy restaurants, visit the jaw-dropping Grand Palace, and shop at Chatuchak Weekend Market or Pathumwan's designer malls. At night there are hip mega-clubs and Patpong's famous red lights.

2 Around Bangkok. Petchaburi has ancient temples and a royal retreat, while Thailand's oldest city, Nakhon Pathom, is home to Phra Pathom Chedi, the world's largest Buddhist structure. You'll find Damnoen Saduak's famous floating market, as well as smaller but more authentic markets near Samut Songkram. Kanchanaburi Province has Erawan National Park, a temple that adopts tigers, and several notable World War II–related sights, including the infamous Death Railway.

3 The Central Plains. Take a riverboat to the remains of Ayutthaya, the ancient capital sacked by the Burmese in 1767. Then visit Lopburi, with its Khmer, Thai, and French architecture. Thailand's first capital, Sukhothai, has carefully restored ruins; Si Satchanalai offers secluded meditation in hilltop temples; and Tak Province has river gorges with white-water rafting.

4 The Southern Beaches. Thailand's two shores have alternating monsoon seasons, so there's great beach weather *somewhere* year-round. The Gulf has Pattaya's raunchy nightlife and the island trio of Koh Samui (good sailing), Koh Pha Ngan (full-moon revelry), and Koh Tao (diving). Andaman Coast highlights include Phuket, Phan Nga Bay (James Bond Island), and Krabi, which is a paradise for divers and rock climbers.

5 Northern Thailand. Chiang Mai's lovely moat-encircled old city is riddled with temples and markets. Smaller Chiang Rai is a chilled-out regional center and the gateway to the Golden Triangle, where Laos, Myanmar (Burma), and Thailand meet. Northern Thailand is also known for mouth-watering regional cuisine and remote luxury resorts.

6 Isan. If you want to immerse yourself in Thai culture with few fellow tourists around, visit Thailand's poorest and most populous region. Check out 4,000-year-old cave paintings and ceramics in Udon Thani and silk weaving centers in Khon Kaen; trek through the Khao Yai National Park; or enjoy Isan's distinctive music and cuisine at Mekong River restaurants.

7 Cambodia. No Southeast Asia trip is complete without a visit to the spectacular ruins of Angkor Wat. The capital, Phnom Penh, is an up-and-coming city with a thriving food scene and the country's only national museum. Cross Lake Tonle Sap to communities living in floating houses or laze on Cambodia's as yet unspoiled coastline.

8 Laos. Photogenic rivers, mountainous countryside, and the dreamy feeling of going back in time are major reasons to make the trip across the border. World Heritage sites Luang Prabang and Champasak both have beautiful temples and centuries-old charm. River-rafting on an inner tube in Vang Vieng will appeal if you're looking for a little adventure along with sightseeing.

Jinghong
VIETNAM
Phongsali
Dien Bien Phu
HANOI
Hai Phong
Gulf of Tonkin
Muang Sing
Luang Namtha
Xam Nua
Mae Sai
Chiang Khong
MYANMAR (BURMA)
Chiang Rai
Luang Phrabang
8
LAOS
Mae Hong Son
5
Phayao
Muang Xaignabouri
Vinh
Chiang Mai
Nan
Lamphun
VIENTIANE
Lampang
Phrae
Nong Khai
Muang Khammouan
Nakhom Phanom
Uttaradit
Loei
Udon Thani
6
Savannakhet
Hue
Sukhothai
Phitsanulok
Khon Kaen
Kalasin
Phetchanburi
Saravan
Da Nang
Roi Et
3
Yasothon
Chaiyaphum
Pakxé
THAILAND
Champasak
Gulf of Martaban
Nakhon Sawan
Buriram
Ubon Ratchathani
Attapu
Sangklaburi
Surin
Lopburi
Nakhon Ratchasima
Ayutthaya
2
1
Angkor Wat
Kanchanaburi
7
Stoeng Treng
Nakhon Pathom
BANGKOK
Siem Reap
CAMBODIA
Ratchaburi
Chon Buri
Batdambang
Samut Sakhon
Kampong Thum
Kracheh
Petchaburi
Pattaya
Phet Buri
Chanthaburi
Pouthisat
Rayong
Kampong Cham
Trat
Gulf of Thailand
Ko Chang
PHNOM PENH
Mergui
Svay Rieng
Ko Kut
Krong Kaoh Kong
Prachuap Khiri Khan
Kaoh Kong
Takev
Ho Chi Minh City
Kampot
Mekong Delta
ISTHMUS OF KRA
MERGUI ARCHIPELAGO
Chumphon
VIETNAM
Lang Suan
Ko Tao
Ranong
Ao Ban Dan
Koh Pha Ngan
Ko Samui
Ko Surin Nua
Surat Thani
SIMILAN ISLANDS
Hon Khoai
4
Andaman Sea
Phangnga
Nakhon Si Thammarat
SOUTH CHINA SEA
Ko Similan
Krabi
Phuket
Ko Phuket
Phatthalung
Ko Lanta Yai
Trang
Songkhla
0
200 mi
Pattani
Satun
Narathiwat
Yala
0
200 km
MALAYSIA
Strait

THAILAND PLANNER

Visitor Info

The Web site of the Tourism Authority of Thailand (TAT), *www.tourismthailand.org*, has details of events, festivals, and transportation options, plus feature articles and brief destination guides. On the ground, it has branches in many tourist towns, although outside the major cities sporadic opening hours can be frustrating and the information often a little sparse. The TAT Call Centre (☎1672) is open daily 8 AM–8 PM. The Tourist Police also have a hotline: ☎1155.

National Parks

Thailand has 103 land and marine national parks with many rare species of flora and fauna. The Web site of the National Park Wildlife and Plant Conservation Department (*www.dnp.go.th*) is a good resource for getting the lowdown on all facilities (including food and drink vendors), animal-spotting opportunities, notable features like waterfalls, and available cabin rentals or camping areas (you can book accommodation online), plus weather news and updates on which areas are closed.

Travel Agents

Thailand-based travel agents can be useful if you're trying to pack a lot into a short trip. The 24-hour support many agents offer is particularly helpful if things go wrong, such as when internal flights are delayed. The following are a few reputable companies; others are covered in regional chapters.

Asian Oasis (☎ *66/2655–6246* *www.asian-oasis.com*). **Asian Trails** (☎ *66/2626–2000* *www.asiantrails.net*). **Circle of Asia** (☎ *66/2651–9780* *www.circleofasia.com*). **Diethelm Travel** (☎ *66/2660–7000* *www.diethelmtravel.com*). **Exotissimo** (☎ *925/937–4550 in the U.S., 66/2636–0360 in Bangkok* *www.exotissimo.com*). **Queen Bee** (☎ *66/5327–5525* *www.queenbeetours.com*).

When to Go

Thailand has three seasons: rainy (June–mid-November), cool (late November–February), and hot (March–May). In central Thailand temperatures average 73°F to 90°F in the rainy season; 68°F to 86°F in the cool season; and 77°F to 95°F in the hot season. The north is a bit cooler, the south a bit hotter.

City sightseeing is okay during the rainy season: downpours lower the temperature, and storms, though fierce, don't last all day. But flooding can make rural areas inaccessible, and it's not a reliable time to plan a trek. The south gets wet by May, but the Gulf islands generally have decent weather until August.

Cool-season weather, which is less humid, is perfect for everything: the beaches, Luang Prabang, Angkor Wat, trekking, or exploring Bangkok. But accommodation rates sometimes double and rooms can be scarce in hot spots like Phuket. The northern nights are chilly in winter—generally in the 50s, but as low as freezing.

By April, you can find good hotel deals, if you can stand the heat, though some hotels in less touristy areas shut down for the hot season.

With Kids

Thais dote on kids, so chances are you'll get extra help and attention when traveling with them, and the experience should be relatively problem free. Powdered milk is readily available. Stomach bugs and infections thrive in the tropical climate. Basic cleanliness—washing hands frequently and making sure any cuts are treated with antibacterial ointment and covered—is the best protection against bacteria. Don't let children play with or touch street animals; they may have rabies. Be careful while walking along sidewalks, where open manhole covers and people riding motorbikes can be hazardous. (*For more about health,* ⇨ *Health in Travel Smart.*)

What it Costs

Despite rapid development, Thailand is still a relatively cheap destination. You'll spend the most getting here: at this writing, fares start at around $950 from the West Coast of the U.S. and are a few hundred dollars more from New York. Traveling within Thailand is a bargain. You can cross Bangkok in a taxi for $5, while a third-class train to Ayutthaya, 45 mi away, costs 50¢. Budget accommodation runs from as low $4 a night, and even five-star is available at $250. One of the reasons people dine out regularly is the cost: A street food meal might set you back $1.50, while a blow-out Thai restaurant meal with a beer would be about $10. High-end international dining starts at around $35, though imported wine could easily double that.

What It Costs in Baht

¢	$	$$	$$$	$$$$
Restaurants				
under B100	B100–B200	B201–B300	B301–B400	over B400
Hotels				
under B1,000	B1,000–B2,000	B2,001–B4,000	B4,001–B6,000	over B6,000

Restaurant prices are for a main course, excluding tax and tip. Hotel prices are for two people in a standard double room in high season, excluding service charges and tax.

Health

Vaccinations aren't required to enter Thailand, but cholera, hepatitis A and B, and tetanus shots are a good idea. The mosquito-born illness dengue fever is a problem, even in Bangkok, and malaria is present, though not prevalent, in some outlying regions. It's best to drink bottled water.

Hospitals and dentists in major cities are of a good standard. They may even accept your health insurance, so carry proof with you (and if you know your insurance doesn't cover you abroad, buy travel insurance before you go just in case). (*For more about health,* ⇨ *Health in Travel Smart.*)

Safety

Thailand is very safe for tourists, but it still pays to take sensible precautions. Be careful about accepting food or drinks from strangers (spiking is not uncommon) and don't flash money around. Though women generally travel without hassle, it's advisable to avoid walking alone in secluded areas after dark. Pickpockets and conmen (and women) patrol some touristy areas. The police contact number is 191, but better communication will be had with the Tourist Police, police officers who speak English and are assigned to deal with tourists. They're reachable on their 1155 hotline. (*For more about safety,* ⇨ *Safety in Travel Smart.*)

THAILAND TODAY

Today's Thailand . . .

. . . is politically divided. For several years, three major political parties have been at violent odds with one another: the TRT, the PPP, and the PAD. In 2005, when prime minister Thaksin Shinawatra of the populist Thai Rak Thai (TRT) party was found guilty of tax evasion, the People's Alliance for Democracy (PAD) led demonstrations against him. In 2006, Thaksin was overthrown in a bloodless military coup and fled to London with his wife. A general election in 2007 brought in the People's Power Party (PPP), a civilian government let by Samak Sundaravej. The TRT was banned the same year. But some Thais believed Thaksin still controlled the new government, and PAD demonstrations resumed. In August 2008, demonstrators occupied Government House; in September the government declared a state of emergency and Samak was forced to step down. PPP member Somchai Wongsawat, Thaksin's brother-in-law, replaced Samak but protests continued. In November PAD protesters shut down Bangkok's international airport—a blow to tourism and the economy. The following month the courts removed Somchai from power, ruled that the PPP was guilty of electoral fraud, and ordered the PPP and two affiliated parties to dissolve. In mid-December, Abhisit Vejjajiva of the Democrat Party became prime minister. In early 2009 the political situation continued to be deeply unsettled. Politics in Thailand is closely tied to business and family relationships rather than ideology, and one common view is that the current conflicts are a power struggle between "new money" families like Thaksin's and the traditional elite.

. . . is ethnically diverse. Throughout its history, Thailand has absorbed countless cultural influences, and is home to groups with Chinese, Tibetan, Lao, Malaysian, Burmese, and other origins. Migrating tribes from modern-day China, Cambodia, Myanmar, and the Malay Peninsula were the region's earliest inhabitants. Ancient trade routes meant constant contact with merchants traveling from India, China, and other parts of Southeast Asia. Conflicts and treaties have continued to alter the country's borders—and ethnicity—into the 20th century. Contemporary Thailand's cultural richness comes from its ethnic diversity. Though Buddhism is the predominant religion, Hindu and animist influences abound

WHAT'S HOT IN THAILAND NOW

Sophisticated Thai architects and designers, historically obsessed with European classical forms, are increasingly turning to their own heritage for inspiration. Hip new hotels and restaurants are now choosing contemporary indigenous fabrics and traditional painted ceramics, not faux Doric columns and Louis XIV furniture.

Young Thais love all things Japanese. Teenagers lounging in Bangkok's Siam Square and other hangouts around the country are filling breaks from school with Japanese comics and tapping their feet to J-Pop, the latest hits from Tokyo. Japanese TV series and accessories are all the rage with the young crowd, as are Thai-language magazines with articles on sushi joints, tea drinking ceremonies, and the Japanese art of gift wrapping.

and there's a significant Muslim majority in the south. Malay is spoken in the southern provinces; Lao and Khmer dialects of Thai are spoken in the northeast; and the hill tribes have their own dialects as well. You're sure to experience Thailand's diverse cuisine, which includes heavy Indian-style curries, delicate Chinese noodles, Lao meat salads, and Indonesian saté.

. . . is steeped in mysticism. Many Thais believe in astrology and supernatural energy. The animist element of Thai spirituality dictates that everything, from buildings to trees, has a spirit. With so many spirits and forces out there, it's no surprise that appeasing them is a daily consideration. Thais often wear amulets blessed by monks to ward off evil, and they believe that tattoos, often of real or mythical animals or magic spells, bring strength and protect the wearer. Car license plates with lucky numbers (such as multiple nines) sell for thousands of baht; important events, such as weddings, house moves, and even births, are arranged, when possible, to fall on auspicious days, which are either divined by shamans or consist of lucky numbers. Newspapers solemnly report that politicians have consulted their favorite astrologers before making critical policy decisions. Businesses erect shrines to powerful deities outside their premises, sometimes positioned to repel the power of their rivals' shrines. In 2008, during a territorial dispute with Cambodia, Thais performed a ceremony to counteracts rituals across the border they believed contained black magic.

. . . is fun-loving. Even in daily life, Thais are guided by a number of behavior principles. Many, such as *jai yen* (cool heart) and *mai pen rai* (never mind), are rooted in the Buddhist philosophies of detachment, and result in a non-confrontational demeanor and an easy-going attitude. Perhaps most important of all is *sanuk* (fun). Thais believe that every activity should be fun—work, play, even funerals. Of course, this isn't always practical, but it's a worthy aim. Thais enjoy being together in large parties, making lots of noise, and—as sanuk nearly always involves food—eating. With their emphasis on giving and sharing, these group activities also reflect elements of Buddhist teaching; being generous is an act of merit making, a way of storing up points for protection in this life and in future lives.

In a high-end housing craze, developers are building sky-scraping condominiums in Bangkok and tourist destinations like Phuket and Pattaya. But there's a lot of debate over who will buy all the new condos. Rents start at around $300 a month, $50 more than the average Thai salary. Foreigners, who aren't allowed to buy land but can own condo units, will fill some of the slots. But foreigners are only allowed to own 49% of the units in a building, so developers are offering significant discounts to Thais. Still, there may not be enough money around to fill all these pricey new homes, and many pundits were warning of a crash even before the global economic downturn in the fall of 2008.

TRANSPORTATION, THAI STYLE

With reasonably priced internal flights and reliable train and bus service, getting around Thailand can be efficient and straightforward. Taxis are often happy to travel distances of around 100 mi, and you can hire a car and driver for a fraction of what it would cost back home. But several quirkier modes of transport have true local color (though sometimes not much regard for safety).

Samlor

The quaint *samlor* (literally meaning "three wheels") is a variation on a rickshaw: the driver pedals a three-wheeled bicycle, pulling an open carriage with room for two in back. It's a slow, quiet, and cheap way to travel short distances, and samlors are still common on the streets of provincial towns. Often, street vendors will attach the carriage to the front of the vehicle instead of the back and use it to display their wares.

Songthaew

Songthaews are converted pick-up trucks with two benches in the back and a metal roof. Thais ride songthaews both within a town and between towns. They aren't cheaper than local buses, but they are more frequent and will sometimes drive slightly out of their way to drop you nearer your destination. Just stick out your hand as one passes, negotiate a price, and climb in back. Songthaews are often packed, and if all the seats are taken, Thais will just climb on the back and hang onto the railings. It's a bumpy ride on rural roads; for longer trips, you'll be more comfortable on the bus.

Motorcycle

In cities, there are so many motorcycles skittering between cars it seems every resident must own one. And no wonder: in the gridlocked traffic, they're often the only way to get anywhere on time. Consequently, people frequently abandon taxis or cars and hop on motorcycle taxis (called "motorcy"), the drivers of which are notorious for two things: shady dealings and scary driving. Yet it's not uncommon to see entire families piled helmet-less on a single vehicle. Women passengers usually ride sidesaddle, with both hands clasped between their knees to preserve modesty—a balancing act of high skill and great faith.

Tuk-Tuk

Although the *tuk-tuk* is practically Thailand's icon, it is in fact a Japanese import. This three-wheeled motorized taxi with open sides is a logical progression from the samlor. It's an atmospheric—i.e., fume-filled, hot, and noisy—way to get around city streets, and a more pleasant ride on rural lanes, although you have to hunker down in the seat to actually see much, and you'll definitely feel every bump in the road. Tuk-tuks come in a variety of styles, including bullet-nosed models in Ayutthaya, elongated "hot rods" on the Eastern Gulf, and elevated versions nicknamed "Skylabs" in the northeast.

Longtail Boat

The slim longtail boat gets its name from the huge V8 car engine that protrudes on an elongated pole from the back of the craft. Catch one of these brightly colored, 40-foot monsters to navigate the river in Bangkok for a bumpy, noisy, and exhilarating ride. When the going gets choppy, passengers huddle behind plastic sheeting. Garlands wrapped around the prow, dedicated to Mae Yanang, the goddess of travel, are also there for your protection.

TOP EXPERIENCES

Street Food

The rich and poor mingle over bowls of herb-laden soups and curries at Thailand's street stalls. Many vendors are famous for a particular dish, whether pad Thai; the spicy, sour shrimp soup *tom yum goong*; or duck with noodles. It's a wonderful journey of discovery, where you can chomp on seemingly anything, from deep-fried flowers to a mixed bag of insects.

Chatuchak Market

There are almost 10,000 stalls at Chatuchak Market, which operates in northern Bangkok each Saturday and Sunday. The world's biggest market is great for ethnic textiles, jewelry, books, funky clothes, food, plants, Buddha statues, and pretty much anything else you can think of.

Songkran Festival

Each April, during Thai New Year celebrations (Songkran), the country becomes a three-day street party of riotous water fights. Participants go armed with cups, buckets, and water guns, and tourist centers like Khao San Road are impassable with hordes of happily drenched merrymakers. Traditionalists complain it's a far cry from the festival's origins—it began as a genteel bathing ritual to honor elders.

Beach Life

Thailand's beach culture is world class. The famous Full Moon Parties on Koh Pha Ngan heave with all-night raves; you may be happier lazing under coconut palms with a gentle massage between dips, or having a beach barbecue with fresh seafood on Koh Chang.

Diving

For unforgettable underwater theater, head to one of Thailand's top dive sites, where facilities range from beginner courses of a few hours to live-aboard boats that stay out several days. Koh Tao, in the Gulf of Thailand is popular, but the best locations are the Similan and Surin islands, where you meet nomadic island-hopping people known as Sea Gypsies and swim with whale sharks, clownfish, and leatherback turtles.

Phuket Vegetarian Festival

Each November religious devotees known as *Ma Song* walk on hot coals and drive a variety of metal objects through their bodies. These feats are believed to deflect evil, and are part of a Chinese Buddhist–Taoist period of spiritual cleansing, when adherents abstain from meat, alcohol, and sex.

Muay Thai

With fighters allowed to inflict damage with anything but the head, *muay thai* (Thai boxing) is reputed to be the most brutal of all martial arts. But it's also a fine spectacle of ritual, in which boxers initially perform a *wai kru* (a bow to their trainer) followed by a *ram muay* (literally, "boxing dance") to warm up, seal the ring from evil spirits, and honor their families and gods.

Phi Ta Khon

This eerie festival is held in Dan Sai, in Loei Province, every June or July. Men dressed as ghosts parade through the streets waving phalluses dipped in red paint. Phi Ta Khon is both an animist fertility rite and a celebration of the Buddha's penultimate incarnation, when ghosts greeted him on his return to his hometown.

TOP THAILAND ATTRACTIONS

A

B

C

D

The Grand Palace

(A) Bangkok's Grand Palace and the adjacent royal temple, Wat Phra Kaew, appear like a fairy tale castle of golden domes and glittering spires within white fortified walls. They were the centerpiece of the new capital when it was built more than 200 years ago, and they still form Bangkok's most impressive architecture. Wat Phra Kaew contains the Emerald Buddha, Thailand's most revered religious image.

Ancient Sukhothai

(C) Sukhothai is recognized as the first independent kingdom in what would eventually become Thailand. Its 13th-century ascendancy is referred to as the country's Golden Age: religion was codified; a writing system was introduced; and the arts flourished. The city's impressive ruins are preserved in Sukhothai Historical Park.

The Ruins of Ayutthaya

(B) Thailand second capital, destroyed by the Burmese in 1767, Ayutthaya had 2,000 gold temples and a population greater than London in its heyday. The Ayutthaya Historical Park has many Thai- and Khmer-style ruins that evoke the city's lost grandeur.

Chiang Mai

(D) Chiang Mai was the capital of the ancient kingdom of Lanna, which grew to prominence in the 13th century. Even after it became part of Siam, Lanna was largely independent until the early 20th century, due to its mountainous terrain, and it retains a distinct culture. Chiang Mai was located on historically important trade routes and still has a varied ethnic population and significant old temples. It's the gateway for jungle and hill tribe treks.

Phimai

(E) Phimai was once the center of an important province in the Khmer empire, which at its height stretched over large parts of Thailand. The northeastern town's Prasat Hin Phimai National Historical Park has ruins of a Hindu-Buddhist temple complex that predates Angkor Wat, in Cambodia, and is thought to have inspired some aspects of it.

Khao Yai National Park

(G) While the chances of seeing a tiger are remote, there's plenty of other wildlife in Khao Yai National Park, home to the waterfall from the film *The Beach.* The park's inhabitants include Malayan sun bears, Indian civets, and three million wrinkle-lipped bats that hunt for food together in a long cloud each evening.

Wat Po

(F) Wat Po is Bangkok's oldest temple and is sometimes called the country's first university. It has lessons in history and astrology inscribed on the walls, and people still come here to learn traditional medicine. Of the many buildings and images onsite, pride of place goes to the 45-meter-long (147-foot-long) Reclining Buddha, which shows the Buddha ascending into Nirvana after reaching enlightenment.

Ao Phang Nga

(H) One of the most arresting natural sights in Thailand is formed by the jungle clad limestone karsts and islands that rise like towers around the waters of Ao Phang Nga, a marine national park close to Phuket. The most famous of the islands is Koh Ping Kan, which was featured in the film *The Man With The Golden Gun,* and is hence better known as James Bond Island.

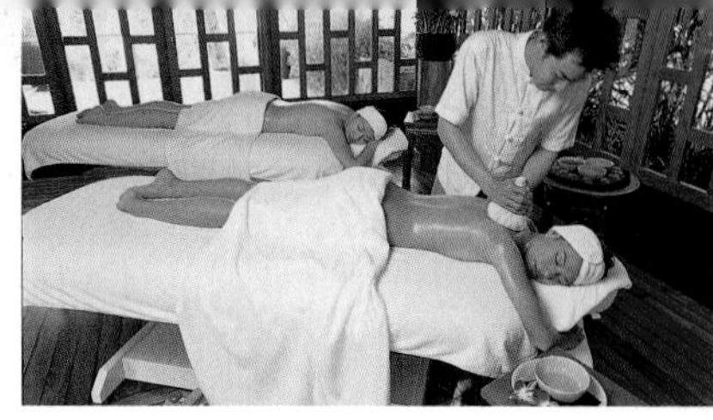

THAI MASSAGE

Thai massage, once only available at temples or tiny shophouses, has become much more popular in recent years. You'll find masseurs and masseuses at work all over the country—in bustling markets, at boutique spas, and in jungle hideaways.

Today massage is a pleasant and relaxing part of Thai culture, and you may see locals giving casual shoulder, back, and arm massages to their friends. But *nuad paen boran* (ancient massage) is also a branch of traditional Thai medicine. Originally it was taught and performed in Thai temples, which were historically places of physical as well as spiritual healing.

Traditional massage combines acupressure, reflexology, yoga, and meditation. Practitioners believe that ten energy lines, called *sip sen,* link the body's meridian points. Blocked lines may lead to physical or spiritual ailments. Massage is thought to unblock the energy lines, clearing toxins and restoring balance to the body.

Where to Get Massage

Temples: Some temples still have massage facilities, and massages are often provided to the elderly for no charge. At Wat Po in Bangkok, you can receive a massage in an open-air pavilion for B250 an hour.

Shophouses: These ubiquitous massage parlors offer no-frills service. Expect to share a room with other patrons (curtains separate the cots); if you're getting a foot massage, you may be seated in the shop window. There's often music, TV, or chatter in the background. A two-hour massage costs at least B250. Though many shophouses are legitimate businesses, some offer "extra" sexual services. To avoid embarrassing misunderstandings, steer clear of treatments with suggestive names, like "special" or "full body" massage. You can also ask the concierge at your hotel to recommend a reputable place.

Outdoors: At markets, on beaches, and at temple fairs, masseurs and masseuses set up shop alongside street vendors. On the beach you'll lie on a mat; at the market you'll probably be seated in a streetside plastic chair set up for foot massage. Prices varies—a one-hour foot massage might cost as little as B100 at a temple fair, or B250 on a popular beach.

Urban Spas: A growing phenomenon, urban spas are more upscale than shophouse parlors. They're often located in old Thai houses, with contemporary–Asian-style private treatment rooms. You'll have more options here: simple Thai massage is still on the menu (for B1,000 and up per hour), along with body scrubs, facials, and various other treatments.

Resort & Hotel Spas: For five-star pampering, head to upscale hotels and resorts whose luxurious, tranquil spas offer an extensive array of massages, including Swedish massage, plus other treatments like tai chi and new-age therapies. Expect to pay at least B2,500 for an hour-long massage at a top Bangkok hotel—a lot by Thai standards but still less than what you'd pay back home.

Restrooms: In a few clubs and bars (both gay and straight), some visitors are alarmed when men's restroom attendants start massaging their shoulders as they stand at the urinal. If you don't like it, ask them to stop (*mai ow, kup*). Otherwise, a B10 tip is welcome.

The Moves

Thai massage is an extremely rigorous, sometimes painful experience, and people with back or joint problems should not undergo it without seeking medical advice first. But it's can also be very pleasurable. It's okay to ask if you want softer pressure (*bow bow, kup/ka*).

Massage artists primarily work with their hands, but they sometimes use elbows, knees, and feet to perform deep-tissue kneading. They occasionally apply balm to ease muscle aches, but they traditionally don't use oil. They may push and pull your body through a series of often contorted yogic stretching movements. There's normally a set sequence: You start lying on your back and the massage artist will work from your feet through your legs, arms, hands, and fingers. Then you turn over for legs, back, neck, head, and face. At the end the masseur will stretch your back across his or her upturned knees. Some people find that they have better flexibility after a massage, in addition to relief from muscular aches.

Massages are booked by the hour, and aficionados say two hours is best to get the full benefit. In most shop-house parlors, the masseuse will first bathe your feet and then give you a pair of pajamas to wear. Spas have shower facilities. You can remove your underwear or not—whatever makes you comfortable.

The standard varies enormously. If you find a masseur or masseuse you like, take their name (sometimes they'll have an identifying number as well) and return to them next time.

Tipping

Tipping is customary. There aren't hard and fast rules about how much to tip, but B50 to B150 at a shophouse, and 10% to 20% in a spa, is about right.

BATHHOUSE "MASSAGE"

Often classically ornate, with names like Poseidon, barn-like bathhouses and saunas are fronts for prostitution. They offer the euphemistic "massage" for which Thailand has had a reputation since the Vietnam War. Luckily, they're fairly easy to avoid—masseuses are usually on display behind a glass partition, and the treatment menu will include options like "soapy massage."

Alternative Massage

Foot massage: This popular treatment is typically an hour-long massage of the feet and lower legs, usually with oil or balm. Foot massage is based on the reflexology principle that manipulating pressure points in the feet can relieve disorders in other parts of the body.

Oil Massage: Most parlors and spas now offer oil massage, which is a gentler treatment based on Swedish massage and doesn't involve stretching. Masseurs will sometimes use oils with delicious aromas, such as lemongrass or jasmine.

Learn the Art of Massage

Bangkok's Wat Po is an acknowledged instruction center with an almost 200-year pedigree. A five-day, 30-hour course costs B8,500. You can get more information on their Web site, 🌐*www.watpomassage.com*. The Thai Massage School in Chiang Mai (🌐*www.tmcschool.com*) is also good. Many shophouse parlors in both cities now also offer courses (a one-hour session at a Khao San Road shophouse costs about B250).

IF YOU LIKE

Ancient Cities and Ruins

Prior to its current incarnation as a unified modern state, Thailand consisted of a series of smaller kingdoms. While some of these kingdoms were destroyed when neighboring armies invaded, others merely lost influence as they merged with other Siamese cities and remained beautifully intact.

Angkor Wat. Yes, it's actually in Cambodia, not Thailand—but this massive ancient city, built by a succession of Khmer kings between the 9th and 13th centuries, which has miraculously survived the ravages of time and the Khmer Rouge, is Southeast Asia's most spectacular architectural site.

Sukhothai. Thailand's first capital, Sukhothai was established in 1238 and saw over 100 years of prosperity and artistic development known as Thailand's Golden Age. Sukhothai began to lose its regional influence in the 14th century, ultimately falling under Ayutthaya's control. Its Khmer- and Hindu-influenced sculpture and architecture are relatively unspoiled by the ages.

Chiang Mai. The Old City of Chiang Mai has continued to develop so that today its streets include bars and minimarts. Regardless, a stroll through the back alleys, both inside and outside the old walls, reveals centuries-old masterpieces of Thai art and architecture.

Ayutthaya. After a number of unsuccessful attempts, the Burmese sacked and brutally destroyed this city, which was the second Siamese capital, in 1767. The redbrick foundations of the Old City and its remaining stupas and wats are now beautiful ruins to explore.

Beaches

Thailand's clear turquoise waters and soft, white, palm-fringed sands are stunning, and they offer plenty more to do than sunbathing and sunset strolls.

Koh Samui. The beaches of Samui offer something to suit most travelers' moods: bustling Chaweng Beach, the fishermen's village of Bophut, the scented oils of spa retreats, and the briny aromas of beachfront shacks. Serious divers head for neighboring island Koh Tao.

Nang Cape/Railay Beach. These four connected beaches are only accessible by boat, but it's an easy 15-minute trip from Krabi Town on the mainland. Two of the beaches, Tonsai and East Railay, are rock-climbing centers; West Railay is known for its gorgeous sunsets; and beautiful Phra Nang has a cave with phallic offerings left for a fabled princess.

Koh Phi Phi. These six islands have some of the best diving and snorkeling in Thailand. Crowds flock to Maya Bay both for its spectacular scenery and because it's where the movie *The Beach* was filmed; Loh Samah Bay is more secluded.

Phang Nga Bay. This national marine park is an eerily beautiful landscape dotted with limestone islands and karsts that rise like vertical sculptures from the sea. Many people come to kayak, to visit James Bond Island, or explore sea caves with prehistoric rock art.

Similan Islands. These nine islands in the Andaman Sea, part of the Mu Koh Similan National Marine Park, are considered Thailand's best dive sites. Visibility is exceptional, and encounters with whale sharks are not uncommon. The isolation heightens the appeal.

Shopping

The first time you set foot in one of Thailand's ubiquitous markets you'll be absolutely mesmerized by the variety of goods, from hand-carved figurines to polo shirts with the alligator slightly askew. In larger cities, malls sell international brands at prices significantly lower than in Singapore or Hong Kong.

Chatuchak Weekend Market. Also called "JJ," this is one of the world's largest markets. Every weekend, thousands of locals and tourists flock to northern Bangkok to navigate the mazes of stalls shopping for pets, clothing, souvenirs, and almost anything else imaginable.

Bangkok's Shopping Streets. Bangkok's glitziest megamalls are located on a section of Thanon Rama I and Thanon Ploenchit. A skywalk links the malls, including upscale Siam Paragon and Central World and mid-range Siam Center, allowing you to bypass the heat and congestion of the busy streets below. There's a lot more than clothing here, too—great bookshops, fabrics, electronics, Ferraris.... Siam Paragon mall even has an aquarium where you can scuba dive.

Night Markets. Put on your best bargaining face and hit the streets of Silom, Patpong, Sukhumvit, and Khao San for the best night-market shopping in Bangkok. Most towns, including Chiang Mai, Pattaya, and Hua Hin, have great souvenirs available after dark.

Bangkok's Chinatown. In Bangkok, if you ask where you can buy something, the answer is usually, "Try Chinatown." Anything goes in this labyrinthine quarter, equally flush with gold shops and grubby souvenir stalls.

Trekking

Thailand's mountain forests would make for good trekking for their rugged beauty alone, but this terrain is also home to various hill tribes—Karen, Hmong, Yao, and many others—that maintain their own traditional languages and cultures. The more remote the village, the more authentic the experience (and the more challenging the trek).

Chiang Mai. The city of Chiang Mai is one of two northern centers for both easygoing and adventurous tours to hill tribe villages, some of which accommodate overnight visitors. Elephant rides and bamboo rafting are often included. From here, it's easy to get to departure points in Pai and Mae Hong Son.

Luang Prabang. Treks in northern Laos practically transport you back in time. In some villages, the only apparent connections to the outside world are discharged Vietnam War–era bombs used as water troughs.

Chiang Rai. Another northern gem for soft adventure enthusiasts, the city of Chiang Rai has many tour operators and individual guides. Lahu, Akha, and Lisu villages are all easily accessible from here. There's a growing number of eco-conscious initiatives and it pays to shop around, both here and in Chiang Mai. Guesthouses can often recommend operators and guides.

Kanchanaburi. Though Kanchanaburi itself is a touristy town, the surrounding area offers some of the most untouched landscape in the country, most of it in national parks. Parts of Sai Yok National Park, with its Kitti's Hog-nosed Bats (the world's smallest mammal), are easy to reach from Kanchanaburi, as is seven-tiered Erawan Waterfall.

WHERE TO STAY BEACHSIDE

Thailand's beaches are so inviting you might be tempted to sleep under the stars. And you can do that if you like, but there are tons of other surfside lodging choices. So even if you're on a budget, there's no need to camp out—or move inland.

Resorts

Luxury Living: There's no shortage of exclusive beach resorts, and though these getaways have traditionally been part of large chains, smaller players—some of them independent—are becoming more common. A number of resorts, such as **Pimalai Resort** on Koh Lanta (*www.pimalai.com*) and **Amanpuri Resort** on Phuket (*www.amanpuri.com*), are offering villa-type accommodations for those who want resort amenities but more privacy than hotel rooms afford. Spas like **Chiva-Som** in Hua Hin (*www.chiva-som.com*) are luring pop stars and models through their doors.

Thai Style: In Thailand, the term *resort* is often used for any accommodation that's not in an urban area—it doesn't necessarily mean there are extra facilities. That said, some of these lower-key Thai-style resorts are worth checking out. Though they're not as sumptuous as luxury resorts, they're often tastefully executed and come with a moderate price tag. At friendly **Sarikantang Resort & Spa** on Koh Phangan (*www.sarikantang.com*), the priciest bungalows are around $120 in high season; **Black Tip Dive Resort** on Koh Tao (*www.blacktipdiving.com*) runs a great diving school.

Eco: At earth-friendly resorts, the emphasis is on using natural materials and preserving resources and land. **Chumphon Cabana Beach Resort** (*www.cabana.co.th*) uses bacteria to clean wastewater and produce organic fertilizer.

Private Houses

Rental houses are much less pricey than resort villas and come in all sorts of styles. A few Web sites to check are *www.thailandretreats.com*; *www.worldvacationrentals.net;* and *www.raileibeachclub.com*. Newspapers like the *Bangkok Post* and the *Pattaya Mail* often list rentals and agents.

Stilt Houses

Bungalows and houses built on stilts above the water make romantic, exotic accommodations. Some are custom built for tourist luxury; others, like **Koh Mak Panorama Resort** near Koh Chang and **SB Cabana** on Koh Tao are rustic but still breathtaking.

Budget Bungalows

Warm weather and beautiful palm-fringed beaches mean you can spend just a few dollars on a room and still be in paradise. **Somewhere Else** on Koh Lanta has funky huts and friendly staff; **Smile Bungalows** on Koh Phangan has great ocean views. At the cheapest places you'll share a bathroom, have cold showers, and sleep to the whirring of a rickety fan (unless the power's out).

Rangers Huts

Many national parks, including the Surin Islands and Similan Islands, have accommodation in rangers' huts, bookable through the national park authorities (*www.dnp.go.th/parkreserve/*) or Thai Forest Booking (*www.thaiforestbooking.com*). Prices start at around B100 per person in a very basic hut that sleeps up to 10 people.

GREAT ITINERARIES

HIGHLIGHTS OF THAILAND: BANGKOK, BEACHES & THE NORTH

10 days

To get the most out of your Thailand vacation, decide what you'd particularly like to do—party in the big city, lie on the beach, go trekking, etc.—and arrange your trip around the region best suited for that activity. Every region has so much to offer, you'll barely scratch the surface in two weeks. However, if you don't know where to start, the following itinerary will allow you see three very different areas of the country without requiring too many marathon travel days.

Almost every trip to Thailand begins in Bangkok, which is a good place to linger for a day or two, because some of the country's most astounding sights can be found in and around the Old City. You'll probably be exhausted by the pace in a few days, so head down to the beach, where you can swim in clear seas and sip cocktails on white sands. After relaxing for a few days, you'll be ready for more adventures, so head to Thailand's second city, Chiang Mai. The surrounding countryside is beautiful and even a short stay will give you a chance to visit centuries-old architecture and the Elephant Conservation Center.

Days 1 & 2: Bangkok

Experience the old Thailand hiding within this modern megalopolis by beginning your first day with a tour of Bangkok's Old City, with visits to the stunning Grand Palace and Wat Po's Reclining Buddha. Later in the day, hire a longtail boat and spend a couple of hours exploring the canals. On the river, you'll catch a glimpse of how countless city people lived until not long ago, in wooden stilt houses along the water's edge. For a casual evening, head to the backpacker hangout of Khao San Road for cheap dinner, fun shopping, and bar hopping. For something fancy, take a ferry to the Oriental Hotel for riverside cocktails and dinner at Le Normandie.

GREAT ITINERARIES

Start Day 2 with the sights and smells of Chinatown, sampling some of the delicious food along the way. Then head north to silk mogul Jim Thomson's House, a fine example of a traditional teak abode, with antiques displayed inside. If you're up for more shopping, the malls near Siam Square are great browsing territory for local and international fashion, jewelry, and accessories. The malls also have a couple movie theaters and a bowling alley—Siam Paragon even has an aquarium with sharks. Later, grab a meal at Ban Khun Mae, then if you've got any energy left, head over to Lumphini Stadium for a Thai boxing match.

Days 3 to 5: The Beaches

Get an early start and head down to the beaches regions. Your choices are too numerous to list here, but Koh Samui, Phuket, and Krabi are all good bets if time is short because of the direct daily flights that connect them with Bangkok. Peaceful Khao Lak is only a two-hour drive from the bustle of Phuket, and Koh Chang is just a couple of hours by ferry from Trat airport. Closer to Bangkok, Koh Samet and Hua Hin are just three hours away by road. But if you have at least three days to spare, you can go almost anywhere that peaks your interest—just make sure the time spent traveling doesn't overshadow the time spent relaxing.

Samui, Phuket, and Krabi are also good choices because of the variety of activities each offers. Though Samui has traditionally been backpacker terrain, there are now a number of spa retreats on the island. You can also hike to a waterfall, careen down a treetop zip line, or take a side trip to Angthong National Marine Park. Phuket is the country's main diving center, offering trips to many nearby reefs. There's great sailing around Phuket, too. On Krabi, you can enjoy a relaxing afternoon and cheap beachside massage at gorgeous Phra Nang Beach; go rock-climbing on limestone cliffs; kayak from bay to bay; and watch the glorious sunset from nearby Railay Beach.

Day 6: Chiang Mai

Though it shouldn't be a terribly taxing day, getting to Chiang Mai requires some travel time, so you should get an early start. Wherever you are, you'll have to make a connecting flight in Bangkok; if you're pinching pennies, this actually works in your favor because it's cheaper to book two separate flights on a low-cost airline than to book one ticket from a more expensive airline "directly" from one of the beaches airports to Chiang Mai—you'll have to stop in Bangkok anyway. If you play your cards right, you should be in Chiang Mai in time to check into your hotel and grab a late lunch. Afterwards, stroll around the Old City, and in the evening go shopping at the famous night market.

Day 7: Chiang Mai

Spend the day exploring the city and visiting the dazzling hilltop wat of Doi Suthep. Ring the dozens of bells surrounding the main building for good luck. On the way back to Chiang Mai, drop in to the seven-spired temple called Wat Chedi Yot or check out the pandas at the zoo. Chiang Mai is famous for its massage and cooking schools, so if you're interested in trying a class in either—or just getting a massage—this is the place to do it.

Day 8: Lampang

An easy side trip from Chiang Mai, Lampang has some beautiful wooden-house architecture and a sedate way of getting around, in horse-drawn carriages.

A short ride out of town is northern Thailand's most revered temple, Wat Phra That Lampang Luang, which contains the country's oldest wooden building. At the Elephant Conservation Center, between Chiang Mai and Lampang, you can take elephant rides, watch the pachyderms bathing in the river, and hear them playing in an orchestra. Proceeds go to promoting elephant welfare.

Day 9: Around Chiang Mai

Your last day in the region can be spent in a variety of ways. Shoppers can takes taxis to the many nearby crafts villages, such as Ban Tawai or Baan Mai Kham, or to Lamphun, which has some pre-Thai-era temple architecture from the 7th century. Active types can head to Doi Inthanon National Park, where there are great views across the mountains towards Myanmar (Burma), plus bird-watching, hiking to waterfalls, and wildlife that includes Asiatic Black Bears.

Day 10: Bangkok

Head back to Bangkok. If you're not flying home the moment you step off the plane from Chiang Mai, spend your final day in the city doing some last-minute shopping around the city's numerous markets, such as Pratunam, Pahuraht, and the weekend-only Chatuchak. Or just relax in Lumphini Park.

TIPS

Temples and royal buildings, such as Bangkok's Grand Palace, require modest dress.

Take a taxi to the Grand Palace or an Express Boat to nearby Tha Chang Pier. Wat Po is a ten-minute walk south. Hire a longtail boat to get to the canals and back at Tha Chang Pier. Khao San Road is a short taxi ride from the pier.

Bangkok Airways owns the airport at Koh Samui and flights there are relatively expensive due to taxes, but if you book online directly from Bangkok Airways, you'll get reduced airfare on the first and last flight of the day. Nok Air and Air Asia also offer cheap flights.

Late November through April is the best time to explore the Andaman Coast. For the Gulf Coast there's good weather from late November until August.

Hotels in the south are frequently packed during high season and Thai holidays, so book in advance.

A great alternative to heading north to Chiang Mai is to use Bangkok as a base to explore the Central Plains. Sukhothai Historical Park isn't as famous as Ayutthaya, but it is even more spectacular, and it and the surrounding region would make an excellent two- to three-day side trip from Bangkok.

ECOTOURISM IN THAILAND

Though the tourism boom has been great for Thailand's economy, it has had many negative effects on Thai culture and natural resources. These problems, which range from water pollution to sex tourism to the transformation of hill tribe villages into virtual theme parks, are difficult to rein in. The good news is that a growing number of tour operators and hotel proprietors are addressing these issues, and are therefore worthy of your support.

Planning Your Trip

Though the worldwide eco trend is catching on in Thailand, truly eco-friendly companies are still thin on the ground. Many businesses describe themselves as "eco," so ask some tough questions about what the company does to preserve the environment and help local communities before you book. And as always, don't be afraid to shop around. Your critical eye will help raise standards. Here are a few questions you might ask.

Accommodations: Ask whether the hotel or resort is energy efficient. Does it use alternative power sources? What steps does it take to conserve water and reduce waste? Does it recycle? Is the building made with any natural or recycled materials? Does it employ members of the local community? Does it contribute any percentage of profits to health, education, or wildlife preservation initiatives?

Elephant Treks: It's important to find out how tour operators treat their elephants. You might ask how many hours a day the elephants work, and whether you'll be riding in the afternoon heat, or resting until its cooler.

Hill Tribe Tours & Other Expeditions: How much the operator knows about the village or wilderness area you'll be visiting is often telling, so ask for details. Also, does the operator work with any NGOs or other interest groups to protect the culture and/or the environment?

Resources

The umbrella group **Thailand Community Based Tourism Institute** (🌐 *www.cbt-i.org*) is a good place to start. They provide information about tour agencies and community programs that promote culturally sensitive tourism.

"Voluntourism"—travel that includes an effort to give back to local communities—is a growing trend in Thailand, and a number of organizations are now offering educational travel programs that incorporate some volunteer work. Lots of businesses are offering eco-minded tours; here are a few reputable ones to get you started:

East West Siam's Himmapaan Project (🌐 *www.ewsiam.com*) is a reforestation initiative near Chiang Mai. Participants work alongside tribespeople and forestry experts to promote biodiversity.

The **Educational Travel Center** (🌐 *www.etc.co.th*) organizes cultural exchanges and eco tours, as well as volunteer programs at a variety of destinations.

North by North East Tours (🌐 *www.north-by-north-east.com*) works in both Thailand and Laos, offering homestays and volunteer work such as building schools, teaching English, and providing medical care.

Lost Horizons (🌐 *www.losthorizonsasia.com*) runs several thematic eco-tourism trips in Thailand, including jungle treks, kayaking, beach retreats, and animal conservation.

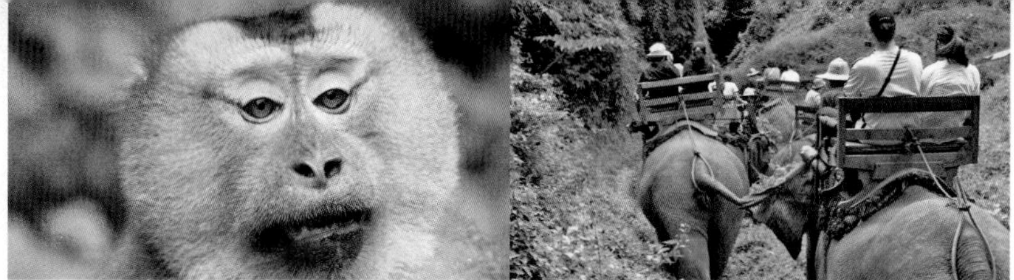

Animal Rights

Though preserving wildlife habitats is a priority in Thailand's national parks, illegal poaching is still rampant. There's such high demand for tiger products (not only skins, but also teeth, bones, and penises, which are used as charms or in traditional medicines) that tigers are now virtually extinct in Thailand.

Elephants are revered in Thailand, where they have a long history as laborers. But mechanization has made elephants' traditional timber-hauling jobs obsolete, and elephant handlers (*mahouts*) now rely on elephant shows, treks, and other tourism-related business for their livelihood. Unfortunately, these endeavors often lead to mistreatment. Yet if there's no work, handlers can't afford the 550 pounds of food and 60 gallons of water an elephant consumes each day; malnutrition is another problem for Thai elephants. Organizations like **Peunpa** (🌐*www.peunpa.org*) focus on broader issues, including educating village communities on the importance of wildlife conservation and how to combat problems like illegal trafficking of endangered species.

What You Can Do

Whatever kind of trip you're planning, there are a few simple things you can do to ensure that you're part of the solution, not part of the problem.

Don't litter. Sadly, garbage is a common sight on Thailand's once-pristine beaches. Litter is hazardous to marine life. You can help by disposing of your rubbish properly; you can also pay a little extra for bio-degradable glass water bottles. If you plan to travel regularly in the developing world, consider buying a hand-pump water purifier, available at many sporting goods stores for $20 and up. You can make your own clean water wherever you go, instead of generating a trail of disposable water bottles.

Don't disturb animal and plant life. Whether you're trekking or snorkeling, be as unobtrusive as possible. Don't remove plants or coral for souvenirs, and don't feed fish or other animals, even if your guide says it's OK.

Respect local customs. Though it may seem like a matter of etiquette, demonstrating respect for a culture is part of ecotourism. Thais tend to be exceedingly tolerant of Western behavior, but tourists who are ignorant about basic customs have a negative effect on the communities they encounter. Take a little time to learn about major cultural mores (especially those related to Buddhism). Thais will appreciate your efforts.

ECOTOURISM VS. SUSTAINABLE TOURISM

Ecotourism is travel to natural areas to observe and learn about wildlife, tourism that refrains from damaging the environment, or tourism that strengthens conservation and improves the lives of local people.

Sustainable tourism has a wider scope that encompasses the definition of ecotourism but also includes increased ecological responsibility throughout the entire travel industry, in everything from city hotels to cruise shops. Not all ecotourism is sustainable tourism.

BUDDHISM IN THAILAND

Today almost 95% of Thailand's population are Buddhist (4% are Muslims, and the remaining 1% are Taoists, Confucianists, Hindus, Christians, and Sikhs). Buddhism is considered one of the foundations of Thai nationhood and is represented on the flag by two white bars between red bars for the people and a central blue bar for the monarchy. Thai kings are required to be Buddhist: King Rama IV spent 27 years as a forest monk before ascending the throne in 1851. The country has 400,000 monks and novices, many of whom take alms bowls into the street at dawn each day to receive food from laypeople.

Origins

Buddhism first showed up in Thailand in the Dvaravati Mon kingdom between the 6th and 9th centuries. The Dvaravati capital of Nakhon Pathom, 34 mi west of Bangkok, was the region's first Buddhist center. In the 14th century, Buddhism became the official religion of Sukhothai, the first Thai kingdom. In 1997, it was written into the constitution as the state religion of modern Thailand. There are two main branches of Buddhism in Asia: Theravada, found today in Thailand, Myanmar (Burma), and Sri Lanka; and Mahayana, which spread northward from India to China, Korea, Vietnam, and Japan. The Mahayana movement emerged from Theravada, the original teachings of the Buddha, in the 1st century. It's a less austere doctrine and therefore more accessible than Theravada, which stresses devotion to study and meditation. (*For more on Buddhism The Buddha in Thailand, Chapter 4.*)

Practice & Rituals

Thai children learn Buddhist teachings (Dhamma) in school, and most males will at some time ordain as a bhikku (monk). Some only do this for a few days, but many join the monkhood each July for the three-month Rains Retreat (a religious retreat, sometimes referred to as Buddhist Lent, when monks are required to remain in their wats for the duration of the rainy season) in July, which is marked by major festivals, such as the Candle Parade, in Nakhon Ratchasima. Joining the monkhood, even for a short time, is such an important event that employers grant time off work for the purpose. Women wanting to devote their lives to Buddhism may become white-robed nuns, known as mae chi. However, women aren't allowed to be officially ordained in Thailand, though a growing feminist lobby questions their lower status. Although most Thais don't visit temples regularly, wats are the center of community life and sometimes serve as schools, meeting halls, and hospitals. Alongside spiritual guidance and funeral rites, monks provide ceremonies in houses and businesses to bring good fortune, and will even bless vehicles to keep drivers safe from accidents. They are also traditional healers and created many of the herbal remedies that now form the basis for New Age spa treatments.

Modern Concerns

Many Thai commentators fear that rapid modernization is eroding Thailand's traditional Buddhist values and that material rewards will overshadow the Buddha's teachings. It's true that greater personal wealth has brought consumerism to the middle classes, and young Thais are exposed to western culture through foreign education, TV, and the Internet. However, Buddhism continues to be the dominant influence on the national psyche.

COUPS & THE KING

THAILAND'S TURBULENT HISTORY

by Karen Coates

Thais share a reverence for their king, Bhumibol Adulyadej, who has been the nation's moral leader and a unifying figure since 1946. Thais are also united by a deep pride in their country, a constitutional monarchy and the only Southeast Asian nation never colonized by Europeans. But this hasn't stopped political turmoil from roiling beneath the surface and erupting.

Though northeastern Thailand has been inhabited for about 2,500 years, it wasn't until 1238 that Thai princes drove the Cambodian Khmers out of central Thailand and established Sukhothai, the first centralized Thai state. There was conflict again in the late 14th century, when the rival state of Ayutthaya conquered Sukhothai. After over 400 years of power, Ayutthaya in turn was defeated by the Burmese in the late 18th century, and the Thais established a new capital in Bangkok.

As European influence in Southeast Asia grew, Thailand alternated between periods of isolation and openness to foreign trade and ideas. Western-style democracy was one idea that took hold in the early 20th century. But since then a pattern has emerged in Thai politics: a prime minister is elected, allegations of corruption surface, the public protests, and the leader is ousted.

King Rama V (1853–1910) and family

(top) Pottery found at Ban Chiang; (left) stone face at Bayon in Angkor Thom, Cambodia; (bottom) Khmer elephant-shaped box.

4000–2000 BC

Bronze & Rice

Scientists think that northeastern Thailand was a hotbed for agricultural innovation. In fact, the Mon people from modern-day Myanmar who settled in Ban Chiang may have been Asia's first farmers. Archaeologists have found ancient pottery, bronze rings, spearheads, bracelets, and axes.

■ Visit:
Ban Chiang archaeological site (⇨ Ch. 7).

500–1400

Great Migrations

Historians believe the Thais' ancestors were the ethnic Tai people of southern China. The Tai migrated south into modern-day Thailand in waves, but the biggest southern push came after the Mongols invaded their kingdom in the 13th century. The fleeing Tai settled in the Mekong River Valley, inventing elaborate agricultural systems to farm rice. Around this time, the Khmers of what is today called Cambodia were extending the Angkor empire west into Thailand.

■ Visit:
Prasat Hin Phimai; Prasat Khao Phra Wihan (⇨ Ch. 7).

1238–1438

Sukhothai & the Golden Age

In 1238 chieftains established the first Thai kingdom at Sukhothai in central Thailand, kicking out the Khmer overlords. The Sukhothai kingdom united many Thai settlements and marked the beginning of a prosperous era when, legend has it, the rivers were full of fish, and the paddies were lush with rice. In the late 13th century, King Ramkhamhaeng created a writing system that is the basis of the modern Thai alphabet.

■ Visit:
Sukhothai (⇨ Ch. 4).

1511 Portuguese arrive
1767 Ayutthaya falls to Burmese invaders
1782 Capital moves to Bangkok

1500 1600 1700 1800

(left) Interior of Wat Po, Bangkok; (top) Royal jewelry from Ayutthaya; (bottom) Buddha statue from Ayutthaya.

1350–1767 Ayutthaya Kingdom

King Ramathibodi founded the kingdom of Ayutthaya, 45 miles up the Chao Phraya River from Bangkok, in 1350 and took over Sukhothai 25 years later. The king made Theravada Buddhism the kingdom's official religion and established the Dharmashastra, a legal code with roots in Hindu Indian texts. Ayutthaya, a city of canals and golden temples, became wealthy and prominent.

■ Visit:
Ayutthaya (⇨ Ch. 4).

1511–1800s European Influence

The Portuguese were the first Europeans to arrive in Thailand, establishing an embassy in Ayutthaya in 1511. But they brought more than ambassadors: The Portuguese also brought the first chilies to the country, making a huge contribution to Thai cuisine.

Over the following centuries of European trade and relations, Thailand's kings charted a sometimes tenuous course of autonomy as their neighbors were colonized by the Portuguese, Dutch, English, and French.

■ Visit:
National Museum (⇨ Ch. 2).

1767–1809 Burmese Invasion & New Beginnings

In 1767 the Burmese sacked Ayutthaya, destroying palaces, temples, artwork, and written records. But within two years, General Phraya Taksin ran out the Burmese and established a new capital at Thonburi, which is today a part of Bangkok. Taksin became king but was forced from power and executed in 1782. After this coup, Buddha Yodfa Chulaloke the Great (known as Rama I) took control. He moved the capital across the river, where he built the Grand Palace in the image of past Thai kingdoms.

■ Visit:
Thonburi; Grand Palace (⇨ Ch. 2).

1850 | 1875 | 1893–1907 Territory ceded to French | 1900

(left) King Mongkut with queen;
(top) *The King and I;*
(bottom) 19th-century tin coin.

1851–1931 *The King and I* & Beyond

In 1862, Anna Leonowens, an English schoolteacher, traveled to Bangkok with her son to serve as royal governess to King Mongkut's wives and children. Leonowens's memoirs inspired Margaret Landon's controversial novel *Anna and the King of Siam,* which in turn was the basis for the well-known Broadway musical *The King and I* and the subsequent film.

Thais were deeply offended by the film, which portrays the king as foolish and barbaric; *The King and I* was consequently banned in Thailand. A 1999 remake, *Anna and the King,* followed Leonowens's version of the story more closely, but Thais, who are extremely devoted to their royal family, still found this version culturally insensitive.

Mongkut (or Rama IV) earned the nickname "Father of Science and Technology" for his efforts to modernize the country. He signed a trade treaty with Great Britain, warding off other colonial powers while opening Thailand to foreign innovation.

After Rama IV's death in 1868, his son Chulalongkorn became king. Also called "Rama the Great," Chulalongkorn is credited with preserving Thailand's independence and abolishing slavery.

■ Visit:
The Grand Palace (⇨ Ch. 2).

1932–41 Constitutional Era

Thailand moved toward Western-style democracy when young intellectuals staged a bloodless coup against King Prajadhipok (Rama VII) in 1931. Thailand's first constitution was signed that year and parliamentary elections were held the next. In the new system—a constitutional monarchy similar to England's—the king is still head of state, but he doesn't have much legal power.

In 1939 the government changed the country's name from Siam to Thailand. The new name refers to the Tai people; Tai also means "free" in Thai.

■ Visit:
Kukrit Pramoj Heritage House (⇨ Ch. 2).

(left) Bridge over the River Kwai; (top) U.S. pilot in Vietnam; (bottom) Postage stamp c. 1950 featuring king Bhumibol Adulyadej.

World War II

1941–46

In 1941, Japan helped Thailand win a territorial conflict with France over parts of French Indochina (modern-day Cambodia, Laos, and Vietnam.) Later that year, the Japanese demanded free passage through Thailand so that they could attack Malaya and Burma. In 1942, under the leadership of Phibun, a military general elected prime minister in 1938, Thailand formed an alliance with Japan.

The Japanese conquered Burma and began to construct the Thailand–Burma "Death Railway," so named because over 100,000 Asian forced-laborers and Allied POWs died while working on it. Meanwhile, an underground resistance called Seri Thai gathered strength as Thais turned against the Phibun regime and the Japanese occupation. Phibun was ousted in 1944 and replaced by a government friendly to the Allies.

In 1946 King Rama VIII was murdered. He was succeeded by his brother, the beloved Bhumibol Adulyadej (Rama IX), who is currently the world's longest-serving head of state.

■ Visit:
Bridge on the River Kwai; Kanchanaburi War Cemetery; Chong-Kai War Cemetery; Thailand-Burma Railway Center (⇨ Ch. 3).

The Vietnam War

1961–75

While publicly staying neutral, the Thai government let the U.S. Air Force use bases throughout Thailand to bomb Laos and Cambodia between 1961 and 1975. Meanwhile, Bangkok and Thailand's beaches became playgrounds to thousands of soldiers on leave. The Westernization of Thai popular culture has roots in the Vietnam era, when restaurants and bars catered to beer- and Coke-drinking Americans.

■ Visit:
Udon Thani (⇨ Ch. 7); National Museum; Plain of Jars (⇨ Ch. 9).

(left) Protesters occupying the Government House garden. Bangkok, September 3rd 2008; (top) Banner demanding that ousted P.M. Thaksin Shinawatra and his wife return to Thailand to stand trial; (bottom) Samak Sundaravej.

Unrest

A new democracy movement gained force in 1973, when protesters charged the streets of Bangkok after students were arrested on antigovernment charges. On October 14, protests erupted into bloody street battles, killing dozens. More violent outbreaks occurred on October 6th, 1976, and again in "Black May" of 1992, when a military crackdown resulted in more than 50 deaths.

In 2001, billionaire Thaksin Shinawatra was elected prime minister on a platform of economic growth and rural development. The year after he was elected, he dissolved the liaison between the Muslim southern provinces and the largely Buddhist administration in Bangkok, rekindling bloody unrest after years of quiet. The situation escalated until insurgents attacked a Thai army arsenal in early 2004; at this writing, over 3,000 people have been killed in frequent outbursts of violence in southern Thailand.

Meanwhile, Thaksin and his family were railed with corruption and tax-evasion charges. In September 2006 he was ousted by a junta, which controlled the country until voters approved a new constitution and elected Samak Sundaravej prime minister. Samak took office in early 2008, but in September, after months of protests, the Consitutional Court demanded his resignation because he had accepted money for hosting a televised cooking show (it's illegal for a prime minister to have other income). Parliament quickly elected Somchai Wongsawat, Thaksin's brother-in-law, to replace Samak.

The protests did not end there, since many Thais believed Somchai's government to be aligned with Thaksin's. In late 2008 Somchai was forced to step down, and Parliament voted in Abhisit Vejjajiva, leader of the opposition party. Thailand's long voyage towards democracy is ongoing.

■ Visit:
Democracy Monument and October 14 Monument (⇨ Ch. 2).

Bangkok

WORD OF MOUTH

"Bangkok is everything you think it is and the complete opposite, simultaneously. It is noisy and crowded, yet serene and spiritual. It is old and traditional, and very sleek and modern. It is incredibly poor and impossibly wealthy. Expensive, and dirt cheap. Well-managed chaos. Easy to navigate, and even easier to get lost.

—ms_go

WELCOME TO BANGKOK

TOP REASONS TO GO

★ **The Canals:** They don't call it "Venice of the East" for nothing. Sure, boat tours are touristy, but the sights, from Khmer wats to bizarre riverside dwellings, are truly unique.

★ **Street Food:** Bangkok may have the best street food in the world. Don't be afraid to try the weird stuff—it's often fresher and better than the food you'd get at a hotel restaurant.

★ **Shopping Bargains:** Forget Hong Kong and Singapore: Bangkok has the same range of high-end designer goods at much lower prices.

★ **Sky-High Sipping:** "Bar with a view" is taken to the extreme when you sip martinis in open-air spaces that are 70 stories high.

★ **Temple-Gazing:** From the venerable Wat Po to the little wats that don't make it into the guidebooks, Bangkok's collection of temples is hard to top.

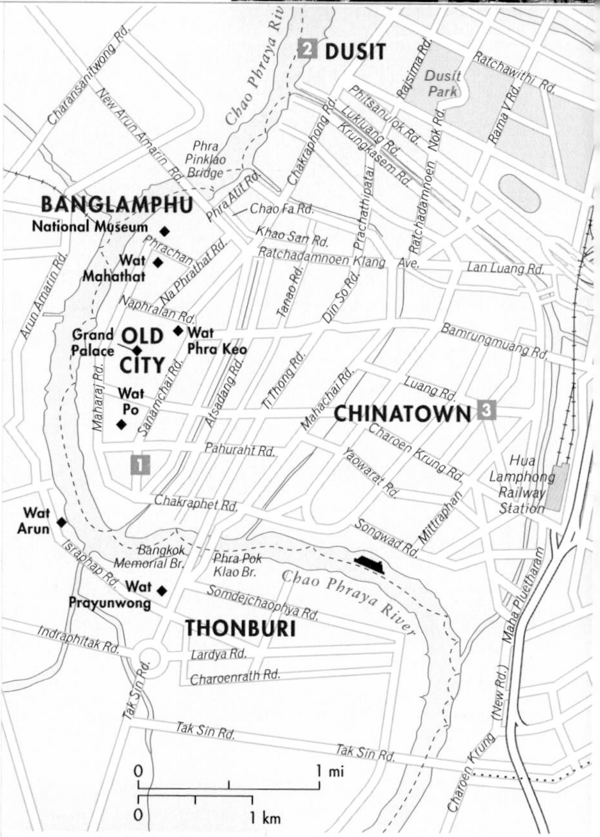

Khao San Road backpacker area

1 The Old City, Thonburi & Banglamphu. The Old City is home to opulent temples like Wat Po. Across the river is Thonburi, a mostly residential neighborhood, where you can find Wat Arun. Banglamphu, north of the Old City, is mostly residential; it's known for famous backpacker street Khao San Road, but it has much more to offer than just touristy kicks with fellow foreigners.

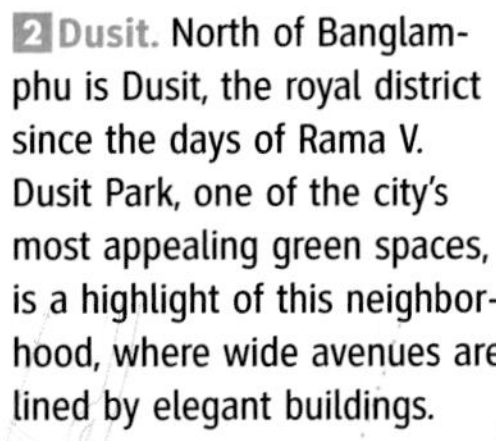

2 Dusit. North of Banglamphu is Dusit, the royal district since the days of Rama V. Dusit Park, one of the city's most appealing green spaces, is a highlight of this neighborhood, where wide avenues are lined by elegant buildings.

Central station, Bangkok.

GETTING ORIENTED

Bangkok's endless maze of streets is part of its fascination and its complexity—getting around a labyrinth is never easy. Although the *S* curve of the Chao Phraya River can throw you off base, it's actually a good landmark. Most of the popular sights are close to the river, and you can use it to get swiftly from one place to another. Also look at the Skytrain and subway to help you navigate and get around quickly.

3 Chinatown. East of the Old City is Chinatown, a labyrinth of streets with restaurants, shops, and warehouses. Within its legendary bustle, you'll find an impressive array of Buddhas for sale, spice boutiques, and open-air fruit and vegetable markets that are among Bangkok's most vibrant. Nearby is the notorious red-light district of Patpong.

4 Downtown Bangkok. "Downtown Bangkok" is actually several neighborhoods in one, and it's truly a mixed bag. In this busy area you'll find Lumphini Park, Bangkok's largest park and a pleasantly green space to escape from the harried pace of the city; Sukhumvit Road, a bustling district filled with restaurants, hotels, shops, tourists, and a famous red-light district; and the riverbank that's home to some of the city's leading hotels.

BANGKOK PLANNER

When to Go

Late October to late March is the best time to visit. The city is at its coolest (85°F) and driest. In April the humidity and heat build up to create a sticky stew until the rains begin in late May.

Visitor Information

The **Tourist Authority of Thailand** (✉ *1600 New Phetchaburi Rd., Sukhumvit* ☎ *02/250–5500* 🌐 *www.tourismthailand.org* Ⓜ *Subway: Sukhumvit; Skytrain: Asok*), open daily 8:30 to 4:30, has more colorful brochures than hard information, but it can supply material on national parks and out-of-the-way destinations. A 24-hour hotline provides information on destinations, festivals, and the arts. You can use the hotline to register complaints or request assistance from the Tourist Police.

Getting Here

By Air: Bangkok's Suvarnabhumi airport (pronounced "Su-wan-na-poom") is 30 km (18 mi) southeast of the city. Bangkok's old international airport, Don Muang (now dubbed DMK), which is 25 km (16 mi) north of the city, now offers domestic flights.

Taxis, cheap and available 24 hours, are the most convenient way to get between downtown and the airport. Get your taxi by taking the free airport shuttle to the airport's Public Transportation Center, then heading to one of the taxi counters on Level 1, near Entrances 3, 4, 7, and 8. State your destination to the dispatcher at the counter, who will lead you to your taxi. Allow 30 minutes to 1½ hours for the trip to or from your hotel, depending on traffic. ■ **TIP→ Don't forget to get Thai baht at the airport, as you'll need it to pay for your taxi.**

The Airport Bus Express is fully operational, and it costs about 40% less than a taxi. The bus runs from 5 AM to midnight. Head to the Airport Bus Counter on Level 1, near Entrance 8 of the Public Transportation Center. The service, which costs B150, operates four routes; ask at the bus terminal which route to take to reach your hotel. Route AE1 serves the Silom neighborhood. Route AE2 serves Khao San Road and the Old City. Route AE3 serves Sukhumvit, and Route AE4 serves Hua Lumphong, the city's main railway station (⇨ *By Air in Travel Smart for more info*).

By Bus: Bangkok has three major terminals for buses headed to other parts of the country. The Northern Bus Terminal, called Mo Chit, serves Chiang Mai and points north. The Southern Bus Terminal, in Thonburi, is for buses bound for Hua Hin, Koh Samui, Phuket, and points south. The Eastern Bus Terminal, called Ekkamai, is for buses headed to Pattaya, Rayong, and Trat provinces.

Bus companies generally sell tickets on a first-come, first-served basis. This is seldom a problem, as the service is so regular that the next bus is sure to depart before long. The air-conditioned orange 999 buses are the most comfortable. Blue VIP buses, though not quite as luxurious, are the next-best option (⇨ *By Bus in Travel Smart*).

By Train: (⇨ *By Train in Travel Smart.*)

2

Getting Around

Bangkok is large, so remember to pace yourself, and take a break to escape the midday heat. ■TIP→**Don't bother driving in Bangkok.** Traffic is unbearable.

By Boat: (⇨ *Roaming the Waterways box, below.*)

By Bus: For a fare of B8 on non-air-conditioned buses and B12 to B40 on air-conditioned ones, you can travel virtually anywhere in the city. Air-conditioned microbuses charge B25. Most buses operate from 5 AM to around 11 PM, but a few routes operate around the clock. You can pick up a route map at most bookstalls for B35.

By Skytrain & Subway: Although the Skytrain (*Bangkok's Skyways, below*) covers just a fraction of the capital (it bypasses the Old City and Dusit, for example), it is surprisingly convenient for visitors, with routes above Sukhumvit, Silom, and Phaholyothin roads. ■TIP→**If you are traveling between two points along the route, the Skytrain is by far the best way to go.** Rates run between B15 and B40. Like the Skytrain, the subway covers only a small section of the city, but it's a great way to get from the city center out to the train stations. The subway runs daily from 6 AM until midnight. Adult fares are B15 to B50. Although the Skytrain and subway are separate entities and use different fare and ticketing systems, the two connect at three points: Sala Daeng Station and Silom Station, Asok Station and Sukhumvit Station, and Mo Chit Station and Chatuchak Station.

By Taxi: Taxis can be an economical way to get around, provided you don't hit gridlock. Most taxis have meters, so avoid those that lack one or claim that it is broken. The rate for the first 1 km (½ mi) is B35, with an additional baht for every 55 yards after that; a 5 km (3 mi) journey runs about B60. ■TIP→**Ask your concierge to write the name of your destination and its cross streets in Thai.**

WHAT IT COSTS IN BAHT

¢	$	$$	$$$	$$$$
Restaurants				
under B100	B100–B200	B201–B300	B301–B400	over B400
Hotels				
under B1,000	B1,000–B2,000	B2,001–B4,000	B4,001–B6,000	over B6,000

Restaurant prices are for a main course, excluding tax and tip. Hotel prices are for a standard double in high season, excluding service charge and tax.

Safety

For a city of its size, Bangkok is relatively safe; however, you still need to practice common sense. Don't accept food or drinks from strangers, as there have been reports of men and women being drugged and robbed. If you have a massage in your hotel room, put your valuables in a safe; likewise, don't take anything but a bit of cash with you when visiting massage parlors. Bangkok is no more dangerous for women than any other major city, but it's still best to avoid walking alone at night (take a taxi if you're out late).

⚠**Beware of hustlers at the airport who claim your hotel is overbooked.** They'll try to convince you to switch to one that pays them a commission. Also avoid anyone trying to sell you on an overpriced taxi or limo. Proceed to the taxi stand; these taxis will use a meter.

Contact the Tourist Police first in an emergency. For medical attention, Bunrungrad Hospital and Bangkok Nursing Hospital are considered the best.

Emergency Services **Ambulance** (☎ *1669*). **Fire** (☎ *199*). **Police** (☎ *191*). **Tourist Police** (☎ *1155* Ⓜ).

Hospitals **Bangkok Nursing Hospital** (✉ *9 Convent Rd., Silom* ☎ *02/686–2700* Ⓜ *Subway: Silom; Skytrain: Sala Daeng*). **Bumrungrad Hospital** (✉ *33 Sukhumvit Soi 3, Sukhumvit* ☎ *02/667–2525* Ⓜ *Subway: Sukhumvit; Skytrain: Ploenchit*).

EXPLORING BANGKOK

Updated by Robin Goldstein & Alexis Herschkowitsch

THE OLD CITY IS A major destination for travelers, as it's home to opulent temples like Wat Po and Wat Phraw Kaew. Across the river is Thonburi, a mostly residential neighborhood, where you can find Wat Arun. At the northern tip of the Old City is Banglamphu, one of Bangkok's older residential neighborhoods. It's best known now for Khao San Road, a backpacker hangout, though the neighborhood has much more to offer, especially as far as street food goes. North of Banglamphu is Dusit, the royal district since the days of Rama V.

East of the Old City is Chinatown, a labyrinth of streets with restaurants, shops, and warehouses. Patpong, the city's most famous of several red-light districts, is also here, as are some of the city's leading hotels: the Oriental, the Peninsula, the Royal Orchid Sheraton, and the Shangri-La. To the north of Rama IV Road is Bangkok's largest green area, Lumphini Park. Continue north and you reach Sukhumvit Road, once a residential area. More recently, Thonglor, farther east along Sukhumvit, has become the "in" neighborhood for those want to see and be seen and is now home to even busier red-light activity than Patpong.

THE OLD CITY

The Old City, which also includes Banglamphu on the north and Thonburi across the Chao Phraya River on the west, is the historical heart of Bangkok, where you can find most of the ancient buildings and the major tourist attractions. Because of the city's conscious decision to preserve this historic area, it's the largest part of Bangkok to escape constant transformation. Much of the residential sections look rundown, but the whole area is safe and it's one of the best in the city for a stroll.

The Grand Palace and other major sights are within a short distance of the river and close to where express boats stop. There is a Skytrain station next to a boat pier downriver from the Old City as well, making the Chao Phraya convenient no matter where you're staying.

Of course, the magnificence of the sights, and the ease in reaching them, make them rather crowded. During rainstorms is about the only time you find few people at the sights. ■ **TIP→ The palace and the temples are busy every day, but you might have better luck earlier in the morning, when it's also cooler, and before some of the tour buses arrive.**

WHAT TO SEE

Democracy Monument and October 14 Monument. Democracy Monument is one of Bangkok's biggest and best-known landmarks. It was built after the military overthrew the absolute monarchy in 1932 and Thailand became a constitutional monarchy. Just to the south of the road that circles the Democracy Monument is the October 14 Monument, honoring the Thais killed during the student-led uprising against the military government that started on October 14, 1973, and left dozens dead. Tributes to those killed in October 1976 and May 1992, in other protests against military rule, are also part of the monument. Although mostly written in Thai, it's a sobering sight, especially so close to the Democracy Monument. Traffic is always whizzing about, the gate is often closed, and there seem to be no regular hours, but there are painting exhibitions on display at times. ✉ *Ratchdamnoen Rd. at Thanon Din So* Ⓜ *Skytrain: Hua Lamphong.*

❶ **Grand Palace & Wat Phraw Kaew** *(Temple of the Emerald Buddha).*
Fodor's Choice ★ ⇨ *The Grand Palace, below.*

❻ **National Gallery.** Though it doesn't get nearly as much attention as the National Museum, the gallery's permanent collection (modern and traditional Thai art) is worth taking the time to see; there are also frequent temporary shows from around the country and abroad. The easiest way to find out what's showing is to ask your hotel's concierge to call, as you're not likely to get an English-speaker on the phone. To get to the gallery, walk down Na Phra That Road, past the National Theater and toward the river. Go under the bridge, then turn right and walk about 100 yards; it's on your left. The building used to house the royal mint. ✉ *Chao Fa Rd., Old City* ☎ *02/281–2224* 🎟 *B30* ⏲ *Wed.–Sun. 9–4* Ⓜ *Skytrain: Hua Lamphong.*

NEED A BREAK?

Taking in all the sights can be exhausting, especially on a hot-and-muggy day. Fortunately two parks by the Grand Palace provide some respite from the heat. Sanam Luang is north of the palace and Wat Phraw Kaew. Trees offer shade and benches offer a place to sit with a cold drink and a snack from one of the vendors. You can also buy bread if you want to feed the numerous pigeons. Suan Saranrom, across from the southeast corner of the palace, is smaller but just as pleasant. It's surrounded by well-kept old government buildings. In the late afternoon you can join the free community aerobics sessions.

❺ ★ **National Museum.** There's no better place to acquaint yourself with Thai history than the National Museum, which also holds one of the world's best collections of Southeast Asian art. Most of the masterpieces from the northern provinces have been transported here, leaving up-country museums looking a little bare. You have a good opportunity to trace Thailand's long history, beginning with the ceramic utensils and bronze ware of the Ban Chiang people (4000–3000 BC). **TIP→ There are free guided tours in English on Wednesday and Thursday; they're usually given at 9:30 AM, though sometimes the time changes.** ✉ *Na Phra That Rd., Old City* ☎ *02/224–1333* 🌐 *www.thailandmuseum.com* 🎟 *B50* ⏲ *Wed.–Sun. 9:30–4* Ⓜ *Skytrain: Hua Lamphong.*

❷ ★ **Wat Po** *(Temple of the Reclining Buddha).* The city's largest wat has what is perhaps the most unusual representation of the Buddha in Bangkok. The 150-foot sculpture, covered with gold, is so large it fills an entire viharn. Especially noteworthy are the mammoth statue's 10-foot feet, with the 108 auspicious signs of the Buddha inlaid in mother-of-pearl. Many people ring the bells surrounding the image for good luck.

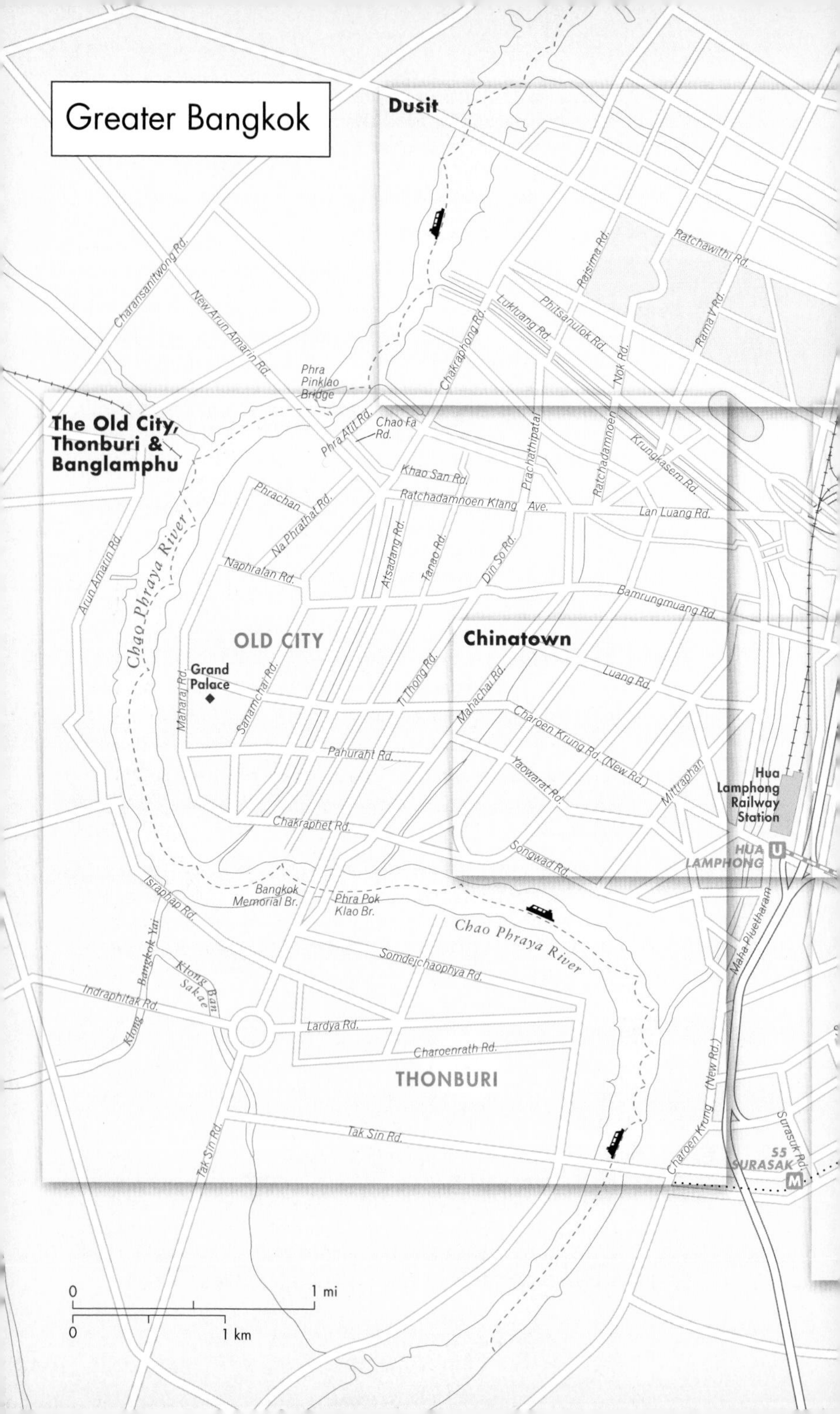

Greater Bangkok
Dusit
The Old City, Thonburi & Banglamphu
Chinatown
OLD CITY
THONBURI
Grand Palace
Phra Pinklao Bridge
Chao Phraya River
Bangkok Memorial Br.
Phra Pok Klao Br.
Hua Lamphong Railway Station
HUA LAMPHONG
SURASAK
Charansanitwong Rd.
New Arun Amarin Rd.
Arun Amarin Rd.
Chakraphong Rd.
Lukluang Rd.
Phitsanulok Rd.
Rajsima Rd.
Ratchawithi Rd.
Rama V Rd.
Nok Rd.
Phra Atit Rd.
Chao Fa Rd.
Khao San Rd.
Ratchadamnoen Klang Ave.
Prachathipatai
Ratchadamnoen
Krungkasem Rd.
Lan Luang Rd.
Phrachan
Na Phrathat Rd.
Naphralan Rd.
Atsadang Rd.
Tanao Rd.
Din So Rd.
Bamrungmuang Rd.
Maharaj Rd.
Sanamchai Rd.
Ti Thong Rd.
Mahachai Rd.
Luang Rd.
Charoen Krung Rd. (New Rd.)
Yaowarat Rd.
Mittraphan
Pahurant Rd.
Chakraphet Rd.
Songwad Rd.
Israphap Rd.
Bangkok Yai
Klong Ban Sakae
Klong
Indraphitak Rd.
Somdejchaophya Rd.
Lardya Rd.
Charoenrath Rd.
Tak Sin Rd.
Charoen Krung (New Rd.)
Maha Pluetharam
Surasuk Rd.
0
1 mi
0
1 km

KEY
Rail lines
MRTA (subway)
BTS Sky Train
River Bus
Downtown Bangkok
Klong Samsen
Ratchawithi Rd.
Rama VI Rd.
Dindaeng Rd.
Rajadapisek Rd.
THAI CULTURAL CENTER
PHRA RAMA 9
Phraram Kao
(Rama IX)
N3 VICTORY MONUMENT
N2 PHAYA THAI
Sri Ayutthaya Rd.
Phayathai Rd.
Ratchaprarop Rd.
Expressway
DOWNTOWN
PETCHABURI
Royal City Ave. (RCA)
Phetchburi Rd.
PRATUNAM
N1 (NORTH) RAJADAPISEK
New Phetchburi Rd.
Klong San Sab
W1 (WEST) NATIONAL STADIUM
SIAM
Siam Square
Ploenchit Rd.
E1 (EAST) CHITLOM
(Rama 1 Rd.)
E2 PHLOENCHIT
Soi 11
Soi 13
Soi 15
E3 NANA
Soi 23
SUKHUMVIT
E4 ASOK
Phayathai Rd.
Henri Dunant Rd.
Ratchadamri Rd.
(Wireless Rd.)
S1 (SOUTH) RATCHADAMRI
Sarasin Rd.
Witthayu
LUMPHINI PARK
SAM YAN
Phraram See
SILOM
(Rama 4 Rd.)
Siphraya Rd.
Patpong 2
Patpong 1
Suriwong Rd.
S2 SALA DAENG
LUMPHINI
Sukhumvit Rd.
Soi 31
E5 PHROM PHONG
Soi 39
Soi 20
Soi 24
E6 THONG LO
QUEEN SIRIKIT
KLONG TOEI
Silom Rd.
SILOM
S3 CHONG NONSI
N. Sathorn Rd.
S. Sathorn Rd.
Soi Suanplu
Phraram See
(Rama IV Rd.)
Soi 26
Aj-Narong Rd.

Behind the viharn holding the Reclining Buddha is Bangkok's oldest open university. A century before Bangkok was established as the capital, a monastery was founded here to teach traditional medicine. Around the walls are marble plaques inscribed with formulas for herbal cures, and stone sculptures squat in various postures demonstrating techniques for relieving pain. The monks still practice ancient cures, and the **massage school** is now famous. A Thai massage (which can actually be painful, though therapeutic) lasts one hour and costs less than B200 (you should also tip B100) Appointments aren't necessary—you usually won't have to wait long if you just show up. Massage courses of up to 10 days are also available.

PHONY GUIDES

One downside to the surge of tourism in this area is the presence of phony tour guides, who will most likely approach you by offering tips about undiscovered or off-the-beaten-path places. Some will even tell you that the place you're going to is closed, and that you should join them for a tour instead. Often their "tours" (offered at too-good-to-be-true prices) include a "short" visit to a gem shop for more than a bit of arm-twisting. The situation got bad enough in the mid-1990s that the government stepped in and distributed fliers to passengers on inbound flights warning of these gem scams.

At the northeastern quarter of the compound there's a pleasant three-tier temple containing 394 seated Buddhas. Usually a monk sits cross-legged at one side of the altar, making himself available to answer questions (in Thai, of course). On the walls, bas-relief plaques salvaged from Ayutthaya depict stories from the *Ramakien,* a traditional tale of the human incarnation of Vishnu. Around the temple area are four tall chedis decorated with brightly colored porcelain. Each chedi represents one of the first four kings of the Chakri Dynasty. Don't be perturbed by the statues that guard the compound's entrance and poke good-natured fun at farang. These towering figures, some of whom wear farcical top hats, are supposed to scare away evil spirits—they were modeled after the Europeans who plundered China during the Opium Wars. ✉ *Chetuphon Rd., Old City* *B50* *Daily 8–6* Ⓜ *Skytrain: Hua Lamphong.*

7 **Wat Rachanada** *(Temple of the Metal Castle).* This wat was built to resemble a mythical castle of the gods. According to legend, a wealthy and pious man built a fabulous castle, Loha Prasat, from the design laid down in Hindu mythology for the disciples of the Buddha. Wat Rachanada, meant to duplicate that castle, is the only one of its kind remaining. Outside there are stalls selling amulets that protect you from harm or increase your chances of finding love. These souvenirs tend to be expensive, but that's the price of good fortune. ✉ *Mahachai Rd. near Ratchadamnoen Rd., Old City* *Free* *Daily 8–5* Ⓜ *Skytrain: Hua Lamphong*

8 **Wat Saket.** A well-known landmark, the towering gold chedi of Wat Saket, which is also known as the Golden Mount, was once the highest point in the city. King Rama III began construction of this temple,

The Old City, Thonburi and Banglamphu

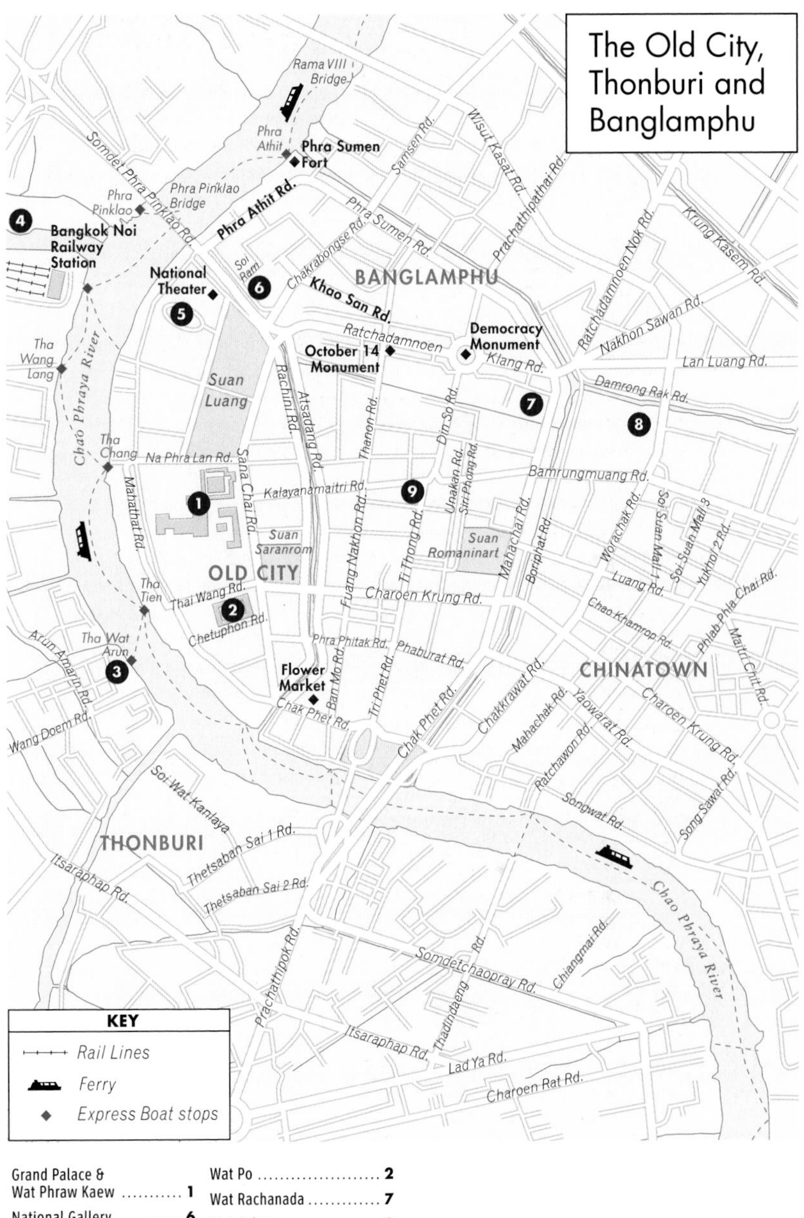

Grand Palace & Wat Phraw Kaew	1
National Gallery	6
National Museum	5
Royal Barge Museum	4
Wat Arun	3
Wat Po	2
Wat Rachanada	7
Wat Saket	8
Wat Suthat & the Giant Swing	9

TWO DAYS IN BANGKOK

You could spend weeks in Bangkok and not get bored. Especially if you only have a few days, planning around Bangkok's traffic is a must, so look for sights near public transportation or close enough to one another to visit on the same day, and don't assume that taxis will be faster than the Skytrain. You can see a lot in a few days. Below is a sample two-day itinerary.

Start your first day with the most famous of all Bangkok sights, the Grand Palace. In the same complex is the gorgeously ornate Wat Phraw Kaew. Not far south of the Grand Palace is Bangkok's oldest and largest temple, Wat Po, famous for its enormous Reclining Buddha and for being the home of the development of traditional Thai massage. Don't miss the chance to try at least a 45-minute massage, which might leave you a bit sore. Later, head toward Banglamphu to take the river walk from Pinklao Bridge to Santichaiprakarn Park. That will put you on Phra Athit Road, where you can find many good restaurants and bars. If you feel up for more after that take a tuk-tuk the short distance to Khao San Road for some shopping and more strolling.

The next day, start out in Chinatown, where you can spend hours browsing the food and spice markets, peeking into temples and shops, and just absorbing the atmosphere. Next, work your way to the Chao Phraya River and take a *klong* (canal) tour, which will give you a glimpse of the fascinating canal life in Bangkok. Then, if it's a weekend head to Kukrit Pramoj Heritage House; if it's a weekday, visit Jim Thompson's House. Take the Skytrain in the evening to Sukhumvit Road, where there are many good restaurants.

but it wasn't completed until the reign of Rama V. ⚠ **To reach the gilded chedi you must ascend an exhausting 318 steps, so don't attempt the climb on a hot afternoon.** On a clear day the view from the top is magnificent. Every November, at the time of the Loi Krathong festival, the temple hosts a popular fair with food stalls and performances. ✉ *Chakkaphatdi Phong Rd., Old City* 🎫 *B20* ⏲ *Daily 8–5* Ⓜ *Skytrain: Hua Lamphong.*

9 **Wat Suthat & the Giant Swing.** Wat Suthat is known for the 19th-century murals in the main chapel, but the numerous statues around the spacious tiled grounds are quite striking, too. There are rows of statue horses along one side of the wat. The Giant Swing (Sao Ching Cha) just outside Wat Suthat (but not part of it) was replaced to great fanfare in late 2006 for the first time in a generation. But it will not be used as it was in ancient times for Brahmanic ceremonies. Apparently, several people were killed in a swing-related accident in the early 20th century and it has been out of service since. It is in a public area that is free to visit. ✉ *Bamrung Muang Rd., Old City* 🎫 *B20* ⏲ *Daily 8:30–9* Ⓜ *Skytrain: Hua Lamphong.*

TUK-TUKS

Though colorful three-wheeled tuk-tuks are somewhat of a symbol of Bangkok, they're really only a good option when traffic is light—otherwise you can end up sitting in gridlock, sweating, and sucking in car fumes. They're also unmetered and prone to overcharging; unless you are good at bargaining you may well end up paying more for a tuk-tuk than for a metered taxi. Some tuk-tuk drivers drive like madmen, and an accident in a tuk-tuk can be scary.

⚠ **Watch out for unscrupulous tuk-tuk drivers who offer tours at a bargain rate, then take you directly to jewelry shops and tailors who pay them a commission.** If a trip to Bangkok does not seem complete without a tuk-tuk adventure, pay half of what the driver suggests, insist on being taken to your destination, and hold on for dear life.

THONBURI

Thonburi is largely residential, including fascinating areas where people still live on the klongs, which are worth a day trip if you have the time. Most of Thonburi beyond the riverbank is of little interest to visitors. Many locals claim it retains more "Thai-ness" than the rest of Bangkok, but you'd have to live there, or visit for a long time, to appreciate that.

WHAT TO SEE

4 ★ **Royal Barge Museum.** These splendid ceremonial barges are berthed on the Thonburi side of the Chao Phraya River. The boats, carved in the early part of the 19th century, take the form of mythical creatures in the *Ramakien*. The most impressive is the red-and-gold royal vessel called *Suphannahongse* (Golden Swan), used by the king on special occasions. Carved from a single piece of teak, it measures about 150 feet and weighs more than 15 tons. Fifty oarsmen propel it along the river, accompanied by two coxswains, flag wavers, and a rhythm-keeper. ✉ *Khlong Bangkok Noi, Thonburi* ☎ *02/424–0004* 🎟 *B30* ⏲ *Daily 9–5* Ⓜ *Skytrain: Hua Lamphong.*

3 Fodor's Choice ★ **Wat Arun** *(Temple of Dawn)*. If this riverside spot is inspiring at sunrise, it's even more marvelous toward dusk when the setting sun throws amber tones over the entire area. The temple's design is symmetrical, with a square courtyard containing five Khmer-style prangs. The central prang, which reaches 282 feet, is surrounded by four attendant prangs at each of the corners. All five are covered in mosaics made from broken pieces of Chinese porcelain. Energetic visitors can climb the steep steps to the top of the lower level for the view over the Chao Phraya; the less ambitious can linger in the small park by the river, a peaceful spot to gaze across at the city. Festivals are held here occasionally; check the Web site for upcoming events. ✉ *Arun Amarin Rd., Thonburi* ☎ *02/466–3167* 🌐 *www.watarunfestival.com* 🎟 *B20* ⏲ *Daily 8:30–5:30* Ⓜ *Skytrain: Hua Lamphong.*

BANGLAMPHU

In the north part of Old City, Banglamphu offers pleasant walks, markets, and Khao San Road, one of the world's best-known backpacker hubs. Khao San has become a truly international street with visitors from dozens of countries populating the scene year-round, and an equally diverse selection of restaurants and street vendors. During the high season up to 10,000 people a day call the area home.

WHAT TO SEE

Khao San Road. Khao San, which means "Shining Rice," has been the heart of the international backpacking scene for decades. In the past few years it's made an attempt at trendiness with new outdoor bars, a glut of terrible Western restaurants, and hotels sharing the space with the ubiquitous low-budget guesthouses, some of which aren't actually budget anymore. **■TIP→The road is closed to traffic at night, making early evening the best time to stroll or sit back and people-watch.** It has become popular with Thais as well, who frequent the bars and watch the *farang* (foreigners). Nightfall also marks the start of a busy street market, where you can find clothing, Thai goods, bootleg CDs, fake IDs, used Western books, cheap street food, and more. The frenetic activity can, depending on your perspective, be infectious or overwhelming. During Songkran, the Thai New Year in mid-April, Khao San turns into one huge wet-and-wild water fight. Only join the fun if you don't mind being soaked to the bone.

Phra Athit Road. A more leisurely neighborhood stroll is the river walk off Phra Athit, which runs between Pinklao Bridge, near the National Museum, and Santichaiprakarn Park. The concrete walkway along the Chao Phraya is cooled by the river breeze and offers views of the life along the water. **Phra Sumen Fort,** one of the two remaining forts of the original 14 built under King Rama I, is in Santichaiprakarn Park. The park is a fine place to sit and watch the river. Phra Athit Road itself is an interesting street with buildings dating back more than 100 years. It has some good cafés, and at night the street comes alive with little bars and restaurants with live music. It's a favorite among university students. Ⓜ *Skytrain: Hua Lamphong.*

DUSIT

More than any other neighborhood in the city, Dusit, north of Banglamphu, seems calm and orderly. Its tree-shaded boulevards and elegant buildings truly befit the district that holds Chitlada Palace, the official residence of the king and queen. The neighborhood's layout was the work of King Rama V, the first of the country's monarchs to visit Europe. He returned with a grand plan to remake his capital after the great cities he had visited. Dusit is a rather big area, but luckily the major attractions—the Dusit Zoo and the numerous museums on the grounds of the Vimanmek Mansion—are close together.

Chitlada Palace 3
Dusit Zoo 2
Vimanmek Palace 1
Wat Benjamabophit 4

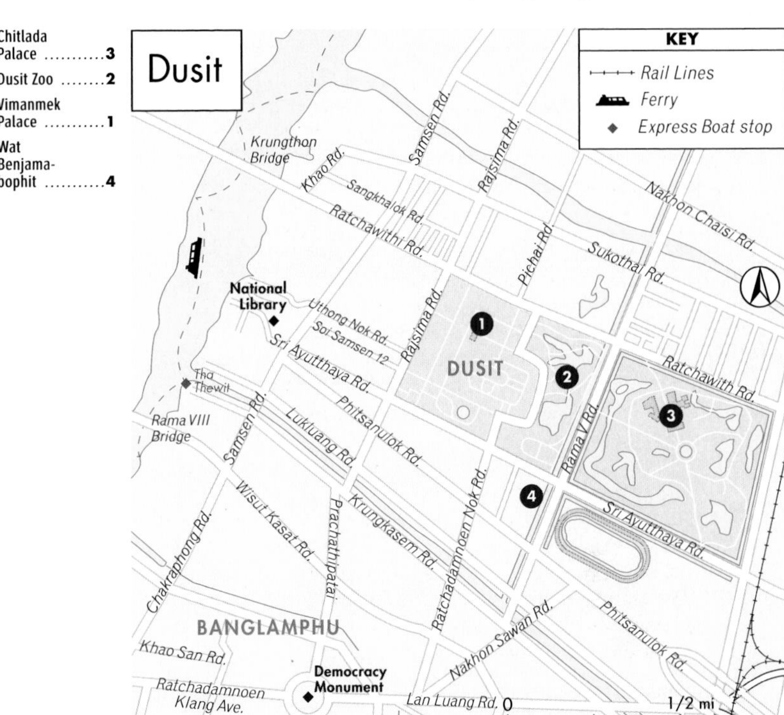

WHAT TO SEE

❸ **Chitlada Palace.** When in Bangkok, the king resides here, an area that takes up an entire block across from Dusit Park. Although the palace is closed to the public, the outside walls are a lovely sight, especially when lighted to celebrate the king's birthday on December 5. The extensive grounds are also home to a herd of royal white elephants, though it's difficult to arrange to see them. ✉*Ratchawith Rd. and Rama V Rd., Dusit* Ⓜ*Skytrain: Victory Monument (take a taxi from the station).*

❷ **Dusit Zoo.** Komodo dragons and other rarely seen creatures, such as the Sumatran rhinoceros, are on display at this charming little zoo. There are also the usual suspects like giraffes and hippos from Africa. (If you've heard about the pandas China gave Thailand, they are in Chiang Mai, not Bangkok.) While adults sip coffee at the cafés, children can ride elephants. ✉*Ratchawith Rd. and Rama V Rd., Dusit* ☎*02/281–0000* *B30* *Daily 8–6* Ⓜ*Skytrain: Victory Monument (take a taxi from the station).*

❶ ★ **Vimanmek Palace.** The spacious grounds within Dusit Park include 20 buildings you can visit, but Vimanmek, considered the largest golden teak structure in the world, is truly the highlight. The mansion's original foundation remains on Koh Si Chang two hours south of Bangkok in the Gulf of Thailand, where it was built in 1868. In 1910 King

Continued on page 62

the Grand Palace

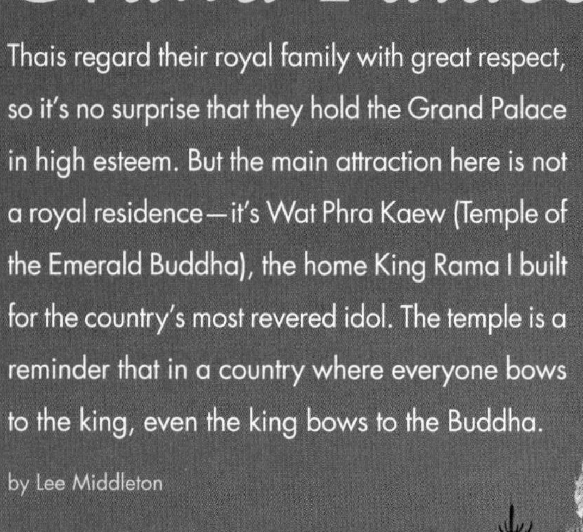

Thais regard their royal family with great respect, so it's no surprise that they hold the Grand Palace in high esteem. But the main attraction here is not a royal residence—it's Wat Phra Kaew (Temple of the Emerald Buddha), the home King Rama I built for the country's most revered idol. The temple is a reminder that in a country where everyone bows to the king, even the king bows to the Buddha.

by Lee Middleton

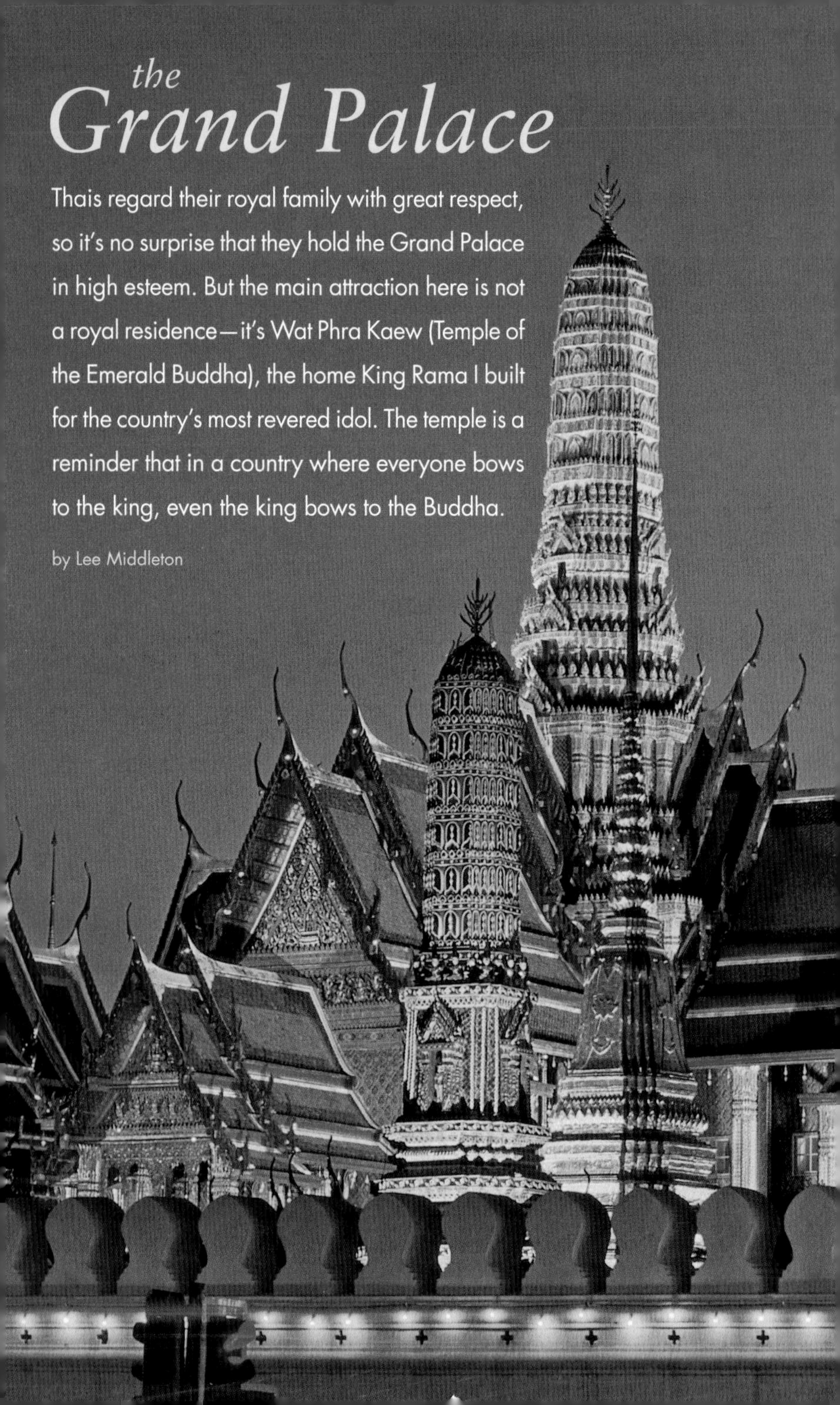

When Rama I was crowned in 1782, he wanted to celebrate the kingdom's renewed power. He moved the capital to Bangkok and set out to exceed the grandeur of Ayutthaya, once one of Asia's finest cities. The result was the dazzling Grand Palace compound, protected by a high white wall over a mile long. Rama I both ruled from and lived in the palace. Indeed, the royal family resided here until 1946, and each king who came to power added to the compound, leaving a mark of his rule and the era. Although the Grand Palace compound still houses the finance ministry, its only other official use is for state occasions and ceremonies like coronations. The current monarch, King Bhumibol (Rama IX), lives in Chitralada Palace which is closed to the public and is in Bangkok's Dusit District, northeast of the palace.

GRAND PALACE COMPOUND

Mural at the Grand Palace.

The palace grounds and Wat Phra Kaew are open to visitors, but many of the buildings in the complex are not. If you arrive by boat, you will land at Chiang Pier (tha Chang). Make your way to the main entrance on Na Phra Lan Road. **Wat Phra Kaew** is the best place to begin your tour. Other highlights are **Phra Thinang Amarin Winichai Mahaisun** (Amarinda Winichai Throne Hall), **Chakri Maha Prasat** (Grand Palace Hall), **Dusit Maha Prasat** (Audience Hall), **Phra Thinang Borom Phiman** (Borom Phiman Mansion), and the **Wat Phra Kaew Museum**.

Phra Thinang Borom Phiman
5
1
Wat Phra Kaew
PRASAT PHRA DHEPBIDORN
HOR PHRA MONTHIAN DHARMA
PHRA MONDOP
PHRA WIHARN YOD
PHRA SIRATANA CHEDI
HOR PHRA NAGA
Shop
SALA SAHADAYA

1 Wat Phra Kaew. King Rama I built Wat Phra Kaew—now regarded as Thailand's most sacred temple—in 1785. The main building, called *ubosoth*, houses the Emerald Buddha. The ubosoth has three doors; only the king and queen are allowed to enter through the central door.

Wat Phra Kaew.

2 Phra Thinang Amarin Winichai Mahaisun. The only part of Rama I's original residence that's open to visitors is used today for royal events such as the king's birthday celebration. Inside this audience hall are an antique boat-shaped throne from Rama I's reign that's now used to hold Buddha images during ceremonies, and a second throne with a nine-tiered white canopy where the king sits. At the entrance, you'll see gold-topped red poles once used by royal guests to tether their elephants.

Golden statue.

3 Chakri Maha Prasat. Rama V's residence, built in 1882, is the largest of the palace buildings. The hybrid Thai–European style was a compromise between Rama V, who wanted a neoclassical palace with a domed roof, and his advisors, who thought such a blatantly European design was inappropriate. Rama V agreed to a Thai-style roof; Thais nicknamed the building farang sai chada or "the westerner wearing a Thai hat.

4 Dusit Maha Prasat. Built in 1784, the Audience Hall contains Rama I's original teak and mother-of-pearl throne. Today the hall is where Thais view royal remains, which are placed here temporarily in a golden urn.

5 Phra Thinang Borom Phiman. King Rama V built this French-style palace for his son (the future Rama VI) in 1903. Though later kings did not use the palace much, today visiting dignitaries stay here.

6 Wat Phra Kaew Museum. Stop by after touring the compound to learn about the restoration of the palace and to see the seasonal robes of the Emerald Buddha. Labels are in Thai, but free English tours occur regularly.

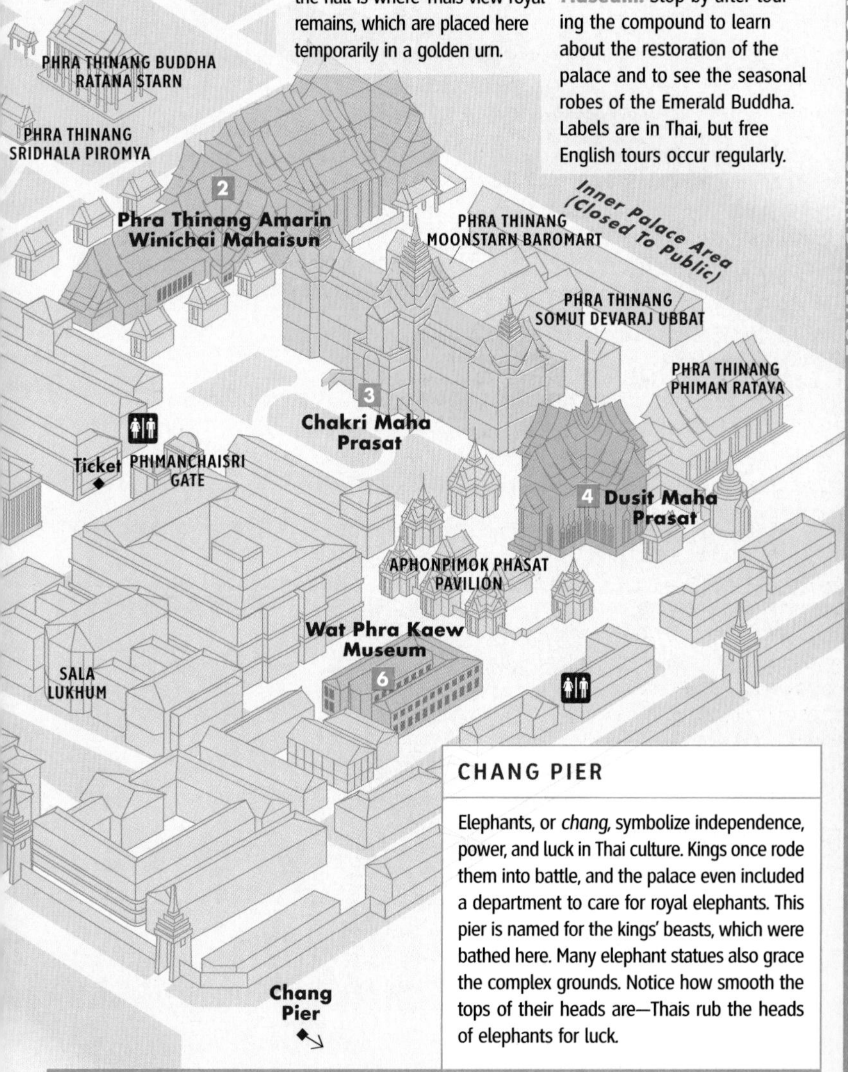

CHANG PIER

Elephants, or *chang*, symbolize independence, power, and luck in Thai culture. Kings once rode them into battle, and the palace even included a department to care for royal elephants. This pier is named for the kings' beasts, which were bathed here. Many elephant statues also grace the complex grounds. Notice how smooth the tops of their heads are—Thais rub the heads of elephants for luck.

TOURING TIPS

■ Free guided tours of the compound are available in English at 10:00, 10:30, 1:30, and 2:00 daily; personal audio guides are available for B100 plus a passport or credit card as a deposit.

■ The best way to get here is to take the Skytrain to Taksin Station and then board the Chao Phraya River Express boat to Chang Pier. It's a short walk from the pier to the palace entrance. You can also take a taxi to the Grand Palace but you may end up wasting time in traffic or getting ripped off.

■ Admission includes a free (though unimpressive) guidebook and admission to the Vimanmek Palace in Dunsit (⇨ above), as long as you go within a week of visiting the compound.

■ Don't listen to men loitering outside the grounds who claim that the compound is closed for a Buddhist holiday or for cleaning, or who offer to show you the "Lucky Buddha" or take you on a special tour. These phony guides will ultimately lead you to a gift shop where they receive a commission.

■ Allow half a day to tour the complex. You'll probably want to spend three hours in Wat Phra Kaew and the other buildings, and another half-hour in the museum.

■ Wat Phra Kaew is actually worth two visits: one on a weekday (when crowds are thinner and you can explore at a leisurely pace) and another on a Sunday or public holiday, when the smell of flowers and incense and the murmur of prayer evoke the spirituality of the place.

✉ Na Phra Lan Rd., Old City
Ⓜ **Skytrain:** Taksin Station (then express boat to Chang Pier).
☎ 02/224-1833
B350 for foreigners (free for Thais).
⏲ Daily 8:30–3:30 except during state functions; some halls are closed on weekends.

The Grand Palace.

WAT PHRA KAEW

As you enter the temple compound, you'll see 20-foot-tall statues of fearsome creatures in battle attire. These are *yakshas*—guardians who protect the Emerald Buddha from evil spirits. Turn right to see the murals depicting the *Ramakien* epic. Inside the main chapel, which is quiet and heavy with the scent of incense, you'll find the Emerald Buddha.

Yaksha.

THE RAMAKIEN

The *Ramakien* is the 2,000-year-old Thai adaptation of the famous Indian epic the *Ramayana,* which dates from around 400 BC. Beginning at the temple's north gate (across from Phra Wihan Yot [the Spired Hall]) and continuing clockwise around the cloister, 178 mural panels illustrate the story, which, like most epics, is about the struggle between good and evil. It begins with the founding of Ayutthaya (City of the Gods) and Lanka (City of the Demons) and focuses on the trials and tribulations of Ayutthaya's Prince Rama: his expulsion from his own kingdom; the abduction of his wife, Sita; and his eventual triumph over the demon Tosakan.

Section of *Ramakien.*

Sita's Abduction

Rama's wife Sita is abducted by the evil demon king, Tosakan, ruler of Lanka. Disguising himself as a deer, Tosakan lures Sita to his palace. A battle ensues, forming a large part of the long and detailed epic, which concludes when Rama rescues Sita.

THE APSONSI

The beautiful gilded figures on the upper terraces of Wat Phra Kaew are *apsonsi*—mythical half-angel, half-lion creatures who guard the temple. According to Thai mythology, apsonsi inhabit the Himavant Forest, which is the realm between earth and the heavens.

Ramakien battle scene.

Aponsi.

THE EMERALD BUDDHA

Thailand's most sacred Buddha image is made of a single piece of jade and is only 31 inches tall. The statue, which historians believe was sculpted in Thailand in the 14th or 15th century, was at one point covered in plaster; in 1434 it was discovered in Chiang Rai as the plaster began to flake.

When the king of nearby Chiang Mai heard about the jade Buddha, he demanded it be brought to him. According to legend, the statue was sent to the king three times, but each time the elephant transporting it veered off to Lampang, 60 miles southeast of Chiang Mai. Finally the king came to the Buddha, building a temple at that spot.

The Buddha was kept at various temples in northern Thailand until Laotian invaders stole it in 1552. It stayed in Laos until the 18th century, when King Rama I captured Vientiane, the capital, reclaimed the statue, and brought it to Bangkok.

Perched in a gilded box high above the altar, the diminutive statue is difficult to see. This doesn't deter Thai Buddhists, who believe that praying before the Emerald Buddha will earn them spiritual merit, helping to ensure a better rebirth in the next life.

The king is the only person allowed to touch the Emerald Buddha. Three times a year, he changes the Buddha's robes in a ceremony to bring good fortune for the coming season. The Buddha's hot season attire includes a gold crown and jewels; in the rainy season, it wears a headdress of gold, enamel, and sapphires; and, in the cool season, it's adorned in a mesh robe of gold beads.

Emerald Buddha in hot season outfit.

Most Thais make an offering to the Buddha when they visit the temple. Inexpensive offerings, for sale outside the temple, generally include three joss sticks, a candle, and a thin piece of gold leaf stuck on a sheet of paper. At some wats, Thais stick gold leaves on the Buddha, but since that's not possible here, keep it as a souvenir or attach it to another sacred image (some elephant statues have gold leaves on their heads.) Light the candle from others that are already burning on the front alter, then light the incense with your candle.

WHAT'S A WAT?

A *wat* is a Buddhist temple or monastery, typically made up of a collection of shrines and structures in an enclosed courtyard, rather than a single building. Traditionally, monks reside in wats, but Wat Phra Kaew is a ceremonial temple, not a place of Buddhist study, so monks don't live here.

HONORING THE EMERALD BUDDHA

Thais usually follow an offering with three prostrations, or bows, to the Buddha. To prostrate, sit facing the Buddha with your legs folded or your feet tucked under you—then follow the sequence below. After prostrating you can sit in fromt of the Buddha in prayer or meditation for as long as you like.

1) Hold your hands together in a *wai* (palms together, fingers pointing up) at your heart.

2) Bring the wai up to touch your forehead,

3) Place your palms on the ground and bow your forehead until it's touching the ground between them.

4) Sit up, bring your hands back into a wai in front of your heart, and repeat.

TEMPLE ETIQUETTE

Even if you don't want to make an offering, pray, or prostrate, it's OK to linger in the temple or sit down. Here are a few other things to keep in mind:

- Appropriate dress—long-sleeved shirts and long pants or skirts—is required. Open-toed shoes must be "closed" by wearing socks. If you've come scantily clad, you can rent a sarong at the palace.
- Never point—with your hands or your feet—at the Emerald Buddha, other sacred objects, or even another person. If you sit down in the temple, make sure not to accidentally point your feet in the Buddha's direction.
- When walking around religious monuments, try to move in a clockwise direction. Thais believe that the right side of the body is superior to the left, so it's more respectful to keep your right side closer to sacred objects.
- Keep your head below the Buddha and anything else sacred. Thais will often bend their knees and lower their heads when walking past a group of older people or monks; it's a gesture of respect even if their heads aren't technically below the monks'.

Offerings.

Rama V had the rest of the structure moved to its present location and it served as his residence for five years while the Grand Palace was being fixed up. The building itself is extensive, with more than 80 rooms. The exterior was spruced up in 2006. The other 19 buildings include the **Royal Family Museum,** with portraits of the royal family, and the **Royal Carriage Museum,** with carriages and other vehicles used by the country's monarchs through the ages. There are several small air-conditioned restaurants offering a limited menu of Thai food. Admission includes everything on the grounds and the classical Thai dancing shows that take place mid-morning and mid-afternoon (10:30 AM and 2 PM, but these times are subject to change). English-language tours are available every half hour starting at 9:15. ■ **TIP→ Admission is free if you have a ticket less than one week old from the Grand Palace.** ✉ *Ratchawith Rd., Dusit* ☎ *02/281–1569* 🎟 *B100* ⏲ *Daily 8:30–4:30* Ⓜ *Skytrain: Victory Monument (take a taxi from the station).*

❹ ★ **Wat Benjamabophit** *(Marble Temple)*. This is a favorite with photographers because of its open spaces and light, shining marble. The wat was built in 1899, statues of the Buddha line the courtyard, and the magnificent interior has crossbeams of lacquer and gold. But Wat Benjamabophit is more than a splendid temple—the monastery is a seat of learning that appeals to Buddhist monks with intellectual yearnings. ✉ *Nakhon Pathom Rd., Dusit* 🎟 *B20* ⏲ *Daily 8–5:30* Ⓜ *Skytrain: Victory Monument (take a taxi from the station).*

CHINATOWN

Almost as soon as Bangkok was founded, Chinatown started to form; it's the city's oldest residential neighborhood. Today it's an integral part of the city, bustling with little markets (and a few big ones), teahouses, restaurants tucked here and there, and endless traffic. Like much of the Old City, Chinatown is a great place to explore on foot. Meandering through the maze of alleys, ducking into herb shops and temples along the way, can be a great way to pass an afternoon, though the constant crowd, especially on hot days, does wear on some people.

Bustling Yaowarat Road is the main thoroughfare. It's crowded with gold shops and excellent restaurants. Pahuraht Road, which is Bangkok's "Little India," is full of textile shops, some quite literally underground; many of the Indian merchant families on this street have been here for generations.

■ **TIP→ Getting to Chinatown is easiest by boat—simply get off at one of the nearby piers and walk into the morass. But you can also start at the Hua Lamphong subway station and head west to the river.** The amount of traffic in this area cannot be overemphasized: avoid taking a taxi into the neighborhood if you can help it.

Another worthy stop is the Flower Market, but it is a bit of a distance, and more in between Chinatown and the Old City.

2

WHAT TO SEE

1 **Flower Market.** The flower market is more a street full of shops than one destination. It's open 24/7, but it's most interesting at night when more deliveries are heading in and out. This is where restaurants, hotels, other businesses, and individuals come to buy their flowers. Just stroll into the warehouse areas and watch the action. Many vendors only sell flowers in bulk, but others sell small bundles or even individual flowers. As everywhere else where Thais do business, there are plenty of street stalls selling a vast array of food. Though the area is not as busy as Chinatown proper, the traffic here can still be overbearing. Then again, one can say that about everywhere in Bangkok. ✉ *Chakraphet Rd. between Pripatt and Yod Fa Rds., Chinatown* Ⓜ *Subway: Hua Lamphong.*

2 **Thieves Market** *(Nakorn Kasem).* The Thieves Market was once known for its reasonable prices for antiques, but stolen goods are no longer the order of the day. It's not worth a visit on its own, but as part of a greater Chinatown walk having a look in the covered lanes of stalls is interesting—like a rabbit warren of little shops. Mostly electronic goods are sold and it really starts slowing down about 5 in the afternoon. For shopping, Chatuchak weekend market is much better. ✉ *Yaowarat Rd. and Chakraphet Rd., Chinatown* Ⓜ *Subway: Hua Lamphong.*

❸ **Wat Mangkorn** *(Neng Noi Yee).* Unlike most temples in Bangkok, Neng Noi Yee has a glazed ceramic roof topped with fearsome dragons. Although it's a Buddhist shrine, its statues and paintings incorporate elements of Confucianism and Taoism as well. It's open daily from early to very late. ✉ *Charoen Krung (New Rd.), Chinatown* Ⓜ *Subway: Hua Lamphong.*

❹ ★ **Wat Traimit** *(Temple of the Golden Buddha).* The actual temple has little architectural merit, but off to its side is a small chapel containing the world's largest solid-gold Buddha, cast about nine centuries ago in the Sukhothai style. Weighing 5½ tons and standing 10 feet high, the statue is a symbol of strength and power that can inspire even the most jaded person. It's believed that the statue was brought first to Ayutthaya. When the Burmese were about to sack the city, it was covered in plaster. Two centuries later, still in plaster, it was thought to be worth very little; when it was being moved to a new Bangkok temple in the 1950s it slipped from a crane and was simply left in the mud by the workmen. In the morning, a temple monk who had dreamed that the statue was divinely inspired went to see the Buddha image. Through a crack in the plaster he saw a glint of yellow, and soon discovered that the statue was pure gold. ✉ *Tri Mit Rd., Chinatown* 🎫 *B30* ⏲ *Daily 8–5* Ⓜ *Subway: Hua Lamphong.*

SOI BOYS

At many *sois* (or side streets) you will find groups of motorcycle taxis. Their drivers, called "soi boys," will take you anywhere in Bangkok. Fares are negotiable—usually about the same as or a little less than a taxi. Motorcycles can be dangerous; helmets, when available, are often nothing more than a thin piece of plastic without a chin strap, but most locals take these taxis regularly. Many soi boys know their way around the city better than taxi drivers. The risks and discomforts limit their desirability, but motorcycles can be one of the best ways to get around Bangkok, especially if you're in a hurry.

DOWNTOWN BANGKOK

Bangkok has many downtowns that blend into each other—even residents have a hard time agreeing on a definitive city center—and so the large collective area considered "downtown" is actually seven neighborhoods. Most of the tourist attractions are in the adjacent neighborhoods of Silom and Pratunam. The other neighborhoods (Lumphini Park, Siam Square, Victory Monument, Sukhumvit, and the rather up-and-coming Rajadapisek) are residential areas, business centers, shopping districts, or all the above.

PRATUNAM

Pratunam, north of Silom, is a large neighborhood that competes with Chinatown for the worst traffic in the city. There are numerous markets here, including those in the garment district (generally north of Phetchaburi Road). Pratunam's Panthip Plaza is Thailand's biggest computer center and an overwhelming shopping experience, with five floors

2

BANGKOK'S SKYWAYS

The Skytrain transformed the city when it opened on the king's birthday in 1999. It now has 25 stations on two lines that intersect at Siam Square. Although the Skytrain bypasses parts of the city entirely, it is the speediest way to travel when its route coincides with yours. The fare is B10 to B40, depending on how far you travel, and trains run from 5 AM to midnight. Since they are relatively new, trains are still impressively clean, quiet, and efficient.

The sights in downtown Bangkok are spread out, but most are near Skytrain stations. Stations are generally half a mile (and less than three minutes) apart, so Chong Nonsi to National Stadium, which is four stations, will take less than 12 minutes. At three stations—Chatuchak Park, Sukhumvit, and Saladaeng—the Skytrain intersects with the subway, which is very convenient for some inter-city travel.

of computer stores. North of Pratunam is Victory Monument, which remains predominantly residential except for Phayathai Road, which is home to many businesses. Sukhumvit, east of Pratunam, is a mixed bag, with countless hotels and restaurants (many expat Westerners and Japanese live in the area, so restaurant pickings tend to be expat-oriented and of spotty quality), as well as many entertainment spots. Traffic is often gridlocked, but, fortunately, the neighborhood has good Skytrain service. Bangkok's newest high-society or yuppie area, called Thonglor (often spelled Thong Lo), is a bit east. For upmarket nightlife this is the current hotspot.

WHAT TO SEE

1 **Erawan Shrine** *(San Phra Phrom)*. Completed in 1956, this is not a particularly old shrine by Bangkok standards, but it's one of the more active ones, with many people stopping by on their way home to pray to Brahma. Thai dancers and a small traditional orchestra perform for a fee to increase the likelihood that your wish will be granted. Its location at one of Bangkok's most congested intersections, next to the Grand Hyatt Erawan and near the Chitlom Skytrain station, detracts a bit from the experience. Even with a traffic jam right outside the gates though, the mix of burning incense, dancers in traditional dress, and many people praying is a memorable sight. Entry is free, but many people leave small donations. A crazed man smashed the main statue in early 2006 and then was beaten to death by people outside the shrine. The statue has since been repaired and is more popular than ever. ✉ *Ratchadamri and Ploenchit Rds., Pratunam* Ⓜ *Skytrain: Chitlom.*

2 **Jim Thompson's House.** Formerly an architect in New York City, Jim Thompson ended up in Thailand at the end of World War II, after a stint as an officer of the OSS (an organization that preceded the CIA). After a couple of other business ventures, he moved into silk and is credited with revitalizing Thailand's moribund silk industry. The success of this project alone would have made him a legend, but the house he left behind is also a national treasure. Thompson imported

Fodor's Choice ★

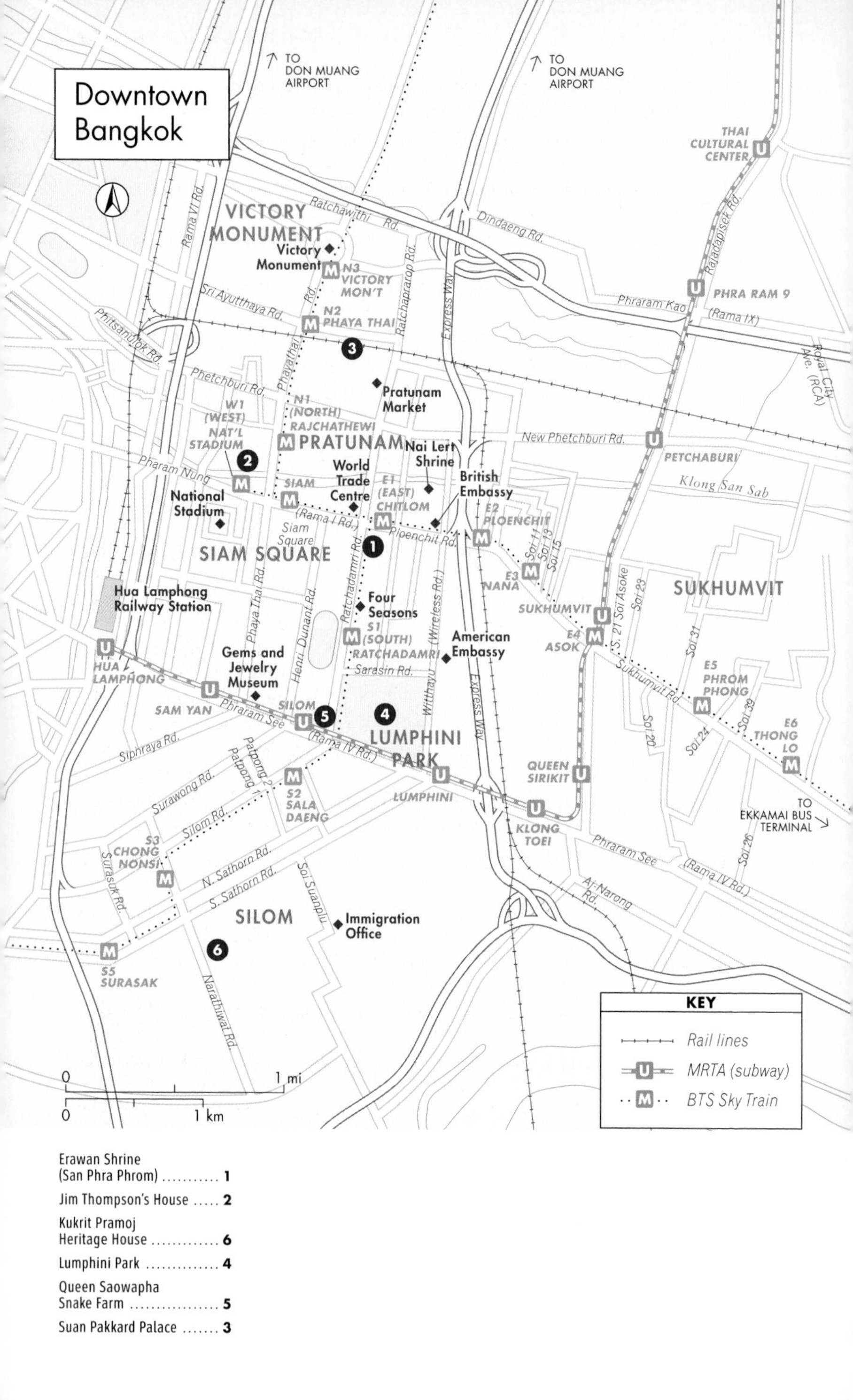

Erawan Shrine (San Phra Phrom) **1**

Jim Thompson's House **2**

Kukrit Pramoj Heritage House **6**

Lumphini Park **4**

Queen Saowapha Snake Farm **5**

Suan Pakkard Palace **3**

parts of several up-country buildings, some as old as 150 years, to construct his compound of six Thai houses (three are still exactly the same as their originals, including details of the interior layout). With true appreciation and a connoisseur's eye, Thompson then furnished them with what are now priceless pieces of Southeast Asian art. Adding to Thompson's notoriety is his disappearance: in 1967 he went to the Malaysian Cameron Highlands for a quiet holiday and was never heard from again. The entrance to the house is easy to miss—it's at the end of an unprepossessing lane, leading north off Rama I Road, west of Phayathai Road (the house is on your left). A good landmark is the National Stadium Skytrain station—the house is north of the station, just down the street from it. An informative 30-minute guided tour starts every 15 minutes and is included in the admission fee. **■ TIP→ The grounds also include a two-story silk and souvenir shop and a restaurant in the reception building that is great for a coffee or cold-drink break.** ✉ *Soi Kasemsong 2, Pratunam* ☎ *02/216–7368* *B100* *Daily 9–5:30* Ⓜ *Skytrain: National Stadium.*

4 **Lumphini Park.** Two lakes enhance this popular park, one of the few and the biggest in the center of the city. You can watch children feed bread to the turtles, or see teenagers taking a rowboat to more secluded shores. During the dry season (November through February) keep an eye and an ear out for Music in the Park, which starts around 5 PM each Sunday on the Singha stage; there are different bands each week playing classical and Thai oldies. The adjacent night market is also a must-see. There are many embassies in the immediate vicinity, and the Bangkok Royal Sports Club is just west of the park. A little farther west, but still within walking distance, is **Siam Square,** home to Thailand's most prestigious university, Chulalongkorn. Siam Square is also one of Bangkok's biggest shopping areas. ✉ *Rama IV Rd., Pratunam* Ⓜ *Subway: Silom and Lumphini stations; Skytrain: Sala Daeng.*

3 ★ **Suan Pakkard Palace.** A collection of antique teak houses, built high on columns, complement undulating lawns and shimmering lotus pools at this compound. Inside the Lacquer Pavilion, which sits serenely at the back of the garden, there's gold-covered paneling with scenes from the life of the Buddha. Academics and historians continue to debate just how old the murals are—whether they're from the reign of King Narai (1656–88) or from the first reign of the current Chakri Dynasty, founded by King Rama I (1782–1809). Whenever they originated, they are worth a look. Other houses display porcelain, stone heads, traditional paintings, and Buddha statues. ✉ *352 Sri Ayutthaya Rd., Pratunam* ☎ *02/245–4934* *B100* *Daily 9–4* Ⓜ *Skytrain: Phaya Thai (10-min walk from station).*

SILOM

The Silom area, with a mix of tall buildings, residential streets, and entertainment areas, is Bangkok's busiest business district. Some of the city's finest hotels and restaurants are in this neighborhood, which retains some charm despite being so developed and chock-full of concrete.

CLOSE UP

Roaming the Waterways

Bangkok used to be known as "Venice of the East," but many of the *klongs* (canals) that once distinguished this area have been paved over. Traveling along the few remaining waterways, however, is one of the city's delights. The water has been cleaned up and is no longer so black and smelly. You'll see houses on stilts, women washing clothes, and kids going for a swim. A popular trip to the Royal Barge Museum and the Khoo Wiang Floating Market starts at the Chang Pier near the Grand Palace.

Ferries (sometimes called "river buses") ply the river. The fare for these express boats is based on the distance you travel; the price ranges from B10 to B32. The river can be an efficient way to get around as well as a sightseeing opportunity. Under the Saphan Taksin Skytrain stop, there is a ferry stop where passengers can cross the river to Thonburi for B3, saving themselves an hour's drive. Many hotels run their own boats from the pier near the Oriental. From here, you can get to the Grand Palace in about 10 minutes and the other side of Krungthon Bridge in about 15 minutes. Local line boats travel specific routes from 6 AM to 6 PM. If you are on Sukhumvit, Phetchaburi Road is a good place to catch them. These boats stop at every pier and will take you all the way to Nonthaburi, where you'll find a little island with vendors selling pottery—a pleasant afternoon trip when the city gets too hot.

A Chao Phraya Tourist Boat day pass is a fun introduction to the river. They are a bargain at B70 for the whole day. One advantage of the tourist boat is while traveling from place to place there's a running commentary in English about the historical sights along the river and how to visit them. The tourist boat starts at the pier under Saphan Taksin Skytrain station, but you can pick it up at any of the piers where it stops, and you can get on and off as often as you like.

Longtail boats (so called for the extra-long propeller shaft that extends behind the stern) operate like taxis. Boatmen will take you anywhere you want to go for B200 to B300 per hour. It's a great way to see the canals. The best place to hire these boats is at the Central Pier on Sathorn Bridge. Longtails often quit running at 6 PM.

For a blast into Bangkok's transportation past, traditional wooden canal boats are a fun (though not entirely practical) way to get around town. Klong Saen Saep, just north of Ploenchit Road, is the main boat route. The fare is a maximum B15, and during rush hour, boats pull up to piers in one-minute intervals. Klong boats provide easy access to Jim Thompson's House and are a handy alternative way to get to Khao San Road during rush hour.

WHAT TO SEE

★ **Kukrit Pramoj Heritage House.** Former Prime Minister Kukrit Pramoj's house reflects his long, influential life. After Thailand became a constitutional monarchy in 1932, he formed the country's first political party and was prime minister in 1974 and 1975. (Perhaps he practiced for that role 12 years earlier when he appeared with Marlon Brando as a Southeast Asian prime minister in *The Ugly American.*) He died in 1995 and much of his living quarters—five interconnected teak houses—has been preserved as he left it. Throughout his life, Kukrit was dedicated to preserving Thai culture, and his house and grounds are monuments to a bygone era; the place is full of Thai and Khmer art and furniture from different periods. The landscaped garden with its Khmer stonework is also a highlight. It took Pramoj 30 years to build the house, so it's no wonder that you can spend the better part of a day wandering around here. ✉ *19 Soi Phra Pinit, S. Sathorn Rd., Silom* ☎ *02/286–8185* 🎫 *B50* ⏲ *Weekends and official holidays 10–5* Ⓜ *Skytrain: Chong Nonsi (10-min walk from station).*

5 **Queen Saowapha Snake Farm.** The Thai Red Cross established this unusual snake farm in 1923. Venom from cobras, pit vipers, and some of the other 56 types of deadly snakes found in Thailand is collected and used to make antidotes for snakebite victims. There are milking sessions at 10:30 AM on weekends and 10:30 AM and 2 PM weekdays, where you can watch the staff fearlessly handle these deadly creatures. They sometimes change the milking times, so you might want to have your hotel call and ask when it is. There are a few displays that can be viewed any time, but the milking sessions are the big reason to come here. ✉ *1871 Rama IV Rd., Silom* ☎ *02/252–0161* 🎫 *B70* ⏲ *Weekdays 8:30–4, weekends 8:30–noon* Ⓜ *Subway: Silom; Skytrain: Sala Daeng.*

WHERE TO EAT

Thais are passionate about food and love discovering out-of-the-way shops that prepare unexpectedly tasty dishes. Nowhere is this more true—or feasible—than in Bangkok. The city's residents always seem to be eating, so the tastes and smells of Thailand's cuisine surround you day and night. That said, Bangkok's restaurant scene is also a minefield, largely because the relationship between price and quality at times seems almost inverse. For every hole-in-the-wall gem serving the best *larb,* sticky rice, and *som tam* (the hot-and-sour green-papaya salad that is the ultimate Thai staple) you've ever had, there's an overpriced hotel restaurant serving touristy, toned-down fare. In general, the best Thai food in the city is generally at the most bare-bones, even run-down restaurants, not at famous, upscale places.

If you want a break from Thai food, plenty of other world cuisines are well represented. Best among them is Chinese, although there's decent Japanese and Korean food in Bangkok as well. The city's ubiquitous noodle shops, though by all means Thai, also have their roots in China, as do roast-meat purveyors, whose historical inspiration was Cantonese. Western fare tends to suffer from the distance.

As with anything in Bangkok, travel time is a major consideration when choosing a restaurant. If you're short on time or patience, choose a place that's an easy walk from a Skytrain or subway station. **■ TIP→Note that often the easiest way to reach a riverside eatery is by taking the Skytrain to the Saphan Taksin station (next to the Shangri-La Hotel).** From there you can take an express boat upriver to a number of the restaurants listed below.

BEST BETS FOR BANGKOK DINING

Fodor's writers and editors have selected their favorite restaurants by price, cuisine, and experience in the lists below. In the first column, the Fodor's Choice properties represent the "best of the best" across price categories. You can also search by area for excellent eats—just peruse our complete reviews on the following pages.

DINNER CRUISES

Though they're definitely very touristy, lunch or dinner cruises on the Chao Phraya River are worth considering. They're a great way to see the city at night, although the food is often subpar. You might even want to skip the dinner, just have drinks, and dine at a real Thai restaurant afterward. Two-hour cruises on modern boats or refurbished rice barges include a buffet or set-menu dinner and often feature live music and sometimes a traditional dance show. Many companies also offer a less expensive lunch cruise, though the heat can make these a little unpleasant. In general, it's wise to reserve a few days in advance, and reservations are a must for some of the more popular dinner cruises.

The **Horizon** (✉*Shangri-La Hotel, 89 Soi Wat Suan Phu, Charoen Krung [New Rd.], Silom* ☎*02/236–7777*) departs each evening at 7:30 PM and costs B2,200 per person. Four days a week there's also a day trip by bus to Ayutthaya with a cruise back for B1,800. It departs at 8 AM and returns around 5 PM. The **Manohra Song** (✉*Marriott Royal Garden Riverside Hotel, 257/1–3 Charoen Krung [New Rd.], Thonburi* ☎*02/476–0021* 🌐*www.manohracruises.com*) has both lunch and dinner cruises. It is the most beautiful dinner boat on the river, but it's smaller than most of the others, with less space to walk around. A mediocre set-price dinner is B1,850 per person. The **Yok Yor** (✉*Wisutikasat Rd. at Yok Yor Pier, across from River City Shopping Complex, Thonburi* ☎*02/863–0565*) departs each evening at 8 PM. The boat ticket costs B140; food is ordered à la carte, which in this case is a plus.

COOKING CLASSES

Culinary tourism is all the rage, and Bangkok is keeping up with the times. A Thai cooking class can be a great way to spend a half day—or longer. You won't be an expert, but you can learn a few fundamentals and some of the history of Thai cuisine. You can also find specialty classes that focus on things like fruit carving (where the first lesson learned is that it's more difficult than it looks) or hot-and-spicy soups. All cooking schools concentrate on practical dishes that students will be able to make at home, usually with spices that are internationally available, and all revolve around the fun of eating something you cooked (at least partly) yourself. ■ **TIP→ Book cooking classes ahead of time; this is one activity that definitely requires advance planning.** Most classes are small enough to allow individual attention and time for questions. Prices vary from B2,000 to more than B10,000.

The **Blue Elephant Cooking School** (✉*233 S. Sathorn Rd., Silom* ☎*02/673–9353* 🌐*www.blueelephant.com* Ⓜ*Skytrain: Surasak*) is a longstanding favorite, connected with the restaurant of the same name, but the Thai dishes here are heavily Westernized. However, at about B3,200 per day, it's cheaper than the others, and the staff is very friendly.

The **Landmark Hotel Cooking School** (✉*138 Sukhumvit Rd., Sukhumvit* ☎*02/254–0404 Ext. 4823* 🌐*www.landmarkbangkok.com*) is also good. Daylong, weeklong, and half-day courses are offered.

The **Oriental Cooking School** (✉ *48 Oriental Ave., across from Oriental Hotel, Thonburi* ☎ *02/659–9000 Ext. 7120*) is the most established and expensive school (B4,000 for a half day), but far from being stuffy, it's fun and informative, and its dishes tend to be more interesting and authentic than those at other schools. Classes are taught in a beautiful century-old house.

NORTH & WEST BANGKOK

DUSIT & NORTH BANGKOK

North Bangkok is worth dining in only if you happen to be in the neighborhood for sightseeing, or really want to get to a part of the river that's off the beaten track.

¢ THAI **Aw Taw Kaw Market.** Bangkok's best food bargains are found at this legendary spot in the Chatuchak market. It's noisy, and you'll be inundated with sights and smells in the rows of food stalls; walk around and let your senses take over. The seafood, like raw crab, curried crab, or steamed whole fish with garlic and chili, is especially tasty. Items are dished out in plastic baggies; finding a seat and utensils can be a challenge. The trick is to buy something small at one of the few café-like establishments that offers seats, plates, and cutlery—then open your bags and feast. ✉ *Phaholyothin Rd., Chatuchak, North Bangkok* Ⓜ *Subway: Chatuchak Park; Skytrain: Mo Chit.* ✣ *D1*

$$$$ CHINESE **Dynasty.** This restaurant has long been a favorite among government ministers and corporate executives both for its outstanding Cantonese cuisine and for its 11 private areas, which are good for business lunches or romantic dinners. The main dining room is elegant with crimson carpeting, carved screens, lacquer furniture, and porcelain objets d'art. The Peking duck is among the draws (as are the jellyfish salad and drunken chicken), but the seasonal specialties include everything from hairy crabs (October and November) to Taiwanese eels (March). The service is efficient and friendly without being obtrusive. The restaurant is in Chatuchak, north of Pratunam. ✉ *Sofitel Centara Grand Bangkok, 1695 Phaholyothin Rd., Chatuchak, North Bangkok* ☎ *02/541–1234* ⚠ *Reservations essential* ▭ *AE, DC, MC, V* Ⓜ *Subway: Phahon Yothin.* ✣ *E1*

$$ THAI **Kaloang Seafood.** An alley near the National Library leads to this off-the-beaten-track restaurant on the Chao Phraya. Kaloang might not look like much, with its plastic chairs and simple tables on a ramshackle pier, but it's a local favorite and worth the effort—and leap in imagination—for fantastic seafood on the river. Breezes coming off the water keep things comfortably cool most evenings. The generous grilled seafood platter is a bargain, as is the plate of grilled giant river prawns. Try the *yam pla duk foo,* a grilled fish salad that's rather spicy, but goes great with a cold beer. Also notable is the *larb goong,* spicy ground shrimp salad with banana blossoms. ✉ *2 Sri Ayutthaya Rd., Dusit* ☎ *02/281–9228 or 02/282–7581* ▭ *AE, DC, MC, V* Ⓜ *Subway: Phahon Yothin.* ✣ *C2*

2

THE OLD CITY & BANGLAMPHU

The Old City has every type of restaurant, including a huge proliferation of holes-in-the-wall, many with excellent food. Touristy Khao San Road is also in this part of town, though the tame Thai food available in this backpacker mecca is nothing to go out of your way for. Don't limit yourself to the listings here, and don't be afraid to eat the street food—it often makes for some of your most memorable meals in Bangkok.

$$ THAI **Chote Chitr.** A favorite of legendary Bangkok food writer Bob Halliday, this simple, diminutive restaurant near Wat Suthat specializes in seafood. Notable in a constellation of superstar dishes are banana-blossom salad (here it's made with shrimp, chicken, tamarind pulp, chili, and coconut cream); perfectly balanced red curry shrimp; and *makheua yao* (a smoky green eggplant salad with shrimp, shallots, palm sugar, fermented shrimp, and lime juice). Come here for the food, not the atmosphere, and you'll be blown away. ✉ *146 Phraeng Phuton, Old City* ☎ *02/221–4082* ▭ *No credit cards.* ⊕ *B3*

¢ THAI **Krua Noppharat.** Though it's nothing fancy, this eatery has a friendly and inviting feel, an English-language menu, and air-conditioning. If you come for the food rather than the creature comforts, you won't be disappointed: the authentic Isan menu includes regional specialties like fried snakehead fish with spicy sauce, banana-flower salad, raw shrimp, fried morning glory, and Isan sausage. Those who have traveled in northeastern Thailand will be overcome with nostalgia. ✉ *130–132 Phra Athit Rd., Banglamphu* ☎ *02/281–7578* ⊙ *Closed Sun.* ⊕ *B2*

$$ THAI **Raan Jay Fai.** "Cult following" would be putting it mildly: it is said that there are people that come to Thailand just for a serving of the *pad khee mao* (drunken noodles) at this small open-air eatery with cafeteria-style tables, green bare lightbulbs, and a culinary wizard presiding over a charcoal-fired wok. The dish, which is all anyone gets here, is a rice noodle preparation with seafood including basil, crabmeat, giant shrimp, and hearts of palm. At around B250, this is a major splurge by Bangkok noodle standards—and the deal of the century for visiting foodies. The lump crabmeat fried with curry powder, though not as wildly popular, is also recommended. ✉ *327 Maha Chai Rd., Old City* ☎ *02/223–9384* ▭ *No credit cards* ⊙ *Closed some Sat.* ⊕ *C3*

THONBURI

Thonburi has restaurants boasting unparalleled river views, along with dinner cruises (⇨ *above*).

$$$$ STEAK HOUSE **Prime.** Though it's just a toddler in restaurant years, this spot in the gleaming new Hilton Millennium has already attained the title of best steak house in Bangkok. It all begins with the groundbreaking interior architecture, which skillfully blends sweeping river and city views with the restaurant's open kitchen while still managing to feel intimate—an almost alchemical feat. Start with one of the signature martinis, and move on to the Caesar salad prepared tableside and perhaps a magnificent shellfish platter with fresh, briny oysters and lobster tails. Then there is the meat—whether it's Wagyu beef flown in from Australia or USDA Prime, no expense is spared in the kitchen (nor on the bill). The

grilling is done over an extremely hot open flame. The wine list is also one of the best in the city, with lower than normal markups. ✉ *Hilton Millennium Hotel, 123 Charoennakorn Rd., Thonburi* ☎ *02/442–2000* 🌐 *www.hilton.com* ▭ *AE, DC, MC, V.* ✥ *C5*

$$$ THAI ✕ **Sala Rim Naam.** The main reason to come here is for the atmosphere, so skip the Thai dancing show and grab a table outside overlooking the river. As it gets dark and cools down, the twinkling lights of passing boats set quite a romantic scene. The restaurant itself is touristy, with westernized renditions of Thai food. Be pushy and demand your food spicy if you want it to resemble anything authentic. ■ **TIP→ To get here, take a boat across the Chao Phraya River from the Oriental Hotel.** ✉ *48 Oriental Ave., across from Oriental Hotel, Thonburi* ☎ *02/437–3080 or 02/437–6211* ✍ *Reservations essential* ▭ *AE, DC, MC, V* Ⓜ *Skytrain: Saphan Taksin.* ✥ *C6*

CHINATOWN

Bangkok's Chinatown is impressive, to say the least, in large part for its food; it draws huge crowds of Thais who spend big bucks on specialties like shark's fin and bird's nest (which you'll see advertised on almost every single restaurant's storefront). Most of the food is Cantonese; many of these restaurants are indistinguishable from what you'd find in Hong Kong. In the middle of Chinatown, just off Yaowarat, there's a massive Indian cloth market and unique local Indian restaurants dot the area outside the market. Don't overlook the delicious street food, the noodle and dumpling shops, and the fruit and spice markets.

$$$ CHINESE ✕ **Hua Seng Hong Restaurant.** This expensive but worthwhile Chinatown classic takes you straight to China, or more specifically, to Hong Kong, with excellent Cantonese roast meats—try the deliciously fatty duck—and soft, delicious goose foot–and–abalone stew. Don't pass up the delectable fried pancake with eggs and plump oysters; dim sum is also impressive. The restaurant is crowded and bustling, and service is authentically brusque. Like many of the neighboring Chinatown restaurants, the place hawks the inexplicably prized shark's fin and bird's nest dishes, but here as elsewhere, they're not worth the sky-high prices—both taste essentially like slightly more resilient glass noodles. ✉ *371–373 Yaowarat Rd., Chinatown* ☎ *02/222–0635* ▭ *MC, V.* ✥ *C4*

$ THAI ✕ **Nai Sow.** Many regulars say this Chinese-Thai restaurant, next door to Wat Plaplachai, has the city's best *tom yum goong* (spicy shrimp soup). Chefs may come and go, but the owner somehow manages to keep the recipe to this signature dish a secret. The food here is consistently excellent; try the *naw mai thalay* (sea asparagus in oyster sauce), the *phad kra prao kai, moo, goong* (spicy chicken, pork, and shrimp with basil leaves), the curried beef, or the sweet-and-sour mushrooms. Simpler options, like fried rice, are also very good. The fried taro is an unusual and delicious dessert. ✉ *3/1 Maitrichit Rd., Chinatown* ☎ *02/222–1539* ✍ *Reservations not accepted* ▭ *MC, V* Ⓜ *Subway: Hua Lamphong.*

$ CHINESE ✕ **Noodle 'N More.** This famous noodle shop would be at home in Tokyo or Hong Kong, with its three narrow floors, the top one a no-shoes-allowed tearoom with sofas and floor seating. The second floor has regular table

Continued on page 79

BANGKOK STREET FOOD

by Robin Goldstein & Alexis Herschkowitsch

In Thailand a good rule of thumb is, the less you pay for food, the better it is. And the food offered by street vendors is very cheap and very good. At any hour, day or night, Thais crowd around sidewalk carts and stalls, slurping noodles or devouring fiery *som tam* (green papaya salad) all for just pennies.

The cooks at street stalls are Thailand's true culinary giants.

If you only eat at upscale restaurants geared to foreigners, you'll miss out on the chili, fish sauce, and bright herbal flavors that define Thai cuisine. Even if you're picky, consider trying simple noodle dishes and skewered meats.

A typical meal costs between B20 and B50 (you pay when you get your food), and most stalls have a few tables and chairs where you can eat.

Street food in Bangkok.

Vendors don't adhere to meal times, nor are different foods served for breakfast, lunch, or dinner, as Thais often eat multiple snacks throughout the day rather than full meals. It's OK to combine foods from more than one cart; vendors won't mind, especially if they're selling something like a curried stew that comes in a plastic bag with no utensils. Find a different stall that offers plates and cutlery, order rice, and add your curry to the mix. Enjoy!

SOM TAM

Thai chefs use contrasting flavors to create balance in their cuisine. The popular green papaya salad is a good example, with dried shrimp, tart lime, salty fish sauce, crunchy peanuts, and long thin slices of green papaya. Pair it with sticky rice for a refreshing treat on a hot day.

SOUR Lime adds a welcome tartness to salads and other dishes, counteracting sweetness.

SPICY Thais like it hot, sometimes using more than 10 fiery chili peppers per dish.

SALTY Instead of salt, Thais often use fish sauce and fermented shrimp paste, which have more nuanced flavors.

BITTER Roasted peanuts add a pleasant bitterness and crunch.

SWEET Palm sugar, a dark brown, natural, aromatic sweetener—will make you wonder why you've been using refined sugar all your life.

STAYING HEALTHY

Sanitary standards in Thailand are far higher than those in many developing countries. By taking a few precautions, you can safely enjoy this wonderful cuisine.

- Avoid tap water. It's the bacteria in the water supply that causes most problems. The water on the table at stalls and restaurants is almost always purified, but stick with bottled water to play it safe.
- Lots of flies are never a good sign. Enough said.
- Know your stomach. Freshly cooked, hot food is least likely to contain bacteria. Steer clear of raw foods and fruits that cannot be peeled if you know you're sensitive.
- Use common sense when selecting a street vendor or a restaurant. Crowds mean high turnover, which translates into fresher food.

Fruit from Chatusak Market, Bangkok.

WHAT SHOULD I ORDER?

Locals will probably be eating the cart's specialty, so if you're not sure what to order, don't be afraid to point. The following are a few common and delicious dishes you'll find in Bangkok.

LARB Another refreshing and flavorful shredded salad, larb (pronounced lahb) consists of ground meat or fish, lime, fish sauce, and a generous helping of aromatic kaffir lime leaves.

PAD Noodles come in many varieties at street carts, and vendors add their own twists. Noodle soups with meat or innards, though traditionally Chinese or Vietnamese, are common in Bangkok, as are *pad khee mao* (drunken noodles) with vegetables, shellfish, or meat, wok-singed and served without broth. If you're in the Old City, stop by Raan Jay Fai (⇨Ch. 2), an open-air restaurant with legendary *pad khee mao*—decadently big rice noodles with river prawns and basil.

TOM YUM This delicious and aromatic water-based soup—flavored with fish sauce, lemongrass, kaffir lime leaves, and vegetables—is a local favorite. *Tom yum goong,* with shrimp, is a popular variation.

YANG Thais love these marinated meat sticks, grilled over charcoal. Pork is usually the tastiest.

Larb.

Pad Thai.

Tom yum.

WILL IT BE TOO SPICY?

Because most Thai cooks tone things down for foreigners, the biggest battle can sometimes be getting enough heat in your food. To be sure that your dish is spicy, ask for it *phet phet* (spicy); if you want it mild, request *mai phet* (less spicy). If you get a bite that's too spicy, water won't help—eat a bite of rice or something sweet to counteract the heat.

Food on sale at Damnoen Saduak floating market.

WHAT ARE ALL THE CONDIMENTS FOR?

At some street stalls, particularly soup and noodle shops, you'll be offered an array of seasonings and herbs to add to your dish: chilies marinated in salty fish sauce or soaking in oil; fresh herbs like mint, cilantro, and Thai basil; crunchy bits of toasted rice, peanuts, or fried onions; and lime wedges. Although it's a good idea to taste things you don't recognize so you don't over-flavor your meal, our advice is to pile it on!

Though it has a bad rap, the flavor enhancer MSG is sometimes used at street stalls and restaurants in Thailand. You can ask for food without it *(mai sai phong chu rat)* if it doesn't agree with you. You may also see MSG, a crystal that looks like white sugar, in a little jar on your table, along with sugar, chili paste, and fish sauce.

Two varieties of Thai basil.

YOU WANT ME TO EAT WHAT?

Pan-fried, seasoned insects such as ants, grasshoppers, and cockroaches, are popular snacks in Thailand. A plastic bag full of these crunchy delicacies will cost you about B20 or 50¢. To try your hand at insect-eating, start small. Little guys like ants are the most palatable, since they really just taste like whatever they've been flavored with (lime or chili, for example). Cockroaches have a higher squeamish factor: You have to pull the legs and the wings off the larger ones. And stay away from the silkworm cocoons, which do not taste any better than they sound.

At fruit stalls in Bangkok you may find the durian, a husk-covered fruit famous for its unpleasant smell. In fact the scent, which is a bit like spicy body odor, is so overpowering that some Thai hotels don't let you keep durians in your room. But don't judge the durian by its smell alone: Many love the fruit's pudding-like texture and intense tropical flavor, which is similar to passion fruit. Buy one at a fruit stand, ask the seller to cut it open, and taste its yellow flesh for yourself.

(above) Deep fried bugs (actual size).
(below) Durian.

seating and a counter with benches along the window that offer great people-watching on the street below. It's a little more chic than your average noodle stand, and its location near the Hua Lamphong subway station makes it a good place to refuel before exploring the neighborhood or while waiting for your train. As the name implies, you can find plenty of noodle dishes here, but the rice dishes are equally good. ✉*513–514 Rong Muang Rd., at Rama IV, Chinatown* ☎*02/613–1992* ▭*No credit cards* Ⓜ*Subway: Hua Lamphong.* ✣ *D4*

¢ INDIAN ✕**Punjab Sweets.** This vegetarian South Indian restaurant is always jam-packed with members of the local Indian community enjoying delicately crispy *pani poori* (crispy shells filled with potato and onion) or earthy samosas. Lighting is low and the place is a bit drab, but the food here is top-notch. There's an adjacent restaurant under the same management that serves meat, too. ✉*3/1 Maitrichit Rd., Chinatown* ✉*436/5 Soi ATM Chinatown* ☎*02/623–7457* ▭*MC, V* Ⓜ*Subway: Hua Lamphong.* ✣ *D4*

$$–$$$ CHINESE ✕**T & K Seafood.** Proudly displaying the freshest catches on ice out front, this enormous and popular seafood restaurant begins luring in customers daily at 4:30 PM and serve as late as 1:30 AM. Whole fish is always a good option, and generally cheaper than the crustaceans, which are also tasty. They also offer both shark's fin and bird's nest soup, but if you've had either of these once, that's probably enough. Stick with sea creatures here, and you'll be happiest. ✉*Thong Suphan 453, Chinatown* ☎*02/223–4519* ▭*MC, V* Ⓜ*Subway: Hua Lamphong* ⊗*No lunch.* ✣ *C4*

$ CHINESE ✕**Tang Jai Yoo.** This open-air ground-floor seafood restaurant, full of festive round tables, is a great Chinatown find. Whole crabs, lobsters, or sea leech come live from tanks inside the restaurant; stewed turtle soup is a fun departure from mainstream Thai cuisine. Roasted pig skin is one of the best terrestrial options. The set menus are the best way to sample a variety of dishes. ✉*85–89 Yaowapanich Rd., Chinatown* ☎*02/224–2167* ▭*MC, V* Ⓜ*Subway: Hua Lamphong.* ✣ *C4*

WORD OF MOUTH

"Finding [Chote Chitr] is an adventure and well worth it. In our hour walk, we saw only one other farang, and none were eating at the restaurant when we were there. It was perhaps the best Thai food I've ever eaten. The flavors were astounding. . . . We had mee grob (a revelation!), banana flower salad, red curry with duck, and a stunning eggplant dish. It takes about 20 minutes from the time you order for the food to begin to arrive, as everything is made just for you. Our bill was something like 270 baht. We will return!" —Kathie

DOWNTOWN BANGKOK

PRATUNAM & SIAM SQUARE

Unimaginably busy Pratunam and Siam Square have a little bit of everything, although many of the restaurants cater to the business crowd. These can range from humble lunch stops to power-dining extravaganzas.

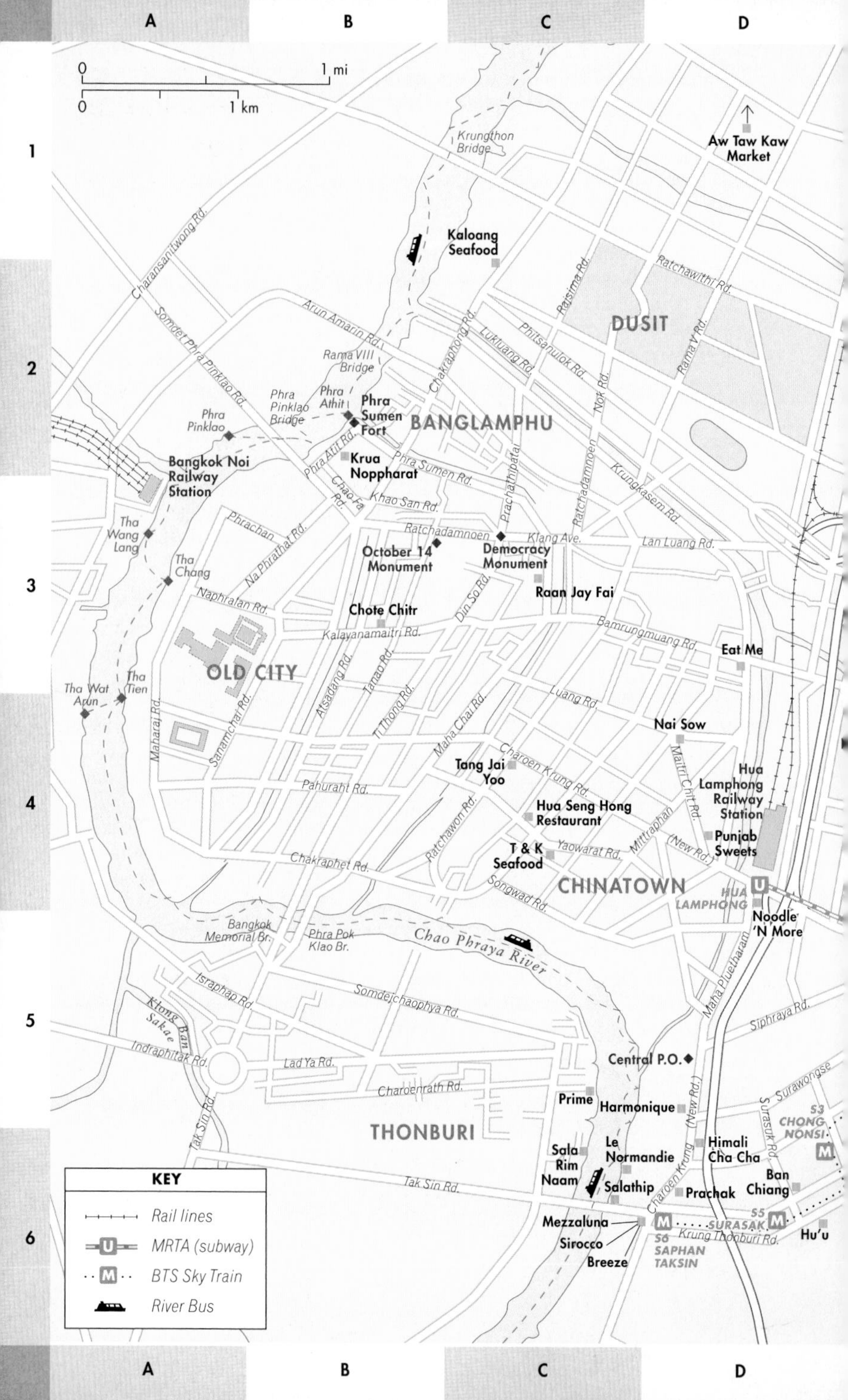
A
B
C
D
1
2
3
4
5
6
0
1 mi
0
1 km
Krungthon Bridge
Aw Taw Kaw Market
Charansanitwong Rd.
Kaloang Seafood
Ratchawithi Rd.
Rajsima Rd.
DUSIT
Arun Amarin Rd.
Somdet Phra Pinklao Rd.
Chakraphong Rd.
Lukluang Rd.
Phitsanulok Rd.
Rama V Rd.
Rama VIII Bridge
Phra Pinklao Bridge
Phra Athit
Phra Sumen Fort
Nok Rd.
Phra Pinklao
BANGLAMPHU
Prachathipatai
Bangkok Noi Railway Station
Krua Noppharat
Phra Atit Rd.
Phra Sumen Rd.
Ratchadamnoen
Krungkasem Rd.
Chao Fa Rd.
Khao San Rd.
Tha Wang Lang
Phrachan
Na Phrathat Rd.
Ratchadamnoen
Klang Ave.
Lan Luang Rd.
October 14 Monument
Democracy Monument
Tha Chang
Naphralan Rd.
Raan Jay Fai
Din So Rd.
Chote Chitr
Kalayanamaitri Rd.
Bamrungmuang Rd.
Eat Me
OLD CITY
Atsadang Rd.
Tanao Rd.
Tha Wat Arun
Tha Tien
Maharaj Rd.
Sanamchai Rd.
Ti Thong Rd.
Maha Chai Rd.
Luang Rd.
Nai Sow
Tang Jai Yoo
Charoen Krung Rd.
Maitri Chit Rd.
Hua Lamphong Railway Station
Pahurant Rd.
Hua Seng Hong Restaurant
Ratchawon Rd.
Mittraphan
Punjab Sweets
T & K Seafood
Yaowarat Rd.
(New Rd.)
Chakraphet Rd.
CHINATOWN
HUA LAMPHONG
Songwad Rd.
Noodle 'N More
Bangkok Memorial Br.
Phra Pok Klao Br.
Chao Phraya River
Maha Pluetharam
Israphap Rd.
Somdejchaophya Rd.
Siphraya Rd.
Klong Ban Sakae
Indraphitak Rd.
Lad Ya Rd.
Central P.O.
Charoenrath Rd.
Surawongse
Prime
Harmonique
Surasuk Rd.
S3 CHONG NONSI
Tak Sin Rd.
THONBURI
(New Rd.)
Charoen Krung
Sala Rim Naam
Le Normandie
Himali Cha Cha
Ban Chiang
Salathip
Prachak
Tak Sin Rd.
Mezzaluna
S5 SURASAK
Sirocco
Krung Thonburi Rd.
Hu'u
Breeze
S6 SAPHAN TAKSIN
KEY
Rail lines
MRTA (subway)
BTS Sky Train
River Bus
A
B
C
D

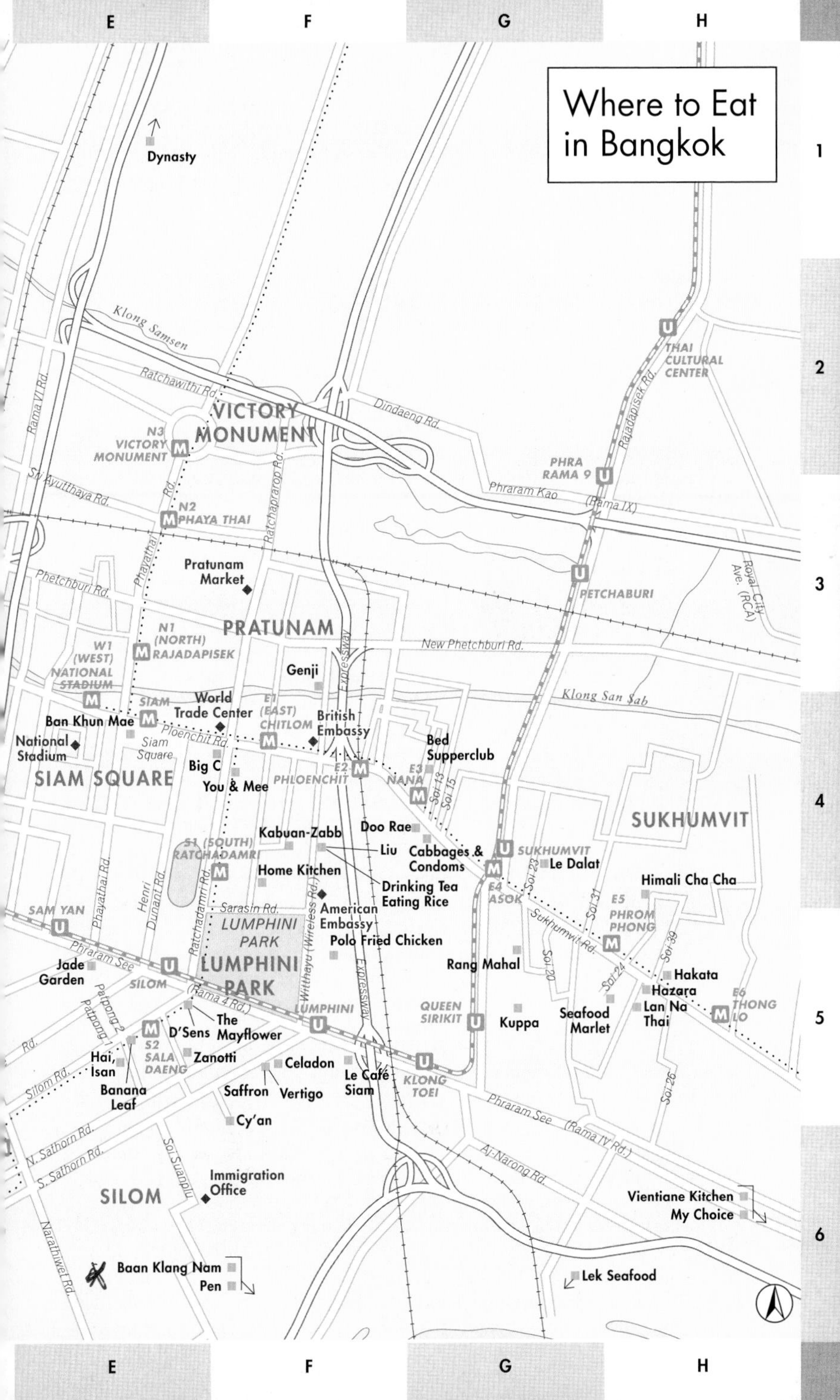

Where to Eat in Bangkok
E
F
G
H
1
2
3
4
5
6
Dynasty
Klong Samsen
Ratchawithi Rd.
VICTORY MONUMENT
N3 VICTORY MONUMENT
Dindaeng Rd.
Rama VI Rd.
Sri Ayutthaya Rd.
N2 PHAYA THAI
Phayathai Rd.
Ratchaprarop Rd.
THAI CULTURAL CENTER
Rajadapisek Rd.
PHRA RAMA 9
Phraram Kao (Rama IX)
Pratunam Market
Phetchburi Rd.
PETCHABURI
Royal City Ave. (RCA)
PRATUNAM
N1 (NORTH) RAJADAPISEK
W1 (WEST) NATIONAL STADIUM
New Phetchburi Rd.
Genji
Expressway
Klong San Sab
SIAM
World Trade Center
E1 (EAST) CHITLOM
British Embassy
Ban Khun Mae
Ploenchit Rd.
National Stadium
Siam Square
Bed Supperclub
Big C
E2
PHLOENCHIT
E3 NANA
Soi 13
Soi 15
SIAM SQUARE
You & Mee
SUKHUMVIT
Doo Rae
Kabuan-Zabb
S1 (SOUTH) RATCHADAMRI
Liu
Cabbages & Condoms
SUKHUMVIT
Le Dalat
Home Kitchen
Drinking Tea Eating Rice
E4 ASOK
Soi 23
Soi 31
Himali Cha Cha
American Embassy
Sarasin Rd.
SAM YAN
Phayathai Rd.
Henri Dunant Rd.
Ratchadamri Rd.
LUMPHINI PARK
Witthayu (Wireless Rd.)
E5 PHROM PHONG
Sukhumvit Rd.
Polo Fried Chicken
Soi 20
Soi 39
Jade Garden
Phraram See
SILOM
Rang Mahal
Soi 24
Hakata
Patpong 2
Patpong
(Rama 4 Rd.)
Hazara
Lan Na Thai
E6 THONG LO
Rd.
D'Sens
The Mayflower
LUMPHINI
QUEEN SIRIKIT
Kuppa
Seafood Marlet
S2 SALA DAENG
Zanotti
Celadon
Le Café Siam
KLONG TOEI
Hai, Isan
Silom Rd.
Banana Leaf
Saffron
Vertigo
Soi 26
Phraram See (Rama IV Rd.)
Cy'an
N. Sathorn Rd.
S. Sathorn Rd.
Soi Suanplu
Aj-Narong Rd.
SILOM
Immigration Office
Vientiane Kitchen
My Choice
Narathiwat Rd.
Baan Klang Nam
Pen
Lek Seafood

$$ Fodor's Choice ★ THAI ✕ **Ban Khun Mae.** This casually upmarket Siam Square restaurant is where the locals go if they want to enjoy skillful, authentic Thai cuisine in an atmosphere that's a couple of notches above that of the simple family restaurants. The room is dark, comfortable, and inviting, filled with big round tables. Start with the sensational *khung sa oug* (a plate of sweet and silky raw shrimp delightfully balanced with chili and garlic), and continue with *pla rad pig* (deep-fried grouper with sweet-and-sour hot sauce). Finish with the unique *tum tim krob* (water chestnut dumpling in coconut syrup with tapioca). ✉ *458/7–9 Siam Sq., Soi 8, Pratunam* ☎ *02/658–4112 up to 13* ▭ *MC, V.* ✣ *E4*

¢ THAI ✕ **Big C.** The food court on the fifth floor of the Big C shopping mall offers a staggering selection of authentic Thai (and a few Chinese) dishes at rock-bottom prices, with virtually nothing exceeding B80. Service is cafeteria-style: you choose, point, and then bring your tray to one of the tables in the middle of the bustling mall. Before you order, you'll prepay at the cashier station and receive a debit card; your selections are deducted from the balance. B200 should be plenty for two, and you can get a refund on any unspent baht after you're done. Highlights include a good version of *som tam,* very spicy chicken with ginger, Cantonese-style honey-roasted pork with crackly skin, and excellent sweetened Thai iced tea with milk. ✉ *97/11 Ratchadamri Rd., opposite Central World Plaza, Pratunam* ☎ *02/250–4888* ▭ *AE, MC, V* Ⓜ *Skytrain: Chitlom.* ✣ *E4*

$$$$ JAPANESE ✕ **Drinking Tea Eating Rice.** This upscale Japanese restaurant serves top-notch sushi, and the sake selection will please almost anyone. Service is almost uncomfortably deferential but never pompous. Not surprisingly, the tea is delicious, and the sushi rice is expertly vinegared; you might find yourself ordering it as a side and eating it plain. Their prized Matsuzaka beef dish is good, with an almost overwhelming surfeit of fat marbled throughout the meat. Dinner prices are sky-high, but set lunches are cheaper. ✉ *Conrad Hotel, 87 Wittayu [Wireless Rd.], Pratunam* ☎ *02/690–9999* ▭ *AE, DC, MC, V* Ⓜ *Skytrain: Ploenchit.* ✣ *F4*

$$$ JAPANESE ✕ **Genji.** Bangkok has plenty of good Japanese restaurants, but many can be a bit chilly toward newcomers. Genji is the happy exception, and the staff is always pleasant. There's an excellent sushi bar and several small private rooms where you can enjoy succulent grilled eel or grilled Kobe beef roll with asparagus and fried bean curd. Set menus for lunch and dinner are well conceived, and are a nice change from typical Thai fare. Lunch seats fill up quickly and dinner sometimes requires a wait. ✉ *Nai Lert Park Hotel Bangkok, 2 Wittayu [Wireless Rd.], Pratunam* ☎ *02/253–0123* ▭ *AE, DC, MC, V* Ⓜ *Skytrain: Ploenchit.* ✣ *F3*

$ Fodor's Choice ★ THAI ✕ **Home Kitchen.** A true hole-in-the-wall across the street from Langsuan Soi 6, this kitchen shines as one of the best places in the city for authentic local cuisine; it's where many local groups of friends go to celebrate the simple act of eating delicious food. Don't miss the *tom yum goong* (hot-and-sour soup with giant river prawns), which is redolent of lemongrass, Kaffir lime leaves, and galangal; a delicately crispy oyster omelet; crispy catfish salad with green mango; or the fried whole fish in chili-and-lime sauce. Such classics simply excel here, and you owe it to yourself to try all of them before leaving Bangkok. ✉ *94 Langsuan Rd., Pratunam* ☎ *No phone* ▭ *No credit cards* Ⓜ *Subway: Lumphini.* ✣ *F4*

¢ THAI ✕**Kabuan-Zabb.** Though Bangkok is filled with open-air holes-in-the-wall serving local staples, this casual eatery is one of the few with English menus and an English-speaking staff. Come here for outstanding versions of the classics: spicy *som tam, larb* (Northeastern salad of minced pork with cilantro, mint, lime juice, fish sauce, and ground toasted rice), and of course, sticky rice. Kabuan-Zabb caters to the local lunch crowd and prices are unbelievably low. ✉*Wittayu (Wireless Rd.), across from U.S. Embassy, Pratunam* ☎*02/253–5243 or 02/253–5244* ▭*No credit cards* ⌚*No dinner.* ✥ *F4*

$$$$ CHINESE ✕**Liu.** You'll want to be spotted at this swanky Chinese restaurant, whose concept and design comes from the creator of the equally snazzy Green T. House in Beijing. The interior is dominated by light-colored wood, and the overall effect is soothing, especially given the high level of service you'll receive here. The cuisine, which Liu calls "Neo Classic Chinese," is a fusion of different regional styles; they are especially proud of the fried frogs' legs. Reserve well in advance, especially for the always-overbooked dim sum lunches. ✉*Conrad Hotel, 87 Wittayu [Wireless Rd.], Pratunam* ☎*02/690–9999* ▭*AE, DC, MC, V* Ⓜ*Skytrain: Ploenchit.* ✥ *F12*

¢–$ Fodor's Choice ★ THAI ✕**Polo Fried Chicken.** After offering only a lunch menu for decades, Polo Fried Chicken finally responded to its unwaning popularity by expanding its hours until 10 PM. The addition of an air-conditioned dining room is also a recent concession to its loyal clientele. Here you'll get world-class fried chicken, flavored with black pepper and plenty of golden-brown garlic; the best way to sample it is with sticky rice and a plate of *som tam,* all for only B170. The place is a bit hard to find—as you enter Soi Polo, it's about 50 yards in on your left. At lunchtime, you need to get here before noon to snag a table before the office workers descend. The restaurant will deliver to your hotel (if you're reasonably close to Lumphini Park) for B30. ✉*137/1–2 Soi Polo, off Wittayu [Wireless Rd.], Pratunam* ☎*02/251–2772 or 02/252–0856* ✍*Reservations not accepted* ▭*No credit cards* Ⓜ*Subway: Lumphini.* ✥ *F5*

$$$$ THAI ✕**You & Mee.** Since hotel restaurants in Bangkok are often disappointing, You & Me, located in the Grand Hyatt Erawan, is a pleasant surprise: quality is high, but the prices aren't too high, and the atmosphere is relaxed and casual, with simple colors and largely unadorned tables. Come for the good selection of noodles or the *khao tom* (rice soup). **■ TIP→There's a buffet at dinner, but you're better off sticking to the dishes on the menu.** ✉*494 Ratchadamri Rd., Pratunam* ☎*02/254–1234* ▭*AE, DC, MC, V* Ⓜ*Skytrain: Ratchadamri.* ✥ *E4*

SILOM

Silom has Bangkok's biggest proliferation of restaurants, period. Many of them are in hotels, on the upper floors of skyscrapers, or around Patpong. You can find a vast variety of ethnic cuisines and restaurant styles in this district, from authentic, humble northern Thai to elaborate, wallet-busting preparations of foie gras.

$$$$ THAI ✕**Baan Klang Nam.** This clapboard house is right on the Chao Phraya River, and if you cruise the river at night, you'll probably end up gazing upon it, wishing you were among the crowd dining at one of Bangkok's

most romantic spots. Happily, the place is less touristy than other restaurants of this type, most of which are part of big hotels. Spicy fried crab with black pepper, steamed fish with soy sauce, river prawns with glass noodles, and stir-fried crab with curry powder are excellent choices from the seafood-centric menu. ✉ *288 Rama III, Soi 14, Yannawa, south of Silom* ☎ *02/292–0175* ▭ *AE, MC, V* Ⓜ *Skytrain: Chong Nonsi.* ✥ *E6*

$ THAI ✕ **Ban Chiang.** This old wooden house is an oasis in the concrete city; the decor is turn-of-the-20th-century Bangkok, with antique prints and old photographs adorning the walls. The place is popular with the *farang* (foreigners) set, and your food won't come spicy unless you request it that way. Try the salted prawns or deep fried grouper with garlic and white pepper, or dried whitefish with mango dip; and finish with banana fritters with coconut ice cream. ✉ *14 Srivieng Rd., Silom* ☎ *02/236–7045 or 02/266–6994* ▭ *AE, MC, V* Ⓜ *Skytrain: Surasak.*

$ THAI ✕ **Banana Leaf.** If you need a break from shopping on Silom Road, stop here for delicious and cheap eats. Try the baked crab with glass noodles, grilled black band fish, deep-fried fish with garlic and pepper, or grilled pork with coconut milk dip. The menu also offers 11 equally scrumptious vegetarian selections. Note that there's a B400 minimum to pay by credit card. ✉ *Silom Complex, Silom Rd., Silom* ☎ *02/231–3124* ▭ *AE, MC, V* Ⓜ *Skytrain: Sala Daeng.* ✥ *E5*

$$$$ SEAFOOD ✕ **Breeze.** The newest restaurant to arrive at the State Tower (home of some of Bangkok's priciest restaurants), this ultra-hip, sky-high spot is where you'll spot Bangkok's moneyed set as well as international jetsetters. The shockingly futuristic design will have you thinking it's 2060, an effect that's most pronounced at night when the dining roomglows with purple neon. The menu includes a mix of Asian- and international-style meat dishes in addition to seafood, often in over-the-top preparations such as silver cod caramelized with Laurent Perrier Champagne. The environmentally controversial shark's fin soup is served with free-range eggs and organic greens—an ironic juxtaposition. ✉ *52nd fl., State Tower, 1055 Silom Rd., Silom* ☎ *02/624–9999* ▭ *AE, DC, MC, V* Ⓜ *Skytrain: Saphan Taksin.* ✥ *C6*

$$$$ THAI ✕ **Celadon.** Lotus ponds reflect the city's beautiful evening lights at this romantic restaurant. The upmarket Thai food is good, with elegant touches that cater to locals as well as foreigners. The extensive menu includes preparations of enormous river prawns, excellent red duck curry, stir-fried morning glory, and a good version of banana-blossom salad. Some of the seafood dishes can be prepared in different styles; the best is with chili and basil. Ask for your dishes spicy if you want the more authentic Thai balance of flavors; sometimes their dishes are too sweet. ✉ *Sukhothai Hotel, 13/3 S. Sathorn Rd., Silom* ☎ *02/344–8888* 🌐 *www.sukhothai.com* ▭ *AE, DC, MC, V* Ⓜ *Subway: Lumphini; Skytrain: Sala Daeng.* ✥ *F5*

$$$$ FRENCH ✕ **D'Sens.** Bangkok's first Michelin three-star chefs arrived in 2004 in the form of brothers Jacques and Laurent Pourcel, executive chefs of Le Jardin des Sens in Montpellier, France. Granted, they only came to set things up, but they also installed a veteran of their restaurant to stay in Bangkok, and the results are delicious. Skip the dishes with prestige

ingredients like foie gras and lobster, and choose instead to appreciate the subtlety of the kitchen in such dishes as mussel soup with saffron, Parmesan crisps, and orange cream or a delicate preparation of roast turbot. The prices and the views from the 22nd floor are both sky-high. Set menus are available at both lunch and dinner. ✉ *Dusit Thani Bangkok Hotel, 946 Rama IV Rd., Silom* ☎ *02/200–9000 Ext. 2499* ⊕ *www.dusit.com* ▭ *AE, DC, MC, V* Ⓜ *Subway: Lumphini; Skytrain: Sala Daeng* ⊙ *Closed Sun. No lunch Sat.* ✥ *E5*

2

$$ THAI ✕ **Eat Me.** Though this café-like establishment serves a smattering of above-average Thai dishes, the main attraction is the young and laid-back crowd, not the food. The atmosphere is decidedly chill, with tables scattered about. Stop by if you're in the neighborhood to people watch and see who you can meet. (Hint: it will most likely be an expat.) ✉ *Soi Pipat 2, Silom* ☎ *02/238–0931* ▭ *AE, MC, V* Ⓜ *Skytrain: Chong Nonsi.* ✥ *D3*

$ THAI ✕ **Hai, Isan.** A sure sign of quality, Hai is packed with Thais sharing tables filled with northeast favorites like grilled chicken, spicy papaya salad, and spicy minced pork. The open-air dining area can be hot and is often crowded and noisy, but that's part of the fun. The staff doesn't speak English, so the best way to order is to point to things that look good on neighboring tables. ✉ *2/4–5 Soi Convent, off Silom Rd., Silom* ☎ *02/631–0216* ▭ *No credit cards* Ⓜ *Subway: Silom; Skytrain: Sala Daeng.* ✥ *E5*

$$ THAI ✕ **Harmonique.** Choose between tables on the terrace or in the dining rooms of this small house near the river. Inside, Thai antiques, chests scattered with bric-a-brac, and bouquets that seem to tumble out of their vases create relaxing clutter, as though you're dining at a relative's house. The staff is very good at assisting indecisive diners choose from the small menu. The *Massaman* (Muslim-style, peanut sauce–based curry) pork spareribs, the mild crab curry, and the deep-fried fish with lemongrass sauce are all excellent. *Chu-chee* prawns or *larb moo* are slightly more interesting dishes, as is the *hoa mouk*—fish curry in a banana leaf. Over the years the crowd has become increasingly tourist-heavy, but there are still Thais who eat here regularly. ✉ *22 Charoen Krung (New Rd.), Soi 34, Silom* ☎ *02/237–8175* or *02/630–6270* ▭ *AE, DC, MC, V* ⊙ *Closed Sun.* Ⓜ *Skytrain: Saphan Taksin.* ✥ *D5*

$$ INDIAN ✕ **Himali Cha Cha.** Cha Cha, who cooked for Indian Prime Minister Jawaharlal Nehru, died in 1996, but his recipes live on and are prepared with equal ability by his son Kovit. The tandoori chicken is locally famous, but the daily specials, precisely explained by the staff, are usually too intriguing to pass up. The breads and the mango *lassi* (yogurt drinks) are delicious. The northern Indian cuisine includes garlic naan and cheese naan, served with various dishes—the mutton tandoori is particularly good. The typical Indian-themed decor sets the scene for this oldie but goodie. A branch on Convent Soi in Silom serves the same food in a more spacious dining area. ✉ *1229/11 Charoen Krung (New Rd.), Silom* ☎ *02/235–1569 or 02/630–6358* Ⓜ *Skytrain: Saphan Taksin.* ✉ *Sukhumvit Soi 31* ☎ *02/258–8843* ✉ *Silom Soi Convent, Silom* ☎ *02/238–1478* ▭ *AE, MC, V.*

$$$ ECLECTIC ✕ **Hu'u.** One of Bangkok's hippest drinking spots is worth checking out for dinner as well. The menu hops from sashimi to cheeseburgers to

A street vendor prepares spicy mango salad in Bangkok.

fried wontons, but the best choices are the pasta dishes, such as homemade ravioli. Seared foie gras atop a toasted brioche is good, too. The place is dark, trendy, and modern; for a better atmosphere, you might choose to dine in the bar area downstairs, where many patrons come just for delicious pre- or post-dinner cocktails. ✉ *The Ascott, Levels 1–2, 187 S. Sathorn Rd., Silom* ☎ *02/676–6677* 🌐 *www.huuinasia.com* 💳 *AE, DC, MC, V* Ⓜ *Skytrain: Chong Nonsi.* ✣ *D6*

$$$$ CHINESE ✕ **Jade Garden.** You won't find a better dim sum brunch than the one at Jade Garden. The decor is more understated than at many expensive Chinese restaurants, with a remarkable wood-beam ceiling and softly lighted Chinese-print screens. Private dining rooms are available with advance notice. Two good dinner specials are fried Hong Kong noodles and pressed duck with tea leaves. Look for the monthly "special promotion" dish featuring seasonal ingredients. ✉ *Montien Hotel, 54 Surawong Rd., Silom* ☎ *02/233–7060* 💳 *AE, MC, V* Ⓜ *Skytrain: Sala Daeng.* ✣ *E5*

$$$$ THAI ✕ **Lan Na Thai.** This hangout's hip bar scene attracts a cool, mainly international clientele. The reasonably authentic Thai menu includes the ubiquitous som tam, steamed freshwater prawns, and duck with kaffir lime leaf; sea bass wrapped in banana leaf and pork belly in Chiang Mai–style curry paste are two more exciting options. Though the beautiful setting (think comfy, plush seating and large tapestries) and toned-down dishes are geared toward foreigners, sometimes that's just what you're in the mood for after a long day of exploring. ✉ *Sukhumvit Soi 38, Silom* ☎ *02/713–6048* 💳 *AE, MC, V* ⏲ *No lunch* Ⓜ *Skytrain: Hua Lamphong.* ✣ *H5*

$$$ ECLECTIC **Le Café Siam.** This quiet restaurant, in a pleasant old house far from traffic noise, offers a successful mix of spicy Thai and subtle French cuisines. It's really like two restaurants in one, perfect for a group with disparate tastes. Some might find the portions small, but the quality of the food more than makes up for this, and, at any rate, it's worth saving room for the magnificent desserts. Many of the objects and artwork that decorate the house are for sale, so do some browsing while you eat. It's best to arrive by taxi as this place can be difficult to find on your own; if you call the restaurant, they will help arrange transportation for you. ✉ *4 Soi Sri Akson, Silom* ☎ *02/671–0030* 🌐 *www.lecafesiam.com* 💳 *AE, MC, V* ⏲ *No lunch* Ⓜ *Subway: Klong Toei.* ✥ *F5*

$$$$ FRENCH **Le Normandie.** Perched atop the Oriental Hotel, this legendary restaurant commands an impressive view of the Chao Phraya. France's most highly esteemed chefs periodically take over the kitchen, often importing ingredients from the old country to use in their creations. Even when no superstar is on the scene, the food is remarkable; the pricey menu (it's hard to get away with spending less than B5,000 on a meal) often includes classic dishes like slow-cooked shoulder of lamb. ✉ *48 Oriental Ave., Silom* ☎ *02/659–9000 Ext. 7670* ✍ *Reservations essential, jacket required* 💳 *AE, DC, MC, V* ⏲ *No lunch Sun.* Ⓜ *Skytrain: Saphan Taksin.* ✥ *C6*

$$ Fodor's Choice ★ THAI **Lek Seafood.** This unassuming storefront beneath an overpass is the sort of establishment that brings international foodies to Bangkok in droves. They come for the spicy crab salad with lemongrass, spicy catfish with toasted rice salad, or fried grouper topped with a spicy chili sauce—all expertly cooked and perfectly balanced between the five flavors. The interior here is nothing special, with poor lighting and bluish colored walls, but the lively buzz makes up for it. ✉ *156 Soi Phiphat, Narathiwat Ratchanakharin Rd.* ☎ 02/636–6460 💳 *AE, MC, V* Ⓜ *Skytrain: Chong Nonsi.* ✥ *G6*

$$$$ Fodor's Choice ★ CHINESE **The Mayflower.** Regulars at this top Cantonese restaurant include members of the Thai royal family, heads of state, and business tycoons. These VIPs favor the six opulent private rooms (one-day advance notice required), but the main dining room is equally stylish, with carved wood screens, porcelain vases, and an air of refinement that complements the outstanding Cantonese food. Delicious Peking duck skin is served without a shred of meat, with roti-like pancakes, plum sauce, and fresh onions. Dim sum options are also stellar, especially the fried taro and pork rolls and the green tea steam rolls. The wine list is excellent but pricey. ✉ *Dusit Thani Bangkok, Rama IV Rd., Silom* ☎ *02/200–9000* 💳 *AE* Ⓜ *Subway: Silom; Skytrain: Sala Daeng.* ✥ *E5*

$$$ Fodor's Choice ★ THAI **Pen.** This spacious restaurant has little atmosphere, but it's where the true seafood aficionados go to splurge. Though it's expensive by Thai restaurant standards, it's still a bargain compared to hotel restaurants, and many dishes here cannot be found outside of Thailand: deep-fried parrot fish served with shallots, sliced green mango in tamarind sauce, delectable mud crabs, enormous charcoal-grilled river prawns, Chinese-style mantis prawns, and raw crab. Even though it's a little out of the way, this temple to seafood is not to be missed. ✉ *2068/4*

Chan Rd., Chongnonsee, Yannawa, south of Silom ☎02/287–2907 or 02/286–7061 ▭MC, V. ✣ F6

$$ CHINESE ✕**Prachak.** This little place with bare walls and tile floor serves superb *ped* (roast duck) and *moo daeng* (red pork) and is a favorite of many locals. Wealthy Thai families will send their maids here to bring dinner home; you may want to follow their lead, as it can get crowded. Whether you eat in or take out, get here early—by 6 PM there's often no duck or pork left, and by 9 PM it's closed. Finding Prachak is a bit challenging. It's on busy Charoen Krung (New Road), across the street from the big Robinson shopping center near the Shangri-La Hotel. ✉*1415 Charoen Krung (New Rd.), Silom Bangrak, Silom* ☎*02/234–3755* ▭*No credit cards* Ⓜ*Skytrain: Saphan Taksin.* ✣ *D6*

$$$ THAI ✕**Saffron.** The creative modern Thai menu here is even more exciting than the stunning views from the 52nd floor of the towering Banyan Tree Hotel. Start with a banana-blossom salad with chicken, which mixes chili paste, dried shrimp paste, and cilantro for brightness. Then try the *phad pak kana moo grib* (stir-fried crisp pork belly with kale), a Chinese-influenced gem, or fried crab in Indian curry powder. ✉*Banyan Tree Hotel, 21/100 S. Sathorn Rd., Silom* ☎*02/679–1200* ▭*AE, MC, V* Ⓜ*Subway: Lumphini; Skytrain: Sala Daeng.* ✣ *F5*

$$$$ THAI ✕**Salathip.** On a veranda facing the Chao Phraya River, this restaurant's setting practically guarantees a romantic evening. Be sure to reserve an outside table so you can enjoy the breeze. Although the food may not have as many chilies as some would like, the Thai standards are represented on the menu. Good among those are Phuket lobster dishes and curried river prawns. Set menus make sampling many different things easy. The live traditional music makes everything taste even better. ✉*Shangri-La Hotel, 89 Soi Wat Suan Phu, Charoen Krung (New Rd.), Silom* ☎*02/236–7777* ✍*Reservations essential* ▭*AE, DC, MC, V* ⏲*No lunch* Ⓜ*Skytrain: Saphan Taksin.* ✣ *C6*

$$$$ ASIAN ✕**Sirocco.** The most memorable, impressive atmosphere of any restaurant in Bangkok—perhaps in all of Asia—is unfortunately diminished by the unimpressive food coming out of its kitchen. On the 63rd floor of one of Bangkok's tallest buildings, this is said to be the tallest open-air restaurant in the world. Its shockingly expensive, haphazard fusion menu includes many imported prestige ingredients, but it stumbles from lamb to lobster with scarcely any success. If you don't want to put up with the bad food, you can come just for a drink at the apocalyptic Sky Bar, which juts out at a gravity-defying angle; however, keep in mind that the bar doesn't offer seating. Perhaps the best strategy is to sit in the restaurant and just order something small. Be forewarned that the whole rooftop closes for windy weather from time to time. ✉*63rd fl., State Tower, 1055 Silom Rd., Silom* ☎*02/624–9999* ▭*AE, DC, MC, V* Ⓜ*Skytrain: Saphan Taksin* ⏲*No lunch.* ✣

$$$$ SEAFOOD ✕**Vertigo.** You'll dine on top of it all at this classy lounge, bar, and eatery—it's one of the tallest open-air restaurants on the planet. Tables are set near the roof's edge for maximum effect; there are also comfy white couches and low-lying tables at the adjacent Moon Bar, if you prefer to come just for drinks. In spite of its name, Vertigo doesn't induce quite as much acrophobia as its competitor Sirocco atop the State Tower, and the

international menu here, which focuses on barbecued seafood, is better, and the service is less pompous. Due to its altitude, the restaurant frequently closes when there are high winds, so you should have a backup plan in mind. Note that it doesn't open until 6:30 PM daily. ✉ *Banyan Tree Hotel, 21/100 S. Sathorn Rd., Silom* ☎ *02/679–1200* ▭ *AE, MC, V* ⏲ *No lunch* Ⓜ *Subway: Lumphini; Skytrain: Sala Daeng.* ✣ *F5*

$$$$ Fodor's Choice ★ ITALIAN

✕ **Zanotti.** Everything about this place is top-notch, from the attentive service to the extensive menu focusing on the regional cuisines of Piedmont and Tuscany. You can find anything from pizza and pasta to fish and steak, but the traditional osso buco served with gremolata and saffron risotto is recommended, though it's the priciest option on the menu. There's an unusually broad Italian wine list with selections by the bottle, glass, or carafe. The prix-fixe lunches are a bargain. The low ceilings and closely grouped tables give the place some intimacy, but the vibe is more lively than romantic, especially during the lunch and dinner rushes. ✉ *Saladaeng Colonnade Condominium, 21/2 Soi Saladaeng, off Silom Rd., Silom* ☎ *02/636–0002 or 02/636–0266* 🌐 *www.zanotti-ristorante.com* ▭ *AE, DC, MC, V* Ⓜ *Skytrain: Sala Daeng.* ✣ *E5*

SUKHUMVIT

Sukhumvit is Bangkok's hippest area for dining and going out, and as such, many of the restaurants have more style than substance, although there's good food to be had.

$$$$ ECLECTIC

✕ **Bed Supperclub.** You have to be 20 years old to get in here, even for dinner. Don't wear sandals or shorts if you're a man; make sure to bring a picture ID with you, no matter what your age; and be prepared for police drug raids, which are frequent. And whatever you do, make a reservation well in advance. But don't let any of that scare you away—this unique modern restaurant is worth the headaches. The "tables" consist of long beds with white sheets, lined up along the walls. The eclectic Mediterranean and Asian fusion menu changes every two weeks, and the food can be hit-or-miss (salmon with Gorgonzola?), but the experience is still worthwhile for a taste of Bangkok's trendiest side, especially if you stick around after dinner, when the place turns into one of the city's hottest nightclubs. ■ **TIP→ Coming for dinner is a much easier way to get in than trying to impress the velvet-rope bouncers later in the evening.** Every Monday is "Black Market Monday," when the club is lighted entirely with candles, and there's a fashion show every Wednesday. ✉ *26 Sukhumvit Soi 11, Sukhumvit* ☎ *02/651–3537* 🌐 *www.bedsupperclub.com* ▭ *AE, DC, MC, V* Ⓜ *Skytrain: Nana.* ✣ *G4*

$$ THAI

✕ **Cabbages & Condoms.** Don't be put off by the restaurant's odd name and the array of contraceptive devices for sale. This popular place raises funds for the Population & Community Development Association, Thailand's family-planning program. The food here is Westernized but competently prepared; standouts are the deep-fried chicken wrapped in pandanus leaves, fried fish with mango sauce, and crispy duck salad. The eatery is comfortable and funky, with Christmas lights strung about, and it serves up good food for a good cause. ✉ *10 Sukhumvit Soi 12, Sukhumvit* ☎ *02/229–4610* ▭ *AE, DC, MC, V* Ⓜ *Subway: Sukhumvit; Skytrain: Asok.* ✣ *G4*

$$$$ KOREAN **Doo Rae.** While there are many authentic Korean restaurants in the Sukhumvit Plaza, this barbecue joint is one of the best. Even though there are three stories of tables, there's often a wait, even at 9 PM on a weeknight. Table barbecue—you cook the meat yourself over a grill at your table—featuring hearty *bulgogi* (thin slices of beef in a tasty marinade) is a good way to go, as are the substantial tofu stews. Drinks include a larger selection of sake and *soju* (a rice-based Korean drink similar to vodka, but with a lower alcohol content) than you'll find elsewhere in the city. ✉ *212/15 Sukhumvit Soi 12, Sukhumvit* ☎ *02/653–3815* ▭ *AE, MC, V* ✥ *F4*

$$ JAPANESE **Hakata.** Although there are many good Japanese restaurants in the Sukhumvit area near the Emporium shopping center, Hakata is a step above most. The main dining area and sushi bar are spacious and relaxing, and there are private rooms available as well. Sushi prices run a little high, but the regular dishes like tempura and *katsu-don* (fried pork strips) are reasonably priced and tasty. ✉ *4 Sukhumvit Soi 39, Sukhumvit* ☎ *02/259–9154* ▭ *MC, V* Ⓜ *Skytrain: Phrom Phong.* ✥ *H5*

$$$$ INDIAN **Hazara.** After a long day of sightseeing, the atmosphere at this upscale Indian eatery simply can't be beat. Plush couches and beautiful drapes create a chic-cozy feel, and there's a great drink list. Some may feel the food itself doesn't hold a candle to the cheap Indian street food you can find elsewhere in the city. It's true that the menu isn't too creative, but there are some interesting options, such as the Dahl Hazara, a dark dahl. Tandoor items are especially good. There's a large array of vegetarian dishes and different types of naan, and Hazara does not cook with MSG. ✉ *Sukhumvit Soi 38, Sukhumvit* ☎ 02/ 713–6048 ▭ *AE, MC, V* Ⓜ *Subway: Sukhumvit.* ✥ *H5*

$$ ECLECTIC **Kuppa.** This light and airy space maintains the aura of its former life as a warehouse, but it's certainly more chic than shabby these days, with polished metal and blond wood adding a hip counterpoint to cement floors. An advantage to such a space is that, unlike many downtown eateries, each table has plenty of room around it. Kuppa offers traditional Thai fare as well as many international dishes, and it has a dedicated following because of its coffee (roasted on the premises) and its impressive desserts. The one drawback is that the portions are somewhat small for the price. ✉ *39 Sukhumvit Soi 16, Sukhumvit* ☎ *02/663–0450 or 02/258–0194* ▭ *AE, DC, MC, V* ⊙ *Closed Mon.* Ⓜ *Subway: Sukhumvit; Skytrain: Asok.* ✥ *G5*

$$ VIETNAMESE **Le Dalat.** This classy restaurant, a favorite with Bangkok residents, consists of several intimate dining rooms in what was once a private home. Don't pass up the *naem neuang,* a garlicky grilled meatball you place on a piece of rice paper before piling on bits of garlic, ginger, hot chili, star apple, and mango and then wrapping the whole thing in a lettuce leaf and popping it in your mouth. Seafood dishes—which are among the pricier options here—include *cha ca thang long,* Hanoi-style fried fish with dill. ✉ *47/1 Sukhumvit Soi 23, opposite Indian Embassy, Sukhumvit* ☎ *02/260–1849* ✍ *Reservations essential* ▭ *AE, DC, MC, V* Ⓜ *Subway: Sukhumvit; Skytrain: Asok.* ✥ *G4*

$ THAI **My Choice.** Thais with a taste for their grandmothers' traditional recipes have flocked to this restaurant off Sukhumvit Road since the mid-'80s. The *ped aob,* whole roasted duck, is particularly popular. The interior is plain, so when the weather is cool most people prefer to sit outside. ✉*Sukhumvit Soi 36, Sukhumvit* ☎*02/258–6174 or 02/259–9470* ▭*AE, DC, MC, V* Ⓜ*Skytrain: Thong Lo.* ⊕ *H6*

$$$$ INDIAN ✕ **Rang Mahal.** Savory food in a pleasant setting with great views of the city brings people back to this upscale Indian restaurant. *Bindi do piaza* with okra is interesting, *rogunjosh kashmiri* (mutton curry) is a hit, and the homemade naan breads are top-notch. The main dining room has Indian music, which can be loud to some ears, but there are smaller rooms for a quieter meal. Take a jacket—the air-conditioning can be overpowering—and ask for a window seat for a great view of the city. ✉*Rembrandt Hotel, 19 Sukhumvit Soi 18, Sukhumvit* ☎*02/261–7100* ✍*Reservations essential* ▭*AE, DC, MC, V* Ⓜ*Subway: Sukhumvit; Skytrain: Asok.* ⊕ *G5*

$$$$ THAI ✕ **Seafood Market.** Although it's miles from the ocean, the fish here are so fresh it feels like the boats must be somewhere nearby. Like at a supermarket, you take a small cart and choose from an array of seafood—crabs, prawns, lobsters, clams, oysters, and fish. The waiter then takes your selections to the chef, who cooks it however you like. Typically, your eyes are bigger than your stomach, so select with prudence, not gusto. Unfortunately, the 1,500-seat setting and fluorescent lighting add to the supermarket feel, but it's a fun and unique dining experience. ✉*89 Sukhumvit Soi 24, Sukhumvit* ☎*02/661–1255 up to 59* 🌐*www.seafood.com.th* ✍*Reservations not accepted* ▭*AE, DC, MC, V* Ⓜ*Skytrain: Phrom Phong.* ⊕ *G5*

$ LAO ✕ **Vientiane Kitchen.** This open-air restaurant, named for the capital of Laos, is set under thatched roofs has a slightly gritty feel. You can opt for a table or traditional seating on floor mats around a low table. Lao cuisine is similar to northeastern Thai cuisine: Among the Thai-style standards offered here, like traditional grilled chicken, sticky rice, and *som tam* (spicy papaya salad), are a few riskier dishes like *Nam tok* (waterfall), so named because it's hot enough to makes your eyes run like a waterfall (it's actually toned down a bit here by Lao standards). The frog soup and grilled duck beak are actually quite tasty, despite the strange images they conjure up. It's best to go with a group so you can try several dishes. Live Laotian music and dance add to the experience. ✉*8 Sukhumvit Soi 36, Sukhumvit* ☎*02/258–6171* 🌐*www.vientiane-kitchen.com* ▭*DC, MC, V* Ⓜ*Skytrain: Thong Lo.* ⊕ *H6*

WHERE TO STAY

Bangkok offers a staggering range of lodging choices, and even some of the best rooms are affordable to travelers on a budget. The city has nearly 500 hotels and guesthouses, and the number is growing. In fact, the amount of competition has brought the prices down at many of the city's hotels; unfortunately, service has suffered at some as a result of cutting corners to lower prices. Still, you'll feel more pampered here than in many other cities.

For first-class lodging, few cities in the world rival Bangkok. In recent years the Oriental, Peninsula, Four Seasons (formerly the Regent), and

BEST BETS FOR BANGKOK LODGING

Fodor's offers a selective listing of quality lodging experiences at every price range, from the city's best budget guesthouse to its most sophisticated luxury hotels. Here, we've compiled our top recommendations by price and experience. The very best properties—those that provide a particularly remarkable experience in their price range—are designated in the listings with a Fodor's Choice logo.

FODOR'S CHOICE

Chakrabongse Villas, $$$$ p. 94
Conrad, $$$$ p. 97
Hilton Millennium, $$$ p. 97
Peninsula, $$$$ p. 97
Shangri-La, $$$$ p. 106

By Price

¢

Krung Kasem Srikrung Hotel p. 96
River View Guest House p. 96

$

Buddy Lodge p. 93
Ibis Siam Bangkok p. 100
La Residence p. 104
Stable Lodge p. 110

$$

Bel-Aire Princess p. 108
Grand China Princess p. 94
Manohra Hotel p. 104
Reflections p. 93

$$$

Bangkok Marriott Resort and Spa p. 96
Nai Lert Park Bangkok p. 101
Siam Heritage p. 106
Triple Two Silom p. 107

$$$$

Oriental p. 105
Sheraton Grande Sukhumvit p. 110

By Experience

BEST VIEW

Banyan Tree Bangkok, $$$$ p. 103
Grand China Princess, $$ p. 94
Lebua, $$$$ p. 104
Peninsula, $$$$ p. 97
River View Guest House, ¢ p. 96
Shangri-La, $$$$ p. 106

BEST LOCATION

Bangkok Marriott Resort & Spa, $$$–$$$$ p. 96
Shangri-La, $$$$ p. 106
Sheraton Grande Sukhumvit, $$$$ p. 110
Westin Grande Sukhumvit, $$$$ p. 111

BEST SPA

Bangkok Marriott Resort & Spa, $$$–$$$$ p. 96
Four Seasons, $$$$ p. 100
Grand Hyatt Erawan, $$$$ p. 100
Metropolitan, $$$$ p. 104

BEST INTERIOR DESIGN

Chakrabongse Villas, $$$$ p. 94
Metropolitan, $$$$ p. 104
Siam@Siam, $$$ p. 103
Sukhothai, $$$$ p. 107
Triple Two Silom, $$$ p. 107

HOT SCENE

Conrad, $$$$ p. 97
Metropolitan, $$$$ p. 104
Siam@Siam, $$$ p. 104
Triple Two Silom, $$$ p. 107

BEST FOR KIDS

Bangkok Marriott Resort and Spa, $$$–$$$$ p. 96
Banyan Tree, $$$$ p. 103
Hilton Millenium, $$$ p. 97
Marriott Courtyard, $$–$$$ p. 101

BEST POOL

Conrad, $$$$ p. 97
Hilton Millenium, $$$ p. 97
Nai Lert Park Bangkok, $$$ p. 101
Oriental, $$$$ p. 105
Peninsula, $$$$ p. 97

BEST HOTEL BAR

Banyan Tree, $$$$ p. 103
Conrad, $$$$ p. 97
Oriental, $$$$ p. 105
Siam@Siam, $$$ p. 103
Triple Two Silom, $$$ p. 107

a handful of others have been repeatedly rated among the best in the world. And if there were a similar comparison of the world's boutique hotels, Bangkok's selection would be near the top, too. These high-end hotels are surprisingly affordable, with rates comparable to standard hotels in New York or London. Business hotels also have fine service, excellent restaurants, and amenities like health clubs, and many have spas. Even budget hotels have comfortable rooms and efficient staffs.

Wherever you stay, remember that prices fluctuate enormously and that huge discounts are the order of the day. **■ TIP→ Always ask for a better price, even if you have already booked a room (you can inquire about a discount upon check-in).** Deals may be more difficult to come by during the high season from November through February, but that doesn't mean they're impossible to find, and during low season they're certainly plentiful.

Hotels are concentrated in four areas: along Silom and Sathorn roads in Silom (where many of the riverfront hotels are located); clustered in Siam Square and on Petchaburi Road in Pratunam; along Sukhumvit Road, which has the greatest number of hotels and an abundance of restaurants and nightlife; and in the Chinatown and the Old City neighborhoods, which have a smaller number of properties, most of which are very affordable. Backpackers often head to Khao San Road in the Old City and its surrounding streets and lanes. The area has a mix of cheap cafés, secondhand bookstalls, trendy bars, and small guesthouses. It's still possible to get a room in that area for B150; even the newer, more upmarket guesthouses charge only around B500.

NORTH & WEST BANKOK

NORTH BANGKOK

$$ **Reflections.** Depending on your taste, this colorful hotel will be either a bit too kitschy or a refreshing compromise between the tiny guesthouses and giant towers that constitute most of the city's lodgings. Though Reflections moved to a new location in 2007, the decor stayed the same: Each room is decorated by a different Thai artist, with an emphasis on freedom of expression and recycling of old architectural or design materials. There are also innovative products for everyday use on sale at the funky gallery-restaurant. **Pros:** unique hotel; cool gallery on-site; friendly and helpful staff. **Cons:** not convenient to city center; rooms are a bit busy. ✉ *224/2–9 and 11–18 Pradipat Rd., Phaya Thai, North Bangkok,* ☎ *02/270–3344* 🌐 *www.reflections-thai.com* *36 rooms* *In-room: safe, refrigerator, DVD, Wi-Fi. In-hotel: restaurant, room service, spa, no-smoking rooms* *AE, MC, V* Ⓜ *Skytrain:* Sapankwai. ✥ *F1*

THE OLD CITY, BANGLAMPHU & DUSIT

$–$$ **Buddy Lodge.** This boutique hotel, the first on Khao San Road, has contributed greatly to the new trendiness of Bangkok's backpacker center. Standard rooms are very comfortable, but paying the extra B400 (roughly $12) for a deluxe room is worth it, considering the extra space and bigger balcony you get. The decor is bright and cheery, with lots of natural wood. You'll really appreciate the rooftop pool after trekking around the Old City sights all day. The lodge is also close to the river and many attractions like the Grand Palace. **Pros:** inexpensive; happening location; cool clientele. **Cons:** nothing fancy; nicer amenities in many other hotels. ✉ *265 Khao San Rd., Banglamphu,* ☎ *02/629–4477* 🌐 *www.buddylodge.com* *76 rooms* *In-room: safe, refrigerator. In-hotel: restaurant, bars, pool, gym, Wi-Fi, no-smoking rooms* *AE, DC, MC, V* Ⓜ *Skytrain: Hua Lamphong.* ✣ *B3*

NEW AIRPORT DIGS

The stunning **Novotel Suvarnabhumi Airport** (☎ *02/131–1111* 🌐 *www.novotel.com*) is the only hotel at the new airport (it's five minutes away with free shuttle service). The massive 612-room complex has four restaurants, a pool, a gym, and a spa. Although it's too far south of the city to be a logical base of operations, it's important given that so many flights in and out of Bangkok happen in the middle of the night. Rooms start at B5,885 and can get quite expensive; the hotel also rents rooms in four-hour blocks (crucial in the event of an unpleasant layover), starting at B3,600.

$$$$ Fodor's Choice ★ **Chakrabongse Villas.** Located on the banks of the Chao Phraya River in an old part of the city, these three villas are in traditional Thai houses, originally built up-country and then transported to the grounds of the Chakrabongse House, which was built in 1908. They may be the best rooms in the city—the problem is there are only three, and the place is very popular, so you must book well in advance (at least a month). The Riverside Villa and Garden Suite each offer more space and better views—the villa has a view of Wat Arun from the bedroom—but the Thai House is also unique and beautifully furnished. There's a sala next to the river for guests to enjoy, where Thai meals are served upon request. A minimum two-night stay is preferred. **Pros:** unique hotel experience; beautiful surroundings. **Cons:** fills up quickly; feels secluded. ✉ *396 Maharay Rd., Old City,* ☎ *02/622–3356* 🌐 *www.thaivillas.com* *3 rooms* *In-room: safe, refrigerator. In-hotel: restaurant, pool, WiFi, no-smoking rooms* *AE, DC, MC, V* Ⓜ *Subway: Hua Lamphong.* ✣ *A4*

$ **Royal Hotel.** Nearer to the Grand Palace and the Old City than any other of the city's lodgings, this hotel is a carefully kept secret of many frequent visitors. Its clean and comfortable rooms have homey touches like small writing tables. Several banquet rooms on the ground floor are popular with wedding parties. The lobby café is a good place to take a break from sightseeing. **Pros:** close to Old City; inexpensive. **Cons:** room decor a bit drab; beds not that comfortable. ✉ *2 Rajdamnoen Ave., Old City,* ☎ *02/222–9111* *300 rooms* *In-room: refrigerator. In-hotel: 2 restaurants, room service, bar, pool, gym, laundry service, Internet terminal, no-smoking rooms* *AE, DC, MC, V* Ⓜ *Subway: Hua Lamphong.* ✣ *B3*

CHINATOWN

$$ **Grand China Princess.** One good reason for staying in Chinatown is the chance to experience the sights and sounds of the city's oldest neighborhood. Another reason is this hotel, which occupies the top two-thirds of

WHERE SHOULD I STAY?

	NEIGHBORHOOD VIBE	PROS	CONS
North Bangkok	This relatively quiet business and residential neighborhood has plenty of local culture but very few tourist attractions.	This is the closest neighborhood to Don Muang, the domestic airport—helpful if you have an early flight to the north or the beaches.	It's a ways from downtown, which means you'll spend a lot on taxis getting to the city center. Public transportation options are limited.
The Old City, Banglamphu & Dusit	These central neighborhoods are the historical heart of the city. Today they're full of places to stay in all price ranges.	Tons of dining and lodging options here to match any budget; you'll be near many major attractions are here, like the Grand Palace and Wat Benjamabophit.	May feel chaotic to some, and too touristy to others. Not easily accessible by subway or Skytrain. Not the cheapest part of town.
Chinatown	The utter chaos of Chinatown is not for everybody. You'll be inundated by the sights and sounds—expect a lot of neon.	There are some good hotel deals here, the neighborhood is truly unique and the food scene is great, too, and the street markets are fascinating.	Hectic and not the most tourist-friendly part of town. Limited hotel selection, terrible traffic, and public transportation options are not that convenient.
Thonburi	You'll rub elbows with the locals in this mostly residential neighborhood across the river from the Old City.	Tucked away in peaceful seclusion from the noise and chaos of Bangkok; stellar river views.	Everything else is on the other side of the Chao Phraya, so expect to take the ferry a lot and spend more on taxis.
Pratunam	One of the neighborhoods that makes up Bangkok's "downtown," this sprawling area is full of markets and megamalls, plus some other attractions.	A shopper's paradise, and relatively convenient to subway and Skytrain. Lots of super-posh hotels; this is the place to stay if you're traveling in style.	Truly horrible traffic—you'll run up quite a taxi tab sitting in gridlock. Most options are pricey, and may be noisy since there's lots of nightlife nearby.
Silom	Another part of the downtown area, this neighborhood is the city's biggest business hub and also has the greatest concentration of restaurants. Nightlife is fun, too.	Very popular area with travelers, so lots of comfortable restaurants and bars. Convenient subway–Skytrain connection here.	Can be clogged with traffic. Not the most authentic Thai experience, and since it's partially a business district, there's a lot of less-than-charming concrete.
Sukhumvit	This downtown neighborhood is the nightlife area in Bangkok, and you'll find everything from Irish pubs to hostess bars. There's also a good restaurant scene here.	If you want to party, this is the place to be. A wide range of hotels here, from dirt cheap to über-ritzy, and public transit is fairly convenient.	Fast-paced; some areas are noisy well into the night, and you may run into some shady dealings, though there are plenty of classier establishments here as well.

a 25-story tower. The rooms are plain but have panoramic views of the city. The lobby has a bar, lounge, and coffee shop. ■ **TIP→ Siang Ping Loh, which serves Cantonese and Szechuan fare, is well worth a visit.** **Pros:** great city and river views; delicious Chinese food nearby. **Cons:** popular with big groups; not the most tourist-friendly neighborhood. ✉*215 Yaowarat Rd., at Ratchawongse Rd., Chinatown,* ☎*02/224–9977* 🌐*www.grandchina.com* *155 rooms, 22 suites* *In-room: safe, refrigerator, Internet. In-hotel: 2 restaurants, pool, gym, Wi-Fi, no-smoking rooms* ▭*AE, DC, MC, V* Ⓜ*Subway: Hua Lamphong.* ✥ *C4*

¢ **Krung Kasem Sri Krung Hotel.** This hotel, across a canal from Hua Lamphong station and near the Temple of the Golden Buddha, is in its fifth decade and a bit worse for wear. But it's ideally located if you arrive on a late train or are departing early in the morning. The sparsely furnished rooms are air-conditioned, the baths are clean, and the price is right—and that's about all you can say about it. **Pros:** the price is right; it's centrally located. **Cons:** old building; small rooms. ✉*1860 Krung Kasem Rd., Chinatown,* ☎*02/225–0132 or 02/225–8900* *120 rooms* *In-hotel: restaurant, no-smoking rooms* ▭*No credit cards* Ⓜ*Subway: Hua Lamphong.* ✥ *D4*

¢ **River View Guest House.** ■ **TIP→ This family-run hotel is one of the few budget accommodations that overlook the river**, and it's the view that sells it. The accommodations are a bit run-down and may remind you of college dorm rooms, but they're clean and comfortable. The staff will go out of its way for you, even staying up to accommodate late flights (someone sleeps downstairs during the night in case you need something). One drawback is that tuk-tuk drivers sometimes have difficulty finding the place. The easiest way to find it is to head north from the Royal Orchid Sheraton; you can see the guesthouse's sign pointing down a side street. **Pros:** river view; inexpensive. **Cons:** not all rooms have a/c; feels quite cheap. ✉*768 Soi Panurangsri, Songvad Rd., Chinatown,* ☎*02/234–5429* 🌐*www.riverviewbkk.com* *45 rooms* *In-room: no a/c (some), refrigerator, no TV. In-hotel: restaurant, laundry service, Internet terminal, no-smoking rooms* ▭*AE* Ⓜ*Subway: Hua Lamphong; Skytrain: Saphan Taksin.* ✥ *D5*

THONBURI

$$$–$$$$ **Bangkok Marriott Resort & Spa.** Getting to the Marriott is a pleasant adventure in itself—free shuttle boats take you across the Chao Phraya from the Taksin bridge. This is more of a resort than a hotel, with many restaurants and a small mall connected. The big pool and garden area on the riverside make you feel a long way from downtown's bustle. All rooms are spacious and well furnished, but if you want a river view, remember to ask for it. The *Manohra Song*, an ancient rice barge converted into a floating restaurant, is berthed here. The only downside to the hotel is its distance from attractions—the shuttle boats are fun, but the trip will tack about 15 minutes onto your travel time, and traveling by road is even slower. **Pros:** resort feel; lots of activities; great service. **Cons:** a hassle to get into the city; may feel too secluded. ✉*257/1–3 Charoennakorn Rd., Thonburi,* ☎*02/476–0022* 🌐*www.marriott.com* *420 rooms* *In-room: safe, refrigerator, Wi-Fi. In-hotel: 8 restaurants, room service, bars, tennis courts, pool, gym, spa,*

laundry service, no-smoking rooms ▭*AE, DC, MC, V* Ⓜ*Skytrain: Saphan Taksin.* ✣ *C6*

$$$ Fodor's Choice ★ **Hilton Millennium.** Lording over the Chao Phraya in postmillennial splendor, this flagship Hilton—which, like the Peninsula, is reached via hotel-operated ferry service from the downtown riverbank at the end of the Skytrain—offers some of the most cutting-edge room design and hotel facilities in the city, competing successfully with Bangkok's longstanding hotel giants at considerably lower prices. The infinity pool hangs like a waterfall off the edge of the cleverly designed deck, an urban beach overlooking the entire city skyline. Towering above everything else, the 32nd-floor open-air roof deck, executive lounge, and chilled-out bar all have spectacular panoramas. Rooms (aside from suites) are on the small side, but their setups compensate well enough for that, and bathrooms seem 22nd century. Every single room in the hotel has river and city views. **Pros:** snazzy amenities; cool pool area; reasonable prices. **Cons:** rooms somewhat small; across the river from downtown pursuits. ✉*123 Charoennakorn Rd., Thonburi,* ☎*02/442–2000* 🌐*www.hilton.com* *465 rooms, 78 suites* *In-room: safe, refrigerator. In-hotel: 5 restaurants, room service, bars, pool, gym, spa, laundry service, Wi-Fi, no-smoking rooms* ▭*AE, DC, MC, V* Ⓜ*Skytrain: Saphan Taksin.* ✣ *C5*

$$$$ Fodor's Choice ★ **Peninsula.** The rooms at the Peninsula have plenty of gadgets like bedside controls that dim the lights, turn on the sound system, and close the curtains; bathrooms with hands-free phones; and TVs with mist-free screens at the end of the tubs. Because the hotel is in Thonburi, its spacious rooms have views of the impressive Bangkok skyline; a free shuttle across the river to the nearest Skytrain station is provided. The restaurants serve Cantonese and Pacific Rim cuisine, as well as a very westernized version of Thai. There's a long swimming pool with private gazebos. **Pros:** beautiful pool; exceptional service; awesome views. **Cons:** most attractions are across the river; onsite dining not very good. ✉*333 Charoen Krung (New Rd.), Klonsan, Thonburi,* ☎*02/861–2888* 🌐*www.peninsula.com* *313 rooms, 67 suites* *In-room: safe, refrigerator. In-hotel: 4 restaurants, room service, bar, pool, gym, spa, laundry service, Wi-Fi, no-smoking rooms* ▭*AE, DC, MC, V* Ⓜ*Skytrain: Saphan Taksin.* ✣ *C6*

DOWNTOWN BANGKOK

PRATUNAM

$$$$ Fodor's Choice ★ **The Conrad.** Though this hotel is one of the largest in the city, service doesn't suffer—the staff is attentive and the rooms and other facilities are well maintained. It's connected to All Seasons Place, which has dozens of restaurants and shops. More importantly, on-site entertainment is top-notch; two great restaurants, Liu and Drinking Tea Eating Rice, are in the hotel (⇨ *Where to Eat, above*). And you can dance the night away at 87 Plus or have a drink and listen to live jazz at the Diplomat Bar. A hotel shuttle bus is available to and from the Skytrain. **Pros:** good restaurants; fun nightlife; sprawling pool area. **Cons:** huge hotel; not on the river. ✉*All Seasons Place, 87 Wittayu (Wireless Rd.), Pratunam,* ☎*02/690–9999* 🌐*www.conradhotels.com* *342 rooms, 49 suites*

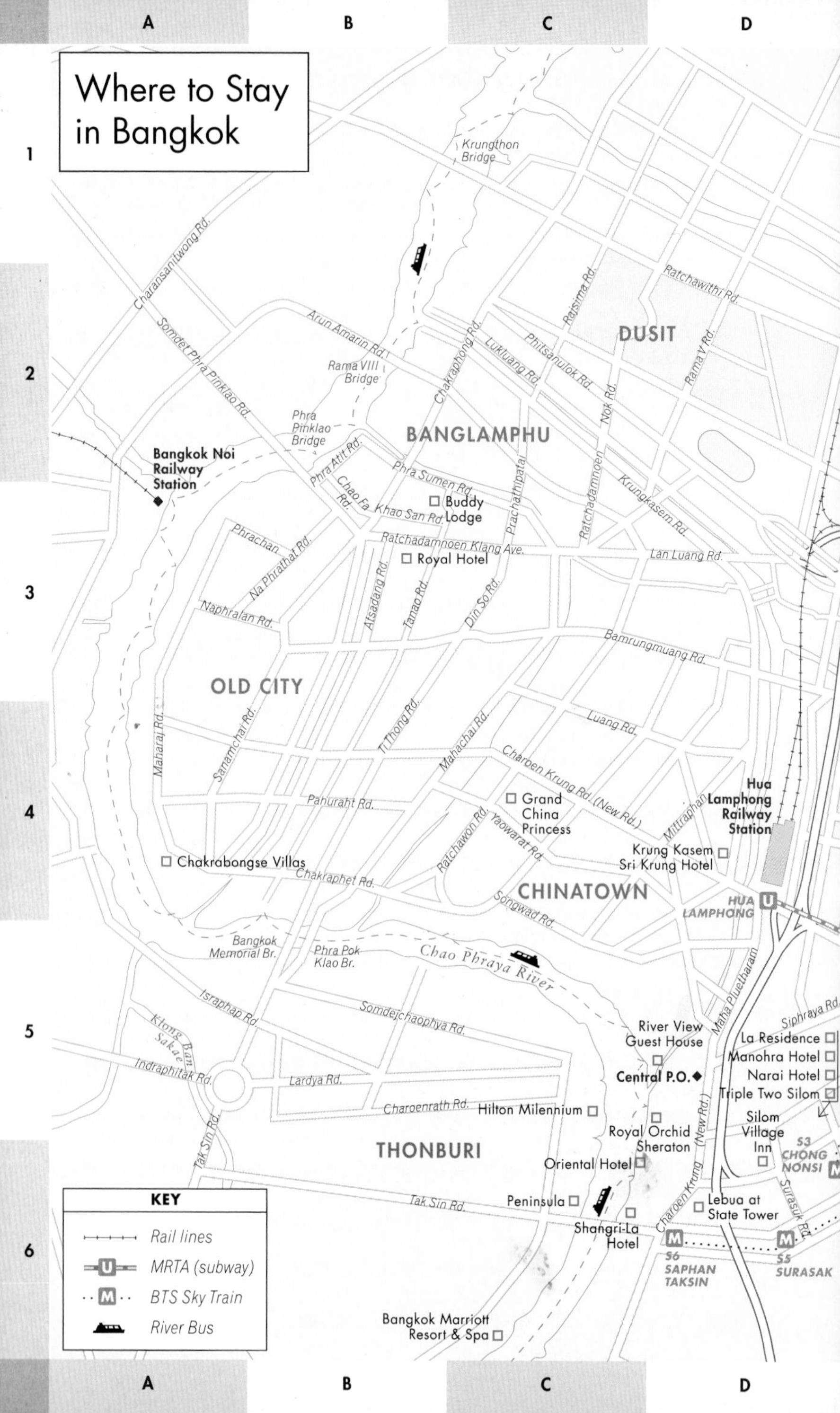

Where to Stay in Bangkok
A
B
C
D
1
2
3
4
5
6
Krungthon Bridge
Charansanitwong Rd.
Ratchawithi Rd.
DUSIT
Rajsima Rd.
Rama V Rd.
Arun Amarin Rd.
Somdet Phra Pinklao Rd.
Rama VIII Bridge
Chakraphong Rd.
Lukluang Rd.
Phitsanulok Rd.
Nok Rd.
Phra Pinklao Bridge
BANGLAMPHU
Bangkok Noi Railway Station
Phra Atit Rd.
Phra Sumen Rd.
Chao Fa Rd.
Khao San Rd.
Buddy Lodge
Prachathipatai
Ratchadamnoen
Krungkasem Rd.
Phrachan
Na Phrathat Rd.
Ratchadamnoen Klang Ave.
Royal Hotel
Lan Luang Rd.
Naphralan Rd.
Atsadang Rd.
Tanao Rd.
Din So Rd.
Bamrungmuang Rd.
OLD CITY
Ti Thong Rd.
Mahachai Rd.
Luang Rd.
Maharaj Rd.
Sanamchai Rd.
Charoen Krung Rd. (New Rd.)
Grand China Princess
Hua Lamphong Railway Station
Pahurat Rd.
Ratchawon Rd.
Yaowarat Rd.
Mittraphan
Krung Kasem Sri Krung Hotel
Chakrabongse Villas
Chakraphet Rd.
CHINATOWN
HUA LAMPHONG
Songwad Rd.
Bangkok Memorial Br.
Phra Pok Klao Br.
Chao Phraya River
Maha Pluetharam
Israphap Rd.
Somdejchaophya Rd.
Siphraya Rd.
River View Guest House
La Residence
Klong Ban Sakae
Manohra Hotel
Indraphitak Rd.
Central P.O.
Narai Hotel
Lardya Rd.
Triple Two Silom
Charoenrath Rd.
Hilton Milennium
Silom Village Inn
Royal Orchid Sheraton
(New Rd.)
Tak Sin Rd.
THONBURI
S3 CHONG NONSI
Oriental Hotel
Charoen Krung
Surasak Rd.
Peninsula
Tak Sin Rd.
Lebua at State Tower
Shangri-La Hotel
S6 SAPHAN TAKSIN
S5 SURASAK
KEY
Rail lines
MRTA (subway)
BTS Sky Train
River Bus
Bangkok Marriott Resort & Spa

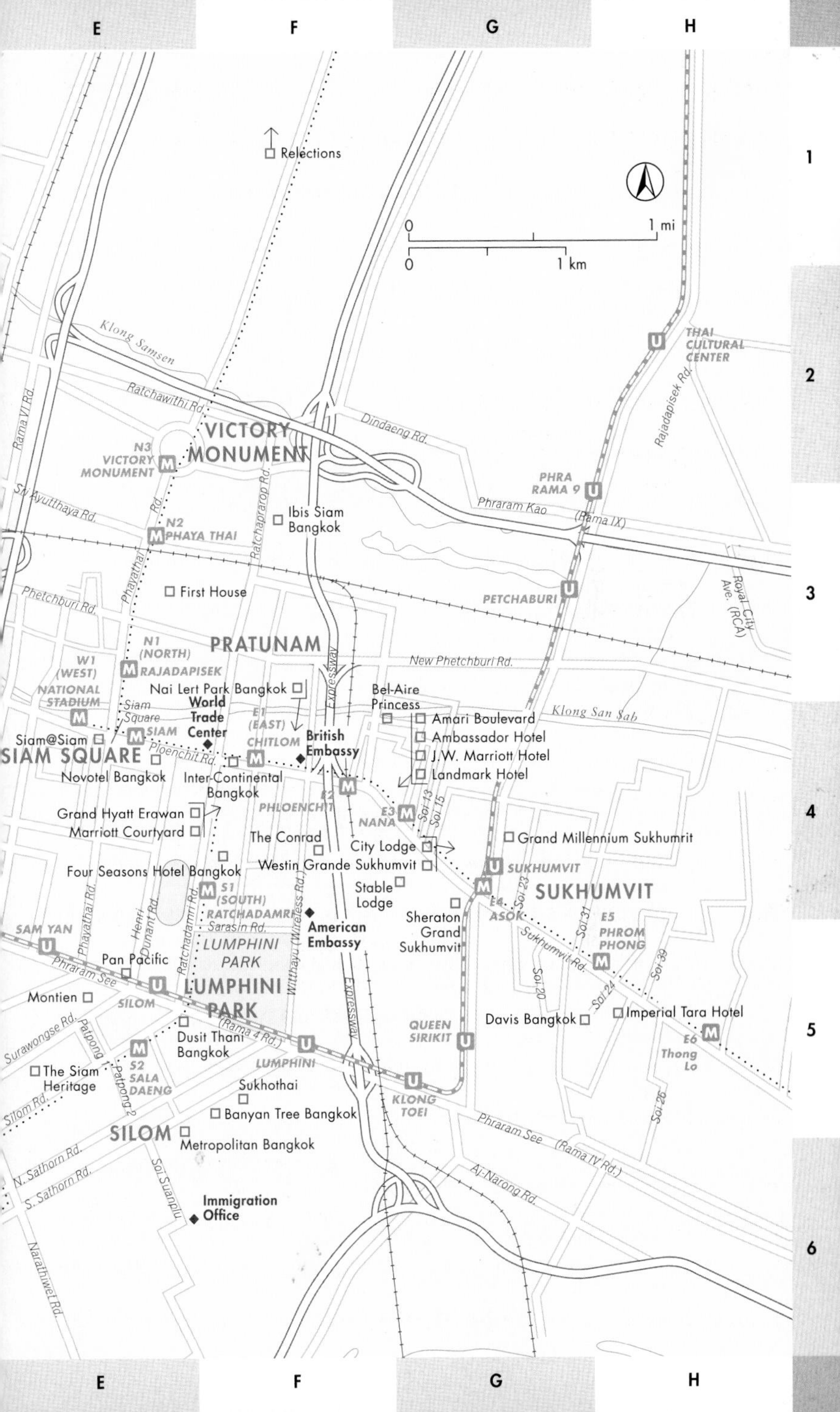

E
F
G
H
1
2
3
4
5
6
Relections
0
1 mi
0
1 km
Klong Samsen
Ratchawithi Rd.
Rama VI Rd.
VICTORY MONUMENT
N3 VICTORY MONUMENT
Dindaeng Rd.
THAI CULTURAL CENTER
Rajadapisek Rd.
PHRA RAMA 9
Phraram Kao
(Rama IX)
Sri Ayutthaya Rd.
Ibis Siam Bangkok
N2 PHAYA THAI
Rd.
Ratchaprarop Rd.
First House
Phetchburi Rd.
Phayathai
PETCHABURI
Royal City Ave. (RCA)
PRATUNAM
N1 (NORTH)
W1 (WEST)
RAJADAPISEK
New Phetchburi Rd.
NATIONAL STADIUM
Nai Lert Park Bangkok
Expressway
Bel-Aire Princess
Siam Square
World Trade Center
E1 (EAST)
Amari Boulevard
Klong San Sab
Siam@Siam
SIAM
CHITLOM
British Embassy
Ambassador Hotel
SIAM SQUARE
Ploenchit Rd.
J.W. Marriott Hotel
Novotel Bangkok
Inter-Continental Bangkok
Landmark Hotel
E2
PHLOENCHIT
E3 NANA
Soi 13
Soi 15
Grand Hyatt Erawan
Marriott Courtyard
The Conrad
Grand Millennium Sukhumrit
City Lodge
Westin Grande Sukhumvit
SUKHUMVIT
Four Seasons Hotel Bangkok
Stable Lodge
SUKHUMVIT
S1 (SOUTH)
RATCHADAMRI
Sheraton Grand Sukhumvit
E4 ASOK
Soi 23
Henri Dunant Rd.
Ratchadamri Rd.
Sarasin Rd.
American Embassy
Soi 31
E5 PHROM PHONG
SAM YAN
Phayathai Rd.
LUMPHINI PARK
Witthayu (Wireless Rd.)
Sukhumvit Rd.
Soi 39
Pan Pacific
Phraram See
Soi 20
Montien
SILOM
LUMPHINI PARK
Soi 24
Imperial Tara Hotel
Surawongse Rd.
Patpong 1
Expressway
Davis Bangkok
(Rama 4 Rd.)
QUEEN SIRIKIT
Dusit Thani Bangkok
E6 Thong Lo
S2 SALA DAENG
LUMPHINI
The Siam Heritage
Silom Rd.
Patpong 2
Sukhothai
KLONG TOEI
Soi 26
Banyan Tree Bangkok
Phraram See
(Rama IV Rd.)
SILOM
Metropolitan Bangkok
N. Sathorn Rd.
S. Sathorn Rd.
Soi Suanplu
Aj-Narong Rd.
Immigration Office
Narathiwat Rd.
E
F
G
H

In-room: safe, refrigerator, Internet (some). In-hotel: 5 restaurants, bars, pool, spa, 2 tennis courts, laundry service, Wi-Fi, no-smoking rooms ▭ *AE, DC, MC, V* Ⓜ *Skytrain: Ploenchit.* ✣ *F4*

$ **First House.** Tucked behind the Pratunam Market in the bustling garment district, the First House is an excellent value for a hotel in this price range. The compact guestrooms are nicely furnished, bright, and cheery. In the small lobby you can catch up on the latest with the complimentary newspapers, and there's a 24-hour coffee shop that serves Thai dishes. **Pros:** reasonably priced; attractive furniture. **Cons:** not much natural light in rooms; neighborhood a bit busy and loud. ✉ *14/20–29 Phetchburi Soi 19, Phaya Thai, Pratunam,* ☎ *02/254–0300* 🌐 *www.firsthousebkk.com* *100 rooms* *In-room: refrigerator. In-hotel: restaurant, room service, spa, laundry service, no-smoking rooms* ▭ *AE, MC, V* Ⓜ *Skytrain: Rajchathewi.* ✣ *E3*

$$$$ **Four Seasons Hotel Bangkok.** Formerly called the Regent, this has been one of Bangkok's leading hotels for many years and has arguably the city's best pool. Local society meets for morning coffee and afternoon tea in the formal lobby, where a string quartet plays most afternoons. There are plenty of shops to browse in off the courtyard. The large rooms are decorated with silk-upholstered furniture. The best rooms overlook the racetrack, but ask for a high floor so that the Skytrain doesn't block the view. The quartet of pricier "cabana rooms," with private patios which look onto a small garden with a lotus pond, are exquisite. Be sure to indulge in the Four Season's signature fragrant-oil massage while you're here. **Pros:** easily accessible location; great pool. **Cons:** decor verges on stuffy; not all rooms have nice views. ✉ *155 Ratchadamri Rd., Pratunam,* ☎ *02/250–1000* 🌐 *www.fourseasons.com/bangkok* *353 rooms, 19 suites* *In-room: safe, Wi-Fi. In-hotel: 7 restaurants, bar, pool, gym, spa, Wi-Fi, no-smoking rooms* ▭ *AE, DC, MC, V* Ⓜ *Skytrain: Ratchadamri.* ✣ *E4*

$$$$ **Grand Hyatt Erawan.** This stylish hotel hovers over the auspicious Erawan Shrine. The impressive atrium, with an extensive modern art collection, soars four stories high to a glass roof. Rooms are spacious; the wood floors are strewn with tasteful rugs, the walls are hung with original art, and a desk and a couple of chairs are positioned directly in front of bay windows. There are plenty of high-tech accoutrements, too. Baths have separate showers, oversize tubs, and private dressing areas. **TIP→ The Italian fare at Spasso, created by a Milanese chef, is especially creative; come for lunch even if you aren't staying here.** Spasso is also a lively nightclub. A new Skytrain walkway system connects the hotel to many more places. **Pros:** easy access to many points in the city; world-class spa. **Cons:** not on the river; expensive. ✉ *494 Ratchadamri Rd., Pratunam,* ☎ *02/254–1234* 🌐 *www.bangkok.grand.hyatt.com* *380 rooms, 44 suites* *In-room: safe, refrigerator, Internet. In-hotel: 6 restaurants, bar, tennis courts, pool, gym, spa, laundry service, Wi-Fi, no-smoking rooms* ▭ *AE, DC, MC, V* Ⓜ *Skytrain: Ratchadamri.* ✣ *E4*

$ **Ibis Siam Bangkok.** Ibis is a popular hotel chain in Asia, and the Bangkok branch lives up to the global reputation: It's clean, efficiently run, and well managed. Rooms don't have many frills but are slightly more attractive than most budget digs, decorated in *au courant* warm browns, golds, and oranges. The Ibis is a 10-minute walk from the Skytrain station. **Pros:** good value; clean and comfortable; close to public transportation. **Cons:** no pool; service isn't as doting as at the big chains. ✉*97 Ratchaprarop Rd., Pratunam,* ☎*02/209–3888* 🌐*www.ibissiam.com* *180 rooms* *In-room: safe, Wi-Fi. In-hotel: restaurant, bar, laundry service, Wi-Fi, no-smoking rooms* *AE, DC, MC, V* Ⓜ*Skytrain: Victory Monument.* ✥ *F3*

2

$$$$ **Inter-Continental Bangkok.** This fine hotel is in one of the city's prime business districts and does a good job of catering to its corporate clientele. Club Inter-Continental rooms have 24-hour butler service. The lounge on the 37th floor has great city views to gaze at while you sip evening cocktails (complimentary for Club-floor guests). The rooftop pool is rather small but feels cozy rather than cramped. The popular Summer Palace restaurant serves Cantonese cuisine. **Pros:** walking distance from many sights; good fitness room; executive floor. **Cons:** small pool; many business travelers. ✉*973 Ploenchit Rd., Pratunam,* ☎*02/656–0444* 🌐*www.intercontinental.com* *381 rooms, 39 suites* *In-room: safe, refrigerator, DVD, Internet. In-hotel: 3 restaurants, room service, pool, gym, spa, laundry service, Wi-Fi, no-smoking rooms* *AE, DC, MC, V* Ⓜ*Skytrain: Chitlom.* ✥ *F4*

$$–$$$ **Marriott Courtyard.** This hotel opened in early 2008, and though its decor is uninspired, its newness shows—in fact, you might not even realize that it comes from the lower end of the Marriott family. It's located right behind the Four Seasons, and while it doesn't have the luxury of some of Bangkok's highest-priced hotels, it does have all the basic amenities. **Pros:** good value; accommodating to families with children. **Cons:** unexciting room decor; not as luxurious as other Marriotts. ✉*155/1 Soi Mahadlekluang 1, Rachadamri Rd., Silom,* ☎*02/690–1888* 🌐*www.marriott.com* *315 rooms* *In-room: safe, refrigerator, Wi-Fi. In-hotel: 7 restaurants, bar, pool, gym, laundry service, Wi-Fi, no-smoking rooms* *AE, DC, MC, V.* ✥ *E4*

$$$ **Nai Lert Park Bangkok.** The best thing about this hotel, part of the Swissotel chain, is the garden, so be sure to ask for a room that faces it. The rooms are large, and the baths have showers and bathtubs. The on-site Japanese restaurant, Genji *(above)*, is excellent. Note that this is a popular hotel for weddings, conferences, and parties, so it may not be the most tranquil of retreats. **Pros:** lush, tropical garden vegetation; beautiful pool; executive floor. **Cons:** sometimes overrun with groups; not on river. ✉*2 Wittayu (Wireless Rd.), Pratunam,* ☎*02/253–0123* 🌐*www.nailertpark.swissotel.com* *301 rooms, 37 suites* *In-room: safe, refrigerator, Internet. In-hotel: 5 restaurants, bars, tennis courts, pool, spa, fitness room, Wi-Fi, no-smoking rooms* *AE, DC, MC, V* Ⓜ*Skytrain: Ploenchit.* ✥ *F3*

$$$$ **Novotel Bangkok on Siam Square.** This big hotel is convenient to shopping, dining, and entertainment. It's also a short walk from the Skytrain central station, which puts much of the city within reach. The rooms are comfortable and functional. Despite the size of the hotel, there are always plenty of staff members around to help you. One of Bangkok's top nightclubs, CM2, is in the basement. **Pros:** good service; convenient location. **Cons:** not many in-room amenities; pricey. ✉*Siam Sq. Soi 6,*

Fodor'sChoice ★

Peninsula

Chakrabongse Villas

Hilton Millenium

Conrad

Shangri-La

Pratunam, ☎02/209–8888 🌐www.novotel-asia.com ↩429 rooms, 43 suites ♿In-room: safe, refrigerator, Wi-Fi. In-hotel: 3 restaurants, room service, bars, pool, gym, laundry service, Wi-Fi, no-smoking rooms ▭AE, DC, MC, V Ⓜ Skytrain: Siam. ✦ E4

$$$ **Siam@Siam.** It's probably safe to say that this hotel has eclipsed the Metropolitan in hipness. It's definitely the place where the cool kids stay—but that doesn't mean you won't feel welcome if you're traveling with children. Rooms are decked out in mod furniture with lots of blacks, whites, and reds, with tile floors. Party House One has comfy chairs and low lighting, and it's open and serving food and drinks all day long. **Pros:** great location; super-hip crowd; beautifully decorated rooms. **Cons:** can be noisy; some rooms have little natural light. *✉865 Rama I Rd., Pratunam, ☎02/217–3000 🌐www.siamatsiam.com ↩203 rooms ♿In-room: safe, refrigerator, Wi-Fi. In-hotel: restaurant, bar, pool, gym, no-smoking rooms ▭AE, DC, MC, V Ⓜ Skytrain: Siam. ✦ E4*

SILOM

$$$$ **Banyan Tree Bangkok.** After checking in on the ground floor, you soar up to your room at this 60-story hotel. The light-filled suites in the impossibly slender tower all have sweeping views of the city. The generous use of native woods in everything from the large desks to the walk-in closets gives each room a warm glow. A fully equipped spa offers the latest treatments, and a sundeck on the 53rd floor beckons with a relaxing whirlpool. For meals or a drink in the evening there's the rooftop Vertigo, which the hotel claims is Asia Pacific's highest alfresco eatery. Each September you can test your fitness in the annual "vertical marathon" up the hotel's stairs; the event is a fundraiser for HIV education. **Pros:** wonderful views; open-air bars feel on top of the world. **Cons:** some on-site construction; very expensive, especially for Silom area. *✉21/100 S. Sathorn Rd., Silom, ☎02/679–1200 🌐www.banyantree.com ↩216 suites ♿In-room: safe, refrigerator, Internet. In-hotel: 6 restaurants, room service, bars, pool, gym, spa, water sports, laundry service, Internet terminal, no-smoking rooms ▭AE, DC, MC, V Ⓜ Subway: Lumphini. ✦ F5*

$$$$ **Dusit Thani Bangkok.** This high-rise hotel has a distinctive pyramid shape that makes it immediately identifiable. The reception area, where a sunken lounge overlooks a small garden and waterfall, is one floor up. Rooms here are spacious, especially the high-price suites. The Dusit's proximity to the Skytrain and subway stations makes it a convenient base for exploring the city. It's also across the street from Lumphini Park, Bangkok's best public park. The pool is in a central courtyard filled with trees, making it a peaceful oasis from the heat and humidity. The Devarana Spa offers an impressive menu of treatments from herbal steam baths to body scrubs with unusual ingredients to a signature massage that combines several different styles including Thai massage. The hotel's popular Chinese restaurant, Mayflower, is worth a visit even if you don't stay here. **Pros:** delicious Chinese restaurant; a stone's throw from subway and Skytrain stations. **Cons:** small pool; feels past its prime. *✉946 Rama IV Rd., Silom, ☎02/200–9000 🌐www.dusit.com ↩487 rooms, 30 suites ♿In-room: safe, refrigerator, Internet.*

In-hotel: 8 restaurants, room service, bar, pool, gym, spa, laundry service, Wi-Fi, no-smoking rooms ▭*AE, DC, MC, V* Ⓜ*Subway: Silom; Skytrain: Sala Daeng.*

$ **La Residence.** You'd expect to find this charming little hotel on the Left Bank of Paris. It's one of the few low-key lodgings in an area dominated by office towers. The rooms are small but comfortable and each is individually decorated; styles vary, so ask to look at a few rooms to decide which you like best. The seven suites are very big and have kitchenettes. A ground-floor restaurant serves Thai food and doubles as a sitting room for guests. The hotel entrance is just down Soi Anuman Rojdhon off Surawongse. **Pros:** cozy and elegant atmosphere; quiet surroundings. **Cons:** rates slowly increasing; rooms a bit small. ✉*173/8–9 Surawongse Rd., Silom,* ☎*02/233–3301* 🌐*www.laresidencebangkok.com* *19 rooms, 7 suites* *In-room: safe, refrigerator, DVD. In-hotel: laundry service, Wi-Fi, no-smoking rooms* ▭*AE, MC, V* Ⓜ*Skytrain: Surasak.* ✥ *D5*

$$$$ **Lebua at State Tower.** The Lebua is a comfortable hotel with great restaurants, a beautiful rooftop bar, and more than a bit of flare. The rooms are spacious and have views of the city. The staff is efficient and helpful. It's at the end of Silom Road near the river, which makes it convenient to most attractions; it's a five-minute walk from the nearest Skytrain station. **Pros:** Bulgari products in rooms; breathtaking views from Sky Bar. **Cons:** may feel a bit pompous; popular with see-and-be-seen crowd. ✉*1055 Silom Rd., Silom,* ☎*02/624–9999* 🌐*www.lebua.com* *198 rooms* *In-room: safe, refrigerator, DVD, Wi-Fi. In-hotel: 6 restaurants, room service, bars, pool, gym, laundry service, Wi-Fi, no-smoking rooms* ▭*AE, DC, MC, V* Ⓜ*Skytrain: Saphan Taksin.* ✥ *D6*

$$ **Manohra Hotel.** An expansive marble lobby is your first clue that this hotel is head and shoulders above others in its price range. Rooms have pleasant furnishings and spotless baths. There's a rooftop garden for sunbathing and a very small indoor pool next to the lobby. The best asset, though, may be the friendly staff. A lot of Asian tour groups stay here. The Skytrain is a 15-minute walk from the hotel. **Pros:** good value; short walk from river. **Cons:** pool is indoors; popular with tour groups. ✉*412 Surawongse Rd., Silom,* ☎*02/234–5070 up to 88* 🌐*www.manohrahotel.com* *200 rooms* *In-room: safe, refrigerator. In-hotel: restaurant, bar room service, pool, gym, Internet terminal, no-smoking rooms* ▭*AE, DC, MC, V* Ⓜ*Skytrain: Surasak.* ✥ *D5*

$$$$ **Metropolitan Bangkok.** The Metropolitan has all the elements of hip: a crisp, modern esthetic; a pop-star clientele; a sexy staff; and an ironic location in a refurbished YMCA. Some of the rooms are a bit small, but they're smartly turned out—dark woods and deep browns are offset by cream-color walls, pillows, and rugs. Though the rooms aren't dripping with high-tech gadgetry, they do have 25-inch flat-screen TVs with DVD players. Breakfast at Glow, the hotel's all-organic restaurant, is surprisingly good; indulge in one of their healthy smoothies. A recently launched program, Touchdown at the Met, is ideal for spa-loving travelers with a fairly short (minimum five-hour stay) stopover in Bangkok: For $200, you get picked up and dropped off at the airport in a limousine; use of spa facilities; a signature massage; and a meal at Glow.

Pros: very hip without sacrificing high level of service; nice city views; free yoga and Pilates classes for guests. **Cons:** has declined in popularity; not on river. ✉*27 S. Sathorn, Silom,* ☎*02/625–3333* 🌐*www.metropolitan.como.bz* *159 rooms, 12 suites* *In-room: safe, refrigerator, DVD, Wi-Fi. In-hotel: 2 restaurants, room service, bar, pool, spa, laundry service, Wi-Fi, no-smoking rooms* *AE, DC, MC, V* *M Subway: Lumphini; Skytrain: Sala Daeng or Chong Nonsi.* *E5*

$$$ **Montien.** This hotel, within stumbling distance of Patpong, has been remarkably well maintained since it was constructed in 1970. Prices are slightly higher than you would expect for the area, but the rooms are spacious and discounts are often available. In-house fortune-tellers, who will read your palm for a small fee, are one sign of the quirky neighborhood a few doors down. **Pros:** regal room decor; fun and happening neighborhood. **Cons:** not the most modern hotel; popular with tour groups. ✉*54 Surawongse Rd., Silom,* ☎*02/233–7060 up to 69* 🌐*www.montien.com* *475 rooms* *In-room: safe, Internet. In-hotel: 2 restaurants, bar, pool, gym, Internet terminal, no-smoking rooms* *AE, DC, MC, V* *M Subway: Silom; Skytrain: Sala Daeng.* *E5*

$$$ **Narai Hotel.** Dating back to 1969, this is one of Bangkok's older hotels, but it's well kept up and conveniently located by the business district on Silom Road. It has basic but comfortable rooms and friendly service. This hotel's name refers to the god Vishnu (Narai is the Thai name for Vishnu), and an elegant bas-relief of the Hindu deity can be seen on the wall in front of the main staircase. Unfortunately, the hotel is a hike to the nearest Skytrain station. **Pros:** fun neighborhood; short walk to river. **Cons:** unexciting pool and decor; far from Skytrain. ✉*222 Silom Rd., Silom,* ☎*02/237–0100* 🌐*www.naraihotel.co.th* *474 rooms* *In-room: safe, refrigerator. In-hotel: 3 restaurants, bar, pool, gym, laundry service, Wi-Fi, no-smoking rooms* *AE, DC, MC, V* *M Skytrain: Chong Nonsi.* *D5*

$$$$ **Oriental Hotel.** This hotel on the Chao Phraya, popular with visiting celebrities, used to set the bar for high-end Bangkok accommodations. These days, although it still attracts some impressive names, its opulence feels a little stuffy, and younger travelers tend to prefer hotels with more of a built-in nightlife scene. The four suites in the original building, now called the Author's Residence, offer superlative service in big historical rooms—but you'd better have a superlative pocketbook to match. The hotel's cooking classes instruct in the secrets of Thai cuisine, and the spa across the river will pamper you with all sorts of luxurious treatments—Ayurvedic massage, facials, soothing herbal and milk baths—in your own private suite. And it's a real treat to sip a cocktail at the riverside bar. **Pros:** posh pool; giant breakfast spread. **Cons:** one of Bangkok's priciest hotels; dated decor. ✉*48 Oriental Ave., Silom,* ☎*02/659–9000* 🌐*www.mandarinoriental.com/bangkok* *358 rooms, 35 suites* *In-room: safe, refrigerator, Internet. In-hotel: 6 restaurants, room service, bar, tennis courts, pool, gym, spa, laundry service, Internet terminal, no-smoking rooms* *AE, DC, MC, V* *M Skytrain: Saphan Taksin.* *C6*

$$–$$$ **Pan Pacific.** Though the Pan Pacific chain is particularly popular with Asian and business travelers, its appeal extends to American vacationers as well. The decor at the Bangkok branch is a little dated, but the

hotel gets a lot of other things right: it's in the middle of the city; it has a beautiful pool; and there are a number of very nice (though pricey) suites on the Pacific Floor. At this writing, some ongoing construction was due to end in 2009, but it's worth checking when you book to be sure they're running on schedule. **Pros:** very friendly, helpful staff; convenient location. **Cons:** attracts a business crowd. ✉ *952 Rama IV Rd., Silom* ☎ *02/632–9000* 🌐 *www.panpacific.com/Bangkok* *235 rooms* *In-room: safe, refrigerator. In-hotel: 3 restaurants, room service, bars, pool, gym, Wi-Fi, no-smoking rooms* ▭ *AE, DC, MC, V* Ⓜ *Skytrain: Sala Daeng.* ✥ *E5*

$$$$ **Royal Orchid Sheraton.** Of the luxury hotels along the riverfront, this 28-story palace is most popular with tour groups. All the well-appointed rooms face the river, but standard rooms tend to be long and narrow, making them feel cramped. The Thai Thara Thong restaurant is memorable, with subtle classical music accompanying your meal. Indian and Italian cuisine are also available here. A glassed-in bridge leads to the adjacent River City Shopping Complex. The hotel runs a free shuttle bus service to the Skytrain every 30 minutes and free boat service to Saphan Taksin station. **Pros:** nice river views; very comfortable beds. **Cons:** often busy with groups and events; tired room decor. ✉ *2 Captain Bush La., Silom* ☎ *02/266–0123* 🌐 *www.sheraton.com/bangkok* *480 rooms, 26 suites* *In-room: safe, refrigerator, Internet. In-hotel: 4 restaurants, room service, bars, tennis court, pools, gym, spa, laundry service, Wi-Fi, no-smoking rooms* ▭ *AE, DC, MC, V* Ⓜ *Skytrain: Saphan Taksin.* ✥ *C5*

$$$$ Fodor's Choice ★ **Shangri-La Hotel.** Utterly cutting edge, yet with an extraordinary sense of calm, the Shangri-La has emerged as one of Bangkok's very best hotels, surpassing the more-famous Oriental. The palatial marble lobby here is illuminated by crystal chandeliers; the adjacent lounge offers a marvelous view of the Chao Phraya River through floor-to-ceiling windows. The peace of the gardens is interrupted only by the puttering of passing boats. Many of the rooms, decorated in soothing pastels, are beginning to show their age, however. In the luxurious Krungthep Wing, a separate tower across the garden, the slightly more expensive rooms are larger and quieter, with balconies overlooking the river—a surprisingly rare thing in Bangkok. **Pros:** breathtaking lobby; private balconies available. **Cons:** some construction in older wing; restaurants not top-notch. ✉ *89 Soi Wat Suan Plu, Charoen Krung (New Rd.), Silom* ☎ *02/236–7777* 🌐 *www.shangri-la.com/bangkok* *747 rooms, 52 suites* *In-room: safe, refrigerator. In-hotel: 5 restaurants, bars, 2 tennis courts, pools, gym, spa, laundry service, no-smoking rooms* ▭ *AE, DC, MC, V* Ⓜ *Skytrain: Saphan Taksin.* ✥ *C6*

$$$ **Siam Heritage.** The family that runs the Siam Heritage has created a classy boutique hotel with a purpose—to preserve and promote Thai heritage. Each room is individually furnished, mostly with pieces from northern Thailand. The bedrooms have wood floors and the bathrooms have stonework in place of tiling. There's attention to detail here, like painted elevator doors and colorful woven bedspreads. **Pros:** well priced; cool Thai decor. **Cons:** not on river; rooms and pool a bit small. ✉ *115/1 Surawong Rd., Silom* ☎ *02/353–6101* 🌐 *www.*

thesiamheritage.com ⇨*59 rooms, 16 suites* ♿*In-room: safe, refrigerator, Wi-Fi. In-hotel: restaurant, bar, pool, spa, laundry service, Wi-Fi, no-smoking rooms* ▭*AE, DC, MC, V* Ⓜ*Subway: Silom; Skytrain: Sala Daeng.* ✥ *E5*

2

$ **Silom Village Inn.** Reasonable rates are just one of the draws at this small hotel. It's also well run, with rooms that are as neat as a pin. The king-size beds leave just enough space for a desk and a couple of chairs, but the 20 new rooms added in 2005 are a little bigger (and more expensive). Ask for a room at the back of the hotel to avoid the ruckus on Silom Road. The staff at the reception desk is helpful and reliable at taking messages. A small restaurant serves Thai food, but many other choices are just outside your door. **Pros:** lively neighborhood; very cheap. **Cons:** lots of street noise; not hip. ✉*Silom Village, 286 Silom Rd., Silom* ☎*02/635–6810 up to 16* ⇨*80 rooms* ♿*In-room: safe, refrigerator. In-hotel: restaurant, room service, no-smoking rooms* ▭*AE, DC, MC, V* Ⓜ*Skytrain: Surasak.* ✥ *D5*

$$$$ **Sukhothai.** On 6 landscaped acres near Sathorn Road, the Sukhothai has numerous courtyards that make the hustle and bustle of Bangkok seem worlds away. Standard rooms are spacious but not exceptionally well furnished. The one-bedroom suites, in contrast, are exquisite and have oversized teak-paneled baths and dual washbasins and mirrors. The hotel's well-regarded continental restaurant is set in a pavilion on an artificial pond. **Pros:** beautiful Thai room decor in suites; spacious grounds. **Cons:** expensive hotel and restaurant; standard rooms may not be worth the price. ✉*13/3 S. Sathorn Rd., Silom,* ☎*02/344–8888* 🌐*www.sukhothai.com* ⇨*140 rooms, 78 suites* ♿*In-room: safe, refrigerator, Internet. In-hotel: 3 restaurants, bar, tennis court, golf, pool, gym, spa, no-smoking rooms* ▭*AE, DC, MC, V* Ⓜ*Subway: Lumphini.* ✥ *F5*

$$$ **Triple Two Silom.** This trendy hotel is the sister property of the Narai Hotel next door (*above*); guests here can use the Narai's pool and fitness center. Spacious rooms have wood floors and modern fittings in what seem to be the standard hip colors these days: deep brown, cream, black, and red. Unfortunately, the windows are small, so don't expect a lot of natural light. There's a courtyard in the center of the hotel, and a restaurant and bar with indoor and outdoor seating. **Pros:** tasteful decor; very friendly and helpful staff. **Cons:** some rooms can be a bit noisy; not great option for kids. ✉*222 Silom Rd., Silom* ☎*02/627–2222* 🌐*www.tripletwosilom.com* ⇨*75 rooms* ♿*In-room: safe, refrigerator, DVD, Internet. In-hotel: restaurant, room service, bar, pool, gym, laundry service, Internet terminal, no-smoking rooms* ▭*AE, DC, MC, V* Ⓜ*Skytrain: Chong Nonsi.* ✥ *D5*

SUKHUMVIT

$$$$ **Amari Boulevard.** This pyramid-shaped tower certainly has a dashing profile. Rooms in the newer glass tower are modern and airy, with plenty of amenities. The use of dark wood in the older rooms lends them a more traditional ambience. Particularly attractive are those rooms overlooking the pool in the older building. The ground-floor lobby is vast, with plenty of places to have a quiet conversation. The casual Peppermill restaurant serves a range of Thai and Japanese dishes. The hotel is on a one-way soi near Sukhumvit Road; it's convenient to

shops and restaurants, but it can be noisy at night because there are also several bars on this street. **Pros:** interesting architecture; close to Skytrain. **Cons:** uninspired restaurant, lacking service. ✉ *2 Sukhumvit Soi 5 Sukhumvit* ☎ *02/255–2930* 🌐 *www.amari.com* *315 rooms* *In-room: safe, refrigerator, Internet. In-hotel: 2 restaurants, room service, bar, pool, gym, laundry service, Internet terminal, no-smoking rooms* ▭ *AE, DC, MC, V* Ⓜ *Skytrain: Nana.* ✥ *G4*

$$ **Ambassador Hotel.** The Ambassador has three wings, a dozen restaurants, a shopping center with scores of stores, and even a bird sanctuary. Its size makes it a bit impersonal, and the rooms are compact and decorated in standard-issue pastels. The Tower Wing is more comfortable, with newer and nicer facilities, but more expensive. The Sukhumvit Wing overlooks a busy street, so you might encounter some noise problems. **Pros:** lots of activity; relatively cheap. **Cons:** not unique; staff not the most helpful. ✉ *171 Sukhumvit Soi 11–13, Sukhumvit* ☎ *02/254–0444* 🌐 *www.amtel.co.th* *813 rooms, 17 suites* *In-room: safe, refrigerator. In-hotel: 5 restaurants, room service, bar, tennis courts, pool, gym, spa, laundry service, Internet terminal, no-smoking rooms* ▭ *AE, DC, MC, V* Ⓜ *Skytrain: Nana.* ✥ *G4*

$$ **Bel-Aire Princess.** This well-managed hotel, part of the respected Dusit chain, is steps from clamorous Sukhumvit Road—thankfully, it's on the quiet end of a bustling street, away from the bars. It gets its fair share of tour groups, but for the most part the lobby and lounge are peaceful retreats. Bowls of fruit on each floor are a thoughtful touch. Rooms at the back of the hotel look down on Soi 7, while those at the front have pool views. **Pros:** quieter than most hotels in neighborhood; sleek lobby. **Cons:** feels expensive for what it is; overpriced, mediocre restaurant. ✉ *16 Sukhumvit Soi 5, Sukhumvit* ☎ *02/253–4300* 🌐 *www.bel-aireprincess.com* *160 rooms* *In-room: safe, refrigerator. In-hotel: restaurant, room service, bar, pool, gym, laundry service, Wi-Fi, no-smoking rooms* ▭ *AE, DC, MC, V* Ⓜ *Skytrain: Nana.* ✥ *G3*

$$ **City Lodge.** Of the two City Lodges off Sukhumvit (the other is on Soi 9), this is the better choice because of its location. The compact rooms are functional, designed to fit a lot into a small space, and each has a balcony with a view of Sukhumvit and the nearby Skytrain. Business services here are minimal, but you can use those, along with other facilities like the pool, at its nearby sister hotel, the Amari Boulevard. The restaurant, La Gritta, specializes in Italian food. **Pros:** close to subway and Skytrain; economical; super-friendly staff. **Cons:** looks like a dump from outside; rooms can be noisy. ✉ *Sukhumvit Soi 19, Sukhumvit* ☎ *02/253–7710* 🌐 *www.amari.com/citylodge* *34 rooms* *In-room: safe, refrigerator, Wi-Fi. In-hotel: restaurant, room service, pool, gym, laundry service, no-smoking rooms* ▭ *AE, DC, MC, V* Ⓜ *Subway: Sukhumvit; Skytrain: Asok.* ✥ *G4*

$$$–$$$$ **Davis Bangkok.** This fine medium-size hotel is actually two buildings: the main one and the Corner Wing, which is two doors down the street and has a separate reception and lobby. Rooms in both buildings have the same decor and amenities. The showpiece of the Davis is two Thai villas—separate houses with modern amenities, but built in traditional Thai style with beautiful wood—both top-of-the-line two- and three-

bedroom structures with all the amenities, their own pool, and a price tag of B25,000 to B30,000 per day (there are big discounts for monthly stays). For humbler budgets, the rooms in the main buildings are comfortable and classy, individually decorated in styles that vary from Bali and Bombay to Thai, and even Florida. **Pros:** uniquely decorated rooms; beautiful pool area. **Cons:** not that close to public transit; uninteresting view from rooms. ✉ *80 Sukhumvit Soi 24, Sukhumvit* ☎ *02/260–8000* 🌐 *www.davisbangkok.net* *247 rooms, 2 villas* *In-room: Internet. In-hotel: 2 restaurants, bar, pool, spa, Wi-Fi, no-smoking rooms* ▭ *AE, DC, MC, V* Ⓜ *Skytrain: Phrom Phong.* ✣ *G5*

2

$$$$ **Grand Millennium Sukhumvit.** This recent addition to Bangkok's upscale hotel market opened in 2007, although it looks like it might have come from the future, with an interesting look and feel (think soaring glass and odd angles). Another advantage of its relative youth is the amenities; you'll find cutting edge technology, but the whole experience still manages to be quite comfortable. The hotel wears yet another cap, as it also caters to a business clientele. **Pros:** beautiful modern decor throughout; interesting exterior architecture. **Cons:** lots of business travelers; bathrooms lack privacy. ✉ *30 Sukhumvit Soi 21, Sukhumvit* ☎ *02/204–4000* 🌐 *www.millenniumhotels.com/th/grandmillennium sukhumvitbangkok* *325 rooms* *In-room: safe, refrigerator, Wi-Fi. In-hotel: 2 restaurants, room service, bar, pool, gym, spa, laundry service, Wi-Fi, no-smoking rooms* ▭ *AE, DC, MC, V* Ⓜ *Subway: Sukhumvit; Skytrain: Asok.* ✣ *G4*

$$ **Imperial Tara Hotel.** This hotel is on a side street near Sukhumvit Road, which means restaurants and clubs are practically at your doorstep. Enjoy a cup of tea in the spacious lobby lined with teak carvings while you check in. Rooms, all of which are on the small side, have cool marble floors and nice views. Many overlook the eighth-floor terrace with a swimming pool. The hotel shares amenities with its sister property, the Imperial Impala. **Pros:** relatively cheap; lively location. **Cons:** not as luxurious as some options; not the most formal service. ✉ *18/1 Sukhumvit Soi 26, Sukhumvit* ☎ *02/665–6300* 🌐 *www.imperialhotels.com/tara* *196 rooms* *In-room: safe, refrigerator. In-hotel: restaurant, pool, gym, spa, no-smoking rooms* ▭ *AE, DC, MC, V* Ⓜ *Skytrain: Phrom Phong.* ✣ *H5*

$$$$ **J.W. Marriott Hotel.** Sukhumvit's Marriott is conveniently located, with many restaurants and businesses nearby, but it's also around the corner from Nana Plaza, one of the city's biggest red-light districts, which might turn some people off as much as it turns others on. Rooms have the standard amenities, with firm beds that make for a good night's sleep. It's worth a few extra baht to stay on the executive floors, which have a separate lounge with complimentary breakfast, afternoon tea, and evening cocktails. The fitness center is superb, with the latest equipment and saunas. Restaurants include Man Ho, serving Cantonese fare; the White Elephant, specializing in Thai favorites; and the New York Steakhouse. **Pros:** very friendly staff; nice gym. **Cons:** not as nice as Marriott in Thonburi; close to red-light district. ✉ *4 Sukhumvit Soi 2, Sukhumvit* ☎ *02/656–7700* 🌐 *www.marriott.com* *441 rooms* *In-room: safe, refrigerator. In-hotel: 5 restaurants, room service, bar, pool,*

gym, laundry service, Wi-Fi, no-smoking rooms ▭*AE, DC, MC, V* Ⓜ*Skytrain: Nana.* ✣ *G4*

$$$ **Landmark Hotel.** The generous use of polished wood in the reception area may suggest a grand European hotel, but the Landmark actually prides itself on being thoroughly modern, and rooms, though elegant enough to satisfy leisure travelers, are geared to corporate types, with good-size desks and business amenities. For a little extra, guests can stay on one of the executive floors, which have more business services and complimentary breakfast and cocktails. There's a staff of nearly 700, so it's no surprise that the service is attentive. There are shops and restaurants in the basement and first floors of the hotel building. At this writing, two of the hotel's restaurants, Nipa and Kiku No Hana, were closed for renovations. **Pros:** attractive discount packages frequently available; very modern amenities. **Cons:** may be too formal for families; some rooms a bit noisy. ✉*138 Sukhumvit Rd., Sukhumvit* ☎*02/254–0404* 🌐*www.landmarkbangkok.com* *273 rooms, 39 suites* *In-room: safe, refrigerator, Internet. In-hotel: 8 restaurants, bar, pool, gym, laundry service, no-smoking rooms* ▭*AE, DC, MC, V* Ⓜ*Skytrain: Nana.* ✣ *G4*

$$$$ **Sheraton Grand Sukhumvit.** The Sheraton soars 33 floors above the noisy city streets, and the suites on the upper floors get tons of natural light. Standard rooms are a bit formulaic—you won't find any Thai-influenced accoutrements—but they're pleasant enough. You never go hungry here: on street level is Basu, serving sushi, while the Orchid Café on the second floor lays out an international buffet. In the afternoon you can enjoy tea in the lounge or cocktails in the rotunda. On the third floor, the health club and the serpentine swimming pool are laid out amid a lovely garden. Here you can also find a Thai restaurant and, during the dry months, a barbecue. The Skytrain is connected to the hotel via a covered walkway from the station to the lobby, and the subway station is next door (and below) the Skytrain station. **Pros:** very close to fun nightlife and public transportation; impressive views from most rooms. **Cons:** somewhat impersonal due to size; pricey. ✉*250 Sukhumvit Rd., Sukhumvit* ☎*02/649–8888* 🌐*www.starwoodhotels.com/bangkok* *420 rooms, 36 suites* *In-room: safe, refrigerator, DVD, Wi-Fi (fee). In-hotel: 4 restaurants, room service, bar, pool, gym, spa, laundry service, Wi-Fi, no-smoking rooms* ▭*AE, DC, MC, V* Ⓜ*Subway: Sukhumvit; Skytrain: Asok.* ✣ *G4*

$ **Stable Lodge.** On a residential street off Sukhumvit Road, this small hotel feels more like a guesthouse. The rooms are basic but clean and comfortable. Each has a balcony where you can have your breakfast, and most, but not all, have private bathrooms. The rooms at the back are the quietest. The pool in front is a delightful place to relax in the afternoon. Make sure to return in the evening for the nightly barbecue, in the garden. The lobby restaurant serves Thai and Danish food. **Pros:** fun atmosphere; close to Skytrain. **Cons:** room and building decor past their prime. ✉*39 Sukhumvit Soi 8, Sukhumvit* ☎*02/653–0017 up to 19* 🌐*www.stablelodge.com* *41 rooms* *In-room: refrigerator. In-hotel: restaurant, pool, Wi-Fi, no-smoking rooms* ▭*AE, DC, MC, V* Ⓜ*Skytrain: Nana.* ✣ *F4*

$$$$ **Westin Grande Sukhumvit.** The Westin is fancy-schmancy, with lots of sleek surfaces and neon lighting, and bright and shiny modern decor in the somewhat futuristic bathrooms—well, maybe not futuristic by Bangkok standards. Still, it's all quite comfortable. For those who'd prefer to workout in the privacy of their own room, the Westin offers a "Workout Deluxe Room," with a treadmill and weights. The pool is clean and simple, not the urban oasis that some hotels have, but still refreshing after a hot day. And there's definitely something to be said for staying along Sukhumvit, with all the entertainment possibilities. **Pros:** right near Skytrain, subway, and nightlife; very comfortable beds. **Cons:** on-site restaurants not great; feels overpriced compared to other nearby options. ✉ *259 Sukhumvit Rd., Sukhumvit* ☎ *02/207–8000* 🌐 *www.starwoodhotels.com/westin* *302 rooms* *In-room: safe, refrigerator. In-hotel: 2 restaurants, room service, bar, pool, gym, spa, laundry service, Wi-Fi, no-smoking rooms* 💳 *AE, DC, MC, V* Ⓜ *Subway: Sukhumvit; Skytrain: Asok.* ✥ *G4*

NIGHTLIFE & THE ARTS

The English-language newspapers the *Bangkok Post* and the *Nation* have the latest information on current festivals, exhibitions, and nightlife. The Tourist Authority of Thailand's weekly *Where* also lists events. Monthly *Metro* magazine has extensive listings and offers reviews of new hot spots.

NIGHTLIFE

Bangkok's nightlife truly runs the gamut: You'll find swanky velvet-rope club scenes, beer bars doubling as brothels, and everything in between. The curfew might be 2 AM, but this city never sleeps; after-hours clubs and restaurants stay open for late-night carousing until 5 or 6 AM. Of the many great above-board nightlife neighborhoods, some of the most notable are the area off Sukhumvit Soi 55 (also called Soi Thonglor), which is full of bars and nightclubs; Soi Sarasin, across from Lumphini Park, with friendly pubs and cafés frequented by yuppie Thais and expats; and Narathiwat Road, which starts at Surawong, intersects Silom, then runs all the way to Rama III, where trendy new bars and restaurants are opening every month. If you want to meet young locals, head to the mega-discos on RCA, which stands for Royal City Avenue. **TIP→The minimum drinking age in Thailand is now 20**; it was raised from 18 in 2006.

In addition to plenty of above-board entertainment, there's also an undeniably smutty side to Bangkok's nightlife. The city's famous red-light district is actually not one but three areas: Patpong, Soi Cowboy, and Nana Plaza. Though live sex shows are officially banned, they are still prevalent in these parts of town, as is prostitution, which is also illegal. Patpong is the largest and most touristy, and it includes three streets that run between Surawong and Silom roads. Lining Patpong 1 and 2 are go-go bars with hostesses by the dozen. Shows are generally found one flight up. The Patpong area is well patrolled by police, so it is quite safe, and there's a night market patronized by Thais.

Soi Cowboy, off Sukhumvit Road at Soi 21, is a less raunchy, easier-going version of Patpong, frequented more by locals. Some bars have go-go dancers, while others are good for a quiet beer (with or without a temporary companion, who is paid by the drink). Nana Plaza, at Soi 4, is popular with expats. The plaza is packed with three floors of hostess bars. The newest bars have spilled out along Soi 4. ⚠ **Those who pay for sex in Thailand risk contracting HIV or another STD; being robbed; and even incarceration**, despite the common notion that the government turns a blind eye.

LADYBOYS

One of the most surprising (and often misunderstood) aspects of Thai culture to first-time visitors is the "ladyboy." These men act, dress, and make themselves up to look—often quite convincingly—like women. Many are found in districts catering to salacious foreign visitors, but this doesn't mean they are sex workers or gay. In fact, many Thais refer to them as a "third sex," Thai men with feminine characteristics and mannerisms, more so than most women. You may hear them referred to as "katoey," but that is a derogatory term—they prefer to be called "ladyboy."

Most gay bars and clubs happen to be located near Patpong on a pair of dead-end alleys off Silom Road. Soi 2 is filled with thumping discos. Other gay establishments are found near Sukhumvit Road.

BARS & PUBS

THONBURI

Though it's neither particularly authentic nor groundbreaking, the Marriott Resort's **Longtail Bar** (✉ *Bangkok Marriott Resort & Spa, 257 Charoennakorn Rd., Samrae Thonburi, Thonburi* ☎ *02/476–0022* 🌐 *www.marriott.com*) distinguishes itself with a tropical getaway feel that is elusive in the hubbub of Bangkok—this place will really make you want to sip a mai tai by the breezy river. In return, though, you'll have to sail about 30 minutes downriver from the Saphan Taksin Skytrain stop on one of the resort's dedicated boats, not an entirely unpleasant prospect on a nice night.

PRATUNAM

The glass-enclosed **Roof Top Bar** (✉ *Baiyoke Sky Hotel, 222 Ratchaprarop Rd., Pratunam* ☎ *02/656–3000* 🌐 *www.baiyokehotel.com* Ⓜ *Subway: Silom; Skytrain: Sala Daeng*), in Thailand's tallest building, is kitschier and more Old Bangkok than newer, hipper rooftop competitors like Vertigo and Skybar, with lounge singers and neon Heineken signs. It's also one of the highest drinking spots in the city, on the 88th floor.

PATPONG

The crowd at the **Barbican** (✉ *9/4–5 Soi Thaniya, off Silom Rd., Silom* ☎ *02/234–3590* 🌐 *www.greatbritishpub.com* Ⓜ *Subway: Silom; Skytrain: Sala Daeng*), a split-level contemporary bar smack-dab in the middle of the Japanese soi, is a bit more stylish and hip than at other pubs. It's popular among expats and a great place to hang out with

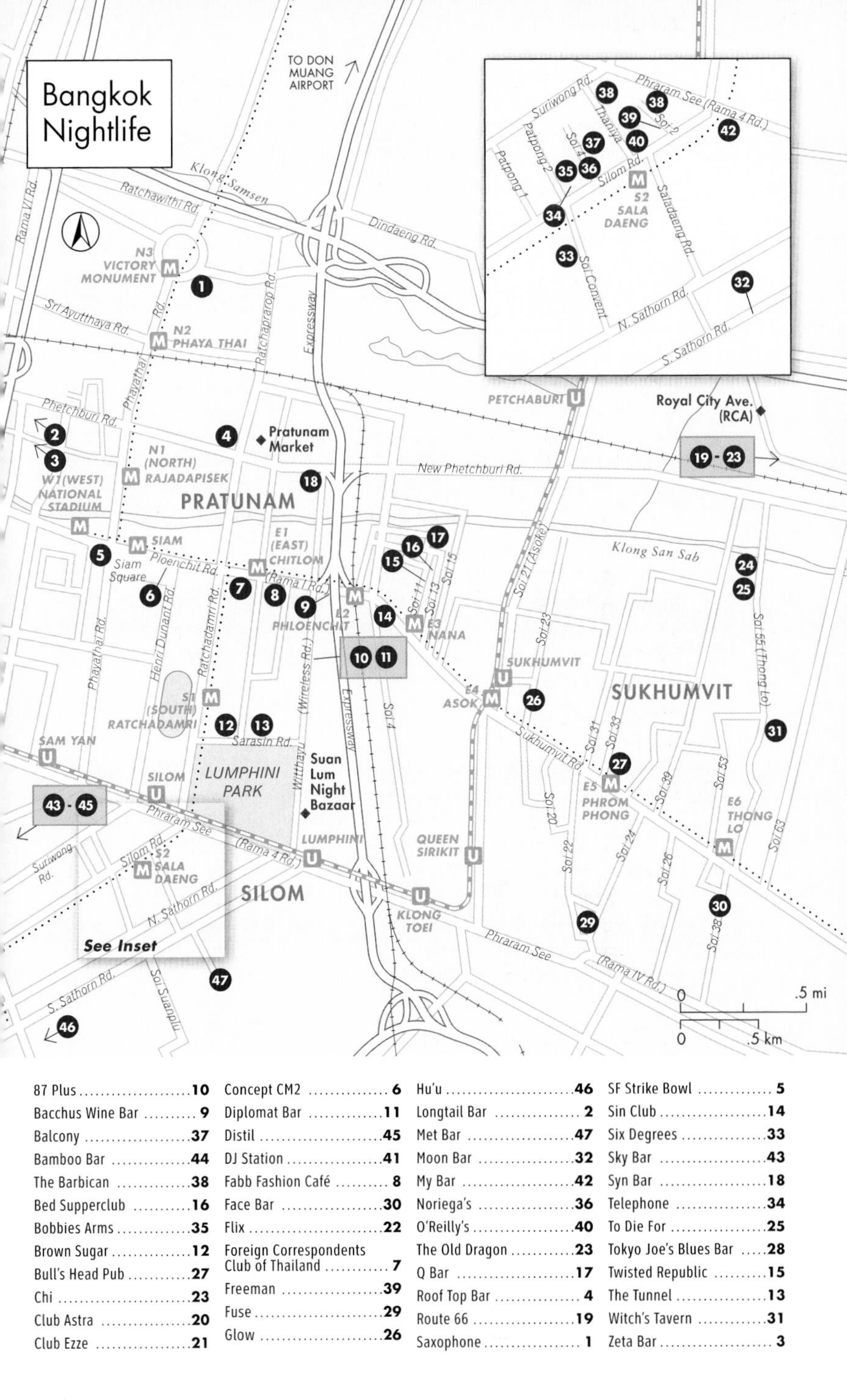

87 Plus **10**	Concept CM2 ..... **6**	Hu'u **46**	SF Strike Bowl **5**
Bacchus Wine Bar **9**	Diplomat Bar **11**	Longtail Bar **2**	Sin Club **14**
Balcony **37**	Distil **45**	Met Bar **47**	Six Degrees **33**
Bamboo Bar **44**	DJ Station **41**	Moon Bar **32**	Sky Bar **43**
The Barbican **38**	Fabb Fashion Café **8**	My Bar **42**	Syn Bar **18**
Bed Supperclub **16**	Face Bar **30**	Noriega's **36**	Telephone **34**
Bobbies Arms **35**	Flix **22**	O'Reilly's **40**	To Die For **25**
Brown Sugar **12**	Foreign Correspondents Club of Thailand **7**	The Old Dragon **23**	Tokyo Joe's Blues Bar **28**
Bull's Head Pub **27**	Freeman **39**	Q Bar **17**	Twisted Republic **15**
Chi **23**	Fuse **29**	Roof Top Bar **4**	The Tunnel **13**
Club Astra **20**	Glow **26**	Route 66 ..... **19**	Witch's Tavern **31**
Club Ezze **21**		Saxophone **1**	Zeta Bar **3**

friends. You can get a decent pint of beer at **Bobbies Arms** (✉*Patpong 2, Silom* ☎*02/233–6828* Ⓜ*Subway: Silom; Skytrain: Sala Daeng*), a rough approximation of an English pub. This longtime favorite remains popular even with the proliferation of new pubs.

The lively **O'Reillys** (✉*62/1–4 Silom Rd., Silom* ☎*02/632–7515* Ⓜ*Subway: Silom; Skytrain: Sala Daeng*) sometimes has live music. Its convenient location, near the Skytrain and the gateway to Patpong, means that the place is always jumping. If you're a Beatles fan, check out the Betters on Friday night.

SILOM

Thai A-listers and entertainers have made **Distil** (✉*State Tower, 1055 Silom Rd., Silom* ☎*02/624–9555* Ⓜ*Skytrain: Surasak*), on the 64th floor of one of Bangkok's tallest buildings, their stomping grounds. It's done in black, coffee, and slate tones, and a full-time sommelier is on staff to take care of your wine desires. **Hu'u** (✉*The Ascott, Levels 1–2, 187 S. Sathorn Rd., Silom* ☎*02/676–6677* 🌐*www.huuinasia.com* Ⓜ*Skytrain: Chong Nonsi*) is a hip restaurant and bar that's famous for its inventive cocktails. It's most popular for predinner drinks.

★ With a sister establishment in London, **Met Bar** (✉*27 S. Sathorn Rd., Silom* ☎*02/625–3333* 🌐*www.metropolitan.como.bz/bangkok* Ⓜ*Subway: Lumphini; Skytrain: Sala Daeng*) is all done up in sleek dark red and black, with patrons chilling out on comfortable couches. It used to be *the* place to go out in Bangkok, but those glory days seem to be over. Now it's more akin to a slightly empty club. Still, the decor is fun.

My Bar (✉*946 Rama IV, Silom* ☎*02/200–9000* Ⓜ*Subway: Lumphini*), a minimalist lounge-style bar, is in the Dusit Thani Bangkok hotel. It serves up signature drinks, hand-rolled Cuban cigars, and the finest single malt whiskey in town. **Noriega's** (✉*Silom Soi 4, Silom* ☎*02/233–2813* Ⓜ*Subway: Sala Daeng*) is the place to go when you're in the mood for some expat fun. A live music venue too, it often has performances by rock bands. The food here isn't special—it's meant for the truly drunk. **Moon Bar** (✉*Banyan Tree Hotel, 21/100 S. Sathorn Rd., Silom* ☎*02/679–1200* Ⓜ*Subway: Lumphini; Skytrain: Sala Daeng*) at Vertigo restaurant is appropriately named: It's an open-air bar perched high atop the Banyan Tree hotel. You can eat here, or just lounge around the sofas and low-lying tables with a drink (it's open at 5 PM). If the weather is clear, do some stargazing with the bar's telescope, but if the weather's bad at all, the place will be closed.

A few blocks down, off Sathorn, **Six Degrees** (✉*Soi Convent, Silom* ☎*02/632–2995* Ⓜ*Skytrain: Sala Daeng*) restaurant and bar has a simple, minimalist style offering a variety of smooth cocktails. The bar crowd starts to filter in after 10 PM. You'll find the chic, black-and-red **Zeta Bar** (✉*Hilton Millenium, 123 Charoennakorn Rd. Thonburi* ☎*02/442–2000*) in the Hilton Millenium. The crowd here is as swanky as the place itself, which has sister locations in London, Sydney, and Kuala Lampur.

Busy Q Bar in Sukhumvit has international DJs and a spacious outdoor terrace.

Fodor'sChoice ★ There's nothing else quite like **Sky Bar** (⊠*State Tower, 1055 Silom Rd., Silom* ☎*02/624–9999* Ⓜ*Skytrain: Surasak*), on the 65th floor of one of Bangkok's tallest buildings. Head toward the pyramid-like structure emitting eerie blue light at the far end of the restaurant and check out the head-spinning views. You'll feel like you're on top of the world.

SUKHUMVIT

Wine bars are slowly popping up around the city, and one worth mentioning is **Bacchus Wine Bar & Cafe Lounge** (⊠*20/6–7 Ruam Rudee Village, Soi Ruam Rudee, Sukhumvit* ☎*02/650–8986* Ⓜ*Skytrain: Ploenchit*). Here you'll find four floors of laid-back ambience and, well, wine. The popular **Bull's Head Pub** (⊠*595/10–11 Sukhumvit Soi 33, Sukhumvit* ☎*02/259–4444* ⊕*www.greatbritishpub.com* Ⓜ*Subway: Sukhumvit; Skytrain: Phrom Phong*) is very British and a good place for serious beer drinkers. There are also lots of activities to keep you entertained, including monthly Pub Quiz Night and disco night. Check their Web site for event schedules.

Chi (⊠*998 Sukhumvit Soi 55, Sukhumvit* ☎*02/381–7587* Ⓜ*Skytrain: Thong Lo*), a Pan-Asian eatery with a bar and lounge, attracts a quirky mix of upscale diners and imbibers, including Thai designers, interior decorators, high-society folks, artists, and, of course, a few foreigners. Each room has a different theme—the living room has an eclectic range of chairs, cushions, and sofas to lounge about on. The Conrad Hotel's **Diplomat Bar** (⊠*All Seasons Pl., 87 Wittayu [Wireless Rd.], Sukhumvit* ☎*02/690–9999* Ⓜ*Skytrain: Ploenchit*) epitomizes the grown-up lounge: warm lighting, brown colors, smooth music, a sophisticated crowd, and a splendid selection of scotch and cigars—cigar makers are sometimes brought in from Cuba just to roll at the Diplomat.

Though it might not be the most happening place in town, **Face Bar** (✉ *29 Sukhumvit Soi 38, Sukhumvit* ☎ *02/713-6048*) is a comfortable spot for a couple of drinks. A strong Indian theme—the bar shares the space with Hazara, an Indian restaurant—makes for pretty surroundings. Seating is on cushy pillows in semi-private areas. **Fuse** (✉ *Camp Davis, Sukhumvit Soi 24, Sukhumvit* ☎ *02/204–0970* Ⓜ *Skytrain: Phrom Phong*) is a low-ceilinged, wood-paneled cocktail bar that draws in Thais, expats, and models.

Celebrating the famous American highway, **Route 66** (✉ *29/37 Royal City Ave., Sukhumvit* ☎ *02/203–0407* Ⓜ *Subway: Petchaburi*) is often packed. It's one of the best places in Bangkok to hear R&B and socialize with locals. Hip **Syn Bar** (✉ *Swissotel, Nai Lert Park, 2 Wittayu [Wireless Rd.], Sukhumvit* ☎ *02/253–0123* Ⓜ *Skytrain: Ploenchit*), with its selection of pretty cocktails, is decorated in cool shades of gray and red. It's got some creative design elements like floating seating. DJs start spinning at 9 PM every day except Sunday.

To Die For (✉ *998 Sukhumvit Soi 55, Sukhumvit* ☎ *02/381–4714* Ⓜ *Skytrain: Thong Lo*) has an exquisitely manicured garden, perfect for sipping fancy drinks on brightly colored Moroccan seats. Situated in the midst of Japanese nightclubs, **Tokyo Joe's Blues Bar** (✉ *25/9 Sukhumvit Soi 26, Sukhumvit* ☎ *02/661–0359* 🌐 *www.tokyojoesbkk.com* Ⓜ *Skytrain: Phrom Phong*) stands out with its rustic interior and live music. Littered with blues mementos, vintage guitars, and stereos, this cozy bar has live music every night.

SIAM SQUARE

If you're searching for something more than just a typical cocktail bar, look no farther than **SF Strike Bowl** (✉ *MBK Shopping Center, Phayathai Rd., Victory Monument* ☎ *02/611–4555* Ⓜ *Skytrain: National Stadium*). One of the city's hottest nightspots, this futuristic bowling alley, lounge, and bar (all set in mega-mall MBK) has a sleek style that rivals most nightclubs in Asia. A DJ spins house tunes above the clatter of falling pins.

VICTORY MONUMENT

The **Old Dragon** (✉ *29/78–81 Royal City Ave., Victory Monument* ☎ *02/203–0972* Ⓜ *Skytrain: Victory Monument*) is filled with oddities, from wooden cinema seats to old mirrors etched with Chinese characters. The owner claims that little here besides the clientele is less than 50 years old. The snacks served are a mix of Chinese and Thai. **Saxophone** (✉ *3/8 Victory Monument, Phayathai Rd., Victory Monument* ☎ *02/246–5472* 🌐 *www.saxophonepub.com* Ⓜ *Skytrain: Victory Monument*) is popular with locals and expats. Live blues, R&B, jazz, rock, reggae, and even ska house bands perform seven nights a week.

LUMPHINI PARK

Suan Lum Night Bazaar (✉ *Rama IV and Wittayu [Wireless] Rds., Lumphini Park* Ⓜ *Subway: Lumphini*) has grown into one of Bangkok's most happening night markets, which is a big tourist draw. It offers an all-in-one experience: shopping, eating, massage, and drinking. There are three beer gardens, with good German beers on tap, and free nightly concerts performed by various bands from 6:30 PM to midnight.

CLUBS

ROYAL CITY AVENUE

Since the enactment of the stricter curfew laws in Bangkok, **RCA** (Royal City Avenue), formerly just a hangout for teens, has turned into one of the city's hottest nightlife areas, staying open until 2 AM and sometimes later. It's north of Downtown and only accessible by taxi.

★ There are many clubs on the RCA pedestrian street, but **Club Astra** (✉*29/53–64 Soi Soonvijai, Rama IX Rd., Huay Kwang* ☎*09/497–8422*) might be the best place to dance. Throbbing with good music, its dance floor fills up every night of the week. Bottle service is popular; get here before 11 PM to secure a table. And bring your ID—they card to make sure you're over 20. **Club Ezze** (✉*Royal City Ave., Rama IX Rd., Huay Kwang* ☎*No phone*) is a different sort of choice in RCA: a smaller venue focusing exclusively on techno music. Like the other RCA venues, it packs them in nightly. Best of all the RCA joints is the chandelier-heavy **Flix** (✉*Royal City Avenue, Rama IX Rd., Huay Kwang* ☎*No phone*), far and away the most popular, and deservedly so. The multiple rooms each have their own feel and style of music, and attract different crowds. The size of Flix is staggering and the number of beautiful people equally so.

SUKHUMVIT & SIAM SQUARE

On the more grown-up and trendier side of things, **Bed Supperclub** (✉*26 Sukhumvit Soi 11, Sukhumvit* ☎*02/651–3537* Ⓜ*Skytrain: Nana*) is Bangkok's answer to cool (*Where to Eat, above*). The futuristic Jetsons-like bar and supper club has been the rage since its inception. Grab a drink and sprawl out on an enormous bed while listening to a rotating cast of DJs mix hip-hop, house, and a variety of other music. You must be 20 years old to get in here.

Concept CM2 (✉*Novotel Siam, 392/44 Rama I, Soi 6, Siam Square* ☎*02/209–8888* Ⓜ*Skytrain: Siam*) is a flashy, energetic club with live pop bands every night. Be prepared to pay a B550 entrance fee on weekends (B220 on weekdays). For something sleek, try the Conrad's **87 Plus** (✉*All Seasons Pl., 87 Wittayu [Wireless Rd.], Sukhumvit* ☎*02/690–9999* Ⓜ*Skytrain: Ploenchit*), where the dance floor meanders throughout the bar, instead of concentrating in front of the DJ booth. Music is thumping, and the crowd is super trendy and very well-to-do. There is now live music Tuesday through Sunday. Prices are through the roof. **Glow** (✉*96/4–5 Sukhumvit Soi 23, Sukhumvit* ☎*02/261–3007*), in a space formerly known as Faith Club, lights up Sukhumvit with an eternally trendy, beautiful crowd dancing to techno. It's got the biggest vodka selection in the city.

★ **Q Bar** (✉*34 Sukhumvit Soi 11, Sukhumvit* ☎*02/252–3274* Ⓜ*Skytrain: Nana*) consistently plays quality music and regularly features international DJs. Upstairs there's a romantic lounge and a huge outdoor terrace perfect for any mood. Between the casually hip crowd, the reasonable door policy (you don't have to be a supermodel, although you won't get in wearing shorts and sneakers either), and the effortlessly energetic scene here, this is perhaps the best and most balanced nightclub in town. Epitomizing the nightclub spirit of thumping music and trippy lights, **Twisted Republic** (✉ *Sukhumvit Soi 11, Sukhumvit* ☎ *02/651–0800* Ⓜ *Skytrain: Nana*) keeps the music going (only until 2 AM, of course) and packs in the beautiful people.

AFTER-HOURS CLUBS

With Bangkok's harsh 2 AM curfew, after-hours bars are key to really making a night of it. Keep in mind that these underground parties can change from week to week, so always ask around before hitting them up—bartenders at upscale bars and clubs are a good resource. This is all technically illegal, but it's unlikely that you (as opposed to the bar) will get in any trouble even if there is a bust.

Sin Club (✉ *Sukhumvit Soi 2, Sukhumvit* ☎ *No phone* Ⓜ *Skytrain: Nana*) stays pumping as late as 5:30 AM on nights when the police don't shut it down. It's in the Rajah hotel complex, on the third floor—just follow the crowds. **The Tunnel** (✉ *Langsuan Soi 5, Sukhumvit* ☎ *No phone* Ⓜ *Skytrain: Nana*) is a veritable who's who of the Bangkok scene these days. Expect to pay B1,000, which includes two drinks, to join the beautiful people. The place will stay open until 3 AM or 3:30 AM, depending on police activity week to week.

GAY BARS

Silom Soi 2 and Silom Soi 4 are the center of Bangkok's gay scene, with every establishment from restaurants to bars to clubs all catering to a gay clientele. **Balcony** (✉ *86–88 Silom Soi 4, Silom* ☎ *02/235–5891* Ⓜ *Subway: Silom; Skytrain: Sala Daeng*) does indeed look out over the street. It has one of the best happy hours on the soi. On crowded Silom Soi 2, the sleek and pleasantly modern **DJ Station** (✉ *8/6–8 Silom Soi 2, Silom* ☎ *02/266–4029* Ⓜ *Subway: Silom; Skytrain: Sala Daeng*) packs absolutely full with a young crowd. The cover charge is B200 on weekends and B100 on weekdays. Around the corner from DJ Station, **Freeman** (✉ *60/18–21 Silom Rd., Silom* ☎ *02/632–8033* Ⓜ *Subway: Silom; Skytrain: Sala Daeng*) has a famous drag show every night at midnight and a balcony where you can watch the dance floor.

The most venerable of Bangkok's gay bars, the friendly, pub-style **Telephone** (✉ *114/1 Silom Soi 4, Silom* ☎ *02/234–3279* Ⓜ *Subway: Silom; Skytrain: Sala Daeng*) is hopping every night of the week. There are telephones on the table so you can chat up your neighbors.

JAZZ BARS

To hear easy-on-the-ears jazz, try the Oriental Hotel's **Bamboo Bar** (✉ *Oriental La., Silom* ☎ *02/236–0400 Ext. 7690* Ⓜ *Skytrain: Saphan Taksin*). This legendary bar features international jazz musicians. A good place to carouse over live jazz, and occasionally blues, is the smoky **Brown Sugar** (✉ *231/19–20 Soi Sarasin, Silom* ☎ *02/250–0103* Ⓜ *Subway: Silom; Skytrain: Ratchadamri*). **Fabb Fashion Café** (✉ *Mercury Tower, 540 Ploenchit Rd., Sukhumvit* ☎ *02/843–4946* Ⓜ *Skytrain:*

Ploenchit) is a great place to start your night with some live jazz just about every night.

The **Foreign Correspondents Club of Thailand** (✉*Penthouse, Maneeya Center, 518/5 Ploenchit Rd., Sukhumvit* ☎*02/652–0580* Ⓜ*Skytrain: Chitlom*) is open to the public only on Friday nights, when there's live music. **Witch's Tavern** (✉*Sukhumvit Soi 55, Sukhumvit* ☎*02/391–9791* Ⓜ*Skytrain: Thong Lo*) recently received a much-needed face-lift and has musicians on Friday, Saturday, and Sunday. The bar also serves hearty English fare.

THE ARTS

A contemporary arts scene is relatively new to Thailand, but the last decade has seen great changes in the fine arts: artists are branching out into all kinds of media, and modern sculpture and artwork can be increasingly found decorating office buildings, parks, and public spaces. Bangkok also offers an eclectic range of theater and dance performances such as traditional *khon* (drama dances), and masterful puppet shows (⇨*Thai Puppetry, below*). Music options range from piano concertos and symphonies to rock concerts and blues-and-jazz festivals.

ART GALLERIES

Today, artists use various media, often melding international art trends with distinctly Thai craftsmanship. To keep up with the pace of an emerging movement, galleries are popping up all over Bangkok. Exhibitions are now held in cafés, restaurants, shopping malls, foreign clubs, and even bars.

Eat Me (✉*Soi Phi Phat 2, off Convent Rd., Silom* ☎*02/238–0931* Ⓜ*Skytrain: Sala Daeng*) is a restaurant-cum-art space. By day this split-level space features a variety of exhibitions from both Thai and foreign artists. In the evening it morphs into a fusion eatery.

The lovely courtyard at the **Four Seasons Hotel Bangkok** (✉*155 Ratchadamri Rd., Siam Square* ☎*02/250–1000* Ⓜ*Skytrain: Ratchadamri*) rotates their exhibits frequently and features paintings in different media, with a greater emphasis on photos. **H Gallery** (✉*201 Sathorn Rd. Soi 12, Silom* ☎*01/310–4428* Ⓜ*Skytrain: Surasak*) often shows solo exhibitions from renowned artists. They are open every day except Tuesday from 10 AM–6 PM.

Tadu Contemporary Art (✉*Barcelona Motors Bldg., 99/2 Tiam Ruammit Rd., North Bangkok* ☎*02/645–2473* 🌐*www.tadu.net*) exhibits dynamic, powerful work in a variety of media by an eclectic group of contemporary artists. **Tang Gallery** (✉*B29, 919/1 Silom Rd., Silom* ☎*02/630–1114* Ⓜ*Skytrain: Sala Daeng*) features works by Chinese artists, including contemporary oil and watercolor paintings and ceramic sculptures.

THEATER & DANCE

For Thais, classical dance is more than graceful movements. The dances actually tell tales from the religious epic *Ramakien*. Performances are accompanied by a woodwind called the *piphat,* which sounds like an oboe, as well as a range of percussion instruments. Many restaurants also present classical dance performances.

The **Chalerm Krung Royal Theater** (☒*66 Charoen Krung [New Rd.], Wang Burapha, Phirom, Old City* ☎*02/222–0434* Ⓜ*Skytrain: Hua Lamphong*) was designed in 1933 by a former student of the Ecole des Beaux-Arts in Paris. The design is Thai Deco, and it hosts traditional khon performances, a masked dance-drama based on tales from the *Ramakien.*

A visit to the Suan Lum Night Bazaar would not be complete without stopping at the **Joe Louis Puppet Theatre** (☒*Suan Lum Night Bazaar, Lumphini Park* ☎*02/252–9683* Ⓜ*Subway: Lumphini; Skytrain: Ploenchit*). Master Sakorn Yangkhiawsod grew up in the theater and is a versatile performer and puppet maker. He has passed on the dying tradition to his nine children and two dozen grandchildren; his family is the only troupe left in Thailand keeping the art alive. Performances take place every night at 7:30 PM. Tickets are B600.

At the **National Theatre** (☒*Na Phra That Rd., Old City* ☎*02/224–1342* Ⓜ*Skytrain: Hua Lamphong*), classical dance and drama can usually be seen here on the last Friday and Saturday of each month. Finding a schedule is a challenge, though. If you're interested in seeing a show, the best bet is to ask your hotel whether they can call and ask for a schedule.

Across the river, **Patravadi** (☒*69/1 Soi Wat Rakang, Thonburi* ☎*02/412–7287*) offers a dance show during dinner. There's also a theater in the restaurant showing performances, from classical to contemporary.

At the Oriental Hotel, **Sala Rim Naam** (☒*Oriental La., Silom* ☎*02/236–0400 Ext. 7330* Ⓜ*Skytrain: Saphan Taksin*) stages a beautiful dance show nightly at 8:30, accompanied by a touristy dinner. **Siam Niramit** (☒*19 Tiamruammit Rd., Huay Kwang* ☎*02/649—9222*) is the largest theater in Thailand, with 2,000 seats and 150 actors and actresses. Their world-class show, "Journey to the Enchanted Kingdom of Siam," is a brief history of Thailand told in words and music. The 80-minute performance starts at 8 PM nightly. Tickets are B1,500.

Silom Village (☒*286 Silom Rd., Silom* ☎*02/234–4448* Ⓜ*Skytrain: Sala Daeng*) appeals mostly to foreigners, but it also draws many Thais. The block-size complex, open daily 10 AM–10 PM, features performances of classical dance.

The **Thailand Cultural Center** (☒*Ratchadaphisek Rd., North Bangkok, Huay Kwang* ☎*02/247–0028* Ⓜ*Subway: Thai Cultural Center*) hosts local and international cultural events, including opera, symphony orchestras, modern dance, and ballet. You can ask your concierge to find out what performance is showing while you're in town.

SHOPPING

Each year, more and more tourists are drawn to the Thai capital for its relatively cheap silk, gems, and tailor-made items. But there are a slew of other goods worth discovering: quality silverware, furniture, fine porcelain, and handmade leather goods—all at prices that put Western shops to shame. Plus, already low prices can often be haggled down even further (haggling is mainly reserved for markets, but shopkeepers will let you know if they're willing to discount, especially if you started walking away). ⚠ **A word to the wise: to avoid getting scammed when shopping for bigger-ticket items (namely jewelry), be sure to patronize reputable dealers only.** Don't be fooled by a tuk-tuk driver offering to take you to a shop. This is a popular con perpetrated by shop owners, who in turn pay drivers a commission to lure in unsuspecting tourists.

The city's most popular shopping areas are Silom Road and Surawong Road, where you can find quality silk; Sukhumvit Road, which is rich in leather goods; Yaowarat Road in Chinatown, where gold trinkets abound; and along Oriental Lane and Charoen Krung (New Road), where there are many antiques shops. The shops around Siam Square and at the World Trade Center attract both Thais and foreigners. Peninsula Plaza, across from the Four Seasons Hotel Bangkok in the embassy district, has very upscale shops. If you're knowledgeable about fabric, you can find bargains at the textile merchants who compete along Pahuraht Road in Chinatown and Pratunam Road off Phetchaburi Road. You can even take the raw material to a tailor and have something made.

You can reclaim the 10% V.A.T. (Value-Added Tax) at the airport if you have a receipt. Ask shopkeepers about the V.A.T. refund—you must fill out the proper forms at the time of purchase. If you still want the convenience of duty-free shopping, try **King Power International Group** (☒*King Power Complex, Rangnam Rd.* ☎*02/205–8888* ☒*Suvarnabhumi Airport, 2nd–4th fls.* ☎*02/134–8888*). The branch at the airport is open 24 hours. You pay for the items at the shop, then pick them up at the airport (or simply take them with you) when you leave. You need your passport and an airline ticket, and you need to make your purchase at least eight hours before leaving the country.

MARKETS

Fodor's Choice ★ You can purchase virtually anything at the sprawling **Chatuchak Weekend Market** (☒*Phaholyothin Rd., Chatuchak, North Bangkok* Ⓜ*Subway: Chatuchak Park; Skytrain: Mo Chit*), including silk items in a *mudmee* (tie-dyed before weaving) design that would sell for five times the price in the United States. Strategically placed food vendors mean you don't have to stop shopping to grab a bite. It's open on weekends from 9 AM to 7 PM, and the city's (some say the world's) largest market is best in the morning before it gets too crowded and hot. It's easy to reach, across the street from the northern terminus of the Skytrain and near the Northern Bus Terminal. Just follow the crowd.

An afternoon at JJ, as it is known by locals ("ch" is pronounced "jha" in Thai, so phonetically Chatuchak is Jatujak), is not for the faint of heart: up to 200,000 people visit each day and there are more than 8,000 vendors. But what's a little discomfort when there are such fantastic bargains to be had? Go prepared with bottles of water, comfortable shoes, and, if you can get a copy, *Nancy Chandler's Map of Bangkok,* which has a helpful, color-coded, stall-by-stall rendering of the market. It's best to order the map online before your trip at 🌐*www.nancychandler.net,* though you may be able to find one at bookstores and tourism businesses.

WORD OF MOUTH

"The market was a joy, and far less hot, crowded, and difficult to navigate than I had feared. I had a Nancy Chandler map but did not use it as I found it delightful just to wander around . . . you guessed it . . . aimlessly. I spent about three hours in the market. My two "major" purchases were a silk ikat jacket for B480 and a pair of wonderful leather sandals that cost about $20. I wish I had purchased another pair or two of the sandals as the workmanship is excellent and they have an artisanal look that reminds me of the sandals my Mom used to bring back from Capri in the 50s!" –ekscrunchy

The borders between the market's many sections can be a bit hazy (for example, the animal section—which includes some bizarre pets like squirrels—spills into the silverware section), but you can keep your bearings by remembering that the outer ring of stalls has mainly new clothing and shoes, with some plants, garden supplies, and home decor thrown in for good measure. The next ring of stalls is primarily used (and some new) clothing and shoes plus accessories like jewelry, belts, and bags. Farther in are pottery, antiques, furniture, dried goods, and live animals. No trip to JJ is complete without a meal at the **Aw Taw Kaw food market** (*Where to Eat, above*).

Even with a map, it's easy to get turned around in the mind-boggling array of goods, but this is also part of the joy that Chatuchak has to offer—wandering through the maze of vendors and suddenly stumbling upon the beautiful teak table, handmade skirt, or colorful paper lamp you'd been seeking.

Khao San Road (⊠*Yaowarat Rd. and Charoen Krung [New Rd.], Banglamphu* Ⓜ*Subway: Hua Lamphong*), in the middle of backpacker central in Banglamphu, is closed to cars, and has some of the finest and most fun street shopping in the city. If the hip clothes, cheesy Thai souvenirs, used books, and delicious B10 pad Thai doesn't make the trip to Khao San worth it, the people-watching and energy of the place will.

Pahuraht Market (⊠*Near Yaowarat Rd., Chinatown* Ⓜ*Subway: Hua Lamphong*) is known for its bargain textiles. A man with a microphone announces when items at a particular stall will be sold at half price, and shoppers surge over to bid. It's best to come in the evening when it's cooler and many street vendors are out selling food.

CLOSE UP

Bargaining in Bangkok

Even if you've honed your bargaining skills in other countries, you might still come up empty-handed in Thailand. The aggressive techniques that go far in say, Delhi, won't get you very far in Bangkok. One of the highest compliments you can pay for any activity in the Land of Smiles is calling it *sanuk* (fun), and haggling is no exception. Thais love to joke and tease, so approach each bargaining situation playfully. However, be aware that Thais are also sensitive to "losing face," so make sure you remain pleasant and respectful throughout the transaction.

As you enter a market stall, smile and acknowledge the proprietor. When something catches your eye, inquire politely about the price, but don't immediately counter. Keep your voice low—you're more likely to get a deal if it's not announced to the whole shop—then ask for a price just slightly below what you want. Don't get too cavalier with your counteroffer—Thai sellers generally price their wares in a range they view as fair, so asking to cut the initial price in half will most likely be seen as an insult and might end the discussion abruptly. In most cases, the best you can hope for is 20%–30% discount.

If the price the shopkeeper offers in return is still high, turn your smile up another watt and say something like, "Can you discount more?" If the answer is no, your last recourse is to say thank you and walk away. If you are called back, the price is still negotiable; if you aren't, maybe B500 wasn't such a bad price after all.

–Molly Petersen

2

Hundreds of vendors jam the sidewalk each day at **Pratunam Market** (✉*Phetchaburi and Ratchaprarop Rds., Pathumwan* Ⓜ*Subway: Phetchaburi; Skytrain: Asok*). The stacks of merchandise consist mainly of inexpensive clothing. It's a good place to meet Thais, who come in the evening to sample the inexpensive Thai and Chinese street food.

Soi Sampeng (✉*Parallel to Yaowarat Rd., Chinatown* Ⓜ*Subway: Hua Lamphong*) also has lots of fabrics—it's Bangkok's best-known and oldest textile center.

Asking a taxi driver to take you to **Patpong** (✉*Silom Rd. at Soi 2, Silom* Ⓜ*Subway: Silom; Skytrain: Sala Daeng*) may prompt a smirk, but for fake Rolex watches, imposter Louis Vuitton handbags, and Western-size clothing there's no better place than this notorious red light district street. You can easily make a night of Patpong's great shopping, good restaurants, and happening bars and clubs.

SHOPPING CENTERS

Bangkok's glittering high-end shopping centers stand in stark contrast to its gritty, chaotic markets. Most of these malls are located close to Siam and Chidlom Skytrain stations, and there's a network of overhead walkways that links several of them between Mah Boon Krong and Gaysorn. **Mah Boon Krong (MBK)** (✉*Phaya Thai and Rama I, Siam Square* Ⓜ *Subway: Silom; Skytrain: Siam*), an impressive seven sto-

CLOSE UP

Thai Puppetry

For hundreds of years, Thailand's puppeteers have entertained both royal courts and village crowds with shadow puppets and marionettes. Historically the *Ramakien,* Thailand's version of the ancient Indian *Ramayana* epic, provided puppeteers with their subject matter. Today, performances are more varied: many stick to the *Ramakien* or other Thai folklore and moral fables; some are contemporary twists on the classic material; and some depart from it entirely. It's an art form that exemplifies Thailand's lively blend of tradition and innovation.

SHADOW PUPPETS

Shadow puppets—carved animal hide stretched between poles—showed up in Thailand during the mid-13th century. Historians believe the art form originated in India over 1,000 years ago and traveled to Thailand via Indonesia and Malaysia. By the 14th century shadow puppetry had become a leading form of entertaining in Ayutthaya, where it acquired the name *nang yai* or "big skin," which is also what large shadow puppets are called.

Today nang yai troupes perform at village festivals, temple fairs, marriages, and royal ceremonies, as well as in theaters. Puppeteers maneuver colorful, intricately carved leather puppets behind a transparent backlit screen. A narrator and musicians help tell the story. A classical music ensemble called a *piphat* adds to the charged dramatic atmosphere with rapid-paced *ranat* (xylophone-like instrument), drums, and haunting oboe.

Large puppets (*nang yai*) are used to form the set at shadow puppet performances, while smaller puppets called *nang thalung* are the characters. There are some macabre traditions about how shadow puppets should be made, though it's unclear how often, if ever, these customs are followed today. Nang yai are supposed made with the hide of a cow or buffalo that has died a violent and accidental death, while nang thalung should be made with the skin from the soles of a dead puppet master's feet, so that the puppets are literally walking in the footsteps of the former artist. Clown characters' lips should be formed from a small piece of skin from the penis of a deceased puppeteer.

Wherever the animal skin comes from these days, it must be carefully prepared. The hide is cured and stretched, then carved (puppet makers use stencils to outline the intricate, lacey designs) and painted. Puppet makers then mount the leather on sticks. You won't see shadow puppets for sale much, though some markets sell greeting cards with paper cut to resemble shadow puppets. You may see an authentic shadow puppet for sale at an antique market.

Though today, shadow puppetry is much more common in Thailand's south, the largest shadow-puppet troupe in Thailand, **Nang Yai Wat Khanon Troupe,** performs in Damnoen Saduak, at Wat Khanon (✉ *T. Soifah., Amphur Photharam, Rachburi* ☎ *03/223–3386*), next to the floating market (⇨ *Damnoen Saduak, Chapter 3*). Performances, which are on Saturdays at 10 AM and cost B200, are hour-long versions of Ramakien stories performed in Thai.

MARIONETTES

Marionettes, born from a blend of shadow puppets and *khon,* a traditional form of Thai dance, entered the scene at the beginning of the

20th century when Krae Saptawanit, a renowned khon performer, began to make them. Krae's first two-foot-tall puppet was a miniature version of his own stage persona, with an elaborate costume, a golden mask, and long, curling finger extensions. Soon after, Krae formed a touring troupe of khon puppet performers.

Marionette choreography is highly stylized and symbolic. It takes three experienced puppeteers to manipulate each doll into a series of gymnastic twists and graceful dances moves. Puppeteers dance alongside and behind the puppets, but they remain in shadow; the dramatically lit and costumed dolls take center stage. As in nang yai, classical Thai music adds to the intense atmosphere and indicates the mood of the story.

The art of puppetmaking—or *hadtasin*—requires great attention to detail. Marionettes consist of a frame covered with papier-mâché. Most of the frame is made of wood. Parts that must be able to move independently—like the head, neck, and hands—are made of aluminum and wire, which are more malleable. The hand joints require the most attention, since they must be capable of intricate khon movements. Puppet makers must also attach the sticks the puppeteers will use to make the puppets move.

Once the frame is constructed, the puppet maker adds layers of papier-mâché and then paints the top layer, paying particular attention to the face. The puppets wear ornate costumes of silk and gold leaf. According to tradition, the puppet maker must clap three times to create the completed marionette's soul.

At the **Baan Tookkatoon Hookrabok Thai Puppet Museum** (✉ *Soi Vibavhadi 60, Laksi, Bangkok* ☎ *02/579-8101* 🌐 *www.tookkatoon.com* ⏲ *Mon.–Fri. 9–5*), you can watch marionette-makers at work and purchase puppets. There's also a substantial private collection in the museum, which is a beautiful wooden house. You may even catch an impromptu show. Admission is free but advance booking is required.

The **Joe Louis Puppet Theatre** (⇨ *above*) offers nightly shows with a live orchestra, professional singers, and elaborate sets. You can visit the theater's workshop and gallery before the show.

WHERE ELSE TO SEE SHOWS

Chiang Mai is a hotspot for contemporary puppet troupes. **Hobby Hut** (🌐 *www.cmaipuppet.com*) and **Wandering Moon** (🌐 *www.wanderingmoontheatre.com*) are both based here.

In the southern province of Nakhon Si Thammarat, about three hours by bus from Krabi or Surat Thani, national artist and puppeteer Suchart Sapsin's house has been turned into the **Shadow Puppet Museum** (✉ *10/18 Si Thammarat Rd., Soi 3, Nakhon Si Thammarat* ☎ *07/534-6394*) with regular 20-minute performances (B100) in a small theater; a workshop; and a gallery.

Keep an eye out for performances at fringe festivals and temple fairs throughout the country. A few Web sites may have information about upcoming shows: 🌐 *www.patravaditheater.com*, 🌐 *www.semathai.com*, and 🌐 *www.montaart.com*. Also check the Tourism Authority of Thailand's site, 🌐 *www.tourismthailand.org*.

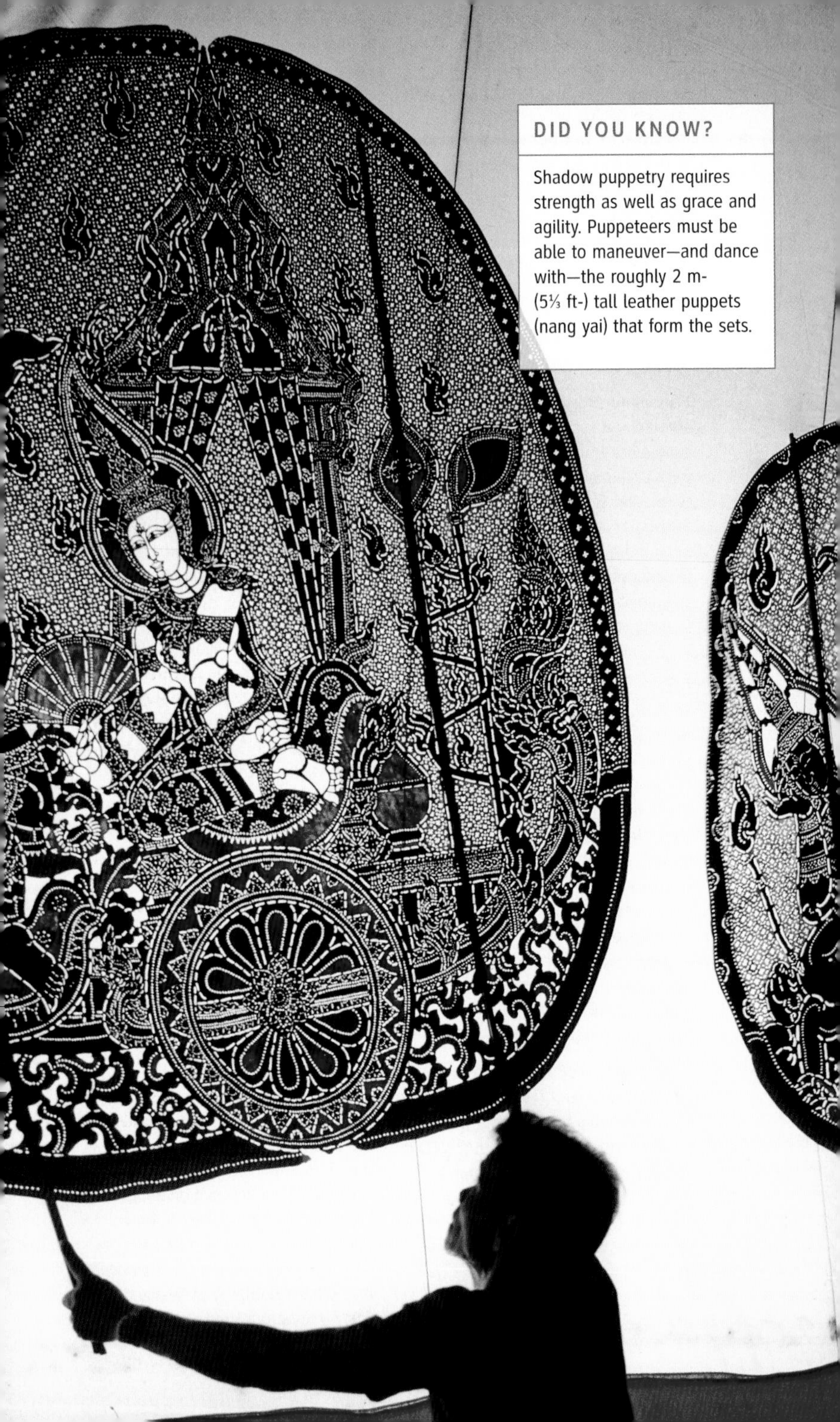

DID YOU KNOW?

Shadow puppetry requires strength as well as grace and agility. Puppeteers must be able to maneuver—and dance with—the roughly 2 m- (5⅓ ft-) tall leather puppets (nang yai) that form the sets.

ries high, is one of the busiest malls in the city. It's not as stylish as Siam Centre—the main attractions are cheap clothes and electronics—but tons of shops plus an IMAX movie theater and a bowling alley mean you can get lost here for hours. **Siam Discovery** (✉ *989 Rama I Rd., Siam Square* 🌐 *www.siamdiscoverycenter.co.th* Ⓜ *Subway: Silom; Skytrain: Siam*) is full of international labels, but has the added bonus of the most grandiose movie theater in Thailand, the Grand EGV. Next door, **Siam Centre** (✉ *Phaya Thai and Rama I, Siam Square* Ⓜ *Subway: Silom; Skytrain: Siam*) is where Bangkok's young hipsters come for the latest fashion trends. With one-of-a-kind handmade clothing, shoes, and accessories, Siam Centre oozes style, but be forewarned that the clothes are all made to Thai proportions, and as such are often small. **Siam Paragon** (✉ *991/1 Rama 1 Rd., Siam Square* 🌐 *www.siamparagon.co.th* Ⓜ *Subway: Silom; Skytrain: Siam*) has 250 stores including all the big international designers, from Porsche to Chanel, along with a multiplex cinema, tons of restaurants, and an underwater marine park where you can swim with the sharks.

The next stop along the walkway is **Central World** (✉ *4/1–2 Ratchadanri Rd., Siam Square* 🌐 *www.centralworld.co.th* Ⓜ *Subway: Silom; Skytrain: Siam*). This monster, at over one million square meters (about 10,760,000 square feet), claims to be Southeast Asia's biggest mall. It's packed with local and international labels plus a multiplex cinema, a hotel, and lots of dining options.The next stop on the line, Siam, is pay dirt for shoppers. **Gaysorn** (✉ *Ratchaprasong Intersection, Siam Square* 🌐 *www.gaysorn.com* Ⓜ *Subway: Silom; Skytrain: Siam*) may outshine all the other posh centers with its white marble and chrome fixtures. You'll find all the requisite European labels as well as local designers, such as Fly Now, Senada, and Stretsis (⇨ *below*).

East of Gaysorn is **Central Chitlom** (✉ *1027 Ploenchit Rd., Sukhumvit* Ⓜ *Subway: Sukhumvit; Skytrain: Chitlom*). The flagship store of Thailand's largest department store chain has a good selection of clothing, fabric, and jewelry, including a Jim Thompson silk shop. Four Skytrain stops beyond Chitlom is the **Emporium** (✉ *622 Sukhumvit, between Sukhumvit Sois 24 and 26, Sukhumvit* 🌐 *www.emporiumthailand.com* Ⓜ *Subway: Sukhumvit; Skytrain: Phrom Phong*). It's glitzy, but often has sales. There's a little area on the sixth floor full of beautiful Thai silks, incense, and glassware, which are all reasonably priced.

Pantip Plaza (✉ *Phetchaburi Rd., Sukhumvit* Ⓜ *Subway: Petchaburi; Skytrain: Asok*) exists for the computer nerd in everyone. Multiple stories high, it houses an enormous collection of computer hardware and software (some legal, some not). Shopping here can be overwhelming, but if you know what you're looking for, the bargains are worth it. ⚠ **Not all electronics will be compatible with what you have in the U.S., so research brands and models ahead of time.**

SPECIALTY STORES

ANTIQUES

Thai antiques and old images of the Buddha require a special export license; check out the Thai Board of Investment's Web site at *www.boi.go.th/english/* for rules on exporting, and applications to do so. Surawongse Road, Charoen Krung (New Road), and the Oriental Plaza (across from Oriental Hotel) have many art and antiques shops, as does the River City Shopping Complex. Original and often illegal artifacts from Angkor Wat are sometimes sold there as well.

> **A UNIQUE SOUVENIR**
>
> One of the famous artisanal products of Bangkok is the steel **monk's bowl,** handmade by monks in the area of tiny alleyways around Soi Banbat (near Wat Suthat). The unique bowls, which resonate harmonically when tapped, are made out of eight strips of metal—one for each Buddhist stage—and are traditionally used by the monks to collect donations. At the shop at 14 Soi Banbat (02/621–2635), you can purchase one for around B500, which will also buy you a look at the workshop.

As you wander around the Old City, don't miss the small teak house that holds **123 Baan Dee** (*123 Fuengnakorn Rd., Old City 02/221–2520 Subway: Hua Lamphong*). Antique silks, ceramics, beads, and other fascinating artifacts fill two floors. If you need sustenance, there's a small ice-cream parlor at the back. **Peng Seng** (*942 Rama IV, at Surawongse Rd., Silom 02/234–1285 Subway: Sam Yan; Skytrain: Sala Daeng*) is one of the city's most respected dealers of antiquities. Prices may be high, but articles will most likely be genuine. **Rasi Sayam** (*32 Sukhumvit Soi 23, Sukhumvit 02/258–4195 Subway: Sukhumvit; Skytrain: Asok*), in an old teak house in a garden, has a wonderful collection of fine Thai crafts.

CLOTHING & FABRICS

Thai silk gained its reputation only after World War II, when technical innovations made it less expensive. Two fabrics are worth seeking out: mudmee silk, produced in the northeastern part of the country, and Thai cotton, which is soft, durable, and easier on the wallet than silk (*Silkworms & Cocoons, Chapter 7*).

B. Tanika (*1348 Charoen Krung, Bangrak 02/237–5280 Skytrain: Saphan Taksin*) sells quality silk and cotton; the linen clothing is especially nice. Many things you can simply buy from the rack, but others can be tailor-made for you.

Design Thai (*304 Silom Rd., Silom 02/235–1553 Subway: Silom; Skytrain: Chong Nonsi*) has a large selection of silk items in all price ranges. If you ask, you can usually manage a 20% discount. **Greyhound** (*Unit 1-22 1st Fl., Siam Paragon, 991/1 Rama 1 Rd., Siam Square 02/129–4358 www.greyhound.co.th Subway: Silom; Skytrain: Siam*) sells casual yet chic street wear. For factory-made clothing, visit the **Indra Garment Export Centre** (*Ratchaprarop Rd. behind Indra Regent Hotel, Pathumwan Skytrain: Phaya Thai*), where hundreds of shops sell discounted items. This rabbit warren of a place is kind of

CLOSE UP

Bangkok Spas

Venues offering traditional massage are quite common in Bangkok—you can even pamper yourself while sightseeing at Wat Po. The staff at your hotel can recommend reputable therapists. If you have the time, pull out all the stops with a two-hour massage. ⚠ **Spa treatments at top hotels tend to fill up at least a day in advance, so plan ahead.**

The treatments at ★ **Being Spa** (✉ *88 Sukhumvit Soi 51, Sukhumvit* ☎ *02/258–7906* Ⓜ *Skytrain: Thong Lo*) take place in a Thai-style house. Among the inventive treatments are a coffee-bean body scrub and detoxifying algae and green-tea body wraps.

COMO Shambhala (✉ *Metropolitan Hotel, 27 S. Sathorn, Silom* ☎ *02/625–3355* Ⓜ *Subway: Lumphini; Skytrain: Sala Daeng*) is the ultimate urban escape. The Metropolitan Bath starts with an invigorating salt scrub, followed by a bath and relaxing massage. Relax with some of their delicious ginger lemongrass tea.

A relaxing massage with deliciously warm oils is available at the **Four Seasons Hotel Bangkok** (✉ *155 Ratchadamri Rd., Siam Square* ☎ *02/250–1000* Ⓜ *Skytrain: Ratchadamri*). You can even get a poolside massage if you like. The new **I. Sawan Spa** (✉ *Grand Hyatt Erawan, 494 Ratchadamri Rd., Pratunam* ☎ *02/254–6310* Ⓜ *Skytrain: Ratchadamri*) offers massage rooms and other facilities that are among the city's most cutting-edge, relaxing, and beautiful. Day passes cost B500, not including any treatments. There are also "residential spa cottages," suites clustered around a courtyard adjacent to the spa with their own treatment spaces; reasonably priced spa packages are available. The small **Jivita Spa House** (✉ *57/155 Silom Terrace Bldg., Saladaeng Soi 2, Silom* ☎ *02/635–5422* Ⓜ *Subway: Silom*) is an oasis of calm and regeneration. There is a variety of treatments here, but the most unusual is the Japanese Healing Stone (using crystals, not stones).

A gentle massage in genteel surroundings is what you'll get at **Oriental Spa** (✉ *Oriental Hotel, 48 Oriental Ave., Silom* ☎ *02/236–0400* Ext. 7440 Ⓜ *Skytrain: Saphan Taksin*). Amid the wood-panel sophistication you can treat yourself to facials, wraps, and massage. The Oriental's "Ayurvedic Penthouse" is a major addition to the Bangkok spa scene, with Ayurvedic massage treatments, that focus on holistic treatment. You'll sit for a quick quiz of sorts, which tells the masseuse how to treat your body based on your lifestyle.

A more low-key, inexpensive, but excellent option for traditional Thai massage is **Ruen Nuad** (✉ *Soi Convent, Silom* ☎ *02/632–2662*). A 90-minute massage will cost B700. Be aware that the place closes by 8 PM (actually a sign that it's legitimate and not a front for nefarious activities like many massage parlors). The Conrad Hotel's **Seasons Spa** (✉ *Conrad Hotel, All Seasons Place, 87 Wittayu [Wireless Rd.], Sukhumvit* ☎ *02/690–9999* Ⓜ *Skytrain: Ploenchit*) has 11 treatment rooms with views that are among the city's finest.

Bangkok offers massage at every turn—in swanky resort spas, tiny shophouses, and everything in between.

fun to hunt around in, and bargains can be found. The heat and humidity can be oppressive during the hot and rainy seasons, though. There are a few little restaurants tucked here and there for when you need a break. Check out **Issue** (✉*226/10 Siam Square, Soi 3, Siam Square* ☎*No phone* Ⓜ *Subway: Silom; Skytrain: Siam)* for chic, impeccably tailored, Indian-influenced designs.

The **Jim Thompson Thai Silk Company** (✉*9 Surawongse Rd., Silom* ☎*02/632–8100* 🌐*www.jimthompson.com* Ⓜ*Subway: Silom; Skytrain: Sala Daeng*) is a prime place for silk by the yard and ready-made clothes. The prices are high, but the staff is knowledgeable. There are numerous other locations throughout the city, such as in the Oriental Hotel, Four Seasons Hotel, Peninsula Hotel, and Central Chitlom shopping center.

Napajaree Suanduenchai studied fashion design in Germany and more than two decades ago opened the **Prayer Textile Gallery** (✉*Phayathai Rd. near Siam Sq., Siam Square* ☎*02/251–7549* Ⓜ*Subway: Sukhumvit; Skytrain: Siam*) in her mother's former dress shop. She makes stunning items in naturally dyed silks and cottons and in antique fabrics from the farthest reaches of Thailand, Laos, and Cambodia.

Many people who visit Bangkok brag about a custom-made suit that was completed in just a day or two, but the finished product often looks like the rush job that it was. If you want an excellent cut, give the tailor the time he needs, which could be up to a week at a reputable place. One of the best custom tailor shops in Bangkok is **Marco Tailor** (✉*430/33 Siam Sq., Soi 7, Siam Square* ☎*02/252–0689* Ⓜ*Subway: Sukhumvit; Skytrain: Siam*), which sews a suit equal to those on London's Savile Row. It's not cheap, but still cheaper than what you'd pay in London—expect to pay in the low triple digits.

Check out photographs of former heads of state modeling their new suits made by **Raja Fashions** (✉*Sukhumvit Soi 4, Sukhumvit* ☎*02/253–8379* Ⓜ*Subway: Sukhumvit; Skytrain: Nana*). Raja has the reputation for tailoring some of the finest men and women's fashions in Bangkok. For women's apparel, **Stephanie Thai Silk** (✉*55 Soi Shangri-La, New Rd., Sukhumvit* ☎*02/233–0325* Ⓜ*Subway: Sukhumvit; Skytrain: Nana*) is among the city's finest shops. A skirt with blouse and jacket made of Thai silk starts at B5,000. Three Thai sisters, darlings of the local design scene, created **Sretsis** (✉*Gaysorn Plaza, 2nd Fl., Ratchaprasong Intersection, Siam Square* ☎*02/656–1125* *www.sretsis.com* Ⓜ*Subway: Silom; Skytrain: Siam*), a feminine design label that have fashionistas around the world raving.

JEWELRY

Thailand is known for its sparkling gems, so it's no surprise that the country exports more colored stones than anywhere in the world. You'll find things you wouldn't find at home, and prices are far lower than in the U.S., too. There are countless jewelry stores on Silom and Surawongse roads. Scams are common, so it's best to stick with established businesses. ■ **TIP→ As usual, deals that seem too good to be true probably are.**

A long-established firm is **Johny's Gems** (✉*199 Fuengnakorn Rd., Old City* ☎*02/224–4065* Ⓜ*Subway: Hua Lamphong*). If you call first, they'll send a car (a frequent practice among the city's better stores) to take you to the shop near Wat Phraw Kaew. They have a massive selection and will also custom design pieces for you. You can rest assured you are getting a genuine piece from **Lin Jewelers** (✉*Soi 38 Charoen Krung [New Rd.], Old City* ☎*02/234–2819* Ⓜ*Subway: Hua Lamphong*), though their prices are a bit more expensive than average. **Oriental Lapidary** (✉*116/1 Silom Rd., Silom* ☎*02/238–2718* Ⓜ*Subway: Silom; Skytrain: Sala Daeng*) has a long record of good service. **Than Shine** (✉*199 Sukhumvit Soi 22, Sukhumvit* ☎*02/261–900 Ext. 5093* Ⓜ*Subway: Sukhumvit; Skytrain: Thong Lo*), run by sisters Cho Cho and Mon Mon, offers classic and modern designs. They're closed on Sunday. With top-quality gems, reliable service, and hordes of repeat clients, it's no wonder you need an appointment to peruse the huge inventory at **Uthai's Gems** (✉*28/7 Soi Ruam Rudi, Sukhumvit* ☎*02/253–8582* Ⓜ*Subway: Sukhumvit; Skytrain: Ploenchit*).

LEATHER

It's easy to find good buys on leather goods in Bangkok, which has some of the lowest prices in the world for custom work. Crocodile leather is popular, but be sure to obtain a certificate that the skins came from a domestically raised reptile; otherwise, U.S. Customs may confiscate the goods. The River City Shopping Complex, next to the Royal Orchid Sheraton Hotel, has a number of leather shops. There are some great leather bags for under $100.

The **Chaophraya Bootery** (✉*116 Silom Soi 4, Silom* Ⓜ*Subway: Silom; Skytrain: Sala Daeng*) will custom-make cowboy boots for around $200 in four or five days. They also have a large inventory of ready-made leather shoes, boots, and accessories. **North City** (✉*66 Phra Athit, Old City* Ⓜ*Skytrain: Hua Lamphong*) carries some of the city's best leather goods, especially bags. The lack of pushiness here makes for a pleasant shopping experience. North City also has a stall at the Chatuchak Weekend Market *(⇨ Markets, above)*.

For shoes and jackets, try 25-year-old **Siam Leather Goods** (✉*River City Shopping Complex, 23 Trok Rongnamkhaeng, Silom* ☎*02/237–0077 Ext. 118* Ⓜ*Subway: Sam Yan; Skytrain: Saphan Taksin*).

PORCELAIN, CERAMICS & CELADON

Benjarong (✉*River City Shopping Complex, 3rd floor, Yotha Rd., Thonburi* ☎*02/237–0077 Ext. 325*) is a massive store with a huge inventory, and will make to-order dining sets, bowls, and vases. The pale green ceramic that will remind you of Thailand for years to come can be found in abundance at the **Celadon House** (✉*8/3 Ratchadaphisek Rd., Sukhumvit* Ⓜ*Subway: Sukhumvit; Skytrain: Asok*). This retailer carries some of the finest celadon tableware found in Bangkok. The blue-and-white porcelain may look more Chinese than Thai, but a lovely selection of dishes and more can be found at **Siamese D'art** (✉*264 Sukhumvit Rd., Sukhumvit* Ⓜ*Subway: Sukhumvit; Skytrain: Phrom Phong*).

PRECIOUS METALS

Chinatown is the place to go for gold. There's no bargaining, but you're likely to get a good price anyway—about 25% less than what you'd pay in the U.S. Just around the corner from Lin Jewelers is its sister shop **Lin Silvercraft** (✉*14 Soi Oriental, Charoen Krung [New Rd.], Silom* Ⓜ*Subway: Sam Yan; Skytrain: Saphan Taksin*). Among all the knickknacks stacked from floor to ceiling, this shop has some of the most finely crafted silver cutlery in town. For bronze try **Siam Bronze Factory** (✉*1250 Charoen Krung [New Rd.], Silom* ☎*02/234–9436* Ⓜ*Subway: Sam Yan; Skytrain: Saphan Taksin*). It's near the Oriental Hotel and not far from Lin Silvercraft.

SOUVENIRS

For a one-stop souvenir shop, go to **Narayana Phand Pavilion** (✉*127 Ratchadamri Rd., Sukhumvit* Ⓜ*Subway: Sukhumvit; Skytrain: Ratchadamri*). Thai silk, ceramics, lacquerware, and hand-tooled leather are all under one roof. It was established by the Thai government in 1941; expect to find high-quality goods, low prices, and half the crowds of the packed markets.

SPORTS

Although Thailand is home to an abundance of adventure and water sports, trekking, and boat racing, it's often difficult to find outdoor activities within Bangkok. Due to elevated temperatures, Bangkok residents generally head to malls on weekends where they can cool off, but the city does have golfing, jogging, and cycling options.

Thai boxers strike their opponents with their hands, elbows, knees, and shins.

Bangkok offers visitors one of the most intense spectator sports in the world, *muay thai* (Thai kickboxing). This is the national sport of Thailand and a quintessential Bangkok experience.

MUAY THAI

The national sport of Thailand draws enthusiastic crowds in Bangkok. Unlike some shows you can see in the resort areas down south, which feel touristy, Bangkok has the real thing. Daily matches alternate between the two main stadiums. Ticket prices range from about B500 to B1,500 for the more expensive seats. The older **Lumphini Stadium** (✉ *Rama IV Rd., Lumphini Park* ☎ *02/251–4303* Ⓜ *Subway: Lumphini*) has matches Tuesday, Friday, and Saturday, starting at around 6:30 PM. The newer and larger **Ratchadamnoen Stadium** (✉ *Ratchadamnoen Nok Rd., Banglamphu* ☎ *02/281–4205* Ⓜ *Skytrain: Hua Lamphong*) has bouts on Monday, Wednesday, Thursday, and Sunday from 6:30 PM to 10 PM. Tickets may be purchased at the gate.

Avoid the hawkers outside the stadiums who will try to sell you pricey ringside seats—you'll be able to see all the action very well and get food-and-drink service at the mid-price seats in the bleachers. The only thing you're getting with the pricier tickets is a little more comfort (a folding chair versus bleacher seating or standing room). In both stadiums there are sections that seem solely reserved for the most manic of Thai gamblers; if you find yourself accidentally sitting in one of these sections, you'll be politely redirected to the *farang* section.

CLOSE UP

Muay Thai, the Sport of Kings

Thais are every bit as passionate about their national sport as Americans are about baseball. Though it's often dismissed as a blood sport, muay thai is one of the world's oldest martial arts, and it was put to noble purposes long before it became a spectator sport.

Muay thai is believed to be over 2,000 years old. It's been practiced by kings and was used to defend the country. It's so important to Thai culture that until the 1920s, muay thai instruction was part of the country's public school curriculum.

Admittedly, some of the sport's brutal reputation is well-deserved. There were very few regulations until the 1930s. Before then, there were no rest periods between rounds. Protective gear was unheard of—the exception was a groin protector, an essential item when kicks to the groin were still legal. Boxing gloves were introduced to the sport in the late 1920s. Hand wraps did exist, but some fighters actually dipped their wrapped hands in resin and finely ground glass to inflict more damage on their opponent.

Techniques: Developed with the battlefield in mind, its moves mimic the weapons of ancient combat. Punching combinations, similar to modern-day boxing, turn the fists into spears that jab relentlessly at an opponent. The roundhouse kick—delivered to the thigh, ribs, or head—turns the shinbone into a devastating striking surface. Elbow strikes to the face and strong knees to the abdomen mimic the motion of a battle-ax. Finally, strong front kicks, using the ball of the foot to jab at the abdomen, thigh, or face, mimic an array of weapons.

Rules: Professional bouts have five three-minute rounds, with a two-minute rest period in between each round. Fights are judged using a points system, with judges awarding rounds to each fighter, but not all rounds are given equal weight—the later rounds are more important as judges view fights as "marathons," with the winner being the fighter who's fared best throughout the entire match. The winner is determined by majority decision. Of course, a fight can also end decisively with a knockout or a technical knockout (wherein a fighter is conscious, but too injured to continue).

Rituals: The "dance" you see before each match is called the *ram muay* or *wai kru* (these terms are often used interchangeably, though the wai kru really refers to the homage paid to the *kru* or trainer). The ram muay serves to honor the fighter's supporters and his god, as well as to help him warm up, relax, and focus. Both fighters walk around the ring with one arm on the top rope to seal out bad spirits, pausing at each corner to say a short prayer. They then kneel in the center of the ring facing the direction of their birthplace and go through a set of specific movements, often incorporating aspects of the *Ramakien*. Fighters wear several good-luck charms, including armbands (*kruang rang*) and a headpiece (*mongkron*). The music you hear during each bout is live. Though it may sound like the tune doesn't change, the musicians actually pay close attention to the fight and they will speed up to match its pace—or to encourage the fighters to match theirs.

3

Around Bangkok

TRIPS TO DAMNOEN SADUAK FLOATING MARKET, PHETCHABURI, KANCHANABURI, AND SANGKLABURI

WORD OF MOUTH

"I only planned on three days [in Kanchanaburi] but I extended my stay a day because I liked it so much! I did . . . rent a motorbike and explore the area each day. The town itself is sleepy with some great restaurants and casual bars. I found the people in Kanchanaburi to be some of the most friendly in all of Thailand."

—eurotraveller

WELCOME TO AROUND BANGKOK

River Kwai, Kanchanaburi

TOP REASONS TO GO

★ **Heading into the Wild:** There's a huge expanse of untouched jungle around Kanchanaburi, which is the kickoff point for trekking, elephant riding, and river-rafting adventures.

★ **Floating Markets:** This area has more floating markets than anywhere else in Thailand. The most famous is at Damnoen Saduak—it's the only daily floating market left in the region.

★ **Seeing Old Siam:** History awaits outside Bangkok at a Neolithic site, the remains of a Khmer temple (Muang Singh Historical Park in Kanchanaburi), and in Nakhon Pathom, Thailand's oldest seat of Buddhist learning.

★ **Bridge on the River Kwai:** For a glimpse of more recent history, visit what remains of the "Death Railway" in Kanchanaburi and walk across the bridge made famous by the movie of the same name.

★ **Converging Cultures:** The area around Sangklaburi on the Thai–Myanmar (Burma) border is a mix of Thai, Burmese, and hill tribe communities like the Mon and Karen.

1 Day Trips from Bangkok. When most people head south, it's to make for Thailand's famous beaches, but along the way are the floating market at Damnoen Saduak, and Muang Boran, a huge park with replicas of the country's landmarks. To the west of Bangkok is Nakhon Pathom, keeper of Thailand's biggest stupa.

Damnoen Saduak's floating market

2 Phetchaburi. Phetchaburi has many interesting temples and a few royal summer palaces. Three hours south of Bangkok, it makes for a long day trip, so either hire a car and driver to make the trip easier or visit as part of a one- or two-day trip to the coastal resort of Hua Hin.

3 Kanchanaburi & Environs. Kanchanaburi, two hours west of Bangkok, is best known as the site of the famous Bridge on the River Kwai. If you're not in a hurry to get back to Bangkok, you can continue your exploration of stunning Kanchanaburi Province, with day trips to 13th-century Khmer ruins and two national parks containing waterfalls.

Kanchanaburi War Cemetery

4 Sangklaburi. Kanchanaburi Province's farthest attraction is the city of Sangklaburi, which is on Myanmar's doorstep. Here Thai, Mon, Karen, and Bangladeshi communities mix, and boats take you to see a village submerged in a reservoir.

An offering of alms at dawn on the King's Birthday.

GETTING ORIENTED

If you need respite from the heat, noise, and pollution of Bangkok, the surrounding countryside offers many possibilities. There are several sights directly outside the city, easily reached in a few hours by bus, train, or taxi. Kanchanaburi Province can become a mini-vacation all on its own, with Kanchanaburi city being the gateway to a first glimpse of Thailand's wilderness.

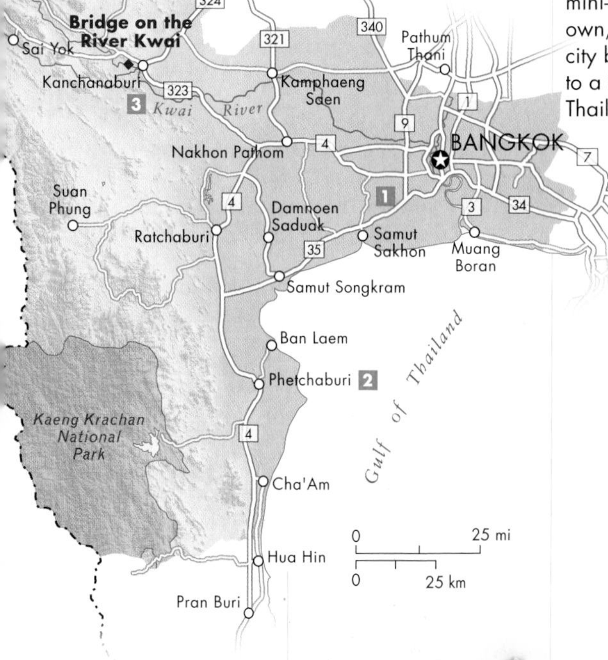

AROUND BANGKOK PLANNER

When to Go

On weekends and national holidays (particularly during the mid-April Buddhist New Year water festival), Kanchanaburi and the restaurants at Samut Songkram are packed with Thais. In high season (November–March) the floating market in Damnoen Saduak has more tourists than vendors. The waterfalls of Kanchanaburi Province are at their best during or just after the rainy season (June–November). The fossil shells in Don Hoi Lod in Samut Songkram are best seen in dry season or at low tide in rainy season. See the fireflies in Ampawa between May and October.

Health & Safety

The region is generally very safe, and the towns mentioned in this chapter have hospitals. Take normal precautions and keep valuables on your person at all times when traveling by bus or train. Deals—particularly involving gems—that sound too good to be true are *always* a rip-off. On a more amusing note, the monkeys of Phetchaburi are cute but cunning, and may relieve you of your possessions, especially food.

Tourist Police (☎ *1155*).

Getting Around

By Bus: Most buses depart from Bangkok's Southern Bus Terminal; tickets are sold on a first-come, first-served basis, but services are so frequent that it's seldom a problem finding an empty seat.

By Car: Distances from Bangkok are short enough to drive, though it's more relaxing to hire a car and driver (⇨ *By Car in Travel Smart*).

By Taxi & Songthaew: Bangkok's air-conditioned taxis are an often-neglected way of accessing sights outside the city. It can be worth it to use them to explore Nakhon Pathom, Samut Songkram, and Muang Boran. Estimate around B500 per hour, depending on your bargaining skills.

Outside Bangkok, songthaews (pickups with wooden benches in the truck bed) are often the closest thing to taxis.

Visitor & Tour Info

It's easy to get around on your own, but both **Asian Trails** (☎02/626–2000 🌐www.asiantrails.net) and **Diethelm Travel** (☎02/660–7000 🌐www.diethelmtravel.com), in Bangkok, organize trips to the floating markets as well as trekking trips, homestays, and bicycle tours.

The **Tourism Authority of Thailand (TAT)** (✉ *325 Saengchuto Rd., Kanchanaburi* ☎ *034/623691* ✉ *Floating market, Damnoen Saduak* ☎ *032/241023* ✉ *500/51 Phetkasem Rd., Ch'am* ☎ *032/471005 up to 6* 🌐 *www.tourismthailand.org*) has several branches and is the main source for tourist information in the region.

WHAT IT COSTS IN BAHT				
¢	$	$$	$$$	$$$$
Restaurants				
under B100	B100–B200	B201–B300	B301–B400	over B400
Hotels				
under B1,000	B1,000–B2,000	B2,001–B4,000	B4,001–B6,000	over B6,000

Restaurant prices are for a main course, excluding tax and tip. Hotel prices are for a standard double in high season, excluding service charge and tax.

DAY TRIPS FROM BANGKOK

MUANG BORAN

Updated by Emmanuelle Michel

20 km (12 mi) southeast of Bangkok.

Muang Boran (Ancient City) is a park with more than 100 replicas and reconstructions of the country's most important architectural sites, monuments, and palaces. The park is shaped like Thailand, and the attractions are placed roughly in their correct geographical position. A "traditional Thai village" within the grounds sells crafts, but the experience is surprisingly un-touristy. The park stretches over 320 acres, and takes about four hours to cover by car. Or you rent a bicycle at the entrance for B50. Small outdoor cafés throughout the grounds serve decent Thai food. ✉ *Km 33, Old Sukhumvit Rd., Samut Prakan* ☎ *02/224–1057* *B300* *Daily 8–5.*

GETTING HERE & AROUND

BY BUS For buses from Bangkok to Muang Boran (2 hours, B30), take the air-conditioned 511, which leaves every half hour from Bangkok's Southern Bus Terminal, to the end of the line at Pak Nam. You can also catch this bus on Sukhumvit Road. Then transfer to songthaew 36 (B5), which goes to the entrance of Muang Boran.

BY CAR Driving to Muang Boran means a trip through heavy and unpredictable Bangkok traffic. It should take 1½–2 hours. Take the Samrong–Samut Prakan expressway and turn left at the Samut Prakan intersection onto Old Sukhumvit Road. Muang Boran is well signposted on the left at Km 33.

ESSENTIALS

Visitor & Tour Info **Ancient City** (✉ *78/1 Democracy Monument cycle, Ratchadamnoen Ave., Bangkok* ☎ *02/224–1057* *www.ancientcity.com*).

DAMNOEN SADUAK

109 km (68 mi) southwest of Bangkok.

The colorful Damnoen Saduak floating market is a true icon of Thai tourism. The image is so evocative that it's become an ad agency favorite. Today the market, which sells mostly produce and other foods, has taken on a bit of the Disneyland effect as it is often infested with tourists and it bears only passing resemblance to the authentic commercial life of this canal-strewn corner of Thailand. On the other hand, even though it feels a bit like a theater production, this is one of the only opportunities to witness a fading Thai tradition (⇨ *Thai Markets, below*). The best way to enjoy the market is to hire a boat; after seeing the market, you can also arrange to tour the wider countryside, taking in local temples and gardens, or even travel back to Bangkok.

GETTING HERE & AROUND

BY BUS Buses to Damnoen Saduak (2 to 3 hours, B73) leave Bangkok's Southern Bus Terminal every 20 minutes starting at 5 AM. From the station in

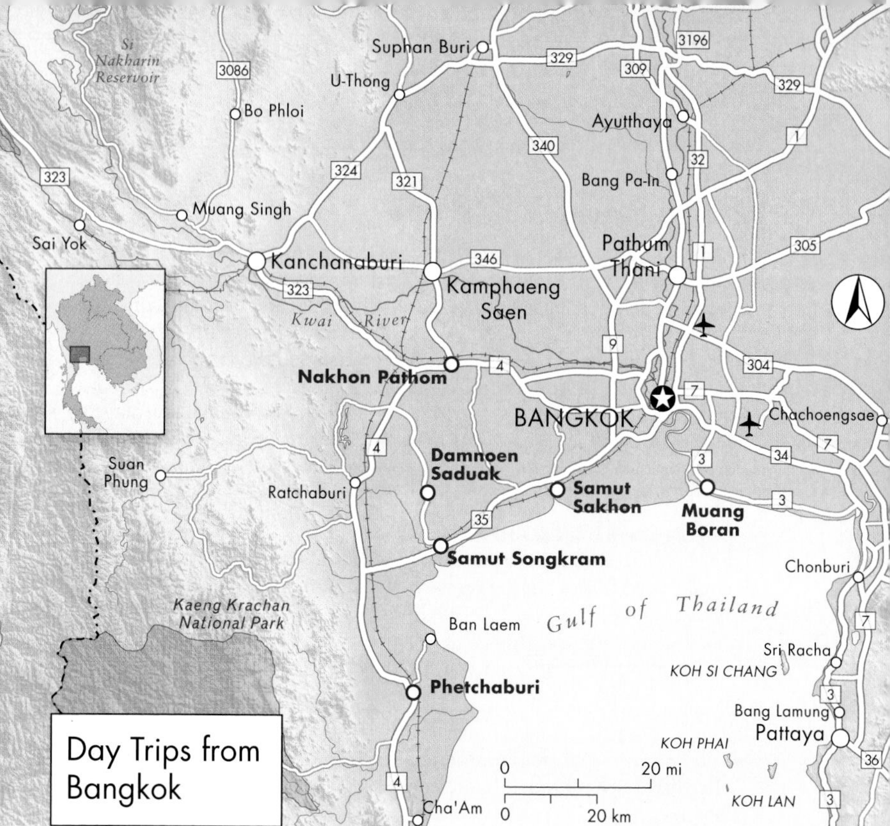

Damnoen Saduak, walk or take a songthaew along the canal for 1½ km (1 mi) to the floating market. Buses also run from Nakhon Pathom and between Samut Songkram.

BY CAR Via car from Bangkok (about 2 hours), take Highway 4 (Phetkasem Road) and turn left at Km 80. Continue for 25 km (16 mi) along the Bang Phae-Damnoen Saduak Road. The half-hour drive from Samut Songkram to Damnoen Saduak, along Route 325, is pleasant, particularly if you go via Ampawa.

ESSENTIALS

WHERE TO STAY

You'll find plenty of food stalls and small street restaurants, as well as fruits and vegetables, along the main road.

¢ **Little Bird Hotel.** Convenience is the top selling point of this hotel just a 10-minute walk to the boats for the floating market and close to banks, stores, and cafés. The plain, municipal-looking building with large, basic rooms is unattractive, but it's set back from the main road and it's quiet. **Pros:** the most convenient hotel to the floating market; arranges market tours. **Cons:** no hot water. ✉ *Moo 1/8, Damnoen Saduak* ☎ *032/254382 or 081/587–4519* *30 rooms* *In-room: no a/c (some)* *No credit cards.*

SAMUT SONGKRAM

72 km (45 mi) south of Bangkok.

The provincial town of Samut Songkram has little to recommend it, but it has many nearby attractions that make it an enjoyable day trip from Bangkok. There are terrific seafood restaurants along the waterfront at Don Hoi Lod; the area is also a good base for exploring some of the surrounding villages on the canal network, such as Ampawa, with its small floating market.

> **WORD OF MOUTH**
>
> "The Floating Market was the next stop . . . we cruised along the canals, tasting various treats prepared by the floating vendors. The food was excellent . . . noodle soups, grilled pork and chicken bits on sticks, fried bananas, mango, pomelo, and pineapple. As time passed the canals became clogged with boats packed with tourists. I would recommend arriving here as early as possible to avoid some of the larger tour groups that descend as the morning wears on." —ekscrunchy

GETTING HERE & AROUND

BY BUS Buses depart from Bangkok's Southern Bus Terminal for Samut Songkram (1½ hours, B45) every hour from 3 AM to 6:30 PM. Bus 996 can drop you off at Ampawa.

BY CAR Route 35, the main road south to Samut Songkram (1 hour) is mainly a two-lane highway that can be slow going if there's heavy traffic. Add an extra half hour to all trip times for possible delays.

BY SONGTHAEW In town, there are frequent songthaews to Don Hoi Lod and Ampawa (10 minutes, B15).

ESSENTIALS

Emergencies **Mae Khlong Song Hospital** (*✉ Ratrasit Rd., Samut Songkram ☎ 034/715001 up to 3*).

EXPLORING SAMUT SONGKRAM

If you want to see both Don Hoi Lod and Ampawa, you'll need a full day. If you don't have a car and want to go on the fireflies tour in Ampawa, you'll have to stay overnight.

WHAT TO SEE

On weekends, Thai families flock to the village of **Don Hoi Lod,** about 3 km (2 mi) south of Samut Songkram to eat the clams (try them with garlic and pepper) and other seafood dishes at the restaurants nestled between the trees at the mouth of the Mae Khlong River. The village is named after a local clam with a tubular shell, the fossilized remains of which are found on the riverbanks here. ■ **TIP→ The best times to view the fossils are March and April, when the water is low.** The rest of the year you can also see the fossils in the early mornings and in the evenings at low tide.

The charming village of **Ampawa** is 10 km (7 mi) by songthaew from Samuk Songkram and has a **floating market** similar to (but smaller than) that in Damnoen Saduak on Friday, Saturday, and Sunday evenings from 5 to 9. The food market in the street adjacent to the canal starts at around 1 PM. **Fireflies tours,** which allow you to enjoy both the market and the beautifully insect-lighted trees, are increasingly popular. The bugs are best seen from May to October and in the waning moon. The hour-long tours usually run every half-hour from 6:30 to 9 PM. You can arrange a tour directly at the pier (B600 for a boat) or through your hotel (around B60 per person). Unless you have private transportation, you'll have to spend the night in Ampawa, as the last bus back to Bangkok is in the early evening.

WHERE TO EAT & STAY

There are many homestay options in Ampawa for every budget. Call the TAT office in Phetchaburi or Kanchanaburi for more details.

$–$$ SEAFOOD **Koon Pao.** One of the last in a long row of seafood places in Don Hoi Lod, this restaurant on wooden stilts is usually packed with Thai families who come to enjoy the nice breeze, the fried sea perch, horseshoe-egg spicy salad, and grilled prawns. The atmosphere is both busy and relaxed. Try to get one of the few sit-on-the-floor tables directly above the water. There's a playground for kids. ⊠ *1/3 Moo 4, Bangyakang, Don Hoi Lod* ☎ *034/723703* ▭ *MC, V.*

Thanicha Boutique Resort. Right by the main canal in an old wooden house close to the market, this lovely boutique hotel is a perfect countryside weekend escape from Bangkok. The rooms are simply but tastefully decorated and overlook a small garden. The staff can arrange boat tours (including fireflies tours). Book ahead if you go on weekends. Rates are cheaper on weekdays. **Pros:** nice café and restaurant in front; free Wi-Fi. **Cons:** busier and more expensive on weekends. ⊠ *261, Ampawa* ☎ *034/725511* ⊕ *www.thanicha.com* *12 rooms* *In-room: refrigerator, Wi-Fi. In-hotel: restaurant* ▭ *No credit cards.*

NAKHON PATHOM

56 km (35 mi) west of Bangkok.

Reputed to be Thailand's oldest city (it's thought to date from 150 BC), Nakhon Pathom was once the center of the Dvaravati kingdom, a 6th- to 11th-century affiliation of Mon city-states. It marks the region's first center of Buddhist learning, established about a millennium ago. Today, there would be little reason to visit if it weren't for the Buddhist monument Phra Pathom Chedi.

GETTING HERE & AROUND

BY BUS Buses depart from Bangkok's Southern Bus Terminal for Nakhon Pathom (1 hour, B34) every hour from 5:30 AM to 4 PM.

BY CAR Driving west from Bangkok, allow an hour to get to Nakhon Pathom on Route 4.

BY TRAIN Ten trains a day run at regular intervals to Nakhon Pathom (1½ hours, B14 to B20). Some of the Nakhon Pathom trains continue on to Phetchaburi (4 hours, B94 to B114) and points farther south. Trains to Kanchanaburi also stop in Nakhon Pathom.

Continued on page 148

THAI MARKETS

by Hana Borrowman

For an authentic Thai shopping experience, forget air-conditioned malls and head to the traditional markets, or *talaats*. Take a deep breath and prepare for an intoxicating medley of colors, sounds, smells, and tastes.

Entrepreneurs set up shop wherever there's an open space—roadsides, footbridges, and bustling waterways. You'll find all sorts of intriguing items: caramelized crickets and still-wriggling eels; "potency" potions made from pigs' feet; fierce-looking hand weapons like elegant samurai swords and knife-edged brass knuckles; temple offerings; plastic toys; and clothing.

Markets are an integral part of Thai life. Locals stop by for a meal from their favorite food vendor or to sit at a coffee stall, gossiping or discussing politics. Whole families take part: You might see an old woman bargaining with a customer at a hardware stall while her grandchild sleeps in a makeshift hammock strung up beneath the table.

Damnoen Saduak's floating market.

GREAT FINDS

Low prices make impulse buys almost irresistible. Here are a few things to keep your eyes out for while you shop.

Housewares. You'll find metal "monks' bowls" like those used for alms-collection, cushions, wicker baskets, carved tables, and ornate daybeds. Polished coconut-shell spoons and wooden salad servers are more practical if you're not up for shipping home your wares. Small wooden bowls and utensils start at around B150.

Memorabilia. Toy *tuk-tuks* (three-wheeled cabs) made from old tin cans, sequined elephants sewn onto cushion covers, satin Muay Thai boxer shorts, wooden frogs that croak—all make great and inexpensive souvenirs, and most Thai markets have them in droves.

Jewelry. Throughout the country, hill-tribe women sell beautiful silver and beaded jewelry. Silver bangles start at B250 and chunky silver rings with semiprecious stones like opal and mother-of-pearl are B350 and up. You'll also find "precious" gemstones and crystals, but you're better off making serious purchases at reputable shops in Bangkok.

Silk. Thailand is famous for its bright, beautiful silks. Raw Thai silk has a relatively coarse texture and a matte finish; it's good value, and wonderful for curtains and upholstery. You'll also find bolts of less expensive shimmering satins, and ready-made items like pajamas, purses, and scarves.

Prices vary enormously—depending on quality and weight—from B100 to upwards of B700 a meter. To test for authenticity, hold the fabric up to the light: If it's pure silk, the color changes, but fake silk shines a uniformly whitish tone. You can also ask for a swatch to burn—pure fibers crumble to ash, while synthetics curl or melt.

Clothes. Markets have tons of clothing: the ubiquitous Thai fisherman pants; factory seconds from The Gap; knockoff designer jeans; and, invariably, frilly underwear. But some of Thailand's edgiest designers are touting more modern apparel at markets as well. It's hard to say whether these up-and-comers are following catwalk trends or vice-versa. Bangkok fashion houses like **Sretsis** (feminine dresses; www.sretsis.com), **Greyhound** (casual, unisex urbanwear; www.greyhound.co.th), and **Issue** (bohemian chic; no Web) are good places to scope out styles beforehand (⇨ *Shopping in Chapter 2*). Prices vary greatly—a cheaply made suit could cost as little as B1,000, while an expertly tailored, high-quality version might be B20,000 or more. But it's difficult to determine quality unless you're experienced.

FLOATING MARKETS

Sunday morning at Damnoen Saduak.

Floating markets date from Bangkok's "Venice of the East" era in the 19th century, when canal-side residents didn't have to go to market—the market came to them. Many waterways have been filled in to create roads, so there are only a handful of floating markets left. These survivors have a nostalgic appeal, with vendors in straw hats peddling produce, flowers, snacks, and crafts against a backdrop of stilt houses and riverbanks.

Thailand's original floating market in Damnoen Saduak (⇨ *above*) is very famous, but it's also crowded and overpriced. Still, you can get a taste of the old river life here, in addition to lots of touristy souvenirs. If you visit, try to stay nearby so that you can arrive near dawn; the market is open from 6 AM till noon, but by 9 it's usually swarming with sightseers.

The Amphawa Floating market near Samut Songkram (⇨ *above*), set on a leafy waterway dotted with temples and traditional Thai homes, is less crowded and more authentic.

LOGISTICS

Many hotels and guesthouses can arrange a longtail boat and an oarsman for you. You can also just head to the pier, though it's a good idea to ask your hotel what going rates are first. Private boats start at around B500 an hour, but oarsmen may try to charge much more. Haggle hard, and don't get in a boat before you've agreed on price and duration. If you join a group of locals in a boat, you'll often pay a set rate per person.

Longtail boat.

SHOPPING KNOW-HOW

Most markets begin to stir around dawn, and morning is the best time to visit—it's not too hot, and most Thais do their marketing early in the day, so you'll get to watch all the local action. Avoid rainy days: The scene loses a lot of its allure when everything's covered in plastic sheets.

Flower market in Bangkok.

SHOPPING TIPS

■ Check prices at less touristy spots—Chinatown, Pratunam Market, and MBK in Bangkok—to get a sense of cost (⇨ *Shopping in Chapter 2*).

■ Keep money and valuables like cell phones tucked away.

■ Avoid tuk-tuk drivers who offer you a shopping tour. They'll pressure you to drop a lot of cash at their friends' stalls.

■ Look for the One Tambon One Product (OTOP) government stamp on market goods. A tambon is a subdistrict—there are over 7,000 in the country, and one handmade, locally sourced product is selected from each.

■ Steer clear of exotic animal products, such as lizard skins, ivory, tortoiseshell, and anything made of tiger. These products may come from endangered animals; if so, it's illegal to leave Thailand with them or bring them into the U.S. If not illegal, they may be counterfeit.

■ Only buy antiques at reputable shops; real Thai antiques cannot be exported without a license, which good shops provide. Most so-called antiques at markets are knockoffs.

■ Thai markets are full of counterfeits—DVDs, computer software, and designer clothes and accessories. In addition to being illegal, these items vary in quality, so examine the products and your conscience carefully before you buy.

Straw hats for sale.

HOW TO BARGAIN

Thais love theatrical bargaining, and it's customary to haggle over nearly everything. Here are some tips for getting a fair price. The most important thing is to have fun!

DO

- Decide about how much you're willing to pay before you start bargaining.
- Let the vendor set the opening price. This is the standard etiquette; vendors who make you go first may be trying to take you for a ride. Vendors who don't speak English may type their price into a calculator, and you can respond in kind.
- Come equipped with a few Thai phrases, such as "How much is this?" *(anee tao rai [kaa/krap]?)*, "A discount?" *(Lod mai?)*, and "Expensive!" *(Paeng!)*.
- Bargain quietly, and if possible, when the vendor is alone. Vendors are unlikely to give big discounts in front of an audience.
- Be polite, no matter what. Confidence and charming persistence are winning tactics in Thailand—not hostility.
- Honor your lowest bid if it's accepted.

DON'T

- Don't lose your temper or raise your voice. These are big no-no's in the land of smiles.
- Don't hesitate to aim low. Your opening counteroffer should be around 50% or 60% of the vendor's price, and you can expect to settle for 10% to 30% off the initial price. If you're buying more than one item, shoot for a bigger discount.
- Don't be afraid to walk away. Often the vendor will call you back with a lower price.
- Don't get too caught up in negotiating. It's OK to back down if you really want something.
- Don't bargain for food—prices are fixed.

Woman displaying Thai silk.

ESSENTIALS

Emergencies **Sanam Chan Hospital** (*1194 Petchkasem Rd., Nakhon Pathom 034/219600*).

Visitor & Tour Info (*Kanchanaburi, below*).

EXPLORING NAKHON PATHOM

Seeing all the sights here will take you a full day, but the bus ride from Bangkok is only an hour, so it's doable as a day trip.

WHAT TO SEE

The tallest Buddhist monument in the world, **Phra Pathom Chedi** stands at 417 feet, just higher—but less ornate—than the chedi at Shwe Dagon in Myanmar.

Erected in the 6th century, the site's first chedi was destroyed in a Burmese attack in 1057. Surrounding the chedi is one of Thailand's most important temples, which contains the ashes of King Rama VI.

The terraces around the temple complex are full of fascinating statuary, including Chinese figures, a large reclining Buddha, and an unusual Buddha seated in a chair. By walking around the inner circle surrounding the chedi, you can see novice monks in their classrooms through arched stone doorways. Traditional dances are sometimes performed in front of the temple, and during Loi Krathong (a festival in November that celebrates the end of the rainy season) a fair is set up in the adjacent park. *½ km (¼ mi) south of train station B40 Daily 5 AM–6 PM.*

Next to Phra Pathom Chedi is the **Phra Pathom Chedi National Museum,** which contains Dvaravati artifacts such as images of the Buddha, stone carvings, and stuccos from the 6th to the 11th centuries. *Khwa Phra Rd. B30 Wed.–Sun. 9–noon and 1–4.*

On the Bangkok Road out of Nakhon Pathom (toward Bangkok) is the **Rose Garden,** which is actually a park complex where herbs, bananas, and various flowers, including orchids and roses, flourish. Within the complex are traditional houses and a performance stage, where shows include dancing, Thai boxing, sword fighting, and even wedding ceremonies (daily at 2:45 PM). **TIP→ The park is popular with Thai families and has restaurants and a nice hotel with rooms starting at B3,130.** *Km 32, Petchkasem Rd. 034/322588 www.rose-garden.com B20, B480 with lunch and show Daily 6–6.*

WHERE TO EAT

The road from Nakhon Pathom train station has several cafés, and a market where food stalls sell one-plate Thai meals. Similar dining options are at the entrance of the chedi. Keep an eye out for Nakhon Pathom specialties such as *kao larm* (sticky rice, palm sugar, and black beans grilled in hollowed-out bamboo sections) and sweet, pink-flesh pomelo (a large citrus fruit).

PHETCHABURI

132 km (82 mi) south of Bangkok.

This small seaport town with many wats once linked the old Thai capitals of Sukhothai and Ayutthaya with trade routes on the South China Sea and Indian Ocean. Phetchaburi is famous for *kao chae,* a chilled rice dish with sweetmeats once favored by royals that has become a summer tradition in posh Bangkok hotels. You can find it around the day market on Phanit Charoen Road (look for people eating at stalls from small silver bowls), along with *khanom jeen thotman* (noodles with curried fish cake). The city was also a royal retreat during the reigns of Rama IV and Rama V (1851–1910) and has two palaces open to the public. ⚠ **Watch out for the gangs of monkeys that roam the streets of the town, particularly around Khao Wang.** Do not get close to them with food in your hands.

GETTING HERE & AROUND

BY CAR Via car (1½ hours), take Route 35, the main road south from Bangkok then continue on Highway 4 to Phetchaburi province. On the way back to Bangkok, there are two possible routes. Follow signs to Samut Songkram for the shorter distance (Route 35).

BY BUS Buses depart Bangkok's Southern Bus Terminal for Phetchaburi (2 hours, B126) every 30 minutes from 5 AM to 9 PM. The bus station is north of town, near the night market. All trains to southern Thailand stop at Phetchaburi (3 hours, B94–B114). The train station is north of town on Rot Fai Road. You can hire motorbikes taxis or tuk-tuks from the train or bus station to get to sights and/or downtown.

BY BIKE Renting a bike or a motorbike at Rabieng Guesthouse (B120 per day for a bike, B200 per day for a motorbike) is a good way to get around town.

ESSENTIALS

Emergencies **Meung Phet Thonburi Hospital** (✉ *Phetkasem Rd., Phetchaburi* ☎ *032/415191 up to 9*).

EXPLORING PHETCHABURI

Phetchaburi's many wats are within, or easily accessible on foot from, the town center, particularly along Matayawong, Pongsuriya, and Phrasong roads. Two days are sufficient to visit all the sights.

WHAT TO SEE

Built in 1910 as a rainy season retreat by King Rama V, **Phra Ram Ratchaniwet** was modeled on a palace of Germany's Kaiser Wilhelm, and consequently has grand European architecture with art-nouveau flourishes. The dining room has ornate ceramic tiles. ✉ *Thai Military Base, Ratchadamnoen Rd.* ☎ *No phone* *B50* *Daily 9–4.*

The 800-year-old Khmer-influenced **Wat Mahathat Worawihan,** on the western side of the Phetchaburi River, is a royal temple. Besides the magnificent architecture and main Buddha statue, an interesting feature of this wat is a subtle political joke. Look around the base of the Buddha statue outside the main temple. A ring of monkeylike Atlases

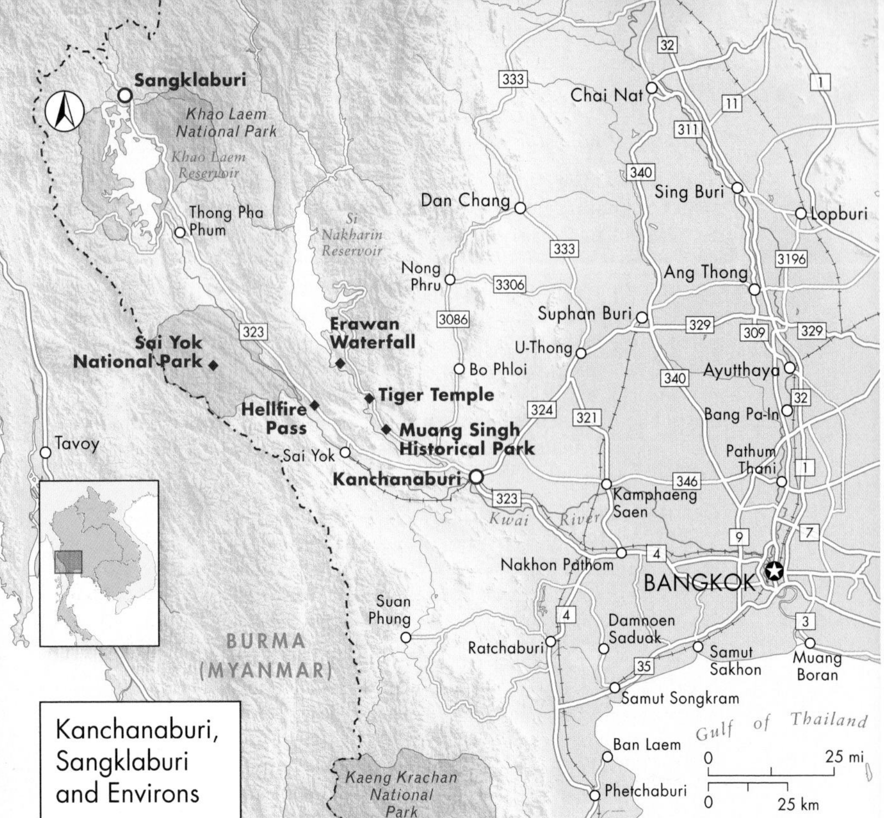

supports the large Buddha image, but one of the monkeys is not like the others. See if you can find him! ✉ *Banda-it and Damnoen Kasem Rds.* ⏲ *Daily 6–6*

Wat Yai Suwannaram, built during the Ayutthaya period by skilled craftsman, has a 300-year-old painting in its main hall, a library on stilts above a fishpond (to deter termites), and an ax mark above one of the temple doors, said to have been left by a Burmese invader. ✉ *Phongsunyia Rd., about 500 meters after crossing the river, on the eastern side* ⏲ *Daily 5 AM–6 PM.*

Phra Nakhon Khiri Historical Park (Khao Wang) is a forested hillside area on the edge of Phetchaburi with one of King Rama IV's palaces and a series of temples and shrines. Many of these are set high on the hilltop and have good views. Monkeys are a major shoplifting hazard around the gift shops at the foot of the hill. There's a cable car (B30) for those who don't fancy the strenuous walk. ✉ *Khao Wang, entrance off Phetkasem Rd.* ☎ *032/401006 or 032/425600* 🎟 *B40* ⏲ *Daily 9–4.*

Khao Luang Cave is filled with stalactites and religious objects, Buddha images and chedis of different sizes, including a 10-meter-long reclining Buddha. Most of them were put in place by kings Rama IV and Rama V. The cave is accessed via a two-minute walk from the parking lot and some steep stairs. Watch out for the monkeys. ■ **TIP→The cave is best appreciated on a clear morning, between 9 and 10, when the sun shines in and reflects off the brass Buddha images.** For a donation of B20 or so (to pay for the electricity), the nun will light up the rear of the cave for you. A large monastery, Wat Tham Klaep, at the bottom of the hill below the cave, is open to the public. ✉ *5 km (3 mi) north of Phra Nakhon via Rot Fai Rd.* ☎ *No phone* ⏲ *Daily 9–4.*

WHERE TO EAT & STAY

¢ THAI **Rabieng Restaurant.** By the river in a small wooden house, this family-run restaurant offers a wide range of classic Thai dishes, as well as a few Western dishes and breakfast, with American music classics playing in the background. It's attached to Rabieng Guesthouse. Try the spicy banana blossom salad or the delicious stuffed chicken with pandanus leaves. It's open daily 8 AM–1 AM. ✉ *1 Shesrain Rd.* ☎ *032/425707* ▭ *No credit cards.*

¢ **Khao Wang Hotel.** This Chinese guesthouse hotel opposite a 24-hour Internet café has simple rooms. You may or may not enjoy the added spectacle of monkeys climbing all over your room's window grates. **Pros:** close to Khao Wang Hill; many street food stalls nearby. **Cons:** quality of some bathrooms in most expensive rooms doesn't match the price; no hot water in some rooms. ✉ *123 Ratchawithi Rd.* ☎ *032/425167* *58 rooms* *In-room: no a/c (some), no TV (some). In-hotel: restaurant* ▭ *No credit cards.*

¢ **Rabieng Guesthouse.** A cluster of small dark-wood plank buildings holds a few basic rooms just big enough for beds. The restaurant serves Thai and Western food. The hotel arranges treks of varying length to Kaeng Krachan National Park, Thailand's largest national park and home to Karen villages, and wildlife such as bears, tigers, leopards, and more than 250 bird species. **Pros:** nice restaurant overlooking the river; bikes and motorbikes for rent; walking distance to bus terminal. **Cons:** along noisy road; shared bathrooms. ✉ *1 Shesrain Rd.* ☎ *032/425707* *9 rooms with shared bath* *In-room: no a/c, no TV. In-hotel: restaurant, laundry service* ▭ *No credit cards.*

¢ **Royal Diamond Hotel.** It's about 3 km (2 mi) northwest of town, but the Royal Diamond is Phetchaburi's only choice for those seeking a hotel instead of a guesthouse. It's close to Khao Wang park and there are a few decent cafés nearby: try Puong Petch for sizzling seafood with hot Kariang chilies or Kway Tiao Pla VIP for a variety of fish noodle dishes. **Pros:** close to Khao Wang. **Cons:** out of town. ✉ *555 Moo 1, Phetkasem Rd., Tambon Rai-Som* ☎ *032/411061 up to 70* *58 rooms* *In-room: refrigerator. In-hotel: restaurant, bar, Internet terminal* ▭ *MC, V* *BP.*

KANCHANABURI & ENVIRONS

Within and around Kanchanaburi are cave temples, museums, tribal villages, waterfalls, hikes, elephant riding, and rafting; it's also the main access point to the large national parks of western Thailand. The city of Kanchanaburi is home to interesting and sometimes moving World

Chong-Kai War Cemetery 4
Jeath War Museum 3
Kanchanaburi War Cemetery ...2
Thailand-Burma Railway Centre ..1
Wat Tham Khao Pun 5

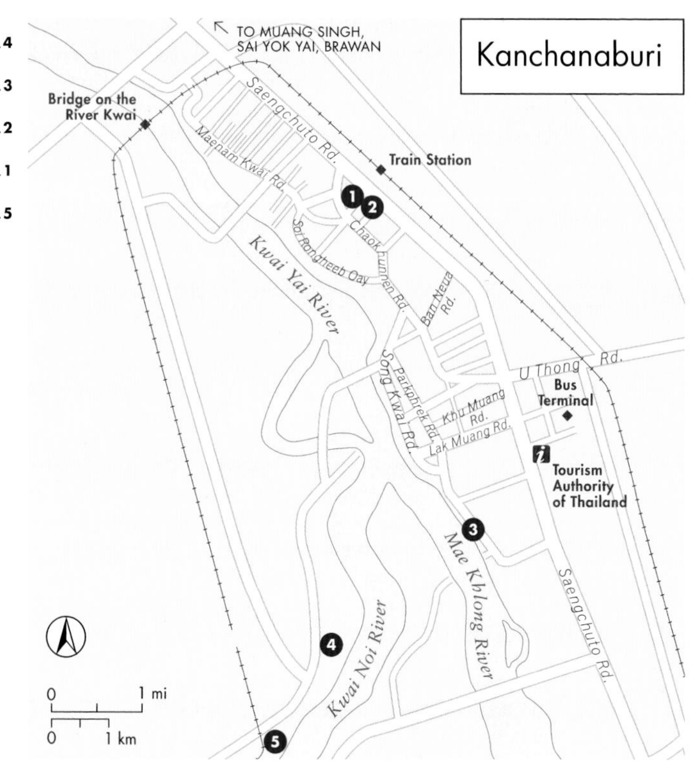

War II historical sites: the bridge on the River Kwai (local people actually call it "Kwaa") and several war cemeteries.

KANCHANABURI

140 km (87 mi) west of Bangkok.

The city is most famous as the location of the **Bridge on the River Kwai**—a piece of the World War II Japanese "Death Railway" and the subject of the 1957 film of the same name starring Alec Guinness and Richard Holden (though the film was shot in Sri Lanka).

During World War II, the Japanese, with whom Thailand sided, forced about 16,000 prisoners of war and 50,000 to 100,000 civilian slave laborers from neighboring countries to construct the "Death Railway," a supply route through the jungles of Thailand and Myanmar. It's estimated that one person died for every railway tie that was laid. Surefooted visitors can walk across the Bridge on the River Kwai, of which the arched portions are original. In December there's a big fair with a sound-and-light show depicting the Allied bombing of the bridge. Next to the bridge is a plaza with restaurants and souvenir shops.

GETTING HERE & AROUND

BY BUS Air-conditioned buses leave from Bangkok's Southern Bus Terminal for Kanchanaburi (2 hours, B79) every 20 minutes from 5 AM to 10:30 PM. Buses also leave eight times a day from Mo Chit Northern Bus Terminal (3 hours, B108).

BY CAR Allow two hours to Kanchanaburi along Route 4. The first half is on a busy truck route that continues to southern Thailand, but the second half is more pleasant, through agricultural land. The road to Kanchanaburi passes through Nakhon Pathom.

BY TAXI & SONGTHAEW In town, options for getting around include pedicabs and motorcycles with sidecars. Songthaews are better for longer forays out of town and can be flagged down. A few tuk-tuks and taxis are in town, but they are harder to find.

BY TRAIN Trains to Kanchanaburi leave from Bangkok Noi Railway Station, on the Thonburi side of the Chao Phraya River. There are two daily trains (3 hours, B100), plus a tourist train (B100) that stops at the province's main sights on weekends and holidays, leaving Hua Lamphong Station at 6:30 AM, returning at 7:30 PM, and stopping at Nakhon Pathom and Kanchanaburi.

ESSENTIALS

Emergencies **Thanakan Hospital** (✉ *Saengchuto Rd., Kanchanaburi* ☎ *034/622366 up to 75*).

EXPLORING KANCHANABURI

Three to four days can easily be spent exploring the town and the surrounding areas. If you're in a rush, you can see the main sights in one or two days by booking package tours.

TOP ATTRACTIONS

3 A bit more than 2 km (1 mi) downriver from the bridge is the **JEATH War Museum** (*JEATH* is an acronym for *J*apan, *E*ngland, *A*merica, *A*ustralia, *T*hailand, and *H*olland). The museum, founded in 1977 by a monk from the adjoining Wat Chaichumpol, is housed in a replica of the bamboo huts that were used to hold prisoners of war. On display are railway spikes, clothing, aerial photographs, newspaper clippings, and original sketches by ex-prisoners depicting their living conditions. ✉ *Wat Chaichumpol, Bantai* ☎ *034/515203* 🎫 *B40* ⏲ *Daily 8–4:30*

1 The **Thailand-Burma Railway Centre,** next to the Kanchanaburi War Cemetery, is the best museum in town. It's small, well designed, and packed with informative displays. A walk through the chronologically arranged nine galleries gives a good overview of the railway's history. At the end of the exhibits is a coffee shop on the second floor that has a view of the cemetery. ✉ *73 Jaokunnen Rd.* ☎ *034/512721* 🌐 *www.tbrconline.com* 🎫 *B100* ⏲ *Daily 9–5.*

ALSO WORTH SEEING

4 The **Chong-Kai War Cemetery,** on the grounds of a former hospital for prisoners of war, is serene and simple, with neatly organized grave markers of the soldiers forced to work on the railway. It's a little out of the way, and therefore rarely visited. To get there, hire a tuk-tuk or

moto-taxi for about B40. ✉ *Western side of river, 3 km (2 mi) from town; take bridge near Wat Nua and follow signs.*

> **WORD OF MOUTH**
>
> "I defy anyone not to have a tear in your eye when reading the inscriptions on the graves at the War Cemetery." —Fiona

2 The **Kanchanaburi War Cemetery,** next to noisy Saengchuto Road just south of the train station, has row upon row of neatly laid-out graves: 6,982 Australian, British, and Dutch prisoners of war were laid to rest here. (The remains of the American POWs were returned to the United States during the Eisenhower administration.) A remembrance ceremony is held every April 25, ANZAC (Australia and New Zealand Army Corps) Day. ✉ *Saengchuto Rd., across from train station.*

5 Less than 1 km (½ mi) southwest of the Chong-Kai War Cemetery you'll find **Wat Tham Khao Pun,** one of the best cave-temples in the area. A guide at the small shrine outside the cave will direct you on where to go. Inside the cave, between the stalagmites and stalactites, are Buddhist and Hindu statues and figurines. During WWII, the Japanese used the cave complex as a series of storerooms. ✉ *Western side of river, 4 km (2½ mi) from town; take bridge near Wat Nua and follow signs to the Chong-Kai War Cemetery* ⏲ *Daily 9–4.*

WHERE TO EAT

Kanchanaburi is laid out along the Mae Khlong and Kwai Yai rivers. The main road commercial district has a few mid-range hotels; the south end of the river, has a popular Thai weekend retreat with raft house accommodations, floating restaurants, and loud disco boats; and the northern riverbank is geared more toward backpackers, with guesthouses, bars, and Internet cafés. **■ TIP→ The city is busy on long weekends and holidays, so book ahead for hotels and resorts.**

¢–$ THAI ✕ **Apple's Restaurant.** The massaman curry at this quiet garden restaurant and guesthouse (⇨ *below*) is very popular with backpackers; it's made with heaps of palm sugar, and is a good balm for stomachs struggling with chili overdose. More authentic (hotter) dishes are available on request. Try the whole fish with lemongrass, lime juice, and crushed chili. ✉ *153/4 Moo 4, Thamakhan Muang* ☎ *034/512017 or 081/948–4646* 🌐 *www.applenoi-kanchanaburi.com* ▭ *MC, V.*

¢–$ ★ THAI ✕ **Keereetara.** This classy restaurant from the owners of the Resort (F *below*) is farther upriver and has a great views of the bridge from its terraces. It caters mostly to Thais, so the food can be quite spicy—ask them to tone the heat down ("mai phet") if you can't handle it. They serve many Thai dishes, but the fish soups and curries are the best choices. ✉ *43/1 River Kwai Rd.* ☎ *034/624093* ▭ *MC, V.*

¢–$ THAI ✕ **Maenam.** This is the busiest of the floating restaurants—built on a network of moored rafts—at the south end of the River Kwai Yai, where it merges with the Kwai Noi. Maenam serves Thai seafood standards, such as red curry with "serpent head fish" (a freshwater relative of the catfish) and char-grilled prawns. The riverfront serenity is disrupted periodically by the loud music of the disco and karaoke boats that meander past. A singer performs each night. The restaurant has no

English sign, but it's next to the Café de Paradiso. ✉ *5/7 Song Kwai Rd.* ☎ *034/514318* ▭ *MC, V.*

¢–$ THAI ✕ **The Resort.** This bar-restaurant occupies a white Thai-style house and draws a mostly Thai clientele. Red clay-tile floors and a low-lighted covered courtyard lend a casual elegance; the garden is particularly lovely, with tables shaded by white canvas umbrellas and palm trees. The menu is standard Thai, except for the deer and fried pig's appendix with garlic. ✉ *318/2 River Kwai Rd.* ☎ *034/624093* ▭ *MC, V.*

CHEAP EATS

For cheap eats, visit the **night market** on Saengchuto Road (next to the train station) that sets up early each evening, offering a variety of Thai soups, rice dishes, and satays. The blended frozen fruit drinks are particularly good. After you grab a bite, you can peruse the market's clothes, CDs, and electronics.

$ SEAFOOD ✕ **River Kwai Floating Restaurant.** This crowded open-air restaurant is in the shadow of the railway bridge. Fish dishes (fried with pungent spices or lightly grilled), soups, and curries dominate the menu. The local specialty is *yeesok*, a fish caught fresh from the Kwai Yai and Kwai Noi rivers. Another tasty choice is the *tom yum goong*, hot-and-sour shrimp soup. ■ **TIP→ The food is toned down for foreigners, so if you want it spicy tell them so.** ✉ *River Kwai Bridge* ☎ *034/512595* ▭ *No credit cards.*

WHERE TO STAY

¢–$ **Apple's Guesthouse.** Owners Apple and Noi, of Apple's Restaurant moved their clean and friendly guesthouse, along with Apple's Restaurant, to a new location in 2008. Rooms face a central courtyard. They also opened a 20-room boutique hotel, Apple's Retreat, on the opposite riverbank in November 2008. ■ **TIP→ The owners teach a one-day Thai cooking course, which starts off with a market visit by bicycle and ends with six prepared dishes.** Apple runs two-day treks (minimum four people; B2,550 per person) that include a stay in a Karen village. They can also pick you up at the train or bus station. **Pros:** good restaurant; knowledgeable owners. **Cons:** can fill quickly in high season. ✉ *153/4 Moo 4, Thamakhan Muang* ☎ *034/512017 or 081/948–4646* ⊕ *www.applenoi-kanchanaburi.com* ▭ *MC, V.*

$$–$$$ **Felix River Kwai Resort.** Kanchanaburi's first luxury hotel is a bit faded now, but it's still a good value. Polished wood floors and wicker headboards decorate the cool, airy rooms. The large pool (with a shallow end for kids) set amid tropical gardens is a great place to relax. The hotel is within walking distance of Kanchanaburi; the River Kwai bridge is 300 meters from the hotel. Rates include a buffet breakfast. **Pros:** right by the famous bridge; wonderful tropical garden. **Cons:** you'll have to take a taxi to the city center. ✉ *9/1 Moo 3, Tambon Thamakham,* ☎ *034/551000, 02/634–4111 in Bangkok* ⊕ *www.felixriverkwai.co.th* *255 rooms* *In-room: safe. In-hotel: 2 restaurants, tennis courts, pool, gym, spa* ▭ *AE, DC, MC, V* *CP.*

¢–$ **Kasem Island Resort.** On an island in the middle of the river, this resort has one of the area's most enviable locations. Choose between bungalows with air-conditioning and bathrooms with hot water, or cheaper bamboo huts on rafts, with fans and cold-water bathrooms. All have balconies and river views. There are two connecting rooms for families. Limited parking is available on the mainland; the island is accessible by taxi or ferry (free for guests). **Pros:** nice view; unique location. **Cons:** isolated. ✉ *44–48 Chaichumpol Rd.* ☎ *034/513359, 02/255–3603 in Bangkok* *18 bungalows, 15 raft houses* *In-room: no a/c (some), no phone, no TV (some). In-hotel: restaurant, pool* *No credit cards.*

¢ ★ **Little Creek.** The tribal-chic bungalows and chalets with thatched roofs, verandas, and open-air showers come in styles ranging from a petite four-by-four hut with cold water and fans to a spacious mini-house with air-conditioning and hot water. Also available are cheaper rooms with fans and cold water and tents with mattresses and bedding (B200). The owner plans to build twice as many bungalows in the years to come and to host monthly "full-moon" parties. The lakeside restaurant (¢–$) has a wood-fired pizza oven and charcoal grill and serves Western and Thai food. The resort provides free taxi rides to town and rents motorcycles or bicycles. **Pros:** quiet; various types of accommodations. CONS: 10-minute drive from town; garden needs better upkeep. ✉ *155 Moo 6, Parkphrek Rd.,* ☎ *034/513222* *www.littlecreekhideawayvalley.com* *31 chalets, 24 bungalows* *In-room: no a/c (some). In-hotel: restaurant, bar, pool, Internet terminal* *MC, V.*

$$–$$$ **Pavilion Rim Kwai Thani Resort.** This resort near the Erawan Waterfall caters to wealthy Bangkok residents who want to retreat into the country without giving up creature comforts (bathtub and shower in each room, TV, air-conditioning). Tropical flora surrounds the complex, and the River Kwai flows serenely past. The minimally furnished rooms have polished wood floors and balcony views. The large dining room serves Thai and western dishes. **Pros:** some rooms have great views; huge pool and garden. **Cons:** far from town; a bit outdated. ✉ *79/2 Moo 4, Km 9, Ladya-Erawan Rd., Tambon Wangdong* ☎ *034/513800* *195 rooms* *In-hotel: restaurant, pools* *MC, V* *BP.*

$$ **River Kwai Village.** In the jungles of the River Kwai Valley, this resort organizes elephant riding and rafting trips, as well as the usual city excursions. Most of the simple rooms are in five single-story log cabins. The more adventurous "raftels" (rooms on rafts floating in the river) have similar amenities to the rooms on dry land. The cafeteria-style restaurant offers a combination of Thai and Western dishes, but it's more fun to eat at the raft restaurant. Package tours come with transport to and from Bangkok. **Pros:** jungle location; raftels are as comfortable as standard rooms. **Cons:** 72 km (45 mi) away from town; no nighttime entertainment. ✉ *72/12 Moo 4, Tambon Thasaso, Amphoe Sai Yok,* ☎ *034/634454, 02/251–7828 in Bangkok* *www.riverkwaivillage.com* *191 rooms, 24 raftels* *In-room: refrigerator. In-hotel: 2 restaurants, room service, pool, laundry service* *AE, MC, V.*

¢ **Sam's House.** This property is a popular launching pad for treks, which the staff can arrange. The air-conditioned floating rooms are nice but a bit cramped and more expensive than those set away from the river. Motorbikes (B150 per day) and cars (B1,200 per day) are available for rent. Fifteen new rooms with TVs are being built at this writing and should be completed by mid-2009. **Pros:** some rooms have nice river views; can arrange tours. **Cons:** more expensive than other "budget" options. ✉*14/2 River Kwai Rd.* ☎*034/515956* 🌐*www.samsguesthouse.com* *39 rooms* *In-room: no a/c (some), no TV. In-hotel: restaurant* *No credit cards.*

SPORTS & THE OUTDOORS

RAFTING

Day-long rafting trips on the Kwai Yai or Mae Khlong rivers let you venture far into the jungle. The mammoth rafts, which resemble house-boats, are often divided into separate sections for eating, sleeping, and sunbathing. ⚠ **Be careful when taking a dip—the currents can sometimes suck a swimmer down.** The cost of a one-day trip starts at about B300. Longer trips are also available. Either your hotel or the tour companies below can help you arrange rafting trips. The Tourism Authority of Thailand office (⇨ *Planner, above*) can also be of assistance.

TREKKING

Jungle treks of one to four days are possible all over the region. They typically include bamboo rafting, elephant riding, visits to Karen villages, sampling local food, and sometimes a cultural performance. Stick to tour companies with Tourism Authority of Thailand licenses, which will be prominently displayed on the premises.

Good Times Travel (✉*63/1 River Kwai Rd.* ☎*034/624441* 🌐*www.good-times-travel.com*) has trips that take in all the usual highlights, including national parks, rafting, caves, Karen village stays, and the Tiger Temple.

RSP Jumbo Travel (✉*3/13 Chao Kun Nen Rd.* ☎*034/514906* 🌐*www.jumboriverkwai.com*) offers everything from day trips to weeklong itineraries that include rafting, elephant riding, and off-road adventures. Some tours are combined with stays at upmarket hotels for those who like more comfort with their adventure.

SHOPPING

Blue sapphires from the Bo Phloi mines, 45 km (28 mi) north of Kanchanaburi town, are for sale at many shops and stalls in the plaza near the bridge. The price is determined by the size and color of the stone, and, as usual, your bargaining skills. You'll do the best when there are few tourists around and business is slow. Stick to stalls with licenses.

AROUND KANCHANABURI PROVINCE

The third-largest province in Thailand, Kanchanaburi has scenic jungles, rivers, waterfalls, and mountains, especially near Sangklaburi, as you approach the Myanmar border. For centuries, it was a favorite invasion route into Siam for the Burmese. Today, it is home to Karen and Mon communities, whose villages can be visited.

GETTING HERE & AROUND

The region is easily accessible by car. Roads 323 and 3199 take you to the main sights. It's also quite easy to travel around by public transportation, although package tours can be helpful if you have limited time. Reaching less-popular sights, such as Muang Singh Historical Park, is complicated if you don't have private transportation. Consider hiring a songthaew (around B500 for half a day). Public buses from Kanchanaburi leave the bus station, or from Saengchuto Road, close to the guesthouse area on River Kwai Road. There's also a private minibus office near the main bus station; minibuses go to many places in the province but are more expensive than public buses and fill up quickly. Sai Yok Noi National Park is accessible by train.

MUANG SINGH HISTORICAL PARK

45 km (28 mi) northwest of Kanchanaburi.

King Chulalongkorn reportedly discovered this 13th- to 14th-century Khmer settlement while traveling along the Kwai Noi River. The restored remains of the city range from mere foundations to a largely intact, well-preserved monument and building complex. There are also examples of Khmer statues and pottery and a prehistoric burial site. You can drive or cycle around the large grounds of Muang Singh Historical Park with the aid of taped commentary in English, Thai, or French, available at the park's entrance. Bicycle rentals cost around B20 per hour. If you don't want to make the 45-minute drive from Kanchanaburi, take the train to Tha Kilen station (B10, one hour); the park is a 1-km (½-mi) walk (turn right when leaving the station) away. There are lodgings and a small café on the grounds. ✉ *Tha Kilen* ☎ *034/591122 or 034/591334* 🎟 *B40* ⏲ *Daily 9–6.*

TIGER TEMPLE

25 km (15 mi) northwest of Kanchanaburi.

Tiger Temple (or Wat Pa Luanta Bua Yannasampanno) is a forest monastery that houses several kinds of animals on its grounds, most notably tigers that have been cared for since 1999. At 3 PM every day the 30 or so tigers are let out of their cages into a canyon. Visitors are lined up for a photo op that lasts no more than a minute. The rest of the day, you can see some of the tigers in their cages, as well as peacocks, wild boars, and water buffaloes. Controversy surrounds the sight—locals are concerned about visitor safety (though no injuries have been reported), suspicions that tigers are drugged, and the presence of commercialism unbefitting a temple, in light of steadily increasing entry fees. (Temple officials say the price hikes are necessary to fund the creation of a larger environment for the tigers.) Many tour operators claim they'd rather not promote the sight, but can't afford to lose customers. To get here, look for the sign posted on the right of the road to Sai Yok National Park or book a tour with one of the private agencies in town. ✉ *Rte. 323, Km. 21* ☎ *034/531557* 🎟 *B300* ⏲ *Daily 9–4.*

ERAWAN NATIONAL PARK

65 km (40 mi) northwest of Kanchanaburi.

Some of the most spectacular scenery of Kanchanaburi Province can be found in Erawan National Park. The main attraction is **Erawan Waterfall,** which has seven tiers; the topmost supposedly resembles the mythical three-headed elephant (Erawan) belonging to the Hindu god Indra. You'll need to make a rather steep 2-km (1-mi) hike to get to the top (it should take about two hours). ⚠ **Comfortable footwear is essential, and don't forget to bring water!** You can swim at each level of the waterfall (levels 2 through 5 are the most popular). The first tier has a small café, and there are several others near the visitor center. There are also accommodations (bungalows from B800 to B2400, sleeping up to eight, or tents from B270, sleeping up to four) in two locations—the ones nearest the waterfall are quieter.

The park is massive; the waterfall is near the main entrance—so too are the visitor center and accommodations. Other highlights of the park include five caves. One of them, **Ta Duang,** has wall paintings, and another, **Ruea,** has prehistoric coffins. The caves are much farther away and are accessed via a different road. About 2 km (1 mi) from the park is Erawan Village; songthaews leave from its market and travel to the park entrance and the caves (B500–B600).

The bus (#8170) to Erawan leaves Kanchanaburi's bus station every 50 minutes; the trip takes 90 minutes. ✉ *Rte. 3199, Km. 44* ☎ *034/574222 or 034/574234* 🌐 *www.dnp.go.th* 🎫 *B200* 🕘 *Daily 8–4:30.*

HELLFIRE PASS

70 km (43 mi) northwest of Kanchanaburi.

The museum at Hellfire Pass is a moving memorial to the Allied prisoners of war who built the River Kwai railway, 12,399 of whom died in the process. Along with a film and exhibits, there's a 4½-km (3-mi) walk along a section of the railway, including the notorious Hellfire Pass, one of the most grueling sections built. The pass got its name from the fire lanterns that flickered on the mountain walls as the men worked through the night. ■ **TIP→ Many people do the walk in the early morning before the museum opens, and before it gets too hot.** Allow 2½ hours round-trip for the walk. Take plenty of water and a snack; there's a small shack near the museum that sells drinks, but not much food. The pass can be busy on weekends (when an average of 500 people a day visit), and on ANZAC Day (April 25). Bus 8203 (2 hours) makes the trip here. The bus stops in front of the museum compound. The last bus back to Kanchanaburi is at 4 PM. The drive by car is about an hour. ✉ *Rte. 323, Km 66* ☎ *081/754–2098* 🎫 *Museum and trail free* 🕘 *Museum daily 9–4. Trail 24 hrs.*

SAI YOK NATIONAL PARK

97 km (60 mi) northwest of Kanchanaburi.

The main attraction in Sai Yok National Park is **Sai Yok Yai waterfall,** which flows into the Kwai Noi River. The waterfall, an easy walk from the visitor center, is single tier and not nearly as spectacular as Erawan's. More unique are the **bat caves,** 2 km (1 mi) past the waterfall, that house the thumb-size Kitti's Hog-nosed bat, the world's smallest mammal, found only in these caves. You can rent flashlights at the visitor center.

The park has accommodations in tents and guesthouses. The private raft houses on the Kwai Noi River are more scenic options. There's no electricity—light is provided by oil lamp. **Sai Yok View Raft** (☎ *081/857–2284* *www.saiyokviewraft.com*) has more isolated raft houses upstream. The raft houses near the waterfall have cheap restaurants that are more pleasant than the food stalls near the visitor center.

Buses to Sai Yok Yai leave Kanchanaburi every 30 minutes from 6 AM to 6:30 PM; it's a two-hour trip. The main entrance for the national park (and the Sai Yok visitor center) is near Sai Yok Yai. Coming from Bangkok and Kanchanaburi on Road 323, you also pass **Sai Yok Noi waterfall,** which is about 40 km (25 mi) before Sai Yok Yai, but within the park's boundaries.

Despite being higher than Sai Yok Yai, Sai Yok Noi waterfall has less water, but there's enough to swim in from June to November, and the area is often packed with Thai families on weekends. Several limestone caves can also be visited in the area.

Sai Yok Noi is 2 km (1 mi) from Nam Tok Station, the terminus of the Death Railway. Motorbike taxis are sometimes available, otherwise you'll have to walk. Trains leave Kanchanaburi each day at 5:52 AM and 10:20 AM, passing through agricultural areas then into thick jungles and past the rushing Kwai Noi as they cling to the mountainside; the journey takes two hours. The trip by bus, which leaves every 30 minutes from Kanchanaburi (6 AM to 5 PM), takes two hours. If you're driving, take Route 323; Sai Yok Noi is at Km 65.

Caves in the park worth visiting include Tham Wang Badan and Lawa Cave, near Sai Yok Noi, and Dowadeung Cave, near Sai Yok Yai. *Park headquarters: Sai Yok Yai, Rte. 323, Km 97 034/516163 up to 64 www.dnp.go.th B200 Daily 7–6.*

SANGKLABURI

203 km (126 mi) northwest of Kanchanaburi.

Sangklaburi is a sleepy town on a large lake created by the Khao Laem Dam. There was once a Mon village here, but when the dam was built in 1983, it was almost completely covered by water. (Some parts, including a temple, are still visible beneath the surface.) The Mon were relocated to a village on the lakeshore opposite Sangklaburi. The Mon arrived in the area 50 years ago from Myanmar, seeking religious sanctuary.

The village has a temple with Indian and Burmese influences and a bronze-color pyramid chedi that's illuminated beautifully at night. A dry-goods market in the village sells Chinese and Burmese clothes and trinkets, with Mon dishes available at nearby food stalls. You can reach the village by car or boat or you can walk from Sangklaburi across the country's longest wooden bridge.

Due to its closeness to Myanmar's border, Sangklaburi is also home to Karen and Bangladeshi communities, and its small **night market** (4 PM–7 PM) attracts itinerant ethnic stalls selling food, clothing, and trinkets. Jungle trekking and visits to Karen villages are popular activities for visitors; trips can be arranged through guesthouses (⇨ *Where to Eat & Stay,* *below*). You can also cross into Myanmar at Three Pagodas Pass with a passport photo and US$10 (U.S. currency only—there's an exchange facility at the border), but you cannot renew Thai visas at this checkpoint, so you won't be allowed to go any farther than the Myanmar border town, Phayathonzu.

GETTING HERE & AROUND

BY BUS Air-conditioned buses from Bangkok's Northern Bus Terminal leave for Sangklaburi four times a day (6½ hours, B330). The last direct bus to Bangkok leaves Sangklaburi early in the afternoon. Air-conditioned buses from Kanchanaburi (3 hours) leave hourly between 7:30 AM and 4:30 PM. The guesthouses are accessible by motorcycle taxi (B10) or songthaew (B60) from the bus station.

BY CAR The 2½- to 3-hour drive from Kanchanaburi, on Route 323, is along good roads beside fields of pomelo, corn, and banana palms, with Myanmar's mist-shrouded mountains in the distance, then winding through the mountains.

BY MOTORCYCLE TAXI Motorcycle taxis (B10–B20) are the favored way to get around this sprawling provincial town. For longer trips, ask your hotel or guesthouse to arrange car transport.

ESSENTIALS

Emergencies **Sangklaburi Hospital** (✉ *Sukhaphiban 2, Sangklaburi* ☎ *034/595058*).

WHERE TO EAT & STAY

Six or seven guesthouses are on the lakeside road, all with views of the wooden bridge and the Mon village. The temple's lights shimmer on the water at night. They all have restaurants, and most offer Burmese and Mon food such as *haeng leh curry* (a country dish made of whatever ingredients are on hand, but often including pork) and the coconut-and-noodle dish *kao sawy,* usually made with chicken. Nightlife consists of a shop-house karaoke bar on the same road as the guesthouses, and a single noodle soup stall at the market that sells beer and local whiskey until 2 AM.

¢–$ THAI ✕ **Burmese Inn Restaurant.** The terrace restaurant of this guesthouse (⇨ *below*) has fish dishes and other Thai and Burmese options, including laphae to, a salad of nuts, beans, and fermented tea leaves. It also serves Western breakfasts, salads, and sandwiches and has a view of the wooden bridge and the Mon village. Service is quite laid-back. ✉ *52/3 Moo 3, Tambon Nongloo* ☎ *034/595146* ▭ *No credit cards.*

¢ **Burmese Inn.** These homey bungalows, run by an Austrian and his Thai wife are on a garden hillside above the lake. The rooms are filled with pictures and knickknacks and some are directly over the water. The room TVs have only Thai-language stations. **Pros:** close to the wooden bridge; lots of information on the region. **Cons:** cheapest rooms are tiny, dark, and far from clean—spring for the pricier options. ✉ *52/3 Moo 3, Tambon Nongloo* ☎ *034/595146 or 086/168–1801* 🌐 *burmeseinn@yahoo.com* *19 rooms* *In-room: no a/c (some). In-hotel: restaurant* ▭ *No credit cards.*

¢ **P Guest House.** Stone bungalows with narrow log ceilings are in a stepped garden that leads down to the lakeside. Rooms are mainly fan-cooled with shared bathrooms, but three have air-conditioning, private bathrooms, and lake views. You can rent kayaks (B100/hour) and motorcycles (B200/day), and the owners organize treks that include a longtail boat ride on the lake to see the submerged temple, elephant riding, and rafting. The large terrace restaurant has an inexpensive Thai menu with a few Burmese dishes, as well as pastas, sandwiches, and Western breakfasts. **Pros:** wooden deck for sunbathing and swimming; all rooms are very clean. **Cons:** no a/c in most rooms. ✉ *81/2 Moo 1, Tambon Nongloo* ☎ *034/595061* 🌐 *www.pguesthouse.com* *20 rooms* *In-room: no a/c (some), no TV (some) In-hotel: restaurant* *No credit cards.*

¢–$ **Pornphailin Riverside.** The bungalows are on the water's edge, but the guesthouse is a long walk from town. All rooms have balconies and panoramic views of the lake; yet some have more windows than others. Larger rooms are less expensive on weekdays. The huge terrace restaurant serves Thai food and a nightclub has regular karaoke. **Pros:** stunning view on the lake. **Cons:** away from town. ✉ *60/3 Moo 1, Soi Tonpeung* ☎ *034/595322* *53 rooms* *In-room: refrigerator. In-hotel: restaurant, bar, laundry service, Internet terminal* *MC, V.*

4

The Central Plains

AYUTTHAYA, SUKHOTHAI, AND TAK PROVINCE

WORD OF MOUTH

"I would include at least one day at Sukhothai ruins. We went there, as well as to Angkor Wat . . . and found Sukhothai to be very different from Angkor Wat visually, culturally, and experientially."

—Shelleyk

WELCOME TO CENTRAL PLAINS

TOP REASONS TO GO

★ **Sukhothai's Monuments:** It is easy to spend days of speechless soul-searching after encountering the mystical monuments of Thailand's 13th-century capital.

★ **River Views in Ayutthaya:** This city, which can be visited as a day trip from Bangkok, combines great river views—most of its hotels offer them—with an island full of fascinating wats.

★ **Loi Krathong:** The Central Plains, Sukhothai in particular, is one of the best areas to experience this festival. Thais set elaborate candle-bearing floats out into the river, creating a memorable light display.

★ **Myanmar for a Day:** Myanmar (Burma), a country ruled by a military junta with a bad human rights record, is a mystery to most people. A day trip across the border from Mae Sot may not provide a deep understanding of the country's situation, but it's a start.

Buddha image at Wat Yai Chaya Mongkol Ayuthaya Historical Park

1 Ayutthaya & Environs. Within easy reach of Bangkok, Ayutthaya is a historically significant ruin, and once one of the country's most important. Nearby Bang Pa-In, with its famous Royal Palace, and Lopburi, with its monkey-infested temples, are a bit farther off the beaten track.

2 Sukhothai & Environs. To history buffs, the soul of the country is to be found in the cities of Sukhothai and Si Satchanalai. These strongholds of architecture and culture evoke Thailand's ancient civilizations, while Sukhothai's well-developed tourist industry makes it the modern-day hub for exploring the region.

Wat Sri Sawai Sukhothai

3 Tak Province. Journeying farther north, by combinations of minibus, bus, and songthaews, will take you from historic to geographic majesty. Within the cooler climes of the north are Mae Sot, a frontierlike city bordering Myanmar, and Umphang, with its mountainous, forested isolation, natural grandeur, hill tribe villages, and ecotourism opportunities.

GETTING ORIENTED

4

The Central Plains is one of the most overlooked regions of Thailand. Some people take a side trip from Bangkok to the ancient capital of Ayutthaya, but fewer venture farther north to the even older cities at Sukhothai and Si Satchanalai, both of which have some of the most breathtaking ruins in the country. Although some sights are decidedly off the beaten track, it isn't difficult to reach the Central Plains. If you have more than a passing interest in Thailand's history, you should make this part of your itinerary.

CENTRAL PLAINS PLANNER

When to Go

The coolest and driest months in central Thailand—between November and February—are also the busiest, since lower temperatures attract travelers. From March to June, the Central Plains, like much of Thailand, becomes almost unbearably hot, with temperatures often exceeding 90 degrees. During the rainy season (June to early October), temperatures a slightly cooler, but frequent flooding in the Central Plains makes a rainy-season visit risky.

The Tak Province's higher elevations mean this region is often cooler than the rest of the country; winter temperatures are often in the 60s or cooler.

During the Loi Krathong festival (usually November), both Ayutthaya and Sukhothai's historical parks explode with orchestrated light-and-sound shows. Tourists fill the towns' guesthouses and hotels; it's a fun time to visit, but be sure to book your accommodations as early as possible.

Getting Around

By Air: There are small airports in Phitsanulok and Sukhothai. There are several flights a day to and from Bangkok, and less frequent flights to and from Chiang Mai. Thai Airways services both airports; Bangkok Airways, which actually owns the Sukhothai airport, does not fly to Phitsanulok. There is no commercial air service to Tak Province.

By Bus: Buses run between Bangkok's Mo Chit Northern Bus Terminal to every major town in the region. Buses also run between Phitsanulok and Sukhothai and from Tak to Sukhothai and Phitsanulok.

By Car: The main road in the region is Highway 1, which runs from Bangkok to Chiang Rai. After traveling north on Highway 1, you'll take Highways 32 to Ayutthaya, Highway 101 to Sukhothai, and Highway 117 to Phitsunalok; you can follow Higway 1 all the way to Tak Province.

By Train: The rail system is rapidly aging, with antiquated trains sluggishly making trips between Ayutthaya, Sukhothai, Kanchanaburi, Lopburi, and Phitsunalok. Trains depart for these destinations 11 times per day between 7 AM and 10 PM (⇨ *By Train in Travel Smart Thailand*).

By Tuk-Tuk & Songthaew: Songthaews travel between towns in central Thailand, but are not usually as efficient or comfortable as taking the bus. Once you're in town, tuk-tuks are a convenient way to get around.

Visitor & Tour Info

The Tourist Authority of Thailand (TAT) has offices in Ayutthaya, Lopburi, Phitsanulok, and Sukhothai.

TAT (Ayutthaya) (✉ *Si Sanphet Rd., Ayutthaya* ☎ *035/246076* ⏲ *Daily 8:30–4:30*).

TAT (Lopburi) (✉ *Rajawatprathat Rd., Tambol Tahin, Amphoe Meuang, Lopburi* ☎ *036/422768* ⏲ *Daily 8:30–4:30*).

TAT (Phitsanulok) (✉ *209/7–8 Boromtrailokanat Rd., Phitsanulok* ☎ *055/231063* ⏲ *Daily 8:30–4:30*).

TAT (Sukhothai) City Hall (✉ *Tambol Thani, Amphoe Meuang, Sukhothai* ☎ *55/611-196* ⏲ *Daily 8:30–4:30*).

Hotel Know-How

Because relatively few tourists visit the Central Plains, most hotels and guesthouses cater chiefly to a business clientele. There are some top-class hotels, but most accommodations are much more modest than in Bangkok or Chiang Mai. As elsewhere in Thailand, standards of cleanliness are high and even the most basic room will invariably have fresh linen and towels.

A new phenomenon is the appearance of lodgings run by hospitable and knowledgeable local people anxious to help visitors get to know this seemingly remote region. They open up their homes to paying guests and show them around for a modest fee. Listed in this chapter are a few of the most reputable.

For budget-conscious travelers, rooms in the Central Plains are truly a bargain—even the most expensive hotels charge less than US$60 a night. Don't expect the full range of facilities, however. Such refinements as room phones and TVs can be rare outside the cities.

Ayutthaya or Sukhothai?

Visitors to the Central Plains often wonder if it's worth visiting both Ayutthaya and Sukhothai. Assuming your time is fairly limited, seeing one or the other of these historic Thai capitals is probably enough. Ayutthaya, an easy day trip from Bangkok, is the more convenient option. You'll see a few ancient Thai temples, and you can stop in Bang Pa-In for a little more sightseeing and some shopping enroute.

Though much farther from Bangkok, Sukhothai's historical park is beautiful and less crowded than Ayutthaya. Outside the main park are other ruin, many of which are within biking or hiking distance. If you have time to stay for at least one night, it's a more interesting choice than Ayutthaya.

WHAT IT COSTS IN BAHT

¢	$	$$	$$$	$$$$
Restaurants				
under B100	B100–B200	B201–B300	B301–B400	over B400
Hotels				
under B1,000	B1,000–B2,000	B2,001–B4,000	B4,001–B6,000	over B6,000

Restaurant prices are for a main course, excluding tax and tips. Hotel prices are for two people in a standard double room in high season, excluding service charges and tax.

Health & Safety

The cities are pretty safe, with common sense being the only precaution needed. However, do watch out for the monkeys in Lopburi. They are a cheeky bunch and have been known to steal anything that you can't hold onto, from your coffee cup to your camera.

Rubies, brought in from Burmese mines, are a big draw at Mae Sot, but unless you know what you're looking at, you might find yourself with substandard or fake gems, as scams on unsuspecting visitors are common.

Periodic clashes between the Thai army and the government of Myanmar (Burma) occasionally result in the closure of areas along Thailand's western border. Check the State Department's Web site (*travel.state.gov/travel/travel_1744.html*) for updates.

Motorcycle thieves who ride up alongside other motorcyclists and snatch their bags are a problem in central Thailand.

In an emergency, contact the Tourist Police first at ☎1155.

EATING & DRINKING WELL IN THE CENTRAL PLAINS

Tom yum goong *(pictured* above).

Considered by some to be the most balanced of Thailand's regional cuisines, central Thai fare includes the mouthwatering coconut-milk curries that show up on Thai menus in the west.

Like most Thai food, typical Central Plains dishes rely on contrasting spicy, sweet, sour, and bitter flavors. *Prik kii nu* (small red chilies) are a key ingredient in most dishes, though generally food here is a bit less spicy than that of other regions. In addition to *lathi* (coconut milk), many recipes use *naam manao* (lime juice), mara (bitter gourd), and soy sauce for salt. Central Plains cooks take advantage of the region's several rivers; giant river prawns, which can grow to be a foot long, are a regional delicacy, served steamed or added to soups. River fish, including *bla chon* (snakehead fish) and several varieties of catfish, are also popular.

Traditional markets or simple, canteen-style restaurants are the most common eateries you'll find in central Thailand. These venues often consist of little more than a corrugated steel roof held up with salvaged lumber, but don't be put off by appearances—even these modest kitchens can turn out surprisingly tasty meals.

DINING WITH YOUNG CHILDREN

Thai kids begin eating spicy food when they're 3 or 4 years old, and also develop a taste for garlic and other flavors that put off many young westerners.

A few options likely to appeal to children are *kuay tiew luck chin bla* (noodles with boiled or fried fish balls, a Thai equivalent to chicken nuggets), *gaeng jeut woon sen* (noodle consommé), and *kai jiao* (a Thai omelet that typically includes minced pork). Be sure to order their dishes "not spicy" (*mai phet*). You can also always feed the kids rice, perhaps lightly flavored with some of whatever you're eating.

HA MOK

This fiery dish gets high marks for presentation—it's served wrapped in a banana leaf or foil. Inside is steamed red curry mixed with an assortment of seafood such as squid, shrimp, and crab. On top is a pool of coconut milk, which has been simmered to make it thick and creamy. Even in the Central Plains, this dish is usually hot and spicy.

GENG KYAW WAN

This thin, soup-like sweet green curry is usually served with an assortment of vegetables and chicken. Though similar dishes are popular in Thai restaurants all over the world, the local version includes two varieties of eggplants that are not common in the West: a pea-like eggplant called *makheuua phuang* (devil's fig) and *makheuua bpraw* (kermit eggplants roughly the size and shape of a golf ball). The eggplants add a slightly bitter taste to this otherwise sweet dish. You can sometimes find green curry with beef or pork instead of chicken.

TOM YUM

Tom yum soup is famous for its hot and sour flavor, which is complemented by lemongrass, onion, and coconut milk. It can be served with many types of meat and seafood; the most popular addition is shrimp (tom yum *goong*).

KHAO OP SAPHAROT

This sweet dish is prepared in a pineapple husk: the pineapple flesh is carved out and the shell is filled with cooked rice. Vegetables and spices are mixed in, along with pineapple chunks. It is then baked so that the rice can absorb the pineapple juices; after it comes out of the oven, cashews and tiny shrimp are often sprinkled on top as garnish. It arrives at your table inside the pineapple skin.

YAM BLA DUK FU

Though it does not actually contain any vegetables, Thais refer to this dish as a salad. Usually eaten as an appetizer, yam bla duk fu consists of raw green mango slices in a sweet and spicy sauce, and crispy, shredded catfish. The mango is served in a separate bowl, and Thais spoon it onto the fried fish.

AYUTTHAYA & ENVIRONS

Updated by Brian Thomson

WITH 92% OF ITS LAND used for agriculture, it isn't surprising that Ayutthaya is known as Southeast Asia's rice field. To its west is the Suphan Buri and its continuing rice paddies, while to the northeast the region borders with Lopburi, approaching the northeastern plateau with rising forested hills. The bountiful plain has been home to Thailand's most influential and ancient Kingdoms: Lopburi and Ayutthaya.

Ayutthaya and its environs represent an important historical journey that traces Thailand's cultural developments from Buddhist art and architecture to modern government and language. Ayutthaya gets the most attention, drawing day-trippers from Bangkok, but a visit to Lopburi, with its Khmer temples and French-influenced Royal Palace, lends even more historical context to the museums and ransacked ruins found at Ayutthaya's historical park and the 18th-century Royal Palace in nearby Bang Pa-In.

AYUTTHAYA

72 km (45 mi) north of Bangkok.

★ Ayutthaya was named by King Ramatibodi after a mythical kingdom of the gods portrayed in the pages of the Ramayana. The city was completed in 1350 and was a powerhouse of Southeast Asia. The city was originally chosen as a capital for its eminently defendable position: it lies in a bend of the Chao Phraya River, where it meets the Pa Sak and Lopburi rivers—to completely surround their capital with water, early residents dug a curving canal along the northern perimeter, linking the Chao Phraya to the Lopburi. However, Ayutthaya quickly changed from being essentially a military base to an important center for the arts, medicine, and technology. Trade routes opened up Siam's first treaty with a Western nation (Portugal, in 1516) and soon after, the Dutch, English, Japanese and, most influentially, the French, accelerated Ayutthaya's role in international relations under King Narai the Great. After Narai's death in 1688 the kingdom plunged into internal conflict.

Today Ayutthaya is a carefully preserved World Heritage Site and a visit provides a fascinating snapshot of ancient Siam. Scattered ruins lay testament to the kingdom's brutal demise at the hands of the Burmese in 1767. Although the modern town is on the eastern bank of the Pa Sak, most of the ancient temples are on the island. An exception is Wat Yai Chai Mongkol, a short tuk-tuk ride away.

■ **TIP→ Ayutthaya is best appreciated in historical context, and a visit to the Historical Study Center can improve the experience for a first-time visitor.** Certain sites are guaranteed to take your breath away, with Wat Phra Si Sanphet, Wat Yai Chai Mongkol, Wat Phra Mahathat, and Wat Ratchaburana being the best. Aside from the temples, Ayutthaya's friendly guesthouses, welcoming people, and floating restaurants make for a refreshing change from Bangkok. However, because Ayutthaya is in such easy reach of Bangkok, hordes of day-trippers roam the city

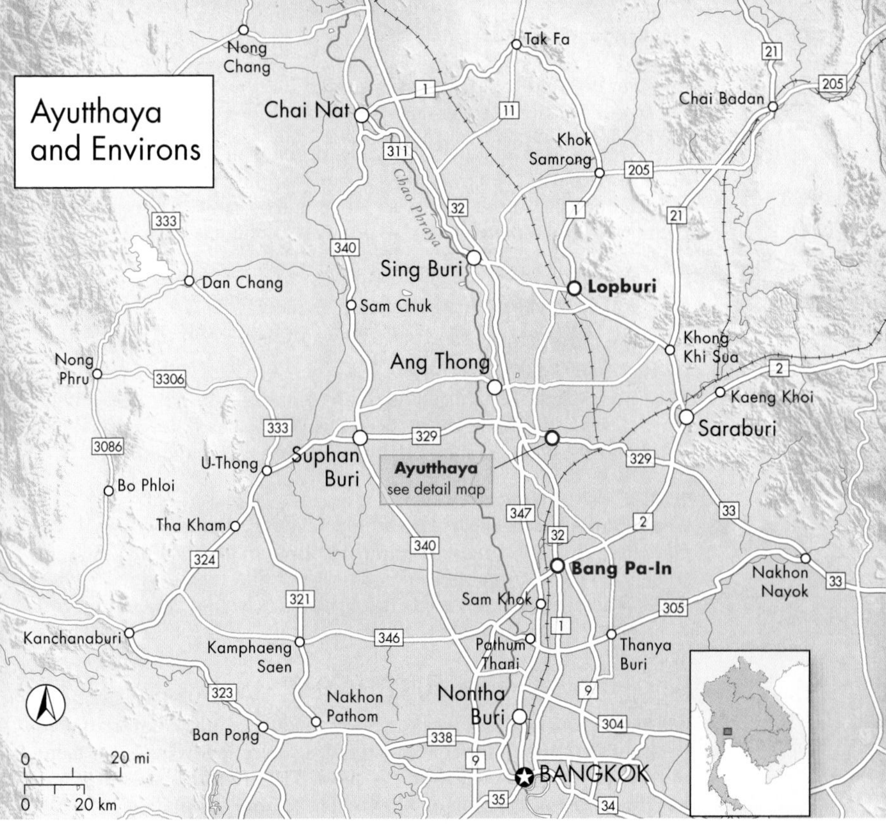

during daylight hours, making Ayutthaya feel somewhat more touristy than the rest of the region—at least until the sun sets.

GETTING HERE & AROUND

BY BOAT **River King Cruise** (☎*02/673–0966* 🌐*www.riverkingcruise.net/*) runs daytrips to Ayutthaya. You'll take the bus there early in the morning (they'll pick you up from most Bangkok hotels at around 6:30 AM), stopping at Bang Pa-In Palace, and return to Bangkok by boat at 4 PM. The B1,700 ticket price includes lunch.

BY BUS Buses to Ayutthaya (1½ hours) leave Bangkok's Mo Chit Northern Bus Terminal about once an hour between 6 AM and 7 PM. Tickets are B50 baht for the 1½-hour trip.

BY CAR Driving to Ayutthaya from Bangkok is an easy day trip once you're out of the congestion of the big city. Kanchanaphisek Road, Bangkok's outer ring road, is the best route to take, costing around B120 in tolls. Following this road will drop you into Bang Pa-In—a good opportunity to visit the Royal Palace before continuing to Ayutthaya.

BY TAXI & TUK-TUK All forms of local transport are available from samlors to a few songth-aews, but the brightly colored tuk-tuks are more frequently used. Tuk-

tuks can be hired for an hour for around B200 or the day for around B600 to B700 and make easier work of Ayutthaya's historical sites.

BY TRAIN The Northeastern Line, which heads all the way up to Isan, has frequent service from Bangkok to Ayutthaya. Beginning at 4:30 AM, trains depart frequently (roughly every 40 minutes) from Bangkok's Hua Lamphong Station, arriving in Ayutthaya 80 minutes later.

ESSENTIALS

Emergencies **Ayutthaya Tourist Police** (☎*035/241446 or 1155*). **Ratcha Thani Hospital** (✉*111 Moo 3, Rotchana Rd., Ayutthaya* ☎*035/335555*).

EXPLORING AYUTTHAYA

Most people find that a morning or afternoon is sufficient to see Ayutthaya. For a three-hour tour of the sites, tuk-tuks can be hired for about B700; a three-wheel samlor (small bicycle cab) costs about B500.

TOP ATTRACTIONS

❻ **Viharn Phra Mongkol Bopitr.** This is one of the modern structures in the Old City. The site's original temple was built in 1610. When the roof collapsed in 1767, one of Thailand's biggest and most revered bronze Buddha images was revealed. It lay here uncovered for almost 200 years before the huge modern viharn was built in 1951. Historians have dated the image back to 1538. ✉*Off Naresuan Rd.* *Free* *Weekdays 8–4:30, weekends 8–5:30.*

❼ ★ **Wat Phanan Choeng.** This bustling merit-making temple complex on the banks of the Lopburi River is an interesting diversion from the dormant ruins that dominate Ayutthaya. A short B3 ferry ride across the river sets the scene for its dramatic origins. The temple was built in 1324 (26 years before Ayutthaya's rise to power) by a U-Thong king in atonement for the death of his fiancée. Instead of bringing his bride, a Chinese princess, into the city himself, the king arranged an escort for her. Distraught at what she interpreted to be a lackluster welcome, the princess threw herself into the river (at the site of the current temple) and drowned. ✉*East of the Old City* *Free* *Daily 8–5.*

❺ **Wat Phra Si Sanphet.** This wat was the largest temple in Ayutthaya, and where the royal family worshipped. The 14th-century structure lost its 50-foot Buddha in 1767, when the invading Burmese melted it down for its 374 pounds of gold. The trio of chedis survived and are the best existing examples of Ayutthaya architecture; enshrining the ashes of several kings, they stand as eternal memories of a golden age. If the design looks familiar, it's because Wat Phra Si Sanphet was the model for Wat Phra Keo at the Grand Palace in Bangkok. Beyond the monuments you can find a grassy field where the Royal Palace once stood. The foundation is all that remains of the palace that was home to 33 kings. ✉*Naresuan Rd.* *B30* *Daily 7–6:30.*

ALSO WORTH SEEING

❶ **Ayutthaya Historical Study Center.** This educational center, financed by the Japanese government, houses fascinating audiovisual displays about Ayutthaya. Models of the city as a rural village, as a port city, as an

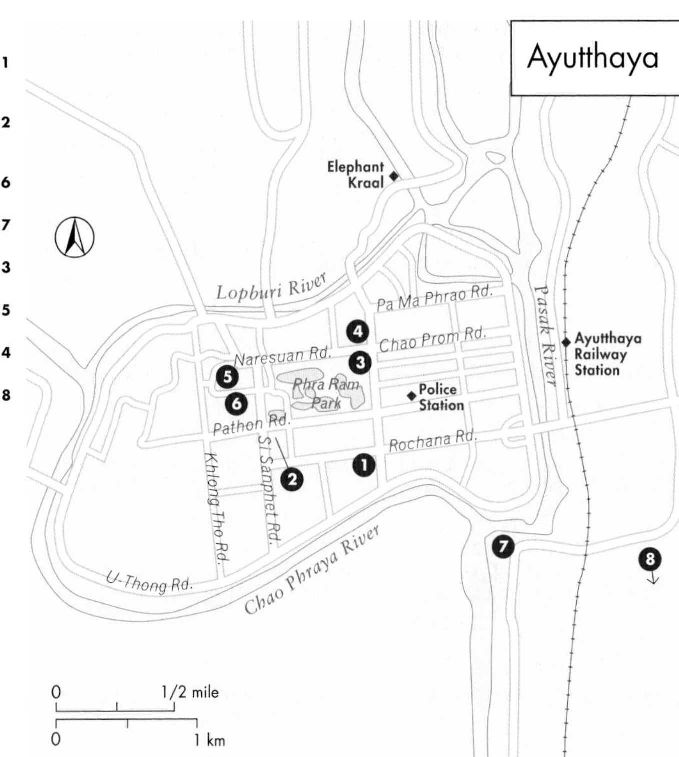

administrative center, and as a royal capital reveal the site's history. ✉ *Rotchana Rd. between Si San Phet and Chikun Rds.* ☎ *035/245124* 🎫 *B100* 🕑 *Weekdays 9–4:30, weekends 9–5.*

❷ **Chao Sam Phraya National Museum.** This dated museum on spacious grounds is ostensibly a showcase of Buddhist sculpture, including Dvaravati (Lamphun), Lopburi, Ayutthayan, and U-Thong styles. In truth, the artifacts are poorly presented, and the best attraction is an upstairs vault in the first building, which has relics (such as a jewel-covered sword) of two of Wat Ratchaburana's original princes. ✉ *Rotchana Rd. at Si San Phet Rd.* ☎ *035/241587* 🎫 *B30* 🕑 *Wed.–Sun. 9–4.*

Elephant Kraal. Thailand's only intact royal kraal was built to hold and train elephants for martial service; it was last used during King Chulalongkorn's reign in 1903. The restored teak stockade acts as little other than a gateway to the Royal Elephant Kraal Village behind it, which cares for about 100 elephants. Though it looks like a working village, it's primarily a business—rehabilitating and parenting elephants for work on tours around Ayutthaya and also for TV and film productions (most recently Oliver Stone's *Alexander*). ✉ *5 km (3 mi) north of Ayutthaya, on Hwy. 3060 to Panead* ☎ *035/321982* 🕑 *Daily 8–5.*

3 **Wat Phra Mahathat.** Building began on this royal monastery in 1374 and was completed during the reign of King Ramesuan (1388–95). Today, tree-shaded grounds contain what's left of its 140-foot brick prang. The prang collapsed twice between 1610 to 1628, and again in the early 20th century, and today barely reflects its former glory. The stunted ruins and beheaded Buddhas that remain in Wat Phra Mahathat are a result of the Burmese sacking this once revered temple in 1767. ✉ *Naresuan Rd. at Chee Kun Rd.* 🎟 *B30* ⏲ *Daily 8–6:30.*

WORD OF MOUTH

"My wife, daughter and I spent the better part of a week in Ayutthaya. I found the temples there to be beautiful, inspiring, and largely deserted. Perhaps not quite in the league with Bagan or Angkor, but nearly so, and easier to access."
—minkyhcmc

4 **Wat Ratchaburana.** Directly north across the road from Wat Phra Mahathat is Wat Ratchaburana, its Khmer-style prang dominating the skyline. King Borommaracha II (Chao Sam Phraya) built this temple in 1424 to commemorate the death of his two older brothers, whose duel for the throne ironically left their younger brother as king. Their relics were buried in a crypt directly under the base of the prang, which was looted in 1957. Arrests were made, however, and the retrieved treasures can now be seen in the Chao Sam Phraya National Museum. ✉ *Naresuan Rd. and Chee Kun Rd.* 🎟 *B30* ⏲ *Daily 8:30–4:30.*

8 **Wat Yai Chai Mongkol.** The enormous chedi at Wat Yai Chai Mongkol, the largest in Ayutthaya, was constructed by King Naresuan after he defeated the Burmese crown prince during a battle atop elephants in 1593. (A recent painting of the battle is one of the highlights of the temple.) The chedi is now leaning quite a bit, as later enlargements are weighing down on the foundation. The complex, dating from 1357, was totally restored in 1982. Linger a while to pay your respects to the huge reclining Buddha or climb to the top for a spectacular view. ■ **TIP→ The site closes at 5 PM, but you can enter after that if the gates are left open, as they often are. The view at sunset is beautiful, and you'll completely escape the crowds.** ✉ *About 5 km (3 mi) southeast of the Old City on the Ayutthaya to Bang Pa-In Rd.* 🎟 *B20, free after 5 PM* ⏲ *Daily 8–5.*

WHERE TO EAT

$ THAI ✕ **Pae Krung Kao.** If you can't resist dining outdoors beside the Pa Sak River, this good option is near the Pridi Damrong Bridge. You can also drop by for a beer. ✉ *4 U-Thong Rd.* ☎ *035/241555* 💳 *MC, V.*

$$$ ★ THAI ✕ **Pasak River Queen.** Enjoy a leisurely two-hour ride along the Pa Sak River while filling your belly with grilled seafood and some fantastic Thai dishes. The 350-passenger boat departs nightly at 6:30 PM. There's a B79 cover charge and dishes are ordered à la carte. The dock's a bit outside town; it's worth booking transportation to and from the dock ahead of time. During the summer rains, boats sometimes do not run in high-water conditions. ✉ *116 Moo 2, Borpong* ☎ *035/724520, 035/724504, or 035/724519* 💳 *AE, DC, MC, V.*

WHERE TO STAY

If you're a romantic, a stay in Ayutthaya allows you to wander among the ruins at night. Since most tourists leave Ayutthaya by 4 PM, those who stay are treated to genuine Thai hospitality. Don't expect luxury, however; Ayutthaya has only modest hotels.

$ **Krungsri River Hotel.** This hotel near the train station has a refreshingly cool and spacious marble-floor lobby. The rooms, although not distinguished, are clean and filled with modern furnishings. For the best views, choose a room overlooking the river. Because Ayutthaya has few overnight visitors, try to negotiate a discounted rate. Rates include a buffet breakfast. The hotel also operates river cruises. **Pros:** near the train station; river views. **Cons:** no Wi-Fi in rooms. ✉*27/2 Moo 11, Rojana Rd., Ayutthaya* ☎*035/244333* 🌐*www.krungsririver.com* *200 rooms* *In-room: refrigerator. In-hotel: 2 restaurants, bar, pool, gym, no-smoking rooms* 💳*AE, DC, MC, V.*

$–$$ ★ **River View Place Hotel.** There may be no other hotel in Thailand that offers so much space for such a small price: the Majesty Suites, with kitchenettes and about 1,000 square feet of space, go for B2,000. An even better value at this hotel on the Pa Sak River are the more-than-adequate 700-square-foot Senior Suites. Riverview suites, meanwhile, have enormous balconies. Rooms are so spacious and sparsely furnished that they can feel somewhat empty, but facilities are brand new. The hotel operates a dinner cruise as well. All in all, it's the best lodging choice in Ayutthaya. **Pros:** Spacious rooms; ample free parking; river views. **Cons:** Wi-Fi only available in the lobby and costs B10 per 5 minutes. ✉*K. 35/5 Horatanachai, U-Thong Rd., Ayutthaya* ☎*035/241444* 🌐*riverview05@hotmail.com* *71 suites* *In-room: safe, refrigerator. In-hotel: 2 restaurants, room service, bar, pool, gym, laundry service, Wi-Fi, no-smoking rooms* 💳*MC, V.*

$ **U-Thong Inn.** If the gilded lobby is grandiose bordering on gaudy, the clean, tasteful rooms with firm beds and modern bathrooms make up for it. The Tower Wing has much better rooms, so make sure you ask for one there. The suites are really just higher-end versions of the double rooms in the tower. The hotel is not far from Wat Yai Chai Mongkol. **Pros:** close to tourist sights; clean. **Cons:** gaudy lobby. ✉*210 Rojana Rd., Ayutthaya* ☎*035/212531* 🌐*www.uthonginn.com* *77 rooms, 132 suites* *In-room: refrigerator. In-hotel: 2 restaurants, bars, pool, gym, room service, no-smoking rooms* 💳 *MC, V.*

BANG PA-IN

20 km (12 mi) south of Ayutthaya.

This village, a popular stopping point between Bangkok and Ayutthaya, has a few architectural sights of note, a Thai palace, a European-style temple, and a Chinese pagoda. These buildings are set around a large pond and open fields with bushes trimmed in the shapes of various animals.

GETTING HERE & AROUND

BY BUS Buses regularly leave from Bangkok's Northern Bus Terminal (Mo Chit) to Bang Pa-In Bus Station, which is located just 500 meters from

DID YOU KNOW?

Wat Phanan Choeng's central Buddha is surrounded by hundreds of small Buddha figures, which sit in niches along the temple walls. Each figure honors someone who has made a substantial donation to the temple.

BOAT TOURS TO BANG PA-IN

The **Chao Phraya Express Boat Company** (✉ *Maharat Pier, 2/58 Aroon-Amarin Rd., Bangkok* ☎ *02/222–5330*) runs a Sunday excursion from Bangkok to Bang Pa-In Summer Palace. It departs at 8 AM and arrives in time for lunch. On the return trip, the boat stops at the Bang Sai Folk Arts and Craft Centre before arriving in Bangkok at 5:30 PM. The trip costs B350.

Another option is the **Manohra Song** (✉ *Marriott Royal Garden Riverside Hotel, 257/1–3 Charoen Nakorn Rd., Bangkok* ☎ *02/476–0021 or 02/276–0022* 🌐 *www.manohracruises.com*) cruise; for a day and a half or longer, you can relax in suites decorated with rich woods like mahogany and teak and yards of flowing silks, and you are pampered by a private chef.

the Palace. Fares are B46 for an air-conditioned bus. Buses leave from the bus station on Naresuan Road in Ayutthaya.

BY CAR Once you get out of Bangkok's labyrinthine roads, it is also easy to get to Bang Pa-In by car. Get on Highway 1 (Phahonyothin Road) to Highway 32 toward Ayutthaya. It's a 30-minute drive here from Ayutthaya along Highway 32.

BY SONGTHAEW Songthaews travel between the bus stations in Bang Pa-In and Ayutthaya regularly.

BY TAXI One-way taxi fares from Bangkok to Bang Pa-In should be B800, but be sure that the driver agrees to this fare before departing, or you may be charged more upon arrival.

BY TRAIN Trains from Bangkok's Hua Lamphong Station regularly make the hour-long trip to Bang Pa-In Station, where you can catch a minibus to the palace. Fares range from B12 to B54. It is necessary to take a tuk-tuk from the station in Bang Pa-In to the palace.

EXPLORING BANG PA-IN

Most visitors spend about two hours at the palaces and topiary gardens before heading for Ayutthaya. However, there's enough here to warrant a longer stay if you have the time.

Bang Pa-In's extravagant **Royal Palace** is set in well-tended gardens. The original structure, built by King Prusat on the banks of the Pa Sak River, was used by the Ayutthaya kings until the Burmese invasion. After being neglected for 80 years, it was rebuilt during the reign of Rama IV and became the favored summer palace of King Rama V until tragedy struck. When the king was delayed in Bangkok, he sent his wife ahead on a boat that capsized. Although she could easily have been rescued, people stood by helplessly because a royal could not be touched by a commoner on pain of death. The king built a pavilion in her memory; be sure to read the touching inscription engraved on the memorial.

King Rama V was interested in the architecture of Europe, and many Western influences are evident here. The most beautiful building, however, is the **Aisawan Thippaya,** a Thai pavilion that seems to float on a small lake. A series of staggered roofs lead to a central spire. The structure is sometimes dismantled and taken to represent the country at worldwide expositions.

Phra Thinang Warophat Phiman, nicknamed the Peking Palace, is a replica of a Chinese imperial court palace. It was built from materials custom-made in China—a gift from Chinese Thais eager to win the king's favor. It contains a collection of exquisite jade and Ming-period porcelain.

Take the cable car across the river to **Wat Nivet Thamaprawat,** built in Gothic style. Complete with a belfry and stained-glass windows, it looks like a Christian church masquerading as a Buddhist temple. *B100 Tues.–Thurs. and weekends 8–3.*

MONKEY BUSINESS

Lopburi has an unusually large monkey population: They cluster around the monuments, particularly Phra Prang Sam Yot. Each November, the Lopburi Inn organizes a monkey banquet, in which a grand buffet is laid out for the monkeys and much of the town's population comes out to watch them feast.

SHOPPING

The **Bang Sai Folk Arts and Craft Centre** was set up by Queen Sirikit in 1982 to train farming families to make traditional crafts for extra income. Workers at the center regularly demonstrate their techniques and a small souvenir shop offers a chance to buy their crafts. *24 km (14½ mi) south of Bang Pa-In 035/366090 or 035/366666 B100 Weekdays 9–5, weekends 9–6.*

LOPBURI

75 km (47 mi) north of Ayutthaya, 150 km (94 mi) north of Bangkok.

One of Thailand's oldest cities, Lopburi has been inhabited since the 4th century. After the 6th century, its influence grew under the Dvaravati rulers, who dominated Northern Thailand until the Khmers swept in from the east. From the beginning of the 10th century until the middle of the 13th, when the new Thai kingdom drove them out, the Khmers used Lopburi as their provincial capital. During the Sukhothai and early Ayutthaya periods, the city's importance declined until, in 1664, King Narai made it his second capital to escape the heat and humidity of Ayutthaya. He employed French architects to build his palace; consequently, Lopburi is a strange mixture of Khmer, Thai, and Western architecture.

GETTING HERE & AROUND

BY BUS Buses to Lopburi leave Bangkok's Mo Chit Northern Bus Terminal (Mo Chit) about every 20 minutes between 6 AM and 7 PM. Tickets for the three-hour journey start at B142 for air-conditioned buses. Lopburi is an hour and a half from Ayutthaya on the green 607 bus from Ayutthaya's bus terminal. Lopburi's bus station is located about 6 km (3.7 mi) from town, making it necessary to take a tuk-tuk or songthaew into town.

BY CAR If you're driving from Bangkok, take Highway 1 (Phahonyothin) north via Salaburi. The trip will take up to two hours.

BY TRAIN The Northeastern train line has frequent service from Bangkok to Lopburi. Three morning and two afternoon trains depart for the three-hour trip from Bangkok's Hua Lamphong Station. Trains back to Bangkok run in the early and late afternoon. Since Lopburi is such a short distance from Bangkok, advance tickets aren't necessary. Fares for air-conditioned cars on the express train are B344. Lopburi's station is located downtown near historic sites and lodgings on Na Phra Kan Road.

ESSENTIALS

Hospital **Lopburi Hospital** (✉ *206 Phahonyothin Rd., Amphoe Muang, Lopburi* ☎ *036/621537 up to 45).*

EXPLORING LOPBURI

Lopburi is relatively off the beaten track for tourists, who are generally outnumbered by the city's famous monkey population. Some foreigners show up on their way to or from Ayutthaya, but few stay overnight. The rarity of foreigners may explain why locals are so friendly and eager to show you their town—and to practice their English. Samlors are available, but most of Lopburi's attractions are within easy walking distance.

Wat Phra Si Rattana Mahathat, built by the Khmers, is near the railway station. It underwent so many restorations during the Sukhothai and Ayutthaya periods that it's difficult to discern the three original Khmer prangs—only the central one is intact. Several Sukhothai- and Ayutthaya-style chedis are within the compound. ✉ *Na Phra Karn Rd.* *B30* ⏲ *Daily 6–6.*

Past Wat Phra Si Rattana Mahathat is **Phra Narai Ratchaniwet.** The palace's well-preserved buildings, completed between 1665 and 1677, have been converted into museums. Surrounding the buildings are castellated walls and triumphal archways grand enough to admit an entourage mounted on elephants. The most elaborate structure is the Dusit Mahaprasat Hall, built by King Narai to receive foreign ambassadors. The roof is gone, but you can spot the mixture of architectural styles: the square doors are Thai and the domed arches are Western. North of Phra Narai Ratchaniwet is the restored Wat Sao Thong Thong. ✉ *Ratchadamneon Rd.* *B30* ⏲ *Daily 8:30–4:30.*

North of Wat Sao Thong Thong is **Vichayen House,** built for French King Louis XIV's personal representative, De Chaumont. The house was later occupied by King Narai's infamous Greek minister, Constantine Phaulkon, whose political schemes eventually caused the ouster of all Westerners from Thailand. When King Narai was dying in 1668, his army commander, Phra Phetracha, seized power and beheaded Phaulkon. ✉ *Vichayen Rd.* ⏲ *Wed.–Sun. 9–noon and 1–4.*

East on Vichayen Road is a Khmer shrine called **Phra Prang Sam Yot,** Lopburi's most famous landmark. The three prangs symbolize the sacred triad of Brahma, Vishnu, and Shiva. King Narai converted the shrine into a Buddhist temple, and a stucco image of the Buddha sits serenely before the central prang. The most memorable aspect of the monument is its hundreds of resident monkeys, including mothers and nursing babies, wizened old males, and aggressive youngsters. ⚠ **Hold tight to your possessions, as the monkeys love to steal anything that looks vulnerable, from a map of the city to your digital camera.** But most tourists wind up having a blast with the monkeys. Approach them and stand still for a minute, and you'll soon have monkeys all over your head, shoulders, and just about everywhere else—a perfect photo-op. ✉ *Vichayen Rd.*

WHERE TO EAT

$ ★ THAI ✕ **Bualuang Restaurant.** This is the sort of local restaurant that you shouldn't miss on your travels, a place for trying true regional specialties, including spicy salted soft-shell crab, charcoal-grilled or steamed blue crabs, mussels in a hot pot, and charcoal-grilled cottonfish and snakehead fish. There are also multicourse Chinese-style set meals for six or more people. ✉ *46/1 Moo 3, T. Tasala, A. Muang* ☎ *036/614227* *up to 30* 💳 *V.*

$ THAI ✕ **White House.** A popular haunt for travelers, the White House offers a standard range of Thai and seafood dishes, including a good crab in yellow curry, with an easy-to-use English-language menu. The location is prime, right next to the night market, and the second-floor terrace is both lively and romantic, as is the tree-shaded garden below. The owner, Mr. Piak, is a good source of information on the area. Make sure to flip through his guest book. ✉ *18 Phraya Kumjud Rd.* ☎ *036/413085* 💳 *MC, V.*

WHERE TO STAY

¢ **Lopburi Inn Hotel.** This hotel has achieved a certain amount of fame by hosting the annual banquet for the town's resident monkeys each November. It is, however, awkwardly located between the old and new cities and dated rooms and cluttered corridors mean that it's not necessarily worth it. The dining room serves Thai and Chinese food; a buffet breakfast is included in the rates. **Pros:** in-room Wi-Fi; close to public pool and tennis courts. **Cons:** inconvenient location; dated room decor. ✉ *28/9 Narai Maharat Rd.* ☎ *036/412300* 🌐 *www.lopburiinnhotel.com* *130 rooms* *In-room: Wi-Fi. In-hotel: restaurant, room service, bar, laundry service, Internet terminal, no-smoking rooms* 💳 *AE, MC, V.*

$ **Lopburi Inn Resort.** This monkey-theme retreat is the best value in Lopburi, with stylish rooms decorated in a modern Thai style, a good range of facilities including a pleasant pool, and a generous buffet breakfast. The only drawback is its distance from the Old City and main sights—10 km (6 mi)—but samlors to the sights are easy enough to arrange. Note that the hotel, like many properties, charges foreigners B250 (about $7) more per night than Thais. **Pros:** pool; Wi-Fi; gym. **Cons:** far from main sights. ✉ *17/1–2 Ratchadamnoen Rd.,*

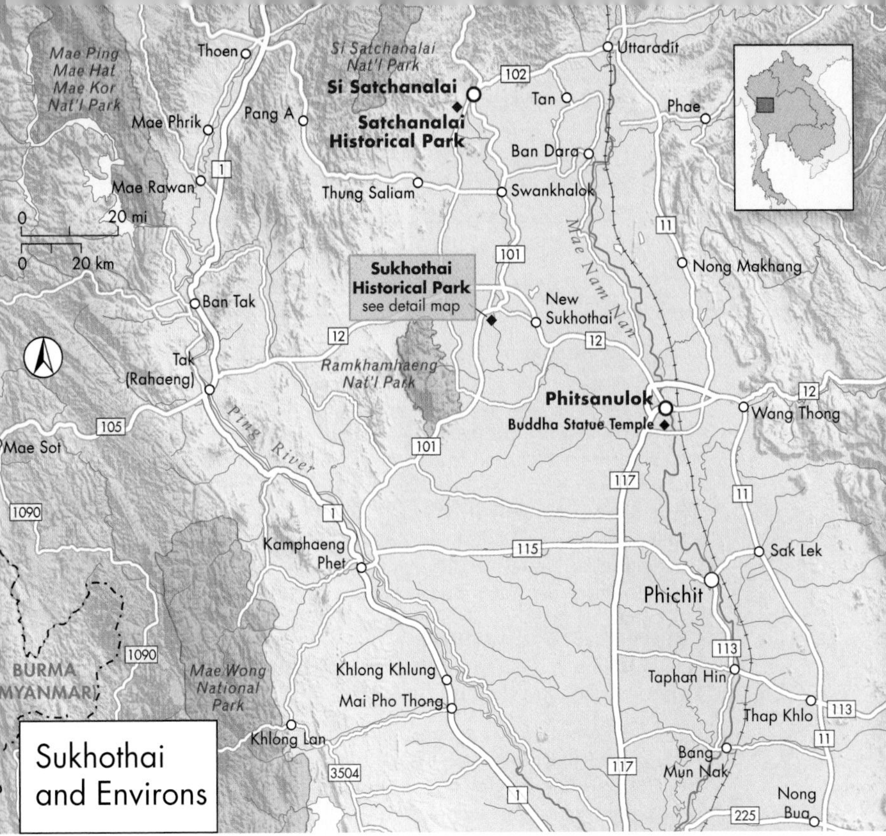

☏036/614790, 036/420777, or 036/421453 🌐*www.lopburiinnresort.com* ⇆*100 rooms* ⛉*In-hotel: restaurant, room service, bars, pool, gym, no-smoking rooms* ▭*AE, MC, V.*

SUKHOTHAI & ENVIRONS

In the valley of the Yom River, protected by a rugged mountain range in the north and rich forest mountains in the south, lies Sukhothai. Here, laterite (red porous soil that hardens when exposed to air) ruins signify the birthplace of the Thai nation and its emergence as a center for Theravada Buddhism.

North of Sukhothai is its sister city of Si Satchanalai, which is quieter and more laid-back, but no less interesting—its historical park has the remains of more than 200 temples and monuments.

Before you reach Sukhothai and Si Satchanalai, you'll come across Phitsanulok, which in many ways makes the best base for exploring the area. Despite its historical relevance as Sukhothai's capital for 25 years, the birthplace of King Narai the Great, and residence of the Ayutthayan Crown Princes, Phitsanulok has grown away from its roots. This onetime military stronghold has stamped over its past, with only a few reminders, like Wat Phra Si Rattana Mahathat and the revered

Buddha Chinnarat image. Phitsanulok now serves as a center for commerce, transportation, and communication. In addition, its blend of entertainment and access to outward-bound excursions make it an enjoyable diversion.

PHITSANULOK

377 km (234 mi) north of Bangkok, 60 km (37 mi) southeast of Sukhothai.

For a brief span in the 14th century, after the decline of Sukhothai and before the rise of Ayutthaya, Phitsanulok was the kingdom's capital. Farther back in history, Phitsanulok was a Khmer outpost called Song Kwae—today only an ancient monastery remains of that incarnation. The new city, which had to relocate 5 km (3 mi) from the old site, is a modern provincial administrative seat with few architectural blessings. There are outstanding attractions, however, such as the Phra Buddha Chinnarat inside Wat Phra Si Rattana Mahathat. And make sure to walk along the Nan River, lined with tempting food stalls in the evening. On the far side are many houseboats, which are popular among Thais.

GETTING HERE & AROUND

BY AIR Thai Airways has daily flights from Bangkok and Chiang Mai. The airport is just 1 km (½ mi) from town.

BY BUS Buses to Phitsanulok regularly leave Bangkok's Northern Terminal. Fares on a 44-seat air-conditioned bus start at B259 for the six-hour trip. Phitsanulok's main bus terminal, on Highway 12, is the stop before Sukhothai, shaving 1½ hours off the journey and around B40 off the ticket price. The terminal also has buses for travel to and from Chiang Mai via Lampang or via Phrae and Phayao, and to Khon Kaen via Lomsak. The terminal is located downtown, just 1 km (½ mi) from Wat Phra Si Mahatat (known locally as Wat Yai).

Between Phitsanulok and Sukhothai there are regular, non-air-conditioned buses for pennies, which depart roughly every hour; the trip takes about 1½ hours.

BY CAR A car is a good way to get around the region. Highway 12 from Sukhothai is a long, straight, and reasonably comfortable 59-km (37-mi), one-hour drive. To get to the Phitsanulok from Bangkok, take the four-lane Highway 117; the drive from Bangkok takes about 4½ hours. Both Avis and Budget have desks at the Phitsanulok airport. Costs for renting economy cars up to SUVs range from B1,500 to B3,500 per day without drivers; count on an additional B1,000 a day for a car and driver. Make sure to request an English-speaking driver. Bigger hotels in Phitsanulok offer chauffeur services at similar prices, but are more tour-oriented and generally offer no more than a one-day trip.

BY SAMLOR There's a cheap, cramped, tin-can bus service within Phitsanulok, but unless ovens are your thing, you're best off using the motorized samlors or the more eco-friendly pedal-powered ones.

ESSENTIALS

Bus Contacts **Bus station** (✉ *Mittaparp Rd.* ☎ *055/242430 or 055/242030*).

Emergencies **Phitsanuwej Hospital** (✉ *Khun Piren Rd.* ☎ *055/21994*). **Police** (☎ *055/258777*).

EXPLORING PHITSANULOK

With modern conveniences, Phitsanulok is an ideal base for exploring the region. Most of the sights in Phitsanulok are within walking distance, but samlors are easily available. Bargain hard—most trips should be about B20. Taxis are available for longer trips; you can find a few loitering around the train station.

4

Naresuan Road runs from the railway station to the Nan River. North of this street you can find **Wat Phra Si Rattana Mahathat,** a temple commonly known as Wat Yai. Built in the mid-14th century, Wat Yai has developed into a large monastery with typical ornamentation. Particularly noteworthy are the viharn's wooden doors, inlaid with mother-of-pearl in 1756 at the behest of King Boromkot. Behind the viharn is a 100-foot prang with a vault containing Buddha relics. The many religious souvenir stands make it hard to gain a good view of the complex, but the bot is a fine example of the traditional three-tier roof with low sweeping eaves, designed to diminish the size of the walls, accentuate the nave, and emphasize the image of the Buddha.

Within the viharn is what many consider the world's most beautiful image of the Buddha, Phra Buddha Chinnarat. It was probably cast in the 14th century, during the late Sukhothai period. Its mesmerizing beauty and the mystical powers ascribed to it draw streams of pilgrims—among the most notable of them was the Sukhothai's King Eka Thossarot, who journeyed here in 1631. According to folklore, the king applied with his own hands the gold leaf that covers the Buddha. Many copies of the image have been made, with the best known residing in Bangkok's Marble Temple. ✉ *Off Ekethosarot Rd.* ⏲ *Daily 8–6.*

★ Phitsanulok also has a little-known museum, **Pim Buranaket Folkcraft Museum,** that alone would justify a visit to the city. In the early 1980s, Sergeant-Major Khun Thawee traveled to small villages, collecting traditional tools, cooking utensils, animal traps, and handicrafts that were rapidly disappearing, and crammed them into a traditional house and barn. For a decade nothing was properly documented; visitors stumbled around tiger traps and cooking pots, with little to help them decipher what they were looking at. But Khun Thawee's daughter came to the rescue and now the marvelous artifacts are systematically laid out. You can now understand the use of everything on display, from the simple wood pipes hunters played to lure their prey, to elaborately complex rat guillotines. The museum is a 15-minute walk south of the railway station, on the east side of the tracks. ✉ *Wisut Kasat Rd.* *B50* ⏲ *Tues.–Sun. 8:30–4:30.*

WHERE TO EAT

Phitsanulok has a good range of dining options, from its popular pontoon and riverside restaurants to some great little daytime canteen-style restaurants near the central clock tower on Phayalithai Road.

The Muslim restaurants on Pra Ong Dam Road, opposite the town's mosque, are great for curry and roti breakfasts. The night bazaar promenade banking the Nan River contains some basic early-evening places to enjoy the sunset, including the infamous "flying vegetable restaurant," where you can have the province's famed *pak bung fire dang* (stir-fried morning glory). And the veggies do fly here—when the cooks fling the morning glory to waiters, who deftly catch the food on their plates. Akathodsarod Road near Topland Hotel is a good bet for late-night noodles.

$$–$$$$ SEAFOOD **Boo Bpen Seafood.** Although not on the river, this upbeat seafood restaurant has the edge on the competition because of its spacious bench seating and garden atmosphere. Live bands play on a small central stage. House specialties include *gai khua kem* (roasted chicken with salt) and *boo nim tort gratium* (crab fried in garlic) and are worth a nibble, but for something more substantial, the barbecue prawns are a must, sampled with the chili, lime, and fish sauce dip. ✉*Sanambin Rd.* ☎ *055/211110* ▭*No credit cards.*

$ SEAFOOD **Phraefahthai.** This floating teak Thai-style house on the Nan River is the more popular of the two pontoon eateries in Phitsanulok; it draws the majority of tourists, as well as local businessmen and their families. It's strikingly lighted up at night, impossible to miss from anywhere on the river. An extensive menu in English makes it the most comfortable riverside experience. The emphasis is on fresh seafood—the *pla taptim* (St. Peter's fish, a delicious freshwater fish) is particularly recommended, served steamed with a spicy lemon-and-lime sauce. ✉*100/49 Phutabucha Rd.* ☎*055/242743* ▭*AE, DC, MC, V.*

WHERE TO STAY

$ **Grand Riverside Hotel.** The new kid on the block is a fine-looking hotel. The foyer is grand, with a spiral staircase leading to well-appointed rooms. It's a great base for Phitsanulok and is within walking distance of restaurants, bars, and the city's main temple. **Pros:** free Wi-Fi in lobby; plentiful free parking. **Cons:** no Wi-Fi in rooms. ✉*59 Praroung Rd.,* ☎*055/248333* *81 rooms* *In-room: safe, refrigerator. In-hotel: restaurant, room service, bar, Wi-Fi, laundry service, parking (free), no-smoking rooms* ▭*MC, V.*

¢–$ **La Paloma.** This vast complex is Phitsanulok's best value high-end option. Rooms are clean and comfortable, with soft floral upholstery against classic dark-wood stain. A good selection of English-language TV channels help make it a comfy retreat. The location, however, isn't the best, with the center of the city a brisk 20-minute walk away and few independent dining or drinking options nearby. **Pros:** clean and comfortable rooms. **Cons:** far from city center. ✉*103 Srithumtripdork Rd.* ☎*055/217930* *239 rooms, 10 suites* *In-room: refrigerator. In-hotel: restaurant, pool, laundry service, Internet terminal, Wi-Fi, no-smoking rooms* ▭*MC, V.*

$ **Pailyn Hotel.** The rooms at this white high-rise are quite large, with picture windows adding plenty of light—rooms on the higher floors have the best view of the river. The large lobby and coffee shop are busy in the morning as tour groups gather, and in the evening when the disco attracts the local teenagers. It's in downtown Phitsanulok, within walking distance of most city attractions. **Pros:** convenient location. **Cons:** no Wi-Fi in rooms. ✉ *38 Boromatrailokart Rd.,* ☎ *055/252411, 02/215–7110 in Bangkok* *125 rooms* *In-room: refrigerator. In-hotel: 2 restaurants, room service, bar, Internet terminal, laundry service, no-smoking rooms* *MC, V.*

$ **Phitsanulok Thani Hotel.** This fresh-faced hotel has a friendly staff and a nicely designed foyer based around a small fountain leads to less attractive, though comfortable, rooms. Although away from the town center, the area around the hotel has plenty of good restaurants and pubs to choose from. Local transport to other areas of the city is easy to find. **Pros:** friendly staff; close to airport. **Cons:** far from town. ✉ *39 Sanambin Rd.,* ☎ *055/211065 up to 69, 055/212631 up to 34* *www.phitsanulokthani.com* *110 rooms* *In-room: refrigerator, Wi-Fi. In-hotel: restaurant, bar, spa, laundry service, no-smoking rooms* *MC, V.*

4

SUKHOTHAI

★ *56 km (35 mi) northwest of Phitsanulok, 427 km (265 mi) north of Bangkok; 1 hr by bus from Phitsanulok.*

Sukhothai, which means "the dawn of happiness," holds a unique place in Thailand's history. Until the 13th century most of Thailand consisted of many small vassal states under the thumb of the Khmer Empire based in Angkor Wat. But the Khmers had overextended their reach, allowing the princes of two Thai states to combine forces. In 1238 one of the two princes, Phor Khun Bang Klang Thao, marched on Sukhothai, defeating the Khmer garrison commander in an elephant duel. Installed as the new king of the region, he took the name Sri Indraditya and founded a dynasty that ruled Sukhothai for nearly 150 years. His youngest son became the third king of Sukhothai, Ramkhamhaeng, who ruled from 1279 to 1299. Through military and diplomatic victories he expanded the kingdom to include most of present-day Thailand and the Malay Peninsula.

By the mid-14th century Sukhothai's power and influence had waned, and Ayutthaya, once its vassal state, became the capital of the Thai kingdom. Sukhothai was gradually abandoned to the jungle, and a new town grew up about 14 km (9 mi) away. In 1978 a 10-year restoration project costing more than $10 million created the Sukhothai Historical Park. The vast park (70 square km [27 square mi]) has 193 historic monuments. Sukhothai is the busiest during the Loi Krathong festival, which is celebrated in the historical park each year on the full moon in November. Its well-orchestrated, three-day light-and-sound show is the highlight. At this time the town's hotels and guesthouses are booked weeks in advance.

New Sukhothai, where all intercity buses arrive, is a quiet town where most inhabitants are in bed by 11 PM. Its many guesthouses are a magnet for tourists coming to see the ruins, and as such, you'll see quite a few *farang* (foreigners), especially young British, German, and American couples, wandering around amid the locals, drinking at the bars or browsing the sidewalk food stalls. New Sukhothai's night market is sleepy by the standards of the region, and in short, you can't expect much of an urban cultural experience here.

GETTING HERE & AROUND

BY AIR Thai Airways flies daily from Chiang Mai to Sukhothai. There are several Thai Airways flights daily from Bangkok to Sukhothai. Sukhothai is roughly equidistant between its own airport (a beautiful open-air terminal) and the one in Phitsanulok, which is less than an hour away by taxi or bus. Bangkok Airways also serves Sukhothai. Two flights go between Bangkok and Sukhothai daily (1 hour 20 minutes), with fares starting at about B2,000.

BY BUS Buses to Sukhothai depart from Bangkok's Northern Bus Terminal (Mo Chit) daily from 7 AM to 11 PM, leaving roughly every 20 minutes. There are five main companies to choose from but all charge about the same, most with prices under B300. The journey takes about seven hours. Buses from Sukhothai's new bus terminal on the bypass road depart at the same times and for the same prices.

BY CAR Highway 12 from Phitsanulok leads to Sukhothai and is a long, straight, and reasonably comfortable 59-km (37-mi), one-hour drive. Car rentals are available at Sukhothai airport. The drive from Bangkok, along the four-lane Highway 117, is about 440 km (273 mi), or roughly seven hours.

BY SAMLOR & SONGTHAEW Sukhothai does not have local buses, and most of the population gets around in souped-up samlors or songthaews.

ESSENTIALS

Emergencies **Police** (☎*055/613611*). **Sukhothai Hospital** (✉*Jarodvithithong Rd., Sukhothai* ☎*055/611782*).

Visitor & Tour Info **Dhanasith ("Tom") Kampempool** (✉*49 Moo 3, Jarodvithithong Rd., next to Vitoon Guesthouse, Sukhothai* ☎*055/697045 or 055/633397* ✉*vitooninn@yahoo.com*), a fluent English-speaking guide, offers custom tours.

EXPLORING SUKHOTHAI

Because the sights are so spread out, the best way to explore the park is by bicycle; you can rent one along the main street. You can also book a tour with a guide. Either way, bring a bottle of water with you—the day will get hotter than you think.

Depending on your means of transportation, a tour of the city could take a few hours or the better part of a day. It's best to come in the late afternoon to avoid the midday sun and enjoy the late evening's pink-and-orange hues. Crowds generally aren't a problem.

TOP ATTRACTIONS

1 **Ramkhamhaeng National Museum.** Most of the significant artifacts from Sukhothai are in Bangkok's National Museum, but this open, airy museum has more than enough fine pieces to demonstrate the gentle beauty of this period. You can learn how refinements in the use of bronze let artisans create the graceful walking Buddhas.

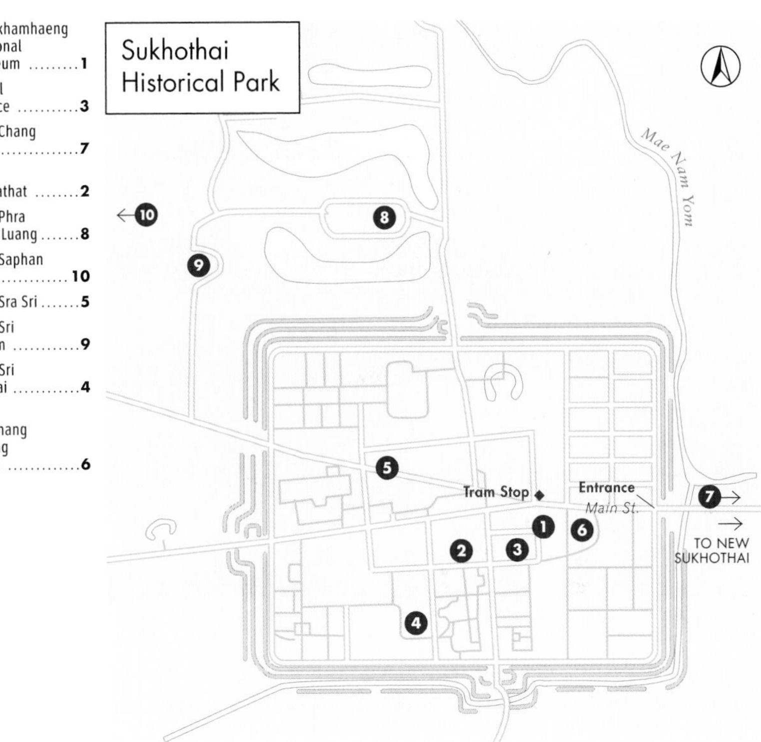

Jarodvithithong Rd., just before entrance to historical park B30 Daily 9–4.

2 **Wat Mahathat.** Sitting amid a tranquil lotus pond, Wat Mahathat is the largest and most beautiful monastery in Sukhothai. Enclosed in the compound are some 200 tightly packed chedis, each containing the funeral ashes of a nobleman. Towering above them is a large central chedi, notable for its bulbous, lotus-bud prang. Wrapping around the chedi is a frieze of 111 monks, their hands raised in adoration. Probably built by Sukhothai's first king, Wat Mahathat owes its present form to King Lö Thai, who in 1345 erected the lotus-bud chedi to house two important relics brought back from Sri Lanka by the monk Sisatta. This Sri Lankan–style chedi became the symbol of Sukhothai and classical Sukhothai style. Copies of it were made in the principal cities of its vassal states, signifying a magic circle emanating from Sukhothai, the spiritual and temporal center of the empire. *In the Old City B40 for all sights inside the Old City walls Daily 8:30–4:30.*

9 **Wat Sri Chum.** Like many other sanctuaries, Wat Si Chum was originally surrounded by a moat. The main structure is dominated by a breathtaking statue of the Buddha in a seated position. The huge but elegant stucco image is one of the largest in Thailand, measuring 37 feet from

Sukhothai declined in power in the 15th century but its temples and palaces were left intact.

knee to knee. Enter the mondop through the passage inside the left inner wall. Keep your eyes on the ceiling: more than 50 engraved slabs illustrate scenes from the *Jataka,* which are stories about the previous lives of Lord Buddha. The monument is open all the time, but you'll have to pay B30 if you visit before 4 PM. ✉*East of Old City walls* 🎫*B30, free after 4* PM.

ALSO WORTH SEEING

❸ **Royal Palace.** Thais imagine Sukhothai's government as a monarchy that served the people, stressing social needs and justice. Slavery was abolished, and people were free to believe in their local religions, Hinduism and Buddhism (often simultaneously), and to pursue their trade without hindrance. In the 19th century a famous stone inscription of King Ramkhamhaeng was found among the ruins of the palace across from Wat Mahathat. Sometimes referred to as Thailand's Declaration of Independence, the inscription's best-known quote reads: "This city Sukhothai is good. In the water there are fish, in the field there is rice. The ruler does not levy tax on the people who travel along the road together, leading their oxen on the way to trade and riding their horses on the way to sell. Whoever wants to trade in elephants, so trades. Whoever wants to trade in horses, so trades." ✉*In the Old City* 🎫*B40 for all sights inside the Old City walls* ⏲*Daily 8–4:30.*

❼ **Wat Chang Lom.** South of the park off Chotwithithong Road is one of Sukhothai's oldest monasteries. Its bell-shaped pagoda, thought to have been built in the latter part of the 14th century, is of Sri Lankan influence and is perched on a three-tiered square base atop damaged elephant buttresses. In front of the chedi are a viharn and solitary pillars; the remains of nine other chedis have been found within this complex. ✉ *Chotwithithong Rd., about 4 km (2½ mi) before entrance to historical park, reached by turning north down a small lane over a smaller bridge.*

10 **Wat Saphan Hin.** This pretty wat is reached by following a slate pathway and climbing a 656-foot hill. It's famous for its standing Buddha, an imposing sculpture whose hand is about as tall as you. ✉ *North of Old City walls* 🎟 *Free.*

8 **Wat Phra Phai Luang.** This former Khmer structure, once a Hindu shrine, was converted to a Buddhist temple. Surrounded by a moat, the sanctuary is encircled by three laterite prangs, similar to those at Wat Sri Sawai—the only one that remains intact is decorated with stucco figures. In front of the prangs are the remains of the viharn and a crumbling chedi with a seated Buddha on its pedestal. Facing these structures is the *mondop,* a square structure with a stepped pyramid roof, built to house religious relics. ✉ *North of Old City walls on Donko Rd., opposite Tourist Information Center* 🎟 *B30* ⏲ *Daily 8:30–4:30.*

5 **Wat Sra Sri.** This peaceful temple sits on two connected islands within a lotus-filled lake. The lake, called Traphong Trakuan Pond, supplied the monks with water and served as a boundary for the sacred area. A Sri Lankan–style chedi dominates six smaller chedis, and a large, stucco, seated Buddha looks down a row of columns, past the chedis, and over the lake to the horizon.

Especially wondrous is the walking Buddha beside the Sri Lankan–style chedi. The walking Buddha is a Sukhothai innovation and the most ethereal of Thailand's artistic styles. The depiction of the Buddha is often a reflection of political authority and is modeled after the ruler. Under the Khmers, authority was hierarchical, but the kings of Sukhothai represented the ideals of serenity, happiness, and justice. The walking Buddha is the epitome of Sukhothai's art; he appears to be floating on air, neither rooted on Earth nor placed on a pedestal above the reach of the common people. ✉ *In the Old City* 🎟 *B40 for all sights inside the Old City walls* ⏲ *Daily 8:30–4:30.*

4 **Wat Sri Sawai.** Sukhothai's oldest structure may be this Khmer-style one, which has three prangs—similar to those found in Lopburi—surrounded by a laterite wall. The many stucco Hindu images and scenes suggest that Sri Sawai was probably first a Hindu temple, later converted to a Buddhist monastery. ✉ *In the Old City* 🎟 *B40 for all sights inside the Old City walls* ⏲ *Daily 8:30–4:30.*

6 **Wat Traphang Thong Lang.** The square mondop of Wat Traphang Thong Lang is the main sanctuary, the outer walls of which boast beautiful stucco figures in niches—some of Sukhothai's finest art. The north side depicts the Buddha returning to preach to his wife. On the west side he preaches to his father and relatives. Note the figures on the south wall, where the story of the Buddha is accompanied by an angel descending from Heaven. ✉ *Just north of Old City walls* 🎟 *B30* ⏲ *Daily 8:30–4:30.*

Continued on page 198

THE BUDDHA IN THAILAND

Buddhism plays a profound role in day-to-day Thai life. Statues of the Buddha are everywhere: in the country's 30,000 *wats* (temples), in sacred forest caves, in home shrines, and in cafés and bars. Each statue is regarded as a direct link to the Buddha himself and imparts its own message—if you know what to look for.

by Howard Richardson

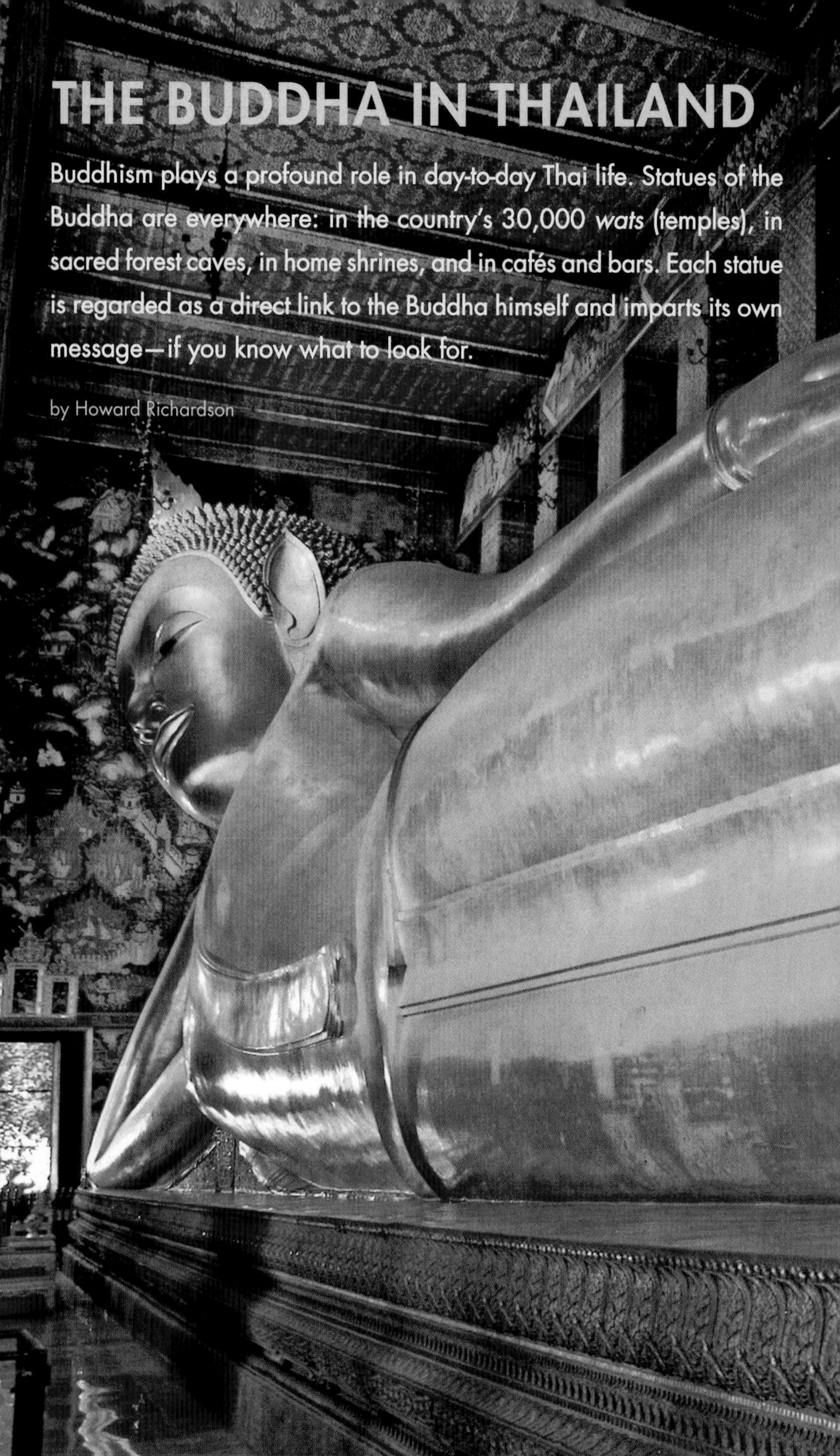

The origins of Buddhism lie in the life of the Indian prince Siddhartha Gautama (563 BC – 483 BC), who became the Buddha (which simply means "awakened"). Statues of the Buddha follow ancient aesthetic rules. The Buddha must be wearing a monastic robe, either covering both shoulders or leaving the right shoulder bare. His body must display sacred marks, or *laksanas,* such as slender toes and fingers, a full, lion-like chest, and long eyelashes. Many statues also have elongated earlobes, a reminder of the Buddha's original life as a prince, when he wore heavy earrings. Buddha statues are in one of four positions: sitting, standing, walking, or reclining.

Statues of the Buddha have their hands arranged in a *mudra* or hand position. The mudras, which represent the Buddha's teachings or incidents in his life, were created by his disciples, who used them to enhance their meditation. There are about 100 mudras, but most are variations on six basic forms.

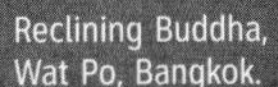

Reclining Buddha, Wat Po, Bangkok.

Detail of Reclining Buddha's head.

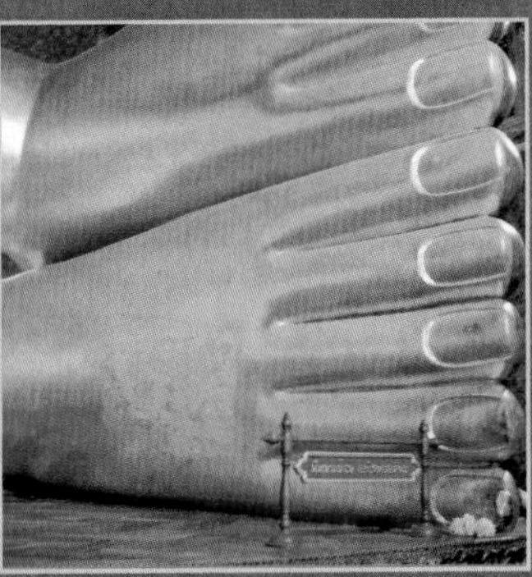

Detail of top of Reclining Buddha's feet.

Detail of bottom of Reclining Buddha's foot.

WHAT THE BUDDHA TAUGHT

Gautama taught that there are three aspects to existence: *dukkha* (suffering), *anicca* (impermanence), and *anatta* (the absence of self). He believed that unfulfilled desire for status, self-worth, and material possessions creates dukkha, but that such desire is pointless because anicca dictates that everything is impermanent and cannot be possessed. Therefore, if we can learn to curb desire and cultivate detachment, we will cease to be unhappy.

The ultimate goal of Buddhism is to reach enlightenment or nirvana, which is basically the cessation of struggle—this happens when you have successfully let go of all desire (and by definition, all suffering). This signals the end to *samsara*, the cycle of reincarnation that Buddhists believe in. Buddhists also believe in karma, a law of cause and effect that suggests that your fate in this life and future lives is determined by your actions. Among the ways to improve your karma—and move toward nirvana—are devoting yourself to spirituality by becoming a monk or a nun, meditating, and *tham boon*, or merit making. Making offerings to the Buddha is one form of tham boon.

Thai painting of monks listening to the Buddha speak at a temple.

THE MIDDLE WAY

Gautama's prescription for ending dukkha is an attitude of moderation towards the material world based on wisdom, morality, and concentration. He broke this threefold approach down further into eight principles, called the Noble Eightfold Path or the Middle Way.

Wisdom:

Right Understanding: to understand dukkha and its causes.

Right Thought: to resist angry or unkind thoughts and acts.

Morality:

Right Speech: to avoid lying, speaking unkindly, or engaging in idle chatter.

Right Action: to refrain from harming or killing others, stealing, and engaging in sexual misconduct.

Right Livelihood: to earn a living peacefully and honestly.

Concentration:

Right Effort: to work towards discipline and kindness, abandoning old, counterproductive habits.

Right Mindfulness: to be aware of your thoughts, words, and actions; to see things as they really are.

Right Concentration: to focus on wholesome thoughts and actions (often while meditating.)

DID YOU KNOW?

Burmese invaders damaged many Buddha statues when they sacked Ayutthaya in 1767. The head of one statue became lodged in the roots of a tree at Wat Phra Mahathat, where it remains today.

THE BUDDHA'S POSITIONS

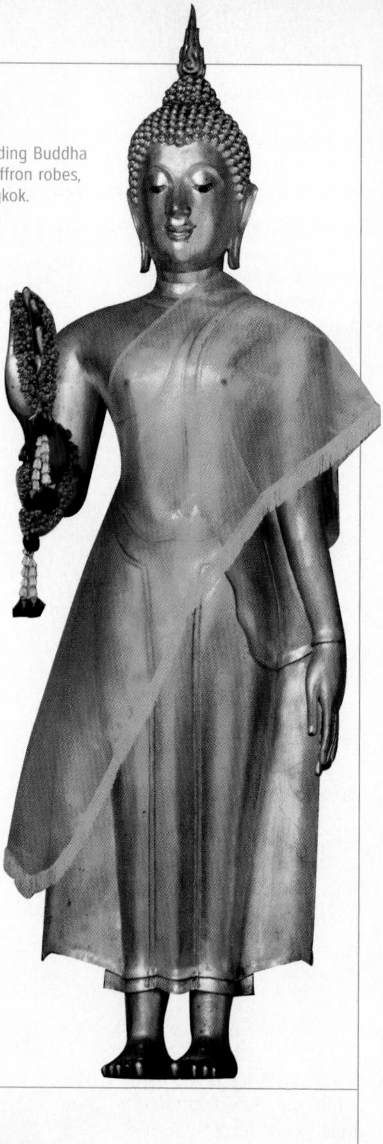

Standing Buddha in saffron robes, Bangkok.

STANDING

The Buddha stands either with his feet together or with one slightly in front of the other. The standing posture is often accompanied by certain hand positions to signify driving away fear or appealing to reason.

⇨ Wat Phra Mahathat, Sukhothai, Ch. 4; Wat Benjamabophit, Bangkok, Ch. 2.

RECLINING

Many scholars believe that reclining sculptures depict the Buddha dying and simultaneously reaching nirvana. According to another story, the Buddha is showing a proud giant who has refused to bow to him that he can lie down and still make himself appear larger than the giant. The Buddha then took the giant to the heavens and showed him angels that made the Buddha himself appear small, teaching the giant that there are truths beyond the realm of our own experience.

⇨ Wat Po, Bangkok, Ch. 2.

Reclining Buddha ornament.

SITTING

Seated Buddhas are the most common. The Buddha can sit in three different postures: adamantine or lotus, with legs crossed and feet resting on opposite thighs; heroic, a half-lotus position with one leg folded over the other; or western, with legs hanging straight down, as if sitting in a chair.

⇨ Wat Suthat, Bangkok (heroic style), Ch. 2.

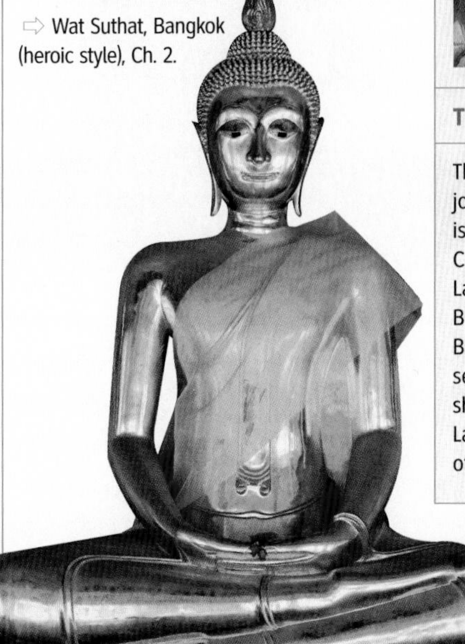

Seated Buddha, Wat Suthat, Bangkok.

THE LAUGHING BUDDHA

The Laughing Buddha, whose large belly and jolly demeanor make him easy to recognize, is a folkloric character based on a 9th century Chinese monk known for his kindness. The Laughing Buddha does not figure into Thai Buddhism but you may see him at temples in Bangkok's Chinatown. And because he represents good fortune and abundance, some Thai shops sell Laughing Buddhas as lucky charms. Laughing Buddha statues often carry sacks full of sweets to give to children.

WALKING

Walking statues represent the Buddha going into the community to spread his teachings. Traditionally, walking Buddhas were constructed in relief. The first walking-Buddha statues were created in Sukhothai, and you can still see a few in the city's ruins.

⇨ Wat Sra Sri, Sukhothai and Wat Phra Phai Luang, Sukhothai, Ch. 4.

Walking Buddhas, Wat Phra Mahathat, Sukhothai.

WHAT DO THE BUDDHA'S HANDS MEAN?

SETTING THE WHEEL IN MOTION

In this mudra, the Buddha's thumbs and forefingers join to make a circle, representing the Wheel of Dharma, a symbol for Buddhist law.

⇨ Cloisters of Wat Benjamabophit, Bangkok, Ch. 2; Phra Pathom Chedi, Nakhon Pathom, Ch. 3.

MEDITATION

The Buddha's hands are in his lap, palms pointing upwards. This position represents a disciplined mind.

⇨ National Museum, Bangkok, Ch. 2; Phra Pathom Chedi, Nakhon Pathom, Ch. 3.

REASONING

This posture, which signifies the Buddha's preference for reason and peace rather than hasty or thoughtless action, is similar to the absence of fear mudra, but the Buddha's thumb and forefinger are touching to form a circle.

⇨ Cloisters of Wat Benjamabophit, Bangkok, Ch. 2; Sukhothai Historical Park, Ch. 4.

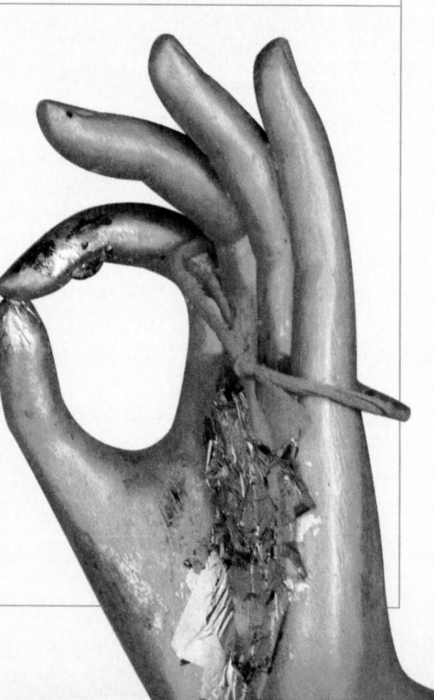

SUBDUING MARA

Mara is a demon who tempted the Buddha with visions of beautiful women. In this posture, the Buddha is renouncing these worldly desires. He sits with his right hand is on his right thigh, fingers pointing down, and his left hand palm-up in his lap.

⇨ Wat Suthat, Bangkok, Ch. 2; Wat Mahathat, Sukhothai, Ch. 4; Phra Pathom Chedi, Nakhon Pathom, Ch. 3.

Hand and alms bowl detail; Nakhon Pathom Chedi, Nakon Pathom.

CHARITY

Buddhas using this mudra are usually standing, with their right arm pointing down, palm facing out, to give or receive offerings. In some modern variations, the Buddha is actually holding an alms bowl.

⇨ National Museum, Bangkok, Ch. 2.

ABSENCE OF FEAR

One or both of the Buddha's arms are bent at the elbow, palms facing out and fingers pointing up (like the international gesture for "Stop!") In this attitude the Buddha is either displaying his own fearlessness or encouraging his followers to be courageous.

⇨ Cloisters of Wat Benjamabophit, Bangkok Ch. 2.

WHERE TO EAT

Some of the best food in town can be found at the local food stalls that line the main street before and after the bridge. If you're in the mood for something sweet, look for the stand selling delicious Thai crepes filled with condensed milk, right at the bridge on the city-center side. But it's hard to go wrong almost anywhere in or near the night market or along that street.

THE TRACES OF A NATION

The optimism that accompanied the birth of the nation at Sukhothai is reflected in the art and architecture of the period. Strongly influenced by Sri Lankan Buddhism, the monuments left behind by the architects, artisans, and craftsmen of those innovative times had a light, often playful touch. Statues of the Buddha show him as smiling, serene, and confidently walking toward a better future. Note the impossibly graceful elephants portrayed in supporting pillars.

$ THAI **Dream Café.** While waiting for your meal, feast your eyes on the extraordinary collection of antiques that fill this charming restaurant, which is in its third decade of existence. The rustic tile floor, the glowing teak tables and chairs, and the nooks and crannies packed with fascinating odds and ends—everything from old lamps to fine ceramics—combine in a perfect harmony to endow the Dream Café with a superlative atmosphere. The modified Thai food is not quite up to snuff, however; be sure to tell your waiter you want things spicy, not farang-style, and even then, don't expect much. Behind the restaurant are four rustic but romantic rooms ($), aptly named Cocoon House, set in a fairy-tale garden. *86/1 Singhawat Rd. 055/612081 sinwatmaykin@yahoo.com MC, V.*

WHERE TO STAY

$$–$$$ Fodor's Choice ★ **Ananda Museum Gallery Hotel.** The Ananda has redefined the concept of luxury lodging in Sukhothai. As you might expect from a hotel that is also an art gallery, room design is informed by a deep sense of minimalism along with a healthy dose of feng shui. The hotel's open-air Celedon restaurant ($$), set in a lovely garden, is a relaxing place to dine. The hotel is 1 km (½ mi) from the city center and 15 minutes from the historical park. **Pros:** attractive hotel and restaurant. **Cons:** remote location. *Jarodvithithong Rd. 055/622428 up to 31 www.anandasukhothai.com 32 rooms, 2 suites In-room: safe, refrigerator. In-hotel: restaurant, room service, bar, gym, spa, Internet terminal, no-smoking rooms AE, MC, V.*

¢–$ **Lotus Village.** The lotus-flower ponds that dot the lush gardens of this attractive Thai-style lodging give the place its name. It's run by a charming French-Thai couple who are happy to help organize tours of Sukhothai and the surrounding area. The teak bungalows—some with fans, others with air-conditioning—are comfortably furnished and have private verandas. The inn is tucked away near the Yom River. It's best reached via Rajuthit Road, which runs along the river from the center of town. There's a breakfast room but no restaurant. **Pros:** helpful owners; lovely grounds. **Cons:** no restaurant; some bungalows lack a/c.

CLOSE UP

Loi Krathong

On the full moon of the 12th lunar month, when the tides are at their highest and the moon at its brightest, the Thais head to the country's waterways to celebrate Loi Krathong, one of Thailand's most anticipated and enchanting festivals.

Loi Krathong was influenced by Diwali, the Indian lantern festival that paid tribute to three Brahman gods. Thai farmers adapted the ceremony to offer tribute to Mae Khlong Kha, the goddess of the water, to thank her for blessing the land with water.

Ancient Sukhothai is where the festival's popular history began, with a story written by King Rama IV in 1863. The story concerns Naang Noppamart, the daughter of a Brahman priest who served in the court of King Li-Thai, grandson of King Ramkhamhaeng the Great. She was a woman of exceptional charm and beauty who soon became his queen. She secretly fashioned a krathong (a small float used as an offering), setting it alight by candle in accordance with her Brahmanist rites. The king, upon seeing this curious, glimmering offering embraced its beauty, adapting it for Theravada Buddhism and thus creating the festival of Loi Krathong.

Krathong were traditionally formed by simply cupping banana leaves and offerings such as dried rice and betel nut were placed at the center along with three incense sticks representing the Brahman gods. Today krathong are more commonly constructed by pinning folded banana leaves to a buoyant base made of a banana tree stem; they're decorated with scented flowers, orange candles (said to be representative of the Buddhist monkhood), and three incense sticks, whose meaning was changed under Li-Thai to represent the three forms of Buddhist existence.

Today, young Thai couples, "loi" their "krathong" to bind their love in an act almost like that of a marriage proposal, while others use the ceremony more as a way to purge any bad luck or resentments they may be harboring. Loi Krathong also commonly represents the pursuit of material gain, with silent wishes placed for a winning lottery number or two. The festival remains Thailand's most romantic vision of tradition, with millions of Thais sending their hopes floating down the nearest waterway.

Although it's celebrated nationwide, with events centered around cities such as Bangkok, Ayutthaya, Chiang Mai, and Tak, the festival's birthplace of Sukhothai remains the focal point. The historical park serves as a kind of Hollywood back lot, with hundreds of costumed students and light, sound, and pyrotechnic engineers, preparing for the fanfare of the annual show, which generally happens twice during the evening. With the historical park lighted and Wat Mahathat as its stage, the show reenacts the story of Sukhothai and the legend of Loi Krathong; then, governors, dignitaries, and other celebrity visitors (which recently included a former Miss USA who is idolized in Thailand) take part in a spectacular finale that includes sending off the krathong representing the king and queen, and fireworks.

–Warwick Dixon

✉170 Ratchathani Rd., ☎055/621484 ⊕www.lotus-village.com ⇨10 rooms ♿In-hotel: laundry service, Internet terminal, no-smoking rooms ▭No credit cards.

$ **Pailyn Hotel.** The staff is proud to point out that King Bhumibol Adulyadej has spent the night here. It's a vast building with a subtle contemporary Thai look, including a typical stepped roof. Rooms are large, comfortable, and reasonably decorated, though the highly varnished rattan bed frames and chairs look kind of tacky. The airy central atrium and the pool are a welcome sight after a day exploring the dusty ruins. It's halfway between New Sukhothai and the Old City, so transport can be a problem. **Pros:** attractive modern decor. **Cons:** inconvenient location. *✉10/2 Moo 1, Jarodvithithong Rd., ☎055/633336 up to 39, 02/215–5640 in Bangkok ⇨230 rooms ♿In-room: refrigerator, Wi-Fi. In-hotel: 2 restaurants, room service, bar, pool, no-smoking rooms ▭MC, V.*

¢ **Rajthanee Hotel.** The traditional Thai entrance of this well-run hotel leads into a modern building. There's a terrace where you can also enjoy a Thai whiskey and a stylish restaurant that serves good Asian cuisine. Comfortable rooms (standards and slightly larger deluxe rooms) are clean and practically furnished with a few trimmings such as woven headboards, which help soothe the eyes from the ever-present glare of lacquer. The swimming pool is proving a welcome addition to this hotel as is its karaoke bar that lights up like a lava lamp at night. **Pros:** reasonable prices. **Cons:** no credit cards. *✉229 Jarodvithithong Rd., ☎055/611031 or 055/611308 ⇨83 rooms ♿In-room: refrigerator. In-hotel: restaurant, pool, no-smoking rooms ▭No credit cards.*

NIGHTLIFE

Of the many bars and pubs that cater to tourists in Sukhothai, **Chopper Bar** (*✉96/1 Pawee Nakhon ☎055/611190*) is one of the best. It's on the main street, with open-air tables laid out amid twinkling lights; there's a fun garden in the back and a terrace in the front with rustic tables, shrines, greenery, flowing water, and live music. Skip the Western food.

SI SATCHANALAI

80 km (50 mi) north of Sukhothai.

Si Satchanalai, a sister city to Sukhothai, was governed by a son of Sukhothai's reigning monarch. Despite its secondary position, the city grew to impressive proportions, and no less than 200 of its temples and monuments survive, most of them in a ruined state but many well worth seeing.

GETTING HERE & AROUND

Most visitors to Si Satchanalai reach it as part of a tour from Sukhothai (most hotels can set you up with a guide). If you want to go on your own, hop on a bus bound for the town of Sawankhalok. The ride from Sukhothai takes 1½ hours and costs B36. Take a taxi to the historical park, asking the driver to wait while you visit the various temples. You can also tour the site by bicycle or on top of an elephant, if that's your choice of transportation.

SHOPPING

Because a relatively small number of travelers venture this way, fewer crafts are for sale here than elsewhere in the country. One notable exception is around Sukhothai and Si Satchanalai, where you can find reproductions of the pottery made here when this was the capital of the country.

EXPLORING SI SATCHANALAI

With its expanse of neatly mowed lawns, Sukhothai is sometimes criticized for being too well groomed. But Si Satchanalai, spread out on 228 acres on the banks of the Mae Yom River, remains a quiet place with a more ancient, undisturbed atmosphere. It isn't difficult to find the ruins of a temple where you won't be disturbed for hours. Accommodations near the park are only relatively expensive bungalows, so most visitors stay in Sukhothai.

Near the entrance, **Wat Chang Lom** shows strong Sri Lankan influences. The 39 elephant buttresses are in much better condition than at the similarly named temple in Sukhothai. The main chedi was completed by 1291. As you climb the stairs that run up the side, you can find seated images of the Buddha.

The second important monument, **Wat Chedi Jet Thaew,** is to the south of Wat Chang Lom. The complex has seven rows of ruined chedis, some with lotus-bud tops that are reminiscent of the larger ones at Sukhothai. The chedis contain the ashes of members of Si Satchanalai's ruling family.

Wat Nang Phya, to the southeast of Wat Chedi Jet Thaew, has well-preserved floral reliefs on its balustrade and stucco reliefs on the viharn wall.

As you leave the park, stop at **Wat Suam Utayan** to see a Si Satchanalai image of Lord Buddha, one of the few still remaining.

Sukhothai grew wealthy on the fine ceramics it produced from the rich earth around the neighboring town of Sawankhalok. The ceramics were so prized that they were offered as gifts from Sukhothai rulers to the imperial courts of China, and they found their way as far as Japan. Fine examples of 1,000-year-old Sawankhalok wares are on display at the **Sawankhalok Museum,** about 1 km (½ mi) from the town. ✉ *Phitsanulok Rd., Sawankhalok* 🎫 *B40* ⏲ *Weekdays 10–6, weekends 10–8.*

TAK PROVINCE: MAE SOT & ENVIRONS

Often overlooked, Tak Province is finally finding its feet as a destination, mainly because of the wonderful trekking opportunities on offer in the region, and the opportunity to cross the border into Myanmar. Most of the eco-trekking centers around Umphang's Thee Lor Su waterfall, but you can also raft and ride elephants, taking in Karen villages, caves, mountains, and waterfalls.

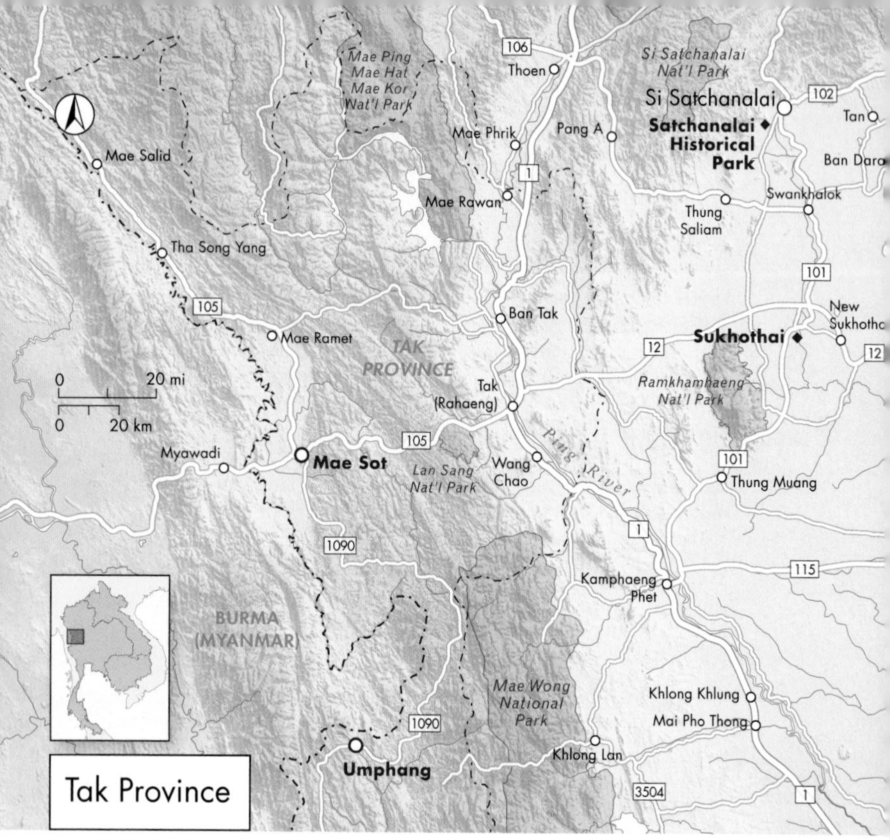

Famed for its teak forests, the province is home to an incredible number of plants and animals, including Thailand's last remaining wild cattle and the last 50 wild water buffalo. Umphang National Park and Thung Yai Naresuan Wildlife Sanctuary are two definite highlights in this, Thailand's largest forest region.

Although the provincial hub city of Tak has little of interest for travelers, it's an inevitable transit point coming from other provinces in the Central Plains. From here, you can head off to Mae Sot and Umphang, where you have the opportunity to sample some of the country's more diverse cultural mixes, and outstanding natural beauty.

Mae Sot borders Myanmar and is a cultural melting pot, with Karen and Burmese peoples creating a vibrant mix rarely seen elsewhere in Thailand. It's also the best place to base yourself, with a range of guesthouses and tour companies preparing you for further exploration of Umphang's natural riches.

Umphang is the key to this area's spectacular tourist attractions; the small, peaceful town is your launching pad for white-water rafting tours that take you through national parks and along gorges and ravines, passing hill tribe communities on your way to the Thee Lor Su waterfall.

MAE SOT

83 km (51 mi) west of Tak city, 506 km (312 mi) north of Bangkok.

At Mae Sot, which borders Myanmar to its west, you can find an interesting mix of local Thais, a dominant Burmese workforce, and the Karen refugees who live an ambiguous life in their 10,000-strong community, stuck between two worlds. It's definitely a frontier town, complete with black-market gems and timber smuggling, but it also provides the gateway for the natural sights of Tak Province.

GETTING HERE & AROUND

BY BIKE & MOTORBIKE This is a good way to see Mae Sot. Bai Fern Guesthouse (⇨*Car Contacts, below*) rents bicycles for B50 a day and 100cc motorbikes for B100 a day. A passport will be required as a deposit for motorbikes.

BY BUS Mae Sot only has bus service to and from Bangkok. Cherd Chai Travel has first-class air-conditioned buses that leave from the new bus station at the rotary at the terminus of Asia Road, just outside town, for the eight-hour journey to Bangkok (B350); the bus also stops outside the Siam Hotel in town. It also has smaller second-class air-conditioned buses departing at 5:40 PM (6 PM outside Siam Hotel) for B241. Tanjit Tour provides a luxury 38-seat VIP bus for B450 that leaves from the Northern Bus Terminal (Mo Chit) in Bangkok and arrives at Intarakeeree Road, 50 feet from the police station in Mae Sot.

Minibuses are the main link between Tak city and Mae Sot. For B56 they take you from the Tak bus terminal to the old bus station on Chidwana Road, downtown Mae Sot. Going both ways, minibuses depart every 30 minutes between 6:30 AM–6 PM; the journey takes 1½ hours.

BY CAR Bai Fern Guesthouse in Mae Sot rents pickup trucks for B1,200 per day.

BY SONGTHAEW This is the main form of travel in and around Mae Sot. Blue songthaews to Umphang can be found on Ratchaganratchadamri 2 Road, about ½ km (1/3 mi) from the Telecommunications Building. The long four-hour ride is around B100; songthaews leave every hour from 7:30 AM to 5:30 PM. Orange songthaews from the old bus station on Chidwana Road go to Mae Sariang, making stops in Mae Hong Son and Chiang Mai, but it's an arduous six-hour trip (though it is very cheap). They run from 6:30 AM to 5:30 PM.

If you're looking to get to the Thai/Myanmar border, jump on a songthaew at Prahsartwithee Road, 60 feet from the Siam Hotel. Hop on as they come along and expect to pay B30. For around B100 you can charter one privately.

ESSENTIALS

Bus Contacts **Cherd Chai Travel** (☎ *055/546856 or 09/708–9448*). **Tanjit Tour** (✉ *Intarakeeree Rd., 50 feet from the police station, Mae Sot* ☎ *055/531835*).

Car Contacts **Bai Fern** (✉ *660 Intarakeeree Rd., Mae Sot* ☎ *055/533343 or 09/858–4186*).

Emergencies **Police** (☎055/563937). **Mae Sot Hospital** (✉*175/16 Seepharnit Rd., Mae Sot* ☎*055/531229 or 055/531224*).

Visitor & Tour Info Both the No. 4 Guesthouse and Max One Tour have a wealth of local information, maps, and advice, and both specialize in trips along the Mae Sot to Kee District white-water rafting route, and to the Thee Lor Su waterfall. One-day or half-day tours around Mae Sot are also available and typically cost B1,500 for a full day or B350 for a half day. **Max One Tour** (✉*269/2 Intarakeeree Rd., Mae Sot* ☎*055/542941 or 055/542942* 🌐*www.maxonetour.com*). **No. 4 Guesthouse** (✉*736 Intarakeeree Rd., Mae Sot* ☎*055/544976 or 01/785–2095* 🌐*www.geocities.com/no4guesthouse*).

EXPLORING MAE SOT

Mae Sot is known for its ethnically diverse inhabitants, who include Chinese, Burmese, Karen, and Mon. It is also a base of operations for Burmese civil rights groups who are working to help refugees from across the border.

Wattanaram Monastery, a Tai Yai temple dating back to 1867, was built in Myanmar by a merchant from Tongchai. A typically Burmese wat, it's notable chiefly for its ornate gold-plate bronze Buddha image (Phra Phutta Maha Muni), which measures 6½ feet by 6½ feet and is encrusted with small precious stones, adding to its prestige. There's also a long 90-foot white concrete reclining Buddha behind the ordination hall. For men, there's an herbal sauna service available daily from 8 to 7. The temple is 3 km (2 mi) west of Mae Sot on Route 1085.

Aside from its miniature Mon-style pagoda—precariously mounted on a boulder and overhanging a 984-foot cliff—the forest temple of **Wat Phra That Hin Kew** is not really much to look at. There is, however, a fantastic view out over the Moei River and Myanmar's forested bank, which you'll feel you've earned after a good 20-minute hike up the complex's 413 stairs. It's about 11 km (7 mi) north of town; take the 1085 road heading north and follow the signs.

OFF THE BEATEN PATH

Wat Don Kaeo. In Ban Maetao, 33 km (20 mi) north of Mae Sot, Wat Don Kaeo houses one of only three white-marble Buddha images in the world. This beautifully crafted sculpture is approximately 50 inches wide and 60 inches tall and is an example some of Myanmar's finest craftsmanship. It was supposedly bought by a villager for 800 rupees and, via boat, horse cart, and mountain passes, was brought to this temple in 1922.

Fodor's Choice ★

The second Thai-Myanmar Friendship Bridge, built in 1996, is 6 km (4 mi) east of town. Crossings into the eastern frontier town of **Myawady** give a brief taste of Myanmar, but with no safe access routes in-country, return to Thailand is unavoidable. The border is open daily 8–6. No visa is required, but you will be required to pay a B500 fee upon arrival in Myanmar, and you'll have to leave your passport with the border officials for the entire duration of your stay. Myawady is quite a change from Thailand, noticeable as soon as you cross: men wearing sarongs, women and children with their faces colored in sun-screening chalk, and unpaved streets will welcome you to this less developed land. Warm welcomes in English greet you, too, along with motorbikes with homemade sidecars. Guided tours of the nominal attractions here, which can be arranged either at one of the tourist agencies that cluster on the Thai side of the border or through one of the taxi drivers on the other side, are fairly cheap at around B500. They'll take you to the Shwe Muay Wan, the city's most prominent temple; to a hilltop monastery where, if you time it right, you might be invited to lunch with the monks; and to the uniquely shaped crocodile temple, the Myikyaungon. The town occasionally erupts into a political flash point as the KNU slug it out with the Yangon-based government, sometimes resulting in the temporary closure of the bridge, but this hasn't happened in a while. The crossing is absolutely worthwhile, and not to be missed if you're in Mae Sot.

Tens of thousands of Karen have been driven into **refugee camps** in Northern Thailand by the Burmese government-backed military attacks on their Burmese villages. Karen villagers live in terror of these attacks, as they're generally being presented with two simple options: stay and work in labor camps on the government's oil pipelines or flee into the forest, where they'll be branded as enemies of the state and consequently hunted and killed. Some stand up and fight as guerrillas for the KNU, but the majority try to cross the border into Thailand, where they are recognized as political refugees. The largest Karen camp, **Bargor,** is about 40 km (25 mi) north of Mae Sot on the 1085 road to Mae Rammat. It's an arresting sight, with thousands of traditional split-bamboo huts staggered (some on stilts) over a hill range that stretches for 4 km (2½ mi). There are small checkpoints at each end, but villagers are allowed to leave during the day to farm the fields and travel into Mae Sot. You won't be able to visit this town without a guide.

WHERE TO EAT

$ THAI ✕**Khaomao Khaofang.** The location, about 5 km (3 mi) from the town center, really shouldn't dissuade you from enjoying one of the most beautiful restaurants in Thailand. This is like a national park of restaurants with spacious, forested grounds—thick-cut varnished teak wood tables are arranged under a variety of open-air pavilions, which are nearly buried in lush vegetation. It's a stunner, but the food is pricey and doesn't match up to the quality setting. The house specialties are all appetizers such as *moo khao mao* (fried pork with rice grain), *muang gai gorp* (crispy chicken wrapped in pendant leave), and *gai tort grua* (deep-fried chicken with salt). ✉ Thanon Mae Sot-Mae Ramad *382 Moo 9, Maepa* ☎*055/532483 or 055/533607* ▭*MC, V.*

¢–$ THAI ✕**TK Restaurant.** Don't be put off by the bright lighting, the linoleum floors, or the vaguely communist feel—this restaurant is justly popular for its hot-pot specialties such as sukiyaki (there are hot pots at the tables) and for its Chinese-influenced Thai food, which might include fresh fish from the tank in back. About half the menu is translated into English, but that half only covers the Westernized dishes, which are not recommended. ✉*68 Prasartwithee Rd.* ☎*No phone* ▭*No credit cards.*

WHERE TO STAY

Mae Sot is often used as a one- or two-night stopover for trips into Umphang and therefore has a good range of cheap, friendly guesthouses, as well as some not-so-special mid-range hotels.

¢ **Ban Thai Guesthouse.** Follow the signpost down a small lane past the Fortune guesthouse and you can find this converted white wooden Thai house. Rooms are very clean and surprisingly cool, with dark varnished floors and furniture. It's popular with expats and long-term tourists, and it's a good spot to pick up some info on the area. **Pros:** clean rooms. **Cons:** no a/c; no Internet. ✉*740/1 Intarakeeree Rd.,* ☎*055/531590, 02/941–8878 in Bangkok* *12 rooms* *In-hotel: laundry service, no-smoking rooms* *No credit cards.*

$$ **Centara Mae Sot Hill Hotel.** The biggest and brightest hotel in Mae Sot has spacious rooms done in a contemporary Thai design, with nice wood furnishings and marble-trim bathrooms. The courtyard surrounding the large pool is a pleasant place to get a massage or to just relax with a cocktail in hand. **Pros:** kids' pool; movies in rooms. **Cons:** pricey for Mae Sot. ✉*100 Asia Rd.,* ☎*055/532601 up to 08* *www.centralhotelsresorts.com* *113 rooms* *In-room: refrigerator. In-hotel: 2 restaurants, room service, bar, tennis courts, pool, gym, Internet terminal, no-smoking rooms* *AE, DC, MC, V.*

STREET FOOD

Mae Sot is famous for its street food, centered around Intarakeeree and Prasartwithee roads. **Tui Khaosoi** (✉*65 Prasartwithee Rd.*) is a famous Muslim noodle joint that serves delicious *khao soi,* noodles with chicken or beef in a thick coconut milk broth.

Another notable noodle stand is at **115/1 Prasartwithee Road.** Don't miss the *kuay tiew tai yai* (Burmese-style glass noodles). Also try *maing kum,* a Thai wrap, with *wai* (betel leaf) wrapped around lemongrass, dried salted shrimp, peanuts, and red onions. All this should set you back only B20 or so.

UMPHANG

164 km (100 mi) south of Mae Sot, 249 km (150 mi) southeast of Tak city

Umphang is Tak Province's largest district. It's landlocked in the Tano Thongchai mountain range, with the high mountains making up 97% of the area; there's only one access road to it from Mae Sot. Dense rain forest rich with bamboo and teak abuts the Thung Yai Naresuan and Huai Kha Kaeng wildlife sanctuaries, as part of the Western Forest range (the largest in Southeast Asia), which due to its importance as a conservation area was classified as a World Heritage Site.

The district's distinct geography and culture is ever present. The town is a center for eco-treks to hill tribe villages and some of the oldest remaining rain forest left in the country, as well as rafting expeditions along the Mekong River to Thailand's largest and most spectacular waterfall, Thee Lor Su.

"Umphang," adapted from the Karen word "umpha," refers to the border pass that the Burmese were required to have to trade with this Thai village. The document was folded, sealed, and placed inside a bamboo cane to prevent wear; its story has become an important part of Umphang's heritage. Today, rubber boats and canoes have replaced the bamboo rafts once used on the rivers and local Karen guides are employed counteracting logging activities.

GETTING HERE & AROUND

BY BUS Service to Umphang leaves from Chitlom Road and Siri Wiang Road in Mae Sot.

BY SONGTHAEW Songthaews from Mae Sot to Umphang are blue and can be found on Sri Panit Road in Umphang. The long four-hour ride is around B100; songthaews leave regularly throughout the day.

ESSENTIALS

Visitor & Tour Info Thee Lor Su waterfall trekking trips range from two-day to seven-day tours and cost B5,500 to B19,000. **Max One Tour** (Mae Sot, above) and **Thee Lor Su Riverside Resort** (below) offer tours.

EXPLORING UMPHANG

Umphang town itself is a sleepy and seasonal one with 3,000 residents of mainly Karen, Mon, and Thai descent. The small cluster of streets is a sight for sore eyes after a twisting four-hour songthaew ride from Mae Sot.

At almost 6 km (4 mi), **Tham Takobi** (meaning "Flat Mangoes" in Karen dialect) is Thailand's fourth-longest cave complex. The cave has three levels; the lowest and narrowest is for the more adventurous (it gets very dark and narrow in parts) and follows an active stream through the system's entire length. The main tourist cave, on the other hand, is 82 feet above the streamline; it's a big, comfortable space to explore, plastered with stalagmites and stalactites, which are lighted up. There's also another cave 98 feet above the main one. There are a total of 15 entrances poking out of the caves but the well-marked tourist entrance is the recommended choice.

Takobi is an easy 2-km (1-mi) walk from Umphang town, making it an accessible and enjoyable half-day excursion. If you intend to walk the full lower level, make sure to give yourself an early start as it will take most of the day. Also take into account that the stream is seasonal: the chambers are flooded from June through December, rendering the lower cave inaccessible. Good shoes, plenty of bottles of water, and a flashlight are essential. *Free* *Daily 8:30–5.*

Fodor's Choice ★ Considered one of Southeast Asia's most spectacular falls and Thailand's largest, **Thee Lor Su Waterfall** is in the Umphang Wildlife Conservation Area. The valley's river, tracking its way from Huai Klotho, cascades down a 984-foot limestone cliff into a green translucent pool; the clearing is surrounded by virgin mountain forest. The waterfall is a 30-minute walk from the conservation area's headquarters. Note that though the conservation area is open year-round, the best time to go rafting is during the rainy season from July through October. Rafting tours are the most rewarding means of seeing Thee Lor Su and its surrounding area, with programs readily available from agents in Umphang, as well as in Mae Sot.

Thee Lor Su Riverside Resort (✉ *Hwy. 1090, Umphang* ☎ *055/561010, 038/312050, or 01/862–0533*) has a unique tour of Thee Lor Su waterfall involving an initial flight over the falls and its surrounding area in a Cessna. After the first night's stay, you leave early and the rafting begins. A three-day/two-night program costs B5,500, but there has to be a minimum of five people for the trip to happen. Book well in advance. The one disadvantage is that, unlike its competitors, the resort can't guarantee English-speaking guides. ✉ *27 km (17 mi) east of Umphang* *B300* *Daily 8:30–6:30.*

WHERE TO STAY

Umphang's about as basic as it gets when it comes to eating options. Noodle soup and basic rice dishes are the staples, and the market adjacent to the main road can supply you with some good Umphang home cooking.

¢–$ **Thee Lor Su Riverside.** This resort 3 km (2 mi) uphill from town is set in spacious, beautifully tended gardens, and is a great way to start your Umphang experience. There are 25 log bungalows of varying sizes for groups as small as 2 or as large as 10. Rooms are cozy, with glowing varnished wood and plenty of blankets and cushions on long communal mattresses. Gas-powered hot-water heaters in the tiled bathrooms mean you're guaranteed a hot shower on a cool morning. The larger Lagato house, where evening barbecues take place, is the center of activities—here you can arrange one of their popular rafting tours (one includes a flight over Thee Lor Su in a Cessna before your rafting begins). **Pros:** beautiful gardens; cheap package deals; close to Thee Lor Su waterfall and river. **Cons:** no Internet, phones, or TV. ✉ *Hwy. 1090,* ☎ *038/312050, 01/278–9292, or 01/862–0533* *www.theelorsuriverside.com* *15 bungalows* *In-room: no a/c, no TV, no-smoking rooms* *No credit cards.*

¢–$ **Tukasu Cottage.** Even from the stylish green sign, you can tell that something special awaits. Flowering plants and lush foliage lead you along the grounds to contemporary hill tribe–inspired bungalows. A combination of split-bamboo and dried-grass roofs covers cozy brick-and-wood rooms. The proximity to town and smart accommodations make it a good choice. **Pros:** close to town; cozy atmosphere. **Cons:** no TV, a/c, or phones in rooms. ✉ *7 Moo 4, Tambol Mae Kong Mai,* ☎ *055/561295, 01/819–0304, or 01/825–8238* *12 bungalows* *In-room: no a/c, no phone, no TV. In-hotel: restaurant, no-smoking rooms* *No credit cards.*

5

The Southern Beaches

WORD OF MOUTH

"If you go to Phuket, you MUST take a tour of Phang Nga Bay—by sea canoe is the best option. In Samui, same goes for Angthong Marine Park."

—MichaelBKK

WELCOME TO THE SOUTHERN BEACHES

TOP REASONS TO GO

★ **Sunsets at Railay Beach:** The sunsets here are unbeatable, however you choose to view them: floating in a kayak, strolling along the sand, or lounging in a beachfront bungalow.

★ **Boating Around Koh Tao:** Don't miss snorkeling at Shark Island, stopping for lunch at Mango Bay, and climbing to the lookout on Koh Nang Yuan.

★ **Kayaking Phang Nga Bay:** Phang Nga Bay's maze of islands is ideal for gliding alongside towering cliffs.

★ **Camping at Koh Similan:** This gorgeous national park has a handful of tents for rent. Hire a longtail boat to do some snorkeling while you're here.

★ **Exploring Koh Phi Phi:** The jewel of Phang Nga Bay cannot be truly appreciated from one beach. Make day trips aboard a longtail boat: Maya Bay is a must-see and quieter Loh Samah Bay is magical.

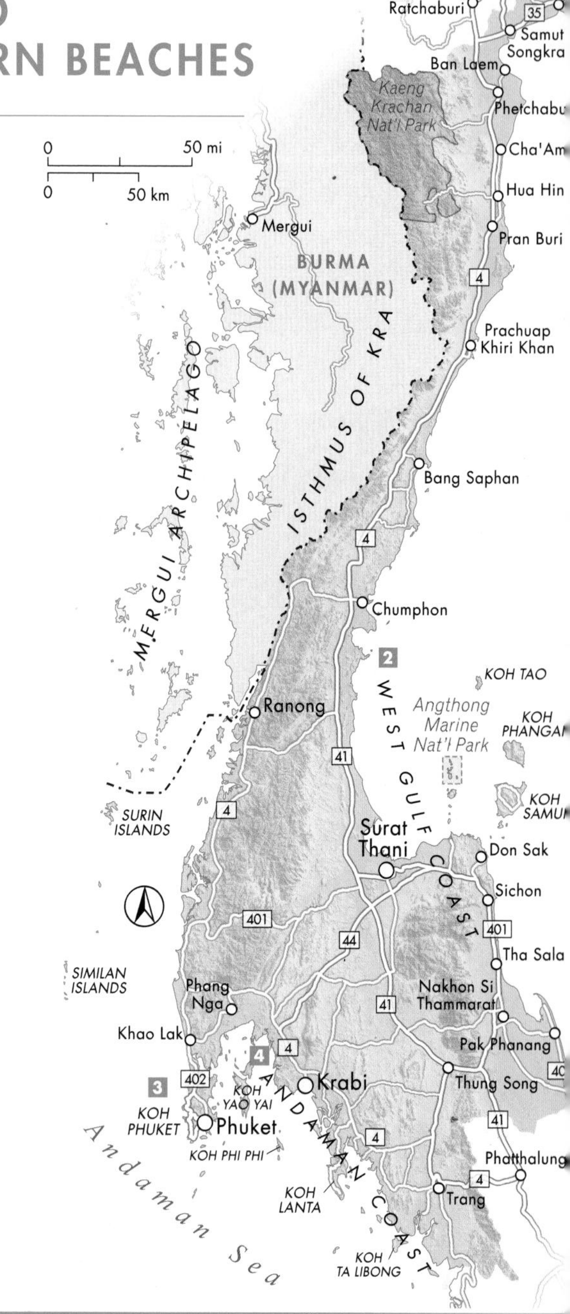

GETTING ORIENTED

In the miles of sandy beaches in Southern Thailand, there is pretty much something for everyone, from secluded spots in the marine National Parks to loud and gaudy resort towns, where the bar scene is a bigger draw than the beach. Thailand has two shores: the eastern shore faces the Gulf of Thailand—also sometimes referred to as the Gulf of Siam—and includes the well-known destinations of Pattaya, Koh Chang, and Koh Samui, among others; the western shore fronts the Andaman Sea, where you'll find the islands of Phuket, Koh Phi Phi, Koh Lanta, and various marine parks.

1 The Eastern Gulf. Several spots are close enough to Bangkok to be easy weekend trips. Gaudy Pattaya is a wild and crazy place, but it also has a few resorts that are secluded from the insanity. Farther south are some great islands, including longtime escape-from-Bangkok favorite, Koh Samet. Koh Chang has also seen considerable growth in the past few years.

2 The Western Gulf. Cha-am and Hua Hin fill up with Bangkok escapees on weekends and holidays. The beaches only get better as you continue south along the narrow peninsula; they're all reachable from Surat Thani. Koh Samui is very developed, but still not too crazy, and daily flights from Bangkok make it very easy to reach.

3 Koh Phuket. Phuket is the hub of the western coast, with daily flights from Bangkok landing in its airport and ferries to Koh Phi Phi, Krabi, and the Similan and Surin islands departing from its docks. Though it's got its share of overdevelopment issues, Phuket has many beautiful beaches.

4 The Andaman Coast. Krabi has beautiful limestone cliffs shooting straight up out of the water that have become popular with rock-climbers. Koh Phi Phi suffered severe damage from the 2004 tsunami, but it has quickly resumed its status as a prime destination for snorkeling and diving.

5

THE SOUTHERN BEACHES PLANNER

When to Go

December to March is the best time to visit the Eastern Gulf: the seas are mostly calm and the skies mostly clear. Pattaya and Koh Samet are year-round destinations. Many places on Koh Chang and the other islands in its archipelago close down during the rainy season. The big car ferries, however, continue to run on a limited schedule, and the larger resorts and many hotels stay open, offering cheaper rates.

On the Western Gulf side the monsoon season runs from late October through December; prices can be halved (except between Christmas and New Year's). Peak season in the Western Gulf runs from January through early July. But even during the off-season flying to Koh Samui is still convenient, and the island is beautiful even with cloudiness and rain. Cha-Am and Hua Hin are busy year-round, particularly Hua Hin, a historical city that has more to offer than just the beach.

The peak season on the Andaman Coast is November through April. The monsoon season is May through October, during which high seas can make beaches unsafe for swimming, though hotel prices are considerably lower.

Getting Here & Around

By Air: There are daily, relatively inexpensive flights from Bangkok to all of the major beach destinations: Surat Thani, Trat, Koh Samui, Phuket, Pattaya, and Krabi. It is generally less expensive to fly to Phuket and Surat Thani than to other southern airports. There are some flights from Chiang Mai to the beaches. Thai Airways, Bangkok Airways, and Phuket Air have regular flights, as do the budget carriers Air Asia and Nok Air (⇨ *By Air in Travel Smart Thailand*). All of the airports in this region are small and much easier to deal with than Bangkok's Suvarnabhumi.

By Boat & Ferry: Boats depart from the mainland to the islands from Chumporn and Surat Thani. There are a number of ferry services, including high-speed catamarans, slower passenger ferries, and "speed boats," as well as large "slow boats," which are car ferries. The main boat operators are Lomprayah, SeaTran, Songserm, and Raja.

Contact **Lomprayah** (☎ *02/629–2569, 02/629–2570 in Bangkok, 077/427765 in Samui, 077/456176 on Koh Tao* 🌐 *www.lomprayah.com*). **Raja Ferry** (☎ *077/471151 up to 53 Donsak Pier, 077/377452 up to 53 Koh Phangan*). **Seatran Ferry & Express** (☎ *02/240–2582 in Bangkok, 077/275060 Surat Thani, 077/471174 Donsak Pier, 077/426000 up to 02 Koh Samui, 077/238679 Koh Phangan* 🌐 *www.seatranferry.com*). **Songserm** (☎ *02/280–8073 up to 74 in Bangkok, 077/377704 Tha Thong Pier in Surat Thani, 077/420157 Koh Samui* 🌐 *www.songserm-expressboat.com*).

By Bus: Buses travel regularly between Bangkok and all major destinations in southern Thailand. There's also good bus service within the south. ⚠ **Private buses are less reputable than public buses.**

By Car: Eastern Gulf resorts are fairly close to Bangkok, making a car trip here reasonable (assuming you can get out of Bangkok). It's a long and potentially exhausting drive farther south to Chumphon, Surat Thani, or Krabi. Most hotels and tour operators can arrange car rentals. However, it may be cheaper, safer, and more convenient to hire a car and driver. It's easiest to arrange this while in Bangkok; you can also ask your hotel to help make arrangements (⇨ *By Car in Travel Smart Thailand*).

By Motorcycle: Scooters are a fun way to explore the islands and beaches, but think twice before renting one. Every year hundreds of foreigners are injured in accidents on Phuket. Remember that a small wreck is much worse if you're only wearing shorts and flip-flops. If you've never driven a motorcycle before, this is not the time to learn.

By Songthaew, Taxi & Tuk-Tuk: Most areas of the south have a variety of motorized taxi services from samlors to tuk-tuks to songthaews. "Metered" taxis can be found in the larger towns and on Samui. They don't actually run their meters, however, and are unscrupulous bargainers.

By Train: Bangkok is connected to Sri Racha and Pattaya via one daily train; there are more frequent trains to Hua Hin, Chumphon, and Surat Thani. Trains leave Bangkok's Hua Lamphong Station (⇨ *By Train in Travel Smart Thailand*). There are also express trains to Surat Thani, which is the closest station to Phuket. In general, bus travel is a better way to go in southern Thailand.

Money & Prices

Hotel prices in beach areas are generally lower than what you'd pay in Bangkok but higher than in other parts of the country. There are budget bungalows and guesthouses everywhere, though many aren't air-conditioned. At the other end of the spectrum are upscale resorts that run over $1,000 a night—though they are some of the most luxurious resorts in the world.

Banks and ATMs are becoming increasingly prevalent, but it's still always a good idea to carry some extra cash. Remote islands do not widely accept credit cards, but have many eager currency exchangers. Some places add a small service charge, typically 3%, when you pay with a credit card.

WHAT IT COSTS IN BAHT

¢	$	$$	$$$	$$$$
Restaurants				
under B100	B100–B200	B201–B300	B301–B400	over B400
Hotels				
under B1,000	B1,000–B2,000	B2,001–B4,000	B4,001–B6,000	over B6,000

Restaurant prices are for a main course, excluding service charge and tips. Hotel prices are for two people in a standard double room in high season, excluding service charges and tax.

Health & Safety

Try the Tourist Police first in an emergency: ☎1155.

Malaria is very rare, but not unheard of in Thailand's southeast. Health authorities have done a great job controlling mosquitoes around the southern resorts, but you'll still need a good supply of repellent.

Be careful at the beach, as the sun is stronger than you think. Wear a hat and plenty of sunscreen. Protective clothing while diving or snorkeling is a good idea, as accidentally brushing against or stepping on coral can be painful. Keep an eye out for dangerous creatures like jellyfish and sea urchins. If you are stung, seek medical attention immediately.

Strong undertows often develop during monsoon season, especially along the west coast. Pay attention to posted warnings and listen if locals tell you not to swim.

Condoms are available in southern Thailand; not all brands are equally reliable, so it may be simpler to bring any you'll need.

In 2004, nearly two dozen tourists were killed in two separate ferry accidents. In both cases, the boats were ill equipped and overloaded (60 people in a boat made for 22, for example). Don't take overcrowded boats; you can often hire speedboats to travel ferry routes. If you do take a ferry, travel during the day, when rescue operations are easier.

5

EATING AND DRINKING WELL IN SOUTHERN THAILAND

Spicy seafood salad *(pictured above)*.

Get ready for the south's distinctive flavors. Turmeric, peanuts, and coconut milk are a few ingredients that play larger roles here than they do in the north. And, of course, there's no shortage of delicious fresh seafood.

Southern Thailand has a larger Muslim population than the rest of the country, and you'll taste this diversity in southern cuisine, along with Malaysian, Lao, and even Indian influences. You won't find many pork dishes here; since the south is less influenced by China than other regions, you also won't find many noodle dishes. Spiciness is a defining characteristic of southern food, though as in other regions, restaurants that cater to tourists sometimes tone down the chilies. And of course, there's no shortage of delicious fresh seafood.

A meal in the south is all about the experience. Though you'll run into some tourist traps in areas like Phuket, in general you're likely to find the real deal—authentic cuisine at rock-bottom prices. It's hard to beat a Singha beer and fresh crab with curry powder just steps from the edge of the turquoise Andaman Sea.

SEAFOOD

In the south, it's all about plentiful fresh seafood. Beachside shacks serve all sorts of aquatic treats, from octopus to crab—and foodies will absolutely love the prices. Imagine a heaping plate of *uni* (sea urchin) for just a few dollars; that same dish stateside would have a couple more zeros attached to it. Raw shrimp is another silky southern treat. And freshness can't be overestimated; you'll often get your pick of seafood from a boat that has just returned with the day's bounty.

GAENG MASAMAN

A Muslim dish by origin (its named is derived from Musulman, an older version of the word "Muslim"), Massaman curry has a distinct flavor that's somewhat reminiscent of Indian cuisine. It's not usually a spicy dish, but peanuts add a big burst of flavor and an even bigger crunch. Coconut milk softens everything, and the result is a soupy and comforting curry. It's made with a variety of meats but rarely fish.

GAENG SOM

Known as sour curry, this dish is usually spicy as well as tart. It's made with fish sauce instead of coconut milk, and the flavor can take some getting used to. It's typically made with fish (gaeng som pla) and green vegetables, such as cabbage and beans. Sour curry is runnier than coconut-milk curries—more like a sauce—and tends to acquire a greenish hue from all the vegetables it contains.

KHAO MOK KAI

This simple but delicious chicken and rice dish is a Thai version of Indian chicken *biryani,* which means "fried" or "roasted." Chicken—which is usually on the bone—lies under a fragrant mound of rice, which owes its bright yellow color to a liberal amount of turmeric. Though turmeric often shows up in Indian cuisine, this is one of its few cameos in southern Thailand food.

Deep-fried shallots add another element of textural complexity.

BOO PAHT PONG KAREE

Curry-powder crab is not a traditional, soupy curry: whole crab is fried in a mixture of curry powder and other spices. The piquant curry is a perfect counterpoint to the sweet crabmeat. Coconut milk is often used to moisten the mix and moderate the spiciness. You'll find other kinds of seafood prepared this way in the south, but crab is particularly tasty.

PLA

Whole fish such as garoupa (grouper) is often on the menu in the south and is so much more flavorful than fillets. Garlic and chilies are common seasonings, and the skin is usually cooked until it's deliciously crispy. It may be spicy, but whole fish is definitely a treat you don't get too often stateside. You can also find steamed versions and less spicy seasonings like ginger.

THE EASTERN GULF

Updated by Robin Goldstein, Alexis Herschkowitsch & Simon Stewart

THE EASTERN GULF HAS LONG been a favorite escape from the heat and humidity of Bangkok. Its proximity to the capital means that weekend trips are possible, which in turn means that the area is overrun with sunseekers during long or holiday weekends. As the capital becomes more and more congested and its residents more affluent with disposable income, the region is growing rapidly. Some of the closer beaches have become so crowded that people now continue down the coast to quieter shores.

Many people go no farther than the coastal city of Pattaya, less than two hours south of Bangkok, which is both a notorious commercial sex hub and a popular weekend beach retreat for Bangkok residents. Pattaya is the most highly developed area in the Eastern Gulf—too much so, it seems, as two consecutive prime ministers have pointed to the area as an example of the evils of unchecked development. For years now the city has been cleaning up its beaches and its act, but it remains an eyesore to many people. But if you're looking for raucous entertainment, this is the spot, and the new world-class Sheraton resort just outside the city provides some isolation from the seedy, frenetic face of Pattaya.

Head farther south and east for more tranquil environs. Koh Chang, Thailand's second-largest island after Phuket, has started to experience the tourism onslaught. The incentives to overbuild are strong, but for the time being it is a charming and beautiful island.

PATTAYA

147 km (88 mi) southeast of Bangkok.

Pattaya proponents like to boast that their city has finally shed its longstanding image as the hub of Thailand's prostitution industry and emerged as a legitimate upscale beach destination. This is partly true: recent years have seen the opening of chic new restaurants and the classy Sheraton resort. Still, Pattaya remains a city as divided as ever between sand and sex—and the emphasis still falls clearly on the latter. ⚠ **If you can't handle being surrounded by live sex shows and smut shops at every turn, then avoid Pattaya—unless you're planning to spend your stay at a luxury resort.** Understand, however, that commercial sex is not just a reality here: it is the lifeblood of the city.

That said, Pattaya was not always like this. Until the end of the 1950s, it was a fishing village sitting on an unspoiled natural harbor. Even after it was discovered by affluent Bangkok residents, it remained rather small and tranquil. Then came the Vietnam War, with thousands of American soldiers stationed at nearby air and naval bases. They piled into Pattaya, and the resort grew with the unrestrained fervor of any boomtown. But the boom eventually went bust. Pattaya was nearly abandoned, but its proximity to Bangkok and the beauty of the natural harbor ensured that it didn't crumble completely. In the late 1990s, after much talk and government planning, Pattaya started regaining

popularity. Two expressways were finished, making the trip from Bangkok even easier. Now that Bangkok's international airport is located on the southeast side of the capital, it is even more convenient to visit Pattaya.

GETTING HERE & AROUND

Buses to Pattaya leave from Bangkok's Eastern Bus Terminal on Sukhumvit at least every hour daily. The journey takes about an hour and a half, and bus fares are quite cheap—usually around B35. You can also drive from Bangkok.

ESSENTIALS

Hospital **Bangkok Hospital Pattaya** (✉ *301 Moo 6, Sukhumvit Rd., Km 143, Banglamung, Chonburi* ☎ *038/259911 emergency, 66/3825–9999*).

Tourist Information **Tourism Authority of Thailand (Pattaya Office)** (✉ *382/1 Moo 10, Chaihat Rd.* ☎ *038/427667 or 038/428750*).

EXPLORING

The curving bay, along which runs Beach Road, with palm trees on the beach side and modern resort hotels on the other, is the central part of the city. By the old pier are pedestrian streets where bars, clubs, and open-air cafés proliferate. South of this area is Jomtien, a beach that is somewhat overdeveloped but still pleasant enough. The northern part of the bay, over steep hills, is the quietest, most easygoing section of Pattaya. Lately, water quality in the bay is improving with the introduction of modern water- and sewage-treatment plants. Pattaya has a big water-sports industry, with a beach full of Jet Skis, paragliders, and even water-skiers.

BEACHES

Some resorts, like the Royal Cliff Beach Hotel and the Sheraton, have their own beaches—rocky outcroppings around the resorts make them more secluded and more private. In addition to those smaller beaches, Pattaya has two big ones: **Pattaya Beach** on Pattaya Bay is the more active beach with Jet Skis, paragliders, and other water sports on offer all day. The bay is usually crowded with small boats. There's a nice landscaped walkway between the beach and Pattaya Beach Road. The other beach, of a bit south of the city proper, is **Jomtien Beach.** It's a long, narrow beach with grainy sand, and is quieter than Pattaya.

A third and better option is **Koh Lan,** an island 45 minutes by ferry or 15 minutes by speedboat from Pattaya Bay. The beaches here have nice white sand and the water is cleaner. There are many water sports here, too, which means that this is not where you can find that quiet place to sun and read a book. Ferries leave South Pattaya Pier daily from 10 AM to 6:30 PM and cost B20. Speedboats on Pattaya Beach are available for B1,800 round-trip, which isn't a bad deal if you have a few people to split the cost.

WHAT TO SEE

The **Bottle Museum** is certainly unique. Dutchman Pieter Beg de Leif created more than 300 miniatures—tiny replicas of famous buildings and ships—in bottles. ✉ *297/1–5 Moo 6, Sukhumvit Rd.* ☎ *038/422957* 🎫 *B200* 🕓 *Daily 9–6:30.*

Though it's more famous for its nightlife, Pattaya also has quite a few activities designed for families. Children love the **Elephant Kraal,** where a few dozen pachyderms display their skills in a two-hour show. There are demonstrations of everything from their part in ceremonial rites to their usefulness in construction. Everything is staged, but it's always fun to see elephants at work and at play. It's a bit unsettling to see these gentle giants languishing in the city, but the Elephant Kraal has a good reputation as one of the few places that doesn't mistreat the animals. One-hour elephant rides are available for an extra B1,000 between 8 and 5. For tickets, go to the Tropicana Hotel on Pattaya 2 Road. ✉ *5 km (3 mi) from Pattaya* ☎ *038/249818 or 038/249853* 🌐 *www.elephant-village-pattaya.com* 🎫 *B650* 🕓 *Daily shows at 2:30* PM.

Also popular with kids is the **Pattaya Monkey Training Center.** The pig-tailed monkeys, who live about 40 years, are adept at harvesting coconuts, a skill they are taught over the course of a year. This training is not just for show; once schooled in coconut collecting, the monkeys are each worth several thousand dollars to resorts that want their coconut trees harvested. But at this training center they are also taught a few other entertaining tricks that bring a smile to the face of even the most jaded traveler. ✉ *Km 151, Sukhumvit Rd., Soi Chaiyapruk* ☎ *038/756367 or 038/756570* 🎫 *B250* ⏲ *Daily shows at 9, 11, noon, 1, 2, and 5.*

The **Ripley's Believe It or Not** is the same one you can find in America with its collection of curiosities from all corners of the world. There's an extensive collection of both authentic items and replicas here in 250 categories ranging from peculiar lifestyles to optical illusions. ✉ *2nd fl., Royal Garden Plaza, 218 Moo 10 Beach Rd.* ☎ *038/710294 up to 98* 🌐 *www.ripleysthailand.com* 🎫 *B380* ⏲ *Daily 10 AM–10 PM.*

★ The **Sanctuary of Truth** is probably the most interesting place in Pattaya. The late tycoon Lek Wiriyaphen started building this massive teak structure in 1981—it's still not finished but it's open. The aim of the building, which looks like an intricate collection of carvings, was to make a statement about the balance of different cultures, mixing modern and traditional arts. The setting right next to the water north of Pattaya is pleasant, too. ✉ *206/2 Moo 5, Naklua 12, Naklua Rd., Banglamung* ☎ *038/367229 or 038/367230* 🌐 *www.sanctuaryoftruth.com* 🎫 *B600* ⏲ *Daily 8 AM–6 PM.*

SPORTS & THE OUTDOORS

Pattaya Beach is the action center for water sports. Just go to the beach and you'll easily find plenty of vendors. Jet skiing is generally B600 for 30 minutes, parasailing B500 for 15 minutes, and waterskiing starts at B1,000 for 30 minutes. All activities are available from 7 AM to 4 PM. Big inflatable bananas, yet another thing to dodge when you're in the water, hold five people and are towed behind a speedboat. They cost B1,000 or more for 30 minutes. For windsurfing, it's best to try Jomtien Beach, where you won't have to deal with all the motorized activities on Pattaya Beach. ■ **TIP→ Pattaya offers scuba diving, but many other beaches have much better diving.**

WHERE TO EAT

Much of Pattaya feels like Little America, with a McDonald's, a Burger King, *and* a KFC lined up next to each other in the Royal Gardens Plaza mall. But Pattaya is also near Thailand's major fruit-producing provinces, as well as many fishing grounds in the Gulf, so you'll have no trouble finding fresh local food. There are also fancier (though not necessarily better) full-scale restaurants here, which can be a refuge if you get weary of the noise and crowds at the simple beachside places.

$$$ ITALIAN ✕ **The Bay.** Giuseppe Zanotti's flashy new restaurant represents well the hip, modern side of Pattaya. Here you can dine at sleek modern tables overlooking the Dusit Resort's expansive pool and (you guessed it) the bay. The menu isn't just luxe (as in a rack of venison with porcini mushrooms and juniper berries), it's also unusually authentic (as in *gnochetti sardi,* Sardinian gnocchi). ✉ *Dusit Resort, 240/2 Pattaya Beach Rd.* ☎ *038/425611* 🌐 *www.dusit.com* 💳 *AE, MC, V* ⏲ *Closed Sun.*

$$$ SWISS ✕ **Bruno's.** This restaurant and wine bar has built up a good reputation among the local expat community since it opened in 1986. The lunchtime set menus for B370 are a real bargain, and the set dinner menu is popular, too. The international cuisine here leans toward Swiss recipes,

Restaurants ▼

The Bay **3**

Bruno's **7**

Mantra **4**

Mum Aroi Gourmet Seafood **1**

Nang Nual **6**

Pic Kitchen **2**

Vientiane Restaurant **5**

Hotels ▼

Amari Orchid Resort & Tower .. **2**

Dusit Resort **1**

Montien **3**

Roayl Cliff Beach Resort **4**

Sheraton Pattaya Resort **5**

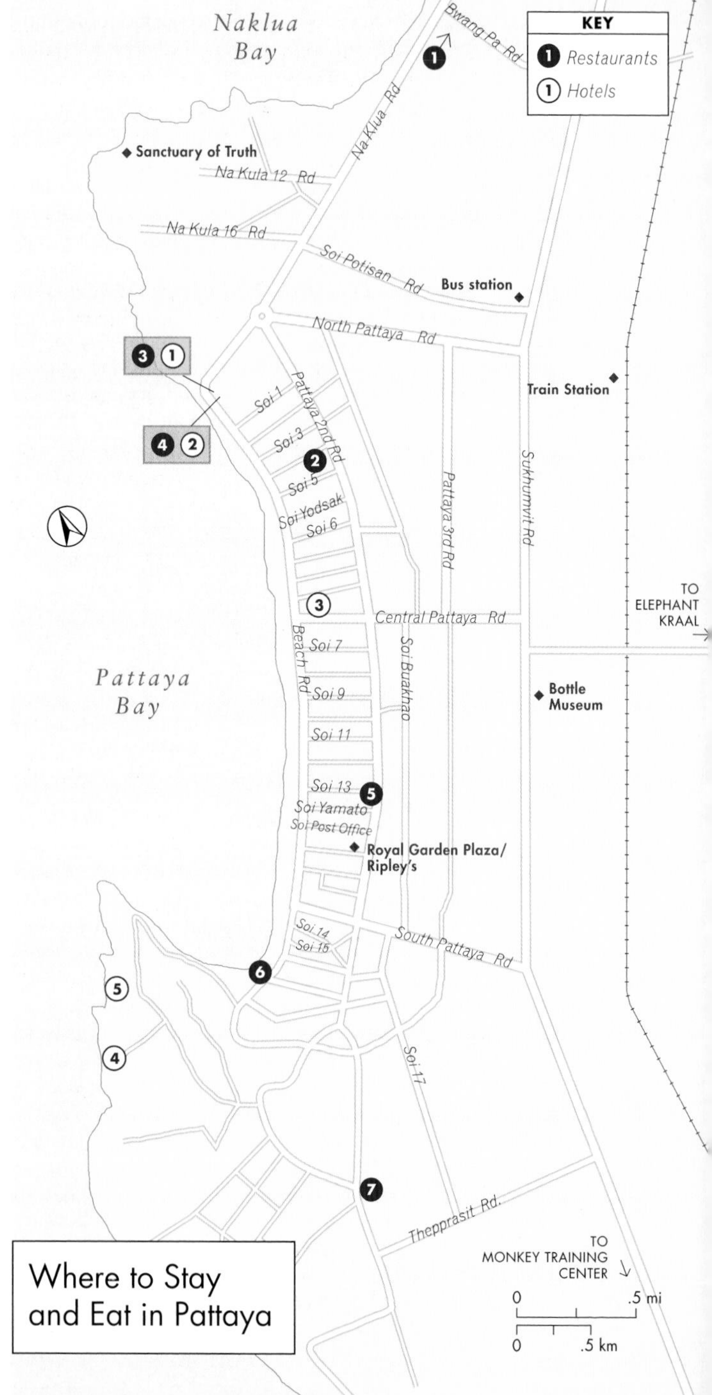

Where to Stay and Eat in Pattaya

but you can also find a wide range of American staples. ■ **TIP→ Though the seafood and Western specialties can be pricey at dinner, the menu also includes pasta and Thai favorites that are far cheaper.** The wine list is extensive enough to necessitate a walk-in wine cellar. ✉ *306/63 Chateau Dale Plaza, Thappraya Rd.* ☎ *038/364600 or 038/364601* 🌐 *www.brunos-pattaya.com* 💳 *AE, DC, MC, V.*

$$$ ECLECTIC ✕ **Mantra.** This enormous, ultramodern restaurant is one of the most talked-about eateries in Pattaya. The menu tries to cover too much geographical territory, from sushi to Italian, but at least some of the cuisines are finely realized: brick-oven pizza with taleggio, Gorgonzola, ricotta, pecorino, and arugula, for instance, or Wagyu beef sizzled on a lava stone. Oddly enough, about the only cuisine you won't find here is Thai. Mantra's Kasbah-meets-soaring-wine-bar-meets-alien-invasion atmosphere is stunning. ✉ *Amari Orchid Resort, Pattaya Beach Rd.* ☎ *038/429591* 🌐 *www.mantra-pattaya.com* 💳 *AE, MC, V* ⊙ *No lunch Mon.–Sat.*

5

$$ SEAFOOD ✕ **Mum Aroi Gourmet Seafood.** For a very different side of Pattaya, head a bit north of the city and seek out this beautiful, romantic outdoor waterfront seafood restaurant. The almost exclusively Thai customers choose their lobsters, giant tiger prawns, crawling crabs, fresh oysters, lobster, and whole fish from a series of huge tanks and enjoy them amid shimmering pools, palm trees, and sweeping views of the bay. There is no English-language menu, so you will have to point to the seafood you want. Prices are very reasonable, especially given the upmarket feel of the place. ✉ *83/4 Na Klua Rd., near Ananya Beachfront Condominium* ☎ *038/223252* 💳 *MC, V.*

$$ SEAFOOD ✕ **Nang Nual.** At the southern end of Pattaya Beach Road amid the bar scene is one of the city's best places for seafood. A huge array of freshly caught fish is laid out on blocks of ice at the entrance; point to what you want, explain how you'd like it cooked (most people get it grilled), and ask for some fried rice on the side. A menu filled with photographs of the dishes overcomes the language barrier, and they will understand the type of cooking as long as you don't make it too complicated. For meat lovers, the huge steaks are an expensive treat. There's a dining room upstairs, but ask for a table on the terrace overlooking the ocean. A newer branch is across from Jomtien Beach, near the Sigma Resort. ✉ *214–10 S. Pattaya Beach Rd.* ☎ *038/428177* ✉ *1 25/24–26 Moo 1, 2 Jomtien Beach Rd.* ☎ *038/231548* 💳 *AE, MC, V.*

$$ THAI ✕ **Pic Kitchen.** This restaurant is actually a series of classic teak pavilions. You can dine inside or outside, and you can choose from table seating, floor seating, or sofas in Pic's jazz pit. The Thai dishes are consistently good, especially the deep-fried crab claws and spicy eggplant salad, as well as the ubiquitous *som tam* (green-papaya salad). All food can be made mild or spicy; if you're really adverse to chilies, try the mild ginger-scented white snapper. ✉ *255 Soi 5 Pattaya 2 Rd.* ☎ *038/428374* 🌐 *www.pic-kitchen.com* 💳 *AE, DC, MC, V.*

$ ASIAN ✕ **Vientiane Restaurant.** This restaurant, named after the capital of Laos, serves Lao, Thai, Chinese, and Western cuisine. The dishes from Thailand's northeastern province of Isan include arguably the best som tam in Pattaya. For something less spicy try the *gai yang* (roast chicken) with sticky rice. Dishes are usually very spicy here, so be sure to specify if you prefer gentler use of chilies. There's an air-conditioned dining room if it's too hot out for comfort, but if it's a pleasant evening, ask for a table outside on the terrace. The restaurant is near the Marriott Resort. ✉*485/18 2nd Rd.* ☎*038/411298* ▭*MC, V.*

WHERE TO STAY

Only Bangkok beats Pattaya in number of hotel rooms. Many places cater primarily to the weekend crowd, many others (though not the ones listed here) to the sex trade, and still more to group tours.

For seclusion, you have to do some spending, but there are some excellent high-end places to stay. ■ **TIP→ Be sure to ask about packages and discounts, as they'll save you a chunk of change.**

$$$ ★ **Amari Orchid Resort and Tower.** Step into this open-air, modern Thai-style lobby, and you'll immediately be transported into a tropical paradise that's worlds away from the hectic streets of Pattaya. Classy "deluxe" rooms are comfortable and spacious, with impeccable furnishings and pleasant views of the free-form pool (or partially obstructed ocean views if you don't mind a third-floor walk-up). The gleaming and newer Ocean Tower wing might well vault Amari to the top of downtown Pattaya's hotel lineup. The tower sports a spa, executive lounge, and all rooms will have ocean-view balconies. The Orchid's buzz-worthy Mantra restaurant/bar has also fueled the resurgence of this grande dame. **Pros:** new, luxurious Ocean Tower; superb service. **Cons:** not all rooms have great views; building looks a bit imposing. ✉*Pattaya Beach Rd.* ☎*038/428161* 🌐*www.orchid.amari.com* *513 rooms, 14 suites* *In-room: safe, refrigerator, Internet. In-hotel: 3 restaurants, bars, pool, gym, spa, water sports, laundry service, no-smoking rooms* ▭*AE, MC, V.*

$$$$ **Dusit Resort.** Located at the northern end of Pattaya Beach, this large hotel has superb views. The beautifully kept grounds, with a lap pool and a free-form pool with a swim-up bar, are on the tip of a promontory. The rooms have comfortable sitting areas and private balconies, and the lobby is a light-soaked atrium complete with waterfalls. For a bit more you can book one of the larger "Landmark" rooms. The resort's good Cantonese and modern Italian restaurants have expansive bay views, and the Bevarana spa is a luxurious, cutting-edge facility. This retreat is only a short songthaew ride from Pattaya attractions. **Pros:** not too wild and crazy; many rooms have private balconies. **Cons:** very expensive; feels a bit large and impersonal. ✉*240/2 Pattaya Beach Rd.* ☎*038/425611, 02/2636–3333 in Bangkok* 🌐*www.dusit.com* *442 rooms, 15 suites* *In-room: safe, refrigerator, DVD, Internet. In-hotel: 3 restaurants, bars, tennis courts, pools, water sports, Wi-Fi, no-smoking rooms* ▭*AE, DC, MC, V.*

$$$ **Montien.** Although it couldn't be described as plush, this centrally located hotel has a laid-back atmosphere that many people prefer, and all but 17 of its rooms have terraces facing the sea. Standard rooms are aging, but the more modern "deluxe" rooms are worth the extra cost. The Montien is across from the beach, and the ocean breezes cool the hotel. The Garden Restaurant has a dance floor and stage for entertainment, which features classically kitschy Thai lounge singers each night. The hotel tends to get tour groups, but it's not overrun by them. **Pros:**

on a pretty part of the beach; spacious rooms. **Cons:** some complaints about outside noise; feels a little dated. ✉ *Pattaya 2nd Rd., Chonburi* ☎ *038/428155, 02/233–7060 in Bangkok* 🌐 *www.montien.com* *293 rooms, 7 suites* *In-room: safe, refrigerator. In-hotel: 3 restaurants, bars, tennis courts, pool, Wi-Fi* *AE, DC, MC, V.*

$$$ **Royal Cliff Beach Resort.** This self-contained resort, actually a cluster of four well-kept hotels, is nothing less than an institution in Thailand. The Royal Cliff is known for its staggering size and its setting, perched high on a bluff overlooking the gulf; most rooms gaze down at the shore. But time has not been kind to the Royal Cliff: the place is starting to feel dated and impersonal, in stark contrast with the new Sheraton next door, which has easily eclipsed the Royal Cliff for best-in-Pattaya honors. On the plus side, even the standard rooms here are big and well furnished, and most have ocean-view terraces (request one ahead of time). Some lavish suites have two bedrooms, which is good for families. There are several swimming pools, each with a view. The beach is nice, but it's a bit of a hike down some stairs. The resort is about 1½ km (1 mi) south of town. **Pros:** attractive Thai decor; beautiful views. **Cons:** tricky to get to beach; so-so dining. ✉ *Jomtien Beach, 353 Phra Tamnak Rd.* ☎ *038/250421, 02/282–1737 in Bangkok* 🌐 *www.royalcliff.com* *966 rooms, 162 suites* *In-room: refrigerator. In-hotel: 10 restaurants, room service, bars, tennis courts, pools, beachfront, water sports, laundry service, Wi-Fi* *AE, DC, MC, V.*

$$$$ Fodor's Choice ★ **Sheraton Pattaya Resort.** The 2005 opening of this spectacular Sheraton, 1½ km (1 mi) south of town next to the Royal Cliff Beach Hotel, established a new standard not just for Pattaya, but for all of the Eastern Gulf. A paradisiacal village of rooms and separate cabanas rings a series of free-form pools. The grounds are shaded by palm trees and the resort is framed by the views of the brilliant waters of the gulf. The complex includes several excellent high-concept bars and restaurants. What further sets this resort apart are its relatively intimate size and degree of personal service—not to mention the most luxurious spa in the region. Don't miss the amazing cuisine at Papaya. **Pros:** spectacular spa; still feels shiny and new. **Cons:** expensive; rooms a bit small for price. ✉ *437 Phra Tamnak Rd.* ☎ *038/259888, 02/2639–1734 in Bangkok* 🌐 *www.sheraton.com/pattaya* *114 rooms, 40 cabanas, 2 villas* *In-room: safe, refrigerator, DVD. In-hotel: 4 restaurants, room service, bar, pools, gym, spa, beachfront, laundry service, Wi-Fi, no-smoking rooms* *AE, DC, MC, V.*

NIGHTLIFE

Nightlife in Pattaya centers on the sex trade. Scattered throughout town (though mostly concentrated on Sai Song) are hundreds of beer bars, which are low-key places where hostesses merely want to keep customers buying drinks. The raunchy go-go bars are mostly found on the southern end of town. But Pattaya's, and perhaps Thailand's, most shockingly in-your-face red-light district is on Soi 6, about a block inward from the beach. Whether you find it intriguing or sickening, the street is a sight to behold, with hundreds of prostitutes lined up shoulder-to-shoulder at all hours, spilling out of bars and storefronts

5

and catcalling to every male passerby. Gay bars are in the sois between Pattaya Beach Road and Pattaya 2 Road called Pattayaland.

■ TIP→ **The only bars in town that are somewhat removed from the commercial sex trade are in pricey hotels.** Below we've listed a few alternatives to the red-light district scene.

In the Pattaya Marriott Resort & Spa, **Shenanigans** (✉ *399/9 Moo 10* ☎ *038/723939*) tries hard to conjure up an Irish pub by serving favorite brews like Guinness. There's Irish food, too, at sky-high prices. A few large-screen TVs make this popular with sports fans. For live music, try **Tony's** (✉ *Walking Street Rd., South Pattaya* ☎ *038/425795*) in the heart of the nightlife district. Grab a beer and head to the outdoor terrace.

Even if you're not staying in the new Sheraton resort, it's worth the five-minute trip from town to have a drink at its bar, **Latitude** (✉ *437 Phra Tamnak Rd.* ☎ *038/259888*). Here you'll get a great view of the sunset over the Gulf of Thailand—through plate-glass windows or, better yet, alfresco—while sipping wines or well-crafted cocktails, perhaps accompanied by tapas. There's a small library adjacent to the wine bar as well. The sleek blockbuster, **Mantra** (✉ *Amari Orchid Resort, Pattaya Beach Rd.* ☎ *038/428–1611*) is as popular for drinks as it is for food; this is the see-and-be-seen spot for businesspeople and visiting jet-setters. Don't miss the secluded table surrounded by Oriental curtains.

To get a glimpse at Pattaya's raunchier side in a way that might be more fun than strolling hostess bar–lined streets, check out one of the city's famous cabaret shows. There are memorable dance shows at **Tiffany** (✉ *464 Moo 9, Pattaya 2nd Rd.* ☎ *038/421711* 🌐 *www.tiffany-show.co.th*), a cabaret that's famous all over Thailand. All the beautiful dancers on stage are really boys, but you'd never know it.

KOH SAMET

30 mins by passenger ferry from Ban Phe, which is 223 km (139 mi) southeast of Bangkok.

Koh Samet's beautiful beaches are popular with Thais and Bangkok expats, especially on weekends. Many people thought that the development of Koh Chang, a couple of hours east, would pull business away from Koh Samet, but that has yet to happen. People are not giving up on Samet just yet and it remains popular, mostly with people looking for a bit of peace and quiet and clean air. It's for the laid-back traveler who just wants to sunbathe and read on the beach.

GETTING HERE & AROUND

Koh Samet is a 30-minute, B150 passenger ferry ride from one of three piers in the small village of Ban Phe, east of Pattaya. Frequent (and cheap) minibuses travel between Ban Phe and Pattaya; the trip takes about an hour and a half. Ferries go to Na Duan on Samet's north shore and An Vong Duan, halfway down the eastern shore. The islands' beaches are an easy walk from either village; you can also take a songthaew from Na Duan down to the center of the island. It's a three-hour walk from the southern to the northern tip.

EXPLORING

Kot Samet is a national marine park, so there's a B200 entrance fee. The government has been unable (or unwilling) to control development on the 3-mi-long island, and although Jet Skis are prohibited in national parks, some find their way to Samet. But there are no high-rises, and there is just one rutted road for songthaews. Most goods are brought straight to the resorts by boat.

BEACHES

Koh Samet is known for its sugary beaches. The island's other name is Koh Kaeo Phitsadan (Island with Sand Like Crushed Crystal), so it isn't surprising that its fine sand is in great demand by glassmakers. The smooth water is another attraction. The beaches are a series of little bays, with more than 10 of them running along the east side of the island. The west side is mostly rocky and offers fewer accommodations.

5

The beaches are busier on the northern tip near Na Duan and become less so as you go south, with the exception of a congregation of bungalows near An Vong Duan, the second ferry stop.

All the beaches have licensed massage ladies walking around offering one- and two-hour Thai massages, which generally cost B50 an hour (not including tip).

Much of the north shore of the island, before the series of little bays down the east side, is rocky, but **Nanai Beach** is a nice little sandy stretch. The view is toward the mainland; the Samed Cliff Resort is just above this beach.

Fodor's Choice ★ **Ao Vong Duan** is a beautiful half-moon bay, but its beach is packed with bungalows, and it's the place where you can find many Jet Skis, sailboats, and windsurfers, as well as more than a few restaurants. For a little more seclusion, two beaches—Ao Cho to the north and Ao Thian to the south—flank Ao Vong Duan. They're both a pleasant five-minute walk away.

Ao Kiu, near the southern end of the island, is beautiful and even more secluded. From here it's an easy walk around the southern end of the island, where you can watch the sunset. The Paradee Resort is here.

Haad Sai Kaew, the island's longest beach, is also its busiest, with many restaurants and bars. It's not the place to come for peace and quiet.

WHERE TO STAY

The island has many bungalows and cottages, with and without electricity. Though the resorts below have good restaurants, you'll have a more memorable experience at one of the delicious seafood joints that sets up along the beach near Au Vong each afternoon. While you dine, the sounds of the surf are soothing, and sometimes waves even splash your feet.

Continued on page 232

Thailand's Beaches

Thailand is a beach-lover's paradise, with nearly 2,000 miles of coastline divided between two stunning shores. Whether you're looking for an exclusive resort, a tranquil beach town, an island with great rock-climbing, or a secluded cove, you can find the right atmosphere on the Andaman or the Gulf coast.

by Martin Young

With so many beaches to choose from, deciding where to go can be overwhelming. What time of year you're traveling helps narrow things down, since the two coasts have different monsoon seasons. In general, the Andaman Coast has bigger waves and better water clarity, although the Gulf Coast has some great snorkeling and diving spots too, particularly around the islands. On both coasts there are windy spots ideal for wind- and kitesurfing, and peaceful bays that beckon swimmers and sunbathers.

Sea temperature averages near a luxurious 80 degrees on both coasts, and almost all beaches are sandy; Andaman beaches tend to have more powdery sand, while Gulf sand is a bit grainier. Though the 2004 tsunami devastated some Andaman beaches, affected areas are now thriving again, and you probably won't even see traces of damage. Developed beaches on both coasts offer tons of activities like sailing, fishing, and rock climbing.

Ao Nang beach, Krabi.

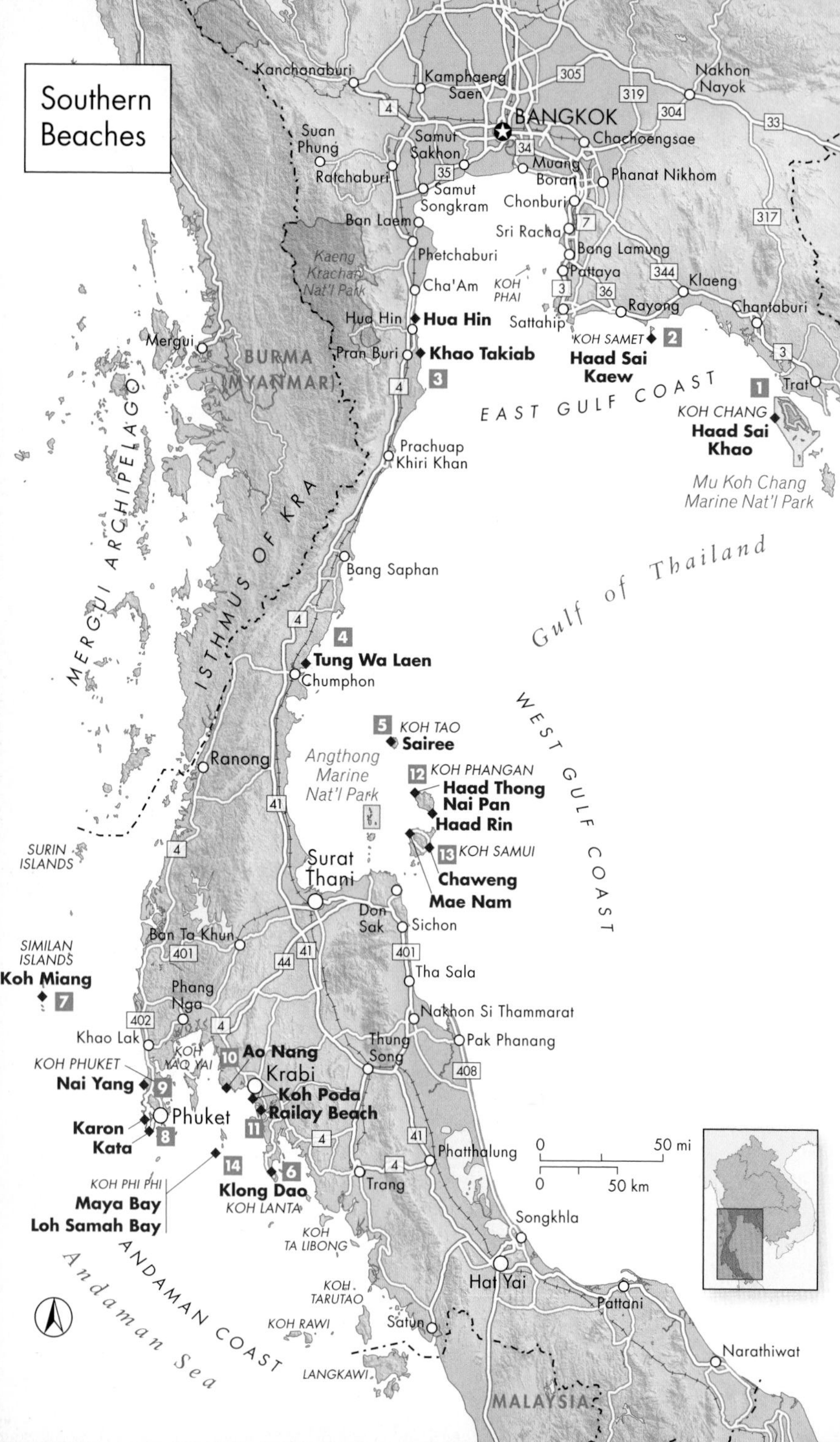

Southern Beaches
Kanchanaburi
Kamphaeng Saen
Nakhon Nayok
BANGKOK
Suan Phung
Samut Sakhon
Chachoengsae
Ratchaburi
Samut Songkram
Muang Boran
Phanat Nikhom
Chonburi
Ban Laem
Sri Racha
Phetchaburi
Bang Lamung
Kaeng Krachan Nat'l Park
Pattaya
Cha'Am
KOH PHAI
Klaeng
Hua Hin
Hua Hin
Sattahip
Rayong
Chantaburi
Mergui
KOH SAMET
2
Pran Buri
Khao Takiab
Haad Sai Kaew
BURMA (MYANMAR)
3
Trat
1
EAST GULF COAST
KOH CHANG
Haad Sai Khao
Prachuap Khiri Khan
Mu Koh Chang Marine Nat'l Park
MERGUI ARCHIPELAGO
ISTHMUS OF KRA
Bang Saphan
Gulf of Thailand
4
Tung Wa Laen
Chumphon
WEST GULF COAST
5
KOH TAO
Sairee
Angthong Marine Nat'l Park
Ranong
12
KOH PHANGAN
Haad Thong Nai Pan
Haad Rin
13
KOH SAMUI
SURIN ISLANDS
Surat Thani
Chaweng
Mae Nam
Don Sak
Sichon
Ban Ta Khun
SIMILAN ISLANDS
Koh Miang
7
Tha Sala
Phang Nga
Nakhon Si Thammarat
Khao Lak
Pak Phanang
KOH YAO YAI
10
Ao Nang
Thung Song
KOH PHUKET
Krabi
Nai Yang
9
Koh Poda
Railay Beach
Phuket
Karon
Kata
8
11
Phatthalung
0
50 mi
0
50 km
14
6
KOH PHI PHI
Maya Bay
Loh Samah Bay
Klong Dao
KOH LANTA
Trang
Songkhla
KOH TA LIBONG
ANDAMAN COAST
Andaman Sea
Hat Yai
KOH TARUTAO
Pattani
KOH RAWI
Satun
Narathiwat
LANGKAWI
MALAYSIA
305
319
304
33
4
34
35
7
317
344
3
36
3
4
4
41
4
401
41
44
401
402
4
408
4
41
4

TOP SPOTS

(left) Kata beach, Phuket (right) Maya Bay, famous from the Hollywood film *The Beach*.

1 On mountainous **Koh Chang**, hillside meets powdery white sand and calm, clear water at **Haad Sai Khao.**

2 **Koh Samet** is famous for its sugary beaches and crystal-clear water; there's room for everyone on **Haad Sai Kaew,** the island's longest beach.

3 Water sports enthusiasts like **Hua Hin's** wide, sandy beach. Just south, **Khao Takiab's** longer, wider beach is more popular with locals, but gets busy on weekends and holidays.

4 Kitesurfers love long, quiet **Tung Wa Laen** beach for its winds and shallow water.

5 **Koh Tao's** most developed beach, **Sairee,** is *the* place to learn to dive and has gorgeous sunsets.

6 Laid-back **Klong Dao** on **Koh Lanta** has long expanses of palm-fringed white sand and azure water.

7 The clear water around the nine **Similan Islands** is Thailand's best underwater playground. **Koh Miang** has some basic bungalows and tranquil white-sand beaches.

8 On **Phuket**, neighboring beaches **Karon** and **Kata** have killer sunsets, great waves, and plenty of daytime and nighttime activities.

9 **Nai Yang,** a tranquil, curving beach on northern **Phuket**, is a pretty place to relax.

10 **Ao Nang** has a nice strip of shops and restaurants and stunning views of the islands in Phanga Bay from its beach. Boats to **Koh Poda**—a small island with white coral sand, hidden coves, and jaw-dropping views—leave from here.

11 **Railay Beach** peninsula has limestone cliffs, knockout views, and crystal-clear water.

12 Backpackers flock to **Haad Rin** for **Koh Phangan's** famous full-moon parties. To get away from the crowds, head north to **Haad Thong Nai Pan,** a beautiful horseshoe bay on **Phangan's** more remote east coast.

13 **Chaweng, Koh Samui's** busiest beach, has gently sloping white sand, clear water, and vibrant nightlife. On the north coast, less developed **Mae Nam** beach is a natural beauty.

14 On **Koh Phi Phi,** breathtaking **Maya Bay,** where the movie *The Beach* was shot, gets very crowded; small but beautiful **Loh Samah Bay** on the other side of the island is less hectic.

KEY

- Diving
- Fishing
- Kayaking
- Land Sports
- Sailing
- Snorkeling
- Surfing

BEACH FINDER

BEACH	NATURAL BEAUTY	DESERTED	PARTY SCENE	THAI CULTURE	RESORTS	BUNGALOWS	GOLF	SNORKELING/ DIVING	SURFING	KITEBOARDING/ WINDSURFING	ACCESSIBILITY
EASTERN GULF											
Pattaya	□		■		□	□		□	□	■	■
Koh Samet	■	■		□		□					□
Koh Chang	□		□		□	■		■			□
Koh Si Chang	□	□		□		□					□
WESTERN GULF											
Cha-am	□	□		■		□		□	□	□	■
Hua Hin	■		■	□	□	□		□	□	□	■
Takiab Beach	□	□		□	□	□		■	□	■	■
Koh Samui	■	□	□	□	■	□	□	□	□	□	■
Koh Phangan	■	□	□	□		■		□	□	□	□
Koh Tao	■	□	□	□	□	■		■	□	□	□
KOH PHUKET											
Mai Khao Beach	□	■		□	■	□	□	□			■
Nai Yang Beach	□	■		□	■	□	□				■
Nai Thon & Layan Beaches	□	■		□	■	□	□	□			■
Bang Thao Beach	□	■	□	□	■	□	□	□		■	□
Pansea, Surin & Laem Beaches	□	□		□	□	□	□				□
Kamala Beach	■	□	□	□	□	□	□	□			□
Patong	■		■	□	■	■	□	□		□	■
Karon Beach	■	□	□	□	■	■	□				□
Kata Beach	□	□	■	□	■	■	□	□	■	□	□
Nai Harn	□	■		■	□	□	□				□
Chalong		■		■			□				□
ANDAMAN COAST											
Phang Nga Bay	■		■					■			
Koh Yao	□	■		□	□	□		■			
Khao Lak	■		□	□	□	□		■			□
Similan Islands	■	□		□		□		■			
Surin Islands	■	□		□		□		■			
Ao Nang	□		■	□	■	■		■	□		□
Nang Cape/Railay Beach	■	□	■	□	■	■		■			
Koh Phi Phi	■	□	■	□	■	■		■			
Koh Lanta	□	□	□	□	■	■		□			□

KEY: □ = Available ■ = Exceptional

GOOD TO KNOW

WHAT SHOULD I WEAR?

On most beaches, bikinis, Speedos, and other swimwear are all perfectly OK. But wear *something*—going topless or nude is generally not acceptable. Women should exercise some caution on remote beaches where skimpy attire might attract unwanted attention from locals.

Once you leave the beach, throw on a cover up or a sarong. Unbuttoned shirts are fine, but sitting at a restaurant or walking through town in only your bathing suit is tacky, though you'll see other travelers doing it.

Beachside dining on Khao Lak.

WHAT TO EXPECT

Eating & Drinking: most popular beaches have a number of bars and restaurants.

Restrooms: few beaches have public facilities, so buy a drink at a restaurant and use theirs.

Rentals & Guides: You can arrange rentals and guides once you arrive. A dive trip costs B2,000 to B3,000 per person; snorkeling gear starts at about B300 a day; a surfboard or a board and kite is B1,000 to B1,500 a day; and a jet-ski rental runs around B500 for 15 minutes.

Hawkers: Vendors selling fruit, drinks, sarongs, and souvenirs can become a nuisance, but a firm "No, thank you" and a smile is the only required response.

Beach chairs: The chairs you'll see at many beaches are for rent; if you plop down in one, someone will usually appear to collect your baht.

WHAT TO WATCH OUT FOR

- **The tropical sun.** Wear strong sunscreen. Drink lots of water. Enough said.
- **Undertows** are a danger, and most beaces lack lifeguards.
- **Jellyfish** are a problem at certain times of year, usually before the rainy season. If you are stung, apply vinegar to the sting—beachside restaurants will probably have some. ("Jellyfish sting" in Thai is *maeng ga-proon fai,* but the locals will probably understand your sign language.)
- **Nefarious characters,** including prostitutes and drug dealers, may approach you, particularly in Patong and Pattaya. As with hawkers, a firm "No, thank you" should send them on their way.

BEACH VOCABULARY

Here are a few words help you decipher Thai beach names.

Ao means "bay."
Haad means "beach."
Koh means "island."
Talay means "sea."

$$$$ **Paradee Resort.** The beach here is tops—the Paradee actually spans beaches on both the east and west coasts of Samet—and it's more secluded than others. Each unique bungalow has a terrace, and most have a private pool. There's also a larger pool complete with a pool bar. ⚠ **The resort caters to couples; bringing small children is discouraged.** **Pros:** beautiful grounds; lots of privacy. **Cons:** very pricey; may feel isolated; not for families. ✉ *76 Moo 4, Rayong* ☎ *038/644283 up to 88* *40 bungalows* *In-room: safe, refrigerator, DVD. In-hotel: restaurant, room service, bar, pool, gym, Wi-Fi, no-smoking rooms* *AE, MC, V.*

$$ **Samed Cliff Resort.** The rooms at this little cluster of bungalows are simply furnished, but they're clean and comfortable and have the requisite amenities, including hot water and air-conditioning. Out front is a small beach with white sand and calm surf. The restaurant serves Thai food, as well as a few other dishes. For dinner, venture out to one of the grills set up on the beach. This place is popular, so make reservations in advance. They offer all-inclusive packages, too. **Pros:** beachside dining; on scenic stretch of beach. **Cons:** pricey for what it is; not many creature comforts. ✉ *Nanai Beach* ☎ *016/457115, 02/635–0800 in Bangkok* *www.samedcliff.com* *38 bungalows* *In-room: refrigerator. In-hotel: restaurant, pool* *MC, V.*

$$ **Vong Deuan Resort.** This resort offers the best bungalows on Ao Vong Duan Beach and is near much of the island's activity. The best rooms are the superior ones with air-conditioning (B3,500); the other bungalows are smaller, but otherwise offer the same amenities. **Pros:** well located; fun atmosphere. **Cons:** not all bungalows have a/c; pricey for what it is. ✉ *Ao Vong Duan* ☎ *01/446–1944, 038/651777 in Ban Phe* *www.vongdeuan.com* *45 bungalows* *In-room: no a/c (some), refrigerator. In-hotel: restaurant* *MC, V.*

CHANTHABURI

100 km (62 mi) east of Rayong, 180 km (108 mi) east of Pattaya.

Chanthaburi has played a big role in Thai history. It was here that the man who would become King Taksin gathered and prepared his troops to retake Ayutthaya from the Burmese after they sacked the capital of Siam in 1767. The King Taksin Shrine, shaped like a house-size helmet from that era, is on the north end of town and it's where locals hold a celebration in his honor from December 28 to early January annually.

The French occupied the city from 1893 to 1905 and some architecture from that time is still evident, particularly along the river where the city was concentrated during those years. The French influence is also evident in Thailand's largest Catholic church, the Cathedral of Immaculate Conception, which is across the river from the center of town and an easy stroll from Gem Street. A footbridge to the cathedral was washed away by a flood in 2002, but there's some chatter of rebuilding it. The walk to the next bridge is a bit farther now, but still an easy motorcycle-taxi ride away. First built in 1711 by Christian Vietnamese who migrated to the area, the cathedral has been rebuilt four times since, and the present building was completed in the early 1900s when the city was under French control. The best time to visit the church is during the morning market on the grounds when local foods, fruits, and desserts are sold. But it's good for peaceful solitude anytime.

GETTING HERE & AROUND

Buses from Rayong and Ban Phe make the 90-minute journey here. There's also a bus from Bangkok's Eastern Bus Terminal (also called Ekamai) on Sukhumvit, which takes four to five hours.

EXPLORING

Most visitors stop here on the way to Koh Chang, attracted by either gem shopping or the fruit season in May and June. The mines are mostly closed, but Chanthaburi is still renowned as a center for gems. Rubies and sapphires rule, but you'll find stones from all corners of the world. On Gem Street, in the center of town, you can see traders sorting through gems and making deals worth hundreds of thousands of baht. The street becomes a gem market on Friday and Saturday.

The province of Chanthaburi has few beach resorts of note, and those cater mostly to Thais, so you won't see any crazy over-development here. Laem Sadet, 18 km (11 mi) from Chanthaburi, is the most popular, and its accommodations range from small bungalows to low-rise hotels. Chanthaburi is once again becoming a gateway to western Cambodia as Thailand's neighbor opens its borders.

KOH CHANG

★ *1 hr by ferry from Laem Ngop, which is 15 km (9 mi) southwest of Trat; Trat is 400 km (250 mi) southeast of Bangkok.*

Koh Chang, or Elephant Island, is the largest and most developed of the 52-island archipelago that was made into Mu Koh Chang National Park in 1982 (many of these islands are not much more than sandbars). Most of Koh Chang is mountainous and it has only a few small beaches. The 30-km-long (18-mi-long) island has only nine villages and 24 km (15 mi) of road linking them, with a few villages accessible only by boat. But this little paradise has been the focus of rapid development in the past few years and the number of resorts is increasing exponentially.

GETTING HERE & AROUND

To get to Koh Chang you first have to get to Trat, on Thailand's easternmost shore, 96 km (60 mi) southeast of Chanthaburi. The easiest way is on one of Bangkok Airway's daily flights. There are also air-conditioned buses from Bangkok's Eastern and Northern bus terminals; the trip takes a little over five hours and costs about B200.

BY BOAT Take a ferry from one of three piers in Trat (Laem Ngop, Center Point, or Ao Thammachat) to one of two piers on Koh Chang. The trip takes a little more than half an hour, and the fare is roughly B30.

BY SONGTHAEW If your resort doesn't arrange transfer from the Trat airport to the pier, take a songthaew to the pier and then another songthaew to your hotel once you've arrived on Koh Chang. Once you're on the island, songthaew are the easiest way to get around; just flag one down on the road. They cost between B30 and B50, or more if you venture toward the eastern part of the island.

ESSENTIALS

Emergencies **Bangkok Trat Hospital** (✉ *376 Moo 2, Sukhumvit* ☎ *039/532735*)

Tourist Information **Tourism Authority of Thailand (Trat Office)** (✉ *100 Moo 1, near Laem Ngop pier* ☎ *039/597255 or 039/597259 up to 60*) has information about the other islands in the archipelago.

EXPLORING

The island is certainly in for more development. Exactly how this will all play out is unknown, but it seems like every beach has something being built or renovated, and those construction sites can certainly ruin your serenity as crews blast electric drills and saws early and late in the day. ■ TIP→ **Make sure that there's no major construction project near your hotel.** The places listed below are well established and should remain largely the same for the next few years.

Beautiful, albeit somewhat inaccessible rain forest, covers a chunk of this territory, making this a great destination if you want more than just sun and sand. But the island is also a good bet for simple beachside relaxation: beaches are picturesque lack the party scene that turns some people off destinations like Pattaya.

BEACHES

Koh Chang's best beaches are found on the western shore. Haad Sai Khao (White Sand Beach) is the farthest north and the most developed. A few miles south is the more serene Haad Khlong Phrao, a long, curving beach of pale golden sand. Nearby Haad Kai Bae is a mix of sand and pebbles. It has a gentle drop-off, making it safe for weak swimmers. Still farther south is Haad Ta Nam (Lonely Beach), which is perhaps the most picturesque beach. But it's also the smallest one and therefore more crowded. Farther along on the southwest corner of the island is the fishing village Bang Bao, which is also experiencing development, with restaurants, dive shops, and cheap bungalows popping up.

Though the east coast is beautiful, it's mostly rugged rain forest, and beaches are in short supply.

SPORTS & THE OUTDOORS

Ban Kwan Chang (☎ *01/919–3995 or 09/815–9566*), in Klongson Village on the north end of the island, offers a trekking program supported by the Asian Elephant Foundation, so you can trust that the elephants are treated more humanely than at many businesses. Half-day tours (from 8:30 AM until around noon; B900 per person) include a bathing and feeding session and a 90-minute trek into the jungle, plus transportation from your hotel. There are shorter treks as well. Most hotels can arrange trips for you, if you don't want to call yourself.

Hiking trips, particularly to some of the island's waterfalls, are gaining popularity. It's a good idea to hire a guide if you plan to venture farther than one of the well-traveled routes, as good maps of the mostly jungle terrain are unheard of. One such provider is **Jungle Way** (☎*09/223–4795*), based in the northern village of Klongson.

Scuba diving, including PADI courses, is readily available. Divers say that the fish are smaller than in other parts of Thailand, but the coral is better, there are no sharks, and most of the dives are less than 54 feet. Prices generally run from B3,200 for a two-day PADI introductory course to more than B20,000 for dive-master certification.

Ploy Scuba Diving (☎*039/558033* 🌐*www.ployscuba.com*) is one of the big names in the business. They offer a full range of dives and internationally recognized PADI courses, from beginner to dive master. Their main office is on Bang Bao Pier on the south of the island. There are offices on many of the beaches around the island, too.

5

OK Diving (☎*09/936–7080*), which has offices on White Sand Beach and Haad Khlong Phrao, offers day dives, PADI courses, and snorkeling excursions

Water World Diving (✉*Koh Chang Plaza, Khlong Phrao Beach* ☎*09/224–1031*) offers day dives, certification courses, and snorkeling.

Snorkeling off a boat costs as little as B500 a day. Snorkelers usually just tag along on dive boats, but boat excursions that feature snorkeling are available. **Thai Fon** (☎*06/141–7498*) leaves White Sand Beach each morning for a 10-hour, 15-island tour of the marine park. The trip includes stops at two or more islands (skirting the shores of the others), a buffet lunch, and two snorkeling stops. The cost is around B800. It's a good way to see some of the archipelago, including uninhabited islands, but it makes for a long day.

WHERE TO EAT

★ For seafood and skewers of chicken, pork, or beef, neighbors **Mac Resort Hotel** and **Koh Chang Lagoon Resort,** on White Sand Beach, excel. Both set up barbecues on the beach just before sunset. Koh Chang Lagoon Resort also offers a reasonable vegetarian selection. The only real problem is deciding which one, but you can't miss with either.

$$ ECLECTIC ✕**Cookies.** The best part of Cookies Hotel & Bungalows is its beachfront restaurant. The Thai food is consistently good and inexpensive. There's also okay Western backpacker fare. The *tom yum talay* (hot-and-sour seafood soup) could be hotter but is definitely a standout; the banana shakes and the banana pancakes alone are worth a visit. The concrete bungalows ($) are somewhat worn and basic, but they're close to the beach and prices are reasonable, even during high season. ✉*7/2 Moo 4, Band Haad Sai Khao, White Sand Beach, Koh Chang* ☎*039/551107* 💳*MC, V.*

¢ SEAFOOD ✕**Magic Resort.** The restaurant at this resort is a rather worn wooden structure that sits over the water. A pleasant breeze usually cools the open-air dining area and there are good views of the coastline and Koh

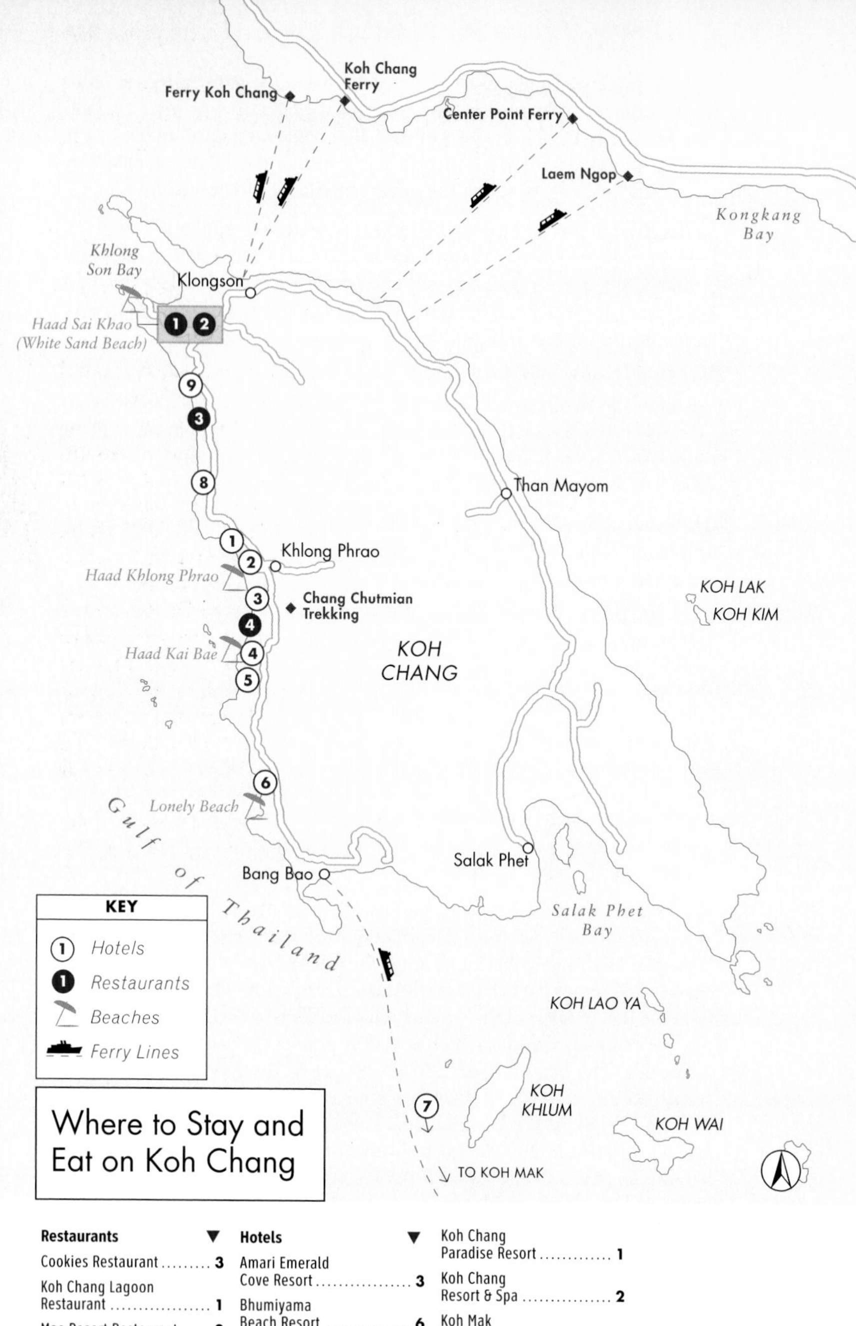

Restaurants

- Cookies Restaurant **3**
- Koh Chang Lagoon Restaurant **1**
- Mae Resort Restaurant **2**
- Magic Resort Restaurant ... **4**

Hotels

- Amari Emerald Cove Resort **3**
- Bhumiyama Beach Resort **6**
- Kai Bae Hut Bungalows **4**
- KC Grande Resort **9**
- Koh Chang Paradise Resort **1**
- Koh Chang Resort & Spa **2**
- Koh Mak Panorama Resort **7**
- Mac Resort Hotel **8**
- Sea View Resort & Spa Koh Chang **5**

Chang's high hills. The Thai seafood is very good—try the crab if you want something spicy. There's also a reasonable Western menu. Breakfast is available all day. ✉*34 Moo 4, Haad Khlong Phrao Beach, Koh Chang* ☎*039/557074* ▭*MC, V.*

WHERE TO STAY

As the tourism industry grows on Koh Chang, mid-level resorts are becoming more common than expensive upscale establishments. Resorts are being built on some of the other islands in the marine park, including Koh Mak, and you can find a few bungalows for rent there. Trat's TAT office (⇨*above*) has information.

$$$$ ★ **Amari Emerald Cove Resort.** This is currently the island's top hotel, and it lives up to its five-star standards with spacious and tastefully decorated rooms. The well-kept grounds include a 50-meter lap pool and numerous fountains, plants, and trees. With a 200-plus staff, service is exemplary, too. However, the beach is rather small and can get crowded. **Pros:** fancy feeling; high level of service. **Cons:** expensive; unexciting dining. ✉*88/8 Moo 4, Haad Khlong Phrao, Koh Chang* ☎*039/552000, 02/255–3960 in Bangkok* 🌐*www.amari.com* *165 rooms* *In-room: safe, refrigerator, DVD (some), Wi-Fi. In-hotel: 3 restaurants, bars, pools, gym, spa, laundry service, no-smoking rooms* ▭*AE, MC, V.*

$$ ★ **Bhumiyama Beach Resort.** The two-story bungalows here are modern and classy, with white walls and a lot of polished wood. The resort has two pools, one spilling into the other below, and landscaped grounds with several fountains and sculpture. It's next to Lonely Beach, which is beautiful, but rather small and, ironically, often crowded. **Pros:** good deal; interesting decor. **Cons:** some rooms lack sea views; may be past its prime. ✉*Haad Tah Nam, Koh Chang* ☎*039/558067 up to 69, 02/266–4388 in Bangkok* 🌐*www.bhumiyama.com* *43 rooms* *In-room: safe, refrigerator. In-hotel: restaurant, bar, pools, no-smoking rooms* ▭*MC, V.*

$ **Kai Bae Hut Bungalows.** There are many sets of bungalows on Kai Bae Beach, which has been backpacker central on Koh Chang for awhile, but this property is the most established and reliable. One-room bungalows have fans or air-conditioning. There are a few air-conditioned hotel rooms in an adjacent building, but the bungalows are closer to the beach. With so many other resorts around, you can easily wander over to nearby restaurants for a meal. **Pros:** fun people; central location. **Cons:** some rooms far from beach; no a/c in some bungalows. ✉*10/3 Moo 4, Kai Bae Beach, Koh Chang* ☎*09/936–1149 or 01/862–8426* *24 bungalows, 30 hotel rooms* *In-room: no a/c (some). In-hotel: restaurant, diving* ▭*No credit cards.*

$$$ ★ **KC Grande Resort.** The bungalows here vary greatly, from spacious multiroom air-conditioned ones with all the amenities, to small one-room, fan-cooled huts (though even these have a minibar and TV). This is the first property you see on the west side of the island as you drive in from the piers, and its location between a nice beach and a steep jungle-covered hill is certainly a plus. You can get a bungalow right on the beach or a row or two back. **Pros:** beautiful location; bungalows feel very private. **Cons:** atmosphere may feel stuffy; least expensive rooms not so desirable. ✉*1/1 Moo 4, Band Haad Sai Khao, White Sand*

Beach, Koh Chang ☎ *039/551199, 02/539–5424 in Bangkok* 🌐 *www.kcresortkohchang.com* *61 bungalows* *In-room: no a/c (some), refrigerator. In-hotel: restaurant, pool, diving, laundry service, no-smoking rooms* ▭ *No credit cards.*

$$$ **Koh Chang Paradise Resort.** The bungalows here are spacious and include porches and all the amenities expected in a big city hotel. They're simply furnished with a few wood accents that offset the white walls and fabrics. The pool is beachside, and some trees along the beach have swings attached to them—at high tide, you can swing out over the surf. The resort is close to Koh Chang Plaza, which has an ever-growing number of stores. **Pros:** cool pool; lovely location. **Cons:** not that luxurious; subpar food. ✉ *39/4 Moo 4, Haad Khlong Phrao, Koh Chang* ☎ *039/551100 or 039/551101* 🌐 *www.kohchangparadise.com* *69 bungalows* *In-hotel: restaurant, pool, no-smoking rooms* ▭ *MC, V.*

$$ **Koh Chang Resort & Spa.** This self-contained complex on the edge of the bay has a long history—it was one of the first major lodgings built on Koh Chang in the late 1980s. Rustic bungalows line the beach and the hillside, and a newer hotel building sits between the bungalows and Koh Chang's one road. The bungalows closest to the beach are nice, but they're more expensive and get more foot traffic than the hillside ones as other guests pass by to get to the beach. There's a spa offering treatments such as traditional Thai massage (B300 an hour) and two-hour packages with sauna and body scrubs (B2,000). ■ **TIP→** **The spa is open to nonguests—there are free transfers from any Koh Chang resort.** **Pros:** good for couples; nice spa. **Cons:** rooms small and tired; bad food. ✉ *Klong Prao Beach, Koh Chang* ☎ *039/551082, 02/692–0094 in Bangkok* 🌐 *www.kohchangresortandspa.com* *145 rooms* *In-room: refrigerator. In-hotel: 2 restaurants, pool, spa* ▭ *AE, MC, V.*

$ ★ **Koh Mak Panorama Resort.** If the bungalows here look more like something you'd find on safari in Africa, it's thanks to owner Khun Luang, a Chanthaburi gem dealer who spent many years on the continent searching for rough stones. Most of the bungalows are clustered in a coconut grove above a slope that leads down to a man-made river. Bungalows have many amenities—cable TV, phone, hot water—but no air-conditioning. A few two-room bungalows on stilts right on the shoreline are a better option, but pricey at B12,000. Most of the coastline is rocky, but there's a small sandy beach near the bungalows. The sprawling open-air restaurant serves wonderful Thai food (a good thing since there's no other place to eat in the immediate vicinity). The resort can arrange transportation to Koh Mak, a small island south of Koh Chang, via speedboat from the pier at Laem Ngop. **Pros:** unique look; great price. **Cons:** isolated; could use more amenities. ✉ *44 Moo 1, Koh Mak* ☎ *02/630–5768 up to 69 in Bangkok, 01/858–8468 mobile* *108 bungalows* *In-room: no a/c. In-hotel: restaurant, bar, public Internet, no-smoking rooms* ▭ *MC, V.*

$$ **Mac Resort Hotel.** A deluxe room with Jacuzzi and a balcony overlooking the beach or one of the bungalows clustered around the big, beachfront pool is the way to go at the Mac. It's a friendly place, and there's a nightly barbecue on the beach. **Pros:** cheap; generally cool guests. **Cons:** not for the older crowd; not fancy. ✉ *7/3 Moo 4, Haad Sai Khao,*

Koh Mak, an island just south of Koh Chang, is known for its spectacular sunsets.

White Sand Beach, Koh Chang ☎*039/551124 or 01/864–6463* *25 rooms* *In-hotel: restaurant, pool, Wi-Fi, no-smoking rooms* *AE, MC, V.*

$$ **Sea View Resort & Spa Koh Chang.** This resort is at the far end of Kai Bae Beach, which means it's quieter than most. Choose between bungalows just beyond the sand or rooms in the hotel section back and above the beach. The grounds include a big beachside pool and an attractive terrace restaurant. A spa offers everything from haircuts to three-day B14,600 packages. **Pros:** nice beach; beautiful grounds. **Cons:** removed from action; food options limited. ✉*10/2 Moo 4, Kai Bae Beach, Koh Chang* ☎*039/529022* *www.seaviewkohchang.com* *74 rooms, 2 suites* *In-room: refrigerator. In-hotel: 2 restaurants, bar, pool, gym, spa, laundry service, no-smoking rooms* *MC, V.*

KOH SI CHANG

40 mins by ferry from Sri Racha, which is 100 km (62 mi) southeast of Bangkok.

For centuries Koh Si Chang was considered a gateway to Thailand, the spot where large ships stopped and loaded goods bound for Bangkok and Ayutthaya onto smaller barges. This practice still occurs, and ships and barges are anchored between the island the mainland. Unfortunately, rubbish from the shipping and fishing industries that lines the coast creates a bit of an eyesore, but it's a clean island otherwise.

Koh Si Chang has been a popular retreat for three generations of royalty. In the 1800s King Rama IV noticed that people on this island lived longer than most Thais (to 70 and 80 years). He concluded that this phenomenon had something to do with the island's climate and he started to spend time here. His son, King Rama V, went one step further and built a summer palace on the island, and King Rama VI would spend up to eight or nine months a year here.

GETTING HERE & AROUND

To get here, first take a bus to Sri Racha, less than three hours by bus from Bangkok's Eastern Terminal for around B100. In Sri Racha, head to the pier at the end of Soi 14, where ferries head to Koh Si Chang hourly between 9 AM and 6 PM. The ride is less than an hour, and it's B40 each way. Transportation around the island is limited to motorcycle taxis, which will take you to most places for B20, and the island's unique "stretch tuk-tuks," which cost about B50 to most spots. Bicycles are not widely available.

EXPLORING

Koh Si Chang is not known for its beaches—most of the coast is rocky—but it's off the main tourist routes, so it has an easygoing pace that makes it a real escape. It's still relatively close to Bangkok, so Thais flood the island on weekends. During the week, however, it's peaceful. Foreign visitors have increased but the development mania that has taken hold of Koh Chang has not found its way here yet. This is a great island for people who want to fill their days with little more than a long stroll. All the sights on the island are within easy walking distance of each other, and there aren't many cars around.

WHAT TO SEE

Most people visit Koh Si Chang to relax in a friendly, nontourist-oriented community, but there are a few places worth visiting, too.

After his father King Mongkut (Rama IV) first realized that people on the island lived longer here than anywhere else in Thailand, King Chulalongkorn (Rama V) built **Chudhadhuj Palace** (named after Prince Chudhadhuj who was born on the island on July 5, 1893), but the palace was abandoned in 1894 when France blockaded the Gulf of Thailand during a political crisis. Few buildings remain today, but the palace gardens are great for strolling around in, and the grounds are only about 2 km (1 mi) south of town. Vimanmek Mansion was originally started here before being moved to Bangkok in 1901, and its beachside foundation remains. Nearby, an old wooden pier has been restored to its former glory.

On the north side of town is **Khao Yai Temple,** which attracts hordes of weekend visitors from Bangkok. The temple is actually a real hodgepodge of shrines and stupas that line a 400-step walkway up a steep hillside. It's an arduous climb to the main temple building, but the view of the northern half of the island, the mainland, and the rows of barges and ships is worth the effort. (Koh Si Chang has no natural water sources, and you can see from above that the reservoir just below the temple can't seem to hold water even with a plastic lining. Nearly every roof on the island has a big water collection jar underneath.)

Wat Yai Prik, just west of town, can be seen as you near the island by boat—it's on the top of a hill and has eight 40-foot reservoirs, as well as many smaller ones. Much of the land around the wat is covered in concrete so the rain runoff can be more easily collected. It seems that everywhere you turn you see pipes linking the roof collection funnels to the concrete reservoirs. The wat often donates drinking water to villagers when they need it. But Yai Prik is equally dedicated to the spiritual as it is to the practical. Meditation courses are available; signs throughout the grounds explain Buddhist principles. It's worth a look for folks interested in the many conservation practices the residents (22 monks, one novice, and 22 nuns) employ, as well as to see a wat where simplicity rules—though donations are accepted, they don't collect wealth to build ornate temples.

WHERE TO EAT & STAY

The island caters to mostly Thai weekend visitors, and therefore has a limited selection of guesthouses and hotels. You need to book ahead for a weekend stay, but getting a room during the week is no problem.

¢ SEAFOOD ✕ **Lek Noi.** Lek Noi doesn't look like much—it's little more than a shack with plastic chairs and simple wooden tables—but many locals cite this as the best place for seafood on the island, and its reputation is growing. It's a little more than a kilometer (½ mi) out of town on the way to Chudhadhuj Palace. ✉ *Mekhaamthaew Rd.* ☎ *No phone* ▭ *No credit cards.*

$$ ECLECTIC ✕ **Pan & David.** Pan and David are a Thai-American couple, and not surprisingly, their eatery offers a good mix of both Thai and western food, as well as some inventive combinations of the two. Thai dishes are generally cheaper than western fare. The spaghetti with a spicy seafood sauce is tops. The open-air dining area is cooled by ocean breezes. ✉ *167 Moo 3, Mekhaamthaew Rd.* ☎ *038/216629* ▭ *MC, V.*

$ **Rim Talay Resort.** For something a little different, stay in one of these three boats that have been converted into bungalows. They're air-conditioned and sit on the beach, overlooking the rocky coast. The resort also has a hotel building, but it's rather bare bones, and rooms aren't as comfortable or novel as those in boats. Pan & David is next door. **Pros:** unique concept; cheap. **Cons:** rooms could be more comfy; non-boat accommodations aren't as fun. ✉ *130 Moo 3, Mekhaamthaew Rd.* ☎ *038/216116* *20 bungalows* ▭ *No credit cards.*

$ **Sichang Palace Hotel.** This is the island's biggest hotel. There's nothing particularly special about it, but it's comfortable enough and centrally located. It's often full on weekends, but nearly empty during the week. The pool is great for an afternoon dip after walking around the island. **Pros:** well located; reliable option. **Cons:** can feel too empty; doesn't have many amenities. ✉ *81 Atsadang Rd.* ☎ *038/216276 up to 78* *56 rooms* *In-hotel: restaurant, pool* ▭ *No credit cards.*

THE WESTERN GULF

South of Bangkok lies the Western Gulf coast, hundreds of miles of shoreline where resort towns are the exception rather than the rule. Most towns along the gulf are either small fishing villages or culturally and historically significant towns, such as Surat Thani. Some touristy areas have grown up out of the smaller villages, but they are considerably less developed than some of their counterparts in the other coastal areas. Thus, the allure of the Western Gulf is its charming towns, spectacular beaches, and not-yet-overgrown tourist destinations.

About three hours south of Bangkok are the laid-back beaches of Cha-am and Hua Hin. Popular with families and weekend warriors escaping from the bustling capital, these nearby towns offer visitors quiet beaches and lots of great seafood restaurants. Bangkok residents have traveled to Hua Hin since the 1920s, when King Rama VII built a palace here. Where royalty goes, high society inevitably follows, but despite the attention the city received, Hua Hin was spared the pitfalls of rapid development, though it's beginning to develop its own party scene. The Eastern Gulf city of Pattaya received most of the development dollars, as well as most of the woes of overdevelopment, while Hua Hin retained its tranquil beauty.

Another 483 km (300 mi) south is Surat Thani, the former capital of an ancient Siamese kingdom. As the center of its own civilization, Surat Thani developed its own artistic and architectural style. In modern times it has remained an important commercial and historic Thai city, and the province is home to one of the most pristine tropical forests in Thailand, Khao Sok National Park. However, most travelers know Surat Thani only as a departure point for the islands off its coast, primarily Koh Samui.

Koh Samui is the most popular tourist destination on the Western Gulf coast, which isn't surprising, considering Samui's gorgeous beaches, perfect weather, and sparkling blue, almost turquoise, water. Samui has been developed quite rapidly since the mid 1990s, but there's still a good variety of experiences to choose from. You can find beaches in all stages of development and hotels in all price ranges. If you can't find what you want on Samui, take a boat to Koh Phangan, a more natural island that draws backpackers, new-age types, hippies, and just about everyone to its Full Moon Festival, or to Koh Tao, a scuba hot spot.

CHA-AM

163 km (101 mi) south of Bangkok, 40 km (25 mi) from Petchaburi.

It may not be the cleanest or most picturesque seaside town, but Cha-am does offer an authentic Thai-style beach experience. The main pier is the center of this small, quiet town; its main street, full of restaurants, bars, guesthouses, and hotels, lies along a tree-lined strip of beach. You can often see Bangkok families here—gathered at large, umbrella-covered tables for all-day meals, stocking up on fresh seafood and beer from wandering vendors.

GETTING HERE & AROUND

Buses leave Bangkok's Southern Bus Terminal every 30 minutes between 6:30 AM and 7 PM; the 2½-hour trip costs around B120. Once you're

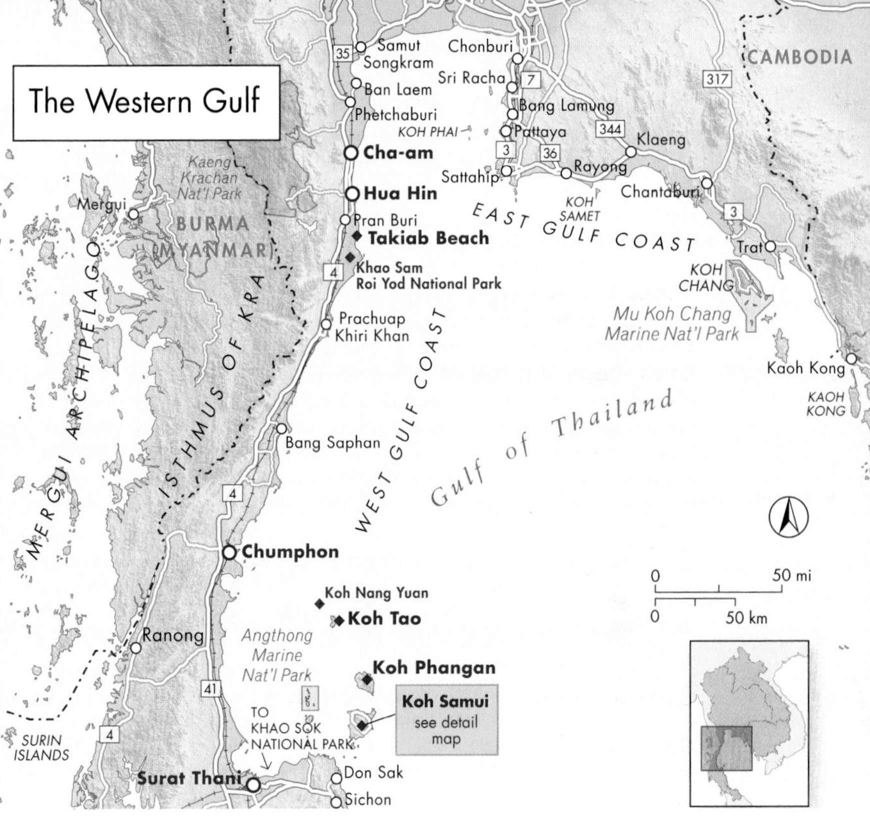

here, tuk-tuks are the best way to get around. It's a small, sleepy place, so you won't be jetting about too much.

VISITOR INFORMATION

Tourist Information **TAT Central Region Office** (✉ *Petchkasem Rd., Petchaburi, Cha-am* ☎ *032/471005 up to 06 or 032/471502* 🌐 *www.tourismthailand.org*).

EXPLORING

Around the pier there are beach chairs, Jet Skis, Windsurfers, and banana-boat rides for hire, but the beach here has fairly dark and dirty sand. Most visitors head to one of the many all-inclusive resorts farther from the town beach, where the sand is prettier and the water better for swimming. Other than during occasional festivals, such as the seafood festival in September, there isn't a whole lot going on in Cha-am town.

WHERE TO EAT & STAY

Fresh seafood is available at small cafés along Ruamchit (Beach) Road, the main drag, where there are also stalls selling trays of deep-fried squid, shrimp, and tiny crab (for around B25). A steadily improving mix of small hotels and guesthouses for all budgets lines this road, while a string of luxury hotels and resorts runs along the main highway south of town to Hua Hin.

$$ SEAFOOD **Poom Restaurant.** The seafood here is perhaps the best in town, evidenced by a steady stream of locals. Try the charcoal-barbecue whole fish, large prawns, crab, and squid—all fresh and accompanied by delicious chili-sauce dip. The decor is nothing special—of the metal-table-and-plastic-chair variety—but there's some outside seating under the trees. The restaurant next door (owned by the same people) has an air-conditioned dining area, if you really can't take the heat. ✉*274/1 Ruamchit Rd., Cha-am* ☎*032/471036* ▭*V.*

$ **Kaenchan Beach Hotel.** Chinese box lanterns and Thai teak benches with silk cushions fill this boutique hotel's modern entrance hall and open-front bar and lounge. Some rooms have ocean views, and garden bungalows are also available. The price drops by 25% during the week, which is when you'd want to come anyway. The Thai and international restaurant specializes in seafood. **Pros:** super-cool decor; inexpensive. **Cons:** not all rooms have sea views; no fancy amenities. ✉*241/4 Ruamchit Rd., Cha-am* ☎*032/470777* *73 rooms* *In-hotel: restaurant, bar, pool, no-smoking rooms* ▭*MC, V.*

$$ **Regent Cha-am.** Taking a swim couldn't be easier than at the Regent Cha-am, which has a quartet of pools spread among the dozens of bungalows that face the beach. The Lom Fang restaurant, overlooking a lake, grills up excellent fish accompanied by a spiced curry-and-lime sauce. The more formal restaurant, the Tapien Thong Grill Room, serves seafood and steak. In the evening live musicians sing all your favorite pop songs in Thai. The hotel has its own car service from Bangkok. **Pros:** pretty layout; fun nightlife. **Cons:** drab room decor; unpredictable availability. ✉*849/21 Cha-am Beach, Cha-am* ☎*032/451240 up to 49, 02/251–0305 in Bangkok* *www.regent-chaam.com* *630 rooms, 30 suites* *In-room: safe, refrigerator. In-hotel: 7 restaurants, room service, tennis court, pools, gym, spa, water sports, no-smoking rooms* ▭*AE, DC, MC, V.*

$$ ★ **Sabaya Jungle Resort.** Whether you're relaxing in your room or chilling out in the common area, you can feel at home at this cute, personable resort. Rooms are either "Tropical"—wooden bungalows with comfortable mattresses on the floor and stylish bathrooms with bamboo walls—or "Madagascar," with regular beds and TVs, in a concrete building alongside the pool. The common area has comfortable chairs to relax in and have coffee or tea. Sabaya also has a competent spa staff. The resort is not on the beach, but it's only about a block away from a swimmable beach. Water sports can be found a short walk down the beach toward town. Driving to Sabaya, turn left at the 208-km mark along Highway 4 south. **Pros:** nice spa; cool concept rooms. **Cons:** not on the beach; unexciting pool. ✉*304/7 Nong Chaeng Rd., Cha-am* ☎*032/470716 or 032/470717* *www.sabaya.co.th* *16 bungalows* *In-room: refrigerator, no TV (some). In-hotel: restaurant, spa, laundry service, no-smoking rooms* ▭*MC, DC.*

HUA HIN

66 km (41 mi) from Cha-am, 189 km (118 mi) south of Bangkok.

Before the introduction of low-cost air carriers in 2003, Bangkokians had few choices for weekend getaways. One of the preferred destinations has been the golden sand near the small seaside city of Hua Hin, and Bangkok's rich and famous are still frequent visitors here. The most renowned visitors are the King and Queen of Thailand, who now use the Klai Kangwol Palace north of Hua Hin town as their primary residence. The palace was completed in 1928 by King Rama VII, who gave it the name Klai Kangwol, which means "Far From Worries."

GETTING HERE & AROUND

The bus is the most convenient way to get here from Bangkok. Buses leave hourly from the Southern Bus Terminal; the trip takes three hours and costs about B130. Minivans (B150) travel to Hua Hin from Bangkok's Khao San Road and are generally faster than buses, though some operators may try to squeeze in too many passengers, making the journey uncomfortable. If you really want to explore you can rent a car, but it's not imperative that you have one.

EXPLORING

Hua Hin's beach is the nicest of those along this part of the coast, but it's also the most popular. The sand is soft enough for sunbathing, though wandering hawkers will frequently disrupt your solace with silk cloth and fresh fruit for sale. You can get away from them figuratively by booking a relaxing beach massage or literally by taking a horseback ride to less populated parts of the beach. Jet Skis, kayaks, Windsurfers, and all other water sports can be arranged at various areas along the beach or through any tour agent or through some hotels.

Hua Hin town, which has many hotels and guesthouses, is also a great place to try fresh Thai seafood dishes. Many of these restaurants are on wooden piers, allowing you to dine above the sea.

The town also has a vibrant night market where souvenirs and local foods are available in abundance. The **Chatchai Street Market** is fun to explore. In the morning vendors sell meats and vegetables. From 5 PM to 11 PM daily, stalls are erected along Dechanuchit Street. You can practice your haggling skills over goods as diverse as jewelry, clothes, vases, lamps, toys, and art. You can also sample a variety of Thai delicacies, exotic fruits, desserts, pancakes, barbecue chicken, and just about anything that can be skewered on a stick, including the local favorite, squid.

When the upper classes from the capital followed the royal family to Hua Hin, they needed somewhere to stay. The Royal Hua Hin Railway Hotel was constructed to give these weary travelers somewhere to rest their heads. Near the intersection of Damnernkasem and Naresdamri roads you can still see the hotel, now called the **Sofitel Central Hua Hin Resort.** The magnificent Victorian-style colonial building was a stand-in for the hotel in Phnom Penh in the film *The Killing Fields*. Be sure to wander through its well-tended gardens and along the lovely verandas.

OFF THE BEATEN PATH

Khao Sam Roi Yod National Park. You'll pass rice fields, sugar palms, pineapple plantations, and crab farms as you make your way to this park, about 63 km (39 mi) south of Hua Hin. The park has two main trails and is a great place to spot wildlife, especially monitor lizards and barking deer. With a little luck you can see the dusky langur, a type of monkey also known as the spectacled langur because of the white circles around its eyes. About a kilometer (½ mi) from the park's headquarters is Khao Daeng Hill, which is worth a hike up to the viewpoint, especially at sunrise. Another 16 km (10 mi) from the headquarters is Haad Laem Sala, a nice white-sand beach—you can pitch a tent here or stay in a guesthouse. Near the beach is Phraya Nakhon Cave, once visited by King Rama V. The cave has an opening in its roof where sunlight shines through for a beautiful effect. If you don't have a car (or haven't hired one), you'll have to take a bus to the Pranburi District in Prachuab Kiri Khan Province. From here, you'll be able to get a songthaew to take you to the park. ☎*066/3261–9078* 🌐*www.dnp.go.th.*

WHERE TO EAT

$ SEAFOOD

✕ **Hua Hin Restaurant (KOTI).** A longtime local favorite for Thai-style seafood, Koti has a no-nonsense decor and typically full tables that attest to its primary focus: good food. A large menu (in English) includes fried fish with garlic and pepper, and *hor mok talay* (steamed seafood curry). ✉*61/1 Petchkasem Rd., Hua Hin* ☎*032/511252* ▭*No credit cards* ⏲*No lunch.*

$$ ASIAN

✕ **Monsoon Restaurant & Bar.** Monsoon serves tasty tapas, afternoon tea (3–7), and a full menu of Thai and Vietnamese cuisine, including vegetarian entrées and a daily set menu. To wash down dishes such as *luc lac* (sautéed beef) and *tom yam goong* (spicy shrimp soup), Monsoon serves up creative cocktails like the Tonkin Wave (Midori, Creme de Banana, and pineapple juice). The restaurant is in a two-story colonial-style building, which has an elegant open-air dining room and garden terrace. ✉*62 Naresdamri Rd., Hua Hin* ☎*032/531062* ✍*Reservations essential* ▭*MC, V.*

$ SEAFOOD

✕ **Sang Thai.** Ignore the ramshackle surroundings and floating debris in the water—for interesting seafood dishes from grilled prawns with bean noodles to fried grouper with chili and tamarind juice, this open-air restaurant down by the wharf can't be beat. It's popular with Thais, which is always a good sign. Don't miss the *kang* (mantis prawns). ✉*Naresdamri Rd.* ☎*032/512144* ▭*AE, DC, MC, V.*

WHERE TO STAY

$$$$ ★

Anantara. The whole resort is surrounded by a 10-foot-tall terra-cotta wall, and it feels like you are entering an ancient Thai village, rather than a beach resort. The lobby, like much of the resort, features numerous works of Thai art, furniture, and flowers. All rooms are within two-story brown-and-burnt-orange structures that are surrounded by five distinct gardens and a lagoon; the color scheme is so complementary and the grounds so beautiful you could spend a whole day taking photographs. When you need actual rest, you can always head back to your

Seven acres of tropical gardens surround Chiva-Som in Hua Hin.

room and collapse on the huge, comfy sofa on your balcony. At night, tiki torches light up the walkways that connect the rooms with the restaurants. Activities include Thai cooking classes, croquet, and elephant-riding classes in the resort's elephant camp. For large groups, there are even elephant polo lessons! **Pros:** lots of elephants; inspiring setting. **Cons:** verges on stuffy; expensive. ✉ *43/1 Phetkasem Beach Rd., Hua Hin* ☎ *032/520250* 🌐 *www.anantara.com* *187 rooms* *In-room: safe, refrigerator, Internet. In-hotel: 4 restaurants, bars, tennis courts, pools, gym, spa, water sports, bicycles, laundry service, no-smoking rooms* ▭ *AE, MC, V.*

$$$$ **Chiva-Som.** Even with the proliferation of spas in Hua Hin, Chiva-Som has not been toppled from its lofty position as one of best destination spa-resorts in the region—and, possibly, in the world. The resort focuses on holistic healing and a wholesome diet, but the setting on the beach will do you a world of good, too. Personalized programs begin with a questionnaire upon arrival, addressing diet, detoxification needs, or any other physical or mental health concerns. For the remainder of your stay obsequiously courteous staff (six per guest room) will help you heal, through educational talks in the library, Watsu treatments (shiatsu massage while floating in a body-temperature pool), and individually tailored diets. The tasteful and comfortable rooms have lots of natural woods and some have private terraces that overlook the ocean. **Pros:** unique spa program; high level of service. **Cons:** not for partiers; expensive. ✉ *73/4 Petchkasem Rd., Hua Hin* ☎ *032/536536* 🌐 *www.chivasom.com* *57 rooms* *In-room: DVD. In-hotel: restaurant, pool, spa* ▭ *AE, DC, MC, V.*

Fodor'sChoice ★

$$$$ **Evason Hideaway and Evason Hua Hin Resort.** These neighboring properties are both located on a quiet beach in Pranburi, approximately 20 minutes south of Hua Hin. The newer Hideaway resort has villas and suites, all of which have private plunge pools and outdoor tubs, along with lounging areas with comfy daybeds shaded by umbrellas. The older Evason Resort has a few pool suites as well as more standard hotel rooms. The resorts share facilities, so there are two spas to choose from, both soft and hard tennis courts, several restaurants, and a gorgeous beachside swimming pool. Daily activities include morning tai chi and afternoon Tibetan Healing Breathing Technique classes, as well as sports like archery and windsurfing. **Pros:** super-comfortable accommodations; access to double the amenities. **Cons:** out of the way; too quiet for some. ✉ *9/22 Moo 5 Paknampran, Pranburi, Prachuap Kiri Khan* ☎ *032/618200 Hideaway, 032/632111 Resort* 🌐 *www.sixsenses.com* *Hideaway: 38 villas, 17 suites; Resort: 185 rooms, 40 villas* *In-room: safe, refrigerator, DVD (some). In-hotel: 3 restaurants, room service, bar, tennis courts, pool, gym, spa, water sports, Wi-Fi, no-smoking rooms* *AE, DC, MC, V.*

¢ ★ **Fulay Guesthouse.** This unique guesthouse is built on a pier that juts out over the gulf. The Cape Cod–blue planks of the pier match the color of the trim around the whitewashed walls; rooms have kitschy (or tacky, depending on your taste) touches like seashell-framed mirrors and sand-encrusted lamps. Two large, private houses claim prime real estate toward the end of the pier, with private wooden decks ideal for sipping afternoon drinks or watching the sun rise. If you prefer not to sleep to the sound of the sea beneath your bed, opt for the more modern but reasonably priced **Fulay Hotel** across the street. Only the more expensive rooms have air-conditioning, but it's an easy cost to justify. **Pros:** hard to beat price; cool location. **Cons:** questionable decor; some rooms lack a/c. ✉ *110/1 Naresdamri Rd., Hua Hin* ☎ *032/513145 or 032/513670* 🌐 *www.fulay-huahin.com* *In-room: no a/c (some), no TV (some). In-hotel: restaurant, bar, laundry service, Internet terminal* *No credit cards.*

$ **Jed Pee Nong.** This complex of bungalows and a small high-rise building is on one of the main streets leading down to the public entrance to the beach. The bungalows are clustered around a swimming pool, but most rooms are in the hotel building. Rooms have huge beds and not much else, but the price can't be beat. The terrace restaurant facing the street stays open late. **Pros:** relatively cheap; prime location. **Cons:** nothing fancy; lots of nearby foot traffic. ✉ *17 Damnernkasem Rd., Hua Hin* ☎ *032/512381* *baanjedpeenong@thaimail.com* *40 rooms* *In-room: safe. In-hotel: 2 restaurants, pool* *MC, V.*

¢ **Pattana Guesthouse.** Two beautiful teakwood houses are hidden down a small alley in the heart of Hua Hin. The main house used to be a fisherman's residence and now holds a variety of clean, simple rooms facing a small garden bar and café. Rooms with fans have either private or shared bathrooms. **Pros:** ideal for budget travelers; cute for what it is. **Cons:** few amenities; no adjacent beach. ✉ *52 Naresdamri Rd., Hua Hin* ☎ *032/513393* *13 rooms* *In-room: no a/c. In-hotel: restaurant, bar, laundry service* *No credit cards.*

$$$$ **Sofitel Central Hua Hin Resort.** Even if you don't stay at this local landmark, its old-world charm makes it worth a visit. Originally built in 1923 for visitors to King Rama VII's summer palace, the hotel has wide verandas that open onto splendid gardens leading down to the beach. More than two dozen gardeners take their work very seriously, caring for the topiaries that look like shadows at night. The lounges on either side of the reception area are open to let in sea breezes. The best rooms are those on the second floor—they have unforgettable views of the ocean. **TIP→ Stay here during the low season, when rates are almost half of what they are the rest of the year.** On-site activities include badminton and two putting greens. **Pros:** pretty grounds; cool atmosphere. **Cons:** pricey; not a party destination. *1 Damnernkasem Rd., Hua Hin 032/512021 up to 38, 02/541–1125 in Bangkok www.sofitel.com 207 rooms, 30 suites In-room: safe, refrigerator, Wi-Fi. In-hotel: 3 restaurants, bar, tennis courts, pools, gym, spa, water sports, no-smoking rooms AE, DC, MC, V.*

5

TAKIAB BEACH

4 km (2½ mi) south of Hua Hin.

Khao Takiab, the beach directly to the south of Hua Hin, is a good alternative for people who wish to avoid Hua Hin's busier scene; tourists who stay in Takiab are mostly well-off Thais who prefer Takiab's exclusivity to Hua Hin's touristy atmosphere, and you can find many upscale condos and small luxury hotels here. The beach itself is wide and long, but the water is quite murky and shallow, and not very suitable for swimming.

GETTING HERE & AROUND

To get to Takiab, flag down a songthaew (B10) on Petchkasem Road in Hua Hin. You can also take a horseback ride from Hua Hin's and trot along the coast to Takiab (horses are available on Takiab, too).

EXPLORING

Sunbathing is the ideal activity here, especially during the low tide when the golden, sandy beach is flat and dry. The usual water activities like jet skiing and banana-boating are available here, and are more enjoyable than in Hua Hin, as the beach and water are less crowded. The southern part of the beach ends at a big cliff, which has a tall, standing image of the Buddha. You can hike to the top of the hill, where you find a small Buddhist monastery and several restaurants with excellent views.

WHERE TO EAT & STAY

$$ THAI **Supatra-by-the-Sea.** The outdoor seating at this restaurant on the southern end of the beach allows you to dine beneath the tranquil gaze of the standing Buddha on the adjacent hillside. The dining room is exquisitely designed in Lanna-style and has water-lily ponds beside several tables. Entrées are mainly seafood-based, such as prawn sour soup with deep-fried green omelet, although other Thai dishes and vegetarian dishes are included on the extensive menu. The full bar serves

inventive cocktails, which may be enjoyed beside the beach. ✉ *122/63 Takiab Beach* ☎ *032/536561* ▭ *AE, MC, V.*

$$$$ **Kaban Tamor Resort.** Rooms at this stylish resort are inside two-story structures that were designed to look like seashells but actually look more like mushrooms. The spacious, round rooms have white walls and pale wooden floors and are filled with plenty of natural light. A small pool and soft grass are alongside the beach. The open-air restaurant serves tasty Thai food. Guests at Kaban Tamor get a 20% discount at Smor Spa next to the resort. **Pros:** easy beach access; cute rooms. **Cons:** tacky exterior; not the hippest place. ✉ *122/43–57 Takiab Beach* ☎ *032/521011 up to 13* ⊕ *www.kabantamor.com* *23 rooms* *In-room: refrigerator. In-hotel: restaurant, room service, bar, pool, laundry service* ▭ *AE, MC, V.*

$$$ **Smor Spa Village & Resort.** Smor's accommodations are nearly identical in design to neighboring Kaban Tamor Resort—spacious, single-story, mushroomlike bungalows—but the rooms at Smor have private outdoor Jacuzzis. The spa has several treatment rooms, saunas, and steam rooms. Sun beds are available on the lawn adjacent to the beach, which is convenient when all of the sand is submerged at high tide. **Pros:** pleasant spa; private Jacuzzis. **Cons:** rooms uninspired; beach not always accessible. ✉ *122/64 Takiab Beach* ☎ *032/536800* ⊕ *www.smorspahuahin.com* *14 rooms, 1 suite* *In-room: refrigerator. In-hotel: restaurant, spa, laundry service* ▭ *MC, V.*

CHUMPHON

400 km (240 mi) south of Bangkok, 211 km (131 mi) south of Hua Hin.

Chumphon is regarded as the gateway to the south, because trains and buses connect it to Bangkok in the north, to Surat Thani and Phuket to the south, and to Ranong to the southwest. Ferries to Koh Tao dock at Pak Nam at the mouth of the Chumphon River, 11 km (7 mi) southeast of town. Most of the city's boat services run a free shuttle to the docks.

GETTING HERE & AROUND

Buses leave regularly from Bangkok's Southern Terminal. The journey takes between six and nine hours; most buses leave at night so you'll arrive early in the morning, and tickets are between B300 and B600. Though buses are cheaper and more reliable, the *Southern Line* train from Bangkok's Hualamphong Station stops here, too. In Chumphon proper, tuk-tuks are a ubiquitous and easy way to get around.

EXPLORING

If you're overnighting here or have a couple of hours to spare before catching a bus, visit the night market. If you have more time, just north of Chumphon there's an excellent beach, **Ao Thong Wua Laen.** You can catch a songthaew on the street across from the bus station. The curving beach is 3 km (2 mi) of white-yellow sand with a horizon dotted by small islands that make up one of the world's strangest bird sanctuaries. Vast flocks of swifts breed here, and their nests are harvested (not without controversy) for the bird's nest soup served up in Chinese restaurants of Southeast Asia. It's such a lucrative business that the concessionaires patrol their properties with armed guards.

WHERE TO STAY

$ **Chumphon Cabana Beach Resort.** This friendly resort at the south end of Chumphon's Thong Wua Beach is a great place to stay if you want to make brief visits to Koh Samui and other nearby islands. The hotel wins top marks for its eco-friendly program, designed to save water and power and keep the beach free of the litter that too often disfigures Thai resorts. Accommodations are in bamboo-wall bungalows hidden in the lush foliage and rooms with private balconies in several low-rise buildings. Furnishings are simple but tasteful. **Pros:** convenient for island-hopping; eco-friendly. **Cons:** you won't be fawned over; rooms are nothing too special. ✉ *69 Thung Wua Laen Beach* ☎ *077/560245 up to 49* 🌐 *www.cabana.co.th* *73 rooms* *In-room: refrigerator. In-hotel: restaurant, bar, diving, laundry service* ▭ *MC, V.*

¢ **Marokot Hotel.** This is not the most luxurious hotel in Chumphon, but the rooms are comfortable (even though not all of them are air-conditioned) and the baths have plenty of hot water. The hotel is a short walk from the night market. Best of all, the rates are among the lowest in town. **Pros:** cheap; centrally located. **Cons:** a/c and other amenities are in short supply. ✉ *102/112 Taweesinka Rd.* ☎ *077/503628 up to 32* *60 rooms* ▭ *No credit cards.*

SURAT THANI

193 km (120 mi) south of Chumphon, 685 km (425 mi) south of Bangkok.

Surat Thani is the main embarkation point for boats bound for Koh Samui. Although it's not a particularly attractive city, don't despair if you have to stay overnight while waiting for your ferry. There are some good restaurants and a handsome hotel.

GETTING HERE & AROUND

You can get here from Bangkok by bus or train, but flying is the most efficient way to go. Thai Air Asia often has low fares here (*By Air in Travel Smart*). Buses from Bangkok's Southern Bus Terminal take about 10 hours and cost B300 to B700. There's also an overnight train here from Bangkok's Hua Lamphong station (*By Train in Travel Smart*).

ESSENTIALS

Emergencies **Surat Thani Hospital** (✉ *Surat-Phun Phin Rd., Surat Thani* ☎ *077/272231*) has a good reputation.

Visitor & Tour Info **Tourism Authority of Thailand** (✉ *5 Talat Mai Rd.* ☎ *077/281828*).

EXPLORING

Surat Thani is a regional hub, so there are a few culturally interesting sights that make it a good destination for those who get easily bored on the beach, and Khao Sok National Park is a few hours away.

Every night, the sleepy downtown turns into an electrifying street fair centered around the **San Chao Night Market,** which is illuminated by the lights of numerous food stalls and shop carts. The market is quite popular with Surat locals, as well as with whatever tourists are in town. Choose from any of the delicious seafood meals you see. Looking for a tasty dessert? Across the street from the market, you can find **Tavorn Roti,** which serves delicious traditional roti.

There's also the possibility of an entertaining excursion to one of Thailand's most unusual educational establishments, the **Monkey Training College** (✉*Km 91, Hwy. 401* ☎*077/273378*). Here, under almost scholastic conditions, monkeys are trained to climb high palms and collect the coconuts that are still an important part of the local economy.

And for those who can't get enough of Thailand's cultural sites, the 1,000-year-old **Wat Phra Barommathat** in the ancient city of Chaiya is the most intriguing one in the area. The simian school and Chaiya are only a short songthaew ride from Surat Thani.

OFF THE BEATEN PATH

Khao Sok National Park. After a few hours by bus south of Surat Thani town, you can find yourself traveling through a different landscape of tall mountain ranges covered with lush greenery and small streams. Soon you reach Ratchabhrapa (Chiew Lan) Dam and Khao Sok National Park, which contains 161,000 acres of the most beautiful forest in Thailand. The park is home to such diverse and rare wildlife as the gaur, banteng, sambar deer, bear, Malayan tapir, macaque, gibbon, serow, mouse deer, and porcupine. It's also one of the few places to see a Raffesia, the world's largest flower, and rare bird species like hornbills. Hiking, boat rides, and night safaris are some of the activities in the park. Rain is inevitable in Khao Sok, as the weather is influenced by monsoon winds from both the northeast and west year-round—the best and driest time to visit Khao Sok is December to April. Both the national park and some private resorts offer various types of lodging, but don't expect too much. Only very basic accommodation can be found in the park. A privately run, funky shaped tree house accommodation is 1 km (½ mi) before the park's entrance. Visit the local TAT office to stock up on info beforehand.

WHERE TO STAY

You'll find good seafood at the simple waterfront restaurants. For fancier dining, try the Wang Tai Hotel's restaurant.

$ **Wang Tai Hotel.** If you find yourself searching for a place to stay in Surat Thani, this modern high-rise offers everything to prepare you for the onward journey. Rooms here overlook the Tapi River. The local tourist office is a few blocks away. The hotel's restaurant ($$) is among the best in Surat Thani, with a predominantly Thai and Chinese menu. The dim sum is excellent. **Pros:** good food; great location. **Cons:** big; doesn't feel particularly Thai. ✉*1 Talad Mai Rd.* ☎*077/283020, 02/253–7947 in Bangkok* *230 rooms* *In-room: refrigerator. In-hotel: 2 restaurants, room service, bar, pool, gym, laundry service* *AE, MC, V.*

KOH SAMUI

20 km (12 mi) by boat east of Don Sak.

Koh Samui is half the size of Phuket, so you could easily drive around it in a day. But Samui is best appreciated by those who take a slower, more casual approach. Most people come for the sun and sea, so they head straight to their hotel and rarely venture beyond the beach where they are staying. And if you're staying at one of the more opulent hotels, you won't want to leave—trust us. However, every beach has its own unique character and with a little exploration, you may find the one most suitable for you.

GETTING HERE & AROUND

BY AIR Bangkok Airways offers multiple daily flights here from Bangkok, and Thai Airways has a morning and an evening flight. At around $200, the hour-long flight is a bit pricier than other flights within Thailand. Some discount fares are available, however, from the Bangkok Airways Web site, and the first and last flights of the day are less than half the cost of the other flights (⇨ *By Air in Travel Smart*).

BY BOAT You can also take a ferry from Surat Thani's Donsak Pier, which takes you to Samui's Na Thon Pier on the west coast; the trip takes roughly two hours. Tour operators in both Surat Thani and Samui can provide ferry schedules, and there's information at the airport as well, but ferries leave every couple of hours throughout the day so you can also just head to the pier. Expect to pay around B200 for the trip.

BY CAR & TAXI Taxis do not normally meet incoming flights at the airport in Koh Samui, but they can easily be called. If you're likely to be needing a taxi throughout your stay on Samui, ask your driver for his card and you can negotiate lower, multiday rates.

Budget and Hertz have counters at the Koh Samui airport, and National has its counter in Samui town. Thai Rent a Car has a counter near the airport, and they'll deliver your car to you when you land. TA Car Rental is a local reputable company based on Samui.

ESSENTIALS

Hospital **Samui International Hospital** (✉ *90/2 Moo 2, North Chawaeng Beach, Koh Samui* ☎ *077/230781*).

Rental Car **TA Car Rental** (✉ *59/8 Moo 5, Choengmon Beach, Koh Samui* ☎ *077/245129*).

Visitor & Tour Info **Tourism Authority of Thailand** (✉ *Na Thon* ☎ *077/421281*).

EXPLORING

Koh Samui is a truly delightful island to explore, and it's one of the few destinations where having a car can come in really handy. A drive along the coastal road will consist of one beautiful view after another; the interior of the island isn't as scenic.

DID YOU KNOW?

Samui is the second-most popular Thai island—only Phuket draws more visits each year. But it's also the third-largest island geographically, which means that it is possible to escape the crowds.

BEACHES

Chawaeng Beach, on Samui's east coast, is the island's primary destination. To the south, Lamai Beach is just as long and nearly as nice. The other coasts are less developed but have plenty of beautiful, quiet beaches.

CHAWAENG Koh Samui's most popular beach is Chawaeng, a fine stretch of glistening white sand, divided into two main sections—Chawaeng Yai (yai means "big") and Chawaeng Noi (noi means "little"). Travelers in search of sun and fun flock here, especially during the high season. You'll find the greatest variety of hotels, restaurants, and bars here. During the day, the beaches are packed with tourists; the ocean buzzes with Jet Skis, parasailers, and banana boats. At night, the streets come alive as shops, bars, and restaurants vie annoyingly for your vacation allowance. But despite the crowds, Chawaeng is no Pattaya or Patong—the mood is very laid-back.

Chawaeng Yai is divided by a coral reef into two sections: the secluded northern half is popular with backpackers, while the noisy southern half is packed with tourists who flock to the big resorts. Many of the women, young and old, wear little to the beach at Chawaeng Yai (note that locals find this display of skin offensive, although they usually say nothing). Chawaeng Noi is not as developed. The salt air has yet to be permanently tainted by the odor of suntan oil, but there are a handful of hotels here, and more in the works.

South of Chawaeng is **Coral Cove**, popular with scuba divers. It's not as idyllic as it once was, because unthinking travelers have trampled the beautiful coral while wading through the water (and worse, many have broken off pieces to take home as souvenirs). To see the lovely formations that still exist a little farther from shore, get a snorkel and swim over the reef—just be careful not to inflict further damage to it or hurt yourself by stepping on it.

LAMAI A rocky headland separates Chawaeng from Koh Samui's second-most-popular beach, Lamai. It lacks the glistening white sand of Chawaeng, but its clear water and long stretch of sand made it the first area to be developed on the island. Lamai does have more of a steeply shelving shoreline than Chawaeng, which makes the swimming a bit better, though it's less suitable for young children. It's not as congested as Chawaeng, though there are plenty of restaurants and bars, many of which are geared to a younger, party-oriented crowd and those who are looking for Thai companions (to put it tactfully).

Chawaeng Beach Road's rampant commercialization is quite a bit more family-friendly than Lamai's semisordid strip. However, if you are young and looking for fun, there are more budget accommodations available here than in Chawaeng, and there are quite a few happening clubs. And the farther from central Lamai you wander, the more likely you are to discover a nice resort with a beautiful beach and a quieter scene than you will find in Chawaeng.

Almost every visitor to Koh Samui makes a pilgrimage to Lamai for yet another reason: at the point marking the end of Lamai Beach stand

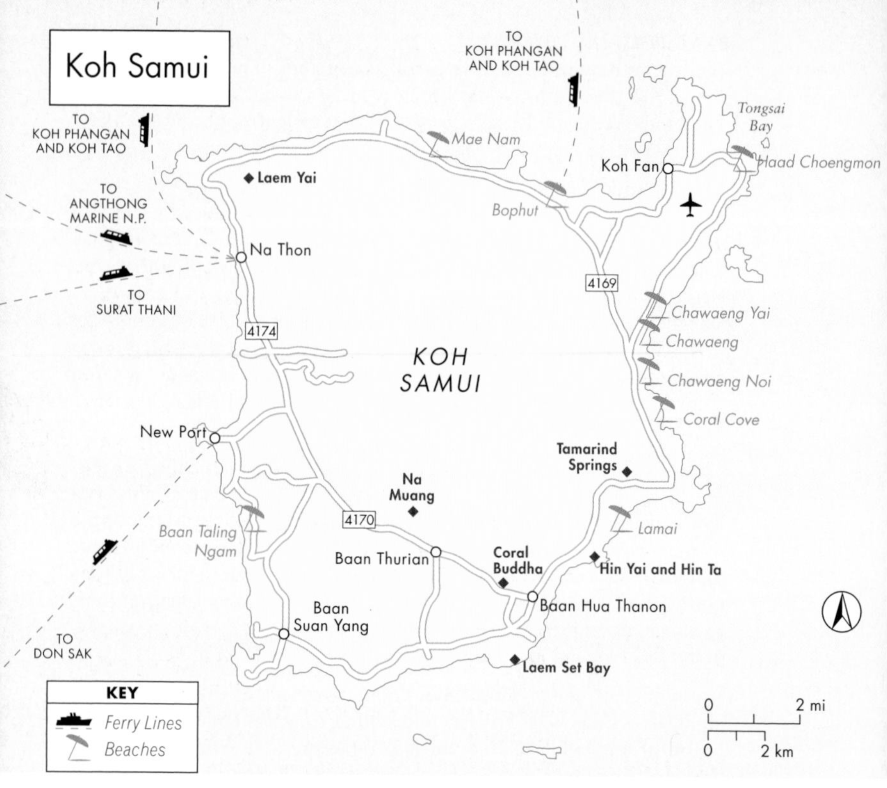

two rocks, named **Hin Yai** (Grandmother Rock) and **Hin Ta** (Grandfather Rock). Erosion has shaped the rocks to resemble weathered and wrinkled private parts. It's nature at its most whimsical.

About 4 km (2½ mi) from Lamai, at the small Chinese fishing village of Baan Hua Thanon, the road that forks inland toward Na Thon leads to the **Coral Buddha,** a natural formation carved by years of erosion.

Beyond the Coral Buddha, toward Na Thon, lies the village of Baan Thurian (famous for its durian trees), where a track to the right climbs up into jungle-clad hills to the island's best waterfall, **Na Muang.** The 105-foot falls are spectacular—especially just after the rainy season—as they tumble from a limestone cliff into a small pool. You are cooled by the spray and warmed by the sun. For a thrill, swim through the curtain of falling water; you can sit on a ledge at the back to catch your breath.

LAEM SET BAY

Laem Set Bay, a small rocky cape on the southeastern tip of the island, is far from the crowds. It's a good 3 km (2 mi) off the main road, so it's hard to reach without your own car or motorbike.

You may want to visit the nearby **Samui Butterfly Garden,** 2 acres of meandering walks enclosed by nets that take you through kaleidoscopic clouds of butterflies. It's open daily 10 to 4.

BAAN TALING NGAM The southern and western coasts are less developed, and with good reason—their beaches are not as golden, the water isn't as clear, and the breezes aren't as fresh. But there's one very good reason to come to Baan Taling Ngam: Le Royal Meridien, a luxury hotel on a pretty stretch of shore with magnificent views of nearby islands and even the mountainous mainland (*Where to Stay, below*).

NA THON TOWN Na Thon, on the west coast of Samui, is the primary port on the island, where ferries and transport ships arrive from and depart to the mainland. Na Thon has the island's governmental offices, including the Tourism Authority of Thailand (TAT). There are also banks, foreign exchange booths, shops, travel agents, restaurants, and cafés by the ferry pier. There are a few places to rent rooms, but there's really no reason to stay in Na Thon—nicer accommodations can be found a short songthaew ride away.

OFF THE BEATEN PATH

Mu Koh Angthong National Marine Park. Although some visitors prefer sunbathing on the white sand and swimming in the blue sea of Samui Island, many choose a trip to Angthong National Marine Park. Angthong is an archipelago of 42 islands, which cover some 250 square km (90 square mi) and lie 35 km (22 mi) northwest of Samui. The seven main islands are Wua Ta Lap Island, which houses the national park's headquarters; Phaluai Island; Mae Koh Island; Sam Sao Island; Hin Dap Island; Nai Phut Island; and Phai Luak Island. The islands feature limestone mountains, strangely shaped caves, and emerald-green water. Most tourists do a one-day trip, which can be arranged from Samui. Prices vary depending on the tour (i.e., some offer kayaking around several islands, while others take you out on small speedboats to do snorkeling or more comprehensive tours of the numerous caves and white-sand beaches). If you're interested in more than a one-day tour, you can hire a taxi-boat to take you out to the national park's headquarters on Wua Talap Island, where there are five huts for rent and a campsite. If you stay overnight you should also have time to hike up to the viewpoint at the top of Wua Talap. The park is open year-round, although the seas can be rough and the waters less clear during the monsoon season (October through December). ☎*077/286025 or 077/420225* 🌐*www.dnp.go.th*.

MAE NAM Mae Nam lies on the northwestern coast of Samui. Its long and narrow curving beach has coarse golden sand shaded by tall coconut trees. Mae Nam town is a relatively busy, local business district along the road from Chawaeng to Na Thon. Mae Nam Beach, on the other hand, is one of the more natural beaches on the island. It's very quiet, both day and night, with little nightlife and few restaurants—though that may not be the case for much longer. The gentle waters here are great for swimming, but water sports are limited to what your hotel can provide. Several inexpensive guesthouses and a few luxurious resorts share the 5-km (3-mi) stretch of sand. Mae Nam is also the departure point for speedboats and Lomprayah Catamaran leaving Samui for Phangan and Koh Tao. Transport on these boats can be arranged from anywhere on the island.

Divers love the clear water and colorful marine life around the nine Similan Islands.

LAEM YAI One the very northwestern tip of the island you'll find Laem Yai. It's also a rather underdeveloped area—for now—that's dotted with a few mega-resorts including the new Four Seasons. But there are also many tiny hole-in-the-wall seaside restaurants with delicious seafood at outrageously low prices.

BOPHUT A small headland separates Mae Nam from the north shore's other low-key community, Bophut. The beach here is quite narrow, but more than wide enough for sunbathing. During the rainy season the runoff waters make the sea slightly muddy. Otherwise, the water is like glass, good for swimming (though it's deep enough to be unsuitable for young children). Lodgings here range from backpacker hangouts to upscale resorts. Unlike ultraquiet Mae Nam, Bophut has a bit more nightlife—Central Bophut, known to everyone as Fishermen's Village, has a beachside strip of old two-story Chinese shophouses that have been converted into restaurants, bars, boutiques, and in one case a hotel. Although the scene is small, there's ample variety, including Italian and French cuisine, English and Australian pubs, and even a few clubs with DJs. Bophut, quaint and romantic, has a devoted following of return visitors who enjoy its compact and quiet environment.

CHOENGMON On the northeast coast of Samui lies Haad Choengmon. A few guesthouses, a handful of luxury resorts, and some restaurants are scattered along the shore of this laid-back beach. The sand is firm and strewn with pebbles and shells, but adequate for sunbathing.

For a little adventure, walk east to the bend in the beach and wade through the water to **Koh Fan Noi**, the small island 30 yards offshore.

The water all along the beach is swimmable, with a shallow shelf, and there are all varieties of water sports to choose from, including catamarans, Sunfish, Windsurfers, and kayaks.

Off the western shore of the northeastern tip of Koh Samui is **Koh Fan** (not to be confused with Koh Fan Noi), a little island with a huge seated Buddha image covered in moss. Try to visit at sunset, when the light off the water shows the statue at its best.

THE SPA LIFE

The ultimate spa experience on the island is at **Tamarind Springs** (✉ *205/7 Thong Takian, Lamai Beach* ☎ *077/424221* 🌐 *www.tamarindretreat.com*). Many different treatments are available, from Thai massage or hot oil massage to herbal relaxation to the "Over the Top" massage package, which lasts 2½ hours. The spa employs the latest treatment trends, including the use of Tibetan singing bowls, and it now has added additional spas, dipping pools, and a tearoom, built harmoniously into Tamarind's boulder-strewn hillside.

SPORTS & THE OUTDOORS

Although many people come to Samui to chill out on the beach, there are dozens of activities, certainly more than one vacation's worth. In addition to the activities listed below, you can arrange paintball, go-karting, shooting, and bungee jumping through most hotels and tour agents on the island.

You can go up into the mountains and explore the jungle and some of the waterfalls by car. If you're more adventurous, you can get a different view of the jungle by sailing through the air on a zipline. **Canopy Adventures** (☎ *077/414150*) will have you zipping among six tree houses on 330 yards of wire strung across the tree canopies. They also offer fun expeditions to waterfalls. If you prefer to stay on the ground, you can arrange a ride at the **Sundowner Horseranch** (☎ *077/424719*) in Ban Thale. Elephant treks are available through **Samui Namuang Travel & Tour** (☎ *077/418680 kwaithaisamui@hotmail.com*).

Finally someone has figured out how to fit an actual golf course on the island: Santiburi Resort has a driving range and an 18-hole course at the **Santiburi Samui Country Club** (☎ *077/421700 up to 08 in Samui, 02/664–4270 up to 74 in Bangkok*), which uses the natural terrain of the Samui mountains to create a challenging multilevel golfing experience. You can play nine holes for half the price. Also, one enterprising company, **Extra Golf Club** (☎ *077/422255*), has built a 3-hole course. Alternatively, you can shoot a round of Frisbee golf (same idea as regular golf, but Frisbees are tossed from the putting area to the "holes," which are actually baskets). Head to **Frisbee Golf** (☎ *091/894–2105*)—not to be confused with nearby Soccer Golf—near Bophut, laugh your way through a round of "golf," and grab an ice-cold beer at the end.

WHERE TO EAT

CHAWAENG

$$$ ★ SEAFOOD

✕ **Eat Sense.** Despite its manicured grounds, this is not a resort—just a restaurant that serves great Thai food. The dining area has several small fountains and towering palms from which hang giant paper lanterns.

Dine on the patio beside the beach or on couches beneath white umbrellas; sip creative cocktails (like the Sabai Sabai Samui, winner of a Samui bartending competition) served in coconut shells; and nosh on exotic seafood creations, such as Phuket lobster with eggplant and Kaffir lime leaves in a green curry paste. Reservations are recommended, particularly during the high season. ✉*Near Central Samui Resort* ☎*077/414242* ▭*MC, V.*

$$ SEAFOOD ✕**Noir Thai.** This restaurant achieves what many Thai restaurants, both here and in the U.S., only attempt: It's simultaneously upscale (well, somewhat) and authentic. You can feel fancy here among the sweeping tapestries and pretty people and still enjoy staples like prawns with chili paste, coconut cream, and Kaffir lime—as well as more interesting options like yam ta krai (yam with dried squid and shrimp). During the nightly happy hour from 6 to 8, cocktails run B120 apiece. ✉*119 Moo 2* ☎*077/230795* ▭*AE, MC, V.*

$$$ THAI ✕**The Page.** Stick to the fun and interesting cocktails here, not the boring wine list, and you'll soon start to feel as hip as your surroundings. The menu is Thai, with all the favorites like prawns with garlic and pepper, and sea bass with chili and basil. The setting is great, overlooking the beach, and it feels much cooler than most of Chawaeng's hectic scene. And it's always nice to be surrounded by such smart and hip design, such as the lounging figurines that dot the property. ✉*14/1 Moo 2, Chawaeng Beach* ☎*077/422767* ▭*AE, DC, MC, V.*

$$$ SEAFOOD ✕**Tarua Samui Seafood.** We don't know which is better here—the view or the food. High up on a mountain, the restaurant juts out above a rocky beach and turquoise waters. The food is also memorable. Raw shrimp have an indescribably silky texture, and the massive (cooked) prawns with garlic or with curry are delicious. Make sure to check the tank as you walk in; you just might see something you can't resist. ✉*210/9 Moo 4* ☎*077/960635* ▭*No credit cards.*

LAMAI

$$$$ MEDITERRANEAN ✕**The Cliff.** Halfway along the road from Chawaeng to Lamai is the Cliff, which is actually perched on a big boulder overlooking the sea. You can have lunch or dinner either inside the spartan dining room or out on the scenic deck. The lunch menu includes sandwiches and hamburgers; dinner features steaks and Mediterranean grill. The prices are a bit high for the small servings, and the service isn't great, but the Cliff is a nice place to stop to have a drink and check out the view. In the evening, cooler-than-thou staff serve cocktails in the enclosed, air-conditioned club. ✉*124/2 Samui Ring Rd., Lamai Beach* ☎*077/414266* 🌐*www.thecliffsamui.com* ✍*Reservations essential* ▭*AE, MC, V.*

$ SEAFOOD ✕**Mr. Pown Seafood Restaurant.** This place is nothing fancy, but it serves up reliable Thai dishes and seafood, as well as some German and English fare. Try the red curry in young coconut (a moderately spicy, not quite "red" curry with cauliflower and string beans served inside a coconut) or the catch of the day. The staff is courteous. ✉*Central Lamai Beach* ▭*No credit cards.*

BAAN TALING NGAM

$$$$ THAI ✕ **Five Islands.** If you truly want to get away from it all, this is the place. There's not much in the immediate vicinity except for the beautiful view—the restaurant faces five islands farther out at sea. Fresh oysters with crispy onion, garlic, and chili are a highlight on the Thai menu, as is the section of meals for two. Packages are also available that include a tour of the islands as well as your meal. ✉*Taling Nam 84320* ☎*077/415359* ▭*AE, DC, MC, V.*

MAE NAM

$ SEAFOOD ✕ **Bang Po Seafood.** Restaurants like Bang Po are almost reason enough to visit the islands. Mere feet away from lapping waves, this shack serves up the freshest seafood at the best of prices. The jarringly purple baby octopus soup and the sour curry with whole fish are two great options. Price-conscious sushi fans will be in love with the sea-urchin salad; $3 gets you more *uni* than one person can possibly eat. ✉*56/4 Moo 6, Mae Nam Beach* ☎*077/420010* ▭*No credit cards.*

5

$ SEAFOOD ✕ **Kohseng.** This two-story seafood restaurant has been feeding Mae Nam locals for decades. The interior is quite simple, with lots of dark wood. Don't be intimidated by the local crowd—menus are in both Thai and English, though the staff's English is a bit rough around the edges. The most famous dish, stir-fried crab with black pepper, is highly recommended. And prices are low, even by Koh Samui standards. ✉*95 Soi Kohseng, Mae Nam Beach* ☎*077/425365* ▭*No credit cards.*

$ SEAFOOD ✕ **Whan Tok.** Perched right on the water, this family-owned joint is often full with locals who come for the seafood—the massive prawns are great, and seafood soups have wonderfully flavorful broths. Finding the place is half the fun; the sign out front has no writing in English, so if you're coming by cab, ask someone at your hotel to write down the name in Thai. The cheap, delicious food is worth the extra effort. ✉*37/1 Moo 5, Mae Nam Beach* ☎*081/719–3595* ▭*No credit cards.*

BOPHUT

$$ SEAFOOD ✕ **Ocean 11.** This restaurant's unapologetically western menu and higher-than-average prices attract Americans and Europeans. Still, soft-shell crab on arugula and white snapper baked in a banana leaf can be a refreshing change of pace. It's all about the atmosphere here: warm, inviting, and right on the beach. So if you're feeling homesick, drop in for a rack of lamb. ✉*23 Moo 4* ☎*077/245134* ▭*AE, MC, V* ⊙*Closed Mon.*

$$$ THAI ✕ **The Pier.** The place is beautifully dressed up and waiting for tourists. The interior is sleek and black, ideal for sipping cocktails by moonlight. Seats out by the water feel more restaurant-like, while the indoor scene is clubbier. The menu here is about two parts Thai, one part international. Of the Thai dishes, catfish salad, wing bean salad, or crispy soft-shell crab are standouts. Modern music sets a nice background for it all. ✉*50 Moo 1* ☎*077/430681* ▭*AE, MC, V.*

$ ECLECTIC ✕ **Villa Daudet.** One of the newest additions to Bophut's dining scene, this French-Thai-Italian restaurant has a solid, continent-hopping menu. Moules marinières (mussels with white wine and garlic) are a good option. Villa Daudet also doubles as a bar, adding a bit to the beach's nightlife scene, which still has nothing on nearby Chawaeng. A cozy interior of warm oranges and paintings done by the owner himself makes the place feel slightly more upscale than its neighbors. ✉ *33/1 Moo 1* ☎ *083/643–6656* ▭ *AE, MC, V* ⊙ *Closed Mon.*

WHERE TO STAY

CHAWAENG

$$$ ★ **AKWA guesthouse.** Rooms at Australian proprietor Timothy Schwan's guesthouse have giant pop-art paintings on the walls, chairs in the shape of giant hands, and kitschy lamps. Smaller details, like a collection of books, including Thai language manuals and beach novels; a stack of DVDs atop the TV; colorful beach towels; and even the odd stuffed animal, really make it feel like you're crashing in a friend's well-designed bedroom. A penthouse room has a huge terrace with two teak sun beds, an outdoor dining area, and a lazy banana bed with a sweeping 180-degree view; indoors, a private bathtub overlooks the terrace towards Chawaeng Beach. ■ **TIP→ Breakfasts are arguably the best on the island**, other meals are decent as well, and the vibe in the lobby's bar-restaurant is friendly and easygoing. **Pros:** hyper-hip feel; fun crowd. **Cons:** can be noisy; not ideal for families. ✉ *28/12 Moo 3, Chawaeng Beach Rd., Chawaeng Beach* ☎ *04/660–0551* ⊕ *www.akwaguesthouse.com* *5 rooms* *In-room: refrigerator, DVD. In-hotel: restaurant, room service, bar, Wi-Fi* ▭ *No credit cards.*

$$ **Al's Hut.** A row of white huts follows a path beneath towering tamarind trees from the entrance of the resort, straight down to the beach. The trees provide a shady, beautiful setting and the huts are set far enough apart to make the resort feel less crowded than many of its neighbors. Doors to the huts have multicolor glass, but the rooms are otherwise simple and cozy. Al's is centrally located, on the nicest section of beach, and close to all the action. In sum, it's a great value. **Pros:** cheap; easy, relaxed vibe. **Cons:** nothing too snazzy; can feel a bit isolated. ✉ *159/86 Moo 2, Chawaeng Beach* ☎ *077/231650* ⊕ *www.alshutsamui.com* *32 rooms* *In-room: refrigerator. In-hotel: restaurant* ▭ *MC, V.*

$$$$ **Buri Rasa.** One of the many hotels along this happening stretch of Chawaeng Beach, Buri Rasa manages to blend in well with the party aspect of the scene while still managing to feel like a bit of a relaxing getaway. The buildings dotting the property look like lodges and are decked out in soothing browns, beiges, and greens. The infinity pool is a great place to hang out with a cocktail and enjoy the ocean view. **Pros:** very chill vibe; fun pool. **Cons:** on party stretch of beach; some foot traffic. ✉ *11/2 Moo 2, Chawaeng Beach* ☎ *077/230222* ⊕ *www.burirasa.com* *32 rooms* *In-room: safe, refrigerator. In-hotel: 2 restaurants, room service, bar, spa, pool* ▭ *AE, DC, MC, V.*

$$$ ★ **Iyara Beach Hotel and Plaza.** The Iyara is a getaway for young, European urbanites who don't want to give up the luxuries of home. The complex includes a maze of boutiques, including Lacoste and Bossini. Bronzed bodies lounge around the beachside pool and book spa treatments at the nearby Four Seasons–operated spa. Iyara studio rooms have peaked ceilings, wooden floors, and large bathtubs with sea views. Superior rooms have mattresses on the floor, Japanese style, but lack sea views. Cabanas, including deluxe pool rooms, are closest to the

beach, and have teak furniture and outdoor daybeds. ■ **TIP→ Particularly in low season, this is one of the most reasonably priced beachfront hotels on Chawaeng.** **Pros:** good deal; close to lots of activities. **Cons:** feels a bit hectic; many rooms lack views. ✉ *90/13–16 Chawaeng Beach, Koh Samui* ☎ *077/231629 up to 41* 🌐 *www.iyarabeachhotelandplaza.com* *75 rooms* *In-room: safe, refrigerator. In-hotel: restaurant, pool, spa, beachfront* ▭ *MC, V.*

The Library. This place is so fun that it's worth a visit even if you don't stay here. The amusingly hip decor will make anyone smile—check out the white figures reading books on the lawn, inviting you to lounge as well. Rooms have modern furniture like long, low tables, but are still quite comfortable. The beachside pool has a red tile base, making it fit in perfectly with the red, black, and white theme that's so prevalent here. The restaurant The Page (*Where to Eat, above*) is worth a visit, too. **Pros:** very stylish; cool, young crowd. **Cons:** pricey; not ideal if you're looking for quiet. ✉ *14/1 Moo 2, Chawaeng Beach,* ☎ *077/422767* 🌐 *www.thelibrary.name* *In-room: safe, refrigerator. In-hotel: restaurant, room service, gym, spa, pool, Internet terminal* ▭ *AE, DC, MC, V.*

5

$$$ **Montien House.** Two rows of charming bungalows line the path leading to the beach at this comfortable little resort. Each modest bungalow has a private patio surrounded by tropical foliage. Rooms are furnished in a spare style, yet are cozy. Penthouses in an adjacent building provide more-luxurious accommodation, with separate living and dining rooms. The management is attentive and helpful. **Pros:** cute; inexpensive. **Cons:** lacks pizzazz and many creature comforts. ✉ *5 Moo 2, Central Chawaeng Beach* ☎ *077/422169* 🌐 *www.montienhouse.com* *57 rooms, 3 suites* *In-room: refrigerator. In-hotel: restaurant, bar, pool, laundry service, Internet terminal* ▭ *MC, V.*

$$$$ **Muang Kulaypan Hotel.** This hotel puts a little more emphasis on design than some of its neighbors. Instead of the teak, antiques, and flowing fabrics you'll find at most resorts going for a "classic Thai" look, here you'll get simple lines, minimal furnishings, and sharp contrasts. There's a sort of subtle Javanese-Thai theme throughout, reflected in the artwork selected for the rooms. The VIP Inao suite allows you to sleep in a bed once used by King Rama IV. Bussaba Thai restaurant ($$$) serves uncommon but authentic Thai food. Note that rooms on the wings, farther from the main road, are considerably quieter. **Pros:** interesting decor; sea views from many rooms. **Cons:** expensive; can be noisy; standard rooms lack sea views. ✉ *100 Samui Ring Rd., North Chawaeng Beach* ☎ *077/230849 or 077/230850* 🌐 *www.kulaypan.com* *41 rooms, 1 suite* *In-room: safe, refrigerator. In-hotel: restaurant, room service, bar, pool, gym, laundry service, Wi-Fi* ▭ *AE, DC, MC, V* *BP.*

$$$$ **Nora Beach Resort and Spa.** An instant plus of this hotel is that 22 of its rooms have sea views. In addition, a large number of rooms look onto the pool, so you're almost guaranteed an aquatic view of some sort. The hotel is only four years old and has comfortable, if unexciting decor. Dark woods contrast beautifully against the golden Buddha images in bedrooms. **Pros:** comfortable surroundings; spacious bathrooms. **Cons:**

a little drab; not cheap. ✉222 Moo 2, North Chawaeng Beach ☎077/413999 or 077/429400 🌐www.norabeachresort.com 113 rooms In-room: safe, refrigerator. In-hotel: restaurant, bar, pool, gym, laundry service, Internet terminal ▭AE, DC, MC, V.

$$$$ ★ **Poppies.** More than 80 competent and friendly employees are on hand to attend to the guests at this romantic beachfront resort on the quieter southern end of Chawaeng. A large number of them are employed by the restaurant, which is as popular and remarkable as the resort itself and serves Thai and seafood under the stars or in the dining room. Cottages have living rooms with sofa beds, making them suitable for families or larger groups. The floors and trim are of handsome teak, and silk upholstery gives the place a decadent feel. Baths have sunken tubs and showers made of marble. The majority of guests are repeat visitors or word-of-mouth referrals. A 2006 renovation gave the resort a face-lift, including new bathrooms, reception area, and spa, and an upgraded pool. **Pros:** snappy service; immediate area not too crazy. **Cons:** not for young partiers; not cheap. ✉*Samui Ring Rd., South Chawaeng Beach* ☎*077/422419* 🌐*www.poppiessamui.net* *24 rooms* *In-room: safe, refrigerator, DVD. In-hotel: restaurant, room service, pool, spa, laundry service, Wi-Fi* ▭*AE, DC, MC, V.*

LAMAI

$$$ **Aloha Resort.** Ask for a room with a view of the ocean at this beachfront resort—many overlook the parking lot. However, all rooms have private terraces or balconies that do face in the general direction of the beach. The rooms are divided between those in the main building and those in attractive, refurbished bungalows, which lack a view but are closer to the beach and pool. The rooms have carpets, furniture, and bedding that appear to have not been replaced since the resort first opened 20 years ago, but Aloha is one of the few family-style accommodations you'll find in Lamai. The popular restaurant, Mai Thai, serves Thai, Chinese, and European food, while the more casual Captain's Kitchen has a nightly barbecue. **Pros:** ideal for families; reasonable price. **Cons:** some rooms not so nice. ✉*128 Moo 3* ☎*077/424014* 🌐*www.alohasamui.com* *74 rooms* *In-room: refrigerator. In-hotel: 2 restaurants, room service, bar, pool, beachfront, laundry service, Wi-Fi* ▭*AE, MC, V.*

$$ ★ **Lamai-Wanta.** Incredibly spartan rooms are kept immaculately clean, which is not surprising considering the owners-managers are a nurse and doctor couple. The two beachfront villas are their private residences, the other 10 bungalows and 40 attached rooms are for guests. Rooms have king-size beds and many tall, thin windows with interior shutters. Another highlight is an infinity-edge swimming pool directly on the beach surrounded by beach chairs, a beach bar, and restaurant. If you have come to Lamai to relax and enjoy the beach, Lamai-Wanta has all that you need, plus a small on-site clinic (in case you crash your motorbike). **Pros:** cool pool; beautiful beach. **Cons:** blah decor; lacks spunk. ✉*Central Lamai Beach* ☎*077/424550* 🌐*www.lamaiwanta.com* *40 rooms, 10 bungalows* *In-room: safe, refrigerator, Wi-Fi. In-hotel: restaurant, bar, pool* ▭*AE, MC, V* *BP.*

$$$$ **Pavilion.** Just far enough from central Lamai, the Pavilion offers a little respite from the downtown hustle and bustle. Rooms in the main building are more modern and more expensive than the stand-alone thatched bungalows, but are not necessarily better. Although Junior Suites have large outdoor daybeds and Jacuzzis, rooms 201 to 208 are the best of the rest. Superior spa rooms have outdoor Jacuzzis and huge wooden-canopy beds. The stylish restaurant serves tasty Thai and Italian, as well as fresh seafood. **Pros:** quiet; Jacuzzis in some rooms. **Cons:** some rooms very pricey; not the most modern hotel. ✉ *124/24 Lamai Beach* ☎ *077/424030* 🌐 *www.pavilionsamui.com* *70 rooms* *In-room: safe, refrigerator, DVD. In-hotel: restaurant, room service, bars, pool, spa, laundry service, Wi-Fi* 💳 *AE, MC, V.*

$$$$ **Renaissance Koh Samui Resort & Spa.** At the far northern end of Lamai, the Renaissance is technically on its own secluded, private beach (two small beaches to be exact). Most rooms are in multistory buildings connected by elevated walkways that pass through tropical gardens. All have outdoor Jacuzzis on terraces with ocean views, opulent decoration, and floor-to-ceiling glass doors leading from the bedroom to the deck. Separate villas have jumbo Jacuzzis, daybeds, fishponds, gardens, and even miniature waterfalls within their private, gated compounds. Shuttle service is available to Chawaeng Beach, where guests are free to use the facilities at the Princess Resort. **Pros:** sprawling grounds; high-end feel. **Cons:** isolated; pricey. ✉ *208/1 North Lamai Beach* ☎ *077/429300* 🌐 *www.renaissancehotels.com/usmbr* *45 rooms, 33 suites* *In-room: safe, refrigerator, DVD (some). In-hotel: 2 restaurants, room service, bar, pools, gym, spa, beachfront, water sports, bicycles, laundry service, Wi-Fi* 💳 *AE, DC, MC, V.*

BAAN TALING NGAM

$$$$ **Le Royal Meridien Baan Taling Ngam.** Its name means "home on a beautiful bank," but that doesn't come close to summing up the stunning location of this luxurious hotel. Most of the rooms are built into the 200-foot cliff, but the beachside villas are even better. The swimming pool is a magnificent trompe l'oeil, looking as if it's part of the ocean far below. There's a second pool by the beach where you can find an activities center. The beach is extremely narrow, so sunbathing is not feasible at high tide, but you can swim here. The southeast corner of the island is also closest to Angthong National Marine Park, making it the best resort from which to explore that island chain. You can dine on Thai and European fare at the Lom Talay ($$$$); seafood is served at the more casual Promenade ($$$). **Pros:** beautiful views; plenty of activities. **Cons:** can't lounge on beach; somewhat isolated. ✉ *295 Taling Ngam Beach* ☎ *077/429100, 02/6532201 up to 07 in Bangkok* 🌐 *www.lemeridien.com* *40 rooms, 30 villas* *In-room: safe, refrigerator, DVD, Internet. In-hotel: 2 restaurants, room service, bar, tennis court, pools, gym, spa, water sports, bicycles, laundry service, Internet terminal* 💳 *AE, DC, MC, V.*

MAE NAM & LAEM YAI

$$ **The Florist.** This guesthouse is quite small, but in a cute and cozy way. Most rooms have balconies with partial sea views, but the huge seafront

room has a full-on view of Phangan from its large deck, outdoor tub, and huge sun bed. Although the rooms in the old wing have aging furniture and a slightly musty smell, they are private enough that you can keep doors open at night to allow the breeze to blow through. Rooms in the new wing have a boutiquey decor, with beautiful wooden furniture and Thai art on the walls. The view from the pool is one of the best around—especially at this price point. **Pros:** good bang for your buck; easy beach access. **Cons:** not as comfy as some megachains; staff not so attentive. ✉ *190 Moo 1, Mae Nam Beach* ☎ *077/425671 up to 72* *32 rooms* *In-room: safe, refrigerator. In-hotel: restaurant, pool, laundry service, no-smoking rooms* ▭ *MC, V.*

$$$$ **Four Seasons Koh Samui.** This is easily one of the most spectacular hotels in the world. Its natural surroundings are breathtaking: turquoise waters, tall palm trees, and not a hint of development in the immediate area. Rooms, too, are impeccably designed, with state-of-the-art amenities. Most rooms have private infinity pools; there's another pool with a bar down by the water if you want to be closer to the action. The only downside is that you'll never want to leave the hotel to explore the island. **Pros:** ultimate luxury and relaxation; cool room design. **Cons:** might break the bank; golf carts necessary to get around. ✉ *219 Moo 5, Laem Yai, Koh Samui* ☎ *077/243000* ⊕ *www.fourseasons.com/kohsamui* *74 villas* *In-room: safe, refrigerator, DVD, Wi-Fi. In-hotel: 2 restaurants, room service, bar, tennis courts, pool, gym, spa, water sports, laundry service, no-smoking rooms* ▭ *AE, DC, MC, V.*

Fodor'sChoice ★

$$$$ ★ **Napasai.** The name means "clear sky," and if you book a beachfront room, you can enjoy the view of both the sky *and* the sea from your outdoor terrace, from inside the room as you lounge on L-shaped floor cushions, or even from your bathtub. Garden spa rooms make up for their lack of views with large living rooms and spacious showers and bathrooms, both adjacent to an outdoor waterfall. Multilevel private pool villas are the epitome of luxury: the bedrooms, the living room and kitchen areas, and the swimming pools are each on different floors. The staff is attentive, and if you should happen to get a rainy day, they'll arrange impromptu bridge games or other activities in the library or bar or outside the resort to help you pass the time. **Pros:** great views; super staff. **Cons:** pricey; some rooms not as nice as others. ✉ *Ban Tai Beach (west of Mae Nam), Koh Samui* ☎ *077/429200* ⊕ *www.napasai.com* *69 rooms* *In-room: safe, refrigerator, DVD. In-hotel: 2 restaurants, room service, bars, tennis courts, pool, gym, spa, laundry service, Wi-Fi, no-smoking rooms* ▭ *AE, DC, MC, V.*

BOPHUT

$$$$ **Anantara Resort Koh Samui.** Anantara captures the essence of Samui: coconut trees dot the grounds, monkey statues and sculptures decorate the entire resort, and, of course, there is a beautiful beach. All rooms have ocean views from their large patios and are designed in a modern Lanna style. Each room also has a tank with several colorful Thai fighting fish. You'll feel like a rock star performing on stage when dining at the Full Moon Italian Restaurant ($$$)—the dining room is a large open platform beside the swimming pool. The High-Tide Thai restaurant ($$$) allows you to interact with your chef, who is working near

your table and will alter any dish to your exact specifications. Booking a treatment at the stylish spa is a must. **Pros:** decent dining; pretty place. **Cons:** feels quite big; not for young party crowd. ✉ *101/3 Samui Ring Rd., Bophut Beach* ☎ *077/428300* 🌐 *www.anantara.com* *82 room, 24 suites* *In-room: safe, refrigerator, DVD, Wi-Fi. In-hotel: 2 restaurants, room service, bar, tennis court, pool, gym, spa, water sports, bicycles, laundry service, Wi-Fi* *AE, DC, MC, V.*

$$$$ **Bandara Resort and Spa.** Bandara gets high marks immediately for convenience: it's on the nicest stretch of Bophut Beach; the resort's facilities will be able to meet nearly all of your needs; and the restaurants, bars, and shops in the fisherman's village are a short walk away. The deluxe rooms in the large, multistory complex aren't particularly special, but they all have decks with daybeds. Rooms smell great—aromas are piped in—and fresh flowers sometimes await you. Private villas have gardens complete with outside tubs and showers, and shady daybeds perfect for massages. Five spa treatment rooms provide a variety of facials, massages, so-called "slimming programs," and aqua therapy. The seaside restaurant ($$) serves seafood and Thai dishes. **Pros:** ideal location; attentive staff. **Cons:** pool not inviting; unexciting room decor. ✉ *178/2 Moo 1, Bophut, Koh Samui* ☎ *077/245795* 🌐 *www.bandararesort.com* *151 rooms* *In-room: refrigerator, DVD, Wi-Fi. In-hotel: 2 restaurants, 3 bars, 2 pools, gym, spa, diving, water sports* *MC, V.*

$$$$ **Bo Phut Resort and Spa.** Though not every Thai beach hotel that claims to be a "resort and spa" really measures up, this place does live up to its name. Massages, scrubs, Thai herbal steams—you'll find it all here in their beautiful facility. Rooms are tasteful and cheery with bright colors and pretty views, and some have cozy balconies. The restaurant, Sala Thai, offers a set menu for B2,000. Don't be surprised if you see a lot of Germans there; the restaurant's sister location is in Hamburg. **Pros:** spectacular spa; nice restaurant. **Cons:** a bit overpriced; not the most happening location. ✉ *12/12 Moo 1, Bophut, Koh Samui* ☎ *077/245777* 🌐 *www.bophutresort.com* *61 rooms* *In-room: refrigerator, safe, DVD, Wi-Fi. In-hotel: restaurant, spa* *MC, V.*

$ **Cactus Bungalows.** Colorful, funky huts are set in an unmanicured, natural environment. Instead of clunky bedsteads, mattresses rest on rounded platforms, giving rooms an organic feel. The bar and restaurant by the beach is pretty basic, but it does have a pool table. As you can imagine, Cactus Bungalows is a pretty laid-back place. **Pros:** interesting decor; laid-back vibe. **Cons:** some rooms lack a/c; not luxurious. ✉ *175/7 Moo 1, Bophut Beach* ☎ *077/245565* 🌐 *www.sawadee.com/hotel/samui/cactus* *13 bungalows, 1 suite* *In-room: no a/c (some). In-hotel: restaurant, bar, laundry service* *MC, V.*

$$$ **Punnpreeda.** This resort is definitely striving for hipness. Though it doesn't achieve quite the effortlessly cool vibe you'll find in some Bangkok hotels, it's still a pleasant little space. Rooms, all of which have balconies, are decked out in pretty colors and have walls that look like hardened clay; 1970s-style beads hang near the beds. For the young set looking for nightlife, there's a shuttle to Chawaeng twice nightly. **Pros:** fun atmosphere; convenient shuttle. **Cons:** not ideal for families; not on

5

Samui's hip strip. ⊠*199 Moo 1, Bang Rak Beach, Koh Samui* ☎*077/246333* 🌐*www.punnpreeda.com* *25 rooms* *In-room: refrigerator, safe, DVD, Wi-Fi. In-hotel: restaurant, bar, pool, water sports* ▭ *AE, MC, V.*

$$ **Red House.** This is no misnomer: The Red House has red walls, red furniture, and red bedding—almost too much red, though considering it's a converted Chinese shophouse, the red lanterns seem particularly appropriate. There is a small seaside patio for snacks and coffee, and a rooftop garden with the best view in Bophut. A small boutique in the front sells mostly cool women's shoes and a few Chinese-style women's tops, and even the library still manages to feel as hip as the rest of the place. All four rooms have sea views—a major plus. **Pros:** charming concept; great views. **Cons:** often fully booked; no easy beach access. ⊠*Fisherman's Village, Bophut, Koh Samui* ☎*077/425686* 🌐*www.design-visio.com* *4 rooms* *In-room: refrigerator. In-hotel: restaurant, room service, bar, laundry service, Wi-Fi* ▭*MC, V.*

$$$$ **Zazen.** The Japanese style of this hotel may be a refreshing change of place if you've been in Thailand for a while. It's a peaceful and relaxing place, especially near the water: the pool is quite striking at night and beautifully lit, and the beach boasts rows of comfy chairs. The spa is first rate, too. Low-slung eastern-style beds, red accents, and panoramic windows are signature elements of the rooms, and bungalows have sliding doors that open the room to the air. **Pros:** on nice stretch of beach; great atmosphere. **Cons:** expensive; not a party destination. ⊠*177 Moo 1, Bophut* ☎*077/425085* 🌐*www.samuizazen.com* *In-room: safe, refrigerator. In-hotel: restaurant, bar, room service, gym, spa, pool, laundry service, Wi-Fi* ▭*AE, DC, MC, V.*

CHOENGMON

$$$$ **Absolute Sanctuary.** If you're looking to detox on vacation, this is the spot—and if you aren't, well, it probably isn't. The hotel offers three different programs of varying intensity: a cleansing program that includes some vegetarian food for newbies; a mostly-raw-foods program; and a fasting regime for the truly committed. You'll find the best yoga on the island here. Rooms here are simple, cute, and—surprise, surprise—relaxing. **Pros:** prime yoga facilities; unique concept. **Cons:** no fun if you're not detoxing; pricey. ⊠*43 Moo 1, Bophut* ☎*077/601190* 🌐*www.absolutesanctuary.com* *38 rooms* *In-room: safe, refrigerator. In-hotel: restaurant, pool, Wi-Fi* ▭*AE, MC, V.*

$$$$ **Kandaburi.** This boutique hotel, though on the large side, is one of the classier options on Samui. Vaguely Balinese in design, it makes use of dark woods—often as a stunning contrast against stark white or shimmering gold. A lotus pond on the grounds doesn't feel the least bit out of place, and the beachside pool almost makes up for the fact that only two rooms have sea views. **Pros:** aesthetically pleasing; pretty beach. **Cons:** most rooms lack beach views; service could be better. ⊠*20 Moo 2, Bophut* ☎*077/428888 or 077/414424* 🌐*www.kandaburi.com* *183 rooms* *In-room: safe, refrigerator. In-hotel: 4 restaurants, room service, bar, spa, pool, gym, laundry service, Internet terminal* ▭ *AE, MC, V.*

$$$$ ★ **SALA Samui.** Bright, nearly all-white rooms have both retractable and open doorways that lead to private courtyards on one side, and curtain-enclosed bathrooms on the other. Only some rooms have small private pools in their courtyards, but all have large oval bathtubs, which are nearly as nice and certainly as romantic. The two-bedroom Presidential Pool Villa has a larger pool and more space to fill with equally lavish accoutrements. SALA restaurant, beside the pool and overlooking the beach, has a wonderful evening atmosphere. **Pros:** lots of privacy; good dining. **Cons:** pricey; beach views could be better. ✉ *10/9 Moo 5, Baan Plai Laem, Koh Samui* ☎ *077/245889* 🌐 *www.salasamui.com* *69 rooms* *In-hotel: restaurant, room service, bar, pools, spa, beachfront, Wi-Fi* *AE, DC, MC, V.*

$$ **Samui Honey Cottages.** The cottages at this small, cozy resort on one of Samui's quieter beaches have glass sliding doors and peaked ceilings, and bathrooms have showers with glass ceilings. Dine alfresco under hanging gardens, or walk down the beach and have fresh seafood at the beachside restaurant across the channel from Koh Fan Lek. **Pros:** well located; welcoming staff. **Cons:** not that special; no real nightlife. ✉ *24/34 Choengmon Beach* ☎ *077/245032 or 077/279093* 🌐 *www.samuihoney.com* *19 bungalows, 1 suite* *In-room: safe, refrigerator. In-hotel: restaurant, laundry service* *MC, V.*

5

$$$$ Fodor's Choice ★ **Six Senses Hideaway Samui.** From the moment you're greeted by the management and introduced to your private butler, you'll realize that this is not just another high-end resort—you're about to embark on an amazing experience. Your butler will escort you via electric car to your private villa. The rooms have plush bedding, tubs arranged near flawless ocean views, separate outdoor showers, and a variety of lighting options. Don't forget to lounge at the 30-meter infinity pool on the cliff. Dining on the Hill serves an exquisite and comprehensive breakfast buffet, and Dining on the Rocks ($$$) has a romantic private terrace perfect for indulging in innovative and exotic cuisine. The resort even employs its own consultants to make sure it is environmentally friendly. **Pros:** butler service; delicious restaurant. **Cons:** expensive; difficult to navigate sprawling hotel. ✉ *9/10 Bay View Bay* ☎ *077/245678* 🌐 *www.sixsenses.com* *66 villas* *In-room: safe, refrigerator, DVD. In-hotel: 2 restaurants, room service, bars, pool, gym, spa, beachfront, laundry service, Wi-Fi* *AE, DC, MC, V* *BP.*

$$$$ ★ **Tongsai Bay.** The owners of this splendid all-suites resort managed to build it without sacrificing even one of the tropical trees that give the place a refreshing and natural sense of utter seclusion. The suites, contained in luxurious wooden bungalows, have large private terraces. They also have outdoor bathtubs or private pools and some have beds outside the rooms, protected by mosquito nets. Furnishings are stunning, with individual touches like fresh flowers. The resort is perfect for honeymooners, as the entire place exudes a "love at first sight" vibe. It's on a private beach just to the north of Choengmon that is suitable for sunbathing. The water is okay for cooling off in, but better for water sports, like windsurfing, which can be arranged through the resort. **Pros:** beautiful exterior and interior. **Cons:** quite secluded; not the best beach for lounging. ✉ *84 Tongsai Bay* ☎ *077/245480 or*

077/245544 ⊕www.tongsaibay.co.th 83 suites In-room: safe, refrigerator, DVD. In-hotel: 3 restaurants, room service, bar, tennis courts, pools, gym, spa, beachfront, laundry service, Internet terminal ▭AE, DC, MC, V BP.

NIGHTLIFE

You'll find the most nighttime action in central Lamai and on Chawaeng's Soi Green Mango—a looping street chockablock with beer bars and nightclubs of all sizes including the enormous Green Mango and trendy DJ club Mint Bar.

CHAWAENG At the corner of Beach Road and Soi Green Mango is the multilevel, open-air, chill-out bar called **The Deck.**

Ark Bar (☎*077/422047 or 077/413798 ⊕www.ark-bar.com*) is one of Samui's original nightlife venues on the beach. They throw a party with free barbecue every Wednesday around sunset. Farther south, across from Central Samui Beach Resort down Soi Coliburi (which looks like an unnamed street) there are several clubs, the most popular and stylish of which is **POD** (☎*018/914042*).

The popular **Reggae Pub** (☎*077/422331*), on the far side of the lagoon opposite Chawaeng's main strip, is a longtime favorite. It has several bars and dance floors.The **Islander Pub & Restaurant** (✉*Central Chawaeng, near Soi Green Mango* ☎*077/230836*) has 11 televisions channeling Thai, Australian, and Malaysian satellites and holds in-house pool competitions and a quiz night.

The hottest place to be on the island is **Q Bar Samui** (☎*081/956–2742* ⊕*www.qbarsamui.com*), an upscale nightclub from the owners of the Q Bar in Bangkok and Singapore. Sexy bartenders pour premium spirits while international DJ's spin. It's high up on the hillside to the north of Chawaeng Lake—the drive home could be disastrous for motorbike riders or anyone unfamiliar with the roads, so plan on a safer form of transportation like a taxi.

LAMAI The one-stop, sprawling party spot **Bauhaus** has foam parties on Monday and Friday nights. In the dead center of town there's a muay thai boxing ring that features women boxers on weekends and *muay thai* (Thai kickboxing) exhibitions staged regularly during the high season. The boxing ring is surrounded by beer bars with highly skilled Connect Four players, and across the street, is the heart of Lamai's club scene: **Fusion,** a dark, chilled-out open-air club spinning hip-hop and progressive house; **SUB,** a huge indoor dance club that also has an outdoor party area with enormous projection TV screen; and **Club Mix,** another megasize club featuring international and local DJs.

KOH PHANGAN

12 km (7 mi) by boat north of Koh Samui.

As Koh Samui developed into an international tourist hot spot, travelers looking for a cheaper and/or more laid-back scene headed for Koh Phangan. Decades ago, the few wanderers who arrived here stayed in fishermen's houses or slung hammocks on the beach. Gradually, simple bungalow colonies sprang up on even the most remote beaches, and investors bought up beach property with plans for sprawling resorts. Although some large commercial development did occur, a funny thing happened on the way to Samui-like development: the allure of Koh Tao's crystalline waters starting drawing away a lot of the attention. While Haad Rin boomed as a result of its world-famous Full Moon Party, most of Koh Phangan's smaller beaches continued to develop, but at a much less rapid pace. For now, most of Phangan remains a destination for backpackers looking for beautiful beaches with budget accommodation and hippies (old-school and nouveau) searching for chilled-out beaches and alternative retreats.

GETTING HERE & AROUND

BY BOAT The best way to get here is by ferry from Koh Samui, or from Surat Thani via Samui. Boats depart hourly from Surat Thani's Donsak Pier to Na Thon Pier in Koh Samui; the price includes the hour bus ride from Surat Thani's airport to the pier. After the 2½-hour voyage to Samui, passengers must disembark and catch a second boat to Koh Phangan's Thong Sala Pier, a 30-minute journey. Seatran boats depart Samui for Phangan daily at 8 AM and 1:30 PM. Return travel from Phangan to Samui is at 10:30 AM and 4:30 PM.

If you take a Songserm ferry instead, you won't have to switch boats on Samui; however, Songserm makes the Surat Thani-Samui-Phangan run only once a day, leaving Surat Thani at 8 AM and returning from Phangan at 12:30 PM.

There are a number of ways to travel between Phangan and either Samui or Koh Tao—Lomphrayah and SeaTran boats are the best options. Boats to and from Koh Tao take 2 to 2½ hours.

ESSENTIALS

Hospital **Haad Rin Inter Clinic** (✉ *116/20 Haad Rin, Haad Rin, Koh Phangan* ☎ *077/375342 or 01/318-5085*).

EXPLORING

Since the island's unpaved roads twist and turn, it's easier to beach-hop via boat, although most beaches are now accessible via songthaew pickup trucks (it's *not* advisable to attempt most of Koh Phangan's curvy roads on motorbike).

BEACHES

If you want to find the beach that most appeals to you, take a longtail boat around the island—the trip takes a full day and stops in many places along the way. Boats from Koh Tao and the mainland alight at Thong Sala, an uninteresting town, where taxis can shuttle you around the island, including to the larger beaches of Chalok Lam, in the north, and Haad Rin, at the southeast tip of the island. Most backpackers and tourists without a game plan head straight to Haad Rin. Haad Sarikantang (Leela Beach), Haad Yuan, and Haad Thien are close to Haad Rin and are good choices for those interested in going to the

Full Moon Party, but who want to stay in a nicer, more relaxing beach environment.

If you aren't here for the Full Moon Party, head up the east coast to quieter Haad Thong Nai Pan, or even farther afield. One of the island's most remote beaches—and the most beautiful—is Haad Kuat (Bottle Beach), which has gorgeous white sand and only five simple accommodations. Haad Salad and Haad Yao, on the northweat coast, are similarly remote beaches for those looking for relaxation.

HAAD RIN Haad Rin Town has many good restaurants, shops, and bars. It's densely built up, and not very quiet, but full of fun. The town is sandwiched between Haad Rin West and Haad Rin East. The west side is where the main pier of the island is located and where literally boatloads of visitors disembark, most of whom stay in Haad Rin town or along the beach on Haad Rin East.

Haad Rin West has swimmable water, but you needn't settle for this beach when Haad Rin East is only a short walk away. Haad Rin East is a beautiful beach lined with bungalows and bars, although the water isn't nearly as pristine as at the more remote beaches. Once a month, Haad Rin East gets seriously crowded when throngs of young people gather on the beach for an all-night Full Moon Party. Check your calendar before heading to Phangan as the island starts to fill up at least a week prior to the big event. Boats from Thong Sala, the major town, take about 40 minutes to reach Haad Rin East, but most people travel on songthaews, which take only 15 minutes. Nearby is the smaller but quieter beach of Haad Sarikantang (Leela Beach) if you want to stay away from the crowds but still want to be close to the party.

HAAD YUAN Haad Yuan is a small, beautiful beach between Haad Rin and Haad Thien. Despite its proximity to Haad Rin (a 10-minute boat ride), Haad Yuan is worlds away: the beach is not built up (there are just a few resorts) and it's extremely quiet most of the month. However, because of its location, the rooms at the resorts fill up quickly about a week prior to the Full Moon Party; ■ TIP→ **in high season you must book in advance.**

HAAD THONG NAI PAN Fodor'sChoice ★ To escape Haad Rin's crowds, take a boat up the east coast to Haad Thong Nai Pan, a horseshoe bay divided by a small promontory. On the beach of the southern half are several guesthouses and restaurants, as well as a convenient ATM. The northern part of the bay, called Tong Nai Pan Noi, has a glistening crescent of sand that curves around the turquoise waters. The best time to visit this long stretch of white-sand beach is from December to August, as the area can be hard to reach by boat during the monsoon months (September–November). However, a bumpy songthaew ride will get you there during those months.

HAAD KUAT The only ways to get to Haad Kuat (Bottle Beach) are by boat from Chalok Lam, on a 20-minute songthaew ride from Thong Sala Pier, or on a longtail boat from nearby Thong Nai Pan. It might be more difficult to get to than other beaches, but it's definitely worth the hassle. The beach itself is about a quarter-mile-long stretch of fine, white sand.

The water is a beautiful sparkling blue, perfect for swimming, especially on the western end of the beach. There are only five resorts on Haad Kuat, so the beach isn't too crowded in the morning or late in the afternoon (though it does receive many day-trippers from the rest of the island midday). The scene is young and fun: each guesthouse blares the latest Western hits in the common areas for travelers chilling out on triangular pillows. If you prefer peace and quiet, stick to the beach or string a hammock up in front of your hut. If you get tired of lounging around, follow the steep trail up to the viewpoint above the western end of the beach.

WHERE TO EAT

Haad Rin has the most restaurants, but you'll find plenty of simple seafood restaurants on other beaches as well.

HAAD RIN

$$ SEAFOOD **Lucky Crab Restaurant.** The extensive menu includes entrées from all around the world, as if trying to please all the island's international visitors. But the specialty at the Lucky Crab is, of course, barbecue seafood, served with 12 different sauces. Select your fish, select your sauce, and then enjoy the breeze from the ceiling fans while you await your tasty food at this fun and friendly eatery. Also worth trying is the sizzling seafood in a hot pan. *94/18 Haad Rin W, Koh Phangan 077/375125 or 077/375498 No credit cards.*

$ CAFE **Nira's Bakery and Restaurant.** As you walk into the restaurant, you'll be bombarded by the mouthwatering smell of fresh-baked goods. The owner picked up his baking skills while living and working in Germany, and then opened this funky bakery in the mid-1980s, before the island even had electricity. Traditional homemade lasagna, fresh fruit juices, and gourmet sandwiches are a few of the specialties available at the juice bar, sandwich bar, and air-conditioned bakery. *130 Central Haad Rin, Koh Phangan No credit cards.*

5

WHERE TO STAY

HAAD RIN

$$–$$$ ★ **Cocohut Resort.** Cocohut Resort is on Leela Beach, a five-minute walk from Haad Rin West. Although Leela Beach is not as beautiful as Haad Rin, it's quieter and much more relaxing. Rooms range from backpacker rooms with a shared bath in a large wood-and-concrete building to cute clapboard huts on the beachfront and hill. Rooms on the beach are either air-conditioned or fan-cooled. Rooms away from the beach are connected by a boardwalk and have ladders leading up to tiny lofts; newer bungalows on the hill have high ceilings and lots of windows with impressive ocean views. The resort provides a slew of services and amenities, including beach volleyball, rafts, and kayaks to keep you busy during the low tide, when the water is too shallow for swimming. **Pros:** good deal; cute quarters. **Cons:** not so scenic; not the best swimming beach. *130/20 Leela Beach, Koh Phangan 077/375368 www.cocohut.com 76 bungalows, 24 rooms In-room: no a/c (some), refrigerator. In-hotel: restaurant, bar, pool, water sports, Wi-Fi MC, V.*

$$$ **Phangan Buri Resort and Health Spa.** This is the latest multimillion-baht, modern hotel development in Haad Rin. What you get is an international-standards hotel room, complete with modern amenities, but sadly lacking the Thai island vibe. Still, rooms have touches of Thai style, including Thai art on the walls. A computer in every room helps e-mail-addicted travelers stay in touch with their less fortunate friends and family back home. Deluxe beachfront rooms have sea views and are next to the seaside swimming pool and spa, where a variety of treatments are available. **Pros:** feels new; nice views. **Cons:** a bit generic; room decor could be nicer. ✉ *120/1 Moo 6, Haad Rin Nai Beach* ☎ *077/375481* 🌐 *www.phanganburiresort.net* *106 rooms* *In-room: safe, refrigerator, Internet. In-hotel: restaurant, bars, pools, spa* *AE, MC, V* *BP.*

$$ ★ **Sarikantang.** This small resort, with both wooden and concrete bungalows on Leela Beach, is a short walk from Haad Rin. All the concrete rooms have outdoor showers and baths, hot water, air-conditioning, and hammocks, while some of the wooden bungalows have only cold water and fans and none of the other standard amenities like TVs or minibars. The rooms are behind the pool, and although none of them are beachfront, almost all have ocean views. The two suites have large stone bathtubs that look over cozy living rooms, across the decks, and out to the sea. The spa, which is right on the beach, provides excellent massages while you listen to the waves lap the shore. This is a family-run resort that genuinely tries to make you feel welcome and help you enjoy your stay. **Pros:** lots of ocean views; friendly place. **Cons:** could be more central; cheapest rooms not comfortable. ✉ *129/3 Leela Beach, Koh Phangan* ☎ *077/375055 or 077/375056* 🌐 *www.sarikantang.com* *47 rooms* *In-room: no a/c (some), safe (some), refrigerator (some), DVD (some), no TV (some). In-hotel: restaurant, pool, spa, laundry service, Wi-Fi* *MC, V.*

¢ **Sea View Haad Rin Resort.** The simple, wooden, fan-cooled huts directly on the beach at the "quieter" northern end of Haad Rin are the best deal in the area—for the best location. In fact, the beachfront rooms with fans and hammocks on their porches are arguably better than air-conditioned huts in the second row. **Pros:** good deal; extremely low-key. **Cons:** not near the action; some rooms lack a/c. ✉ *134 Haad Rin Nok Beach* ☎ *077/375160* *40 rooms* *In-room: no a/c (some), no phone, no TV. In-hotel: restaurant* *No credit cards.*

HAAD YUAN

¢ **Barcelona Resort.** For very few baht you get a private cottage with doors on two walls that fold open to reveal a wraparound deck. Every cottage, large and small, is on the hill overlooking the powdery beach. Rooms are simple, with fans and mosquito nets, but slightly larger and breezier than your average beach bungalow. **Pros:** low price; fun experience. **Cons:** no a/c; few amenities. ✉ *Haad Yuan* ☎ *085/787–2339* *25 rooms* *In-room: no a/c, no TV. In-hotel: restaurant, laundry service* *No credit cards.*

HAAD THONG NAI PAN

¢ **Dolphin.** Dolphin's small, clean, basic bungalows are situated in a veritable Garden of Eden on the southern end of Tong Nai Pan Yai. The rooms are Thai-style huts the way beach bungalows should be designed: built entirely of wood with shuttered windows, fans, mosquito nets, and hammocks slung on the decks. Sadly, they are not beachfront, but sit behind an ultracool beach bar, which has a variety of shady lounge areas for people to relax and play cards, sip cocktails, or just laze away the days. **Pros:** lush grounds; cool crowd. **Cons:** not beachfront; few creature comforts. ✉ *Tong Nai Pan Yai* ☎ *077/445135 kimgiet@hotmail.com* *20 rooms* *In-room: no a/c, no phone, no TV. In-hotel: bar* *No credit cards.*

$$$$ ★ **Panviman Resort.** The big attraction at this friendly resort is its two restaurants ($$), one of which is a circular Thai-style dining area that is open to the ocean breezes; the other is seaside. Superior rooms have hardwood floors, spacious decks with ocean views, and convenient access to the gorgeous, multitiered swimming pool. Superior cottages are more like small wooden houses than bungalows and sit on the hill above the small private beach. Family cottages are enormous, with tall glass windows for walls on both stories. The resort provides shuttle service to Bangkok. **Pros:** good for families; shuttle service. **Cons:** verging on overpriced; not near interesting nightlife. ✉ *22/1 Thong Nai Pan Noi Bay* ☎ *077/445101 up to 09, 077/445220 up to 24* *www.panviman.com* *72 rooms, 14 cottages, 18 deluxe cottages* *In-room: no a/c (some), safe, refrigerator. In-hotel: 2 restaurants, bar, pool, beachfront, laundry service* *MC, V.*

$ **Star Hut Resort.** A friendly and chilled-out resort on Tong Nai Pan Noi, Star Hut has simple wooden huts with rattan walls, thatch roofs, and wraparound decks ideal for enjoying this beautiful and peaceful remote beach. Rooms 1, 110, 210, and 310 are beachfront. The open-air restaurant provides service with a smile. **Pros:** great Thai vibe; cheap. **Cons:** some rooms lack a/c; not all huts beachside. ✉ *Tong Nai Pan Noi* ☎ *077/445085 star_hut@hotmail.com* *26 rooms* *In-room: no a/c (some). In-hotel: restaurant, Wi-Fi* *MC, V.*

HAAD KUAT

¢ **Smile Bungalows.** Of the guesthouses on Haad Kuat, this one, on the western end of the beach, is the best. Huts are on the hillside overlooking the beach and have large wooden decks and bright bathrooms decorated with shells. The bungalows higher up on the hill are duplexes and have great ocean views. The restaurant ($$) has a comfortable seating area with both standard wooden tables, and low tables surrounded by triangular pillows. The staff frequently hangs out with the guests in the evening when the music gets turned up, the lights turned down, and cards and beer bottles cover the tables. The beach in front is also the best spot for swimming. The bungalows only have electricity from 6 PM to 6 AM. **Pros:** cool views; fun staff. **Cons:** no a/c; no electricity during the day. ✉ *Haad Kuat* ☎ *091/780–2881* *25 rooms* *In-room: no a/c, no TV. In-hotel: restaurant, laundry service* *No credit cards.*

5

NIGHTLIFE

Haad Rin East is lined with bars and clubs—music pumps and drinks pour from dusk until dawn, seven days a week, 365 days a year. All this culminates in a huge beach party with tens of thousands of revelers every full moon (or the night after, if the full moon lands on a major Buddhist holiday). Check out *www.fullmoonparty-thailand.com* for details. If you're only here for a night, check out **Cactus** and **Drop In Club,** two of the most popular nightspots, both right on the beach.

KOH TAO

47 km (29 mi) by boat north of Koh Phangan.

Less than a decade ago, the tiny island of Koh Tao could be compared to the one inhabited by Robinson Crusoe: no electricity, no running water, no modern amenities of any kind. Today it's built up with air-conditioned huts with cable TV, tattoo parlors, discos, and a few 7-11s. Dozens of small bungalow colonies offer every level of accommodation, from ultrabasic to modern luxury. The peace and quiet has disappeared from the main beaches, but the primary reason to come here is still the underwater world. **TIP→ Koh Tao is an excellent place to get your scuba certification.** Many operators don't have pools, so the initial dives must be done in the shallow, crystal-clear ocean water. Advanced divers will appreciate the great visibility, decent amount of coral, and exotic and plentiful marine life.

GETTING HERE & AROUND

Getting to Koh Tao is easy—it's on the scheduled ferry routes out of Koh Phangan and Koh Samui, and several boats a day make the trip from Chumphon on the mainland. Catamarans take 1½ hours, high-speed Seatran vessels take 2 hours, and regular ferry service takes 6.

Lomprayah Catamaran (*www.lomprayah.com*) has 1¾-hour trips between Koh Samui and Koh Tao for B500 twice daily, at 7 AM and 5 PM. Lomprayah Catamaran stops at Koh Phangan on their way from Koh Samui (at 8:30 and 12:30), if you wish to jump on or off there. Lomprayah also has boat-and-bus packages available to get you from Bangkok or Hua Hin to Koh Tao. In addition, speedboats leave at 8:30 AM from Bophut Pier on the north side of Koh Samui, taking snorkelers on day trips to the island and its neighbor, Koh Nang Yuan.

ESSENTIALS

Hospital **Mae Haad Clinic** (*Mae Haad Blvd., across from Post Office, Mae Haad, Koh Tao 091/081–7797*).

EXPLORING

Sairee, the island's longest, most popular beach, is a crescent-shaped beach with palm trees arching over the pellucid, aquamarine water as if they are yearning to drink from the sea. Along the thin sliver of golden sand sit rustic, traditional wooden beach huts with bohemian youths lounging in hammocks; novice divers practicing in seaside pools; and European students on holiday, sipping cocktails at basic beach bars. On the far northern end of the beach a few "upscale" resorts provide urban amenities amid manicured landscapes that manage to blend in with their surroundings enough to create idyllic beach environments rather than artificial resort settings. Sairee Beach is west-facing and therefore great for watching the sun set and for kayaking to Koh Nang Yuan. Chalok Baan Kao Beach, on the southern shore, is another nice beach, which is popular with travelers of all stripes. Travelers looking for real peace and quiet head to the smaller, more isolated beaches and bays, which generally have only a few guesthouses each, a more laid-back scene, and nice snorkeling conditions directly offshore.

At high tide the three small islands of Koh Nang Yuan sit beside each other in an obtuse, triangular pattern, separated by shallow, translucent water. At low tide the receding water exposes two narrow sandbars connecting the outer islands where the bungalows are to the central island, which has a lodge, restaurant, and beach bar. The islands are privately owned by the Koh Nang Yuan Dive Resort, and all visitors who wish to set foot on the island must shell out a B100 fee. Although many visitors opt to pay, many others simply dock offshore to snorkel and dive the gorgeous waters surrounding the islands. The islands are quite close to Koh Tao; you can kayak from Sairee Beach, or hire a longtail to ferry you here (it takes about 15 minutes). ■ **TIP→The islands are quite busy throughout the day, so try to visit early in the morning or late in the afternoon.** While you are visiting, take a trip up to the viewpoint on the southern island for some photos to make your friends at home jealous.

5

WHERE TO EAT

$$ ★ TAPAS ✕ **Papa's Tapas.** Low, warm lighting and relaxing music contribute to the upscale feel of Papa's—the elegance of this restaurant is indicative of Koh Tao's growing popularity and prosperity. Each of the five courses on the set menu is served with a luscious beverage, such as a Japanese plum martini, that complements the food. You can also sample delectable seafood, meat, and vegetarian tapas (like lemon-and-tandoori black tiger prawns or coffee-flavored duck breast with a vanilla foam) à la carte. There is also a small hooka lounge where hip patrons lounge on beanbags while puffing on flavored tobaccos or Cuban cigars and sipping on glasses of absinthe. Reservations are recommended during the high season. ✉ *Next to the 7-11 on the northern end of Sairee Beach* ☎ *077/457020* ▬ *No credit cards.*

WHERE TO STAY

$$ **Black Tip Dive Resort and Watersport Center.** This resort is located on Tanote Bay, on Koh Tao's eastern shore. Although the sand here is coarse, the bay is great for snorkeling, full of colorful coral, large fish, and even small black-tip reef sharks that cruise the northern side of the bay around sunset. It's a great place to do your scuba certification. Rooms are set in a nicely landscaped garden on the hill above the bay and are a stylish blend of natural wood and painted, curvaceous concrete walls. A pickup-truck taxi makes the run to Mae Haad five times daily, and a taxi-boat for trips around the island is available from the Mt. Reef Resort at the south end of the bay. Room discounts

CLOSE UP

Diving & Snorkeling Responsibly

Decades of visitors scuba-diving in Thailand's islands and reefs has had far greater negative effects on marine life than the 2004 tsunami. Considering that the number of visitors is quickly returning to pre-tsunami levels, every diver needs to be aware of, and consequently minimize, his or her impact.

As fascinating as something you see may be, **do not touch anything** if possible, and **never stand on anything other than sand.** Coral is extremely fragile, urchins are as painful as they look, and although sharks may be no threat to divers, you can appreciate the foolishness of grabbing one's tail. Other dangers to both you and the environment are less obvious: eels live within holes in rocks and reef; turtles are mammals that require air to breathe and even some dive instructors are guilty of "hitching a ride" on them, causing the turtles to expend precious air. Let instructors know you find this behavior unacceptable. Furthermore, **don't feed fish human food**—feeding the fish bread, peas, or even M&Ms may be entertaining, but it rewards more aggressive fish to the detriment of species diversity.

Divers should also **make sure equipment is securely fastened or stored,** so that no items are lost or scrape against coral. Divers should also **maintain level buoyancy** to prevent inadvertent brushes with coral, as well as to save air. Snorkelers who need to remove their masks should pull them down around their necks rather than up on their foreheads. Masks can fall off and quickly sink, and a mask on the forehead is considered a symbol of distress. When snorkeling, you can **minimize underwater pollution by checking your pockets** before jumping into the water. Conscientious divers can clip a stuffsack to their BCDs to pocket random trash they encounter. Lastly, it seems like a no-brainer, but apparently many people need to be reminded: **don't flick cigarette butts into the water.**

Sunscreen is a must anytime you are exposed to Thailand's tropical sun. Snorkeling unprotected is a guaranteed skin disaster (and painful obstacle to the rest of your holiday); however, sunblock, when dissolving into the water from hundreds of visitors each day, is bound to take its toll on the marine environment. You can limit the amount of sunscreen you must slather on by covering your back with a Lycra Rashguard or a short- or long-sleeve shirt while snorkeling.

Follow the credo: "Leave only footprints, take only memories (or photographs)." Try to minimize your impact on this ecosystem in which you are only a visitor.

are available if you sign up for a dive course. **Pros:** great for divers; transportation around island easily arranged. **Cons:** far from action; some rooms lack hot water or private baths; only deluxe bungalows have TVs and minibars. ✉*40/6 Tanote Bay* ☎*077/456867* 🌐*www.blacktipdiving.com* *25 bungalows* *In-room: no a/c (some), refrigerator (some), no TV (some). In-hotel: restaurant, bar, pool, diving, water sports* 💳*MC, V.*

$$$ Fodor's Choice ★ **Charmchuree Villa.** Whether you opt to stay in one of the uniquely designed tropical villas or in a superior or deluxe room, you'll enjoy a tiny corner of heaven on the private beach at Jansom Bay. Rooms and thatch-roofed villas are built into the landscape, constructed on or around massive boulders and trees, and situated to maximize exposure to the magnificent views of Nang Yuan, Jansom Bay, and Sairee Beach. Indoor-outdoor baths and semidetached living rooms are great features, as is lots of deck space for chairs, hammocks, and triangular pillows. The spa, Elvis Bar, and spectacular snorkeling (free equipment rental for guests) are both found at the beach, which is just a three-minute walk from the farthest rooms. ■ TIP→ **Nonguests can use the beach (not as exotic as Nang Yuan, but quieter and just as satisfying) for B100.** **Pros:** private beach; sweeping views. **Cons:** isolated; feels spread out. ✉ *30/1 Moo 2, Jansom Bay, Koh Tao* ☎ *077/456393 or 077/456394* 🌐 *www.charmchureevilla.com* *40 rooms* *In-room: safe, refrigerator. In-hotel: 3 restaurants, room service, bar, spa, water sports, laundry service, Wi-Fi* *MC, V.*

$$$$ ★ **Koh Tao Cabana.** On the far northern end of Sairee Beach, this is one of the few boutique resorts on the island. Choose between the circular, thatch-roofed White Sand Villas or the more traditional cottages. The Mediterranean-style villas have tile and wood floors, four-poster beds, chill-out nooks, and panoramic windows. The wooden cottages, which are farther up the hill away from the beach, have bamboo-frame beds, native art, and decks that face south towards Sairee Beach. Rooms on the hill have stairs leading down to a snorkeling spot. The stylish restaurant, just above the water, is open for dinner. **Pros:** attractive decor; stylish resort. **Cons:** so-so food; some rooms lack easy beach access. ✉ *16 Moo 1, Baan Hadd Sai Ree, Koh Tao,* ☎ *077/456250 or 077/456504* 🌐 *www.kohtaocabana.com* *33 villas and cottages* *In-room: safe, refrigerator. In-hotel: restaurant, laundry service, Internet terminal* *AE, MC, V* *BP.*

$$$$ **Koh Tao Coral Grand Resort.** This resort, on the quieter, northern end of Sairee, is a great place to get your scuba certification. The colorfully painted, traditional wooden Thai beach huts were built to 21st-century hotel standards, including clean, spacious, sunken bathrooms with stone floors. Air-conditioned standard rooms are similar to deluxe rooms but smaller and without some amenities like phones and minibars. ■ TIP→ **Rooms 304 and 403 are adjacent to the sometimes noisy restaurant and beach bar.** Much cheaper and more basic fan rooms are available for those strictly visiting the resort for its scuba courses. Guests at neighboring resorts, including Koh Tao Cabana, are welcome to take scuba courses here as well. **Pros:** feels peaceful; lots of amenities. **Cons:** can be noisy; some foot traffic. ✉ *15/4 Moo 1, Sairee Beach, Koh Tao, 84280* ☎ *077/456431 up to 33* 🌐 *www.kohtaocoral.com* *42 rooms* *In-room: no phone (some), safe, refrigerator (some). In-hotel: restaurant, room service, bar, pool, beachfront, diving, water sports, laundry service, Internet terminal* *MC, V.*

$$ **Mango Bay Grand Resort.** Mango Bay may not have a beach, but the spectacular view from the enormous deck, spacious restaurant, and cliff-side rooms easily makes up for the lack of a sandy shore. All rooms

Koh Samui's accessibility and beautiful beaches make it a popular destination year-round.

have balconies overlooking the crystalline waters of Mango Bay, a favorite of dive boats and day-trip snorkelers. Air-conditioned rooms are in wooden huts with comfortable beds, mosquito nets, and deck chairs for staring at the amazing hues of the water and reef below. Fan-cooled rooms are smaller and have no amenities but have decks with the same amazing view. Room A9, at the top, is a hike, but the view is the best of the best. **Pros:** pretty bay; comfortable rooms. **Cons:** no beach access; some rooms lack a/c. ✉ *Mango Bay* ☎ *077/456949* 🌐 *www.kohtaomangobay.com* *14 rooms* *In-room: no a/c (some), refrigerator, DVD. In-hotel: restaurant, room service, bar, laundry service, Internet terminal* *No credit cards* *Closed Sept.–Dec. 20.*

$ **SB Cabana.** Certainly not a place for those unaccustomed to roughing it, SB Cabana consists of old-school wooden beach huts. At high tide the ocean laps at the stilts of these simple, wooden structures, which have limited amenities—only a handful have air-conditioning and most have cold-water showers. They may be best for backpackers, but if you're willing to be a little adventurous, you'll find great accommodations here: clean, comfortable, and centrally located. Only a handful of rooms are beachside; the cheapest are around $10. **Pros:** can be a fun experience; cool crowd. **Cons:** no frills; some huts not that cheap. ✉ *Sairee Beach* ☎ *077/456005* *60 huts* *In-room: no a/c, no phone, no TV. In-hotel: restaurant, bicycles* *No credit cards.*

KOH PHUKET

Phuket was one of the region's economic powerhouses—millions of tourists visited the island every year and many beaches were exhibiting the rampant overbuilding that turned Pattaya from peaceful getaway to eyesore. The 2004 tsunami, however, changed all that. Although only a few of the island's many beaches were directly affected (the worst damage actually occurred north of the island along the Andaman Coast), the beaches that were hit were hit really hard, and the island suffered its share of destruction and casualties. But it's important to note that most of the island wasn't hit at all, and the affected areas have, at this writing, completely recovered. In fact, if you've never been to Phuket, you will likely love it; returning visitors will find a new island that eagerly greets its next wave of tourism.

Koh Phuket is linked to the mainland by a causeway, and the rest of the world by an international airport. Its indented coastline and hilly interior make the island seem larger than its 48-km (30-mi) length and 21-km (13-mi) breadth. Before tourism, Koh Phuket was already making fortunes out of tin mining and rubber plantations. Then backpackers discovered Koh Phuket in the early 1970s. Word quickly spread about its white, sandy beaches and cliff-sheltered coves, its plunging waterfalls and impressive mountains, its cloudless days and fiery sunsets.

This love of Phuket has brought serious problems. Entrepreneurs built massive resorts, first at Patong, then spreading out around the island. Before the tsunami, there was no easy way to navigate the island, which was plagued by horrendous traffic and overdevelopment. Some would say Phuket was being loved to death. Now, many hope the tsunami's silver lining will be a bit of thought and reflection as the rebuilding continues.

Even though it may seem like every other business here is a tour operator or dive shop or tailor or jeep rental or pub, there's still a lot to love about the island. The beaches are beautiful and this is a top destination for snorkeling and diving (with more than 180 registered dive shops). The island offers some of the most exclusive resorts and spas in the world yet the food, drink, and accommodations are cheap compared to most visitors' home countries (though Phuket is quite expensive by Thai standards). And direct flights to the island make this a very convenient getaway.

⚠ **When planning your trip, keep in mind that the monsoon season runs from May to October, and swimming on the west side of the coast is not advisable during this time as the current can be dangerous.**

This section starts with Phuket Town, the hub of the island, and is organized counterclockwise from there. It's best to pick one or two choice spots and stick with them. The frazzling travel between destinations can very well undo any relaxation you enjoyed the previous day.

GETTING HERE & AROUND

BY AIR Although flights to Phuket used to be quite expensive, the emergence of discount airlines has dropped prices dramatically. A flight now costs around B1,000 to B2,500, little more than taking the train and a bus from Bangkok—but the trip takes just over an hour, rather than a full day. Bangkok Airways and Thai Airways fly between Bangkok and Phuket daily, as do a couple of newer low-cost airlines including Air Asia and Nok Air. If you are flexible with your dates, then you can find some ridiculously cheap fares on Air Asia; book online for the best deals. Keep in mind that planes fill up fast during the high season, and the lowest fares are mostly available if booked weeks or months in advance (*By Air in Travel Smart*).

Phuket's airport is at the northern end of the island. All hotels are to the south. Check to see if yours offers a free shuttle. Taxis meet all incoming flights. Fares are higher than in Bangkok; expect to pay B700 to Patong, Kata, or Karon, or B400 to Phuket Town. On your way back to the airport, you have to book a taxi for a minimum of B400. Many hotels charge B350 to B400 per person for the journey.

There are also frequent minibus and van services to Phuket Town, Patong, Kata, and Karon that cost between B80 and B120. However, it might be worth springing for a cab as not all van drivers are reputable and might try to take you on an extended detour to a friend's shop or restaurant.

BY BUS Numerous buses leave from Bangkok's Southern Bus Terminal, generally in the late afternoon and evening. The trip takes from 12 to 14 hours, depending on the bus and road conditions. You'll need to go to either a travel agent or to the bus station to check exact times and purchase tickets in advance, especially for VIP buses. Costs run from B278 for a non-air-conditioned bus to B970 for an air-conditioned VIP bus. Most long-haul VIP buses travel overnight, but day trips are recommended as Thailand's highways grow even more dangerous at night.

There are buses from Phuket to pretty much every major destination in Southern Thailand. This includes, but is not limited to: Surat Thani, Krabi, Trang, Hat Yai, Satun, Phang Nga, and the ferry crossing to Koh Samui. You can check departure times at your hotel or the centrally located bus station just east of Montri Road, two blocks north of Phang Nga Road in Phuket Town.

BY CAR You can take Highway 4 from Thonburi in Bangkok all the way to the Causeway at the north end of Phuket Island, where it turns into Highway 402. It's a long drive, but once you're out of the capital all you have to do is follow the compass due south. Follow Highway 4 to Chumphon, where it jogs west and south and follows the Andaman Sea coast to Phuket island. Phuket Town is 862 km (517 mi) from Bangkok; bus companies make the trip in 13–15 hours.

Though roads on Phuket are badly congested and poorly marked, it can be handy to have a car on the island. All hotels can arrange for car rentals. Look for Avis, Budget, and Hertz at the airport. In town you can find rental cars at various private shops near the Pearl and Metropole hotels, as well as shops along all the major beaches. Prices will be a little lower than those at the airport, but not by a lot. If you are driving, make sure you pick up at least two or three tourist maps (available at the airport, travel agencies, and most any tourism-related office), as they differ in details.

BY TAXI, TUK-TUK & SONGTHAEW Taxis aren't common on Phuket. The ones you'll find are usually uninsured, cheaper than tuk-tuks, and quite adventurous. Tuk-tuks are registered, insured, and plentiful; drivers will be happy to take you to your destination for an absurd price. Be ready to bargain hard or simply walk away. Fares within any one town shouldn't be much more than B20 per trip, but drivers will often demand a flat B100. Keep in mind you can catch a minivan from the airport to Phuket Town for B100, a distance of 30 km (19 mi).

Motorcycle taxis—you ride on the back, behind the driver—are cheaper than tuk-tuks and taxis, but much more dangerous.

The best and cheapest way of getting between beaches on the island is by songthaew. You catch songthaews in front of the market on Ranong Road or at the bus stops in the beach towns. These are marked on most maps and locals can help you find them. Prices run from B15 to B30 per trip. They run every half hour from 7 AM to 5 PM. If you miss that last songthaew, you may end up spending B400 on a tuk-tuk. ■ **TIP→You can sometimes arrange a cut-rate ride on the sly with a hotel taxi driver who's heading your way.** If he drives alone, he makes no money. If he takes you for, say, half the normal hotel fare, he gets to keep that, which will probably pay for his dinner.

■ **TIP→Some hotels and resorts provide shuttle service to other beaches—check before you shell out your own money for transportation.**

BY TRAIN Surat Thani, four hours away, is the closest train station to Phuket. From Surat Thani you can take a bus to Phuket. Express trains from Bangkok's Hua Lamphong railway station stop at Surat Thani on their way south. The journey takes 12 hours or so; if you leave Bangkok at 3 PM, you'll arrive to a dark train station in Surat Thani at around 3 AM (*By Train in Travel Smart Thailand*).

PHUKET ESSENTIALS

Emergencies **Fire** (☎ *199*). **Marine Police** (☎ *076/211883*). **Police** (☎ *191*). **Tourist Police** (☎ *1155, 076/219878 in Phuket*). **Bangkok Phuket Hospital** (✉ *2/1 Hongyok Rd., Phuket Town* ☎ *076/254429 or 076/254430*). **Phuket International Hospital** (☎ *076/249400*).

TOUR & VISITOR INFORMATION

As the saying goes, you can't throw a stone at a dog in Phuket without hitting a tour operator. Nearly all of them are selling the same package tours and renting the same cars and motorcycles, so feel free to comparison shop and haggle over prices. Common half-day sightseeing tours include visits to Wat Chalong, Rawai Beach, Phromthep Cape, and Khao Rang.

In general, be wary of what tour operators tell you; they are in business to sell you a trip to the beach, not to tell you how to get there on your own. If you feel you have been ripped off, note the offender's name and other info and report him to the local Tourism Authority of Thailand office. Also let the manager at your hotel know, so he or she can steer other tourists clear.

ELEPHANT SHOWS

On Phuket, there are many opportunities to ride elephants or see them at work. Many were former logging elephants, whose jobs are now to entertain tourists. Before forking over your money, examine how the animals are kept and treated, and whether they show signs of abuse, such as sores on their legs from chains. Even well-respected businesses have been accused of mistreating elephants. If you think chaining an elephant to a concrete slab in a park, or putting him on stage in a show, is wrong, then don't pay to see or ride him. Better yet, write a letter to the establishment and the Tourism Authority of Thailand.

Contacts **Dive Asia** (☎ *076/330598* 🌐 *www.diveasia.com*), on Kata Beach, is a certified PADI instructor and operator that's been in business for more than 20 years. **John Gray's Sea Canoe** (☎ *076/254505* 🌐 *www.johngray-seacanoe.com*) is known internationally for ecotourism trips, including canoeing through Phang Nga Bay. Look for their fliers at travel agencies. **Santana** (☎ *076/294220* 🌐 *www.santanaphuket.com*) is a well-regarded diving and canoeing operator based in Patong. They will pick customers up in Phuket. **Tourism Authority of Thailand** (✉ *73–75 Phuket Rd.* ☎ *076/212213*) in Phuket Town has maps and brochures, as well as information about local excursions.

PHUKET TOWN

862 km (539 mi) south of Bangkok.

Though very few tourists linger here, Phuket Town, the provincial capital, is one of the more interesting places on the island. About one-third of the island's population lives here, and the town is an intriguing mix of old Sino-Portuguese architecture and the influences of the Chinese, Muslims, and Thais that inhabit it. The old Chinese quarter along Talang Street is especially good for a stroll, as its history has not yet been replaced by modern concrete and tile. And this same area also has a variety of antiques shops, art studios, and cafés.

GETTING HERE & AROUND

Phuket Town is in the center of the island. Taxis, tuk-tuks, motorcycles, and local buses will take you from here to the surrounding beaches and to the airport. Expect to pay approximately B400 to travel from the town to the airport or Patong via taxi—a little more to most other southern beaches and a little less to more northern beaches. The price will depend on your negotiation techniques. The best place to pick up transport is at the bus station, located in the center of town. Ranong Road also has a songthaew terminal, where minibuses depart for the most popular beaches every half hour. The fare is B15–B30.

EXPLORING

Phuket town is a nice place to visit for half a day or so, but there's no need to plan on a long visit. Besides Talang, the major thoroughfares are Ratsada, Phuket, and Ranong roads. Ratsada connects Phuket Road (where you'll find the Tourism Authority of Thailand office) to Ranong Road, where there's an aromatic local market filled with fruits, vegetables, spices, and meats.

WHAT TO SEE

The **National Museum,** opposite the Heroines Monument, has an interesting exhibition of the island's culture and history, including its encounter with the Burmese and their defeat by the island's two heroines. ✉ *12 km (7 mi) north of Phuket Town* ☎ *076/311426* *B30* *Daily 9–4.*

South of Phuket Town, not far from Chalong Bay, you'll find **Wat Chalong,** the largest and most famous of Phuket's Buddhist temples. It enshrines gilt statues of two revered monks who helped quell an 1876 Chinese rebellion. They're wrapped in brilliant saffron robes. Wats are generally open during daylight hours, and you can show up at 5 PM to see the resident monks pray. You can take a taxi, tuk-tuk, or motorcycle here from town.

5

WHERE TO EAT

$–$$ INDIAN ✕ **Khanasutra, A Taste of India.** This restaurant's name is not making false promises—the Sikh owner and Indian chef turn out flavorful, authentic Indian cuisine. The fish tikka is recommended. Part of the unique decor is a bedouin-style tent, where you can have a few cocktails after dinner. ✉ *18–20 Takua Pa Rd., Phuket Town* ☎ *091/894–0794* *No credit cards* *No lunch Sun.*

¢–$ CAFE ✕ **Kopi de Phuket.** For a good cup of coffee, try this artistically designed shop, which also serves snacks, sandwiches, breads, and shakes. It's across from the Honda Shop/Nai Yao Restaurant. It opens daily at 9:30 AM. ✉ *Phuket Rd.* ☎ *No phone* *No credit cards.*

¢ THAI ✕ **Wilai.** Thai fast food is served from big vats at this little shop in the heart of the old Sino-Portuguese district. The owner makes different dishes every day to keep her regular customers interested. She focuses on curries, vegetables, fish, and soups, and she'll warn hapless foreigners away from the spicy ones. Try a traditional cup of coffee, made with a cloth bag. Ask the owner about the temple in her backyard. The restaurant closes at 4 PM. ✉ *14 Talang Rd.* ☎ *076/222875* *No credit cards* *No dinner.*

WHERE TO STAY

$$ **Metropole.** The grand old Metropole—the town's first luxury hotel—has a shuttle service to the closest beaches, so you can stay in town and commute to the sea. The advantages are not only cheaper accommodation, but the opportunity to visit more than just one beach. Rooms are bright, with picture windows that let in a lot of sun. A spacious lounge is a cool retreat during the day, and the karaoke bar is fun at night. The hotel's handsome Chinese restaurant serves great dim sum; for Western food, try the Metropole Café. **Pros:** shuttle service to beaches; good

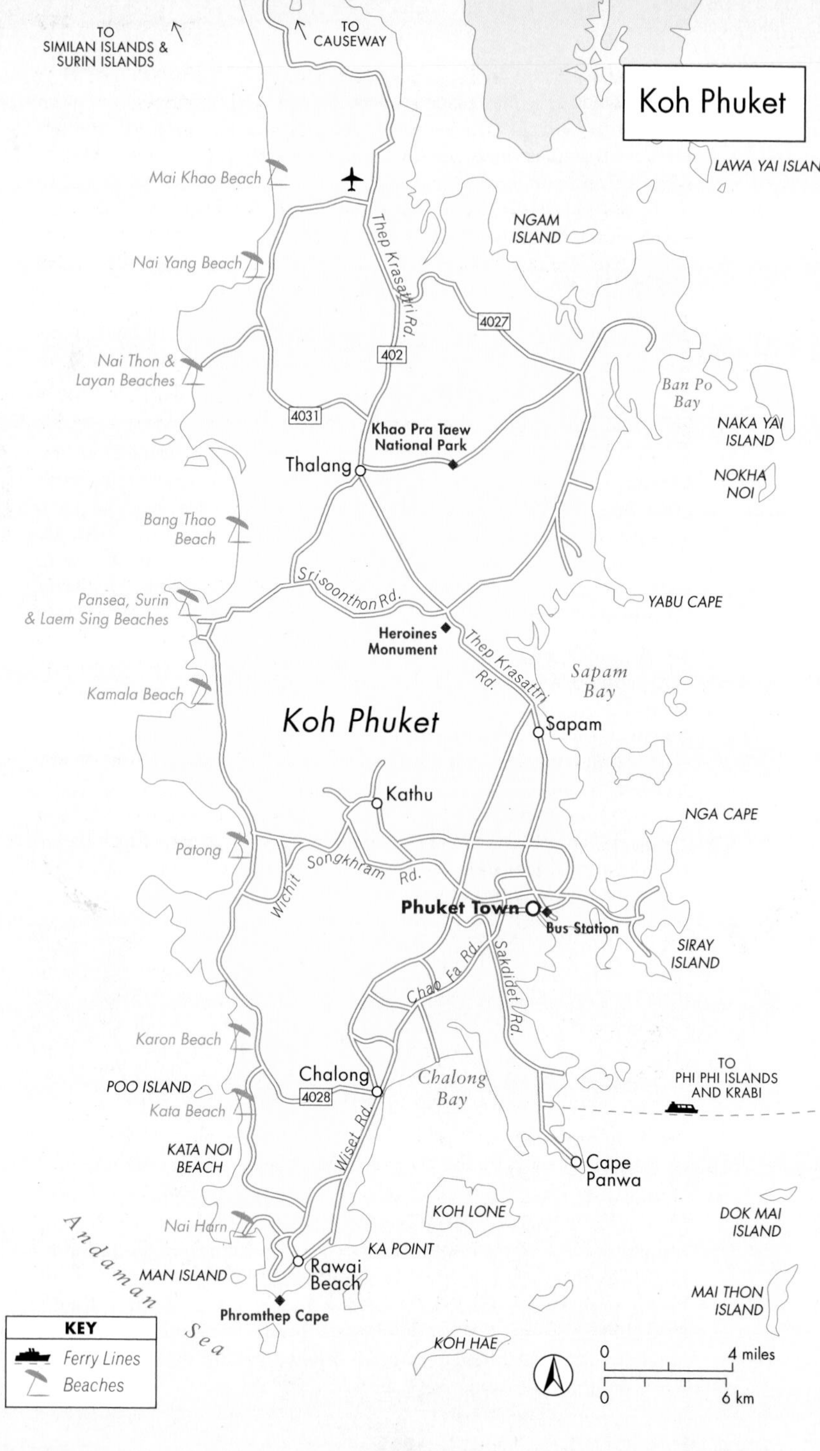

Koh Phuket
TO SIMILAN ISLANDS & SURIN ISLANDS
TO CAUSEWAY
LAWA YAI ISLAND
Mai Khao Beach
NGAM ISLAND
Nai Yang Beach
Thep Krasattri Rd.
4027
402
Nai Thon & Layan Beaches
Ban Po Bay
4031
Khao Pra Taew National Park
NAKA YAI ISLAND
Thalang
NOKHA NOI
Bang Thao Beach
Srisoonthon Rd.
YABU CAPE
Pansea, Surin & Laem Sing Beaches
Heroines Monument
Thep Krasattri Rd.
Sapam Bay
Kamala Beach
Koh Phuket
Sapam
Kathu
NGA CAPE
Patong
Songkhram Rd.
Wichit
Phuket Town
Bus Station
SIRAY ISLAND
Chao Fa Rd.
Sakdidet Rd.
Karon Beach
TO PHI PHI ISLANDS AND KRABI
POO ISLAND
Chalong
Chalong Bay
4028
Kata Beach
Wiset Rd.
KATA NOI BEACH
Cape Panwa
KOH LONE
DOK MAI ISLAND
Andaman Sea
Nai Harn
KA POINT
Rawai Beach
MAN ISLAND
MAI THON ISLAND
Phromthep Cape
KEY
Ferry Lines
Beaches
KOH HAE
0
4 miles
0
6 km

food. **Cons:** no Wi-Fi in rooms. ✉ *1 Montri Rd.* ☎ *076/215050 or 076/214020* 🌐 *www.metropolephuket.com* *248 rooms, 20 suites* *In-room: refrigerator. In-hotel: 2 restaurants, pool, gym, laundry service, Internet terminal, no-smoking rooms* *AE, DC, MC, V* *EP.*

$$–$$$ **Royal Phuket City Hotel.** This is arguably Phuket Town's best address. Rooms are spacious and contemporary, but don't have great views. The large Club Asia health club is popular with locals. The top-floor Thai Thai Room has outdoor seating and great views; the Cappuccino 154 deli on the ground floor caters its baked goods to other coffee shops around town. **Pros:** large rooms. **Cons:** some rooms lack nice views. ✉ *154 Phang Nga Rd., Phuket* ☎ *076/233333* 🌐 *www.royalphuketcity.com* *251 rooms* *In-room: safe, refrigerator. In-hotel: 3 restaurants, bar, pool, gym, spa, laundry service, Internet terminal* *AE, DC, MC, V.*

5

KHAO PRA TAEW NATIONAL PARK

19 km (12 mi) north of Phuket Town.

Thailand's islands have several national parks, and this one is home to Phuket's last remaining virgin forest and populations of endangered animals. The park has two easily accessible waterfalls. The Gibbon Center, which works to protect the primates and educate visitors about them, is part of the park (*The Gibbon Rehabilitation Project box*).

GETTING HERE & AROUND

You can take a taxi, tuk-tuk, or motorcycle here from any of the island's beaches or from Phuket Town. Cost depends on distance—a taxi from Phuket Town would be about B250, a tuk-tuk a little more. If you're driving, take Highway 4027, watch the signs, and turn west toward Bang Pae Waterfall and the Gibbon Rehabilitation Center.

EXPLORING

You'll have to pay the standard foreigner's fee to enter the park: B200 (Thais pay B20). To access **Tonsai Waterfall** on the other side of the park follow the signs and turn east off Highway 402. Here, you can find two trails (600 meters and 2 km [1 mi]), through rich tropical evergreen forest. Expect buckets of rain in the monsoon season. Gibbons, civets, macaques, mouse deer, wild boar, lemurs, and loris live in the park, but spotting one would be a rare and impressive feat.

The park advertises the good deeds of the Gibbon Center, and indeed it's a worthy cause. (What they don't tell you is that the center, which sits near the parking lot at Bang Pae, receives none of your entrance fee.) After visiting the center, follow the paved trail along the waterfall. It's a relatively easy hike, quite lush in the rainy season. Both park entrances have bathrooms, parking lots, and food stalls. If you plan to visit both waterfalls, make sure you get entrance tickets at your first stop—they're good for both sites.

CLOSE UP

The Gibbon Rehabilitation Project

Just inside Khao Pra Taew National Park, between a jungled hillside and a gurgling stream, dozens of gibbons swing from branch to branch, filling the forest with boisterous hooting.

It seems like a happy sign of jungle life, but something is wrong with this picture. These animals are not roaming around free; instead, they live in cages near the park entrance as part of the Gibbon Rehabilitation Project. Most of these small apes were poached from jungles around Thailand and kept as pets or zoo and bar amusements. They were forced to perform shows, do tricks, drink beer, or get their pictures taken with tourists before they were rescued by this project. As a branch of the Wild Animal Rescue Foundation of Thailand, the center aims to rehabilitate the gibbons in their natural habitat, with the intention of releasing the animals into the wild (though some animals that were abused will never be able to live freely again).

The center holds more than 60 gibbons. They're kept in large cages, away from visitors. The idea is to purge them of their familiarity with people, although visitors can hear them in the distance and glimpse their playful leaps through the trees. All gibbons are named, and their life stories are posted at the center for tourists to read: Lamut and Pai Mei were working as tourist attractions at Patong Beach before their rescue. A baby, called Bam-Bam, was found in a cardboard box at a roadside. Saul, a young blonde male, is missing a patch of fur, which researchers think could be the result of bullets that grazed him when his mother was shot.

When new gibbons arrive at the center, they get a complete medical checkup, including tests for HIV, hepatitis, and tuberculosis. It costs $700 a year to treat, feed, and house each animal, and although the center sits within the national park, it receives none of the $5 entrance fee. In fact, the center receives no funding from the Thai government—it survives on donations alone. For B1,500, the price of a good night out in Patong, visitors can "adopt" a gibbon for a year. If you're unable to make it out to the center, the Web site of the **Wildlife Friends of Thailand** (🌐 *www.wfft.org*), has information on how to adopt a gibbon or make a donation.

–Karen Coates

MAI KHAO BEACH

37 km (23 mi) northwest of Phuket Town.

This is Phuket's northernmost beach, still a haven for leatherback turtles that lay their eggs here between November and February. It's an increasingly rare event, but one new nest was found less than two weeks after the tsunami hit.

The Marriott Resort and next-door Sirinath Marine National Park (established to protect the turtles) are the only things to occupy this beach, which connects with Nai Yang Beach, to form Phuket's longest stretch of sand. It's great for running, sunbathing, and swimming (in the hot season, although dangerous during the monsoons).

WHERE TO STAY

$$$$ **J. W. Marriott Resort & Spa.** Wow. This secluded resort offers the longest stretch of sand on the island. It has luxurious rooms with impeccable classic Thai design and an unbeatable spa with amenities that meet or exceed those in the guest rooms. The Marriott is the only thing on this beach, but it has everything you need and then some, including the flagship spa of Marriott Asia and a cooking school. **Pros:** great long and quiet beach; Thai-style rooms. **Cons:** may be too isolated for some; surf sometimes too rough for swimming. ✉ *231 Moo 3, Mai Khao* ☎ *076/338000* 🌐 *www.marriott.com/HKTJW* *265 rooms* *In-room: safe, refrigerator, DVD, Internet. In-hotel: 6 restaurants, room service, bars, tennis courts, pools, gym, spa, laundry service* *AE, MC, V* *EP.*

Fodor'sChoice ★

WORD OF MOUTH

"The J.W. Phuket is a beautiful property. Great pools, very lush landscaping, and lots to do. With dozens of torches lit up at night, it is very impressive. Yet, it is isolated and may be best enjoyed with kids. If you are traveling during a school vacation the hotel will be packed with younguns . . . Most spots are 15+ minutes away. We took taxis for dinner most every night. We had some very good meals and prices were much less then eating at the hotel. Yet, in truth, we much prefer being closer to stores and restaurants."
—tengohambre

NAI YANG BEACH

34 km (20 mi) northwest of Phuket Town.

Nai Yang Beach is really a continuation south of Mai Khao, making a long stretch of sand good for running or swimming in the dry season. Casuarina trees line the gently curving shore. It's a far quieter beach than most, with a strip of trees and a small string of beachside restaurants and bars, tour guides, tailors, and shops. Fishing boats anchor nearby, making for picture-perfect sunrises and sunsets. Nai Yang did suffer some damage from the tsunami, but its businesses were fully operational by that spring.

GETTING HERE & AROUND

Nai Yang Beach is accessible from Highway 4027, the main road running through the island. Taxis, tuk-tuks, and motorcycles will take you to and from other parts of the island. **TIP→Transport to often difficult to find on the road through Nai Yang Beach.** Your hotel may be able to help arrange transportation.

WHERE TO STAY

You can find tasty, fresh seafood at Nai Yang's beachside restaurants.

$$–$$$ **Nai Yang Beach Resort.** These basic bungalows are a short walk from the beach. They surround a small fishpond and come with a variety of amenities—choose between fans or air-conditioning, and with or without TVs and minibars. The higher the price, the better the view, although none of the rooms overlook the sea. **Pros:** choice of in-room amenities; quiet. **Cons:** no sea view. ✉ *65/23–24 Nai Yang Beach Rd., Moo 5, T.*

Sakhu, Thalang, Phuket ☎076/328300 🌐www.naiyangbeachresort.com ⇆36 rooms ♨In-room: no a/c (some), refrigerator (some), no TV (some). In-hotel: restaurant ▭MC, V 🍴EP.

NAI THON & LAYAN BEACHES

30 km (18½ mi) northwest of Phuket Town.

Just a few miles north of Bang Thao Bay, follow a smaller highway off the main routes (4030 and 4031) along a scenic coastline reminiscent of California's Pacific Coast Highway. These beaches are good for swimming in the dry season. There's more development on the way, but for now they're two of the island's quiet gems, with more homes than resorts.

GETTING HERE & AROUND

Nai Thon and Layan beaches are easily accessible from all parts of Phuket island. Taxis, tuk-tuks, and motorcycles will gladly ferry you to and from these quiet beaches.

WHERE TO STAY

You can find fresh seafood and standard Thai and western dishes at most of the beachside restaurants.

$$$$ **Bundarika Villa.** On a quiet, isolated beach, Bundarika has the ideal environment for relaxation; accordingly, the resort has a special focus on wellness for both body and mind. You can begin each day with a tai chi or yoga class. If you need a change of scenery during the day, you can take a stroll across the sandbar at low tide to a small offshore island. In the evening, dine on cuisine designed with your health in mind. All accommodations are private villas with peaked roofs, dark stained wood, and artfully placed flowers, statues, and silk pillows. Within the walls of your private compound, covered sala tables and chairs are set up so you can enjoy afternoon tea or coffee beside your small private pool. **Pros:** focus on wellness; quiet location. **Cons:** not suitable for families. *✉89 Moo 6, Layan Beach ☎076/317200 🌐www.bundarika.com ⇆20 villas ♨In-room: safe, refrigerator, DVD. In-hotel: restaurant, bicycles, laundry service, Wi-Fi ▭AE, MC, V.*

$$$–$$$$ ★ **Layan Beach Resort & Spa Village.** The spa is the focus of this resort, which is tucked away on a hillside overlooking the sea, a small beach, and nearby island. In fact, the spa looks like it's own exclusive set of villas. You won't find much else around here, for now. The standard rooms aren't terribly exciting, but they're spacious and bright. **Pros:** excellent spa; stunning location. **Cons:** isolated; not family-friendly. *✉62 Moo 6, Layan Village ☎076/313412 up to 14 🌐www.layanphuket.com ⇆52 rooms and villas ♨In-hotel: 2 restaurants, pools, gym, spa, bicycles ▭AE, MC, V 🍴EP.*

$$$$ **Pavilions.** Many resorts claim that they're set up so that you never have to leave your villa, but Pavilions really means it. Each private villa here has a pool and a small kitchen. All meals are delivered to your room, as are massages and spa treatments. Rooms have enormous tubs, covered outdoor beds with fans, and ocean views from either the bed

or the pool. It's the ideal honeymoon retreat. **TIP→ If you feel the need to mingle with other guests, at the peak of the hill there is a bar with panoramic views; nonguests often drop in here, too, for tapas and spectacular sunsets.** Note that all rooms are nonsmoking and the resort does not allow children. The beach is a bit far away, but there is shuttle service available on demand. **Pros:** fabulous views from the bar; great amenities. **Cons:** a bit isolated; no children under 14 allowed. *31/1 Moo 6, Cherngtalay, Thalang 076/317600, 091/621–4841 in Bangkok www.pavilions-resorts.com 30 villas In-room: safe, refrigerator, DVD, Wi-Fi. In-hotel: room service, bar, spa AE, DC, MC, V.*

$$$$ **Trisara.** Opulence is the standard at the Trisara resort; rooms feature a variety of Thai wooden art pieces, silk throw pillows on the divans, and 32-inch plasma TVs hidden in the walls. The spacious library contains an abundance of literature, magazines, music, and games for the occasional rainy day. The restaurant serves meals on an enormous wooden deck built over a giant pool, beneath swaying palms and beside the resort's small, private beach. Guests enjoy golf at a 36-hole course just 15 minutes away. If you simply love Trisara (which translates roughly to "inner peace"), then you can purchase one of the villa homes. **Pros:** beautiful Thai decor; golf course. **Cons:** often fully booked. *60/1 Moo 6, Srisoonthorn Rd., Cherngtalay 076/310100 or 076/310355 www.trisara.com 42 rooms In-room: safe, refrigerator, DVD, Wi-Fi. In-hotel: restaurant, room service, bar, tennis courts, pool, gym, spa, beachfront, diving, water sports AE, DC, MC, V.*

BANG THAO BEACH

22 km (14 mi) northwest of Phuket Town.

Once the site of a tin mine, Bang Thao Beach (a resort area collectively called Laguna Phuket) now glistens with the more precious metals worn by its affluent visitors. Due to the ingenuity of Ho Kwon Ping and his family, this area was built nearly 20 years ago in a spot so damaged from mining, most thought it beyond repair. Now it's recovered enough to support an array of accommodations, eateries, and golf courses set around the lagoons. The beach itself is a long stretch of white sand with vendors offering a variety of sports equipment rental, inexpensive seafood, beach massages, and cocktails. The beach is good for swimming in the hot season; the lagoon for kayaking anytime.

GETTING HERE & AROUND

Bang Thao Beach is accessible from Highway 4027. Taxis, tuk-tuks, and motorcycles can all take you to and from the beach. Getting away from the beach is sometimes a little difficult, but if you wait on the beach road a taxi or another form of transport will materialize eventually. If you get stuck, ask for help at one of the resorts. There's a free shuttle service between the resorts along the shore.

5

EXPLORING

The once-quiet bay was one of the island's major destinations, though it's been quieter since the 2004 tsunami. As anywhere on the island, some of the older resorts are showing signs of age and tropical weather damage, despite frequent renovations.

WHERE TO EAT

¢ SEAFOOD ✕ **Seafood.** The friendly women at this popular street-side shanty serve made-to-order seafood, noodles, and stir-fry. Every meal comes with a bowl of aromatic cardamom soup. It's safe for foreign bellies, but if you're wary of street food or spicy food, you probably won't be comfortable here. ✉ *About 5 km (3 mi) east of the resort. Look for a small sign on the left side of the road that says* SEAFOOD. *If you reach the mosque, you've gone too far* ☎ *No phone* ▭ *No credit cards.*

WHERE TO STAY

$$$$ **Allamanda Laguna Phuket.** Unlike the other four resorts in the area, this all-suites property sits on the lagoon instead of the beach and therefore offers lower rates. You definitely get more bang for your buck here than at the other four resorts. Suites come in various configurations (one or two bedrooms), but all have kitchenettes. Shuttle boats between the resort and the beach run every 30 minutes 8–5. The scenic trip across the lagoon takes approximately 10 minutes. **Pros:** good choice of rooms with different amenities; shuttle boat service. **Cons:** not on the beach. ✉ *29 Moo 4, Srisoonthorn Rd., Cherngtalay* ☎ *076/324359* ⊕ *www.allamanda.com* *235 suites* *In-room: kitchen. In-hotel: 2 restaurants, pools, spa, water sports, children's programs (ages 4–14), laundry service* ▭ *AE, MC, V* *EP.*

$$$$ **Banyan Tree Phuket.** Of the quintet of resorts on Laguna Beach, this is the most exclusive—and expensive. Your secluded villa has a bathroom as big as the bedroom; an outdoor shower for rinsing off after a swim is a nice addition. Teak floors and locally woven fabrics remind you that you are in Thailand. The king-size bed is on a raised platform so that you can gaze out onto your garden. The most expensive villas have their own private pools. Rejuvenating treatments in the spa include herbal massages. **Pros:** peaceful setting; traditional Thai decor, children's programs. **Cons:** pricey. ✉ *33 Moo 4, Srisoonthorn Rd., Cherngtalay, Amphur Talang* ☎ *076/324374* ⊕ *www.banyantree.com* *132 villas* *In-room: safe, refrigerator, DVD, Wi-Fi. In-hotel: 3 restaurants, bars, golf course, tennis courts, pool, gym, spa, beachfront, water sports, bicycles, children's programs (ages 3–12), laundry service, Wi-Fi* ▭ *AE, MC, V* *EP.*

$$$–$$$$ **Laguna Beach Resort.** Laguna Beach has a high-end-resort feel but the price is a bit gentler. The resort has traditional Thai and Angkor details, including a vast, meandering pool with replica Angkor Wat wall carvings. In addition, this resort has less of an amusement park feel than its neighbor, but still has plenty of kids' activities. **Pros:** plenty of facilities; family-oriented. **Cons:** slightly off the beaten track. ✉ *Bang Thao Bay, Phuket* ☎ *076/324352* ⊕ *www.lagunabeach-resort.com* *252 rooms* *In-room: safe, refrigerator. In-hotel: 5 restaurants, room service, golf course, tennis courts, pools, diving, water sports, bicycles, children's*

programs (ages 4–12), laundry service, Internet terminal ▭*AE, MC, V* 🍽*EP.*

PANSEA, SURIN & LAEM SING BEACHES

21 km (12 mi) northwest of Phuket Town.

South of Bang Thao is a jagged shoreline with little inlets. Once secluded, these areas are developing quickly with villas, restaurants, high-end resorts, cheap backpacker hotels, and what is becoming the usual Phuket beach development.

GETTING HERE & AROUND

The beaches are accessible from Highway 4027. Taxis, tuk-tuks, and motorcycles can all take you to and from the beach. A taxi to or from Phuket town should cost approximately B250 to B350; expect to pay a little more for a tuk tuk.

5

EXPLORING

Surin Beach is about 550 yards of sand where you can get a beer and pretty much anything else that you want. There's a public parking lot above the beach, which is literally a garbage dump in the off-season. Construction is ongoing here, though post-tsunami developments have been more measured than in the pre-tsunami years.

Head north a bit and things change. On the spit of land separating these beaches from Bang Thao sit two of the island's most luxurious resorts, though you may never find them without careful sleuthing. An overgrown sign points the way up a small road to the Chedi; no sign marks the Amanpuri beyond that.

WHERE TO STAY

There are many little restaurants with cheap and tasty Thai and western food along the shore.

$$$$ ★ **Amanpuri Resort.** You'd be hard-pressed to find a more elegant hotel in Thailand—nor one quite as expensive (the nightly rate for the largest of the villas is more than $8,000!). The reception area, with beautifully polished teak floors, is completely open in the dry season so that you can enjoy the ocean breezes. Here you can find two palm-shaded restaurants overlooking the blue-tiled swimming pool. Choose between rooms in secluded hillside pavilions or immense villas with private swimming pools. Pavilion prices differ according to the view offered; villas have between two and six bedrooms. The split-level bar has stunning sunset views. **Pros:** private beach; great sunsets. **Cons:** staff may not speak adequate English. ✉*Pansea Beach, Phuket* ☎*076/324333* 🌐*www.amanpuri.com* *40 pavilions, 31 villas* *In-room: safe, refrigerator, no TV, Wi-Fi. In-hotel: 2 restaurants, bar, tennis courts, pools, gym, spa, beachfront, water sports, laundry service* ▭*AE, D, MC, V* 🍽*EP.*

$$$$ ★ **Chedi.** Almost completely hidden by a grove of coconut palms, this resort has more than 100 thatch-roof cottages overlooking a quiet beach. You know this place is special when you walk into the lobby, which has a sweeping view of the Andaman Sea. The decor is sleek and

geometric. An octagonal pool is set amid the tropical flora. Each of the cottages has its own sundeck. The interiors, done in wood and stone, with high, pointed ceilings, are simple but elegant. **Pros:** great location; private beach. **Cons:** layout a little confusing; isolated. ✉ *118 Moo 3, Cherngtalay, Phuket* ☎ *076/324017* 🌐 *www.phuket.com/chedi* *108 chalets* *In-room: safe, refrigerator, Wi-Fi. In-hotel: 3 restaurants, bar, tennis courts, pool, spa, beachfront, water sports, laundry service* 💳 *AE, MC, V* *EP.*

$–$$ **Surin Bay Inn.** For cheaper accommodations near Surin Beach (only a few minutes' walk away), try this small hotel. Some rooms have balconies overlooking the street along the beach. This is one of the cleanest, nicest budget options in the area. **Pros:** nice restaurant; nice rooms for moderate price. **Cons:** not on beach. ✉ *106/11 Surin Beach* ☎ *076/271601* 🌐 *www.surinbayinn.com* *12 rooms* *In-room: safe, refrigerator, Internet. In-hotel: restaurant, bar, laundry service, Internet terminal* 💳 *MC, V* *BP.*

KAMALA BEACH

18 km (11 mi) west of Phuket Town.

South of Bang Thao is Kamala Beach, a curving strip of coral sand backed by coconut palms. Unlike the more upscale enclaves to the north, Kamala Beach had some reasonably priced accommodations. The area suffered some of the worst destruction on Phuket during the tsunami but has fully recovered. You won't see many (if any) signs of the damage, but many local taxi drivers and shop owners can give personal accounts of the day the wave hit.

GETTING HERE & AROUND

You can get here from Phuket Town or Patong Beach—a taxi will cost about B200.

EXPLORING

Kamala Beach is quieter and less touristy than neighboring Patong and attracts a more laid-back crowd. The beach is quite small but has a distinct feel to it with mangrove trees and blue water.

WHERE TO STAY

$$ **Baan Chaba.** If you're looking for a bungalow or hotel on the beach, you'll find several options at the north end of Kamala (none of which have views of the beach, some of which are absurdly priced). This one has newly designed concrete, tile, and wood rooms with nicer trimmings than the others, and wood furniture. Each bungalow has a porch. Post-tsunami renovated rooms now feature air-conditioning and hot water. There is no restaurant at the resort, but you'll find plenty of beachside options just a few feet away. **Pros:** spacious bungalows. **Cons:** not beachfront; lacks amenities. ✉ *95/3 Moo 3, Kamala Beach, Kathu, Phuket* ☎ *076/279158* 🌐 *www.baanchaba.com* *8 bungalows* *In-room: refrigerator. In-hotel: laundry service, Internet terminal* 💳 *No credit cards* *EP.*

The 2004 tsunami hit Patong's beach hard, but today the area is rebuilt and hopping.

PATONG

13 km (8 mi) west of Phuket Town.

You'd hardly believe it today, but Patong was once the island's most remote beach, completely cut off by the surrounding mountains and only accessible by boat. In 1959 a highway linked Patong with Phuket Town, and the tranquil beachfront was bought up by developers who knew the beautiful beach wouldn't stay a secret for long. Today, the cat is definitely out of the bag: Patong is a thriving beach resort community frequented by both Bangkokians, down for a weekend of fun in the sun, and international visitors. Patong is a great place for new visitors to Thailand who are looking for a nice beach with characteristic Thai experiences, like muay thai, street shopping, and authentic Thai food, as well as familiar facilities, like Starbuck's, sushi bars, and chain hotels.

GETTING HERE & AROUND

Every street, hotel, and shop in Patong seems to have a ready team of taxis, tuk-tuks, and motorcycles whose drivers are all more than happy to ferry you around. Just pick your vehicle of choice and bargain hard. Tuk-tuks to Phuket Town should cost approximately B400; to Karon will be B150; and to Kamala is around B220. It can be a little frustrating to get to the beach during morning rush hour, since the road from Phuket Town is often congested.

EXPLORING

The beach was hit hard by the 2004 tsunami, and anything close to the water was destroyed. The area has fully recovered, however, and as a result of post-tsunami redevelopment, Patong's beach road has undergone a beautification that includes a mosaic-inlaid sidewalk. You can now stroll along several miles of boutiques, Western restaurants and bars, ice cream parlors, and upscale nightlife venues, interspersed with traditional Thai market stalls selling food, cheap T-shirts, and knockoff goods. Patong has something for travelers of any age or demeanor.

The beach itself, which used to be cluttered with beach umbrellas, now has ample room for both sunbathing and playing soccer or Frisbee on the beach. Every conceivable beach activity from wakeboarding to jet skiing to parasailing is available. Like Chawaeng on Koh Samui, Patong became so popular because it was the nicest beach on the island, and now its popularity has caused some degradation of the environment, particularly noticeable when the monsoon rains wash the grime off the street and onto the beach. That said, it's still a nice stretch of sand for walking, swimming, or sunbathing.

PATONG'S SULLIED REPUTATION

Patong has, on occasion, been portrayed as a sleazy environment crawling with prostitutes, but this is a gross exaggeration. It is a far cry from Pattaya or Patpong in Bangkok, and most visitors are oblivious to anything untoward, spending the majority of their days playing on the beach, and their evenings at the tasteful bars and tasty restaurants along Thaweewong Road. The sex trade does exist here, but Patong is a suitable destination for families and couples, as well as singles.

WHERE TO EAT

$$–$$$$ Fodor'sChoice ★ THAI ✕ **Baan Rim Pa.** If you suffer from vertigo, take a pass on this restaurant. You dine on a terrace that clings to a cliff at the north end of Patong Beach. There are tables set back from the edge, but you'll then miss the gorgeous ocean views. The food is among the best Phuket has to offer. Well-thought-out set menus make ordering simpler for those unfamiliar with Thai food. They've turned down the heat on many favorites, so you may be disappointed if you like spicier fare. The restaurant has a piano bar open Tuesday through Sunday. ✉ *223 Prabaramee Rd., Kalim Beach, Patong, Phuket* ☎ *076/340789* ✍ *Reservations essential* ▭ *AE, MC, V.*

$$$$ JAPANESE ✕ **Otowa.** This Japanese-French fusion restaurant sits between its two other cliff-top neighbors, offering the same spectacular views. The chef has cooked in Tokyo and Monaco before settling in Thailand. Menu items include foie-gras sushi, goose liver, and Kobe beef, and abalone cooked in burgundy butter. ✉ *223 Prabaramee Rd., Kalim Beach, Patong* ☎ *076/344254* ✍ *Reservations essential* ▭ *AE, MC, V.*

WHERE TO STAY

$$$$ ☺ ★ **Holiday Inn.** This is no ordinary Holiday Inn: this stylish, modern hotel exudes the kind of sophistication that most people would never imagine possible from a Holiday Inn or from Patong in general. The

hotel has two wings. In the main wing, the superior rooms above the terrace are nicer. A colorful hallway leads to the Kids' Suites, which have bunk beds and Playstations in the children's room; Family Suites are larger—a king-size parents' room is connected to a pirate-theme kids' room that has two separate beds. The hotel has two activities centers for kids (featuring Thai culture, arts, and crafts classes), as well as a children's pool with a waterfall. The Busakorn wing has a separate reception area; Thai-style, peaked-roof rooms; and an adults-only swimming pool surrounded by Singha and elephant sculptures and fountains. The main swimming pool, like the rest of the resort, is across the road from the beach but is buffered from the street by an Italian café, which is a great place to watch the sun set. **Pros:** central location; children's programs. **Cons:** family atmosphere not ideal for everyone. ✉*52 Thaweewong Rd., Patong Beach* ☎*076/340–0608* 🌐*www.phuket.com/holidayinn* *405 rooms* *In-room: safe (some), refrigerator, DVD (some). In-hotel: 4 restaurants, room service, bars, pools, gym, spa, concierge, children's programs (ages 5–12), laundry service* 💳*AE, MC, V.*

5

$$–$$$ ★ **Impiana Phuket Cabana.** This hotel's chief attraction is its unbeatable location, right in the middle of the city facing the beach. Furthermore, post-tsunami renovations have made it the nicest resort in Patong. Towering flower displays stand in the lobby, where Buddhist Thai art adorns the walls, and large sliding glass doors exit to the beachside bar and adjacent pool. Among the hotel's other highlights are good travel services, a reputable dive shop, an outstanding restaurant, and a festive cigar/tapas bar, La Salsa, with pictures of Che smoking stogies and Fidel hamming it up with Hemingway. The beachside spa has glass doors and windows so that you can enjoy the view while having your treatments or massages. **Pros:** great beachfront spa; good restaurant and bar; best location in Patong. **Cons:** busy beach road traffic. ✉*41 Taweewong Rd.* ☎*076/340138* 🌐*www.impiana.com* *70 rooms* *In-room: safe, refrigerator. In-hotel: 3 restaurants, room service, bars, pool, spa, laundry service, Wi-Fi* 💳*AE, MC, V* *EP.*

$$ **QVC Patong Beach Resort.** This small beach hotel is at the southern end of Patong Beach, away from the noise, but close enough to the action. The beach, just across a relatively quiet road, is narrow at high tide, but lacks the clutter of boats and Jet Skis found along the main stretch of Patong. Rooms have either sea views or no views; sea-view rooms have balconies. All guest rooms have Thai-style wooden bed frames and silk throw pillows, which are a nice touch. There is no pool on-site, but guests can use the pool at the hotel next door. The restaurant serves breakfast only, which is included in the price of the room. **Pros:** nice location on beach. **Cons:** lacks hotel facilities. ✉*22–26 Thaweewong Rd., Kathu-Patong* ☎*076/342197 or 076/342198* 🌐*www.qualityvacationclub.com* *18 rooms* *In-room: safe, refrigerator, Wi-Fi. In-hotel: restaurant, Internet terminal, Wi-Fi* 💳*MC, V* *BP.*

NIGHTLIFE

The vast majority of tourists only venture as far as Bang La Road, a walking street that is more of a carnival atmosphere than something disturbingly sleazy; children pose for photos with flamboyant and friendly transvestites, honeymooning couples people-watch from numerous beer bars along the traffic-free promenade, and everyone else simply strolls the strip, some stopping to dance or play Connect Four, Jenga, or a curiously popular nail-hammering game with friendly Thai hostesses.

Patong has a reputation for its happening nightlife, and the seedy side of it is easily avoidable. Some of the more tasteful nightlife venues are on Thaweewong Road, including **Saxophone** (✉*188/2 Andaman Bazaar, Thaweewong Rd.* ☎*076/346167*), a branch of the legendary Bangkok jazz and blues bar, and the neighboring **Rock City,** both of which provide live music nightly, and a number of pubs and bars, some of which have live music and other shows.

With the varied nightlife in Patong, it's no surprise to find a sensational drag show here. The famous **Simon Cabaret** (✉*8 Sirirach Rd.* ☎*076/342011*) treats you to a beautifully costumed and choreographed show. There are two shows daily, at 7:30 and 9:30.

There are also regularly scheduled muay thai fights at the arena on the corner of Bang La and Rat-U-Thit Songroipee roads.

KARON BEACH

20 km (12 mi) southwest of Phuket Town.

Just south of Patong lie Karon Beach and its smaller northern counterpart, Karon Noi. Bunches of hotels, restaurants, tailors, dive operators, and gift shops have sprung up along the main Karon Beach to accommodate the tourists tempted by this long stretch of white sand and good dry-season swimming (it's good for running year-round).

GETTING HERE & AROUND

Taxis, tuk-tuks, and motorcycles will all take you to and from Karon Beach. A taxi will cost about B100 for the 5 km (3 mi) ride to Patong; a tuk-tuk will be about B150.

EXPLORING

Getting your bearings is easy in Karon. There is a small village just off the traffic circle to your left as you enter town from Patong. For the glut of resorts, just continue your journey down beach road. You will find the beach is more open than most in Phuket—there are no trees covering the beach and precious little shade. The beach is also strewn with a few rocks; however, on the whole, it is a beautiful, clean, and open space that will appeal to those looking to get away from the more frantic pace of Patong.

The Flintstones-style buildings along the road in central Karon village belong to **Dino Park Mini Golf** (✉*Karon Beach* ☎*076/330625* 🌐*www.dinopark.com* *B300 adult* ⏲*Daily 10 AM–midnight*). Street side are a dinosaur-theme bar and restaurant, but the real fun is inside: 18 holes of miniature golf, featuring a swamp, a lava cave, and a real live Tyrannasaurus Rex (well, the kids will think so!).

WHERE TO EAT

$$–$$$$ SEAFOOD ✕ **On the Rock.** Built, you guessed it, on a rock overlooking Karon Beach, this restaurant has great views of the water. Seafood is the specialty, but Italian and traditional Thai dishes are on the menu, too. This restaurant is part of the Marina Cottage hotel. ✉*South end of Karon Beach* ☎*076/330625* ▭*AE, MC, V.*

WHERE TO STAY

A sprawling Meridien resort is wedged into Karon Noi. If none of the following options tickle your fancy, there are literally dozens upon dozens of others.

$ **Fantasy Hill Bungalows.** Set on a hill in-between the two beach areas, these well-situated bungalows are great value. The bungalows are basic but clean, and all rooms have comfortable balconies which overlook a central courtyard area. **Pros:** excellent value; balconies. **Cons:** few amenities. ✉*8/1 Patak Rd., Karon Beach, Phuket* ☎*076/330106* *35 bungalows* *In-room: some a/c. In-hotel: 1 restaurant* ▭*No credit cards.*

$$–$$$ **In On the Beach.** This place way at the north end of Karon is truly on the beach. Many of the rooms have good sea views. It's a quick walk from here to the rest of the sprawl of Karon Beach. **Pros:** beach location. **Cons:** slightly removed from center of town. ✉*Moo 1, Patak Rd., Karon Beach, Phuket* ☎*076/398220* *www.karon-inonthebeach.com* *30 rooms* *In-hotel: restaurant, laundry service, Internet terminal* ▭*MC, V* *CP.*

$$$–$$$$ **Le Meridien.** Between Patong and Karon Beach sits this sprawling resort. There are more bars, cafés, and restaurants in this hotel than in many small towns. Its range of outdoor diversions—everything from tennis to waterskiing—means you never have to leave the property. There are hundreds of guests at any given time, yet the resort never feels too crowded, thanks to its thoughtful design. Two huge wings are where you'll find the sumptuous rooms, which are furnished in teak and rattan. Most have sea views, others overlook the pair of pools. **Pros:** large swimming pool; excellent activities; private beach. **Cons:** too big for some; some rooms lack view. ✉*8/5 Moo 1, Karon, Muang, Phuket* ☎*076/340480* *www.lemeridien-phuket.com* *470 rooms* *In-room: safe, refrigerator, Internet. In-hotel: 7 restaurants, room service, tennis courts, pools, gym, spa, beachfront, diving, water sports, children's programs (ages 3–12), laundry service, Internet terminal* ▭*AE, DC, MC, V* *EP.*

$$$–$$$$ ★ **Marina Phuket Resort.** This surprisingly quiet option has its cottages spread out over a lush hillside separating Karon from Kata Beach. Those cottages higher on the hill are the quietest. A wonderful pool and second restaurant (the first is On the Rock, *above*) are surrounded by more trees and plants. Best of all, Marina Cottage has its own beach access, keeping the hordes at bay. Half of the jungle rooms around the pool have all the latest high-tech amenities, including minicomputers and DVD players; note that some older rooms don't have certain amenities,

5

like TVs. **Pros:** good location; private beach. **Cons:** some rooms lack amenities. ✉ *47 Karon Rd.* ☎ *076/330493 or 076/330625* 🌐 *www.marinaphuket.com* *89 rooms* *In-room: refrigerator, DVD (some), no TV (some), Internet (some). In-hotel: 3 restaurants, pool, diving, Internet terminal* *MC, V* *EP.*

$$$–$$$$ ★ **Moevenpick Resort and Spa.** Live Thai music greets you as you enter an expansive lobby lavishly decorated with Thai art. Six types of rooms include two-bedroom family villas, one-bedroom plunge pool villas, and rooftop villas that have penthouse salas with deck chairs and outdoor Jacuzzis. Wander across the beautifully landscaped grounds, past the jungle gym and volleyball and badminton courts, follow the scent of incense to the spa, or continue toward the sea, where sand has been transported across the road to create an authentic "beach" bar. The main pool has a domed, thatch-roof platform within the water. **Pros:** beachfront location; amazing facilities. **Cons:** slight package-tour feel. ✉ *509 Patak Rd., Karon Beach* ☎ *076/396139* 🌐 *www.moevenpick-phuket.com* *339 rooms* *In-room: safe, refrigerator, Internet. In-hotel: 2 restaurants, room service, bars, tennis courts, pools, gym, spa, diving* *AE, DC, MC, V.*

$$ **Phuket Orchid Resort.** This resort is slightly inland, but the beach is just a short walk away. The lack of a beachfront brings the rates down considerably, but the lower rates make it very popular. A hodgepodge of Thai, Khmer, and Chinese architectural and design flourishes are everywhere, even in the sprawling pool and surrounding patios. And yes, lots of orchids are sprinkled about the main lobby. Some rooms have direct pool access. If you want a no-smoking room, be sure to demand it when booking. **Pros:** interesting design influences including Khmer and Chinese; great pool. **Cons:** not on beach; slightly confused decor. ✉ *34 Luang Pohchuan Rd., Karon Muang, Phuket* ☎ *076/396519* 🌐 *www.katagroup.com* *525 rooms* *In-room: safe, refrigerator. In-hotel: 3 restaurants, room service, bar, pools, spa, laundry service, Internet terminal* *AE, MC, V* *EP.*

KATA BEACH

22 km (13 mi) southwest of Phuket Town.

Of the three most popular beaches on the west coast of Phuket, this is the calmest of the lot. A shady sidewalk runs the length of the beach. Club Med dominates a large hunk of the beachfront, keeping the development frenzy to the southern end. There's also a committed group of regulars here who surf the small local breaks.

GETTING HERE & AROUND

Taxis, tuk-tuks, and motorcycles all vie for your attention to take you to and from Kata Beach. Expect to pay B250 into Phuket Town or B200 into Patong by taxi, and about B50 more for a tuk-tuk.

EXPLORING

Walking around Kata is easy—just follow the beach road from north to south. Kata Yai is the main beach and located near the main shopping street of Thai Na. To the south, Kata Noi is almost exclusively taken

CLOSE UP

A Festival for Health and Purity

During Phuket's annual Vegetarian Festival, devotees perform religious rites, including piercing their bodies with needles.

Phuket's most important festival is its annual Vegetarian Festival, held in late September or early October. Though no one knows the precise details of the event's origins, the most common story is that it started in 1825, when a traveling Chinese opera group fell ill. The Taoist group feared that their illnesses were the result of their failure to pay proper respects to the nine Emperor Gods. After sticking to a strict vegetarian diet to honor these gods, they quickly recovered. This made quite an impression on the local villagers, and the island has celebrated a nine-day festival for good health ever since. Devotees, who wear white, abstain from eating meat, drinking alcohol, and having sex. Along with detoxing the body, the festival is meant to renew the soul—not killing animals for food is supposed to calm and purify the spirit.

The festival involves numerous temple ceremonies, parades, and fireworks. But what most fascinates visitors are the grisly body-piercing rituals. Some devotees become mediums for warrior spirits, going into trances and mutilating their bodies to ward off demons and bring the whole community good luck. These mediums pierce their bodies (tongues and cheeks are popular choices) with all sorts of things from spears to sharpened branches to florescent lightbulbs. Supposedly, the presence of the spirits within them keeps them from feeling any pain.

The events are centered around the island's five Chinese temples. Processions are held daily from morning until mid-afternoon. The Tourism Authority of Thailand office in Phuket Town can provide a list of all activities and their locations. Note that you might want to invest in earplugs—it's believed that the louder the fireworks, the more evil spirits they'll scare away.

up with the very long and expensive Kata Thani Phuket Beach Resort. This is a public beach (as all beaches in Thailand are), so be sure to exercise your beach rights and soak up some sun on delightfully quiet Kata Noi if you're in the area.

WORD OF MOUTH

"Kata Beach on Phuket is my idea of an idyllic beach and you will find plenty of nice little boutique hotels within your price range [in October]. For a big night out, Karon and Patong beaches are a quick taxi ride away and offer plenty of wild and crazy options. Kata itself is nice and relaxed by day and has plenty of little bars and restaurants." —shanek

WHERE TO STAY

¢–$ **Da Bungalows.** Across the street from Mama Tri's Boathouse sits a set of snug, white bungalows high on the hill with views of the beach and ocean. Some of the rooms are surprisingly spacious; all come with pleasant balconies. The friendly owner Da also runs the local surf shop, which doubles as the hotel office. The place is small and popular with the international surfer crowd (they rent boards in the lobby and on the beach by Mom Tri's), so it's best to call in advance about rooms. **Pros:** great views; surfer friendly. **Cons:** rooms are a bit basic; not family friendly. ✉ *235/1 Kohktanode Rd., A. Muang, Phuket* ☎ *076/333055* *8 rooms* *In-room: no a/c (some). In-hotel: laundry service* *No credit cards.*

¢–$ **Kata Noi Bay Inn.** If you want to enjoy the serenity of Kata Noi without draining your wallet, here's the spot. All but a few of the simple, clean rooms have air-conditioning and all have small balconies. Most rooms overlook the Kata Thani across the road, but some manage to squeeze in a small view of the beach. **Pros:** quiet location. **Cons:** poor views; rooms lack amenities. ✉ *4/16 Moo 2, Patak Rd., Kata Noi Beach, Phuket* ☎ *076/333308 up to 09* *22 rooms* *In-room: no a/c (some), refrigerator, no TV. In-hotel: restaurant* *MC, V* *EP.*

$$$$ **Kata Thani Phuket Beach Resort.** This long, sprawling lodge fronts most of the Kata Noi beach. This seems to intimidate day-trippers, whose general absence keeps nearly 1 km (½ mi) of smooth sand delightfully calm. Glass-walled suites in the Thani wing have some of the best ocean views on the island. You can shower and watch the sun set at the same time through huge bathroom windows. Regular rooms (if you can call them that) in the Buri wing are very tastefully furnished, with all the bells and whistles you'd expect in this price range (some have pool views, others ocean views). **Pros:** peaceful beach location. **Cons:** large and rather impersonal touch. ✉ *14 Kata Noi Rd., Karon, Muang, Phuket* ☎ *076/330124* *www.katathani.com* *479 rooms* *In-room: safe, refrigerator, Wi-Fi. In-hotel: 6 restaurants, tennis courts, pools, gym, spa, children's programs (ages 4–12), laundry service, Wi-Fi* *AE, MC, V* *EP.*

NAI HARN

18 km (11 mi) southwest of Phuket Town.

South of Kata Beach the road cuts inland across the hills before it drops into yet another beautiful bay, Nai Harn. On the north side of the bay is the gleaming white Royal Meridien Phuket Yacht Club. On the south side is a nice little beach, removed for now from the tailors and cheap restaurants that have sprung up at the entrance to the Royal Meridien

GETTING HERE & AROUND

This is the southernmost beach on Phuket. You can get here from Phuket Town or along the coastal road through Kata, Karon, and Patong. Taxis, tuk-tuks, and motocycles will all take you to and from Nai Harn; a taxi to or from Phuket Town should be about B400, and it costs B700 to get to the airport.

EXPLORING

From the top of the cliff at **Phromthep Cape,** the southernmost point on Koh Phuket, you're treated to a fantastic, panoramic view of Nai Harn Bay, the coastline, and a few outlying islands. At sunset, you can share the view with swarms of others who pour forth from tour buses to view the same sight. If you're driving, arrive early if you want a parking spot. There's a lighthouse atop the point.

5

WHERE TO EAT & STAY

$–$$$ SEAFOOD ✕ **Phromthep Cape Restaurant.** Although it doesn't look like much from the Phromthep Cape parking lot, views from the tables out back are hard to beat. Just slightly down the hill from the lighthouse, you get unobstructed sights of the cape and coastline. Plus, you get lower prices and better views than most places on the island that boast of their panoramas. The restaurant serves Thai food and some Western fare. ✉*94/6 Moo 6, Rawai Beach* ☎*076/288656* 🌐*www.phuketdir.com/phromthep caperest* 💳*AE, MC, V.*

$$$$ **Royal Meridien Phuket Yacht Club.** This place used to be home to the annual King's Cup Regatta—now the only yachts here are decorative carvings on the walls, but the place is still every inch a luxury destination. Beautifully appointed rooms in a modern Thai style all have balconies overlooking the sea with views of Promthep Cape in the distance. The building's layout has balconies staggered up the hillside. Some would say this is to afford each room a perfect view of the sea. Others would say it allows you to look down and see your sun-tanning neighbors. **Pros:** modern Thai furnishings; great views. **Cons:** isolated location. ✉*Nai Harn Beach, Phuket* ☎*076/380200* 🌐*www.lemeridien.com* *110 rooms and suites* *In-room: safe, refrigerator. In-hotel: 3 restaurants, room service, tennis courts, pool, gym, spa, beachfront, water sports, laundry service* 💳*AE, DC, MC, V* *EP.*

THE ANDAMAN COAST

The Andaman Coast stretches from Ranong Province, bordering Myanmar (Burma) to the north, to Satun Province, flanking Malaysia to the south. Along this shore are hundreds of islands and thousands of beaches. Because of their proximity to Phuket, Phang Nga and Krabi provinces are the two most popular destinations on the Andaman Coast.

The effects from the 2004 tsunami varied greatly around the region. Generally speaking, west-facing coasts were hardest hit, followed by south- and north-facing shores. East-facing beaches and areas shielded to the west by other bodies of land were less harmed.

Cleanup was undertaken almost immediately, and considering the popularity of this region and the inherent economic value of these beautiful beaches and islands, reconstruction proceeded rapidly. In some instances, Khao Lak for example, many resorts built in the year preceding the tsunami were to be rebuilt exactly as they had been the year before, with reopenings occurring regularly. The impact on the beaches and underwater marine life was harmful in some regard and beneficial in others. However, most beaches were not adversely affected by the waves; many areas were actually cleansed by the deep ocean water and are more beautiful than they have been in many years.

Phang Nga Bay National Park is Phang Nga's most heralded attraction, drawing thousands of day-trippers from Phuket. There are dozens of little islands to explore, as well as offshore caves and startling karst formations rising out of the sea. Most visitors make an obligatory stop at Phing Kan Island, made famous by the James Bond movie *The Man with the Golden Gun.*

The Similan and Surin Islands national parks are well known to scuba divers for their crystalline waters and abundant marine life. You can camp or stay in a national park bungalow on either of the islands; no commercial lodging is available in either park. Many divers opt to stay on live-aboard ships departing from Phuket or Khao Lak.

Prior to the tsunami, Khao Lak, the departure point for boats to the Similans, was an up-and-coming beach "town" in its own right. Khao Lak Lamru National Park attracted nature lovers, while the beaches along this coast drew beachgoers who wanted a vibe more tranquil than Phuket has to offer. Although most resorts were destroyed, the "town" was spared and Khao Lak was nearly back to business as usual by 2006. Travelers looking for even greater seclusion head to the Koh Yao Islands, which have cultural tours and homestays that provide insight on southern Thai lifestyles.

Krabi Province lies to the east of Phuket. Its capital, Krabi Town, sits on the northeastern shore of Phuket Bay. Once a favorite harbor for smugglers bringing in alcohol and tobacco from Malaysia, the town has been transformed into a gateway to the nearby islands. Ao Nang, a short distance from Krabi Town, has evolved into a quaint beach town. Ao Nang and nearby Noppharat Thara exist simply to cater to tourists, and restaurants and shopping abound. With its coast lined with longtail boats, Ao Nang is a more convenient base of operations than Krabi Town for exploring nearby islands and beaches. Longtail boats and ferries depart Ao Nang to Koh Phi Phi, Koh Lanta, Nang Cape, and the multitude of smaller islands in eastern Phang Nga Bay.

The islands of Koh Phi Phi were once idyllic retreats, with secret silver-sand coves, unspoiled stretches of shoreline, and limestone cliffs dropping precipitously into the sea. But then the islands were portrayed in *The Beach* (2000). By the time the film had been released on DVD, Phi

Phi was a hot property. Koh Phi Phi was also hit hard by the tsunami, which destroyed many resorts, restaurants, bars, and shops along all but the east-facing beaches. The untouched beaches are certainly still beautiful and the affected areas were quickly cleaned up. By fall 2006, many restaurants, bars, and smaller guesthouses had sprung up to fill the demand for lodging on this ultrapopular tourist destination, and major resorts have reopened. There is still a great deal of development and construction on the island; many of the budget accommodations that sprung up right after the tsunami are now upgrading their facilities.

Farther south, more-adventurous travelers are discovering the relative serenity of Krabi's "hidden" gem, Koh Lanta. Koh Lanta, one of the largest islands in Thailand, has many beautiful beaches, accommodations to please both budget and spendthrift travelers, and a few activities such as elephant trekking in the jungle.

PHANG NGA BAY NATIONAL MARINE PARK

Fodor's Choice ★

100 km (62 mi) north of Phuket, 93 km (56 mi) northwest of Krabi.

From stunning monoliths that rise from the sea to the secluded, crystal-clear bays, Phang Nga Bay is a must see for any nature lover. The only way to visit is by boat. Tours (B800 to B1,300) can be arranged through your hotel or resort if you're staying in the area.

GETTING HERE & AROUND

Many travel agencies in Phuket offer half-day tours of the area, and this is the way most travelers see the park. Another option is to take a bus heading north from Phuket Town (B60) to one of two inlets near the town of Phang Nga, where you can hire a longtail boat and explore at your own pace, but unless you speak Thai or are very intrepid, this is likely to be more of a hassle than it's worth. At the western inlet, you can rent a boat for about B1,300 for two hours. The second inlet sees fewer foreign tourists, so the prices are better—about B800 for three hours. The bay can also be explored via tour boat, speedboat, or sea canoe. Most tourists don't arrive from Phuket until 11 AM, so if you get into the bay earlier, you can explore it in solitude. To get an early start, you may want to stay overnight in the area. Be sure to take time to appreciate the sunsets, which are particularly beautiful on the island of **Koh Mak.**

ESSENTIALS

Hospital **Phang Nga Hospital** (✉ *436 Petchkasem Rd., Phang Nga Town* ☎ *076/412034*).

EXPLORING

There are several key sights around Phang Nga Bay. The island of **Koh Panyi** has a Muslim fishing village consisting of houses built on stilts. Restaurants are no bargain, tripling their prices for tourists. Beautiful **Koh Phing Kan,** now known locally as James Bond Island, is well worth a visit. The island of **Koh Tapu** resembles a nail driven into the sea.

Kao Kien has overhanging cliffs covered with primitive paintings of elephants, fish, and crabs. Many are thought to be at least 3,500 years old. **Tham Lot** is a stalactite-studded cave that has an opening large enough for boats to pass through.

WHERE TO STAY

$$$$ Fodor'sChoice ★ **Aleenta Resort and Spa Phan-Nga.** Stylish design, a romantic atmosphere, and a beautiful beach contribute to the Aleenta experience. Two-story lofts have glass walls overlooking the sea; you can watch the sunset from the bed, the sofa, or from your small poolside deck. Pool suites have outdoor tubs and showers and glass walls that retract so that the rooms are open air. Pool villas don't have sea views, but their retractable glass doors open onto a wooden deck that connects separate bedroom and living room areas to each other and to private pools and large outdoor tubs. Breakfast is served by the beach, as are sunset cocktails. The library has movie nights complete with popcorn. Located just over the Sarasin bridge north of Phuket, Aleenta is on a quiet Phang Nga beach a brief drive to Phuket, Phang Nga Bay, or Khao Lak. **Pros:** great sunset views from some suites; quiet, relaxing location. **Cons:** fills up early in high season. ✉ *33 Moo 5, Khokkloy, Phang Nga* ☎ *076/580333* 🌐 *www.aleenta.com* *15 suites and villas* *In-room: refrigerator, Wi-Fi. In-hotel: restaurant, room service, bars, pool, spa, beachfront, Wi-Fi* 💳 *AE, DC, MC, V.*

¢–$ **Ao Phang Nga National Park.** In addition to the camping grounds (where you can rent tents), the park has a few well-built bungalows within its grounds. The bungalows have one to three bedrooms and are either simple, fan-cooled affairs or plusher, with air-conditioning, TVs, and minibars. Near the bungalows and visitor center are three piers for hiring boats to explore the park. Rates vary based on the number of individuals in your party. **Pros:** excellent location. **Cons:** some rooms are basic and lack amenities. ✉ *80 Ban Tha Dan, Koh Panyi* ☎ *076/522236, 02/562–0760 for reservations* 🌐 *www.dnp.go.th* *15 bungalows* *In-room: no a/c (some), refrigerator, no TV (some). In-hotel: restaurant* 💳 *No credit cards.*

$–$$ **Phang Nga Bay Resort Hotel.** Each of the comfortable rooms at this modern resort has a private terrace overlooking a jungle-ringed estuary. The four levels are set back to ensure picture-perfect views from everywhere. The nearest beaches are more than 1 km (½ mi) away, but the hotel operates a boat to bring you there. Rooms are conventionally but comfortably furnished, with all modern amenities. The restaurant, which has a terrace overlooking the water, serves Thai, Chinese, and Western dishes. **Pros:** good facilities for price range. **Cons:** basic rooms; removed from beaches. ✉ *20 Thaddan Panyee* ☎ *076/411067* *88 rooms* *In-room: refrigerator. In-hotel: 2 restaurants, bar, tennis courts, pool* 💳 *AE, MC, V.*

DID YOU KNOW?

The limestone formations off Railay Beach—called karsts—are the result of a collision between mainland Asia and India about 30 million years ago, which forced limestone deposits to rise from the ocean floor.

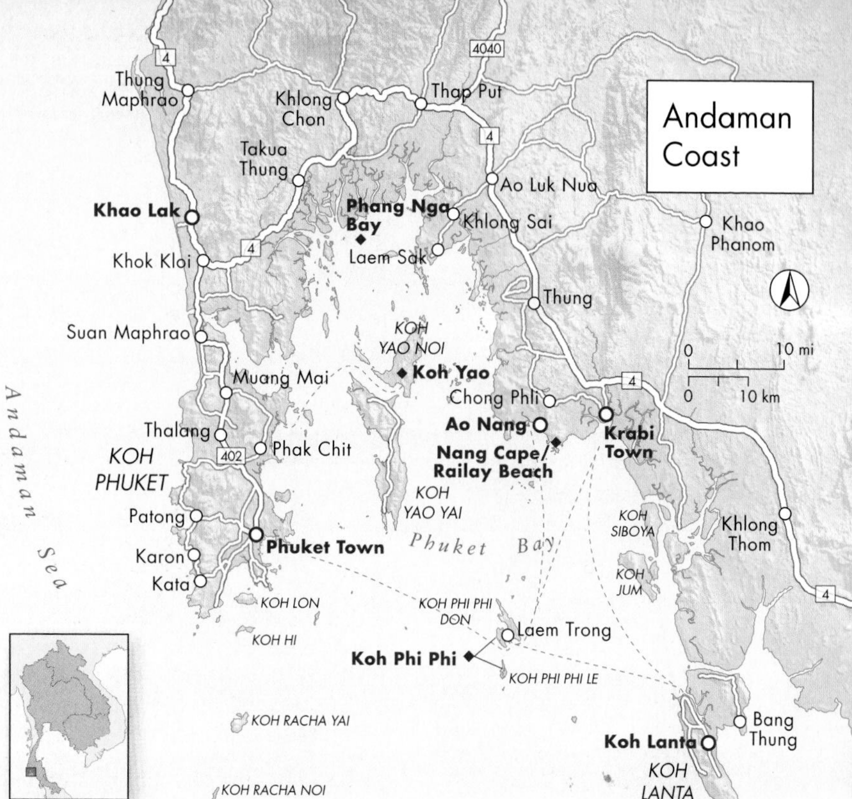

KOH YAO

45 mins by boat from Bangrong Pier, Phuket or 45 mins by boat from Chaofa Pier, Krabi.

Koh Yao Yai and Koh Yao Noi are the two large islands in the center of Phang Nga Bay. Both are quiet, peaceful places, fringed with sandy beaches and clear water. Most inhabitants still make their living through traditional means such as fishing, rubber tapping, and batik-painting. Considering their size and proximity to Phuket and Krabi, it's surprising how little development these islands have seen. During the 1990s many tourists began to discover the islands and the impact was, unsurprisingly, negative. So, to reduce the impact on the land and their culture the villagers residing on Koh Yao organized the "Koh Yao Noi Ecotourism Club" to regulate growth on the islands. They've certainly been successful—they even picked up a 2003 award for tourism development sponsored by Conservation International and *National Geographic Traveler.*

GETTING HERE & AROUND

Public ferry is the easiest, and cheapest, way to get to and from Koh Yao Noi. Most of the tourist developments can be found on Koh Yao

Noi. Ferries from Bangrong Pier to the north of Phuket leave regularly throughout the day and cost B100 per person. You can also travel from Chaofa Pier in Krabi for B100.

EXPLORING

A visit to Koh Yao will allow you to experience the local culture and customs while exploring the beauty of the islands (kayak and mountain bike are popular transportation options). The Ecotourism Club provides homestays if you really want the full experience of the islands; otherwise, most resorts provide day tours or information for self-guided exploration.

WHERE TO STAY

¢ **Koh Yao Homestay.** Koh Yao Homestay is organized by a community of Koh Yao residents who welcome tourists to share their way of life. The community provides visitors with lodging in their own homes, meals (consisting primarily of fish caught by village fishermen), and knowledge about their local customs. Visitors learn about rubber-tapping, batik-dying, fishing, rice-farming, coconut-harvesting, and other traditional trades from the people who have practiced them for centuries. More environmentally friendly and less invasive on the island's indigenous people than resort development, the homestay program is a unique way to learn about local people while helping to preserve their way of life. **Pros:** up-close cultural experience; eco-tourism at its best. **Cons:** homestay accommodations don't suit everyone. ✉ *Baan Laem Sai, Koh Yao Noi, Phang Nga* ☎ *076/597428* 🌐 *www.kohyaohomestay.com* ▭ *No credit cards.*

$$$$ Fodor's Choice ★ **Koyao Island Resort.** Koyao Island Resort has arguably the best view of any beach resort in Thailand. From east-facing Haad Pa Sai you have a panoramic vista of a string of magnificent islands. The bungalows are almost entirely open-air, so you not only admire the surroundings, you're part of them—you can even throw open the doors and watch the sunrise from your bed! An ideal romantic hideaway, Koyao Island Resort even arranges private beach barbecues. Although the beach is not great for swimming or sunbathing, there are beach chairs on the grass beside the sea, and kayaks and mountain bikes are available for use around the island. Boats can be hired to visit nearby islands for diving or snorkeling, and day trips, including cultural tours to batik-dying and fishing villages, can be arranged. The restaurant ($$) serves great fresh seafood; you select your meal from the saltwater pond. **Pros:** captivating panoramas of nearby islands. **Cons:** not family-oriented. ✉ *24/2 Koh Yao Noi, Phang Nga* ☎ *076/597474 up to 76* 🌐 *www.koyao.com* *15 villas* *In-room: safe, refrigerator, DVD, Internet. In-hotel: restaurant, spa* ▭ *AE, MC, V.*

KHAO LAK

80 km (50 mi) north of Phuket.

The coastal area collectively known as Khao Lak was one of Thailand's hottest new resort destinations prior to the 2004 tsunami. Unfortunately, Khao Lak bore the full brunt of the tsunami, which devastated most of the resorts along the coast, killing thousands of Thais and international tourists. Very few resorts were not completely destroyed. The extent of the destruction also makes Khao Lak the region's greatest success story—only two years after the catastrophe, Khao Lak was amazingly back on its feet. Today, aside from a few abandoned buildings, there's no physical evidence of the damage that occurred. But the tsunami has not been forgotten by the locals, many of whom lost friends and family.

GETTING HERE & AROUND

VIP and first-class buses leave for Khao Lak from Bangkok's Southern Bus Terminal each evening around 6 or 7 PM. The journey takes at least 12 hours. There's also regular bus service here from other beach areas. The journey to Phuket takes about two hours and costs about B200. There is no direct bus from Phuket to Khao Lak, but you can take a local bus that is bound for Ranong, Surat Thani, or Kuraburi and ask to get dropped off in Khao Lak.

The usual array of motorcycles, songthaews, and taxis will shuttle you around the area.

EXPLORING

Khao Lak Beach proper lies to the south of the national park, while most resorts and dive operators purporting to hail from "Khao Lak" actually line the coasts of Nang Thong, Bang Niang, Khuk Khak, and Bang Sak beaches to the north. As a result of Khao Lak's (once again) booming popularity, many properties are beginning to stay open more during the low season; however, Khao Lak is best visited near or during the high season (November to May) when you can be sure that all businesses are in full operation.

Khao Lak Lamru National Marine Park's rolling green hills and abundant wildlife is a primary attraction. The park grounds cover more than 325 square km (125 square mi) from the sea to the mountains, including a secluded sandy beach and several waterfalls. The park preserves some pristine tropical evergreen forest that is often supplanted in the south by fruit and rubber trees. Wildlife includes wild pigs, barking deer, macaques, and reticulated pythons. Walking trails lead to waterfalls with swimmable pools. Three rudimentary cabins are available for overnight stays, as are tent rentals for visitors who do not have their own. The park headquarters, on the road from Khao Lak Beach to Khao Lak town, provides information about exploring or staying in the park. ☎*076/720023, 02/579–0529 National Park Division in Bangkok* 🌐*www.dnp.go.th*.

WHERE TO EAT

$ THAI ✕ **Jai Restaurant.** This simple restaurant in central "Khao Lak town" pleases locals and visitors alike; the presence of locals in a restaurant is always a good sign in a tourist town. Choose your own fish or jumbo prawns from the display boat and select a cooking style. The deep-fried snapper with chili sauce (not spicy) and the spicy vegetable salad with cashew nuts are both highly recommended. ✉*5/1 Moo 7, Khao Lak* ☎*076/485390* ▭*No credit cards*.

WHERE TO STAY

$$$–$$$$ **Baan Krating.** Baan Krating was one of the few properties that didn't have to rebuild—it has a fortunate (and wonderful) location on a cliff above a rocky beach. The beautiful view and a path to the beach that travels within Khao Lak Lamru National Park give the resort a quiet, natural atmosphere. Rooms are in wooden cottages that are "rustic" in the sense that they do not have the usual explosion of silk fittings and Thai art that most resorts of this class have, but you'll hardly have to sacrifice any comfort here. Each room has a few deck chairs out front for gazing at the sea. **Pros:** quiet, relaxed atmosphere; great views. **Cons:** spartan rooms; slightly worn. ✉ *28 Khao Lak, Takuapa, Phang Nga* ☎ *076/423088* 🌐 *www.baankrating.com* *24 cottages* *In-room: safe, refrigerator. In-hotel: restaurant, pool, laundry service, Internet terminal* *MC, V.*

$ **Green Beach Resort.** Standard clapboard bungalows have wooden floors, rattan walls, and bamboo furniture. The brick-enclosed outdoor showers in deluxe rooms have semi-incongruous wooden sinks—the only boutique-style element in otherwise generic bathrooms. Sea-view bungalows have much better locations than the standard ones, which are located beside a barren lot. All bungalows have decks and chairs. Budget rooms can have the air-conditioning shut off for discounted rates. **Pros:** inexpensive. **Cons:** slightly tacky exterior; bland feeling. ✉ *13/51 Moo 7, Haad Nangtong, Khuk Khak* ☎ *076/420046 greenbeach_th@yahoo.com* *40 bungalows* *In-room: refrigerator. In-hotel: restaurant, Internet terminal* *MC, V* *Closed May–Nov.*

¢ **Khao Lak Nature Resort.** The best budget option in the area is near the Khao Lak Lamru National Park. Basic wooden huts have rattan walls and many windows that look out into the surrounding forest. A trail leads to a small sandy beach within the national park. Newer huts have a/c and balconies. **Pros:** budget accommodation; close to the national park. **Cons:** lacking amenities and pool. ✉ *26/10 Khao Lak, Takuapa, Phang Nga* ☎ *084/7440520* *39 huts* *In-room: no a/c (some), no phone, no TV. In-hotel: restaurant* *No credit cards* *Closed May–Nov.*

$$$–$$$$ **Khao Lak Seaview Resort and Spa.** Seaview Resort's stunning tiered swimming pool epitomizes the luxury available to its guests. Octagonal villas have high ceilings, four-poster beds, and whirlpool tubs. The resort's small private stretch of sand is nice, but the beach and the ocean are slightly better at beaches farther north. Regardless, the water is swimmable and, as Seaview is situated on the south end of Nang Thong Road, the resort is ideally located for romantic beach walks. That is, if you can tear yourself away from the stunning tiered swimming pool long enough to explore the beach. **Pros:** great pool; luxurious feel. **Cons:** not the best views. ✉ *18/1 Moo 7 Petchkasem Rd., Khuk Khak* ☎ *076/420625* 🌐 *www.khaolak-seaviewresort.com* *156 rooms, 41 villas* *In-room: safe, refrigerator. In-hotel: 2 restaurants, room service, bars, tennis court, pools, gym, spa, beachfront, laundry service, Internet terminal* *AE, DC, MC, V.*

$$$–$$$$ **Le Meridien Khao Lak Beach & Spa Resort.** Le Meridien is on an isolated 12-km (7-mi) stretch of beach to the north of Khao Lak town. Most

rooms are either in the Family wing or Spa wing, the former having connecting parents' and kids' rooms and views of the pool and "kids beach," the latter positioned closer to the spa and adults-only swimming pool. Beautifully furnished villas have peaked roofs, spacious baths with tubs and outdoor showers, and comfortable sofas from which to watch the plasma TVs. Beachside villas have long, thin pools ending in Jacuzzis beside the beach. Le Spa earned the resort the 2006 World Travel Award for Asia's and Thailand's Leading Spa Resort. **Pros:** great for kids; nice spa facilities. **Cons:** not for romantic getaways. ✉*9/9 Moo 1, Tambol Kuk Kak, Amphur Takua Pa, Phang Nga* ☎*076/427500* 🌐*www.starwoodhotels.com* *243 rooms* *In-room: safe, refrigerator, DVD, Internet. In-hotel: 4 restaurants, room service, bars, pools, gym, spa, diving, concierge, children's programs (ages 3–12), laundry service* 💳*AE, D, MC, V.*

$$$$ **Mukdara Beach Resort.** This expansive resort was hit hard by the tsunami but has been rebuilt to look almost identical to how it looked before: gorgeous. Accommodations are in large, Thai-style, peaked-roof villas in landscaped tropical gardens or in rooms in a three-story building farther from the beach (only the top floor has an ocean view). Deluxe rooms are luxurious, with hardwood floors, glass-enclosed baths that see through to the living room, and sundecks. Villas have canopy beds, triangular floor pillows, lounge areas, and outdoor rain showers. **Pros:** on beach; tasteful Thai furnishings. **Cons:** large resort, so not intimate. ✉*26/14 Moo 7, Thanon Khuk Khak, Takuapa, Phang Nga* ☎*076/429999* 🌐*www.mukdarabeach.com* *70 rooms, 64 villas, 7 suites* *In-room: safe, refrigerator, Internet. In-hotel: 6 restaurants, bars, tennis court, gym, spa, laundry service, Internet terminal* 💳*AE, D, MC, V.*

$–$$ ★ **Nang Thong Bay Resort.** The majority of rooms here are surprisingly inexpensive cottages that face the beach and are surrounded by manicured gardens. White concrete beachfront cottages have contemporary Thai interiors, outdoor garden showers, and decks with sun chairs. Beyond the pool (which has a great pool bar) and garden stands two modern, two- and three-story complexes with studios and roomy one-bedroom suites. Long walks along the beach are magical at sunset. Reasonably priced spa services are available next door at the Seaview Resort. **Pros:** good value. **Cons:** disappointing restaurant. ✉*Khao Lak, Takuapa, Phang Nga* ☎*076/485088 up to 89* 🌐*www.nangthongbayresort.de/enangthongbayresort.htm* *82 rooms* *In-room: refrigerator. In-hotel: restaurant, bar, pool, laundry service, Internet terminal* 💳*MC, V.*

SIMILAN ISLANDS

Fodor's Choice ★ *70 km (45 mi) 1½ hrs by boat from Thaplamu Pier.*

The Mu Koh Similan National Marine Park consists of the nine Similan Islands, as well as Koh Tachai and Koh Bon, which are located farther north. The diving around the Similan Islands is world class, with visibility of up to 120 feet; abundant blue, green, and purple coral; and rare marine life, such as the whale shark, the world's largest fish. In

Tropical forest meets powdery white sand on the Similan Islands.

addition to sparkling, crystal-clear water, the Similan Islands also have ultrafine, powdery white-sand beaches and lush tropical forests. The national park service allows visitors to stay on the beaches of Koh Miang (Island 4) and Koh Similan (Island 8).

GETTING HERE & AROUND

BY BOAT Speedboats to Similan National Park leave from Thaplamu Pier in Tai Muang District just south of Khao Lak beach at 8:30 AM when the park is open to the public (November–May). Once you reach Koh Similan, motorboats will take you to other islands for between B150 and B400 depending on distance.

You can also take a private tour boat from Thaplamu Pier for around B2,000 per person. The tour boat departs from Thaplamu at 8 AM daily and returns at 2 PM. Direct tickets, booked through the national parks, will cost B1,800; however, private tours are better value.

EXPLORING

The tsunami had a considerable effect on the islands. Shallow reefs were particularly hard hit, and as of this writing islands 1, 2, and 3 were indefinitely closed to divers, snorkelers, and visitors. However, many reefs were less affected and the underwater experience on the Similan Islands is fantastic. ■ TIP→ **If you plan to dive, contact a dive operator in Phuket or Khao Lak; there are no dive shops on the islands, though snorkeling gear is available for rent from the ranger stations.**

Koh Miang, where the park headquarters is located, has bungalows with 24-hour electricity and even some with air-conditioning (B2,000 with air-conditioning, B1,000 without); some bungalows have ocean views as well. Beachside camping is also available on Koh Miang (the park rents out roomy tents, large enough to stand in, which have two camping cots, for B450). Koh Similan has no bungalows, but has the same large tents for rent (B450), as well as an area for visitors to set up their own tents for B80 per person. If you choose to visit the island to stay at the park, expect to pay B1,800 to B2,000 for a round-trip boat transfer. Once on the island, you can hire a longtail boat to explore the other islands for about B500 per day. Alternatively, tour groups, such as **Jack's Similan** (☎ *076/443205* 🌐 *www.jacksimilan.com*), have their own smaller tents set up in this area and rent them out for the same fee charged by the national park. There are also overnight packages, which include tours of the islands, as well as camping and food. **■ TIP→ The park is extremely popular with Thais, so book well in advance if you're planning a visit during a Thai holiday. The islands are more enjoyable, and more explorable, if visited midweek.** The park entrance fee is B200 per visit. Note that the islands are normally closed to visitors from mid-May until early November. ☎ *076/595045 for campsite reservations, 02/562–0760 for bungalow reservations* 🌐 *www.dnp.go.th*.

SURIN ISLANDS

60 km (37 mi), 2 hrs by boat from Kuraburi Pier.

Mu Koh Surin National Marine Park is a remote island paradise practically unknown to anyone other than adventurous scuba divers and Thais. Five islands make up the national park, each with sea turtles, varieties of shark, and plentiful coral. If you get tired of sun and sea, there are several hiking trails that lead to waterfalls and a sea gypsy village.

GETTING HERE & AROUND

Khuraburi Pier, north of Khao Lak beach, is the departure point for boats to the Surin Islands and can be reached by any bus going to or from Ranong (about B100 from Phuket or Krabi). Songthaews will take you to the pier, approximately 9 km (5½ mi) out of town. Expect to pay B150 to B400 for boat trips to the various islands. Negotiating prices is not really an option here. An easier option is to book a trip through your resort. They will arrange your transportation to Khuraburi and your boat ticket.

EXPLORING

The tsunami hit the Surin islands quite hard, damaging shallow reefs and destroying all park structures. Coral at snorkeling sites in shallow water received considerable damage, but most dive sites were protected by their deeper water and were generally unaffected. All dive sites have reopened and conditions are good—reefs have recovered and there aren't any visual reminders of the tsunami today. The visibility and diversity of marine life is spectacular, and this is arguably the most unspoiled Thai island retreat, owing to its remote location and low number of visitors. Note that the park is normally closed during the rainy season (June–November).

There are 15 newly built, comfortable fan-cooled wooden huts on Koh Surin Nua (B2,000), and tent camping is allowed at a site that has decent facilities, including toilets and showers. You may bring your own tent and camp for B80, or rent one that sleeps two from the national park for B450. ☎*02/562–0760 inquiries and bungalow reservations* 🌐*www.dnp.go.th*.

KRABI TOWN

814 km (506 mi) south of Bangkok, 180 km (117 mi) southeast of Phuket, 43 km (27 mi) by boat east of Koh Phi Phi.

Krabi is a major travel hub in southern Thailand. Travelers often breeze through without stopping to enjoy the atmosphere, which is a shame, because Krabi is a laid-back town with great food and charming people. Locals are determined to keep Phuket-style development at bay, and so far—despite the opening of an airport 12 km (7 mi) from town—they are succeeding.

5

GETTING HERE & AROUND

BY AIR Flying is the easiest way to get here from Bangkok. Thai Airways, Bangkok Airways, and Air Asia all have daily flights to Krabi International Airport. One-way prices from Bangkok range from B1,000 to B3,500; the flight takes about an hour.

AIRPORT TRANSFERS The airport is a 20-minute ride from Krabi Town, and there are taxis (B35) and minibuses (B100) waiting outside the airport. These vehicles are also available to take you to other nearby (and not-so-nearby) beach areas. Minivans don't leave until they're full, which can happen very quickly or after a long wait. Your best bet is to check in with the minivans first to make sure you get a seat if one is about to depart—if not, you can opt for a taxi.

BY BUS & SONGTHAEW Buses from Bangkok to Krabi leave from Bangkok's Southern Bus Terminal and take at least 12 hours. VIP and first-class buses leave once every evening around 6 or 7 PM. Public buses leave Krabi for Bangkok at 8 AM and 4 and 5:30 PM. First-class buses travel between Phuket and Krabi (a three-hour journey) every hour. Getting around town or to Ao Nang is best done by songthaew. You can find songthaews at the corner of Maharat Soi 4 and Pruksa Uthit Road.

Bus and boat combination tickets are available from Krabi to Koh Samui and Koh Phangan.

There are a few bus terminals in Krabi, but if you don't arrive at the pier, songthaews can take you there; if you've purchased a combination ticket, this transfer is included.

BY CAR The airport has Avis, National, and Budget rental counters. Prices start at about B1,200 per day; for the same price, you can also rent a four-wheel-drive jeep in town.

ESSENTIALS

Hospital **Krabi Hospital** (✉ *325 Uttarakit Rd., Krabi Town* ☎ *075/631768, 075/631769, or 075/611210*).

VISITOR INFORMATION

Krabi has its own small Tourism Authority of Thailand (TAT) offices, where you can pick up maps and brochures, as well as information about local excursions. Tour operators and your hotel's tour desk are also good sources of information.

Information **Krabi** (✉ *Uttarakit Rd.* ☎ *075/622163*).

EXPLORING

There are a few good restaurants in town and there's excellent seafood at the night market, which also sells souvenirs. Still, there's no reason to spend more than a night or two here.

Just 3 km (2 mi) from Krabi Town is **Wat Tham Sua.** Built in 1976 as a monastery and meditation retreat, Wat Tham Sua is both respected by the local population and popular with tourists. Locals come to participate in Buddhist rituals, tourists to climb the 1,277 steps to panoramic views of the cliffs, Krabi Town, Krabi River, and the Panom Benja mountain range. There's also a cave with many chambers, which can be fun to explore, though it's not terribly attractive. A really large tree grows outside the entrance. The wat is between Krabi Town and the airport. ✉ *Tambon Muang Chum, 4 km (2½ mi) after Wachiralongkorn Dam.*

OFF THE BEATEN PATH

Than Bokkharani National Park. Between Krabi and Phang Nga is this forested park, which has several emerald-green ponds surrounded by tropical foliage, including wild gardenia and apocynaceae. The pools are filled with refreshing cool water, fed by a mountain spring 4 km (2½ mi) away. The largest pond is 130 feet by 100 feet, deep and suitable for swimming. The pools are best visited in the dry season, as they get quite murky when it rains. There's a B200 admission fee. ✉ *From Krabi: take Hwy. 4 to Ao Luek, then turn onto Rte. 4039* ☎ *075/681071*

WHERE TO EAT

¢–$ THAI ✕ **Chao Fa Pier Street Food Stalls.** Looking for local quality food at a low price? This strip of street-side food stalls serves everything from simple fried rice to more sophisticated southern delicacies such as *kanom jeen* (rice noodles topped with whatever sauces and vegetables you want). Open from nightfall until midnight, these stalls serve as an excellent opportunity to discover some exotic and enjoyable Thai foods. ✉ *Chao Fa Pier, Khong Kha Rd.* ▭ *No credit cards.*

¢ ★ CAFE ✕ **Relax Coffee and Restaurant.** The menu at this street-side café includes more than 10 different breakfast platters; a number of sandwiches, such as chicken satay, served on freshly baked brown bread, baguette, or ciabatta; many Thai dishes, including 10 different barracuda dishes; and, not surprisingly, a huge variety of coffee drinks, like raspberry latte frappés. ✉ *7/4 Chaofa Rd.* ☎ *075/611570* ▭ *No credit cards* ⏲ *Closed 2nd and 4th Fri. of each month.*

¢–$ SEAFOOD **Ruen Pae.** This massive floating restaurant aboard a large, flat barge serves Thai standards, with an emphasis on seafood dishes. It's at the Chao Fa Pier beside the night market. *Ut-tarkit Rd. 076/611956 No credit cards.*

WHERE TO STAY

¢–$ **City Hotel.** Rooms in the old wing of this hotel are simple but very clean and come with air-conditioning or fans; rooms in the new wing are standard, modern hotel rooms with carpeting and air-conditioning. Both buildings are near the night market and the river. **Pros:** central location; cheap rooms. **Cons:** basic. *15/2–4 Sukon Rd. 075/611961 or 075/621280 124 rooms In-room: no a/c (some). In-hotel: laundry service No credit cards.*

¢–$ **Krabi City Seaview Hotel.** This resort could have also added "riverside" to its name, as only a walking path separates it from the Krabi River. However, not all rooms have either river or sea views. Top-floor rooms have carpeted floors and small balconies, but the two second-floor rooms have large picture windows with the best views. The cheapest, ground-floor rooms have tile floors and no views. The resort is a five-minute walk from Chao Fa Pier. Another five minutes along the walking path to the south leads to Thara Nature Park. **Pros:** riverside location; close to Chao Fa Pier. **Cons:** rooms on lower floor unimpressive. *77/1 Kohngka Rd. 075/622885 up to 88 www.krabicityseaviewhotel.com 30 rooms In-room: refrigerator. In-hotel: bar, Internet terminal MC, V.*

5

$$–$$$$ **Krabi Maritime Park and Spa Resort.** This resort extends over 25 acres, and features a mangrove forest, a sprawling lagoon, a large swimming pool, and views of Krabi's signature limestone cliffs. A recent refurbishment has added a touch of class. The spa has a Jacuzzi that sits upon small tented piers above the lagoon. The large rooms look out over water, forest, and stunning cliffs. **Pros:** impressive views over the mangroves and forest. **Cons:** staff inattentive at times. *1 Tungfa Rd. 075/620028 up to 46 www.maritimeparkandspa.com 221 rooms In-room: refrigerator. In-hotel: restaurant, room service, bar, pool, gym, spa, laundry service AE, MC, V.*

EN ROUTE

Shell Cemetery is a pleasant beach park between Ao Nang and Krabi Town. It has a small information center explaining how snails from tens of millions of years ago were preserved for us to wonder about today. The fossils are probably not that interesting to most people, but the beach here is pleasant for a dip (although sunbathing in skimpy suits would be inappropriate, as many Thai families picnic on the hill above). Also, the view from the hill is quite nice, and if you're cruising on a motorbike, this is a fine place to get some shade in between destinations.

AO NANG

★ *20 km (12 mi) from Krabi Town.*

Although Ao Nang Beach is not much of an attraction, the strip facing it underwent a face-lift in 2002 that transformed it into a pleasant promenade of hotels, shops, and restaurants. In the evening, storefronts light up the sidewalk and open-air restaurants provide excellent venues to kick back with a beer and watch the crowd go by. For a more romantic atmosphere, head to the half dozen seafood restaurants atop a pier extending from the bend in Liab Chai Haad Road in between Ao Nang and Noppharat Thara beaches.

WORD OF MOUTH

"I would second the vote for Krabi—specifically Ao Nang or Railay. In terms of scenic beauty right on your doorstep, it's hard to beat. There are also quite a few interesting things to see and do away from the beaches, including hot springs, mangrove forests, and elephant treks." —MichaelBKK

GETTING HERE & AROUND

Buses from Bangkok headed to Krabi stop here. If you fly into Krabi, it takes about 45 minutes to Ao Nang in a taxi. Songthaews travel between Ao Nang and Krabi Town regularly. The fare shouldn't be more than B60; you can find them on the main road, displaying Krabi–Ao Nang signs.

EXPLORING

During the day, longtail boats depart Ao Nang for the more spectacular beaches and waters of Hong, Poda, Gai, Lanta, and the Phi Phi Islands, as well as nearby Railay Beach. Less adventurous types can find nicer sand and better water for swimming on the far eastern end of the beach or at Noppharat Thara Beach National Park to the west.

BEACHES

Noppharat Thara Beach, a 15-minute walk from central Ao Nang, is quiet and relaxing. The renovated walking path was extended here from Ao Nang in 2004, but as of this writing, the development had not yet followed it. The national park at the western end has shady casuarina trees and a clean, quiet beach.

A narrow river pier delineates the western edge of Noppharat Thara National Park. Here you can catch boats departing from the pier to Railay, Phi Phi, and Lanta, or simply cross to the other side and enjoy the unspoiled natural beauty of **Laem Son Beach.**

Farther north are the beaches of **Klong Muang** and **Tubkaak,** beautiful stretches of sand with amazing views that are occupied by upmarket resorts.

WHERE TO EAT

$–$$ THAI ✕ **Ao Nang Cuisine.** Believe the hype! The sign outside the restaurant brags that its chef, Mrs. Phaichat, is world famous, having worked at several well-known Thai eateries, including Chao Phraya Restaurant in Hollywood, California. The melt-in-your-mouth chicken satay (curry chicken skewers), an otherwise ordinary dish, is prepared superbly here, with a side of spicy peanut sauce. More elaborate Thai dishes are available for tourists who are tired of street-side barbecue seafood. ✉ *245/4 Liab Chai Haad Rd.* ☎ *075/695399* ▭ *MC, V.*

WHERE TO STAY

$$–$$$ ★ **Alis Hotel and Spa.** Whitewashed walls and red, ceramic tile floors contribute to the Morrocan design at Alis Hotel. The top-floor club rooms and honeymoon suite have blue wooden doors facing a two-story atrium hallway. Inside, wood-frame beds and small tables and chairs are nice, but the real treat lies up a flight of stairs that leads to a private sunbathing deck with a large, round wooden tub. The honeymoon suite has mosaic-style tile floors, bead curtains, and an atmosphere worthy of the extra baht. The minitheater beside the lobby is ideal for rainy days. **Pros:** polite, helpful staff; good facilities for the price. **Cons:** whitewash needs to be reapplied. ✉ *125 Moo 3, Ao Nang* ☎ *075/638000, 02/801–0760 in Bangkok* 🌐 *www.alisthailand.com* *34 rooms* *In-room: refrigerator. In-hotel: restaurant, bars, pool, spa, laundry service, Wi-Fi* ▭ *MC, V* *BP.*

$$ **Best Western Anyavee Ao Nang Resort & Spa.** The resort is a cluster of four-story buildings in Thai design, including northern-style peaked roofs. The large swimming pool has a waterfall you can swim through to have a drink at the pool bar. Rooms are contemporary Thai, austere but tastefully trimmed with hardwood. The resort is on a small rise a bit far from the sea, but that means it overlooks the hills and water around (and below) it. **Pros:** good selection of facilities. **Cons:** a bit removed from beach; exterior needs some renovation. ✉ *31/3 Liab Chai Haad Rd., Ao Nang* ☎ *075/695051 up to 54* 🌐 *www.anyavee.com* *71 rooms* *In-room: safe, refrigerator. In-hotel: restaurant, pool, spa, laundry service, Wi-Fi* ▭ *AE, DC, MC, V.*

$$$$ **The Cliff.** You can get a good view of the cliff that inspired the hotel's name as soon as you enter the lobby. But then your attention will quickly shift to burned bricks, charred wooden tiles, and natural wooden beams that create an atmosphere reminiscent of ancient Srivijaya Period of Siam. The Cliff's villas are set around a nonchlorinated, ozone-treated swimming pool. The rooms, each with outdoor shower, feature glass bay doors on two sides. The suite is on stilts above a small private fishpond and is particularly popular with honeymooners. **Pros:** atmospheric design; stunning location. **Cons:** not on beach. ✉ *85/2 Liab Chai Haad Rd., Ao Nang* ☎ *075/638117 up to 18* 🌐 *www.k-bi.com* *20 rooms, 1 suite* *In-room: refrigerator. In-hotel: restaurant, room service, pool* ▭ *AE, DC, MC, V.*

¢–$ ★ **Emerald Bungalow.** On isolated Laem Son Beach, this family-run resort offers genuine Thai hospitality. Tall pines, arching coconut trees, flowers, and ferns abound, and many birds, including a few chickens, inhabit the grounds. Budget-conscious travelers can enjoy proximity to the beach from basic wooden huts. Larger air-conditioned villas have individually designed layouts and interior design, but all include some Thai art. The resort is across the river from Noppharat Thara National Park. **Pros:** close to national park; great, relaxed atmosphere. **Cons:** a bit pricey for basic lodgings. ✉ *Noppharat Thara Beach* ☎ *091/892–1072 or 091/956–2566* *In-room: no a/c (some). In-hotel: restaurant, laundry service* ▭ *No credit cards.*

¢ **J Mansion.** Top-floor rooms peek out over surrounding buildings for a nice view of the sea. The primary reason to stay here is to save money

5

for day trips and nightlife—the view is a nice bonus. Large, bright rooms have tile floors, and all rooms are available without the air-conditioning turned on for an extra discount. The hotel is very close to the action in town, as well as to the minibus and longtail boat junction. **Pros:** large rooms; good views from top floor; friendly staff. **Cons:** slow Internet connection. ✉ *23/3 Moo 2, Ao Nang Beach* ☎ *075/637878* *21 rooms* *In-room: refrigerator. In-hotel: restaurant, Internet terminal* ▭ *AE, DC, MC, V.*

$$–$$$ ★ **Phra Nang Inn.** When selecting a room at this inn on the shore of Ao Phra Nang Beach, you can choose between the coconut wing and the betel-nut wing. The difference? Well, the rooms in the former are constructed from coconut palms, while those in the latter . . . well, you get the picture. The resort has a wonderfully kooky vibe—you might find headboards decorated with bright paintings of seashells and fish in the coconut wing and a few pieces of furniture might look like they're made from tree branches in the betel-nut wing. Even the bar, called the 75 Million Year Pub, is a little odd. The central location is also a big plus. **Pros:** airport shuttle available; central location. **Cons:** decor not for everyone. ✉ *119 Liab Chai Haad Rd., Ao Nang* ☎ *075/637130* ⊕ *www.phrananginn.com* *74 rooms* *In-room: safe, refrigerator. In-hotel: 2 restaurants, bar, pools, spa, laundry service, Internet terminal* ▭ *AE, DC, MC, V.*

$$$–$$$$ **Sheraton Krabi Beach Resort.** The Sheraton Krabi is built around an expansive mangrove forest, and there's a wide, sandy beach on the premises. All of the contemporary and colorful standard rooms overlook the forest, while the six suites have views of the sea. There are many activities to keep guests occupied, including aerobics, sailing, and tennis on lit courts. The pool, restaurants, and bar are down by the beach, where various water sports are available, and the sunbathing and swimming are great. **Pros:** beachfront location; great amenities. **Cons:** location may disappoint beach purists—water isn't crystal clear. ✉ *155 Klong Muang Beach, Nongtalay* ☎ *075/628000* ⊕ *www.sheraton.com* *246 rooms, 6 suites* *In-room: safe, refrigerator. In-hotel: 2 restaurants, room service, bars, tennis court, pool, gym, diving, water sports, bicycles, laundry service, Internet terminal* ▭ *AE, DC, MC, V.*

$$$$ ★ **The Tubkaak.** The elegant wooden buildings here each resemble a *kor lae,* a traditional Southern Thai fishing boat. Tubkaak Beach is calm and lovely, and the rooms have spectacular views of the Hong Islands. All superior and deluxe rooms are a few steps from the free-form swimming pool, while sea-view villas are only steps from the beach. A cozy library and bar has books and games for rainy days and relaxing evenings. The small size of the Tubkaak makes you feel at home and friendly staff make everyone feel like family. **Pros:** relaxed environment; beach location. **Cons:** disappointing restaurant. ✉ *123 Taab Kaak Beach, Nongtalay* ☎ *075/628400* ⊕ *www.tubkaakresort.com* *44 rooms, 2 suites* *In-room: safe, refrigerator. In-hotel: restaurant, pool, spa, water sports, laundry service* ▭ *AE, MC, V.*

NIGHTLIFE

Funky tunes and an extremely inviting atmosphere courtesy of proprietors Oil (a native Southerner) and Jeff (her Canadian husband) make most people become repeat customers at the aptly named **Bad Habit Bar** (✉*Noppharat Thara Beach, Liab Chai Haad Rd., Ao Nang* ☎*075/637882 or 06/279–2712*). Drink prices are reasonable (beer for B50 and cocktails for B100). It's one of the nicest pubs in the area and good times are pretty much guaranteed. The bar is midway down Noppharat Thara Beach directly across from the beach and next to the Andaman Spa. Upstairs at **The Loft** restaurant enjoy the view of the beach and dine on the small specials menu, changed weekly, featuring fusion Thai-Western food like pasta and Thai green curry sauce.

Encore Café (✉*245/23 Liab Chai Haad Rd., Nang Beach, Ao Nang* ☎*075/637107*) has live music five to seven nights a week from prominent local and expat musicians who play rock, reggae, blues, jazz, funk, folk, and fusion Western-Thai tunes. Hidden back behind the main road in Central Ao Nang, Encore Café is one of the few places to hear quality music while knocking back some beers and eating Thai and Western pub grub.

5

NANG CAPE/RAILAY BEACH

★ *15 mins by longtail boat east of Ao Nang.*

Don't strain your neck admiring the sky-scraping cliffs as your longtail boat delivers you to Nang Cape, four interconnected beaches collectively referred to as Railay Beach; the isolated beaches of Tonsai, Phra Nang, East Railay, and West Railay, only accessible by boat, are sandy oases surrounded by vertical sandstone cliffs.

GETTING HERE & AROUND

Longtails will ferry you here from Ao Nang. Prices vary depending on time of day and which beach you're headed to, but expect to pay around B60 or B70 each way. Prices can rise dramatically in the evening so leave early to save money.

EXPLORING

The four beaches are connected by walking paths and each have their own attractions. Tonsai Beach, with a pebble-strewn shore and shallow, rocky water, caters to budget travelers and rock-climbers. West Railay has powdery white sand, shallow but swimmable water, gorgeous sunset views, and many kayaks for hire. East Railay, a mangrove-lined shore unsuitable for beach or water activities, draws rock-climbing enthusiasts, as well as younger travelers looking for late-night drinks and loud music. Phra Nang Beach, one of the nicest beaches in all Krabi, is ideal for swimming, sunbathing, and rock-climbing.

SPORTS & THE OUTDOORS

ROCK-CLIMBING

Climbers discovered the cliffs around Nang Cape in the late 1980s. The mostly vertical cliffs rising up out of the sea were, and certainly are, a dream comes true for hard-core climbers. Today, anyone daring enough can learn to scale the face of a rock in one of the most beautiful climbing destinations in the world. There are 500 to 600 established routes. Notable climbs include the Tonsai Beach overhang and Thaiwand Wall, where climbers must use lanterns to pass through a cave and then rappel down from the top. Beginners can learn some skills through half-day or full-day courses for fixed rates of B800 or B1,500, respectively. Most climbing organizations are found on East Railay. **Cliffs Man** (☎*075/621768*), **Tex** (☎*075/631509*), and **King Climbers** (☎*075/637125* 🌐*www.railay.com*) are a few of the originals. King Climbers provides rescue services, though hopefully you won't need them.

Slightly less adventurous, or more spendthrift, types can try the free climb to "the lagoon." The lagoon isn't all that impressive, but the view from the top is spectacular. The trailhead for the fairly arduous climb up the occasionally near-vertical mud, rock, vine, and fixed-rope ascent is along the path to Phra Nang Beach, immediately across from the gazebo. Watch out for monkeys!

WHERE TO STAY

There are plenty of bars and restaurants along the beaches. Most restaurants serve standard Thai and Western fare. As you move away from the beach, you'll find less expensive and more atmospheric places, including some climber hangouts.

$$$ **Koh Jum Lodge.** Located on the island of Koh Jum, in Phang Nga Bay between Krabi, Phi Phi, and Koh Lanta, Koh Jum Lodge has rooms in 16 wooden cottages designed in traditional Thai architectural style. Bungalows are on the grounds of a coconut palm plantation in a tropical garden setting. All cottages are near the beach, facing Phi Phi Island to the west, each benefiting from sunset and sea views. Although the resort is open all year, public boats do not service it year-round. During the high season (November to mid-May), boats from Krabi to Koh Lanta stop offshore, where longtail boats ferry you to the island. The remainder of the year you must contact the resort to hire a B2,500 longtail for the 40-minute ride out to the island from Krabi. **Pros:** traditional Thai design; helpful staff. **Cons:** a bit isolated from resort towns. ✉*286 Moo 3, Koh Siboya, Kua Klong, Krabi* ☎*075/618275* 🌐*www.kohjumlodge.com* *16 bungalows* *In-room: no a/c, no phone, no TV. In-hotel: restaurant, pool, Internet terminal* *MC, V.*

$$ **Railay Bay Resort and Spa.** Great Thai food ($$) and a beachside patio and bar from which you can watch the sunset are a few good reasons to visit Railay Bay Resort and Spa. Basic cottages and rooms in a row of modern two-story buildings are suitable reasons to lodge here, also. Get a massage in a room overlooking the beach and pool and you may never want to leave. This resort in the center of West Railay appeals to people who like a natural environment—one that comes with plenty of amenities, such as a minimart, Internet, and air-conditioning. A walking path connects West and East Railay for easy access to Phra Nang Beach. **Pros:** great sunset views; central location. **Cons:** staff may not speak great English. ✉*145 Moo 2, Railay West Beach, Krabi* ☎*075/622570 up to 72* 🌐*www.krabi-railaybay.com* *141 rooms, 10 suites* *In-room: safe, refrigerator. In-hotel: restaurant, pool, spa, Wi-Fi* *MC, V.*

Railay Beach's dramatic limestone formations attract rock-climbers; there are courses and routes for novices.

¢ **Railay Highland Resort.** While admiring the sweeping view of the towering limestone cliffs, take a closer look and you may see teeny people scaling the rock face. Awake early and you can witness the sunrise over the distant bay. The restaurant and bar have amazing views, the rooms are set back in the hillside, spread out among the trees. Basic huts with rattan walls and thatched roofs have mattresses on the floor with mosquito nets. There's no hot water, but electricity runs 24 hours. This is a great spot for rock-climbers or people who want to chill out and don't mind roughing it a bit. **Pros:** inexpensive. **Cons:** no pool; lacking some other facilities. ✉ *Moo 1, Railay East Beach, Krabi* ☎ *075/621731* *20 bungalows* *In-room: no a/c, no TV. In-hotel: restaurant, bar, diving, laundry service* *No credit cards.*

$$ **Railay Princess Resort and Spa.** Thai-style lamps and silk throw pillows on the beds and sofas are nice touches at this quiet retreat located midway between East and West Railay beaches. All rooms have balconies that look out over the pool and the lotus- and fishpond to the surrounding cliffs. A teak walkway connects the restaurant to the swimming pool. **Pros:** quiet location; great value. **Cons:** not on beach; furniture looks cheap. ✉ *145/1 Moo 2, Railay Beach, Ao Nang* ☎ *075/622605 or 075/624356* *www.railayprincessresortandspa.com* *59 rooms* *In-room: refrigerator. In-hotel: restaurant, pool, spa, water sports, laundry service* *MC, V.*

$$ **Railei Beach Club.** Each of the 24 privately owned homes here is individually designed (and named), giving each its own unique character.
Fodor'sChoice ★ Solly's house, a two-story glass house on the beach, is particularly popular. The houses sleep between two and eight persons and most have large decks and kitchens. Powdery white sand is a short walk away and kayaks

are available. Feeling lazy? The staff can go into town and shop for you. Really lazy? A cook can be arranged. Two small rooms are available in the clubhouse, next to the common area and reception; they have no kitchens, so you must have your meals down the beach at other resorts, but they are the best deal on all of Nang Cape. Booking ahead is a must. Note that there's no electricity from 6 AM to 6 PM. **Pros:** great choice of accommodation and prices. **Cons:** fills up early in high season. *Box 8, Krabi Town, 81000 075/622582 www.raileibeachclub.com 24 houses In-room: no a/c, safe, kitchen No credit cards.*

$$$$ ★ **Rayavadee Premier Resort.** Scattered across 26 landscaped acres, this magnificent resort is set in coconut groves with white-sand beaches on three sides. The lobby faces East Railay, the pool looks out over West Railay Bay, and the beach bar and restaurant are the only structures on Phra Nang Beach—Rayavadee has the only direct access to this beautiful stretch of sand. Circular pavilions built in traditional Thai style have spacious living rooms with curving staircases that lead up to opulent bedrooms and baths with huge, round tubs. Some of the best rooms have secluded gardens with private hot tubs. Four restaurants assure variety—the beachfront Krua Pranang ($$$), set in a breezy pavilion, serves outstanding Thai food. **Pros:** great dining variety; intricate room design; plenty of facilities. **Cons:** notably non-eco-friendly use of wood. *214 Railay Beach, Ao Nang 075/620740 www.rayavadee.com 98 rooms, 5 suites In-room: safe, refrigerator, DVD. In-hotel: 4 restaurants, room service, bar, tennis court, pool, gym, spa, beachfront, water sports, laundry service, Internet terminal AE, DC, MC, V.*

¢ **YaYa Resort.** This large complex of three- and four-story wooden buildings looks like a small village—something like the castaways on Gilligan's Island would have developed after three or four generations. In fact, it's one of the oldest resorts on the cape and has undergone several renovations over the years. Well . . . some of the rooms have. Newer rooms have tile floors, air-conditioning, and standard amenities. Older ones have moldy wood and dodgy bedding. Nonetheless, the resort has a funky, tropical vibe, and is centrally located on East Railay Beach, a short walk from everything including beaches, climbing, and nightlife. **Pros:** inexpensive rooms available. **Cons:** parts of resort need renovation. *1 Moo 2, Railay Beach, Ao Nang 075/622593 www.yayaresort.com 86 rooms In-room: no a/c (some), refrigerator (some), no TV (some). In-hotel: restaurant, laundry service, Internet terminal No credit cards.*

KOH PHI PHI

48 km (30 mi) or 90 mins by boat southeast of Phuket Town; 42 km (26 mi) or 2 hrs by boat southwest of Krabi.

The Phi Phi Islands consist of six islands. **Phi Phi Don,** the largest of the islands, is shaped like a butterfly: The "wings," covered by limestone mountains, are connected by a flat 2-km (1-mi) narrow body featuring two opposing sandy beaches. Phi Phi Don is the only inhabited island.

The tsunami affected Phi Phi Don enormously. However, a huge rebuilding program has left the island looking remarkably developed. If you were unaware that such a catastrophe had taken place, you would think it was a beautiful island under a lot of development, rather than one that was destroyed and has been rebuilt. There's quite a bit of construction these days, as resorts as well as budget accommodations update and renovate their facilities. Several of the finest hotels on the island, Phi Phi Cabana, Charlies, and Phi Phi Princess, all of which were devastated by the tsunami, have taken their time rebuilding and just reopened in 2008.

GETTING HERE & AROUND

Seatran and Royal Fern Ferry depart from Ratsada Pier on Phuket—usually once in the morning and once in the early afternoon—and reach Phi Phi Don two hours later. PP Cruiser also takes two hours to reach Phi Phi Don, but departs from Phuket's Makham Pier. A one-way ticket is about B400. Ferries traveling to Phuket from Ao Nang or Koh Lanta stop at Koh Phi Phi in the high season (November to April) as well.

EXPLORING

The popularity of the Phi Phi Islands stems from the outstanding scuba diving; leopard sharks, turtles, and sea horses are some species still frequenting popular reefs. The tsunami actually had surprisingly little effect on the dive sites here, with 75% of coral reefs sustaining low to no impact. The best dive sites were relatively unaffected and those hardest hit were not good snorkeling sites to begin with.

Since the tsunami, farther-flung beaches on Phi Phi Don have been getting the attention that they deserve. Before Tonsai Beach was rebuilt, visitors who were forced to look elsewhere for lodging discovered the magic of sandy and swimmable Laem Tong Beach and beautiful, peaceful Long Beach.

A popular day trip from Phi Phi Don is a visit to nearby **Phi Phi Lae** via longtail or speedboat. The first stop is Viking Cave, a vast cavern of limestone pillars covered with crude drawings. Most boats continue on for an afternoon in **Maya Bay,** aka "The Beach." If you don't mind huge crowds (the snorkelers practically outnumber the fish), Maya Bay is a spectacular site. If you get a really early jump on everyone, cruise into a secluded bay, and leave first tracks along the powdery sand beach, you've done it right; otherwise, head to secluded **Loh Samah Bay,** on the opposite side of the island. Loh Samah Bay may, in fact, be the better option. Though smaller, it is as beautiful as Maya Bay but receives less attention.

Alternatively, you can take a 45-minute trip by longtail boat to circular **Bamboo Island,** with a superb beach around it. The underwater colors of the fish and the coral are brilliant. The island is uninhabited, but you can spend a night under the stars if you're adventuresome. You can also hike up to a series of viewpoints toward the 1,030-foot peak on the east side of the island. The trailhead is near Tonsai Bay; ask your hotel for directions.

CLOSE UP

The Tsunami

The waves from the 2004 tsunami were cataclysmic, but to a far greater extent on land than underwater. Shallow reefs were upturned and countless fish were left stranded far ashore, but the underwater impact was relatively mild. Official reports found 13% of coral reefs sustained severe damage, while 40% had no noticeable impact at all. Almost immediately after the event, more than 200 experts had examined over 300 dive sites to asses the damage. Their reports indicate that within 5 to 10 years, depending on the level of impingement by divers and fishermen, damaged reefs will have naturally regrown.

Shallow dive sites, such as Similan Island's Snapper Alley, were most affected by the waves. The waves primarily upturned table coral and buried shallow reefs with a blanket of sand, causing greater harm to crustaceans than to fish. As many dive sites are in deeper water, they were generally unaffected. That said, Similan and Surin islands accounted for half of the severely damaged sites.

Damage off Phi Phi Island was a combination of ocean surge and debris from the island. At Lanah Bay, up to 90% of the coral was destroyed. Most damaged reefs, with the exception of Bamboo Island, were not in popular snorkeling areas. Hard coral around the islands was particularly hard hit, but numerous volunteers contributed to cleaning up tons of debris and turning table coral over to its original upright position. Phi Phi dive sites are more renowned for the variety of marine life, such as leopard sharks, and this is still the case, although turtles and other marine life that feed off coral may see reduced numbers.

Phi Phi Dive Camp (🌐 *www.phiphidivecamp.com*) has established a floating coral nursery and deployed cement blocks near Viking Cave by Phi Phi Ley. The cement blocks have been positioned into formations that will be seeded by coral fragments from the nursery to develop artificial reefs. The dive camp provides a four-day reef-monitoring course that is educational to the diver, promotes responsibility regarding reef treatment, and collects useful for data for its ongoing reef-monitoring program.

Recent reports cite a greater diversity of fish around the Similan Island's reefs than before the tsunami. Experts from the Global Coral Reef Monitoring Network postulate that much-needed coastal management implemented as a result of the tsunami may have a long-term benefit on the ecosystem. Prior to the tsunami, nearly 50% of Thailand's reefs were considered deteriorated and less than 20% were in good or excellent shape. This trend has been reversed and a greater emphasis on conservation permeates Thailand's diving community these days.

With the exception of those around Similan Islands 1, 2, and 3 (closed prior to the tsunami), all dive sites in Thailand are open to divers, some indisputably beautiful. Especially around the Similan and Surin islands, there are many dive spots that remain world class.

THE POST-TSUNAMI RECOVERY

Both of Thailand's coasts had been experiencing a tourism boom for years—with many places facing the consequences of overdevelopment—when the tsunami hit the Andaman Coast on December 26, 2004. Several beaches on Phuket, the beach area

of Khao Lak, and much of Koh Phi Phi were devastated by the waves, and although many areas on the Andaman Coast were unaffected by the tsunami, tourism on that shore came to a near standstill in the months following the disaster.

More than four years later, the situation is considerably different. Phuket's affected beaches have been completely redeveloped, including much improved beachfront sidewalks, street lighting, restaurants, bars, and cafés on par with Western beach destinations. Phi Phi Island has rebuilt a bit more slowly. Most development along Tonsai and Loh Dalam initially focused on upgrading salvageable budget accommodation to nicer, mid-range standards to fill the void left as the largest resorts planned their reconstruction. The middle and high end resorts have now re-entered the market and Phi Phi is once again booming, with plenty of bars and restaurants. Khao Lak has more hotels, restaurants, and activities than it did before to 2004. These days the tsunami's lasting effects are not visible to the naked eye, but many Andaman Coast locals lost friends and family, and their lives have been irrevocably altered.

Overdevelopment is an issue, as it was before the disaster. Once adventurous travelers find a new, secluded, undeveloped beach and start talking about it, rapid development follows at a frightening pace. In many spots this development hasn't been regulated or monitored properly and the country is now pulling in the tourist dollar at the expense of the environment. It's a cycle that's hard to stop. Redevelopment in the tsunami areas began quite slowly, while developers and local businesses awaited government regulations. In some instances, the planning paid off (Phi Phi now has much-needed waste-water treatment facilities), but as most areas waited for regulations that never arrived, no-holds-barred development quickly followed.

CLOSE UP

Tsunami Memorials

On the eastern end of Loh Dalam Beach is the Phi Phi Tsunami Memorial Park, a tiny garden with a small plaque listing some of the names of those who lost their lives in the 2004 tsunami. Several benches have been dedicated to the memory of others lost in the disaster. The memorial is a little sad because it seems so small in relation to the devastation that claimed 5,395 lives. Regardless, it is a nice little park, and looking out across the beach and sea, one cannot help but be moved.

Another memorial, this one underwater, is located 66 feet deep, off the coast of Monkey Beach. The granite memorial consists of three pyramid-shaped plaques arranged in the shape of an equilateral triangle; the plaques are the exact number of centimeters apart as the number of victims taken by the sea. The bases of the pyramids contain philosophical quotations, and the three markers symbolize the elements of land, water, and air, in which humans must learn to live in balance. In the center of the triangle rests a single granite stand that describes the tsunami's occurrence. In addition, 2,874 (the number of missing persons) centimeters from the memorial is a traditional Thai sala made from tsunami debris. It is the first underwater memorial monument on earth.

WHERE TO EAT

$–$$ SEAFOOD **Chao Koh Restaurant.** As you stroll Tonsai's walking path, you'll surely notice the catches of the day on display in front of Chao Koh Restaurant. Kingfish, swordfish, and barracuda, grilled with garlic and butter, white wine, or marsala sauce, and served with rice or a baked potato, is a mere B200. Clams, crabs, shrimp, Phuket lobster, and live rock lobsters are priced by weight. Chao Koh also serves a variety of Thai salads, appetizers, noodles, and curry dishes, but seafood is their specialty. ✉ *Tongsai Bay* ☎ *075/620800* ▭ *No credit cards.*

¢–$ THAI **Pearl Restaurant.** Nothing fancy here, just genuine Thai food prepared and served by genuinely friendly Thai people. They also serve breakfast and a few Western dishes, including pizza. ✉ *Next to Cosmic Restaurant, Tonsai Village* ☎ *07/164–5716* ▭ *No credit cards.*

¢ CAFE **Phi Phi Bakery.** Craving fresh baked donuts, Danish, croissants, or real coffee rather than Nescafé? Check out Phi Phi Bakery, which serves American, Continental, and Thai breakfast specials and freshly baked pastries. They also serve Thai and Western standards for lunch and dinner. ✉ *97 Moo 7, Tonsai Village* ☎ *091/894–0374* ▭ *No credit cards.*

¢–$$ SEAFOOD **Thai Cuisine.** Fresh seafood is not hard to come by on Phi Phi, but even so, Thai Cuisine's selection of white shark, barracuda, swordfish, lobster, and crab have people lining up outside to get a table. In addition to finely cooked fish, Thai Cuisine makes great fried rice. Look for the restaurant with all rattan walls and ceiling across from Phi Phi Bakery in the middle of Tonsai's beach road, near the pier. ✉ *Central Tonsai Beach, Koh Phi Phi* ☎ *091/979–2525* ▭ *No credit cards.*

WHERE TO STAY

$$–$$$ **Bay View and Arayaburi Resorts.** All rooms at these two neighboring resorts are on a hill at the far eastern end of Tonsai Bay. Every bungalow has a large deck with a great view of both Phi Phi Lae and Tonsai Bay. These two resorts share everything but their names. The only difference between them is the room decor: Bay View is older and its rooms have hardwood floors, whereas Arayaburi is newer and its rooms have tile floors—the wood-floor rooms feel more traditional and natural, which suits the environment better. Arayaburi rooms are closer to the small "private" beach, which is slightly better than the water in front of the reception area, which is quite shallow and not great for swimming. The resort is on the quietest spot along Laem Hin Beach and it's only a short (although sometimes slippery) 15-minute walk along the rocks to gorgeous Long Beach. Electric cars transfer guests from distant rooms to the reception and restaurant areas. **Pros:** quiet location; great views; breakfast included. **Cons:** removed from main village; not on best beach. ✉*69 Laem Hin Beach* ☎*076/281360 up to 64* 🌐*www.phiphibayview.com* *109 bungalows* *In-room: safe, refrigerator. In-hotel: restaurant, room service, pool, Internet terminal* *AE, D, MC, V.*

5

$–$$ **Chao Koh Phi Phi Lodge.** Chao Koh Phi Phi Lodge is a collection of basic but comfortable bungalows near Tonsai Bay. A swimming pool and family-style suites were added in 2005 renovations. Several simple fan huts survived both the tsunami and the renovation, so the place still welcomes budget travelers. Evenings, the lodge runs a popular seafood restaurant by the sea, with a nice view of the bay. **Pros:** budget accommodation with a lot of amenities. **Cons:** bungalows have gaudy exteriors. ✉*Tongsai Bay* ☎*075/620800* 🌐*www.chaokohphiphi.com* *44 bungalows* *In-room: no a/c (some), safe, refrigerator (some). In-hotel: restaurant, pool, diving, Internet terminal* *MC, V.*

$$$$ Fodor's Choice ★ **Holiday Inn Resort.** The Holiday Inn couldn't have a better location—it's on more than 50 acres of tropical gardens along a private beach, which has gorgeous blue water with a sandy sea floor, where you can swim and snorkel year-round. Most bungalows have identical design with parquet floors, comfortable indoor daybeds, and decks with lounge chairs. However, a few rooms are family-style duplexes; those numbered 100–118 are also beachfront. A late 2007 expansion of the resort has added more beachfront rooms, hillside rooms with spectacular beach views, and an additional pool, bar, and restaurant. The Terrace Restaurant ($$$$), which serves Thai and international cuisines, has splendid views of the sea, and the cliff-side satay bar is one of the few sunset viewpoints on the island. Classes in Thai culture, arts, cooking, and language are offered throughout the week. The resort offers boat service from Phuket. **Pros:** secluded, private beach. **Cons:** set away from the main part of Koh Phi Phi. ✉*Cape Laemtong* ☎ *075/627300* 🌐*www.phiphi-palmbeach.com* *130 bungalows* *In-room: safe, refrigerator. In-hotel: 4 restaurants, room service, bars, tennis courts, pools, gym, spa, beachfront, diving, water sports, laundry service* *AE, MC, V.*

¢–$ **Maprao Resort.** If you don't mind a few geckos in your room, this resort is a great place to stay. Six styles of bungalows are available, from the two-story, beachfront Holy Tree, which has a large deck and breezy sea view, to the Roof Terrace Bungalows, which feature rooftop sun chairs. Bamboo bungalows on stilts with shared baths are available for budget travelers; newer concrete bungalows have small lofts above the baths with fans and mosquito nets for families with adventurous kids. Maprao is on a small private beach between Tonsai and Long Beach, accessible only by foot or by boat. **Pros:** private beach. **Cons:** no frills. ✉ *Between Tonsai and Long beaches* ☎ *075/622486* 🌐 *www.maprao.com* *25 rooms* *In-hotel: restaurant, bar, diving* *No credit cards.*

$ **Paradise Resort.** Book ahead (it's popular) and don't settle for less than beachfront. These are the best beachfront rooms on Long Beach and the other rooms aren't all that special. All rooms have tile floors and are relatively characterless, though superior rooms are slightly better than family rooms, which are far from the beach. You probably won't spend much time in your room, though, as the beach is gorgeous and there are many trees in front of the resort that provide much-needed shade. **Pros:** budget rooms with great location. **Cons:** some rooms lack a/c; unexciting restaurant. ✉ *Long Beach* ☎ *091/968–3982 up to 89* 🌐 *www.paradiseresort.co.th* *25 rooms* *In-room: no a/c (some). In-hotel: restaurant, water sports, laundry service* *No credit cards.*

$$–$$$ **Phi Phi Erawan Palm Resort.** Erawan Palm is a small, comfortable resort in the middle on Laem Tong Beach, next to the sea gypsy village. The spacious cottages all have wooden floors and ceilings with golden curtains and comforters. The beach bar is great for lazy afternoon cocktails and there is a small museum about the sea gypsy community that you can check out when you need a break from the beach. **Pros:** relaxed resort feel; interesting museum. **Cons:** boat ride away from main village; decor shows some age. ✉ *Moo 8, Laem Tong Beach* ☎ *075/627500* 🌐 *www.pperawanpalms.com* *18 cottages* *In-room: refrigerator, Internet. In-hotel: restaurant, room service, bar, pool, diving, laundry service, Internet terminal* *AE, MC, V.*

$$–$$$ **Phi Phi Natural Resort.** Beautiful sunrise views from the deluxe seaside bungalows are this resort's biggest draw. The 20 deluxe rooms along the rocky shoreline have wooden floors and Thai arts and crafts. The resort is on a hill between the north end of Laem Tong Beach and a smaller secluded beach, which is quite private, but less than ideal for swimming. Budget rooms also have good views, as they are high up on the hill. **Pros:** daily boat service to Phuket and Krabi; good views at moderate prices. **Cons:** lacks amenities compared to other resorts in price range. ✉ *Moo 8, Laem Tong Beach* ☎ *075/613000* 🌐 *www.phiphinatural.com* *70 rooms* *In-room: safe (some), refrigerator. In-hotel: restaurant, room service, bar, pool, public Internet* *MC, V.*

$–$$ **Phi Phi Viewpoint Resort.** On the western hillside overlooking Loh Dalam Bay, Phi Phi Viewpoint Resort was the sole survivor of the tsunami that devastated the resorts on this beautiful beach. Although the hillside huts are stacked pretty tightly next to and on top of each other, the six beachfront huts will give you a little more breathing room and privacy. The outdoor bar and the pool also have outstanding views of the beach and bay. Note that some huts don't have hot water. **Pros:**

good location overlooking bay. **Cons:** some huts are basic for the price. *107 Loh Dalam Bay 075/618111 www.phiphiviewpoint.com 54 huts, 1 suite In-room: no a/c (some), refrigerator. In-hotel: restaurant, bar, pool, diving, water sports, Wi-Fi MC, V.*

¢–$ ★ **Phi Phi Villa Resort.** Large, thatch-covered huts in a natural setting give Phi Phi Villa a relaxing island feeling quite different from bustling Tonsai Bay, a short walk away. All bungalows have small patios with wooden handrails, and interiors large enough to fit desks, chairs, wardrobes, and enormous bathrooms. The resort is on a stretch of private beach where boats are prohibited from landing; the absence of longtails that clutter Tonsai's shore makes the beach here more suitable for swimming, although it's still shallow and quite rocky. It's great for travelers who want to stay close to the action without being a part of it. The cheapest rooms lack air-conditioning, hot water, and basic amenities, but they do have access to everything else, including a new yoga center, the first on Phi Phi. ⚠ Rooms closest to the beach are only for sound sleepers or night owls; the reverberations from Hippies Bar and Carpe Diem beach bar can be heard late into the night. **Pros:** budget prices. **Cons:** noise from nearby bars; rocky beach not great for swimming. *Tonsai Bay 075/601100 www.phiphivillaresort.com 55 bungalows In-room: no a/c (some), refrigerator (some), no TV (some). In-hotel: restaurant, room service, bars, pool, diving, laundry service MC, V.*

¢–$ **Twin Palm Bungalow.** It doesn't get more basic than these small bamboo bungalows (nor does it need to). Were the island covered with these, it couldn't be more ideal. Thrown up in a sandy field, just off the beach, which once housed larger bungalows prior to the tsunami, they will inevitably be replaced by more permanent structures that may be "nicer" and more expensive, though not necessarily better. Check 'em out while you can. Reception is in the minimart on Loh Dalam Beach. Some rooms have shared bathrooms. **Pros:** cheap accommodation. **Cons:** prices increase dramatically November to May. *Central Loh Dalam Beach 084/185–8296 24 bungalows In-room: no a/c, no phone, no TV. In-hotel: restaurant No credit cards.*

$$$$ ★ **Zeavola.** Zeavola takes its name from a flower, the name of which translates in Thai to "love of the sea." That certainly is fitting, as the water off the powdery white-sand Laem Tong Beach is simply stunning. From the beach, sandy garden paths meander between semisecluded teak villas with outdoor sala entryways. Though the resort has modern amenities, there's a decided old-world charm to the place: baths have small mirrors and exterior iron plumbing and beds have cream-color mosquito nets. Chill out by the sea to relaxing tunes piped through all-weather Bose speakers. You can even relax on a simple mat outside your villa while fresh coffee percolates. Need privacy? Flick a switch and bamboo shades enclose your sala. **Pros:** stunning beach location; tasteful design. **Cons:** doubled service charge on food. *11 Moo 8, Laem Tong, Koh Phi Phi 075/627000 www.zeavola.com 52 villas In-room: safe, refrigerator, DVD. In-hotel: 2 restaurants, spa, beachfront, diving, laundry service AE, MC, V BP.*

5

DID YOU KNOW?

Koh Phi Phi is actually six islands, though only the largest, Phi Phi Don, is inhabited. Phi Phi Leh, is home to the famous Maya Bay; the other islands are really just large limestone outcroppings.

NIGHTLIFE

Many people come to Phi Phi for two reasons only: to go to Maya Bay during the day, and to party in Tonsai Bay at night. As a result, a large number of bars were constructed, primarily out of concrete, most of which were strong enough to survive the impact from the waves. Once you head down the side streets away from the beach there are mazes of bars and clubs competing in stereo wars, filled with young travelers eager to drink and dance the night away. If you like Khao San Road in Bangkok, you will love Tonsai Bay at night. The most popular of these bars, located near the 7-11 in the center of "town," are **Tiger Bar** and **Reggae Bar.** Along the path running parallel to the sea, there are several popular bars, notably **Apache Bar,** which has an impressive "katoey" (drag cabaret) show, and farther to the east are fire shows at the popular beach bars **Hippies Bar** and **Carpe Diem.** More remote beaches around the island have more subdued nightlife, primarily centered around resort restaurants and bars. One of the best of these is **Sunflower Bar,** which is on the eastern end of Loh Dalam Beach, next to the Tsunami Memorial Park. Constructed almost entirely of driftwood or old wooden bungalows, this laid-back beach bar often has local reggae bands jamming beneath the stars.

KOH LANTA

70 km (42 mi) south of Krabi Town.

Long, uncrowded beaches, crystal-clear water, and a laid-back natural environment are Koh Lanta's main attractions. Although "discovered" by international travelers in early 2000, Koh Lanta remains fairly quiet. Early development resulted in the construction of hundreds of budget bungalows and several swanky resorts along the west coast of Lanta Yai (Lanta Noi's coast is less suitable for development); however, as one of the largest islands in Thailand, Lanta was able to absorb the "boom" and therefore remains relatively uncluttered. In addition, Lanta is approximately 70 km (44 mi) south of Krabi Town, far enough outside established tourist circuits that visitor arrivals have increased more slowly than at other Krabi and Phang Nga beaches and islands.

GETTING HERE & AROUND

Krabi's airport is about two hours from Koh Lanta by taxi (B2,300) or minibus (B300 to B400). Minibuses depart from Krabi Town and Ao Nang, not the airport. There's no direct bus service from Bangkok to Koh Lanta; you'll have to take the bus to Trang or Krabi and then continue on in a minivan (songthaews will take you from the bus station to the minivans bound for Koh Lanta.) Two ferries travel between Lanta and the mainland. There is one main road running through the island that will take you to all major resorts. Pick-up trucks masquerading as taxis and motorcycles with sidecars will take you wherever you want to go. Negotiate hard for good fares; prices start at about B40 for a short ride of 1 km (1/3 mi).

ESSENTIALS

Hospital **Koh Lanta Hospital** (✉ *Lanta Old Town* ☎ *075/697068*).

EXPLORING

The tsunami was a mixed blessing for Koh Lanta. It had a small effect on the buildings along the coast, and most damage was repaired within months of the disaster. However, it had a beneficial effect on the environment, cleansing the beaches and replenishing the shore with clear deep-ocean water. Before the tsunami it was hard to imagine how Koh Lanta could be any more beautiful, but afterwards the water was bluer and more sparkling, the sand whiter and softer. Though the huge decrease in visitor arrivals to the island initially caused its share of economic hardship, it wasn't long before word of Koh Lanta's renewal spread and lucky travelers again found their way to its shores.

Most smaller resorts are closed during the low season (May though October). However, some do open in late October and remain open until mid-May—during these (slightly) off times, the weather is still generally good, and you can find that the rates are much lower and the beaches much less crowded.

BEACHES

Klong Dao Beach and Phra Ae Beach, both on Lanta Yai's west coast, are the most developed. If you head south, you'll reach calmer Klong Nin Beach and southern Lanta's quiet, scenic coves.

KLONG DAO Klong Dao Beach is a 2-km-long (1-mi-long) beach on the northern coast of Lanta Yai, the larger of the two islands that comprise Koh Lanta. Most resorts along Klong Dao are larger facilities catering to families and couples looking for a quiet environment. The water is shallow but swimmable, and at low tide the firm, exposed sand is ideal for long jogs on the beach.

PHRA AE Long and wide, Phra Ae Beach (aka Long Beach) is Lanta Yai's main tourist destination. The sand is soft and fine, perfect for both sunbathing and long walks. The water is less shallow than at other Lanta beaches, and therefore more suitable for diving in and having a swim. However, kayaks, catamarans, and other water activities, while available, are not as ubiquitous as on other islands. Although most lodging consists of simple budget bungalows, the beachfront does have several three- and four-star resorts. Along the beach and on the main road are many restaurants, bars, Internet cafés, and dive operators.

KLONG NIN Klong Nin Beach, approximately 30 minutes south of Long Beach by car or boat, is one of the larger, nicer beaches toward the southern end of Lanta Yai. Klong Nin is less developed and more tranquil than Long Beach. A typical day on Klong Nin could consist of a long walk on the silky soft sand interrupted by occasional dips in the sea, a spectacular sunset, a seaside massage, and a candlelit barbecue beneath a canopy of stars. Central Klong Nin, near Otto bar, is the best for swimming, as rocks punctuate the rest of the shoreline. Kayaks are available from some resorts and longtail boat taxis are for hire along the sea. Most resorts here rent motorbikes as well, as the road to the south is much smoother than the road from Long Beach.

SOUTHERN LANTA Southern Lanta beaches consist of several widely dispersed small coves and beaches ending at Klong Chak National Park. Immediately south of Klong Nin the road suddenly becomes well paved (much smoother than the road from Long Beach to Klong Nin), making the southern beaches accessible by road as well as by taxi boat. The nicest of the southern beaches is Bakantiang Beach, a beautiful one to visit on the way to the national park.

SPORTS & THE OUTDOORS

Diving, snorkeling, hiking, and elephant trekking are a few activities available on Koh Lanta and the nearby islands. Diving and snorkeling around Koh Lanta can be arranged through dive and tour operators, though most people choose to book through their own resort. Popular nearby dive sites are **Koh Ha** and **Koh Rok** off Koh Lanta. If you would like to enjoy Koh Lanta from another viewpoint, elephant trekking is available near Phra Ae (Long) Beach. A boat trip to the famous **Emerald Cave** on **Koh Muk** is a worthwhile experience; it's easiest to inquire at your resort about day trip options.

5

WHERE TO EAT

KLONG DAO BEACH

$ THAI ✕ **Picasso Restaurant.** Once you spot the giant mushrooms, you'll know you've arrived at this comfortable restaurant at the **Chaba Guesthouse** ($). Thai people believe that southerners make the best food, and Picasso Restaurant lives up to this southern reputation. Proprietor and artist Khun Toi creates pastel-color oil paintings incorporating shells and driftwood from Klong Dao Beach. Finished products adorn the walls of the restaurant, which itself is a Monet-inspired swirl of impressionist pastels and sculpture. Toi's style of art has even been granted a patent by the Thai government. The guesthouse offers comfortable bungalows. ✉ *Klong Dao Beach, Lanta Yai* ☎ *075/684118 or 099/738–7710* ▭ *No credit cards.*

$ THAI ✕ **Time for Lime.** Time for Lime is a large, open-air kitchen right off the beach where you can learn to cook Thai food (with Chinese, Malaysian, and Indian twists), using fresh seafood and vegetables. Instruction is provided in selecting the best ingredients and then cooking and presenting your own visual feast. It's fun, easy, and taught in a great environment. Spartan but cozy accommodations (¢) are available for those who wish to take multiple classes or just enjoy the smell of Thai cooking. Each night, the restaurant serves a different three-course set menu for B600, and reclining chairs are placed on the recessed sandbar while music plays and cocktails are served. Note that you should reserve workshops at least two days in advance. ✉ *72/2 Klong Dao Beach, Lanta Yai* ☎ *075/684590 or 089/967–5017* 🌐 *www.timeforlime.net.*

PHRA AE BEACH

¢–$ PIZZA ✕ **Funky Fish Bar and Bungalows–Mr. Wee Pizzeria.** Feeling funky? Dine while you recline on a triangular Thai pillow atop one of dozens of elevated wooden platforms. Mr. Wee serves thin-crust pizzas that should satisfy both American and Italian palates. The pizza Raul, with mozzarella, tomato, mushroom, and shrimp, is recommended. They also serve Thai and Italian food as well as ice cream and other desserts. Funky Fish is a happening bar at night, and they rent simple wood and rattan bungalows (¢) with thatched roofs and tile baths. ✉ *241 Moo 3, Phra Ae Beach, Lanta Yai* ☎ 081/2759501 ▭ *No credit cards* ⊙ *Closed June–Sept.*

KLONG NIN BEACH

$ Fodor's Choice ★ THAI

✕ **Cook Kai.** From the outside, the restaurant appears to be a standard, wooden Thai beach restaurant. Once inside, fairy lights along the ceiling light up your eyes and the food does likewise to your taste buds. Sizzling "hotpan" dishes of seafood in coconut cream and sweet-and-sour shrimp are succulent. Specials, such as duck curry served in a hollowed-out pineapple, change daily. Everything on their extensive menu tastes amazing. They even share their recipes, offering cooking classes upon request. ✉ *Moo 6, Klong Nin Beach* ☎ *091/606–3015* ▭ *No credit cards.*

SOUTHERN LANTA

¢–$ ★ THAI

✕ **Same Same But Different.** This restaurant is tucked away in a shady grove near the southern end of Bakantiang Beach. The "dining room" is very Robinson Crusoe, enclosed by a rudimentary roof with a dozen tables on the sand and wood bar. Have your longtail boat drop you off here and pick you up on the northern end of the beach an hour or so later, so you have time for a swim before you eat, and a nice walk on the beach when you're done. Same Same serves some southern Thai dishes, typically spicy. We recommend the fried prawns with tamarind sauce topped with fried shallot and chili. Smoothies and ice-cold beer are perfect for combating the afternoon heat. ✉ *85 Moo 5, Bakantiang Beach, Lanta Yai* ☎ *091/787–8670* ▭ *No credit cards.*

WHERE TO STAY

KLONG DAO BEACH

$$$$ ★

Costa Lanta. The coolest thing about Costa Lanta is the room design; each room at this trendy boutique resort is a convertible box, so if you're too hot you can open up the "walls" and allow the breeze to blow through your room. The resort keeps the design elements minimal, so as to place an emphasis on nature. The result? "Camping" for people who don't want to camp without air-conditioning and a nice bathroom. Even the water in the swimming pool appears greenish and pondlike. The resort is at the northern end of Klong Dao Beach—the quiet end of an already quiet beach. Isolation is a blessing here, as the resort has almost everything you might need, including a pool table and a spa. The water here is swimmable, and snorkeling around Kaw Kwang Cape, while not exceptional, is pleasant and there are fish to be seen. **Pros:** quiet location; art deco design. **Cons:** not great value; not on best beach. ✉ *212 Klong Dao Beach, Lanta Yai* ☎ *075/618092* 🌐 *www.costalanta.com* *22 rooms* *In-room: safe, refrigerator. In-hotel: restaurant, bar, pool, spa* ▭ *AE, DC, MC, V.*

$ **Southern Lanta.** With a fun-slide plunging into a big pool and several two-bedroom villas (each with large multibed rooms), Southern Lanta is quite popular with families. Standard rooms are bungalows built closely to each other with slightly run-down exteriors, but comfortable interiors. Seaside rooms are newer and have sofas indoors and deck chairs outdoors for maximum lounging. **Pros:** family-friendly; great pool. **Cons:** needs some redecoration. *105 Klong Dao Beach, Lanta Yai 075/684175 up to 77 www.southernlanta.com 80 rooms, 10 suites In-room: refrigerator. In-hotel: 2 restaurants, bar, pools, gym, spa, Internet terminal MC, V.*

$$$$ ★ **Twin Lotus Resort and Spa.** Twin Lotus is as much an architectural and interior-design exhibition as it is a sophisticated and tranquil retreat. At times the resort seems traditionally tropical (Thai massage is offered on thatched sala islands in a lotus pond), but at other times, it's creatively modern (the swimming pool is fringed with waterfalls). Occasionally, the two styles meld: deluxe superior rooms have colorful tile floors, but incredibly romantic outdoor baths. The resort's main dining area is a feast for the eyes as well as the palate, and the two bars make up for the fairly isolated location on the quiet northern end of Klong Dao Beach. **Pros:** great dining; romantic. **Cons:** not ideal for families. *199 Moo 1, Klong Dao Beach, Koh Lanta Yai 075/607000, 02/361–1946 up to 49 in Bangkok www.twinlotusresort.com 78 rooms In-room: safe, refrigerator, DVD. In-hotel: 2 restaurants, room service, pools, spa, diving, water sports, Internet terminal AE, MC, V.*

PHRA AE BEACH

¢–$ **Best House.** The entry to Best House is an inviting high-ceiling room with many comfortable chairs, white tile floors, and wooden beams, trim, and hand railings. The rooms are spacious and comfortable, the closest thing to "normal" Western hotel rooms on an island of bungalows and upscale spa-resorts. The place isn't on the beach, but it's very close to it. All rooms are equally nice, but air-conditioned rooms have the added luxury of hot water, which is unavailable in cheaper, fan rooms. **Pros:** inexpensive; close to the beach. **Cons:** some rooms very basic; no pool. *5/1 Moo 3, Phra Ae Beach, Lanta Yai 091/174–0241 www.krabidir.com/besthouse 40 rooms In-room: no a/c (some). In-hotel: laundry service No credit cards Closed June–Sept.*

$–$$ **Lanta Long Beach Resort.** The exteriors of the thatched roof wooden huts appear weathered and worn and the restaurant is now a short walk away at the neighboring, co-owned Nakara, but the resort's simplicity is its charm. The rooms are rustic—floors and walls are made of wood the way Thai huts should be, natural, but airtight, to keep the mosquitoes out. Some huts, however, have a few amenities like air-conditioning, large windows, and decks with roll-down wind-rain screens. Years of expansion have resulted in a variety of rooms for the thriftiest backpacker as well as the spendthrifty hippie. Construction of the "nicer" Nakara resort benefits L.L.B Resort guests, who may now use the swimming pool next door. **Pros:** nice selection of accommodations. **Cons:** must go to neighboring resort for some facilities. *172 Moo 3, Phra Ae Beach, Lanta Yai 075/684178 www.lantalongbeach.com 95* *rooms* ♿*In-room: no a/c (some), refrigerator (some), no TV (some). In-hotel: restaurant, bar, pool, laundry service, Wi-Fi* ▭*MC, V.*

$$ **Lanta Nakara.** If you're staying in a resort on a beautiful, white-sand beach with crystal-clear, blue water you should treat yourself to a room with a view. Fortunately, if you stay at Lanta Nakara (formerly Lanta Resortel), you will have such a view, even if you get stuck in a room at the back—most wooden bungalows are positioned so that you can look down a sandy walkway to the beach. So whether lying in bed and looking through the picture window, or lounging on one of two daybeds on the deck, you'll appreciate the tranquility of the Andaman Sea. Ask for one of the rooms away from the restaurant and pool to ensure quiet. When it gets too hot, retreat to the air-conditioned bliss of your cottage, which has wooden floors and rattan walls—a perfect blend of island design and modern amenities. **Pros:** friendly staff; great views. **Cons:** bland design. ✉*172 Moo, Phra Ae Beach* ☎*075/684178* 🌐*www.lantalongbeach.com/nakara.php* *44 cottages* *In-room: refrigerator. In-hotel: restaurant, bar, pool, laundry service, Wi-Fi* ▭*MC, V.*

$$$$ **Layana Resort and Spa.** The majority of rooms are in two-story garden pavilions set around a football field–size grass clearing that opens to the sea. The ocean and beach suites are the finest rooms here, the former featuring rooftop, open-air salas with large desks and mosquito net–enclosed daybeds ideal for afternoon lounging or romantic evenings. Beach suites have beds in the center of the rooms looking directly out to sea. The suites also have outdoor rainfall showers and glass-enclosed garden bathtubs. **Pros:** nice design. **Cons:** some bungalows lack sea views. ✉*272 Moo 3, Saladan, Phra Ae Beach, Koh Lanta* ☎*075/607100, 02/713–2313 in Bangkok* 🌐*www.layanaresort.com* *50 rooms* *In-room: safe, refrigerator, DVD, Wi-Fi. In-hotel: restaurant, bar, pool, spa, beachfront, diving, water sports* ▭*AE, DC, MC, V.*

¢ **Somewhere Else.** If you like your huts to be innovative, check out Somewhere Else. The six octagonal rooms in the front of the clearing are particularly cool. They have fold-down windows, wooden floors, and loose-pebble bathroom floors. This resort is nothing fancy (expect cold water and fans) but it has a great vibe, and you'll enjoy playing Ping-Pong with friendly staff in the common room or just watching the sunset on the chill-out pillows strewn on various wooden platforms. Note that there's no hot water. **Pros:** friendly and helpful staff; great beach location. **Cons:** no hot water or TV. ✉*253 Moo 3, Phra Ae Beach, Lanta Yai* ☎*091/536–0858 or 089/731–1312* *16 rooms* *In-room: no a/c. In-hotel: restaurant, laundry service* ▭*No credit cards* ⏲*Closed June–Sept.*

KLONG NIN BEACH

¢–$ **Lanta Miami Bungalows.** The Lanta Miami is on the beach, it's affordable, and the staff are incredibly friendly—you truly need little more. The rooms are spacious, and have big beds and tile floors, though you can probably spend your days on the beach or under a shady palm. Note there's no hot water or air-conditioning in some rooms. **Pros:** great location at low prices. **Cons:** some rooms lack amenities. ✉*13 Moo 6, Klong Nin Beach, Lanta Yai* ☎*075/662559* 🌐*www.lantamiami.com*

22 rooms In-room: no a/c (some), refrigerator. In-hotel: restaurant, laundry service No credit cards Closed June–Sept.

$ **Lanta Paradise Resort.** It's only a short walk along the beach to the best swimming spot, but the sand gets so hot you'll be glad to have the pool outside your room. Bungalows come in all permutations from fan-cooled and cold-water-only to air-conditioned, with hot water and all the standard amenities. The beachfront rooms are the best of the lot and have the most amenities (even TVs). Shady twin massage beds and southern Thai–style elevated dining tables with chill-out pillows and peaked roofs (both by the beach) help you keep your cool. There's even a hip little hippie beach bar that sells shell necklaces. **Pros:** good choice of accommodations; good Western food at restaurant. **Cons:** not the best value. *67 Moo 6, Klong Nin Beach, Lanta Yai 089/473–3279 www.lantaparadiseresort.com 35 rooms In-room: no a/c (some), refrigerator (some), no TV (some). In-hotel: restaurant, bar, pool, laundry service, Internet terminal No credit cards Closed June–Sept.*

$$$$ **Rawi Warin Resort and Spa.** This enormous resort encompasses an entire hillside along the road from Klong Khong Beach to Klong Nin and makes great use of the land to create a comprehensive vacation retreat. In addition to its luxuriously outfitted rooms, the resort features, among many other things, a 24-seat minitheater, a music room, a video game room, a dive shop, and a beautiful private beach. Landscaping marvels include wooden walkway bridges that cross a lagoon to several gazebos. Hotel and room decor is Thai style with an emphasis on the sea; the restaurant-bar area attempts to resemble a fishing village. **Pros:** large resort with many amenities; helpful staff; family-friendly. **Cons:** big resort feel not for everyone. *139 Moo 8, Lanta Yai Island, Krabi 075/607400 up to 48, 02/434–5526 in Bangkok www.rawiwarin.com 186 rooms In-room: safe, refrigerator. In-hotel: 3 restaurants, room service, bars, tennis court, pools, gym, spa, diving, bicycles, children's programs (ages 5–10), laundry service, Wi-Fi AE, DC, MC, V.*

$$–$$$ **Srilanta.** One of the first upscale resorts in the area to market the "less is more" philosophy, Srilanta remains a cool yet classy island getaway for trendy urbanites. Breezy rooms are primitive but have comfortable lounging areas and are tastefully decorated with flowers. Unfortunately, most rooms have no view, and the beach is a short walk down the hill. Suites, in addition to having larger rooms, also feature cable TV and in-room DVD players. The beachside pool, sunbathing lawn, spa, and common areas follow stylish Hindu and Balinese themes. The spa has massage tables on a platform above a large fishpond. Srilanta is reasonably priced for what you get (one of the nicest resorts on one of the nicest beaches), but the service is quite ordinary for such an extraordinary resort. **Pros:** great in-room amenities. **Cons:** staff a bit standoffish. *111 Moo 6, Klong Nin Beach, Lanta Yai 075/697288, 02/712–8858 in Bangkok www.srilanta.com 49 rooms, 3 suites In-room: refrigerator, no TV (some). In-hotel: 2 restaurants, bar, pool, spa, beachfront, laundry service, Internet terminal AE, DC, MC, V.*

5

SOUTHERN LANTA

$–$$ ★ **Narima Resort.** The owners staggered the bungalows when they were built so that almost all could enjoy the awesome view of Koh Ha. If that were not enough, they strung hammocks on each deck and threw in a couple of palm-straw rocking chairs. The rooms have cloth canopy ceilings and rattan walls. It almost doesn't matter that the shore here is rocky rather than sandy. The guests do not seem to mind; many take courses with the in-house dive shop, practicing in the pool or the crystal-clear sea. Others snorkel or just soak up the view from the large Jacuzzi. Owner-manager Dr. Jotiban is a doting, pleasant host. **Pros:** great views; good dive school. **Cons:** poor restaurant. ✉ *98 M. 5 Klong Nin Beach, Lanta Yai* ☎ *075/662668 or 075/662670* 🌐 *www.narima-lanta.com* *32 rooms* *In-room: refrigerator. In-hotel: restaurant, pool, laundry service, Internet terminal* 💳 *MC, V.*

$$$$ **Pimalai Resort and Spa.** Pimalai Resort and Spa is a premier resort encompassing hundreds of acres of beachfront and hillside along southern Bakantiang Beach. Standard rooms are luxurious enough, but exclusive villas have full kitchens, private pools, and drivers to shuttle you to the spa, beach, or other facilities around the sprawling resort. The spa was carefully landscaped with tall palms and sloping trails. The soothing sounds of streams and waterfalls around the spa and classical Thai music in the lobby are just as tranquilizing as the treatments. Thai royalty and celebrities have been guests here. Booking ahead is essential. **Pros:** exclusive resort; first-rate service. **Cons:** prices also exclusive; fills up fast. ✉ *99 Moo 5, Bakantiang Beach, Lanta Yai* ☎ *075/607999* 🌐 *www.pimalai.com* *79 rooms, including 7 suites, 40 private houses* *In-room: safe, refrigerator, DVD. In-hotel: 3 restaurants, room service, bars, pool, gym, spa, beachfront, diving, Internet terminal* 💳 *AE, DC, MC, V.*

6

Northern Thailand

WORD OF MOUTH

"I'd opt for north—I think you would see more 'real' Thailand . . . hill tribes, elephant rides, rafting, boats along the Ping River, hiking, and a much quieter style. Chiang Mai and Chiang Rai have more tuk-tuks and motorcyle taxis than BKK, which I think the kids would enjoy (okay, we're in our 50s and enjoyed them!)"

—kywood1955

WELCOME TO NORTHERN THAILAND

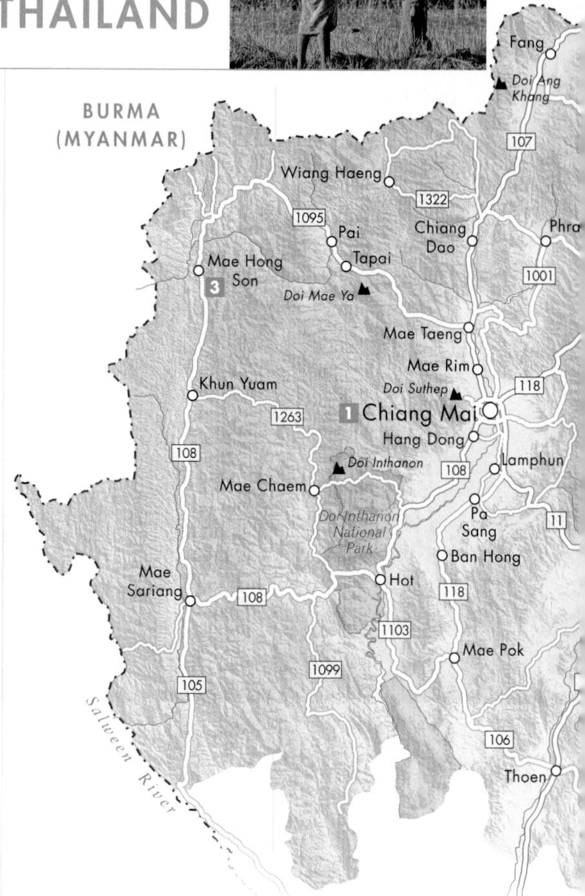

TOP REASONS TO GO

★ **Natural Wonders:** You don't have to venture far from Chiang Mai to see the region's natural beauty. You can hike to spectacular waterfalls and be back in the city in time for dinner.

★ **Shopping:** The region is world famous for its silks, and the night markets of Chiang Mai and Chiang Rai have an astonishing range of handicrafts, many of them from hill tribe villages.

★ **Eating:** The region's cuisine is said to be the country's tastiest. Chiang Mai has excellent restaurants, but even the simplest food stall can dish up delicious surprises.

★ **Temples:** The golden spires of thousands of temples dot the region. Each can tell you volumes about Buddhist faith and culture.

★ **Sports:** The country's most beautiful golf courses are here, and nongolfers have an almost unlimited variety of sports to choose from—rock climbing, white-water rafting, and paragliding are just a few.

1 Chiang Mai & Environs. Northern Thailand's principal city is a vibrant regional hub, modern and expanding rapidly outside its historic, moat-ringed, and partially walled center. Its famous Night Bazaar attracts shoppers from around the world, who are catered to with world-class hotels and restaurants.

2 Nan & Environs. Northern Thailand's most remote provincial capital is a fascinating destination. Nan is reached by a long but worthwhile drive from Chiang Mai along empty highways lined by fruit orchards, paddy fields, and jungle-clad uplands. The city's Pumin temple and its unique frescoes are reason enough to tackle the journey.

GETTING ORIENTED

A journey through Northern Thailand feels like venturing into a different country from the one ruled by far-off Bangkok: the landscape, the language, the architecture, the food, and even the people of this region are quite distinct. Chiang Mai is the natural capital of the north. The city is not a smaller version of Bangkok, but a bustling metropolis in its own right. Just beyond the city rises the mountain range that forms the eastern buttress of the Himalayas, and the region overall has some of the country's most dramatic scenery. The northernmost part of the region borders both Myanmar (Burma) and Laos, and improved land crossings into Laos from here have made forays into that country popular side trips.

Elephants in Chiang Mai.

Tachilek
Golden Triangle
Mae Sai
4
Chiang Saen
Houay Say (Houayxay)
Doi Mae Salong
Chiang Khong
Mae Chan
1089
1
LAOS
1020
Chiang Rai
Wiang Chai
Mekong River
Thoeng
Mae Suai
Phan
118
1
Song Khwae
Wang Nua
Phayao
Tha Wang Pha
1120
Chae Son National Park
2
Nan
Ngao
1035
101
Wiang Sa
1
103
Lampang
101
Phrae
11
Wiang Kosai National Park
11
0 30 mi
0 30 km
101
Uttaradit

3 The Mae Hong Son Loop. Set two or three days aside for traveling Thailand's famous tourist trail, which begins and ends in Chiang Mai, winding through spectacular mountain scenery for much of the way. Although the route is named after its principal town, Mae Hong Son, the quiet village of Pai has become a major destination.

4 The Golden Triangle. The northernmost region of Thailand is mostly known for its former role as the center of the opium trade; it has a museum devoted to the subject that's a worthy side trip. Beyond its fascinating past, the area has much to recommend it: mountain scenery, boat trips on the Mekong River, and a few luxurious resorts.

NORTHERN THAILAND PLANNER

Visitor Info

In Chiang Mai you can find an office of the Tourist Authority of Thailand on Chiang Mai–Lamphun Road. It's in a small building on the eastern bank of the Mae Ping River, opposite the New Bridge, and opens daily 8:30 to 4:30.

Lampang's tourist office is on Thakhraonoi Road near the clock tower. The TAT office in Lamphun, opposite the main entrance to Wat Hariphunchai, has irregular hours, but is generally open weekdays 9 to 5.

Tourist information about Nan Province, Nan itself, and Phrae is handled by the Tourism Authority of Thailand's regional office in Chiang Rai.

Tourist Information **Tourist Authority of Thailand (Chiang Mai)** (✉ *105/1 Chiang Mai–Lamphun Rd., Chiang Mai* ☎ *053/248604* 🌐 *www.tourismthailand.org*).

Tourist Authority of Thailand (Chiang Rai) (✉ *448/16 Singhaklai Rd., Chiang Rai* ☎ *053/744674 or 053/744675* 🌐 *www.tourismthailand.org*).

Getting Around

Northern Thailand appears to be a very remote area of Asia, nearly 700 km (420 mi) from the country's capital, Bangkok, and far from other major centers. In fact, this region——bounded on the north, east, and west by Myanmar (Burma) and Laos—is easily accessible. Chiang Mai is Northern Thailand's hub.

By Air. Main cities and towns are linked to Bangkok by frequent and reliable air services. There are several flights a day from Bangkok to Chiang Mai and Chiang Rai, and regular flights from the capital to Lampang, Mae Hong Son, and Nan.

By Bus & Car. An excellent regional bus service links town and villages, however remote, via a network of highways. The country's main north–south artery, Highway 1, bypasses Chiang Mai but connects Bangkok with Chiang Rai and the Golden Triangle. Highway 11 branches off for Chiang Mai at Lampang, itself a major transport hub with a long-distance bus terminal, railroad station, and airport. From Chiang Mai you can reach the entire region on well-paved roads, with travel times not exceeding eight hours or so. The journey on serpentine mountain roads to Mae Hong Son, however, can be very tiring, requiring a stopover in either the popular resort town of Pai or quieter Mae Sariang. Chiang Rai is a convenient stopover on the road north to the Golden Triangle.

Lampang is less than two hours' drive south from Chiang Mai, and is also a convenient and comfortable center from which to explore the nearby national parks and lakes. Nan sits in a remote valley with few routes in and out—if you're traveling there from Bangkok, it's advisable to do one leg of the journey by air.

Driving in Thailand is not for the faint of heart; hiring a car and driver is usually a better option (*By Car in Travel Smart*). ⚠ **Between Christmas and New Year's the highway between Chiang Mai, Pai, and Mae Hong Son may be packed with bumper-to-bumper traffic.**

By Motorcycle. Motorcycles are a cheap and popular option for getting around cities and towns. Rental agencies are numerous, and most small hotels have their own.

When to Go

Northern Thailand has three seasons. The region is hottest and driest from March to May. The rainy season is June to October, with the wettest weather in September. Unpaved roads are often impassable at this time of year. November to March is the best time to visit, when days are warm, sunny, and generally cloudless, and nights pleasantly cool. (At higher altitudes, it can be quite cold in the evening.) Book hotel accommodation a month or two ahead of the Christmas and New Year holiday periods and the Songkran festival (Thai New Year festival; also known as the Water Festival, because revelers douse each other with water), in mid-April.

Temple Know-How

Most temple complexes open about 6 AM and don't close until 6 or 8 PM, although the hours can be irregular and the doors may be locked for no reason. If that's the case, approach any monk and explain you'd like to visit. He'll normally open up the temple. There's no admission charge, but leave some change in one of the collection boxes. (By making a donation you're also "making merit" and easing your journey to the hereafter.) In some temples, caged birds are for sale—you're expected to set them free, another means of making merit.

WHAT IT COSTS IN BAHT

¢	$	$$	$$$	$$$$
Restaurants				
under B100	B100–B200	B201–B300	B301–B400	over B400
Hotels				
under B1,000	B1,000–B2,000	B2,001–B4,000	B4,001–B6,000	over B6,000

Restaurant prices are for a main course, excluding service charge and tips. Hotel prices are for two people in a standard double room in high season, excluding service charges and tax.

Health & Safety

Malaria and other mosquito-borne diseases are virtually unknown in northern cities, but if you're traveling in the jungle during the rainy season (June to October), consider taking antimalarials. If you're trekking in the mountains or staying at hill tribe villages, pack mosquito repellent. Spray your room about a half hour before turning in, even if windows have screens and beds have mosquito nets.

Chiang Mai and other communities in northern Thailand are generally safe. However, it's a good idea to leave your passport, expensive jewelry, and large amounts of cash in your hotel safe. Keep a copy of your passport with you at all times, as police can demand proof of identification and levy a fine if you don't produce it. Always walk holding bags on the side of you facing away from the street, as Chiang Mai has its share of motorcycle thieves who snatch your bag as they drive by. In a medical emergency, head to Chiang Mai. The police hotline is ☎191.

Chiang Mai's **Tourist Police** (*☎1699 for emergencies, 053/248130 information*) can be helpful in dealing with minor emergencies, thefts, or shady antiques dealers. Expatriate volunteers now assist the Tourist Police—they wear black uniforms and a TOURIST POLICE badge. The volunteers' powers are limited, but they can at least direct you to someone who can assist you further.

EATING AND DRINKING WELL IN NORTHERN THAILAND

Snakehead fish with mango salad.

To most foodies, the north of Thailand is the country's most interesting culinary hotbed. The distinctive Laotian and Burmese influences, spicy salads, and grilled river fish are unlike any Thai food you've tasted in the west.

Through rice paddies, across plains, and along the majestic Mekong, a healthy peasant's diet of fresh river fish, sticky rice, sausage, and spicy salads replace the richer shellfish and coconut curries of Thailand's center and south.

Thailand's expansive north encompasses various ethnicities and immigrant groups, making it hard to pigeonhole the food. Universal, however, are searingly sour curries centering around sharp herbs and spices rather than coconut milk; salt-rubbed river fish grilled over open coals; and salads integrating lime, fermented shrimp, and dried chili. The fish-sauce fire of these amazingly fresh creations is extinguished by the bamboo-wrapped sticky rice that follows you everywhere in this region with miles upon miles of rice paddies. And adventurous eaters shouldn't miss the famous northern insect cuisine, which you'll find at regional markets.

CLEVER COOKING IN NORTHERN THAILAND

The food of the far north of Thailand is an adventure—distinctly different from that of the rest of Thailand, and in many ways resourceful. In this poorer region of the country, cooks are sometimes inspired by whatever's on hand. Take, for instance, salted eggs, a common condiment. The eggs are soaked in salt and then pickled, preserving a fragile food in the hot environment and adding another tasty salty and briny element to Thai dishes. Less appealing to the Western palate is rat, which is often eaten as part of a spicy curry.

BLA DUKG YANG

You'll find grilled river fish throughout the north, and snakehead fish is one of the region's most special treats. Unlike in the south, where fish is sometimes deep-fried or curried, here it is usually stuffed with big, long lemongrass skewers and grilled over an open fire, searing the skin. Add the spicy, sour curry that's served atop the fish—and throw in *som tam* and sticky rice for good measure—and you've got a quintessential Northern meal.

SOM TAM

Som tam, a classic, ragingly hot green-papaya salad prepared with a mortar and pestle is found all over Thailand, but its homeland is really the north. Tease out the differences between three versions: *som tam poo*, also found in Burma, integrating black crab shells (a challenging texture, to say the least); *som tam plara*, an Isan version with salt fish and long bean; and the traditional Thai *som tam*, ground with peanuts and tiny dried and fermented shrimp.

KHAO LAM

On highways, meandering rural roads, and at most markets you find women selling tubes of bamboo filled with sticky rice. The rice is steamed in bamboo, which adds a woodiness to the rice's rich, sweet, salty flavor. (Slowly peel off the bamboo to eat it.) The rice

can be black or white, and sometimes is cooked with minuscule purplish beans. In mango season, *khao neaw ma muang* (mango with sticky rice) is the ultimate salty-sweet dessert.

KHAO SOI

This comforting concoction of vaguely Burmese, vaguely Laotian, vaguely Muslim origins is ubiquitous in Chiang Mai. Noodles swim in a hearty, meaty broth fortified with coconut milk and perked up with chili and lime. It's a lovely textural experience, especially when the noodles are pan-fried: they become soggy in the broth—great for slurping. Get it from a street food vendor, where portions are incredibly cheap.

GAENG LAY

Another Northern favorite, this mild pork curry gets its flavor comes not from chilies but from tamarind. The result is a fairly sweet curry, but with sour back notes, and chunks of pork. There's no coconut milk in the mix, but then again, it's not needed to temper any flames in this curry. It's almost always served with a side of sticky rice.

CHIANG MAI & ENVIRONS

Updated by Robert Tilley

CHIANG MAI, KNOWN AS THE "Rose of the North," has ambitious plans: it wants to expand beyond its role as a provincial capital to become a gateway to Myanmar, Laos, and western China. Since the late 1990s, luxury hotels have been shooting up, attracting more business and leisure travelers. The airport is being expanded to accommodate more and larger airplanes, and already there has been an increase in the number of direct flights from Europe and Asia. And although the country's main highway, Highway 1, bypasses Chiang Mai as it runs between Bangkok and Chiang Rai, officials have made sure the city is at the center of a spider's web of highways reaching out in all four directions of the compass, with no major city or town more than a day's drive away. Two newly constructed ring roads, complete with underpasses, keep traffic flowing around the city center.

CHIANG MAI

696 km (430 mi) north of Bangkok.

Chiang Mai's rich history stretches back 700 years to the time when several small tribes, under King Mengrai, banded together to form a new nation called Anachak Lanna Thai. Their first capital was Chiang Rai, but after three decades they moved it to the fertile plains near the Mae Ping River to a place they called Napphaburi Sri Nakornping Chiang Mai.

The Lanna Thai eventually lost their independence to Ayutthaya and, later, to Myanmar. Not until 1774—when the Burmese were finally driven out—did the region revert to the Thai kingdom. After that, the region developed independently of Southern Thailand. Even the language is different, marked by a more relaxed tempo. In the last 50 years the city has grown well beyond its original moated city walls, expanding far into the neighboring countryside.

First impressions of modern Chiang Mai can be disappointing. The immaculately maintained railroad station and the chaotic bus terminal are in shabby districts, and the drive into the city center is far from spectacular. First-time visitors ask why they can't see the mountains that figure so prominently in the travel brochures. But once you cross the Ping River, Chiang Mai begins to take shape. The Old City is roughly 2½ square km (1 square mi), bounded by a moat where fountains splash and locals stroll along a flower-bordered promenade. Much of the wall that once encircled the city has been restored, and the most important of its five original gates, called Pratou Tha Phae, fronts a broad square where markets and festivals are constantly in full swing. Chiang Mai's brooding mountain, Doi Suthep, is now in view, rising in steps over the Old City.

Enter the Old City and you're in another world. Buildings more than three stories high have been banned, and guesthouses and restaurants vie with each other for the most florid decoration. Many of the streets and *sois* (alleys) have been paved with flat, red cobblestones. Strolling these

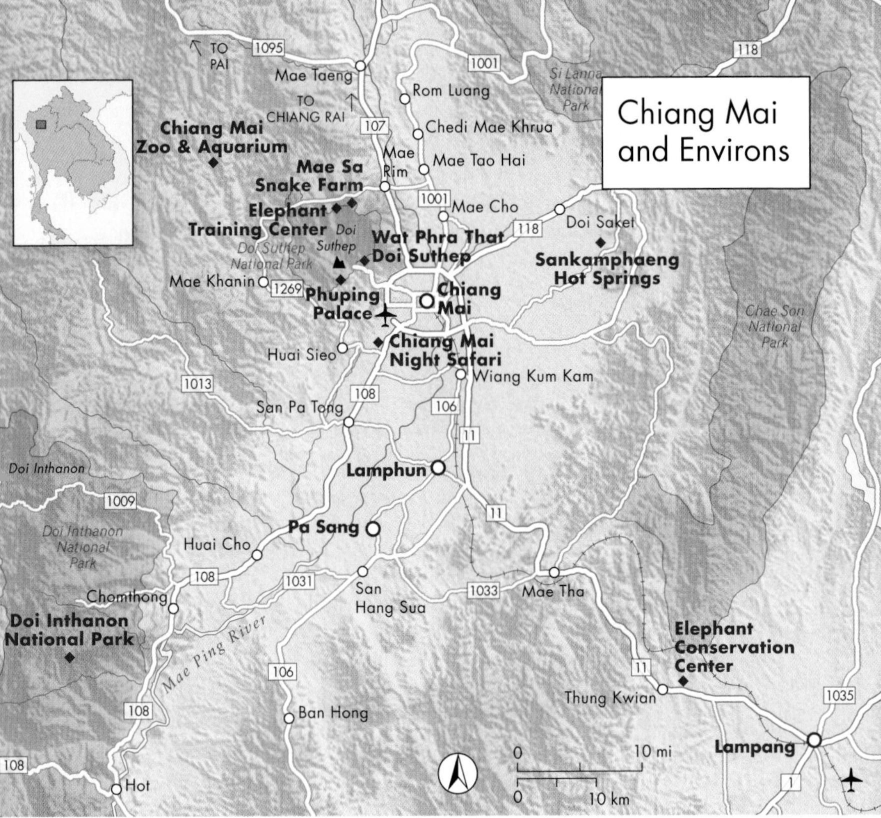

narrow lanes, lingering in the quiet cloisters of a temple, sipping hill tribe coffee at a wayside stall, and fingering local fabrics in one of the many boutiques are among the chief pleasures of a visit to Chiang Mai. And whenever you visit, there's bound to be a festival in progress.

GETTING HERE & AROUND

The compact Old City can be explored easily on foot or by bicycle. The system of one-way streets can be confusing for newcomers, but the plan keeps traffic moving quite effectively around the moat, which is crossed by bridges at regular intervals.

BY AIR Thai Airways has frequent daily flights to Chiang Mai from Bangkok (1 hour 10 minutes) and two direct flights daily from Phuket (1 hour 50 minutes). In peak season, flights are heavily booked. Bangkok Airways has near-daily flights here from Bangkok. Three budget airlines offer flights for as little as US$50: Orient Thai Airlines, Air Asia, and Nok Air. Chiang Mai International Airport is about 10 minutes south of downtown and a B100 taxi ride. Songthaews run to the city center for around B50.

BY BUS VIP buses ply the route between Bangkok's Northern Bus Terminal and Chiang Mai, stopping at Lampang on the way. For around B400 to B600 you get a very comfortable 10-hour ride in a modern bus with reclining seats, blankets and pillows, TV, onboard refreshments, and lunch or dinner at a motorway stop. You can take cheaper buses, but the faster service is well worth a few extra baht.

Chiang Mai's Arcade Bus Terminal serves Bangkok, Mae Hong Son, and destinations within Chiang Rai Province. Chiang Phuak Bus Terminal serves Lamphun, Chiang Dao, Tha Ton, and destinations within Chiang Mai Province.

BY CAR The well-paved roads around Chiang Mai are no problem for most drivers—even the mountainous Mae Sa route north of Chiang Mai is perfectly drivable. However, Thai drivers are notoriously reckless and accidents are frequent. Two major car-rental agencies in Chiang Mai are Avis and Hertz; Budget has a good range of four-wheel-drive vehicles. Many hotels have motorcycle rentals.

Avoid driving in the city during rush hours, which start as early as 7 in the morning and 3 in the afternoon, and pay special attention to no-parking restrictions (usually 9 AM to noon and 3 PM to 6 PM). Parking is prohibited on many streets on alternate days, but the explanatory signs are mostly in Thai. Your best bet is to note on which side of the street vehicles are parking. Chiang Mai's traffic police are merciless and clamp and tow away vehicles parked illegally. Parking lots are numerous and charge as little as B20 for all-day parking.

A car and driver is the most convenient way to visit the hard-to-find temples outside the city. Car-rental agencies also handle car-and-driver hires.

BY TAXI, TUK-TUK & SONGTHAEW Metered taxis, which can be flagged down on the street, are being introduced gradually in Chiang Mai, replacing the noisier, dirtier songthaews. The basic taxi charge is B30; you'll pay around B50 for a ride across the Old City. Tuk-tuks are generally cheaper, but you are expected to bargain—offer B20 or so less than the driver demands. The songthaews that trundle around the city on fixed routes are the cheapest form of transport—just B15 if your destination is on the driver's route. If he has to make a detour, you'll be charged an extra B20 or so. Settle on the fare before you get in. If your Thai is limited, just hold up the relevant number of fingers. If you hold up three and your gesture evokes the same response from the driver, you'll be paying B30.

BY TRAIN The State Railway links Chiang Mai to Bangkok and points south. As the uninteresting trip from Bangkok takes about 13 hours, overnight sleepers are the best choice. The overnight trains are invariably well maintained, with clean sheets on rows of two-tier bunks. ■ **TIP→ Spending a few extra baht for a first-class compartment is strongly recommended. In second class, you may be kept awake by partying passengers.** Trains for the north depart from Bangkok's Hualamphong Railway Station and arrive in the Chiang Mai Railway Station. First-class fares from Bangkok to Chiang Mai range from B1,300 for a sleeper to B600 or B800 for a day train (*By Train in Travel Smart*).

CHIANG MAI TOURS

Every other storefront in Chiang Mai seems to be a tour agency, and not all of them are professionally run. Pick up a list of agencies approved by the Tourism Authority of Thailand before choosing one. Prices vary quite a bit, so shop around, and carefully examine the offerings. Each hotel also has its own travel desk with ties to a tour operator. The prices are often higher, as the hotel adds its own surcharge.

Chiang Mai's **Trekking Club** (✉ *181 Loy Kroh Rd., opposite Downtown Inn Hotel, Chiang Mai* ☎ *053/818519*) is an association of 87 licensed guides with enough experience among them to manage the most demanding customer. The club has its own café where you can meet the guides over a drink. **World Travel Service** (✉ *100/16 Huay Kaew Rd., Chiang Mai* ☎ *053/217850 and 053/217851*) is another reliable operator. **Chiangmai Cattleya Tour & Travel Services** (✉ *Hillside Plaza and Condotel 4, 50 Huay Kaew Rd., Chiang Mai* ☎ *053/223991*) has morning and afternoon tours of Wiang Kum Kam for B700. **Chiangmai Tic Travel** (✉ *147/1 Ratchadamnoen Rd., Chiang Mai* ☎ *053/814174*) arranges custom tours of Northern Thailand, ranging from day trips to weeklong holidays; ask for Pom or Tinar. **Boutique Travel Service** (✉ *44/3 Sridonchai Rd., Chiang Mai* ☎ *053/284042*)—is a realiable and helpful agency—ask for Boong. TAT-registered **Nathlada Boonthueng** (☎ *081/531–6884*), who works from her home, is an English-speaking guide with a deep knowledge of the region and one of the best local independent operators; she's known as Timmy. **Top North** (✉ *15 Soi 2, Moon Muang Rd., Chiang Mai* ☎ *053/278532*) arranges various one-day mountain tours and multiday trekking tours to hilltribe villages.

6

ESSENTIALS

Emergencies **Lanna Hospital** (✉ *103 Super Hwy., Chiang Mai* ☎ *053/357234*). **Police** (☎ *191*). **Tourist Police** (✉ *105/1 Chiang Mai–Lamphun Rd., Chiang Mai* ☎ *1699 or 053/248130*).

EXPLORING: THE OLD CITY & ENVIRONS

Covering roughly 2½ square km (1 square mi), the patchwork of winding lanes that make up Chiang Mai's Old City is bounded by remains of the original city wall and a wide, water-filled moat. Start any tour of the Old City at the Tha Pae Gate, which leads through the ancient city walls into the oldest part of Chiang Mai. Heading west on Ratchadamnoen Road and turning north on Ratchaphakhinai Road will bring you to the first of the area's major sights, Wat Chiang Man, the oldest temple in Chiang Mai. Backtracking down Ratchaphakhinai Road and heading west on Ratchadamnoen Road will bring you to Wat Chedi Luang and Wat Phra Singh. Several other worthwhile temples are outside the city walls. To the east is the serene Wat Chaimongkol. It's an easy walk from the Tha Pae Gate if the sun isn't too strong. You'll want to take a tuk-tuk to Wat Suan Dok, one of the largest temples in the region. A bit farther away are the verdant grounds of Wat Umong.

TOP ATTRACTIONS

11 **Chiang Mai Tribal Museum.** The varied collection at this museum, of more than 1,000 pieces of traditional crafts from the hill tribes living in the region, is one of the finest in the country and includes farming implements, hunting traps, weapons, colorful embroidery, and musical instruments. The museum is in Ratchangkla Park, off the road to Mae Rim, about 1 km (½ mi) from the National Museum. ✉ *Ratchangkla Park, Chotana Rd.* ☎ *053/210872* 🎫 *Free* ⏲ *Daily 9–4.*

10 **National Museum.** This Northern Thai–style building contains many statues of Lord Buddha, including a bust that measures 10 feet high. There's also a huge Buddha footprint of wood with mother-of-pearl inlay. The exhibits have been skillfully arranged into topics such as the early history of the Lanna region, the founding of Chiang Mai, and the development of city's distinctive art forms. The centerpiece of one display is a regal bed covered with mosquito netting that was used by an early prince of Chiang Mai. ✉ *Super Hwy. (Chiang Mai–Lampang Rd.)* ☎ *053/221308* 🎫 *B30* ⏲ *Daily 9–4.*

2 **Wat Chedi Luang.** In 1411 King Saen Muang Ma ordered his workers to build a chedi "as high as a dove could fly." He died before the structure was finished, as did the next king. During the reign of the following king, an earthquake knocked down about a third of the 282-foot spire, and it's now a superb ruin. The parklike grounds contain a variety of assembly halls, chapels, a 30-foot-long reclining Buddha, and the ancient city pillar. The main assembly hall, a vast, pillared building guarded by two nagas (mythical snakes believed to control the irrigation waters in rice fields), has been restored and was reopened to the public in 2008. ✉ *Phrapokklao Rd., between Ratchamankha and Ratchadamnoen Rds.*

Fodor'sChoice ★

1 **Wat Chiang Man.** Chiang Mai's oldest monastery, dating from 1296, is typical of Northern Thai architecture. It has massive teak pillars inside the bot, and two important images of the Buddha sit in the small building to the right of the main viharn. ■ TIP→ **The Buddha images are supposedly on view only on Sunday, but sometimes the door is unlocked.** ✉ *Ratchaphakhinat Rd.*

4 ★ **Wat Phra Singh.** In the western section of the Old City stands Chiang Mai's principal monastery, Wat Phra Singh, which was extensively renovated in 2006. The beautifully decorated wat contains the Phra Singh Buddha, with a serene and benevolent expression that is enhanced by the light filtering in through the tall windows. Note the temple's facades of splendidly carved wood, the elegant teak beams and posts, and the masonry. Don't be surprised if a student monk approaches you to practice his English. ✉ *Phra Singh Rd. and Singharat Rd.*

ALSO WORTH SEEING

3 **Chiang Mai City Art & Cultural Center.** The handsome city museum is housed in a colonnaded palace that was the official administrative headquarters of the last local ruler, Chao (Prince) Inthawichayanon. Around its quiet central courtyard are 15 rooms with exhibits documenting the history of Chiang Mai. ■ TIP→ **In another small, shady courtyard is a**

delightful café. The palace was built in 1924 in the exact center of the city, site of the ancient city pillar that now stands in the compound of nearby Wat Chedi Luang. In front of the museum sit statues of the three kings who founded Chiang Mai. ✉ *Phrapokklao Rd.* ☎ *053/217793 or 053/219833* *B90* *Tues.–Sun. 8:30–5.*

8 **Museum of World Insects & Natural Wonders.** Save a visit to this offbeat museum for a rainy day. Children love its oddball display of creepy-crawlies, which include enormous centipedes, beetles, moths, gaudy butterflies, and the world's largest collection of individual mosquito species. ✉ *72 Soi 13, off Nimmanhemin Rd.* ☎ *053/211891* *B200* *Daily 8:30–4:30.*

5 ★ **Wat Chaimongkol.** Although rarely visited, this small temple is well worth the journey. Its little chedi contains holy relics, but its real beauty lies in the serenity of the grounds. Outside the Old City near the Mae Ping River, it has only 18 monks in residence. ✉ *Charoen Prathet Rd.*

9 **Wat Chedi Yot.** Wat Photharam Maha Viharn is more commonly known as Wat Chedi Yot, or Seven-Spired Pagoda. Built in 1455, it's a copy of the Mahabodhi temple in Bodh Gaya, India, where the Buddha is said to have achieved enlightenment. The seven intricately carved spires represent the seven weeks that he subsequently spent there. The sides of the chedi have striking bas-relief sculptures of celestial figures, most of them in poor repair but one bearing a face of hauntingly contemporary beauty. The temple is just off the highway that circles Chiang Mai, but its green lawns and shady corners are strangely still and peaceful. ✉ *Super Hwy., between Huay Kaew and Chang Puak Rds.*

6 **Wat Suan Dok.** To the west of the Old City is one of the largest of Chiang Mai's temples, Wat Suan Dok. It's said to have been built on the site where bones of Lord Buddha were found. Some of these relics are believed to be inside the chedi; others were transported to Wat Phra That Doi Suthep. At the back of the viharn is the bot housing Phra Chao Kao, a superb bronze Buddha figure cast in 1504. Chiang Mai aristocrats are buried in stupas in the graveyard. ✉ *Suthep Rd.*

7 **Wat Umong.** The most unusual temple in Chiang Mai is Wat Umong, dating from 1296. According to local lore, a monk named Jam liked to go wandering in the forest. This irritated King Ku Na, who often wanted to consult with the sage. So he could seek advice at any time, the king built this wat for the monk in 1380. Along with the temple, tunnels were constructed and decorated with paintings, fragments of which may still be seen. Beyond the chedi is a pond filled with hungry carp. Throughout the grounds the trees are hung with snippets of wisdom such as "Time unused is the longest time." ✉ *Off Suthep Rd., past Wat Suan Dok.*

EXPLORING: NEAR CHIANG MAI

Beyond the highway that surrounds Chiang Mai you will find plenty to hold your attention. The most famous sight is Wat Phra That Doi Suthep, the mountaintop temple that overlooks the city. The mountain road that skirts Doi Suthep, winding through the thickly forested Mae

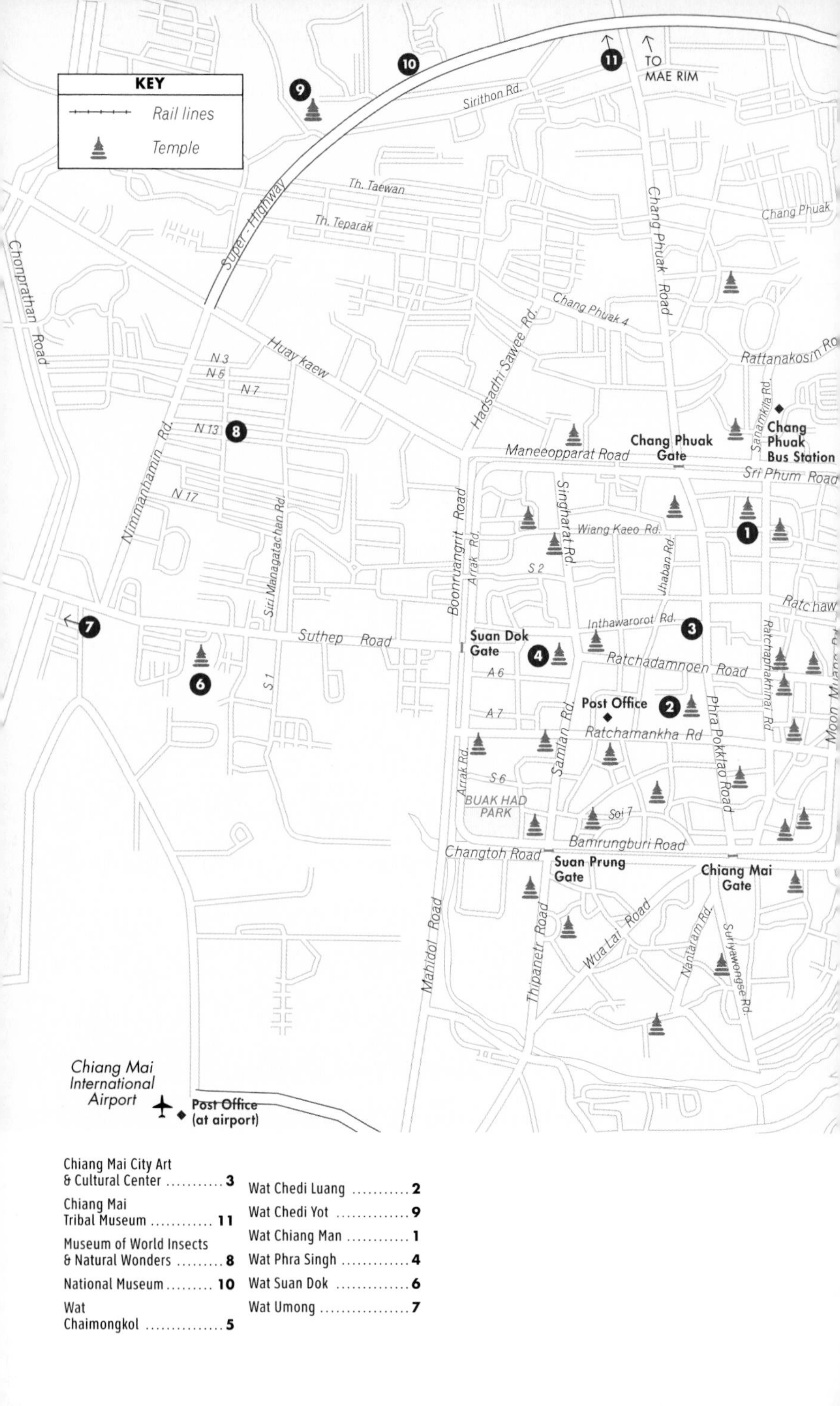

Chiang Mai City Art & Cultural Center **3**

Chiang Mai Tribal Museum **11**

Museum of World Insects & Natural Wonders **8**

National Museum **10**

Wat Chaimongkol **5**

Wat Chedi Luang **2**

Wat Chedi Yot **9**

Wat Chiang Man **1**

Wat Phra Singh **4**

Wat Suan Dok **6**

Wat Umong **7**

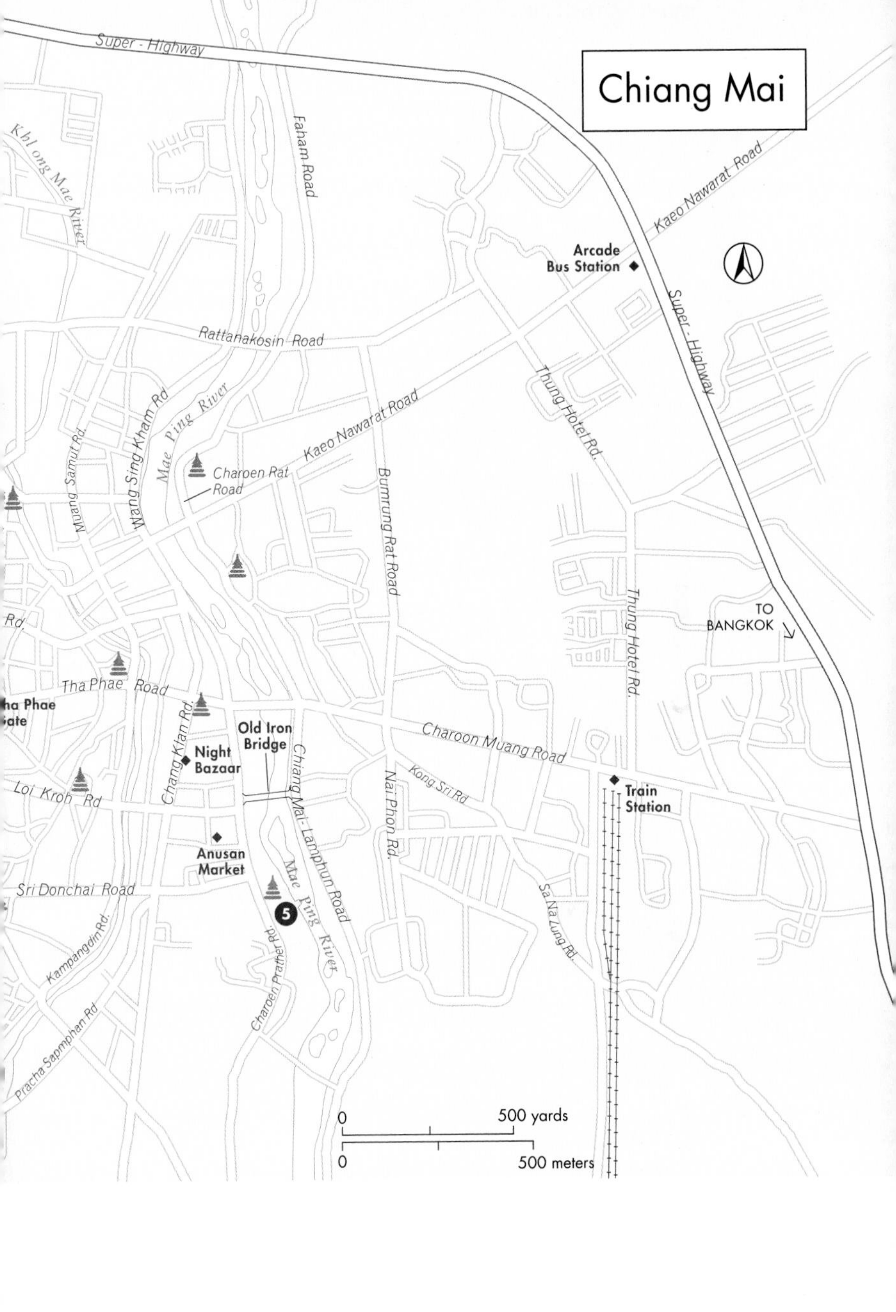

Chiang Mai
Super - Highway
Faham Road
Khl ong Mae River
Kaeo Nawarat Road
Arcade
Bus Station
Super - Highway
Rattanakosin Road
Wang Sing Kham Rd
Mae Ping River
Muang Samut Rd.
Charoen Rat Road
Kaeo Nawarat Road
Thung Hotel Rd.
Bumrung Rat Road
Thung Hotel Rd.
TO
BANGKOK
Rd.
Tha Phae Road
ha Phae
ate
Chang Klan Rd.
Old Iron
Bridge
Night
Bazaar
Chiang Mai-Lamphun Road
Charoon Muang Road
Kong Sri Rd
Nai Phon Rd.
Train
Station
Loi Kroh Rd
Anusan
Market
Sri Donchai Road
Mae Ping River
5
Sa Na Lung Rd.
Kampangdin Rd.
Charoen Prather Rd.
Pracha Sapmphan Rd
0
500 yards
0
500 meters

CLOSE UP

Monk Chat

If you're like most people, a visit to Chiang Mai's numerous temples is likely to leave you full of unanswered questions. Head to Wat Suan Dok or Wat Chedi Luang, where help is at hand. The monks and novice monks who reside in the two temples eagerly welcome foreign visitors for chats about the history of their temples, the Buddhist faith, and Thai history and culture. Their enthusiasm isn't totally altruistic—they're keen to practice their English.

The talkative monks at Wat Suan Dok are all students of a religious university attached to the temple. Their "monk chat" takes place 5:30 to 7:30 PM on Monday, Wednesday, and Friday. Their counterparts at Wat Chedi Luang can be approached Monday to Saturday noon to 6:30 PM as they relax under the trees of their parklike compound. They urge foreign visitors to converse with them about Lanna culture, life in a monastery, or, as one monk put it, "anything at all."

Sa Valley, is lined with tourist attractions for much of its way, from bungee-jumping towers to orchid farms.

TOP ATTRACTIONS

Chiang Mai Aquarium. Asia's biggest aquarium opened in Chiang Mai in 2008. The vast project, on a four-acre plot next to the city's zoo, features a walk-through underwater tunnel more than 160 yards long. About 8,000 aquatic creatures, embracing 250 species, stock the aquarium. Several varieties of sharks, including the Great White, swim around visitors as they make their way through the viewing tunnel. ✉ *Chiang Mai Zoo, Huay Kaew Rd.* ☎ *053/221179* 🌐 *www.chiangmaiaquarium.com* 🎫 *B450* 🕐 *Daily 9–9.*

Chiang Mai Night Safari. Modeled on Singapore's famous game park, the Chiang Mai Night Safari realized a long-held dream of Thaksin Shinnawatra, the country's former prime minister (he was deposed in a military coup in September 2006). The 100-acre reserve on the edge of the Doi Suthep-Pui National Park, 10 km (6 mi) from downtown Chiang Mai, has more than 100 species of wild animals, including tigers, leopards, jaguars, and elephants. For a real thrill, board one of the special trams and tour the grounds after dark. ✉ *Km 10, Chiang Mai–Hod Rd.* 🎫 *B100 until 4* PM, *B500 after 6* PM 🕐 *Weekdays 1* PM*–4* PM *and 6* PM*–midnight, weekends 10–4 and 6* PM*–midnight.*

Phuping Palace. The summer residence of the royal family is a serene mansion that shares an exquisitely landscaped park with the more modest mountain retreats of the crown prince and princess. The palace itself cannot be visited, but the gardens are open to the public. Flower enthusiasts swoon at the sight of the roses—among the lovely blooms is a variety created by the king himself. A rough, unpaved road left of the palace brings you after 4 km (2½ mi) to a village called Doi Pui Meo, where most of the Hmong women seem busy creating finely worked textiles (the songthaew return fare there is B300). On the mountainside above the village are two tiny museums documenting hill tribe life and the opium trade. ✉ *Off Huay Kaew Rd., 6 km (4 mi) past Wat Phra*

Most boys are ordained as monks at least temporarily, often for the three-month Rains Retreat.

That Doi Suthep ☎*No phone* *Gardens free* *Gardens daily 9–5, except when royal family in residence (usually in Jan.).*

Fodor's Choice ★ **Wat Phra That Doi Suthep.** As in so many chapters of Thai history, an elephant is closely involved in the legend surrounding the foundation of Wat Phra That, Northern Thailand's most revered temple and one of only a few enjoying royal patronage. The elephant was dispatched from Chiang Mai carrying religious relics from Wat Suan Dok. Instead of ambling off into the open countryside, it stubbornly climbed up Doi Suthep. When the elephant came to rest at the 3,542-foot summit, the decision was made to establish a temple to contain the relics at that site. Over the centuries the temple compound grew into the glittering assembly of chedis, bots, viharns, and frescoed cloisters you see today. The vast terrace, usually smothered with flowers, commands a breathtaking view of Chiang Mai. Constructing the temple was quite a feat—until 1935 there was no paved road to the temple. Workers

THE MAE SA VALLEY

This beautiful upland valley winds behind Chiang Mai's Doi Suthep and Doi Pui mountain range. A well-paved 100-km (60-mi) loop begins and ends in Chiang Mai, and is lined by resorts, country restaurants, tribal villages, an elephant center, a snake farm, a monkey colony, orchid hothouses, and the Queen Sirikit Botanical Gardens. The route follows Highway 1001 north from Chiang Mai, turning left at Mae Rim onto Highways 1096 and then 1269, returning to Chiang Mai from the south on Highway 108. Contact **Nakornlanna C. Ltd** (☎*053/279291 or 053/271242*) for taxi service or rentals.

King Saen Muang Ma designed Wat Chedi Luang to house his father's ashes.

and pilgrims alike had to slog through thick jungle. The road was the result of a vast community project: individual villages throughout the Chiang Mai region contributed the labor, each laying 1,300-foot sections.

You can find songthaews to take you on the 30-minute drive to this temple at Chuang Puak Gate, the Central Department Store on Huay Kaew Road, or outside the entrance to Wat Phra Singh. When you arrive, you are faced with an arduous but exhilarating climb up the broad, 304-step staircase flanked by 16th-century tiled balustrades that take the customary form of *nagas* (mythical snakes believed to control the irrigation waters in rice fields). **TIP→ A funicular railway provides a much easier way to the top.** But the true pilgrim's way is up the majestic steps. ✉ *Huay Kaew Rd.* ☎ *No phone* 🎫 *B70 (includes funicular)* ⏲ *Daily 6–6.*

ALSO WORTH SEEING

Chiang Mai Zoo. On the lower slopes of Doi Suthep, this zoo's cages and enclosures are spaced out along paths that wind leisurely through shady woodlands. If the walk seems too strenuous, you can hop on an electric trolley that stops at all the sights. The most popular animals are two giant pandas, Lin Hui and Chuang Chuang—the only ones in captivity in Southeast Asia. ✉ *100 Huay Kaew Rd.* ☎ *053/221179* 🎫 *B100, plus B100 to view pandas* ⏲ *Daily 8–9.*

Doi Suthep National Park. You don't have to head to the distant mountains to go trekking during your stay in Chiang Mai. Doi Suthep, the 3,542-foot peak that broods over the city, has its own national park with plenty of hiking trails to explore. One of these, a path taken by pilgrims over the centuries preceding the construction of a road, leads up to the gold-spired Wat Phra That Doi Suthep. **TIP→ It's a half-day hike from the edge of the city to the temple compound. Set off early to avoid the heat of the midday sun.** If it's not a public holiday, you'll probably be alone on the mountain. The trail begins at the entrance of the national park, reached by a five-minute ride in one of the songthaews that wait for passengers at the end of Huay Kaew Road, near the entrance to Chiang Mai Zoo.

An easy hike lasting about 45 minutes brings you to one of Chiang Mai's least known but most charming temples, Wat Pha Lat. This modest ensemble of buildings is virtually lost in the forest. Make sure to explore the compound, which has a weathered chedi and a grotto filled with images of the Buddha. After you leave Wat Pha Lat, the path becomes steeper. After another 45 minutes you emerge onto the mountain road, where you can flag down a songthaew if you can't take another step. Otherwise follow the road for about 200 yards; a break in the forest marks the uphill trail to Wat Phra That. ✉ *Huay Kaew Rd.* ☎ *053/210244* *B400* *Daily 6–6.*

6

Elephant Training Center. The pachyderms here are treated well and seem to enjoy showing off their skills. They certainly like the dip they take in the river before demonstrating log-rolling routines and giving rides. ✉ *Mai Sa Valley road, between Mae Rim and Samoeng* ☎ *053/206247* *B150, B800 for ½-hr elephant ride* *Shows daily at 8 AM, 9:40 AM, noon, and 1:30.*

Mae Sa Snake Farm. If you're fascinated by slithering creatures, you'll find them not only at Chiang Mai Zoo but at this snake farm on the Mae Sa Valley road. There are cobra shows at 11:30 AM, 2:15 PM, and 3:30 PM, during which the snakes are "milked" for their venom. ✉ *Mae Rim–Samoeng Rd.* ☎ *053/860719* *B400* *Daily 9–5.*

NEED A BREAK?

If you're visiting the Elephant Training Center or the Mae Sa Snake Farm, stop for lunch at Mae Sa Valley Resort (✉ *Mae Rim–Samoeng Rd.* ☎ *053/291051*). It's a pretty place, with thatched cottages in beautifully tended gardens. The owner's honey-cooked chicken with chili is particularly good.

Sankamphaeng Hot Springs. Among the most spectacular in Northern Thailand, these hot springs include two geysers that shoot water about 32 yards into the air. The spa complex, set among beautiful flowers, includes an open-air pool and several bathhouses of various sizes. There's a rustic restaurant with a view over the gardens, and small chalets with hot tubs are rented either by the hour (B200) or for the night (B800). Tents and sleeping bags can also be rented for B80. The spa is 56 km (35 mi) north of Chiang Mai, beyond the village of San Kamphaeng. Songthaews bound for the spa leave from the riverside flower market in Chiang Mai. ✉ *Moo 7, Tambon Ban Sahakorn, Mae-On* ☎ *053/929077 or 053/929099* *B20* *Daily 8–6.*

CLOSE UP

Northern Thailand Then and Now

As late as 1939, Northern Thailand was a semiautonomous region of Siam, with a history rich in tales of kings, queens, and princes locked in dynastic struggles and wars. The diversity of cultures you find here today is hardly surprising, since the ancestors of today's Northern Thai people came from China, and the point where they first crossed the mighty Mekong River, Chiang Saen, became a citadel-kingdom of its own as early as 773. Nearly half a millennium passed before the arrival of a king who was able to unite the citizens of the new realm of Lanna ("a thousand rice fields").

The fabled ruler King Mengrai (1259–1317) also established a dynasty that lasted two centuries. Mengrai's first capital was Chiang Rai, but at the end of the 13th century he moved his court south and in 1296 founded a new dynastic city, Chiang Mai. Two friendly rulers, King Ngarm Muang of Phayao and King Rama Kampeng of Sukhothai, helped him in the huge enterprise, and the trio sealed their alliance in blood, drinking from a chalice filled from their slit wrists. A monument outside the city museum in the center of Chiang Mai's Old City commemorates the event. Nearby, another monument marks the spot where King Mengrai died, in 1317, after being struck by lightning in one of the fierce storms that regularly roll down from the nearby mountains.

Lanna power was weakened by waves of attacks by Burmese and Lao invaders, and for two centuries—from 1556 to the late 1700s—Lanna was virtually a vassal Burmese state. The capital was moved south to Lampang, where Burmese power was finally broken and a new Lanna dynasty, the Chakri, was established under King Rama I.

Chiang Mai, nearby Lamphun (also at the center of Lanna-Burmese struggles), and Lampang are full of reminders of this rich history. Lampang's fortified Wat Lampang Luang commemorates with an ancient bullet hole the spot where the commander of besieging Burmese forces was killed.

To the north is Chiang Rai, a regal capital 30 years before Chiang Mai was built. This quieter, less-developed town is slowly becoming a base for exploring the country's northernmost reaches. In the far north, the Chiang Saen, site of the region's first true kingdom, is being excavated, its 1,000-year-old walls slowly taking shape again. Chiang Saen is on the edge of the fabled Golden Triangle. This mountainous region, bordered by Myanmar to the west and Laos to the east, was once ruled by the opium warlord Khun Sa, whose hometown, Ban Sop Ruak, has a magnificent museum, the Hall of Opium, that traces the story of the spread of narcotics.

Chiang Mai and Chiang Rai are ideal bases for exploring the hill-tribe villages, where people live as they have for centuries. The communities closest to the two cities have been overrun by tourists, but if you strike out on your own with a good map you may still find some that haven't become theme parks. Most of the villages are bustling crafts centers where the colorful fabrics you see displayed in Bangkok shop windows take shape before your eyes. The elaborately costumed villagers descend into Chiang Mai and Chiang Rai every evening to sell their wares in the night markets that transform thoroughfares into tented bazaars.

WHERE TO EAT

All of the city's top hotels serve reasonably good food, but for the best Thai cuisine go to the restaurants in town. The greatest variety—from traditional Thai to French nouvelle cuisine—are to be found within the old city, although Nimmanhemin Road, about 1½ km (1 mi) northwest of downtown, is rapidly becoming a star-studded restaurant row. The best fish restaurants, many of them Chinese-run, are found at the Anusan Market, near the Night Bazaar. Chiang Mai also has Northern Thailand's best European-cuisine restaurants, and some of its French, Italian, and Mediterranean fusion restaurants rival those of Bangkok.

$ ★ THAI ✕**Antique House.** Built in 1870, this teak-beamed home is one of Chiang Mai's true treasures. It's furnished with antiques from the area's finest shops. If you like the chair you're sitting on or the table in front of you, it's possible to add to your (surprisingly modest) bill an order for a replica from a local workshop. The menu is authentic Northern cuisine—try the Hang Led pork curry, spiced up with ginger, or the grilled chicken in pandanus leaves. A big surprise is the wine list—small but with some rare finds and unusual selections. ✉*71 Charoen Prathet Rd.* ☎*053/276810* 💳*MC, V.*

¢ THAI ✕**Arun Rai.** This simple, open-sided restaurant has prepared such traditional Northern dishes as frogs' legs fried with ginger for more than 30 years. Try the *tabong* (boiled bamboo shoots fried in batter) and *sai ua* (pork sausage with herbs). There's also a takeout service for customers in a hurry. ✉*45 Kotchasarn Rd.* ☎*053/276947* *Reservations not accepted* 💳*No credit cards.*

$$–$$$ ITALIAN ✕**Buonissimo.** The name means "very good," and it's no idle boast. Owner Sergio has moved his popular restaurant from the suburbs to an attractive riverside location, with a view of the old city and the mountains beyond. It's a huge barn of a place, so intimate dining is out, although cool breezes from the river are welcome compensation in summer. Traditional Italian pasta dishes and pizzas share menu space with fish specialties that include local trout and a magnificent sole Luguria-style, swimming in a sauce enriched with olives and capers. ✉*425 Charoen Rat Rd.* ☎*053/266431 or 053/266432* 💳*MC, V.*

$$–$$$ FRENCH ✕**Chez Daniel.** Although Chiang Mai has fancier French restaurants, none can match the value offered by Daniel at his charming restaurant on the airport road. A typical three-course lunch menu of salad, home-cured charcuterie, and crepes in Daniel's own alcohol-laced orange sauce costs less than B200, while the B350 menu often features free-range chicken and duck from royal project farms (agricultural projects designed to give hill tribes an alternative to opium production). The dining room is classic French, with Gallic attention to table settings and tableware. ✉*251/18 Mahidol Rd.* ☎*053/204800* 💳*MC, V.*

$ THAI ✕**Chiengmai Gymkhana Club.** The son of the author of *Anna and the King of Siam* was among the founders of this delightfully eccentric place in 1898. Polo isn't played as often now, but a country-club crowd gathers regularly at the restaurant for lunch and dinner. The food is remarkably good, with a variety of local and foreign dishes—the traditional fish-and-chips are among Chiang Mai's tastiest. Sporty types can enjoy a

CLOSE UP

Back to School

If spending time in monasteries makes you wonder about the lives of the monks, or if you find yourself so enthralled by delicious dishes that you want to learn how to prepare them, you're in luck. Chiang Mai has hundreds of schools offering classes in anything from aromatherapy to Zen Buddhism. Alternative medicine, cooking, and massage are the most popular courses, but by no means the most exotic. In three weeks at the Thailand's Elephant Conservation Center near Lampang you can train to become a fully qualified mahout.

Cooking: Chiang Mai has dozens of classes—some in the kitchens of guesthouses, others fully accredited schools—teaching the basics of Thai cuisine. Courses cost B800 to B1,000 a day. Among the best cooking classes is the **Baan Thai Home Cooking Course** (✉ *11 Ratchadamnoen Rd., Soi 5* ☎ *053/357339*). **Chiang Mai Cookery School** (✉ *42/7 Moon Muang Rd.* ☎ *053/206388* 🌐 *www.thaicookery-school.com*) is attached to one of the city's best Thai restaurants, The Wok. One of the city's most popular budget lodgings, **Gap's House** (✉ *4 Ratchadamnoen Rd., Soi 3* ☎ *053/278140*), runs an excellent cooking school. A trek through the mountains usually involves eating simple meals cooked over an open fire. One Chiang Mai cooking course teaches how to prepare these simple, flavorful meals. The so-called "jungle course" is organized by **Smile House** (✉ *5 Rachamankha Rd., Soi 2* ☎ *053/208661*) and costs about B800.

Dancing: Surprise your friends by learning the ancient art of Thai dancing at the **Thai Dance Institute** (✉ *53 Kohklong Rd., Nonghoy* ☎ *053/801375*). A two-hour course teaching you a few of the graceful movements costs B900.

Jewelry: One- to five-day courses in jewelry making are offered at **Nova Artlab** (✉ *201 Tha Pae Rd.* ☎ *053/273058* 🌐 *www.nova-collection.com*). You can also study sculpture, leatherwork, painting, and photography—all for B1,100 a day.

Language: The **American University Alumni** (✉ *73 Ratchadamnoen Rd.* ☎ *053/278407*) has been around for more than 20 years. Charges vary according to the duration of the course and the number of pupils. **Corner Stone International** (✉ *178/233 Moo 7, Nhongkwai, Hang Dong* ☎ *053/430450*) has both group and individual instruction.

Massage: Held at the Chiang Mai University Art Museum, the **Thai Massage School** (✉ *Nimmanhemin Rd.* ☎ *053/907193* 🌐 *www.tmcschool.com*) is authorized by the Thai Ministry of Education. Courses lasting two to five days cost B2,560 to B4,800. The **Chetawan Thai Traditional Massage School** (✉ *Opposite Rajabhat University, on Pracha Uthit Rd.* ☎ *053/410360* 🌐 *www.watpomassage.com*) is affiliated to Bangkok's famous Wat Po massage school. Courses cost B800 a day. The school has accommodation for female students.

Yoga: The **Yogasala** (✉ *48/1 Rachamankha Rd.* ☎ *05/208452* 🌐 *www.cmyogasala.com*) has a five-day yoga course that costs B1,500. The **Yoga Center** (✉ *65/1 Arak Rd.* ☎ *061/927375*) has five-day workshops costing B1,800. The 90-minute "open classes" on Tuesday, Thursday, and weekends cost B200.

round of golf on the 9-hole course or a set or two of tennis. ☒*349 Chiang Mai–Lamphun Rd.* ☎*053/241035 or 053/247352* ▭*MC, V.*

$–$$ ★ ECLECTIC ✕ **The Gallery.** Awards have been heaped on this very attractive riverside restaurant, both for its architecture (a combination of Chinese and Lanna styles) and its cuisine, which embraces dishes from Asia, Europe, and the U.S. Guests enter through a gallery (a small exhibition of local antiques and handicrafts), cross a secluded courtyard with an open-air barbecue, and proceed into a teak-floored dining area with eggplant linens. A Northern Thai string ensemble plays in the evening, and a subtly integrated bar-café offers some of Chiang Mai's best jazz and blues. ☒*25–29 Charoen Rat Rd.* ☎*053/248601* ▭*AE, DC, MC, V.*

$ ECLECTIC ✕ **The Good View.** The name of this waterfront restaurant is an homage to its sweeping view of the Ping River, which, along with the food and live music, attracts a big nightly crowd. It's no place for a quiet evening—partying Thais tend to occupy the maze of tables. Stick to the excellent Thai menu rather than settling for the rather indifferent Western cuisine—the pad thai and grilled perch are particularly recommended. *23 Charoen Rat Rd., Ping River* ☎*053/241866* ▭*MC, V.*

$$$ ECLECTIC ✕ **The House.** A white stucco city mansion is home to central Chiang Mai's most elegant restaurant and bar. Reserve a table either inside the teak-floored, chandelier-lighted dining room, where a guitarist plays nightly, or in the neighboring tapas bar, a sybaritic den of plump cushions and oriental carpets. The plate of mixed tapas is a meal in itself, and the accompanying Spanish wines are superb (but expensive). The restaurant's comprehensive menu is made up of mainly Continental cuisine, with some Thai dishes; the steaks are said to be among Chiang Mai's best. ☒*199 Moon Muang Rd.* ☎*053/419011 up to 14* ✍*Reservations essential* ▭*AE, MC, V.*

¢–$ ★ THAI ✕ **Huen Huay Kaew.** Thai families escape the heat of the city by dining at this rustic restaurant built of bamboo and ancient teak and perched by the edge of a waterfall at the base of Doi Suthep mountain. Some of the tables in the multitiered dining area are so close to the cascade that diners are cooled by the spray. The Thai food is outstanding—the *gaeng som* fish curry is cooked in a delicious tamarind reduction, and the deep-fried pork ribs come with a sauce that blends several flavors of the Thai kitchen. ☒*31/2 Moo 2, Huay Kaew Rd.* ☎*053/892698* ▭*No credit cards.*

¢ ★ THAI ✕ **Huen Phen.** The small rooms in this restaurant, once a private home, are full of handicrafts that are typical of the region. Select a table in any of the dining rooms or out among the plants of the garden. The house and garden are open only in the evening; lunch is served in a street-front extension packed daily with hungry Thais. The *kaeng hang led* (pork curry) with *kao nio* (sticky rice) is a specialty. The *larb nua* (spicy ground beef fried with herbs) and deep-fried pork ribs are two more dishes you won't want to miss. ☒*112 Rachamankha Rd.* ☎*053/814548* ▭*MC, V.*

$ THAI ✕ **Just Khao Soy.** Northern Thailand's favorite dish, khao soy, has been turned into a work of art at Shane Beary's stylish, brick-floored restaurant one block from the river. The bowl of meat soup topped with crispy fried noodles is served on an artist's palette, with the various condiments

6

Restaurants ▼

Antique House **14**
Arun Rai **8**
Buonissimo **11**
Chez Daniel **3**
Chiengmai Gymkhana Club **18**
The Gallery **12**
The Good View **13**
The House **7**
Huen Huay Kaew **1**
Huen Phen **4**
Just Khao Soy **15**
Mi Casa **5**
Ratana's Kitchen **9**
Tea House Siam Celadon **10**
Tha Nam **17**
Whole Earth **16**
The Wok **6**
The Writers Club & Wine Bar **5**

Hotels ▼

The Chedi **15**
Chiang Mai Orchid **1**
Dusit D2 Hotel **19**
Eurana Boutique Hotel **9**
Four Seasons **7**

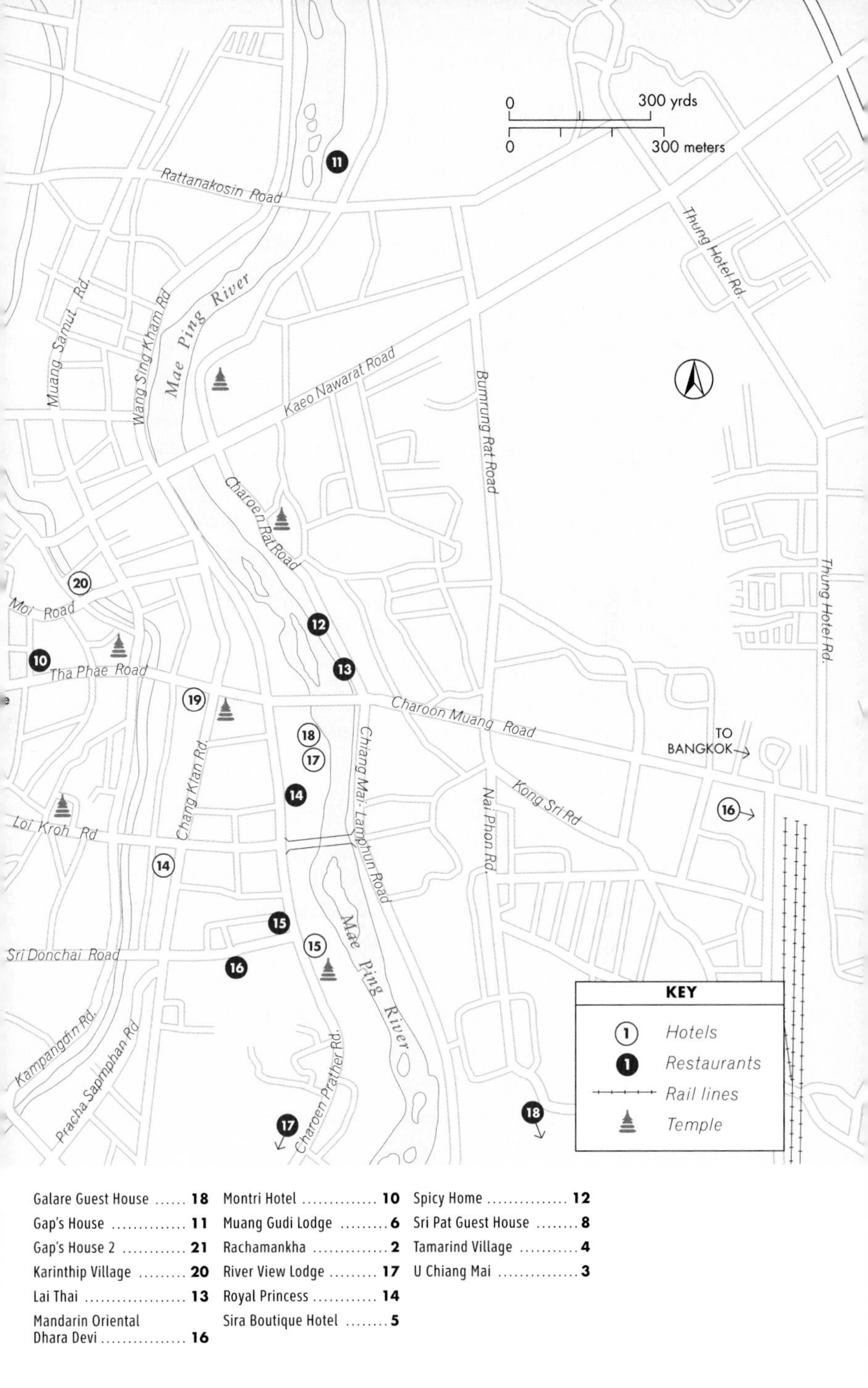

Galare Guest House **18**
Gap's House **11**
Gap's House 2 .... **21**
Karinthip Village **20**
Lai Thai **13**
Mandarin Oriental
Dhara Devi **16**

Montri Hotel **10**
Muang Gudi Lodge **6**
Rachamankha **2**
River View Lodge **17**
Royal Princess **14**
Sira Boutique Hotel **5**

Spicy Home **12**
Sri Pat Guest House **8**
Tamarind Village **4**
U Chiang Mai **3**

taking the place of the paint. Diners are issued aprons—eating khao soy can be messier than tackling lobster. ✉ *108/2 Charoen Prathet Rd.* ☎ *053/818641* ▭ *DC, MC, V.*

$$–$$$ MEDITERRANEAN ✕ **Mi Casa.** The Basque chef and his charming Hong Kong–born wife offer an eclectic international menu with distinctly Spanish and Italian emphasis at their appealing restaurant, which is in a converted Thai house tucked away near the Chiang Mai University campus. The mixed tapas (B280) are an Iberian dream and would serve as a meal for two. A B250 lunchtime set menu includes imaginatively prepared prime beef, pork, and fish creations, such as lobster-filled ravioli. ✉ *60 Moo 6, Suthep Rd.* ☎ *053/810088* ▭ *MC, V* ⊙ *Closed Mon.*

¢–$ BRITISH ✕ **Ratana's Kitchen.** Looking rather like an English village tearoom, with a white clapboard facade and a rustic door that chimes as you enter, this friendly little restaurant on Chiang Mai's main shopping street draws in tourists with a menu packed with more than 50 low-priced U.K. favorites, including bangers and mash, beans on toast, and a big, British-style breakfast. ✉ *320–322 Tha Pae Rd.* ☎ *053/874173* ▭ *No credit cards.*

¢–$ ★ ECLECTIC ✕ **Tea House Siam Celadon.** Escape the hustle and bustle of busy Tha Pae Road by stepping into the cool interior of this exquisitely restored century-old Chinese merchant's house. You enter through a showroom of fine celadon pottery and an adjoining courtyard flanked by tiny boutiques selling Lanna fabrics. The fan-cooled tearoom is a teak-floored salon furnished with wrought iron and glass. The menu is limited, mostly sandwiches and salads (try the avocado and prawns), but the pastries and fruitcake are among Chiang Mai's best. It opens at 9 AM. ✉ *158 Tha Pae Rd.* ☎ *053/234518 or 053/234519* ▭ *AE, MC, V* ⊙ *No dinner.*

¢–$ THAI ✕ **Tha Nam.** The Ping River meanders past the outdoor terrace of this rambling old Thai house. The upper floor, where a classical trio plays for evening diners, is so old and creaking that it tilts like the main deck of a schooner in a storm. The lower terrace is a lush tropical garden, shaded by enormous trees older than the house itself. The extensive menu is packed with Thai specialties—try the *hang led* (pork curry with ginger) or the chicken wrapped in pandanus leaves. ✉ *43/3 Moo 2, Chang Klan Rd.* ☎ *053/275125* ▭ *AE, MC, V.*

$ VEGETARIAN ✕ **Whole Earth.** On the second floor of an attractive old house, this long-time favorite serves delicious and healthy foods. It's mostly vegetarian fare, but there are a few meat dishes for the carnivorous, such as *gai tahkhrai* (fried chicken with lemon and garlic). Many of the favorites here, including the tasty eggplant masala, are Indian dishes. The dining room is air-conditioned, and the garden terrace that surrounds it takes full advantage of any breezes. The service is sometimes slow. ✉ *88 Sri Donchai Rd.* ☎ *053/282463* ✍ *Reservations not accepted* ▭ *MC, V.*

¢–$ THAI ✕ **The Wok.** One of Chiang Mai's best cooking schools is fronted by this excellent restaurant. If the ancient teak house at the heart of the establishment is crowded, grab a table in the shrub-festooned garden. The menu is packed with local specialties like *nam prik ong* (minced pork dip), and the puddings are a delight—particularly the black rice and the pumpkin in coconut milk. ✉*44 Rachamankha Rd.* ☎*053/208287* ▭*AE, MC, V* ⏲*No lunch Mon.*

¢–$ ECLECTIC ✕ **Writers Club & Wine Bar.** You don't have to be a journalist to dine at Chiang Mai's unofficial press club—the regulars include not only media types but also anyone from hard-up artists and eccentric local characters to successful entrepreneurs. Local venison, wild boar, and rainbow trout frequently appear on the ever-changing menu, which also has an extensive Thai section. The house wines are good and sensibly priced. Reservations are essential on Friday and Sunday. ✉*141/3 Ratchadamnoen Rd.* ☎*053/814187* ▭*No credit cards* ⏲*Closed Sat.*

WHERE TO STAY

Fears of a tourist slump due to soaring oil prices, a strong Thai currency, and political uncertainty failed to put the brakes on the hotel building boom in Chiang Mai, and several grand establishments opened in 2007 and 2008. The most luxurious rival those in Bangkok and one, the Mandarin Oriental Dhara Devi, justly claims to be among Asia's finest. Prices are nonetheless far lower than in the capital (outside the December to February high season). Charming, modestly priced guesthouses and small hotels abound, and some are right on the water. ⚠ **Watch out for guesthouses that advertise cheap room rates and then tell you the accommodation is only available if you book an expensive tour.** Always ask if there's any tour requirement with your room rate.

$$$$ **The Chedi.** The city's newest waterfront hotel sits in isolated splendor between the Mae Ping River and one of the city's busiest streets. Rooms and suites are styled and furnished in an eclectic mix of traditional styles and fabrics and sleek modern lines. Private terraces overlook either the river or the gardens. The hotel was built on the grounds of the former British consulate, which has been restored to its original 1920s appearance, although it now houses a smart bar and restaurant and is fitted with gleaming teak and leather. Lotus ponds border the 25-meter pool, giving the impression of bathing in a Thai jungle clearing. **Pros:** faultless service; riverside location; traditional "English" afternoon teas on the terrace. **Cons:** some find the metallic, rust-colored facade ugly; nearby streets dingy. ✉*123 Charoen Prathet Rd.* ☎*053/253333* 🌐*www.ghmhotels.com* *84 rooms* *In-room: safe, DVD, Wi-Fi. In-hotel: restaurant, room service, pool, gym, spa, laundry service, parking (free), no-smoking rooms* ▭*AE, DC, MC, V* *BP.*

$$ **Chiang Mai Orchid.** With teak pillars lining the lobby, the Chiang Mai Orchid is a grand hotel in the old style. The rooms are tastefully furnished and trimmed with hardwoods. The lavish honeymoon suite is often used by the crown prince. You can dine at either the formal Le Pavillon, which serves French fare, or at Phuping, where you can enjoy Chinese favorites. The more informal Mae Rim Café features a buffet. Stop for a cocktail in the lobby bar where a pianist plays nightly, or the cozy Opium Den. The hotel is a 10-minute taxi ride from the center of Chiang Mai. **Pros:** busy shopping street Huay Kaew Road is on the doorstep; lively in-house bar scene. **Cons:** pool and exercise room used by outsiders; some rooms in need of renovation. ✉*23 Huay Kaew Rd.* ☎*053/222099, 02/714–2521 in Bangkok* 🌐*www.chiangmaiorchid.*

com ⇆*266 rooms* ♁*In-room: safe (some). In-hotel: 2 restaurants, room service, bars, pool, gym, spa, laundry service, Internet terminal, parking (free), no-smoking rooms* ▭*AE, DC, MC, V.*

$$$–$$$$ **Dusit D2 Hotel.** The sturdy old Chiang Inn has been demolished to make way for Chiang Mai's most daringly modern hotel, a complete break from the traditional Lanna style that's been so in vogue. Clean lines, brushed steel and glass surfaces, and cubist upholstery dictate the interiors, from the vast, airy, and light lobby to the beautifully lighted rooms, where a wealth of cushions compensate for the somewhat minimalist look. The hotel abuts Chiang Mai's famed Night Bazaar and is surrounded by bars and restaurants. **Pros:** in the thick of the nightlife scene; short stroll to night market. **Cons:** small pool; rooms aren't spacious; modern aesthetic won't to those looking for traditional Thai charm. ✉*100 Chang Klan Rd., T. Chang Klan, A. Muang* ☎*053/999999* ⊕*www.dusit.com* ⇆*131 rooms* ♁*In-room: safe, DVD, Wi-Fi. In-hotel: restaurant, room service, bar, pool, gym, spa, laundry service, Internet terminal, parking (free), no-smoking rooms* ▭*AE, MC, V.*

$ **Eurana Boutique Hotel.** The former S.P. Hotel has blossomed into one of Chiang Mai's most attractive boutique hotels, a haven of peace and understated luxury on a quiet lane near busy Sompet Market. You step through an archway, walk along a winding path lined with tropical shrubs and into a courtyard atrium ringed by rooms furnished in homey Lanna style. The Violet restaurant is among the best in this corner of the Old City. **Pros:** secluded Old City location; cool and leafy garden; nearby market. **Cons:** noisy neighborhood dogs. ✉*Moon Muang Rd., Soi 7* ☎*063/214522* ⊕*www.euranaboutiquehotel.com* ⇆*72 rooms* ♁*In-room: refrigerator. In-hotel: restaurant, pool, spa* ▭*MC, V.*

$$$$ Fodor'sChoice ★ **Four Seasons.** One of the finest hotels in Southeast Asia, the magnificent Four Seasons commands 20 acres of tropical countryside above the lush Mae Rim Valley. Its terraces, pools, and huge suites have views of verdant mountains, tropical gardens, and its own manicured rice paddies. The accommodations are in clusters of Lanna-style buildings. Each suite has an outdoor *sala* (gazebo) ideal for breakfast or cocktails. Rooms of polished teak are furnished with richly colored fabrics and traditional art. Both restaurants, which serve beautifully presented Thai dishes and Italian specialties, overlook the valley. The spa, with an open-air massage salon surrounded by rice paddies and lotus ponds, is one of Asia's best. **Pros:** peaceful mountain setting; idyllic pool; impeccable, attentive service. **Cons:** terraced landscape and access to many rooms is challenging for those with mobility problems. ✉*Mae Rim–Samoeng Old Rd.* ☎*053/298181, 800/545–4000 in U.S.* ⊕*www.fourseasons.com/chiangmai* ⇆*64 suites* ♁*In-room: safe, DVD, Wi-Fi. In-hotel: 2 restaurants, room service, bar, tennis courts, pool, gym, spa, laundry service* ▭*AE, DC, MC, V.*

¢ ★ **Galare Guest House.** The location is the envy of many of the city's top hotels—its gardens lead right down to the Mae Ping River. Even better, it's a short walk to the Night Bazaar. The teak-paneled rooms are simply but adequately furnished and overlook a tidy garden. The terrace restaurant faces the river. The staff is happy to assist with all travel requirements, from bus, train, and plane tickets to visas for Myanmar and

DID YOU KNOW?

There are almost 22,000 known orchid species (about four times the number of mammal species) and more than 1,000 grow in Thailand. January and August are the best times to catch them in bloom.

Laos. **Pros:** riverside location; airy terrace restaurant; secluded garden. **Cons:** lots of insects, especially around restaurant; no pool; many rooms overlook busy parking lot. ✉ *7 Charoen Prathet Rd., Soi 2* ☎ *053/818887* 🌐 *www.galare.com* *35 rooms* *In-room: refrigerator. In-hotel: restaurant, room service, laundry service, Internet terminal, parking (free)* 💳 *MC, V.*

¢ **Gap's House.** This inn is both well placed for exploring the Old City and removed from the hustle and bustle, sunk dreamily in a backstreet tropical oasis. Tours are reliable; classes can be booked at one of Chiang Mai's leading cooking schools. **Pros:** luxuriant garden; total seclusion. **Cons:** moody owner; lots of insects; noisy plumbing; no parking. ✉ *3 Ratchadamnoen Rd., Soi 4* ☎ *053/278140* 🌐 *www.gaps-house.com* *18 rooms* *In-room: safe, refrigerator, Wi-Fi. In-hotel: restaurant, room service, bar, pool, laundry service, Internet terminal* 💳 *No credit cards.*

¢ **Gap's House 2.** The very popular Gap's House has spawned this second guesthouse on the western edge of the city moat. It lacks some of the rustic charm of the original and the clientele is a bit more boisterous, but the service is friendlier and more efficient, and bicycle rental is included in the very reasonable room rate. Like the original Gap's House, this inn is in a central Old City location and has an excellent tour service. **Pros:** airy, comfortable lobby-lounge; Internet café; great tours. **Cons:** fronts a busy street with traffic noise; small rooms; no pool. ✉ *43/2 Arak Rd., A. Muang* ☎ *053/274277* 🌐 *www.gaps-house2.com* *21 rooms* *In-room: no a/c (some), safe, no TV (some), Wi-Fi. In-hotel: bicycles, laundry service* 💳 *No credit cards* 🍽 *BP.*

$$ **Karinthip Village.** A statue of a mythical winged elephant welcomes you at the entrance of the Karinthip, one of many traditional Lanna touches that distinguish the hotel from others in this otherwise rather shabby corner of town. Chinese influences are also present, particularly in the furnishings of many of the rooms. For an extra B1,000 or so you can sleep in a Lanna-style four-poster bed; suites have whirlpool bathtubs and crimson-and-pink bedrooms complete with Chinese-style lounge chairs. **Pros:** flexible room rates; helpful tour desk. **Cons:** in a rundown neighborhood; small pool. ✉ *50/2 Changmoikao Rd.* ☎ *053/235414 or 053/874302* 🌐 *www.karinthipvillage.com* *62 rooms, 5 suites* *In-hotel: restaurant, bar, pool, laundry service, parking (free)* 💳 *AE, DC, MC, V.*

¢ ★ **Lai Thai.** This rambling guesthouse on a busy thoroughfare just outside the moat is a budget traveler's favorite, so book far ahead. If it's full you'll be offered a nearby guesthouse under the same management, the Rux-Thai, which has little of the Lai Thai's charm but is an acceptable alternative nearer the city night market. Lai Thai rooms, newly renovated (in 2006) and with air-conditioning, are huddled around a courtyard with a small swimming pool. **TIP→ The adjacent open-air restaurant is also always buzzing with activity—this is the place to pick up helpful hints from seasoned travelers.** The staff is happy to arrange excursions in the area, but the prices are a bit higher than you'll find at nearby travel agencies. **Pros:** efficient travel service; courtyard pool. **Cons:** rooms have thin walls; some night noise also from partying backpackers. ✉111/4–5 Kotchasarn Rd. ☎053/271725 🌐www.laithai.com 110 rooms In-room: refrigerator. In-hotel: restaurant, pool, laundry service, Internet terminal, parking (free). AE, DC, MC, V.

$$$$ ★ **Mandarin Oriental Dhara Devi.** A Thai billionaire has turned 60 acres of farmland on the eastern outskirts of Chiang Mai into one of Asia's most extraordinary hotels, recreating a walled Lanna city surrounded by a moat. Guests can sip their evening cocktails while watching farmers work the rice paddies with buffaloes. Various traditional buildings house hotel amenities—the spa, for instance, is an exact replica of the royal palace in Mandalay, Myanmar. The suites and the regal, two-story "residences," with private gardens, are the last word in luxury; the most expensive even have pianos. U.S. President George W. Bush stayed here during his Chiang Mai visit in July 2008. **TIP→ Even if you're not staying the night, book a table for dinner and visit the pavilion-like restaurant;** it's known as the "king's room," because the king once dined here. **Pros:** total seclusion; beautiful grounds; spa treatments. **Cons:** shabby neighborhood; getting around the complex can be difficult, despite the buggy and horse-drawn carriage transport system. ✉51/4 Chiang Mai–San Kampaeng Rd., Moo 1, Tambon Tasala ☎053/888888 or 053/888929 🌐www.mandarinoriental.com/chiangmai 101 suites, 34 residences In-room: safe, kitchen, DVD, Wi-Fi. In-hotel: 3 restaurants, room service, bars, tennis courts, pools, gym, spa, children's programs (ages 6–14), laundry service, no-smoking rooms AE, DC, MC, V.

¢ **Montri Hotel.** Next to the Tha Pae Gate, this hotel's central location, bordering the moat and Pratou Tha Phae, makes up for what it lacks in creature comforts. It's adjacent to the bars and restaurants on Tha Pae and Loi Khroh roads and is an easy walk to the Night Bazaar. Most of the rooms lack a view of the moat, but they are quiet. **Pros:** central location; cozy rooms; bright ground-floor café. **Cons:** no pool; some traffic noise in rooms facing moat; no parking. ✉2–6 Ratchadamnoen Rd. ☎053/211069 or 053/418480 🌐www.hotelthailand.com/chiangmai/montri 75 rooms In-room: safe, refrigerator. In-hotel: restaurant, laundry service, Internet terminal MC, V.

$$–$$$ Fodor's Choice ★ **Muang Gudi Lodge.** Lanna-style boutique resorts are springing up throughout Chiang Mai and beyond, so it's a delight to find a mountain retreat designed in the more graceful Sukhothai fashion. Two finely tapering Sukhothai chedis guide the way to this exquisitely conceived and furnished hotel in the hills north of Chiang Mai. The Sukhothai style is maintained throughout the breathtakingly beautiful ensemble, from the arabesque arches of the interior galleries to the airy, luxuriously appointed bedrooms. Even the courtyard swimming pool is a small replica of the pools that cooled Sukhothai more than eight centuries ago. **Pros:** striking architecture; forest setting. **Cons:** far from town; no public transport. ✉815 Mae Rim-Samoeng Rd., Tambon Rim Tai ☎053/299900 🌐www.muanggudilodge.com 26 rooms In-room: safe. In-hotel: restaurant, room service, pool, gym, spa, bicycles, laundry service, Internet terminal, no-smoking rooms AE, MC, V.

$$$$ ★ **Rachamankha.** On a quiet lane near Wat Pra Singh, the Rachamankha is one of the newest of the city's luxury resorts. Visually an extension

of the temple compound, the hotel is a series of hushed brick courtyards enclosed by triple-eaved Lanna-style buildings. Most of the rooms, all furnished with Lanna or Chinese antiques, are set along green lawns planted with tall palms and fragrant frangipani. Collections of rare 19th-century Lanna scripture boxes and Burmese manuscript chests stand guard outside the rooms. The peaceful courtyard swimming pool is embraced by a tropical, walled garden. **Pros:** cool, peaceful setting; helpful receptionists very knowledgeable about local attractions. **Cons:** shabby neighborhood; noisy temple dogs; rooms too spartan for some. ☒*Rachamanka Rd., Soi 9* ☎*053/904111* 🌐*www.rachamankha.com* *21 rooms, 1 suite* *In-room: safe. In-hotel: restaurant, room service, bar, pool, laundry service, parking (free), no-smoking rooms* ▭*AE, DC, MC, V* *CP.*

$–$$ ★ **River View Lodge.** Facing a grassy lawn that runs down to the Mae Ping River, this lodge lets you forget the noise of the city. The restful rooms have terra-cotta floors and wood furniture; some have private balconies overlooking the river. The terrace and gazebo overlooking the secluded riverside pool are pleasant retreats for an afternoon coffee or tea or an evening cocktail. It's an easy 10-minute walk to the Night Bazaar. **Pros:** riverside location, breezy poolside gazebo. **Cons:** small pool; small parking lot with narrow access. ☒*25 Charoen Prathet Rd., Soi 4* ☎*053/271109* 🌐*www.riverviewlodgch.com* *33 rooms* *In-room: refrigerator. In-hotel: restaurant, pool, laundry service, Internet terminal, parking (free).* ▭*MC, V.*

$ **Royal Princess.** This centrally located hotel is ideal if you'd like to step out of the lobby and right into the tumult of downtown Chiang Mai. The bustling Night Market is at the front door and the famous Night Bazaar is barely a block away. Rooms have been upgraded and reflect the light, airy atmosphere of the lobby, where a pianist or a Thai trio plays nightly. The swimming pool and its tropical garden terrace and bar are a welcome retreat after a day of sightseeing or shopping. **Pros:** central location; close to Night Bazaar; helpful travel desk. **Cons:** noisy street scene; package-tour clientele. ☒*112 Chang Klan Rd.* ☎*053/281033* 🌐*chiangmai.royalprincess.com* *182 rooms, 16 suites* *In-room: safe, Wi-Fi. In-hotel: 4 restaurants, room service, bars, pool, gym, laundry service, no-smoking rooms* ▭*AE, DC, MC, V.*

$ **Sira Boutique Hotel.** British-run, and therefore serving an excellent English-style breakfast, this attractive, Lanna-style hotel stands on the edge of the northern section of Chiang Mai's moat. The dark woods and cream fabrics of the airy lobby set the style for the decor of the guest rooms. Two of them are teak-walled, with massive four-poster beds and bathroom Jacuzzis. A front terrace is a shady place for a morning coffee or evening cocktail. **Pros:** friendly British owners with in-depth local knowledge; lively neighborhood restaurant-and-bar scene. **Cons:** steep, narrow stairs from second to third floors. ☒*85/5 Sriphoom Rd. 50200* ☎*053/287555* 🌐*www.sirahotel.com* *17 rooms* *In-room: DVD (some), Wi-Fi. In-hotel: bar, bicycles, laundry service, Internet terminal, parking (free)* ▭*MC,V.*

¢ **Spicy Home.** The incredibly low rates at this very friendly little timber-built guesthouse include an evening meal, making this an incredible deal.

Kun Mim, who runs the place, is an excellent cook and has a small business on the side teaching Thai cooking. The evening meals around her dining table attract not only paying guests but friends as well, so they are a great way of breaking the ice on a first visit to Chiang Mai. There are only five rooms (basic but functional and clean, sharing two bathrooms), so it's essential to book ahead. **Pros:** authentic Thai atmosphere. **Cons:** shared bathroom; insects a problem. ✉*42/1 Rachamankha Rd.* ☏*09/5566727* *5 rooms with shared bath* *No credit cards.*

¢ **Sri Pat Guest House.** This family-run establishment is one of the best deals in the Old City. The spotlessly clean and stylishly furnished little hotel sits on a cobbled lane a short walk from the moat. The light and airy rooms have twin beds with crisp linens and tiled baths. Sompet Market, with its jumble of stalls selling every kind of fresh produce, is just around the corner. **Pros:** friendly, helpful Thai owner; lively village street scene (locals on porches, chatting and playing cards or strumming guitars). **Cons:** noisy neighborhood dogs; no double beds; no parking. ✉*16 Moon Muang Rd., Soi 7* ☏*053/218716* *sri-pat@sri-patguesthouse.com* *18 rooms* *In-hotel: restaurant* *No credit cards.*

$$$$ **Tamarind Village.** A canopy of towering, interlaced bamboo leads to the main entrance of this stylish, village-style hotel in the center of the Old City. Beyond the entrance is a blue pool, embraced by whitewashed corridors that lend a feeling of contemplative peace. Rooms (renovated in 2006) are furnished in teak and tones of cream and surround a garden dominated by a venerable 200-year-old tamarind tree. **Pros:** quiet, secluded location; short walk to center of Old City. **Cons:** relatively small rooms. ✉*50/1 Ratchadamnoen Rd.* ☏*053/418898* *www.tamarindvillage.com* *40 rooms* *In-room: safe, Wi-Fi. In-hotel: restaurant, room service, pool, spa, laundry service, parking (free), no-smoking rooms* *AE, MC, V.*

$$$ **U Chiang Mai.** Chiang Mai's newest Lanna-style boutique hotel, opened in June 2008, was constructed around a century-old teak house, which now serves as the lobby, spa, and reading room. Rooms, with traditional Lanna-style fabrics and furnishings, overlook a courtyard swimming pool and shady terrace. The stylish bar is open-fronted and a comfortable place from which to view the busy street scene below. **Pros:** 24-hour room rate, so if you arrive at 10 PM, you don't have to leave until the same time the next day. **Cons:** exposed pool that's open to view from most rooms; no parking. ✉*70 Ratchadmanoen Rd. 50200* ☏*053/327000* *www.uchiangmai.com* *41 rooms* *In-room: safe, DVD, Wi-Fi. In-hotel: restaurant, room service, bar, pool, gym, spa, bicycles, laundry service, Internet terminal, no-smoking rooms* *MC, V.*

NIGHTLIFE

This being Thailand, Chiang Mai has its share of Bangkok-style hostess bars. If you don't want to be hassled, there are also dozens of places where you can grab a beer and listen to live music. Many restaurants, such as the Good View, double as bars later in the evening.

6

The Four Seasons' spa offers body treatments and massage in luxurious open-air suites.

BARS

The western end of Loi Khroh Road, the southern end of Moon Muang Road, and the vast **Bar Beer Center** next to the Top North Hotel on Moon Muang Road have bars where the "working girls" usually outnumber the customers, but pool tables and dartboards are valid rival attractions. Step through the gnarled door of **The Pub** (✉ *189 Huay Kaew Rd.* ☎ *053/211550*) and you could be anywhere in rural England. The bar area is hung with the usual pub paraphernalia and there's a large hearth where a log fire burns on cold evenings. The clientele is drawn mostly from Chiang Mai's large expat community.

O'Malley's Irish Pub (✉ *Anusarn Market, Chang Klan Rd.* ☎ *053/271921*) serves draught Guinness. Regulars say it's Chiang Mai's most authentic Irish bar. **U.N. Irish Pub & Restaurant** (✉ *24 Ratvithee Rd.* ☎ *053/214554*) has a nightly entertainment program, varying from live music quiz games and live sports broadcasts. The upstairs bar, with French doors onto the street, and a small side garden are cool places to while away a warm evening.

Most bars serve wine, but two have made it their specialty: **Darling** (✉ *49/21 Huay Kaew Rd.* ☎ *053/227427*) is a chic place on a busy main road, compared by many to a smart New York bar but run by a British couple. The **Writers Club & Wine Bar** (✉ *141/3 Ratchadamnoen Rd.* ☎ *053/814187*) is Chiang Mai's unofficial press club but open to anyone who enjoys networking in good company. The decor is "eclectic colonial."

DANCE CLUBS

Local tuppies (Thai yuppies) crowd the discotheques and music bars of the Nimmanhemin Road area, fast becoming Chiang Mai's major night scene. Visiting ravers under 40 won't feel out of place in haunts like **Warm Up** (✉ *251 Nimmanhemin Rd.*). The **Monkey Club** (✉ *Soi 9, Nimmanhemin Rd.*) has a large, shady garden, packed most nights with young Thais, and an indoor music stage and bar. If you prefer to remain anonymously unobtrusive on the disco floor, then **Bubbles** (✉ *Charoen Prathet Rd.* ☎ *053/270099*) is the place to be, where the spotlights pierce the gloom only at 2 AM closing time. It adjoins the Pornping Tower Hotel. The **Horizon Club** (✉ *Loy Kroh Rd.* ☎ *053/905000*), in the basement of the Central Duang Tawan Hotel, is a popular addition to the local night scene.

In the Chiang Mai Orchid Hotel, **The Opium Den** (✉ *23 Huay Kaew Rd.* ☎ *053/222099*) caters to a stylish, sophisticated crowd. The stylish **Empress Hotel lobby bar** (✉ *199/42 Chang Klan Rd.* ☎ *053/270240*) has live music every night.

KHANTOKE

Khantoke (or kantoke) originally described a revolving wooden tray on which food is served, but it has now come to mean an evening's entertainment combining a seemingly endless menu of Northern cuisine and presentations of traditional music and dancing. With sticky rice, which you mold into balls with your fingers, you sample delicacies like *kap moo* (spiced pork skin), *nam prik naw* (a spicy dip made with onions, cucumber, and chili), and *kang kai* (a chicken and vegetable curry).

Among the best of places offering khantoke is the sumptuously temple-like **Khum Khantoke** (✉ *Chiang Mai Business Park, 139 Moo 4, Nong Pakrung* ☎ *053/30412 up to 31*). Another popular place for khantoke is **Kantoke Palace** (✉ *288/19 Chang Klan Rd.* ☎ *053/272757*). The **Vista Hotel** (✉ *252 Phrapokklao Rd.* ☎ *053/210663*) has a nightly khantoke show and dinner in its **Khum Kaew Palace,** costing B160 for hotel guests and B260 for other visitors. The **Old Chiang Mai Cultural Center** (✉ *185/3 Wualai Rd.* ☎ *053/275097*), a fine ensemble of traditional teak-built houses, accompanies a multicourse dinner with traditional music and dancing. The B320 charge includes transport to and from your hotel.

MUSIC

Jazz aficionados call Chiang Mai Thailand's New Orleans, and some say it offers better quality music at lower prices than Bangkok. A West Virginian jazz multi-instrumentalist has created the city's best hangout, the **North Gate** (✉ *Sriphum Rd., opposite the Chiang Phuak gate* ☎ *No phone*). Tuesdays are jam session nights. The **Rasta Art Bar** (✉ *Sriphum Rd., between Sois 1 and 2*) is also fun, with mostly reggae and some soft rock.

A rough, unnamed alleyway off Ratchaphakinai Road has become a magnet for local night owls, who nightly pack the dozen or so open-air or open-sided music bars. The best of them are **Babylon** (formerly the Rasta Café) and **Heaven Beach.** Follow the alley at the western side of the U.N. Irish Pub; take the second lane on the left.

Thai rock is the specialty of the vast beer hall called **Sai Lom Joi** (✉*125 Chang Klan Rd.* ☎*053/247531*). **Tha Nam** (✉*43/3 Moo 2, Chang Klan Rd.* ☎*053/275125*) has nightly performances of Thai classical music.

The east bank of the Ping River between Nawarat Bridge and Nakorn Ping Bridge resounds nightly with live music. Most of the decibels come from the **Good View** (✉*13 Charoen Rat Rd.* ☎*053/241866*), which has a variety of bands that play nightly. Farther along the riverbank, the **Gallery** (✉*31–35 Charoen Rat Rd.* ☎*053/248601*) has a café-bar adjacent to its restaurant where some of the city's best jazz can be heard Thursday to Sunday nights. A few doors down, crowds pack in late every night to hear one of Chiang Mai's finest guitarists, Lek, at the **Brasserie** (✉*31 Charoen Rat Rd.* ☎*053/241665*). Jazz jam sessions also attract big crowds of fans nightly at **Guitarman** ✉*68/5–6 Loy Kroh Rd.* ☎*053/818110*).

SPORTS & THE OUTDOORS

BOATING

Book ahead for boat tours via phone if possible.

Two-hour **Chiang Mai Ping River cruises** depart daily between 8:30 AM and 5 PM from the **River Cruise Seafood Restaurant** (✉*Charoen Prathet Rd.* ☎*053/274822 booking*) landing at Wat Chai Mongkol, Charoen Prathet Road. A dinner cruise sets off nightly at 7:30.

For a taste of how the locals used to travel along the Ping River, take a ride in a scorpion-tail boat. Two companies operate services from the east bank of the river, between Nawarat Bridge and Rattanakosin Bridge. The large rudder at the stern of this sturdy Siamese craft gives it its name. **Scorpion-tail boat tours** (✉*Charoen Rat Rd.* ☎*081/885–0663 or 081/884–4621*) has several trips daily between 10 and 5:30, and there are dinner cruises at 7 PM.

GOLF

Chiang Mai is ringed by championship golf courses that challenge players of all levels. The **Chiengmai Gymkhana Club** (☎*053/241035*) has a 9-hole course just 1 mi from the city center; green fees are B400 per day. Farther out, on the road north to San Khamphaeng, is the city's principal championship course, the **Chiang Mai-Lamphun Golf Club** (☎*053/880880* 🌐*chiangmaigolf.com*). **Northern Express Tour** (✉*Chiang Mai–Lamphun Rd., Soi 9, Nong Hoi* ☎*09/850–7344*) has a "tee-off service" that delivers golfers to any one of four courses near Chiang Mai for B800. Between the airport and the city center, near the junction of Hangdong and Mahidol roads, there's a two-tier driving range, with a good restaurant and coffee shop.

HORSEBACK RIDING

North of Chiang Mai, **J & T Happy Riding** (✉*Mae Rim–Samoeng Rd.* ☎*05/036–1227*) sponsors trail rides through the beautiful Mae Sa Valley. Beginners are welcome. The stables are opposite the Mae Sa Orchid Farm.

ROCK CLIMBING

You can go rock climbing right in the center of Chiang Mai at The Peak, a three-story-tall artificial rock face. **The Peak Rock Climbing School** (✉*282 Chang Klan Rd.* ☎*053/820777* 🌐*www.thepeakadventure.com*) offers climbs for first-timers costing B300 and three-day courses for more advanced climbers costing B5,800. A four-day tour that includes climbs

CLOSE UP

Massages & Spa Treatments

Chiang Mai has no shortage of massage parlors (the respectable kind) where the aches of a day's strenuous sightseeing can be kneaded away with a traditional massage. Your hotel can usually organize either an in-house massage or recommend one of the city's numerous centers.

Good massages with or without accompanying herbal treatments are given at **Rada** (✉ *2/2 Soi 3, Nimmanhemin Rd.* ☎ *053/220407*). A two-hour full-body massage costs B300. If you want to do a good deed for Thai society as well as enjoy a great massage, stop by Chiang Mai's **women's prison** (✉ *115 Ratvithee Rd.*). Female inmates trained in Thai massage are allowed to practice their trade in a room adjoining the prison's shop (where handicrafts from the prison workshops are sold). A two-hour Thai massage costs B150—money well spent in assuring these remarkably cheerful women a solid foundation for life outside the prison walls.

Chiang Mai also has dozens of spas specializing in Thai massage and various treatments involving traditional herbs and oils. **Oasis Spa** (✉ *102 Sirimungklajan Rd.* ✉ *Samlan Rd.* ☎ *053/815000* 🌐 *www.chiangmaioasis.com*) has two first-class establishments in Chiang Mai. Both offer a full range of different types of massage from Swedish to traditional Thai and a slew of mouthwatering body scrubs like Thai coffee, honey and yogurt, or orange, almond, and honey.

At the **Ban Sabai Spa Village** (✉ *216 Moo 9, San Pee Sua* ☎ *053/854–7789*) you can get your massage in a wooden Thai-style house or in a riverside sala. Treatments of note include a steamed herb massage, wherein a bundle of soothing herbs is placed on the body, and various fruit-based body masques like honey-tamarind or pineapple.

6

up rock faces in the Pai and Mae Hong Son areas costs B7,100. The facility is on Chang Klan Road behind the Night Bazaar.

THAI BOXING Professional muay thai (Thai boxing) contestants square off every Thursday night at the **Tha Pae Boxing Stadium** (✉ *Beer Bar Center, Moon Muang Rd., behind True Blue Pub*). The program starts at 9 PM; admission is B400.

SHOPPING

Day-to-day life in Chiang Mai seems to revolve around shopping. The delightful surprise is that you don't have to part with much of your hard-earned money—even the most elaborately crafted silver costs a fraction of what you'd expect to pay at home. Fine jewelry, weighed and priced at just above the current market value, pewter, leather, and silk are all on display all around the city.

Fodor'sChoice ★ The justifiably famous **Night Bazaar,** on Chang Klan Road, is a kind of open-air department store filled with stalls selling everything from inexpensive souvenirs to pricey antiques. In the afternoon and evening traders set up tented stalls, confusingly known as the Night Market, along Chang Klan Road and the adjoining streets. You're expected to bargain, so don't be shy. Do, however, remain polite. ■ **TIP→ Many vendors**

believe the first and last customers of the day bring good luck, so if you're after a real bargain (up to 50% off) start your shopping early in the day.

Another permanent bazaar, the **Kalare Night Bazaar,** is in a big entertainment complex on the eastern side of the Night Market on Chang Klan Road; it's clearly marked. It's packed with boutiques, stalls, cheap restaurants, and a beer garden featuring nightly performances of traditional Thai dances. Chiang Mai has two so-called **"walking streets,"** closed off to traffic to make way for weekly markets. One is held on **Wualai Road** (the "silver street") on Saturday evening. The other, much larger one, takes up the whole of **Ratchadamnoen Road** and surrounding streets on Sunday. Both are cheaper and far more authentic than the market on Chang Klan Road.

SHOPPING GUIDES

Before setting off on a shopping expedition in Chiang Mai, buy a copy of *Shopping Secrets of Chiang Mai,* a comprehensive 280-page visitors' guide containing in-depth information on virtually everything the city has to offer. It's available in most bookstores. Or page through the local English-language monthlies *Guidelines* or *Art & Culture Lanna,* available free of charge in most hotels. Both are packed with information and feature an astonishing variety of local crafts by trustworthy dealers.

ANTIQUES If you follow certain common-sense rules—examine each item very carefully for signs of counterfeiting (new paint or varnish, tooled damage marks) and ask for certificates of provenance and written guarantees that the goods can be returned if proved counterfeit—shopping for antiques should present few problems. ■ **TIP→ Reputable stores will always provide certificates of provenance,** aware that penalties for dishonest trading are severe (if you're ever in doubt about a deal contact the Tourist Police).

The Night Bazaar in Chiang Mai has two floors packed with antiques, many of which were manufactured yesterday (and hence come with no guarantee of authenticity). Some stalls have the genuine article, among them **Lanna Antiques** (✉ *Chang Klan Rd.*). It's the second booth on the second floor.

The road south to Hang Dong (take the signposted turn before the airport) is lined with antiques shops. Just outside Hang Dong you'll reach the craft village of Ban Tawai. You could spend an entire morning or afternoon rummaging through its antiques shops and storerooms.

ART Chiang Mai has a vibrant artists' scene, and several small galleries dot the city. **La Luna** (✉ *Charoen Rat Rd.* ☎ *053/306678* 🌐 *www.lalunagallery.com*) has regular exhibitions by top local and regional artists. The **Writers Club and Wine Bar** (✉ *141/3 Ratchadamnoen Rd.*) has a permanent, rotating exhibit of work by Myanmar artists, many of whom are political dissidents and unable to show in their native country. A number of other restaurants feature displays of Thai art. The best of them is **The Gallery** (✉ *25–29 Charoen Rat Rd.* ☎ *053/248601*).

HANDICRAFTS For local handicrafts, head to two of Chiang Mai's main shopping streets, Tha Pae Road and Loi Kroh Road. On Tha Pae Road **Living Space** (✉ *276–278 Tha Pae Rd.* ☎ *053/874156* 🌐 *www.livingspacedesigns.com*) is worth seeking out for its very original and aesthetic collection of home decor items. Across the Nawarat Bridge, Charoen Rat Road is home to a row of refurbished old teak houses with a handful of boutiques selling interesting crafts such as incense candles and carved curios. Farther afield, along Nimmanhemin Road near the Amari Rincome Hotel, a whole neighborhood of crafts shops has developed. The first lane on the left, Soi 1, has some of the most rewarding.

OTOP

To encourage each *tambon* (community) to make the best use of its special skills, the government set up a program called **OTOP** (✉ *29/19 Singharat Rd.* ☎ *053/221174 or 053/223164* 🌐 *www.depthai.go.th*). The program, which stands for "One Tambon, One Product," has been a great success. Its center has a two-story showroom with a collection that rivals many of the city's galleries and museums. The ground floor has an exquisite display of furniture and decorative items. Upstairs are smaller items—baskets, carvings, ceramics, and textiles.

6

The money you pay for a woven mat or carved mask goes directly to the local communities at the **Hilltribe Products Promotion Center** (✉ *21/17 Suthep Rd.* ☎ *053/277743*), a government supported crafts store. Here you can discover a wide range of handicrafts made by Akha, Hmong, Karen, Lahu, Lisu, and Yao people in their native villages. **Hill Tribes Handicraft Center** (✉ *1 Moon Muang Rd.,* ☎ *053/274877*), Chiang Mai's second government-supported store, stocks a very wide range of products, from elaborate silver jewelry to key-rings. Fine examples of hill tribe textiles hang in frames on the center's walls and can be bought for around B2,000. **Thai Tribal Crafts** (✉ *208 Bumrungrat Rd.* ☎ *053/241043* 🌐 *www.ttcrafts.co.th*) has more than 25 years' experience in retailing the products of Northern Thailand's hill tribe people. Chiang Mai's largest handicrafts retail outlet is called the **Northern Village** (✉ *Hang Dong and Mahidol Rds.*). The massive store takes up two floors of the Central Airport Plaza Shopping Center. The selection here is astounding: silks and other textiles, ceramics, jewelry, and carvings.

For two of Chiang Mai's specialties, lacquerware and exquisite paper products, take a taxi or songthaew to any of the outlets along San Kamphaeng Road (also known as the Golden Mile). Large emporiums that line the 10-km (6-mi) stretch sell a wide variety of items. Whole communities here devote themselves to their traditional trades. One community rears silkworms, for instance, providing the raw product for the looms humming in workshops. Among the crafts you can find are hand-painted umbrellas made from lacquered paper and tree bark. Hundreds of these are displayed at the **Umbrella Making Center** (✉ *11/2 Moo 3, Bor Sang* ☎ *053/338324*). The artists at the center will paint traditional designs on anything from a T-shirt to a suitcase—travelers have discovered that this is a very handy way of helping identify their luggage on an airport carousel.

Outside the city center, the highways running south and east of Chiang Mai—those leading to Hang Dong and San Kamphaeng—are lined for several miles with workshops stocked with handicrafts of every description. They're a favorite destination for tuk-tuk drivers, who receive a commission on goods bought by their passengers. ⚠ **Be very specific with tuk-tuk drivers about what you're looking for before setting out—otherwise you might find yourself ferried to an expensive silverware outlet when all you want to buy is an inexpensive souvenir.**

Near Hang Dong, 12 km (7 mi) from the city center, is the crafts village of **Ban Tawai,** whose streets are lined with antiques shops. Four kilometers (2½ mi) beyond Ban Tawai is the **Ban Tawai Tourist Village,** an entire community of shops dealing in antiques and handicrafts. At workshops you can see teak, mango, rattan, and water hyacinth being worked into an astonishing variety of attractive and unusual items. If you end up buying a heavy teak piece of furniture, the dealers here will arrange for its transport. Beyond the Hang Dong–Ban Tawai junction is a large Lanna-style crafts center called **Baan Mai Kham** (⊠ *122 Chiang Mai–Hod Rd.* ☎ *04/040–5007*).

JEWELRY Chiang Mai is renowned for its gems and semiprecious stones. ⚠ **Avoid the unscrupulous dealers at the Night Market and head to any of the more reputable stores.** If gold is your passion, make for the Chinese district. All the shops that jostle for space at the eastern end of Chang Moi Road are reliable, invariably issuing certificates of authenticity. The city's silver district, Wualai Road, is lined for several hundred yards with shops where you can sometimes see silversmiths at work. **Hirunyakorn Silverware** (⊠ *27–29 Wualai Rd.* ☎ *053/272750*) has one of the street's best selections of hand-crafted silver.

A very attractive Chiang Mai specialty features orchid blooms or rose petals set in 24-karat gold. There's a spectacular selection at the **Royal Orchid Collection** (⊠ *94–120 Charoen Muang Rd., 2nd fl.* ☎ *053/245598*). **Eaze** (⊠ *Central Airport Plaza, 2nd fl.*) also has a good selection of these blooms in gold.

Nova (⊠ *201 Tha Pae Rd.* ☎ *053/273058*) is a reliable jewelry shop with an attached jewelry school. **Shiraz** (⊠ *170 Tha Pae Rd.* ☎ *053/252382*) is a long-established and reliable shop. Ask for Mr. Nasser. **Sherry** (⊠ *59/2 Loi Kroh Rd.* ☎ *053/273529*) is a small treasure trove of a boutique crammed in between the bars and restaurants of one of the city's busiest streets.

The **Orchid Jade Factory** (⊠ *7/7 Srivichai Rd., opposite the entrance to Doi Suthep* ☎ *053/295021 up to 23*) claims to be the world's largest retailer of jadeite. The hard-sell tactics here can be slightly annoying, but the showrooms are truly a treasure trove of fabulous jade jewelry and ornaments, and visitors are invited to watch the craftspeople at work.

PAPER The groves of mulberry trees grown in Northern Thailand aren't only used to feed the silkworms—their bark, called *saa,* produces a distinctive, fibrous paper that is fashioned into every conceivable form: writing paper and envelopes, boxes, book covers, and picture frames. In Chiang Mai, **HQ PaperMaker** (✉*3/31 Samlan Rd.* ☎*053/814717*) is the biggest and best outlet. Its first floor is a secluded gallery whose works include paintings done by elephants at the Elephant Conservation Center near Lampang. **Siam Promprathan** (✉*95/3 Moo 4, Ratchawithi Rd., San Kamphaeng* ☎*053/331768 or 053/392214*) also has a wide selection of saa paper products.

TEXTILES Chiang Mai and silk are nearly synonymous, and here you can buy the product *and* see it being manufactured. Several companies along San Kamphaeng Road open their workrooms to visitors and explain the process of making fine silk, from the silkworm to the loom. ⚠ **These shops are favorite destinations of package tours, so prices tend to be higher than in other parts of town or at the Night Market.**

Silk and other local textiles can be reliably bought at **Shinawatra Thai Silk** (✉*18 Huay Kaew Rd.* ☎*053/221076 or 053/888535* ✉*Mandarin Oriental Dhara Devi, 51/4 Chiang Mai–San Kampaeng Rd., Moo 1, Tambon Tasala* ☎*053/888535*).

Studio Naenna (✉*Soi 8, 138 Huay Kaew Rd.* ☎*053/226042*), tucked on a heavily forested slope of Doi Suthep mountain, is run by a renowned authority on local textiles, Patricia Naenna.

Vaniche (✉*133 Boonraksa Rd.* ☎*053/262786*) complements its wide selection of silk and other textiles with its own individually designed jewelry.

Eaze (✉*2nd fl., Airport Plaza* ☎*053/262786*) in a leading Chiang Mai shopping mall, has an eclectic display of textiles and decorative items.

Textiles woven in hill tribe villages can be found at **Nicha** (✉*86/1 Charoen Rat Rd.* ☎*053/288–0470*).

DOI INTHANON NATIONAL PARK

90 km (54 mi) southwest of Chiang Mai.

Doi Inthanon, Thailand's highest mountain (8,464 feet), rises majestically over a national park of staggering beauty. Many have compared the landscape—thick forests of pines, oaks, and laurels—with that of Canada. Only the tropical vegetation on its lower slopes, and the 30 villages that are home to 3,000 Karen and Hmong people, remind you that this is indeed Asia. The reserve is of great interest to nature lovers, especially birders who come to see the 362 species that nest here. Red-and-white rhododendron run riot, as do other plants found nowhere else in Thailand.

Hiking trails penetrate deep into the park, which has some of Thailand's highest and most beautiful waterfalls. The Mae Klang Falls, just past the turnoff to the park, are easily accessible by foot or by vehicle, but the most spectacular are more remote and involve a trek of 4 to 5 km (2½ to 3 mi). The Mae Ya Falls are the country's highest, but even more spectacular are the Siribhum Falls, which plunge in two parallel cataracts from a 1,650-foot-high cliff above the Inthanon Royal Research Station. The station's vast nurseries are a gardener's dream, filled with countless varieties of tropical and temperate plants. Rainbow trout—unknown in the warm waters of Southeast Asia—are raised here in tanks fed by cold streams plunging from the mountain's heights, then served at the station's restaurant. The national park office provides maps and guides for trekkers and bird-watchers. ■ **TIP→ Accommodations are available: B1,000 for a two-person chalet, B6,500 for a villa for up to eight people.** The park admission fee is collected at a tollbooth at the start of the road to the summit. ✉ *Amphur Chomthong* ☎ *053/28678 or 053/286730* 🌐 *www.dnp.go.th* 🎫 *B400 per person, plus B30 per car* ⏲ *Daily 9–6.*

GETTING HERE & AROUND

Although there are minibus services from the nearest village, Chom Tong, to the summit of Doi Inthanon, there is no direct bus route from Chiang Mai. So the most convenient way to access the park is either to book a tour with a Chiang Mai operator or to hire a car and driver in Chiang Mai for around B2,000. If you're driving a rental car (about B1,000 per day), take Highway 108 south (the road to Hot) and after 36 km (22 mi) turn right at Chom Thong onto the minor road 1099, a sinuous 48-km (30-mi) stretch winding to the mountain's summit. ■ **TIP→ The ashes of Chiang Mai's last ruler, King Inthawichayanon, are contained on road 1099 in a secluded stupa that draws hundreds of thousands of pilgrims annually.**

LAMPHUN

26 km (16 mi) south of Chiang Mai.

Lamphun claims to be the oldest existing city in Thailand (but so does Nakhon Pathom). Originally called Nakhon Hariphunchai, it was founded in AD 660. Its first ruler was a queen, Chamthewi, who has a special place in Thailand's pantheon of powerful female leaders. There are two striking statues of her in the sleepy little town, and one of its wats bears her name. Queen Chamthewi founded the eponymous dynasty, which ruled the region until 1932. Today the compact little city is the capital of Thailand's smallest province, and also a textile and silk production center.

GETTING HERE & AROUND

BY BUS The provincial buses from Chiang Mai to Lampang stop at Lamphun, a 40-minute drive south on Highway 106, a very busy but beautiful and shady road lined by 100-foot-tall rubber trees. The buses leave half-hourly from Chiang Mai's city bus station and from a stop next to the TAT office on the road to Lamphun. Minibus songthaews also operate a service to Lamphun. They leave from in front of the TAT office. Fares for all services to Lamphun are about B20. Lamphun has no bus station; buses stop at various points around town, including at the TAT office and outside Wat Haripunchai.

BY TRAIN One slow daily Bangkok–Chiang Mai train stops at Lamphun, where a samlor (pedicab) can take you the 3 km (2 mi) into town for about B30. But the bus is more practical.

BY TUK-TUK & SONGTHAEW It's a compact city, easy to tour on foot, although Wat Chamtewi is on the outskirts and best visited by tuk-tuk or songthaew.

LAMPHUN'S NATIVE FRUIT

The countryside surrounding Lamphun is blanketed with orchards of *lamyai*, a sweet cherry-size fruit with a thin, buff-color shell. The annual lamyai festival brings the town to a halt in the first week of August with parades, exhibitions, a beauty contest, and copious quantities of lamyai wine. The lamyai-flower honey is reputed to have exceptional healing and aphrodisiacal powers. You can buy lamyai at the market stalls along the 100-yard covered wooden bridge opposite Wat Phra That Hariphunchai.

EXPLORING LAMPHUN

Lamphun has two of northern Thailand's most important monasteries, dating back more than 1,000 years. The smallest of them guards the remains of the city's fabled 8th-century ruler, Queen Chamthewi. The other, Wat Phra That Hariphunchai, is a walled treasure house of ancient chapels, chedis, and gilded Buddhas.

WHAT TO SEE

★ Lamphun's architectural treasures include two monasteries. About 2 km (1 mi) west of the town's center is **Wat Chamthewi**, often called the "topless chedi" because the gold that once covered the spire was pillaged sometime during its history. Work began on the monastery in AD 755, and despite a modern viharn added to the side of the complex, it retains an ancient, weathered look. Suwan Chang Kot, to the right of the entrance, is the most famous of the two chedis, built by King Mahantayot to hold the remains of his mother, the legendary Queen Chamthewi. The five-tier sandstone chedi is square; on each tier are Buddha images that get progressively smaller. All are in the 9th-century Dvaravati style, though many have obviously been restored. The other chedi was probably built in the 10th century, though most of what you see today is the work of 12th-century King Phaya Sapphasit. ■ **TIP→ You probably want to take a samlor down the narrow residential street to the complex. Since this is not an area where samlors generally cruise, ask the driver to wait for you.** ✉ *Lamphun–San Pa Tong Rd.*

Fodor's Choice ★ The temple complex of **Wat Phra That Hariphunchai** is dazzling. Through the gates guarded by ornamental lions is a three-tier, sloping-roof viharn, a replica of the original that burned down in 1915. Inside, note the large Chiang Saen–style bronze image of the Buddha and the carved *thammas* (Buddhism's universal principals) to the left of the altar. As you leave the viharn, you pass what is reputedly the largest bronze gong in the world, cast in 1860. The 165-foot Suwana chedi, covered in copper and topped by a golden spire, dates from 847. A century later, King Athitayarat, the 32nd ruler of Hariphunchai, added a nine-tier umbrella, gilded with 14 pounds of gold. At the back of the compound—where you can find a shortcut to the center of town—there's another viharn

Elephants embrace at the Anantara Golden Triangle's elephant camp.

with a standing Buddha, a sala housing four Buddha footprints, and the old museum. ✉ *Inthayongyot Rd.* ⏲ *Wed.–Sun. 8:30–4.*

Just outside Wat Phra That Hariphunchai, the **National Museum** has a fine selection of Dvaravati-style stuccowork. There's also an impressive collection of Lanna antiques. ✉ *Inthayongyot Rd.* ☎ *053/511186* 🎫 *B30* ⏲ *Wed.–Sun. 9–4.*

WHERE TO EAT & STAY

¢–$ THAI ✕ **Add Up Coffee Bar.** This attractive riverside haunt, next door to the visitor information center, is more than just a coffee shop. The menu has the usual Thai dishes, but its list of Western specialties is full of surprises—pork chops, for instance, served with garlic-apple compote. The ice cream is made under American license and is delicious. A vegetarian-only annex under the same management, Spa Food, opened next door in 2008. ✉ *22 Lobmuangnai Rd.* ☎ *053/530272* 💳 *MC, V.*

¢–$ ASIAN ✕ **Lamphun Ice.** The odd name of this restaurant seems to come from its origins as an ice-cream parlor. The interior has cozy booths that give it the feel of a vintage soda fountain. The Chinese, Thai, and Indian food served here is the real thing—try the sensational Indian-style crab curry. ✉ *Chaimongkon Rd., opposite southern gate of Wat Phra That Hariphunchai* ☎ *053/511452* 💳 *MC, V.*

¢–$ THAI ✕ **Ton Fai.** This restaurant, named for the colorful flame tree, occupies an ancient house and its shady backyard. Inside you can climb the stairs to a teak-floored dining room with tables set beneath the original rafters. The river breeze wafting in through the shuttered windows cools the room. The menu is simple, but has plenty of tasty Northern Thai specialties. ✉ *183 Chaimongkol Rd., Tambon Nai Muang* ☎ *053/530060* ▭ *No credit cards.*

¢ **Supamit.** From this hotel's fifth-floor restaurant you have fine views of Wat Chamthewi, on the opposite side of the street. Lamphun's best hotel, the Supamit has simple but adequately furnished and clean rooms. After a day touring the city's temples, the airy lobby offers a cool and soothing retreat. **Pros:** opposite Lamphun's most beautiful wat. **Cons:** impersonal atmosphere and hotel service. ✉ *Chamthewi Rd.* ☎ *053/534865* *50 rooms* *In-room: refrigerator. In-hotel: restaurant, bar* ▭ *MC, V.*

SHOPPING

Lamphun's silk and other fine textiles make a visit to this charming city worthwhile. It has its own version of Venice's Rialto Bridge, a 100-yard-long covered wooden bridge lined on both sides with stands selling mostly silk, textiles, and local handicrafts. The bridge is opposite the main entrance to Wat Phra That Hariphunchai, Inthayongyot Road. The market is open daily 9 to 6. Eight kilometers (5 mi) from Lamphun on the main Lampang highway is one of the area's largest silk businesses, **Lampoon Thai Silk** (✉ *8/2 Panangjitawong Rd., Changkong* ☎ *053/510329* 🌐 *www.thaisilk.th.com*), where you can watch women weave at wooden looms.

6

LAMPANG

65 km (40 mi) southeast of Lamphun, 91 km (57 mi) southeast of Chiang Mai.

At the end of the 19th century, when Lampang was a thriving center of the teak trade, the well-to-do city elders gave the city a genteel look by buying a fleet of English-built carriages and a stable of nimble ponies to pull them through the streets. Until then, elephants had been a favored means of transport—a century ago the number of elephants, employed in the nearby teak forests, nearly matched the city's population. The carriages arrived on the first trains to steam into Lampang's fine railroad station, which still looks much the same as it did back then. More than a century later, the odd sight of horse-drawn carriages still greets visitors to Lampang. The brightly painted, flower-bedecked carriages, driven by hardened types in Stetson hats and cowboy boots, look very touristy, but the locals also use them to get around the city, albeit for considerably less than the B150 visitors are charged for a short city tour.

GETTING HERE & AROUND

BY AIR Lampang Airport, which handles domestic flights, is just west of downtown. Songthaews run to the city center for around B50. A privately operated carrier, PBair operates daily flights from Bangkok to Lampang (one hour), costing around B2,000 one-way and B4,000 round-trip.

BY BUS Buses from Chiang Mai to Lampang (stopping at the Elephant Conservation Center) leave every half hour from near the Tourism Authority of Thailand office on the road to Lamphun. Lampang's bus station is 2 km (1 mi) south of the city, just off the main highway to Bangkok.

Faster VIP buses from Bangkok to Chiang Mai—operated by various companies—stop at Lampang; they leave Chiang Mai's Arcade Bus Station about every hour throughout the day. Fares from Chiang Mai range from about B40 to B150.

BY TRAIN All Bangkok–Chiang Mai trains stop at Lampang, where a samlor (pedicab) can take you the 3 km (2 mi) into town for about B30. By train, Lampang is about 2½ hours from Chiang Mai and 11 hours from Bangkok. First-class fares from Bangkok range from B1,300 (for a sleeper) to B600 or B800 (for a day train).

BY SONGTHAEW & CARRIAGE Within Lampang, songthaews are the cheapest way of getting around, though traveling via the city's horse-drawn carriages is much more thrilling. Carriages are at various city stands, most of them outside the Wiengthong Hotel.

EXPLORING LAMPANG

Apart from some noteworthy temples, not much else remains of Lampang's prosperous heyday. An ever-dwindling number of fine teak homes can be found among the maze of concrete. Running parallel to the south bank of the Wang River is a narrow street of ancient shops that once belonged to the Chinese merchants who catered to Lampang's prosperous populace. ■ **TIP→ The riverfront promenade is a pleasant place for a stroll; a handful of cafés and restaurants have terraces overlooking the water.**

WHAT TO SEE

Workers from Myanmar were employed in the region's rapidly expanding logging business, and these immigrants left their mark on the city's architecture. Especially well preserved is **Wat Sri Chum,** a lovely Burmese temple. Pay particular attention to the viharn, as the eaves are covered with beautiful carvings. Inside you can find gold-and-black lacquered pillars supporting a carved-wood ceiling. To the right is a bronze Buddha cast in the Burmese style. Red-and-gold panels on the walls depict temple scenes. ⊠*Sri Chum Rd.*

Near the banks of the Wang River is **Wat Phra Kaew Don Tao,** dominated by its tall chedi, built on a rectangular base and topped with a rounded spire. More interesting, however, are the Burmese-style shrine and adjacent Thai-style sala. The 18th-century shrine has a multitier roof. The interior walls are carved and inlaid with colored stones; the ornately engraved ceiling is painted with enamel. The sala, with the traditional three-tier roof and carved-wood pediments, houses a Sukhothai-style reclining Buddha. Legend has it that the sala was once home to the Emerald Buddha, which now resides in Bangkok. In 1436, when King Sam Fang Kaem was transporting the statue from Chiang Rai to Chiang Mai, his elephant reached Lampang and refused to go farther. The Emerald Buddha is said to have remained here for the next 32 years, until the succeeding king managed to get it to Chiang Mai. ⊠*Phra Kaew Rd.*

Fodor's Choice ★ Near the village of Ko Khang is **Wat Phra That Lampang Luang,** one of the most venerated temples in the north. It's also one of the most striking.

Surrounded by stout laterite defense walls, the temple has the appearance of a fortress—and that's exactly what it was when the legendary Queen Chamthewi founded her capital here in the 8th century. The Burmese captured it two centuries ago, but were ejected by the forces of a Lampang prince (a bullet hole marks the spot where he killed the Burmese commander). The sandy temple compound has much to hold your interest, including a tiny chapel with a hole in the door that creates an amazing, inverted photographic image of the Wat's central, gold-covered chedi. The temple's ancient viharn has a beautifully carved wooden facade; note the painstaking workmanship of the intricate decorations around the porticoes. A museum has excellent woodcarvings, but its treasure is a small emerald Buddha, which some claim was carved from the same stone as its counterpart in Bangkok. ✉ *15 km (9 mi) south of Lampang* ⏲ *Tues.–Sun. 9–4.*

Fodor's Choice ★ On the main highway between Lampang and Chiang Mai is Thailand's internationally known **Elephant Conservation Center.** So-called training camps are scattered throughout the region, but many of them are little more than overpriced sideshows. This is the real thing: a government-supported research station. Here you can find the special stables that house the white elephants owned by the king, although only those who are taking the center's mahout training course are allowed to see them. The 36 "commoner" elephants (the most venerable are over 80 years old) get individual care from more than 40 mahouts. The younger ones evidently enjoy the routines they perform for the tourists—not only the usual log-rolling, but painting pictures (a New York auction of their work raised thousands of dollars for the center). There's even an elephant band—its trumpeter is truly a star. The elephants are bathed every day at 9:30 and 1:15, and perform at 10, 11, and 1:30. You can even take an elephant ride through the center's extensive grounds, and if you fancy becoming a mahout you can take a residential course in elephant management. The center's hospital, largely financed by a Swiss benefactor, is a heart-rending place, treating elephants injured by mines sown along the Burmese border. Its latest mine victim won international renown in 2008 by becoming the first elephant in the world to be fitted successfully with an artificial leg. ✉ *Baan Tung Kwian* ☎ *054/228034 or 054/229042* 🎫 *B70* ⏲ *Daily 8–4.*

WHERE TO EAT

¢–$ THAI **✕ Aroi Sep.** Sep is the new Thai owner of this popular, formerly Vietnamese restaurant, and he's added "Aroi" (meaning "delicious") to the name because of the praise his exclusively Thai menu wins among the locals. You dine either indoors beneath massive teak beams and slowly revolving fans or on the tree-shaded flagstone terrace overlooking the Wang River. ✉ *340 Tipchang Rd.* ☎ *054/310103* 💳 *AE, MC.*

¢–$ THAI **✕ Riverside.** A random assortment of wooden rooms and terraces gives this place an easygoing charm. Perched above the sluggish Wang River, it's a great place for a casual meal. The moderately priced Thai and European fare is generally excellent (although the steak, from local beef, is to be avoided), and on weekends the chef serves up a very passable pizza. Most nights a live band performs, but there are so many quiet

CLOSE UP

Thailand's Elephants

The United States has its eagle. Britain acquired the lion. Thailand's symbolic animal is the elephant, which has played an enormous role in the country's history through the ages. It even appeared on the national flag when Thailand was Siam. It's a truly regal beast—white elephants enjoy royal patronage and several are stabled at the National Elephant Institute's conservation center near Lampang.

But the elephant is also an animal of the people, domesticated some 2,000 years ago to help with the heavy work and logging in the teak forests of Northern Thailand. Elephants were in big demand by the European trading companies, which scrambled for rich harvests of teak in the late 19th century and early 20th century. At one time there were more elephants in Lampang than people.

Early on, warrior rulers recognized their usefulness in battle, and "Elephants served as the armored tanks of pre-modern Southeast Asian armies," according to American historian David K. Wyatt. The director of the mahout training program at the Lampang conservation center believes he is a reincarnation of one of the foot soldiers who ran beside elephants in campaigns against Burmese invaders.

While many of Thailand's elephants enjoy royal status, the gentle giant is under threat from the march of progress. Ivory poaching, a cross-border trade in live elephants, and urban encroachment have reduced Thailand's elephant population from about 100,000 a century ago to just 2,500 today. Despite conservation efforts, even these 2,500 face an uncertain future as mechanization and a 1988 government ban on private logging threw virtually all elephants and their mahouts out of work. Hundreds of mahouts took their elephants to Bangkok and other big cities to beg for money and food. The sight of an elephant begging for bananas curbside in Bangkok makes for an exotic snapshot, but the photo hides a grim reality. The elephants are kept in miserable urban conditions, usually penned in the tiny backyards of city tenements. It's been estimated that the poor living conditions, unsuitable diet, and city pollution combine to reduce their life expectancy by at least five years.

A nationwide action to rescue the urban elephants and resettle them in the country—mostly in Northern Thailand—is gathering pace. The National Elephant Institute near Lampang is a leader in this field, thanks largely to the efforts of an American expert, Richard Lair, and two young British volunteers. The 40 or so elephants that have found refuge at the center actually pay for their keep by working at various tasks, from entertaining visitors with shows of their logging skills to providing the raw material (dung) for a papermaking plant. The center has a school of elephant artists, trained by two New York artists, and an elephant orchestra. The art they make sells for $1,000 and more on the Internet, and the orchestra has produced two CDs. Several similar enterprises are dotted around Northern Thailand. All are humanely run. The alternative—a life on the streets of Bangkok—is just too depressing to consider.

—Robert Tilley

corners that you can easily escape the music. ✉*328 Tipchang Rd.* ☎*054/221861* ▭*AE, MC, V.*

> **WORD OF MOUTH**
>
> "The Thai elephant training camp in Lampang was special. The two-day mahout camp gave us a real taste for the animals—they are obviously well treated. The best part was the morning of the second day—you wake up very early, and take a long walk in the forest to get your elephant. You feed him snacks and then ride him back to camp as the mist lifts up from the forest. Fabulous." —4bams

WHERE TO STAY

¢ **Asia Lampang.** Although this hotel sits on a bustling street, most of the rooms are quiet enough to ensure a good night's sleep. Extensive renovation has given most of the rooms a sleek, modern look, and all have blue satin bedspreads and curtains. The airy terrace is just the place to relax on a warm evening. If you fancy singing along with the locals, head for karaoke in the Sweety Music Room. **Pros:** central location; open-sided restaurant with view of busy street scene. **Cons:** dismal lobby; some rooms need refurbishing. ✉*229 Boonyawat Rd.* ☎*054/227844 up to 47, 02/642–5497 Bangkok reservations* ⊕*www.asialampang.com* *71 rooms* *In-room: refrigerator (some). In-hotel: restaurant, bar, laundry service, parking (free)* ▭*MC, V.*

$$ **Lampang River Lodge.** Facing the Wang River, this lodge is in a forest. The simple but comfortable rooms are in Thai-style wooden pavilions near a small lake where you can untie a dinghy from the jetty and row around among the lotus blossoms, the ducks, and the noisy geese. The large, airy restaurant is often crammed with tour groups, but you shouldn't have a problem securing a quiet corner. To get away from the crowds, totter over the swaying bridge to the riverside restaurant and bar. The complex is 6 km (4 mi) south of Lampang. **Pros:** beautifully landscaped grounds. **Cons:** far from Lampang city center and shuttle bus is infrequent. ✉*330 Moo 11, off Chiang Mai-Lampang Hwy. 11, Tambon Champoo* ☎*054/336640* ⊕*www.lampangriverlodge.com* *60 rooms* *In-hotel: restaurant, bar, pool, laundry service* ▭*AE, MC, V.*

¢–$ **Lampang Wiengthong.** One of the city's best hotels, this modern high-rise has a number of luxuriously appointed rooms and suites. Its Drinks Palace bar features live music most nights. ■ **TIP→ The Wiengthip coffee shop and Wiengpana restaurant rank among Lampang's smartest eateries.** **Pros:** central location; bathrooms with tubs; horse-carriage stand in front of hotel. **Cons:** chain hotel atmosphere; package tour groups. ✉*138/109 Phaholyothin Rd.* ☎*054/225801* ⊕*www.lampangwiengthonghotel.com* *235 rooms* *In-hotel: 2 restaurants, bar, pool, laundry service, parking (free)* ▭*AE, MC, V.*

¢ **Riverside Guest House.** Under the same management as the nearby Riverside restaurant (⇨ *above*), this utterly enchanting little place has the same rustic coziness. Most of the snug, teak rooms overlook the Wang River—ask for Room 4, which is especially attractive, with its Northern Thai style. The Italian owner, Lorenza, has lived in Lampang for nearly 30 years and has a deep knowledge of the area, which she gladly shares with guests. **Pros:** homey atmosphere; garden hammocks.

Cons: noisy neighborhood dogs; insects. ✉ *286 Talad Kao Rd.* ☎ *054/227006* 🌐 *www.theriverside-lampang.com* ⇨ *19 rooms* ♿ *In-hotel: parking (free)* ▭ *MC, V.*

SHOPPING

Lampang is known for its blue, white, and orange pottery, much of it incorporating the image of a cockerel, the city's emblem. ■ **TIP→ You can find the best bargains at markets a few miles south of the city on the highway to Bangkok, or north of the city on the road to Chiang Mai.** The biggest pottery outlet is 2 km (1 mi) west of the city center, on the road to Phrae, at **Indra Ceramic** (✉ *382 Vajiravudh Damnoen Rd. [Lampang–Phrae Hwy.], 2 km [1 mi] from Lampang* ☎ *054/315591*). You can see the ceramics being made and also paint your own designs. The extensive showrooms feature a ceramic model city. In Lampang proper, Phaholyothin Road has several small showrooms. The best place for pottery is **Srisawat Ceramics** (✉ *316 Phaholyothin Rd.* ☎ *054/225931*).

NAN & ENVIRONS

Visitors looking for off-the-beaten-track territory usually head north from Chiang Mai and Chiang Rai to the Golden Triangle or west to Mae Hong Son. Relatively few venture east, toward Laos, but if time permits, it's a region that's well worth exploring. The center of the region is a provincial capital and ancient royal residence, Nan, some 70 km (42 mi) from the Laotian border. The city is very remote; roads to the border end in mountain trails and there are no frontier crossings, although there are ambitious, long-term plans to run a highway through the mountains to Luang Prabang.

Two roads link Nan with the west and the cities of Chiang Mai, Chiang Rai, and Lampang—they are both modern highways that sweep through some of Thailand's most spectacular scenery, following river valleys, penetrating forests of bamboo and teak, and skirting upland terraces of rice and maize. Hill tribe villages sit on the heights of the surrounding Doi Phu Chi (Phu Chi Mountains), where dozens of waterfalls, mountain river rapids, and revered caves beckon travelers with time on their hands. Here you can find Hmong and Lahu villages untouched by commercialism, and jungle trails where you, your elephant, and mahout beat virgin paths through the thick undergrowth.

The southern route from Chiang Mai to Nan passes through the ancient town of Phrae, the center of Thailand's richest teak-growing region and a pleasant overnight stop. The region has three wild, mountainous national parks: Doi Phak Long, 20 km (12 mi) west of Phrae on Route 1023; Doi Luang, south of Chiang Rai; and Doi Phukku, on the slopes of the mountain range that separates Thailand and Laos, some 80 km (48 mi) northeast of Nan.

CLOSE UP

Trekking

In the 1960s a few intrepid people in Northern Thailand started wandering through the countryside, finding rooms at the hill-tribe villages. By 1980 tour companies were organizing guided groups and sending them off for three- to seven-day treks. The level of difficulty of a Northern Thailand trek varies: you might traverse tough, hilly terrain for several hours or travel mostly by pickup and hike just the last few miles. Days are spent walking forest trails between villages, where you can sleep overnight. Accommodations are in huts, where the bed can be a wooden platform with no mattress. Food is likely to be a bowl of sticky rice and stewed vegetables. Travel light, but be sure to wear sturdy hiking shoes and to pack a sweater. Mosquito repellent is a must.

Always use a certified guide with papers stamped by the TAT. It's important to pick one who's familiar with local dialects and who knows which villages are not overrun with tour groups. It's also imperative that you discuss the route; that way you'll know what to expect. You can usually tell whether the guide is knowledgeable and respects the villagers, but question him thoroughly about his experience before you sign up. The best way to select a tour that is right for you is to talk to other travelers. Guides come and go, and what was true six months ago may not be today. The charge for a guided trek is around B800 per day.

Try to avoid the hot months of April and May, when trekking can be sweaty work even at high altitudes. The best time of year to make for the hills is the cool, dry season, between November and March.

Trekking is more than a popular pastime in Northern Thailand—it's big business. Some of the more accessible villages, particularly those inhabited by the long-necked women of the Karen people, have consequently come to resemble theme parks. Be clear about what you expect when booking a trek. Insist on the real thing, perhaps offering a bit more to achieve it. Better still, ask your hotel to recommend a good local guide. Gather as much information as you can from those who have just returned from a trek. Their advice will save you time, money, and frustration.

NAN

318 km (198 mi) southeast of Chiang Mai, 270 km (168 mi) southeast of Chiang Rai, 668 km (415 mi) northeast of Bangkok.

Near the border of Laos lies the city of Nan, a provincial capital founded in 1272. According to local legend, Lord Buddha, passing through Nan Valley, spotted an auspicious site for a temple to be built. By the late 13th century Nan was brought into Sukhothai's fold, but it maintained a fairly independent status until the last few decades.

GETTING HERE & AROUND

BY AIR A privately operated carrier, PBair, flies from Bangkok to Nan on Monday, Tuesday, Friday, and Sunday. Prices range from about B2,500 to B5,000; the flight takes 80 minutes. Songthaews meet incoming

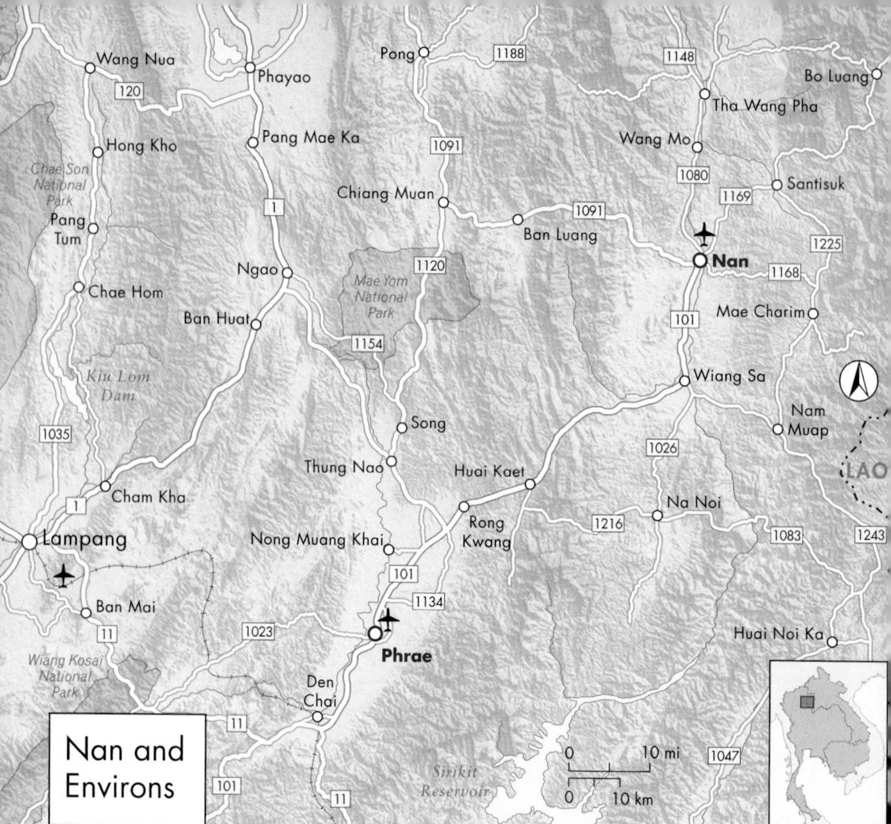

and charge about B50 for the 3-km (2-mi) drive south into central Nan.

BY BUS Several air-conditioned buses leave Bangkok and Chiang Mai daily for Nan, stopping en route at Phrae. The 11-hour journey from Bangkok to Nan costs B400–B600; it's eight hours from Chiang Mai to Nan and the cost is B300–B400. Air-conditioned buses also make the five-hour journey from Lampang to Nan. There's local bus service between Nan and Phrae.

BY CAR Hiring a car and driver is the easiest way to get to Nan from Lampang or Chiang Mai, but it will cost about B1,000 per day.

BY TAXI & TUK-TUK City transport in Nan is provided by a combination of tuk-tuks, songthaews, and samlors. All are cheap and trips within a city should seldom exceed B30.

BY TRAIN Nan is not on the railroad route, but a comfortable way of reaching the city from Bangkok is to take the Chiang Mai–bound train and change at Den Chai to a local bus for the remaining 146 km (87 mi) to Nan. The bus stops en route at Phrae.

ESSENTIALS

Emergencies **Nan Hospital** (✉ *Thawangpha Rd., Nan* ☎ *054/77160*).

Visitor & Tour Info Trips range from city tours of Nan and short cycling tours of the region to jungle trekking, elephant riding, and white-water rafting. (⇨ *Tourist information is available from the TAT office in Chiang Rai.)* **Fhu Travel** (✉*453/4 Sumondhevaraj Rd., Nan* ☎*054/710636* 🌐*www.fhutravel.com*). **Inter Tours** (✉*10/10 Khaluang Rd., Nan* ☎*054/710195*). **River Raft** (✉*50/6 Norkam Rd., Nan* ☎*054/710940*).

EXPLORING NAN

Nan is rich in teak plantations and fertile valleys that produce rice and superb oranges. The town of Nan itself is small; everything is within walking distance. Daily life centers on the morning and evening markets. ■ **TIP→ The Nan River, which flows past the eastern edge of town, draws visitors at the end of Buddhist Lent, in late October or early November, when traditional boat races are held.** Each longtail boat is carved out of a single tree trunk, and at least one capsizes every year, to the delight of the locals. In mid-December Nan honors its famous fruit crop with a special Golden Orange and Red Cross Fair—there's even a Miss Golden Orange contest. It's advisable to book hotels ahead of time for these events.

6

WHAT TO SEE

To get a sense of the region's art, visit the **National Museum,** a mansion built in 1923 for the prince who ruled Nan, Chao Suriyapong Pharittadit. The house itself is a work of art, a synthesis of overlapping red roofs, forest green doors and shutters, and brilliant white walls. There's a fine array of wood and bronze Buddha statues, musical instruments, ceramics, and other works of Lanna art. The revered "black elephant tusk" is also an attraction. The 3-foot-long, 40-pound tusk is actually dark brown in color, but that doesn't detract at all from its special role as a local good luck charm. ✉*Phalong Rd.* ☎*054/710561* 🎫*B30* ⏲*Daily 9–5.*

Fodor's Choice ★ Nan has one of the region's most unusual and beautiful temples, **Wat Pumin,** whose murals alone make a visit to this part of Northern Thailand worthwhile. It's an economically constructed temple, combining the main shrine hall and viharn, and qualifies as one of Northern Thailand's best examples of folk architecture. To enter, you climb a short flight of steps flanked by two superb nagas, their heads guarding the north entrance and their tails the south. The 16th-century temple was extensively renovated in 1865 and 1873, and at the end of the 19th century murals picturing everyday life were added to the inner walls. Some have a unique historical context—like the French colonial soldiers disembarking at a Mekong River port with their wives in crinolines. A fully rigged merchant ship and a primitive steamboat are portrayed as backdrops to scenes showing colonial soldiers leering at the pretty local girls corralled in a palace courtyard. Even the conventional Buddhist images have a lively originality, ranging from the traumas of hell to the joys of courtly life. The bot's central images are also quite unusual—four Sukhothai Buddhas locked in conflict with the evil Mara. ✉*Phalong Rd. Daily 8–6.*

Nan is dotted with other wats. **Wat Hua Wiang Tai** is the gaudiest, with a naga running along the top of the wall and lively murals painted on the viharn's exterior. ✉*Sumonthewarat Rd.*

Wat Suan Tan has a 15th-century bronze Buddha image. It's the scene of all-night fireworks during the annual Songkran festival in April. ✉*Tambon Nai Wiang.*

Wat Ming Muang contains a stone pillar erected at the founding of Nan, some 800 years ago. ✉*Suriyaphong Rd.*

Wat Chang Kham has one of only seven surviving solid-gold Buddha images from the Sukhothai period. Its large chedi is supported by elephant-shaped buttresses. ✉*Suriyaphong Rd.*

WHERE TO EAT

¢–$ THAI **Ruen Kaew.** Its name means Crystal House, and this riverside restaurant really is a gem. Guests step in through a profusion of bougainvillea onto a wooden deck directly overlooking the Nan River. A Thai band and singers perform from 6:30 PM every night. The Thai menu has some original touches—the chicken in a honey sauce, for instance, is a rare delight. ✉*1/1 Sumondhevaraj Rd.* ☎*054/710631* ▭*V.*

¢–$ THAI **Suriya Garden.** This substantial restaurant on the banks of the Nan River is a larger version of the nearby Ruen Kaew, with a wooden deck overlooking the water. Like its neighbor, it has added some interesting specialties to its conventional Thai menu—Chinese-style white bass or pig's hooves, for instance. A band and solo vocalists perform nightly. ✉*9 Sumondhevaraj Rd.* ☎*054/710687* ▭*MC, V.*

WHERE TO STAY

$ **City Park Hotel.** Nan's top hotel is a low-rise, ranch-style complex of buildings on the outskirts of the city, set in 12 acres of gardens. Rooms overlook either the gardens or the landscaped pool, and all have private balconies. The Chumpoo-Thip restaurant serves fresh produce from the hotel's own kitchen garden, where guests can walk and learn about the herbs and spices that season Thai cuisine. **Pros:** clean, well-maintained pool. **Cons:** far from town center. ✉*99 Yantarakitkosol Rd.* ☎*054/741343 up to 52* 🌐*www.thecityparkhotel.com* *129 rooms* *In-room: refrigerator. In-hotel: restaurant, room service, tennis court, pool, laundry service, Internet terminal, parking (free)* ▭*AE, MC, V.*

¢–$ **Dhevaraj.** Built around an attractive interior courtyard, which is romantically lighted for evening dining, the Dhevaraj has all the comforts and facilities of a top-class hotel. Rooms are cozily furnished and the bed linen is high quality. The location couldn't be better, across from the city market and within a short walk of all the sights. A welcome plate of fresh fruit in your room is a nice touch, but **TIP→ shun the complimentary "American" breakfast** (congealed fried eggs, warped ham, and tasteless sausage) in favor of a cup of Thai rice soup at the market. **Pros:** cool interior courtyard. **Cons:** lousy breakfast; some rooms need refurbishing. ✉*466 Sumondhevaraj Rd.* ☎*054/751577* 🌐*www.dhevarajhotel.com* *160 rooms* *In-room: refrigerator. In-hotel: 2 restaurants, pool, laundry service* ▭*MC, V.*

¢ **Nan Fah Hotel.** A reminder of the past, this old wooden Chinese hotel is worth a visit even if you're disinclined to stay in its rather dark rooms. The wide-plank floors are of a bygone age. A balcony overlooking the street is a great place to take in the town. Marvelous antiques are scattered around the hotel, and the delightful owner is happy to sell you some in the shop in the lobby. A live band plays in the restaurant most nights, so if you're planning on turning in early, ask for a room at the back of the hotel. **Pros:** central location, opposite market. **Cons:** creaking wood floors and eccentric plumbing. ✉ *436–440 Sumondhevaraj Rd.* ☎ *054/710284* *14 rooms* *In-hotel: restaurant, bar* *No credit cards.*

SPORTS & THE OUTDOORS

Nan is the ideal center from which to embark on treks through the nearby mountains, as well as raft and kayak trips along the rivers that cut through them. Khun Chompupach Sirsappuris has run Nan's leading tourist agency, **Fhu Travel and Information** (✉ *453/4 Sumondhevaraj Rd.* ☎ *054/710636 or 081/287–7209* 🌐 *www.fhutravel.com*), for 20 years and knows the region like her own backyard. She speaks fluent English, and has an impressive Web site describing tours and prices.

6

PHRAE

110 km (68 mi) southeast of Lampang, 118 km (73 mi) southwest of Nan.

A market town in a narrow valley, Phrae is well off the beaten path. It's a useful stopover on the 230-km (143-mi) journey from Lampang to Nan, but has little to offer the visitor apart from ruined city walls, some attractive and historic temples, and sturdy teak buildings that attest to its former importance as a center of the logging industry.

GETTING HERE & AROUND

Daily air-conditioned buses from Bangkok and Chiang Mai headed for Nan stop at Phrae. It's a 10-hour journey from Bangkok and five hours from Chiang Mai. Fares are B400 to B600. Air-conditioned buses travel between Lampang and Phrae (3 hours) daily. There's local bus service between Phrae and Nan, an uncomfortable but cheap journey of two to three hours between each center. Hiring a car and driver in Lampang or Chiang Mai is the easiest way to get here (about B1,000 per day).

EXPLORING PHRAE

The town's recorded history starts in the 12th century, when it was called Wiang Kosai, the Silk City. It remained an independent kingdom until the Ayutthaya period. Remains of these former times are seen in the crumbling city walls and moat, which separate the Old City from the new commercial sprawl.

WHAT TO SEE

On the northeastern edge of town stands **Wat Chom Sawan,** a beautiful monastery designed by a Burmese architect and built during the reign of King Rama V (1868–1910). The bot and viharn are combined to make one giant sweeping structure. ✉ *Yantrakitkoson Rd.*

Phrae's oldest building is **Wat Luang,** within the Old City walls. Although it was founded in the 12th century, renovations and expansions completely obscure so much of the original design that the only original section is a Lanna chedi with primitive elephant statues. A small museum on the grounds contains sacred Buddha images, swords, and texts. ✉ *Kham Lue Rd.*

Phrae is renowned in Northern Thailand for its fine teak houses. There are many to admire all over the city, but none to match what is claimed to be the world's largest teak structure, the **Ban Prathap Chai,** in the hamlet of Tambon Pa Maet near the southern edge of Phrae. Like many such houses, it's actually a reconstruction of several older houses—in this case, nine of them supported on 130 huge centuries-old teak posts. The result is remarkably harmonious. A tour of the rooms open to public view gives a fascinating picture of bourgeois life in the region. The space between the teak poles on the ground floor of the building is taken up by stalls selling a variety of handicrafts, including much carved teak. ✉ *Hwy. 1022, 10 km (5 mi) east of Phrae* ☎ *No phone* *B40* ⏲ *Daily 8–5.*

WHERE TO EAT & STAY

For a quick bite, there's a night market at Pratuchai Gate with numerous stalls offering cheap, tasty food.

¢ THAI ✕ **Ban Jai.** For authentic Lanna cuisine, you can't do better than this simple but superb restaurant. You're automatically served *kanom jin* (Chinese noodles) in basketwork dishes, with a spicy meat sauce, raw and pickled cabbage, and various condiments. If that's not to your taste, then order the *satay moo,* thin slices of lean pork on wooden skewers, served with a peanut sauce dip. In the evenings, every table has its own brazier for preparing the popular northern specialty, *moo kata,* a kind of pork stew. The open-sided, teak-floored dining area is shaded by ancient acacia trees, making it a cool retreat on warm evenings. ✉ *Chatawan Rd. 3* ☎ *No phone* ▭ *No credit cards.*

¢ **Nakorn Phrae Tower.** A curious but effective combination of a conventional high-rise and a Lanna-style aesthetic distinguishes this very comfortable central Phrae hotel. Traditionally dressed staff (the women in sarongs) offer a friendly welcome, and the Lanna touches extend to decorative features of the rooms, where local woods frame the beds and work areas. Phrae has very little nightlife, so the piano player in the lounge bar is a very popular local performer. **Pros:** center of Phrae's muted nightlife. **Cons:** favored by tour groups. ✉ *3 Muanghit Rd.* ☎ *054/521321* *139 rooms* *In-room: safe, refrigerator. In-hotel: restaurant, bar, laundry service, Internet terminal, parking (free)* ▭ *AE, DC, MC, V.*

THE MAE HONG SON LOOP

If you're driving to Mae Hong Son, the best way to get there is along a mountainous stretch of road known to travelers as "The Loop." The route runs from Chiang Mai to Mae Hong Son via Pai if you take the northern route, and via Mae Sariang if you take the southern one.

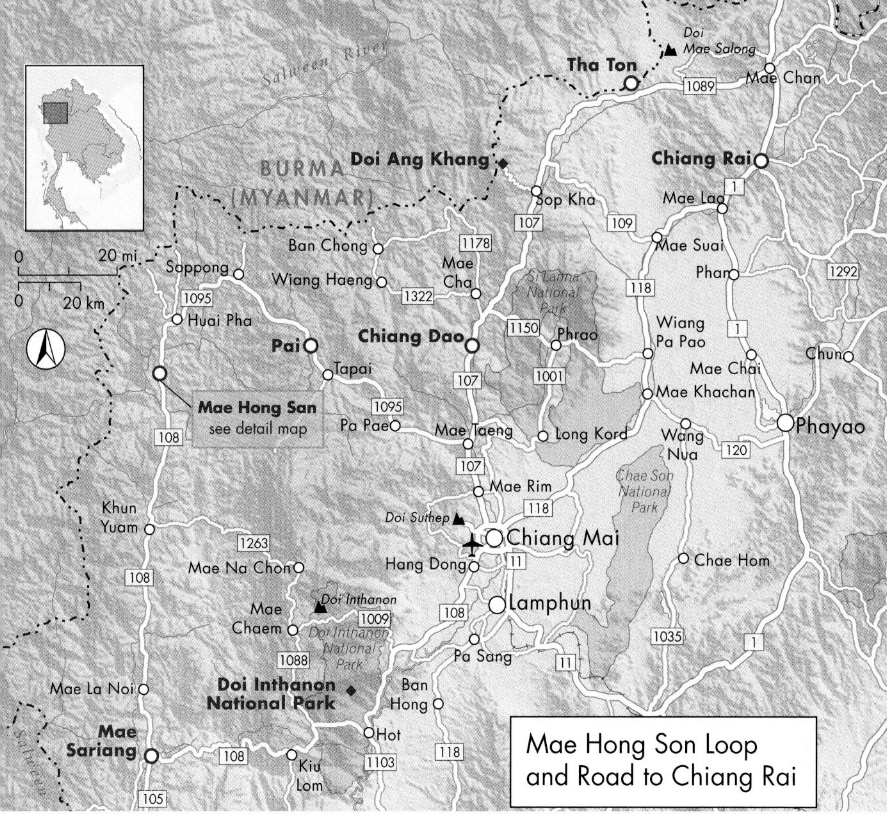

Which route offers the best views is the subject of much heated debate. The entire Loop is 615 km (382 mi) long. **TIP→ Allow at least four days to cover it—longer if you want to leave the road occasionally and visit the hot springs, waterfalls, and grottos found along the way.**

PAI

160 km (99 mi) northwest of Chiang Mai, 110 km (68 mi) east of Mae Hong Son.

Disastrous floods and mud slides in the surrounding mountains devastated this very popular tourist haunt in 2005, but the town rapidly recovered and now the only reminders of the catastrophe are a few high-water marks on the walls of some buildings and empty swathes of riverside land. A building boom is again in full swing as the former market town struggles to cope with another annual flood—the thousands of visitors who outnumber the locals in high season.

It was exhausted backpackers looking for a stopover along the serpentine road between Chiang Mai and Mae Hong Son who discovered Pai in the late 1980s. In 1991 it had seven modest guesthouses and three restaurants; now its frontier-style streets are lined with restaurants and bars of every description, cheap guesthouses and smart hotels, art

DID YOU KNOW?

Remote Mae Salong, home to the Princess Mother Pagoda, was a major opium production area until the late 1980s. Today the mountainous region, nicknamed Little Switzerland, is popular with backpackers; its notable crop is high-quality oolong tea.

galleries, and chic coffeehouses, while every class of resort, from back-to-nature to luxury, nestles in the surrounding hills. Thus far, Pai has managed to retain its slightly-off-the-beaten-path appeal, but that may change as Bangkok property investors pour money into its infrastructure and flights arrive daily from Chiang Mai.

GETTING HERE & AROUND

BY AIR A daily air service between Chiang Mai and Pai, operated by SGA, uses 12-seater aircraft for the 20-minute flight. It's an excellent alternative to the long, tortuous drive.

BY BUS Buses traveling between Mae Hong Son and Chiang Mai stop in Pai. They take four hours for the 120-km (75-mi) journey from Chiang Mai and an additional five hours to cover the 130-km (81-mi) from Pai to Mae Hong Son. Fares for each stretch vary from about B100 to B200. Buses stop in the center of Pai.

BY CAR A hired car does the trip from Chiang Mai to Pai one hour faster than the buses and cuts the journey time from Pai to Mae Hong Son by about the same margin.

EXPLORING PAI

Although Pai lies in a flat valley, a 10-minute drive in any direction brings you to a rugged upland terrain with stands of wild teak, groves of towering bamboo, and clusters of palm and banana trees, hiding out-of-the-way resorts catering to visitors who seek peace and quiet. At night, the surrounding fields and forest seems to enfold the town in a black embrace. As you enter Pai from the direction of Chiang Mai, you'll cross the so-called World War II Memorial Bridge, which was stolen from Chiang Mai during the Japanese advance through Northern Thailand and rebuilt here to carry heavy armor over the Pai River. When the Japanese left, they neglected to return the bridge to Chiang Mai. Residents of that city are perfectly happy, as they eventually built a much more handsome river crossing.

WHERE TO EAT

¢–$ CAFE ✕ **All About Coffee.** One of Pai's historic merchant houses has been converted into a coffee shop that could grace any fashionable city street in the world. More than 20 different kinds of java are on the menu, which is also packed with delicacies from the café's own bakery. The mezzanine floor has a gallery of works by local artists. ✉ *100, Moo 1, Chaisongkram Rd.* ☎ *053/699429* ▭ *No credit cards* ⏲ *Closes at 6 PM.*

¢–$ THAI ✕ **Baan Pai.** The town's central meeting point is this airy, teak restaurant. Dishes such as spaghetti tend to crowd out the Thai specialties, but the customers seem to come to this friendly hangout more for the atmosphere than for the food. ✉ *7 Moo 3, Rungsiyanon Rd., Baan Pakham, Tambon Viengtai* ☎ *053/699912* ▭ *MC, V.*

$ ECLECTIC ✕ **Café del Doi.** There's nowhere better in Pai to watch the sun sink over the surrounding mountains than this bustling bar-restaurant on a hillside just outside the town limits. The owners ran a similarly successful establishment in Chiang Mai before settling in Pai, and many of their old regulars join the nightly crowds drawn by the live bands that perform regularly. The menu is eclectic—ranging from hill-tribe food to Tex-Mex and Italian. In winter months underfloor heating is provided by water from the nearby hot springs. ✉*Pai–Chiang Mai Rd., Km 5* ☎*09/851–9621 or 053/693230* *Reservations not accepted* *No credit cards.*

¢–$ CAFE ✕**Edible Jazz.** The international menu at this friendly little café, which includes chili con carne and good burritos, matches the flavor of the music. It's one of few places in Pai where you can hear live jazz. ✉*Tambon Viengtai* ☎*053/232960* *No credit cards.*

$ THAI ✕**House of Glass.** Glass isn't much in evidence at this open-air roughly built shack of a place. The buffet is an unbeatable value—pumpkin soup, various curries, fish-and-chips, and fresh fruit, all for B69. ✉*Down an unnamed alley in Tambon Viengtai* ☎*No phone* *No credit cards.*

PAI: DEMURE HAMLET OR PARTY TOWN?

Pai has a sizable Muslim population, which is why some of the guesthouses post notices asking foreign visitors to refrain from public displays of affection. Immodest clothing is frowned upon, so bikini tops and other revealing items are definitely out. The music bars close early, meaning that by 1 AM the town slumbers beneath the tropical sky. Nevertheless, quiet partying continues behind the shutters of the teak cabins that make up much of the tourist lodgings. This is, after all, backpacker territory.

$–$$ ECLECTIC ✕**Pai Corner.** German Thomas Casper ("Tom" to his regulars) has been running this simple, thatch bar and restaurant for more than 15 years, and he's such a mine of information that he wrote the town's definitive guidebook. German specialties figure largely (literally) on the menu, but classic Northern Thai dishes such as *khao soy* (spicy soup with crispy noodles and chicken) can also be found. ✉*53 Moo 4, Raddamrong Rd.* ☎*010/303195* *No credit cards.*

WHERE TO STAY

$–$$ Fodor's Choice ★ **Belle Villa.** This appealing little resort's 24 teak chalets (traditional outside, pure luxury inside) are perched on stilts in a tropical garden that blends seamlessly with the neighboring rice paddies and the foothills of the nearby mountains. A thatched-roof reception area adds an additional exotic touch. The terrace restaurant ($$), overlooking the pool and a lotus-covered pond, is one of the region's best, serving fish from the Pai River and lamb from New Zealand. **Pros:** infinity pool, giving impression of swimming in a rice paddy; horse-and-buggy transport to town. **Cons:** 15-minute drive from town. ✉*113 Moo 6, Huay Poo-Wiang Nua Rd., Tambon Wiang Tai* ☎*053/698226, 02/693–2895 in Bangkok* *www.bellevillaresort.com* *24 chalets* *In-room: safe, refrigerator, Wi-Fi. In-hotel: restaurant, room service, bar, pool, laundry service* *AE, DC, MC, V.*

¢–$ **Brook View.** The brook babbles right outside your cabin window if you ask for a room with a view at this well-run little resort. The teak cabins are tiny, but scrupulously clean. Those at the water's edge have terraces where you can soak up the uninterrupted view of sugarcane fields and the mountains beyond. **Pros:** near town, but still "away from it all." **Cons:** some cabins are small, with no river view; staff keep a very low profile. ✉132 Moo 1, Tambon Wiang Tai ☎053/699366 ✉brookviewpai@yahoo.com 12 rooms In-room: refrigerator. In-hotel: parking (free) No credit cards.

> **WORD OF MOUTH**
>
> "We stayed in Pai about two years ago when driving the [Mae Hong Son] loop from Chiang Mai and loved it. There were a few hippy types about but it was nothing like the Khao San Road. There are quite a few backpackers hostels in the center but we stayed just outside of town at the Belle Vista and it was very peaceful. A great place to stay for a few days. In fact I preferred it to MHS." —crellston

¢ **Cave Lodge.** The chatter of gibbons wakes you up at this remote mountain lodge between Pai and Mae Hong Son. The cave after which it is named, just a short walk from the lodge, is one of the region's most spectacular caverns, with wall paintings and prehistoric coffins. The Australian owner of the lodge organizes treks and river tours in the surrounding jungle. **Pros:** the lodge's bread and pastries, cooked in its wood-fired oven. **Cons:** snakes lurk in the grounds; Pai is an hour's drive away. ✉*90 Moo 2, 15 Moo 1, Pang Mapa, Mae Hong Son* ☎*053/617203* *www.cavelodge.com* *10 rooms* *In-hotel: restaurant, bar* *AE, MC, V.*

$–$$ **Paivimaan Resort.** Vimann means "heaven," and this fine resort, opened in 2006, certainly commands a heavenly spot on the banks of the Pai River. Deluxe rooms in the main house, a stately building constructed almost entirely of teak, are enormous and opulently furnished in Lanna style. Two-story villas are arranged along a path that leads down to the river. The hotel has its own motorcycle taxi service to ferry guests around Pai. **Pros:** friendly family welcome; four-poster beds in "deluxe" rooms. **Cons:** villa rooms are small. ✉*Moo 3, Tetsaban Rd.* ☎*053/699403* *www.paivimaan.com* *12 rooms* *In-room: refrigerator. In-hotel: restaurant, room service, bar, parking (free)* *AE, MC, V.*

¢ **Tree House.** The rooms with the best views at this riverside "hotel" outside Pai are only for the most adventurous travelers—they're nestled in the upper branches of an enormous rain tree. There are three of these wooden cabins, which are simply furnished and share two bathrooms. For those who prefer to keep their feet on the ground, there are seven simple bungalows on the riverbank. **Pros:** terrace bar-restaurant with fine river views. **Cons:** 20-minute drive from town; popular for seminars so can get crowded. ✉*90 Moo 2, Tambon Machee* ☎*081/911–3640* *www.paitreehouse.com* *10 rooms* *In-hotel: restaurant, bar* *AE, MC, V.*

NIGHTLIFE

In high season, Pai is packed with backpackers looking for a place to party. Pai's top music bar is **Bepop** (✉*188 Moo 8, Tambon Viengtai* ☎*053/698046*), which throbs nightly to the sounds of visiting bands. At popular backpacker hangout **Phu Pai Art Cafe** (✉*21 Rangiyanon Rd., Tambon Viangtai* ☎*084/2098169*), bands perform every night beginning at 9:30. A good place to chill out in the early evening is the aptly named **Ting Tong ("crazy") Bar** (✉*55 Moo 4, Tambon Viengtai*

☎*048/073781*). On warm, rainless evenings you can lie on cushions and count the stars.

SPORTS & THE OUTDOORS

While in Pai, you can join a white-water rafting trip sponsored by **Pai in the Sky Rafting** (✉*114 Moo 4, Tambon Viengtai* ☎*053/699145 or 084/174–6157*). The two-day outing on the Khong River sends you through steep-sided gorges, past spectacular waterfalls, and over 15 sets of rapids. An overnight stop is made at the Pai in the Sky camp, near the confluence of the Pai and Kohong rivers, before reaching the end point outside Mae Hong Son. The trips, costing B2,000, are made daily June to February, when the rivers are at their peak.

MAE SARIANG

175 km (109 mi) southwest of Chiang Mai, 140 km (87 mi) south of Mae Hong Son.

The southern route of the Loop runs through Mae Sariang, a neat little market town that sits beside the Yuam River. With two very comfortable hotels and a handful of good restaurants, the town makes a good base for trekking in the nearby Salawin National Park or for boat trips on the Salawin River, which borders Myanmar.

GETTING HERE & AROUND

Buses from Chiang Mai's Chiang Phuak bus station take about four hours to reach Mae Sariang. Fares range from B200 to B300. A few songthaews ply the few streets of Mae Sariang, but the town is small and compact and can be covered very easily on foot.

EXPLORING MAE SARIANG

Near Mae Sariang, the road winds through some of Thailand's most spectacular mountain scenery, with seemingly endless panoramas opening up through gaps in the thick teak forests that line the route. You'll pass hill tribe villages where time seems to have stood still and Karen women go to market proudly in their traditional dress.

WHAT TO SEE

In the village of Khun Yuam, 100 km (62 mi) north of Mae Sariang, you can find one of the region's most unusual and, for many, most poignant museums, the **World War II Memorial Museum.** The modest little building commemorates the hundreds of Japanese soldiers who died here on their chaotic retreat from the Allied armies in Myanmar. Locals took in the dejected and defeated men. A local historian later gathered the belongings they left behind: rifles, uniforms, cooking utensils, personal photographs, and documents. They provide a fascinating glimpse into a little-known chapter of World War II. Outside is a graveyard of old military vehicles, including an Allied truck presumably commandeered by the Japanese on their retreat east. ✉*Mae Hong Son Rd.* 🎫*B10* ⏲*Daily 8–4.*

WHERE TO EAT & STAY

¢–$ THAI **Riverside.** This restaurant, on the open-air terrace of an inexpensive guesthouse, is on a bend of the Yuam River, commanding an impressive view of rice paddies and the mountains beyond. The menu is simple, but the panoramic view is reason enough to eat here. The guesthouse, a rambling wooden building cluttered with antique bits and bobs ranging from worm-eaten farm implements to antlers, has 18 reasonably comfortable rooms (B180 to B350). *85 Langpanich Rd. 053/681188 or 053/682592 No credit cards.*

¢ **Riverhouse Hotel.** Cooling breezes from the Yuam River waft through the open-plan reception area, lounge, and dining room of this attractive hotel. Rooms are a simple but elegant synthesis of white walls, dark woods, and plain cotton drapes, with small terraces overlooking the river (Room 23 has a lamyai tree growing through its outside deck). The 12 rooms are quickly taken in high season, so **TIP→ if the hotel is full, the nearby, larger Riverhouse Resort (under the same management) is recommended.** It's more expensive (B1,550–B2,700) but has more facilities. **Pros:** cozy, timber-walled bathrooms. **Cons:** limited restaurant menu. *77 Langpanich Rd. 053/621201 www.riverhousehotels.com 12 rooms In-hotel: restaurant, bar No credit cards.*

6

MAE HONG SON

245 km (152 mi) northwest of Chiang Mai via Pai, 368 km (229 mi) via Mae Sariang.

Stressed-out residents of Bangkok and other cities have transformed this remote, mountain-ringed market town into one of Northern Thailand's major resort areas. Some handsome hotels have arisen in recent years to cater to them. Overseas travelers also love the town because of its easy access to some of Thailand's most beautiful countryside.

GETTING HERE & AROUND

BY AIR SGA Airlines flies five times a week between Chiang Mai and Mae Hong Son (40 minutes; about B1,700). The Mae Hong Son Airport is at the town's northern edge. Songthaews run to the city center for around B50. In March and April, smoke from slash-and-burn fires often causes flight cancellations.

BY BUS Chiang Mai's Arcade Bus Terminal serves Mae Hong Son. Several buses depart daily on an eight-hour journey that follows the northern section of the Loop, via Pai. Buses stop in the center of town.

BY CAR If you choose to rent a car, you'll probably do it in Chiang Mai, but Avis also has an office at Mae Hong Son Airport, if needed.

TIP→ The road to Mae Hong Son from Chiang Mai has more than 1,200 curves, so make sure your rental car has power steering. The most comfortable way to travel the route and enjoy the breathtaking mountain scenery is to let somebody else do the driving. The Loop road brings you here from either direction; the northern route through Pai (six hours) is a more attractive trip; the southern route through Mae Sariang (eight hours) is easier driving.

ESSENTIALS

Emergencies **Tourist Police** (✉ *Rajadrama Phithak Rd., Mae Hong Son* ☎ *053/611812*).

VISITOR & TOUR INFO

A tourist info kiosk (with erratic hours) lies on the corner of Khunlum Prapas and Chamnan Salit roads.

EXPLORING MAE HONG SON

For a small town, Mae Hong Son has some notable temples, thanks to immigrants from nearby Myanmar, where Burmese architecture and decorative arts were historically more advanced. Two of the temples, Wat Chong Kham and Wat Kham Klang, sit on the banks of a placid lake in the center of town, forming a breathtakingly beautiful ensemble of golden spires. Within a short drive are dozens of villages inhabited by the Karen, the so-called "long-neck" people. Fine handicrafts are produced in these hamlets, whose inhabitants trek daily to Mae Hong Son to sell their wares at the lively morning market and along the lakeside promenade.

Although Mae Hong Son offers a welcome cool retreat during the sometimes unbearably hot months of March and April, the mountains can be obscured during that part of the year by the fires set by farmers to clear their fields. One of the local names for Mae Hong Son translates as "City of the Three Mists." The other two are the clouds that creep through the valleys in the depths of winter and the gray monsoons of the rainy season.

TOP ATTRACTIONS

❷ **Wat Chong Klang.** This temple is worth visiting to see a collection of figurines brought from Myanmar more than a century ago. The teak-wood carvings depict an astonishing range of Burmese individuals, from peasants to nobles. ✉ *Chamnansathit Rd.*

❹ **Wat Hua Wiang.** Mae Hong Son's most celebrated Buddha image—one of the most revered in Northern Thailand—is inside this temple. Its origins are clear—note the Burmese-style long earlobes, a symbol of the Buddha's omniscience. ✉ *Panishwatana Rd.*

❶ **Wat Phra That Doi Kong Mu.** On the top of Doi Kong Mu, this temple has a remarkable view of the surrounding mountains. The temple's two chedis contain the ashes of 19th-century monks. ✉ *West of Mae Hong Son*

ALSO WORTH SEEING

❺ ★ **Thampla-Phasua Waterfall National Park.** About 16 km (10 mi) from Mae Hong Son, this park has one of the region's strangest sights—a grotto with a dark, cisternlike pool overflowing with fat mountain carp. The pool is fed by a mountain stream that is also full of thrashing fish fighting to get into the cave. Why? Nobody knows. It's a secret that draws thousands of Thai visitors a year. Some see a mystical meaning in the strange sight. The cave is a pleasant 10-minute stroll from the park's headquarters. ✉ *70 Moo 1, Huay Pa* ☎ *053/619036* *Free.*

Thampla-Phausa Waterfall N.P. **5**
Wat Chong Kham **3**
Wat Chong Klang **2**
Wat Hua Wiang . . **4**
Wat Phra That Doi Kong Mu **1**

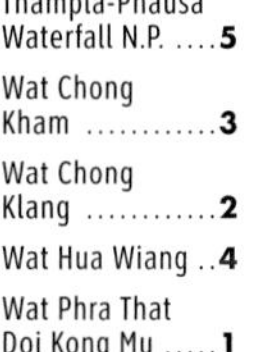

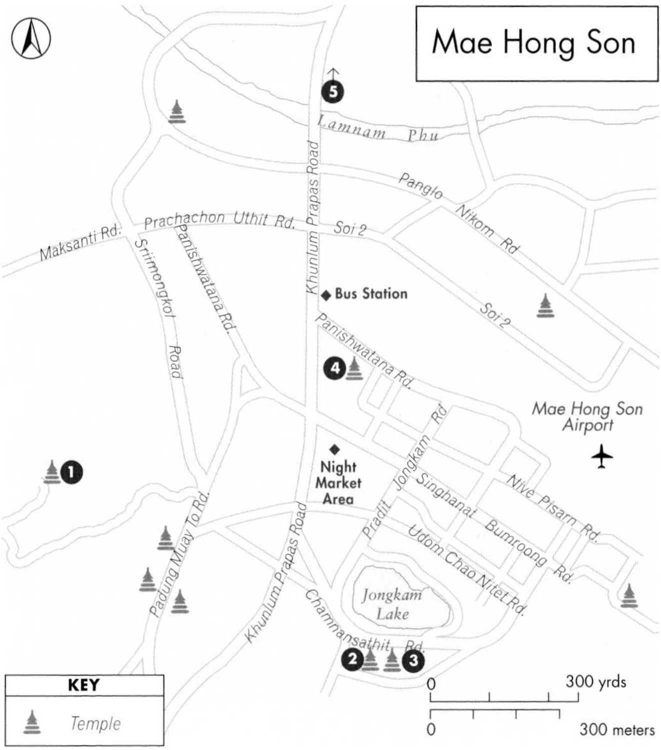

❸ ★ **Wat Chong Kham.** A wonderfully self-satisfied Burmese-style Buddha, the cares of the world far from his arched brow, watches over the temple, which has a fine pulpit carved with incredible precision. ✉ *Chamnansathit Rd.*

WHERE TO EAT

¢–$ THAI ✕ **Bai Fern.** Mae Hong Son's main thoroughfare, Khunlum Prapas Road, is lined with inexpensive restaurants serving local cuisine. Bai Fern is among the best. In the spacious dining room you eat in typical Thai style, amid solid teak columns and beneath whirling fans. Among the array of Thai dishes, pork ribs with pineapple stands out as a highly individual and tasty creation. ✉ *87 Khunlum Prapas Rd.* ☎ *053/611374* ▭ *MC, V.*

$ THAI ✕ **Lakeside Bar and Restaurant.** This is the best of the restaurants that border Mae Hong Son's city lake, and its terrace is an ideal place to

SUNSET VIEWS

For a giddy view of Mae Hong Son and the surrounding mountains, take a deep breath and trudge up Doi Kong Mu, a hill on the western edge of town. It's well worth the effort—from here you can see the mountains on the border of Myanmar (it's particularly lovely at sunset). There's another shade of gold to admire—a flame-surrounded white-marble Buddha in a hilltop temple called Wat Phra That Doi Kong Mu.

sit and watch the sun drop over the nearby mountains. Northern Thai dishes dominate the menu—try *hang led*, a delicious pork curry spiced with ginger. ✉ *2/3 Khunlum Prapas Rd.* ☎ *053/611779* ▭ *MC, V.*

WHERE TO STAY

$$ **Fern Resort.** The room rate is relatively expensive but it buys unexpected luxury in the midst of beautiful countryside outside Mae Hong Son. Thirty bungalows in steep-eaved Shan style are scattered over a valley of former rice paddies. They are all comfortably furnished in bamboo and teak, and have private terraces. The rooms have no TVs or telephones—the owners of this "eco-resort" want to guarantee an away-from-it-all experience. **Pros:** regular barbecue nights. **Cons:** 15-minute drive from town, although resort does have a shuttle bus; mosquitos. ✉ *10 Ban Hua Nam Mae Sakut, Tambon Pha Bong* ☎ *053/686110 or 053/686111* 🌐 *www.fernresort.info* *30 rooms* *In-hotel: restaurant, pool, laundry service* ▭ *MC, V.*

$$ ★ **Imperial Tara Mae Hong Son.** Set amid mature teak trees, this fine hotel was designed to blend in with the surroundings. Bungalows in landscaped gardens have both front and back porches, giving the teak-floored and bamboo-furnished rooms a light and airy feel. Golden Teak, which serves excellent Thai, Chinese, and European dishes, has a glassed-in section for chilly mornings and evenings. The restaurant and bar face the valley, as does the beautifully landscaped pool area. **Pros:** pleasant walks in the grounds. **Cons:** some rooms need refurbishing; long walk from town, although hotel offers regular shuttle-bus service. ✉ *149 Moo 8, Tambon Pang Moo* ☎ *053/611473, 02/261–9000 in Bangkok* 🌐 *www.imperialhotels.com/taramaehongson* *104 rooms* *In-room: refrigerator. In-hotel: restaurant, bar, pool, gym, laundry service* ▭ *AE, DC, MC, V.*

¢ **Panorama Hotel.** This centrally located hotel lives up to its name with upper-floor rooms that have sweeping views of the mountains surrounding the city. Twenty of the rooms are in a guesthouse annex. All rooms are simply but comfortably furnished, decorated with Northern Thai handicrafts. **Pros:** central location; helpful tour desk. **Cons:** some rooms are showing their age; cleaning service could be more efficient. ✉ *51 Khunlum Prapas Rd.* ☎ *053/611757 up to 62* *463 rooms* *In-room: no a/c (some), refrigerator. In-hotel: restaurant, room service, bar, Internet terminal* ▭ *MC, V.*

¢ **Rim Nam Klang Doi.** This retreat, about 7 km (4 mi) outside Mae Hong Son, is an especially good value. Some of the cozy rooms overlook the Pai River, while others have views of the tropical grounds. A minivan shuttles you to town for B100. **Pros:** helpful tour service; fine local walks. **Cons:** shuttle-bus service to town is erratic. ✉ *108 Ban Huay Dua* ☎ *053/612142* *39 rooms* *In-room: no a/c (some). In-hotel: restaurant, pool* ▭ *MC, V.*

THE ROAD TO CHIANG RAI

Winding your way from Chiang Mai to Chiang Rai, the hub of the fabled Golden Triangle, will take you past Chiang Dao, best known for its astonishing cave complex; Tha Ton, a pretty riverside town on the Myanmar border, which has many outdoor activities; and Doi Ang Khang, a small, remote settlement—with one very fancy resort.

CHIANG DAO

★ *72 km (40 mi) north of Chiang Mai.*

The dusty, rather delapidated village of Chiang Dao has two claims to fame: Thailand's third highest mountain, 7,500-foot Doi Chiang Dao, which leaps up almost vertically from the valley floor, and the country's most spectacular caves, which penetrate more than 10 km (6 mi) into the massif. If you want to explore more of the mountain, hire a guide.

GETTING HERE & AROUND

Hourly bus services run from Chiang Mai's Chiang Phuak Bus Terminal. The fare is B100 to B200, depending on the type of service (express, air-conditioned, etc.). Buses stop right on the main road in town.

6

EXPLORING CHIANG DAO

Caves have a mystic hold over Buddhist Thais, and foreign visitors to Chiang Dao's famous caverns find themselves vastly outnumbered by the locals. If you're at all claustrophobic, join a group of Thais to explore the caves, which are thought to penetrate more than 10 km (6 mi) into the small town's guardian mountain, Doi Chiang Dao. Only a few hundred meters are lit; if you want to explore further, hire a local guide with a lantern (about B100). The mountain can be scaled without difficulty in a day, but even just an hour or two of tough walking can bring you to viewpoints with amazing panoramas.

Thailand's most famous caves, the **Chiang Dao Caves,** run deep into the mountain that broods over the small town of Chiang Dao. The caverns, only some of which are lit, contain spectacular stalagmites and stalagtites and hundreds of Buddha statues and other votive items, placed there by devout Buddhists, for whom caves have a deep religious significance. ■ TIP→ **About half the caves have electric lights, but make sure you have a flashlight in your pocket in case there's a power failure.** ✉ *About 3 km (2 mi) west of town* ☎ *053/248604* 🎫 *B10* ⏲ *Daily 8–5.*

WHERE TO STAY

¢–$ **Chiang Dao Nest.** For a back-to-nature experience, this remote little resort can't be beaten. Chalets cluster at the foot of Chiang Dao's spectacular mountain, so great upland views are guaranteed. The chalets are simple but clean, and visitors don't stay long in their rooms anyway—the stunning surrounding countryside offers unlimited walking and biking trails. The British owner's Thai wife, Wicha, runs the best restaurant between Chiang Mai and Chiang Rai. **Pros:** total seclusion; great food; new pool installed in 2008. **Cons:** some rooms need refurbishing; insects. ✉*144/4 Moo 5, Chiang Dao* ☎*053/456242* 🌐*www.chiangdao.com/nest* *16 chalets* *In-room: no a/c (some). In-hotel: restaurant, pool, bicycles, laundry service, Wi-Fi* *No credit cards.*

¢ **Rim Doi Resort.** Rim Doi means "on the edge of the mountain," so it's fitting that two extraordinary peaks loom over this peaceful little resort near Chiang Dao. After a day exploring the nearby caves or venturing into the mountains, it's just the place to relax and prepare for the journey farther north. You'll probably be tempted to stay longer than one night. Just B350 buys you a comfortable bed in a rustic bungalow, while a more stylish room in a modern extension overlooking a placid lake is an unbeatable B800. **Pros:** pleasant walks on the grounds; anglers can hire a rod and fish for perch in the resort's well-stocked lake. **Cons:** staff have limited English-language skills. ✉*46 Moo 4, Muang Ghay* ☎*053/375028* 🌐*www.rimdoiresort.com* *40 rooms* *In-room: refrigerator. In-hotel: restaurant, bar* *MC, V.*

DOI ANG KHANG

60 km (36 mi) north of Chiang Dao.

Ang means "bowl," and that sums up the mountaintop location of this remote corner of Thailand. A tiny, two-street settlement shares the small valley with the orchards and gardens of a royal agricultural project, which grows temperate fruits and vegetables found nowhere else in Thailand.

GETTING HERE & AROUND

From Chiang Dao take highways 1178 and 1340 north to Doi Ang Khang. Local bus services connect the two towns, stopping in the center of Doi Ang Khang.

EXPLORING DOI ANG KHANG

The orchards, gardens, and hothouses of the royal project are open to the public, and at various times of the year you can buy pears, apples, plums, and peaches harvested directly from the trees. Not many tourists find their way into this border territory, so you'll get a warm welcome from the people who inhabit the dusty little village.

WHERE TO STAY

$$$ **Ang Khang Nature Resort.** Amari, which normally runs luxurious city hotels, manages this stylish country resort in the mountains near Doi Ang Khan. Rooms have all the comforts of Amari's downtown digs, with teak furnishings and locally woven fabrics. All rooms have private balconies, many of them with spectacular views of the mountains. **Pros:** good restaurant, the Camellia, with first-class cuisine; open log fire in the lobby in cool season. **Cons:** 2 km (1 mi) from the village center. ✉*1/1 Moo 5 Baan Koom, Tambon Mae Ngon, Amphoe Fang, Doi Ang Khang* ☎*053/450110* 🌐*www.amari.com/angkhang* *72 room. In-hotel: restaurant, bicycles, laundry service, Internet terminal* *AE, DC, MC, V.*

THA TON

90 km (56 mi) north of Chiang Dao.

North of Chiang Dao lies the pretty resort town of Tha Ton, which sits on the River Kok right across the border from Myanmar. The local temple, Wat Tha Ton, is built on a cliff overlooking the town. From the bridge below, boats set off for trips on the River Kok, some of them headed for Chiang Rai, 130 km (81 mi) away.

Tha Ton is a pleasant base for touring this mountainous region. The 1089 and 1130 highways that run north, close to the Burmese border, pass through villages that are more Chinese than Thai, inhabited by descendants of Kuomintang nationalist forces who fled here from Mao Tse Tung's army in the civil war that gave birth to the People's Republic of China. The largest community is Mae Salong (⇨ *Chiang Rai, below*).

GETTING HERE & AROUND

Six buses a day leave Chiang Mai's Chiang Phuak bus station for the four-hour journey to Tha Ton. Fares range from B150 to B250. Boats leave Chiang Rai for the four-hour upstream journey to Tha Ton at 10:30 AM. The single fare is B350.

WHERE TO STAY

$$ **Maekok River Village Resort.** This remarkable resort, a combination of hotel and outdoor education center is in a beautiful location on the Kok River, with sweeping views of the winding waterway, rice paddies, maize fields and orchards, and the mountains beyond. Accommodation is in modern rooms and villas, with teak built-in furniture. An outdoor education center, which attracts young people from throughout the world, is part of the complex but with separate facilities and grounds. **Pros:** snug bar with open fireplace for winter evenings; friendly and knowledgeable British management. **Cons:** kids at the education center can be noisy. ✉ *1 km from Tha Ton on road to Chiang Rai* ✉ *Box 3, Mae Ai, Chiang Mai, 50280* ☎ *053/459355* 🌐 *www.maekok-river-village-resort.com* *36 rooms* *In-room: refrigerator. In-hotel: restaurant, room service, bars, pool, water sports, laundry service, Internet terminal, no-smoking rooms.*

CHIANG RAI & THE GOLDEN TRIANGLE

This fabled area is a beautiful stretch of rolling uplands that conceal remote hill tribe villages and drop down to the broad Mekong, which is backed on its far side by the mountains of Laos. Although some 60 km (37 mi) to the south, Chiang Rai is its natural capital and a city equipped with the infrastructure for touring the entire region.

The region's involvement in the lucrative opium trade began in the late 19th century, when migrating hill tribes introduced poppy cultivation. For more than 100 years the opium produced from poppy fields was the region's main source of income. Even today, despite vigorous official suppression and a royal project to wean farmers away from the opium trade, the mountains of the Golden Triangle conceal isolated poppy plantations. Scarcely a week goes by without a bloody clash between Thai police and suspected opium traders.

Despite its associations with the opium trade, the Golden Triangle is still regarded as a geographical area, varying in size and interpretation from the few square yards where the borders of Thailand, Myanmar, and Laos actually meet to a 40,000-square-km (15,440-square-mi) region where the opium-yielding poppies are still cultivated. That region includes much of Thailand's Chiang Rai Province, where strenuous and sometimes controversial police raids have severely curbed opium production and trade. The royal program to encourage farmers to plant alternative crops is also paying dividends.

THE RUBBER TRIANGLE

En route to the Golden Triangle you'll pass through a small area known as the Rubber Triangle—and not because of any rubber trees. It's an offshoot of Bangkok's famous Cabbages and Condoms restaurant, which was founded by Thai politician Mechai Viravaidya, who led a successful campaign to combat AIDS. The **Cabbages and Condoms Inn and Restaurant** (✉ *Wiang Pa Pao, Chiang Rai* ☎ *053/952312* 🌐 *www.pda.or.th*) is about halfway between Chiang Mai and Chiang Rai, and is identified by a sign: YOU HAVE ARRIVED AT THE RUBBER TRIANGLE. Proceeds go toward funding development programs.

Whatever the size of the actual triangle is thought to be, its apex is the riverside village of Ban Sop Ruak, once a bustling center of the region's opium trade. An archway on the Mekong riverbank at Ban Sop Ruak invites visitors to step symbolically into the Golden Triangle, and a large golden Buddha watches impassively over the river scene. In a nearby valley where poppies once grew stands a huge museum, the Hall of Opium, which describes the history of the worldwide trade in narcotics.

CHIANG RAI

180 km (112 mi) northeast of Chiang Mai, 780 km (485 mi) north of Bangkok.

Once again, an elephant played a central role in the foundation of an important Thai city. Legend has it that a royal elephant ran away from its patron, the 13th-century king Mengrai, founder of the Lanna kingdom. The beast stopped to rest on the banks of the Mae Kok River. The king regarded this as an auspicious sign and in 1256 built his capital, Chiang Rai, on the site. But little is left from those heady days: the Emerald Buddha that used to reside in Wat Phra Keo is now in Bangkok's Grand Palace, and a precious Buddha image in the 15th-century Wat Phra Singh has long since disappeared.

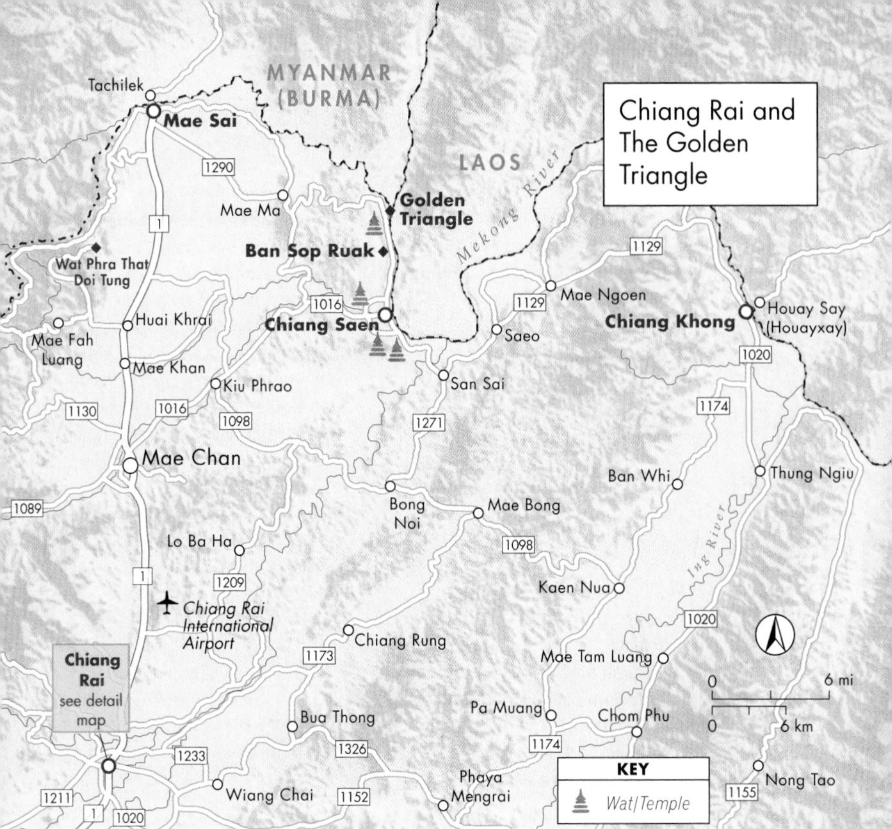

GETTING HERE & AROUND

BY AIR Thai Airways has three daily flights from Bangkok to Chiang Rai. SGA Airlines flies twice daily from Chiang Mai to Chiang Rai. The single fare is B1,690. Chiang Rai International Airport is 6 km (4 mi) northeast of the city. Incoming flights are met by songthaews and tuk-tuks, which charge about B50 for the journey to central Chiang Rai.

BY BOAT & FERRY Longtail boats and rafts set off daily from Tha Ton for the 130-km (81-mi) trip downstream to Chiang Rai. (⇨ *Boating in Sports & the Outdoors, below.*)

BY BUS Chiang Rai is served by buses that leave regularly from Chiang Mai's two terminals (3 to 4 hours; B80 to B200). Buses to Chiang Rai also leave regularly between 8 AM and 7:15 PM from Bangkok's Northern bus terminal (12 hours; B600 to B700). Express buses also leave hourly from Chiang Mai's Arcade terminal. The fare is B180.

BY CAR Roads are well paved throughout the Golden Triangle, presenting no problem for drivers. The area is bisected by the main north–south road, Highway 110, and crisscrossed by good country roads. In Chiang Rai, the most prominent companies are Avis, National, and Budget.

BY TAXI & TUK-TUK Tuk-tuks are the common way of getting around Chiang Rai, and a trip across town costs B40 to B50. Songthaews can also be hailed on the street and hired for trips to outlying areas. The fare inside the city is B15—farther afield is a matter of negotiation.

THE STORY OF THE NAME

U.S. Assistant Secretary of State Marshall Green coined the term "Golden Triangle" in 1971 during a preview of the historic visit by President Richard Nixon to China. The Nixon Administration was concerned about the rise of heroin addiction in the United States and wanted to stem the flow of opium from China, Thailand, Myanmar, and Laos. The greatest source of opium was the wild territory where the Mekong and Ruak rivers formed porous borders between Thailand, Myanmar, and Laos—the "golden triangle" drawn by Green on the world map.

ESSENTIALS

Emergencies **Overbrooke Hospital** (✉ *Singhaklai Rd., Chiang Rai* ☎ *053/711366*). **Police** (☎ *053/711444 in Chiang Rai*).

VISITOR & TOUR INFORMATION

The major hotels in Chiang Rai and the Golden Triangle Resort in Chiang Saen also organize minibus tours of the region and their travel desks will arrange treks to the hill-tribe villages. The TAT's Chiang Rai branch (*above*) is a good resource.

Contacts **Dapa Tours** (✉ *115 Moo 2, Rimkok Rd., Chiang Rai* ☎ *053/711354* ♁ *Nonprofit run by Akha people*). **Golden Triangle Tours** (✉ *590 Phaholyothin Rd., Chiang Rai* ☎ *053/711339*). **Track of the Tiger** (✉ *Maekok River Village Resort, Box 3, Mae Ai, Chiang Rai* ☎ *053/459355* 🌐 *www.maekok-river-village-resort.com* ♁ *Pioneer of soft-adventure tourism, from rock climbing and biking to cooking and golf*).

EXPLORING CHIANG RAI

Chiang Rai attracts more and more visitors each year, and it's easy to see why. Six hill tribes—the Akha, Yao, Meo, Lisu, Lahu, and Karen—all live within Chiang Rai Province. Each has different dialects, customs, handicrafts, and costumes, and all still venerate animist spirits despite their increasing acquaintance with the outside world. As in Chiang Mai, they make daily journeys to the markets of Chiang Rai. The best of these is a night bazaar, just off Phaholyothin Road, which has a cluster of small restaurants and food vendors.

■ TIP→ **Climbing to the top of Doi Tong, a modest hill on the northeastern edge of Chiang Rai, is a great way to learn the lay of the land.** From the grounds of a 13th-century temple called Wat Doi Tong, you have a fine view of the Mae Kok River and the mountains beyond. Chiang Rai has very few sights of note, so a leisurely walk around town will take at most a few hours.

WHAT TO SEE

1 **Wat Doi Tong.** Near the summit of Doi Tong, this temple overlooks the Mae Kok River. The ancient pillar that stands here once symbolized the center of the universe for devout Buddhists. The sunset view is worth the trip. ✉ *Winitchaikul Rd.*

2 **Wat Phra Keo.** The Emerald Buddha, which now sits in Thailand's holiest temple, Wat Phra Keo in Bangkok, is said to have been discovered when

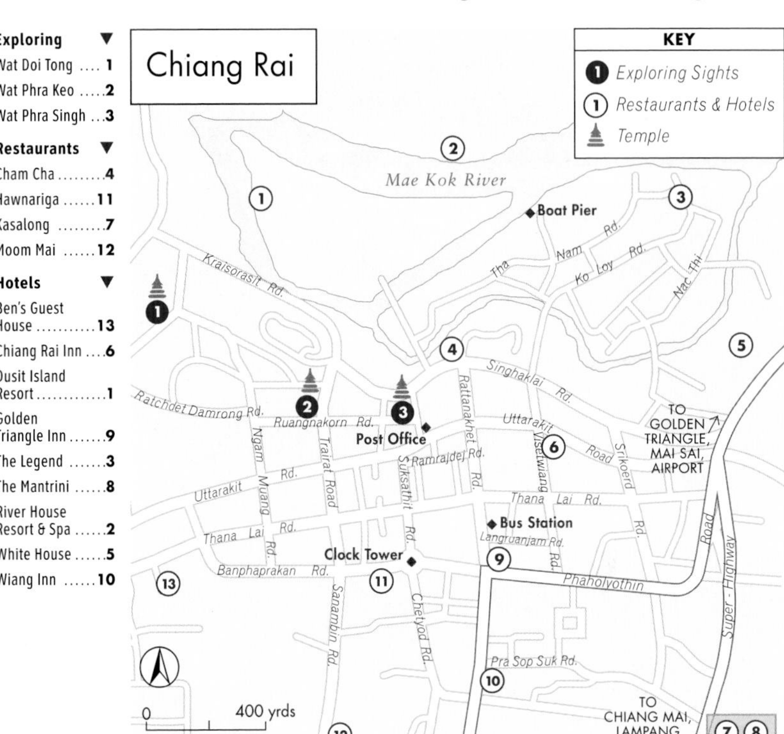

lightning split the chedi housing it at this similarly named temple at the foot of the Doi Tong. A Chinese millionaire financed a jade replica in 1991—although it's not the real thing, the statuette is still strikingly beautiful. ✉ *Trairat Rd.*

3 **Wat Phra Singh.** This 14th-century temple is worth visiting for its viharn, distinguished by some remarkably delicate woodcarving and for colorful frescoes depicting the life of Lord Buddha. A sacred Indian Bhoti tree stands in the peaceful temple grounds. ✉ *Singhaklai Rd.*

OFF THE BEATEN PATH

The journey to the village of **Mae Salong,** near the top of a mountain and along slopes covered with fruit orchards and coffee plantations, may alone be worth the trip. Visit in December and January and you can find the area swathed in cherry blossoms. A local bus service runs from Chiang Rai to Mae Salong via Highway 1234.

WHERE TO EAT

¢–$ THAI

✕ **Cham Cha.** Climb the stairs at this busy restaurant to avoid the lunchtime crowds and take a first-floor table overlooking a garden dominated by the handsome cham cha tree that gives the place its name. Avoid the Western dishes on the menu and go for traditional Northern Thai specialties such as *tom djuet,* a delicious soup laced with tofu and tiny pork dumplings. You can find the restaurant next to the Chiang Rai tourist

Continued on page 421

HILL TRIBES
OWNERS OF THE MOUNTAINS

by Robert Tilley

Thailand's hill tribes populate the remote, mountainous regions in the north. They welcome visitors, and their villages have become major attractions—some are even dependent on tourist dollars. But other villages, especially those that are harder to reach, have retained an authentic feel; a knowledgeable guide can take you to them.

Hill tribes are descendants of migratory peoples from Myanmar (Burma), Tibet, and China. There are at least 10 tribes living in northern Thailand, and they number a little over half a million, a mere 1% of Thailand's population. The tribes follow forms of ancestral worship and are animists: that is, they believe in a world of spirits that inhabit everything—rivers, forests, homes, and gardens. Historically, some tribes made a living by cultivating poppies for opium, but this practice has mostly died out.

Many tribespeople claim to be victims of official discrimination, and it is indeed often difficult for them to gain full citizenship. Although the Thai government has a program to progressively grant them citizenship, the lack of reliable documentation and the slow workings of the Bangkok bureaucracy are formidable obstacles. However, Thais normally treat hill tribe people with respect; in the Thai language they aren't called "tribes" but Chao Khao, which means "Owners of the Mountains."

Visiting the Chao Khao is a matter of debate. Some of the more accessible villages have become Disneyland-like, with tribespeople, clad in colorful costumes, who are eager to pose in a picture with you—and then collect your baht. In general, the farther afield you go, the more authentic the experience.

Even if you don't visit a village, you'll likely encounter tribespeople selling their crafts at markets in Chiang Mai, Chiang Rai, and Mae Hong Son.

The four tribes you're likely to encounter in northern Thailand are the Karen, Hmong, Akha, and Lisu.

(left) Long neck woman, Chiang Mai; (top) Akha girls wearing ornate headdresses.

KAREN

ORIGINS: Myanmar

POPULATION: 400,000

DID YOU KNOW? The famous "long necks" are actually the Paduang tribe, a subdivision of the Karen.

CRAFTS THEY'RE KNOWN FOR: weaving, beaded jewelry, handmade drums.

The majority of Thailand's hill tribe population is Karen, and there are an estimated 7 million of them living in Myanmar as well. The Karen are the most settled of the tribes, living in permanent villages of well-constructed houses and farming plots of land that leave as much of the forest as possible undisturbed. Though Karen traditionally hold Buddhist and animist beliefs, many communities follow Christianity, which missionaries introduced in colonial Burma.

(top) Karen woman weaving; (bottom) Padaung girls.

LONG NECKS

Traditionally, Paduang women have created the illusion of elongated necks—considered beautiful in their culture—by wrapping brass coils around them. The process begins when a girl is about 5 years old; she will add rings each year. The bands, which can weigh up to 12 lbs, push down on the collarbone, making the neck appear long.

Some human rights groups call the Paduang villages "human zoos" and say that you should not visit because tourism perpetuates the practice of wearing neck coils, which can be harmful. But, most of Thailand's Paduang are refugees who have fled worse conditions in Myanmar, and Thailand's three Paduang villages depend on tourism. Some Paduang women object not to tourism but to the fact that they earn as little as $50 a month from tour operators who profit handsomely. If you go, try to find an operator who treats the Paduang equitably.

HMONG

ORIGINS: China

POPULATION: 80,000

DID YOU KNOW? The Hmong wear elaborate silver lockets to keep their souls firmly locked into their bodies.

CRAFTS THEY'RE KNOWN FOR: needlework, batik, decorative clothing and headdresses.

(right) Hmong children.

At the night markets of Chiang Mai and Chiang Rai, you'll recognize Hmong women by their colorful costumes and heavy silver jewelry. There are two divisions of Hmong, White and Blue; White Hmong women wear baggy black pants and blue sashes, while Blue Hmong women wear knee-length pleated skirts. But the divisions "white" and "blue" don't refer to traditional Hmong costumes. "Blue" is a translation of the Hmong word "ntsuab," which also means "dark," a description given to a branch of Hmong whose members once practiced cannibalism. Hmong communities that rejected cannibalism were described as "dlawb," which means "innocent" or "white."

AKHA

ORIGINS: Tibet

POPULATION: 33,000

DID YOU KNOW? Akha villages are defined by a set of wooden gates, often decorated with charms meant to ward off evil spirits.

CRAFTS THEY'RE KNOWN FOR: silver belt buckles and bracelets, decorative hats and clothing, *saw oo* (fiddles).

The Akha once thrived on opium production, shielded from outside interference by the relative inaccessibility of the remote mountaintop sites they chose for their settlements. Today, all but the most remote communities grow alternative crops, such as rice, beans, and corn. They're a gentle, hospitable people whose women wear elaborate headdresses decorated with silver, beads, and feathers. Akha men wear hollow bracelets containing a silver bead, which they believe keeps them in touch with ancestral spirits.

Akha women wearing traditional headdresses.

LISU

ORIGINS: Tibet

POPULATION: 25,000

DID YOU KNOW? The Lisu pass their history from generation to generation in the form of a song.

CRAFTS THEY'RE KNOWN FOR: silver belt buckles, saw oo, large beaded hats.

Though they're not the most numerous, the business-like Lisu are the tribe you're most likely to meet on day trips out of Chiang Mai and Chiang Rai. More than any other hill tribe, the Lisu have recognized the earning power of tourism. As tourist buses draw up, women scramble to change from their everyday clothes into the famous multicolored costumes they normally wear only on high days and holidays.

Lisu women.

THE SHAN

Though sometimes referred to as a hill tribe, the Shan, who live predominantly in Myanmar, are actually a large minority (there are an estimated 6 million) who have been fighting for their own state for decades. They have lived in the area for 1,000 years and are believed to be descendents of the Tai people, the original inhabitants of the region. The Shan who reside in Thailand have fled persecution in Myanmar. Unlike the hill tribes, the Shan are predominantly Buddhist. Shan craftspeople make some of the silver jewelry and ornaments you'll find at markets.

Shan women wearing traditional bamboo hats.

VISITING HILL TRIBE COMMUNITIES

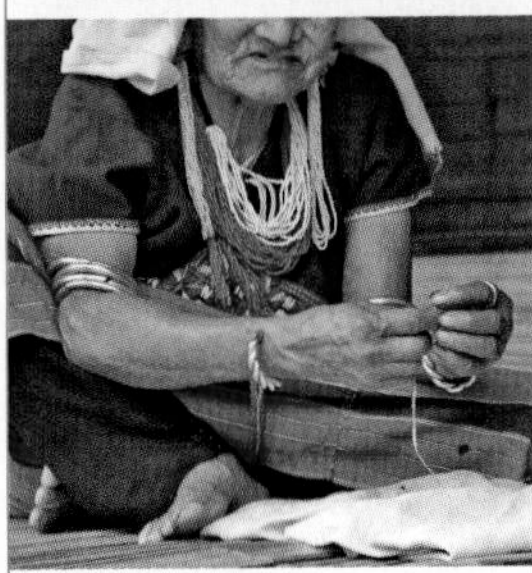

(top) Akha woman with children; (bottom) Karen woman.

ETIQUETTE

Hill-tribe people tend to be conservative, so do follow a few simple guidelines on your visit.

- Dress modestly.
- Keep a respectful distance from religious ceremonies or symbols, and don't touch any talismans without asking first.
- Avoid loud or aggressive behavior and public displays of affection.
- Always ask permission before taking a person's picture.

TREKKING

Meeting and staying with tribespeople is one of the main attractions of trekking in northern Thailand. Some day trips include brief stops at villages, which are often little more than theme parks. But if you book a trek of three days or more you're sure to encounter authentic hill tribes living as they have for centuries.

Chao Khao are hospitable to westerners, often organizing spontaneous parties at which home-brewed rice whiskey flows copiously. If you stay overnight, you'll be invited to share the community's simple food and sleep on the floor in one of their basic huts.

Virtually all travel operators offer tours and treks to hill tribe villages. The **Mirror Foundation** (✉*106 Moo 1, Ban Huay Khom, T. Mae Yao, Chiang Rai,* ☎*053/737412* 🌐*www.mirrorartgroup.org*), an NGO that works to improve the lives of hill tribes near Chiang Rai, can arrange culturally respectful tours. The foundation's current projects include bringing volunteer teachers to tribal villages and preventing the exploitation of hill tribe women and children.

■ **TIP→To avoid being taken to a tourist trap instead of an authentic village, ask the operator to identify the tribes you'll visit and to describe their culture and traditions.** It's a good sign if the operator can answer your questions knowledgeably; the information will also add greatly to the pleasure of your trip.

DAY TRIPS

You can also take daytrips to see hill tribes from Chiang Mai, Chiang Rai, or Mae Hong Son. The villages appear on few maps, so it's not advisable to set out on your own; a guide or driver who knows the region well is a better bet. You can easily hire one for about B1,000 per day; ask the TAT in Chiang Mai or Chiang Rai for recommendations.

Several Chiang Mai operators offer "three country" one-day tours of the Golden Triangle: a boat trip to a Laotian island in the Mekong River; a brief shopping trip to the tax-free Burmese border town of Tachilek; and a stop at a Thai hill tribe village on the way home. The fare of B800 to B1,000 includes lunch. These tours are likely to feel fairly touristy.

SHOPPING FOR HILL TRIBE CRAFTS

Embroidered textiles at a market near Chiang Mai.

Over the past few decades, the Thai royal family has worked with the government to wean hill tribe farmers off cultivating opium poppies. One initiative has been financing workshops for manufacturing traditional handicrafts, such as basketry, weaving, and woodworking. Some of these royal projects, located near hill tribe villages, offer both employment and on-site training. The workshops also prevent the crafts from dying out and create a market for products that were originally only distributed within the tribal communities.

WORKSHOPS

The Doi Tung mountain, 40 km (25 mi) north of Chiang Rai, is home to 26 hill tribe villages as well as the **Doi Tung Development Project** (☎*053/767001* 🌐*www.doitung.org*), a royal project based at the late Queen Mother's former summer palace. The tribes living in the mountain villages produce handicrafts; the project workshops also employ hill tribe craftsmen and women. Both the villages and the project welcome visitors. Daily tours of the project grounds are available for B100; tribespeople sell crafts at a shop and at stalls on the grounds.

Though it's not for the faint of heart, a very curvy 16-km (10-mi) road leads to the top of Doi Tung from the village of Huai Krai, 20 km (12 mi) south of Mae Sai via Highway 101. Local buses and songthaews from Huai Krai will take you here; you can also hire a driver or a guide.

MARKETS & STORES

Although hill tribe crafts are abundant at the night markets in Chiang Mai, Chiang Rai, and Mae Hong Son, serious collectors prefer government-run stores whose products come with certificates of authenticity. There are two stores in Chiang Mai—the **Thai Hill Tribe Products Promotion Foundation**, and the **Hill Tribes Handicraft Center** (⇨*Shopping in Chiang Mai, above*). Prices are fixed at these stores but are comparable to what you'll pay at markets (upscale hotel boutiques, however, inflate prices substantially). Expect to pay at least B500 for a silver ring or belt buckle and as much as B2,500 for a bracelet or necklace; around B300 for a meter of woven cloth; and B300 to 400 for a simple wooden instrument like a bamboo flute.

office. ✉447/17 Singhaklai Rd. ☎053/744191 ▭No credit cards ⏲Closed Sun. No dinner.

¢–$ THAI ✕**Hawnariga.** The name of this traditional Thai restaurant means "clock tower," and that's just where it's located, in the center of town. Orchids hang from the thatched palm-leaf roof of the large, open-sided restaurant. Two fishponds are connected by a brook that skirts the tables, and they provide fat tabtim for the menu. ✉*402/1–2 Banpapragarn Rd.* ☎*053/711062* ▭*V.*

¢–$ CHINESE ✕**Kasalong.** Chiang Rai's best seafood restaurant is a 15-minute tuk-tuk drive south of the city, but the journey is worth it. A large variety of seafood and lake fish is prepared according to Thai or Chinese recipes. The *tabtim* (sweet-tasting lake fish) in garlic-and-pepper sauce is particularly recommended. Although the restaurant sits on the busy superhighway, opposite the Big C megastore, you dine in a pleasant garden setting. ✉*556/13 Super Hwy. Rd.* ☎*053/754908* ▭*MC, V.*

$ THAI ✕**Moom Mai.** One of Chiang Rai's most popular restaurants, the large and friendly Moom Mai has live Thai folk music most nights. You eat at closely packed teak tables, where contact with the locals is guaranteed. The menu features Northern Thai specialties and Chinese-influenced dishes such as deep-fried chopped prawns in dumplings. ✉*64 Sankhonluang Rd., Moo 16, Tambon Robwiang* ☎*053/716416* ▭*No credit cards.*

WHERE TO STAY

¢ **Ben's Guest House.** This family-run inn has repeatedly won accolades for its comfortable and extremely reasonable accommodations. The steep-eaved Lanna-style home and an annex are at the end of a quiet lane on the western edge of town. Transportation into Chiang Rai is easy to arrange. **Pros:** friendly staff with deep knowledge of the region; lively evening scene, as backpackers gather around the pool and exchange tour tips. **Cons:** cheaper rooms are very basic; thin walls. ✉*35/10 San Khon Noi Rd., Soi 4* ☎*053/716775* *28 rooms* *In-room: refrigerator. In-hotel: restaurant, pool, gym, Internet terminal, no-smoking rooms* ▭*No credit cards.*

¢ **Chiang Rai Inn.** All the accommodations at this Lanna-style hotel, near the bus station, look out over a cool, palm-shaded courtyard. Some of the comfortable rooms have sitting areas. The casual restaurant, furnished in cane and bamboo, serves an excellent choice of Northern Thai dishes. **Pros:** friendly staff, central location. **Cons:** some rooms need a lick of paint; thin walls. ✉*661 Uttarakit Rd.* ☎*053/71700 up to 03* *77 rooms* *In-room: refrigerator. In-hotel: restaurant, laundry facilities* ▭*MC, V.*

$$ ★ **Dusit Island Resort.** This gleaming white high-rise, which sits on an island in the Mae Kok River, has tons of amenities, including the largest outdoor pool in Northern Thailand. The complex's three wings all have spacious rooms overlooking the river and filled with modern renditions of traditional Thai furnishings and unexpected extras like large marble baths. The Peak grills up delicious steaks, while Chinatown stir-fries Cantonese fare. The casual Island Café serves Thai food all day and has a breakfast buffet. All three dining rooms have impressive views. **Pros:** great breakfast; bathrooms with tubs. **Cons:** some guests say it's

showing its age. ✉ *1129 Kraisorasit Rd.* ☎ *053/715777, 02/238–4790 in Bangkok* 🌐 *chiangrai.dusit.com* *270 rooms* *In-room: safe, Wi-Fi. In-hotel: 3 restaurants, room service, bars, tennis courts, pool, gym, laundry service, no-smoking rooms* ▭ *AE, DC, MC, V.*

¢ **Golden Triangle Inn.** Don't confuse this cozy guesthouse with the backpackers' hangout at Ban Sop Ruak. ■ **TIP→ This comfortable little place is all too popular—advance reservations are necessary due to its ideal location in the center of town.** Wood-ceiling rooms are cooled by slowly turning fans. The café serves Thai and Western fare, while the terrace bar has a wide range of fruity drinks. Next door is a travel agency that arranges treks into Laos. **Pros:** central location; good travel service. **Cons:** bathrooms need upgrading; thin walls. ✉ *590–2 Phaholyothin Rd.* ☎ *053/711339* *39 rooms* *In-room: no a/c (some). In-hotel: restaurant, bar* ▭ *No credit cards.*

$$$–$$$$ **The Legend.** This newer hotel (opened in 2004) could truly become something of a local legend. It's built in exclusively Lanna style on an island in the Mae Kok River, just a short walk from the city center. Rooms are furnished with exquisite Northern Thai antiques and reproductions, while public areas are a Lanna-style mixture of whitewashed walls, brickwork, and dark teak. The airy restaurant and landscaped swimming pool are on the riverbank, with views of the mountains beyond. For real seclusion, book one of the villas, which have their own private pools. **Pros:** elegant, peaceful, and impeccably designed; reliable airport pickup. **Cons:** some rooms in need of refurbishing; unreliable hot water. ✉ *124/15 Kohloy Rd., A. Muang* ☎ *053/910400 or 053/719649, 02/642–5497 in Bangkok* 🌐 *www.thelegend-chiangrai.com* *79 rooms* *In-room: safe, refrigerator, DVD, Wi-Fi. In-hotel: 3 restaurants, bar, pool, spa, laundry service, parking (free), no-smoking rooms* ▭ *AE, DC, MC, V.*

$$ **The Mantrini.** Only the tropical vegetation hints that this highly stylish hotel is in Thailand and not a boutique establishment in central Milan or Munich. Rooms are furnished in a modern Italian style, with retro-looking Mondriani primary colors, crisp white linens, and claw-footed, stand-alone bathtubs in some of the suites. Most rooms are grouped around a secluded pool and a large wooden sundeck. **Pros:** beautifully designed; shady pool area. **Cons:** shabby neighborhood, with cheap, noisy bars. ✉ *292/13 Moo 13, Robwiang, A. Muang* ☎ *053/601555 up to 9* 🌐 *www.mantrini.com* *63 rooms* *In-room: Wi-Fi. In-hotel: restaurant, bar, pool, laundry service, parking (free), no-smoking rooms* ▭ *MC, V.*

$$$$ **River House Resort & Spa.** A lofty, spacious lobby that also serves as an art gallery sets the tone for this elegant new hotel (opened in 2008) on the banks of the Kok River. Rooms are teak-floored and decorated with a generous use of Thai silk. The resort's own minibuses ferry guests in and out of the town center. **Pros:** views across the Kok River to Chiang Rai; infinity swimming pool; excellent restaurant. **Cons:** loud golfers tend to take over the bar. ✉ *482 Moo 4, Mae Kok Rd., Rimkok, A. Muang, city outskirts* ☎ *053/750829 up to 34* 🌐 *www.riverhouse-chiangrai.com* *36 rooms* *In-room: Wi-Fi. In-hotel: restaurant, bar, pool, no smoking rooms* ▭ *MC, V.*

¢ ★ **White House.** The charming Indian-Thai couple who run this attractive, Mediterranean-style inn are justifiably proud of their homey place. Rooms are huddled around a courtyard. Nearby is a small pool and an open-air café. The owners also run an efficient travel service and a modest business center. **Pros:** secluded but central location. **Cons:** pool, with faded and grimy tiles, needs attention. *789 Phaholyothin Rd. 053/713427 or 053/744051 36 rooms In-room: no a/c (some), refrigerator, no TV (some). In-hotel: 2 restaurants, pool, laundry service, Internet terminal MC.*

$ **Wiang Inn.** In the heart of downtown, this sleek, modern hotel is among the best in central Chiang Rai. Spacious rooms are decked out in dark woods and fine fabrics. Outside is a small outdoor pool surrounded by exotic greenery. The Golden Teak restaurant serves Thai, Chinese, and other fare. The hotel has a fun, plush karaoke room. **Pros:** best facilities of in-city hotels; good restaurant; central location. **Cons:** standard rooms have only single beds. *893 Phaholyothin Rd. 053/71151 up to 33 www.wianginn.com 260 rooms In-room: refrigerator. In-hotel: restaurant, room service, pool, gym, Internet terminal, no-smoking rooms DC, V.*

6

SHOPPING

Chiang Rai has a **night market,** on Robviang Nongbua Road, and although it's much smaller than Chiang Mai's, there are a large variety of handicrafts and textiles on offer. **T.S. Jewelry & Antiques** (*877–879 Phaholyothin Rd. 053/711050*) has a very large selection of jewelry and antiques from Northern Thailand and neighboring Myanmar and Laos.

SPORTS & THE OUTDOORS

Chiang Rai is an excellent base from which to set out on tours trekking through the nearby mountains or canoeing and rafting on the region's rivers. Tour operators charge about B800 a day (including overnight stops in hill tribe villages).

Some 90 km (56 mi) due east of Chiang Rai is perhaps the region's most beautiful national park, **Phu Sang,** which has one of Thailand's rarest natural wonders, cascades of hot water. The temperature of the water that tumbles over the 85-foot-high falls never drops below 33°C (91°F), and a nearby pool is even warmer. The park has some spectacular caves and is crisscrossed by nature trails teeming with birdlife. One hour's drive north lies the mountainous border with Laos, straddled by 5,730-foot-high Phu Chee Fah, a favorite destination for trekkers and climbers. You reach the Phu Sang National Park via Thoeng, 70 km (43 mi) east of Chiang Rai on Route 1020. The park rents lodges for B800 to B1,000 a night. Entrance to the park costs B400, and B30 for a vehicle. Call 054/401099 for reservations.

BOATING For something adventurous, catch a bus to the border town of Tha Thon and board a high-powered longtail boat there and ride the rapids 130 km (81 mi) to Chiang Rai. Boats leave from a pier near the town bridge at 12:30 PM and take about three to four hours to negotiate the bends and rapids of the river, which passes through thick jungle and past remote hill tribe villages. The single fare is B350. For a more leisurely ride to Chiang Rai, board a raft, which takes two days and nights to reach the city, overnighting in hill tribe villages. Fares start at B1,000. ■ **TIP→ Take bottled water, an inflatable cushion, and (most important) a hat or umbrella to shade you from the sun.** The best time to make the trip is during October and November, when the water is still high but the rainy season has passed.

You can book the trip through **Four Lens Tour** (✉ *131/6 Moo 13, Mae Korn Intersection* ☎ *053/700617 to 20* 🌐 *www.4lens.com*) or **Inbound-Outbound Tour Service** (✉ *199/38 Phaholyothin Rd.* ☎ *053/715690*).

GOLF

Chiang Rai has one of Northern Thailand's finest golf courses, the **Santiburi Country Club** (✉ *12 Moo 3, Huadoi-Sobpao Rd.* ☎ *053/662821 up to 26* 📠 *053/717377*), laid out by the celebrated Robert Trent Jones, Jr. The par-72, 18-hole course is set among rolling hills 10 km (6 mi) outside Chiang Rai. The ranch-style clubhouse has an excellent restaurant and coffee shop and the facilities also include a sauna. Visitors are welcome and clubs, carts, and shoes can be rented. Reservations are requested.

EN ROUTE

If you're traveling north from Chiang Rai on Highway 110, watch for the left-hand turn at Km 32 to **Doi Tung.** The road winds 42 km (26 mi) to the summit, where an astonishing view opens out over the surrounding countryside. The temple here, Wat Phra That Doi Tung, founded more than a millennium ago, is said to be the repository of some important relics of Lord Buddha, including a collarbone. The shrine attracts pilgrims from as far away as India and China, for whom its huge Chinese Buddha figure is a vastly important symbol of good fortune. On the mountain slopes below the temple is the summer home built for the king's late mother. The fine mansion is closed to the public, but the gardens, an explosion of color in all seasons, are often open.

CHIANG SAEN

59 km (37 mi) north of Chiang Rai, 239 km (149 mi) northeast of Chiang Mai, 935 km (581 mi) north of Bangkok.

On the banks of the Mekong River sits Chiang Saen, a one-road town that in the 12th century was home to the future king Mengrai. Only fragments of the ancient ramparts survived the incursion by the Burmese in 1588, and the rest of the citadel was ravaged by fire when the last of the Burmese were ousted in 1786. Chiang Saen is now being developed as a major Mekong River port, and it's the embarkation point for river trips to Myanmar, Laos, and China.

GETTING HERE & AROUND

The ubiquitous songthaews provide the local transport service. They charge B15, although it's usual to round up to B20. Two buses daily run between Chiang Mai's Chiang Phuak bus station and Chiang Saen, taking 4½ hours. The fare is about B150; buses stop in the center of town and at the boat piers.

EXPLORING CHIANG SAEN

Only two ancient chedis remain standing to remind the visitor of Chiang Saen's ancient glory, although government-financed excavation is gradually uncovering evidence of the citadel built here in the 12th century by King Mengrai, who later founded Chiang Mai. Ancient flooring and walls have been exposed and give a fascinating idea of the extent of what was one of the region's first royal palaces.

WHAT TO SEE

Just outside the city walls is the oldest chedi, **Wat Pa Sak,** whose name refers to the 300 teak trees that were planted in the surrounding area. The stepped temple, which narrows to a spire, is said to enshrine holy relics brought here when the city was founded.

Inside the city walls stands the imposing octagonal **Wat Phra That Luang.** Scholars say it dates from the 14th century.

Next door to Wat Phra That Luang is the **National Museum,** which houses artifacts from the Lanna period, as well as some Neolithic discoveries. The museum also has a good collection of carvings and traditional handicrafts from the hill tribes.

✉ *Road to Chiang Rai, 1 km (½ mi) from town center* ☎ *053/777102* *B30* ⏲ *Wed.–Sun. 9–4.*

6

WHERE TO STAY

¢ ★ **Gin's Guest House.** Local lawyer Khun Gin and his wife run this charming guesthouse, which is a true home away from home. Rooms are as you'd expect to find in your favorite aunt's country retreat. Some have large hearths for chilly nights. Kun Gin is a mine of local information and can organize everything from a trip across the nearby Mekong to a two-night cruise to China. If the house is full in high season, you'll be lodged in bivouac-style wooden chalets in the extensive, tree-shaded garden, so early booking is recommended. **Pros:** friendly and helpful owners who are steeped in knowledge of the area; riverside walks. **Cons:** 10-minute drive from Chiang Saen. ✉ *Ban Sop Ruak Rd.* ☎ *053/650847* *9 rooms* *In-room: refrigerators. In-hotel: parking (free)* *No credit cards.*

CHIANG KHONG

53 km (33 mi) northeast of Chiang Rai.

This small Mekong River town is gearing up to become a main waystation on the planned Asian Highway, and a bridge is being built across the Mekong River to the Laotian harbor town of Houayxay. Until its completion (held up because of budgetary problems) small skiffs carry people across the Mekong between Chiang Khong and Houayxay, from whose pier daily boats set off for the two-day trip to the World Heritage town of Luang Prabang in Laos. Chiang Khong is a convenient overnight stop before boarding.

A 15-day Laos visa can be acquired in Chiang Khong from **Ann Tour** (✉ *6/1 Moo 8, Saiklang Rd.* ☎ *053/655198*).

GETTING HERE & AROUND

The paved road east out of Chiang Saen parallels the Mekong River en route to Chiang Khong. Songthaews ply the route for about B100, but you can also hire a speedboat (B500) to go down the river, a thrilling three hours of slipping between the rocks and rapids. Not too many tourists make the journey, especially to villages inhabited by the local Hmong and Yao tribes. The rugged scenery along the Mekong River is actually more dramatic than that of the Golden Triangle.

EXPLORING CHIANG KHONG

Chiang Khong has little to attract the visitor apart from magnificent vistas from its riverside towpath to the hills of Laos across the Mekong. Its one 300-year-old temple has an interesting Chiang Saen–style chedi but is in need of repair. Textiles from China and Laos can be bought cheaply in the town's market.

WHERE TO STAY

$ **Nam Khong River Side.** Chiang Khon's best hotel sits on the south bank of the Mekong River, commanding unobstructed views to the hills of Laos on the other side. Extensive gardens drop to the water's edge and are a pleasant spot for an evening stroll. **Pros:** airy dining room. **Cons:** small bothrooms; unreliable shower. ✉*174–176 Moo 8, Tambon Wiang* ☎*053/791796* 🌐*www.namkhongriverside.com* *40 rooms* *In-hotel: restaurant, bar, no smoking rooms* 💳*MC, V.*

BAN SOP RUAK

8 km (5 mi) north of Chiang Saen.

Ban Sop Ruak, a village in the heart of the Golden Triangle, was once the domain of the opium warlord Khun Sa. More than a decade ago, government troops forced him back to Burmese territory, but his reputation still draws those eager to see evidence of the man who once held the region under his thumb.

GETTING HERE & AROUND

Songthaews (about B50) are the only transport service from Chiang Saen to Ban Sop Ruak.

EXPLORING BAN SOP RUAK

This simple riverside town has one main street, 1 km (½ mi) in length, that winds along the southern bank of the Mekong River and is lined with stalls selling souvenirs and textiles from neighboring Laos. Waterfront restaurants serve up fresh catfish and provide vantage points for watching the evening sun dip over the mountains to the west.

WHAT TO SEE

Opium is so linked to the history of Ban Sop Ruak that the small town now has two museums devoted to the subject. The smaller one, **Opium Museum,** is in the center of town. A commentary in English details the growing, harvesting, and smoking of opium. Many of the exhibits, such as carved teak opium boxes and jade and silver pipes, are fascinating. ✉*Main street* ☎*No phone* *B30* *Daily 7–6.*

Fodor's Choice ★ Opened in 2004, the magnificent **Hall of Opium** is a dazzling white stucco, glass, marble, and aluminum building nestling in a valley above the Mekong. The site of the museum is so close to former poppy fields that a plan is still being considered to extend the complex to encompass an "open-air" exhibit of a functioning opium plantation. The museum traces the history of the entire drug trade (including a look at how mild stimulants like coffee and tea took hold in the West). It even attempts to give visitors a taste of the "opium experience" by leading them through a 500-foot-long tunnel where synthetic aroma traces of the drug and atmospheric music waft between walls bearing phantasmagoric bas-relief scenes.

The entrance tunnel emerges into a gallery of blinding light, where the nature of the opium-producing poppy is vividly described on an information panel erected in front of an imitation field of the insidiously beautiful flower. It's an arresting introduction to an imaginatively designed and assembled exhibition, which reaches back into the murky history of the opium trade and takes a long, monitory look into a potentially even darker future. **TIP→ The Hall of Opium is so large in scope and scale that two days are hardly enough to take it all in. A visit is ideally combined with an overnight stay** at one of two hotels within walking distance: the Hall's own Greater Mekong Lodge (double rooms from B1,800 including breakfast) or, for a sheer splurge, at the luxurious Anantara, just across the road. ✉ *Main street* ☎ *053/784444* 🌐 *www.maefahluang.org* 🎫 *B300* ⏲ *Tues.–Sun. 10–3:30.*

Even if you don't stay overnight, pay a visit to the sumptuous **Imperial Golden Triangle Resort,** which has the best views over the confluence of the Mae Sai, Ruak, and Mekong rivers.

Longtail excursion boats captained by experienced river men tie up at the Ban Sop Ruak jetty, and the B500 fee covers a 90-minute cruise into the waters of Myanmar and Laos and a stop at a Laotian market. You can take a short trip into Myanmar by visiting the Golden Triangle Paradise Resort, which sits in isolated splendor on the Burmese bank of the Mekong, about 1 km (½ mi) upstream from the Golden Triangle. The Thai immigration office at the Ban Sop Ruak jetty makes a photocopy of your passport for the Burmese authorities for B200.

WHERE TO STAY

$$ Fodor's Choice ★ **Anantara Golden Triangle.** The Anantara is one of the Golden Triangle's top addresses. Mythical figures line the way to a palatial entrance, which leads into a vast, open-plan, two-floor area encompassing an excellent restaurant, opulently furnished lounge, and reputedly the longest bar in Northern Thailand. Rooms are luxuriously furnished in indigenous woods and draped with handmade Thai fabrics. Louvered glass doors lead to bathrooms with terra-cotta tubs big enough for a pool party. Picture windows opening onto private balconies command spectacular views of the confluence of the Mekong and Ruak rivers. **TIP→ The former Opium Den Bar has become the best Italian restaurant north of Chiang Mai.** **Pros:** truly stunning place to stay; great restaurant. **Cons:** access to most of the rooms involves much stair climbing;

Elephants flank the ruined chedi at Wat Chedi Luang.

bathrooms are separated from rooms by only a glass partition. ✉ *Chiang Saen* ☎ *053/784084, 02/476–0022 in Bangkok* 🌐 *www.anantara.com* *106 rooms, 4 suites* *In-room: safe, Wi-Fi. In-hotel: 2 restaurants, room service, bars, tennis courts, pool, gym, spa, laundry service* *AE, DC, MC, V.*

$ **De River Boutique Resort.** Rooms at this small, Lanna-style hotel, halfway between Chiang Saen and Ban Sop Ruak, directly overlook the Mekong, with sweeping views across its swirling waters to the hills of Laos on the opposite bank. The hotel is comfortable and scrupulously clean, and run by a very friendly local family. Rooms are furnished in light veneers and pastel-shaded textiles. **Pros:** sunrise over the Mekong from one's private balcony; riverside walks. **Cons:** staff have poor English skills; no transport to either Chiang Saen or Ban Sop Ruak, both a 15-minute drive away. ✉ *455 Moo 1 Chiang Saen* ☎ *053/784477 or 053/784488* *18 rooms* 🌐 *www.deriverresort.com* *In-hotel: restaurant, bar* *MC, V.*

$$$ **Four Seasons Tented Camp.** Modeled on an African safari camp, this collection of canvas-roof bungalows sits in thick jungle in Northern Thailand's famed Golden Triangle. It combines a touch of soft adventure with all the comforts of a luxury hotel. The "tents" are floored with polished teak and furnished with Thai silks; hand-hammered copper bathtubs with room for two dominate the bedrooms. Activities include elephant riding, boat trips on the Mekong River, jungle treks, and Thai cooking classes. Evenings are spent over sundowners and opulent dinners. **Pros:** sweeping views of Gold Triangle confluence of Mekong and Sop Ruak rivers; unlimited gin or whisky at sundowner

time. **Cons:** impersonal service; not much feeling of true adventure. ✉*Transport leaves from Anantara hotel* *Box 18, Chiang Saen Post Office, Chiang Saen, 57150* ☎*053/784477* 🌐*www.fourseasons.com/goldentriangle* *15 tents* *In-room: safe, refrigerator, Wi-Fi. In-hotel: restaurant, bar, spa, laundry service* ▭*AE, DC, MC, V.*

> **WORD OF MOUTH**
>
> "I recommend against the day trips to Laos and Burma. Both are trips to border towns that will give you no real feel for the country. I'd recommend taking a full day to do things away from Anantara, and spend the rest of your time there, interacting with the elephants, enjoying the gorgeous scenery, [and] the pool and the spa. Oh, do venture . . . to the Opium Museum. It's very well done." —Kathie

¢ **Golden Home.** The Mekong River is just across the road from this small resortlike guesthouse. There are just seven wooden cabins, each with a tiny terrace overlooking a flower-covered yard. The night market that borders the river is a short walk away. **Pros:** central location, near restaurants and shopping. **Cons:** small, basic rooms. ✉*41 Moo 1, Wiang, Chiang Saen* ☎*053/784205* *7 cabins* *In-room: refrigerator. In-hotel: parking (free)* ▭*No credit cards.*

$$ **Imperial Golden Triangle Resort.** From the superior rooms in this high-eaved, Lanna-style hotel you are treated to magnificent views of three rivers rushing together. The smart restaurant, the Border View, lives up to its name, but the best way to enjoy the panorama is to soak it up with a glass of Mekong whiskey on the terrace. Classical Thai dance is performed in the evening during high season. **Pros:** spectacular sunsets over the Mekong from the restaurant terrace; excellent travel service. **Cons:** access to many rooms involves climbing flights of stairs. ✉*222 Ban Sop Ruak* ☎*053/784001 up to 5, 02/261–9000 reservations* 🌐*www.imperialhotels.com* *73 rooms* *In-room: refrigerator. In-hotel: 2 restaurants, pool, laundry service* ▭*AE, DC, MC, V.*

MAE SAI

25 km (16 mi) west of Ban Sop Ruak, 60 km (37 mi) north of Chiang Rai.

From Ban Sop Ruak you can travel west on a dusty road to Mae Sai, a town that straddles the Mae Sai River. At this market town the merchants trade goods with the Burmese.

GETTING HERE & AROUND

Buses leave six times daily from Chiang Mai's Chiang Phuak bus station for the five-hour journey to Mae Sai. The fare is about B150. Regular bus service also runs between Chiang Rai and Mae Sai (1 hour; B50). Around town, songthaews are the only means of getting around.

EXPLORING MAE SAI

Mae Sai attracts a steady flow of foreign residents of Thailand who cross the Myanmar border on the edge of the town in order to renew their visas. But the cross-border trip is also the town's main tourist attraction. The market that nestles next to the border bridge is packed with jewelry stalls, where the careful buyer can find some bargains, including rubies and jade from Myanmar.

WHAT TO SEE

For the best view across the river into Myanmar, climb up to **Wat Phra That Doi Wao**—the 207-step staircase starts from behind the Top North Hotel.

Foreigners may cross the river to visit **Thachilek** on a one-day visa, obtainable at the bridge for US$10. It's a smaller version of Mae Sai, but with no less than three casinos, packed with Thai gamblers.

For $30 you can get a three-night visa that lets you travel 63 km (39 mi) north to **Kengtung,** a quaint town with colonial-era structures built by the British alongside old Buddhist temples.

WHERE TO EAT & STAY

¢ THAI **Rabiang Kaew.** Set back from the main road by a wooden bridge, this restaurant built in the Northern style has an unmistakable charm. Antiques adorning the dining room add to its rustic style. The Thai fare is tasty and expertly prepared. *356/1 Phaholyothin Rd. 053/731172 MC, V.*

¢ **Piyaporn Place.** Mae Sai's top hotel is a long walk from the center of town and the markets, but the friendly staff arranges transport to both. The newly refurbished (in 2007) rooms are decorated in soothing pastel colors and many have fine views of the town and neighboring Myanmar. **Pros:** pleasant riverside walks; helpful travel desk. **Cons:** staff have limited English-language skills. *77/1 Moo 1, Wiang Pang Khamm 57130 053/734511 up to 13 or 053/642113 up to 15 www.piyaporn-place.com 78 rooms In-hotel: restaurant, bar, pool MC, V.*

¢ **Wang Thong.** This riverside hotel was originally intended to cater to business executives trading across the nearby Thai-Burmese border, but now the guests are mostly travelers. Choose a room high up on the river side so you can spend an idle hour or two watching the flowing waters and the flowing pedestrian traffic across the bridge. Its modern rooms are neutral and sparsely furnished. **Pros:** pleasant riverside walks. **Cons:** bland room decor; room-cleaning service could be more thorough. *299 Phaholyothin Rd.57130 053/733388 150 rooms In-room: refrigerator. In-hotel: 2 restaurants, bars, pool, laundry service MC, V.*

SHOPPING

Thais take household goods and consumer products across the river, where the Burmese trade them for sandalwood, jade, and rubies. Though you may want to see Myanmar, the prices and quality of the goods will not be better than in Mae Sai. Near the bridge, **Mengrai Antique** (*Phaholyothin Rd. 053/731423*) has a matchless reputation.

TIP→ Rubies aren't the only red gems here. Mae Sai is also justifiably proud of its sweet strawberries, which ripen in December or January, found at local markets and as far away as Chiang Rai and Chiang Mai.

7

Isan

WORD OF MOUTH

"We spent three days in Khao Yai National Park. What a gem for outdoors lovers! One evening, we climbed a rocky hill to see bats swarm out of their caves. The next day we took a moderate hike through the forest. . . . What a treat—climbing along elephant trails, seeing wild orchids and beautiful tropical birds."

—Kay

WELCOME TO ISAN

TOP REASONS TO GO

★ **Roads Less Traveled:** Tour buses are rare on the roads of the sprawling northeast plateau, and you'll probably only run into a few other *farang (foreigners)*.

★ **Khmer ruins:** Thailand's finest Khmer temples are living histories, too, with Hindu shrines sometimes supplanted by Buddhist monuments.

★ **Nature Preserves:** Two of the country's most popular national parks are here, including Phu Kradueng, where you can find a profusion of wildflowers in spring.

★ **Drifting down the Mekong:** The Mekong's murky waters are a fixture in the eastern landscape. Take a boat trip, dine in a floating restaurant, or just take in the views from a waterfront hotel.

★ **Som Tam:** This spicy-and-sour green-papaya salad is a staple of the entire country, but its birthplace is Isan, and that's where it's still the best.

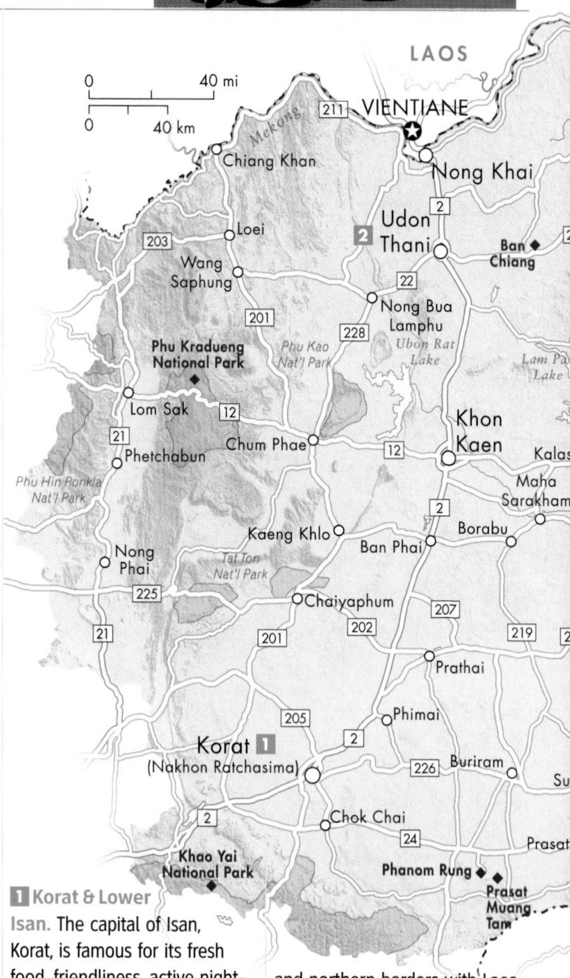

1 Korat & Lower Isan. The capital of Isan, Korat, is famous for its fresh food, friendliness, active nightlife, and the impressive Khao Yai National Park, nearby. But the real gems of this region are its ancient Khmer temples, which often share Hindu and Buddhist histories. The legendary Mekong River forms Thailand's eastern and northern borders with Laos, and along its banks are some beautiful and off-the-beaten-path towns: a great opportunity to see unchanged rural farming and fishing communities. Ubon Ratchathani is the major metropolis of this region.

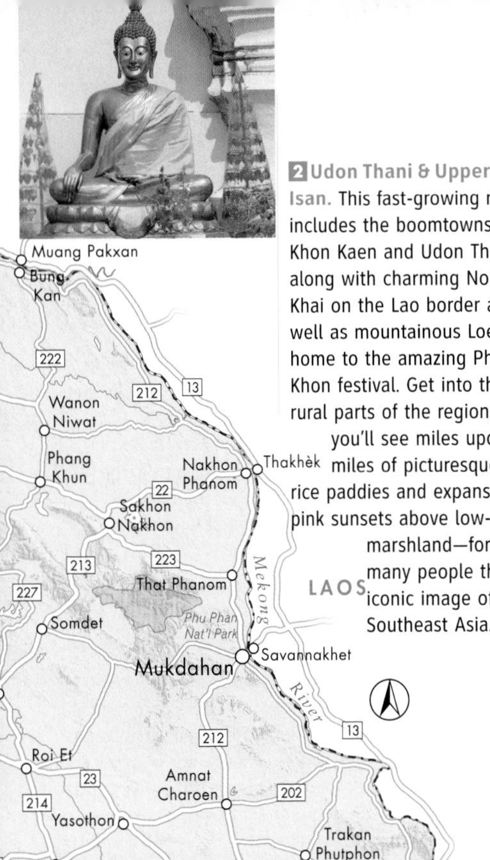

2 Udon Thani & Upper Isan. This fast-growing region includes the boomtowns of Khon Kaen and Udon Thani, along with charming Nong Khai on the Lao border as well as mountainous Loei, home to the amazing Phi Ta Khon festival. Get into the rural parts of the region, and you'll see miles upon miles of picturesque rice paddies and expansive, pink sunsets above low-lying marshland—for many people the iconic image of Southeast Asia.

GETTING ORIENTED

The vast swath of Thailand known as Isan has often been characterized, if not stigmatized, by the existence of the Korat plateau, which makes up a good portion of the region. If much of Isan's landscape is flat and featureless, this is hardly true of the region's culture. Travelers to Isan have the option of visiting the mountains around Korat and Loei, experiencing the traditional life of the provinces along the length of the Mekong River from Nong Khai, or visiting the wealth of Khmer architecture found in the southern stretch of the region bordering Cambodia. The best way to approach the region is from one of the major cities, Korat or Udon Thani.

Phimai, Isan.

ISAN PLANNER

When to Go

The ideal time to visit Isan is during the cooler winter months between late October and February, when the rains stop, the temperatures are more agreeable, and the flora more abundant. But this major rice bowl of Thailand looks its best when the vast plains are filled with the calming sight of rice fields in full production, which happens August through December.

The region is not affected by the traditional high season, either in terms of costs or volume of visitors, but you should be prepared for crowds and steep accommodation price rises during major public festivals. Discounts are prevalent during the off-season, particularly the rainy season, June through October.

Crossing into Laos

Foreigners can cross into Laos at Nong Khai, Nakhon Phanom, Chong Mek (near Ubon Ratchathani), and Mukdahan. You'll need a Lao visa ($36), which can be obtained from the Laotian Embassy in Bangkok, the consulate in Khon Kaen, or directly at the border crossings. Some hotels and guesthouses in Nong Khai can also arrange visas for an added fee.

How Much Can You Do?

In the best of all possible worlds, you'd take two weeks in order to visit the whole region on a circular route. The good news is that even on a short trip you can get a sense of the region. If you are short on time, you may want to base yourself in Korat, a four-hour journey by train from Bangkok. The town can serve as a base for trips to the nearby Khmer ruins at Phimai. Surin, Buriram, and Si Saket, a little farther away, are also good bases from which to visit more ruins.

Tour & Visitor Info

Tour packages are not common in Isan, but travel agents and guesthouses in most major towns may be able to offer services. The harder to get to Khmer ruins near Surin and Si Saket would be the best places to make use of a tour or rental car. Recommended operators are listed in the appropriate region. ■ TIP→ **English-speaking guides are few in number, so be sure to specify that you require one. Otherwise, you may find yourself paying for a driver and pointer.**

The Tourism Authority of Thailand (TAT ⊕ *www.tourismthailand.org*) has branches in most cities and is a good source of information. Most branches are open daily from; typical hours are 8:30 to 4:30.

TAT (Korat) (✉ *2102–2104 Mittraphap Rd.* ☎ *044/213666*).

TAT (Surin) (✉ *Th. Thessaban 1 and Sirirat Rd., Krungsurinnork* ☎ *044/514447 or 089/201–7985*).

TAT (Ubon Ratchathani) (✉ *264/1 Khuan Thani Rd.* ☎ *045/243770*).

TAT (Udon Thani) (✉ *16/5 Mukmontri Rd.* ☎ *042/325406*).

TAT (Khon Kaen) (✉ *15/5 Prachasamosorn Rd.* ☎ *043/244498 or 043/244499*).

TAT (Loei) (✉ *Charoenrat Rd.* ☎ *042/812812*).

TAT (Nong Khai) (✉ *Thai-Laos Friendship Bridge Rd.* ☎ *042/467844*).

Getting Around

By Bus: All of Isan is accessible by bus from Bangkok; outlying areas can be accessed from the major centers of Korat, Udon Thani, and Ubon Ratchathani.

By Car: Tour companies are not common in the area, but it's possible to rent a car or hire a driver in the larger cities. Driving from Bangkok is feasible, but public transport is cheap and efficient, and most cities in Isan are within three or four hours of each other. If you do drive, to get to the Mekong towns, use the faster Highway 2 until Khon Kaen and then backtrack.

Rentals are about B1,000 to B1,500 per day. Hiring a private driver for your whole trip costs a bit more (at least B2,000 per day) but is safer and more relaxing, especially if you're able to find an English-speaking driver.

By Moto, Samlor, Songthaew & Tuk-Tuk: Cities in this part of the country do not have taxis like in Bangkok (though most of Bangkok's taxi drivers come from Isan). The most common means of getting around is by tuk-tuk, samlor (a three-wheel pedicab), or motorbike taxi. In all cases, you'll negotiate the price when you get in. Generally speaking, fares within city limits range from B30 to B60.

The cheapest (though not the most direct) means of getting around town and often between small towns is by songthaew—prices can be as low as B10 for a short trip. Public songthaews have fixed prices, whereas hired ones (on which you are the only passenger) need the price negotiated before boarding. Fellow passengers can typically help you determine where to get off.

By Train: There are two train routes from Bangkok, both running through Korat, where the line splits—one way to Udon Thani and Nong Khai via Khon Kaen, the other to Ubon Ratchathani via Buriram, Surin, and Si Saket.

WHAT IT COSTS IN BAHT

¢	$	$$	$$$	$$$$
Restaurants				
under B100	B100–B200	B201–B300	B301–B400	over B400
Hotels				
under B1,000	B1,000–B2,000	B2,001–B4,000	B4,001–B6,000	over B6,000

Restaurant prices are for a main course, excluding tax and tip. Hotel prices are for two people in a standard double room in high season, excluding service charges and tax.

Safety

The national tourist police can be contacted in emergency at 1155, possibly your best bet at finding an English speaker.

Theft isn't particularly common in the region, but it's not unheard of, so it's advisable to take the normal precautions like ensuring rental cars are locked and possessions are out of sight. Motorbikes are more prone to theft than cars.

The strong currents of the Mekong River can be dangerous. Swimming, diving, or kayaking is not recommended.

Hotel Tips

Because relatively few tourists visit Isan, most hotels and guesthouses cater chiefly to a business clientele. There are some top-class hotels in larger towns like Korat, Khon Kaen, and Udon Thani, but most accommodations are much more modest. As elsewhere in Thailand, standards of cleanliness are high and even the most basic room will invariably have fresh linen and towels.

Isan is a bargain—with the exception of Khon Kaen's Sofitel, it is difficult to spend more than US$50 a night even at the top-end hotels. Remember that such refinements as room telephones, TVs, and even hot water, can be rare outside the cities.

7

EATING & DRINKING WELL IN ISAN

Som tam.

Eating in Isan is all about spice and simplicity, and cooks are renowned for creating exquisite dishes with minimal preparation and fresh ingredients.

Restaurants here are often nothing more than a few tables and chairs, but the lack of elegance is made up for by what comes out of the kitchen. Cooks combine chilies, shallots, garlic, lime juice, and dried shrimp together for a number of *yum* (salads), and for *larb* (grilled-meat, -poultry, or -fish salads, often with mint). The mortar and pestle play a leading role in the kitchen, where cooks pound abundant chilies and grilled meat and fish—the stables on most menus in Isan. Meanwhile, the grill is kept full of charcoal for roasting fresh pork, chicken, and salted river fish, all of which are served with chili dip and sticky rice, and washed down with beer or Thai whiskey.

MEETING AND EATING

Udon Thani is home to Isan's premiere night market, a lively insight into northeastern food and culture. It seems that 80% of the city turns out on any given evening, as couples and families swoop in on their motorcycles and settle in for a few hours of alfresco dining. Just about any type of Isan specialties are available, with vendors dishing out heaping plates of som tam, roast chicken, spicy yum salads, and grilled fish served with chili and lemon sauce. At the back of the market there's a large beer garden serving cold beverages and playing Thai rock music.

SOM TAM

Savory *som tam*—a salad of green papaya crushed with tomatoes, shallots, peanuts, dried shrimp, palm sugar, lime, garlic, fish sauce, and plenty of fiery chilies—may be the most quintessential of Thai dishes. But in Isan it takes on a special flavor: it's often eaten with small crabs or with *pla raa* (fermented mud fish), a real acquired taste.

NAM PRIK PLA RAA

Nose-numbing *nam prik* (literally, "chili water") is made by combining garlic, fresh chilies, fish sauce, lime juice, and fish paste. It's eaten all over Thailand, but in Isan, the fish paste is made with *pla raa,* freshwater fish that has been fermented from six months to two years. *Pla raa* translates directly as "moldy fish." It is served with fresh vegetables, eaten as a dip, or for poorer folks, often eaten as the sole topping on rice.

LARB PHET

Larb, or spicy meat salads, are an Isan staple, and *larb phet* (spicy duck salad) is one of the tastiest. The duck meat is boiled, than chopped into small pieces, and combined with fish sauce, lemongrass, roasted and dried chilies, kaffir lime leaves, lime juice, roasted rice powder, red onions, and mint leaves to create a powerful mix of exquisite flavors. Look for this northeastern treat at small local restaurants or in night markets.

GAI YANG AND KAO NIAO

Gai yang (roast chicken) is served everywhere in Isan, from fancy restaurants to vendors coming on buses and trains. Every city will have several places that locals tout as the "best" due to the garlic and chilies used in grilling or the sweet-and-sour sauce it's served with. And eating gai yang without a ball of *kao niao* or sticky rice (traditionally served in a bamboo basket) is a faux pas in northeastern Thailand.

SUP NORMAI

If you partake of this dish in Isan, locals will embrace you as a family member. Not only is it extremely spicy, but *sup normai* (bamboo salad) is considered a working-class staple due to the cheap cost of bamboo. You can usually find it in open-air restaurants and in places where papaya salad is served. A basket or two of sticky rice to moderate the heat is advised.

KORAT & LOWER ISAN

Updated by Dave Stamboulis

THE PROVINCES STRETCHING FROM KORAT through Buriram, Surin, Si Saket, and on to Ubon Ratchathani are known as Lower Isan. The area is particularly renowned for its Khmer architecture; its delicious cuisine based on pungent spices, vegetables, and river fish; and the continued influence of Khmer culture, particularly with regard to minority dialects and a musical style called *kantrum* (traditional music with singing in the Khmer language), which can be found east of Korat.

A trip to this part of the country would not be complete without visiting the famous Khmer prasats (ornate, towered temples of religious and royal significance) in Phimai, Buriram, Surin, and Si Saket. Here, ruins have intricate engravings cut from sandstone and towering structures fashioned in laterite, which are somewhat more imposing than the soft touches of limestone stucco and red brick found in equivalent historical sites in the Central Plains.

Khao Yai National Park offers some variety to your trip, and while on your travels you may want to take the opportunity to buy the fine silks produced here or enjoy some of the local Thai folk rock ballads, known as *pleng pheua chiwit* (songs for life). The food will take chili lovers to paradise. If you're lucky enough to be here during the rice production period, the harmonious pace of rural life among the rice fields will provide you with an unforgettable image of traditions in practice.

KORAT

259 km (160 mi) northeast of Bangkok.

Considered the gateway to the Northeast, Korat is the largest city in Isan and the one of the largest cities in Thailand. Its size resulted from the need for a strong frontier city to govern the towns of the vast northeastern plateau. Korat is a modern mini-metropolis, complete with huge shopping malls, a few high-rise hotels, and a wonderful bustling night market, which serves as a good introduction to Isan's lively, friendly, local feel.

The city also has a very distinct culture from the rest of Isan (its own dialect and musical style, for example) and a strong sense of self, which grew out of its prestigious past. Indeed, many people in the city will describe themselves as Korat people as opposed to Isan people. Above all, the city reveres its beloved *Ya Mo*, short for Thao Suranaree, a local woman who led her people to victory over the invading Laotians. Her monument can be found in front of Phratu Chumpol, one of the four gates leading into the Old City, and homage is paid to her throughout the city.

Korat itself does not have tourist "sights" per se, but the nearby restored Khmer ruins at Phimai and the natural wonders of nearby Khao Yai National Park make it a great base for exploring the region. Addition-

ally, the city provides a perfect introduction into Isan culture and has excellent food and accommodation choices.

GETTING HERE & AROUND

BY BUS Korat is a major transport hub for Isan, with bus services to and from Bangkok, Pattaya, Chiang Mai, Udon Thani, and Phitsanulok. A bus journey from Bangkok's Northern Bus Terminal will take roughly four hours and cost B250; from Chiang Mai it will take roughly 11 hours, costing around B450, depending on the standard of the bus.

Korat has two bus stations—the older Terminal 1 in the city center and the newer Terminal 2 north of Mittraphap Road. Buses going outside the province use Terminal 2, while buses to local destinations use Terminal 1 (Phimai being the exception). Bangkok buses can be found at both stations.

BY CAR Korat is about a three-hour drive from Bangkok up Highway 2. The city itself is small and somewhat laid out on a grid so easy to navigate.

BY TAXI, TUK-TUK & SONGTHAEW Public songthaews run everywhere in Korat and cost B9—just wave them down and ask if they are going where you want. Private tuk-tuks and samlors will take you anywhere in town for B40–B60; agree on a price before embarking.

BY TRAIN Korat is best served by train from Bangkok. Train 71 leaves Hualamphong Station at 10:05AM and arrives in Korat at 2:27 PM, and train 233 departs at 11:40 AM, arriving at 4:50 PM; there are several late afternoon departures as well. Seats are B325–B1,010. The trip takes about 4½ hours. From Korat station, tuk-tuks will take you the short distance into town for B60.

THE NAME GAME

It's easy to get confused by the name of the city: Korat's official name is Nakhon Ratchasima, and it's labeled as such on maps and many highway signs, but Thai people call the city Korat.

ESSENTIALS

Car-Rental Agency **Fodo Car Rent** (*✉The Mall, Mitthapap Rd., Korat ☎044/256773 or 081/977–0320*).

Emergencies **General Emergencies** (*☎191*). **Police** (*☎044/242010*). **Bangkok Ratchasima Hospital** (*✉130 8/9 Mitthapap Rd., Korat ☎044/262000*).

Visitor & Tour Info **Greenleaf Travel** (*✉51/1 Moo 2, Tessaban 15 Rd., Pakchong District, Korat ☎044/280285*). **Nanta Travel** (*✉334 Suranari Rd., Korat ☎044/251339*).

WHERE TO EAT

$–$$ THAI ✕**Korat Buri.** On Korat's busiest nightlife street is this romantic restaurant, where you can enjoy real local food (there's no English menu) while being serenaded by live music in a garden that's decked out with lanterns and shaded by big, arching trees. Try the *pla chon samunprai* (snakehead fish deep-fried with lemongrass, ginger, crispy chilies, and spicy sauce) or the *kha mu tod krob* (pork leg with a sweet-and-spicy sauce). *✉268 Yommarat Rd. ☎044/269108 ▭MC, V ⊙No lunch.*

$–$$ ★ THAI ✕**Nai-Ruen.** Nai-Ruen may be in the basement of the Sima Thani Hotel, but it elevates the all-you-can-eat buffet concept to a new level. Throw out all of your preconceived notions about buffets (quantity over quality, lack of freshness, and so on), because everything at this one is spot-on and impeccably fresh. It's a great opportunity to sample dozens of Isan specialties at once. The Thai food is best, but also decent are the Chinese food, the sushi, the noodle soups, and the steak. (Yep, they're all included.) The B165 lunch buffet is easily the top value in town, especially if you're hungry. *✉Sima Thani Hotel, 2112/2 Mittraphap Rd. ☎044/213100 ▭MC, V.*

¢–$ THAI ✕**Rabieng-Pa.** The name means "forest terrace," which makes sense given the amount of greenery surrounding the courtyard's fountain. Rabieng-Pa's food is Isan to the core, and you'll find some unique dishes here; for example, try the *lahp plah-chaun taut* (fried snakehead fish with ground rice and mint), and don't miss the *poo-mah daung* (fresh raw blue swimming crabs in a hot chili sauce). Prices are more than fair, and another advantage of the place is its English-language menu. However, the atmosphere here isn't as charming as at Korat Buri. *✉284 Yommarat Rd. ☎044/243137 ▭MC, V.*

¢ THAI ✕**Samranlap Suansim Restaurant.** Popular with locals, this restaurant serves up a selection of Isan dishes, of which *larb phet,* a spicy minced

Restaurants ▼
Korat Buri 3
Nai-Ruen 1
Rabieng-Pa 4
Samranlap Suansim Restaurant 2

Hotels ▼
Dusit Princess 2
Rachaphruk Grand Hotel......1
Sima Thani.......3

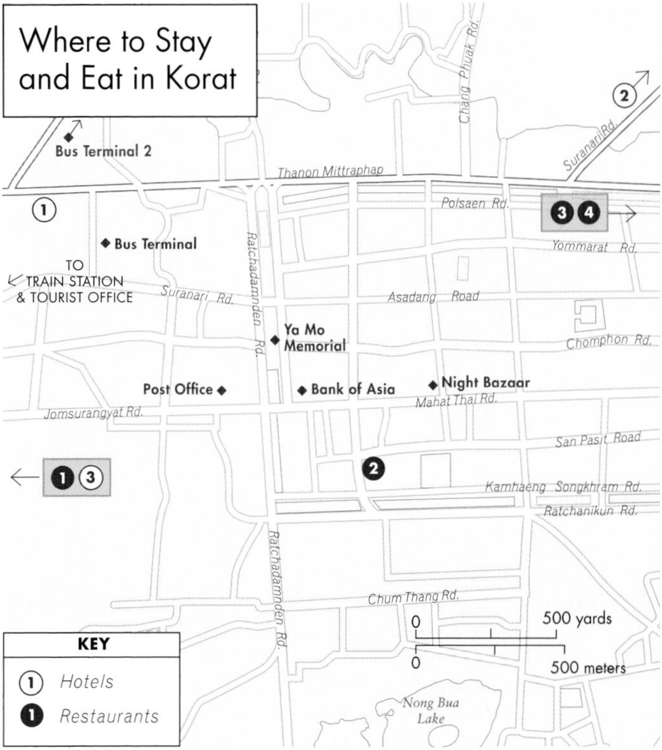

Where to Stay and Eat in Korat

Bus Terminal 2
Thanon Mittraphap
Chang Phuak Rd.
Suranari Rd.
Polsaen Rd.
Yommarat Rd.
Bus Terminal
TO TRAIN STATION & TOURIST OFFICE
Suranari Rd.
Ratchadamnden Rd.
Asadang Road
Chomphon Rd.
Ya Mo Memorial
Post Office
Bank of Asia
Night Bazaar
Mahat Thai Rd.
Jomsurangyat Rd.
San Pasit Road
Kamhaeng Songkhram Rd.
Ratchanikun Rd.
Chum Thang Rd.
0 500 yards
0 500 meters
Nong Bua Lake

KEY
① Hotels
❶ Restaurants

duck salad, is a particular hit. The restaurant has basic furnishings and cement floors, but the fine fare at very reasonable prices more than makes up for the lack of ambience. If you feel brave, you can try the bull penis salad (be sure to let us know what it's like). ✉*163 Watcharasarit Rd.* ☎*044/243636* ▭*No credit cards.*

WHERE TO STAY

The city, which is home to the Thai Second Army and air force, hosts annual U.S. army exercises, called Cobra Gold, in November and December. If you're traveling during this time, make your reservations in advance, as the city's hotels fill up.

$–$$ ★ **Dusit Princess.** This gleaming nine-story showplace has finely furnished guest rooms complete with executive desks and comfortable chairs. The expansive lobby has eye-catching silk in its souvenir shops. A small garden and pool offer some relief from the glare of the noonday sun. ■ **TIP→ The formal restaurant serves the best Cantonese food in town.** **Pros:** elegant spa opened in 2008; dim sum buffet on Sunday; spacious and opulent suites. **Cons:** away from downtown; often full with conference and seminar groups; on very busy road. ✉*1137 Suranari Rd.,* ☎*044/256629* 🌐*www.royalprincess.com* *186 rooms, 9 suites* *In-room: refrigerator, Wi-Fi. In-hotel: 2 restaurants, bars, pool, gym, laundry service* ▭*AE, DC, MC, V.*

$ **Rachaphruk Grand Hotel.** The dark, polished-granite lobby of this modern high-rise leads to a relaxing lounge. Check out the signed photos of Thai celebrity guests behind the front desk. The light and airy rooms are decorated mostly in primrose and pale woods; Japanese-style window screens can be opened to provide a commanding view of the city. The hotel is popular with visiting U.S. servicemen and women in November and December. **Pros:** nice city views; eclectic choice of international buffet restaurants; massage parlor on premises. **Cons:** small pool; walk-in booking often not available; far from main restaurants and bars. ✉*311 Mittraphap Rd.,* ☎*044/26122* 🌐*www.rachaphruk.com* *159 rooms* *In-room: refrigerator. In-hotel: restaurant, room service, bar, pool, gym, laundry service* *AE, MC, V* *BP.*

PLENG KORAT

On the west side of Ratchadamnoen Road, across from the Chumpol Gate, you can find regular performances of *Pleng Korat*, an oratory sung on request here in a style unique to the province. Performers wear traditional costumes and can be enticed into singing for about B400 for a half-hour performance. *Pleng Korat* was a favorite of the famous Suranaree and is still popular with merit-making Buddhists, as well as passing tourists. The performers usually pack up by 6 PM.

$$ **Sima Thani.** At one of Korat's most distinguished hotels, a soaring lobby features fountains with rushing water and a tastefully executed elephant theme. Go for one of the deluxe rooms, which have beautiful bedding and Asian flair. Most high-end hotels in Isan have Chinese restaurants and this one is no exception. **Pros:** spacious rooms; gorgeous Atrium bar in lobby; separate smoking/no-smoking floors. **Cons:** rooms musty; carpet and furniture old and drab; on busy road. ✉*2112/2 Mittraphap Rd.,* ☎*044/213100, 02/253–4885 in Bangkok* 🌐*www.simathani.com* *245 rooms, 20 suites* *In-room: refrigerator, Wi-Fi. In-hotel: 3 restaurants, room service, bars, pool, gym, laundry service* *MC, V.*

NIGHTLIFE

Korat has a lively nightlife, much of which is concentrated on Jomsurangyart Road, near the edge of the Old City. Another good street to try is Yommarat Road, within the Old City, where you can find a number of bars and restaurants.

Bule's Saloon Pub and Restaurant (✉*264 Yommarat Rd.* ☎*044/256538*) is a longtime favorite for Western rock music lovers in the city. You'll feel like you're in a mountain lodge as you sit back and listen to the fine guitar licks of the owner. It's one of the few places outside Bangkok where you can hear bands play a repertoire that includes Pink Floyd, Led Zeppelin, and the Rolling Stones.

You spot the lively **Coco Beet Pub and Restaurant** (✉*Yommarat Rd.* ☎*044/247993*) by its waterfall-effect windows. Inside you'll be wowed by the owner's unique decorating taste—a kitschy mishmash of decors—and the fine covers of Thai and Western pop songs coming from the marvelous live band. The crowd is mainly made up of the well-to-do local party set.

Pub-restaurant **Long Tiem** (✉ *38 Suranari Rd.* ☎ *044/272198*) is in a wooden Thai-style house and has an enormous beer garden. It's a great choice for those who prefer local Thai live folk-rock, known as pleng pheua chiwit. A resident dreadlocked tattoo artist to the rear of the establishment can provide you with the ultimate souvenir.

Living Bar (✉ *Rachaphruk Grand Hotel, 311 Mittraphap Rd.* ☎ *044/261222* 🌐 *www.rachaphruk.com*) is a happening disco-bar where foreigners and locals hit the dance floor together.

SHOPPING

Between 6 and 9 PM head to Korat's **Night Bazaar,** on Mahadthai Road in the center of town. A block-long street is taken over by food stands and vendor stalls and is crowded with locals. If you're looking to buy local products during the day, head to the **Suranaree Monument.** The shops facing the monument sell souvenirs at reasonable prices, including locally produced silks, pottery, and *kao tang* rice snacks.

A side trip to **Pak Thong Chai Silk and Cultural Centre,** 32 km (20 mi) south of Korat, offers a chance to see how locals make silk, from the raising of silkworms to the spinning of thread and the weaving of fabric. You can buy silk at some 70 factories in the area. From Bus Terminal 1, buses to Pak Thongchai leave every hour (B50 one-way). They drop you at the market, from where you can explore the surrounding lanes for silk outlets and factories. The most interesting shop is **Machada Thai Silk Machada** (✉ *118/1 Sabesiri Rd.* ☎ *044/441684 or 081/976–4378*), which has weaving demonstrations. For ceramics, drive out to the village of **Ban Dan Kwian,** 15 km (10 mi) southwest of Korat. The rust-color clay here is used for reproductions of classic designs. The village can be easily reached by taking a songthaew from Kamhang Songkram Road, near the police station. Trucks leave every 20 minutes and the trip costs a nominal B30.

KHAO YAI NATIONAL PARK

130 km (80 mi) southwest of Korat.

Khao Yai is Thailand's oldest national park (established in 1962). The reserve covers 2,168 square km (833 square mi) and spreads over four provinces. It's a frequent destination for Thais seeking to escape Bangkok and on weekends the park can feel crowded.

On entering the park and winding your way up into the forested hills, you'll soon find yourself confronted by hordes of pleading macaque monkeys loitering on the road in search of handouts. But these are not the only wildlife you'll likely to encounter here—of particular note are the wild elephants, tigers, leopard cats, and barking deer that can sometimes be observed at the salt licks. Elephants generally roam only at night, but occasionally one pops out during the day.

Trekking trails, bicycle paths, viewpoints, and bird-watching towers are prolific in this huge evergreen forest, and many of the park's splendid waterfalls are easily accessible by car or bicycle. ■ **TIP→ Leech socks, which can be purchased at the visitor center, are advised when walking on the trails between May and October to keep the minuscule but annoying leeches off your ankles.** The park is particularly easy to get around, and frequent information points and warning signs such as "Cobra Crossing" will help keep you from harm's way (though evening strolls are still not advised). Hiking trails from the park headquarters are 1 km to 8 km (½ mi to 5 mi). ✉ *Moo 4, Thanarat Rd., Km 17, Amphur Pak Chong, Korat* ☎ *044/297297* 🎫 *B400 per person plus B150 per car* ⏲ *Daily 6 AM–9 PM.*

The otherwise undistinguished **Jungle House resort,** along the road into Khao Yai, operates **elephant rides** around the surrounding forest. ✉ *Khao Yai National Park, Pakchong District* 🎫 *B300* ⏲ *Daily dawn–dusk.*

GETTING HERE & AROUND

BY BUS Buses leave frequently from Bangkok's Mo Chit Bus Station, taking about 2½ to 3 hours to Pak Chong (B200). There are also many departures by train from Hualamphong Station to Pak Chong, which take slightly longer.

From Korat you can take a bus from Bus Station 1 to Pak Chong for B70; buses leave hourly for the 1½-hour trip. At Pak Chong take a local songthaew to the park's entrance. Note that it's another 14 km (9 mi) from the park entrance to the visitor center, so it's best to negotiate a ride into the heart of the camp or else you'll need to hire an additional taxi at the entrance.

BY CAR As Khao Yai and its surroundings are vast, with minimal public transport, the best way to get around the park is by rental car or hired driver from Korat or Bangkok, which will also allow you to stop along the way at one of the many roadside fruit stalls (look for custard fruit) or curry puff vendors. If driving from Bangkok, take Hwy. 305 (Rangsit to Nakhon Nayok), then switch to Hwy. 33 at Naresuan Junction, and then turn left onto 3077 leading to the park headquarters after 40 km (25 mi; about 2½ hours). F See *Essentials in Korat and Bangkok, for car rentals and drivers.*

ESSENTIALS

Emergencies **Pak Chong Nana Hospital** (✉ *Mittraphap Rd., Pak Chong* ☎ *044/311856*).

Visitor & Tour Info **Greenleaf Tours** (✉ *52 Moo 6, Tanat Rd., Km 7.5, Pak Chong* ☎ *044/365073 or 044/365024* 🌐 *www.greenleaftour.com*).

WHERE TO EAT

$$–$$$ STEAK ✕ **Chokchai Steakhouse.** It's not surprising that this steak house has American pretensions: it's near a cattle ranch, started by an American nicknamed the "Little Cowboy," which provides the restaurant's meat. Don't expect world-class cuts here, but Chokchai does about as well with the genre as the budget-busting spots in Bangkok that import their

meat from Australia. ✉ *170 Moo 2, Mittraphap Rd.* ☎ *044/328553 or 044/328232* ▭ *No credit cards.*

$–$$ ★ THAI **Ya Ka Restaurant.** Most people come to this casual, open-air restaurant along the road into Khao Yai for one reason: the show-stopping grilled snakehead fish, which comes fresh out of the tanks and is then salted, skewered, and grilled over an open fire. But equally worth trying are the deep-fried, ground snakehead fish with a spicy salad and the pork leg with red gravy. Enjoy it all with sticky rice, spicy som tam, and friendly smiles from the staff. ✉ *101/3 Khao Yai Rd.* ☎ *044/297151* 🌐 *www.yakarestaurant.com* ▭ *No credit cards.*

THE PRASAT

The Khmer influence is evident in the occasional *prasat*, or towered temple, that dots the region. The prasat wasn't a royal residence, but rather a retreat for those traveling from the Khmer temple of Angkor in present-day Cambodia.

WHERE TO STAY

The park provides a variety of cabin accommodations at reasonable rates, though many prefer to camp at one of the park's two designated sites. Tents and bedding, along with bicycles, are available for hire on-site. If you don't wish to sleep under the stars, there are several resorts and plenty of pleasant restaurants located along Thanarat Road, which leads to the park entrance. ■ **TIP→ The park's headquarters, next door to the informative visitor center, can help arrange lodgings and treks.**

$–$$ ★ **Juldis.** A luxurious resort set back from an unassuming road leading to Khao Yai, the Juldis is ideal if you're devoting a full day to exploring the park. It has a spa and pool, and the gardens in back create a wonderfully isolated feeling. Skip the steak house (which becomes a pub at night) and try the Thai-Chinese restaurant instead. The "deluxe" rooms, with balconies overlooking the forest, are a better deal for only a few baht more. The lovely houses and bungalows in the garden are much pricier. **Pros:** beautiful, natural location just outside national park; many activities (tennis, bicycles, swimming); on-site spa. **Cons:** far from town; no off-site restaurants nearby; many Thai tour groups. ✉ *54 Moo 4, Thanarat Rd., Km 17, Thambol Moo-Sri, Pakchong,* ☎ *044/297297* 🌐 *www.khaoyai.com* *156 rooms* *In-room: refrigerator. In-hotel: 2 restaurants, room service, bars, tennis courts, pool, gym, spa, bicycles, laundry service* ▭ *AE, DC, MC, V.*

PHIMAI

60 km (37 mi) northeast of Korat.

The town of Phimai boasts a verdant city square, an energetic market, tough muay thai boxers, and locally produced noodles, but it is most famous for its magnificent Khmer architecture at the Prasat Hin Phimai, right in the middle of it all. The town's quiet streets come to life with the arrival of tour buses ferrying tourists to the site, but it's still possible to rent a bicycle and explore the area in relative peace. Phimai is dotted with the remnants of ancient edifices, walls, and gates, and the sense of history surrounding this friendly town will not be lost on you. ■ **TIP→ The Phimai festival, held on the second weekend of November, brings the crowds to see boat races and cultural shows, so it's best to book in advance if you wish to stay overnight at this time.**

GETTING HERE & AROUND

Phimai is small enough to walk around. It can easily be reached by bus from Bus Station 2 in Korat. Bus 1305 leaves every 30 minutes and costs B60, arriving in Phimai 75 minutes later.

ESSENTIALS

Emergencies In an emergency, head for the Bangkok-Ratchasima Hospital in Korat (⇨ *above*).

Visitor & Tour Info **Boonsiri Guest House** (✉ *Th. Chomsudasadej,Phimai* ☎ 089/424–9942 🌐 *www.boonsiri.net*).

EXPLORING PHIMAI

Prasat Phimai sits in the center of the tiny town, and takes a few hours to explore in full. The only other major sight here is the banyan tree, and as it's only 2 km (1 mi) away, it makes sense to rent a bicycle, and explore the beautiful rice fields surrounding town while you're at it.

WHAT TO SEE

Bicycles, which come with maps highlighting points of interest, can be rented from the **Boonsiri Guest House** (✉ *Th. Chomsudasadej, Phimai* ☎ *089/424–9942* 🌐 *www.boonsiri.net*), around the corner from Prasat Phimai, for B20 an hour.

★ **Prasat Hin Phimai,** in the center of town, is one of the great Khmer structures in Isan. Built sometime in the late 11th or early 12th century (believed to predate Angkor Wat), it has been carefully restored and frequently appears in music videos and movies. To enter the prasat is to step back eight centuries. Most fascinating, perhaps, is that the temple was first Hindu when founded by Jayavarman V, then was adapted into a Buddhist temple in the 11th century, when Jayavarman VII of Angkor Thom himself converted to Buddhism. Buddhist images replaced Hindu ones. Some Hindu iconography remains, but a giant phallus at the entrance of the temple, for one, was covered up.

By the time you pass through the external sandstone wall and the gallery, you're swept up in the creation and destruction of the Brahman gods engraved on the lintels. A quartet of *gopuras* (gate towers) guards the entrances, with the main one facing south toward Angkor. The central white sandstone prang, towering more than 60 feet, is flanked by two smaller buildings, one in laterite, the other in red sandstone. The principal prasat is surrounded by four porches whose external lintels depict Hindu gods and scenes from the Ramayana. Inside, the lintels portray the religious art of Mahayana Buddhism. ✉ *Tha Songkhran Rd.* ☎ *044/471568* 🎟 *B40* ⏲ *Daily 7:30–6.*

The excellent **Phimai National Museum,** adjacent to the site, contains priceless treasures from the Dvaravati and Khmer civilizations—notably great works of Khmer sculpture. The museum's masterpiece is a stone

Sticky rice is Isan's major crop; rice paddies constitute about 60% of the region's farmland.

statue of King Jayavarman VII found at Prasat Hin Phimai. ✉ *Tha Songkhran Rd.* ☎ *044/471167* *B30* *Daily 9–4.*

The village of **Sai Ngam** is home of the world's largest banyan tree, said to be more than 350 years old, which is easy to believe if you examine its mass of intertwined trunks. Walk along the raised footpaths in the shade of this vast natural phenomenon; it was once believed that the roots of the tree stretched as far as the center of town. The adjoining food stalls make it a favorite picnic spot for Thai families, and across the lake you'll see a faithful reconstruction of a traditional Northeastern Thailand house. To get to Sai Ngam, 2 km (1 mi) take a tuk-tuk (B60–B80) from downtown or rent a bicycle for B20 an hour from Boonsiri Guest House.

WHERE TO EAT & STAY

¢–$ ★ THAI **Bahn Muong Restaurant.** In Phimai, the Thais like to eat at the seafood restaurants out by the lake, and you shouldn't pass up the chance to do so, too. At Bahn Muong, the freshwater "catch of the day" takes on new meaning: when you order a fish, they row out to a netted-in area in the lake and come back with the catch. Enjoy your *pla nin tap tim pao* (grilled snakehead fish with a spicy dipping sauce) in one of the thatched-roof cabanas, reached by walking across rickety wooden planks. ✉ *Bahn Samitt Rd.* ☎ *081/997–4970* *No credit cards.*

¢–$ THAI **Baitoey Restaurant.** This wonderful, relaxing restaurant has a quiet location 10 minutes out of town. The theme here is ancient Khmer: The walls are made of local laterite bricks, the ceiling is made of bamboo, and Khmer designs and engravings are all around. The restaurant serves traditional Thai fare with some emphasis on local dishes, such as stir-fried Phimai noodles. ✉*Phimai-Chumpuang Rd.* ☎*044/287103* ▭*MC, V.*

¢ **Phimai Inn Hotel.** This friendly hotel is a good value; however, ask to look at several rooms as there is a tremendous difference in quality, not always dictated by price. "VIP" rooms have carpeting and minibars. There's an enormous pool in the middle of it all, possibly the largest in Isan. The hotel is on the bypass at the edge of town. **Pros:** giant swimming pool; VIP rooms very spacious; poolside restaurant. **Cons:** far from town and from shops and restaurants; hard to find transport into town at night. ✉*33/1 Bypass Rd.,* ☎*044/287228 or 044/287229* *80 rooms* *In-room: no a/c (some), refrigerator (some). In-hotel: 2 restaurants, pool, laundry service* ▭*MC, V.*

BURIRAM

151 km (94 mi) east of Korat.

The provincial capital of Buriram lies between Korat and Surin and is a good gateway for those visiting the nearby Khmer prasats, some of the finest in the country. Founded in the late 18th century by the first king of the Chakri dynasty, this somewhat neglected city, which translates as "City of Pleasantness," is turning a corner, as evidenced by the $1 million conversion of an ancient moat into an attractive public park.

More peaceful than its neighboring cities, Buriram provides an opportunity to pick up some bargain silk products and sample the Isan lifestyle by eating local specialties such as larb at the bustling Night Bazaar, or listening to local folk rock in one of the city's live country music venues.

GETTING HERE & AROUND

BY AIR PB Air has flights from Bangkok to Buriram. Buriram's airport is 30 km (18 mi) northeast of town.

BY BUS Buses from Korat to Buriram leave hourly, cost B120, and take around two hours. Bangkok buses to Buriram leave as frequently and are B333 or B515 (for VIP service with air-conditioning), and take six hours to reach Mo Chit Station. Buriram's bus station is about 2 km (1 mi) west of downtown.

BY CAR Buriram is on Highway 226, which runs directly from Korat, continuing on toward Surin.

BY TAXI & TUK-TUK Tuk-tuks and motorcycle taxis can take you anywhere in town for B40–B60.

BY TRAIN The Northeastern Line runs frequent service from Bangkok to Buriram, on the line that terminates at Ubon Ratchathani. The most convenient train departs Bangkok at 10:05 arriving in Buriram at 4:14. Prices from Bangkok range from about B375 to B1,150, depending on class; from Korat prices are approximately B200–B875. Buriram's train station is less than 1 km (½ mi) north of downtown on Nasathanee Road.

ESSENTIALS

Emergencies **Buriram Hospital** (✉ *Nasathanee Rd., Buriram* ☎ *044/615001*).

VISITOR & TOUR INFO Tour companies can arrange for car rentals. **Buriram Expats** (✉ *Buriram* ☎ *044/621962 or 081/070–4750*). **Thepnakorn Hotel** (✉ *139 Jira Rd., Buriram* ☎ *044/613400 up to 02*).

WHERE TO EAT & STAY

If you really want to mix it up with the locals and get a sense of how people dine out in Buriram, head to the Night Bazaar (daily 4 PM–11 PM) at the end of Romburi Road. It has plenty of cheap, ready-to-order food, along with fresh produce. It's at its best after 6 PM.

¢–$ AMERICAN–CASUAL **Bamboo Bar & Restaurant.** This simple country-style restaurant in the heart of town is only minutes from the train station and even closer to the city's nightspots. You'll find such Western dishes as ploughman's lunch (a cheese sandwich with a salad) and fish-and-chips; the ham-and-cheese baguettes are particularly popular. It's a good place to meet the local expat crowd, kick back in front of some cable TV, and get some tips on what to do and see in the area. ✉ *14/13 Romburi Rd.* ☎ *044/625577* *No credit cards.*

¢–$ THAI **Phu Tawan.** A popular evening eatery, Phu Tawan is a must for Thai folk-rock-music lovers. A booming band plays to an excitable local crowd, who spend all evening jumping up to dance and sing along with the musicians. It's only a minute's walk from the Thepnakorn Hotel. Recommended dishes are the local spicy minced pork dish larb moo and *yum takrai,* a lemongrass-and-dried-shrimp salad. ✉ *99 Jira Rd.* ☎ *044/617123* *No credit cards* *No lunch.*

$–$$ **Thepnakorn Hotel.** This is as close as Buriram has to a top-end hotel and a serviceable place to rest up while investigating the nearby ruins. The English-speaking staff will give you a warm welcome, though the aesthetic and quite drab look of the place lends a slightly depressing tone to it all. The value is good by Western standards, but not by the standards of Buriram. It's a 5- to 10-minute tuk-tuk ride from the center of town. **Pros:** can arrange transport/tours to Phanom Rung; nice swimming pool; English spoken; superior rooms include buffet breakfast. **Cons:** far from center of town; carpets in rooms old and worn; cigarette smell in some rooms. ✉ *139 Jira Rd.,* ☎ *044/613400 up to 02* *169 rooms* *In-room: refrigerator (some). In-hotel: restaurant, room service, bars, pool, gym, spa, laundry service* *MC, V.*

PHANOM RUNG

65 km (41 mi) south of Buriram.

Occupying a majestic spot on top of a 4,265-foot-tall mountain, Phanom Rung is not only a great vantage point for looking out at the plains of Isan, but is also the site of the best Khmer ruins in Thailand. Its 12th-century Angkorian temples have been fully restored and the site they occupy is a quiet and peaceful respite from the towns and heat of the plains below.

7

Elephants and mahouts (handlers) play soccer during the Elephant Roundup festival in Surin.

GETTING HERE & AROUND

BY BUS From Buriram, bus 522 to Chantaburi leaves every 45 minutes and stops in Ban Ta Pek (B60); from there you can get a songthaew or motorcycle taxi on to the ruins.

BY CAR Phanom Rung is reached by taking Road 218 south from Buriram 45 km (28 mi) to Nang Rong, then following Highway 24 east 14 km (9 mi) to Ban Tako, and then turning onto Road 2117 south another 15 km (9 mi) to the park. The total driving time from Buriram is about one hour.

EXPLORING PHANOM RUNG

The temple area of Phanom Rung is quite large, and taking in the ruins can be exhausting if done in the midday heat. Best to start early, when there are few tourists and good light.

WHAT TO SEE

Fodor's Choice ★ The restored hilltop shrine of **Prasat Hin Khao Phanom Rung,** 65 km (40 mi) from Buriram, is a supreme example of Khmer art. The approach to the prasat sets your heart thumping—you cross an imposing bridge and climb majestic staircases to the top, where you're greeted by a magnificent reclining Vishnu lintel. This architectural treasure hit the headlines when it mysteriously disappeared in the 1960s, then reappeared at the Chicago Art Institute. After 16 years of protests it was finally returned to its rightful place. Step under the lintel and through the portal into the double-walled sanctuary. Intricate carvings in a style similar to those found in Lopburi cover the interior walls, and in the center of the prasat stands the great throne room dedicated to the Hindu Lord Shiva.

Built in the 12th century under King Suriyaworamann II, one of the great Khmer rulers, it was restored in the 1980s at a cost of $2 million. It's one of the few Khmer sanctuaries without later Thai Buddhist additions. **TIP→ For insight into this and other nearby Khmer architecture it's well worth having a look in the visitor center,** which can be found beyond the souvenir stalls, along the shaded path where you catch your first glimpse of the prasat. The center has commendably clear information; the exhibits that shed light on the magnificent stone carvings found at Phanom Rung are particularly recommended. In the gardens outside the temple area, don't miss the huge bamboo tree creaking in the wind. ✉ *Phanon Rung Historical Park, Chaleum Prakiat, Buriram* ☎ *044/631746* 🎫 *B40* ⏲ *Prasat daily 6–6, visitor center 9–4.*

Scattered around the area are other Khmer prasats in various stages of decay, many of them overgrown by vegetation. One of these has been rescued by Thailand's Department of Fine Arts. **Prasat Muang Tam** is only a couple of miles from the base of Phanom Rung hill. It's estimated to be 100 years older than its neighbor, starting off as a 10th-century Hindu sanctuary. Its main building symbolically represents the universe, with lesser towers emanating from the center. Today four towers remain, all containing carvings of Shiva and his consort Uma, Varuna on a swan, Krishna with cows, and Indra on the elephant Erawan. The complex is flanked by ceremonial ponds, with five-headed nagas (water serpents that appear in Buddhist folklore) lying alongside it. ✉ *8 km (5 mi) southeast of Prasat Hin Khao Phanom Rung* ☎ *044/631746* 🎫 *B40* ⏲ *Daily 6–6.*

7

WHERE TO EAT

¢–$ THAI ✕ **Kam Khum.** Of the several casual open-air restaurants lined up outside the entrance to Phanom Rung, this is one of the most reliable choices. Ignore the dumbed-down English menu and go straight for the local specialty, pla nin pao, a whole river fish covered with salt, stuffed with lemongrass, and grilled over an open fire. Try the delicious *larb moo* spicy salad. If you're standing with your back to the park, Kam Khum is to the left of the restroom complex. ✉ *Phanom Rung Historical Park* ☎ *081/878–7148* 💳 *No credit cards* ⏲ *No dinner.*

SURIN

52 km (32 mi) east of Buriram, 198 km (123 mi) east of Korat.

With its Phanom Don Rak mountain range bordering Cambodia to the south, Surin has always been heavily influenced by Cambodian culture, and a large proportion of the local population speaks a Khmer dialect. Its strategic location also made Surin an assembly point for the elephant armies during the early Rattanakosin period; to this day the city is best known for its elephants. Everywhere you look in this bustling city you'll see homage paid to these noble creatures in the form of sculptures, artwork, and even streetlamp motifs. In addition, Surin shares with its neighboring provinces a wealth of ancient Khmer structures, found outside the city in varying states of decay or restoration.

Surin is famous, above all, for its annual Elephant Roundup (*box, below*), held the third week of November. Surin has also become something of a year-round expat center, full of *farang* (westerners) who have married Thais—it's a good place to absorb that subculture, perhaps over a beer at Farang Connection (⇨ *Where to Eat, below*).

THE ELEPHANT ROUNDUP

Surin's Elephant Roundup, held the third week in November, is an impressive show in which *mahouts* (handlers) lead elephants in performing tricks, playing polo and soccer, and reenacting scenes of old military battles. The main show (B300–B500) is held at the Sri Narong Stadium, and starts at 7:30 AM. For a small fee, you can take a short elephant ride after the performance or hand-feed the elephants. The town is packed with visitors at Roundup time, so make sure you have a hotel reservation.

GETTING HERE & AROUND

BY BUS Korat to Surin takes around three hours by bus and costs B140; departures are frequent. From Bangkok, there are many services (7 hours, B280). Surin's bus station is right downtown.

BY CAR Road 226 leads to Surin from Buriram, a 30- to 40-minute drive.

BY TUK-TUK The center of Surin can be walked, but if you need a tuk-tuk or samlor to your hotel from the station, they are plentiful and cost B40–B50.

BY TRAIN The Northeastern Line runs frequent service from Bangkok to Korat, continuing east to Surin (via Buriram) on the line terminating at Ubon Ratchathani. It is 8½ hours from Bangkok and there are daytime departures as well as sleeper trains that cost B429–B1,200, depending on class. Surin's train station is on Nong Toom Road, five minutes from the heart of downtown.

ESSENTIALS

Emergencies **Surin Hospital** (✉ *Th. Thessaban 1, Surin* ☎ *044/511757*).

Visitor & Tour Info **Saren Travel** (✉ *202/1–4 Th. Thessaban 2, Surin* ☎ *044/520174 or 089/949–1185* ♿ *English-language tours to Preah Wihan, Prasat Ta Muan, Phanom Rung, Laos, elephant camps, villages; car and car-and-driver rental*).

EXPLORING SURIN

In addition to the temples and ruins around Surin, be sure to visit the Queen Sirikit Silk Center just west of town for a fascinating insight into traditional Isan and Thai crafts.

WHAT TO SEE

Prasat Sikhoraphum, a five-prang Khmer pagoda built in the 12th century, is 36 km (24 mi) east of Surin. The central structure has engraved lintels depicting Shiva, as well as carvings of Brahma, Vishnu, and Ganesha. The bus (No. 3) from Korat stops at Surin bus station, which has a regular bus service to the prang's adjoining village. ✉ *Road between Si Saket and Surin* ☎ *No phone* 🎫 *B40* ⏲ *Daily 6–6.*

Nestled amid thick vegetation beside the Cambodian border, 75 km (47 mi) from the far south of Surin, is a series of three prasats collectively known as **Prasat Ta Muean.** All lie on an ancient road stretching from Phimai to Angkor. The first prasat you see is **Prasat Ta Muean,** built in the Jayavarman VII period of the late 12th century and believed to be one of 17 rest stops made for pilgrims traveling the route. The second, smaller, site, **Prasat Ta Muean Tot,** acted as an ancient hospital and was also constructed in the 12th century. But these are only teasers for what lies farther on, directly beside the Cambodian border: **Prasat Ta Muean Thom.**

Thom means big, and Prasat Ta Muean Thom is indeed the largest of the three sites. It was constructed in the 11th century, making it the oldest of the sites as well. The contrasting textures and colors of the pink sandstone towers and the rugged gray laterite of the viharns set against the backdrop of the forest are something to behold.

The prasat's survival over the ages is made particularly poignant by the existence of unexploded grenades and land mines in the vicinity, left over from more troubled times. Some have even reported the distant crack of gunfire, and the area is kept a close eye on by the Thai army, whose checkpoints you'll pass on your approach to the area. For these reasons, ⚠ **don't wander off into the forest, and admire the structures at Prasat Ta Muean Thom from cleared paths only.**

Prasat Ta Muean is on a newly surfaced road, but it's still a bit isolated and is often a difficult place to get to via public transportation (at any rate, it can be a slow trip). Therefore, it's best to drive or take a tour provided by Saren Travel. ✉ *75 km (47 mi) south of Surin* ☎ *081/730–5811* B30 ⏲ Daily 6–6.

7

The best place to see the silk process in its entirety is the **Queen Sirikit Silk Center** just west of Surin. The agro-tourism project includes a mulberry plantation, cocoon development, silk extraction, dying, and weaving. There's also a silk museum and a shop that sells silk and mulberry products. A pink songthaew runs here regularly from the Surin Market (B12), but taking a tour with Saren Travels (*above*) is a better bet; the center's workers, though eager to show visitors around, do not speak much English. ✣ *3.5 km (2 mi) west of Surin on Hwy. 226 to Buriram* ☎ *044/511393* *B40* ⏲ *Daily 6–6.*

WHERE TO EAT

The small but busy provincial capital of Surin has plenty of standard shophouse-style eateries (restaurant downstairs, living quarters upstairs) where you can order basic rice or noodle dishes. Sirirat Road has many late-night dining spots, but if you want to mix with the locals in the evenings, head to the Night Bazaar on Krung Sri Nai Road between 5 PM and 11 PM.

$ AMERICAN ✕ **Farang Connection.** If you have a craving for some Western fare (and company), this foreigner-run restaurant is the place to go. The small restaurant acts as a meeting point for expats and provides additional services such as motorbike rental, Internet, and tour services. The newer **Farang Connection 2** across the street has a big-screen TV showing Premiership (English soccer matches), and a dartboard; the menu includes cottage pie, bangers-and-mash, and Cornish pasties. The beer

Continued on page 458

SILKWORMS & COCOONS:

SILK-MAKING IN THAILAND

by Dave Stamboulis

According to legend, the Chinese empress His-Ling discovered silk nearly 5,000 years ago when a cocoon fell into her teacup, and she watched it unwind into a fine filament. As China realized the value of these threads, the silk trade was born, spreading through Asia, along what became known as the Silk Road.

For centuries, the Chinese protected the secret of silk production, beheading anyone who tried to take silkworm eggs out of the country. But, eventually, smuggled worms, along with silk-making knowledge, made it to other parts of Asia. As the demand for silk grew, Chinese traders searched for the best climates in which to cultivate worms; historians believe that these traders brought sericulture, or silk-making, to Thailand about 2,000 years ago. Archaeologists have found silk remnants in the ruins of Baan Chiang near Udon Thani.

Though silkworms thrived, the silk business did not take on a large scale in Thailand, because Buddhist Thais were reluctant to kill the silkworms—an unavoidable part of the process. But a few families in Isan did continue to produce silk, using native plants like Palmyra Palm and jackfruit to make natural bleaches and dyes. After World War II, American businessman Jim Thompson discovered Thailand's cottage industry and helped expand it, founding the Thai Silk Company in 1951 (⇨ *Jim Thompson Thai Silk Company, Chapter 2*). Queen Sirikit, King Bhumibol's wife, has also been a long-term supporter of sericulture through her SUPPORT organization, which teaches traditional crafts to rural Thais.

Silk cocoons in the final stage of incubation, Surin.

HOW SILK IS MADE

Adult female bombyx mari.

Female moth laying eggs.

Larvae eating mulberry leaves.

Silkworms are really the caterpillars of bombyx mari, the silk moth. The process begins when a mature female moth lays eggs—about 300 at once. When the eggs hatch 10 days later, the larvae are placed on trays of mulberry leaves, which they devour. After this mulberry binge, when the worms are approximately 7 cm (2.75 in) long, they begin to spin their cocoons. After 36 hours the cocoons are complete.

Before the worms emerge as moths—destroying the cocoons in the process—silk makers boil the cocoons so they can unravel the intact silk filament. The raw silk, which ranges in color from gold to light green, is dried, washed, bleached, and then dyed before being stretched and twisted into strands strong enough for weaving. The course, knotty texture of Thai silk is ideal for hand-weaving on traditional looms—the final step to creating a finished piece of fabric.

Silk cocoons.

Boiling cocoons to remove silk.

DID YOU KNOW?

Thai silk moths reproduce 10 or more times per year—they're much more productive than their Japanese and Korean counterparts, which lay eggs only once annually.

A worm can eat 25,000 times its original weight over a 30-day period, before encasing itself in a single strand of raw silk up to 900 m (3,000 ft) long.

Woman sifting through cocoons.

CHECK IT OUT

SILK IN ISAN

Queen Sirikit focused on strengthening the silk cottage industry in Isan in part because the region's climate was not ideal for rubber and fruit trees, two lucrative crops in other parts of the country. Isan is Thailand's poorest, least-developed region; sericulture provides jobs to its inhabitants while keeping a traditional craft alive.

The Queen Sirikit Silk Center just west of Surin is an excellent place to learn about silk production (⇨ *above*). Near Khon Kaen, the weaving village of Chonnabot is renowned for mudmee silk. There's an excellent exhibition center here and households of weavers welcome visitors (⇨ *below*). The town of Pak Thong Chai, south of Korat, is full of silk factories and shops (⇨ *above*).

Man works a traditional loom.

VARIETIES OF THAI SILK

Most Thai silk is a blend of two different colors, one for the warp (threads that run lengthwise in a loom) and the other for the weft (strands that are woven across the warp.) Smoother silk, made with finer threads, is used for clothing, while rougher fabric is more appropriate for curtains. To make "striped" silk, weavers alternate course and smooth threads. Isan's famous mudmee silk, which is used mainly for clothing, consists of threads that are tie-dyed before they are woven into cloth.

Mudmee silk.

SHOPPING TIPS

Appraising silk quality is an art in itself. But there are a few simple ways to be sure you're buying pure, handmade fabric.

- Examine the weave. Hand-woven, authentic silk has small bumps and blemishes—no part of the fabric will look exactly like any other part. Imitation silk has a smooth, flawless surface.
- Hold it up to the light. Imitation silk shines white at any angle, while the color of real silk appears to change.
- Burn a thread. When held to a flame, natural fibers disintegrate into fine ash, while synthetic fabrics melt, smoke, and smell terrible.
- Though this isn't a foolproof method, consider the price. Genuine silk costs five to 10 times more than an imitation or blended fabric. You should expect to pay between B250 and B350 a meter for high-quality, clothing-weight silk. Men's shirts start at B800 but could be more than B2,000; women's scarves run from B350 to B1,500. At Bangkok shops that cater to westerners, you'll pay considerably more, though shops frequented by Thais have comparable prices throughout the country.

Fine Thai silk on bobbins.

list, which features such gems as John Smith's Smooth Bitter, is perhaps the best in Thailand. ✉ *257/11 Chitbamrung Rd.* ☎ *044/511509* 🌐 *www.farangconnection.com* 💳 *No credit cards.*

¢ THAI **Je Took Restaurant.** With a constant stream of customers passing underneath its thatched-straw roof, Je Took is a bit frenetic. But it's popular for a reason: it's won many awards for its food, which includes fish dishes from Isan and other Thai provinces. ✉ *805 Lakmuang Rd.* ☎ *086/865–8893* 💳 *No credit cards* ⏲ *Closed Mon.*

¢–$ ★ THAI **Larn-Chang.** This delightful, wooden house restaurant is by a pond. You can have a relaxing Thai meal in the restaurant's garden. Try the spicy manta ray soup. The restaurant has an English-language menu and is open until midnight. ✉ *199 Seepatai Samon Rd.* ☎ *044/512869* 💳 *No credit cards.*

WHERE TO STAY

¢–$ **Majestic.** Though the furnishings are fairly standard, the level of amenities and comfort is slightly higher here than at most other Surin hotels. All rooms have terraces, most overlooking a big lagoon. **Pros:** DVD players in superior rooms; free Internet; nice swimming pool. **Cons:** rooms looking worn for a new hotel; better value to be found at Thong Tarin; very few computers for Internet use. ✉ *99 Chitbamrung Rd.,* ☎ *044/713980* *69 rooms, 3 suites* *In-room: refrigerator, DVD (some). In-hotel: restaurant, bar, pool, laundry service, Internet terminal, Wi-Fi* 💳 *AE, MC, V.*

¢–$ **Thong Tarin Hotel.** Surin's most stylish hotel is popular with those looking for a night on the town, as it's only minutes from local watering holes. The hotel's beer garden, nightclub with live music, and Big Bite Restaurant attract their own crowds every evening. Rates leap during Elephant Roundup week. **TIP→ Ask for a corner room—they're larger and have commanding views of the city.** **Pros:** deluxe rooms are best value in town; great local nightlife; fantastic city views from upstairs rooms. **Cons:** noisy at night; no Internet access in rooms; often crowded with convention and conference groups. ✉ *60 Sirirat Rd.,* ☎ *045/514281 to 88* 🌐 *www.thongtarinhotel.com* *212 rooms, 11 suites rooms* *In-room: refrigerator. In-hotel: 2 restaurants, bar, pool, spa, laundry service, Internet terminal* 💳 *AE, DC, MC, V.*

SHOPPING

About 15 km (9 mi) north of Surin a small road leads to **Khwao Sinarin,** a village famous for its excellent silk. Silver jewelry is now made here as well, and you can find bargains for bracelets and necklaces with a minimal amount of negotiation. You can detour south to **Ban Butom,** 12 km (7 mi) from Surin, where villagers weave the straw baskets sold in Bangkok. They'll be happy to demonstrate their techniques.

NIGHTLIFE

Surin hops at night, especially on weekends. Most of the activity centers around Sirirat Road, about a block from the Thong Tharin Hotel. The best strategy is to cruise this strip, known as Soi Cola, which is full of discos, karaoke bars and other clubs.

PRASAT KHAO PHRA WIHAN

Fodor's Choice ★ *94 km (58 mi) southeast of Si Saket, 101 km (63 mi) southwest of Ubon Ratchathani.*

It's not only the ruins of Khao Phra Wihan that make this a must-visit, but also the ruins' beautiful, remote, and eerie location, as well as the interesting history of the spot, both ancient and recent. The 1963 resolution of a contentious territorial dispute between Thailand and Cambodia, the World Court awarded these spectacular mountaintop Khmer ruins to Cambodia. Ironically, however, even after the border was redefined, the temple, which sits on a cliff high above the rest of Cambodia, could only be accessed from a Thai road. The site later became a Khmer Rouge stronghold, and even after the Cambodian government opened the ruins again in the early 1990s, access to the area was only intermittent until the fall of Pol Pot in 1998. ⚠ **In 2008, protests broke out over the wording and monitoring of the UNESCO treaty between the two countries, and Thai and Cambodian troops exchanged fire on the border, killing several soldiers.** At this writing, though there have not been further outbreaks of violence, the ruins are closed, but signs point to the dispute being resolved soon. Check with the TAT before venturing out.

The long period of neglect now forms part of Khao Phra Wihan's unique allure. Admire the ornate 12th-century Khmer lintels in red laterite honoring Shiva and other Hindu icons, and you will revel in the fact that the temples have for the most part not been reconstructed. As you wander through the temple complex, which proudly stretches along a misty bluff for more than a kilometer, you'll step over column fragments that seem to have crumbled only days earlier.

Aside from the steep entrance fee, crossing the border into Cambodia presents no obstacles other than showing your passport at a checkpoint. They won't stamp it, as no visa is required to make this trip. You'll leave your car at the Thai side of the checkpoint, which has a basic information booth, restrooms, and such, then walk across the border for about a kilometer along a paved road. The road gives way to an area of lava-like sandstone before descending into a large market area where fried bananas, drinks, and replicas of brand-name consumer products (from watches to cigarettes) are sold. The ruins are spread over four levels, with the access to the first level having the steepest ascent (after this the going gets a little easier). You pass *gopura* (gateways) and naga-lined terraces on your ascent through this compound, which was adapted to suit the landscape, utilizing the natural bedrock of the mountain to form the base of causeways and courtyards. The principal temple structure is on the steepest level, perched on a cliff that plunges into thick rain forest. It's a long climb to the top, but the effort is rewarded with a truly breathtaking view of the jungle beyond. On a clear day you can see not just Cambodia and Thailand but also Laos.

You'll also see some grim reminders of the Khmer Rouge regime that killed 1.7 million people over the course of two horrific decades in Cambodia. A cannon that was once used by Khmer Rouge guerrillas to patrol the jungle from the cliff top is still relatively intact; behind its shield, you can operate a crank that raises and lowers the barrel. ⚠ **Minefields in the brush outside the temple area have been cleared through French efforts, but it's still not a good idea to wander in the unmarked areas outside the site itself and its access paths.**

✉ *Khao Phra Wihan National Park, Hwy. 221, Kantharalak District, Jangwat Si Saket* ☎ *045/816071* 🌐 *www.dnp.go.th* 🎟 *B400* ⏲ *Daily 7:30–4:30, last entry at 3* PM.

GETTING HERE & AROUND

Phra Wihan is off the beaten track and hard to get to. ■ **TIP→ Be sure to check with the TAT to make sure the ruins are open before you go.** Public transport runs to the ruins but is time-consuming; your best bet may be taking a tour with Saren Travel in Surin, Sakda Travel in Ubon, or Nakhorn Angkor Travel in Si Saket. A car with driver can be arranged to tour all Khmer ruins in the vicinity for about B2,500 to B3,000.

BY BUS You can take a local bus to Kantharalak, 80 km (50 mi) from Si Saket, and then seek out a songthaew or local van to the border from there. The bus to Kantaralak leaves hourly from Si Saket's bus terminal and costs B50.

BY CAR Road 221 runs from Si Saket 100 km (62 mi) south to the ruins.

BY TAXI & SONGTHAEW Songthaews and motorcycle taxis can be found in Kantharalak, about 20 km (12 mi) from Phra Wihan.

SI SAKET

312 km (194 mi) east of Korat, 61 km (38 mi) west of Ubon Ratchathani.

With the exception of a newly constructed temple, **Phrathat Ruang Rong,** which is said to be one of the biggest in the northeastern part of the country, the provincial, unexciting town of Si Saket is best known for its pickled garlic and onions. However, it is a convenient place to overnight if visiting the ruins at Phra Wihan (*above*). In early March, when the lamduan flower blooms, the town comes alive in a riot of yellows and reds. Locals celebrate with a three-day festival, the **Lamduan Ban Fair,** which centers around the beautiful Somdej Sri Nakharin Park.

GETTING HERE & AROUND

The best way to reach Si Saket is by train, as the rail station is centrally located and service frequent. The town is small enough to cover on foot, but samlors are available for B20 to B30.

BY BUS The trip to Si Saket from Korat by bus takes about five hours and costs B250. There are better and more convenient connections by rail.

BY CAR Si Saket lies on Route 226 from Korat to Ubon, and is about four hours by car from Korat.

BY TRAIN The Northeastern Line runs frequent service from Bangkok to Korat, and then east to Si Saket on the line terminating at Ubon Ratchathani.

Service to Bangkok costs B450–B1,300, depending on class or type of train. As it is an eight- to nine-hour journey, a sleeper may be preferable. Si Saket's train station is on Ratchagarn Rot Fai Road, a five-minute walk from the Phrompiman Hotel and downtown.

ESSENTIALS

Emergencies **Si Saket Hospital** (✉ *Kasikum Rd., Si Saket* ☎ *045/611434*).

Visitor & Tour Info **Nakhorn Angkor Travel** (✉ *Phrompiman Hotel, Si Saket* ☎ *045/622456 or 081/999–1488*) can arrange cars to Phra Wihan. **Si Saket Tourism Center** (✉ *Thepa and Lakmuang Rds., Si Saket* ☎ *045611283*).

WHERE TO EAT

¢–$ THAI **Somkid Restaurant.** Dishes at this Chinese-style Thai eatery are served with a thick rice soup. The plain plastic seating and wooden tables don't do justice to the quality of the food. The restaurant receives regular customers into the wee hours—it's open until 3 AM. ✉ *332/1–3 Ratchagarn Rot Fai Rd.* ☎ *085/015–4429 or 045/614195* ▭ *No credit cards.*

WHERE TO STAY

¢ **Phrompiman Hotel.** Near the train station, the night market, and the city's main restaurant and bar district, this hotel is probably the best positioned in the city, and it is the largest hotel in Si Saket. The superior air-conditioned rooms are very reasonably priced and are decorated with Thai mural reproductions. However, its sparse lobby area does feel kind of lonely. **Pros:** excellent value for the money; travel agency on premises; in-room Wi-Fi. **Cons:** noisy nightclub next door; minimal English spoken; located next to railway line. ✉ *849/1 Lakmuang Rd.,* ☎ *045/612677* *192 rooms* *In-room: Wi-Fi. In-hotel: 2 restaurants, laundry service, Wi-Fi* ▭ *MC, V.*

7

UBON RATCHATHANI

227 km (141 mi) east of Surin.

Ubon Ratchathani, known as the "Royal City of the Lotus," is Eastern Isan's largest city, but there is a positively provincial air about the place, especially at night, when, aside from the night markets, mostly quiet pervades. Although you'll find pockets of hipness and the occasional fusion restaurant, Ubon is nowhere near as lively as its neighbors of Surin or Udon Thani and doesn't have many sights to see. Ubon is, however, considered the gateway to the "Emerald Triangle," the verdant region where Thailand, Laos, and Cambodia meet.

Ubon was established on the bank of the Mun River in the late 18th century. Ubon is famous for its political heritage, musical performers, and *moo yor* (processed pork wrapped in a banana leaf and steamed), but is best known for its Candle Procession in late July. Candles are traditionally offered to monks at the start of Buddhist Lent, Kao Pansaa, and villages throughout the area compete to produce the finest float adorned with huge beeswax sculptures of Buddhist mythical figures and towering candles. The floats are paraded through the downtown area accompanied by musicians and local dancers. The festival is held over two days and is centered at Thung Sri Muang Park.

GETTING HERE & AROUND

Due to the distance from Bangkok, train travel is more comfortable and preferable to taking the bus. Ubon is rather sprawled out so make use of the good public songthaew system and the hundreds of friendly rickshaw drivers.

BY AIR Thai Airways and Air Asia fly daily from Bangkok to Ubon Ratchathani. Ubon's airport is a few kilometers north of downtown; tuk-tuks will get you there for B80–B100.

BY BUS Buses to Ubon Ratchathani from Korat take upward of six hours and cost around B250. The best company for this trip is Nakornchai Air (🌐*www.nca.co.th*), which has luxury coaches between Ubon Ratchathani, Bangkok, and Chiang Mai (around B650), and elsewhere, though you will need a Thai speaker (or the TAT) to make arrangements. The Nakornchai Air bus station is 2 km (1 mi) south of the Moon River on the Upparat–Warin Market main road. All other buses leave from the main bus terminal slightly north of town on Thanon Chayangkun, accessible by songthaews 2, 3, and 11, or by tuk-tuk (B50–B80 for either). For access from Udon, Khon Kaen, and Upper Isan, the bus is your best and often only bet, whereas for Korat, Buriram, and Surin, the train has convenient services.

BY CAR Ubon lies at the end of Highway 226 from Korat. Budget has a rental-car desk at the airport in Ubon Ratchathani.

BY TUK-TUK & SONGTHAEW Public songthaews run throughout town for B12 (get a bus map from the TAT office), and tuk-tuks and samlors will ferry you around for B30 to B60.

BY TRAIN The Northeastern Line runs frequent service from Bangkok to Korat, continuing east to Buriram, Surin, and Si Saket before terminating at Ubon Ratchathani. Trains bound for Ubon leave from Hualamphong Station in Bangkok several times daily; the trip is approximately 11 hours and costs around B330 to B1,300, depending on class. The train station is not in Ubon Ratchathani itself, but directly across the river in Warinchamrab (on Sathanee Road), a 15-minute, B12 songthaew ride or B60 tuk-tuk trip away.

ESSENTIALS

Emergencies **Police** (☎*045/254216*). **Rajavej Ubol Hospital** (✉*999 Chayangkul Rd., Ubon Ratchathani* ☎*045/280040*).

Visitor & Tour Info **Sakda Travel** (✉*150/1 Kantalak Rd., Ubon Ratchathani* ☎*045/321937* 🌐*www.sakdatour.com* *Visas and trips to Laos; transport and guides to Phra Wihan*).

EXPLORING UBON RATCHATHANI

Although short on tourist attractions, Ubon Ratchathani is one of the few cities in Thailand with large sidewalks and quiet side streets, so it makes for a pleasant spot for wandering around on foot, slipping into one of the many local eateries and coffee shops.

WHAT TO SEE

In the northern reaches of Ubon you can find the Indian-style pagoda **Wat Nong Bua,** a copy of the famous one in India where the Buddha attained enlightenment more than 2,500 years ago. The rectangular white chedi is breathtaking. Take the white No. 10 songthaew. ✉ *Thamma Withi Rd., Prathat Nong Bua* ⏲ *Daily 6–6.*

More wax candles, as well as comprehensive and interactive exhibits concerning the history of the province and its makeup, can be found at Rajabhat University of Ubon's **Culture and Art Centre.** This unique white building houses in its basement an interesting museum that celebrates the lives of local wax sculptors, as well as musicians and singers who perform in the famous Isan *morlam* style. Morlam is traditional Laotian music with strong rhythms and dynamic vocals. The genre has been augmented with electronic keyboards, helping to keep it alive and as popular, nationally, as ever. ✉ *Changsanit Rd.* ☎ *045/352000* 🎫 *Free* ⏲ *Mon.–Sat. 8:30–4.*

WHERE TO EAT

Locals love the evening food stalls along Ratchabut Road, beside Thung Sri Muang Park. Another popular spot is Haad Ku Dua, a beach along the banks of the Mun River about 7 km (4½ mi) out of town. Here you walk out over wooden gangways to thatched rafts, where your food is brought to you as you recline on reed mats. Try such favorites as *pla chon* (snakehead fish, which is white with a size, texture, and flavor similar to mullet) or the ubiquitous roast chicken. Back in town, Sappasit Road also offers a good selection of eateries.

¢ THAI ✕ **Dee Amnuay Choke.** This bustling, friendly Chinese-style restaurant has an extensive menu and speedy service. This is arguably the most popular restaurant in town for late-evening diners (it's open until 3 AM), and you'll literally be rubbing shoulders with locals. The place feels like a big warehouse, but the food is outstanding and great value for the money. Try the *phad poo pong garee,* a crab curry, which, like other dishes here, you can select straight from a massive bowl. Order by pointing to what looks good—it's hard to go wrong. ✉ *377–379 Sappasit Rd.* ☎ *045/241809* 💳 *No credit cards* ⏲ *No lunch.*

¢ ✕ **Indochine.** This long-established Vietnamese restaurant is showing its age, but it's still a favorite for both visitors and locals. The exquisite wooden entrance leads to a treasure trove of rooms with regional decor and antiques from around Southeast Asia. The more-luxurious upstairs dining area is reminiscent of a piano bar. A popular dish is *nem nuong,* minced pork balls on skewers. There's an illustrated English-language menu with good explanations of the dishes. ✉ *168–170 Sappasit Rd.* ☎ *045/245584 or 045/254126* 💳 *MC, V.*

$–$$ Fodor's Choice ★ THAI ✕ **Jumpa-Hom.** It is refreshing to find a fusion restaurant that expands upon its own regional culinary traditions, rather than jumping from one world cuisine to the next. At Jumpa-Hom, in the midst of an urban jungle full of palms, lanterns, and flowing fountains full of floating reeds, you can try such Thai-Chinese creations as "noodle envelopes" (like dim sum rice noodles) stuffed with Chinese sausage and served in a sweet soy sauce. White deep-sea tiger prawns are baked in a casserole with *woon sen* (glass noodles) and tender whole garlic cloves. Although most customers are locals, there is an English-language menu that may just be the most eloquent in all of Thailand. ✉ *49/3 Phichit Rangsan Rd., Nai Muang, 34000* ☎ *045/265671* ▭ *MC, V* ⊙ *No lunch.*

WHERE TO STAY

$ **Laithong Hotel.** Locally made crafts and colorful textiles decorate the basic but comfortable rooms at this popular high-rise hotel. Don't expect luxury amenities or out-of-the-ordinary service here, but it's a reasonable higher-end choice near downtown. There's a lobby pub where you can relax with a beer. **Pros:** bicycles for rent; deluxe rooms are spotless and spacious; complimentary shuttle to airport. **Cons:** long walk to night markets and sights; 7% VAT charged to all rooms; small pool. ✉ *50 Pichit Rangsan Rd.,* ☎ *045/264271* *124 rooms* *In-room: refrigerator, DVD (some), Wi-Fi. In-hotel: restaurant, room service, bars* ▭ *AE, DC, MC, V.*

$–$$ **Tohsang City Hotel.** The elegant lobby, decorated with Thai flair in subdued shades of purple and beige, feels more refined than its surroundings. The suites are quite chic, spacious, and artsy, and far more furnished than the "superior rooms," which don't deserve their moniker. (Apart from the suites, Laithong is a better choice for lodging.) The hotel also has a mellow restaurant and piano bar—useful since the hotel is far from the city center. **Pros:** opulent suites with suave design; cool lobby; more like a private residence than hotel. **Cons:** non-suite rooms dark; far from town; no elevator. ✉ *251 Palochai Rd., Muang District,* ☎ *045/245531* ⊕ *www.tohsang.com* *74 rooms, 2 suites* *In-room: refrigerator. In-hotel: restaurant, bar, laundry service, Internet terminal* ▭ *MC, V.*

SHOPPING

Punchard (✉ *Ratchabut Rd.* ☎ *045/243433* ⊕ *www.punchard.net*) is a popular handicraft shop with an extensive collection of crafts from around the region.

NIGHTLIFE

Although Ubon tends to be quieter by night than its neighbors of Korat and Surin, there is one world-class nightspot. At **U-Bar** (✉ *97/8–10 Pichit Rangsan Rd.* ☎ *045/265141*), yuppie twentysomethings gather to listen to live Thai rock music while sipping mojitos, kamikazes, or bottles of Johnnie Walker. The upstairs lounge has a playful Austin Powers feel, with faux-vintage furniture and a little outdoor terrace.

KHONG JIAM

77 km (48 mi) east of Ubon Ratchathani

If you're heading east from Ubon to the Mekong, Khong Jiam is the first town you'll hit. It's a sleepy village (technically a so-called "district" of Ubon) notable for its pretty, flag-lined boardwalk along the Mekong River, which has food stalls and other vendors, and for its spectacular luxury hotel, the Tohsang. At the boardwalk, which overlooks the bend in the Mekong famous for its two colors (the uncharitable might call them yellow and brown), is a point where the River Mae Nam Moon, which begins in the Khao Yai forest and winds its way through much of Isan, past Ubon, Phimai, and Korat, empties into the Mekong. Here you can wander along the riverbank and take in the views or hire a local boatman to float you around for a bit; you can also enjoy a fresh fish lunch for pennies at one of the delicious open-air restaurants.

GETTING HERE & AROUND

BY BUS The bus from Ubon to Khong Jiam takes two hours and costs B60. Khong Jiam itself is tiny and pleasant for strolling. If staying at the Tohsang, call ahead for pickup as they are outside of town.

BY CAR From Ubon, take Road 2222; the drive is an hour to 90 minutes.

WHERE TO EAT & STAY

¢ THAI **Chuan Chom.** This is the northernmost, and most elaborate, of the string of food stalls and restaurants along Khong Jiam's boardwalk; it's near the District Office, right where the unpaved road for vehicles ends. Beneath a green corrugated tin roof, at simple picnic tables overlooking the Mekong, you can enjoy local river fish such as *lod pla nua orn gra thiem,* a plate of battered, deep-fried whisker snapper, which are meant to be eaten whole, head, tail, and all (you might want to remove the dorsal bone on the larger ones). Also good is *pla buek phad cha* (spicy stir-fried giant catfish with ginger and sweet basil). And it all costs only pennies. *Khong Jiam 042/351334 No credit cards.*

$$ Fodor's Choice ★ **Tohsang Khongjiam.** The finest resort along the Mekong River in Thailand is an all-encompassing experience in relaxation. The pool and hot tub are encircled by a lush, exotic garden; meals or drinks can be taken on tables spectacularly perched above expanses of river with views of Laos beyond. In the resort's manicured jungle you can enjoy an outdoor Thai massage, mineral bath, or herbal steam treatment; lounge in front of the river amid palm fronds; or take one of the Tohsang's kayaks out along the Mekong. Private villas are posh, but the "deluxe" corner rooms have sizable terraces with better views. **Pros:** excellent Web specials including spa and meals; elegance in a fantastic location; Isan's most romantic spot. **Cons:** far from town and local restaurants; poor breakfast buffet if low occupancy; many guests say water pressure and hot water is lacking. *68 Moo 7, Huay Mak Tay 045/351174 up to 76 www.tohsang.com 48 rooms, 7 villas In-room: refrigerator. In-hotel: 2 restaurants, bars, pool, gym, spa, water sports, bicycles, Internet terminal AE, MC, V.*

UDON THANI & UPPER ISAN

Prehistory, geography, myth, superstition, and Vietnam War–era boomtowns make this area of Northern Isan one of the richest and most varied destinations in Thailand. Its geography, spreading east from the mountain ranges of Petchabun, through to the rich depths of the Mekong River, give this region one of the most varied terrains in the country.

Thailand's largest fossilized remains have been unearthed in Isan's plateau, along with proof of Southeast Asia's oldest Bronze Age civilization. Although its soils are of archaeological value, the vast waters of the Mekong have been valued even more. During the Ayutthaya period (1350–1758) these small riverside communities saw strategic garrison towns spring up, heralding territorial disputes between Laos and Siam that continued until 1907 and the Siamese-French treaties.

The French colonization of Laos from 1893 to 1953 and its gaining of all territories east of the Mekong River left a strong influence on these bordering towns in the form of architecture and a diversity in culture and surroundings that can be found in few other places in Thailand. The start of the Vietnam War, however, brought this area into the 20th-century with a bang. Thailand's major alliance with the United States during the war helped bring money into this whole region, causing its greatest economic thrust and spawning overnight boomtowns that today stabilize Thailand's poorest reaches.

Most travelers making their way into Laos find themselves spending some time in Nong Khai, the main crossing point into the country. Although Nong Khai has little to offer other than temple tours and the annual, mysterious spectacle of balls of fire rising from the Mekong during the *Bon Fai Naak* festival, the surrounding countryside is beautiful, and it does offer a wide range of accommodation and might be your last chance to immerse yourself in Thailand before you venture into the tropics of Laos.

Udon Thani serves as the best base for this region, with transit links on the way to the lower reaches of the Isan plain, as well as into Laos. And those looking for a bit of Bangkok sophistication (without the grime) enjoy the city's mix of foreign foods and tongues and the pumping bars and clubs, which make for a memorable night out.

Loei is the prime natural attraction for this region, containing the last mountainous ranges of Northern Thailand, culminating in the evergreen heights of its deservedly famous Phu Kradueng National Park. With the Laotian-influenced festival of Phi Ta Khon and the strong French colonial styles of architecture in Chiang Khan, the region is as rich culturally as it is naturally.

Khon Kaen, aside from its Cretaceous bones and wartime legacy, is the quintessential Isan city. It holds the key to Isan's heart with its generous hospitality, wild foods, and royal fabrics. Whether on excursions out to rural Isan communities or scooting around its Bangkok-style pubs and clubs, you're guaranteed a true slice of Isan life.

UDON THANI

564 km (350 mi) northeast of Bangkok, 401 km (249 mi) northwest of Ubon Ratchathani.

As the site of a major U.S. Air Force base during the Vietnam War, Udon Thani quickly grew in size and importance. There are still traces of the massive U.S. presence in its hostess bars and shopping malls, but the independent Thais have managed to keep hold on the city.

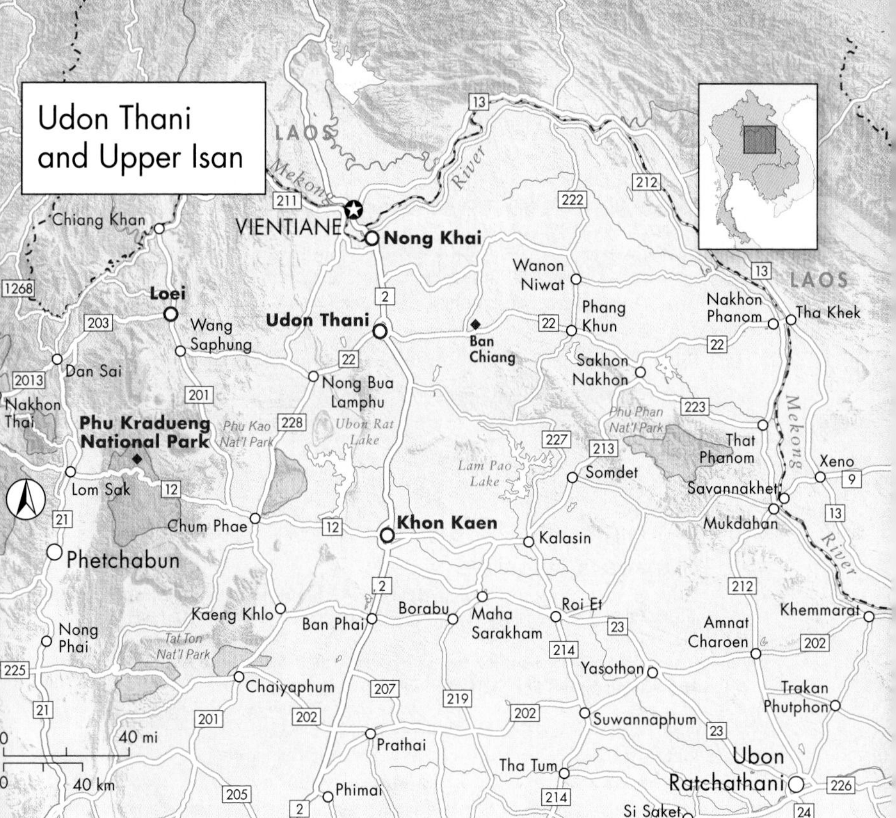

GETTING HERE & AROUND

BY AIR Udon Thani International Airport, the largest major airport in the region, has several daily arrivals from Bangkok. The major carrier is Thai Airways, but a number of budget airlines, such as Air Asia and Nok Air, also service these routes.

BY BUS From Bangkok, buses to Udon (9 hours) depart throughout the day and early evening (B370–B480, depending on class). Udon Thani is usually the starting point for the region and has regular buses to Khon Kaen, Nong Khai, Loei, and Korat.

Nong Khai buses depart from the Nong Khai Bus Terminal, at the northern end of Udon Dutsadi Road (songthaew No. 6); buses to Loei and Chiang Mai use a station on the Ring Road (west end of Srisuk Road, songthaew No. 7); all other buses leave from the main terminal on Sai Uthit Road.

BY CAR Roads are generally in good condition around Udon Thani. The fast, four-lane Highway 2 links Udon with Bangkok, making travel from Khon Kaen and Nong Khai also easy. Highway 22 through Sakhon Nakhon also provides links to the Mekong River towns. Loei's spacious 210 roadoffers easy access to and from Udon, with the optional 211 road being smaller but more scenic as it follows the Mekong River route, swinging through Chiang Khan to Nong Khai. The 212 road follows the Mekong, connecting Nong Khai to Nakhon Phanom and Mukdahan.

Avis, Budget, and Mall Thai (☎*042/346673*), all of which have branches at the Udon Thani Airport, are reliable rental agencies.

BY SAMLOR & SONGTHAEW Songthaew drivers in Udon are relentless sharks—they frequently hound visitors for business and overcharge. You can find one anywhere anytime, but be prepared to bargain hard. You can get to the airport for B80 to B100, and anywhere else for B60 to B80. Coming from the airport, minivans go to all hotels for B80.

BY TRAIN Trains run four times daily from Bangkok's Hua Lamphong train station to Udon Thani (12 hours; around B465 to B1,200 depending on class), departing at 8:20 AM, 6:30 PM, 6:40 PM, and 8:45 PM. Due to the distance, a sleeper train from Bangkok may be preferable to the bus. Udon's train station is on Prajak Road, about 1 km (½ mi) east of the town center.

CONTACTS & RESOURCES

Emergencies **Police** (☎*042/611333*). **Aek Udon International Hospital** (✉*555/5 Th. Phosi, Udon Thani* ☎*042/342555*).

Visitor & Tour Info **Kannika Tours** (✉*36/9 Sisutha Rd., Udon Thani* ☎*042/240443*). **Thorsaeng Travel** (✉*544/3–4 Phosi Rd., Udon Thani* ☎*042/221048*).

EXPLORING UDON THANI

Get an early start in Udon. If taking public transport out to Ban Chiang or Phu Phrabat, it will take up most of your day, as the short distances in Isan don't translate into fast arrivals, and there aren't that many departures.

WHAT TO SEE

The **Udon Thani Provincial Museum,** opened in January 2004, showcases most of the province's sights. The museum occupies the impressive Rachinuthit building, which was built during Rama VI's reign and was originally used as a girls' school. Divided into two floors and seven sections, the museum takes you through the history, geology, archaeology, anthropology, and urban development of the city. Sliding across the buffed golden teak floorboards from one room to the next you pass models of ethnic groups and miniatures of attractions, as well as ethnic artwork. ✉*Phosi Rd.* ☎*No phone* *Free* *Daily 9–4.*

The chief attraction near Udon Thani is **Ban Chiang,** about 60 km (37 mi) east of the city. At this Bronze Age settlement, archaeologists have found evidence to suggest a civilization thrived here more than 7,000 years ago. The United Nations declared it a World Heritage Site in 1992. The peculiar pottery—red-on-cream with swirling geometric spirals—indicates that this civilization was ahead of its time in cultural development. Even more intriguing are the copper bells and glass beads found here, many of which are similar to some found in North and Central America. This poses the question: did Asians trade with Americans 7,000 years ago, or even migrate halfway around the world? You can reach Ban Chiang from Udon Thani on the local bus (50 km [31 mi] on the Sakhon Nakhon Road, then 6 km [4 mi] north by motorbike taxi) or take a car and driver for about B800. ✉ *Via Sakhon Nakhon Rd., Ban Chiang* ☎ *043/208340* *B30* *Daily 8:30–4:30.*

OFF THE BEATEN PATH

Phu Phrabat Historical Park. One hour by bus northwest of Udon Thani is a 1,200-acre mountainside retreat near the village of Ban Phue. It's littered with rocks of all sizes, some in shapes that the faithful say resemble Buddhist and Hindu images. Take the path to the right of the temple and you'll reach a cave with silhouette paintings thought to be 4,000 years old. Local buses from Udon Thani's Nong Khai bus station go to Ban Phue for B55, and a songthaew or motorbike taxi can get you the last few kilometers to the park. ✉ *Ban Tiew,Ban Phue* ☎ *042/222909* *B30* *Daily 8–4:30.*

WHERE TO EAT

Udon Thani is famous for its version of gai yang (roast chicken), which you can try in the night market or at stalls on virtually every street.

¢–$ THAI — **Rabiang Phatchanee.** On the edge of the lake at Nong Prajak Park you find this pleasant, traditional Thai restaurant. An extensive menu features standard favorites alongside some interesting variations. *Pla deuk fu phad phet* (fried crispy catfish with a chili sauce) is fiery but ever so tasty, while *gaeng som pla chon tawt* (sour soup with water mimosa and snakehead fish) is authentic Isan food. Live music plays in the background. ✉ *53/1 Bannon Rd.* ☎ *042/241515 or 042/244015* *MC, V.*

$ AMERICAN — **Steve's Bar and Restaurant.** Steve, an ex-fireman from England, and his Thai wife serve up traditional pub classics at this long-standing expat haunt in the center of town. An indoor air-conditioned dining room fills up with those craving authentic steak-and-kidney pies and fish-and-chips. Portions are large and it's a good spot to catch sports on the big screen. ✉ *254/26 Prajaksilapakom Rd.* ☎ *042/244523* *www.udonmap.com/stevesbar/* *No credit cards.*

WHERE TO STAY

$ — **Ban Chiang Hotel.** Ban Chiang is a nicely furnished hotel, tastefully decorated with local paintings. The rates make it quite a bargain, and you'll be tempted to spend your savings on pampering yourself at the hotel spa. **Pros:** excellent and well-stocked wine cellar; inviting pool and fitness center; traditional Thai spa on premises. **Cons:** not close to bus and train stations; some rooms musty; not convenient for nightlife and night market. ✉ *5 Mookmontri Rd.,* ☎ *042/327911* *149 rooms* *In-room: safe, refrigerator, Wi-Fi. In-hotel: restaurant, pool, gym, spa, Internet terminal* *AE, DC, MC, V.*

$–$$ — **Charoensri Grand Royal.** Just to make sure you get the message, the city's top hotel calls itself both grand *and* royal. It's certainly luxurious, with softly carpeted rooms furnished in pale woods and decorated in restful pastels. The two restaurants serve Thai, Chinese, and Western food, and the pleasant beer garden has a variety of beers on tap. **Pros:** centrally located; pleasant fifth-floor terrace pool with views; rejuvenating spa and fitness center. **Cons:** worn carpeting in rooms; staff and premises a bit impersonal; not the best value in town for price. ✉ *277/1*

7

Restaurants ▼

Rabiang Phatchanee 1

Steve's Bar & Restaurant 2

Hotels ▼

Ban Chiang Hotel 1

Charoensri Grand Royal Hotel 2

City Lodge Hotel 3

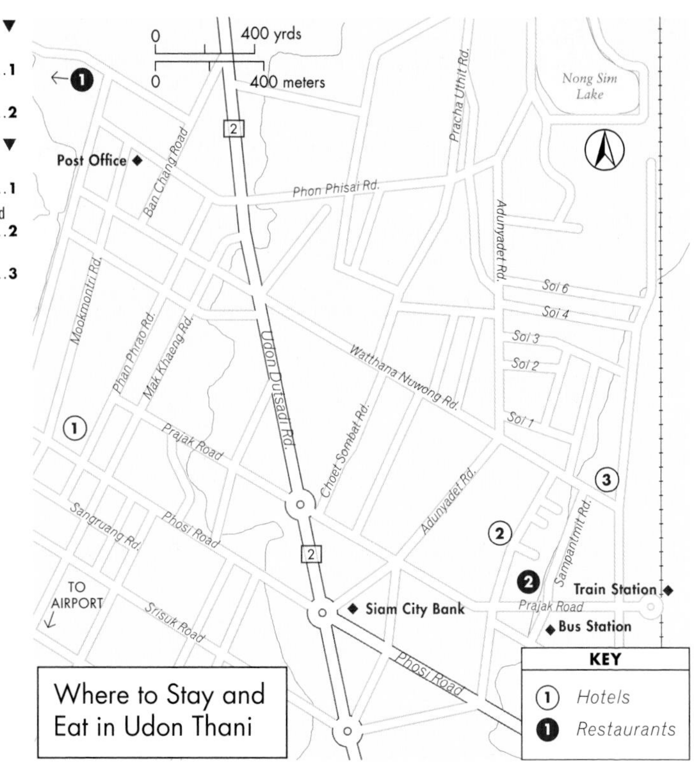

Where to Stay and Eat in Udon Thani

Prajaksilapakom Rd., ☎ *042/343555* ⊕ *www.charoensrigrandroyal.com* *260 rooms* *In-room: refrigerator. In-hotel: 2 restaurants, room service, bars, pool, gym* *AE, DC, MC, V.*

¢ **City Lodge Hotel.** The name is uninspiring, but City Lodge is actually an excellent English-owned boutique hotel. It's tastefully designed with a decidedly modern bent: heavy on pastel shades and chrome fittings, with contemporary furnishings and arresting local art. The hearty complimentary breakfast and well-stocked bar make this place a particularly good value. **Pros:** in nightlife district; Western steak restaurant downstairs; lively pool bar in hotel. **Cons:** no elevator; bar downstairs can be noisy; few rooms so may be hard to book. ✉ *83/14–15 Wattananuwong Rd.,* ☎ *042/224439* ⊕ *www.udonmap.com/thecitylodge* *10 rooms* *In-room: refrigerator, Wi-Fi. In-hotel: restaurant, laundry facilities* *No credit cards.*

NIGHTLIFE

Udon Thani has the most active nightlife in all Isan, with many pubs, clubs, and discos to choose from. Many expat bars can be found on Prajak Road near the night market and on nearby Sampantamit Road. For a traditional Irish pub, try **Molly Malone's** (✉ *56/40–41 Wattananiwong Rd.* ☎ *086/902–1364*), a sports lounge with good pub grub. Also popular is **Mojo's Bar** (✉ *254/24 Prajak Silpakorn* ☎ *042/343401*), a pool bar and restaurant next to Steve's that is crowded each evening.

KHON KAEN

190 km (118 mi) northeast of Korat, 115 km (69 mi) south of Udon Thani.

Thailand's sixth largest city, Khon Kaen has seen rapid growth due to the government's efforts to bolster the economy of the northeastern region. You'll see high-rise hotels shooting up and shopping malls under construction everywhere you look. Khon Kaen has long been renowned for its mudmee silk, celebrated each December with a huge festival. The city can feel chaotic, but its pleasures include dining in seafood restaurants along Lake Bueng Kaen Nakhon and interacting with the city's rousing party scene at one of its hopping nightclubs.

GETTING HERE & AROUND

BY AIR Khon Kaen Airport is one of the region's two major airports (the other is in Udon Thani) and has several daily flights from Bangkok on Thai Airways. The airport is 3 km (2 mi) west of town. Van transfer is available from all the major hotels for B70, and a tuk-tuk costs B100.

BY BUS Khon Kaen has two bus stations in the center of town. The Air-Con Station on Ammart Road has primarily direct buses to and from Bangkok, whereas the Ordinary Station on Prachasamosorn Road has departures to everywhere in the country. Khon Kaen is a central bus hub in Isan, so travel by bus is convenient.

There are regular buses to and from Udon Thani, Ubon Ratchathani, Korat, and Loei (all 2- to 4-hour trips). A bus from Bangkok takes about seven hours and costs from around B300 at the Ordinary Bus Station up to B450 at the Air-Con Terminal, which serves mostly VIP buses.

BY CAR Khon Kaen is a straight shot up Highway 2 from Bangkok (6 hours), continuing on to Udon Thani. Highway 23 runs west from Ubon Ratchathani, meeting up with Highway 2, 25 km (16 mi) south of Khon Kaen. A number of sights in the area aren't easy to reach via public transport; **Narujee Car Rent** (✉*Soi Kosa, Si Chan Rd., Khon Kaen* ☎*043/224220*) does rentals.

BY SAMLOR & SONGTHAEW There are public songthaews running on all the major boulevards in Khon Kaen (B10), stopping at 8 PM, and chartered tuk-tuks can be had for B40–B80, depending on the distance traveled.

BY TRAIN Trains to Khon Kaen depart several times daily from Bangkok's Hua Lamphong train station (9 hours), with the best coach being the 8:45 PM sleeper. Fares run from around B400 to B1,175, depending on class of sleeper. Khon Kaen's train station is on Ruan Rom Road, 15 minutes on foot southwest of the center of town.

ESSENTIALS

Emergencies **Khon Kaen Ram Hospital** (✉*Si Chan Rd., Khon Kaen* ☎*043/333900*).

EXPLORING KHON KAEN

The Beung Kaen Nakhon is a 250-acre lake located almost in the center of Khon Kaen, and is a great escape from the hustle and bustle of the city. Walking paths and eateries surround the lake, and there are paddleboats for rent.

WHAT TO SEE

The weaving village of **Chonnabot,** 50 km (31 mi) to the south, is renowned for mudmee (tie-dyed) silk. There are many weaving households to visit in the village. There's also an excellent exhibition center, **Thai Silk Pavilion** (☎*043/286160*), located just outside the village. Take a bus or songthaew from Khon Kaen from the Prachasamosorn bus terminal (B45; 45 minutes).

About 50 km (31 mi) north of Khon Kaen is a small village called **Ban Kok Sa-Nga,** where virtually every household raises king cobras. The practice was started by a local medicine man some 50 years ago, but is now under the strict control of the Thai Tourism Authority. An official king cobra breeding center has been established on the grounds of the local temple, and there are daily snake boxing and dancing matches, as well as several varieties of cobras in cages circling the grounds. Donations are appreciated, and the hourly shows make for ample photo opportunities. To get to the village, take bus 501, which runs every half-hour from the Ordingary Bus Station to the Ban Kok Sa-Nga village turnoff (B35), and then take a motorbike taxi the last few kilometers.

About 80 km (50 mi) west of Khon Kaen is **Phu Wiang National Park,** where the world's oldest fossils of carnivorous dinosaurs, the Siam Mityrennous Esannensil, were discovered. There are dinosaur museums at the park entrance, at Phu Pratu Teema, as well as in the nearby village of Kok Sanambin. To get here from Khon Kaen by car, take Highway 12 (Khon Kaen–Chumpae Road) west for about 50 km (31 mi), until you reach Route 2038; head north for about 40 km (25 mi) until you reach the park. Bus travel to the park is an ordeal: from Khon Kaen go to Phu Wiang village (B60), but you'll need to hire a B250 round-trip motorbike taxi to do the last 20 km (12 mi) to the site. ✉ *Rte. 2038, near Phu Wiang town* ☎*043/259052* *B200* *Daily 6–6.*

WHERE TO EAT

It would be a crime to dine in Khon Kaen without experiencing the romance of a restaurant on Bueng Kaen Nakorn Lake (really a large pond), which is about five minutes south of the city center and has a dozen well-priced seafood restaurants on its banks. In town, there's a wealth of restaurants and cheap food stalls on Klangmuang Road; options along this stretch are as varied as Vietnamese, homemade pizza, and local Isan cuisine. A good late-night food stop is the night market off Namuang Road, which is open until the wee hours.

$–$$ THAI ✕ **Bua Luang.** This enormous, open-plan lakeside restaurant is perched on the northern end of Lake Bueng Kaen Nakhon, extending out into the water. It's the biggest in the city, but the setting justifies the place's renown. The menu is a blend of Isan, Thai, and Chinese. One specialty worth trying is the *tom yam mapow orn* (prawns with coconut palm heart in a spicy hot-and-sour soup). ✉ *Rop Bueng Kaen Nakhorn Rd.* ☎ *043/222504 or 043/320202* ▭ *MC, V.*

¢–$ THAI ✕ **Pla Payai.** Perhaps the best place in town to try true regional Isan food, Pla Payai's open kitchen prepares complex but light dishes like *mok lab pla tong* (lightly grilled minced fish steamed in banana leaf). You also can't go wrong with the *larb ped*—a minced-duck version of the classic salad, with chilies, red onion, lime, fish sauce, rice powder, and cilantro. One of Khon Kaen's many great places to eat on the lake, Pla Payai is a supremely local joint; if you don't speak Thai, you'll have to stumble and bumble through the ordering process. ✉ *Rop Bueng Kaen Nakhorn Rd.* ☎ *043/225411* ▭ *No credit cards.*

$–$$ SEAFOOD ✕ **Samyan Seafood.** This big temple to fresh seafood is renowned for its first-rate preparations, such as *poo phad prong garee* (fried crab in curry), *poo phad prik tai dam* (fried crab with black pepper), and *yam hoi shell* (a mixed shellfish salad). You can also order a whole fresh grouper. All of this is enjoyed in classic Khon Kaen fashion—in the open air on the edge of the lake. ✉ *120/16 Rop Bueng Kaen Nakhorn Rd.* ☎ *043/321847 or 081/873–1202* ▭ *No credit cards.*

WHERE TO STAY

¢–$ **Bussarakam Hotel.** This high-rise in the center of town, opened in 2007, is more affordable than some of its neighbors. The lobby is palatial in the slightly overdone Thai way, and rooms are done in soothing pale earth tones. Rates are different for one or two people, which is not the norm in Thailand. **Pros:** near bus station; centrally located near markets and restaurants; large windows in rooms. **Cons:** rooms on west side of building get tremendous heat and sunshine; worn carpets and sparse furnishings. ✉ *68 Pimpasut Rd.,* ☎ *043/333666* 🌐 *www.bussarakamhotel.com* *155 rooms* *In-room: safe, refrigerator, Wi-Fi. In-hotel: restaurant, room service, laundry service* ▭ *MC, V.*

$–$$ **Charoen Thani Princess.** One of the many bold new additions to the Khon Kaen hotel scene that has accompanied the city's unprecedented business boom, this 19-floor hotel has a multistory lobby full of fountains, a relaxing pool, and a bustling bar, along with the requisite disco-karaoke-snooker entertainment options. Ask for an upper floor to take in great city views, even though Khon Kaen's not much to look at. **Pros:** in heart of nightlife district; lake views from some rooms; spacious and relaxing lobby. **Cons:** basement disco and surrounding area loud at night; small pool; very dirty windows in some rooms. ✉ *260 Sri Chan Rd., Naimuang,* ☎ *043/220400 up to 14* 🌐 *www.royalprincess.com* *320 rooms, 33 suites* *In-room: safe, refrigerator, Wi-Fi. In-hotel: 2 restaurants, room service, bars, pool, gym, laundry service* ▭ *AE, DC, MC, V.*

$$–$$$ Fodor's Choice ★ **Sofitel Raja Orchid.** Khon Kaen's skyline is dominated by the gleaming 25-story facade of the Sofitel Raja Orchid, easily Isan's most luxurious hotel. Everything about it is first-rate—the rooms are elegant, furnished with native woods and handwoven silks. If you're looking to splurge, there's always the 6,500-square-foot royal suite, which has its own helipad. The hotel is like a multistory shopping mall, with numerous restaurants (though none too impressive); Isan's largest karaoke bar, Studio 1; and the Funhouse, a disco that really lives up to its name.

7

During the Phi Ta Khonn ghost festival in Loei, dancers wear painted bamboo masks.

German visitors marvel at Thailand's first microbrewery, the Krönen Brauhaus, where you can even order bratwurst. **Pros:** elegant and top-class rooms; vast array of international restaurants on premises; renovated in 2008; German microbrewery in basement. **Cons:** street fronting the hotel is narrow and congested with traffic; curved and shallow pool not useful for swimming; neighborhood has many noisy bars and clubs. ✉ *9/9 Prachasumran Rd., Amphur Muang,* ☎ *043/322155, 800/ 221–4542 in U.S.* *www.sofitel.com* *293 rooms* *In-room: safe, refrigerator, DVD. Wi-Fi. In-hotel: 5 restaurants, room service, bars, pool, gym, laundry service, Internet terminal* *AE, DC, MC, V.*

SHOPPING

Khon Kaen has many souvenir shops. Locally made woven bamboo products can be found at **Moradok Thai** (✉ *87/26–27 Ammat Rd.* ☎ *043/243827*). Silver trinkets are on sale at the centrally located **Gloom Prae Phaan** (✉ *131/193 Chattaphadoong Rd.* ☎ *043/337216*).

Khon Kaen's most notable products are the province's famed mudmee silks and cottons. If you don't have time to make it to Chonnabot, Ban Muang Pha, or Phu, then pay a visit to the small but well-stocked **Rin Thai Silk** (✉ *412 Namuang Rd.* ☎ *043/220705 or 043/221042*).

LOEI

152 km (94 mi) west of Udon Thani, 43 km (27 mi) south of Chiang Khan.

Loei, one of Thailand's most sparsely populated provinces, is a fertile basin fed by the Loei and Man rivers, tributaries of the Mekong, making it one of the country's most geographically scenic regions. Its unique topography, bordered by the Eastern and Western Phetchabun mountain ranges, and its susceptibility to China's winter winds, result in Loei bearing some of the most dramatic temperatures in the country. Summers can reach 40°C (104°F), while winter nights can drop to freezing.

Once the site of a prehistoric Bronze Age mining settlement, Loei started life in the 15th century when the kingdoms of Ayutthaya and Lan Xang, in Laos, built Phra That Si Song Rak temple in what is now the Dan Sai District. The temple's name literally translates as the "sublime love of two" and served as a sign of beneficial relations between the two kingdoms at a time when Myanmar was infringing on domains based on the Mekong. In 1853, King Rama IV bestowed Muang Loei Thai with town status and present-day Loei achieved its independent provincial status in 1933.

The province is a rare blend of culture and language between its Northern Thai neighbors, Laotian migrations, and northeastern affection. The result is a warm, traditional lifestyle and the unique Thai Loei language. Dan Sai District has its animated Phi Ta Khon festival in June, which is reminiscent of the Puyoe Yayoe festival in Muang Kaen Tao, Laos.

Despite its rich, embracing nature, the town itself is rather drab, with predictable concrete blocks and shophouses lining the streets. As a short stopover, Loei can be useful as a place to gather information, but the places worth exploring lie out of town. Phu Kradueng National Park is Loei's most visited station for its evergreen plateau and views, and Chiang Khan, with its Laotian roots and colonial architecture, is the heart of the province.

GETTING HERE & AROUND

One of the more remote spots in Isan, Loei is only accessible by bus.

BY BUS There are regular buses connecting Udon Thani with Loei (about 3½ hours; B105). Getting to Loei along the Mekong from Nong Khai (5½ hours) means taking a fan-cooled bus. Nong Khai departures (B120) are infrequent; buses usually leave in early morning and stop in Chiang Khan (B40) along the way. You can also connect to Loei from Phitsanulok (F *Chapter 4*), with buses running from 6 AM to 4 PM and costing B160.

To Phu Kradueng National Park from Loei takes around 1½ hours and costs B60. To and from Bangkok takes 10 hours and costs B360 to B730, depending on type of bus and service. Loei's bus station is on Maliwan Road (Highway 201), 10 minutes south of the town center.

CLOSE UP

Thailand's Partying Provinces

In a nation that loves to have a good time, Isan bangs the drum the loudest and puts so much into its festivals that you soon forget this is Thailand's poorest region. Isan treats national celebrations and ceremonies with such gusto and enthusiasm that people flock from around the country to experience them. From the rice paddies to the bustling cities, the region rocks during its festivals, which are often begun as reverent affairs of Buddhist worship, but are more often than not fueled by a simple passion for living—and copious amounts of *sato* (rice whiskey).

Singing and dancing are always major components of any Isan festival. Brass bands often boom in processions and troops of young students in traditional costumes dance in elegant lines. Then come the good ol' boys and their traditional Isan instruments—the *kahn* and *wuud* bamboo organs, the *pin* guitars and *pong larng* xylophones—followed by the *dit hai* performers, traditionally garbed young women who dance as their fingers effortlessly rise and fall to pluck notes from stringed fish pots.

There's a festival in Thailand every month of the year, often called *Heet Sib Song* (The Twelve Customs), and associated with various forms of Buddhist merit-making or ceremony. Of particular note are the third month's *Boon Khao Jee* in Roi Et (usually in February), which features unique roasted rice-and-egg offerings; the *Boon Bung Fai* (usually in May), a rocket festival best known in Yasathon; and *Boon Khao Pansa,* the start of Buddhist Lent (mid-July), marked with the incomparable Candle Procession in Ubon Ratchathani. But what also makes the region stand out are some of the more unique parties found here. These include the Elephant Roundup of Surin during the third weekend in November for its shows and spectacle, and the Phi Ta Khonn ghost festival of Dan Sai District in Loei, which is held at the end of June or early July. This festival includes a procession of dancers wearing ghoulish masks made from bamboo rice baskets holding elongated wooden phalluses that they lightheartedly poke at the giggling onlookers. Their antics follow the awakening of the spirit of a monk, Pra Ub Pa Kud, which resides in a stream in the form of white marble. Once his spirit is led back to the local temple it's believed he'll protect the village from harm for another year.

But the pièce de résistance has to be the Bon Fai Naak festival in Nong Khai in late October. Thousands of onlookers crowd the banks of the mighty Mekong in anticipation of the supernatural conflagrations of the mythical (or not so mythical) *nagas,* water serpents that appear in so much Buddhist folklore. All eyes are focused on the waters of this famous river. Anticipation rises and then the whoops and cheers erupt as into the night sky from the very depths of the waters ascend multicolor balls of fire and light. The nagas have not disappointed and have breathed their mysterious life into another moon-drenched night. The authenticity of these annual, unearthly fireballs has been the matter of much speculation, but that fails to stop the throngs who come for the wonder and pure fun of it. This is Isan—suspend your disbelief and have a thumping good time.

–Ivan Benedict New

BY CAR Loei's spacious 210 road offers easy access to and from Udon, with the optional 211 road being smaller but more scenic as it follows the Mekong River route, swinging through Chiang Khan to Nong Khai.

BY SAMLOR & SONGTHAEW Public songthaews run the short distance from the bus station into town for B10, and tuk-tuks can be hired here or in town for B30 to B40.

ESSENTIALS

Emergencies **Loei Ram Hospital** (*Maliwan Rd., Loei 042/833400*).

WHERE TO EAT & STAY

¢–$ THAI **Can Can.** Conveniently attached to the Kings Hotel, Can Can is a cute and comfortable family-style diner serving tasty Thai food, along with some Western and Chinese selections. Popular with locals and visitors, the cozy eatery has an English menu, and utilizes the freshest of ingredients in preparing dishes like kana moo krop (watercress with dried, fried pork), yam pla meuk (spicy squid salad), and a piquant tom klong pla chon tawt (snakehead fish soup). Can Can also serves American breakfasts and filter coffee. *11/9–12 Chumsai Rd. 042/815180 No credit cards.*

¢ **Kings Hotel.** This central hotel represents Loei's best value. An unassuming entrance leads into a modest five-floor, atrium-style complex with a small square garden at its base. The rooms are clean and white, with functional wood furnishings. Cheaper fan-cooled rooms are also available by way of a thigh-burning hike up to the fifth floor. Prices and cleanliness undercut the competition, making it a good deal downtown. **Pros:** best value and most centrally located hotel in town; renovated in 2008. **Cons:** no elevator; cheapest rooms often full; not much English spoken. *11/9–12 Chumsai Rd., 042/811701 or 042/811225 50 rooms In-room: refrigerator, Wi-Fi. In-hotel: restaurant, laundry service, Internet terminal MC, V.*

$$ **Loei Palace.** The sinuous white facade of the massive Loei Palace dominates the city's skyline. Surrounded by well-tended gardens, the pool is a welcome sight after a day exploring the mountains. The excellent restaurant, serving Thai, Chinese, and other dishes, reassures you that sophisticated cuisine is still to be found in this remote region. An interesting outing offered by the hotel is to the Chateau de Loei, Thailand's top vineyard. Come during low season (May–November) when prices drop 50%. **Pros:** large pool and fitness center; inviting and spacious lobby; dedicated smoking/no-smoking floors. **Cons:** overpriced in high season; superior rooms have worn furniture; poor value compared to other choices. *167/4 Charoenrat Rd., 042/815668 www.amari.com 156 rooms, 33 suites In-room: refrigerator. In-hotel: restaurant, bar, pool, gym, laundry service, Wi-Fi AE, DC, MC, V.*

$$ **Phu Pha Nam Resort.** With the exception of the rustic tiled floors of its pavilion-style restaurant and the stone walls in the billiards room, this entire hotel seems to be constructed of richly colored teak. You sleep on carved teak beds in teak-floor rooms, all of which have sitting areas with picture windows framing views of the nearby hills. The resort is on a 52-acre estate about 70 km (43 mi) south of Loei. **Pros:** beautiful natural surroundings; complimentary kayaks and mountain bikes for

use; pampering Japanese spa. **Cons:** far out in countryside; not convenient for getting around without car; no other restaurants nearby. ✉*252 Moo 1, Koakngam Amphur Dansai,* ☎*042/078078, 02/254–3000 in Bangkok* 🌐*www.phuphanamresort.com* *71 rooms* *In-room: refrigerator. In-hotel: restaurant, pool, gym, water sports, bicycles, Internet terminal* 💳*AE, MC, V.*

PHU KRADUENG NATIONAL PARK

★ *78 km (48 mi) south of Loei.*

This was supposed to be Thailand's first national park, but lack of funding prevented that from happening. It wasn't until 1949 that government funds were finally allocated, and it took another 10 years before Phu Kradueng was finally granted national park status, becoming Thailand's second (after Korat's Khao Yai). Regardless of the slow start, it has become one of Thailand's most visited destinations.

The park consists of a lone, steep-sided mountain, which rises out of a flat plain that sprawls over 348 square km (134 square mi), and is crowned by a 60-square-km (23-square-mi) plateau. It takes four hours to hike the 5 km (3 mi) to the top, but there's a spectacular panorama at 4,265 feet above sea level waiting for you.

The mountaintop is usually covered in mist from October to February, when the temperature can drop as low as freezing. The summit, full of rich flora year-round, is mostly a combination of dense evergreen forest and equally dense pine forest, but from February onward color begins to saturate the park. The rainy season brings out the mountain's famed red-and-white rhododendrons and flowering grasses such as Pro Phu and Ya Khao Kam. In winter the park is ablaze with lush green mosses and ferns, set against the reddening of maple tree leaves. More than 276 animal species have been identified here, such as serows (a type of Asian goat), Asiatic elephants, tigers, bears, and boars, plus 171 species of birds including silver pheasants, black hawks, and red jungle fowl.

Main tourist attractions are well marked. Trails take you through forest vegetation and vast grasslands, and along streams to waterfalls, caves, and overhanging cliffs (perfect for taking in a sunrise or sunset). There's plenty to do, and the park is equally good for a day trip or extended exploration. The park headquarters at the base of the mountain has maps and information for you to plan your wanderings.

Accommodation, food, and conveniences are readily available from top to bottom. Most people bring their own tents (there's a B30 pitching fee). There are also bungalows (B1,200 to B3,600). **■ TIP→ The crowds are out in force from late November through mid-January, so unless you're bringing you own tent, be sure to contact the park headquarters to reserve accommodation as soon as possible.**

Note that they stop letting visitors into the park at 2 PM—the climb to the top takes a long time and they don't want people tackling it in the dark. If you are already inside the park, however, you don't need to be worried about being ushered out. ✉*Hwy. 201, Loei-Phu Kradueng Rd.* ☎*042/871333* 🌐*www.dnp.go.th/national_park.asp* *B400* ⏲*Oct.–May, daily 7–4; last entry at 2.*

GETTING HERE & AROUND

Buses from Loei (B71) stop in the town of Phu Kradueng, 70 km (43 mi) south of Loei, and it is a short songthaew ride (B30) to the park entrance from there. If driving, take Highway 201 from Loei to the Phu Kradueng turnoff and then 2019 west for the last 8 km (5 mi) to the park.

VISITOR & TOUR INFO

Kannika Tours (✉*36/9 Sisutha Rd., Udon Thani* ☎*042/240443*). **Thorsaeng Travel** (✉*546/1 Phosi Rd., Udon Thani* ☎*042/221048*).

EN ROUTE

Chiang Khan, 235 km (146 mi) east of Nong Khai, 43 km (27 mi) north of Loei, is a sleepy town set on the banks of the Mekong. With old wooden houses along the river, the community retains much of its rural charm, and the village makes for a nice break if traveling between Nong Khai and Loei. There are many simple yet atmospheric guesthouses lining the Mekong, and on the eastern edge of town are scores of restaurants with seating areas facing the river and Laos. At the impressive Kaeng Khut rapids, 6 km (4 mi) east of town, you can have a picnic provided by local vendors. The peaceful **Chiang Khan Hill Resort** (☎*042/821285*) has comfortable and peaceful lodgings (B800 to 1000) with plenty of creature comforts.

NONG KHAI

51 km (32 mi) north of Udon Thani.

Nong Khai is literally the end of the line—it's the country's northernmost railhead and bus terminus. To the east and west, the mighty Mekong meanders through largely uncharted territory, while across the river to the north lies Laos. The French influence that is still evident in the Laotian capital of Vientiane can also be seen in Nong Khai. The architecture of the town has noticeable Gallic touches, particularly the governor's residence on Meechai Road. Running parallel to Meechai Road is Rim Khong Road, lined by small guesthouses and restaurants. Laotian goods, mostly textiles, are cheap and plentiful at Nong Khai's lively market.

GETTING HERE & AROUND

Nong Khai is a major crossing point into Laos (F*Friendship Bridge, below*).

BY BUS Buses run from Udon Thani to Nong Khai every hour from the bus stand at the northern end of Udon Dutsadi Road (1 hour; B40). There are also frequent departures from Nong Khai back to Udon, and on to Khon Kaen and Bangkok (B400). But it's best to take a sleeper train if you're heading back to Bangkok. Only fan-cooled coaches are available to or from Loei (4 hours; B100). The bus station is downtown, at the Pho Chai market just off Prajak Road.

BY CAR The fast, four-lane Highway 2 links Nong Khai to Udon and on to Bangkok, making driving here easy. The small but scenic 211 road follows the Mekong River route to Nong Khai from Chiang Khan and points west. The 212 road follows the Mekong east from Nong Khai, connecting to Nakhon Phanom and Mukdahan.

BY SAMLOR & SONGTHAEW A songthaew will ferry you around town and to the Friendship Bridge and train station for B30 to B80, depending on your destination and bargaining skills.

BY TRAIN Three Nong Khai sleepers depart daily from Bangkok's Hua Lamphong station, at 6:30 PM, 7:40 PM, and 8:45 PM. The return trip leaves Nong Khai at 6:20 PM and 7:15 PM. The trip is around B500 to B1,250, depending on type of sleeper. The train station is 2 km (1 mi) west of town, near the Friendship Bridge, on Sadet Road.

CONTACTS & RESOURCES

Emergencies **Police** (☎ *042/411020*). **Nong Khai Provincial Hospital** (✉ *1669 Meechai Rd., Nong Khai* ☎ *042/411504*).

EXPLORING NONG KHAI

Nong Khai is one of the few Thai towns that haven't been overdeveloped with shopping malls and department stores. Lots of traditional homes and shops line the Mekong, and the waterfront area is wonderful for strolling around.

WHAT TO SEE

One of the main draws to Nong Khai is access to Laos via the **Friendship Bridge.** The 1-km-long (½-mi-long) bridge, which opened in 1992, has brought Nong Khai and its province a boost in tourist traffic, which means you can find accommodations here that rival those of bigger towns. To cross into Laos, you must buy a visa for US$36. From the Laotian side it's a 25-km (16-mi) samlor ride to the immensely charming capital city of Laos, Vientiane. The best way to get to Vientiane is to take the hourly bus from either Nong Khai or Udon's bus terminals into downtown Vientiane; however, you must have a visa in advance to use this service. Without a visa, take a tuk-tuk to the border (B50 to B60), then the public bus that crosses the Friendship Bridge (B15), and then either a tuk-tuk or public bus on the Lao side.

Wat Po Chai is Nong Khai's best-known and most attractive temple, easily accessible by way of Prajak Road. It houses a revered gold Buddha image, Luang Pho Phra Sai, which was lost for many centuries after capsizing in a storm and falling to the muddy bottom of the Mekong. Its rediscovery, part of the local lore, is displayed in a number of beautiful murals seen spread over the *ubosot* (ordination hall) walls. ✉ *Th. Phochai, Ban Pho Chai* ⏲ *Daily 6–6.*

Thailand's strangest temple grounds are 5 km (3 mi) west of town on the Nong Khai–Phon Pisai Road at **Wat Khaek,** better known as Sala Kaew Koo. The temple's gardens, created by an ecumenically minded monk, have an extraordinary collection of immense (and immensely bizarre) statues representing gods, goddesses, demons, and devils from many of the world's faiths, though the emphasis is on Hindu gods. ✉*Hwy. 212, Ban Wat Kaek* ☎*081/369–5744* *B10* ⏲*Daily 6–6.*

Wat Noen Pranao is in a shaded forest, and makes for an interesting excursion. The central ubosot is the dominating structure, with its rich motifs and gold stenciling, but the aging wooden hall to its east and the small courtyard bungalows are also worth investigating. This is Nong Khai's leading meditative retreat and is serious business for those involved, who practice meditation and abstinence to heal their troubled souls. You can reach the center on the Nong Khai–Phon Pisai Road by songthaew, which costs around B70. ✉*Noen Pranao, Ban Noen Pranao* ⏲*Daily 6–6.*

WHERE TO EAT & STAY

There are plenty of nice eateries along the Mekong, throughout the Lao market area. Most are similar in menu and price—find the one with biggest crowd and join in.

¢–$ THAI ✕**Nagarina.** On an old barge in the Mekong in front of the Mut Mee Guesthouse, the Nagarina is a charming place to while away the afternoon or evening over tasty Thai dishes. The menu is extensive, with plenty of curries and noodles, and there is often live music to accompany a meal, as you gaze out at Laos across the river. ✉*Haisok Pier* ☎*089/861–3474 or 042/412211* ▭*MC, V.*

$–$$ **Mae Khong Royal.** The main attraction of this Western-style lodging, also known as the Royal Mekong, is its large pool, which is a godsend in the hot summer season. The terrace, cooled by breezes off the Mekong River, is also pleasant. Rooms have great views of the Friendship Bridge and Laos. The hotel's only disadvantage is its isolated location about 3 km (2 mi) outside town. **Pros: enormous pool, one of the best in Thailand;** deluxe and suite rooms are huge; great river and Lao views. **Cons:** very far out of town; no other eating options close by; worn carpets and furniture in standard rooms. ✉*222 Panungchonprathan Rd., Jommanee Beach,* ☎*042/465777 up to 81 or 042/420024* *183 rooms, 15 suites* *In-room: refrigerator. In-hotel: restaurant, room service, bars, laundry service, Internet terminal* ▭*DC, MC, V.*

¢ ★ **Mut Mee Guesthouse.** A wonderful little oasis of charm and friendliness right on the banks of the Mekong River, this great find seems to be the heart of a seasonal community that includes artists and qualified yoga, fitness, and Reiki instructors. Rooms are scattered around a tropical garden and are stylishly decorated with terra-cotta tiles, stone-slab bathrooms, and antique four-poster beds. Steel-welded Buddha images add a nice touch to the window grates and local artwork hangs on the walls. The small pavilion restaurant and lounge serve up healthful dishes and juices. **Pros:** excellent location on the Mekong; patio area with free Wi-Fi right on the river; very clean. **Cons:** low door frames everywhere (watch your head!); often full; limited number of rooms with private bathrooms. ✉*1111/4 Kaeworawut Rd.,* ☎*042/460717 or 081/261–2646* 🌐*www.mutmee.net* *27 rooms, 20 with bath* *In-hotel: restaurant, laundry service, Wi-Fi* ▭*No credit cards.*

¢–$ **Ruan Thai Guesthouse.** An ornate wooden house set in lush green gardens makes this one of the more attractive guesthouses along Rimkhong

7

Road. The original house and additional two-story wooden chalets mean plenty of rooms and a range of prices. Rooms are comfortable, with cozy plaid bedding and chunky wooden furniture. Even though there are no views of the Mekong River, it's only a few feet away. **Pros:** quiet and charming garden; deluxe rooms are homey and spacious; bicycle rental available. **Cons:** no views whatsoever; standard rooms rather small; better value for standard rooms can be found elsewhere. ✉ *1126/2 Rimkhong Rd.,* ☎ *042/412519 or 089/186–7227* *18 rooms* *In-hotel: bicycles, laundry service, Internet terminal* *No credit cards.*

SHOPPING

Village Weaver Handicrafts (✉ *1020 Prajak Rd.* ☎ *042/422651 up to 53*) is an inviting converted shophouse rich with woodwork and vibrant fabrics. It was established as an outlet for the Village Weaver Handicrafts Self-Help Project, which supports local women villagers in a network of about 50 villages, helping them earn personal income to counter the constant threat of poverty. The store has a small workshop down the street on Soi Jittapunya, where skilled seamstresses weave high-quality mudmee fabric. The center is open daily from 9 AM to 7 PM.

EN ROUTE

You can take a marvelous scenic trip on the old road west along the Mekong. Take your own wheels or travel by bus (#507; 1½ hours; B40) to **Si Chiang Mai,** 50 km (31 mi) northwest from Nong Khai. This sleepy backwater is famous for producing spring-roll wrappers—you can see the white translucent rice flour everywhere, spread out on mats to dry. Just out of Si Chiang Mai at road marker 83 you come to Wat Hin Maak Peng, a meditation temple run by *mae chee* (Buddhist nuns).

8

Cambodia

WORD OF MOUTH

"Bottom line: Angkor Wat is a fantastic, 'must see' destination in my book. I highly recommend you go sooner rather than later as it has been 'discovered,' and more and more tourists come each year."

—degas

WELCOME TO CAMBODIA

TOP REASONS TO GO

★ **Angkor Temple Complex:** Hands-down Southeast Asia's most magnificent archaeological treasure, Angkor has hundreds of ruins, many still hidden deep in the jungle.

★ **Education and Enlightenment:** You'll learn a heap about history, warfare and human tragedy, science, and archaeology.

★ **Off-the-Beaten-Path Beaches:** Along the Gulf of Thailand lie some of Southeast Asia's most unspoiled beaches and unpolluted (for now) waters. You'll eat some of the best seafood of your life here.

★ **Philanthropy:** Work with street kids, give blood, buy a cookie to support the arts—if you're looking to do good while you travel, you'll find plenty of interesting opportunities here.

★ **Southeast Asia's Rising Star:** Though it doesn't yet have worldwide attention, Phnom Penh is one of the hippest cities in Southeast Asia.

1 Phnom Penh & Environs. In the capital, you'll find it all: a palace and war monuments, great food and fine wine, and ample opportunities for people-watching along the breezy riverfront. It's an eye-opening place—a city that's come a long way in postwar recovery. And the stories its residents have to tell are both tragic and optimistic.

2 North of Phnom Penh. As you travel north, you'll see some of Asia's last remaining jungles where wildlife populations are actually increasing. Get a glimpse of the rare Irrawaddy dolphin at Kratie. There are still hill tribes in the far north in Ratanakkiri Province.

3 Siem Reap & Angkor Temple Complex. Angkor Wat is the largest religious structure ever built, and it's but one temple in a complex of hundreds. Siem Reap, a rapidly growing city, is the gateway to Angkor and other adventurous excursions.

4 Southern Cambodia. The once-sleepy coast is perking up. Whether you stay at a high-end resort, in a hillside bungalow, or in an island hut, it remains a treat to see such beauty, yet untrammeled. Sihanoukville and Kep are beautiful seaside destinations.

Bayon Temple, Angkor Wat.

Fishing boat, Sihanouk. Opposite: Water festival Phnom Penh.

8

GETTING ORIENTED

Cambodia is one of Southeast Asia's smallest countries—about the size of the state of Washington. The country is bordered by Thailand to the west and northwest, Laos to the northeast, and Vietnam to the east and southeast. In the south, Cambodia faces the Gulf of Thailand, which provides access to the Indian and Pacific oceans. The coastline here is small, largely undeveloped, and isolated by a low mountain range. Much of the country is a low-lying plain dominated by the region's largest lake, the Tonle Sap, and a network of waterways forming the start of the Mekong Delta. Its northern border with Thailand is a remarkable escarpment, rising from the plains to heights of up to 1,800 feet—a natural defensive border and the site of many ancient fortresses.

CAMBODIA PLANNER

When to Go

Cambodia has two seasons, affected by the monsoon winds. The northeastern monsoon blowing toward the coast ushers in the cool, dry season in November, which lasts through February, with temperatures between 65°F (18°C) and 80°F (27°C). December and January are the coolest months. It heats up to around 95°F (35°C) and higher in March and April, when the southwestern monsoon blows inland from the Gulf of Thailand, bringing downpours that last an hour or more most days. This rainy, humid season runs through October, with temperatures ranging from 80°F (27°C) to 95°F (35°C). The climate in Phnom Penh is always very humid. Thanks to climate change, Cambodia now experiences rainstorms in the dry season, cool temps in the hot season, and a lot of unpredictability. Bring your umbrella.

It's important to book in advance if you plan on visiting during mid-April's New Year celebrations or for the Water Festival in Phnom Penh in November. Strangely, the New Year is one of the best times to see the capital—at least in terms of lower rates and crowds—because the majority of Phnom Penh residents come from somewhere else and they all go home for the holidays.

Getting Here & Around

By Air: Regular air service links Phnom Penh and Siem Reap to Bangkok and Vientiane. Domestic flights run between Phnom Penh and Siem Reap. Air Asia, Bangkok Airways, Lao Airlines, Royal Khmer Airlines, Siem Reap Airways, and Thai Airways have flights to Cambodia (⇨ *By Air in Travel Smart*).

By Boat: From Phnom Penh, ferries called "bullet boats" travel along the Tonle Sap to reach Siem Reap and Angkor; they also ply waters between Sihanoukville and Koh Kong. You can buy tickets from a tour operator, your hotel's concierge, or at the port in Phnom Penh. ⚠ **Bullet boats, though fast, can be dangerous.** Smaller ferries travel daily between Siem Reap's port and Battambang, on the Sangker River. Ask about water levels before booking a ticket; in dry season, the water can get so low the boat may get stuck for hours at a time.

Compagnie Fluviale Du Mekong (✉ *30 St. 240, Phnom Penh* ☎ *023/216070* 🌐 *www.cfmekong.com*) offers three-day luxury river excursions between Phnom Penh and Siem Reap. Boats depart Phnom Penh from the municipal port on Sisowath Quay, at Street 84, early in the morning (about $26 one way).

By Bus: Cambodia has a comprehensive bus network, and bus travel is cheap. It's also generally the safest cross-country transportation, aside from flying. Travel from neighboring countries is easy, reliable, and cheap. Buses from Thailand and Vietnam operate daily.

By Car: If you want to get to a destination quickly, hiring a driver with a car is probably the most effective way, but it can be a hair-raising ride. A hired car with a driver costs about $45 a day, but agree on the price beforehand. ⚠ **We strongly advise against driving yourself.** Foreign drivers licenses are not valid here, rules of the road aren't observed, and most drivers drive dangerously.

By Cyclo, Moto & Tuk-Tuk: Within cities and for shorter journeys, *motos* (motorcycle taxis), *tuk-tuks* (three-wheeled cabs), and *cyclos* (pedal-powered trishaws) are the best ways of getting around. Motorcycle taxi drivers, known as *motodops,* will find you at every street corner.

Passports & Visas

At this writing, one-month tourist visas, which cost US$20, are available at all border crossings listed above and at the airports. You'll need two passport photos. ■ **TIP→If you want to cross into Laos from Cambodia, you'll need to secure your visa to Laos in advance, as they are not available at the border.** Border crossings are open daily 7:30–11:30 and 2–5.

Unfortunately, travelers report corruption at many border crossings. Cambodian authorities often will ask for a US$1 fee at the Laos border, or for 1,200 Thai baht or more (well above the legal US$20 fee for a tourist visa) at the Thailand crossings. Often, there's not much you can do to avoid this unless you speak Khmer.

Money Matters

The Cambodian currency is the riel, but the U.S. dollar is nearly as widely accepted, and many high-end businesses actually require payment in dollars. All prices are given in dollars in this chapter. Thai baht are usually accepted in bordering provinces.

The official exchange rate is approximately 4,000 riel to one U.S. dollar and 100 riel to the Thai baht. It's possible to change dollars to riel just about anywhere. Banks and businesses usually charge 2% to cash traveler's checks.

ATMs are available in Phnom Penh, Siem Reap, and Sihanoukville, mostly at ANZ and Canadia banks, although there are a few other banks starting to install them. Credit cards are accepted at major hotels, restaurants, and at some boutiques. Cambodian banking hours are shorter than in many Western countries, generally from 8 AM until 3 or 4 PM. ATMs are available 24 hours.

WHAT IT COSTS IN U.S. DOLLARS

¢	$	$$	$$$	$$$$
Restaurants				
under $5	$5–$8	$8–$12	$12–$16	over $16
Hotels				
under $25	$25–$50	$50–$100	$100–$150	over $150

Restaurant prices are per person for a main course at dinner excluding tax and tip. Hotel prices are for a standard double room, excluding service charge and tax.

Health & Safety

If a real health emergency arises, evacuation to Bangkok is the best option.

Cambodia is safer than many people realize, but you still need to exercise caution. Most violence occurs against Cambodians. However, tourists have been mugged and sometimes killed in Phnom Penh and on the beaches of Sihanoukville. Keep most of your cash, valuables, and your passport in a hotel safe, and avoid walking on side streets after dark. Siem Reap has much less crime than the capital, but that's starting to change. ⚠ **Avoid motos late at night.** Moto theft is one of Cambodia's most widespread crimes, and the unfortunate driver often winds up dead.

Land mines laid during the civil war have been removed from most major tourist destinations. Unexploded ordnance is a concern, however, around off-the-beaten-track temples, where you should only travel with a knowledgeable guide. As a general rule, never walk in uncharted territory in Cambodia, unless you know it's safe.

Cambodia has one of Asia's most atrocious road records. Accidents are common in the chaotic traffic of Phnom Penh and on the highways, where people drive like maniacs. The better the road, the scarier the driving. Unfortunately, chauffeurs are some of the worst offenders. Wear a seatbelt if they're available, and if you rent a moto, wear a helmet.

CAMBODIA PLANNER

Border Crossings

Every few months, it seems, another border crossing opens with a neighboring country. As of this writing, the following border points are open with Thailand (Thai border towns in parentheses): Koh Kong (Hat Lek), Pailin (Ban Pakard), Duan Lem (Ban Laem), Poipet (Aranyaprathet), O'Smach (Chong Jom), and Anlong Veng (Chong Sa Ngam). From Laos you can cross at Dom Kralor (Voeung Kam). Overland crossings through Poipet and Koh Kong are the most popular, but bear in mind that Cambodian roads remain arduous, particularly in the rainy season. Coming from Laos overland, the only way to continue into Cambodia is by boat or bus to Stung Treng, then on from there the following morning.

Beggars

Beggars will approach you in Cambodia. Many NGO workers who work with the homeless advise against giving handouts on the street. Instead, you should acknowledge the people that greet you, politely decline, and make a donation to an organization that operates larger-scale programs to aid beggars and street kids.

Tours & Packages

Hanuman Tourism Voyages (✉ *12 St. 310, Sangkat Tonle Bassac Phnom Penh* ☎ *023/218356 or 012/807657* 🌐 *www.hanumantourism.com*) puts its money into rural development projects. Birders enjoy **oSmoSe Conservation Ecotourism Education** (✉ *0552, Group 12, Wat Bo Village, Siem Reap* ☎ *012/832812* 🌐 *http://jinja.apsara.org/osmose*), which offers tours to the Prek Toal Biosphere Reserve, mainland Southeast Asia's most important waterbird nesting territory. **Wild Asia** (🌐 *www.wildasia.net*) has good information on responsible tourism in Asia. Do a search for Cambodia on the site to see a number of tour possibilities. On the coast, several dive companies have popped up in recent years; **EcoSea Dive** (☎ *012/654104* 🌐 *www.ecosea.com*) is a popular option.

A Rare Opportunity

Should a tuk-tuk driver offer to take you to his home village for a glimpse, consider accepting. The real Cambodian life is nothing like that seen from a tour-bus window, and understanding the greater context of a country that's in tremendous transition will make every experience richer.

Visitor Information

Andy Brouwer (🌐 *www.andybrouwer.blogspot.com*, 🌐 *www.andybrouwer.co.uk*), a longtime traveler to Cambodia, has dedicated a good chunk of his life to informing people about the country. **Tales of Asia** (🌐 www.talesofasia.com) is an excellent source of information, with travelers' stories, road reports, and up-to-date travel information.

Once you arrive, pick up a visitor's guide (separate editions for Phnom Penh, Siem Reap, and Sihanoukville), as well as any of the various Cambodia Pocket Guides, widely available free at airports, hotels, and restaurants.

The **Ministry of Tourism** (🌐 www.mot.gov.kh) has some information on its Web site. **Tourism Cambodia** (🌐 *www.tourismcambodia.com*) has more detailed descriptions of top attractions.

PHNOM PENH & ENVIRONS

Updated by
Simon Stewart

CAMBODIA'S CAPITAL IS ALSO THE country's commercial and political hub, a busy city amid rapid change. Over the past few years, the number of international hotels, large restaurants, sidewalk cafés, art galleries, boutiques, Internet cafés, and sophisticated nightclubs has increased dramatically. So has the city traffic: motorbikes, tuk-tuks, and cyclos (three-wheel pedicabs) fight for space with cars and SUVs.

Phnom Penh is the natural gateway to anywhere in Cambodia: a slew of the north's accessible towns, far-off Ratanakkiri Province in the northeast, the beaches of Sihanoukville and Kep, and Kampot nearby in the south. Cambodia's roads have come a long way in recent years, but many remain potholed and difficult in the rainy season (particularly heading toward the Thai border). Roads heading out of the capital lead to day-trip destinations like the beaches of Tonle Bati, a small lake with a couple of temples nearby, the lovely temple at Phnom Chisor to the south, and the pagoda-topped hill of Udong and the Mekong island of Koh Dach in the north.

PHNOM PENH

The capital of Cambodia, Phnom Penh is strategically positioned at the confluence of the Mekong, Tonle Sap, and Bassac rivers. The city's origins date to 1372, when a wealthy woman named Penh, who lived at the eastern side of a small hill near the Tonle Sap, is said to have found four Buddha statues hidden in a large tree drifting down the river. With the help of her neighbors, she built a hill (a *phnom*) with a temple on top, and invited Buddhist monks to settle on its western slope. In 1434 King Ponhea Yat established his capital on the same spot and constructed a brick pagoda on top of the hill. The capital was later moved twice, first to Lovek and later to Udong. In 1866 during the reign of King Norodom, the capital was moved back to Phnom Penh.

It was approximately during this time that France colonized Cambodia, and the French influence in the city is palpable—the legacy of a 90-year period that saw the construction of many colonial buildings, including the grandiose post office and railway station (both still standing, though the latter is threatened by potential development plans). Some of the era's art-deco architecture remains, in varying degrees of disrepair. Much of Phnom Penh's era of modern development took place after independence in 1953, with the addition of tree-lined boulevards, large stretches of gardens, and the Independence Monument, built in 1958.

Today Phnom Penh has a population of about 2 million people. But during the Pol Pot regime's forced emigration of people from the cities, Phnom Penh had fewer than 1,000 residents. Buildings and roads deteriorated, and most side streets are still a mess. The main routes are now well paved, however, and the city's wats (temples) sport fresh coats of paint, as do many homes. This is a city on the rebound, and its vibrancy is in part due to the abundance of young people, many of whom were born after those war years. Its wide streets are filled

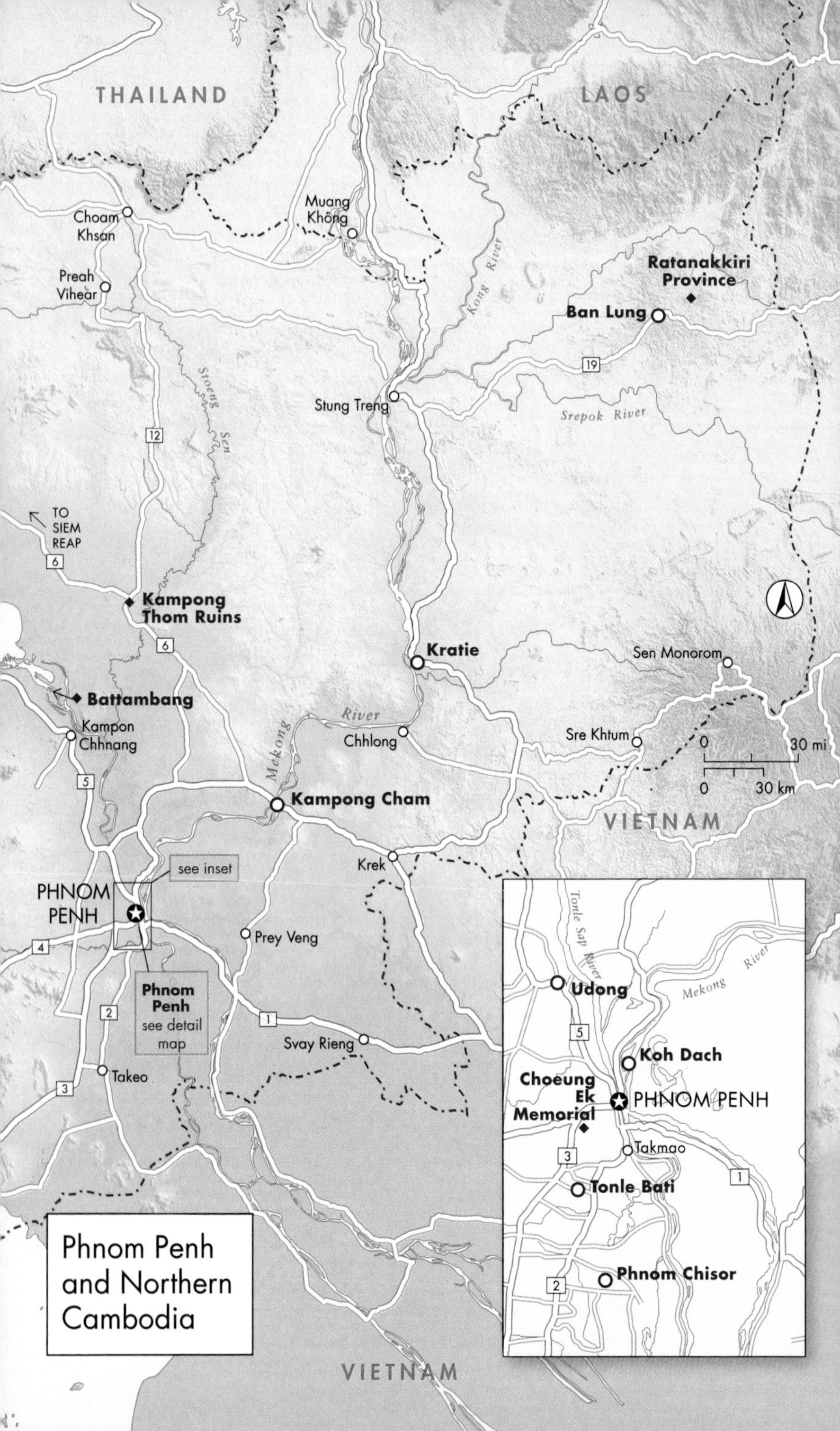

THAILAND
LAOS
Choam Khsan
Muang Không
Preah Vihear
Ratanakkiri Province
Ban Lung
Kong River
19
Stoeng Sen
Stung Treng
Srepok River
12
TO SIEM REAP
6
Kampong Thom Ruins
6
Kratie
Sen Monorom
Battambang
Kampon Chhnang
River
Mekong
Chhlong
Sre Khtum
0
30 mi
0
30 km
5
Kampong Cham
VIETNAM
see inset
Krek
PHNOM PENH
Prey Veng
4
Phnom Penh see detail map
2
1
Svay Rieng
Takeo
3
Tonle Sap River
Mekong River
Udong
5
Koh Dach
Choeung Ek Memorial
PHNOM PENH
Takmao
3
1
Tonle Bati
Phnom Chisor
2
Phnom Penh and Northern Cambodia
VIETNAM

with motorcycles, which weave about in a complex ballet, making it a thrilling achievement merely to cross the street (the best way is to screw up your courage and step straight into the flow, which should part for you as if by magic. If you're not quite that brave (and people have been hit doing this), a good tip is to wait for locals to cross and cross with them.

There are several wats and museums worth visiting, and the old city has some attractive colonial buildings scattered about, though many disappear as time goes on. The wide park that lines the waterfront between the Royal Palace and Wat Phnom is a great place for a sunset stroll, particularly on weekend evenings when it fills with Khmer families, as do the other parks around town: Hun Sen Park, the Vietnamese monument area, and the promenade near the monstrous new Naga Casino. On a breezy evening, you'll find hundreds of Khmers out flying kites.

RESPONSIBLE TOURISM

In the aftermath of Cambodia's civil war foreign aid groups and governments have poured billions of dollars into the country. Hundreds of nonprofit organizations are working toward a better Cambodia on all fronts: health, environment, safety, women's rights, civil rights, children's rights, economy, education. Many nonprofits run hotels, restaurants, and travel agencies that give a chunk of their earnings to development projects and people in need. Do-good travel options are noted in this chapter's listings. It's possible to wine, dine, and shop your way through Cambodia, knowing your money is helping others.

8

GETTING HERE & AROUND

BY AIR Thai International Airways flies twice daily from Bangkok to Phnom Penh, and Bangkok Airways has three flights a day. The trip takes about an hour and costs less than $200 round-trip. Siem Reap Airways and AirAsia also have service between Bangkok and Phnom Penh. Lao Airlines flies from Vientiane and Pakse in Laos to Phnom Penh. Siem Reap Airways and Royal Khmer Airlines provide service between Cambodian cities. (⇨ *See Cambodia Planner for airline contacts.*)

Phnom Penh's modern Pochentong Airport is 10 km (6 mi) west of downtown. The international departure tax is $25, and the charge for domestic departures is $5 to $15. A taxi from the airport to downtown Phnom Penh costs $10. **TIP→ Motorcycles and tuk-tuks are cheaper than taxis (around $3), but it's a long, dusty ride.**

BY BOAT (⇨ *See Cambodia Planner for boat information and contacts.*)

BY BUS Phnom Penh has a half dozen or more private bus companies with regular service from all major Cambodian cities. Major bus stations include the Central Market, Sisowath Quay near the ferry port, and the Hua Lian station near the Olympic Stadium. Mekong Express charges a little more than other bus companies, but routes are direct and buses are clean and comfortable with onboard tour guides and bathrooms. Most long-distance bus tickets cost $3 to $10, depending on the destination and distance.

Tickets can be purchased at the bus companies' offices or through most hotels and guesthouses.

Note that some bus companies advertise a direct Phnom Penh–Bangkok ticket, but that trip takes 20 hours on rough roads, so it's not recommended. Minivans are often a better way to travel, but ensure that the driver doesn't oversell the space and leave you sitting atop assorted produce and livestock. Minivans go to all major, and some minor, destinations within Cambodia. Minivans travel between the Lao border (at the Cambodian immigration point) and Stung Treng (about 2 hours), where you can catch a bus to Phnom Penh.

BY CAR A hired car with a driver costs about $45 a day, but settle on the price before setting off. You can arrange to hire a car with driver through any hotel.

BY TAXI, MOTO & CYCLO The most common forms of transportation are the moto (motorcycle taxi) and tuk-tuk. They cruise the streets in abundance, and gather outside hotels and restaurants—wherever you walk, you'll attract them. The standard fare for a short trip on a moto is 2,000 to 4,000 riel; tuk-tuks run a little higher. Foreigners will always pay more than locals, but the price is generally so cheap it's not worth arguing. Less-abundant cyclos charge the same rates as tuk-tuks. Taxis don't cruise the streets, but there are usually a couple parked outside large hotels, and the receptionist at any hotel can call one. Almost all drivers speak varying degrees of English, some fluently.

ESSENTIALS

Emergencies The International SOS Medical Clinic or Tropical & Travellers Medical Clinic can handle most situations, but if medical evacuation may be required, head to Bangkok Hospital.

Hospitals **Bangkok Hospital Office** (✉ *Hong Kong Center, Sothearos, Phnom Penh* ☎ *023/219422*). **International SOS Medical Clinic** (✉ *161 St. 51, Phnom Penh* ☎ *023/216911 or 012/816911*). **Tropical & Travellers Medical Clinic** (✉ *88 St. 108, Phnom Penh* ☎ *023/366802 or 012/898981*).

Visitor & Tour Info **Diethelm Travel** (✉ *65 240th St., Phnom Penh* ☎ *023/219151* 🌐 *www.diethelm-travel.com*). **Exotissimo** (✉ *46 Norodom, Phnom Penh* ☎ *023/218948* 🌐 *www.exotissimo.com*). **Hanuman Tourism Voyages** (⇨ *Cambodia Planner*).

Guides can also be hired right at the Royal Palace and National Museum.

EXPLORING PHNOM PENH

Phnom Penh is an easy place to navigate and explore. There are markets, museums, and historical sites to visit. You will be able to explore the highlights of the city's tourist attractions in three to four days. All hotels will be able to arrange a range of transport options for your tours around the city.

TOP ATTRACTIONS

9 **Choeung Ek Memorial** *(Killing Fields)*. In the mid- to late 1970s, thousands of Khmer Rouge prisoners who had been tortured at the infamous Tuol Sleng prison were taken to the Choeung Ek extermination camp

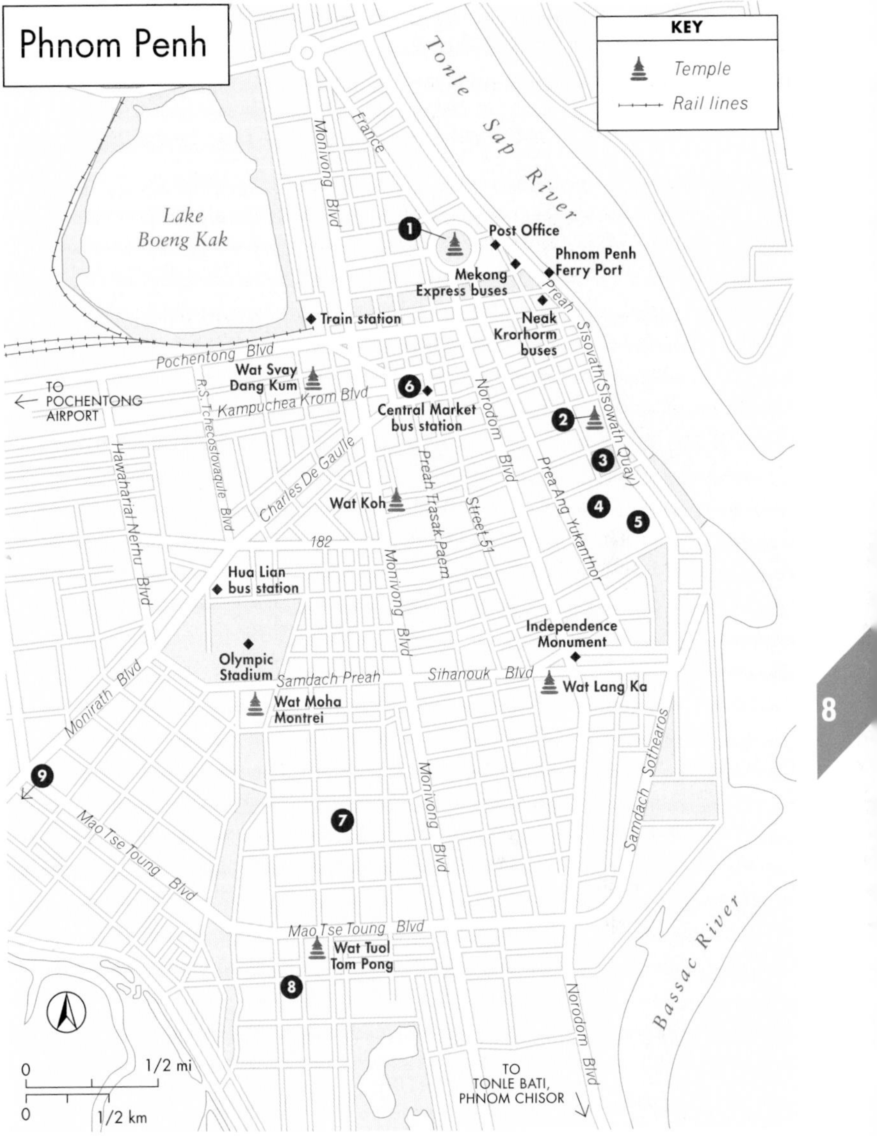

Phnom Penh

KEY

Temple

Rail lines

Choeung Ek Memorial (Killing Fields) **9**

National Museum **3**

Phsar Thmei (Central Market) **6**

Phsar Tuol Tom Pong (Russian Market) **8**

Royal Palace **4**

Tuol Sleng Genocide Museum **7**

Wat Ounalom **2**

Wat Phnom **1**

Wat Preah Keo Morokat **5**

TOURING PHNOM PENH

Start your tour early, just as the sun rises over the Tonle Sap. Take a tuk-tuk to **Wat Phnom**; as you walk in the surrounding gardens, say hello to Sambo, Phnom Penh's only working elephant. She's a gentle creature, and she's had a hard life (someone cut off the end of her tail prior to the 2003 election). Then, climb the staircase and head for the temple, where King Ponhea Yat is venerated. After descending the hill, head east to the Tonle Sap and walk south along the riverfront promenade. Across the street, you are greeted by a plethora of breakfast options; pick the restaurant of your choice. After eating, return to the riverfront, where you have a fine view of the Chroy Changvar Peninsula. The cobbled riverside path leads you to **Wat Ounalom**, one of Phnom Penh's largest and oldest pagodas.

After visiting the wat, continue south on Sisowath Quay, past a busy strip of bars and restaurants, and on to a huge lawn in front of the cheerful yellow **Royal Palace.** On the grounds of the palace is the must-see **Wat Preah Keo Morokat,** aka the Silver Pagoda. The palace closes for lunch from 11 AM to 2 PM, so plan accordingly. On the northern side of the palace, a side street leads to the traditional-style **National Museum,** which is a very peaceful and quiet place to spend an hour or two.

By now you might be hungry again. As you exit the museum, head north on Street 13 to **Friends the Restaurant** for a light lunch and tasty drink. From there, catch a tuk-tuk to the **Tuol Sleng Genocide Museum,** which will require an hour or more with a clear head. It's a somber, sobering experience. If you can handle more, take a tuk-tuk from there to **Choeung Ek,** the Killing Fields, several kilometers outside town.

for execution. Today the camp is a memorial, and the site consists of a monumental glass stupa built in 1989 and filled with 8,000 skulls, which were exhumed from mass graves nearby. It's an extremely disturbing sight: many of the skulls, which are grouped according to age and sex, bear the holes and slices from the blows that killed them. The site is at the end of a rough and dusty road, and can be reached in 30 minutes by motorbike, tuk-tuk, or car. ■ **TIP→ Guides are available, but they are not necessary.** ✉ *15 km (9 mi) southwest of downtown Phnom Penh* ☎ *012/897046* 🎫 *$2* ⏲ *Daily 7–5.*

❸ **National Museum.** Within this splendid, rust-red colonial landmark are many archaeological treasures. Exhibits chronicle the various stages of Khmer cultural development, from the pre-Angkor periods of Fu Nan and Zhen La (5th to 8th century) to the Indravarman period (9th century), classical Angkor period (10th to 13th century), and post-Angkor period. Among the more than 5,000 artifacts and works of art are 19th-century dance costumes, royal barges, and palanquins. A palm-shaded central courtyard with lotus ponds houses the museum's showpiece: a sandstone statue of the Hindu god Yama, the Leper King, housed in a pavilion. Guides, who are usually waiting just inside the entrance, can add a lot to a visit here. ■ **TIP→ This is Cambodia's only national museum, and it's the best place to view archaeological relics that have survived war,**

The Royal Palace's Throne Hall is used today for ceremonies like coronations and royal weddings.

genocide, and widespread plundering. ✉*Junction of Sts. 178 and 13, next to Royal Palace* ☎*023/211755* 🎫*$3* ⏲*Daily 8–5.*

8 **Phsar Tuol Tom Pong** *(Russian Market)*. This popular covered market earned its nickname in the 1980s, when the wives and daughters of Russian diplomats would often cruise the stalls on the lookout for curios and antiques. Today the market has a good selection of Cambodian handicrafts. Wood carvings and furniture abound, as do "spirit houses" used for offerings of food, flowers, and incense. Colorful straw mats and hats, as well as baskets, are in high demand. The market is the city's best source for art objects, including statues of the Buddha and Hindu gods; you can also buy valuable old Indochinese coins and paper money printed during different times of Cambodia's turbulent modern history. A jumble of stalls concentrated at the market's south side sells CDs, videos, and electronics. It's also a great place to buy overstock clothes from Cambodia's numerous garment factories. ✉*South of Mao Tse Tung Blvd., between Sts. 155 and 163* ⏲*Daily 7–5.*

4 **Royal Palace.** A walled complex that covers several blocks near the river, the official residence of current King Preah Norodom Sihamoni and former residence of King Sihanouk and Queen Monineath Sihanouk is a 1913 reconstruction of the timber palace built in 1866 by King Norodom. The residential areas of the palace are closed to the public, but within the pagoda-style compound are a number of structures worth visiting. These include Wat Preah Keo Morokat (⇨ *below*); the Throne Hall, with a tiered roof topped by a 200-foot-tall tower; and a pavilion donated by the Emperor Napoleon III and shipped here from France.

Guides can be hired at the entrance for $5. ✉*Sothearos, between Sts. 184 and 240* ☎*No phone* 🎫*$3* ⏲*Daily 7:30–11 and 2–5.*

7 **Tuol Sleng Genocide Museum.** This museum is a horrific reminder of the cruelty of which humans are capable. Once a neighborhood school, the building was seized by Pol Pot's Khmer Rouge and turned into a prison and interrogation center, the dreaded S-21. During the prison's four years of operation, some 14,000 Cambodians were tortured here; most were then taken to the infamous Killing Fields for execution. Many of the soldiers who did the torturing were children, some as young as 10—many may be walking the streets of Phnom Penh today. The four school buildings that made up S-21 have been left largely as they were when the Khmer Rouge left in January 1979. The prison kept extensive records and photos of the victims, and many of the documents are on display. Particularly chilling are the representations of torture scenes painted by S-21 survivor Vann Nath. ✉*St. 113 (Boeng Keng Kang) and St. 350* ☎*012/927659* 🎫*$2* ⏲*Daily 10–3.*

5 ★ **Wat Preah Keo Morokat** *(Temple of the Emerald Buddha).* Within the Royal Palace grounds is Phnom Penh's greatest attraction: the Temple of the Emerald Buddha, built in 1892–1902 and renovated in 1962. The temple is often referred to as the **Silver Pagoda** because of the 5,329 silver tiles—more than 5 tons of pure silver—that make up the floor in the main vihear. At the back of the vihear is the venerated **Preah Keo Morokat** (Emerald Buddha)—some say it's carved from jade, whereas others maintain that it's Baccarat crystal. In front of the altar is a 200-pound solid-gold Buddha studded with 2,086 diamonds. Displayed in a glass case are the golden offerings donated by Queen Kossomak Nearyreath (King Sihanouk's mother) in 1969; gifts received by the royal family over the years are stored in other glass cases. The gallery walls surrounding the temple compound, which serves as the royal graveyard, are covered with murals depicting scenes from the Indian epic, the *Ramayana.* Pride of place is given to a bronze statue of King Norodom on horseback, completed in Paris in 1875 and brought here in 1892. There's a nearby shrine dedicated to the sacred bull Nandi. ✉*Sothearos, between Sts. 240 and 184* ☎*No phone* 🎫*Included in $3 admission to Royal Palace* ⏲*Daily 7:30–11 and 2–5.*

ALSO WORTH SEEING

6 **Phsar Thmei** *(Central Market).* An inescapable sightseeing destination in Phnom Penh is the colonial-era Central Market, built in the late 1930s on land that was once a watery swamp. This wonderfully ornate building with a large dome retains some of the city's art-deco style. The market's Khmer name, Phsar Thmei, translates as "new" market to distinguish it from Phnom Penh's original market, Phsar Chas, near the Tonle Sap River; it's popularly known as Central Market, however.

You enter the market through one of four great doors that face the directions of the compass. The main entrance, facing east, is lined with souvenir and textile merchants hawking everything from cheap T-shirts and postcards to expensive silks, handicrafts, and silverware. Other stalls sell electronic goods, mobile phones, watches, jewelry, household items, shoes, secondhand clothing, flowers, and just about anything else you can imagine. Money changers mingle with beggars and war veterans with disabilities asking for a few riel. ✉ *Blvd. 128, Kampuchea Krom, at 76 St.* ⏲ *Daily 7–5.*

2 **Wat Ounalom.** The 15th-century Wat Ounalom is now the center of Cambodian Buddhism. Until 1999 it housed the Institute Buddhique, which originally contained a large religious library destroyed by the Khmer Rouge in the 1970s. Wat Ounalom's main vihear, built in 1952 and still intact, has three floors; the top floor holds paintings illustrating the lives of the Buddha. The central feature of the complex is the large stupa, **Chetdai,** which dates to Angkorian times and is said to contain hair from one of the Buddha's eyebrows. Four niche rooms here hold priceless bronze sculptures of the Buddha. The sanctuary is dedicated to the Angkorian king Jayavarman VII (circa 1120–1215). In much more recent times, the wat served as a temporary sanctuary for monks fleeing cops and soldiers in postelection political riots. ✉ *Riverfront, about 250 yards north of National Museum* ☎ *No phone* 🎫 *Free* ⏲ *Daily 7–5.*

1 **Wat Phnom.** According to legend, a wealthy woman named Penh found four statues of Buddha washed up on the banks of the river, and in 1372 she built this hill and commissioned this sanctuary to house them. It is this 90-foot knoll for which the city was named: Phnom Penh means "Hill of Penh." Sixty years later, King Ponhea Yat had a huge stupa built here to house his funeral ashes after his death. You approach the temple by a flight of steps flanked by bronze friezes of chariots in battle and heavenly *apsara* (traditional Khmer dancing figures). Inside the temple hall, the *vihear,* are some fine wall paintings depicting scenes from the Buddha's lives, and on the north side is a charming Chinese shrine. The bottom of the hill swarms with vendors selling everything from devotional candles and flowers to elephant rides. ✉ *St. 96 and Norodom Blvd.* ☎ *No phone* 🎫 *$1* ⏲ *Daily 7:30–6.*

8

WHERE TO EAT

Phnom Penh is quickly becoming one of the top culinary cities in Asia. With delectable Khmer food at all levels, from street stalls to five-star establishments, plus an influx of international restaurants, you'll eat well every night in Phnom Penh. The country's colonial history means you'll find many French-inspired restaurants, too.

$–$$ ECLECTIC ✕ **FCC.** You don't have to be a journalist to join the international crowd gathered here. In fact, it's not really a Foreign Correspondents Club, though it does attract a fair expat following. People drop in as much for the atmosphere of the French colonial building and its river views as for the food, which is as eclectic as the diners. The beer is always cold and you can always grab a reliable burger or pizza. If you find it difficult to leave this pleasant corner of Phnom Penh, you're in luck: there are even rooms for overnight guests. ✉ *363 Sisowath Quay* ☎ *023/724014* 💳 *MC, V.*

¢ TAPAS ✕ **Friends the Restaurant.** Before Romdeng (⇨ *below*), there was Friends the Restaurant. This extremely popular nonprofit café near the National Museum serves a wide range of tapas, fruit juices, salads, and international dishes. Admire the colorful artwork, then visit the Friends store

CAMBODIAN CUISINE

Cambodian cuisine is distinct from that of neighbors Thailand, Laos, and Vietnam, although some dishes are common throughout the region. Fish and rice are the mainstays, and some of the world's tastiest fish are to be had in Cambodia. The country has the benefit of a complex river system that feeds Southeast Asia's largest freshwater lake, plus a coastline famous for its shrimp and crab. Beyond all that, Cambodia's rice paddies grow some of the most succulent fish around. (Besides fish, Cambodians also eat a lot of pork, more so than beef, which tends to be tough.)

Be sure to try *prahok,* the Cambodian lifeblood: a stinky cheeselike fermented fish paste that nourishes the nation. *Amok,* too, is a sure delight. Done the old-fashioned way, it takes two days to make this fish-and-coconut concoction, which is steamed in a banana leaf.

Down south, Kampot Province grows world-renowned pepper. If you're coming from a northern climate, try a seafood dish with whole green peppercorns on the stalk. You won't find them (not fresh, anyway) in your home country.

Generally, the food in Cambodia is not as spicy as that of Thailand or Laos, but flavored heavily with herbs. Curried dishes, known as *kari*, show the ties between Indian and Cambodian cuisine. It is usual in Cambodian food to use fish sauce in soups, stir-fried cuisine, and as a dipping sauces. There are many variations of rice noodles, which give the cuisine a Chinese flavor. Beef noodle soup, known simply as *kuyteav*, is a popular dish brought to Cambodia by Chinese settlers. Also, *banh chiao*, a crepelike pancake stuffed with pork, shrimp and bean sprouts, and then fried, is the Khmer version of the Vietnamese bánh xèo. Cambodian cuisine uses many vegetables. Mushrooms, cabbage, baby corn, bamboo shoots, fresh ginger, Chinese broccoli, snow peas, and bok choy are all found in Cambodian dishes from stir-fry to soup.

Usually, meals in Cambodia consist of three or four different dishes, reflecting the tastes of sweet, sour, salty and bitter. The dishes are set out and you take from which dish you want and mix with your rice. Eating is usually a communal experience and it is appropriate to share your food with others.

next door, filled with souvenirs and trinkets, whose proceeds help the NGO provide much-needed assistance to street children. ✉*215 St. 13* ☎*012/802072* 🌐*www.streetfriends.org* 💳*No credit cards.*

$ JAPANESE ✕**Ginga.** This Japanese spot is on unpleasantly busy Monivong Boulevard, but patrons come here for fresh sushi, not the locale. Along with the usual sushi bar items, Ginga serves great appetizers and plenty of sake and green tea. ✉*295 Monivong Blvd.* ☎*023/217323* 💳*MC, V.*

¢–$ CAMBODIAN ✕**Khmer Borane.** This casual, breezy riverfront café on the bottom floor of an old colonial-era building attracts a steady crowd. Try something from the extensive list of classic Khmer dishes; the pomelo salad and fish soup with lemon and herbs are both good choices. If those don't please your palate, Khmer Borane also offers a wide variety of Western dishes for reasonable prices. ✉*389 Sisowath Quay* ☎*012/290092* 💳*No credit cards.*

Where to Stay and Eat in Phnom Penh

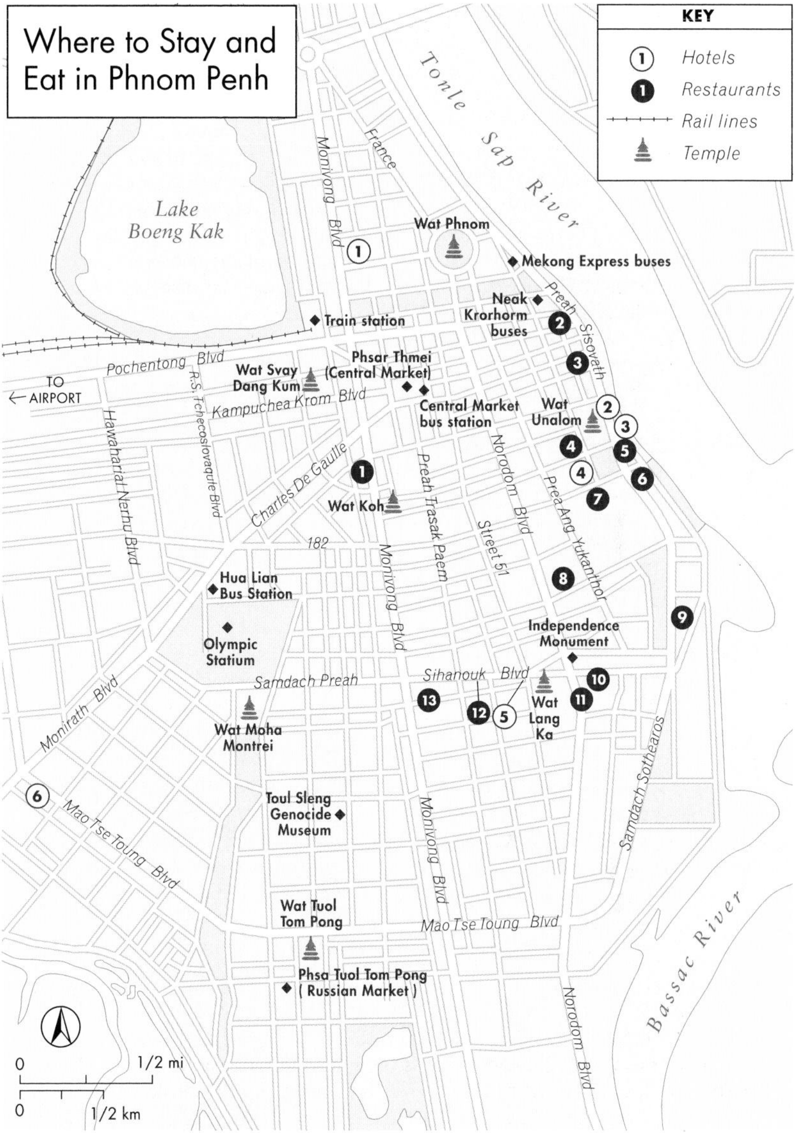

KEY

① Hotels

❶ Restaurants

Rail lines

Temple

Restaurants ▼	
FCC	**5**
Friends the Restaurant	**4**
Ginga	**1**
Khmer Borane	**6**
Malis	**11**
Mount Everest	**12**
Riverhouse Restaurant	**2**
Romdeng	**13**
Sa	**7**
Shiva Shakti	**1**
Tamarind	**8**
Topaz	**9**
Veiyo Tonle	**3**

Hotels ▼	
Amanjaya	**2**
Bright Lotus Guesthouse	**4**
Golden Gate Hotel	**5**
Hotel InterContinental	**6**
Hotel Raffles Le Royal	**1**
Riverside Apartment	**3**

$ THAI ✕ **Malis.** The Phnom Penh elite frequent this upscale traditional Khmer restaurant with outdoor seating. The long menu features lots of fish and seafood, soups and curries, and meats. The prices are right and the place is open all day, starting at 6 AM. ✉ *136 St. 41, Norodom Blvd.* ☎ *023/221022* ▭ *AE, MC, V.*

STOCKING THE FRIDGE

If your room or suite has a kitchenette or an ample mini-fridge, check out **Veggy's** (✉ *23 St. 240* ☎ *023/211534*), which features fine wines, cheeses, and meats from around the world. It also supplies imported dry goods and fresh veggies, as the name indicates.

¢–$ INDIAN ✕ **Mount Everest.** You'll find all the classic Indian and Nepalese dishes at Mount Everest, which has been consistently serving fantastic Indian food for years. Entrées can be ordered as spicy as you like them. ■ **TIP→ The restaurant will deliver to your hotel for free.** ✉ *98A Sihanouk Blvd.* ☎ *023/213821* ▭ *No credit cards.*

$–$$ MEDITERRANEAN ✕ **Riverhouse Restaurant.** The Riverhouse evokes a French bistro, with sidewalk seating and a daily set menu. It's on a corner across the street from the northern end of the waterfront park, with half the tables outside, behind a potted hedge, and half beneath the ceiling fans of the open-air dining room. The menu is eclectic, ranging from couscous to tagines to stewed rabbit. It's a good idea to reserve ahead. ■ **TIP→ With a balcony overlooking the street and river, the upstairs bar is a great place for a drink or a game of pool.** ✉ *Sisowath Quay at 110th St.* ☎ *023/212302* ▭ *AE, MC, V.*

¢–$ ★ CAMBODIAN ✕ **Romdeng.** Some of the country's tastiest provincial Khmer dishes are served at this gorgeously redesigned house in a residential area. The adventurous can try the three flavors of *prahok*, Cambodia's signature fermented fish paste, or even fried spiders. If those don't suit your tastes, Romdeng (which means "galangal" in Khmer) offers plenty of piquant soups, curries, salads, and meat dishes. Have a glass of palm wine to sip with the meal, and enjoy the paintings on the walls—artwork by former street kids. As part of the Mith Samlanh (Friends) group, your dollars will help the former street kids who have been trained to work here. ✉ *21 St. 278* ☎ *092/219565* ▭ *No credit cards.*

$–$$ CAMBODIAN ✕ **Sa.** Restaurants in Phnom Penh don't get much more quaint than Sa, which is in a tiny old colonial building that overlooks the palace park. Sa serves elegant international dishes with Khmer touches, as well as tapas. ✉ *Royal Palace Esplanade* ☎ *012/901822* ▭ *No credit cards* ⊙ *Closed Sun.*

¢–$ INDIAN ✕ **Shiva Shakti.** Succulent samosas, vegetable *pakoras* (fritters), spicy lamb masala, chicken korma, and prawn *biryani* (with rice and vegetables) are among the dishes served at this small Indian restaurant, which is popular with expats. In the pleasant dining room, a statue of the elephant-headed Hindu god Ganesha stands by the door, and reproductions of Mogul art line the walls. There are also a few tables on the sidewalk. It's just east of the Independence Monument. ✉ *70E Sihanouk Blvd.* ☎ *012/813817* ▭ *AE, MC, V* ⊙ *Closed Mon.*

$ MEDITERRANEAN **Tamarind.** The Mediterranean comes east at this popular three-story bar-restaurant in the heart of arty Street 240. The menu extends from North African couscous to Spanish tapas. The wine list is comprehensive and quite good. *31 St. 240 012/830139 MC, V.*

$–$$ FRENCH **Topaz.** The first-class French specialties and extensive wine list at this fine restaurant make it a longtime Phnom Penh favorite. Though it no longer truly stands out in the city's growing restaurant scene, it is a reliable choice for a good, candlelit meal. Note that Topaz is opens for lunch early around 11 AM, but closes again at 2 PM; dinner starts at 6 PM. *100–102 Sothearos 023/211054 AE, MC, V.*

LOCAL EATS

For a local treat, try the afternoon **noodle shops** on Street 178 near the National Museum. These street-side eateries pack in the Khmer crowds, serving quick fried noodles and rice-flour-and-onion cakes. They're very popular among locals, and very cheap (less than a dollar per serving). You won't find the cleanest of restaurants here, but everything is well cooked and you'll get a tasty snack with an eye for what it's like to eat Khmer-style. Don't get here before 4 PM.

¢–$ ★ CAMBODIAN **Veiyo Tonle.** This Khmer-owned and -operated nonprofit restaurant on the riverfront serves excellent traditional Khmer dishes, pizzas (39 varieties!), pastas, and more. Proceeds go toward an orphanage established by the owner. Visit on a Saturday or Monday night and watch the kids perform traditional dances. *237 Sisowath Quay 012/847419 No credit cards.*

WHERE TO STAY

These days, the capital offers a plethora of accommodations for all budgets. Phnom Penh has several international-standard hotels, including the Raffles's refurbishment of a 1929 beauty. Clean and comfortable guesthouses have sprung up across the city, particularly in the Boeung Kak area. Most charge less than $10 a night. If you haven't found what you're looking for, wander the riverfront and its side streets. You're bound to discover something to your liking among the dozens upon dozens of options. **TIP→ When booking a hotel in Cambodia, always ask for the best price. Often, just asking for a discount will yield a rate that's half the listed price. If you're doing business in Cambodia, be sure to say so, as additional discounts may apply.**

$$$$ **Amanjaya.** With tasteful rosewood furnishings and silk textiles, the Amanjaya is the classiest hotel on the banks of the Tonle Sap River. This is an all-suites property and every suite has a balcony with a view of either the river or Wat Ounalom. In-room massage services are available. The price includes your choice of a European- or Asian-style breakfast. **Pros:** glorious riverside location; great restaurant and bar. **Cons:** noisy traffic all day; small rooms. *1 St. 154, Sisowath Quay 023/214747 www.amanjaya.com 21 suites In-room: safe, refrigerator, Wi-Fi. In-hotel: restaurant, room service, bar AE, MC, V.*

¢ **Bright Lotus Guesthouse.** This centrally located guesthouse across from the National Museum is a pleasant and convenient option. Each floor has a balcony with a sitting area. Rooftop rooms offer wide views of the area. Corner rooms are bigger and brighter than the rest of the standard rooms. The restaurant offers tasty Khmer, Mediterranean, and American food at reasonable prices in a shaded area. **Pros:** central location; cheap rooms; good restaurant. **Cons:** on a noisy street; many hawkers at all times of the day. ✉ *22 St. 178* ☎ *023/990446 or 012/676682* *12 rooms* *In-room: no a/c (some), refrigerator (some)* *No credit cards.*

¢–$ **Golden Gate Hotel.** Long popular with long-term and frequent visitors, the Golden Gate offers rooms by the night or by the month. The hotel is located in two separate buildings across the street from each other in a neighborhood with many government and NGO offices and expatriate homes. Laundry service is included in the room price. **Pros:** central location; free airport pick-up; free laundry. **Cons:** facilities in two separate buildings; better suited to long-term business guests than to tourists. ✉ *9 St. 278, Sangkat Bengkengkang 1* ☎ *023/427618 or 012/737319* *www.goldengatehotels.com* *In-room: refrigerator. In-hotel: restaurant, laundry service, Internet terminal* *AE, MC, V. .*

$$$$ **Hotel InterContinental.** One of Phnom Penh's finest hotels is on the far edge of town. For this reason, it may not be the first choice for many tourists. But the InterCon has long been a favorite of business travelers and tycoons requiring VIP treatment. Upper-level rooms offers sweeping views of the flat lands surrounding Phnom Penh. **TIP→ Check out the wine shop in the basement for a unique collection of bottles with prewar labels.** **Pros:** many amenities and services (including a concierge and executive floor); good selection of bars and restaurants at the hotel. **Cons:** location in business district; better suited to business travelers than to vacationers. ✉ *296 Blvd. Mao Tse Tung* ☎ *023/424888* *www.intercontinental.com* *372 rooms* *In-room: safe, refrigerator, Internet. In-hotel: 2 restaurants, bar, tennis courts, pool, gym, spa, laundry service* *AE, MC, V* *BP.*

$$$$ ★ CAMBODIAN **Hotel Raffles Le Royal.** Phnom Penh's best hotel first opened in 1929, was practically destroyed during the Khmer Rouge years, and was meticulously restored by the Raffles group in 1996. A colonial landmark surrounded by gardens, Le Royal has an elegant lobby, a tranquil pool area shaded by massive trees, and various bars and restaurants that are a world apart from this slightly chaotic city. Guest rooms are furnished with fine Cambodian handicrafts in an elegant colonial and art deco style and overlook the pool or gardens. Suites in the main building include claw-foot tubs from the original 1929 hotel. The Elephant Bar is famous for its cocktails (and happy hour), and the sumptuous Restaurant Le Royal ($$–$$$$) serves Khmer haute cuisine. **Pros:** great location; exemplary service. **Cons:** expensive; style may not be to everyone's tastes. ✉ *92 Rukhak Vithei Daun Penh* ☎ *023/981888, 800/637–9477 in U.S., 800/6379–4771 in U.K.* *www.raffles.com* *170 rooms* *In-room: safe, refrigerator, Internet (some). In-hotel: 3 restaurants, bar, pool, gym, spa, laundry service, no-smoking rooms* *AE, MC, V* *BP, MAP.*

$ **Riverside Apartment.** The rooms here are immaculate and surprisingly stylish for a budget property; note that those in the back have no windows. An extra $10 per night gets you a room facing the river—one of the best riverside views you'll find. The Riverside is above the Sunny

Internet Café, which makes up for the lack of Internet access in rooms. **Pros:** river views; stylish rooms. **Cons:** hotel exterior needs renovating. ✉*351 and 353 Sisowath Quay* ☎*012/842036* *lek_sovanarith@yahoo.com* *In-hotel: restaurant, laundry service* *No credit cards.*

NIGHTLIFE & THE ARTS

THE ARTS Various Phnom Penh theaters and restaurants offer programs of traditional music and dancing. Many of these shows are organized by nonprofit groups that help Cambodian orphans and disadvantaged kids. Siem Reap perhaps has more venues, but many there are run by for-profit companies in the tourism industry. The nonprofit **Veiyo Tonle restaurant** (✉*237 Sisowath Quay* ☎*012/847419*) sponsors an orphanage, and twice a week the kids put on beautiful dance performances.

Chaktomuk Theater (✉*Sisowath Quay, north of St. 240* ☎*023/725119*) hosts performances of traditional music and dance. The dates and times of shows are listed in the English-language newspaper *The Cambodia Daily.* Authentic and aesthetically pleasing performances of traditional music and dance are presented every Friday and Saturday at 7:30 PM at the **Sovanna Phum Khmer Art Association** (✉*111 St. 360* ☎*023/987564*).

These days Phnom Penh has a number of remarkably good art and photo galleries to browse. **Le Popil Photo Gallery** (✉*126 St. 19* ☎*012/992750*) exhibits photojournalism and art photography with a focus on Cambodia and the region. **Reyum** (✉*47 St. 178* ☎*023/217149*), a gallery managed by the Institute of Arts and Cultures, offers exhibits on traditional Khmer art and architecture.

8

NIGHTLIFE Phnom Penh's nightlife now rivals that of Bangkok and in many cases exceeds it. What makes the nightlife here so great is how easy it is to get from place to place in this compact city. Most of the dusk-to-dawn nightspots are near the Tonle Sap riverside, along Street 240 and Street 51. Stroll around the riverfront and you'll be duly entertained. ⚠ **Be careful after dark in Phnom Penh—robberies and violence are common, and although foreigners aren't specifically targeted, they are certainly not exempt from the rise in crime.** With its American and Australian music, **Freebird** (✉*69 240th St.* ☎*012/810569*) attracts an expat crowd.

Gone are the legendary Joseph Conrad–inspired days of this popular haunt, but **Heart of Darkness** (✉*26 St. 51* ☎*023/231776*) continues to pack in the crowds.

Phnom Penh Internet Café Pub (✉*No. 219E Sisowath Quay* ☎*012/956292*) is an Internet café, restaurant, and nightspot all in one. It offers great music and cocktails and happy-hour deals, as well as coffee and Khmer and Western food. The Wi-Fi and public computers are available at all times—you get 30 minutes of Internet time free with any drink order.

SHOPPING

The city has many boutiques selling everything from fake antiques to fine jewelry. Prices are generally set at these boutiques, so you won't be able to bargain. The best are on streets 178 and 240.

CLOSE UP

Cambodia's Festivals

Like many Southeast Asian nations, Cambodia celebrates a lot of important festivals. Quite a few of them are closely tied to Buddhism, the country's predominant religion.

Khmer New Year: Celebrated at the same time as the Thai and Lao lunar new year, it's a new-moon festival spread over the three days following the winter rice harvest. People celebrate by cleaning and decorating their houses, making offerings at their home altars, going to Buddhist temples, and splashing lots and lots of water on each other. Be forewarned: Foreigners are fair game.

Bonn Om Touk: The Water Festival ushers in the fishing season and marks the "miraculous" reversal of the Tonle Sap waters. It's celebrated throughout the country: longboat river races are held, and an illuminated flotilla of *naga,* or dragon boats, adds to the festive atmosphere. The biggest races are held in Phnom Penh in front of the Royal Palace, where the King traditionally presides.

Chrat Preah Nongkol: The Royal Ploughing Ceremony, a celebration of the start of the summer planting season, is held in front of the Royal Palace in Phnom Penh in May. The impressive ceremony includes soothsaying rites meant to predict the outcomes for the year's rice harvest.

Meak Bochea: On the day of the full moon in February, this festival commemorates the Buddha's first sermon to 1,250 of his disciples. In the evening, Buddhists parade three times around their respective pagodas.

King Sihanouk's Birthday: The birthday of former King Norodom Sihanouk, born October 31, 1922, in Phnom Penh, is celebrated October 30–November 1; the whole nation joins in to honor him, and a grand fireworks display is held along the riverfront in Phnom Penh.

Pchum Ben (All Souls' Day): In mid-October, the spirits of deceased ancestors are honored according to Khmer tradition. People make special offerings at Buddhist temples to appease these spirits.

Visakha Bochea: This Buddhist festival, on the day of the full moon in May, celebrates the Buddha's birth, enlightenment, and death.

The largest market in Phnom Penh is **Phsar Thmei** (☒*Blvd. 128, Kampuchea Krom, at St. 76*), popularly known as Central Market, an art deco–style structure in the center of the city that sells foodstuffs, household goods, fake antiques, and some silver and gold jewelry. You're expected to bargain—start off by offering half the named price and you'll probably end up paying about 70%. It's busiest in the morning. The **Phsar Tuol Tom Pong** (*Russian Market* ☒*Adjacent to Wat Tuol Tom Pong, at Sts. 155 and 163* ☎*No phone*) sells Cambodian handicrafts, wood carvings, baskets, electronics, clothes, and much more.

ANTIQUES & FINE ART

Bazar Art de Vivre (☒*28 Sihanouk Blvd.* ☎*012/866178*) includes some rare Chinese pieces among its eclectic collection of Asian art and antiques. **Couleurs d'Asie** (☒*19 St. 360* ☎*012/902650*) has regular exhibitions of Asian art and also many fine examples of local artists' work. **Le Lezard Bleu** (☒*61 St. 240* ☎*023/986978*) has a gallery of local artists' work and a collection of small antiques. **Lotus Pond** (✉*57 St. 178* ☎*023/426782*) has a good selection of fine Cambodian silks, carvings and statues, spirit houses, and small furniture items.

> **A SURE SIGN OF CHANGE**
>
> Phnom Penh now has two classy wine shops and tasting bars. **Open Wine** (✉*219 St. 19* ☎*023/223527*) and **Red Apron** (✉*15 and 17E St. 240* ☎*023/990951*), right around the corner, both add a touch of international style to the capital. A decade ago it was hard to imagine such venues in Phnom Penh.

LOCAL CRAFTS **Northeast Cambodia Souvenir Shop** (✉*52 CE0 St. 240* ☎*012/838350*) sells cotton clothing and handicrafts made by the hill tribes of Ratanakkiri Province, many of whom have little contact with the world beyond the forests they live in. **Rajana** (✉*Two locations on St. 450 by the Russian Market* ☎*023/993642* 🌐*www.rajanacrafts.org*) sells unique and interesting handicrafts, jewelry, silks, clothing, and knickknacks. Proceeds go toward the Rajana Association, which trains local artisans. ■ **TIP→ Check out the old war-scrap necklaces and recycled spark-plug figurines.** The store has other locations in Sihanoukville and Siem Reap. **Roth Souvenir Shop** (✉*18 St. 178* ☎*012/603484*) is the outlet for curios, handicrafts, and small decorative items. **Watthan Artisans Cambodia** (✉*Wat Than Pagoda, 180 Norodom Blvd.* ☎*023/216321* 🌐*www.wac.khmerproducts.com*), an organization worth supporting, features silks and other handicrafts made on-site by people with disabilities.

SILK **Kravanh House** (✉*13E St. 178* ☎*012/756631*) has one of the city's best selections of raw silk and silk products. **Sayon Silk Shop** (✉*40 St. 178* ☎*012/859380*) has an exquisite collection of silks and ready-made items.

8

TONLE BATI

33 km (20 mi) south of Phnom Penh.

On weekends, Phnom Penh residents head for this small lake just a half hour's drive south on Highway 2. It has a beach with refreshment stalls and souvenir stands. Note that you'll encounter many beggars and children clamoring for attention here. The nearby, but more remote, **Ta Phrom,** a 12th-century temple built around the time of Siem Reap's Angkor Thom and Bayon, is less chaotic. The five-chambered laterite temple has several well-preserved Hindu and Buddhist bas-reliefs. Nearby is an attractive, smaller temple, **Yeah Peau.** Both temples are free and open to the public at all time. Phnom Tamao, Cambodia's leading zoo, is about 11 km (7 mi) farther south, but it's not worth a detour.

GETTING HERE & AROUND

Hiring a car and driver in Phnom Penh is perhaps the easiest way to visit Tonle Bati, and if you do this, you can easily combine the trip with Phnom Chisor. The drive takes about 30 minutes. Nearly hourly GST

Women parade near the Royal Palace in celebration of Bonn Om Touk, Cambodia's water festival.

and Neak Krorhorm buses head to Tonle Bati. Buses drop you within walking distance of the lake, but there are also moto-taxis available.

Diethelm Travel (⇨ *Essentials in Phnom Penh, above*) arranges tours to Tonle Bati.

PHNOM CHISOR

55 km (34 mi) south of Phnom Penh.

A trip to Phnom Chisor is worth the drive just for the view from the top of the hill of the same name. There's a road to the summit, but most visitors prefer the 20-minute walk to the top, where stunning vistas of the Cambodian countryside unfold. At the summit, the 11th-century temple, which is free and open to the public, is a Khmer masterpiece of laterite, brick, and sandstone.

GETTING HERE & AROUND

Though the bus is dirt cheap, you can combine Tonle Bati and Phnom Chisor in one trip if you hire a car and driver (about $50 per day), perhaps the easiest way to visit Phnom Chisor. The drive from Tonle Bati takes about 20 minutes, or 40 minutes from Phnom Penh. Takeo-bound GST and Neak Krorhorm buses (departing Phnom Penh every hour) stop at Prasat Neang Khmau; from there you can hire a moto to take you up the hill. The whole trip should take no more than an hour.

Diethelm Travel and Hanuman Tourism Voyages (⇨ *Cambodia Planner*) arrange tours to Phnom Chisor.

KOH DACH

30 km (19 mi) north of Phnom Penh.

This Mekong River island's main attractions are its beach and handicrafts community of silk weavers, wood-carvers, potters, painters, and jewelry makers. The beach isn't spectacular by Southeast Asian standards, but it is convenient for Phnom Penh getaways. In all, the trip over to the island is pretty quick; most people spend about half a day on this excursion, but you can dwell longer if you want a relaxing beach day.

GETTING HERE & AROUND

Any tuk-tuk or moto driver can take you to Koh Dach from Phnom Penh. Alternatively, you can hire a car and driver for the day (about $40 per day). The trip takes approximately two hours each way and involves a ferry trip to the island.

Diethelm Travel and Hanuman Tourism Voyages arrange tours to Koh Dach.

UDONG

45 km (28 mi) north of Phnom Penh.

This small town served as the Khmer capital from the early 1600s until 1866, when King Norodom moved the capital south to Phnom Penh. Today it's an important pilgrimage destination for Cambodians paying homage to their former kings. You can join them on the climb to the pagoda-studded hilltop, site of the revered Vihear Prah Ath Roes assembly hall, which still bears the scars of local conflicts from the Khmer Rouge era.

GETTING HERE & AROUND

Udong is best reached by catching a GST or Neak Krorhorm bus to Kampong Chhnang from the Central Bus Station and getting off at the junction at the Km 37 mark. Motos and tuk-tuks will then take you to the temples. The bus costs around $1.

You can also take a boat from Phnom Penh; this can be arranged through your hotel or any travel agent.

Diethelm Travel, Exotissimo, and Hanuman Tourism Voyages arrange tours to Udong.

NORTH OF PHNOM PENH

If you're looking to go even farther afield, you can visit the ancient ruins of Kampong Thom or Kampong Cham; see highly endangered freshwater Irrawaddy dolphins at Kratie; or head to the remote and largely undeveloped provinces of Ratanakkiri or Mondulkiri, both of which offer trekking opportunities among hill tribes. The city of Battambang (Cambodia's second largest) may be closer to Siem Reap on the map, but Phnom Penh is the logical jumping-off point for a visit there. Note that many of these destinations are quite removed from one another or accessed via different routes, and thus can't be combined in one tour. ■ **TIP→ During rainy season the road to Ratanakkiri is often hazardous.**

KAMPONG CHAM

125 km (78 mi) northeast of Phnom Penh.

Cambodia's third-largest city was also an ancient Khmer center of culture and power on the Mekong River, and it has a pre-Angkorian temple, **Wat Nokor.** (Sadly, the temple itself is in a state of disrepair and the US$3 entry fee unmerited.) Just outside town are the twin temple-topped hills, Phnom Pros and Phnom Srei. Ask a local to explain the interesting legend surrounding their creation. In the ecotourism village of Cheungkok, about 5 km (3 mi) south of town, you can see silk-making, carving, and other traditional crafts in progress and also buy the wares directly from villagers. All profits are reinvested in the village.

Kampong Cham can be visited in a few hours, but with Cheungkok it is an all-day trip.

GETTING HERE & AROUND

You can get to Kampong Cham from Phnom Penh by taxi or bus; the trip takes about 3 hours. Any guesthouse or hotel can arrange for a taxi. Expect to pay $5 for a single bus ticket and $50 for a taxi from Phnom Penh. The buses (GST, Hua Lian, Mekong Express, and Neak Krorhorm) leave hourly from the bus station at the Central Market.

WHERE TO STAY

Kampong Cham has the usual local food stalls and shophouses, but no restaurants of note.

¢ **Mekong Hotel.** A Japanese enterprise built this riverside hotel but kept to a high-eaved Cambodian style. The boat pier is close by and rivercraft skippers tend to blast their horns early to announce their departure, so if you like to sleep late, book a room at the back. Rooms are large and smartly furnished in light woods and fabrics. **Pros:** riverside. **Cons:** basic rooms; can be noisy. ✉*River Rd.* ☎*042/941536* *18 rooms* *In-room: refrigerator. In-hotel: restaurant, laundry service* *No credit cards.*

KAMPONG THOM RUINS

160 km (99 mi) north of Phnom Penh.

These ruins, exactly halfway between Phnom Penh and Siem Reap, are even older than those at Angkor. They are all that remain of the 7th-century Sambor Prei Kuk, the capital of Zhen La, a loose federation of city-states. The ruins, which are free and open to the public at all times, are near the Stung Sen River, 35 km (22 mi) northeast of the provincial town of Kampong.

GETTING HERE & AROUND

The ruins are a day trip by taxi from Siem Reap (2 hours; $50) or Phnom Penh (3 hours). The journey can be dusty and hot in the dry season and muddy and wet in the rainy season. You can catch a bus to the town of Kampong Thom from Siem Reap ($4) or Phnom Penh ($10) and arrange local transport via tuk-tuk or moto (about $20 for the full tour of the ruins).

KRATIE

★ *350 km (217 mi) northeast of Phnom Penh.*

Kratie is famous for the colony of freshwater Irrawaddy dolphins *(⇨ Irrawaddy Dolphins box, Chapter 9)* that inhabit the Mekong River some 15 km (9 mi) north of town. ■ **TIP→ The dolphins are most active in the early morning and late afternoon.** Taxis and hired cars from Kratie charge about $10 for the journey to the stretch of river where the dolphins can be observed. You will likely have to hire a local boatman to take you to where the dolphins are, as they move up and down the river.

GETTING HERE & AROUND

Several bus companies from Phnom Penh's Central Bus Station offer regular service to Kratie (6–7 hours; $10). Expect delays in the wet season. You can also get a share taxi or hire your own driver, but buses are a far safer option.

Diethelm Travel (F *Essentials in Phnom Penh, above*) arrange tours to Kratie.

WHERE TO STAY

Kratie has an abundance of local food shops. Most guesthouses have simple menus and there is a lively food-stall scene in town.

¢ **Santepheap Hotel.** Ask for a room with a river view at this hotel across the road from the boat pier. Rooms are simple, with little decoration, but comfortable enough, and the bathrooms are large, with tubs. **Pros:** clean rooms; river views from the front rooms. **Cons:** some might find the accommodation a little basic. ✉ *River Rd.* ☎ *072/971537* *24 rooms* *In-room: no a/c (some), no TV (some). In-hotel: restaurant* *No credit cards.*

8

RATANAKKIRI PROVINCE

Ban Lung is 635 km (395 mi) northeast of Phnom Penh.

Visiting this region makes you feel as if you've arrived at the end of the world. Both Ratanakkiri and neighboring Mondulkiri provinces are mountainous and covered with dense jungle, and together they are home to 12 different Khmer Loeu ethnic-minority groups. The government has borrowed money from the Asian Development Bank and at this writing is developing four community-based projects in the region. The eventual aim (though it's been slow going) is to reinvent large sections of the area as ecotourism destinations, making them self-sufficient and helping the communities reduce the impact on the natural resources by creating an ecotourism destination.

CLOSE UP

Religion in Cambodia

As in neighboring Thailand, Laos, and Vietnam, Buddhism is the predominant religion in Cambodia. But animism and superstition continue to play strong roles in Khmer culture and society. Many people believe in powerful *neak ta,* or territorial guardian spirits. Spirit shrines are common in Khmer houses as well as on temple grounds and along roadsides. The Khmer Loeu hill tribes, who live in the remote mountain areas of Ratanakkiri and Mondulkiri provinces, and some tribes of the Cardamom Mountains are pure animists, believing in spirits living in trees, rocks, and water.

The main layer of Cambodian religion is a mix of Hinduism and Buddhism. These two religions reached the country from India about 2,000 years ago and played a pivotal role in the social and ideological life of the earliest kingdoms. Buddhism flourished in Cambodia in the 12th to 13th century, when King Jayavarman VII embraced Mahayana Buddhism. By the 15th century, influenced by Buddhist monks from Siam and Sri Lanka, most Cambodians practiced Theravada Buddhism.

Cambodian religious literature and royal classical dance draw on Hindu models, such as the *Reamker,* an ancient epic about an Indian prince searching for his abducted wife and fighting an evil king. Brahman priests still play an important role at court rituals.

Cambodia's Muslim Chams, who number a few hundred thousand, are the descendants of the Champa Kingdom that was based in what is today Vietnam. Many have lived in this area since the 15th century when they were forced from the original kingdom. The country's 60,000 Roman Catholics are mainly ethnic Vietnamese. A small Chinese minority follows Taoism.

GETTING HERE & AROUND

From Phnom Penh there's daily bus service to Ban Lung (12+ hours; $10) on GST. The journey is much improved from a few years ago with the opening of the resurfaced road. There are no scheduled flights available, but charter companies do the trip regularly. Visit any travel agent for details. Share taxis are always an option, unattractive as that option may be. It's an arduous drive.

Diethelm Travel arrange tours to Ratanakkiri.

In Ban Lung you can hire a jeep (preferably with a driver-guide) or, if you're very adventurous, a motorcycle, to visit the fascinating destinations an hour or two away.

EXPLORING RATANAKKIRI PROVINCE

Ratanakkiri Province is remote but it is slowly building a reputation as an ecotourism destination, and the government is trying hard to promote tourism to this part of Cambodia. Intrepid travelers will find natural and cultural attractions including waterfalls, jungle treks, lakes, and villages.

The provincial capital of **Ban Lung** is a small, sleepy town. It holds a certain romance as a far-flung capital away from the influence of Phnom

Penh, but otherwise offers little more than slow-paced local life and dust in the dry season, and mud in the wet season. Arrive with everything you need, western goods are sometimes difficult to obtain.

A visit to the gem mines of the **Bo Keo** area, 35 km (22 mi) east of Ban Lung, can be arranged through your hotel, or any moto driver in Ban Lung can take you there. The mines are shallow, mainly for semi-precious stones such as zircon.

Mystical **Yeak Laom Lake,** 5 km (3 mi) from Ban Lung, is sacred to many of the Khmer Loeu hill tribes. Lodged in a volcanic crater, the lake is a half-mile in diameter and 154 feet deep. Take a tuk-tuk or moto from Ban Lung. Admission is $1, but a request for $5 is standard.

The beautiful jungle of **Virachey National Park**, 35 km (22 mi) northeast of Ban Lung, has the two-tiered Bu Sra Waterfall and lots of wildlife. Tuk-tuks and motos will take you there from Ban Lung ($10). Admission is sometimes free, sometimes $3, based on a fickle schedule.

WHERE TO EAT & STAY

¢–$ ASIAN **Terres Rouge Lodge Restaurant.** At this fine restaurant, local flavor is mixed with French cuisine. It knocks the socks off the local competition. ✉ *Beoung Kan Siang* ☎ *075/974051* ▭ *No credit cards.*

$–$$ **Terres Rouge Lodge.** This handsome property on the edge of Ban Lung's Boeung Kan Siang Lake is the region's best. It's a traditional wooden Cambodian country house, decorated in traditional style, with antiques and local artifacts in the spacious rooms. The restaurant is also one of the best of the area. **Pros:** spacious rooms; beautiful, traditional building. **Cons:** few facilities in rooms. ✉ *Boeung Kan Siang Lake, Ban Lung* ☎ *075/974051* *14 rooms* *In-room: refrigerator. In-hotel: restaurant, laundry service* ▭ *No credit cards.*

¢–$ **Yaklom Hill Lodge.** This popular lodge, which prides itself on an eco-friendly philosophy, offers 13 wooden cottages and a traditional hill-tribe house in a jungle setting outside the city (note: no hot water). The lodge arranges tours of the area, and the property itself allows you to enjoy nature—there are several terraces with outstanding views and a few short nature trails. Bicycles and motorcycles are available for rent. **Pros:** great natural location. **Cons:** no hot water; basic facilities only. ✉ *Outside Ban Lung* ☎ *011/725881* 🌐 *www.yaklom.com* *13 cottages, 1 house* *In-room: no a/c, no phone, no TV. In-hotel: restaurant* ▭ *No credit cards.*

BATTAMBANG

290 km (180 mi) northwest of Phnom Penh.

Cambodia's second-largest city straddles the Sanker River in the center of the country's rice bowl. Dusty Battambang is bypassed by most visitors to Cambodia, but it's an interesting city to explore. **■ TIP→ The French left their mark here with some fine old buildings, more than you'll find in most Cambodian cities these days.**

8

GETTING HERE & AROUND

BY BUS All the major bus companies depart daily from Phnom Penh's Central Market to Battambang (5 hours; $8) and in some cases, on to Poipet.

BY CAR A hired car with a driver costs about $45 a day, but settle on the price before setting off.

BY TRAIN The journey to Battambang from Phnom Penh by decrepit once-a-week train takes up to 14 hours, costs 22,000 riel (about $5), and attracts only the poorest of travelers. Trains leave Saturday morning around 6 am and tickets can be purchased at the central train station in Phnom Penh.

ESSENTIALS

Banks **ANZ/Royal Bank Battambang** (⊠ *2, 4, and 6 St. 1, Svay Poa Commune, Battambang).*

Emergencies **Makalin Clinic Branch 1** (⊠ *Rd. No 1, along Maot Steung St., next to old Spean Dek, Battambang* ☎ *012/381376).*

Visitor & Tour Info **Capitol Tours** (⊠ *739 La Er St., near Boeung Chhouk Market, Battambang* ☎ *053/953040).*

EXPLORING BATTAMBANG

The few sights to see in and around town include some Angkor-era temple ruins and the Khmer Rouge "killing caves." The town is walkable, and strolling down to the river in the evening is a pleasant way to pass the time.

WHAT TO SEE

Long before the French arrived, Battambang was an important Khmer city, and among its many temples is an 11th-century Angkorian temple, **Wat Ek Phnom.** The temple has some fine stone carvings in excellent condition. Get here via tuk-tuk or moto (around $15); negotiate a price before you set out.

In the countryside outside the city is the 11th-century hilltop temple **Phnom Banan,** with five impressive towers.

Perhaps Battambang's most interesting site is a mountain, **Phnom Sampeou,** which contains a temple and a group of "killing caves" used by the Khmer Rouge. In one, which contains the skeletal remains of some of the victims, you can stand on the dark floor and look to a hole in the cave ceiling with sunlight streaming through. The Khmer Rouge reportedly pushed their victims through that hole to their deaths on the rocks below.

Phsar Nath Market, like most local markets, is a decent place for souvenir-hunting. The market is known for its gems and Battambang's famous fruit, but it also sells everything from fresh produce to electronics imported from China. Some stalls sell textiles, but most of these are imported. ⊠ *On the Sangker River* ☎ *No phone* ⊙ *Daily 7–5.*

WHERE TO STAY

There is a good selection of restaurants in town, including some Western cuisine. The places to eat here are all at the lower end of the price range. A Khmer food market opens down by the river in late afternoon or early evening.

$$ **La Villa.** This boutique hotel is in a restored 1930s colonial house; rooms have an art-deco feel and antique furnishings. **Pros:** colonial-era design. **Cons:** not many facilities. *E. River Rd. 012/991801 or 012/858571 lavilla@online.com.kh 6 rooms In-room: no a/c (some). In-hotel: restaurant, bar No credit cards.*

$ ECLECTIC **Teo Hotel.** Teo is one of Battambang's best hotels, but it is on a busy main road, so insist on a room at the back. Rooms are reminiscent of French provincial auberges, with lots of fussy chintz and incongruous decorations. There are even floor-to-ceiling French windows. The garden restaurant (¢–$) serves Khmer, Thai, and Western dishes. **Pros:** decent restaurant. **Cons:** street noise; strange decor. *3rd St., Svay Pro Commune 012/857048 81 rooms In-hotel: restaurant MC.*

SIEM REAP & ANGKOR TEMPLE COMPLEX

The temples of Angkor constitute one of the world's great ancient sites and Southeast Asia's most impressive archaeological treasure. The massive structures, surrounded by lush tropical forest, are comparable to Central America's Mayan ruins—and far exceed them in size. Angkor Wat is the world's largest religious structure; so large, it's hard to describe its breadth to someone who hasn't seen it. And that's just one temple in a complex of hundreds.

8

Siem Reap was once a small, provincial town known only for the nearby Angkor ruins. In recent years, it has grown tremendously, becoming a tourism hub critical to the Cambodian economy.

It's well worth spinning through the countryside around Siem Reap to get a feel for the way Cambodian farmers and fishermen live. Take a day to tour floating villages, some of the outlying temples, or Kulen Mountain, a sacred place for modern Cambodians, with tremendous views. Naturalists won't be sorry with a trip to see the birdlife at Prek Toal, near Tonle Sap, especially when birds are nesting (November or December). Local guesthouses and tour companies can arrange most trips.

SIEM REAP

315 km (195 mi) north of Phnom Penh.

Siem Reap, which means "Siam defeated," based on a 15th-century battle with Cambodia's neighbors to the west, is turning into a thriving, bustling city with great shopping, dining, and nightlife options. There's still not much in the town itself to distract you from Angkor, but after a long day at the temples, you'll be happy to spend your evening strolling along the Siemp Reap River, and dining at an outdoor table on a back alley in the hip old French quarter near Pub Street, which is closed to traffic in the evening.

CLOSE UP

Cambodia Then and Now

The Kingdom of Cambodia, encircled by Thailand, Laos, Vietnam, and the sea, is a land of striking extremes. Internationally, it's most well known for two contrasting chapters of its long history. The first is the Khmer empire, which in its heyday covered most of modern-day Southeast Asia. Today, the ruins of Angkor attest to the nation's immutable cultural heritage. The second chapter is the country's recent history and legacy of Khmer Rouge brutality, which left at least 1.7 million Cambodians dead. In 1993, the United Nations sponsored democratic elections that failed to honor the people's vote. Civil war continued until 1998, when another round of elections was held, and violent riots ensued in the aftermath. Cambodia's long-standing political turmoil—both on the battlefield and in much more subtle displays—continues to shape the nation's day-to-day workings. Through decades of war, a genocide, continued widespread government corruption, high rates of violence and mental illness, the provision of billions of dollars in international aid, and the disappearance of much of that money, Cambodia has suffered its demons. It remains one of the poorest, least-developed countries in the world.

Yet Cambodians are an energetic and friendly people, whose quick smiles belie the inordinate suffering their nation continues to endure. Though practically destroyed by the regional conflict and homegrown repression of the 1970s, individual Cambodians have risen from those disasters. The streets of Phnom Penh are abuzz with a youthful vibrancy, and the tourism boomtown of Siem Reap, near the Angkor ruins, is full of construction sites.

More than half of Cambodia was once covered with forest, but the landscape has changed in recent decades thanks to ruthless and mercenary deforestation. The country is blessed with powerful waters: the Mekong and Tonle Sap rivers, and the Tonle Sap lake, which feeds 70% of the nation. The surrounding mountain ranges, protecting Cambodia's long river valleys, are home to hill tribes and some of the region's rarest wildlife species.

The three ranges of low mountains—the northern Dangkrek, the exotically named Elephant Mountains in the south, and the country's highest range, the Cardamoms, in the southwest—formed natural barriers against invasion and were used as fortresses during the war years. Among these ranges is a depression in the northwest of Cambodia connecting the country with the lowlands in Thailand; by allowing communication between the two countries, this geographic feature played an important part in the history of the Khmer nation. In eastern Cambodia, the land rises to a forested plateau that continues into the Annamite Cordillera, the backbone of neighboring Vietnam.

As the seat of the Khmer empire from the 9th to the 13th century, Cambodia developed a complex society based first on Hinduism and then on Buddhism. After the decline of the Khmers and the ascendancy of the Siamese, Cambodia was colonized by the French, who ruled from the mid-1860s until 1953. Shortly after the end of World War II, during which the Japanese had occupied Cambodia, independence became the rallying cry for all of Indochina. Cambodia became a sovereign power with a monarchy ruled by King Norodom Sihanouk, who abdicated in favor of his father in 1955 and entered the public stage as a mercurial politician.

In the early 1970s, the destabilizing consequences of the Vietnam War sparked a horrible chain of events. The U.S. government secretly bombed Cambodia, arranged a coup to oust the king, and invaded parts of the country in an attempt to rout the Vietcong. Civil war ensued, and in 1975 the Khmer Rouge, led by French-educated Pol Pot, emerged as the victors. A regime of terror followed. Under a program of Mao Tse-Tung–inspired reeducation centered on forced agricultural collectives, the cities were emptied and hundreds of thousands of civilians were tortured and executed. Hundreds of thousands more succumbed to starvation and disease. During the four years of Khmer Rouge rule, somewhere between 1 and 2 million Cambodians—almost one-third of the population—were killed.

By 1979, the country lay in ruins. Vietnam, unified under the Hanoi government, invaded the country in response to a series of cross-border attacks and massacres in the Mekong Delta by the Khmer Rouge. The invasion forced the Khmer Rouge into the hills bordering Thailand, where they remained entrenched and fighting for years. United Nations–brokered peace accords were signed in 1991. International mediation allowed the return of Norodom Sihanouk as king and the formation of a coalition government that included Khmer Rouge elements after parliamentary elections in 1993. But civil war continued.

In 1997 Second Prime Minister Hun Sen toppled First Prime Minister Norodom Ranariddh in a coup. During the following year's national elections, Hun Sen won a plurality and formed a new government, despite charges of election rigging. Pol Pot died in his mountain stronghold in April 1998, and the remaining Khmer Rouge elements lost any influence they still had. It has taken years for the United Nations and the Cambodian government to establish a tribunal that will bring to justice the few surviving key leaders of the Khmer Rouge regime. Proceedings began in 2007, but only one former Khmer Rouge leader (Duch, the infamous head of Tuol Sleng) is in jail; Ta Mok, the so-called "Butcher," was the only other Khmer Rouge leader to be imprisoned, but he died in 2006. The others remain free; many have blended with ease into current society, and some remain in the folds of the Cambodian government.

Foreign investment and the development of tourism have been very strong in recent years, but it remains to be seen whether domestic problems can truly be solved by Prime Minister Hun Sen and his hard-line rule.

DID YOU KNOW?

The roots that creep over the ruins of Ta Prohm belong to either silk-cotton trees or thinner strangler fig trees. Strangler figs grow out of crevices in other trees, sometimes smothering their hosts over time.

True, construction sites are common eyesores and disrupters of the peace in this rapidly expanding town, but don't let that deter you from exploring Siem Reap. The Old Market area is a huge draw and the perfect place to shop for souvenirs. Many of the colonial buildings in the area were destroyed during the Khmer Rouge years, but many others have been restored and turned into delightful hotels and restaurants.

You could spend an entire afternoon in the Old Market area, wandering from shop to shop, café to café, gallery to gallery. It changes every month, with ever more delights in store. Long gone are the days when high-end souvenirs (the legal kind) came from Thailand. Today, numerous shops offer high-quality Cambodian silks, Kampot pepper and other Cambodian spices, and herbal soaps and toiletries made from natural Cambodian products.

GETTING HERE & AROUND

BY AIR Bangkok Airways flies six times daily between Siem Reap and Bangkok (1 hour; $250 round-trip). Lao Air flies three times a week to Siem Reap from both Pakse (50 minutes; $150 one way) and Vientiane (80 minutes; $100 one way), in Laos. Royal Khmer Airlines and Siem Reap Airways fly between Phnom Penh and Siem Reap (1 hour; $80 one-way). Siem Reap International Airport is 6 km (4 mi) northwest of town. The taxi fare to any hotel in Siem Reap is $5.

BY BOAT The road to Phnom Penh was upgraded several years ago, but some tourists still prefer the six-hour boat trip on the Tonle Sap. High-speed ferries, or "bullet boats," depart Phnom Penh for Siem Reap daily (⇨ *Cambodia Planner*).

A daily boat travels from Battambang to Siem Reap (3 to 4 hours; $15) on the Tonle Sap. ⚠ **In the dry season, the water level on the Tonle Sap is often low. Passengers may be required to switch boats, or boats might get stuck in the lake, a long ordeal.**

Boats arrive at the ferry port at Chong Khneas, 12 km (7½ mi) south of Siem Reap.

BY BUS Siem Reap is accessible by direct bus to and from Phnom Penh (5 hours; $4 to $9) on all major lines, and to and from Bangkok (10 to 12 hours; $15) over rough roads. The road between Siem Reap and the border is usually a slow-moving morass in the rainy season. Neak Krorhorm Travel (⇨ *Visitor & Tour Info, below*)can help you arrange all bus trips.

BY CAR The road to Siem Reap from Phnom Penh has greatly improved in recent years and the trip by taxi is just four hours. But you'll be putting your life in the hands of daredevil drivers with little care for the rules of the road or the function of the brake pedal. Take the bus instead.

BY MOTO & TUK-TUK Tuk-tuk and moto drivers have kept apace with the growing number of tourists visiting Siem Reap: they'll find you; you won't need to find them. They cost about $1 to $2 for a trip within town, but be sure to settle on the fare before setting off. There are no cruising taxis, but hotels can order one.

Siem Reap, Sihanoukville and Southern Cambodia

ESSENTIALS

Emergencies **Jin Hua international Hospital** (✉ *Airport Rd., Siem Reap* ☎ *063/963299*). **Ly Srey Vyna Clinic** (✉ *Airport Rd., Siem Reap* ☎ *063/965088*).

Visitor & Tour Info **Hanuman Tourism Voyages** (✉ *12 St. 310, Sangkat Tonle Bassac, Phnom Penh* ☎ *023/218356 or 012/807657* ✉ *marketing@hanumantourism.com*). **Neak Krorhorm Travel** (✉ *127 St. 108, Phnom Penh* ☎ *023/219496*). **oSmoSe Conservation Ecotourism Education** (✉ *0552, Group 12, Wat Bo Village, Siem Reap* ☎ *012/832812* 🌐 *jinja.apsara.org/osmose*).

EXPLORING SIEM REAP

Siem Reap is the base to use for exploring the temples at Angkor, however the town does have a few places to see by itself. You can wander around the myriad art galleries, visit the various museums, or take a stroll down the central Pub Street. There is plenty to keep the temple-weary traveler occupied for two or three days.

WHAT TO SEE

★ Be sure to visit the **Cambodia Land Mine Museum,** established by Akira, a former child soldier who fought for the Khmer Rouge, the Vietnamese, and the Cambodian Army. Now he dedicates his life to removing the land mines he and thousands of others laid across Cambodia. His museum is a must-see, an eye-opener that portrays a different picture of Cambodia from the glorious temples and five-star hotels. Any tuk-tuk or taxi driver can find the museum. When in the Old Market area, visit the Akira Mine Action Gallery for more information on land mines and ways to help land-mine victims go to college. ✉ *Off the road to Angkor, 6 km (4 mi) south of Banteay Srey Temple* ☎ *No phone* 🌐 *www.cambodialandminemuseum.org* 🎫 *Donations accepted* ⏲ *Daily 10–6.*

WHERE TO EAT

¢–$ ASIAN ✕ **Blue Pumpkin.** Don't miss this sleek Internet café, bakery, and restaurant near the Old Market. In addition to fresh-baked goods, the Blue Pumpkin serves up interesting salads, mild Asian dishes, and energizing fresh juices. You could easily take a post-meal nap on the big white bed-couches upstairs. ✉ *Old Market* ☎ *063/963574* ▭ *No credit cards.*

¢ CAMBODIAN ✕ **Khmer Kitchen.** Like its neighbor, Traditional Khmer Food, this popular restaurant serves tasty Khmer dishes (and some Thai), but with modern interpretations. Dishes include the traditional amok (fish with coconut sauce steamed in banana leaves) and Khmer curries, as well as an assortment of Thai curries. ✉ *Alley off Pub St.* ☎ *063/964154* ▭ *No credit cards.*

$–$$ ECLECTIC ✕ **Les Carnets d'Asie.** Behind a stylish gallery on Sivatha Road, this restaurant offers a mixture of western and Khmer cuisine. The setting is colorful and relaxing, the mood is calming and the food is well prepared. This is a place for diners who are looking for a cultural experience as well as a meal. ✉ *333 Sivatha Rd.* ☎ *092/746287* ▭ *AE, MC, V.*

$–$$ THAI ✕ **L'Escale des Arts & des Sens.** Siem Reap's dining scene raised several notches with the opening of this restaurant. Chef Didier Corlou, who hails from the Hotel Metropole in Hanoi, has a long, fine tradition of creating modern Indochinese culinary marvels. His menus are specific to the locale, which means you can try his favorite delights from the Tonle Sap, or beef prepared in seven ways (based on an old tiger recipe). You could return every night for a week and still not have sampled everything on offer. ✉ *Oum Khum St.* ☎ *063/761442* ▭ *MC, V.*

$$–$$$$ ASIAN ✕ **Meric.** The best thing on offer at the Hotel de la Paix is its fine Khmer restaurant, named for the famous pepper that grows in Kampot Province. Here, you'll dine in style in the hotel's courtyard. Choose a traditional seven-course meal (set menu), with foods served on clay, stone, or banana leaf, and adorned with local herbs. A pungent ginger fish stew is a highlight. Portions are small, but the point is to savor each bite. ✉ *Sivatha Rd.* ☎ *063/966000* ▭ *AE, MC, V.*

¢–$ CAMBODIAN ✕ **Traditional Khmer Food.** The name says it all—this Khmer-owned and -operated restaurant gives you a hearty introduction to real Khmer cooking. The bright little spot (painted in orange and purple) is along one of the back alleys near Pub Street. It serves a wide selection of Khmer soups, curries, and meat and vegetable dishes. ✉ *Alley off Pub St.* ☎ *015/999909* ▭ *No credit cards.*

8

Where to Stay & Eat in Siem Reap

KEY: Hotels; Restaurants; Temple

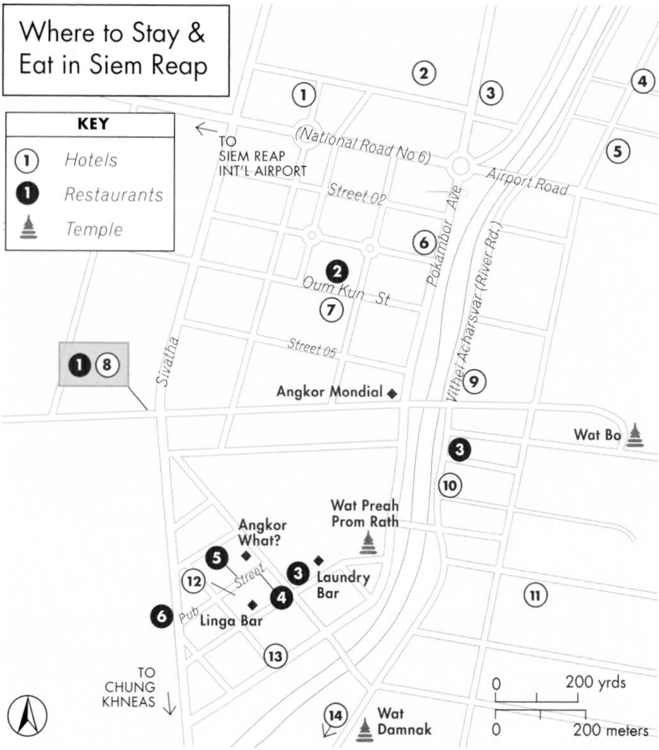

WHERE TO STAY

$$$$ Fodor's Choice ★ **Amansara.** The Amansara is so good it doesn't need to advertise or even post an English-language sign out front. This all-suites retreat is in what was once a guest villa of former King Norodom Sihanouk. Clearly the sleekest of Siem Reap's resorts, it does the minimalist black-and-white and earth-tone decor—something of a trend these days among the city's hotels—just a little better than the competition. Half the suites have private plunge pools; all suites share two resort pools, one for lap swimming. Visit the jasmine-scented spa for a private treatment, followed by a few moments in a private relaxation room. The resort has shuttle service to the temples in private black tuk-tuks and offers cultural tours of the area. Suites have CD players, but no TVs. **Pros:** stylish and well designed; private pools. **Cons:** expensive; not in the center of Siem Reap. ✉ *Road to Angkor, behind the Tourism Department* ✉ *262 Krom 8, Phum Beong Don Pa, Khum Slar Kram, Siem Reap* ☎ *063/760333* 🌐 *www.amanresorts.com* *24 suites* *In-room: safe, refrigerator, no TV,*

GOOD DEEDS

Not far from the Old Market on Achamen Street sits the **Angkor Hospital for Children** (☎ *012/725745* 🌐 *www.fwab.org*), founded in 1999 by Japanese photographer Kenro Izu. It provides pediatric care to more than 100,000 children each year. Give blood, save a life.

There are about 200 faces of Lokesvara, the bodhisattva of compassion, on Bayon's towers.

Internet. In-hotel: restaurant, pools, spa, bicycles, laundry service, Internet terminal ▭*AE, MC, V.*

8

$$$–$$$$ ★ **Angkor Village Hotel.** This oasis of wooden buildings, gardens, and pools filled with lotus blossoms lies a couple blocks from the river on a stone road in a green neighborhood. It's a warm and welcoming place, from the airy teak lobby to the tasteful rooms, all designed like a traditional Khmer village. Standard rooms are small, so it's best to pay a little extra for superior rooms, which are bigger and brighter and overlook the water and greenery. All rooms have Khmer handicrafts. The open-air restaurant, in the middle of a pond, serves French and Asian cuisine. ■ TIP→ **The cultural show performed in the hotel's gorgeous theater, designed like a temple, is a must-see.** A sister property, Angkor Village Resort, is farther from the city and quieter. **Pros:** central location. **Cons:** road leading to the hotel can become a quagmire in the rainy season. ✉ *Wat Bo Rd.* ☎ *063/963361* 🌐 *www.angkorvillage.com* *49 rooms* *In-room: safe, refrigerator. In-hotel: restaurant, bar, pool, laundry service, Internet terminal* ▭*AE, MC, V* *BP.*

$–$$ **Bopha Angkor Hotel.** Across the street from the Siem Reap River's east bank is this small hotel offering quality Khmer cuisine and comfortable rooms at very competitive prices. The guest rooms have tile floors, wood ceilings, local handicrafts, and mosquito nets. ■ TIP→ **The open-air restaurant (¢–$) is a good dinner option even if you stay elsewhere.** Amid gardens and small pools, meals of hot pots and fish dishes, along with tantalizing fresh juices and desserts, are accompanied by live Cambodian traditional music. **Pros:** great restaurant; quiet. **Cons:** lacking some facilities for the price. ✉ *512 Vithei Acharsvar (River Rd., east side)*

☎063/964928 🌐www.bopha-angkor.com ⇨23 rooms ◊In-room: refrigerator. In-hotel: restaurant, laundry service, Internet terminal ▭MC, V.

$ **Borann, l'Auberge des Temples.** The accommodations are attractive and the rates low at this tranquil, small hotel a couple of blocks east of the river. Khmer handicrafts and antiques fill the rooms, which have high ceilings and tile floors. Each one has a large porch or balcony overlooking a nicely planted yard, which holds a small pool and open-air thatched restaurant. Large bathrooms with stone floors have both a shower and the traditional Cambodian bathing option of scooping water out of a giant ceramic urn, which sounds archaic but is thoroughly refreshing after a hot day at the temples. **Pros:** large rooms. **Cons:** small pool. *✉1½ blocks east of river, 1 block north of 6th St., behind La Noria hotel ☎063/964740 🌐www.borann.com ⇨20 rooms ◊In-room: no a/c (some), safe. In-hotel: restaurant, pool, laundry service ▭No credit cards.*

$$$ **FCC Angkor Hotel.** Yet another in a line of resorts with black-and-white decor, the FCC Angkor takes a former French Consulate and turns it into an inviting respite along the river. Rooms and suites, in minimalist contemporary design, with gleaming hardwood floors and modern art on walls, wrap around an attractive pool and gardens. The hotel is far from the noise of the city. **Pros:** sleek contemporary design; riverside location. **Cons:** not within walking distance to town. *✉Pokambor Ave., next to the Royal Palace ☎063/760280 🌐www.fcccambodia.com ⇨29 rooms, 2 suites ◊In-room: DVD, Internet. In-hotel: restaurant, bar, pool, spa ▭MC, V ⍟CP.*

$ **Golden Banana Boutique Hotel and Bed & Breakfast.** When renovation of the new building was completed in summer of 2006, it made this gem of a getaway one of the best budget accommodations in the region. Each room at the hotel is a duplex—bedroom and bathroom downstairs, and a sitting room upstairs. The rooms are grouped around a stone-and-palm-enclosed pool. Just beside the hotel, the original B&B still offers great budget accommodations, too, though with fewer amenities. Both properties emphasize that they are gay friendly, though the clientele is very mixed. **Pros:** good prices; friendly staff. **Cons:** not central; poor road access; small swimming pool. *✉Wat Damnak area ☎012/654638 🌐www.goldenbanana.info ◊In-room: safe, refrigerator, DVD, Internet. In-hotel: restaurant, bar, pool, laundry service ▭MC, V ⍟BP.*

$$$$ **Heritage Suites Hotel.** In a quiet neighborhood but still close to the town center, this boutique hotel offers a calm and relaxing stay. The rooms are tastefully decorated with teak floors, silk curtains, and marvelous marble baths with exposed plumbing. The large windows allow a great deal of light to filter in through the low hanging trees in the garden. The relaxing rooms give you a taste of Khmer culture with a modern design. The saltwater pool and the spa add to the hotel ambience, as does the evening lighting and poolside bar. **Pros:** quiet atmosphere; saltwater pool nicely lit in evening; spa facilities. **Cons:** not suitable for families; hidden in Siem Reap's back streets. *✉Wat Polanka ☎063/969100 🌐www.heritage.com.kh ⇨29 rooms ◊In-room: safe,*

Internet, In-hotel: restaurant, pool, laundry service, Internet terminal ▭ *MC, V.*

$$$$ **Hotel de La Paix.** This much-hyped addition to the city offers boutique rooms in black and white. The hotel's internationally acclaimed design has incorporated all the amenities one would expect of a member of the Small Luxury Hotels of the World: spa suites with in-room massage facilities, terrazzo soaking tubs, preprogrammed iPods, DVD players, and a lot more. Unfortunately, the hotel is on dusty, noisy Sivutha Boulevard, with construction in all directions—however, the disorder outside might accentuate the feeling of exclusive luxury within. Here you can sip a drink poolside or gaze out the windows of your swanky room, thankful you're not parching in the heat like the laundry hung on the neighbors' lines. **Pros:** stunning design; luxurious, excellent spa facilities. **Cons:** dusty and noisy location; expensive. ✉*Sivutha Blvd.* ☎*063/966000* 🌐*www.hoteldelapaixangkor.com* *107 rooms* *In-room: safe, refrigerator, Wi-Fi. In-hotel: restaurant, bar, pool, gym, laundry service* ▭*AE, MC, V.*

¢ **Ivy Guesthouse & Bar.** This charming corner spot in the Old Market area offers clean, comfortable rooms that retain the original colonial ambience of the building: high ceilings, green French doors opening onto balconies, and black-and-white tile floors. **■ TIP→ The restaurant (Western and Khmer) and bar downstairs have long been popular with expats and tourists.** **Pros:** central location; cheap prices; near all local nightlife; downstairs bar. **Cons:** noisy location next to tourist market; some find the accommodation tatty around the edges. ✉*Old Market* ☎*012/800860* *6 rooms* *In-room: no a/c (some). In-hotel: restaurant, room service, bar, laundry service* ▭*No credit cards.*

$$$$ ★ **La Résidence d'Angkor.** Employing ancient Angkor style, this luxury retreat is packed into a central walled compound on the river. The guest rooms are stunning and spacious—subtle mixes of hardwoods, white walls and bedspreads, colorful pillows, and Khmer art. Sliding glass doors open onto balconies, and sliding wooden doors enclose long bathroom/dressing areas that have large round tubs at one end. The gardens, statues, and open-air bar are equally attractive. The restaurant ($$–$$$$), which serves an inventive mix of Asian and western dishes, is one of the town's best. **Pros:** attractive riverside location; excellent restaurant; attentive service. **Cons:** a little distance out of town; some rooms may have less-than-spectacular views. ✉*River Rd. (east side)* ☎*063/963390* 🌐*www.residencedangkor.com* *55 rooms* *In-room: safe, refrigerator. In-hotel: restaurant, bar, pool, laundry service, Internet terminal* ▭*AE, MC, V.*

$$$$ ★ **The One Hotel.** The One Hotel has but one room, but it's on the one street in town where you'd want to be. Across from the affiliated (and equally hip) Linga Bar is this unique option in a renovated colonial shophouse. Inside, you get sleek, modern design with all the trimmings, including an iPod and iBook. Open the balcony doors of your second-story suite, and watch over Siem Reap's new nightlife scene. Take the staircase to the rooftop and indulge in a private Jacuzzi and shower under the moonlight. A personal chef provides your meals. **Pros:** prime location; ultimate in personal attention. **Cons:** must be reserved months in advance.

8

⊠Pub St. area, across from Linga Bar ☎012/755311 ⊕www.theonehotelangkor.com ⇆1 room ♁In-room: safe, refrigerator, Wi-Fi. In-hotel: room service, laundry service ▭AE, MC, V.

NIGHT FLIGHTS

Around sunset, the sky fills with thousands of large bats, which make their homes in the trees behind the Preah Ang Chek Preah Ang Chorm Shrine, near the gardens in front of the Raffles hotel.

$$$$ **Raffles Grand Hotel d'Angkor.** Built in 1932, this grande dame was restored and reopened a decade ago after nearly being destroyed by occupying Khmer Rouge guerillas. The Grand now ranks among the region's finest, and most expensive, hotels. It combines French sensibilities and Cambodian art with Oriental carpets and wicker furniture; rooms are large and elegant, with balconies that overlook the extensive gardens and blue-tile pool. Horticulture is something taken seriously at the Raffles, which has nearly 15 acres of greenery with flowers, shrubs, and local trees. **Pros:** great gardens; excellent restaurant; nicely designed and decorated. **Cons:** more impersonal than smaller hotels; outside the center of Siem Reap. *⊠1 Vithei Charles de Gaulle ☎063/963888 ⊕www.raffles-grandhoteldangkor.com ⇆150 rooms ♁In-room: safe, refrigerator, Wi-Fi. In-hotel: 3 restaurants, room service, bar, pool, gym, spa, laundry service, no-smoking rooms ▭AE, MC, V ⍡BP, MAP.*

$$$–$$$$ ★ **Shinta Mani.** When you spend your money here, you help enrich a young Cambodian's life. The resort, in a laid-back, tree-lined neighborhood, is the flagship of the Institute of Hospitality, which trains young Cambodians to work in the hotel and restaurant industry. Not only will you sleep and eat in style here, your money will also help support projects bringing clean water, transportation, and jobs to underprivileged communities. The spacious rooms are all tastefully designed in dark wood with a traditional Khmer tapestry adorning the walls. You can choose between a poolside room and a garden view. ■ **TIP→ The Shinta Mani's two deluxe rooms are modeled in style after those at the Hotel de la Paix, but cost a fraction of the price.** **Pros:** proceeds go to a charitable cause; good location. **Cons:** the hotel has been squeezed into a relatively small space. *⊠Oun Khum and 14th Sts. ☎063/761998 ⊕www.shintamani.com ⇆18 rooms ♁In-room: safe, refrigerator, Wi-Fi. In-hotel: restaurant, bar, pool, spa ▭AE, MC, V.*

$$$$ **Victoria Angkor Resort & Spa.** Just west of the Raffles botanical gardens is this splendid spread evocative of colonial times. Rooms employ lots of wood and rattan, and have porches with pool or garden views. Enjoy a dip in the sunken pool, surrounded by a wooden deck and a stone wall. **Pros:** attentive service; sunken pool; lots of wood used in design. **Cons:** a bit of a commercial feel. *⊠Central Park ☎063/760428 ⊕www.victoriahotels-asia.com ⇆120 rooms, 10 suites ♁In-room: safe, refrigerator, Internet. In-hotel: 2 restaurants, pool, spa, Internet terminal ▭AE, MC, V ⍡BP.*

NIGHTLIFE & THE ARTS

No matter where you wander in the evening, you're likely to encounter a traditional dance performance; dozens of hotels and restaurants offer them nightly. For a full-blown affair, try the **Angkor Mondial Restaurant** (✉ *Pokambor Ave., Wat Bo Bridge* ☎ *063/966875*), where $12 gets you a Khmer buffet dinner and an apsara show.

Most of Siem Reap's nightlife is concentrated around the Old Market, particularly on vibrant Pub Street, which has become very popular. Just wander around, and you're sure to find a hangout that fits your style. **Angkor What?** (✉ *Pub St.* ☎ *012/490755*) was one of the first nighttime establishments in the old quarter, and it still packs in the crowds until early morning. Write your name and your personal philosophy on the walls. The **Laundry Bar** (✉ *Old Market area* ☎ *016/962026*) is another favorite, popular for its music, which thumps until late. The **Linga Bar** (✉ *Pub St. alley* 🌐 *www.lingabar.com*), across from the affiliated One Hotel, offers stylish cocktails (at stylish prices) in a funky setting.

THE BEST OF THE BEST

Reliable international chains have begun to open along the road to Angkor, and both the dusty airport road and the town's noisy thoroughfares are clogged with upper-end accommodations. However, why settle for a lousy location? Siem Reap offers several superb options in the quaint and quiet river area, where lush gardens are the norm and birds and butterflies thrive. Booking a room in a high-price hotel in this quarter means that your view of the hotel pool won't include the neighbors' laundry line, and your view will delight you with natural splendor instead of traffic jams.

8

AROUND SIEM REAP

TONLE SAP

10 km (6 mi) south of Siem Reap.

Covering 2,600 square km (1,000 square mi) in the dry season, Cambodia's vast Tonle Sap is the biggest freshwater lake in Southeast Asia. Its unique annual cycle of flood expansion and retreat dictates Cambodia's rice production and supplies of fish. During the rainy season, the Mekong River backs into the Tonle Sap River, pushing waters into the lake, which quadruples in size. In the dry season as the Mekong lowers, and the Tonle Sap River reverses its direction, draining the lake. Boats make the river journey to the lake from Phnom Penh and Battambang, tying up at Chong Khneas, 12 km (7½ mi) south of Siem Reap. Two-hour tours of the lake, costing $6, set off from Chong Khneas.

Between Chong Khneas and Battambang is the **Prek Toal Biosphere Reserve,** which is mainland Southeast Asia's most important waterbird nesting site. It's a spectacular scene if you visit at the start of the dry season (November and December) when water remains high and thousands of rare birds begin to nest. Visits can be booked through **oSmoSe Conservation Ecotourism Education** (⇨ *Visitors & Tour Info in Siem*

Reap, above). Day tours and overnight stays at the Prek Toal Research Station can be arranged. Prices vary.

GETTING HERE & AROUND

Boats make the river journey to the lake from Phnom Penh ($26) and Battambang ($15; usually May– to October only), tying up at Chong Khneas, 12 km (7½ mi) south of Siem Reap.

Two-hour tours of the lake ($6) set off from Chong Khneas; arrange them at any travel agent in Siem Reap.

Transport to and from the Tonle Sap can be arranged at any hotel or travel agent. Alternatively, ask any tuk-tuk or moto ($5 to $7).

KULEN MOUNTAIN

50 km (31 mi) north of Siem Reap.

King Jayavarman II established this mountain retreat 50 km (31 mi) northeast of Siem Reap in AD 802, the year regarded as the start of the Angkor dynasty. The area is strewn with the ruins of Khmer temples from that time. The mountain was revered as holy, with a hallowed river and a waterfall. Admission to the area costs $20, and is not included in the ticket price to the Angkor Temple Complex.

GETTING HERE & AROUND

Tuk-tuks, motos, and local taxis can take you to Kulen Mountain; negotiate a price prior to departure, or ask your hotel to handle it. The journey should take no more than 50 minutes. Or go with a Siem Reap tour company.

SIHANOUKVILLE & SOUTHERN CAMBODIA

The beaches of Sihanoukville are quickly becoming a top Cambodian tourist destination (after Angkor, of course). Much of the country's stunning coastal areas remain relatively undiscovered, a natural draw for those who tire of the crowds on neighboring Thai islands. Sihanoukville lies some 230 km (143 mi) southwest of Phnom Penh, a four-hour bus ride from the capital.

THE ROAD TO THE COAST

The four-hour bus journey from Phnom Penh to Sihanoukville along Highway 4 is an interesting one, winding through uplands, rice paddies, and orchards. Once you drive past Phnom Penh's Pochentong Airport and the prestigious Cambodia Golf & Country Club, and on through the area of Kompong Speu, the landscape turns rural, dotted with small villages where a major source of income seems to be the sale of firewood and charcoal. Somewhere around the entrance to Kirirom National Park all buses stop for refreshments at a roadside restaurant.

The halfway point of the journey lies at the top of the **Pich Nil mountain pass,** guarded by dozens of colorful spirit houses. These spirit houses were built for the legendary deity Yeah Mao, guardian of Sihanoukville and the coastal region. Legend has it that Yeah Mao was the wife of a village headman who worked in far-off Koh Kong, an island near today's border with Thailand. On a journey to visit him, Yeah Mao died when the boat transporting her sank in a storm—an all-too-believable story to anyone who has taken the boat from Sihanoukville to Koh Kong. Her spirit became the guardian of local villagers and fisherfolk.

At the small town of Chamcar Luang, a side road leads to the renowned smuggling port of Sre Ambel. The main highway threads along **Ream National Park**, with the Elephant Mountains as a backdrop. The national park is a highlight of Sihanoukville, with its mangroves, forests, waterfalls, and wildlife. The park is, unusually for Cambodia, well protected from the vagaries of modern development. The sprawling Angkor Beer brewery heralds the outskirts of Sihanoukville and the journey's end.

GETTING HERE & AROUND

You can hire a private car and driver through your hotel or guesthouse for the trip to the coast from Phnom Penh. The price varies, but starts at approximately $50. The drive (3 to 4 hours) is often an alarmingly fast and dangerous ride along the well-maintained highway. However, it is common to see tourists who have rented motorcycles in Phnom Penh zipping past.

All major bus companies go to the coast, and Hunaman Tourism Voyages and oSmoSe Conservation (⇨ *Visitor & Tour Info in Siem Reap, above*) do tours.

SIHANOUKVILLE

8

230 km (143 mi) southwest of Phnom Penh.

A half a century ago, Cambodia's main port city, Sihanoukville, was a sleepy backwater called Kampong Som. Then, a series of world-shattering events overtook it and gave rise to the busy industrial center and coastal resort now prominent on every tourist map.

The French laid the foundations of Kampong Som back in the mid-1950s, before they lost control of the Mekong Delta and its ports following their retreat after the French-Indochina War. The town was renamed Sihanoukville in honor of the then king. A decade later, Sihanoukville received a further boost when it became an important transit post for weapons destined for American forces fighting in the Vietnam War. In the mid-1970s, Sihanoukville itself came under American attack and suffered heavy casualties after Khmer Rouge forces captured the SS *Mayaguez,* a U.S. container ship.

Today Sihanoukville presents a relatively peaceful face to the world as Cambodia's seaside playground. It has seven primary tourist beaches, all easily accessible from downtown by motorbike taxi or even a rented bicycle.

GETTING HERE & AROUND

Air-conditioned buses from Phnom Penh run several times daily (4 hours; $5), departing from the Central Market or the Hua Lian

Continued on page 540

ANGKOR

by Christina Knight

The scale of the ruins, the power of the encroaching jungle, and the beauty of the architecture have made Angkor one of the world's most celebrated ancient cities. This was the capital of the mighty Khmer empire (present-day Thailand, Laos, Vietnam, and Cambodia). The vast complex

contains more than 300 temples and monuments that four centuries of kings built to honor the gods they believed they would become after they died. It's not just the size of the structures that takes your breath away; it's the otherworldly setting and a pervading sense of mystery.

THE CITY OF ANGKOR

Silk-cotton tree roots growing over the ruins at Ta Prohm.

CONSTRUCTION

Angkor, which simply means "city," was founded in 839 AD when King Jayavarman II completed the first temple, Phnom Bakheng, using sandstone from the Kulen mountains, northeast of Angkor. Jayavarman II had established the empire in 802, uniting various principalities, securing independence from Java (in present-day Indonesia), and declaring himself the world emperor as well as a "god who is king," or *devaraja*.

Over the next 400 years, each successive Khmer emperor added to Angkor, erecting a *wat*, or temple, to worship either Shiva or Vishnu. The Khmer empire was Hindu except during the rule of Jayavarman VII (1181–1220), who was a Mahayana Buddhist. Theravada Buddhism became the dominant religion in Cambodia after the decline of the Khmer empire, in the 15th century.

Kings situated buildings according to principles of cosmology and numerology, so the center of the city shifted over the centuries. Only the wats, built with reddish-brown laterite, ochre brick, or gray sandstone, have survived; wooden structures perished long ago.

Historians estimate that the royal city had a population of 100,000 in the late 13th century; at that time, London's population was roughly 80,000. The royal city was ringed by a larger medieval city about 3,000 square km (1,150 square mi)—the world's largest pre-industrial settlement and more than twice the size of present-day Los Angeles, with an estimated population of 1 million. At its height, the Khmer empire covered about 1 million square km (400,000 square mi), stretching east from the Burmese border to southern Vietnam and north from Malaysia to Laos.

Archaeologists have only excavated the largest of the hundreds of temples that once dotted the royal city, and even fewer have been restored. The most impressive and best preserved temple, Angkor Wat, is also the world's largest religious monument; it covers approximately 2 square km (¾ square mi), including its moat.

Angkor Wat.

Apsara bas-relief on a wall of Angkor Wat.

DECLINE AND REDISCOVERY

In 1431, Thailand's Ayutthaya kingdom invaded and sacked Angkor. The following year, the declining Khmer empire moved its kingdom to Phnom Penh, 315 km (195 mi) south. Though a handful of foreign adventurers visited Angkor in the following centuries, it wasn't until 1861, when Frenchman and naturalist Henri Mouhot published a book about the site, that Angkor became famous. By this time, looting foreigners and the insistent forces of time and nature had taken a toll on the complex. Restoration efforts began in the early 20th century but were interrupted by the Cambodian Civil War in the 1960s and '70s; in 1992, UNESCO declared Angkor a World Heritage Site. Since that time the number of visitors has risen dramatically to 2 million in 2007. You won't have the place to yourself, but it's unlikely to feel crowded in comparison to famous European sites.

PLANNING YOUR VISIT

The sunset from atop Phnom Bakheng.

You can see most of the significant temples and monuments in a one-day sprint, although a three-day visit is recommended. If you have just one day, stick to a 17-km (11-mi) route that takes in the south gate of Angkor Thom, Bayon, Baphuon, the Elephant Terrace and the Terrace of the Leper King, and Ta Prohm, ending with a visit to Angkor Wat itself in time to catch the sunset. Leave the most time for the Bayon and Angkor Wat.

If you have two or three days, cover ground at a more leisurely pace. You can also tack on additional sites such as Preah Khan, Neak Pean, Pre Rup (a good sunset spot), Phnom Bakheng, or farther-flung Banteay Srei. Another option is East Mebon, a 10th-century ruin in the East Baray, a former reservoir. Alternatively, visit the West Baray, once Angkor's largest reservoir—it still fills with water during the rainy season (June to October).

The best way to experience Angkor is with a guide, who can help you decode the bas-reliefs and architectural styles.

■ TIP→ If you buy your ticket at 5 PM, you'll be admitted for the remaining open hour, in time to see the sunset from Phnom Bakeng or to catch the last rays setting Angkor Wat aglow. Your ticket will also count for the following day.

Elephant statue at East Mebon.

ESSENTIALS

HOURS & FEES The Angkor complex is open from 5:30 AM to 6 PM. Admission is $20 for one day, $40 for three consecutive days, and $60 for a week. You'll receive a ticket with your photo on it. Don't lose the ticket—you'll need it at each site and to access the restrooms.

WHEN TO GO Most people visit the east-facing temples of Bayon and Baphuon in the morning—the earlier you arrive, the better the light and the smaller the crowd. West-facing Angkor Wat gets the best light in the late afternoon, though these temples can also be stunning at sunrise. You can visit the

Eastern entrance to Banteay Srei.

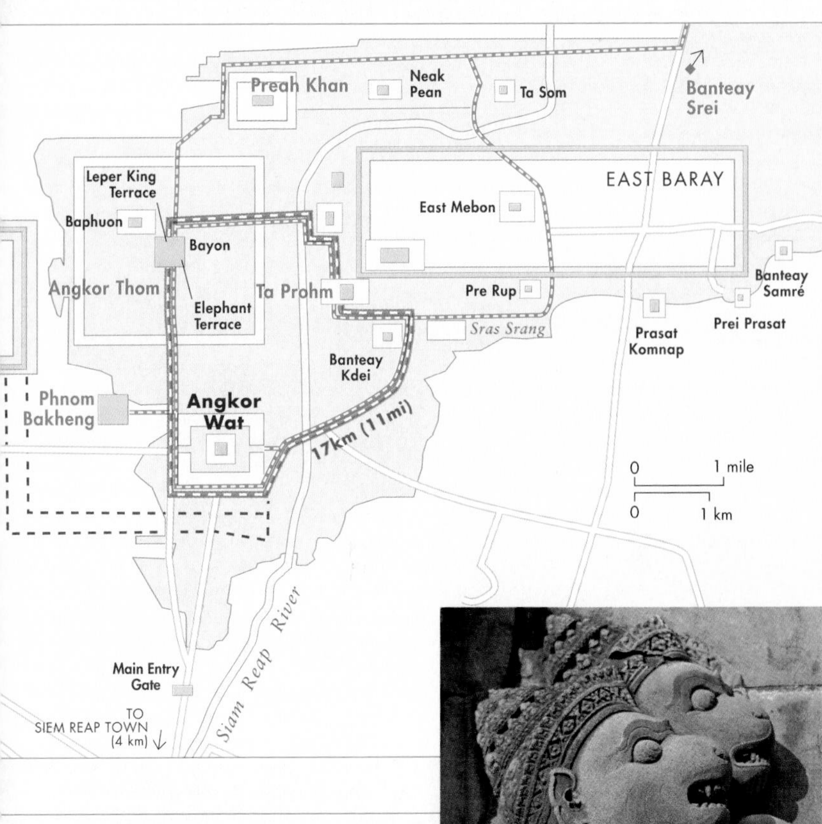

Bas-relief detail in red sandstone at Banteay Srei.

woodland-surrounded Ta Prohm at any time, though photos will turn out best on cloudy days; the distant Banteay Srei is prettiest in late-afternoon light. If quiet is your priority, beat the crowds by visiting sunset spots in the morning and east-facing temples in the afternoon.

GETTING AROUND The entrance to the complex is 4 km (2 ½ mi) north of Siem Reap; you'll need to arrange transportation to get here and around. Most independent travelers hire a car and driver ($20–$25 per day), moto (motorcycle) driver ($8-$10), or tuk-tuk ($10–$15, seats up to four). Renting bicycles ($3–$4) or electric bikes ($5) is also an option if you're up for the exertion in the heat. Tourists may not drive motorized vehicles in the park. If you hire a driver, he'll stick with you for the whole day, ferrying you between the sites. However, going with a guide is strongly recommended.

DRESS Skimpy clothes, such as short shorts and backless tops, violate the park's dress code. Shield yourself from the sun with light fabrics, and bring a wide-brimmed hat or even a shade umbrella. Drivers remain with the vehicle so you can leave items you don't want to carry.

ON THE GROUND You'll find food and souvenir stalls inside the park near the temples; children also roam the sites selling trinkets and guidebooks. But you'll get templed out if you don't take a break from sightseeing; consider breaking up the day by swinging back to Siem Reap for lunch or to your hotel for an afternoon rest. Make sure to drink plenty of water, which you can buy inside the park.

ANGKOR WAT

A monk looking at Angkor Wat across the moat.

The best-preserved temple has become shorthand for the entire complex: Angkor Wat, built by King Suryavarman II in the early 12th century. The king dedicated Angkor Wat to Vishnu (the preserver and protector), breaking with tradition—Khmer kings usually built their temples to honor Shiva, the god of destruction and rebirth, whose powers the kings considered more cosmically essential than Vishnu's.

It helps to think of the ancient city as a series of concentric protective layers: a 190-m- (623-ft-) wide moat surrounds an outer wall that's 1,024 by 802 m (3,359 by 2,630 ft) long—walking around the outside of the wall is a more than 2-mi stroll. A royal city and palace once occupied the space inside the wall; you can still see traces of some streets, but the buildings did not survive. The temple itself sits on an elevated terrace that takes up about a tenth of the city.

APPROACHING THE TEMPLE

You'll reach the temple after crossing the moat, entering the western gateway (where you'll see a 10-foot, eight-armed Vishnu statue), and walking nearly a quarter of a mile along an unshaded causeway. Angkor Wat originally had nine towers (an auspicious number in Hindu mythology), though only five remain. These towers, which took 30 years to complete, are shaped like closed lotuses and

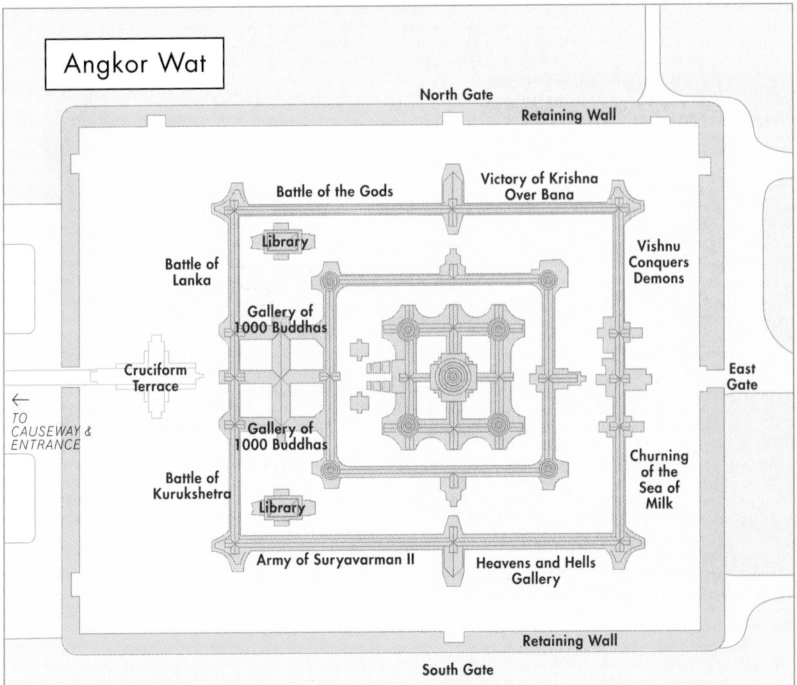

Angkor Wat

North Gate
Retaining Wall
Battle of the Gods
Victory of Krishna Over Bana
Library
Vishnu Conquers Demons
Battle of Lanka
Gallery of 1000 Buddhas
Cruciform Terrace
East Gate
← TO CAUSEWAY & ENTRANCE
Gallery of 1000 Buddhas
Churning of the Sea of Milk
Battle of Kurukshetra
Library
Army of Suryavarman II
Heavens and Hells Gallery
Retaining Wall
South Gate

form the center of the temple complex. Their ribbed appearance comes from rings of finials that also take the form of closed lotuses. These finials, along with statues of lions and multi-headed serpents called *nagas,* were believed to protect the temple from evil spirits.

Like the other major monuments at Angkor, the complex represents the Hindu universe. The central shrines symbolize Mt. Meru, mythical home of the Hindu gods, and the moats represent the seven oceans that surround Mt. Meru.

Bas-relief depicting a historical Khmer battle.

THE GALLERIES

Nearly 2,000 *Apsara*—celestial female dancers—are scattered in bas-relief on the outer entrances and columns of galleries. Inside the shaded galleries, 600 m (2,000 ft) of bas-reliefs tell epic tales from the *Ramayana,* the *Churning of the Sea of Milk* (gods and demons join forces to find the immortality elixir), the punishments of the 32 hells, and the less-imaginative rewards of the 37 heavens.

EXPLORING OTHER ANGKOR TEMPLES

Banteay Srei temple complex.

ANGKOR THOM

King Jayavarman VII built the massive city known as Angkor Thom in 1181 and changed the state religion to Buddhism (although subsequent kings reverted to Hinduism). At the center of the city stands the 12th-century **Bayon,** a large, ornate state temple that rises into many towers (37 remain today), most of which are topped with giant, serene, smiling boddhisattva faces on four sides. These faces, the most photogenic and beatific in all of Angkor, resemble both the king and the boddhisattva of compassion—a Buddhist twist on the king-as-a-god tradition.

On the walls of Bayon's central sanctuary are 1½ km (1 mi) of marvelous bas-relief murals depicting historic sea battles scenes from daily life, and Hindu gods and mythical creatures. You can pick out the Khmers in the reliefs because they are depicted with long earlobes; they frequently warred with the Cham, whose warriors wear headpieces that curl towards the jawline. Jayavarman VIII, a later king, added the Hindu iconography and destroyed some of his predecessor's Buddhist statuary.

Just to the north of the Bayon is the slightly older **Baphuon,** which King Udayadityavarman II built in the mid-11th century as part of a small settlement that predated Angkor Thom. The king built the temple on a hill without proper supports, so it collapsed during a 16th-century earthquake. In that same century, a magnificent reclining Buddha was added to the three-tiered temple pyramid, which was originally a Shiva sanctuary. The temple is undergoing reconstruction and is not open to the public; however, the exterior gate and elevated walkway are open.

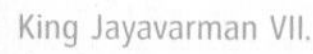

King Jayavarman VII.

Once the foundation of the royal audience hall, the **Elephant Terrace** is adorned with carvings of *garudas* (birdlike creatures), lion-headed figures, and elephants tugging at strands of lotuses with their trunks.

Located at the north end of the Elephant Terrance, the **Terrace of the Leper King** area is named after a stone statue found here that now resides in the National Museum (⇨*Phnom Penh, above*); a copy remains here. Precisely who the Leper King was and why he was so named remains uncertain, though several legends offer speculation. (One theory is that damage to the sculpture made the figure look leprous, leading people in later generations to believe the person depicted had been ill.) Today the terrace's two walls create a maze lined some seven layers high with gods, goddesses, and nagas.

TA PROHM

Jayavarman VII dedicated this large monastic complex to his mother. It once housed 2,700 monks and 615 royal dancers. Today the moss-covered ruins lie between tangles of silk-cotton and strangler fig trees whose gnarled offshoots drape window frames and grasp walls. This gorgeous, eerie spot gives you an idea of what the Angkor complex looked like when westerners first discovered it in the 19th century. Another famous mother—Angelina Jolie—shot scenes of *Lara Croft: Tomb Raider* here.

Sculptures of *devas* leading to Angkor Thom.

Two-storeyed pavilion at Preah Khan.

PHNOM BAKHENG

One of the oldest Angkor structures, dating from the 9th century, Bakheng temple was carved out of a rocky hilltop and occupied the center of the first royal city site. Phnom Bakheng is perhaps the most popular sunset destination, with views of the Tonle Sap Lake and the towers of Angkor Wat rising above the jungle. Climb a shaded trail or ride an elephant up the hill. You'll still have to climb steep stairs to reach the top of the temple.

PREAH KHAN

Dedicated to the Jayavarman VII's father, mossy Preah Khan was also a monastery. Its long, dim corridors are dramatically lit by openings where stones have fallen out. Preah Khan is the only Angkor site with an annex supported by rounded, not square, columns.

BANTEAY SREI

This restored 10th-century temple, whose name means "citadel of women," lies 38 km (24 mi) northeast of Siem Reap. Its scale is small (no stairs to climb), but its dark pink sandstone is celebrated for its intricate carvings of scenes from Hindu tales including the Ramayana. The site is at least a 40-minute, somewhat-scenic drive from other Angkor sites; your driver will charge extra to take you here.

DID YOU KNOW?

Time has erased the red lacquer and gold leaf that originally accented Angkor's many bas-reliefs; oil from the hands of countless visitors has darkened the dancing *Asparas* and warring soldiers.

GOING WITH A GUIDE

A guide can greatly enrich your visit to Angkor's temples, helping you decode action-packed reliefs and explaining the juxtaposition of Hindu and Budhhist elements at sites that were transformed over the centuries. You can always ask your guide for a little free time; another option is to spend two days with a guide and return on the third day with a tuk-tuk driver to wander solo.

HIRING A GUIDE

The tourism office on Pokambor Avenue, across from the Raffles Grand Hotel d'Angkor, can provide a list of English-speaking guides. The best way to find a guide, however, is through word of mouth. Most guides who work for tour companies are freelancers, and you'll usually pay less if you hire them independently. Find a younger staffer at your hotel or guesthouse and tell him or her what you want to learn and any particular interests. You don't need to worry about ending up with an amateur; only certified, highly trained guides are permitted to give tours. Prices usually run around $25 (not including transportation) for eight hours with a very well-informed guide fluent in English. Fancy hotels often have guides who work for them full-time; a day with one of these guides is around $35.

If you feel more comfortable booking through a travel company, Hanuman Tourism Voyages (✉ 12 St. 310,

Bayon temple in Angkor Thom.

Stupa in the center of Preah Khan.

Sangkat Tonle Bassac, Phnom Penh ☎ 023/218356 or 012/807657 🌐 www.hanumantourism.com) is an excellent choice. The company has established a foundation to help eradicate poverty in rural Cambodia. Their guides are $35 per day, but some of your dollars will go towards wells, water filters, and mosquito nets.

WHAT TO EXPECT

Your guide will meet you at your hotel, along with a tuk-tuk or car driver, whom you'll need to pay separately ($12–$15 per day for a tuk-tuk; $25 for a car). Guides, who are almost always men, will typically cater to your interests and know how to avoid crowds. You aren't expected to join your guide for lunch. Don't be surprised to hear your guide speak with disdain about Cambodia's neighbors, particularly Thailand and Vietnam; some Cambodians are bitter about these countries' influence over Cambodian business and politics.

Linga Bar is Siem Reap's first gay-friendly nightlife spot but it attracts a mixed crowd.

station near Olympic Stadium. Buses from Bangkok (10 hours; $35) and other towns on Thailand's eastern seaboard connect to Sihanoukville via Koh Kong.

You can hire a private car and driver through your hotel or guesthouse for the trip to the coast from Phnom Penh (3 to 4 hours; starting at $50). ⚠ **The highway to Sihanoukville is one of the most dangerous in the country.** Buses are almost as quick and often safer.

ESSENTIALS

Banks **Acleda Bank** (✉ *Ekareach St., Sihanoukville* ☎ *034/320232* 👍 *Western Union services*). **ANZ ATM** (✉ *Ekareach St., Sihanoukville* ☎ *No phone*. **Canadia Bank** (✉ *Ekareach St. at Sopheak-Monkoi St., Sihanoukville* ☎ *034/933490*).

Emergencies **International Peace Clinic** (✉ *Ekareach Rd., Sihanoukville* ☎ *012/794269*). **Sihanouk Public Hospital** (✉ *Ekareach Rd., Sihanoukville* ☎ *034/93311*).

EXPLORING SIHANOUKVILLE

Sihanoukville is a beach town without a center. There is a market area with a surrounding business area that has all the banks and other facilities; however, the town's accommodations are spread out along the coast. There is a national park to visit that has mangroves and rivers, and is teeming with birdlife.

Victory Beach is named after the Vietnamese victory over the Khmer Rouge regime in 1979. The beach itself has a few hotels to offer, but the popular spot (for backpackers, especially) sits on a hill overlooking the beach. Known as Victory Hill, or Weather Station Hill, this area has

CLOSE UP

Cambodia's Endangered Species

In an ironic twist to the Khmer Rouge atrocities, at least some of Cambodia's wildlands and wildlife populations emerged from that period intact, and therefore the country has a far different scenario than that faced by neighboring countries where the rarest of species were expunged years ago.

The Prek Toal Biosphere Reserve is Southeast Asia's most important waterbird nesting site, home to several endangered species. Near Sre Ambel, in what was a Khmer Rouge hotbed, conservationists are working to save the Cambodian Royal Turtle, which was thought extinct until early this decade. In Kratie, some of the world's last Irrawaddy dolphins swim the Mekong in another area long held by the Khmer Rouge; and in Mondulkiri, conservationists report an increase in wildlife species in recent years.

The more tourists who express interest in Cambodia's natural environment, the better the outlook for these species and others. The jungles remain threatened by illegal logging (just visit Stung Treng and Ratanakkiri), and poaching is common. But if those in charge begin to see serious tourist dollars connected to conservation, there may be hope yet.

grown from a small Khmer neighborhood 10 years ago to a bustling sprawl of guesthouses, cafés, pubs, and music dens, much like those in neighboring Thai islands.

Hawaii Beach, where the foundations of Sihanoukville were dug in the early 1950s, almost meets the promise of its name. It has one of Sihanoukville's longtime favorite seafood restaurants, the Hawaii Sea View Restaurant. Accommodation on Hawaii Beach is not available at this writing.

Many locals prefer **Independence Beach,** also known as 7-Chann Beach, and on weekends and holidays its long narrow stretch of sand can get crowded. The beach is backed by a neglected little park, where vendors set up food and drink stalls.

Some of the best swimming can be enjoyed at **Sokha Beach,** site of Cambodia's first international-class beach resort, the Sokha Beach Resort (owned and operated by the Cambodian oil giant, Sokimex Group).

Budget beachcombers favor **Ochheuteal Beach,** which offers inexpensive bungalows, in-the-sand dining, and plenty of activities for the young-at-heart. The far southeast end is lined with the homes of fishing families, although the aura of the place is changing quickly with new developments.

Serendipity Beach, neighboring Ochheuteal, is the backpacker's favorite haunt. Over the past few years a slew of bungalows, cheap guesthouses, and earthy restaurants has been added to the landscape. The beach is moving upmarket and there are constant rumors of large-scale development, but so far development has been slow.

KHMER: A FEW KEY PHRASES

A knowledge of French may get you somewhere in francophone Cambodia, but these days it's far easier to find English speakers. The Cambodian language, Khmer, belongs to the Mon-Khmer family of languages, enriched by Indian Pali and Sanskrit vocabulary. It has many similarities to Thai and Lao, a reminder of their years as vassal lands in the Khmer empire.

The following are some useful words and phrases:

Hello: joom reap soo-uh

Thank you: aw-koun

Yes: bah (male speaker), jah (female speaker)

No: aw-te

Excuse me: som-toh

Where?: ai nah?

How much?: t'lay pohn mahn?

Never mind: mun ay dtay

Zero: sohn

One: muay

Two: bpee

Three: bay

Four: buon

Five: bpram

Six: bpram muay

Seven: bpram pull

Eight: bpram bay

Nine: bpram buon

Ten: dop

Eleven: dop muay

Hundred: muay roi

Thousand: muay poan

Food: m'hohp

Water: dteuk

Expensive: t'lay nah

Morning: bprek

Night: youp

Today: tngay nee

Tomorrow: tngay sa-ik

Yesterday: mus'el mun

Bus: laan ch'nual

Ferry: salang

Village: pum

Island: koh

River: tonle

Doctor: bpet

Hospital: moonty bpet

Bank: tia-nia-kia

Post Office: praisinee

Toilet: baan tawp tdeuk

The Sihanoukville coast is flanked by several islands (many untouristed and lightly populated by Khmer fishermen) accessible by boat. **Koh Rong Samlem, Koh Tas,** and **Koh Russei** are popular day-trip destinations for snorkeling and picnicking. ■ **TIP→ Local guides can arrange overnight stays in rustic bungalows on some of these islands.**

Ream National Park encompasses 210 square km (81 square mi) of coastal land 18 km (10 mi) north of Sihanoukville, including mangrove forests, the Prek Tuk Sap estuary, two islands, isolated beaches, and offshore coral reefs. Macaques, pangolin (scaly anteaters), sun bears, and muntjac (barking deer) live in the forest. ✉ *Airport Rd. (near the naga* *statue), across from entrance to airport* ☎*012/875096* *Walking tour $2 per hour, 6-hour boat trip $30* ⏲*Daily 7–5.*

WHERE TO EAT

The most inexpensive guesthouses, restaurants, and other tourist services are on Victory (Weather Station) Hill, Serendipity Beach, and Ochheuteal Beach. Some of the lodgings in these areas are quite attractive, and a few restaurant gems sit amid the masses.

¢–$$ SEAFOOD ✕ **Chhne Meas Restaurant.** Dine on the edge of Victory Beach, close to the crashing waves, at this lovely indoor-outdoor restaurant. All manner of fish and seafood, from stir-frys to clay pots to barbecues and curries, is available. ✉Near the New Beach Hotel and port ☎012/340060 ▭No credit cards.

$–$$ SEAFOOD ✕ **Hawaii Sea View Restaurant.** You can practically dangle your feet in the surf as you tuck into giant prawns and crabs at this beach restaurant. The sunset alone is reason enough to grab a table, which the staff will set up for you right on the beach. ✉*Hawaii Beach* ☎*012/513008* ▭*MC, V.*

$–$$ FRENCH ✕ **La Paillote.** Tucked away in the sprawl of Weather Station Hill is this elegant open-air restaurant whose chef hails from Madagascar. La Paillote serves foie gras and a number of dishes employing distinctly European and imported ingredients; the accompanying wine list is good. ✉*Victory (Weather Station) Hill, between Papagayo and MASH* ☎*012/633247* ▭*No credit cards.*

¢–$ SEAFOOD ✕ **Sea Dragon.** You can start or end the day in style right on the beach at this friendly restaurant, which serves tasty Khmer seafood (try the crab curry with lemongrass or the grilled fish with pepper) as well as Western standbys. ✉*Ochheuteal Beach* ☎*034/933671* ▭*No credit cards.*

¢ CONTINENTAL ✕ **Starfish Bakery & Cafe.** Proceeds from this delightful little garden café go toward the Starfish Project, which supports individuals and families in need. Try a shake or brownie, indulge in a massage, and learn about volunteering opportunities in Sihanoukville. The café has Internet access and a handicrafts shop upstairs. It's not the easiest of places to find—it's hidden down a dirt road behind the Samudera Market in town—but it's well worth the trek. It's open from 7 AM to 5 PM. ✉*On unmarked road off 7 Makara St.* ☎*012/952011* ▭*No credit cards.*

WHERE TO STAY

$ **House of Malibu.** Sihanoukville hotels don't get much more secluded than this. Perched on a hillside overlooking the rocky coastline of Serendipity and Sokha beaches are a handful of tastefully designed bungalows, accessible by a dirt road. Malibu sits away from the growing crowd of Serendipity Beach budget accommodations. Each wood-and-thatch bungalow offers a private porch with views of the sea. A small sunbathing deck awaits you, right on the edge of the water. **Pros:** quiet and secluded; well designed. **Cons:** transport to any other location may be pricey. ✉*Group 14, Mondol 4, Sangkat 4, Khan Mitteapheap* ☎*012/733334 or 016/770277* *In-room: no a/c (some), safe, refrigerator. In-hotel: restaurant, bar, laundry service* ▭*No credit cards.*

8

$$$ **Independence Hotel.** First opened in 1963 with the interior designed by King Sihanouk, the Independence established itself as the premier destination of the era. War and subsequent disrepair left the shell in poor condition until refurbishment a few years ago. Now the rooms once again ooze imperial splendor with beautiful appointments, modern facilities, and a design orchestrated to make the best of stunning views across the water. **Pros:** wonderful mix of historic and modern design; great views. **Cons:** not necessarily family-friendly. ✉ *St. 2 Thnou, Sangkat No. 03, Khan Mittapheap* ☎ *034/934300 up to 3* 🌐 *www.independencehotel.net* *52 rooms* *In-room: safe, refrigerator. In-hotel: restaurant, room service, bar, pool, gym, beachfront, laundry service, Wi-Fi* *AE, MC, V.*

$ **New Beach Hotel.** This modern three-story concrete hotel offers basic, clean rooms that overlook the rocky shoreline of Victory Beach. Some rooms have fine views of the ships entering and exiting Sihanoukville Port. Deluxe rooms have Internet access. **Pros:** Internet access. **Cons:** basic rooms only; a bit close to the heavy industry of the port. ✉ *Victory Beach, opposite Customs office* ☎ *034/933822* 🌐 *www.newbeachhotel.com* *38 rooms* *In-room: refrigerator. In-hotel: restaurant, Internet terminal* *No credit cards.*

¢–$ **Orchidee Guesthouse.** This brick-and-stucco lodging is one of Sihanoukville's oldest and consistently popular choices. To keep up with the times it has recently added a pool and rooms with balconies in a new wing. It's one block, or an easy five-minute walk, from the beach. Rooms are perfectly clean; those in the new wing feature a bit of artwork. The small shrub-enclosed patio is pleasant, particularly in the evening. **Pros:** great facilities for the price. **Cons:** away from the beach. ✉ *Ochheuteal Beach, 23 Tola St.* ☎ *016/867764 or 034/933639* 🌐 *www.orchidee-guesthouse.com* *44 rooms* *In-room: refrigerator. In-hotel: restaurant, bar* *No credit cards.*

¢–$ **Queen's Hill Resort.** If you're looking for a bungalow at an even better price than the House of Malibu, stay here. High on the hill between Ochheuteal and Otres beaches, the Queen's Hill Resort has spectacular views and the chance to sleep to the sound of waves crashing below. Basic wooden bungalows with fans and mosquito nets have up to three beds each. Dine in solitude with your feet in the sand at the resort's restaurant on Otres Beach—for now, it's about the only thing on that beach. **Pros:** great views; calming sounds wash over you. **Cons:** a little isolated; cold-water showers. ✉ *Follow Ochheuteal Beach St. south over the small bridge and up the hill* ☎ *011/937373* *18 bungalows* *In-room: no a/c. In-hotel: restaurant, bar* *No credit cards.*

¢ **Small Hotel.** If you're looking for a budget hotel in Sihanoukville town that doesn't cater to bar girls and their clientele, this is it. Not only is the Small Hotel clean, it's also conveniently close to the bus station. A portion of your payment goes toward the nonprofit children's organization sponsored by the hotel's Swedish owner. **Pros:** small boutique style; clean; close to all town amenities. **Cons:** far from the beach. ✉ *Behind the Caltex station off Sopheakmongkol St.* ☎ *012/487888 or 016/567778* *thesmallhotel@yahoo.com* *In-room: no a/c (some), refrigerator. In-hotel: restaurant, bar, laundry service* *No credit cards.*

$$$ **Sokha Beach Resort.** This is the top address in Sihanoukville, a first-class resort hotel with all the facilities required for a fun-filled beach ★ holiday. The resort takes up 6 acres of landscaped gardens that lead directly to the beach. Rooms have tiled floors, wood and rattan furniture, and French doors leading to small balconies overlooking the pool and the beach. A playground and a special kid's menu at one of the restaurants make this place family-friendly. **Pros:** great for families; large selection of services; nice location. **Cons:** not geared toward romantic getaways; a bit short of the luxury status it claims. ✉ *Sokha Beach* ☎ *034/935999* 🌐 *www.sokhahotels.com* *188 rooms* *In-room: safe, refrigerator. In-hotel: 2 restaurants, room service, bars, tennis courts, pool, gym, spa, beachfront, diving, water sports, laundry service, Internet terminal* ▭ *AE, MC, V* 🍽 *BP.*

SPORTS & THE OUTDOORS

Most hotels and guesthouses arrange boat trips, which include packed lunches, to the many offshore islands. Several companies offer diving and snorkeling; two of the most popular dive centers are EcoSea Dive and Scuba Nation.

EcoSea Dive (✉ *Ekareach St.* ☎ *012/654104* 🌐 *www.ecosea.com*) has eco-friendly instruction. **Scuba Nation Diving Center** (✉ *Weather Station Hill* ☎ *012/715785* 🌐 *www.divecambodia.com*) was Cambodia's first certified PADI dive center.

KAMPOT

8

110 km (68 mi) east of Sihanoukville, 150 km (93 mi) south of Phnom Penh.

This attractive riverside town at the foot of the Elephant Mountain range, not far from the sea, is known for its French colonial architecture remnants—and for salt and pepper. In the dry season, laborers can be seen along the highway to Kep, working long hours in the salt fields; pepper plantations are scattered around the province. Kampot is the departure point for trips to the seaside resort of Kep and Bokor Hill Station. The coastal road from Sihanoukville to Kampot is somewhat rough, but has spectacular views. Several spectacular limestone caves speckle the landscape from Kampot to Kep to the Vietnam border. Plan at least a morning or afternoon excursion to see the cave at Phnom Chhnork.

GETTING HERE & AROUND

To get here, take a taxi or bus, or hire a car and driver through your hotel. The journey from Phnom Penh takes approximately four hours. A single bus ticket is $5 from Phnom Penh's Central Market. Prices for a taxi or a car with driver start at $40. Hotels are the best source for tour information in and around Kampot.

EXPLORING KAMPOT

Kampot has enough to keep the intrepid traveler busy for a couple of days. The town is sleepy and relaxed with a wide, flowing river marking the center of the town's dining and lodging area. Kampot is the stepping-off point for nearby Kep, and it has rapids and a few caves to

Jayavarman VII built Preah Khan in 1191 to commemorate the Khmers' victory over Cham invaders.

explore. Don't forget the world-renowned salt and pepper production. Bokor Hill Station remains the largest draw for visitors.

The limestone **Phnom Chhnork caves** shelter a pre-Angkorian ruin. The stalagmites and stalactites of the caves are slowly growing back into the ruin. The small, 4th-century brick structure is associated with the ancient state of Funan. ✉ *40 minutes west of Kampot via tuk-tuk ($15) or taxi.*

Bokor Hill Station, an early-20th-century, French-built retreat from the heat and humidity of the coast is now a collection of ruins, but it's worth visiting for the spectacular sea views from its 3,000-foot heights. It's 35 km (22 mi) west of Kampot; travel here is extremely rough in the rainy season.

WHERE TO EAT

¢ CAFE ✕ **Epic Arts Cafe.** Order a strong cup of Lao coffee, a banana-cinnamon milk shake, or a slice of cake at this pleasant little nonprofit café on the edge of the Kampot lawn. ✉ *Across from the abandoned market* ☎ *011/376968* 🌐 *www.epicarts.org.uk* ▭ *No credit cards* ⊙ *No dinner.*

¢–$ SEAFOOD ✕ **Phnom Kamchay Thmey.** Cambodia's best seafood is found at local joints like this. The decor consists of plastic chairs and fluorescent lighting, but the beer is cold, the room is bright, the menu's extensive, and the food is delectable. Try the crab curry. ✉ *Riverfront St.* ☎ *No phone* ▭ *No credit cards.*

¢–$ BARBECUE ✕ **Rusty Keyhole.** This is a great spot to watch the sunset as rush hour (three squeaky bikes, a stray dog, and a compact car) hits Kampot's riverfront street. The place has happy-hour specials, and serves standard pub food and nightly barbecues. ✉*Riverfront St.* ☎*012/679607* ▭*No credit cards.*

WHERE TO STAY

¢ **Blissful Guesthouse.** This foreign-run guesthouse is cheap and friendly. The remodeled, two-story house has basic fan-cooled rooms (some with attached bathrooms), a pleasant garden, and a "chill out" TV room where you can trade tales with other travelers. The bar is popular and has great music. **Pros:** friendly atmosphere. **Cons:** away from the riverside; no a/c. ✉*Across from Orchid Guesthouse, near Acleda Bank* ☎*012/513024* *blissfulguesthouse@yahoo.com* *In-room: no a/c. In-hotel: restaurant, bar* ▭*No credit cards.*

¢ **Bokor Mountain Lodge.** In a beautifully restored colonial building on the riverfront, this lodge offers a handful of rooms and a good view. **Pros:** riverside views; great restaurant. **Cons:** more expensive than other options in town. ✉*Riverfront Rd. near the Rusty Keyhole* ☎*033/932314* *www.bokorlodge.com* *6 rooms* *In-room: Wi-Fi. In-hotel: restaurant, bar, laundry facilities* ▭*MC, V.*

¢ **Orchid Guesthouse.** This quiet but quaint little guesthouse on a neighborhood street offers bungalows and a patio in a pleasant garden setting. The staff is very friendly. **Pros:** cheap; friendly staff. **Cons:** away from the river. ✉*Across from Acleda Bank and Blissful Guesthouse* ☎*092/226996* *orchidguesthousekampot@yahoo.com* *In-room: no a/c (some). In-hotel: restaurant, bar, bicycles* ▭*No credit cards.*

KEP

8

25 km (16 mi) east of Kampot; 172 km (107 mi) south of Phnom Penh.

You'll never find another seaside getaway quite like Kep, with its narrow pebble beach bordered by the ghostly villa ruins of the Khmer Rouge era. What once was the coastal playground of Cambodia's elite was destroyed in decades of war. Squatters have taken up residence in the old mansions, and ever so slowly investors are refurbishing what's salvageable. Someday soon, Kep will again bustle with activity—it's already the home of the most expensive hotel in the country. But first, Kep needs the basics, like electricity—if you see an electric light, it's powered by a car battery or a generator. Don't let the mention of squatters scare you away; Kep is not dangerous. When you arrive, moto drivers and tour guides are sure to find you. Not much traffic comes through Kep, so the locals know the bus schedule. They're sure to offer you a tour of the nearby pepper plantation. Take up the offer. Kep grows some of the world's best.

The beach in town is small but sandy. Offshore, **Rabbit Island** is an idyllic spot with nothing but a few huts, a few fishermen, and a few seaweed farmers in residence. You can hire a boat to take you there for $10. Sit in one of the beachside salas to enjoy the afternoon, or take a walk around the island. Hurry, though—a Vietnamese casino is planned for the island, and soon its calm will be lost forever.

GETTING HERE & AROUND

To get here, take a taxi or bus, or hire a car and driver through your hotel. The journey from Phnom Penh takes approximately 3½ hours. A single bus ticket is $4.50 from Phnom Penh's Central Market. Hiring a taxi or a car with driver will cost at least $40.

WHERE TO EAT

¢ SEAFOOD **Thmor Da.** In Kep's seafood market, this little restaurant in a string of several offers superb crab stir-fries and curries, shrimp with Kampot pepper, and a long list of other delectable options. Thmor Da has some of the cheapest, tastiest seafood you'll ever eat and a great waterfront location. *Riverfront St.* *No phone* *No credit cards.*

WHERE TO STAY

$ **Beach House.** A relative newcomer to the Kep scene, this hotel is perched on a hillside overlooking the sea. Rooms are clean and basic and have balconies. The rooms are spartanly decorated with tile floors and a simple bed. **Pros:** good views from the hillside; nice pool; good restaurant. **Cons:** no room TVs. *On beach road in central Kep* *012/240090* *www.thebeachhousekep.com* *16 rooms* *In-room: no TV. In-hotel: restaurant, bar, pool* *No credit cards.*

$ **Champey Inn.** What could easily be called a boutique hotel, the Champey Inn is a laid-back resort with stylish bungalows set in tropical gardens. Rooms are simply but attractively furnished with local dark woods. Power runs on a generator from 5 PM to 7 AM; there is no electricity in the guest rooms during the day. **Pros:** stylish, laid-back. **Cons:** limited electricity. *25 Ave. de la Plage* *012/501742* I*champeyinn@mobitel.com.kh* *12 bungalows* *In-hotel: restaurant, bar, pool* *No credit cards.*

¢ **Kep Seaside Guesthouse.** Rooms are very basic—fan-cooled and cold water only—at this hotel, but its waterfront location is hard to beat. All rooms have balconies. Enjoy a meal in one of the seaside cabanas, which offer some of Kep's best views—and some of its best seafood, too. The staff is exceptionally friendly. **Pros:** waterfront location; balconies in rooms. **Cons:** cold water only; no a/c. *Next to Knai Bang Chatt, not far from the seaside seafood market* *012/858571* *sengbunly@bnckh.com* *20 rooms* *In-room: no a/c, no phone, no TV. In-hotel: restaurant* *No credit cards.*

$$$$ Fodor's Choice ★ **Knai Bang Chatt.** This isn't a hotel per se, but a collection of waterfront villas. You can rent one house, all four houses, or just a single room. A two-night minimum stay is required. Pay extra and have the chef provide a daily menu of your choice. You'll also have help arranging trips to a nearby island, scheduling a spiritual visit with monks, or setting up fishing excursions with locals. A permanent staff of 14 and the participation of a host of local venues mean that you can arrange anything from a massage to a tai chi class to a lecture on Cambodian history. **Pros:** exclusive and luxurious; great waterfront location. **Cons:** a bit isolated; very expensive. *Phum Thmey Sangkat Prey, Thom Khan Kep* *012/879486* *www.knaibangchatt.com* *4 houses* *In-room: safe, Wi-Fi. In-hotel: pool, gym, laundry service* *No credit cards.*

Laos

WORD OF MOUTH

"Luang Prabang is magical. This is the Southeast Asia that I remember from my travels 20 years ago. Tourists are very much in evidence (the majority seemed to be Thai but Europeans and a few North Americans were at the hotel and in town) but they do not, as of yet, seem to overwhelm the place."

—ekscrunchy

WELCOME TO LAOS

Plain of Jars

TOP REASONS TO GO

★ **Natural Beauty:** It may not have the sheer variety of Thailand, but Laos is a beautiful country. Take a multiday trek or bike ride, or enjoy the scenic bus ride from Luang Prabang to Vang Vieng.

★ **Archaeological Wonders:** The country's most unusual attraction is the Plain of Jars, which has 5-ton stone-and-clay jars of mysterious origin. Wat Phu, pre-Angkor Khmer ruins, is Laos's most recent UNESCO World Heritage Site.

★ **Buddhist Customs:** Observing or participating in morning alms in Luang Prabang is a magical experience; so, too, is sitting in a temple to chat with a novice monk, surrounded by the sounds of chanting and chiming bells.

★ **The Mekong:** The Mekong is the lifeline of Laos. You can travel down the mighty river and stop at one of 4,000 islands for a chance to spot freshwater dolphins.

1 Vientiane & Environs. Vientiane is a curiosity—more like a small market town than a national capital—but it has some fine temples, many French colonial buildings, and a riverside boulevard unmatched elsewhere in Laos. Vang Vieng, a short bus ride north, has beautiful mountains, waterfalls, and a laid-back, rural vibe.

Monks collecting morning alms.

2 Luang Prabang & Northern Laos. Luang Prabang is the country's major tourist destination, thanks to its royal palace (now a museum), temples, French colonial architecture, and the village-like ambience it's managed to retain and refine. Hill tribes, Buddhist rituals, and Lao textiles are also major draws of the northern part of the country, as are trekking and river-rafting adventures.

Along the Mekong River.

3 Southern Laos. Few tourists venture to the far south of the country, but Pakse is an interesting town and a convenient base from which to explore ancient Khmer ruins, such as the fabulous Wat Phu. Fishing villages line the lower reaches of the Mekong River, a water wonderland with islands, countless waterfalls, and the rare Irrawaddy dolphin.

Xieng Khaw
Hua Muang
7
Pakxan
8
13
Khamkeut
Mekong
12
Tha Khaek
VIETNAM
9
9
Savannakhet
River
13
3
BOLAVEN PLATEAU
Pakse
0
100 mi
Attapeu
Wat Phu
0
100 km
13
CAMBODIA

GETTING ORIENTED

Boxed in by China, Myanmar (Burma), Thailand, Cambodia, and Vietnam, Laos is geographically divided into three regions, each with its chief city: northern Laos and Luang Prabang, central Laos and Vientiane, southern Laos and Pakse. About 90% of Laos is mountainous, so once you leave Vientiane, Luang Prabang, and the southern lowlands, you're in true off-the-beaten-track territory. Luang Prabang is the best base for single or multiday trekking, biking, and river-rafting expeditions.

LAOS PLANNER

When to Go

Laos has a tropical climate with two distinct seasons: the dry season from November through April, and the rainy season from May to October. The cooler dry season is the more comfortable time to tour Laos. In the rainy season, road and air travel can be slower and days can get very hot and sticky; July and August see the most rain. But the country is greener and less crowded during the rains and prices are much lower.

The yearly average temperature is about 82°F (28°C), rising to a maximum of 100°F (38°C) during the rainy season. In the mountainous areas around Luang Nam Tha and Phongsaly, however, temperatures can drop to 59°F (15°C) in winter and sometimes hit the freezing point at night.

Laos has a busy festival calendar and Vientiane and Luang Prabang, in particular, can get very crowded during the most important of these festivals (such as the That Luang Festival in Vientiane in November), so book your hotel room early.

Getting Here & Around

By Air: Most of the country's mountainous terrain is impenetrable jungle; the only practical way to tour the country in less than a week is by plane. Bangkok Air has daily flights from Bangkok to Luang Prabang; Thai Air flies to Vientiane; and Lao Airlines runs frequent (and cheap) flights from Bangkok to Luang Prabang and Vientiane, as well as provincial cities including Pakse and Savannakhet. Daily flights are also available to Vientiane and Luang Prabang from Chiang Mai. *(⇨ By Air in Travel Smart).*

By Boat: Running virtually the entire length of the country, the Mekong River is a natural highway. Because all main cities lie along the Mekong, boats offer an exotic but practical way to travel. The most popular water route is between Huay Xai (on the Thai border) and Luang Prabang *(⇨ River Journey to Huay Xai, below)*. More adventurous travelers can board boats in Huay Xai or Pak Tha to travel up the Nam Tha River to Luang Nam Tha. Two luxury vessels ply the Mekong: the Wat Phu *(⇨ Pakse, below)* and the Luang-Say *(⇨ River Journey to Huay Xai, below)*.

By Bus: A network of bus services covers almost the entire country. Though cheap, bus travel is slow and not as comfortable as in Thailand. VIP buses, which connect Vientiane, Luang Prabang, and Pakse, are somewhat more comfortable—they have assigned seats and more legroom, and make fewer stops.

By Car: Although it's possible to enter Laos by car or motorbike and drive around on your own, it's not recommended, as driving conditions are difficult: nearly 90% of the country's 14,000 km (8,700 mi) of roads are unpaved; road signs are often indecipherable; and accidents will invariably be considered your fault. A better alternative is to hire a car and driver for about $50 per day.

By Songthaew and Tuk-Tuk: Tuk-tuks and songthaews cruise the streets and are easy to flag down in most towns. Lao tuk-tuk drivers can be unscrupulous about fares, especially in Luang Prabang. ■ **TIP→Never get into a tuk-tuk before you've agreed on a fare; don't negotiate in dollars (get a quote in kip or baht); and don't pay more than you would for a comparable ride in Thailand.**

Border Crossings

In addition to the international airports in Vientiane, Luang Prabang, and Pakse, there are numerous land and river crossings into Laos. The busiest is the Friendship Bridge, which spans the Mekong River 29 km (12 mi) east of Vientiane. Other border crossings from Thailand to Laos are: Chiang Khong to Huay Xai (by ferry across the Mekong River); Nakhon Phanom to Tha Khek; Mukdahan to Savannakhet; and Chongmek to Vang Tao. You can also enter Laos from Cambodia at Voeung Kam; and from Mohan, in China's Yunnan Province at Buten.

Border crossings are open daily 8:30 AM–5 PM, except for the Friendship Bridge, which is open daily 6 AM–10 PM.

Money Matters

The currency is the Lao kip (LAK), which comes in relatively small notes (the largest denomination equals about $6). Since the kip has historically fluctuated quite a bit, all hotel rates are listed in U.S. dollars. The Thai baht is accepted in Vientiane, Luang Prabang, and border towns. It's best to carry most of your cash in dollars or baht and exchange relatively small amounts of kip as you travel. At this writing, the official exchange rate is approximately 243 kip to the Thai baht and 8,500 kip to one U.S. dollar.

There are ATM machines in Vientiane, Luang Prabang, Udomaxay, Vang Vieng, Savannakhet, and Pakse, but not many outside these cities, so plan accordingly. ■ TIP→ **Outside Vientiane and Luang Prabang, it's best to travel with enough cash to cover your expenses.**

Credit cards are accepted in most hotels and some restaurants, but few shops. Banks in major tourist destinations will provide a cash advance on a MasterCard or Visa, typically for a 5% service charge. Western Union has branches in Vientiane and other major towns.

WHAT IT COSTS IN U.S. DOLLARS

¢	$	$$	$$$	$$$$
Restaurants				
under $5	$5–$10	$11–$15	$16–$20	over $20
Hotels				
under $25	$25–$50	$50–$100	$100–$150	over $150

Restaurant prices are per person for a main course at dinner excluding tax and tip. Hotel prices are for a standard double room, excluding service charge and tax.

Health & Safety

⚠ **Laos's health care is not as good as Thailand's.** If you will be traveling extensively, consider buying international health insurance that covers evacuation to Thailand.

Take the same health precautions in Laos that you would in Thailand (*Health in Travel Smart*). Pharmacies are stocked with Thai antibiotics and often staffed with assistants who speak some English. Vientiane is malaria-free, but if you're visiting remote regions, consider taking prophylactics. HIV is widespread in border areas. Reliable Thai condoms are available in Laos.

Laos is fairly free of crime in tourist areas. Pickpocketing is rare, but you should still be careful in crowded areas. Never leave luggage unattended.

Penalties for drug possession are severe. Prostitution is illegal, and $500 fines can be levied against foreigners for having sexual relations with Lao citizens (how this is enforced is unclear, but even public displays of affection may be seen as shady behavior).

⚠ **In the countryside, trekkers should watch out for unexploded ordnance left over from the Vietnam War,** especially in Xieng Khuang and Hua Phan provinces, and in southern Laos. Don't wander off well-traveled trails. Better yet, trek with a qualified guide. Do not photograph anything that may have military significance, like airports or military installations.

LAOS PLANNER

Passports & Visas

You'll need a passport and a visa to enter Laos. Visas are now available on arrival at most entry points, but if you're taking the bus to Vientiane from Udon Than or Nong Khai in Thailand, you'll need to get a visa in advance *(Getting Here & Around in Vientiane, below)*. You can do this at the Lao embassy in Bangkok (begin the process at least two days ahead of time) or through an embassy or travel agency before you leave home. Tourist visas are good for 30 days, cost about $36, and must be paid for in U.S. dollars. You'll need to have two passport-size photos with you—bring these from home or get them in Bangkok. In the past Lao border officials have been able to accommodate travelers who don't have extra photos for an additional fee. Occasionally immigration officials ask to see evidence of sufficient funds and a plane ticket out of the country. Showing them credit and ATM cards should be proof enough of funds. ⚠ **Regulations change without warning, so check with the Lao embassy in your own country before setting out.**

Lao Embassy (Bangkok) (✉ *502/502/1–3, Soi Sahakarnpramoon, Pracha Uthit Rd., Wangthonglang, Bangkok* ☎ *02/539–6667*).

Tours Operators

Tourism professionals in Thailand and Laos have been energetically pushing a joint cooperation program, making it considerably easier for visitors to Thailand to plan a side trip to Laos. Much of the Thai part of this program is based in Chiang Mai, and travel agents there can set you up with a package.

In Chiang Mai, **Nam Khong Travel** (✉ *6 Chaiyaphoom Rd., Chiang Mai, Thailand* ☎ *053/874321*) is the leading specialist in package tours to Laos. **Diethelm Travel** (✉ *Kian Gwan II Bldg., 140/1 Wittayu [Wireless] Rd., Bangkok, Thailand* ☎ *02/255–9150* ✉ *Setthathirat Rd. at Nam Phu Fountain Sq., Vientiane* ☎ *021/215129 or 021/215920* ✉ *Sisavangvong Rd., Luang Prabang* ☎ *071/212277* 🌐 *www.diethelmtravel.com*) is one of the oldest and most-respected travel agencies offering package trips to Laos and a good source of travel information and tours in Laos.

Green Discovery Laos (✉ *54 Setthathirat Rd., Nam Phou, Vientiane* ☎ *021/223022* 🌐 *www.greendiscoverylaos.com*) is the top eco- and adventure-tour operator in Laos and is the best source for local information. **Lao Youth Travel** (✉ *039 Fa Ngum Quay, Ban Mixay, Vientiane* ☎ *021/240939* ✉ *410 Visounnarath Rd., Visoun, Box 1086, Luang Prabang* ☎ *071/253340* 🌐 *www.laoyouthtravel.com*) does tours around Laos and can answer questions.

The **National Tourism Authority of the Lao People's Democratic Republic** (✉ *BP 3556, Ave. Lan Xang, Vientiane* ☎ *021/212248 or 021/250681* 🌐 *www.tourismlaos.gov.la*) has offices in Vientiane and all other provinces in Laos; they provide some printed materials, but little else.

■ TIP→ **The private Web site 🌐 www.laos-hotels.com can provide information on the major hotels in the country.**

VIENTIANE & ENVIRONS

Updated by Dave Stamboulis

VIENTIANE IS NOT ONLY THE capital of Laos but also the logical gateway to the country, as it's far more accessible to the outside world than Luang Prabang. The city sits along the Mekong River, with Thailand just across the water. A 20-minute ride by taxi or *tuk-tuk* brings you to the Friendship Bridge, which links Laos and Thailand. Crossing the bridge is a mere formality. On the Thai side of the bridge is the riverside frontier town of Nong Khai, which has direct rail services to Bangkok and a bus terminus serving the Thai capital and most cities in eastern Isan. Many tourists choose this route from Thailand into Laos, although Vientiane is easily and cheaply reached by air from Bangkok, Chiang Mai, and most Southeast Asian cities.

VIENTIANE

Vientiane is the quietest Southeast Asian capital, with a pace as slow as the Mekong River, which flows along the edge of town. It doesn't have the kind of imposing sights you find in Bangkok, but neither does it have the air pollution and traffic jams. That's not to say that Vientiane isn't changing at all—though there are still many more bicycles and scooters than cars on its streets, several of the main thoroughfares are beginning to bustle.

The abundance of ugly cement-block buildings in urgent need of paint gives the town a superficially run-down appearance, but scattered among these eyesores are some remnants of elegant colonial French architecture. There are also dozens of temples—ornate, historic Buddhist structures that stand amid towering palms and flowering trees. First-time visitors often find Vientiane a drab, joyless city, but you only have to arrive in the midst of the weeklong That Luang Festival in November to be reminded that first impressions can be misleading.

GETTING HERE & AROUND

BY AIR Vientiane's Wattay International Airport is about 4 km (2½ mi) from the city center. You can take a metered taxi from Wattay International Airport into the city for $7; get a taxi voucher from the kiosk in the arrivals hall. The ride to the city center takes about 15 minutes. Alternatively, if you don't have much luggage, walk out of the airport gate and take a tuk-tuk for 40,000 kip (about $5).

BY BUS The best way to get to Vientiane from Thailand via bus is to take one of the hourly buses from either Udon Thani (two hours, B80) or Nong Khai (one hour, B55). These buses take you straight to Talat Sao, Vientiane's morning market, but **■ TIP→ you cannot board them unless you already have a Lao visa.**

If you don't have an advance visa, you can take a bus from Udon Thani to Nong Khai, then a tuk-tuk to the border (B30 to B50), cross the Friendship Bridge on a B20 shuttle bus, and take a taxi (B350), tuk-tuk (B150), or public bus (B20) from the Lao side of the border into Vientiane.

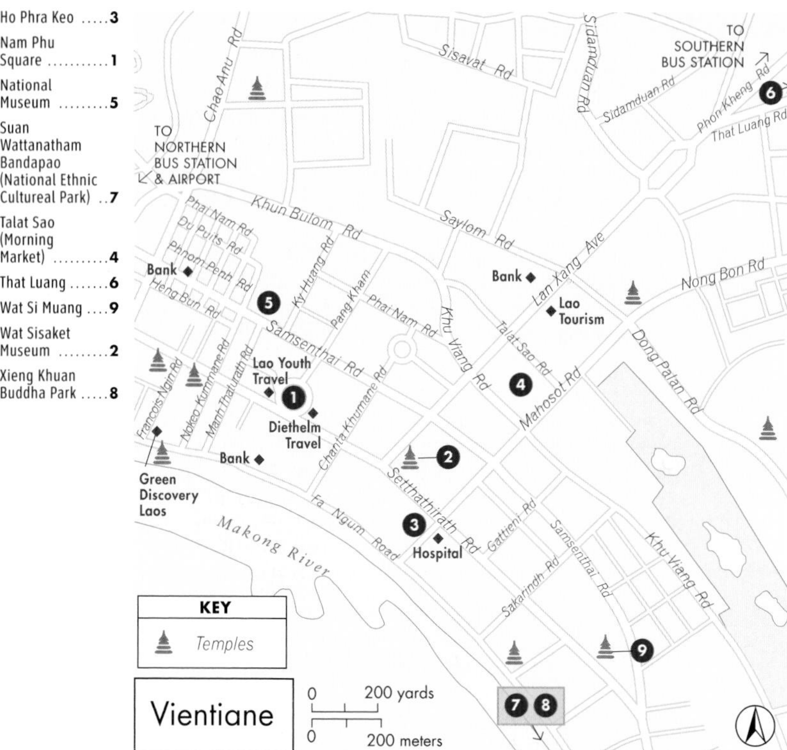

The Northern Bus Terminal for trips to and from northern Laos is 3 km (2 mi) northwest of the center, while southern buses leave from the Southern Bus Station, which is out on Highway 13. The Talat Sao (Morning Market) Bus Station handles local departures.

Although there's city bus service in Vientiane, schedules and routes are confusing for visitors, so it's best to stick to tuk-tuks and taxis. The city bus station is next to the Morning Market.

BY TAXI & TUK-TUK You can cover Vientiane on foot, but tuk-tuks and jumbos, their larger brethren, are easy to flag down. Be sure to negotiate the price before setting off; you can expect to pay about 30,000 kip for a ride within the city if you are a firm negotiator. Taxis are available but must be reserved, which you can do through your hotel or at the Morning Market. For day trips outside the city, ask your hotel or guesthouse to book a car with a driver.

ESSENTIALS

Emergencies Mahosot Hospital International Clinic in Vientiane is the best medical center in the country. **Mahosot Hospital International Clinic** (✉ *Fa Ngum Quay* ☎ *021/214022*). **U.S. Embassy** (✉ *Rue Bartholoni* ☎ *021/267000 or 021/212581*).

CLOSE UP

Etiquette & Behavior

Laotians are generally gentle and polite, and visitors should take their lead from them—avoiding any public display of anger or impolite behavior. Even showing affection in public is frowned upon.

Laotians traditionally greet others by pressing their palms together in a sort of prayer gesture known as a *nop*; it is also acceptable for men to shake hands. If you attempt a nop, remember that it's basically reserved for social greetings; don't greet a hotel or restaurant employee this way. The general greeting is *sabai di* ("good health"), invariably said with a smile.

Avoid touching or embracing a Laotian, and keep in mind that the head has spiritual significance; even patting a child affectionately on the head could be misinterpreted. Feet are considered "unclean," so when you sit, make sure your feet are not pointing directly at anyone, and never use your foot to point in any situation. Shoes must be removed before you enter a temple or private home, as well as some restaurants and offices.

Shorts and sleeveless tops should not be worn in temple compounds. When visiting a temple, be careful not to touch anything of spiritual significance, such as altars, Buddha images, or spirit houses. Ask permission from any individual before taking a photograph of him or her.

EXPLORING VIENTIANE

Laos's capital is a low-key, pleasant city thanks to its small size, relative lack of traffic, and navigable layout. Outside of That Luang, there aren't too many must-sees, but the promenade along the Mekong and the *wats* (temples) scattered throughout town are great to explore by bicycle. Good restaurants and old colonial French architecture make it an enjoyable place to stop for a day or two.

MAIN ATTRACTIONS

3 **Ho Phra Keo.** There's a good reason why Ho Phra Keo, one of the city's oldest and most impressive temples, has a name so similar to the wat in Bangkok's Grand Palace. The original Ho Phra Keo here was built by King Setthathirat in 1565 to house the Emerald Buddha, which he had taken from Chang Mai in Thailand. The king installed the sacred statue first in Luang Prabang and then in Vientiane at Ho Phra Keo, but the Buddha was recaptured by the Siamese army in 1778 and taken to Bangkok. The present temple was restored in 1936, and has become a national museum. On display are Buddha sculptures of different styles, some wonderful chiseled images of Khmer deities, and a fine collection of stone inscriptions. The masterpiece of the museum is a 16th-century lacquered door carved with Hindu images. ✉ *Setthathirat Rd. at Mahosot St.* ☎ *No phone* 🎫 *5,000 kip* ⏲ *Daily 8–4.*

4 **Talat Sao** *(Morning Market)*. To truly immerse yourself in Vientiane, visit this vast indoor bazaar that is, despite its name, actually open all day. The bright, orderly emporium holds everything from handwoven fabrics and wooden Buddha figures to electric rice cookers and sneakers. Most of the shops cater to locals, but there's still plenty to

interest travelers: handicrafts, intricate gold-and-silver work, jewelry, T-shirts, and bags and suitcases to accommodate all your extra purchases. Many products are imported from abroad. Fruits, confections, and noodle soups are sold at open-door stalls outside, where Vietnamese shoemakers also ply their trade. The market, which is near the main post office, is made up of three Lao-style buildings, each with two floors. The funding of the construction (1989–91) came mainly from the market traders themselves. ✉ *Lane Xang Ave. at Khu Vieng St.* ☎ *No phone* ⏲ *Daily 7–6.*

THE RISE OF THE MOON CITY

Originally named Chanthaburi (City of the Moon), Vientiane was founded in the 16th century by King Setthathirat near a wide bend of the Mekong River, on the grounds of a Khmer fortress dating to the 9th to 13th century. In 1828 the Siamese army from Bangkok razed the city. But the old part of Vientiane is still an attractive settlement, where ancient temples that survived the Siamese attack, museums, and parks are all just a short distance from one another.

6 ★ **That Luang.** The city's most sacred monument, this massive, 147-foot-high, gold-painted stupa is also the nation's most important cultural symbol, representing the unity of the Lao people. It was built by King Setthathirat in 1566 (and restored in 1953) to guard a relic of the Buddha's hair and to represent Mt. Meru, the holy mountain of Hindu mythology, the center and axis of the world. Surrounding the lotus-shaped stupa are 30 pinnacles on the third level and a cloistered square on the ground with stone statues of the Buddha. The complex is flanked by two brilliantly decorated temple halls, the survivors of four temples that originally surrounded the stupa. On the avenue outside the west gate stands a bronze statue of King Setthathirat erected in the 1960s by a pious general. ■ **TIP→ That Luang is the center of a major week-long festival during November's full moon.** It's on the outskirts of town (a 10-minute songthaew ride from the center). The monument is also short *songthaew* ride away from the riverside. Be sure to head to the riverbank in the late afternoon to experience one of Vientiane's most spectacular sights—sunset over the Mekong. ✉ *North end of That Luang Rd.* ☎ *No phone* 🎫 *5,000 kip* ⏲ *Daily 8–4.*

8 **Xieng Khuan Buddha Park.** The bizarre creation of an ecumenical monk, Luang Pa Bunleua Sulilat, who dreamed of a world religion embracing all faiths, this park is "peopled" by enormous Buddhist and Hindu sculptures spread among an attractive landscape of trees, shrubs, and flower gardens. Keep an eye out for the remarkable 165-foot-long sleeping Buddha. The park was laid out by the monk's followers in 1958 on the banks of the Mekong, opposite the Thai town of Nong Khai. ✉ *Km 27–28 on Tha Deua Rd.* ☎ *No phone* 🎫 *5,000 kip* ⏲ *Daily 8–4:30.*

ALSO WORTH SEEING

1 **Nam Phu Square** *(Fountain Square).* An attractive square with a nice but nonfunctioning circular fountain in the middle, this is one of several reminders in the city of French colonial influence—reinforced further

CLOSE UP

Lao Festivals

Laos has many fascinating festivals, quite a few of which are steeped in Buddhism. Be sure to book hotels in advance if you're planning on visiting during festival time, particularly in the big cities.

Bun Bang Fai: The Rocket Festival is held in the middle of May. Rockets are fired and prayers are said in the paddy fields to bring rain in time for the planting of the rice seedlings.

Bun Khao Padab Din: This is a special rice ceremony held in August (the exact date depends on the harvest schedule). People make offerings at local temples to keep alive the memory of spirits who have no relatives.

Bun Khao Salak: This is a similar rice ceremony in September (the exact date depends on the harvest schedule), wherein people visit local temples to make offerings to their ancestors. Boat races are held on the Mekong, especially in Luang Prabang and Khammuan Province.

Bun Ok Pansa: The day of the full moon in October marks the end of Buddhist Lent and is celebrated with donations to local temples. Candlelight processions are held, and colorful floats are set adrift on the Mekong River. The following day, boat races are held in Vientiane, Savannakhet, and Pakse.

Bun Pimai: Lao New Year takes place April 13–15. This is a water festival similar to Thailand's celebrated Songkran, when all the important Buddha images get a cleaning with scented water (and the general public gets wet in the bargain). The festivities are particularly lively in Luang Prabang.

Bun Visakhabucha (Buddha Day): On the day of the full moon in May, candlelight processions are held in temples to mark the birth, enlightenment, and death of the Buddha.

That Ing Hang Festival: This takes place in Savannakhet in December and lasts several days on the grounds of the ancient Wat That Inhang, just outside the city. There are performances of traditional Lao music and dance, sports contests, and a spectacular drumming competition.

That Luang Festival: This is a week-long event in Vientiane in November, which ends with a grand fireworks display. Hundreds of monks gather to accept alms. The festival runs concurrently with an international trade fair showcasing the products of Laos and other countries of the Greater Mekong Subregion (GMS).

Wat Phu Festival: Also known as Makhabucha Day, this festival is held during the day of the first full moon in February at Wat Phu, near Champasak. A full schedule of events includes elephant races, buffalo fights, cockfights, and traditional Lao music-and-dance performances.

by the presence on the square's perimeter of some very Gallic restaurants. Nam Phu Square is a convenient meeting or starting point as it is easy to find and is situated in the center of Vientiane's tourist area; restaurants, Internet cafés, travel agents, and massage parlors are all located in this area.

5 **National Museum.** A modern, well-laid-out, two-story building houses interesting geological and historical displays. Exhibits touch on Laos's

Thai invaders destroyed That Luang in 1828; it was restored in the 20th century.

royal history, its colonial years, and its struggle for liberation. The museum also highlights the country's 50 main ethnic groups, and indigenous instruments. ✉*Sam Sen Tai Rd.* ☎*021/212460, 021/212461, or 021/212462* 🎫*5,000 kip* ⏲*Daily 8–noon and 1–4.*

7 **Suan Wattanatham Bandapao** *(National Ethnic Cultural Park).* The attraction at this park near the river is a model village of miniature Lao houses. Sculptures of Lao heroes dot the grounds, which also include a small zoo in one corner. This is a pleasant place to stroll and admire the sleek lines of the Friendship Bridge, just a short distance downstream. A string of restaurants lines the riverbank here. ✉*Km. 20 on Tha Deua Rd.* ☎*No phone* 🎫*3,000 kip* ⏲*Daily 8–6.*

9 **Wat Si Muang.** This wat, built in 1956, guards the original city pillar, a revered foundation stone dating to the 16th century. In a small park in front of the monastery stands a rare memorial to Laos's royal past: a large bronze statue of King Sisavang Vong. ✉*Lan Xang Ave.* ☎*No phone* 🎫*Free* ⏲*Daily 7–5.*

2 **Wat Sisaket Museum.** This interesting museum complex is made up of a crumbling temple and monastery compound across the road from Ho Phra Keo. Built in 1818 by King Anu, the temple survived the destruction of the city by the Siamese army in 1828. The monastery stands intact in its original form and is one of the most frequented in the city. Inside the main compound, the courtyard walls have hundreds of little niches and large shelves displaying 6,840 Buddha statues. Although it's in need of more work, the impressive temple hall underwent some restoration in 1938. The paintings that once covered its interior walls

have largely been destroyed by the ravages of time, but the intricately carved wooden ceiling and doors are still intact. There's also an intriguing wooden library that stores palm-leaf manuscripts. ✉ *Setthathirat Rd. at Mahosot St.* ☎ *No phone* *5,000 kip* ⏲ *Daily 8–4.*

WHERE TO EAT

$ ECLECTIC **Khop Chai Deu.** A French colonial structure houses this very popular downtown restaurant and bar, which serves as an excellent meeting point for happy-hour cocktails or dinner. The long menu is crammed with Lao and international dishes, and a daily buffet is also served. **■ TIP→ For a tasty introduction to traditional Lao cuisine, try the Lao Discovery, a set menu including *larb*, a semi-spicy salad; *tom yum*, a sour chili-and-lemongrass fish soup; *khao niaw*, Lao sticky rice; and a glass of *lao-lao* (rice whiskey).** Draft beer is on tap, live music plays in the bar nightly, and the kitchen is open until 11 PM. ✉ *54 Setthathirat Rd.* ☎ *021/223022* ▭ *MC, V.*

$ LAO **Kualao.** In a fading mansion one block southeast of Nam Phu Square, this is one of Vientiane's best Lao restaurants. The food is quite good, and the vast menu ranges from *mok pa fork* (banana-leaf-wrapped steamed fish cooked with eggs, onions, and coconut milk) to *gaeng panaeng* (a thick red curry with chicken, pork, or beef). Servings are small, so most people order several entrées, or set menus with seven to nine dishes, plus dessert and coffee. Photos and English descriptions facilitate the ordering process. There's Lao folk dancing nightly from 7 to 9. ✉ *134 Samsenthai Rd.* ☎ *021/215777* ▭ *MC, V.*

$ FRENCH **Le Provençal.** A local family that lived in France for many years runs this little bistro behind Nam Phu Square. Chef Daniel's menu is almost exclusively French, although there's a hybrid pizza à la française. Try the beef-based terrine *du maison* to start, then sink your teeth into chicken niçoise, frogs' legs à la lyonnaise, or fillet of fish à la Provençale. Save room for such desserts as crème caramel and chocolate mousse. On sunny days, you can sit on the terrace overlooking the square. ✉ *73/1 Pang Kham Rd.* ☎ *021/219685* ▭ *MC, V* ⏲ *No lunch Sun.*

9

$–$$ ITALIAN **L'Opera.** Vientiane's best Italian restaurant serves authentic pastas, baked entrees, and fresh salads. Try the Pizza de Laos (made with chilies and Lao sausage) if you're in the mood for fusion. There are also espresso and cappuccinos, plus an extensive wine list to choose from. Tables at the small front terrace look out on all the action on Nam Phu Square. ✉ *12 Nam Phu Fountain Sq.* ☎ *021/215099* ▭ *AE, MC, V.*

$–$$ ★ FRENCH **Nam Phu.** A filet mignon as good as any you can find in Paris is one of the specialties at this very French restaurant on central Nam Phu Square. The dish, which comes with a blue-cheese sauce, is one of several savory creations on a menu also distinguished for its seafood and freshwater fish. There's an excellent wine list, with prices for bottles starting at a very reasonable $12. ✉ *99/03 Nam Phu Fountain Sq.* ☎ *021/216248* ▭ *AE, MC, V.*

¢ INDIAN **Nazim.** Mr. Nazim has opened Indian restaurants in Luang Prabang, Vang Vieng, and finally Vientiane. His Indian curries, served with *papadum* (crunchy lentil bread) and thick rounds of nan, are the real deal. Try for one of the few seats on the small terrace; in the evening,

CLOSE UP

Laos: Then & Now

Despite its limited infrastructure, Laos is a wonderful country to visit. The Laotians are some of the friendliest, gentlest people in Southeast Asia—devoutly Buddhist, and traditional in many ways. Not yet inured to countless visiting foreigners, locals volunteer assistance and a genuine welcome. And because this land-locked nation is so sparsely populated—fewer than 6 million people in an area larger than Great Britain—its mountainous countryside has not yet been deforested or overdeveloped. Laos has a rich culture and history, and though it's been a battleground many times in the past, it's a peaceful, stable country today.

Prehistoric remains show that the river valleys and lowland areas of Laos were settled as far back as 40,000 years ago, first by hunters and gatherers and later by more developed communities. The mysterious Plain of Jars—a stretch of land littered with ancient stone and clay jars at least 2,000 years old—indicates the early presence of a sophisticated society skilled in the manufacture of bronze and iron implements and ceramics. Starting in the 3rd century BC, cultural and trading links were forged with Chinese and Indian civilizations.

Between the 4th and 8th century, farming communities along the Mekong River began to organize themselves into communities called "Muang"—a term still used in both Laos and neighboring Thailand. This network of Muang gave rise in the mid-14th century to the first Lao monarchy, given the fanciful name of Lan Xang, or the "Kingdom of a Million Elephants," for the large herds of the pachyderms that roamed the land.

At the start of the 18th century, following fighting over the throne, the kingdom was partitioned into three realms: Luang Prabang, Vientiane, and Champasak. Throughout the latter part of the 18th century Laos was under the control of neighboring Siam. In the early 19th century Laos staged an uprising against the Siamese, but in 1828 an invading Siamese army under King Rama III sacked Vientiane and took firm control of most of Laos as a province of Siam. Siam maintained possession of Laos until the French established the Federation of French Indochina, which included Laos, Vietnam, and Cambodia, in 1893. In 1904 the Lao monarch Sisavang Vong set up court in Luang Prabang, but Laos remained part of French Indochina until 1949. For a brief period during World War II Laos was occupied by Japan, but reverted to French control at the end of the war. In 1953 the Lao PDR became an independent nation, which was confirmed by the passage of the Geneva Convention in 1954. The monarchy was finally dissolved in 1975, when the revolutionary group Pathet Lao, allied with North Vietnam's communist movement during the Vietnam War, seized power after a long guerrilla war.

During the Vietnam War, the U.S. Air Force, in a vain attempt to disrupt the Ho Chi Minh Trail, dropped more tons of bombs on Laos than were dropped on Germany during World War II. Since the end of the Vietnam War, the People's Democratic Party (formerly the Pathet Lao) has ruled the country, first on Marxist-Leninist lines and now on the basis of limited pro-market reforms. Overtures are being made to the outside, particularly to Thailand, Japan, and China, to assist in developing the country—not an easy task.

The Friendship Bridge over the Mekong River connects Vientiane with Nong Khai in northeastern Thailand, making Laos more accessible to trade with neighboring countries.

Decentralization of the state-controlled economy began in 1986, resulting in a steady annual growth rate of around 6%. The country has continued to grow steadily: Vientiane, Luang Prabang, and Pakse have new airports; visitors from most countries can now get a visa upon arrival, and those from some ASEAN (Association of Southeast Asian Nations) countries need no visa at all. New hotels are constantly opening. Nonetheless, infrastructure in the country remains primitive in comparison to the rest of the world. Laos has no railways; communications technology and electricity are common only in more densely populated areas (cell phones outnumber landlines five to one), and only 9 of the country's 44 airports and airstrips are paved. The road from the current capital, Vientiane, to Laos's ancient capital, Luang Prabang, has been paved and upgraded—though it still takes eight hours to make the serpentine, 320-km (198-mi) journey north, and nearly 90% of the nation's roads are unpaved. The upgraded road running south from Vientiane can now accommodate tour buses going all the way to the Cambodian border. Other border crossings have also opened up, especially along the Vietnamese border.

A low standard of living (the GDP per capita of $1,900 is one of the world's lowest, and 34% of the population lives below the poverty line), and a rugged landscape that hampers transportation and communication, have long made the countryside of Laos a sleepy backwater. But Luang Prabang, boosted by its status as a World Heritage Site, has become a busy and relatively prosperous tourist hub. Vientiane, despite its new hotels and restaurants, remains one of the world's sleepiest capital cities.

Despite their relative poverty, Lao people are frank, friendly, and outwardly cheerful people. Although Laos certainly has far to go economically, it is currently a member of the ASEAN trade group, has Normal Trade Relations status with the United States, and receives assistance from the European Union to help it acquire WTO membership. Growing investment in Laos and expanding numbers of tourists to both the main tourist centers and more remote areas should continue to benefit the people of Laos.

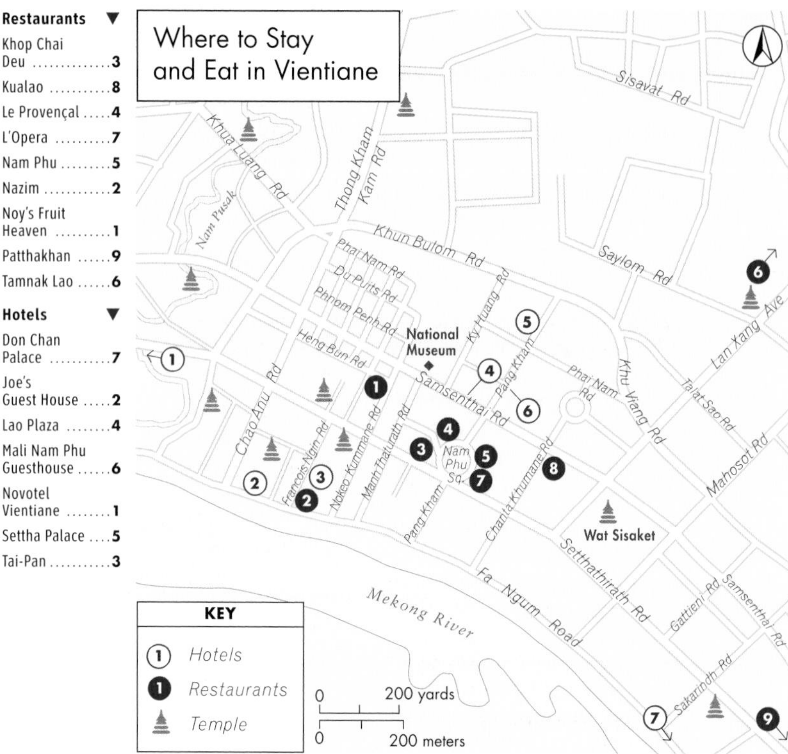

you can watch the sun set over the Mekong, which flows just across the road. ✉*335 Fa Ngum Quay* ☎*021/223480* ▭*V.*

¢ CAFE ✕ **Noy's Fruit Heaven.** This cute little café serves up gourmet sandwiches, such as imported feta, Camembert, or goat cheese melted onto fresh baguette, as well as any sort of tropical fruit smoothie you can dream up. The lively owner Noy also rents bicycles, sells traditional crafts, and gives impromptu Lao lessons upon request. ✉*Heng Boun Rd., Ban Haysok, Vientiane* ☎*030/526–2369* ▭*No credit cards.*

¢ LAO ✕ **Patthakhan.** Vientiane's largest Lao restaurant, on the edge of the city, is a new structure built in traditional style. The extensive menu is dominated by Lao dishes, but it also includes Thai, Chinese, and other Asian food. Freshly caught Mekong fish is a specialty. ✉*Km. 4 on Tha Deua Rd.* ☎*021/312480* ▭*No credit cards.*

¢ LAO ✕ **Tamnak Lao.** Classical Lao dances are performed every evening at this fine outdoor restaurant specializing in the cuisine of Luang Prabang. Many dishes, such as the *pla larb* (minced fish with herbs), are prepared with fish fresh from the Mekong River. Note that dinner service doesn't begin until 6. ✉*308 That Luang Rd., Ban Phon Xay* ☎*021/413562* ▭*MC, V.*

CLOSE UP

Lao Cuisine

It may not be as famous as Thai food, but Lao cuisine is similar and often just as good, though usually not as spicy. Chilies are used as a condiment, but Lao cuisine also makes good use of ginger, lemongrass, coconut, tamarind, crushed peanuts, and fish paste. Because so much of the country is wilderness, there's usually game, such as venison or wild boar, on the menu. Fresh river prawns and fish—including the famous, massive Mekong catfish, the world's largest freshwater fish—are also standard fare, along with chicken, vegetables, and sticky rice.

As in Isan, *larb* (meat salad with shallots, lime juice, chilies, garlic, and other spices) is a staple, as are sticky rice and *tam mak hu,* the Lao version of green-papaya salad. Grilled chicken, pork, and duck stalls can be found in every bus station and market in the country. Northern Laos, especially Luang Prabang, is noted for its distinctive cuisine: specialties include grilled Mekong seaweed, sprinkled with sesame seeds and served with a spicy chili dip; and *orlam,* an eggplant and meat stew with bitter herbs. Sticky rice, served in bamboo baskets, is the bread and butter of Laos. Locals eat it with their hands, squeezing it into a solid ball or log and dipping it in other dishes.

Throughout the country, you'll find *pho,* a Vietnamese-style noodle soup, served for breakfast. Fresh baguettes, a throwback to the French colonial days, are also available everywhere, often made into sandwiches with meat pate, vegetables, and chili sauce. Laotians wash it all down with extra-strong Lao coffee sweetened with condensed milk, or the ubiquitous Beer Lao, a slightly sweet lager.

WHERE TO STAY

$$$–$$$$ **Don Chan Palace.** The tallest building in Laos, Don Chan Palace has spectacular views of Vientiane and of Thailand, across the Mekong River. Otherwise, it is a very typical four-star international hotel, geared mainly to corporate and diplomatic travelers—it has all the expected services and facilities, but very little character. **TIP→ Even if you don't stay here, you might want to use the hotel's open-air fitness center and pool ($10 per day for nonguests), to take in the sunset view at the Sky Lounge, or to party at the popular nightclub.** **Pros:** fantastic river views; best nightclub in town; abundant and attentive staff. **Cons:** pool area is covered and doesn't get sun; isolated. ✉ *Unit 6, Piawat Village* ☎ *021/244288* 🌐 *www.donchanpalacelaopdr.com* *230 rooms* *In-room: safe, Internet. In-hotel: 3 restaurants, room service, bar, pool, gym, spa, laundry service* ▭ *AE, MC, V* *BP.*

¢ **Joe's Guest House.** This is probably the cleanest and friendliest budget guesthouse along the river road. Rooms are very simple and plain, but have crisp, white bedding. Some rooms have shared baths. Larger rooms have air-conditioning and private baths. **Pros:** nice location on Mekong; good source of travel information; cheap. **Cons:** rooms windowless and dark; hard beds; long climb to rooms on upper floors. ✉ *135/01 Fa Ngum Rd.* ☎ *021/241936* *14 rooms* *In-room: no a/c (some). In-hotel: bar, bicycles, no-smoking rooms* ▭ *No credit cards.*

9

$$$ **Lao Plaza.** Something of a local landmark, Lao Plaza stands six stories tall in the center of town. The sleek exterior is a contrast to the old-fashioned comforts within: rooms are furnished with dark woods, shades of powder blue and soft rose, Oriental rugs, and some homey touches like fresh flowers and fluffed pillows. **Pros:** large swimming pool and terrace; enormous beds; great central location. **Cons:** least expensive rooms aren't great value; on very busy street; constant hassle from tuk-tuk drivers outside. ✉ *63 Samsenthai Rd.* ☎ *021/218800 or 021/218801* 🌐 *www.laoplazahotel.com* *142 rooms* *In-room: safe, Internet. In-hotel: 2 restaurants, room service, bar, pool, gym, spa, laundry service, Internet terminal* *AE, MC, V.*

¢ ★ **Mali Nam Phu Guesthouse.** This spotlessly clean, Vietnamese-run guesthouse is a short walk from several restaurants and shopping areas. Rooms are comfortable, although simply furnished. A central garden courtyard offers a quiet place to relax after a day of sightseeing. **Pros:** beautiful, peaceful courtyard; helpful staff; central location. **Cons:** very basic rooms; no Internet. ✉ *114 Pang Kham Rd.* ☎ *021/215093 or 021/263297* 🌐 *www.malinamphu.com* *40 rooms* *In-hotel: restaurant, laundry service, no-smoking rooms* *MC, V.*

$$$ **Novotel Vientiane.** Although Vientiane's Novotel is just a five-minute drive from the airport, it has a pleasant location in front of Fa Ngum Park. The modern building, with a sweeping art nouveau facade, has all the usual Novotel comforts and facilities, including a dance club that is popular with locals. **Pros:** close to airport; tennis courts; one of few hotels in Laos that has all amenities. **Cons:** out of town center; on very busy road; expensive. ✉ *Unit 10, Samsenthai Rd.* ☎ *021/213570* 🌐 *www.novotel.com* *172 rooms* *In-room: safe, Internet. In-hotel: 2 restaurants, bar, tennis court, pool, gym, laundry service, no-smoking rooms* *AE, MC, V.*

$$$–$$$$ ★ **Settha Palace.** This colonial landmark has been through a lot of changes: it was built by the French at the turn of the 19th century, converted into a hotel in the 1930s, and expropriated by the communist government in the 1970s. It became a hotel again in the late 1990s. Although it underwent extensive renovations—the marble floors and fixtures are new—the owners have respected the original design. Rooms have high ceilings, hardwood floors, Oriental rugs, and period pieces; the executive suite has a large and comfortable sitting room as well. All rooms have tall windows that overlook lush gardens surrounding a large pool. The lobby, decorated with fine antiques, is adjacent to a small bar and elegant restaurant, La Belle Epoque, which specializes in Lao and French cuisine. City tours are available via the hotel's London Taxi, and Wi-Fi is available throughout the hotel. **Pros:** elegant and private; gorgeous furnishings; beautiful pool garden. **Cons:** small pool; often fully booked; no elevator. ✉ *6 Pang Kham Rd.* ☎ *021/217581 or 021/217582* 🌐 *www.setthapalace.com* *29 rooms* *In-room: safe, refrigerator, Wi-Fi. In-hotel: restaurant, room service, bar, pool, laundry service, Wi-Fi, no-smoking rooms* *AE, MC, V* *BP.*

$$ **Tai-Pan.** With a convenient location in the heart of town near the Mekong River, and comfort at competitive rates, this hotel is popular with business travelers. Rooms are spacious and have dark par-

quet floors. The ground floor holds the reception area, restaurant, and lounge, which are separated by potted plants and wooden dividers. Behind the building is a narrow garden and a small pool, a nice place to take advantage of the hotel's Wi-Fi. **Pros:** fitness center and hot tub; quiet pool area; great location near river and restaurants. **Cons:** small pool; no views; rooms feel slightly worn. ✉*2–12 Francois Nginn Rd., Ban Mixay* ☎*021/216906 up to 09* 🌐*www.taipanhotel-vientiane.com* *44 rooms* *In-room: safe, refrigerator. In-hotel: restaurant, bar, pool, gym, laundry service, Wi-Fi, no-smoking rooms* *AE, MC, V.*

NIGHTLIFE & THE ARTS

The after-dark scene in Vientiane is very subdued, mostly confined to some of the more expensive hotels and a handful of bars and pubs along the Mekong River boulevard. Otherwise, entertainment in Vientiane means a cultural pursuit.

You can enjoy traditional Lao folk music and dancing on a Mekong River cruise aboard the ***Lane Xang* riverboat** (☎*020/235–8123*). The one-hour cruise is free to board and departs from the jetty at the western end of Fa Ngum Quay at 7:30 PM. Food and drink are available for purchase at reasonable rates.

The **Laos Tradition Show** (✉*National Theater, Manthaturat Rd.* ☎*021/242978*) stages traditional music and dance performances nightly at 8:30.

The crowded and loud **Lunar 36 Disco** (☎*021/244288*), in the Don Chan Palace Hotel, has Vientiane's most happening nighttime action.

The Lane Xang hotel's **Snack Bar** (✉*1 Fa Ngum Quay* ☎*021/214100*) is a popular haunt—a little shady, but interesting.

Vientiane's newest and most popular bar-restaurant, **Bor Pen Yang** (✉*Fah Ngum Quay, Ban Wat Cham* ☎*021/261373*) occupies a prime spot on the Mekong, with great views, good music, international cuisine, and plenty of beer and cocktails. Most nights it's packed with locals and travelers.

Believe it or not, the **bowling alley** on Khun Bulom Road, around the corner from Settha Palace, is a happening after-hours spot, serving food and drinks to a rowdy mix of locals, expats, and travelers until 5 AM.

SHOPPING

With crafts, jewelry, T-shirts, and more, the **Talat Sao** (*Morning Market* ✉*Lane Xang Ave. at Khao Vieng St.*) market should satisfy all your shopping needs.

★ If you're still looking for that something special and you can't find it at Talat Sao, try the **Small and Medium Enterprises Promotion Center** handicrafts center (*SMEPC* ✉*Phokheng Rd.* ☎*021/416736*). **Lao Handicraft Group** (✉*Ban Thongphanthong* ☎*021/416267*), about 2 km (1 mi) north of town, also sells a wide selection of Lao crafts. A tuk-tuk can take you here for about 25,000 kip.

Lao handwoven silk is world renowned; **Carol Cassidy Lao Textiles** (✉ *84–86 Th. Nokeo Khumman* ☎ *021/212123* 🌐 *www.laotextiles.com*), a beautiful weaving studio housed in an old French home, sells some particularly high-quality fabrics, as well as scarves, shawls, and wall hangings.

Phaeng Mai Silk Gallery (✉ *Ban Nongbuathong Tai* ☎ *021/243121*), located in the old weaving district, is another shop with handwoven silk. For wood carvings, head to **Humsinh Craft** (✉ *Ban Dong Miang* ☎ *021/212329*), about 1 km (2/3 mi) north of the river, near Thong Thang Kham market.

NAM NGUM LAKE

90 km (56 mi) north of Vientiane via Phonhong on Hwy. 13.

Forested mountains surround this island-dotted reservoir lake, which is accessible by car from Vientiane. Floating restaurants here serve freshly caught lake fish, and there's a large hotel complex, the Dansavanh Nam Ngum Resort. Visitors who have built substantial amounts of time into their itineraries to explore Laos, may want to skip this trip as there are others that are far better. But those who only have a few days in the country will enjoy this side trip as a way to see a bit of Laos's countryside without having to travel too far from Vientiane. Green Discovery Laos (⇨ *Laos Planner*) offers excellent day trips that include a boat ride on the lake.

GETTING HERE & AROUND

There are morning departures from Talat Sao Bus Station to the Nam Ngum Dam (15,000 kip) that take about three hours, but to really take in the area, it is best to do an adventure tour with Green Discovery Laos. Hiring a car and driver will run upwards of $60 per day. If you're driving, take Highway 10 north from Vientiane to the Lao Zoo; from there, follow the road for the Dansavanh Resort.

PHU KHAO KHOUAY

40 km (25 mi) northeast of Vientiane on Hwy. 10

Phu Khao Khouay, or Buffalo Horn Mountain, lies in a national park—a dramatic area of sheer sandstone cliffs, river gorges, abundant wildlife, and the Ang Nam reservoir. The park's three rivers empty into the Mekong. The banks of the reservoir have several simple restaurants and refreshment stands.

GETTING HERE & AROUND

The park is about three hours from Viantiane, via Highway 13 south to Tha Bok and then via a side road north from there. Green Discovery Laos (⇨ *Laos Planner*) runs reasonably priced one- to two-day treks and homestays; this is a good way to see the park, since hiring a car and driver is pricey. If coming on your own, buses run from Talat Sao to Tha Bok (15,000 kip); from there, songthaew go to Ban Hat Khai, where you can arrange treks.

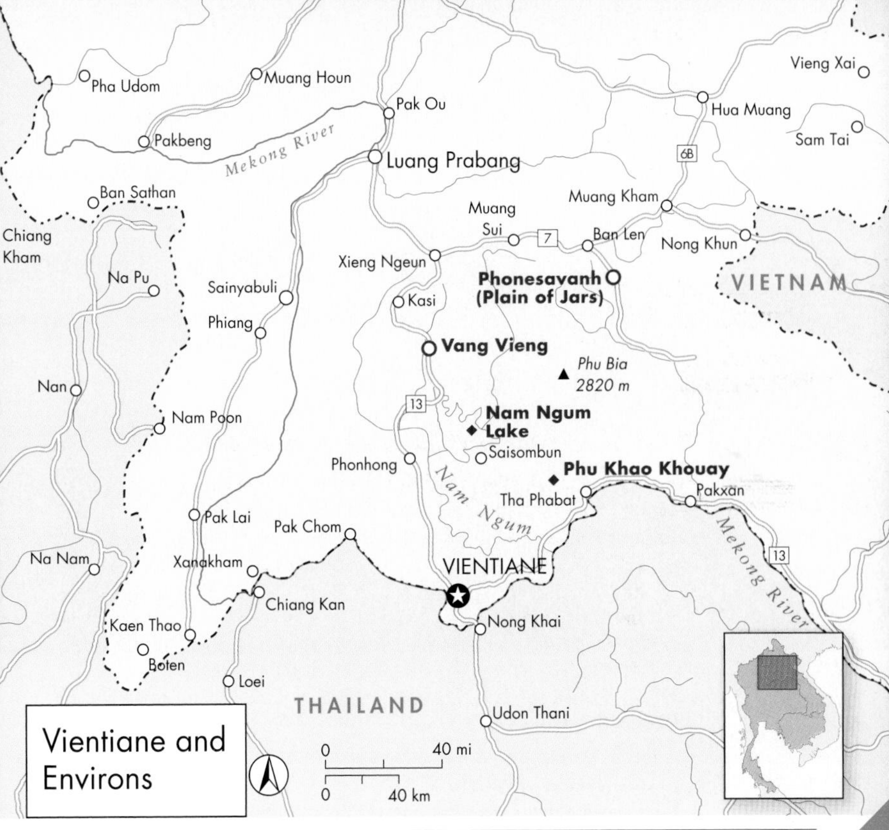

PLAIN OF JARS

9

★ *390 km (242 mi) northeast of Vientiane, 96 km (60 mi) southeast of Luang Prabang.*

One of the world's major archaeological wonders, the Plain of Jars is also one of the world's most tantalizing mysteries. The broad, mountain-ringed plain northeast of Vientiane is littered with hundreds of ancient stone and clay jars, some estimated to weigh 5 or 6 tons. The jars are said to be at least 2,000 years old, but to this day, nobody knows who made them or why. They survived heavy bombing during the Vietnam War, and their sheer size has kept them out of the hands of antiquities hunters.

The jars are scattered over three main areas, but only the Ban Ang site is accessible and worth visiting. Here you can find some 300 jars dotting a windswept plateau about 12 km (7½ mi) from Phonsavanh, capital of Xieng Khuang Province. This is true Hmong territory: you pass Hmong villages on the way from Phonsavanh to Ban Ang and on Highway 7, which leads east to the Vietnamese border at Nong Het. There's much of interest in this remote area along Highway 7, including hot mineral springs at Muang Kham. From Muang Kham, a road leads to Vieng Xay, which has more than 100 limestone caves, some

According to legend, the Plain of Jars was once inhabited by giants who built the jars to brew rice wine.

of them used as hideouts by the revolutionary Pathet Lao during the war years.

GETTING HERE & AROUND

A hard day's drive along Highway 7 from either Vientiane or Luang Prabang, the vast plain is difficult to reach. Travel operators in both cities, such as Diethelm Travel and Lao Youth Travel (⇨ *Laos Planner*), offer tours: You'll fly into Xieng Khuang Airport in Phonsavanh, 30 km (19 mi) away. Lao Airlines does this flight four times weekly for about $100. Most hotels and guesthouses in Phonsavanh can arrange trips to the plain for $10 to $15 per person in a minivan or jeep; you can also take a taxi to the edge of the plain for about $25.

The bus to Phonsavanh from Luang Prabang costs 85,000 kip and takes eight hours. From Vientiane, it is 120,000 kip and is 10 hours or more.

ESSENTIALS

Emergencies **Lao Mongol Hospital** (*Phonsavanh ☎ 061/312018*).

WHERE TO EAT & STAY

$ ECLECTIC ✕ **Maly Restaurant.** Housed in the hotel of the same name, the Maly serves a large selection of both Lao and Western dishes, which are surprisingly good given Phonsavanh's remoteness. Staples include different kinds of larb and decent curries, along with some Western dishes. Street names aren't widely used here, so just ask a local to point you to Maly. ✉ *Phonsavanh* ☎ *061/312031* ▭ *No credit cards.*

$$ **Vansana Plain of Jars.** On a hilltop overlooking Phonsavanh, this is the best hotel in the city. The guest rooms are comfortably furnished and have balconies, minibars, and TVs. **Pros:** great views of surrounding area; large bathtubs; big TVs. **Cons:** isolated from town; popular with tour groups. ✉ *Phonthan Rd., Phonsavanh* ☎ *61/213170 up to 75* *36 rooms* *In-hotel: restaurant, laundry service* *No credit cards* *CP.*

VANG VIENG

★ *160 km (99 mi) north of Vientiane.*

The town of Vang Vieng was discovered in the mid-1990s by backpackers traveling between Vientiane and Luang Prabang on Highway 13. It's not only a convenient stopover, but also a town bordered by an attractive countryside, including the Nam Song River and a dramatic range of jagged limestone mountains. During the Vietnam War, the United States maintained an airstrip in the town center; there are rumors that the abandoned tarmac will soon field direct flights from Luang Prabang. These days the town center is jampacked with bars and backpacker hangouts, but you can escape the noise and the crowds by making for the river, which is lined with guesthouses and restaurants catering to both backpackers and those on a more flexible budget. The river is clean and good for swimming and kayaking, and the mountains beyond are riddled with caves and small pleasant swimming holes. River trips and caving expeditions are organized by every guesthouse and hotel. ⚠ **Note that the treks to the caves can be fairly arduous, and some are only accessible by motorbike.** The less-adventurous adventurer can rent an inner tube for $6 and float down the river for a few hours, starting at the riverside rope swing and ending at one of 10 island bars on the north end of town.

VANG VIENG PADDLING ADVENTURE

Xplore Asia (✉ *Vang Vieng* ☎ *030/5200746* 🌐 *www.xplore-asia.com*) offers a unique way to travel from Vang Vieng to Vientiane. Departing at 9:30 AM, you are transported downstream, where you get in a kayak for the four-hour paddle to Vientiane, stopping for lunch and a 33-foot rock jump into the river. You're picked up riverside outside Vientiane around 4 PM, reunited with your luggage, and dropped off at Nam Phu Fountain Square in Vientiane around 5 PM. The one-way trip costs a reasonable $20.

GETTING HERE & AROUND

BY BUS From Vientiane, you can take the Luang Prabang–bound VIP bus, which runs three times a day, takes three to four hours to reach Vang Vieng, and costs 70,000 kip. You can also take a local bus or songthaew from the northern bus station; it costs 50,000 kip and takes four to five hours.

If you're coming from Luang Prabang, VIP buses headed back to Vientiane stop here three times a day as well—the journey takes seven hours and costs 135,000 kip. Minivans to Vang Vieng can be arranged at travel agencies in both cities for about the same price as a VIP bus ticket.

A daily bus also goes to Phonsavanh (Plain of Jars) for 85,000 kip (9 hours).

BY SONGTHAEW Songthaew run from the bus station, 2 km (1 mi) north of town, to all hotels for 10,000 kip per person. They can also be hired for excursions farther afield; prepare to bargain.

ESSENTIALS

Emergencies **Provincial Hospital** (✉ *Ban Vieng Keo, Vang Vieng* ☎ *023/511604*).

WHERE TO EAT & STAY

$ ECLECTIC **La Verandah Riverside.** In a town noted for extremely bland food, this beautifully situated restaurant right on the river inside the Villa Nam Song Resort serves up a nice blend of Thai, Lao, French, and Western dishes. The *penang* curry is aromatic and full of flavor, as is the spaghetti *pad kee mao* (drunken noodles, with basil and chili sauce). On the French menu, there is coq au vin, ratatouille, and fresh organic salad. A fine French wine list complements the menu, and if you still have room, there is even homemade ice cream. ✉ *Riverside Rd., Ban Viengkeo,Vang Vieng* ☎ *023/511637* ▭ *MC, V.*

$ ★ **Ban Sabai Bungalows.** The chicest rooms in town are in traditional Lao-style thatch-roof bungalows that are raised on stilts. All bungalows have wooden floors, comfortable bedding, modern baths, and glass doors that open onto balconies with river views. The grounds have brick walkways and a pond, and they blend in harmoniously with the river habitat and pastoral fields and mountains across the water. The resort staff provide Laotian hospitality and friendly and competent service. The riverside restaurant has a great view along a quiet stretch of river. Bungalow 14 has the best location—right beside the Nam Song River. **Pros:** rustic rooms; private decks with river views; charming restaurant on river. **Cons:** small rooms; often fully booked; rooms fairly basic for price. ✉ *Nam Song River Rd.* ☎ *023/511088* ⊕ *www.xayohgroup.com* *13 bungalows* *In-hotel: restaurant, no-smoking rooms* ▭ *MC, V.*

$ **Elephant Crossing Hotel.** Every room at this modern four-story hotel has a river view, a balcony, hardwood floors, and wooden trim constructed of recycled bits of old Lao houses. The restaurant spills over onto the lawn and a patio alongside the river, where guests can sip complimentary tea and Lao coffee. A traditional herbal Lao sauna and massage room lie underneath the restaurant, and are a great respite after a day outdoors. ■ TIP→ **The dormitory-style room here is the best value in town (three beds, $10 per person).** **Pros:** excellent river views; free Wi-Fi in lobby; private balcony in each room. **Cons:** small rooms; fair walk to town center; often crowded with tour groups. ✉ *Ban Viengkeo (Namsong Riverside)* ☎ *023/511232 or 020/560–2830* ⊕ *www.theelephantcrossinghotel.com* *32 rooms* *In-hotel: restaurant, Wi-Fi, no-smoking rooms* ▭ *MC, V.*

¢ **Saysong Guest House.** Cheap. Riverside. Did we mention cheap? You won't find a better price ($5–$12) for a riverside location. Most rooms are ultrabasic but clean, and the location just can't be beat. The three rooms that face the river have extras like TVs and minibars; a few more rooms have air-conditioning. **TIP→ Book in advance, especially if you want a river-view room—even in low season this place is normally full.** **Pros:** excellent location in heart of town; river views from some rooms; super value. **Cons:** cheaper rooms rather dark and very basic; west-facing rooms get very hot in afternoon. *Ban Savang 023/511130 koodhangmee@yahoo.com 31 rooms In-room: no a/c (some), no TV (some). In-hotel: laundry service No credit cards.*

LUANG PRABANG & NORTHERN LAOS

For all its popularity as a tourist destination, Luang Prabang remains one of the most remote cities in Southeast Asia. Although a highway now runs north to the Chinese border, the hinterland of Luang Prabang is mostly off-the-beaten-track territory, a mountainous region of impenetrable forests and deep river valleys. Despite Luang Prabang's air links to the rest of the country and the outside world, the Mekong River is still a preferred travel route. Passenger craft and freight barges ply the river's length as far as China in the north and near the Cambodian border in the south.

LUANG PRABANG

390 km (242 mi) north of Vientiane.

This is Laos's religious and artistic capital, and its combination of impressive natural surroundings, historic architecture, and friendly inhabitants make it one of the region's most pleasant towns. The city's abundance of ancient temples led UNESCO to declare it a World Heritage Site in 1995, and since then it's been bustling with construction and renovation activity.

But the charm of Luang Prabang is not exclusively architectural—just as pleasant are the people, who seem to spend as much time on the streets as they do in their homes. Children play on the sidewalks while matrons gossip in the shade, young women in traditional dress zip past on motor scooters, and Buddhist monks in saffron robes stroll by with black umbrellas, which protect their shaven heads from the tropical sun.

⚠ **Despite scores of guesthouses, finding accommodation here can be a challenge in the peak season. And when you visit the main attractions, be prepared for crowds of tourists.**

GETTING HERE & AROUND

BY AIR There are direct flights to Luang Prabang from both Bangkok and Chiang Mai. Lao Airlines operates a thrice-weekly service from Bangkok to Luang Prabang and five flights weekly from Chiang Mai to

9

Luang Prabang. Bangkok Airways flies direct twice daily from Bangkok to Luang Prabang, and onwards to Siem Reap.

Lao Airlines also has several flights a day between Vientiane and Luang Prabang, plus three weekly flights from Vientiane to Huay Xai.

Luang Prabang International Airport is 4 km (2½ mi) northeast of the city. The taxi ride to the city center costs $6.

BY BIKE Biking is one of the best ways to visit all of the interesting sights within Luang Prabang, and many shops in town rent bikes for $5 per day (⇨ *Biking in Luang Prabang, below*).

BY BOAT & FERRY In Luang Prabang you can find a boat for hire just about anywhere along the entire length of the road bordering the Mekong River; the main jetty is on the river side of Wat Xieng Thong.

Buses from Vientiane arrive four to five times daily and take between eight and 11 hours. You have your choice of VIP (usually with a/c and toilets aboard), express, and regular buses; prices range from 100,000 to 135,000 kip. **■ TIP→ You'll pay more if you buy your ticket from an agency in town.** There are also buses to Phonsavanh (8 hours; 100,000 kip), Vang Vieng (5 hours; 135,000 kip), Udomxai (4 hours; 60,000 kip), and Luang Nam Tha (9 hours; 100,000 kip), among other places. There are two bus terminals in Luang Prabang, the northern bus terminal, out near the airport, and the Ban Naluang southern bus terminal, in the south of town, with services to respective destinations.

BY CAR Although you can drive from Vientiane to Luang Prabang, it takes seven to eight hours to make the 242-km (150-mi) trip along the meandering, but paved, road up into the mountains.

BY TAXI, TUK-TUK, & SONGTHAEW Tuk-tuks and songthaews make up Luang Prabang's public transport system. They cruise all the streets and are easy to flag down. Plan on paying around $1 to $2 for a trip within the city. The few taxis in town must be booked through your hotel or guesthouse.

BIKING IN LUANG PRABANG

For years, bicycles have been a popular way to get around Luang Prabang. But in early 2008, for mysterious reasons, the Lao government made it illegal for foreigners to rent motorcycles and bikes in town. At this writing, enforcement of the new law is lax, but the number of rental shops has dwindled and most guesthouses no longer rent bikes. However, it's still legal to go on a bicycle tour with a Lao company or guide.

ESSENTIALS

Emergencies For medical and police emergencies, use the services of your hotel or guesthouse. **International Clinic** (✉ *Ban Thongchaloen, Luang Prabang* ☎ *071/252048 or 071/252049*).

Visitor and Tour Info **Lao Youth Travel** and **Diethelm Travel** *(⇨ Laos Planner)* have Luang Prabang branches. **White Elephant Adventures** (✉ *Sisavangvong Rd., Luang Prabang* ☎ *020/589–4394 or 030/514–0243* 🌐 *www.white-elephant-adventures-laos.com*) runs single and multi-day hiking, biking, and kayaking adventures.

EXPLORING LUANG PRABANG

Some 36 temples are scattered around town, making Luang Prabang a pleasant place to explore on a rented bicycle or on foot. When you need a break from temple-hopping, there are plenty of appealing eateries and fashionable boutiques. Waking early one morning to watch the throngs of monks make their alms runs at dawn is highly recommended. Your hotel should be able to tell you what time to get up and suggest a good viewing spot.

MAIN ATTRACTIONS

4 **Phu Si Hill.** Several shrines and temples and a golden stupa crown this forested hill, but the best reason to ascend its 328 steps is to enjoy the view from the summit: a panorama of Luang Prabang, the Nam Khan and Mekong rivers, and the surrounding mountains. It's a popular spot for watching the sunset (just be sure to bring insect repellent), but the view from atop old Phu Si is splendid at any hour. ■ **TIP→ If you're not up for the steep climb up the staircase, try the more enjoyable hike up the trail on the "back" side of the hill.** ✉ *Rathsavong Rd.* ☎ *No phone* 🎫 *10,000 kip* ⏲ *Daily 6–6.*

A GOOD WALK (OR RIDE)

Touring the city's major sights takes a full day—maybe longer if you climb Phu Si Hill, which has particularly lovely views at sunset. The evening bazaar on Sisavangvong Road starts around 6 PM. Though the distances between these attractions are walkable, you may not want to do this all on foot if it's really hot out. Rent a bike, or break this into a few shorter walks, and stay out of the sun during the heat of the day.

Start your tour of Luang Prabang at the pulsing heart of the city: the **Tribal Market** at the crossroads of Sisavangvong Road and Setthathirat Road. From here, head northeast along Sisavangvong, stopping on the left at one of the city's most beautiful temples, **Wat Mai.** Magnificent wood carvings and golden murals decorate the main pillars and portico entrance to the temple. Continue down Sisavangvong to the compound of the **Royal Palace,** with its large bronze statue of King Sisavangvong. On leaving the palace grounds by the main entrance, climb the staircase to **Phu Si Hill.** The climb is steep and takes about 15 minutes, but you'll be rewarded with an unforgettable view of Luang Prabang and the surrounding countryside.

Back in front of the Royal Palace, follow Sisavangvong toward the confluence of the Mekong and Nam Khan rivers, where you can find another fascinating Luang Prabang temple, **Wat Xieng Thong.** Leaving the compound on the Mekong River side, walk back to the city center along the romantic waterside road, which is fronted by several French colonial houses and Lao traditional homes. Passing the port area behind the Royal Palace, continue on to the crossroads at Wat Phu Xay; turn right here to return to the Tribal Market. Every evening there's a local night bazaar, stretching from the Tribal Market to the Royal Palace.

3 ★ **Royal Palace.** In a walled compound at the foot of Phu Si Hill stands this palace, the former home of the royal Savang family. Built at the beginning of the 20th century, the palace served as the royal residence until the Pathet Lao took over Laos in 1975 and exiled Crown Prince Savang Vatthana and his children to a remote region of the country (their fate has never been established). It still has the feel of a large family home—a maze of teak-floor rooms surprisingly modest in scale. The largest of them is the **throne room,** with its gilded furniture, colorful mosaic-covered walls, and display cases filled with rare Buddha images, royal regalia, and other priceless artifacts.

The walls of the **king's reception room** are decorated with scenes of traditional Lao life painted in 1930 by the French artist Alex de Fautereau. The **queen's reception room** contains a collection of royal portraits by the Russian artist Ilya Glazunov. The room also has cabinets full of presents given to the royal couple by visiting heads of state; a model moon lander and a piece of moon rock from U.S. president Richard Nixon share shelf space with an exquisite Sevres tea set presented by French president Charles de Gaulle and fine porcelain teacups from Chinese leader Mao Tse-tung. Other exhibits in this eclectic collec-

Phu Si Hill 4
Royal Palace 3
Tribal Market 1
Wat Mai 2
Wat Visun 6
Wat Xieng Thong 5

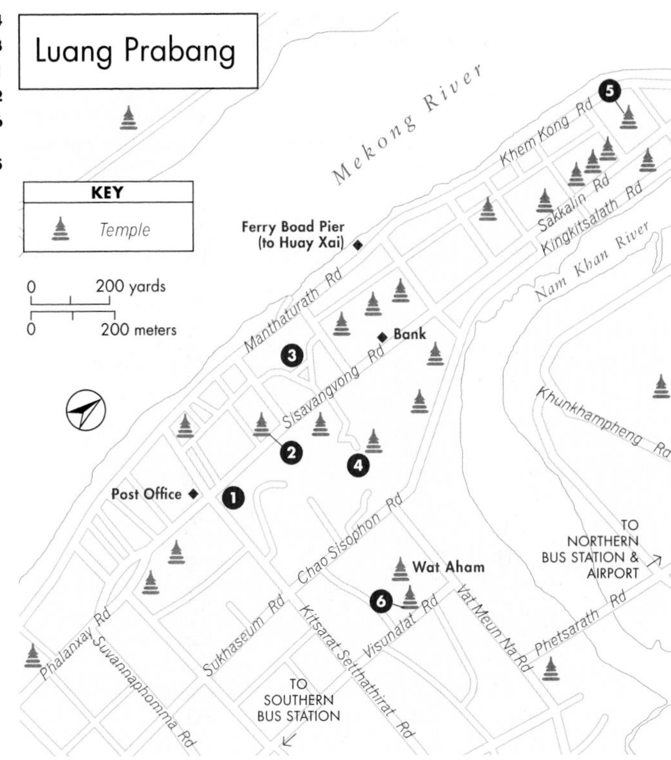

9

tion include friezes removed from local temples, Khmer drums, and elephant tusks with carved images of the Buddha.

The museum's most prized exhibit is the **Pha Bang,** a gold image of the Buddha slightly less than 3 feet tall and weighing more than 100 pounds. Its history goes back to the 1st century, when it was cast in Sri Lanka; it was brought to Luang Prabang from Cambodia in 1353 as a gift to King Fa Ngum. This event is celebrated as the introduction of Buddhism as an official religion to Laos, and Pha Bang is venerated as the protector of the faith. An ornate temple called Ho Pha Bang, near the entrance to the palace compound, is being restored to house the image.

Tucked away behind the palace is a crumbling wooden garage that houses the royal fleet of aging automobiles. **■ TIP→ You'll need about two hours to work through the Royal Palace's maze of rooms.** ✉ *Sisavangvong Rd., across from Phu Si Hill* ☎ *071/212470* *30,000 kip* ⏲ *Weekdays 8:30–11 and 1–4.*

5 ★ **Wat Xieng Thong.** Luang Prabang's most important and impressive temple complex is Wat Xieng Thong, a collection of ancient buildings near the tip of the peninsula, where the Mekong and Nam Khan rivers meet. Constructed in 1559–60, the main temple is one of the

few structures to have survived centuries of marauding Vietnamese, Chinese, and Siamese armies, and it's regarded as one of the region's best-preserved examples of Buddhist art and architecture. The intricate golden facades, colorful murals, sparkling glass mosaics, and low, sweeping roofs of the entire ensemble of buildings (which overlap to make complex patterns) all combine to create a feeling of harmony and peace.

> **WORD OF MOUTH**
>
> "Wat Xiang Thong is an enchanting mélange of buildings capped by sweeping graceful Lao roofs and embellished by glass mosaics, tiles, and black and red walls stenciled in gold leaf. I visited several times during the course of my stay here and it remains the most enduring memory of my time in Luang Prabang." –ekscrunchy

The interior of the main temple has decorated wooden columns and a ceiling covered with wheels of dharma, representing the Buddha's teaching. The exterior is just as impressive thanks to mosaics of colored glass that were added at the beginning of 20th century. Several small **chapels** at the sides of the main hall are also covered with mosaics and contain various images of the Buddha. The bronze 16th-century reclining Buddha in one chapel was displayed in the 1931 Paris Exhibition. The mosaic on the back wall of that chapel commemorates the 2,500th anniversary of the Buddha's birth with a depiction of Lao village life. The chapel near the compound's east gate, with a gilded facade, contains the royal family's funeral statuary and urns, including a 40-foot-long wooden boat that was used as a hearse. ⊠*Sisavangvong Rd.* ☎*071/212470* *20,000 kip* *Daily 6–6.*

ALSO WORTH SEEING

1 **Tribal Market.** A hive of daily activity, this central covered market is usually packed with shoppers sifting through piles of produce and household goods, including textiles and Chinese-made items. Hill tribe people often shop here, particularly during cooler weather, when they journey into town to buy winter blankets and clothing. ⊠*Sisavangvong Rd. at Setthathirat Rd.* *Daily 7–5.*

2 **Wat Mai.** This small but lovely temple next to the Royal Palace compound dates from 1796. Its four-tier roof is characteristic of Luang Prabang's religious architecture, but more impressive are the magnificent wood carvings and gold-leaf murals on the main pillars and portico entrance to the temple. These intricate panels depict the last life of the Buddha, as well as various Asian animals. During the Bun Pimai festival (Lao New Year), the Pha Bang sacred Buddha image is carried from the Royal Palace compound to Wat Mai for ritual cleansing ceremonies. ⊠*Sisavangvong Rd.* ☎*No phone* *10,000 kip* *Daily 6–6.*

6 **Wat Visun.** The 16th-century Wat Visun and neighboring **Wat Aham** play a central role in Lao New Year celebrations, when ancestral masks, called *phu gneu gna gneu*, are taken from Wat Aham and displayed in public. Wat Visun was built in 1503, during the reign of King Visunalat, who had the temple named after himself. Within the

CLOSE UP

The Prabang Buddha

But for a few simple facts, the Prabang Buddha image, the namesake of Luang Prabang, is shrouded in mystery. This much *is* known: the Prabang image is approximately 33 inches tall and weighs 110 pounds. Both hands of the Buddha are raised in double *abhaya mudra* position (the meaning of which has predictably ambiguous symbolic interpretations, including dispelling fear, teaching reason, and offering protection, benevolence, and peace). Historically, the Prabang Buddha has been a symbol of religious and political authority, including the legitimate right to rule the kingdom of Laos. Beyond that, there is much speculation.

It is believed that the image was cast in bronze in Ceylon (Sri Lanka) between the 1st and 9th century, although it has also been suggested that it is made primarily of gold, with silver and bronze alloys. Regardless of its composition, the double-raised palms indicate a later construction (14th century), and a possibly Khmer origin.

Nonetheless, in 1359 the Prabang was given to Fa Ngum, the son-in-law of the Khmer king at Angkor, and brought to Muang Swa, which was subsequently renamed Luang Prabang, the capital of the newly formed kingdom of Lang Xang. The Prabang Buddha became a symbol of the legitimate rule of the king and a device for promoting Theravada Buddhism throughout Laos.

In 1563, the Prabang image was relocated, along with the seat of power, to the new capital city of Vientiane. In 1778, Siamese invaders ransacked Vientiane and made off with both the Prabang and Emerald Buddhas.

The Prabang was returned to Laos in 1782 after political and social unrest in Siam was attributed to the image. Similar circumstances surrounded the subsequent capture and release of the Prabang by the Siamese in 1827 and 1867.

Following its return to Laos, the Prabang was housed in Wat Wisunalat, Luang Prabang's oldest temple, and then at Wat Mai. In 1963, during the reign of Sisavang Vatthana, Laos's final monarch, construction began on Haw Pha Bang, a temple to house the Prabang on the grounds of the palace.

However, in 1975 the communist Pathet Lao rose to power, absolved the monarchy, and installed a communist regime. The communist government, having little respect for any symbol of royalty *or* Buddhism, may have handed over the Prabang to Moscow in exchange for assistance from the Soviet Union. Other accounts of the image have it spirited away to Vientiane for safekeeping in a vault, where it may still reside today.

Regardless, there is a 33-inch-tall Buddha statue, real or replica, housed behind bars in an unassuming room beside the entrance to the Royal Palace Museum (until Haw Pha Bang is completed). On the third day of every Lao New Year (April 13–15), the image is ferried via chariot to Wat Mai, where it is cleansed with water by reverent Laotians.

In regards to its authenticity, a respectable and reliable source told me simply this, "People believe that it is real because the Prabang Buddha belongs in Luang Prabang."

–Trevor Ranges

compound is a large and unusual watermelon-shaped stupa called **That Makmo** (literally Watermelon Stupa). The 100-foot-high mound is actually a royal tomb, where many small precious Buddha statues were found when Chin Haw marauders destroyed the city in the late 19th century (these statues have since been moved to the Royal Palace). The temple hall was rebuilt in 1898 along the lines of the original wooden structure and now houses an impressive collection of Buddha statues, stone inscriptions, and other Buddhist art. ✉ *Visunalat Rd.* ☎ *No phone* 🎟 *10,000 kip* ⏲ *Daily 6–6.*

A JACK OF ALL TRADES

L'etranger Books and Tea (✉ *Ban Aphay, next to Hive Bar*) has a little bit of everything for those in search of a sightseeing break. The first floor contains a collection of new and used books in a variety of languages for sale or for loan (2,000 kip per hour or 5,000 kip per day). Upstairs, 20 years of *National Geographic* magazines line the walls and patrons sip on tea, coffee, and smoothies or nibble on snacks while reclining on comfortable and chic floor pillows. In the evening, the place fills up for nightly DVD screenings. A gallery in an adjoining room on the second floor features local Lao artists.

WHERE TO EAT

$ INTERNATIONAL ✕ **Apsara.** Occupying a lovely spot overlooking the Nam Khan River, the Apsara serves fine western and eastern cuisine, ranging from baguette sandwiches for lunch to elegant set dinners featuring fresh fish and meat dishes such as braised pork belly on roasted pumpkin with eggplant chutney. There's an extensive wine list, and the quiet location is an excellent place for a leisurely meal. In high season you may need a reservation. ✉ *Kingkitsarath St., Baan Wat Sene, Luang Prabang* ☎ *071/254670* ▭ *MC, V.*

¢–$ ECLECTIC ✕ **Indochina Spirit.** For a hearty meal, head to this eclectic Thai-run restaurant, housed in a 1920s residence that once belonged to a royal physician, where a selection of Lao specialties costs just $4. Start with an appetizer of Mekong seaweed or banana flower salad, followed by steak. Italian-style pastas and pizza are also on the menu, and delicious pancakes are served for breakfast. ✉ *50–51 Ban Wat That* ☎ *071/252372* ▭ *MC, V.*

¢ CAFE ✕ **Joma Bakery Cafe.** Canadians run this cheap, friendly self-service restaurant, where an in-house bakery turns out delicious pastries, pizzas, salads, and French bread. The homemade soups are excellent. ✉ *Chao Fa Ngum Rd.* ☎ *071/252292* ▭ *No credit cards* ⏲ *Closed Sun.*

¢–$ CAFE ✕ **Le Café et Restaurant Ban Vat Sene.** Sidewalk seating and a retractable brown-striped awning contribute to the traditional French café atmosphere here. Freshly made quiche, baguettes, and *grandes tartines* (large slices of homemade bread with various toppings) are the highlights of the menu. Across from Villa Santi on the northern end of town, the café is a relaxing place for a meal or simply a cup of coffee and some pastries. ■ **TIP→ A $6 purchase also buys you unlimited Wi-Fi access.** ✉ *Sakkarin Rd.* ☎ *071/252482* ▭ *MC, V.*

$$$ ★ FRENCH **L'Elephant Restaurant Français.** When you can't face another serving of rice or spicy sauces, it's time to walk down the hill from the Villa Santi to this pleasant corner restaurant. The menu is traditional French, with a bit of Lao influence, especially when it comes to the ingredients. Consider, for example, the *chevreuil au poivre vert* (local venison in a pepper sauce). There are always the three-course set meal and several daily specials, which usually include fish fresh from the Mekong. Seating is available in the bright, airy dining room or on the sidewalk, behind a barrier of plants. ✉*Ban Wat Nong* ☎*071/252482* ▭*MC, V.*

COOKING CLASSES

Restaurant **Tamnak Lao** (⇨ *below*) doesn't just serve tasty Laotian food, it also teaches you how to cook it yourself. The restaurant's school comprehensively explains Lao cuisine, cultural influences, and provides ingredients for 12 recipes. Full-day (from 10 to 6) classes of no more than eight students each are held daily. **Tum Tum Cheng** (⇨ *below*) now offers cooking classes as well. You can spend a half day learning one of their 150 recipes, some of which are adapted from the cookbook of Phia Sing, former chef to the Lao royal family.

¢–$ CAFE **Luang Prabang Bakery.** It would be difficult not to eventually wander into Luang Prabang Bakery—it has a great central location and the most enticing atmosphere of the several outdoor-seating restaurants in this part of town. It certainly is a great spot for a cool drink and some prime people-watching. The restaurant also serves more than 20 different Laotian dishes, such as *jo mart len pak lae kout noi* (steamed fresh vegetables with a spicy grilled-tomato sauce), and you can also satisfy a craving for Western food with a tasty hamburger, a pizza, some pasta, or even a steak. The menu includes a variety of French and Australian wines. ✉*Sisavangvong Rd.* ☎*071/252499* ▭*V.*

¢ ASIAN **Pak Huay Mixay.** Venison steak is recommended at this long-established Asian restaurant, a favorite with locals. Start your meal, though, with a more conventional Lao dish, such as tom yum soup (with lemongrass, coriander, chilies, and chicken or fish), and end it with a glass of lao-lao. ✉*75/6 Sothikhoummane Rd., Ban Xieng Muan* ☎*071/212260 or 020/551–1496* ▭*No credit cards.*

$ ★ LAO **Tamnak Lao.** If you're looking for excellent Lao food, this noted restaurant and cooking school is the place to start. Try a set menu to sample a variety of the country's cooking styles or order from the lengthy menu that includes *kaipan,* a crispy dried Mekong River plant covered with sesame seeds and served with a local chutney (the local equivalent of chips and salsa), and *orlam,* an eggplant "casserole" that can be compared to an exotic *gaeng kiew waan* (Thai green curry) and is a local favorite. You can even try venison, wild boar, or kangaroo steaks (the latter arguably not so traditional). ✉*Sakkarin Rd.* ☎*071/252525* ▭*MC, V.*

$ LAO **Tum Tum Cheng.** This popular restaurant also runs a well-known cooking school. Even if you don't take a class (about 250,000 kip per day), come for the delicious citronella Mekong catfish, sautéed chicken in

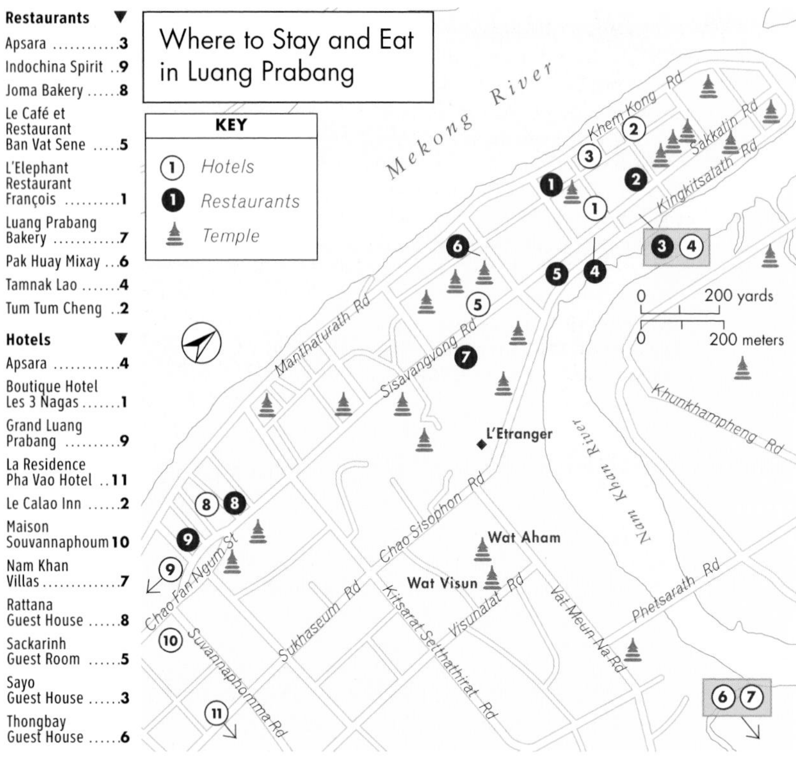

banana leaf, or eggplant with chili sauce. ✉ *Sakkarine Rd, Baan Wat Kily, Luang Prabang* ☎ *071/252019* ▭ *MC, V.*

WHERE TO STAY

New hotels are shooting up in Luang Prabang to accommodate the growing numbers of tourists. Many of the most attractive of them are in converted buildings dating from French colonial days, and two old favorites are former royal properties.

$$–$$$ ★ **Apsara.** With its white facade and balustrades and its riverside location, this French-style *maison* would be at home in southern France; instead, it's the trendiest boutique hotel in Luang Prabang. **TIP→ The plush silk-adorned restaurant ($) is worth a visit, even if you're not staying the night (it claims to serve the driest martini in town).** The reasonably priced rooms have floor-to-ceiling windows that face east, so you can catch the sunrise over the nearby mountains. Rooms 1 through 5 on the second floor have the best river or mountain views. At this writing, a second hotel under the same management, with a swimming pool, was scheduled to open directly across the river from the Apsara in mid-2009. **Pros:** quiet riverside location; beautifully furnished rooms; rain-style showerheads in some bathrooms. **Cons:** downstairs rooms have no views; standard rooms a bit dark; often fully booked. ✉ *Kingkitsarat Rd.* ☎ *071/212420* 🌐 *www.theapsara.com* *13 rooms* *In-room:*

safe, refrigerator. In-hotel: restaurant, bar, laundry service, Wi-Fi, no-smoking rooms ▭*MC, V* 🍽*BP.*

$$$–$$$$ Fodor's Choice ★ **Boutique Hotel Les 3 Nagas.** This turn-of-the-19th-century mansion stands under official UNESCO World Heritage Site protection, thanks in no small measure to the efforts of the French owner to retain its weathered but handsome colonial look. The wooden floors and clay tiles are original, and the large rooms are furnished with dark wood, silks, and homespun local fabrics (you can also buy these fabrics in the hotel shop, along with Lao teas, coffee, and spices). Some rooms have four-poster beds. Superior Room 6 has a balcony like that of the executive suite, ideal for watching the morning alms procession of local monks. **Pros:** private patios; spacious bathrooms with claw-foot tubs. **Cons:** often fully booked; poor lighting around bed; 20% service charge. ✉*Sakkarin Rd., Ban Wat Nong* ☎*071/253888* 🌐*www.alilahotels.com* *15 rooms* *In-room: safe, refrigerator, Wi-Fi. In-hotel: restaurant, room service, laundry service, no-smoking rooms* ▭*MC, V* 🍽*BP.*

$$$ **Grand Luang Prabang.** This Thai-owned hotel occupies the former residence of nationalist hero Prince Petsarath (1890–1959), whose villa stands amid the hotel's new (but traditionally designed) buildings. The hotel has an unmatched location on a bend of the Mekong River, and though guest rooms are set back a bit, most have river views. Rooms are spacious and have hardwood floors, white marble baths, and sliding glass doors that open onto large balconies. It's 5 km (2½ mi) from Luang Prabang, near the village of Xieng Keo; a shuttle provides regular transportation to town and the airport. **Pros:** riverside restaurant; quiet swimming pool; lovely gardens. **Cons:** out-of-the-way location; rather small standard rooms; no Wi-Fi. ✉*Ban Xieng Keo, Khet Sangkalok* ☎*071/253851 up to 57* 🌐*www.grandluangprabang.com* *78 rooms* *In-room: refrigerator. In-hotel: restaurant, bar, bicycles, laundry service, no-smoking rooms* ▭*AE, MC, V* 🍽*BP.*

$$$$ **La Residence Phou Vao Hotel.** Its prime position on Kite Hill gives this sumptuous hotel the best views in town. Traditional Lao touches are everywhere and create a sense of exotic luxury in the rosewood-furnished rooms. In the evening, you can relax over cocktails at the Dok Chama Bar and soak in the restful garden surroundings. The restaurant ($$$$) is among Luang Prabang's best, serving authentic Lao food and rich French dishes. Seven different therapies are available at the spa; guests staying a full week can try a different treatment each day. **TIP→ Nonguests can use the small but picturesque pool area, including the steam room, for $10 per day.** The hotel provides free shuttle service into town for its guests. **Pros:** best views in town; infinity pool; luxury spa. **Cons:** on hill out of town; garden rooms do not have great views; not the best value. ✉*Phu Vao Hill* ☎*071/212530 up to 33* 🌐 *www.residencephouvao.com* *34 rooms* *In-room: safe, refrigerator. In-hotel: restaurant, room service, bar, pool, spa, laundry service, Internet terminal, no-smoking rooms* ▭*AE, MC, V.*

$$ **Le Calao Inn.** Fronting the Mekong and just down the street from Wat Xieng Thong is this small hotel, which was resurrected from a ruined mansion built by a Portuguese merchant in 1904. Four guest

9

Samlors (three-wheeled bicycle carriage) are a leisurely way to get around Luang Prabang.

rooms upstairs open onto a colonnaded veranda to views of the river and the hills beyond. The two rooms on the lower floor are larger—with three beds each—and have private terraces, but are a bit dark. The Buasavan Restaurant on the ground floor serves French and Asian fare. ■ **TIP→ Because of the hotel's small size and popularity, it's highly advisable to book ahead November–April.** **Pros:** quiet spot on the Mekong; lovely Mediterranean restaurant; upstairs rooms have private balconies with river views. **Cons:** almost always booked; interiors not as elegant as exterior; some rooms have unpleasant smell. ✉ *Khem Kong Rd.* ☎ *071/212100* *6 rooms* *In-room: no TV. In-hotel: restaurant, laundry service, no-smoking rooms* *MC, V* *BP.*

$$$$ **Maison Souvannaphoum.** The once-run-down residence of Prince Souvannaphoum, prime minister in the 1960s, has been transformed into one of the top hotels in Luang Prabang. The colonial-style mansion contains the reception area, an open-air restaurant, a bar, and upstairs, the suites; guest rooms occupy a newer building alongside the main building. Rooms are large, bright, and attractively furnished, with small balconies overlooking tropical greenery. Ask for a room at the back, away from the busy street, for more peace and quiet, or opt for the prince's bedroom suite, which is spacious, elegant, and romantic. After Banyan Tree Hotels took over the resort in 2005, they opened the Angsana Spa in the hotel, which offers a variety of luxurious treatments but is unfortunately located along a busy main road. **Pros:** spa; beautiful photo gallery; exclusive, private feel. **Cons:** views not inspiring; long walk from main dining and shopping area; often booked. ✉ *Chao Fa Ngum Rd.* ☎ *071/254609* *www.coloursofangsana.com* *24*

rooms *In-room: refrigerator, Wi-Fi. In-hotel: restaurant, bar, pool, spa, laundry service, no-smoking rooms* *MC, V* *BP.*

$$ ★ **Nam Khan Villas.** Proprietors Graham and Caroline have successfully combined the atmosphere of traditional Laos with the comforts of the Western world; the resort is laid out like a local village, with meandering paths connecting reconstructed 40-year-old Laotian houses set amid local flora and overlooking the Nam Khan River. The Mediterranean-style, open-air **El Gecko restaurant** serves delectable European and Lao tapas (Caroline has 30 years' experience catering to an international clientele in Spain). Although a bit farther from town than the other major hotels, the resort is connected via a walking path to the Ban Phanom weaving village, and tuk-tuks can be readily called for forays into town, plus bicycles are available. **Pros:** airy and cool traditional Lao building style; neat riverside jungle setting; plenty of hot water. **Cons:** rooms a bit dark; frequently booked in high season; no Internet. *Just before the New Bridge on the New Road leading to the airport, turn right onto a small dirt road. Follow the dirt road 100 meters; the hotel is on the right* *071/254631 or 020/777–1305* *www.nkvresort.com* *9 rooms* *In-room: no a/c, no phone, no TV. In-hotel: restaurant, bar, bicycles, no-smoking rooms* *No credit cards.*

¢–$ **Rattana Guest House.** Family-run guesthouses are common in Luang Prabang, but this one certainly makes you feel right at home. The Rattana sisters Somsanith and Somporn, their mother, and their adopted daughter are extremely knowledgeable and helpful (one sister works for an established tour operator, the other is a doctor). Rooms are bright, clean, and comfortable. Rooms 101 and 102 have small balconies; note that 102 has a detached, though private, bath. There's no restaurant, but there is a breakfast room. **Pros:** spotlessly clean; new building with teak floors; firm mattresses. **Cons:** a bit of a walk to main dining and shopping area; rooms in new wing a bit small; no views. *Koksack St., 4/2 Ban What That* *071/252255* *13 rooms* *In-hotel: no-smoking rooms* *No credit cards.*

¢ **Sackarinh Guest Room.** This friendly place in the center of town is the ideal Luang Prabang guesthouse—it's spotless and it's super cheap. Rooms are basic, but furnished with TVs and private bathrooms. Best of all, you are located near a row of bakeries: the Croissant d' Or is right next door, and the Luang Prabang Bakery and Scandinavian Bakery are just across the road. **Pros:** ideal location; very clean; friendly staff. **Cons:** some rooms dark; low ceilings; often booked in high season. *Sisavangvong Rd.* *071/254512 or 020/544–2001* *sackarinh_guestroom@hotmail.com* *11 rooms* *In-room: no phone.* *No credit cards.*

$ **Sayo Guest House.** An elegant white colonial-style hotel with green shutters, Sayo Guest House is almost prototypical Luang Prabang style. Chic yet unpretentious, the hotel consists of rooms with river views, furnishings made from local wood, mosquito nets, and Lao comforters, the combined effect being old-world charm and a relaxed vibe. The second floor has hardwood floors, and rooms 1 and 2 have private balconies, ideal for lazy afternoon river-watching. **Pros:** serene riverside location; spacious, well-furnished rooms; some rooms have balconies.

9

Cons: some rooms lack big windows; often full in high season; a walk from central area. ✉*Kham Kong Rd.* ☎*071/252614* 🌐*www.sayoguesthouse.com* *13 rooms* *In-room: refrigerator. In-hotel: laundry service, no-smoking rooms* ▭*No credit cards.*

$ ★ **Thongbay Guest House.** Thongbay is just outside town, but it's right on the Nam Khan River. The resort is a small village of well-built, comfortable, thatch huts with fans. Stone and tile bathrooms are clean and surprisingly stylish for such a rustic retreat. Every bungalow has a deck with floor pillows and chairs from which to look out over the river or the beautiful gardens. It's about a 10-minute ride into town on a bicycle. **Pros:** relaxing private deck areas; quiet, pretty location; friendly neighborhood. **Cons:** out of town; no a/c; no Internet. ✉*On a small dirt road off 13 North Rd., near the New Bridge Ban Vieng Mai, Vat Sakem* ☎*071/253234* 🌐*www.thongbay-guesthouses.com* *In-room: no a/c, refrigerator. In-hotel: restaurant, laundry service, no-smoking rooms* ▭*No credit cards.*

NIGHTLIFE & THE ARTS

Luang Prabang's nightlife is limited. Monday, Wednesday, and Saturday evenings at 6:30, the **Royal Ballet Theater Phralak-Phralam** (☎*071/253705*) performs at the Royal Palace museum. The program includes local folk songs, a local *bai-si* ceremony, classical dances enacting episodes from the Indian *Ramayana* epic, and outdoor presentations of the music and dances of Lao minorities. Admission is $10.

Locals head to the nightclub **Muong Sua** (✉*Phu Vao Rd.*) for Lao-style folk and rock music. If you need a dancing partner, the waiters will find you one. Otherwise wait until the locals start line-dancing and simply get in line! When Muong Sua shuts down at 11:30 PM the party moves to **Dao Fa** (✉*Across from Southern Bus Terminal*), where Luang Prabang's young "nouveau riche" strut their stuff.

A number of bar-restaurants consisting of simple tables and chairs are set up on the hill above the Mekong River on Souvannakhamphong Road. On the other side of Phousi Hill are **Lao Lao Garden,** a casual, open air restaurant and bar, **L'etranger Books and Tea,** and the **Hive bar,** where young backpackers congregate within a dimly lit interior or around small outdoor "campfires" to mix, mingle, and share tales of the road. The three are located near the corner of Phou Si and Phommathay streets.

SPORTS & THE OUTDOORS

Many of the tour operators in town offer interesting rafting and kayaking trips, plus cycling expeditions. Several shops rent bikes for about $4 a day (*Biking in Luang Prabang, above*).

The owner of **White Elephant Adventures** (✉*Sisavangvong Rd., opposite Nazim Restaurant* ☎*020/589–4394 or 030/514–0243* 🌐*www.white-elephant-adventures-laos.com*), Derek, is as enthusiastic about sharing his adopted home country as he is about making sure each visitor's experiences are authentic and uncrowded and that the impact of these journeys on the local people and their environment is low. The tours are educational, led by local university students, and are constantly exploring new areas to provide a less touristy experience. Single- or multi-day hiking, biking, and kayaking adventures are available for groups of two to six people costing about $35 per head.

SHOPPING

Luang Prabang has two principal markets where you can find a large selection of handicrafts: the Dala Central Market, on Setthathirat Road, and the Tribal Market, on Sisavangvong Road. In the evening, most of Sisavangvong Road turns into an open bazaar, similar to Thailand's night markets. It's a pleasant place to stroll, bargain with hawkers, and stop for a simple meal and a beer at one of many roadside stalls.

Locally worked silver is cheap and very attractive. You can find a good selection at **Thit Peng** (✉ *48/2 Ban Wat That* ☎ *071/212327*).

Pathana Boupha (✉ *29/4 Ban Visoun* ☎ *071/212262*) is an antiques and textile shop and museum. It claims to produce the costumes and ornaments for the Miss New Year pageant in Luang Prabang (a seemingly prestigious endeavor). It has a dizzying array of goods on display, many of which are not for sale. Shoppers *can*, however, purchase textiles produced by a variety of different Laotian ethnic groups.

TAD SAE WATERFALL

15 km (9 mi) east of Luang Prabang.

Accessible only by boat, this spectacular waterfall is best visited in the rainy season, when the rivers are high and their waters thunder over the cascade. The waterfall features multilevel limestone formations divided into three steps with big pools beneath them—don't forget your bathing suit. There are some old waterwheels here and a small, simple resort nearby.

9

GETTING HERE & AROUND

From Luang Prabang, you can take a tuk-tuk east on Highway 13 for 13 km (8 mi) to the turnoff for the pristine Lao Lum riverside village of Ban Aen (15,000–20,000 kip). From Ban Aen, hire a boat (10,000 kip per person) for a two-minute trip upstream to the waterfall. However, it's easier to let one of Luang Prabang's many travel agencies arrange your trip for about 55,000 kip per person, including admission to the falls. Tours leave around 1 PM and return by 5. Adventure-tour agencies like White Elephant (⇨ *Sports & the Outdoors in Luang Prabang, above*) and Green Discovery (⇨ *Laos Planner*) also organize kayaking day trips to the falls.

PAK OU CAVES

25 km (16 mi) up the Mekong from Luang Prabang.

Set in high limestone cliffs above the Mekong River, at the point where it meets the Nam Ou River from northern Laos, are two sacred caves filled with thousands of Buddha statues dating from the 16th century. The lower cave, **Tham Thing,** is accessible from the river by a stairway and has enough daylight to allow you to find your way around. The stairway continues to the upper cave, **Tham Phum,** for which you need a flashlight. The admission charge of 20,000 kip includes a flashlight and a guide.

The town of Pak Ou, across the river from the caves and accessible by ferry, has several passable restaurants.

GETTING HERE & AROUND

It takes 1½ hours to get to Pak Ou by boat from Luang Prabang. Many agencies in town organize tours for 70,000 kip per person, including admission to the caves. Tours leave Luang Prabang around 8 AM and include visits to waterside villages for a perusal of the rich variety of local handicrafts, a nip of lao-lao, and perhaps a bowl of noodles. You can also take a tuk-tuk to the village of Pak Ou, and then a quick boat ride across the Mekong, but few people use this option, as it is less scenic and pricier than taking a tour.

TAD KHUANG SI WATERFALL

★ *29 km (18 mi) south of Luang Prabang.*

A series of cascades surrounded by lush foliage, Tad Khuang Si is a popular spot with Lao and foreigners alike. Many visitors merely view the falls from the lower pool, where picnic tables and food vendors invite you to linger, but a steep path through the forest leads to pools above the falls that are the perfect spot for a swim. The best time to visit the falls is between November and April, after the rainy season.

GETTING HERE & AROUND

Tour operators in Luang Prabang offer day trips that combine Tad Kuang Si with a visit to a Khamu tribal village nearby for 55,000 kip. The drive, past rice farms and small Lao Lum tribal villages, is half the adventure. Taxi and tuk-tuk drivers in Luang Prabang all want to take you to the falls, quoting around $20 round-trip, but unless you have your own group, a tour is a better deal.

BAN MUANG NGOI

150 km (93 mi) northeast of Luang Prabang.

This picturesque river village sits on the eastern side of the Nam Ou River, which descends from Phong Saly Province in the north to meet the Maekong River opposite the famous Pak Ou Caves. The village, populated by Lao Lum and surrounded by unusual limestone peaks, has become a popular traveler hangout spot, with friendly locals, gorgeous scenery, and plenty of treks and river options to stay busy for several days.

GETTING HERE & AROUND

The journey here is an adventure in itself: a minivan takes you from Luang Prabang's Northern Bus Terminal to a pier at Nong Khiaw (4 hours, 50,000 kip), where boats (20,000 kip) continue on a one-hour trip upstream to the village (boats leave Nong Khiaw at 11 AM and 2 PM, and return from Muang Ngoi at 9:30 AM daily, which means that you need to charter your own boat or go on a tour if you don't want to spend the night). Just about any guesthouse or restaurant in Luang Prabang can arrange a guide or a tour, but the local branch of Lao Youth Travel (⇨ *Laos Planner*) is the best-established operator.

WHERE TO STAY

¢ **Ning Ning Guesthouse.** Of the many guesthouses in Ban Muang Ngoi, this is probably the best. It has six clean and spacious bungalows with wooden decks and good mosquito netting to rent for between $8 and $20, depending on the season, plus a great restaurant overlooking the river. **Pros:** good mosquito nets; riverside restaurant. **Cons:** bungalows lack river views; hot water rarely works; no fans or a/c. ✉ *Ban Muang Ngoi* ☎ *030/5140863* *6 bungalows* *In-room: no a/c, no phone, no TV* *No credit cards* *BP.*

LUANG NAM THA

319 km (198 mi) north of Luang Prabang.

The capital of Laos's northernmost province, Luang Nam Tha is the headquarters of the groundbreaking Nam Ha Ecotourism. The program, a model for Southeast Asia, actively encourages the involvement of local communities in the development and management of tourism policies. You can join a two- or three-day trek (organized by Nam Ha Eco Guide, Green Discovery, the Boat Landing Guesthouse, and a few other agencies) through the Nam Ha Protected Area, which shelters numerous animals, including elephants, tigers, and bears. Khamu, Akha, Lanten, and Yao tribes live in the dense forest.

GETTING HERE & AROUND

Luang Nam Tha is tiny and can be navigated on foot, although many places rent mountain bikes (10,000 kip per day) for exploring the surrounding countryside.

9

BY AIR Lao Airlines flies from Vientiane to Luang Nam Tha Monday, Wednesday, and Friday for $100. Tuk-tuks run from the airport and bus station into town for 10,000 kip per person.

BY BOAT Longtail boats can be arranged for the two-day trip on the Nam Tha River, running all the way down to Pak Tha, where the Nam Tha meets the Mekong, and on to Huay Xai. Coming from Huay Xai, boats can be chartered all the way to Luang Nam Tha. A boat costs about $250 and can take four to six passengers. Unless you speak Lao, it's best to make arrangements through The Boat Landing (F *Where to Stay, below*) or Nam Ha Eco Tourism (F*below*).

BY BUS The new Luang Nam Tha Bus Station is 10 km (6 mi) out of town, past the airport. Buses go to Udomxai three times a day (4 hours, 40,000 kip); to Luang Prabang and Vientiane each morning (8 and 19 hours; 90,000 kip and 170,000 kip, respectively); and to Muang Singh hourly (2 hours, 22,000 kip). The mountainous terrain and bad roads, in addition to rental prices, making driving impractical.

ESSENTIALS

Emergencies **Provincial Hospital** (✉ *Nam Tha Rd., Luang Nam Tha* ☎ *086/211752*).

Visitor & Tour Info **Green Discovery Laos** (✉ *Nam Tha Rd., Luang Nam Tha* ☎ *086/211484* 🌐 *www.greendiscoverylaos.com*). **Nam Ha Eco Guide Service and Tourism Center** (✉ *Nam Tha Rd., Luang Nam Tha* ☎ *086/211534*).

WHERE TO STAY & EAT

¢ ASIAN **Heuan Lao.** In a beautiful wooden guesthouse with an open-air dining room, Heuan Lao, at the northern end of Nam Tha Road, has great ambience and is the most popular place in town for officials and businesspeople. The extensive menu has plenty of Thai and Chinese specialties, and they even serve Western breakfasts. ✉ *Nam Tha Rd., Luang Nam Tha* ☎ *086/211111* 💳 *No credit cards.*

$ **Boat Landing Guesthouse.** Comfortable accommodations can be found in the timber-and-bamboo bungalows at this eco-friendly guesthouse run by an American. Rooms are furnished in rattan. The guesthouse organizes two- and three-day treks into the Nam Ha Protected Area. **Pros:** open-air restaurant with traditional food; great source of local information; bicycles available. **Cons:** 6 km (4 mi) out of town; often full in high season. ✉ *Box 28, Ban Kone* ☎ *086/312398* 🌐 *www.theboatlanding.com* *10 rooms* *In-hotel: restaurant, bicycles* 💳 *No credit cards* *BP.*

MUANG SING

60 km (37 mi) north of Luang Nam Tha.

In the late 19th century, this mountain-ringed town on the Sing Mountain River was the seat of a Tai Lue prince, Chao Fa Silino; Muang Sing lost its regional prominence, however, when French colonial forces occupied the town and established a garrison here. Muang Sing is known for its market, which draws throngs of traditionally robed tribespeople. Shoppers from among the 20 different tribes living in the area, and even traders from China, visit the market to buy locally produced goods and handicrafts. The market is open daily 6 AM to 9 AM.

GETTING HERE & AROUND

The only way in and out of Muang Singh is by bus from Luang Nam Tha. There are five to six departures each day; the two-hour journey costs 22,000 kip.

RIVER JOURNEY TO HUAY XAI

297 km (184 mi) up the Mekong from Luang Prabang.

Growing rapidly in popularity is the 300-km (186-mi) Mekong River trip between Luang Prabang and Huay Xai, across the river from Chiang Khong in Thailand. It's a leisurely journey on one of the world's most famous stretches of river. Your boat drifts through the meandering Mekong and a constantly changing primeval scene of towering cliffs, huge mud flats and sandbanks, rocky islands, and riverbanks

Most Lao men, like Thai men, join the sangha (monastic community) at least temporarily.

smothered in thick jungle, passing by swaths of cultivated land, mulberry trees, bananas, and tiny garlic fields. There are no roads, just forest paths linking dusty settlements where the boats tie up for refreshment stops.

The only village of note is a halfway station, Pakbeng, which has many guesthouses and restaurants along its one main street, and seems to exist solely to serve the boat passengers who arrive each night. ■ **TIP→ Once you arrive in Huay Xai (which has little of interest in itself), a good way to return to Thailand is to cross the river to Chiang Khong and then take a bus to Chiang Rai, 60 km (37 mi) inland.**

GETTING HERE & AROUND

There are three ways to make the journey to Huay Xai from Luang Prabang on the river: by regular "slow" boat, which holds about 50 passengers; by speedboat, which seats about four; and by luxury cruise.

The regular boat is at least a 12- to 14-hour journey over two days. You'll spend the night in Pakbeng, in very basic guesthouses whose owners come to meet the boats and corral guests. The fare is about $30 per person; slow boats depart daily from the riverside near the morning market in Luang Prabang.

Speedboats make the journey between Luang Prabang and Huay Xai in six hours. ⚠ **Speedboats may be fun for the first hour, but they are not safe and become extremely uncomfortable after the novelty wears off.** The seats are hard, the engine noise is deafening (earplugs are advised), and the wind and spray can be chilling. If you're determined to take one, bring a warm, waterproof windbreaker, and be sure to get a life jacket and crash helmet with a visor from the boat driver. Speedboats cost $45 per person and leave daily from a pier on the northern outskirts of Luang Prabang.

Much more comfortable than the regular boat and speedboat, but far more expensive, is the ***LuangSay*** luxury boat (✉ *50/4 Sakkarine Rd., Luang Prabang* ☎ *071/252553* 🌐 *www.mekong-cruises.com*), which is specially designed for leisurely river travel. The river cruise includes accommodation in Pakbeng at the very comfortable LuangSay Lodge (*below*). The *LuangSay* departs from Luang Prabang every Wednesday and Saturday (and Tuesday, October through April), and returns from Huay Xai every Monday and Friday (and Thursday, October through April). The cruise costs $413 ($267 from May to September).

ESSENTIALS

Visitor & Tour Info Guesthouses in Huay Xai can answer most questions. If you want to charter a boat to travel up the Nam Tha River to Luang Nam Tha, **Easy Trip** (✉ *Huay Xai* ☎ *084/212111* 🌐 *www.discoverylaos.com/e-version/OurService/NamthaRiverTrip.php*) can be of assistance.

WHERE TO EAT & STAY

HUAY XAI ¢–$ LAO ✕ **Latsuly Restaurant.** Occupying some prime real estate, above the boat landing along the Mekong, this restaurant serves tasty papaya salads, fried catfish, and *larb moo* (spicy pork salads). ✉ *Saykhong Rd.,Huay Xai* 💳 *No credit cards.*

HUAY XAI ¢ **Keo Udomphone Hotel.** This simple old town house is more comfortable than its outside appearance might suggest. The bright guestrooms are furnished in an eclectic mix of styles. Staff go out of their way to give a cheery welcome. **Pros:** spotlessly clean; welcoming staff; lots of light. **Cons:** long walk from town center; not all rooms have a/c. ✉ *Saykhong Rd., Huay Xai* ☎ *084/211405* *20 rooms* *In-hotel: restaurant* 💳 *No credit cards.*

PAKBENG $$ **LuangSay Lodge.** This attractive collection of traditional bamboo huts sits on the riverbank just outside of Pakbeng amid lush green hills. The staff is welcoming, and the resort feels truly isolated. It's the nicest place to stay in Pakbeng and is often fully booked by the luxury cruise boats, but if you arrive on a night in low season when cruise passengers aren't in town, you will have it all to yourself. **Pros:** traditional design; serene surroundings; attentive staff. **Cons:** far from the rest of Pakbeng; if a *LuangSay* cruise is here, rooms will be full; huge flight of steps up from boat dock. ✉ *Pakbeng* ☎ *020/670177, 021/215958 in Luang Prabang, 071/252553 in Vientiane* 🌐 *www.asian-oasis.com* *19 rooms* *In-room: no a/c* 💳 *No credit cards.*

PHONGSALY

425 km (264 mi) north of Luang Prabang.

If you're looking for off-the-beaten-track "soft" adventure, head for the provincial capital Phongsaly, in the far north of Laos. It's a hill station and market town nearly 5,000 feet above sea level in the country's most spectacular mountain range, Phu Fa. Trekking through this

CLOSE UP

Religion in Laos

The overwhelming majority of Laotians are Buddhists, yet, as in neighboring Thailand, spirit worship is widespread, blending easily with temple traditions and rituals. A common belief holds that supernatural spirits called *phi* have power over individual and community life.

Laotians believe that each person has 32 *khwan,* or individual spirits, which must be appeased and kept "bound" to the body. If one of the khwan leaves the body, sickness can result, and then a ceremony must be performed to reattach the errant spirit. In this ritual, which is known as *bai-si,* white threads are tied to the wrist of the ailing person in order to fasten the spirits. Apart from the khwan, there are countless other spirits inhabiting the home, gardens, orchards, fields, forests, mountains, rivers, and even individual rocks and trees.

Luang Prabang has a team of ancestral guardian spirits, the Pu Nyeu Na Nyeu, who are lodged in a special temple, Wat Aham. In the south, the fierce guardian spirits of Wat Phu are appeased every year with the sacrifice of a buffalo to guarantee an abundance of rain during the rice-growing season.

Despite the common belief in a spirit world, more than 90% of Laotians are officially Theravada Buddhists, a conservative nontheistic form of Buddhism said to be derived directly from the words of the Buddha. Buddhism arrived in Laos in the 3rd century BC by way of Ashoka, an Indian emperor who helped spread the religion. A later form of Buddhism, Mahayana, which arose in the 1st century AD, is also practiced in Laos, particularly in the cities. It differs from Theravada in that followers venerate the bodhisattvas. This northern school of Buddhism spread from India to Nepal, China, Korea, and Japan and is practiced by Vietnamese and Chinese alike in all the bigger towns of Laos. The Chinese in Laos also follow Taoism and Confucianism.

Buddhism in Laos is so interlaced with daily life that you have a good chance of witnessing its practices and rituals firsthand—from the early-morning sight of women giving alms to monks on their rounds through the neighborhood, to the evening routine of monks gathering for their temple recitations. If you visit temples on Buddhist holy days, which coincide with the new moon, you'll likely hear monks chanting texts of the Buddha's teachings.

Christianity is followed by a small minority of mostly French-educated, elite Laotians, although the faith also has adherents among hill tribe converts in areas that have been visited by foreign missionaries. Missionary activity has been curbed in recent years, however, as the Lao government forbids the dissemination of foreign religious materials.

Islam is practiced by a handful of Arab and Indian businesspeople in Vientiane. There are also some Muslims from Yunnan, China, called Chin Haw, in the northern part of Laos. More recently, a very small number of Cham refugees from Pol Pot's Cambodia (1975–79) took refuge in Vientiane, where they have established a mosque.

land of forest-covered mountains and rushing rivers may be as close as you'll ever get to the thrill of exploring virgin territory. ■ **TIP→ You can arrange for a guide (a must) through any of the hotels or guesthouses in town, or with Diethelm Travel or Lao Youth Travel back in Luang Prabang.**

GETTING HERE & AROUND

Buses from Udomxai make the nine-hour run to Phongsaly daily at 8 AM (80,000 kip). You can also get here by boat from Muang Khua when the water levels are high enough; the six-hour trip is 150,000 kip per person. In town, tuk-tuks can take you wherever you need to go for 10,000 kip.

EXPLORING PHONGSALY

Trekking is Phongsaly's main attraction.

There are about 25 different ethnic groups in the area, and the local **tribal museum** offers a fascinating look into their lives and culture. Among the exhibits is a kaleidoscopic display of tribal costumes. ☎ *No phone* *5,000 kip* ⊙ *Weekdays 7:30–11:30 and 1:30–4:30.*

WHERE TO EAT & STAY

UDOMXAI ¢ LAO ✕ **Thanousin Restaurant.** You will undoubtedly pass through or get stuck in drab Udomxai going to or from Phongsaly (or Luang Nam Tha), and this small restaurant is a great place to fill up. They serve up excellent larb, and you shouldn't miss sampling the northern specialty of *khao soi,* a slightly spicy handmade noodle dish that Thanousin serves in giant portions. ■ **TIP→ Conveniently, the restaurant is also the office of Udom Xai Tours and Travel.** If you need to stay a day and want to arrange a tour, they can help. ✉ *Road 13, 268/28, Ban Na Lao,Udomxai* ☎ *020/675–2035* ▭ *No credit cards.*

UDOMXAI ¢ **Litthavixay Guesthouse.** Located right between the bus station and market on the main road, this is a good choice if you're spending the night in Udomxai on the way to or from Phongsaly. Rooms are basic, but have refrigerators, TVs, hot showers, a/c, and fans—all luxuries in this neck of the woods. You'll pay an extra few dollars to switch the a/c on. **Pros:** centrally located; bicycle rental; Internet café. **Cons:** noisy street outside; minimal English spoken; few staff around. ✉ *Udomxai (main road)* ☎ *081/212175* *17 rooms* *In-room: refrigerator. In-hotel: restaurant, Internet terminal* ▭ *No credit cards.*

PHONGSALY ¢ **Viphaphone Hotel.** Spacious and furnished rooms make the Viphaphone a luxurious rarity in off-the-beaten-track Phongsaly. **Pros:** spacious rooms; good hot water supply; Western toilets. **Cons:** staff speaks little English; often noisy in street below; no views from corner rooms. ✉ *Phongsaly* ☎ *088/210111* *27 rooms* *In-room: no a/c. In-hotel: restaurant* ▭ *No credit cards.*

SOUTHERN LAOS

In some ways, Laos is really two countries: the south and north are as different as two sides of a coin. The mountainous north was for centuries virtually isolated from the more accessible south, where lowlands, the broad Mekong valley, and high plateaus were easier to tra-

CLOSE UP

Lao: A Few Key Phrases

The official language is Lao, part of the extensive Tai family of languages of Southeast Asia spoken from Vietnam in the east to India in the west. Spoken Lao is very similar to the Northern Thai language, as well as local dialects in the Shan states in Myanmar and Sipsongbanna in China. Lao is tonal, meaning a word can have several meanings according to the tone in which it's spoken.

In tourist hotels, the staff generally speaks some English. You can find a smattering of English speakers in shops and restaurants. A few old-timers know some French.

Here are a few common and useful words:

Hello: sabai di (pronounced sa-bye dee)

Thank you: khop chai deu (pronounced *cop chi dew*; use khop cheu neu in northern Laos)

Yes: heu (pronounced like deux) *or* thia

No: bo

Where?: iu sai (pronounced *you sai*)?

How much?: to dai (pronounced *taw dai*)?

Zero: sun (pronounced *soon*)

One: neung

Two: song

Three: sam

Four: si

Five: ha

Six: hok

Seven: tiet (pronounced *jee-yet*)

Eight: pet

Nine: kao

Ten: sip

Twenty: sao (rhymes with cow; different from Thai "yee sip")

Hundred: neung loi

Thousand: neung phan

To have fun: muan

To eat: kin khao (pronounced *kin cow*)

To drink: kin nam

Water: nam

Rice: khao

Expensive: peng

Bus: lot me (pronounced *lot may*)

House: ban

Road: thanon

Village: ban

Island: don

River: mae nam (pronounced *may nam*)

Doctor: maw

Hospital: hong mo (pronounced *hong maw*)

Post Office: paisani

Hotel: hong hem

Toilet: hong nam

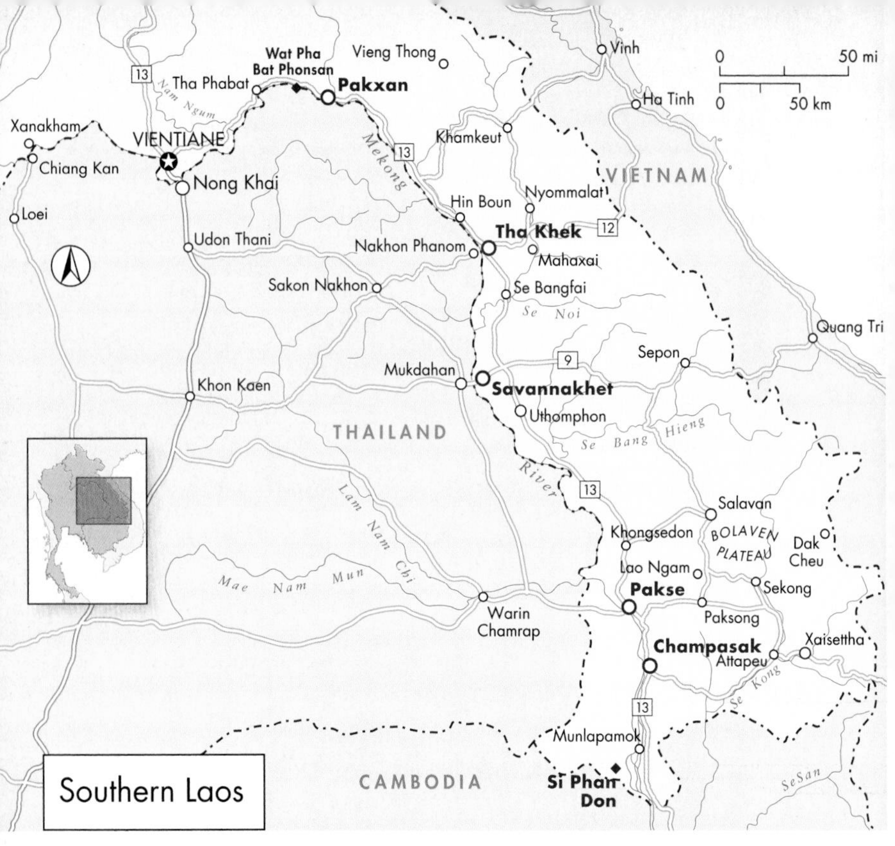

verse and settle. The south does have its mountains, however: notably the Annamite range, called Phu Luang, home of the aboriginal Mon-Khmer ethnic groups who lived here long before Lao farmers and traders arrived from northern Laos and China. The Lao were followed by French colonists, who built the cities of Pakxan, Tha Khek, Savannakhet, and Pakse. Although the French influence is still tangible, the southern Lao cling tenaciously to their old traditions, making the south a fascinating destination.

Pakse is the regional capital and has an international airport with daily flights to Vientiane, as well as to Phnom Penh and Siem Reap in neighboring Cambodia. There's also overnight bus service to Pakse from Vientiane, plus good local service in the area.

SOUTH ALONG THE MEKONG

Highway 13 out of Vientiane penetrates as far as the deep south of Laos and the Cambodian border, a distance of 835 km (518 mi). It's paved all the way. The section between Vientiane and Pakse is not abundant with sightseeing opportunities, but if you have time you can stop to savor the slow-paced, timeless river life here.

The Bolaven Plateau's volcanic soil is ideal for farming.

GETTING HERE & AROUND

BY AIR Lao Airlines flies from Vientiane to Savannakhet several times daily for 850,000 kip.

BY BUS Local bus service connects all the towns on Highway 13, from Vientiane or Pakse. VIP buses traveling the Vientiane–Pakse route do not stop in the small towns; they will stop in Savannakhet and Tha Kaek, but they'll charge you the full fare to Vientiane or Pakse and you'll arrive in the middle of the night. Local buses depart hourly until midday for Savannakhet, Tha Kaek, Paksan and all other destinations along the Mekong from Pakse's northern bus station (about five hours, 45,000 kip) and from Vientiane's southern bus station.

ESSENTIALS

Emergencies **Provincial Hospital** (✉*Kanthabuli Rd., Savannakhet* ☎*041/212051*).

VISITOR & TOUR INFO

Contact **Provincial Tourist Office** (✉*Ratsaphanith Rd., Savannakhet* ☎*041/212755*).

EXPLORING THE ROAD SOUTH TO PAKSE

The first stop of interest on Highway 13, about 80 km (50 mi) northeast of Vientiane, is the pilgrimage temple complex **Wat Pha Bat Phonsan,** which has a revered footprint in stone said to be that of the Buddha.

Pakxan, 150 km (93 mi) south of Vientiane, in Bolikhamxay Province, is a former French colonial outpost, a Mekong River port, and now the center of the Lao Christian community. Traveling south from Pakxan, Highway 13 crosses the Nam Kading River, for which the protected forested NBCA (National Biodiversity Conservation Area Nam Kading) is named. About 90 km (56 mi) south of Pakxan, Highway 13 meets Highway 8, which leads via Lak Sao to Nam Pho on the Vietnamese border. From here the road leads to the Vietnamese coastal city of Vinh and other areas of north Vietnam.

Tha Khek, 350 km (217 mi) south of Vientiane, in Khammuan Province, is a bustling Mekong River port, with some of its ancient city wall still intact. It's surrounded by stunning countryside and karst (limestone caverns and sinkholes). There are some spectacular limestone caves in the area—notably **Tham Khong Lor.** This cave is more than 6½ km (4 mi) long and is so large that the Nam Hin Bun River runs through it. Opposite Tha Khek is Thailand's provincial capital of Nakhon Phanom. Ferries ply the waters between the two cities.

Savannakhet, 470 km (290 mi) south of Vientiane, is a former French colonial provincial center. This pleasant riverside town is today the urban hub of a vast rice-growing plain. It's distinguished by some fine examples of French colonial architecture. One of Savannakhet's curiosities is a **dinosaur museum** (✉ *Khantaburi Rd., Savannakhet* ☎ *No phone* 🎫 *5,000 kip* ⏲ *Weekdays 8–11:30 and 1–3:30*), which displays fossils discovered in the area.

PAKSE

205 km (127 mi) south of Savannakhet, 675 km (420 mi) south of Vientiane.

Pakse is a former French colonial stronghold, linked now with neighboring Thailand by a bridge 40 km (25 mi) away. It plays a central role in an ambitious regional plan to create an "Emerald Triangle"—a trade and tourism community grouping Laos, Thailand, and Cambodia. The city has few attractions but is the starting point for tours to the Khmer ruins at Wat Phu, the 4,000 Islands, and the Bolaven Plateau, which straddles the southern provinces of Saravan, Sekon, Attapeu, and Champasak. The volcanic soil of the plateau makes the vast region ideal for agriculture: it's the source of much of the country's prized coffee, tea, and spices. Despite its beauty and central role in the Lao economy, the plateau has virtually no tourist infrastructure and is very much off-the-beaten-track territory.

GETTING HERE & AROUND

BY AIR There are several Lao Airlines flights each day from Vientiane to Pakse, sometimes routed via Savannakhet; the flight takes an hour and costs $125 one-way.Lao Airlines flights from Siem Reap, Cambodia, arrive every Wednesday, Friday, and Sunday. The price of a one-way ticket is $115. A tuk-tuk from Pakse International Airport (4 km [2 mi] west of town) to the city center costs 30,000 kip to 40,000 kip.

BY BOAT There is one public boat to Champasak each morning at 8 AM for 70,000 kip per passenger. You can charter a boat for $60 to $70 (up to six passengers) from several agencies in town.

BY BUS Pakse is the transportation hub for all destinations in the south. Comfortable VIP buses (using the VIP bus station near the evening market) make the overnight, 11-hour journey to and from Vientiane (180,000 kip). Buses leave Vientiane nightly at 8 or 8:30 PM and arriving in Pakse at 6:30 am; the times are the same from Pakse to Vientiane. Pakse's central bus station, a short walk east of the VIP terminal, has hourly departures to Savannakhet (40,000 kip, 5 hours) and other points north.

CRUISING ON THE MEKONG

A luxurious double-decker houseboat, the *Vat Phou,* operated by **Mekong Cruises** (*23 Ban Anou, Haengboun Rd., Chanthaboury, Vientiane 021/215958 www.mekong-cruises.com*), plies the southern length of the Mekong between Pakse and Si Phan Don. The cruises, which last three days and two nights, depart from Pakse every Tuesday, Thursday, and Saturday in high season, and cost $591.

Buses depart from the southern bus station (known as Lo Lak Pert, due to its location at the 8 km mark on the road east of Pakse) for the Si Phan Don area and Champasak. If you're headed to Si Phan Don, it's more convenient to take a minibus, which will pick you up at your hotel for 60,000 kip; all guesthouses sell tickets.

BY CAR Any travel agent in town can arrange car rental with a driver.

BY TAXI, TUK-TUK & SONGTHAEW Tuk-tuks around town cost 10,000 kip, and a charter out to the southern bus station costs 40,000 kip. Songthaews to Champasak (two hours, 30,000 kip) leave from the Dao Heuang market.

ESSENTIALS

Banks **BCEL** (*11 St.,, Pakse 31/212770*).

Emergencies **Provincial Hospital** (*Ban Pakse, Pakse 031/212018*).

Visitor & Tour Info **Champasak Provincial Tourism** (*Th. 11, Ban Naheak, Pakse 031/212021 ou_thai@hotmail.com*) can organize half-day tours to the Boloven Plateau, ethnic villages, and a tea-and-coffee plantation ($180 for two), and boat trips to Champasak and Wat Phu, and Don Kong for $120.

EXPLORING PAKSE

Pakse's **Historical Heritage Museum** displays stonework from the famous Wat Phu in Champasak, handicrafts from the Bolaven Plateau ethnic groups, and locally made musical instruments. *Hwy. 13 No phone 5,000 kip Daily 8–11:30 and 1–4.*

WHERE TO EAT & STAY

¢ ★ ASIAN **Tour Lao.** This popular corner eatery sets the standard for food in Pakse, and arguably in all of Southern Laos. Made up of an indoor air-conditioned room and a large outdoor venue with wooden tables, Tour Lao is popular with Thai tour groups and locals, as well as foreigners in the know. The kitchen churns out a variety of tasty dishes: fusion-style green curry spaghetti; pork rolls stuffed with Napa cabbage; and spicy favorites like red duck curry or Mekong fish salad. There's plenty of beer to quench your thirst, and a live band plays regularly in high season. ✉ *Th. 9 at Th. 46, Ban Naheak, Pakse* ☎ *031/900388*

¢ **Champa Residence Hotel.** Five handsome traditional-style houses make up this comfortable hotel complex near Pakse's evening market and the Historical Heritage Museum. Rooms have tiny terraces overlooking the leafy grounds. **Pros:** spacious rooms; quiet location; spa and sauna. **Cons:** very far from town center; no real views. ✉ *Champasak Rd.* ☎ *031/212120* *champare@laotel.com* *45 rooms* *In-room: refrigerator. In-hotel: restaurant, bar, laundry service* *MC, V.*

$ **Champasak Palace.** On the banks of the Seddon River on the town's outskirts, this former residence of a local prince is impressive, though scarcely palatial. It's a vast four-story complex with flanking wings and pagoda-like eaves. Guestrooms are royally large and comfortably furnished, with an antique here and there. Rooms in the new wing are in better shape but have less character than those in the old wing. **Pros:** beautiful terrace over the river; huge beds; sauna and fitness center. **Cons:** not central; dirty walls in some rooms; small elevators. ✉ *Ban Prabaht* ☎ *031/212263 or 031/212779* *115 rooms* *In-room: refrigerator, Wi-Fi (some). In-hotel: 2 restaurants, bar, laundry service, Wi-Fi* *AE, MC, V.*

$ **Pakse Hotel.** This recently renovated, central hotel now offers international standards of comfort and service. Its rooftop terrace is a pleasant evening retreat, with a fine view of the town and surrounding countryside. **Pros:** great location in the heart of city; clean, comfortable rooms with big plenty of light; friendly and attentive staff. **Cons:** small elevator; far from bus stations; busy with tour groups. ✉ *Rd. 5, Ban Vat Luang* ☎ *031/212131* *www.paksehotel.com* *65 rooms* *In-room: refrigerator, Wi-Fi. In-hotel: restaurant, bar, laundry service, no-smoking rooms* *AE, MC, V.*

CHAMPASAK

40 km (25 mi) south of Pakse.

In the early 18th century, the kingdom of Laos was partitioned into three realms: Luang Prabang, Vientiane, and Champasak. During the 18th and 19th centuries this small village on the west bank of the Mekong River was the royal center of a wide area of what is today Thailand and Cambodia.

GETTING HERE & AROUND

Songthaew travel here from the Dao Heuang Market in Pakse three times each morning (2 hours, 20,000 kip). Minibuses can be arranged via guesthouses and travel agencies in Pakse for 60,000 kip. A car with a driver can be hired from all tour agencies in Pakse for about $50 to $60. Tuk-tuks run to Wat Phu from Champasak for 10,000 kip per person.

EXPLORING CHAMPASAK

Wat Phu is Champasak's main attraction. **■ TIP→ Every February, at the time of the full moon, the wat holds a nationally renowned festival that includes elephant racing, cockfighting, concerts, and lots of drinking and dancing.**

★ **Wat Phu** sits impressively on heights above the Mekong River, about 8 km (5 mi) south of Champasak, looking back on a centuries-old history that won it UNESCO recognition as a World Heritage Site. Wat Phu predates Cambodia's Angkor Wat—Wat Phu's hilltop site was chosen by Khmer Hindus in the 6th century AD, probably because of a nearby spring of fresh water. Construction of the wat continued into the 13th century, at which point it finally became a Buddhist temple. Much of the original Hindu sculpture remains unchanged, however, including representations on the temple's lintels of the Hindu gods Vishnu, Shiva, and Kala. The staircase is particularly beautiful, its protective *nagas* (mystical serpents) decorated with plumeria, the national flower of Laos. Many of the temple's treasures, including pre-Angkor–era inscriptions, are preserved in an archaeology museum that is part of the complex. ✉ *8 km (5 mi) southwest of Champasak* ☎ *No phone* *30,000 kip* *Daily 8–4:30.*

SI PHAN DON

★ *80 km (50 mi) south of Champasak, 120 km (74 mi) south of Pakse.*

If you've made it as far south as Champasak, then a visit to the Si Phan Don area—celebrated for its 4,000 Mekong River islands and freshwater dolphins—is a must. *Don* means island, and two of them in particular are worth visiting: Don Khong and the similarly named Don Khon, both of which are accessible by boat. Neighboring Don Det, connected to Don Khon by a bridge, attracts the backpacker crowd.

GETTING HERE & AROUND

Any travel agency in Pakse can help you charter a boat to Don Khong or Don Khon for about $140; the trip takes four to five hours. You can charter a boat from Champasak as well.

From Pakse, you can take a minibus, arranged at any travel agency or guesthouse, to the boat crossing at either Hai Sai Khun (for Don Khong) or Nakasang (for Don Khon). The journey takes two to three hours and costs 60,000 kip.

Boat crossings from the mainland to Don Khon (from Nakasang) cost 20,000 kip and take 15 minutes; to Don Khong (from Hat Sai Khun) it's a five-minute trip and costs 5,000 kip.

Visitor & Tour Info Pakse's tourism office can arrange boat and vehicle eco tours to Champasak and Si Phan Don as well as farther afield, with trained guides at competitive prices. Pakse Travel runs similar tours and has excellent transportation options.

Champasak Provincial Tourism (✉ *Th. 11, Pakse* ☎ *031/212021*). **Pakse Travel** (✉ *108 Ban Thaluang, Pakse* ☎ *020/2277277* *paksetravel@yahoo.com*).

9

CLOSE UP

The Irrawaddy Dolphin

The freshwater Irrawaddy dolphin, known as pla ka in Lao, is one of the world's most endangered species; according to a 2008 study, less than 50 now remain in the Mekong. The Irrawaddy has mythical origins. According to Lao and Khmer legend, a beautiful maiden, in despair over being forced to marry a snake, attempted suicide by jumping into the Mekong. But the gods intervened, saving her life by transforming her into a dolphin.

Lao people do not traditionally hunt the dolphins, but the Irrawaddy have been casualties of over-fishing, getting tangled in nets. New dams in the Mekong have altered their ecosystem, further threatening their survival.

Catching a glimpse of these majestic animals—which look more like orcas than dolphins—can be a thrilling experience. The least obtrusive way to visit the Irrawaddy is in a kayak or other non-motorized boat. If you go by motorboat and do spot dolphins, ask your driver to cut the engine when you're still 100 yards or so away. You can then paddle closer to the animals without disturbing them. Do not try to swim with the dolphins, and—of course—don't throw any trash into the water.

EXPLORING SI PHAN DON

Beautiful scenery and laid-back atmosphere are the reasons to come to Si Phan Don. The Khone Phapheng Falls near Don Khon are a highlight, and visiting them can be combined with seeing the Irrawaddy dolphins. (You'll find many boat operators happy to take you on this tour.) Don Khong has scenic rice fields and more upscale lodging choices, but is not as interesting or attractive as Don Khon. Don Det is another island adjoined to Don Khon by an old rail bridge. The two islands are similar, but Don Khon has fewer guesthouses and is slightly more upmarket.

Don Khong is the largest island in the area, inhabited by a community of fisherfolk living in small villages amid ancient Buddhist temples.

You can hike to the beautiful Liphi waterfall on the island known as **Don Khon**, and the even more stunning waterfall, Khone Phapheng, is just east of Don Khon on the mainland. Also on Don Khon (and Don Det) are the remains of a former French-built railway.

Downstream of Don Khon, at the border between Laos and Cambodia, freshwater Irrawaddy dolphins frolic in a protected area of the Mekong. Boat trips to view the dolphins set off from Veun Kham and Don Khon.

WHERE TO EAT & STAY

At this writing, electricity is only available on Don Khon and Don Det until 10 PM.

¢ LAO ✕ **Villa Muong Khong.** Housed in a beautiful old wooden lodge on the river, this restaurant is has great ambience and tasty local food. Soft and succulent grilled fish is a specialty, along with spicy *tom yum* soup

DID YOU KNOW?

Though the government encourages crop diversification, rice still covers about 80% of Laos's cultivated land. However, coffee is the country's only significant agricultural export, and Laos imports much of its food supply.

and papaya salad. Order baskets of sticky rice for a traditional Lao meal. There's also a well-stocked wine rack. ✉ *Don Khong Island* ☎ *031/213011.*

$ ★ **Sala Ban Khon.** This charming resort on Don Khon offers French colonial–style rooms, traditional Lao homes in a garden, or incredibly atmospheric "raftels," bungalows that are actually floating on the Mekong. The attached Bamboo restaurant serves delicious food; a swimming pool is in the works. **Pros:** beautiful riverside location; excellent restaurant; small decks on raftels for swimming. **Cons:** raftels go quickly in high season mosquitoes annoying at sunset. ✉ *Don Khon Island* ☎ *030/5256390* 🌐 *www.salalao.com* *14 rooms, 8 raftels* *In-room: no a/c, no phone. In-hotel: restaurant, bar* *No credit cards.*

$ **Villa Muong Khong Hotel.** At this friendly, family-run hotel on the island of Don Khong, you live alongside local Lao fisherfolk. Rooms are not glamorous, but the location is superb. Not surprisingly, Mekong fish figures prominently at the hotel's open-air restaurant. **Pros:** fantastic location at quiet end of village; owners can arrange boat trips to nearby sights. **Cons:** small baths; dirty shower curtains; bit of a walk from the main boat dock. ✉ *Don Khong Island* ☎ *031/213011* 🌐 *www.khongislandtravel.com* *52 rooms* *In-room: no phone. In-hotel: restaurant, bar* *No credit cards.*

UNDERSTANDING THAILAND

INTRODUCTION TO THAI ARCHITECTURE

Though real architecture buffs are few and far between, you'd be hard pressed to find a visitor to Thailand who doesn't spend at least a little time staring in slack-jawed amazement at the country's glittering wats and ornate palaces—and the elegant sculptures of the mythical beasts that protect them. As befitting this spiritual nation, most of the fanfare is saved for religious structures, but you can find plenty to admire in the much simpler lines of the traditional houses of the Central Plains and Northern Thailand.

Wats

Wat is the Thai name for what can range from a simple ordination hall for monks and nuns to a huge sprawling complex comprising libraries, bell towers, and meditation rooms. Usually the focal point for a community, it's not unusual for a wat to also be the grounds for village fetes and festivals. Although most wats you come across symbolize some aspect of Theravada Buddhism, examples of other architectural styles are relatively easy to find: Khmer ruins dot the Isan countryside to the east, while Northern Thailand is littered with Burmese-style temples.

Wats are erected as acts of merit—allowing the donor to improve his karma and perhaps be reborn as a higher being—or in memory of great events. You can tell much about a wat's origin by its name. A wat *luang* (royal wat), for example, was constructed or restored by royals and may have the words *rat, raja,* or *racha* in its name (e.g., Ratburana or Rajapradit). The word *phra* may indicate that a wat contains an image of the Buddha. Wats that contain an important relic of the Buddha have the words *maha* (great) and *that* (relic) in their names. Thailand's nine major wat mahathats are in Chiang Rai, Chai Nat, Sukhothai, Phisanulk, Ayutthaya, Bangkok, Yasothon, Phetchaburi, and Nakhon Si Thammarat.

Thai wats, especially in the later periods, were seldom planned as entire units, so they often appear disjointed and crowded. To appreciate a wat's beauty you often have to look at its individual buildings.

Perhaps the most recognizable feature of a wat, and certainly a useful landmark when hunting them down, is the towering conelike *chedi.* Originally used to hold relics of the Buddha (hair, bones, or even nails), chedis can now be built by anyone with enough cash, to house their ashes. At the base of the chedi you can find three platforms representing hell, earth, and heaven, while the 33 Buddhist heavens are symbolized at the top of the tallest spire by a number of rings.

The main buildings of a wat are the *bot,* which contains a Buddha image and functions as congregation and ordination hall for the monks, and the *viharn,* which serves a similar function, but will hold the most important Buddha image. Standard bot and viharn roofs will feature three steeply curved levels featuring red, gold, and green tiles; the outer walls range from highly decorated to simply whitewashed.

Other noticeable features include the *mondop, prang,* and *ho trai.* Usually square with a pyramid-shaped roof, the mondop is reminiscent of Indian temple architecture and serves as a kind of storeroom for holy artifacts, books, and ceremonial objects. The prang is a tall tower similar to the chedi, which came to Thailand by way of the Khmer empire and is used to store images of the Buddha. Easily identifiable by its stilts or raised platform, the ho trai is a library for holy scriptures.

Roofs, which are covered in glazed clay tiles or wooden shakes, generally consist of three overlapping sections, with the lower roof set at gentle slopes, increasing to a topmost roof with a pitch of 60 degrees. Eave brackets in the form of a *naga* (snakes believed to control the irrigation waters of rice fields) with its head at the bottom often support the lower edges of the roofs. Along the eaves of many roofs are a row of small brass bells with clappers attached to thin brass pieces shaped like Bodhi tree leaves.

During the early Ayutthaya period (1350–1767), wat interiors were illuminated by the light passing through vertical slits in the walls (wider, more elaborate windows would have compromised the strength of the walls and, thus, the integrity of the structure). In the Bangkok period (1767–1932), the slits were replaced by proper windows set below wide lintels that supported the upper portions of the brick walls. There are usually five, seven, or nine windows on a side in accordance with the Thai preference for odd numbers. The entrance doors are in the end wall facing the Buddha image; narrower doors may flank the entrance door.

Principal building materials have varied with the ages. Khmer and Lopburi architects built in stone and laterite; Sukhothai and Lanna builders worked with laterite and brick. Ayutthaya and Bangkok architects opted for brick cemented by mortar and covered with one or more coats of stucco (made of lime, sand, and, often, rice husks). In early construction, walls were often several feet thick; when binding materials and construction techniques improved they became thinner.

The mid-13th century saw an enormous wave of men entering the monkhood as the Kingdom of Sukhothai adopted Hinayana Buddhism as its official religion. Consequently there was a need for bigger monasteries. Due to the lack of quality stone and brick available, wood became the building material of choice, marking a shift away from the exclusively stone structures of the Khmer period.

Sculpture

The Thai image of the Buddha usually features markedly long ears weighed down by heavy earrings in reference to his royal background, and is caste in bronze and covered in gold leaf by followers. Typically depicted seated or standing, less common images are reclining Buddhas, acknowledging his impending death, and walking Buddhas, which were favored during the Sukhothai period (13th to 15th century). Statues from the Lanna period of the 13th to 15th century and the present Ratanakosin era feature eyes fashioned from colored gems or enamel, while the Lopburi period of the 10th to 13th century favored metal.

A collection of 32 Pali *lakshanas,* descriptions used to identify future incarnations of the Buddha, popularly serve as a kind of blueprint for reproductions. The lakshanas include reference to wedge-shaped heels, long fingers and toes of equal length, legs like an antelope, arms long enough that he could touch either knee without bending, skin so smooth that dust wouldn't adhere to it, a body as thick as a banyan tree, long eyelashes like those of a cow, 40 teeth, a hairy white mole between his eyebrows, deep blue eyes, and an *ushnisha* (protuberance) atop his head—either a turban, a topknot, or a bump on his skull.

Palaces

Although King Bhumibol currently uses Chitlada Palace when in Bangkok, the Chakri Dynasty monarchs who preceded him used the showpiece Grand Palace as their official residence. Shots of the palace with its gleaming spires floodlighted up at night fill every postcard stand, and it's arguably Bangkok's single most important tourist attraction.

Built in 1782 when King Rama I chose Bangkok as Siam's new capital, the Grand Palace is the only remaining example of early Ratanakosin architecture—Ramas II and III chose not to initiate any large-scale construction projects in the face of economic hardship. A primarily functional collection of buildings, the compound contains the Royal Thai Decorations and

Coin Pavilion, the Museum of Fine Art, and the Weapons Museum.

Also worth checking out while in the capital is what is believed to be the world's largest golden teak-wood building. The three-story Vimanmek Palace was moved from Chonburi in the east to Bangkok's Dusit Palace and contains jewelry and gifts given as presents from around the world.

Rama IV led the revival of palace construction in the second half of the 19th century, overseeing the building of several royal getaways. Perhaps the most impressive of these getaways is Phra Nakhon Khiri in the southern town of Phetchaburi. Known locally as Khao Wang, the palace sits atop a mountain with wonderful panoramic views. Sharing its mountain home are various wat, halls, and thousands of macaque monkeys. Klai Kangwon in nearby Hua Hin is still used as a seaside getaway for the royal family and as a base when they visit southern provinces. Built in 1926 by Rama VI, the two-story concrete palace's name translates as Far From Worries and was built in the style of European chateaux.

Houses

Look around many Thai towns and you can see that this is a swiftly modernizing country: whitewashed apartment blocks, everything-under-one-roof shopping malls, and glass-fronted fast-food outlets are testaments to a growing economy and general rush to get ahead (as well as to the disappearance of Thailand's forests, which once provided cheap and sturdy building materials). However, peer a little closer and you will find Thailand's heritage staring right back at you.

Traditional Thai houses are usually very simple and essentially boil down to three basic components: stilts, a deck, and a sloping roof. Heavy, annual monsoon rains all over the country necessitate that living quarters be raised on stilts to escape flooding; in the dry season the space under the house is typically used as storage for farming equipment or other machinery. The deck of the house is essentially the living room—it's where you can find families eating, cooking, and just plain relaxing.

As with wats, it's often the roofs of houses that are the most interesting. Lanna-style (Northern Thailand) roofs, usually thatched or tiled, are thought to have evolved from the Thai people's roots in Southern China, where steeply pitched roofs would have been needed to combat heavy snows. Although there's no real chance of a snowball fight in Thailand, the gradient and overhang allows for quick runoff of the rains and welcome shade from the sun.

These basics are fairly uniform throughout the country, with a few small adjustments to accommodate different climates. For example, roofs are steepest in areas with more intense weather patterns, like the Central Plains, and Northern Thai houses have smaller windows to preserve heat better.

VOCABULARY

Thai has several distinct forms for different social levels. The most common one is the street language, which is used in everyday situations. If you want to be polite, add "khrup" (men) or "kah" (women) to the end of your sentence. For the word "I," men should use "phom" and women should use "deeshan."

Note that the "h" is silent when combined with most other consonants (th, ph, kh, etc.). Double vowels indicate long vowel sounds (uu=oo, as in food), except for "aa," which is pronounced "ah."

BASICS

Hello/goodbye:	Sa-wa-dee-khrup/kah.
How are you?:	Sa-bai-dee-mai khrup/kah.
I'm fine:	Sa-bai-dee khrup/kah.
I'm very well:	Dee-mark khrup/kah.
I'm so so:	Sa-bai sa-bai.
What's your name?:	Khun-chue-ar-rai khrup/kah?
My name is Joe:	Phom-chue Joe khrup.
My name is Alice:	Deeshan chue Alice kah.
It's nice to meet you:	Yin-dee-tee dai ruu jak khun khrup/kah.
Excuse me:	Khor thod khrup/kah.
I'm sorry:	Phom sia jai khrup (M)/Deeshan sia chy kah (F).
It's okay/It doesn't matter:	Mai pen rai khrup/kah.
Yes:	Chai khrup/kah
No:	Mai chai khrup/kah
Please:	Karoona
Thank you:	Khop-khun-khrup/kah.
You're welcome:	Mai pen rai khrup/kah.

GETTING AROUND

How do I get to . . .	Phom/chan ja pai . . . (name of the place).dai yang-ngai khrup/kah?
. . . the train station?	sa-ta-nee rod-fai
. . . the post office?	pai-sa-nee

. . . the tourist office?	sam-nak-ngan tong-teow
. . . the hospital?	rong-pha-ya-barn
Does this bus go to?	Rod-khan-nee bpai-nai khrup/ka?
Where is . . .	Yoo tee-nai khrup/ka?
. . . the bathroom?	hong nam
. . . the subway?	sa-ta-nee rot-fai-tai-din
. . . the bank?	ta-na-kahn
. . . the hotel?	rong ram
. . . the store?	rarn
. . . the market?	talaat
Left:	sai
Right:	kwah
Straight ahead:	trong-pai
Is it far?	Klai mai khrup/kah?

USEFUL PHRASES

Do you speak English?	Khun pood pa-sa ung-grid dai mai khrup/kah?
I don't speak Thai:	Phom/chan pood pa-sa Thai mai dai khrup/kah.
I don't understand:	Phom/chan mai cao jai khrup/kah.
I don't know:	Phom/chan mai roo khrup/kah.
I'm American/British.	Phom/chan pen American/Ung-grid khrup/kah.
I'm sick.	Phom/chan mai sa-bai khrup/kah.
Please call a doctor.	Choo-ay re-ak mor doo-ay khrup/kah.
Do you have any rooms?	Khun-mee hawng-mai khrup/kah?
How much does it cost?	Tao rai khrup/kah?
Too expensive:	pa-eng gern-pai
It's beautiful:	soo-ay.
When?	Muah-rai khrup/kah?
Where?	Tee-nai khrup/kah?

Help!	Choo-ay doo-ay!
Stop!	Yoot!

NUMBERS

1	nueng
2	song
3	sam
4	see
5	hah
6	hok
7	jet
8	bpaet
9	gao
10	sib
11	sib-et
12	sib-song
13	sib-sam
14	sib-see
15	sib-hah
16	sib-hok
17	sib-jet
18	sib-bpaet
19	sib-gao
20	yee-sib
21	yee-sib-et
30	sam-sib
40	see-sib
50	hah-sib
60	hok-sib
70	jet-sib
80	bpaet-sib
90	gao-sib

100	nueng-roy
101	nueng-roy-nung
200	song-roy

DAYS & TIME

Today:	wannee
Tomorrow:	proong nee
Yesterday:	muah-waan-nee
Morning:	thawn-chao
Afternoon:	thawn bai
Night:	thorn muet
What time is it?	gee-mong-laew khrup/kah?
It's 2:00:	song mong.
It's 4:00:	see mong.
It's 2:30:	song moang sarm-sip na-tee.
It's 2:45:	song moang see-sip hah na-tee.
Monday:	wan-jun
Tuesday:	wan-ung-kan
Wednesday:	wan-poot
Thursday:	wan-phra-roo-hud
Friday:	wan-sook
Saturday:	an-sao
Sunday:	an-ar-teet
January:	ok-ka-ra-kom
February:	oom-pha-parn
March:	ee-na-kom
April:	ay-sar-yon
May:	rus-sa-pa-kom
June:	e-tu-na-yon
July:	a-rak-ga-da-kom
August:	ing-ha-kom
September:	un-ya-yon

October:	hu-la-kom
November:	rus-sa-ji-ga-yon
December:	an-wa-kom

MENU GUIDE

The first term you should file away is "aroi," which means delicious. You'll no doubt use that one again and again whether you're dining at food stalls or upscale restaurants. When someone asks "Aroi mai?" that's your cue to practice your Thai—most likely your answer will be a resounding "aroi mak" (It's very delicious).

Another useful word is "Kaw," which simply means "Could I have . . .?" However, the most important phrase to remember may be "Gin ped dai mai?" or "Can you eat spicy food?" Answer this one wrong and you might have a five-alarm fire in your mouth. You can answer with a basic "dai" (can), "mai dai" (cannot), or "dai nit noi" (a little). Most restaurants will tone down dishes for foreigners, but if you're visiting a food stall or if you're nervous, you can ask your server "Ped mai?" (Is it spicy?) or specify that you would like your food "mai ped" (not spicy), "ped nit noi khrup/kah" (a little spicy), or if you have very resilient taste buds, "ped ped" (very spicy). Don't be surprised if the latter request is met with some laughter—and if all Thai eyes are on you when you take your first bite. Remember, water won't put out the fire; you'll need to eat something sweet.

food:	a-harn
breakfast:	a-harn chao
lunch:	a-harn klang wan
dinner:	a-harn yen
eat here:	gin tee nee khrup/kah
take away:	kaw glub baan khrup/kah
"The check, please.:"	Check bin khrup/kah
"More, please.:"	Kaw eek noi khrup/kah
Another please.:	Kaw eek an khrup/kah
"A table for two, please.:"	Kaw toh song tee khrup/kah
vegetarian:	gin jay
spicy:	ped
Is it spicy?:	Ped mai?
not spicy:	mai ped
a little spicy:	ped nit noi khrup/kah
very spicy:	ped ped
steamed:	nueng
stir-fried:	pad

stir-fried with ginger:	pad king
stir-fried hot and spicy:	pad ped
grilled (use phao instead when referring to seafood):	ping
deep-fried:	tawd
boiled:	thom

UTENSILS

spoon:	chawn
fork:	sorm
plate:	jarn
glass:	gaew
knife:	meed
napkin:	par ched park
cup:	tuay
chopsticks:	tha-geab

BASIC INGREDIENTS

rice:	kao
steamed rice:	kao suay
fried rice:	kao pad
sticky rice:	kao niao
rice with curry sauce:	kao gaeng
rice porridge (usually for breakfast):	joke
noodles:	kuay theow
egg noodles:	ba mee
egg:	kai
vegetables:	pak
meat:	nua
pork:	moo
chicken:	gai
roast duck:	bped
beef:	nua (same as meat)

fish:	pla
prawns:	gung
squid:	pla muek
crab:	bpu
vegetarian:	jay
galanga (herb):	ka
ginger:	king
lemongrass:	ta krai
garlic:	kratiam
fish sauce:	nam pla
soy sauce:	see-ew
chili paste (spicy dips usually accompanied by various vegetables):	nam prik
"satay sauce (peanut base sauce made of crushed peanuts, coconut milk, chili, and curry):"	satay

BEVERAGES

Thai iced tea (*cha yen*) is Thai black tea mixed with cinnamon, vanilla, star anise, and food coloring. It's usually served cold, but you might see a hot version being enjoyed at the end of a meal. It's very sweet. Don't buy these from food stalls that are working off a block of ice—there's a good chance that the ice isn't purified.

ice:	nam kang
iced coffee:	ga-fare-yen
coffee with milk:	ga-fare sai noom
whiskey:	wis-gee
tea:	nam charr
plain water:	nam plao
soda water:	nam soda
a sweet drink brewed from lemongrass:	nam takrai
vodka:	what gaa
gin:	gin

APPETIZERS

spring rolls:	por pia tawd
panfried rice noodles:	mee krob
spicy raw papaya salad:	som tam
spicy beef salad:	yum nua

MEAT & SEAFOOD

chicken fried with cashew nuts:	gai pad med mamuang himmapan
spicy chicken with basil:	gai ka-prao
grilled chicken:	gai yang
curry soup:	gaeng ga-ree
green curry soup:	gaeng keow wan
mild yellow curry soup:	gaeng massaman
red curry soup:	gaeng ped
hot and sour curry:	kaeng som
minced meat with chilies and lime juice:	larb
spicy salad:	yum
panfried rice noodles:	pad tai
"soup made with coconut cream, chicken, lemongrass, and chilies:"	tom ka gai
lemongrass soup with shrimp and mushrooms:	tom yum kung

FRUIT

banana:	gluay
tamarind:	ma karm
papaya:	ma la gore
mango:	ma muang
coconut:	ma prao
mangosteen:	mung kood
mandarin orange:	som
pomegranate:	tub tim

DESSERTS

dessert:	ka nom
mango with sticky rice:	kao niao ma muang
grilled bananas:	gluay bping
coconut pudding:	ka nom krog
rice based dessert cooked in coconut milk:	kao larm
spicy raw papaya salad:	som tam
spicy beef salad:	yum nua

Travel Smart Thailand

WORD OF MOUTH

"No question, getting those award tickets nailed down is the first priority (I also use United miles, but to upgrade to Biz) and they are bookable about 330 days in advance. You can wait a while to book your internal flights, but do book them before you go. The price will be the same, and who wants to spend their vacation buying plane tickets?"

—Kathie

www.fodors.com/forums

GETTING HERE & AROUND

Thailand is a long country, stretching some 1,100 mi north to south. Bangkok is a major Asian travel hub, so you'll very likely begin your trip by flying into the capital. Relatively affordable flights are available from Bangkok to every major city in the country, and if you're strapped for time, flying is a great way to get around. But train travel, where available, can be an enjoyable sightseeing experience if you're not in a rush, and Thailand also has a comprehensive bus system.

BY AIR

Bangkok is 17 hours from San Francisco, 18 hours from Seattle and Vancouver, 20 hours from Chicago, 22 hours from New York, and 10 hours from Sydney. Add more time for stopovers and connections, especially if you're using more than one carrier. Thai Airways' new direct flights between Bangkok and New York and Bangkok and Los Angeles are 16½ and 14½ hours, respectively, far and away the quickest trips available.

On popular tourist routes during peak holiday times, domestic flights in Thailand are often fully booked. Make sure you have reservations, and make them well in advance of your travel date. Be sure to reconfirm your return flight when you arrive in Thailand.

Airline Security Issues **Transportation Security Administration** (*www.tsa.gov*) has answers for almost every question that might come up.

AIRPORTS

Bangkok remains Thailand's gateway to the world. The look of that gateway changed a couple of years ago with the opening of the new international Suvarnabhumi Airport, 30 km (18 mi) southeast of town, which is a huge improvement over the old Don Muang International Airport. Unfortunately, the new airport (pronounced *soo-wanna-poom*) is not any closer to the city than the old one—it lies far from downtown and as of yet does not have any decent public transportation links. The government promises eventual subway and light-rail connections.

At Chiang Mai International Airport, work hurries along to finish a large new terminal to handle the recent sharp increases in national and regional air traffic. The airport lies on the edge of town, and taxi service to most hotels costs a flat B120 (about $3).

Perhaps Thailand's third-busiest airport (especially in high season) is the one at Phuket, a major link to the Southern Beaches region, particularly the islands of the Andaman Coast.

Bangkok Airways owns and runs the airports in Sukhothai, Trat, and Koh Samui. They have the only flights to these destinations, which can be expensive in high season. You also have to use the airport transport options they offer unless your hotel picks you up.

Airport Information **Airports of Thailand** (*www.airportthai.co.th*) has information on the country's major airports, though much of it is in Thai. **Suvarnabhumi Airport** (*www.suvarnabhumiairport.com*).

GROUND TRANSPORTATION

At Suvarnabhumi, free shuttle buses run from the airport to a public bus stand, where you can catch a bus into the city.

Meter taxis run between the airport and town and charge a B50 airport fee on top of the meter charge. Be sure to find the public taxi stand upon leaving Suvarnabhumi. Touts are notorious for approaching travelers in the airport and offering rides at rates that far exceed the norm. Taxis in town will often try to set a high flat fee to take you to the airport, though this is technically illegal. If you do talk a taxi driver into charging by the meter, expect a long, scenic trip to the airport.

Suvarnabhumi Airport offers six types of limousines for hire—visit the limo counter on Level 2 in the baggage claim hall.

If possible, plan your flights to arrive and depart outside of rush hours. A trip to Suvarnabhumi from the main hotel strip along Sukhumvit Road can take as little as 25 minutes if traffic is moving, and hours during traffic jams—the same goes for the Khao San Road area.

■ **TIP→ It helps to have a hotel brochure or an address in Thai for the driver.** Also, stop at one of the ATMs in the arrival hall and get some baht before leaving the airport so you can pay your taxi driver.

INTERNATIONAL FLIGHTS

Bangkok is one of Asia's—and the world's—largest air hubs, with flights to most corners of the globe and service from nearly all of the world's major carriers, plus dozens of minor carriers. Most flights from the United States stop in Hong Kong, Tokyo, or Taipei on the way to Bangkok.

Northwest Airlines and Japan Airlines (JAL) are both major carriers with hubs in the United States and offer daily flights between the U.S. and Thailand. JAL is one of the best options, around with a flight time of 17 hours from Dallas including a stopover at Tokyo's Narita airport. East Coast travelers departing from New York or Washington D.C. could also consider using British Airways or Virgin Atlantic/Thai Airways via London or Singapore Airlines from Newark via Amsterdam. From the West Coast, Thai Airways has good connections from Los Angeles, San Francisco, and Seattle. Cathay Pacific often has good fares from San Francisco.

■ **TIP→ Many Asian airlines (Thai Airways, Singapore Airlines, Cathay Pacific, Malaysia Airlines) are rated among the best in the world for their service.** They often have more-comfortable seats, better food selections (still without extra charge), and more entertainment options than do most U.S.-based carriers. Many Asian airlines also allow you to change your bookings for free (or for a nominal charge) if done a week in advance. Lastly, tickets purchased from these carriers are generally no more expensive than those offered by U.S. carriers. And the extra creature comforts these airlines provide can leave you a little less frazzled when you reach your destination, ensuring that you don't spend half your vacation recovering from the trip over.

At this writing, Bangkok Airways offers the only flights between Bangkok and Siem Reap, Cambodia (home of Angkor Wat), and you pay a pretty price for the service. However, several budget airlines now fly other popular routes around Southeast Asia, making short country-hopping excursions far more feasible than before.

Chiang Mai, Thailand's second-biggest city, is slowly becoming an important regional destination and direct flights between here and Hong Kong, Singapore, Tokyo, Taipei, various points in China, Luang Prabang in Laos, and other Asian destinations may be available. However, these routes seem to change with the wind, so check before your trip.

Airline Contacts **Asiana Airlines** (☎ *800/227-4262* ⊕ *us.flyasiana.com*). **British Airways** (☎ *800/247-9297* ⊕ *www.britishairways.com*). **Cathay Pacific** (☎ *800/233-2742* ⊕ *www.cathaypacific.com*). **China Airlines** (☎ *800/227-5118* ⊕ *www.china-airlines.com*). **Continental Airlines** (☎ *800/523—3273 for U.S. and Mexico reservations, 800/231-0856 for international reservations* ⊕ *www.continental.com*). **Delta Airlines** (☎ *800/221-1212 for U.S. reservations, 800/241-4141 for international reservations* ⊕ *www.delta.com*). **EVA Air** (☎ *800/695-1188* ⊕ *www.evaair.com*). **Japan Airlines** (☎ *800/525-3663* ⊕ *www.jal.com*). **Korean Air** (☎ *800/438-5000* ⊕ *www.koreanair.com*). **Lao Airlines** (☎ *21/212-057 in Laos* ⊕ *www.laoairlines.com*). **Malaysia Air-**

lines (☎ *800/552–9264* 🌐 *us.malaysiaairlines.com*). **Northwest Airlines** (☎ *800/225–2525* 🌐 *www.nwa.com*). **Royal Khmer Airlines** (☎ *023/994502* 🌐 *www.royalkhmerairlines.com*). **Siem Reap Airways** (☎ *023/720022* 🌐 *www.siemreapairways.com*). **Singapore Airlines** (☎ *800/742–3333* 🌐 *www.singaporeair.com*). **Thai Airways** (☎ *800/426–5204* 🌐 *www.thaiairwaysusa.com*). **United Airlines** (☎ *800/864–8331 for U.S. reservations, 800/538–2929 for international reservations* 🌐 *www.united.com*).

AIR TRAVEL WITHIN THAILAND

Thai Airways has by far the largest network of any airline in Thailand and connects all major and many minor destinations across the country. Bangkok Airways, which bills itself as a luxury boutique airline with comfy seats and good food, covers many routes and is the only airline to service Koh Samui, Trat, and Sukhothai. Both Thai and Bangkok Airways fly a mix of larger jet aircrafts and smaller turbo-props. For the last few years, buying tickets on the Thai Airways Web site was an act reserved for masochists; at this writing, it is still easier and cheaper to go to a travel agent to get Thai Airways tickets. The Web sites of other Thai airlines generally work well for online bookings.

Budget airlines now cover Thailand's skies and have dramatically lowered the cost of travel. Nok Air (a subsidiary of Thai Airways) and Thai AirAsia are the most well known. As of this writing, another budget carrier, One-Two-Go (owned by Orient-Thai Airlines) has been grounded temporarily by the Thai government following a fatal crash in Phuket.

With budget carriers, you'll save the most by booking online and as far in advance as you can. There's a small fee for booking over the phone, and you may not get an English-speaking operator. The airlines keep their prices low by charging extra for services like food—or not offering it at all. They charge less for flights at odd hours (often late in the day) and change their schedules based on the availability of cheap landing and take-off times. AirAsia, generally the cheapest of the budget carriers, seems to change its flight times and routes every couple of months. **■ TIP→ Delays are more common the later in the day you're flying, so if you need to make an international connection, morning flights are a safer bet.**

Regional Carriers **AirAsia** (☎ *02/515–9999 in Thailand, 603/8660–4343 from all other countries* 🌐 *www.airasia.com*). **Bangkok Airways** (☎ *02/265–5555 in Thailand* 🌐 *www.bangkokair.com*). **JetStar Asia** (☎ *02/267–5125 in Thailand, 800/611–2957 from other countries* 🌐 *www.jetstar.com*). **Nok Air** (☎ *02/627–2000* 🌐 *www.nokair.com*). **Orient Thai Airlines** (☎ *02/2294260* 🌐 *www.orient-thai.com*). **Silk Airlines** (☎ *053/904985 in Thailand* 🌐 *www.silkair.com*). **Thai Airways** (☎ *02/232–8000* 🌐 *www.thaiairways.com*). **Tiger Airways** (☎ *02/975–5333 in Thailand* 🌐 *www.tigerairways.com*).

BY BUS

Thai buses are cheap and faster than trains, and reach every corner of the country. There are usually two to three buses a day on most routes and several (or even hourly) daily buses on popular routes between major towns. Most buses leave in the morning, with a few other runs spaced out in the afternoon and evening. Buses leave in the evening for long overnight trips. Overnight buses are very popular with Thais and they're a more efficient use of time, but they do crash with disturbing regularity and many foreign expats avoid them.

■ TIP→ Avoid taking private bus company trips from the Khao San Road area. The buses are not as comfortable as public buses, they take longer, and they usually try to trap you at an affiliated hotel once you reach your destination. There have also been many reports of rip-offs, scams, and luggage thefts on these buses over the years.

There are, generally speaking, three classes of bus service: cheap, no-frills locals on short routes that stop at every road crossing and for anyone who waves them down; second- and first-class buses on specific routes that have air-conditioning, toilets (sometimes), and loud chop-socky movies (too often); and VIP buses that provide nonstop service between major bus stations and have comfortable seats, drinks, snacks, air-conditioning, and movies (often starring Steven Seagal or Jean-Claude Van Damme). If you're setting out on a long bus journey, it's worth inquiring about the onboard entertainment—14 hours on a bus with continuous karaoke VCDs blasting out old pop hits can be torturous. Air-conditioned buses are usually so cold that you'll want an extra sweater. On local buses, space at the back soon fills up with all kinds of oversize luggage, so it's best to sit toward the middle or front.

Bangkok has three main bus stations, serving routes to the north (Mo Chit), south (Southern Terminal), and east (Ekamai). Chiang Mai has one major terminal. All have telephone information lines, but the operators rarely speak English. It's best to buy tickets at the bus station, where the bigger bus companies have ticket windows. Thais usually just head to the station an hour before they'd like to leave; you may want to go a day early to be sure you get a ticket if your plans aren't flexible. Travel agents can sometimes get tickets for you, but often the fee is more than half the cost of the ticket. All fares are paid in cash.

Many small towns don't have formal bus terminals, but rather a spot along a main road where buses stop. Information concerning schedules can be obtained from TAT offices and the bus stations.

BY CAR

Car travel in Thailand has its ups and downs. Major thoroughfares tend to be congested, but the limited number of roads and the straightforward layout of cities combine to make navigation relatively easy. The exception, of course, is Bangkok. Don't even think about negotiating that tangled mass of traffic-clogged streets. Hire a driver instead.

Cars are available for rent in Bangkok and in major tourist destinations. However, even outside Bangkok, the additional cost of hiring a driver is a small price to pay for peace of mind. If a foreigner is involved in an automobile accident, he or she—not the Thai—is likely to be judged at fault, no matter who hit whom.

If you do decide to rent a car, know that traffic laws are routinely disregarded. Bigger vehicles have the unspoken right of way, motorcyclists seem to think they are invincible, and bicyclists often don't look around them. Few Thai drivers go anywhere anymore without a cell phone stuck to one ear. **TIP→ Drive *very* carefully, as those around you generally won't.**

Police checkpoints are common, especially near international borders and in the restive south. You must stop for them but will most likely be waved through.

Rental-company rates in Thailand begin at about $30 a day for an economy car with unlimited mileage. This includes neither tax, which is 7% on car rentals, nor the collision-damage waiver. It's better to make your car-rental reservations when you arrive in Thailand, as you can usually secure a discount.

Jeeps and other vehicles are widely available for rent in tourist spots—particularly beach areas—and prices generally begin at about $25 a day. But be wary of the renter and any contract you sign (which might be in Thai). Often these vehicles come with no insurance that covers you, so you are liable for any damage incurred.

You must have an International Driving Permit (IDP) to drive or rent a car in Thailand. IDP's are not difficult to obtain, and having one in your wallet may save you from unwanted headaches if you do have to deal with local authorities. Check the AAA Web site for more info as well as for IDPs ($15) themselves.

GASOLINE

A liter of gasoline costs approximately B35. Many gas stations stay open 24 hours and have clean toilet facilities and minimarts. As you get farther away from developed areas, roadside stalls sell gasoline from bottles or tanks.

PARKING

You can park on most streets; no-parking areas are marked either with red-and-white bars on the curb or with circular blue signs with a red "don't" stroke through the middle. The less urban the area, the more likely locals will double- and triple-park to be as close as possible to their destination. Thai traffic police do "boot" cars and motorcycles that are improperly parked, though only when they feel like it. The ticketing officer usually leaves a sheet of paper with a contact number to call; once you call, he returns, you pay your fine (often subject to negotiation), and he removes the boot.

In cities, the larger hotels, restaurants, and department stores have garages or parking lots. Rates vary, but count on B10 or more an hour. If you purchase anything, parking is free, but you must have your ticket validated.

ROAD CONDITIONS

Thai highways and town roads are generally quite good. Byways and rural roads range from good to indescribably bad. In rainy season, expect rural dirt roads to be impassable bogs.

TIP→ Leafy twigs and branches lying on a road are not decorations but warnings that something is amiss ahead. Slow down and proceed with caution.

Thai traffic signs will be familiar to all international drivers, though most roads are marked in Thai. Fortunately, larger roads, highways, and tourist attractions often have English signs, too. Signs aren't always clear, so you may find yourself asking for directions quite often.

If you have a choice, don't drive at night. Motorists out after dark often drive like maniacs and may be drunk. Likewise, if you have a choice, avoid driving during key holidays such as Songkran. The Bangkok newspapers keep tallies of road deaths during each big holiday and the numbers are enough to frighten anyone off the highway. When you are driving anywhere in the country, at all times beware of oxcarts, cows, dogs, small children, and people on bikes suddenly joining the traffic fray.

ROADSIDE EMERGENCIES

Should you run into any problems, you can contact the Tourist Police at their hotline, 1155.

RULES OF THE ROAD

As in the United Kingdom, drive on the left side of the road, even if the locals don't. Speed limits are 60 KPH (37 MPH) in cities, 90 KPH (56 MPH) outside, and 130 KPH (81 MPH) on expressways, not that anyone pays much heed. If you're caught breaking traffic laws, you officially have to report to the police station to pay a large fine. In reality, an on-the-spot fine of B100 or B200 can usually be paid. Never presume to have the right of way in Thailand and always expect the other driver to do exactly what you think they should not.

BY MOTORCYCLE

Many people rent small motorcycles to get around the countryside or the islands. **⚠ A Thai city is not the place to learn how to drive a motorcycle.** Phuket in particular is unforgiving to novices—don't think of driving one around there unless you are experienced. Motorcycles skid easily on wet or gravel roads. On Koh Samui, a sign posts the year's count of foreigners who never made it home from their vacations because of such accidents. In the past people often did not bother to wear a helmet in the evenings, but government crackdowns have made it common practice to drive as safely at night as during the day. Shoes, a shirt, and long pants will also offer some protection in wrecks, which are common. When driving a motorbike, make sure your vehicle has a rectangular sticker showing up-to-date insurance and registration. The sticker should be pasted somewhere towards the front of the bike, with the Buddhist year in big, bold numbers (The year 2010 is 2553 on the Buddhist calendar).

You can rent a smaller 100cc–125cc motorcycles for only a few dollars a day. Dirt bikes and bigger road bikes, 250cc and above, start at $20 per day.

Two-wheeled vacations are a growing segment of Thai tourism, especially in the north. With Thailand's crazy traffic, this is not a good option for first-time tourists to the area. That said, Golden Triangle Rider has a fantastic Web site, *www.gt-rider.com*, on biking in the area, with information on rentals and routes.

BY SAMLOR, SONGTHAEW & TUK-TUK

(⇨ *Transportation, Thai-Style in Chapter 1, Experience Thailand*).

BY TAXI

Most Thai taxis now have meters installed, and these are the ones tourists should take. (However, the drivers of Chiang Mai's small fleet of "meter" taxis rarely offer a meter rate and demand flat fees instead. Bargain.) Taxis waiting at hotels are more likely to demand a high flat fare than those flagged down on the street. **TIP→ Never enter any taxi until the price has been established or the driver agrees to use the meter.** Most taxi drivers do not speak English, but all understand the finger count. One finger means B10, two is for B20, and so on. Whenever possible, ask at your hotel front desk what the approximate fare should be. If you flag down a meter taxi and the driver refuses to use the meter, you can try to negotiate a better fare, or simply get another taxi. If you negotiate too much, he will simply take you on a long route to jack the meter price up.

BY TRAIN

Trains are a great way to get around Thailand. Though they're a bit slower and generally more expensive than buses, they're more comfortable and safer. They go to (or close to) most major tourist destinations, and many go through areas where major roads don't venture. The State Railway of Thailand has four lines, all of which terminate in Bangkok. Hualamphong is Bangkok's main terminal; you can book tickets for any route in the country there. (Chiang Mai's station is another major hub, where you can also buy tickets for any route.)

TRAIN ROUTES

The Northern Line connects Bangkok with Chiang Mai, passing through Ayutthaya, Phitsanulok, and Sukhothai. The Northeastern Line travels up to Nong Khai, on the Laotian border (across from Vientiane), and has a branch that goes east to Ubon Ratchathani. The Southern Line goes all the way south through Surat Thani (get off here for Koh Samui) to the Malaysian border and on to Kuala Lumpur and Singapore, a journey that takes 37 hours. The Eastern line splits and goes to both Pattaya and Aranyaprathet on the Cambodian border. A short line also connects Bangkok with Nam Tok to the west, passing through Kanchanaburi and the bridge over the River Kwai along the way. (There's no train to Phuket; you have to go to the Phun Phin station, about 14 km [9 mi] from Surat Thani and change to a bus.) ⚠ **The Southern Line has been attacked in insurgency-related violence.** Check the security situation before booking a trip to the South.

TICKETS AND RAIL PASSES

The State Railway of Thailand offers two types of rail passes. Both are valid for 20 days of unlimited travel on all trains in either second or third class. The cheaper of the two costs B1,500 and does not include supplementary charges such as air-conditioning and berths; for B3,000, you can get a pass that does. You would need to take several long overnight sleeper trains to get your money's worth on a B3,000 pass, but if the train is your primary mode of transportation, it may be worth it. If you don't plan to cover many miles by train, individual tickets are probably the way to go.

Even if you purchase a rail pass, you're not guaranteed seats on any particular train; you'll need to book these ahead of time through a travel agent or by visiting the advance booking office of the nearest train station. Seat reservations are required on some trains and are strongly advised on long-distance routes, especially if you want a sleeper on the Bangkok to Chiang Mai trip. Bangkok to Chiang Mai and other popular routes need to be booked several days in advance, especially during the popular tourist season between November and January, as well as during the Thai New Year in April. Tickets for shorter, less frequented routes can be bought a day in advance or, sometimes, right at the station before departure. Most travel agencies have information on train schedules, and many will book seats for you for a small fee, saving you a trip to the station.

The State Railway of Thailand's rather basic Web site has timetables, routes, available seats, and other information, but no way to book tickets. The British-based Web site Seat 61 also has lots of helpful information about train travel in Thailand. Train schedules in English are available from travel agents and from major railway stations.

CLASSES OF SERVICE

Local trains are generally pretty slow and can get crowded, but you'll never be lonely! On some local trains there's a choice between second and third class.

Most long-distance trains offer second- or third-class tickets, and some overnight trains to the north (Chiang Mai) and to the south offer first-class sleeping cabins. First-class sleepers have nice individual rooms for two to four people, but they are increasingly rare. If you have the chance, splurging on a first-class overnight cabin can be a unique, almost romantic experience. You'd be hard-pressed to find a first-class sleeper cabin this cheap anywhere else in the world (B1,353 for a Bangkok to Chiang Mai ticket).

Second-class cars have comfy padded bench seats or sleeper bunks with sheets and curtains. Tickets are about half the price of first-class (B881, Bangkok to Chiang Mai), and since the couchettes are quite comfortable, most westerners choose these. Second class is generally air-conditioned, but on overnight journeys you have a choice of air-conditioning or fan-cooled cars. The air-conditioning tends to be freezing (bring a sweater and socks) and leave you dehydrated. Sleeping next to an open train window can leave you deaf and covered in soot. It's your choice. Third-class cars have hard benches and no air-conditioning, but are wildly cheap (B271, Bangkok to Chiang Mai).

Meals are served at your seat in first and second classes.

Information **Chiang Mai Railway Station** (☎ *053/244795*). **Hualamphong Railway Station** (☎ *02/223–3762 or 02/223–0341*). **Seat 61** (🌐 *www.seat61.com/Thailand.htm*). **The State of the Railway of Thailand** (🌐 *www.railway.co.th/english*).

ESSENTIALS

ACCOMMODATIONS

Nearly every town offers accommodation. In smaller towns hotels may be fairly simple, but they will usually be clean and inexpensive. In major cities or resort areas there are hotels to fit all price categories. The least-expensive places may have Asian toilets (squat type with no seat) and a fan rather than air-conditioning. Breakfast is sometimes included in the room rate at hotels and guesthouses.

During the peak tourist season, hotels are often fully booked and rates are at their highest. During holidays, such as between December 30 and January 2, Chinese New Year (in January or February, depending on the year), and Songkran (the Thai New Year in April), rates climb even higher, and reservations are difficult to obtain on short notice. Weekday rates at some resorts are often lower, and virtually all hotels will discount their rooms if they are not fully booked. You can often get a deal by booking mid- to upper-range hotel rooms through Thai travel agents. They get a deeply discounted rate, part of which they then pass on to you.

Don't be reticent about asking for a special rate. Though it may feel awkward to haggle since Western hotel prices aren't negotiable, this practice is perfectly normal in Thailand. Often it will get you nothing, but it can occasionally save you up to 50% if you catch a manager in the right mood with a bunch of empty rooms. Give it a whirl. The worst they can say is "no."

The lodgings we list are the cream of the crop in each price category. We always list the facilities that are available, but we don't specify whether they cost extra; when pricing accommodations, always ask what's included and what costs extra. Hotels have private bath unless otherwise noted.

APARTMENT & HOUSE RENTALS

It is possible to rent apartments or houses for longer stays in most places in Thailand. Bangkok, Chiang Mai, Phuket, and Pattaya in particular have large expat and long-term tourist communities. Also, many hotels and guesthouses are willing to offer greatly reduced rates for long-term guests. Agents are available in all big cities and are used to helping foreigners. Often, they will be the only way to find an affordable place quickly in a city like Bangkok. The *Bangkok Post, Chiang Mai CityLife* magazine, *Chiang Mai Mail, Phuket Gazette,* and *Pattaya Mail* are all good places to begin looking for agents or places for rent.

GUESTHOUSES

Though the "guesthouse" label is tacked onto accommodations of all sizes and prices, guesthouses are generally smaller, cheaper, and more casual than hotels. They are often family run, with small restaurants. The least expensive rooms often have shared baths, and linens may not be included. At the other end of the spectrum, $25 will get you a room with all the amenities—a/c, cable TV, en-suite bathrooms, even Internet access—in just about every corner of the country. **TIP→ Even if you're traveling on a strict budget, make sure your room has window screens or a mosquito net.**

HOTELS

Thai luxury hotels are among the best in the world. Service is generally superb—polite and efficient—and most of the staff speak English. At the other end of the scale, budget lodgings are simple and basic—a room with little more than a bed. Expect any room costing more than the equivalent of US$20 a night to come with hot water, air-conditioning, and a TV. Southeast Asian hotels traditionally have two twin beds. Make sure to ask for one big bed if that is your preference, though this is often two twins pushed together.

Many hotels have restaurants and offer room service throughout most of the day and night. Many will also be happy to make travel arrangements for you—for which they receive commissions. Use hotel safe-deposit boxes if they are offered.

COMMUNICATIONS

INTERNET

Only the largest hotels offer in-room Internet connections, and these are often inconvenient or expensive, although this is slowly starting to improve. It is not uncommon for a hotel to claim to have complimentary Internet access when in reality, you must buy a local dial-up Internet plan which you then connect to via the hotel's phone (incurring extra costs from the hotel in the process). Reliable Wi-Fi connections are very uncommon. Those hotels or businesses that have them tend to have them in one location, such as the lobby. Fortunately, many hotels have business centers that provide Internet access.

Outside of large hotels and business centers, the electrical supply can be temperamental. Surging and dipping power supplies are normal, and power outages are not unheard of.

Even the smallest towns have Internet shops, though the connection can be slow and temperamental. Shops used to dealing with foreigners will often allow you to connect a laptop. The standard price in a tourist area is B1 per minute, while shops aimed at locals can be as cheap as B20 per hour. Larger hotels and resorts usually charge a lot more so make sure to ask in advance.

Contacts **Cybercafes** (*www.cybercafes.com*) lists over 4,000 Internet cafés worldwide.

PHONES

The country code for Thailand is 66. When dialing a Thailand number from abroad, drop the initial 0 from the local area code.

To call Cambodia from overseas, dial the country code, 855, and then the area code, omitting the first "0." The code for Phnom Penh is 023; for Siem Reap it's 063. Unfortunately, Cambodia's international lines are frequently jammed; booking and requesting information through Web sites is consequently the best option. Almost all Internet shops offer overseas calling, which runs about 25¢ to 50¢ a minute. This is the most popular way to make such calls.

To call Laos from overseas, dial the country code, 856, and then the area code, omitting the first 0. The outgoing international code is 00, but IDD phones are rare. If you have to make an international call from Laos, use your hotel's switchboard. This is a good idea even for local calls, as there are few pay phones.

CALLING WITHIN THAILAND

There are three major phone companies and at least four cell phone operators. Pay phones are available throughout the country, and they generally work, though long-distance calls can only be made on phones that accept both B1 and B5 coins.

Many hotels and guesthouses use cruddy third-party pay phones, which rarely work well but make extra money for the hotel. Avoid them if you can.

If you wish to receive assistance for an overseas call, dial 100/233–2771. For local telephone inquiries, dial 100/183, but you will need to speak Thai. In Bangkok, you can dial 1133 for an English-speaking operator.

CALLING OUTSIDE THAILAND

The country code for the United States is 1.

To make overseas calls, you can use either your hotel switchboard—Chiang Mai and Bangkok have direct dialing—or the overseas telephone facilities at the central post office and telecommunications building. You'll find one in all towns. In Bangkok, the overseas telephone center, next to the general post office, is open 24 hours; up-country, the facilities' hours may vary, but they usually open at 8 AM and some stay open until 10 PM.

The cheapest—and often easiest—way to call internationally is on the Internet. Any Internet shop should be able to set you up. You can also start a Skype (or similar) account before leaving home, and use it on the road. It is an increasingly popular option among frequent travelers.

MOBILE PHONES

If you have a GSM cell phone and your operator allows it, your phone may work in Thailand, though the roaming charges can be deadly. Many use their cell phones to send and receive text messages, a cheap way to stay in touch.

Alternately, if you have a GSM phone (and it has not been locked to one number by your phone company), you can buy a SIM card (the chip that keeps your phone number and account) in Thailand for about B800 at one of the ubiquitous cell phone kiosks, pop it into your phone, and have a local number while visiting. Then buy phone cards in B100 to B500 denominations and pay for calls as you go, generally B3 to B10 a minute depending on the time of day and number you are calling. International calls will run about B40 a minute.

It is possible to rent a cell phone through a company, but a week will cost you nearly $30; two weeks nearly $50. At those rates, you can buy a used phone at any cell phone shop (all malls in Thailand have them). If you still prefer to rent, some options:

Contacts **Cellular Abroad** (☎ *800/287-5072* 🌐 *www.cellularabroad.com*) rents and sells GMS phones and sells SIM cards that work in many countries. **Mobal** (☎ *888/888-9162* 🌐 *www.mobalrental.com*) rents mobiles and sells GSM phones (starting at $49) that will operate in 140 countries. Per-call rates vary throughout the world. **Planet Fone** (☎ *888/988-4777* 🌐 *www.planetfone.com*) rents cell phones, but the per-minute rates are expensive.

CUSTOMS & DUTIES

THAILAND

Most people pass through Customs at Suvarnabhumi without even so much as a glance from a Customs officer. The country worries more about people smuggling opium across borders than they do about an extra bottle of wine or your new camera. That said, if you're bringing any foreign-made equipment from home, such as cameras, it's wise to carry the original receipt with you or register it with U.S. Customs before you leave (Form 4457). Otherwise, you may end up paying duty on your return.

One liter of wine or liquor, 200 cigarettes or 250 grams of smoking tobacco, and all personal effects may be brought into Thailand duty-free. Visitors may bring in and leave with any amount of foreign currency; you cannot leave with more than B50,000 without obtaining a permit. Narcotics, pornographic materials, protected wild animals and wild animal parts, and firearms are strictly prohibited.

Some tourists dream of Thailand as a tropical paradise floating on a cloud of marijuana smoke—not so. Narcotics are strictly illegal and jail terms for the transporting or possession of even the smallest amounts are extremely harsh.

If you purchase any Buddha images (originals or reproductions), artifacts, or true antiques and want to take them home, you need to get a certificate from the Fine Arts Department. Taking unregistered or unauthorized antiques out of the country is a major offense to the culture-conscious

Thais. If you get a particularly good reproduction of an antique, get a letter or certificate from the seller saying it is a reproduction, or risk losing it on your way out of the country. Art or antiques requiring export permits must be taken to one of the museums listed below at least a week before the departure date. You will have to fill out an application and provide two photographs—front and side views—of the object as well as a photocopy of your passport information page.

Antiques Permits **Chiang Mai National Museum** (☎ *053/221308*). **National Museum–Bangkok** (☎ *02/224–1370 or 02/224–1333*).

CAMBODIA & LAOS

You are allowed to bring 200 cigarettes or the equivalent in cigars or tobacco and one bottle of liquor into Cambodia. You are not allowed to bring in or take out local currency, nor are you allowed to remove Angkor antiquities. The export of other antiques or religious objects requires a permit. Contact your embassy for assistance in obtaining one before laying out money on an expensive purchase.

Tourists are allowed to bring up to one liter of spirits and two liters of wine into Laos, as well as 200 cigarettes, 50 cigars, or 250 grams of tobacco. Bringing in or taking out local currency is prohibited, as is the export of antiques and religious artifacts without a permit.

Note that the dissemination of foreign religious and political materials is forbidden, and you should refrain from bringing such materials into the country.

Thai Customs Department (🌐 *www.customs.go.th/Customs-Eng/indexEng.jsp*).

U.S. Information **U.S. Customs and Border Protection** (🌐 *www.cbp.gov*).

EATING OUT

Thai food is eaten with a fork and spoon; the spoon held in the right hand and the fork is used like a plow to push food into the spoon. Chopsticks are used only for Chinese food, such as noodle dishes. After you have finished eating, place your fork and spoon on the plate at the 5:25 position; otherwise the server will assume you would like another helping.

If you want to catch a waiter's attention, use the all-purpose polite word, *krup* if you are a man and *ka* if you are a woman. Beckoning with a hand and fingers pointed upward is considered rude; point your fingers downward instead.

MEALS & MEALTIMES

Thai cuisine's distinctive flavor comes particularly from the use of fresh Thai basil, lemongrass, tamarind, lime, and citrus leaves. And though some Thai food is fiery hot from garlic and chilies, an equal number of dishes serve the spices on the side so that you can adjust the incendiary level. Thais use *nam pla,* a fish sauce, instead of salt.

Restaurant hours vary, but Thais eat at all times of day, and in cities, you will find eateries open through the night. In Thailand, breakfast outside the hotel often means noodle soup or curry on the street (or banana pancakes in backpacker areas). Street vendors also sell coffee, although diehard caffeine addicts may not get enough of a fix; Thai coffee isn't simply coffee, but a combination of ground beans with nuts and spices. If you're desperate, look for a western-style espresso machine or a Chinese coffee shop.

The lunch hour is long—roughly 11:30 to 2—in smaller towns and rural areas, a holdover from when Thailand was primarily a country of rice farmers and everyone napped during the hottest hours of the day.

LOCAL DO'S & TABOOS

THE KING

King Bhumibol Adulyadej has ruled Thailand for more than 60 years, and is revered by his people. Any insult against him is an insult against the national religion and patrimony. Lighthearted remarks or comparisons to any other person living or dead are also taboo. If you don't have something nice to say about the king, don't say anything at all.

GOOD MANNERS

Thais aim to live with a "cool heart" or *jai yen*—free from emotional extremes. Since being in a hurry shows an obvious lack of calm, they don't rush and aren't always punctual. Try to leave space in your itinerary for this relaxed attitude, since something will invariably happen to slow your progress.

Always remove your shoes when you enter a home. Do not step over a seated person's legs. Don't point your feet at anyone; keep them on the floor, and take care not to show the soles of your feet (as the lowest part of the body, they are seen by Buddhists as the least holy). Never touch a person's head, even a child's (the head is the most sacred part of the body in Buddhist cultures), and avoid touching a monk if you're a woman.

When possible do not give or receive anything with your left hand; use your right hand and support it lightly at the elbow with your left hand to show greater respect. Don't be touchy-feely in public. Speak softly and politely—a calm demeanor always accomplishes more than a hot-headed attitude. Displays of anger, raised voices, or even very direct speech are considered bad form.

Thais don't like anything done in twos, a number associated with death. Hence, you should buy three mangoes, not two; stairways have odd numbers of stairs; and people rarely want to have their photo taken if there are only two people.

OUT ON THE TOWN

Many Thais drink and smoke, but smoking of late has been banned in public buildings (including restaurants and bars). While you might spot a few drunken Thais stumbling about on a Saturday night, public drunkenness is not any more welcome here than it would be at home. Backpackers who flock to Thailand for cheap beer and beach parties rarely leave a favorable impression on the locals.

DOING BUSINESS

Thais are polite and formal in their business doings, employing the same sense of propriety as in everyday life. In professional settings, it is always best to address people with the courtesy title, *khun* (for males and females). As anywhere, greet a business associate with a Buddhist *wai* (hands clasped, head bowed.)

Business cards are hugely popular in Southeast Asia and it's a good idea to have some on hand. You can have them made quickly and cheaply in Thailand if necessary.

Local copy shops and business centers are about as common as Internet shops—ask around. In the cities, the nearest business-service center is likely a block or two away. Department stores such as Central (🌐 *www.central.co.th/index_en.html*) usually dedicate the majority of a floor to school supplies and business services.

Unless otherwise noted, the restaurants listed in this guide are open daily for lunch and dinner.

PAYING

Expect to pay for most meals in cash. Larger hotels and fancy restaurants in metropolitan areas accept some major credit cards, but they will often charge an extra 2% to 4% for the convenience. If you are at the restaurant of the hotel where you are staying, you can generally just add the bill to your room and leave a cash tip if you desire. Street vendors and small, local restaurants only accept cash. (⇨ *Tipping, below.*)

RESERVATIONS & DRESS

Generally, reservations are not necessary at Thai restaurants, and even then are only accepted at the most expensive and popular ones.

Because Thailand has a hot climate, jackets and ties are rarely worn at dinner except in expensive hotel restaurants. Attire tends to fit the setting: People dress casually at simple restaurants and in small towns, but the Bangkok and Chiang Mai elite love dressing to the hilt for a posh night on the town. We mention dress when men are required to wear a jacket or tie.

WINES, BEER & SPIRITS

Singha, Tiger, and Heineken are at the top end of Thailand's beer market, while Chang, Leo, and a host of other brands fight it out for the budget drinkers. It's also becoming more common to find imports such as Guinness, Corona, Budweiser, and the ever-popular Beer Lao lining the shelves of cosmopolitan bars.

If you want to drink like the hip locals, don't bother with beer. Grab a bottle of whiskey (Chivas Regal, Johnnie Walker, or the very affordable 100 Pipers) to mix with soda.

Rice whiskey, which tastes sweet and has a whopping 35% alcohol content, is another favorite throughout Thailand. It tastes and mixes more like rum than whiskey. Mekong and Sam Song are by far the most popular rice whiskeys, but you will also see labels such as Kwangthong, Hong Thong, Hong Ngoen, Hong Yok, and Hong Tho. Thais mix their rice whiskey with soda water, though it goes great with Coke, too.

Many Thais are just beginning to develop a taste for wine, and the foreign tipples on offer are expensive and mediocre. Thirty years ago, the king first brought up the idea of growing grapes for wine and fruit through his Royal Projects Foundation. Now, both fruit- and grape-based wines are made in various places up-country. Their quality generally does not match international offerings (they tend to taste better if you don't think of them as wines, as such), but some are quite pleasant. International markets often carry them, and they can occasionally be found on the menus of larger restaurants.

ELECTRICITY

The electrical current in Thailand is 220 volts, 50 cycles alternating current (AC); wall outlets take either two flat prongs, like outlets in the United States, or continental-type plugs, with two round prongs, or sometimes both. Plug adapters are cheap and can be found without great difficulty in tourist areas and electrical shops. Outlets outside expensive international hotels are rarely grounded, so use caution when plugging in delicate electronic equipment like laptops.

In both Cambodia and Laos, the electrical current is 220 volts AC, 50 Hz. In Laos, outside of Vientiane and Luang Prabang, electricity is spotty, and even in Luang Prabang there are frequent late-afternoon outages in hot weather.

Consider making a small investment in a universal adapter, which has several types of plugs in one lightweight, compact unit. Most laptops and mobile phone chargers are dual voltage (i.e., they operate equally well on 110 and 220 volts), so require only an adapter. These days the same is true of small appliances such as hair dryers. Always check labels and manufacturer instructions to be sure. Don't use 110-volt outlets marked FOR SHAVERS ONLY for high-wattage appliances such as hair-dryers.

Contacts **Steve Kropla's Help for World Traveler's** (*www.kropla.com*) has information on electrical and telephone plugs around the world. **Walkabout Travel Gear** (*www.walkabouttravelgear.com*) has a good coverage of electricity under "adapters."

EMERGENCIES

Thais are generally quite helpful, so you should get assistance from locals if you need it. The Tourist Police will help you in case of a robbery or rip-off. The Tourist Police hotline is ☎1155.

Many hotels can refer you to an English-speaking doctor. Major cities in Thailand have some of Southeast Asia's best hospitals, and the country is quickly becoming a "medical holiday" destination (i.e., a cost-effective place to have plastic surgery, dental work, etc., done). However, if you are still wary about treating serious health problems in Thailand, you can fly cheaply to Singapore for the best medical care in the region.

Most nations maintain diplomatic relations with Thailand and have embassies in Bangkok; a few have consulates also in Chiang Mai.

In Bangkok **U.S. Embassy** (✉ *120–122 Wittayu (Wireless Rd.)* ☎ *02/205–4000*).

In Chiang Mai **U.S. Consulate** (✉ *387 Wichayanond Rd.* ☎ *053/234472*).

In Phnom Penh, Cambodia **U.S. Embassy** (✉ *No. 1 St. 96, behind Wat Phnom, Phnom Penh* ☎ *023/728000*).

In Vientiane, Laos **U.S. Embassy** (✉ *BP 114, Rue Bartholomié, Vientiane* ☎ *21/267000*).

WORD OF MOUTH

Was the service stellar or not up to snuff? Did the food give you shivers of delight or leave you cold? Did the prices and portions make you happy or sad? Rate restaurants and write your own reviews in Travel Ratings or start a discussion about your favorite places in Travel Talk on www.fodors.com. Your comments might even appear in our books. Yes, you, too, can be a correspondent!

General Emergency Contacts **Police** (☎ *191*). **Tourist Police** (☎ *1155*).

HEALTH

The most common vacation sickness in Thailand is traveler's diarrhea. You can take some solace in knowing that it is also the most common affliction of the locals. It generally comes from eating contaminated food, be it fruit, veggies, unclean water, or badly prepared or stored foods—really anything. It can also be triggered by a change in diet. Avoid ice unless you know it comes from clean water, uncooked or undercooked foods (particularly seafood, sometimes served raw in salads), and unpasteurized dairy products. ■ TIP→ **Drink only bottled water or water that has been boiled for at least 20 minutes, even when brushing your teeth.** The water served in pitchers at small restaurants or in hotel rooms is generally safe, as it is either boiled or from a larger bottle of purified water, though if you have any suspicions about its origins, it's best to go with your gut feeling.

The best way to treat "Bangkok belly" is to wait for it to pass. Take Pepto-Bismol to help ease your discomfort and if you must travel, take Imodium (known generically as loperamide), which will immobilize your lower gut and everything in it. It doesn't cure the problem, but simply postpones it until a more convenient time. Note that if you have a serious stomach sickness, taking Imodium can occasionally intensify the problem, leading to a debilitating fever and sickness. If at any time you get a high fever with stomach sickness, find a doctor.

If you have frequent, watery diarrhea for more than two days, see a doctor for diagnosis and treatment. Days of sickness can leave you seriously dehydrated and weak in the tropics.

In any case, drink plenty of purified water or tea—chamomile, lemongrass, and ginger are good choices. In severe cases, rehydrate yourself with a salt-sugar solution (½ teaspoon salt and 4 tablespoons sugar per quart of water) or rehydration salts, available at any pharmacy.

SHOTS & MEDICATIONS

No vaccinations are required to enter Thailand, but ■ TIP→ **we strongly recommend that the hepatitis A vaccination**, and you should make sure your tetanus and polio vaccinations are up to date, as well as measles, mumps, and rubella.

Malaria and dengue fever are also possible (though remote) risks as you move out of the main tourist areas. There is much debate about whether travelers headed to Thailand should take malarial prophylactics. Though many Western doctors recommend that you take antimalarials, many healthcare workers in Thailand believe they can do more harm than good: They can have side effects, they are not 100% effective, they can mask the symptoms of the disease if you do contract it, and they can make treatment more complicated. Consult your physician, see what medications your insurance will cover, and do what makes you feel most comfortable.

There are no prophylactics available for dengue fever. The best way to prevent mosquito-borne illness is to protect yourself against mosquitoes as much as possible (⇨ *Specific Issues in Thailand, below*).

According to the U.S. government's National Centers for Disease Control (CDC) there's also a risk of hepatitis B, rabies, and Japanese encephalitis in rural areas of Thailand. In most urban or easily accessible areas you need not worry. However, if you plan to visit remote regions or stay for more than six weeks, check with the CDC's International Travelers Hotline.

Health Warnings **National Centers for Disease Control & Prevention** (*CDC* ☎ *800/311–3435 international travelers' health line* 🌐 *www.cdc.gov/travel*). **World Health Organization** (*WHO* 🌐 *www.who.int/en*).

SPECIFIC ISSUES IN THAILAND

The avian flu crisis that ripped through Southeast Asia at the start of the 21st century had a devastating impact on Thailand. Poultry farmers went out of business, tourists stayed away, and each week brought news of a new species found to be infected (including isolated cases of humans contracting the virus). At this writing, the worry has died down as human cases continue to be exceedingly rare. That doesn't mean it won't flare up again, but note that all cases have occurred in rural areas outside the tourist track, and most infected people dealt with large numbers of dead birds.

Malaria and dengue fever, though more common than bird flu, are still quite rare in well-traveled areas. Malarial mosquitoes generally fly from dusk to dawn, while dengue carriers do the opposite; both are most numerous during the rainy season, as they breed in stagnant water.

The best policy is to avoid being bitten. To that end, wear light-color clothing and some form of insect repellent (preferably containing DEET) on any exposed skin when out and about in the mornings and evenings, especially during the rainy season. Make sure that hotel rooms have air-conditioning, mosquito nets over the bed, good screens over windows, or some combination thereof. You can also use a bug spray (available everywhere) in your room before heading out to dinner, and return to a bug-free room. ■ **TIP→ The ubiquitous bottles of menthol-scented Siang Pure Oil both ward off mosquitoes and stop the incessant itching of bites.**

Dengue fever tends to appear with a sudden high fever, sweating, headache, joint and muscle pain (where it got the name "breakbone fever"), and nausea. A rash of red spots on the chest is a telltale sign. Malaria offers a raft of symptoms, including fever, chills, headache, sweating, diarrhea, and abdominal pain. A key sign is the recurrent nature of the symptoms, coming in waves every day or two.

Find a doctor immediately if you think you may have either disease. In Thailand, the test for both is quick and accurate and the doctors are much more accustomed to treating these diseases than are doctors in the United States. Left untreated, both diseases can quickly become serious, possibly fatal. Even when properly treated, dengue has a long recovery period, leaving the victim debilitated for weeks, sometimes months.

Reliable condoms in a variety of brands and styles are available at most 7-Elevens (yes, those have come to Thailand), supermarket, and mini-mart, usually near the check-out counter. ⚠ **Be aware that a high percentage of sex workers in Thailand are HIV positive, and unprotected sex is extremely risky.**

Do not fly within 24 hours of scuba diving, as you may risk decompression sickness.

OVER-THE-COUNTER REMEDIES

Thailand has nearly every drug known to the Western world, and many that aren't. All are readily available at pharmacies throughout the country. They are also often cheaper than in the United States and many drugs don't require the prescriptions and doctor visits needed at home. Be wary, however, of fake medications. It's best to visit larger, well-established pharmacies that locals vouch for.

HOURS OF OPERATION

Thai business hours generally follow the 9 to 5 model, though the smaller the business, the more eclectic the hours. Nearly all businesses either close or slow to a halt during lunch hour—don't expect to accomplish anything important at this time. Many tourist businesses in the north and on the beaches and islands in the south often shut down outside the main tourist seasons of November through January and June through August.

Thai and foreign banks are open weekdays 8:30 to 3:30 (sometimes longer), except for public holidays. Most commercial concerns in Bangkok operate on a five-day week and are open 8 to 5. Government offices are generally open weekdays 8:30 to 4:30, with a noon to 1 lunch break. Generally speaking, avoid visiting any sort of office during the Thai lunch hour—or bring a book to pass the time.

Gas stations in Thailand are usually open at least 8 to 8 daily; many, particularly those on the highways, are open 24 hours a day. Twenty-four hour minimart-style gas stations are growing in popularity. Many also have fast-food restaurants and convenience stores.

Each museum keeps its own hours and may select a different day of the week to close (though it's usually Monday); it's best to call before visiting.

Temples are generally open to visitors from 7 or 8 in the morning to 5 or 6 PM, but in truth they don't really have set hours. If a compound has gates, they open at dawn to allow the monks to do their rounds. Outside of major tourist sights like Wat Po in Bangkok, few temples appear to have fixed closing times.

Most pharmacies are open daily 9 to 9. You'll find a few 24-hour pharmacies in tourist areas.

Most small stores are open daily 8 to 8, whereas department and chain stores are usually open from 10 until 10.

HOLIDAYS

Thailand: New Year's Day (January 1); Chinese New Year (February 14, 2010 and February 3, 2011); Makha Bhucha Day (on the full moon of the third lunar month); Chakri Day (April 6); Songkran (mid-April); Labor Day (May 1); Coronation Day (May 5); Ploughing Day (May 9); Visakha Bucha (May, on the full moon of the sixth lunar month); Buddhist Lent day (July); Queen's Birthday (August 12); Chulalongkorn Memorial Day (October 23); King's Birthday (December 5); Constitution Day (December 10). Government offices, banks, commercial concerns, and department stores are usually closed on these days, but smaller shops stay open.

Cambodia: New Year's Day (January 1); Victory Day (January 7); Meak Bochea Day (February); International Women's Day (March 8); Cambodian New Year (mid-April, depending on the lunar cycle); Labor Day (May 1); Visak Bochea (the Buddha's Birthday, early May); King Sihamoni's birthday (May 13–15); Visaka Bochea (May 19); Royal Ploughing Ceremony (May); International Children's Day (June 1); Queen Mother's birthday (June 18); Pchum Ben (September); Constitution Day (September 24); Anniversary of Paris Peace Agreement (October 23), Coronation Day (October 29); Sihanouk's birthday (October 31); Independence Day (November 9); Water Festival (November); Human Rights Day (December 10).

Laos: New Year's Day (January 1); Pathet Lao Day (January 6); Army Day (late January); International Women Day (March 8); Day of the People's Party (March 22); Lao New Year (Water Festival, April 13–15); Labor Day (May 1); Buddha Day (May 2); Children's Day (June 1); Lao Issara (August 13); Day of Liberation (October 12); National Day (December 2).

LANGUAGE

Thai is the country's national language. It has five tones, which makes it confusing to most foreigners. Thankfully, Thais tend to be patient with people trying to speak their language, and will often guess what you are trying to say, even if it's badly mispronounced. In polite conversation, a male speaker will use the word "krup" to end a sentence or to acknowledge what someone has said. Female speakers use "ka." It's easy to speak a few words, such as "sawahdee krup" or "sawahdee ka" (good day) and "khop khun krup" or "khop khun ka" (thank you).

With the exception of taxi drivers, Thais working with travelers in the resort and tourist areas of Thailand generally speak sufficient English to permit basic communication. If you find yourself truly unable to communicate something important to a Thai, he or she will often start grabbing people from the street at random to see if they speak English to help you out.

MAIL

Thailand's mail service is generally reliable and efficient. It is a good idea—and cheap—to send all packages registered mail. Major hotels provide basic postal services.

If something must get to its destination quickly, send it via FedEx, UPS, or DHL, which have branches in the major tourist centers. "Overnight" shipping time from Thailand to the United States via these international carriers is actually two working days. Expect to pay at least B800 to B1,000 for an "overnight" letter. Major offices of the Thailand Post also offer overseas express mail service (EMS), though it usually takes longer than an international carrier and costs nearly as much.

Letter, packet, and parcel rates through the Thailand Post are low—B30 for a letter to the United States, B25 for a letter to Europe. Allow at least 10 days for your mail to arrive. A sea, air, and land service (SAL) is available for less urgent mail at a much cheaper rate. Note it can take up to three months for packages to reach their destination by this method. Bangkok's central general post office on Charoen Krung (New Road) is open weekdays 8 to 8, weekends and public holidays 8 to 1. Up-country post offices close at 4:30 PM.

Post offices in major towns are often quite crowded. Never go to a post office during lunch hour unless you bring a book and a mountain of patience.

If you need to receive mail in Bangkok, have it sent to you "poste restante" at the following address: Poste Restante, General Post Office, Bangkok, Thailand. There's a small charge for each piece collected. Thais write their last name first, so be sure to have your last name written in capital letters and underlined.

SHIPPING PACKAGES

Parcels are easy to send from Thailand via Thai Post. Rates vary according to weight, destination, and shipping style (air or surface). Expect to pay between B700 and B1,100 for a kilo package shipped by sea, which will take up to three months to arrive in the U.S. and another additional B300 to B350 per additional kilo. Most shops catering to tourists will offer to pack and ship your purchases anywhere in the world, usually at very reasonable rates. If you want to ship a larger piece, most furniture and antiques stores can help with freight shipping.

Although thousands of travelers have had no problems with the Thai Post, there has been at least one major incident of postal larceny in Chiang Mai, so if you're shipping something precious, consider paying the extra money to send it by an international courier like DHL, Federal Express, or UPS.

Express Services **DHL Worldwide** (✉ *22nd fl., Grand Amarin Tower, 1550 Phetburi Tat Mai, Bangkok* ☎ *02/207–0600*). **Federal Express** (✉ *8th fl., Green Tower, Rama IV, Bangkok* ☎ *02/367–3222*). **UPS** (✉ *16/1 Sukhumvit Soi 44/1, Bangkok* ☎ *02/712–3300*).

MONEY

It's possible to live and travel quite inexpensively if you do as Thais do—eat in small, neighborhood restaurants, use buses, and stay at non-air-conditioned hotels. Traveling this way, two people could easily get by on $30 a day or less. Once you start enjoying a little luxury, prices can jump as much as you let them. Imported items are heavily taxed.

Resort areas and Bangkok are much pricier than other parts of the country.

Prices throughout this guide are given for adults. Substantially reduced fees are almost always available for children, students, and senior citizens.

ATMS & BANKS

Your own bank will probably charge a fee for using ATMs abroad; the foreign bank you use may also charge a fee. Nevertheless, you'll usually get a better rate of exchange at an ATM than you will at a currency-exchange office or even when changing money in a bank.

TIP→ PIN numbers with more than four digits are not recognized at ATMs in many countries. If yours has five or more, remember to change it before you leave.

Thankfully, over the last few years, ATMs have sprouted like mushrooms around the country. Only smaller towns don't yet have them, and even that is changing. Most ATMs accept foreign bank cards; all pay in baht. As of this writing, most Thai ATMs do not charge any extra fees, but your home bank may well add extra fees for using a foreign bank and/or converting foreign currency. Do contact your bank and ask about this before leaving to avoid any nasty billing surprises. Some

Thai ATMs take Cirrus, some take Plus, some take both.

CREDIT CARDS

Throughout this guide, the following abbreviations are used: **AE,** American Express; **DC,** Diners Club; **MC,** MasterCard; and **V,** Visa.

It's a good idea to inform your credit-card company and the bank that issues your ATM card before you travel, especially if you don't travel internationally very often. Otherwise, the credit-card company might put a hold on your card owing to unusual activity—not a good thing halfway through your trip. Record all your credit-card numbers—as well as the phone numbers to call if your cards are lost or stolen—in a safe place, so you're prepared should something go wrong. Both MasterCard and Visa have general numbers you can call (collect if you're abroad) if your card is lost, but you're better off calling the number of your issuing bank, since MasterCard and Visa usually just transfer you to your bank; your bank's number is usually printed on your card.

If you plan to use your credit card for cash advances, you'll need to apply for a PIN at least two weeks before your trip. Although it's usually cheaper (and safer) to use a credit card abroad for large purchases (so you can cancel payments or be reimbursed if there's a problem), note that some credit-card companies *and* the banks that issue them add substantial percentages to all foreign transactions, whether they're in a foreign currency or not. Check on these fees before leaving home, so there won't be any surprises when you get the bill.

■ TIP→ **Before you charge something, ask the merchant whether or not he or she plans to do a dynamic currency conversion (DCC). In such a transaction the credit-card *processor* (shop, restaurant, or hotel, not Visa or MasterCard) converts the currency and charges you in dollars. In most cases you'll pay the merchant a 3% fee for this service in addition to any credit-card company and issuing-bank foreign-transaction surcharges.**

Dynamic currency conversion programs are becoming increasingly widespread. Merchants who participate in them are supposed to ask whether you want to be charged in dollars or the local currency, but they don't always do so. And even if they do offer you a choice, they may well avoid mentioning the additional surcharges. The good news is that you *do* have a choice. And if this practice really gets your goat, you can avoid it entirely thanks to American Express; with its cards, DCC simply isn't an option.

Credit cards are almost always accepted at upper-end hotels, resorts, boutique stores, and shopping malls, and that list is slowly expanding. Expect to pay a two percent to four percent service charge. It is illegal, but that's what everyone does.

Reporting Lost Cards **American Express** (☎ *800/992–3404 in the U.S., 336/393–1111 collect from abroad* 🌐 *www.americanexpress.com*). **Diners Club** (☎ *800/234–6377 in the U.S., 303/799–1504 collect from abroad* 🌐 *www.dinersclub.com*). **MasterCard** (☎ *800/622–7747 in the U.S., 636/722–7111 collect from abroad* 🌐 *www.mastercard.com*). **Visa** (☎ *800/847–2911 in the U.S., 410/581–9994 collect from abroad* 🌐 *www.visa.com*).

CURRENCY & EXCHANGE

The basic unit of currency is the baht. There are 100 satang to one baht. Baht come in six different bills, each a different color: B10, brown; B20, green; B50, blue; B100, red; B500, purple; and B1,000, beige. Coins in use are 25 satang, 50 satang, B1, B2, B5, and B10. The B10 coin has a gold-color center surrounded by silver.

Major hotels will convert traveler's checks and major currencies into baht, though exchange rates are better at banks and authorized money changers. The rate tends to be better in any larger city than up-country and is better in Thailand than in the United States.

At this writing, B34.5 = US$1.

Currency Conversion **Google** (www.google.com) does currency conversion. Just type in the amount you want to convert and an explanation of how you want it converted (e.g., "14 Swiss francs in dollars"), and then voilà. **Oanda.com** (www.oanda.com) also allows you to print out a handy table with the current day's conversion rates. **XE.com** (www.xe.com) is a good currency conversion Web site.

TIP→ Even if a currency-exchange booth has a sign promising no commission, rest assured that there's some kind of huge, hidden fee. (Oh . . . that's right. The sign didn't say no *fee*.) And as for rates, you're almost always better off getting foreign currency at an ATM or exchanging money at a bank.

PACKING

Light cotton or other natural-fiber clothing is appropriate for Thailand; drip-dry is an especially good idea, because the tropical sun and high humidity encourage frequent changes of clothing. Avoid delicate fabrics because you may have difficulty getting them laundered. A sweater is welcome on cool evenings or in overly air-conditioned restaurants, buses, and trains.

The paths leading to temples can be rough, so bring a sturdy pair of walking shoes. Slip-ons are preferable to lace-up shoes, as they must be removed before you enter shrines and temples.

Bring a hat and UV-protection sunglasses and use them. The tropical sun is powerful and its effects long-lasting and painful.

Thailand has a huge range of clothing options at good prices, though it may be difficult to find the right sizes if you're not petit.

PASSPORTS & VISAS

U.S. citizens who are arriving by air need only a valid passport, not a pre-arranged visa, to visit Thailand for less than 30 days. Technically, travelers need an outgoing ticket and "adequate finances" for the duration of their Thailand stay to receive a 30-day stamp upon entry, but authorities in Bangkok rarely check your finances, unless you look like the sort who might sponge off Thai society. They do occasionally ask to see an outbound ticket. Scrutiny is inconsistent; authorities periodically crack down on long-term tourists who try to hang out in Thailand indefinitely by making monthly "visa runs" across international borders. ⚠ **As of 2008, tourists who arrive in Thailand by land from a neighboring country are now granted only a 15-day visa.** As of this writing, tourists are not allowed to spend more than 90 days of any six-month period in Thailand, and Immigration officials will count days and stamps in your passport.

If for whatever reason you are traveling to Thailand on a one-way ticket, airline officials might ask you to sign a waiver before allowing you to board, relieving them of responsibility should you be turned away at immigration.

If you want to stay longer than one month, you can apply for a 60-day Tourist visa through a Royal Thai Embassy. The Embassy in Washington, D.C. charges about $35 for this visa, and you'll need to show them a round-trip ticket and a current bank statement to prove you can afford the trip. Be sure to apply for the correct number of entries; for example, if you're going to Laos for a few days in the middle of your stay, you'll need to apply for two Thailand entries.

Tourist visas can also be extended one month at a time once you're in Thailand. You must apply in person at a Thai immigration office; expect the process to take a day. You application will be granted at the discretion of the immigration office where you apply.

If you overstay your visa by a day or two, you'll have to pay a B500 fine for each day overstayed when you leave the country.

Visa Extensions **Bangkok Immigration** (✉ *Soi Suan Phlu, South Sathorn Rd., Bangkok* ☎ *02/287–3101*). **Chiang Mai Immigration** (✉ *71 Airport Road, Chiang Mai* ☎ *053/277510*). **Royal Thai Embassy in Washington, D.C.** (☎ *202/944–3600* 🌐 *www.thaiembdc.org*).

U.S. Passport Information **U.S. Department of State** (☎ *877/487–2778* 🌐 *travel.state.gov/passport*).

RESTROOMS

Western-style facilities are usually available, although you still may find squat toilets in older buildings. For the uninitiated, squat toilets can be something of a puzzle. You will doubtless find a method that works best for you, but here's a general guide: squat down with feet on either side of the basin and use one hand to keep your clothes out of the way and the other for balance or, if you're really good, holding your newspaper. The Thai version of a bidet is either a hose or a big tank of water with a bowl. If you've had the foresight to bring tissues with you, throw the used paper into the basket alongside the basin. Finally, pour bowls of water into the toilet to flush it—and after thoroughly washing your hands, give yourself a pat on the back. Except at plusher hotels and restaurants, plumbing in most buildings is archaic, so resist the temptation to flush your paper unless you want to be remembered as the foreigner who ruined the toilet.

Find a Loo **The Bathroom Diaries** (🌐 *www.thebathroomdiaries.com*) is flush with unsanitized info on restrooms the world over—each one located, reviewed, and rated.

WORST-CASE SCENARIO

All your money and credit cards have just been stolen. These days, this isn't a predicament that should destroy your vacation. First, report the theft of the credit cards. Then get any traveler's checks you were carrying replaced. **Western Union** (☎ *800/325–6000* 🌐 *www.westernunion.com*) sends money almost anywhere. Have someone back home order a transfer online, over the phone, or at one of the company's offices. The U.S. State Department's **Overseas Citizens Services** (☎ *888/407–4747*) can wire money to any U.S. consulate or embassy abroad for a fee of $30. Just have someone back home wire money or send a money order or cashier's check to the state department, which will then disburse the funds.

SAFETY

You should not travel in the four southern provinces closest to the Malaysian border: Yala, Pattani, Songkhla, and Narathiwat. A low-grade and seemingly endless insurgency there, which began in 2004, has led to the deaths of more than 3,000, with thousands more injured. Although the insurgents originally targeted government institutions and officials, they have also bombed tourist centers, shopping malls, restaurants, and the airport at Hat Yai. Fear permeates both Buddhist and Muslim communities in these southern provinces; often, locals have no idea who is attacking or why. Witnesses to drive-bys and bombings are afraid to speak. Residents avoid driving at night, shops close early, and Southern towns turn eerily quiet by sundown.

In the fall of 2008, political demonstrations in Bangkok resulted in some outbreaks of violence. At this writing, the political situation remains tenuous, though day-to-day life in Thailand is not usually affected. Stay informed about local developments as best you can and determine if the possible dangers make you too uneasy to travel or stay in Thailand. The *Bangkok Post* (🌐*www.bangkokpost.net*) and *The Nation* (🌐*www.nationmultimedia.com*) are the best sources of local news.

Thailand is generally a safe country, and millions of foreigners visit each year without incident. That said, every year a few tourists are attacked or raped and murdered, generally either in Bangkok or in the southern beach regions. Be careful at night, particularly in poorly lighted areas or on lonely beaches. Follow other normal precautions: watch your valuables in crowded areas and lock your hotel rooms securely. Thai crooks generally try to relieve you of cash through crimes of convenience or negligence, not violence.

Credit card scams—from stealing your card to swiping it several times when you use it at stores—are a frequent problem. Don't leave your wallet behind when you go trekking and make sure you keep an eye on the card when you give it to a salesperson.

■ **TIP→ A great little invention is the metal doorknob cup that can be found at Thai hardware shops.** It covers your doorknob and locks it in place with a padlock, keeping anyone from using a spare key or even twisting the knob to get into your room. A good B300 investment, it's usable anywhere.

Guesthouses also offer commission for customers brought in by drivers, so be wary of anyone telling you that the place where you booked a room has burned down overnight or is suddenly full. Smile and be courteous, but be firm about where you want to go. If the driver doesn't immediately take you where you want to go, get out and get another taxi.

Watch out for scams while shopping. Bait and switch is common, as is trying to pass off reproductions as authentic antiques. True antique and artifact vendors will gladly help you finish the necessary government paperwork to take your purchase home. Keep in mind that authentic Thai or other Southeast Asian antiques in Thailand are usually stunningly expensive. Thais, Chinese, Malaysians, and Singaporeans are all fanatical collectors themselves, and pay as much as any Western buyer. If you think you're getting a super deal on a Thai antique, think twice.

Thailand offers many adventurous ways to spend your days, few of which include the safety provisions demanded in Western countries. Motorcycle wrecks are a common way to cut a vacation tragically short.

Thailand's most famous danger comes from the ocean. The Asian tsunami hit the Andaman coast in December 2004 and killed more than 5,300 people in Thailand. Reports from the areas hit show that many people could have been saved if they had known how to recognize the signs of an impending tsunami, or if an evacuation plan had been in place. Tsunamis are rare and very unpredictable. It's highly unlikely you'll experience one, but it pays to be prepared. If you plan to stay in a beach resort, ask if they have a tsunami plan in place, and ask what it is. If you feel an earthquake, leave any waterside area. ⚠ **Pay attention to the ocean: if you see all of the water race off the beach, evacuate immediately and head for high ground.** A tsunami could be only minutes away. Remember, a tsunami is a series of waves that could go on for hours. Do not assume it is over after the first wave.

⚠ **Thai beaches almost never have lifeguards, but that doesn't mean they don't have undertows or other dangers.**

FEMALE TRAVELERS

Foreign women in Thailand get quite a few stares, and Thai women as often as Thai men will be eager to chat and become your friend. Although there's no doubt that attitudes are changing, traditional Thai women dress and act modestly, so loud or overly confident behavior from a foreign woman can be a shock to both men and women alike. It's also worth noting that Thai men often see foreign women as something exotic. If you're being subjected to unwelcome attention, be firm, but try to stay calm—"losing face" is a big concern among Thai men and embarrassing them (even if it's deserved) can have ugly repercussions.

Safety **Transportation Security Administration** (*TSA; www.tsa.gov*).

General Information **U.S. Department of State** (*www.travel.state.gov*).

TAXES

A 7% (and sometimes more) Value Added Tax (V.A.T.) is built into the price of all goods and services, including restaurant meals. You can reclaim some of this tax on souvenirs and other high-price items purchased at stores that are part of the V.A.T. refund program at the airport upon leaving the country. You cannot claim the V.A.T. refund when leaving Thailand by land at a border crossing. Shops that offer this refund will have a sign displayed; ask shopkeepers to fill out the necessary forms and make sure you keep your receipts. You'll have to fill out additional forms at the airport.

V.A.T. refund guidelines are particular. The goods must be purchased from stores displaying the V.A.T. REFUND FOR TOURISTS sign. Purchases at each shop you visit must total more than B2,000 before they can fill out the necessary forms. The total amount claimed for refund upon leaving the country cannot be less than B5,000. You must depart the country from an international airport, where you finish claiming your refund at the V.A.T. Refund Counter—allow an extra hour at the airport for this process. You cannot claim V.A.T. refunds for gemstones.

For refunds less than B30,000, you can receive the money in cash at the airport, or have it wired to a bank account or to a credit card for a B100 fee. Refunds over B30,000 are paid either to a bank account or credit card for a B100 fee.

TIME

Thailand is 7 hours ahead of Greenwich Mean Time. It's 12 hours ahead of New York, 15 hours ahead of Los Angeles, 7 hours ahead of London, and 3 hours behind Sydney.

Time Zones **Timeanddate.com** (*www.timeanddate.com/worldclock*) can help you figure out the correct time anywhere.

TIPPING

Tipping is not a local custom, but it is expected of foreigners, especially at larger hotels and restaurants and for taxi rides. If you feel the service has been less than stellar, you are under no obligation to leave a tip, especially with crabby cabbies.

In Thailand, tips are generally given for good service, except when a price has been negotiated in advance. If you hire a private driver for an excursion, do tip him. With metered taxis in Bangkok, however, the custom is to round the fare up to the nearest B5. Hotel porters expect at least a B20 tip, and hotel staff who have given good personal service are usually tipped. A 10% tip is appreciated at a restaurant when no service charge has been added to the bill.

VISITOR INFO

ONLINE TRAVEL TOOLS

All About Thailand A few sites worth checking out are: *www.discoverythailand.com* and *www.sawadee.com*.

Visitor Information **Tourism Authority of Thailand (TAT)** (*212/432–0433 in New York, 323/461–9814 in Los Angeles www.tourismthailand.org*) is a great place to begin research.

INDEX

T

Photo Credits: 1, *Michael Yamashita/Aurora Photos*. 2, *Steven Allan/iStockphoto*. 5, *José Fuste Raga/age fotostock*. Chapter 1: **Experience Thailand:** 10-11, *Ingolf Pompe 17/Alamy*. 12, *SuperStock/age fotostock*. 13 (left), *Sylvain Grandadam/age fotostock*. 13 (right), *SuperStock/age fotostock*. 16, *Travelscape Images/Alamy*. 17 (left), *Kevin O'Hara/age fotostock*. 17 (right), *SuperStock/age fotostock*. 18 and 19, *Dave Stamboulis*. 20 (left), *innocent/Shutterstock*. 20 (top center), *Christine Gonsalves/Shutterstock*. 20 (top right), *John Hemmings/Shutterstock*. 20 (bottom right), *Shenval/Alamy*. 21 (top left), *Aflo Co. Ltd./Alamy*. 21 (bottom left), *iStockphoto*. 21 (top center), *Frank van den Bergh/iStockphoto*. 21 (right), *Bartlomiej K. Kwieciszewski/Shutterstock*. 22, *Tourism Authority of Thailand*. 23 (left), *Phil Date/Shutterstock*. 23 (right), *Tourism Authority of Thailand*. 24, *Bruno Morandi/age fotostock*. 25 (left), *Cris Haigh/Alamy*. 25 (right), *Ben Heys/Shutterstock*. 26, *Hemis/Alamy*. 28, *Dave Stamboulis*. 30, *Cojocaru Emanuela/Shutterstock*. 31 (left), *Dave Stamboulis*. 31 (right), *pambrick/fodors.com member*. 32, *Muellek/Shutterstock*. 33, *North Wind Picture Archives/Alamy*. 34 (left), *Alvaro Leiva/age fotostock*. 34 (top right), *Thomas Cockrem/Alamy*. 34 (bottom right), *Genevieve Dietrich/Shutterstock*. 35 (left), *Juha Sompinmäki/Shutterstock*. 35 (top right), *Thomas Cockrem/Alamy*. 35 (bottom right), *Bryan Busovicki/Shutterstock*. 36 (left), *Mary Evans Picture Library/Alamy*. 36 (top right), *Content Mine International/Alamy*. 37 (left), *Sam DCruz/Shutterstock*. 37 (top right), *Newscom*. 37 (bottom right), *Ivan Vdovin/age fotostock*. 38 (left and top right), *Thor Jorgen Udvang/Shutterstock*. 38 (bottom right), *AFP/Getty Images/Newscom*. **Chapter 2: Bangkok:** 39, *Angelo Cavalli/age fotostock*. 40 (top), *Marco Simoni/age fotostock*. 40 (bottom), *Peter Horree/Alamy*. 41, *Steve Silver/age fotostock*. 42, *Juriah Mosin/Shutterstock*. 54-55, *Chris L Jones/ Photolibrary.com*. 56 (top), *Gina Smith/Shutterstock*. 56 (bottom left), *PCL/Alamy*. 56 (bottom right), *John Hemmings/Shutterstock*. 58, *Andy Lim/Shutterstock*. 59 (top left), *do_ok/Shutterstock*. 59 (center left), *Heinrich Damm*. 59 (bottom left), *Steve Vidler/eStockphoto*. 59 (right), *Plotnikoff/Shutterstock*. 60 (top), *P. Narayan/age fotostock*. 60 (bottom), *Dave Stamboulis*. 61 (bottom), *Wayne Planz/Shutterstock*. 70, *kd2/Shutterstock*. 75, *Travel Pix Collection/age fotostock*. 76 (top), *Juha Sompinmäki/Shutterstock*. 76 (bottom), *SuperStock/age fotostock*. 77 (top), *BlueMoon Stock/Alamy*. 77 (2nd from top), *John Lander/Alamy*. 77 (3rd from top), *kd2/Shutterstock*. 77 (bottom), *Mireille Vautier/Alamy*. 78 (top), *David Kay/Shutterstock*. 78 (center), *ARCO/I Schulz/age fotostock*. 78 (bottom), *jamalludin/Shutterstock*. 86, *iStockphoto*. 102 (top), *The Peninsula Bangkok*. 102 (center left), *Tibor Bognar/Alamy*. 102 (center right), *LOOK Die Bildagentur der Fotografen GmbH/Alamy*. 102 (bottom left), *Shangri-La Hotels and Resorts*. 102 (bottom right), *Hilton Hotels Corporation*. 115, *Ingolf Pompe 6/Alamy*. 126, *Luca Invernizzi Tettoni/Tips Italia/photolibrary.com*. 130, *Tourism Authority of Thailand*. 133, *Dave Stamboulis*. **Chapter 3: Around Bangkok:** 135, *Jon Arnold Images/Alamy*. 136 (top), *Steve Raymer/age fotostock*. 136 (center), *Richard*

Wainscoat/Alamy. 136 (bottom), *Can Sengunes/Alamy*. 137, *Jeremy Horner/Alamy*. 143, *Juriah Mosin/ Shutterstock*. 144 (top right), *Ian Trower/Alamy*. 144 (top left), *Andy Lim/Shutterstock*. 144 (bottom left), *Elena Elisseeva/Shutterstock*. 144 (bottom right), *Robert Fried/Alamy*. 145 (top), *Juriah Mosin/ Shutterstock*. 145 (bottom), *Chris Howey/Shutterstock*. 146 (top), *Asia/Alamy*. 146 (bottom), *Ronald Sumners/Shutterstock*. 147, *dbimages/Alamy*. **Chapter 4: The Central Plains:** 163, *Gonzalo Azumendi/ age fotostock*. 164 (top), *JTB Photo Communications, Inc./Alamy*. 164 (center), *Robert Fried/Alamy*. 164 (bottom), *Peter Treanor/Alamy*. 166, *atikarn/Shutterstock*. 167, *Juha Sompinmäki/Shutterstock*. 168, *Simon Reddy/Alamy*. 169 (top), *Bon Appetit/Alamy*. 169 (bottom), *Timur Kulgarin/Shutterstock*. 176, *Tourism Authority of Thailand*. 188, *Luciano Mortula/Shutterstock*. 190-91, *Juha Sompinmäki/ Shutterstock*. 191 (top), *Chie Ushio*. 191 (center), *Khoo Si Lin/Shutterstock*. 191 (bottom), *N. Frey Photography/Shutterstock*. 192, *Idealink Photography/Alamy*. 193, *Joel Blit/Shutterstock*. 194 (top), *David Halbakken/Alamy*. 194 (bottom), *SteveSPF/Shutterstock*. 195 (left), *javarman/Shutterstock*. 195 (top right), *qingqing/Shutterstock*. 195 (bottom right), *Michele Falzone/Alamy*. 196 (left), *J Marshall - Tribaleye Images/Alamy*. 196 (top right), *Julien Grondin/Shutterstock*. 196 (bottom right), *Juha Sompinmäki/Shutterstock*. 197 (left), *Julien Grondin/Shutterstock*. 197 (top right), *Jon Arnold Images Ltd/ Alamy*. 197 (bottom right), *hfng/Shutterstock*. **Chapter 5: The Southern Beaches:** 209, *travelstock44/ Alamy*. 211 (top), *Angelo Cavalli/age fotostock*. 211 (bottom), *Craig Lovell/Eagle Visions Photography /Alamy*. 214, *Chie Ushio*. 215 (top), *Dave Stamboulis*. 215 (bottom), *William Berry/Shutterstock*. 226-27, *José Fuste Raga/age fotostock*. 229 (left), *Gonzalo Azumendi/age fotostock*. 229 (right), *LOOK Die Bildagentur der Fotografen GmbH/Alamy*. 231 (left), *Gavriel Jecan/age fotostock*. 231 (right) and 239, *Dave Stamboulis*. 247, *Chiva-Som International*. 254, *Dave Smurthwaite/iStockphoto*. 258, *Reinhard Dirscherl/Alamy*. 280, *Franck Guiziou/age fotostock*. 295, *Abigail Silver/TAT*. 301 and 307, *Dave Stamboulis*. 313, *Pichugin Dmitry/Shutterstock*. 323, *OM3/age fotostock*. 327, *David Rydevik*. 332, *Andy Lim/Shutterstock*. **Chapter 6: Northern Thailand:** 341, *Gonzalo Azumendi/age fotostock*. 342, *Mervyn Rees/Alamy*. 343, *Angelo Cavalli/age fotostock*. 344, *Nicky Gordon/iStockphoto*. 345, *Randy Plett/iStockphoto*. 346, *Dave Stamboulis/Alamy*. 347 (top), *kentoh/Shutterstock*. 347 (bottom), *Andrea Skjold/Shutterstock*. 357, *Jean Du Boisberranger/Hemis.fr/Aurora Photos*. 358, *Muellek/Shutterstock*. 369, *Denis Babenko/Shutterstock*. 374, *Four Seasons Hotels & Resorts*. 384, *TC/fodors.com member*. 398, *David South/Alamy*. 414, *Raffaele Meucci/age fotostock*. 415, *Stuart Pearce/age fotostock*. 416 (top and bottom), *SuperStock/age fotostock*. 417 (top), *John Arnold Images Ltd/Alamy*. 417 (bottom), *KLJ Photographic Ltd/iStockphoto*. 418 (top), *SuperStock/age fotostock*. 418 (bottom), *Anders Ryman/ Alamy*. 419 (top), *Val Duncan/Kenebec Images/Alamy*. 419 (bottom), *Simon Podgorsek/iStockphoto*. 420, *Robert Fried/Alamy*. 428, *Valery Shanin/Shutterstock*. **Chapter 7: Isan:** 431, 432, and 433 (top), *Cris Haigh/Alamy*. 433 (bottom), *Pietro Cenini/age fotostock*. 436, *isifa Image Service s.r.o./Alamy*. 437 (top), *Jasna/Shutterstock*. 437 (bottom), *Muellek/Shutterstock*. 447, *mypokcik/Shutterstock*. 450, *Robert Harding Picture Library Ltd/Alamy*. 455, *Dave Stamboulis*. 456 (top and 2nd from top), *wikipedia.org*. 456 (3rd from top), *mediacolor's/Alamy*. 456 (4th from top), *Dave Stamboulis*. 456 (bottom), *Hemis/Alamy*. 457 (top), *Dave Stamboulis*. 457 (center), *Bryan Busovicki/Shutterstock*. 457 (bottom), *David Bleeker Photography.com/Alamy*. 474, *Dave Stamboulis*. **Chapter 8: Cambodia:** 483, *Atlantide S.N.C./age fotostock*. 484 (top), *Roger Hutchings/Alamy*. 484 (bottom), *Gavin Hellier/age fotostock*. 485, *f1 online/Alamy*. 495, *Luciano Mortula/Shutterstock*. 506, *Ryan Fox/age fotostock*. 516, *Evan Wong/Shutterstock*. 521, *Ben Heys/Shutterstock*. 528-59, *Roy Garnier/Alamy*. 530, *José Fuste Raga/age fotostock*. 531 (top), *Luciano Mortula/iStockphoto*. 531 (bottom), *Bruno Morandi/age fotostock*. 532 (top right), *Tito Wong/Shutterstock*. 532 (left), *Danita Delimont/Alamy*. 532 (bottom right) and 533, *Craig Lovell/Eagle Visions Photography/Alamy*. 534 (top), *Jordí Camí/age fotostock*. 534 (bottom), 535, *Brianna May/iStockphoto*. 536 (top), *R. Matina/age fotostock*. 536 (bottom), *Vladimir Renard/wikipedia.org*. 537 (top), *Paul Panayiotou/Alamy*. 537 (bottom), *Bernard O'Kane/ Alamy*. 538, *Joris Van Ostaeyen/iStockphoto*. 539 (top), *Robert Preston Photography/Alamy*. 539 (bottom), *Jie Xu/iStockphoto*. 540, *Linga Bar*. 546, *Vladimir Korostyshevskiy/Shutterstock*. **Chapter 9: Laos:** 549, *Mob Images/Alamy*. 550 (top), *Henry Westheim Photography/Alamy*. 550 (bottom), *Ron Yue/Alamy*. 551, *Travel Ink/Alamy*. 552, *Jean-Michel Olives/Shutterstock*. 554, *Tamara Gentuso/ iStockphoto*. 560, *Juha Sompinmäki/Shutterstock*. 570, *Lucid Images/age fotostock*. 584, *Angelo Cavalli/age fotostock*. 591 and 597, *Dave Stamboulis*. 603, *Gautier Willaume/iStockphoto*.

ABOUT OUR WRITERS

Hana Borrowman lives and breathes Bangkok, along with her journalist husband and one-year-old son. Having met in Bangkok working for *The Nation*, the couple has since traversed Thailand researching various writing projects, as well as buckling on the baby to tackle Malaysia, Indonesia, Cambodia, Egypt, and even their homeland, the U.K. Hana covered markets and puppet theater for *Fodor's Thailand*.

Karen Coates, who updated the Travel Smart Thailand chapter and wrote "Coups & the King," has covered Southeast Asia since 1998, starting with a gig as an editor at the *Cambodia Daily*. She is a correspondent for *Gourmet Magazine* and writes regularly for newspapers, magazines, and journals around the world. She is the author of *Cambodia Now: Life in the Wake of War*, and co-author of *Pacific Lady: The First Woman to Sail Solo Across the World's Largest Ocean*. She also keeps a food blog at www.ramblingspoon.com/blog.

Robin Goldstein, who covered Bangkok for this edition, is an old travel guide pro, having written for more than 30 different books; he's covered destinations for Fodor's ranging from Italy to Argentina to Hong Kong. As founder and editor-in-chief of the Fearless Critic restaurant guide series and author of *The Wine Trials*, a guide to wines under $15, Robin makes far more use of his culinary and wine training than of his law degree.

Alexis Herschkowitsch, who updated Bangkok for this edition, has also covered Mexico and El Salvador for Fodor's. As managing editor of the Fearless Critic restaurant guide series, she has covered the culinary scenes of Austin and Houston, Texas, and Washington, DC. She currently lives in New York, where she spends much of her time searching in vain for authentic Thai insect cuisine.

Christina Knight, a former Fodor's editor, has written about travel for publications in the U.S., U.K., and Germany. She recommends attending a classical dance performance in Cambodia, which is like witnessing Angkor Wat's apsaras set into deliberate, graceful motion.

Emmanuelle Michel tackled the sights and lodging sections of the Around Bangkok chapter. She has lived in the Thai capital since late 2007, when she started covering South East Asia (especially Thailand and Myanmar) for several French newspapers, magazines, and wire services. Before settling in Asia, she traveled across North and South America, and worked in Paris for Radio France Internationale.

Lee Middleton covered the Grand Palace and Wat Phra Kaew for *Fodor's Thailand, 11th Edition*. Lee's various sojourns in Thailand have involved researching the roles of Thai women in Buddhism from Chiang Mai University, working with ceramic artists in Mae Rim, and studying tigers in Khao Yai national park. A freelance journalist since 2000, Lee currently lives in Africa, and writes for several magazines, wire services, and websites. She has covered other destinations for Fodor's, including South Africa and the Seychelles.

Howard Richardson has lived in Bangkok since 1996, exploring Thailand as magazine editor and food and travel writer. Among a wide range of features for international publications, he has written about nightlife for *GQ* and food for the BBC's *Olive* magazine, and had a monthly column for six years covering Bangkok events and trends in *Sawasdee*, the Thai Airways inflight magazine. He was previously the editor of *Bangkok Metro* magazine, for which he instigated the *Bangkok Best Restaurant and Nightlife Awards*. Howard won awards, himself, for Best ASEAN Travel Article 2004, and Best Asian Food Feature, at the 2008 World Gourmet Summit Awards.

ABOUT OUR WRITERS

Dave Stamboulis is a well-worn road veteran who has bicycled over 25,000 miles around the world. The Society of American Travel Writers awarded his book about this adventure, *Odysseus' Last Stand: the Chronicles of a Bicycle Nomad,* the silver medal for travel book of the year in 2006. Originally from Greece, Dave now resides in Bangkok. His photographs and articles have appeared in publications, books, and elsewhere throughout the globe. For this edition, he kept busy running back and forth between Laos and Isan, as well as taking photos.

Simon Stewart has lived in Thailand since 2003 and works as a freelance writer and university lecturer. He writes about traveling and cycle touring in Southeast Asia. He covered Thailand's Andaman Coast and Cambodia for this edition.

Brian Thomson updated the Central Plains section. He has lived in Bangkok for the last four years where he is an researcher and editor. He also spent four years working in Phuket's hotel industry and did a two-year stint in Japan.

Robert Tilley is a veteran Fodor's writer and researcher. He masterminded the first Gold Guide to Germany in 1988 and updated it regularly until 1999, when he left Europe for Asia. From his current base in Chiang Mai, Northern Thailand, he writes for several regional and international publications and is working on his third book. He updated the Northern Thailand chapter.